C000176711

STREET ATLAS
Somerset
North Somerset and
Bath and North East Somerset

www.philips-maps.co.uk

First published in 2002 by Philip's
a division of Octopus Publishing Group Ltd
www.octopusbooks.co.uk
Carmelite House
50 Victoria Embankment
London EC4Y 0DZ
An Hachette UK Company
www.hachette.co.uk

Fourth edition with interim revision 2016
Second impression 2017

SOMDA

ISBN 978-1-84907-427-8 (spiral)

© Philip's 2016

Contents

III	**Key to map symbols**
IV	**Key to map pages**
VI	**Route planning**
X	Major administrative and Postcode boundaries

1	**Street maps** at 3½ inches to 1 mile
122	**Street maps** at 1¾ inches to 1 mile
200	**Street maps** at 3½ inches to 1 mile
226	**Street maps** of Bristol and Bath city centres at 7 inches to 1 mile

| 229 | **Index** of towns, villages, streets, hospitals, industrial estates, railway stations, schools, shopping centres, universities and places of interest |

III

Key to map symbols

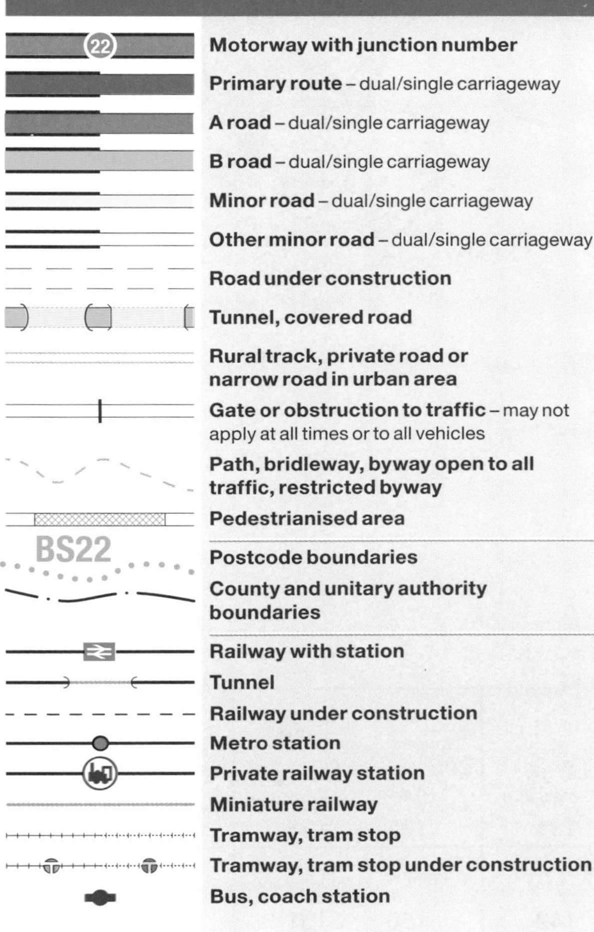

Motorway with junction number

Primary route – dual/single carriageway

A road – dual/single carriageway

B road – dual/single carriageway

Minor road – dual/single carriageway

Other minor road – dual/single carriageway

Road under construction

Tunnel, covered road

Rural track, private road or narrow road in urban area

Gate or obstruction to traffic – may not apply at all times or to all vehicles

Path, bridleway, byway open to all traffic, restricted byway

Pedestrianised area

BS22   Postcode boundaries

County and unitary authority boundaries

Railway with station

Tunnel

Railway under construction

Metro station

Private railway station

Miniature railway

Tramway, tram stop

Tramway, tram stop under construction

Bus, coach station

Ambulance station

Coastguard station

Fire station

Police station

Accident and Emergency entrance to hospital

H   Hospital

Place of worship

i   Information centre – open all year

P   Shopping centre, parking

P&R   PO   Park and Ride, Post Office

Camping site, caravan site

Golf course, picnic site

Church   ROMAN FORT   Non-Roman antiquity, Roman antiquity

Univ   Important buildings, schools, colleges, universities and hospitals

Woods, built-up area

River Medway   Water name

River, weir

Stream

Canal, lock, tunnel

Water

Tidal water

58   **87**   **246**   Adjoining page indicators and overlap bands – the colour of the arrow and band indicates the scale of the adjoining or overlapping page (see scales below)

The dark grey border on the inside edge of some pages indicates that the mapping does not continue onto the adjacent page

The small numbers around the edges of the maps identify the 1-kilometre National Grid lines

Acad	Academy	Meml	Memorial
Allot Gdns	Allotments	Mon	Monument
Cemy	Cemetery	Mus	Museum
C Ctr	Civic centre	Obsy	Observatory
CH	Club house	Pal	Royal palace
Coll	College	PH	Public house
Crem	Crematorium	Recn Gd	Recreation ground
Ent	Enterprise	Resr	Reservoir
Ex H	Exhibition hall	Ret Pk	Retail park
Ind Est	Industrial Estate	Sch	School
IRB Sta	Inshore rescue boat station	Sh Ctr	Shopping centre
Inst	Institute	TH	Town hall / house
Ct	Law court	Trad Est	Trading estate
L Ctr	Leisure centre	Univ	University
LC	Level crossing	W Twr	Water tower
Liby	Library	Wks	Works
Mkt	Market	YH	Youth hostel

Enlarged maps only

Railway or bus station building

Place of interest

Parkland

The map scale on the pages numbered in green is 1¾ inches to 1 mile
2.76 cm to 1 km • 1:36 206

0	½ mile	1 mile	1½ miles	2 miles
0	500m	1 km	1½ km	2km

The map scale on the pages numbered in blue is 3½ inches to 1 mile
5.52 cm to 1 km • 1:18 103

0	¼ mile	½ mile	¾ mile	1 mile
0	250m	500m	750m	1km

The map scale on the pages numbered in red is 7 inches to 1 mile
11.04 cm to 1 km • 1:9 051

0	220yds	440yds	660yds	½ mile
0	125m	250m	375m	500m

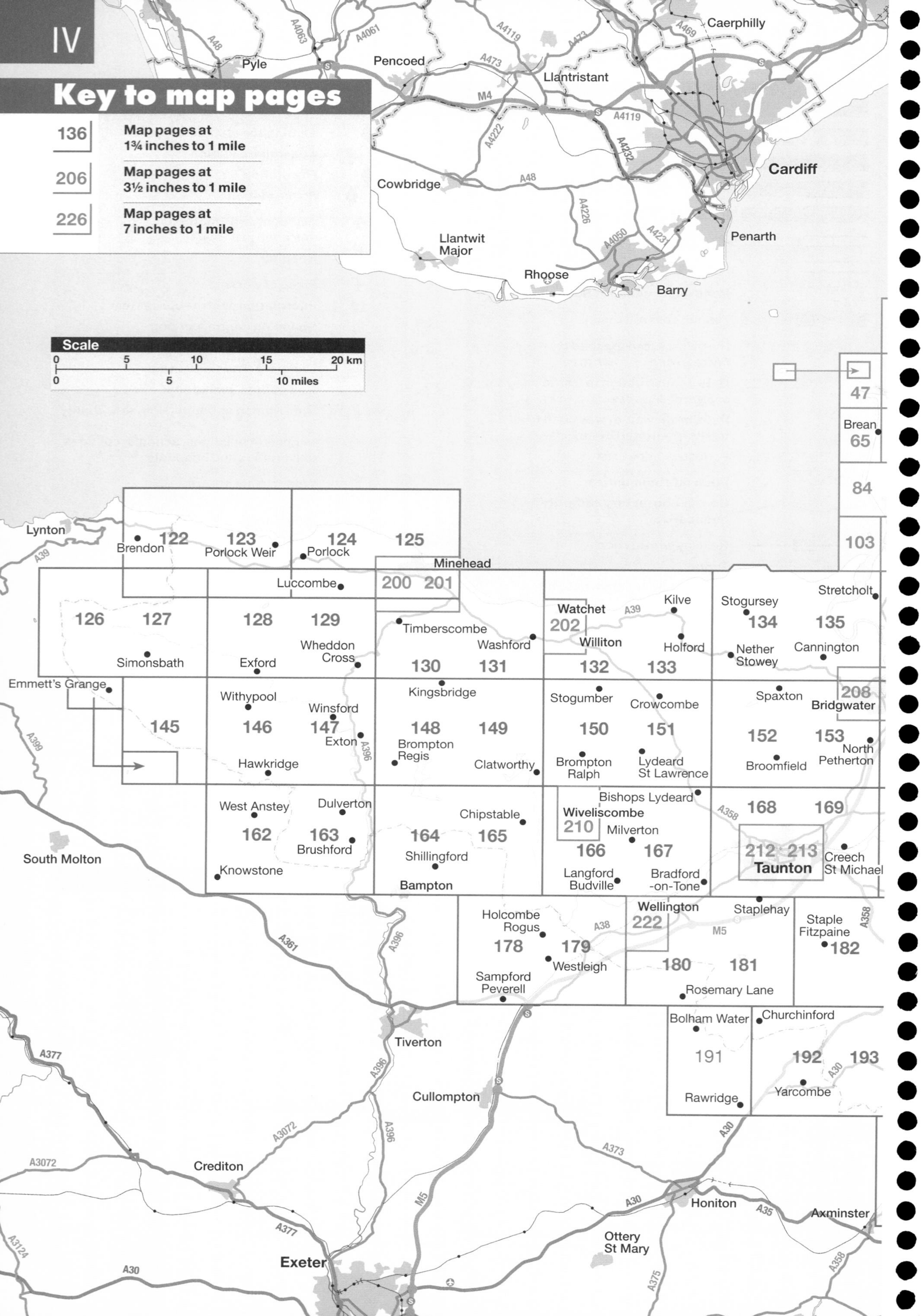

IV
Key to map pages
136 Map pages at 1¾ inches to 1 mile
206 Map pages at 3½ inches to 1 mile
226 Map pages at 7 inches to 1 mile
Scale
0 5 10 15 20 km
0 5 10 miles
Pyle
Pencoed
Caerphilly
Llantristant
Cardiff
Cowbridge
Llantwit Major
Rhoose
Barry
Penarth
A48
A4063
A4061
A4119
A473
A469
M4
A4222
A4232
A4226
A4050
A423
47
Brean
65
84
103
Lynton
A39
Brendon
122
123
Porlock Weir
124
Porlock
125
Minehead
200
201
Luccombe
126
127
Simonsbath
128
Exford
129
Wheddon Cross
Timberscombe
Washford
130
131
Watchet
202
Williton
A39
Kilve
Holford
132
133
Stogursey
134
Nether Stowey
135
Stretcholt
Cannington
Emmett's Grange
145
Withypool
146
Winsford
147
Exton
A396
Hawkridge
Kingsbridge
148
Brompton Regis
149
Clatworthy
Stogumber
150
Brompton Ralph
Crowcombe
151
Lydeard St Lawrence
Spaxton
152
Broomfield
208
Bridgwater
153
North Petherton
A399
West Anstey
162
Dulverton
163
Brushford
Knowstone
164
Shillingford
Bampton
Chipstable
165
Bishops Lydeard
Wiveliscombe
210
Milverton
166
167
Langford Budville
Bradford -on-Tone
A358
168
169
212
213
Taunton
Creech St Michael
South Molton
A361
A396
Holcombe Rogus
178
179
Westleigh
Sampford Peverell
A38
Wellington
222
Staplehay
M5
180
181
Rosemary Lane
Staple Fitzpaine
182
A358
Bolham Water
191
Rawridge
Churchinford
192
193
Yarcombe
A30
Tiverton
Cullompton
A396
A377
A3072
Crediton
A3072
A373
A30
Honiton
A35
Axminster
M5
A377
A3124
Exeter
A30
Ottery St Mary
A375
A358

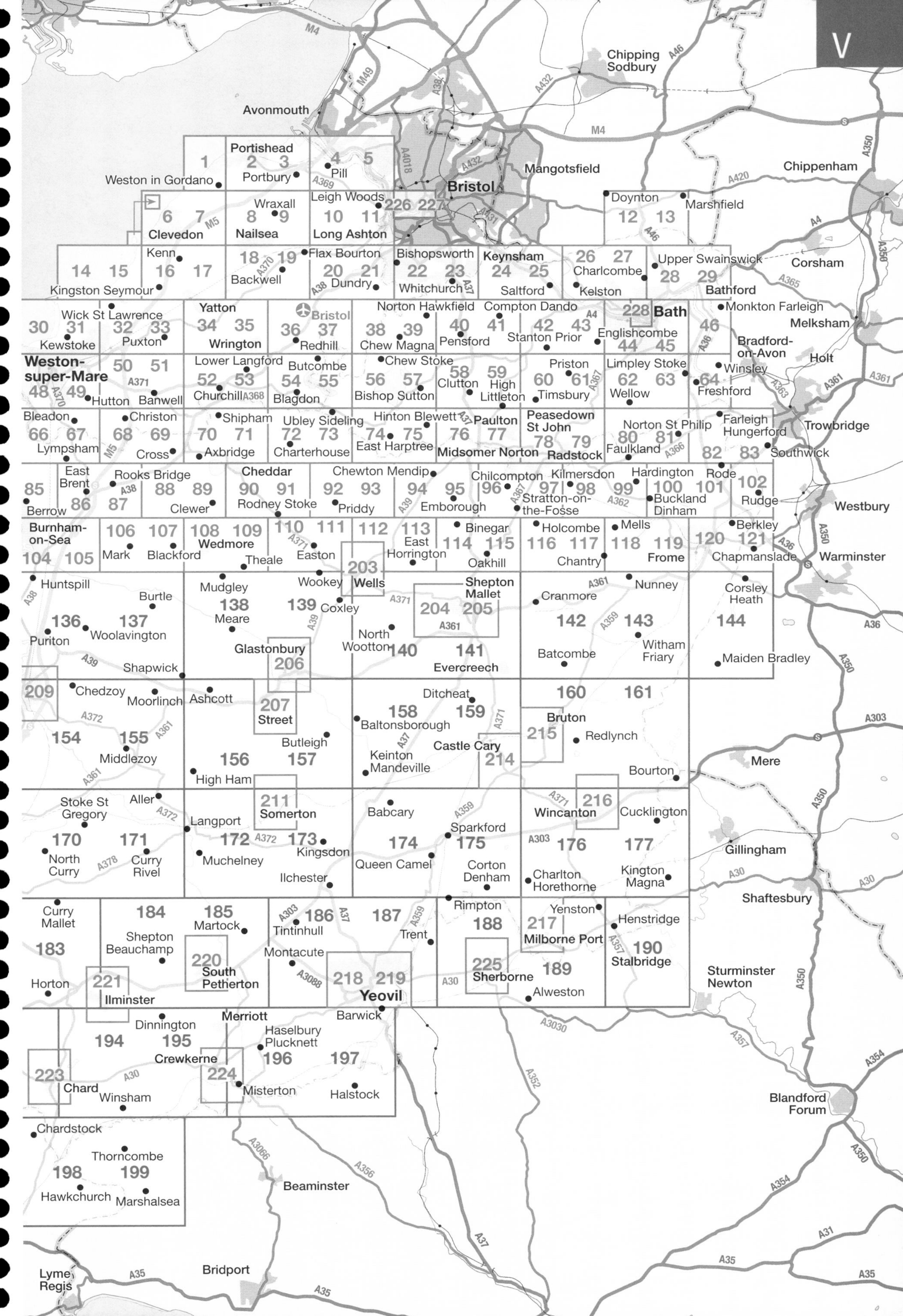

Avonmouth
Chipping Sodbury
Portishead
Portbury
Pill
Weston in Gordano
Bristol
Mangotsfield
Chippenham
Clevedon
Wraxall
Nailsea
Leigh Woods
Long Ashton
Doynton
Marshfield
Kenn
Kingston Seymour
Backwell
Flax Bourton
Dundry
Bishopsworth
Whitchurch
Keynsham
Saltford
Charlcombe
Kelston
Upper Swainswick
Bathford
Corsham
Wick St Lawrence
Kewstoke
Puxton
Yatton
Wrington
Bristol
Redhill
Norton Hawkfield
Chew Magna
Pensford
Compton Dando
Stanton Prior
Englishcombe
Bath
Monkton Farleigh
Melksham
Bradford-on-Avon
Holt
Weston-super-Mare
Hutton
Banwell
Lower Langford
Churchill
Butcombe
Blagdon
Chew Stoke
Bishop Sutton
Clutton
High Littleton
Priston
Timsbury
Limpley Stoke
Wellow
Winsley
Freshford
Bleadon
Lympsham
Christon
Cross
Shipham
Axbridge
Ubley
Sideling
Charterhouse
Hinton Blewett
East Harptree
Paulton
Midsomer Norton
Peasedown St John
Radstock
Norton St Philip
Faulkland
Farleigh Hungerford
Trowbridge
Southwick
East Brent
Berrow
Rooks Bridge
Clewer
Cheddar
Rodney Stoke
Chewton Mendip
Priddy
Emborough
Chilcompton
Stratton-on-the-Fosse
Kilmersdon
Hardington
Buckland Dinham
Rode
Rudge
Westbury
Burnham-on-Sea
Mark
Blackford
Wedmore
Theale
Easton
East Horrington
Binegar
Oakhill
Holcombe
Chantry
Mells
Frome
Berkley
Chapmanslade
Warminster
Huntspill
Burtle
Mudgley
Meare
Wookey
Wells
Coxley
Shepton Mallet
Cranmore
Nunney
Corsley Heath
Puriton
Woolavington
Glastonbury
North Wootton
Evercreech
Batcombe
Witham Friary
Maiden Bradley
Shapwick
Chedzoy
Moorlinch
Ashcott
Street
Ditcheat
Baltonsborough
Bruton
Redlynch
Middlezoy
Butleigh
Keinton Mandeville
Castle Cary
High Ham
Bourton
Mere
Stoke St Gregory
Aller
Langport
Somerton
Babcary
Sparkford
Wincanton
Cucklington
North Curry
Curry Rivel
Muchelney
Kingsdon
Ilchester
Queen Camel
Corton Denham
Charlton Horethorne
Kington Magna
Gillingham
Shaftesbury
Curry Mallet
Shepton Beauchamp
Martock
Tintinhull
Trent
Rimpton
Yenston
Henstridge
Milborne Port
Stalbridge
Horton
Ilminster
South Petherton
Montacute
Yeovil
Sherborne
Alweston
Sturminster Newton
Barwick
Merriott
Dinnington
Haselbury Plucknett
Crewkerne
Chard
Winsham
Misterton
Halstock
Blandford Forum
Chardstock
Thorncombe
Hawkchurch
Marshalsea
Beaminster
Lyme Regis
Bridport

CARDIFF
PENARTH
Lower Penarth
Newton
Avonmouth
Portishead
Redcliff Bay
Shirehampton
Weston-in-Gordano
Clapton-in-Gordano
Walton-in-Gordano
Portbury
Easton-in-Gordano
Pill
Ham Green
Abbots Leigh
Clifton
Leigh Woods
Clevedon
Tickenham
Nailsea
Wraxall
Failand
Long Ashton
Bedminster
North Somerset
Kenn
Flax Bourton
Backwell
Chelvey
Brockley
Barrow Gurney
Bishopsworth
Dundry
Kingston Seymour
Claverham
Yatton
Cleeve
West Town
Lulsgate Bottom
Upper Town
Felton
Winford
Wick St Lawrence
Sand Bay
Hewish
Puxton
Congresbury
Wrington
Kewstoke
Worle
Milton
Weston-super-Mare
Weston Bay
West Wick
Locking
Hutton
Banwell
Churchill
Sandford
Star
Langford
Burrington
Blagdon
Ubley
Redhill
Cowslip Green
Butcombe
Chew Stoke
Chew Magna
Nempnett Thrubwell
Chew Valley Lake
Blagdon Lake
Uphill
Bleadon
Christon
Winscombe
Sidcot
Shipham
Compton Martin
West Harptree
East Harptree
Brean
Loxton
Compton Bishop
Cross
Axbridge
Charterhouse
BERROW FLATS
Lympsham
Eastertown
Biddisham
Lower Weare
Weare
Cheddar
Cheddar Res.
Chewton Mendip
SEDGEMOOR SERVICES
East Brent
Rooks Bridge
Badgworth
Berrow
Brent Knoll
Stone Allerton
Chapel Allerton
Clewer
Draycott
Rodney Stoke
Priddy
Green Ore
Burnham-on-Sea
Edithmead
Cocklake
Westbury-sub-Mendip
STERT FLATS
Highbridge
Mark Causeway
Mark
West Stoughton
Blackford
Wedmore
Latcham
Easton
Wookey Hole
West Horrington
Watchfield
Westham
Theale
Wookey
Wells
Stolford
Steart
Huntspill
Bason Bridge
Heath House
Henton
Mudgley
Dinder
Lilstock
Shurton
Stockland Bristol
Stretcholt
East Huntspill
Burtle
Dulcote
Coxley
Burton
Stogursey
Otterhampton
Polsham
Worminster
Stringston
Combwich
Pawlett
Westhay
Godney
Southway
Puriton
Woolavington
Meare
North Wootton
Pilton
Nether Stowey
Fiddington
Dunball
Cossington
Chilton Polden
Edington
Rodway
Cannington
Bawdrip
Catcott
Glastonbury
Over Stowey
Somerset
Chilton Trinity
Stawell
Shapwick
Northover
West Pennard
Charlynch
Wembdon
Ashcott
Edgarley
Spaxton
Four Forks
Durleigh
Bridgwater
Chedzoy
Sutton Mallet
Moorlinch
Greinton
Pedwell
Walton
Overleigh
Street
West Bradley
Parbrook
Enmore
Lower Aisholt
BRIDGWATER SERVICES
Westonzoyland
Butleigh Wootton
Ham Street
Baltonsborough
Goathurst
West Bagborough
Courtway
North Petherton
Huntworth
Butleigh
Southwood
Compton Dundon
Dundon
Barton St David
West Lydford
East Lydford
East Combe
Cothelstone
Broomfield
Northmoor Green or Moorland
Middlezoy
Henley
Othery
Pathe
High Ham
Littleton
Kingweston
Cushuish
North Newton
Keinton Mandeville
Lydford-on-Fosse
Thurloxton
Bishops Lydeard
Fulford
Pickney
Kingston St Mary
Burrow-bridge
Stathe
Aller
Low Ham
Somerton
Charlton Adam
Babcary
Hedging
Lyng
Athelney
Pitney
Nailsbourne
West Monkton
Charlton Mackerell
South Barrow
Cheddon Fitzpaine
Monkton Heathfield
Durston
West Lyng
Creech Heathfield
Stoke St Gregory
Heathfield
Staplegrove
Bathpool
North End
Meare Green
Langport
Cary Fitzpaine
Norton Fitzwarren
Creech St Michael
Knapp
Hurst Episcopi
Long Sutton
Kingsdon
Bishop's Hull
Taunton
Ruishton
North Curry
Curry Rivel
Drayton
Muchelney
Podimore
Bradford-on-Tone
Thornfalcon
Fivehead
Northover
Bridgehampton
Henlade
Long Load
Ilchester
Yeovilton
Chilton Cantelo
Trull
Stoke St Mary
Staplehay
Orchard Portman
Wrantage
Curry Mallet
Isle Brewers
Isle Abbotts
Stapleton
Limington
West Buckland
TAUNTON DEANE SERVICES
Thurlbear
West Hatch
Hatch Beauchamp
Hambridge
Kingsbury Episcopi
Ash
Ashington
Beercrocombe
Coat
Tintinhull
Pitminster
Corfe
Hatch Green
Westport
West Lambrook
East Lambrook
Martock
Yeovil Marsh
Mudford
Angersleigh
Blagdon Hill
Staple Fitzpaine
Puckington
Chilthorne Domer
Bickenhall
Ilton
Barrington
South Petherton
Bower Hinton
Hurst
Stoke sub Hamdon
Ashill
Curland
STAPLE HILL
Stocklinch
Shepton Beauchamp
Montacute
Preston Plucknett
Yeovil
Windmill Hill
Broadway
Ashwell
Seavington St Michael
Norton sub Hamdon
Over Stratton
Odcombe
Clayhidon
Churchstanton
Horton
Ilminster
Brympton
Fyfett
Seavington St Mary
Lopen
Chiselborough
West Coker
Buckland St Mary
Donyatt
West Chinnock
North Coker
Barwick
Stapley
Churchinford
Crock Street
Kingstone
Dinnington
Stoford

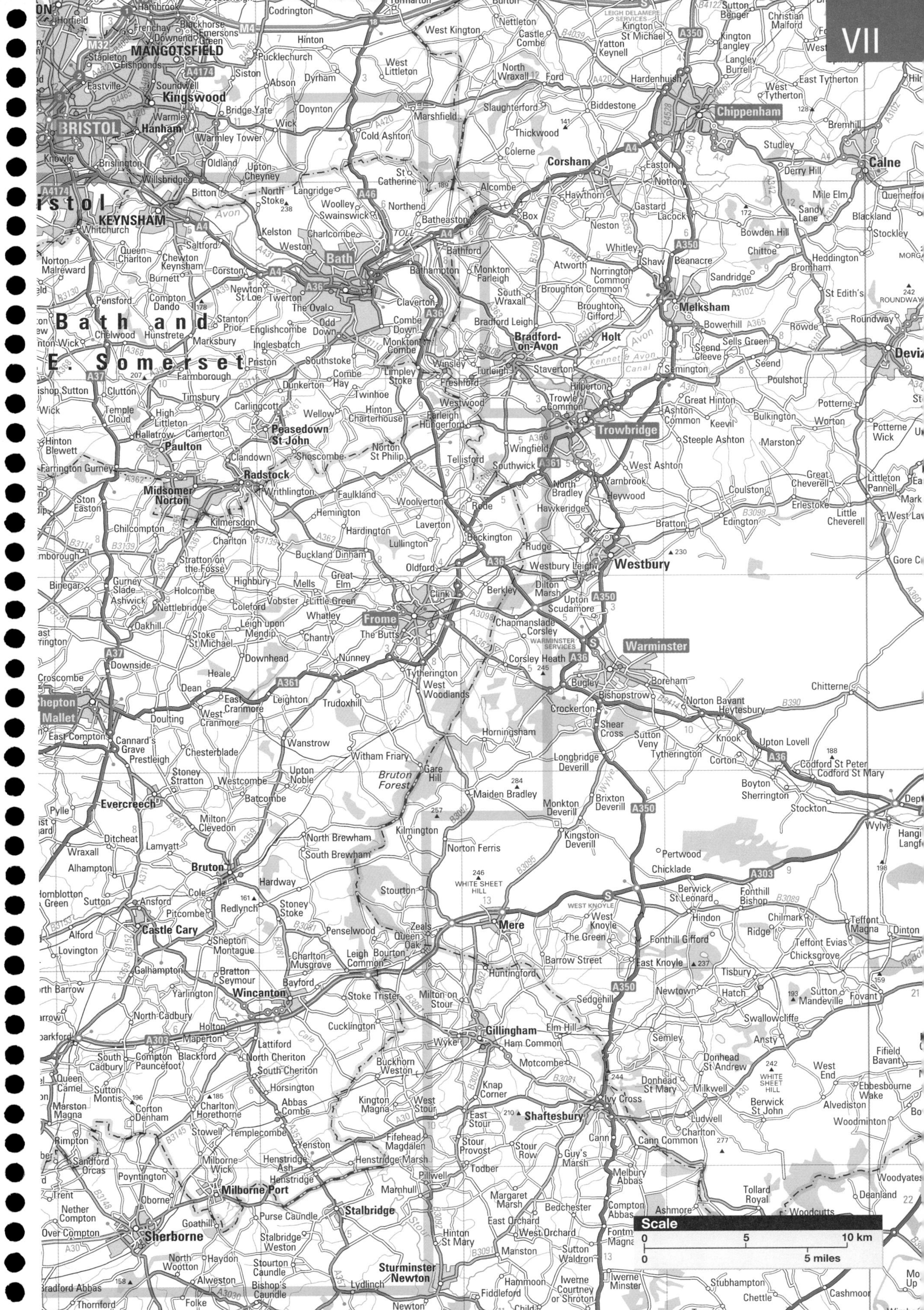
VII
Hambrook
Codrington
Tormarton
Burton
Sutton Benger
Christian Malford
Horfield
Frenchay
Blackhorse
Emersons Green
Downend
M32
M4
Stapleton
Fishponds
MANGOTSFIELD
Pucklechurch
Hinton
West Kington
Nettleton
Castle Combe
Yatton Keynell
LEIGH DELAMERE SERVICES
Kington St Michael
Kington Langley
Langley Burrell
A350
Siston
A4174
Eastville
Soundwell
Kingswood
Abson
Dyrham
West Littleton
North Wraxall
Ford
Hardenhuish
East Tytherton
West Tytherton
Chippenham
BRISTOL
Hanham
Warmley
Bridge Yate
Doynton
Wick
Marshfield
Slaughterford
Biddestone
Bremhill
Warmley Tower
Cold Ashton
Thickwood
Colerne
Studley
Knowle
Brislington
Oldland
Upton Cheyney
St Catherine
Corsham
Easton
Derry Hill
Calne
Willsbridge
Notton
A4174
Bitton
North Stoke
Langridge
Woolley
A46
Alcombe
Hawthorn
Mile Elm
Quemerford
Bristol
KEYNSHAM
Swainswick
Northend
Batheaston
Box
Gastard
Lacock
Sandy Lane
Blackland
Avon
Whitchurch
Kelston
Charlcombe
TOLL
A4
Neston
Bowden Hill
Stockley
Queen Charlton
Saltford
Weston
Bathford
Whitley
Shaw
Beanacre
Chittoe
Heddington
Norton Malreward
Chewton Keynsham
Corston
Bath
Bathampton
Monkton Farleigh
Atworth
Norrington Common
Bromham
Burnett
Newton St Loe
Twerton
A36
Sandridge
Pensford
Compton Dando
The Oval
Claverton
South Wraxall
Broughton Common
Melksham
St Edith's
Combe Down
Odd Down
Broughton Gifford
Roundway
Bath and
Stanton Prior
Englishcombe
Bradford Leigh
Bowerhill
Rowde
Chelwood
Hunstrete
Marksbury
Inglesbatch
Monkton Combe
Bradford-on-Avon
Holt
Sells Green
E. Somerset
Priston
Southstoke
Winsley
Turleigh
Kennet & Avon Canal
Seend Cleeve
Seend
Devizes
A37
Farmborough
Combe Hay
Limpley Stoke
Freshford
Staverton
Semington
Poulshot
Bishop Sutton
Clutton
Timsbury
Dunkerton
Twinhoe
Hilperton
Trowle Common
Great Hinton
Potterne
Temple Cloud
High Littleton
Carlingcott
Wellow
Hinton Charterhouse
Farleigh Hungerford
Westwood
Ashton Common
Keevil
Bulkington
Worton
Potterne Wick
Hinton Blewett
Hallatrow
Camerton
Peasedown St John
Paulton
Norton St Philip
Trowbridge
Steeple Ashton
Marston
Clandown
Shoscombe
Tellisford
Wingfield
West Ashton
Farrington Gurney
Radstock
Southwick
A361
Great Cheverell
Littleton Pannell
Midsomer Norton
Writhlington
Faulkland
North Bradley
Yarnbrook
Heywood
Coulston
Ston Easton
Woolverton
Rode
Hawkeridge
Erlestoke
Little Cheverell
Hemington
Kilmersdon
Laverton
Bratton
Edington
Chilcompton
Hardington
Beckington
Charlton
Lullington
Westbury
Stratton on the Fosse
Buckland Dinham
Rudge
Gore Cross
Oldford
Westbury Leigh
Binegar
Gurney Slade
Holcombe
Highbury
Mells
Great Elm
Berkley
Dilton Marsh
Ashwick
Nettlebridge
Coleford
Vobster
Little Green
Clink
Upton Scudamore
Whatley
Frome
Chapmanslade
Corsley
Oakhill
Leigh upon Mendip
Stoke St Michael
Chantry
The Butts
WARMINSTER SERVICES
Warminster
Downhead
Nunney
Corsley Heath
Downside
Heale
Tytherington
Bugley
Croscombe
Dean
A361
West Woodlands
Boreham
Chitterne
Shepton Mallet
East Cranmore
Leighton
Bishopstrow
Norton Bavant
Heytesbury
Doulting
West Cranmore
Trudoxhill
Crockerton
B390
East Compton
Cannard's Grave
Shear Cross
Sutton Veny
Knook
Upton Lovell
Horningsham
Prestleigh
Chesterblade
Wanstrow
Tytherington
Corton
Witham Friary
Longbridge Deverill
Codford St Peter
Codford St Mary
Stoney Stratton
Westcombe
Upton Noble
Gare Hill
Bruton Forest
Boyton
Sherrington
Evercreech
Batcombe
Maiden Bradley
Brixton Deverill
Pylle
Milton Clevedon
Monkton Deverill
Stockton
Wylye
Ditcheat
North Brewham
Kilmington
Kingston Deverill
Lamyatt
South Brewham
Norton Ferris
Pertwood
Wraxall
Alhampton
Bruton
Chicklade
Hardway
WHITE SHEET HILL
A303
Homblotton Green
Sutton
Cole
Stourton
Berwick St Leonard
Fonthill Bishop
Ansford
Pitcombe
Redlynch
Stoney Stoke
WEST KNOYLE
West Knoyle
Chilmark
Teffont Magna
Dinton
Alford
Castle Cary
Zeals
Mere
Hindon
Ridge
Lovington
Shepton Montague
Penselwood
Queen Oak
The Green
Fonthill Gifford
Teffont Evias
Charlton Musgrove
Leigh Common
Bourton
Barrow Street
Chicksgrove
Galhampton
Bratton Seymour
East Knoyle
Tisbury
Bayford
Huntingford
Newtown
Hatch
Sutton Mandeville
Fovant
North Barrow
Yarlington
Wincanton
Stoke Trister
Milton on Stour
Sedgehill
A350
North Cadbury
Cucklington
Swallowcliffe
Holton
Gillingham
Elm Hill
Ansty
Sparkford
A303
Maperton
Lattiford
Wyke
Ham Common
Semley
Fifield Bavant
South Cadbury
Compton Pauncefoot
Blackford
North Cheriton
Buckhorn Weston
Motcombe
Donhead St Andrew
West End
Queen Camel
South Cheriton
Knap Corner
Donhead St Mary
Milkwell
WHITE SHEET HILL
Ebbesbourne Wake
Sutton Montis
Horsington
Ivy Cross
Marston Magna
Charlton Horethorne
Corton Denham
Abbas Combe
Kington Magna
West Stour
Berwick St John
Alvediston
East Stour
Shaftesbury
Ludwell
Woodminton
Stowell
Templecombe
Charlton
Rimpton
Fifehead Magdalen
Stour Provost
Cann
Cann Common
Yenston
Stour Row
Sandford Orcas
Milborne Wick
Henstridge Ash
Henstridge Marsh
Guy's Marsh
Todber
Henstridge
Pillwell
Melbury Abbas
Woodyates
Poyntington
Marnhull
Trent
Milborne Port
Tollard Royal
Deanland
Oborne
Margaret Marsh
Nether Compton
Compton Abbas
Ashmore
Woodcutts
Goathill
Purse Caundle
Stalbridge
Bedchester
East Orchard
Over Compton
Scale
0
5
10 km
0
5 miles
Sherborne
Stalbridge Weston
Hinton St Mary
West Orchard
Fontmell Magna
North Wootton
Haydon
Stourton Caundle
Manston
Sutton Waldron
Sturminster Newton
Bradford Abbas
Alweston
Bishop's Caundle
Lydlinch
Hammoon
Iwerne Courtney or Shroton
Iwerne Minster
Stubhampton
Chettle
Cashmoor
Thornford
Folke
Fiddleford
Newton
Child

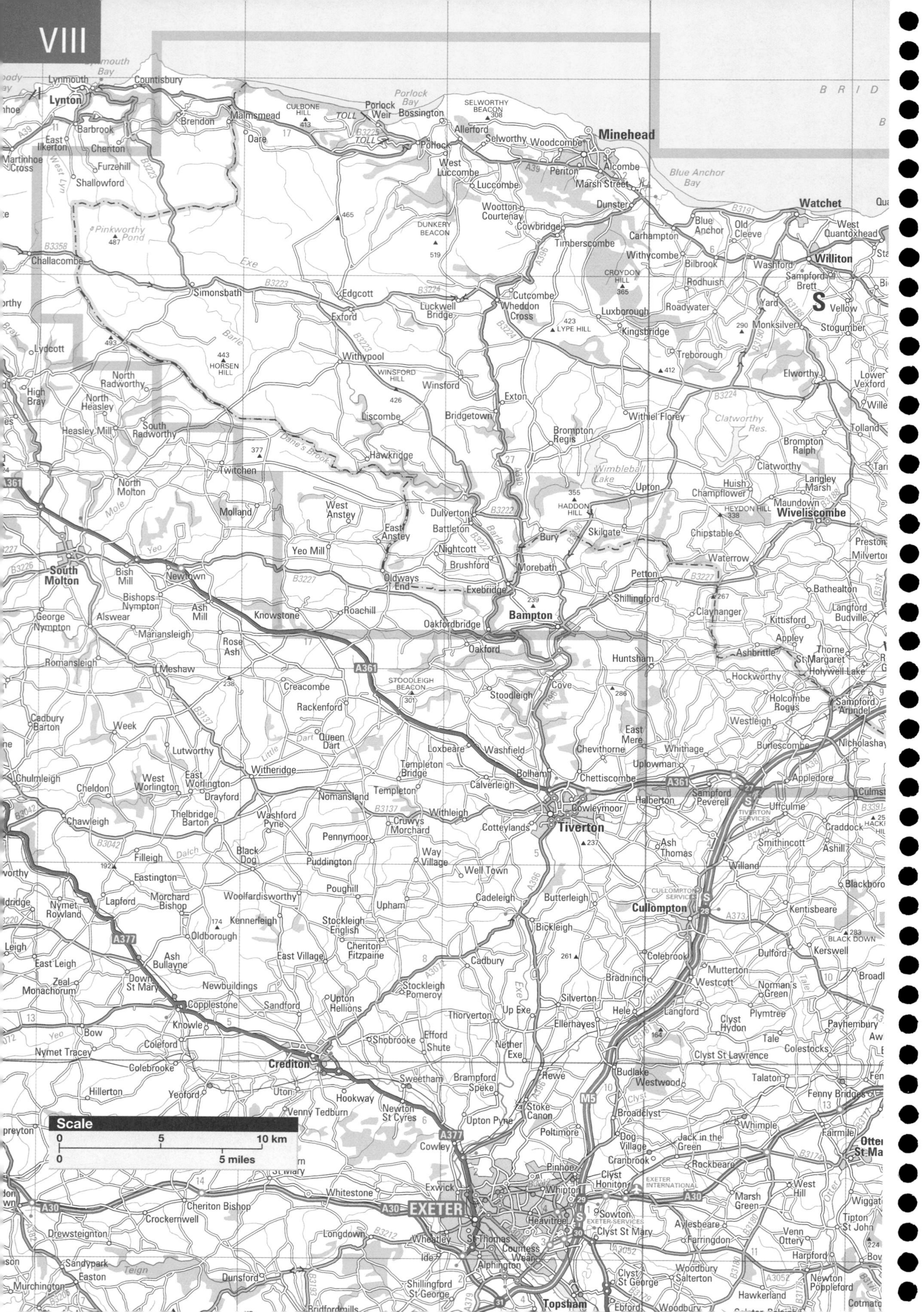
Lynmouth
Lynton
Countisbury
Barbrook
East Ilkerton
Cheriton
Martinhoe Cross
Furzehill
Shallowford
Brendon
Malmsmead
Oare
CULBONE HILL
413
Porlock Bay
Porlock Weir
Bossington
TOLL
Porlock
SELWORTHY BEACON
308
Allerford
Selworthy
Woodcombe
Minehead
West Luccombe
Luccombe
Periton
Alcombe
Marsh Street
Blue Anchor Bay
Dunster
Wootton Courtenay
Cowbridge
DUNKERY BEACON
519
465
Timberscombe
Carhampton
Blue Anchor
Old Cleeve
Watchet
West Quantoxhead
Withycombe
Bilbrook
Washford
Williton
Rodhuish
Sampford Brett
CROYDON HILL
365
Pinkworthy Pond
487
Challacombe
Exe
Simonsbath
B3223
Edgcott
B3224
Luckwell Bridge
Cutcombe
Wheddon Cross
Luxborough
Roadwater
Yard
Vellow
Stogumber
Monksilver
290
423
LYPE HILL
Kingsbridge
Treborough
412
Exford
Lydcott
493
Barle
443
HORSEN HILL
Withypool
WINSFORD HILL
Winsford
426
Elworthy
Lower Vexford
High Bray
North Radworthy
North Heasley
Heasley Mill
South Radworthy
Liscombe
Bridgetown
Exton
Withiel Florey
B3224
Clatworthy Res.
Tolland
Brompton Regis
Brompton Ralph
377
Dane's Brook
Hawkridge
Twitchen
North Molton
Wimbleball Lake
Clatworthy
Huish Champflower
Langley Marsh
Maundown
Upton
355
HADDON HILL
HEYDON HILL
338
Wiveliscombe
Mole
Molland
West Anstey
Dulverton
Battleton
B3222
East Anstey
Bury
Skilgate
Chipstable
Preston
Milverton
South Molton
Bish Mill
Newtown
Yeo
Yeo Mill
Nightcott
Brushford
Morebath
Waterrow
Petton
B3227
Bathealton
Oldways End
Exebridge
267
239
Shillingford
Bishops Nympton
Ash Mill
Knowstone
Roachill
Bampton
Clayhanger
Langford Budville
Kittisford
George Nympton
Alswear
Mariansleigh
Rose Ash
Oakfordbridge
Oakford
Appley
Thorne St Margaret
Huntsham
Ashbrittle
Holywell Lake
Romansleigh
Meshaw
238
A361
STOODLEIGH BEACON
301
Creacombe
Cove
286
Hockworthy
Stoodleigh
Holcombe Rogus
Sampford Arundel
Rackenford
Cadbury Barton
Week
Queen Dart
Little Dart
Westleigh
East Mere
Loxbeare
Washfield
Chevithorne
Whitnage
Burlescombe
Nicholashayne
Lutworthy
Templeton Bridge
Uplowman
Witheridge
Bolham
Chettiscombe
Appledore
Chulmleigh
Cheldon
West Worlington
East Worlington
Calverleigh
Drayford
Templeton
Nomansland
Halberton
Sampford Peverell
Cowleymoor
TIVERTON SERVICES
Uffculme
Chawleigh
Thelbridge Barton
Washford Pyne
B3137
Cruwys Morchard
Withleigh
Cotteylands
Tiverton
237
Craddock
Smithincott
Ashill
B3042
Pennymoor
Way Village
Ash Thomas
Dalch
Black Dog
Filleigh
192
Puddington
Well Town
Willand
Eastington
Poughill
Blackborough
Nymet Rowland
Lapford
Morchard Bishop
Woolfardisworthy
Upham
Cadeleigh
Butterleigh
CULLOMPTON SERVICES
Cullompton
Kentisbeare
A373
174
Kennerleigh
Stockleigh English
Bickleigh
Oldborough
A377
Cheriton Fitzpaine
283
BLACK DOWN
Leigh
East Leigh
Ash Bullayne
East Village
Cadbury
261
Colebrook
Dulford
Kerswell
Zeal Monachorum
Down St Mary
Mutterton
Westcott
Newbuildings
Stockleigh Pomeroy
Bradninch
Norman's Green
Broadhembury
Copplestone
Sandford
Upton Hellions
Silverton
Culm
Hele
Langford
Plymtree
Knowle
Thorverton
Up Exe
Ellerhayes
Clyst Hydon
Payhembury
Bow
Yeo
Coleford
Shobrooke
Efford
Shute
Nether Exe
164
Tale
Colestocks
Nymet Tracey
Crediton
Clyst St Lawrence
Golebrooke
Rewe
Budlake
Talaton
Sweetham
Brampford Speke
Westwood
Hillerton
Yeoford
Uton
Hookway
Fenny Bridges
Newton St Cyres
M5
Stoke Canon
Clyst
Venny Tedburn
Broadclyst
Scale
0
5
10 km
5 miles
Upton Pyne
Whimple
A377
Poltimore
Dog Village
Jack in the Green
Fairmile
Cowley
Cranbrook
Rockbeare
Pinhoe
Clyst Honiton
EXETER INTERNATIONAL
West Hill
Exwick
Whipton
A30
Cheriton Bishop
Whitestone
EXETER
Sowton
EXETER SERVICES
Marsh Green
Wiggaton
Crockernwell
Heavitree
Aylesbeare
Tipton St John
Drewsteignton
Longdown
B3212
Wheatley
St Thomas
Clyst St Mary
Farringdon
Venn Ottery
Countess Wear
Ide
Alphington
Harpford
Sandypark
Teign
Easton
Dunsford
Clyst St George
Woodbury Salterton
Newton Poppleford
Murchington
Shillingford St George
Hawkerland
Topsham
Ebford
Woodbury
Cotmaton
Bridfordmills

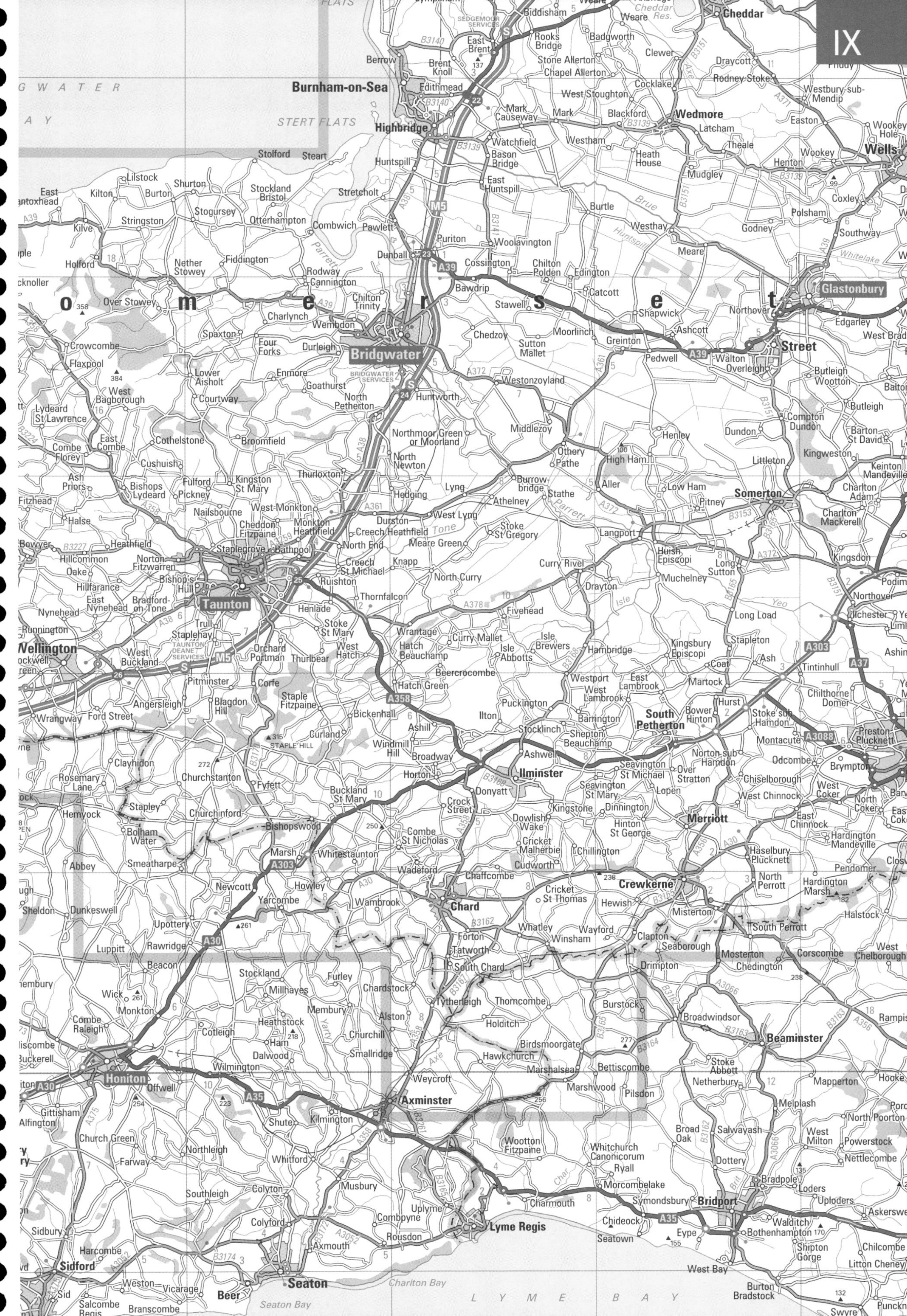

IX
Cheddar
Biddisham
Weare
Rooks Bridge
Badgworth
East Brent
Berrow
Brent Knoll
Stone Allerton
Chapel Allerton
Clewer
Draycott
Rodney Stoke
Burnham-on-Sea
Edithmead
Cocklake
West Stoughton
Westbury-sub-Mendip
Mark Causeway
Mark
Blackford
Wedmore
Easton
Wookey Hole
Highbridge
Watchfield
Westham
Latcham
Theale
Wookey
Wells
STERT FLATS
Stolford
Steart
Huntspill
Bason Bridge
Heath House
Henton
Mudgley
East Huntspill
Lilstock
Kilton
Burton
Shurton
Stockland Bristol
Stretcholt
Coxley
Polsham
Burtle
Stringston
Stogursey
Otterhampton
Combwich
Pawlett
Westhay
Godney
Southway
Kilve
Puriton
Woolavington
Meare
Holford
Nether Stowey
Fiddington
Dunball
Rodway
Cannington
Cossington
Chilton Polden
Edington
Bawdrip
Catcott
Glastonbury
Over Stowey
Chilton Trinity
Charlynch
Stawell
Shapwick
Northover
Wembdon
Spaxton
Edgarley
Four Forks
Durleigh
Chedzoy
Moorlinch
Ashcott
Bridgwater
Sutton Mallet
Greinton
Pedwell
Walton
Overleigh
Street
Crowcombe
Flaxpool
Lower Aisholt
Enmore
Goathurst
Westonzoyland
Butleigh Wootton
West Bagborough
Courtway
North Petherton
Huntworth
Butleigh
Lydeard St Lawrence
Northmoor Green or Moorland
Middlezoy
Compton Dundon
Dundon
Henley
Barton St David
Combe Florey
East Combe
Cothelstone
Broomfield
Othery
Pathe
High Ham
Kingweston
Cushuish
North Newton
Littleton
Keinton Mandeville
Ash Priors
Bishops Lydeard
Fulford
Pickney
Kingston St Mary
Thurloxton
Burrow-bridge
Lyng
Stathe
Aller
Low Ham
Charlton Adam
Fitzhead
Hedging
Athelney
Somerton
Nailsbourne
West Monkton
Pitney
Charlton Mackerell
Halse
Cheddon Fitzpaine
Monkton Heathfield
Durston
West Lyng
Creech Heathfield
Stoke St Gregory
Langport
Bowyer
Heathfield
Staplegrove
Bathpool
North End
Meare Green
Huish Episcopi
Hillcommon
Norton Fitzwarren
Creech St Michael
Knapp
Curry Rivel
Long Sutton
Kingsdon
Oake
Bishop's Hull
North Curry
Hillfarance
Ruishton
Drayton
Muchelney
Podimore
Bradford-on-Tone
East Nynehead
Nynehead
Taunton
Thornfalcon
Henlade
Fivehead
Northover
Ilchester
Long Load
Runnington
Trull
Stoke St Mary
Wrantage
Curry Mallet
Isle Brewers
Wellington
Staplehay
West Buckland
Orchard Portman
Thurlbear
West Hatch
Hatch Beauchamp
Isle Abbotts
Hambridge
Kingsbury Episcopi
Stapleton
Ash
Ashington
Beercrocombe
Coat
Tintinhull
Pitminster
Corfe
Hatch Green
Westport
West Lambrook
East Lambrook
Martock
Angersleigh
Blagdon Hill
Staple Fitzpaine
Puckington
Chilthorne Domer
Wrangway
Ford Street
Bickenhall
Ilton
Barrington
South Petherton
Bower Hinton
Hurst
Stoke sub Hamdon
Ashill
Curland
Stocklinch
Shepton Beauchamp
Montacute
Preston Plucknett
STAPLE HILL
Windmill Hill
Broadway
Ashwell
Norton sub Hamdon
Odcombe
Brympton
Clayhidon
Horton
Ilminster
Seavington St Michael
Over Stratton
Rosemary Lane
Churchstanton
Fyfett
Buckland St Mary
Donyatt
Seavington St Mary
Lopen
Chiselborough
West Coker
Stapley
Crock Street
Kingstone
Dinnington
West Chinnock
North Coker
East Coker
Hemyock
Churchinford
Bishopswood
Combe St Nicholas
Dowlish Wake
Hinton St George
Merriott
East Chinnock
Bolham Water
Cricket Malherbie
Chillington
Hardington Mandeville
Abbey
Smeatharpe
Marsh
Whitestaunton
Cudworth
Haselbury Plucknett
Pendomer
Closworth
Wadeford
Chaffcombe
Newcott
Howley
Cricket St Thomas
Crewkerne
North Perrott
Hardington Marsh
Yarcombe
Wambrook
Chard
Hewish
Sheldon
Dunkeswell
Misterton
Halstock
Upottery
Whatley
Wayford
Forton
Winsham
Clapton
South Perrott
Luppitt
Rawridge
Tatworth
Seaborough
Mosterton
Corscombe
West Chelbourgh
Beacon
South Chard
Drimpton
Chedington
Stockland
Furley
Chardstock
Millhayes
Wick
Tytherleigh
Thorncombe
Burstock
Broadwindsor
Rampisham
Membury
Monkton
Alston
Holditch
Combe Raleigh
Cotleigh
Heathstock
Churchill
Beaminster
Ham
Birdsmoorgate
Buckerell
Dalwood
Smallridge
Hawkchurch
Stoke Abbott
Wilmington
Marshalsea
Bettiscombe
Honiton
Weycroft
Netherbury
Mapperton
Hooke
Offwell
Marshwood
Pilsdon
Axminster
Melplash
Gittisham
Shute
Kilmington
North Poorton
Alfington
Broad Oak
Salwayash
Church Green
Wootton Fitzpaine
Whitchurch Canonicorum
West Milton
Powerstock
Northleigh
Farway
Whitford
Ryall
Dottery
Nettlecombe
Bradpole
Southleigh
Colyton
Musbury
Morcombelake
Loders
Charmouth
Symondsbury
Bridport
Uploders
Uplyme
Askerswell
Sidbury
Colyford
Combpyne
Lyme Regis
Chideock
Eype
Walditch
Bothenhampton
Seatown
Harcombe
Rousdon
Axmouth
Shipton Gorge
Chilcombe
Sidford
Litton Cheney
West Bay
Weston
Vicarage
Beer
Seaton
Charlton Bay
Burton Bradstock
Sid
Salcombe Regis
Branscombe
Seaton Bay
LYME BAY
Swyre
Puncknowle
Somerset

Major administrative and Postcode boundaries

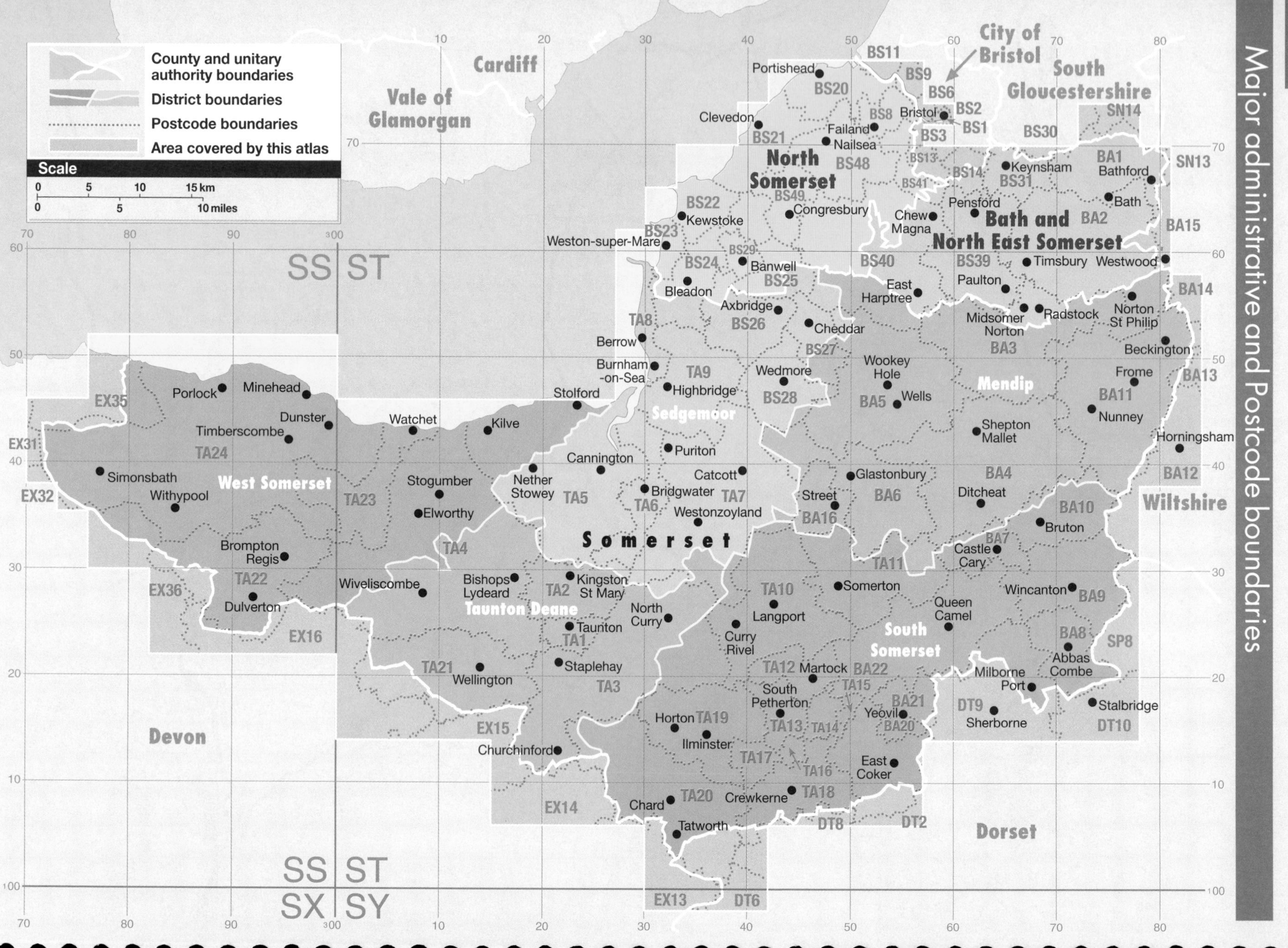
County and unitary authority boundaries
District boundaries
Postcode boundaries
Area covered by this atlas
Scale
0 5 10 15 km
0 5 10 miles
City of Bristol
South Gloucestershire
Bath and North East Somerset
North Somerset
Mendip
Sedgemoor
Somerset
South Somerset
Taunton Deane
West Somerset
Wiltshire
Dorset
Devon
Cardiff
Vale of Glamorgan
SS
ST
SX
SY
Portishead
Clevedon
Nailsea
Failand
Bristol
Keynsham
Bathford
Bath
Pensford
Chew Magna
Congresbury
Kewstoke
Weston-super-Mare
Bleadon
Banwell
Axbridge
Cheddar
East Harptree
Paulton
Midsomer Norton
Radstock
Timsbury
Westwood
Norton St Philip
Beckington
Frome
Nunney
Horningsham
Shepton Mallet
Wookey Hole
Wells
Wedmore
Glastonbury
Street
Ditcheat
Castle Cary
Bruton
Wincanton
Abbas Combe
Stalbridge
Milborne Port
Sherborne
Queen Camel
Somerton
Yeovil
East Coker
Martock
South Petherton
Crewkerne
Langport
Curry Rivel
Ilminster
Horton
Chard
Tatworth
Berrow
Burnham-on-Sea
Highbridge
Puriton
Catcott
Bridgwater
Westonzoyland
Cannington
Stolford
North Curry
Kingston St Mary
Taunton
Staplehay
Churchinford
Nether Stowey
Kilve
Bishops Lydeard
Wellington
Watchet
Stogumber
Elworthy
Wiveliscombe
Minehead
Dunster
Timberscombe
Porlock
Brompton Regis
Dulverton
Withypool
Simonsbath
BS1
BS2
BS3
BS6
BS8
BS9
BS11
BS13
BS14
BS20
BS21
BS22
BS23
BS24
BS25
BS26
BS27
BS28
BS29
BS30
BS31
BS39
BS40
BS41
BS48
BS49
BA1
BA2
BA3
BA4
BA5
BA6
BA7
BA8
BA9
BA10
BA11
BA12
BA13
BA14
BA15
BA16
BA20
BA21
BA22
SN13
SN14
SP8
DT2
DT6
DT8
DT9
DT10
TA1
TA2
TA3
TA4
TA5
TA6
TA7
TA8
TA9
TA10
TA11
TA12
TA13
TA14
TA15
TA16
TA17
TA18
TA19
TA20
TA21
TA22
TA23
TA24
EX13
EX14
EX15
EX16
EX31
EX32
EX35
EX36

A B C D E F

8

7

77

6

Black
Nore

BLACK NORE
POINT

SEAVIEW RD
NICHOL'S RD

NORWOOD

SEVERNMEADE

FEDDEN
VILLAGE

CHAPLAINS
WOOD

BEECHWOOD DR
BEECHWOOD RD

GLENWOOD RISE
MORE PARK DR
IVY CL
RIVER CL

DEVONSHIRE DR
SOMERSET RD

KINGSWAY

Brackenwood
Gdns

BRACKENWOOD GDNS

DENNY VIEW

HAWTHORN

MEADOWS

BEDWIN CL

MONMOUTH CL
NEWPORT CL

MERLIN PK

5

76

SAGE CL
WOODSIDE
CONST

CREST
HEIGHTS

HILLCREST RD

QUEENS

QUEENS
WAY

SEAVIEW RD

KING RD

LINDY CL

Mast

4

Hang
Rock

Redcliff
Bay

Redcliffe
Bay

HILLSIDE RD

HALLIWELL RD

LITTLE HALL

NEWHAVEN PL

ST AUGUSTINE'S CL

QUEENS RD

DOWN RD

HILL GAY CL

RANGEWAYS

HARKWAY

GAUNT'S CL

Mast

WATERSIDE PK

NEWHAVEN RD

PEMBROKE RD

REDCLIFFE CL

CEDARHURST RD

HOMESTEAD

BADGER RISE

WEATHERLEY DR

Police
HQ

NORTHFIELD RD

CHARLCOMBE RISE

CHESLEFIELD
CL

CHESLE

HIGHFIELD DR

BRICK END

NIGHTINGALE RISE

VALLEY CL

BRANSCOMBE
WLK

Nightingale
Valley

3

Charlcombe
Bay

Charlcombe
Wood

Mast

PH

CHARLCOMBE
PK

VALLEY
RD

BLACKBERRY LA

PORTISHEAD

75

Weston
Down

BS20

Quarry

Seven
Acre
Wood

2

Walton
Bay

The
Ripple

Black
Strip

Weston
Lodge

The
Conygar

HILL LA

THE CLOSE

SPRIGG DR
THE TYNINGS

THE MEADOW

B3124

Culver
Cliff

SKYLARK
AVE
WALTON BAY
HOUSE PARK
HOMES

TWO ACRES
CVN PK

BS21

Weston
Wood

SILVER ST

CADBURY LA
WESTON DRO

PH

1

Pigeon House
Bay

COAST
CVN PK

KINGFISHER
WAY

Farley

Signal
Station

Walton
Down

Common Hill
Wood

CLEVEDON ROAD

Weston in
Gordano

Cadbury
Halt

WALTON ST

Canon's
Wood

B3124

74

42 A 43 B C 43 D 44 E F

1

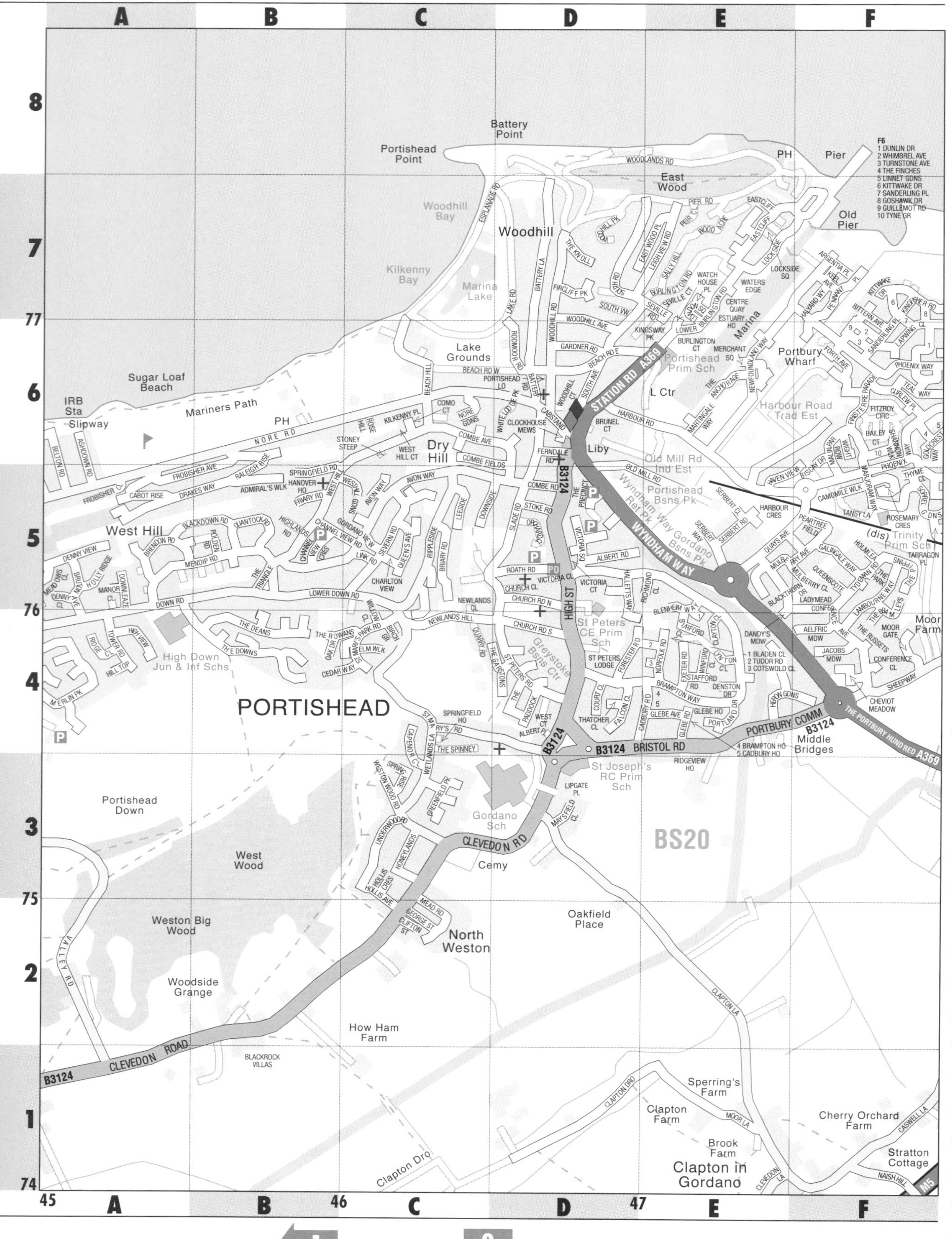

A
B
C
D
E
F
8
7
77
6
5
76
4
3
75
2
1
74
45
46
47
Battery Point
Portishead Point
WOODLANDS RD
East Wood
PH
Pier
Old Pier
F6
1 DUNLIN DR
2 WHIMBREL AVE
3 TURNSTONE AVE
4 THE FINCHES
5 LINNET GDNS
6 KITTWAKE DR
7 SANDERLING PL
8 GOSHAWK DR
9 GUILLEMOT RD
10 TYNE GR
Woodhill Bay
Woodhill
ESPLANADE RD
Kilkenny Bay
Marina Lake
BATTERY LA
LAKE RD
WOODHILL RD
THE KNOLL
FIRCLIFF PK
SOUTH VW
WOODHILL AVE
GARDNER RD
RODMOOR RD
Lake Grounds
BEACH RD W
BEACH RD E
PORTISHEAD LO
LOCKSIDE SQ
WATCH HOUSE PL
WATERS EDGE
CENTRE QUAY
ESTUARY HO
KINGSWAY PK
BURLINGTON CT
MERCHANT SQ
Marina
Portishead Prim Sch
STATION RD A369
L Ctr
Portbury Wharf
Harbour Road Trad Est
Sugar Loaf Beach
IRB Sta
Slipway
Mariners Path
PH
NORE RD
BEACH HILL
KILKENNY PL
COMO CT
NORE GDNS
CLOCKHOUSE MEWS
CABSTAND
HARBOUR RD
BRUNEL CT
Liby
Old Mill Rd Ind Est
OLD MILL RD
Dry Hill
COMBE AVE
COMBE FIELDS
STONEY STEEP
WEST HILL CT
FROBISHER AVE
RALEIGH RISE
SPRINGFIELD RD
HANOVER HO
FRIARY RD
ADMIRAL'S WLK
DRAKES WAY
CABOT RISE
AVON WAY
FERNDALE RD
B3124
COMBE RD
STOKE RD
Portishead Bsns Pk
Wyndham Way Ret Pk
Gordano Bsns Pk
WYNDHAM WAY
HARBOUR CRES
SERBERT RD
CAMOMILE WLK
TANSY LA
ROSEMARY CRES
(dis) Trinity Prim Sch
TARRAGON PL
West Hill
BLACKDOWN RD
QUANTOCK RD
MENDIP RD
BRENDON RD
DENNY VIEW
HOLLY RIDGE
MANOR CL
DOWNLEAZE
THE TRIANGLE
DOWN RD
LOWER DOWN RD
CHARLTON VIEW
QUEEN'S AVE
RIPPLESIDE
BRIARY RD
LEESIDE
DOWNSIDE
SLADE RD
ROATH RD
CHURCH CL
VICTORIA CL
VICTORIA CT
ALBERT RD
HIGH ST
NEWLANDS CL
NEWLANDS HILL
CHURCH RD N
CHURCH RD S
St Peters CE Prim Sch
Greystoke Bsns Ctr
BLENHEIM WAY
BRAMPTON WAY
DANDY'S MDW
1 BLADEN CL
2 TUDOR RD
3 COTSWOLD CL
AELFRIC MDW
JACOBS MDW
CONFERENCE CL
SHEEPWAY
CHEVIOT MEADOW
Moor Farm
THE DEANS
THE DOWNS
High Down Jun & Inf Schs
THE ROWANS
ELM WLK
CEDAR WAY
PORTISHEAD
SPRINGFIELD HO
THE SPINNEY
WEST CT
ALBERT PL
THATCHER CL
GLEBE AVE
GLEBE HO
PORTLAND DR
B3124 BRISTOL RD
PORTBURY COMM
4 BRAMPTON HO
5 CADBURY HO
RIDGEVIEW HO
Middle Bridges
THE PORTBURY HUNDRED A369
St Joseph's RC Prim Sch
LIPGATE PL
Portishead Down
Gordano Sch
MAYSFIELD CL
BS20
CLEVEDON RD
West Wood
Cemy
HOLLIS CRES
HOLLIS AVE
MEAD RD
GEORGE ST
CLIFTON ST
Weston Big Wood
North Weston
Oakfield Place
VALLEY RD
Woodside Grange
How Ham Farm
CLAPTON LA
B3124 CLEVEDON ROAD
BLACKROCK VILLAS
Sperring's Farm
Clapton Farm
CLAPTON DRO
MOOR LA
Brook Farm
Clapton in Gordano
Clapton Dro
Cherry Orchard Farm
CASWELL LA
Stratton Cottage
NAISH HILL
M5
CLEVEDON LA

1
8

4

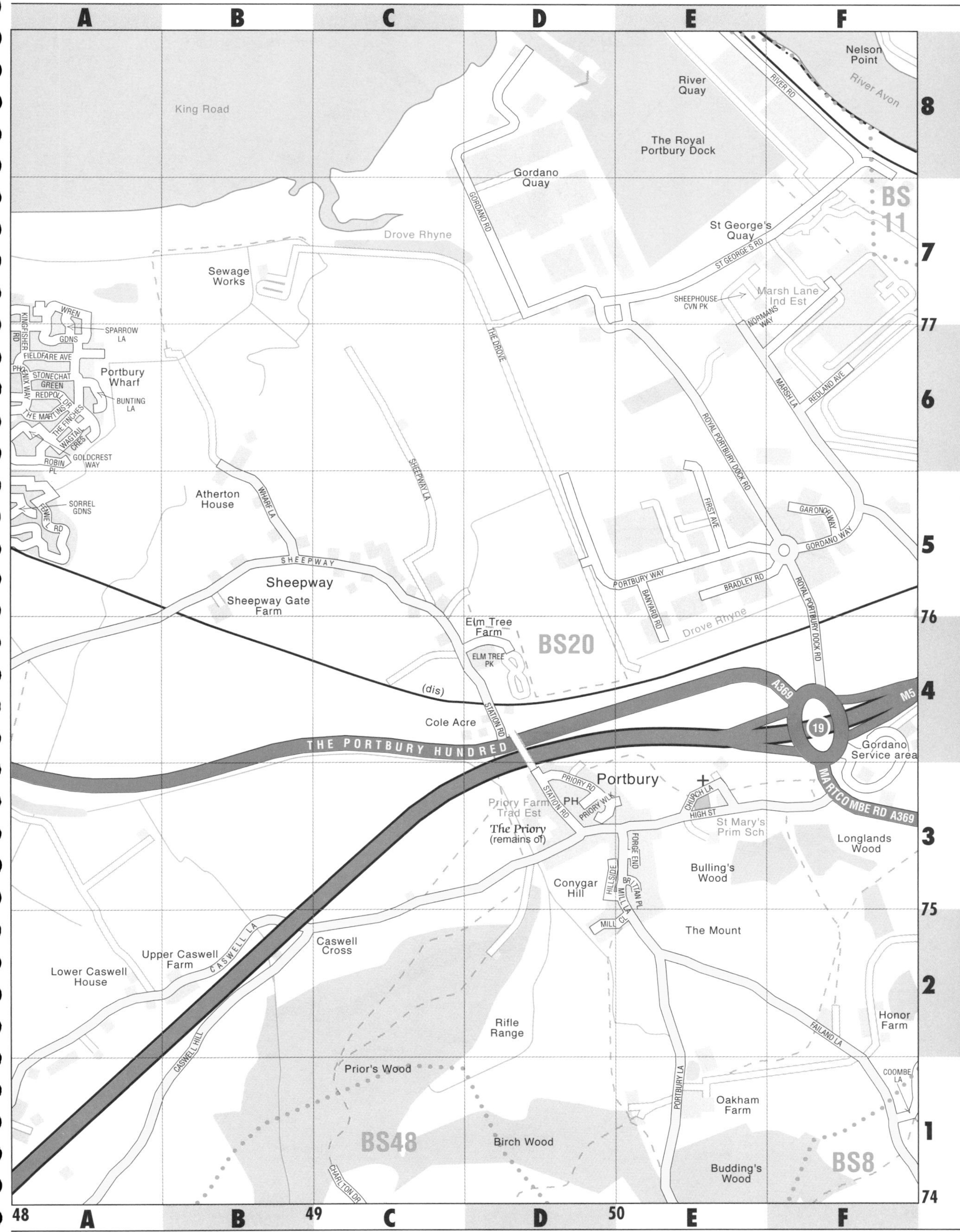
A
B
C
D
E
F
King Road
Nelson Point
River Quay
River Avon
RIVER RD
The Royal Portbury Dock
Gordano Quay
GORDANO RD
BS 11
Drove Rhyne
St George's Quay
ST GEORGE'S RD
Sewage Works
SHEEPHOUSE CVN PK
Marsh Lane Ind Est
NORMANS WAY
WREN GDNS
SPARROW LA
KINGFISHER RD
FIELDFARE AVE
STONECHAT GREEN
REDPOLL DR
THE MARTINS
THE FINCHES
WAGTAIL CRES
ROBIN PL
GOLDCREST WAY
BUNTING LA
Portbury Wharf
THE DROVE
MARSH LA
REDLAND AVE
ROYAL PORTBURY DOCK RD
SHEEPWAY LA
Atherton House
WHARF LA
SORREL GDNS
FENNEL RD
FIRST AVE
GARONOR WAY
GORDANO WAY
SHEEPWAY
Sheepway
Sheepway Gate Farm
PORTBURY WAY
BANYARD RD
BRADLEY RD
Elm Tree Farm
ELM TREE PK
BS20
(dis)
A369
M5
Cole Acre
STATION RD
19
THE PORTBURY HUNDRED
Gordano Service area
Portbury
PRIORY RD
PRIORY WLK
CHURCH LA
HIGH ST
PH
Priory Farm Trad Est
The Priory (remains of)
St Mary's Prim Sch
MARTCOMBE RD A369
Longlands Wood
FORGE END
HILLSIDE
BRITTAN PL
MILL LA
MILL CL
Conygar Hill
Bulling's Wood
The Mount
Caswell Cross
CASWELL LA
Upper Caswell Farm
Lower Caswell House
Rifle Range
FAILAND LA
Honor Farm
CASWELL HILL
Prior's Wood
PORTBURY LA
COOMBE LA
Oakham Farm
BS48
Birch Wood
CHARLTON DR
Budding's Wood
BS8
8
7
77
6
5
76
4
3
75
2
1
74
48
49
50

9
4

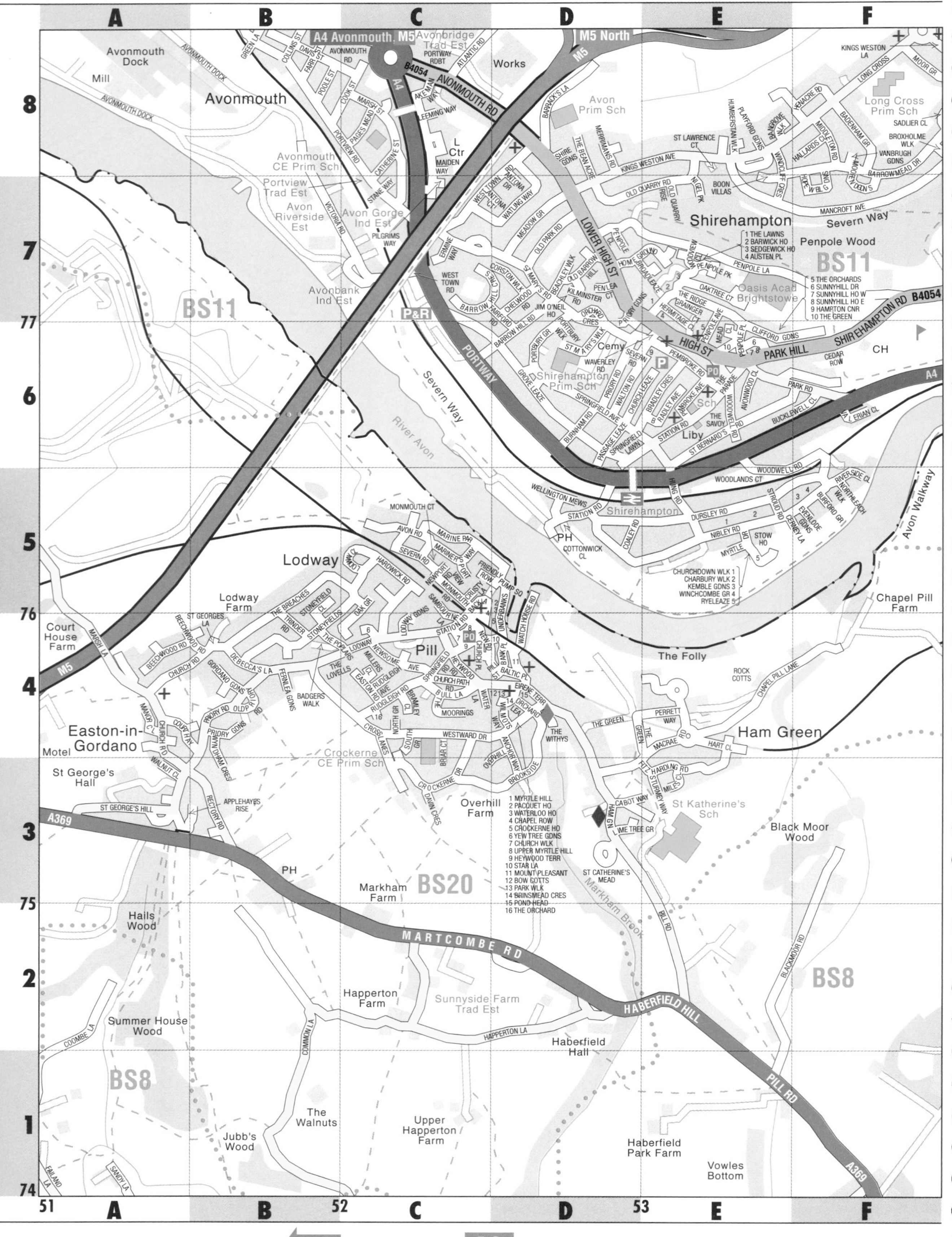

A
B
C
D
E
F
Avonmouth
Avonmouth Dock
Mill
A4 Avonmouth M5
Avonbridge Trad Est
Works
M5 North
B4054
AVONMOUTH RD
Avon Prim Sch
Long Cross Prim Sch
Avonmouth CE Prim Sch
Portview Trad Est
Avon Riverside Est
Avon Gorge Ind Est
Shirehampton
Penpole Wood
Severn Way
BS11
Oasis Acad Brightstowe
SHIREHAMPTON RD B4054
PARK HILL
HIGH ST
LOWER HIGH ST
PORTWAY
Avonbank Ind Est
P&R
Severn Way
River Avon
Shirehampton Prim Sch
Cemy
Liby
Sch
CH
A4
Shirehampton
PH
Lodway
Lodway Farm
Court House Farm
Pill
M5
Easton-in-Gordano
Motel
St George's Hall
Crockerne CE Prim Sch
Overhill Farm
Ham Green
St Katherine's Sch
The Folly
Chapel Pill Farm
Avon Walkway
Black Moor Wood
A369
PH
Markham Farm
BS20
MARTCOMBE RD
Hails Wood
Happerton Farm
Sunnyside Farm Trad Est
HABERFIELD HILL
Haberfield Hall
BS8
Summer House Wood
The Walnuts
Upper Happerton Farm
Jubb's Wood
Haberfield Park Farm
Vowles Bottom
PILL RD
1 THE LAWNS
2 BARWICK HO
3 SEDGEWICK HO
4 AUSTEN PL
5 THE ORCHARDS
6 SUNNYHILL DR
7 SUNNYHILL HO W
8 SUNNYHILL HO E
9 HAMPTON CNR
10 THE GREEN
CHURCHDOWN WLK 1
CHARBURY WLK 2
KEMBLE GDNS 3
WINCHCOMBE GR 4
RYELEAZE 5
1 MYRTLE HILL
2 PACQUET HO
3 WATERLOO HO
4 CHAPEL ROW
5 CROCKERNE HO
6 YEW TREE GDNS
7 CHURCH WLK
8 UPPER MYRTLE HILL
9 HEYWOOD TERR
10 STAR LA
11 MOUNT PLEASANT
12 BOW COTTS
13 PARK WLK
14 BRINSMEAD CRES
15 POND HEAD
16 THE ORCHARD
8
7
77
6
5
76
4
3
75
2
1
74
51
52
53

3
10

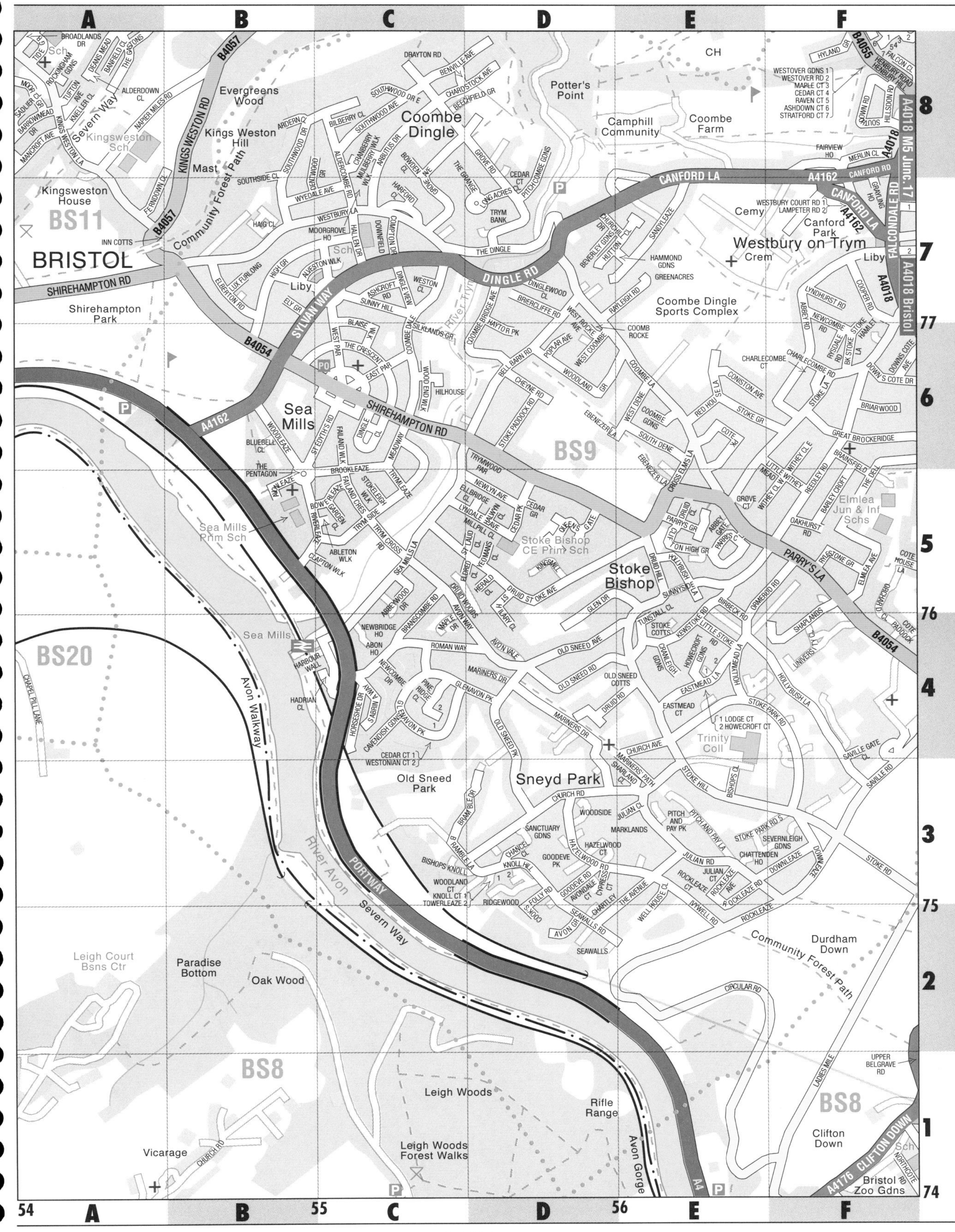

A
B
C
D
E
F
8
7
77
6
5
76
4
3
75
2
1
74
54
55
56
BRISTOL
BS11
BS9
BS20
BS8
BS8
Evergreens Wood
Kings Weston Hill
Mast
Kingsweston House
Kingsweston Sch
Shirehampton Park
SHIREHAMPTON RD
KINGS WESTON RD
B4057
Community Forest Path
Severn Way
Coombe Dingle
Potter's Point
Camphill Community
Coombe Farm
CH
CANFORD LA
A4162
Cemy
Canford Park
Westbury on Trym
Crem
Liby
FALCONDALE RD
A4018 M5 Junc.17
A4018 Bristol
B4055
Coombe Dingle Sports Complex
DINGLE RD
SYLVAN WAY
B4054
Sea Mills
SHIREHAMPTON RD
Sea Mills Prim Sch
Stoke Bishop CE Prim Sch
Stoke Bishop
PARRY'S LA
Elmlea Jun & Inf Schs
Trinity Coll
Sneyd Park
Old Sneed Park
Avon Walkway
River Avon
PORTWAY
Severn Way
River Trym
Community Forest Path
Durdham Down
Leigh Court Bsns Ctr
Paradise Bottom
Oak Wood
Leigh Woods
Rifle Range
Avon Gorge
Leigh Woods Forest Walks
Vicarage
Clifton Down
A4176 CLIFTON DOWN
Bristol Zoo Gdns
A4
LADIES MILE
CIRCULAR RD
STOKE RD
UPPER BELGRAVE RD
CHAPEL PILL LANE

11

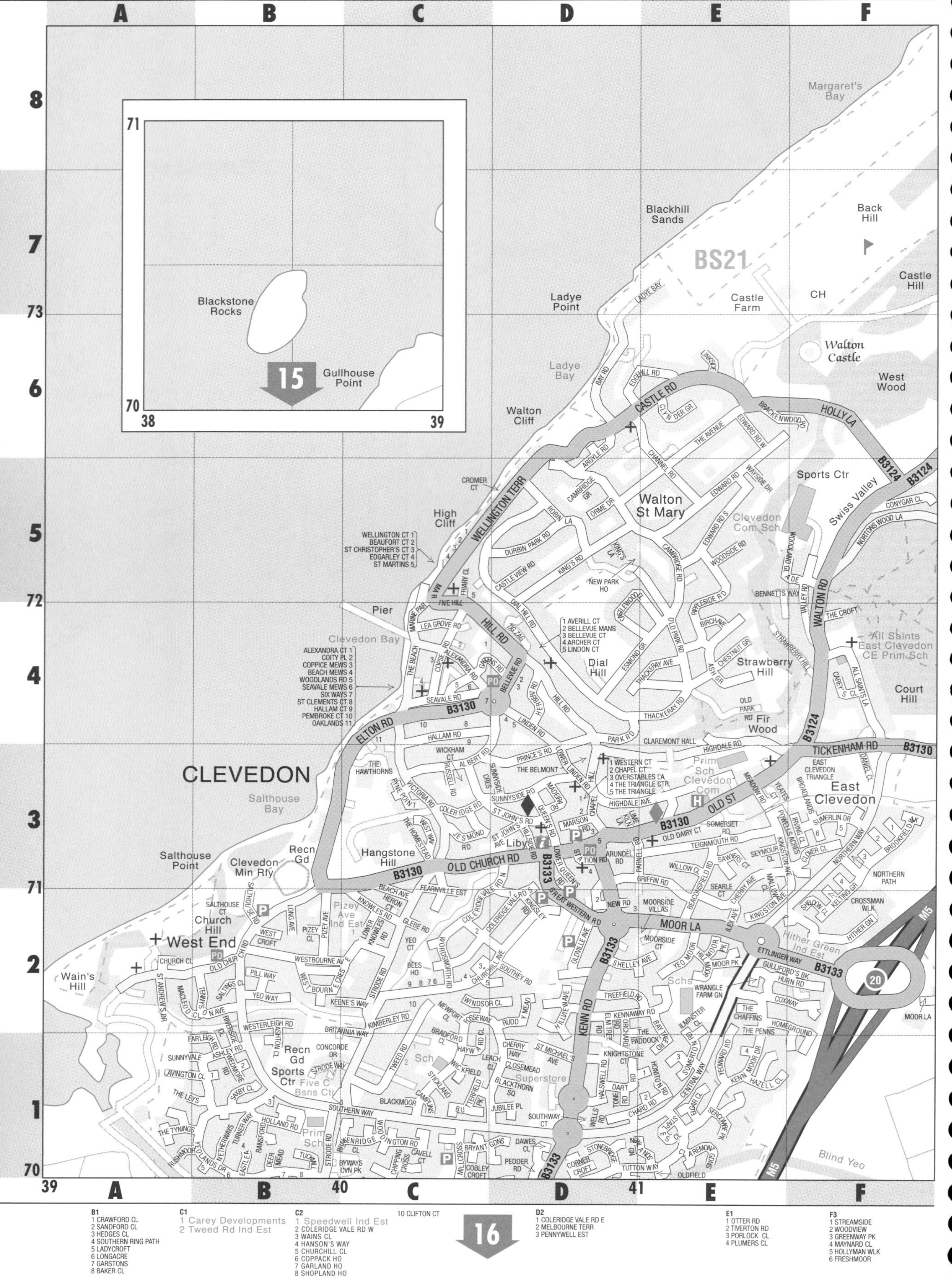

B1
1 CRAWFORD CL
2 SANDFORD CL
3 HEDGES CL
4 SOUTHERN RING PATH
5 LADYCROFT
6 LONGACRE
7 GARSTONS
8 BAKER CL

C1
1 Carey Developments
2 Tweed Rd Ind Est

C2
1 Speedwell Ind Est
2 Coleridge Vale Rd W
3 WAINS CL
4 HANSON'S WAY
5 CHURCHILL CL
6 COPPACK HO
7 GARLAND HO
8 SHOPLAND HO
9 BRIDGE HO

10 CLIFTON CT

D2
1 Coleridge Vale Rd E
2 MELBOURNE TERR
3 PENNYWELL EST

E1
1 OTTER RD
2 TIVERTON RD
3 PORLOCK CL
4 PLUMERS CL

F3
1 STREAMSIDE
2 WOODVIEW
3 GREENWAY PK
4 MAYNARD CL
5 HOLLYMAN WLK
6 FRESHMOOR

1
8

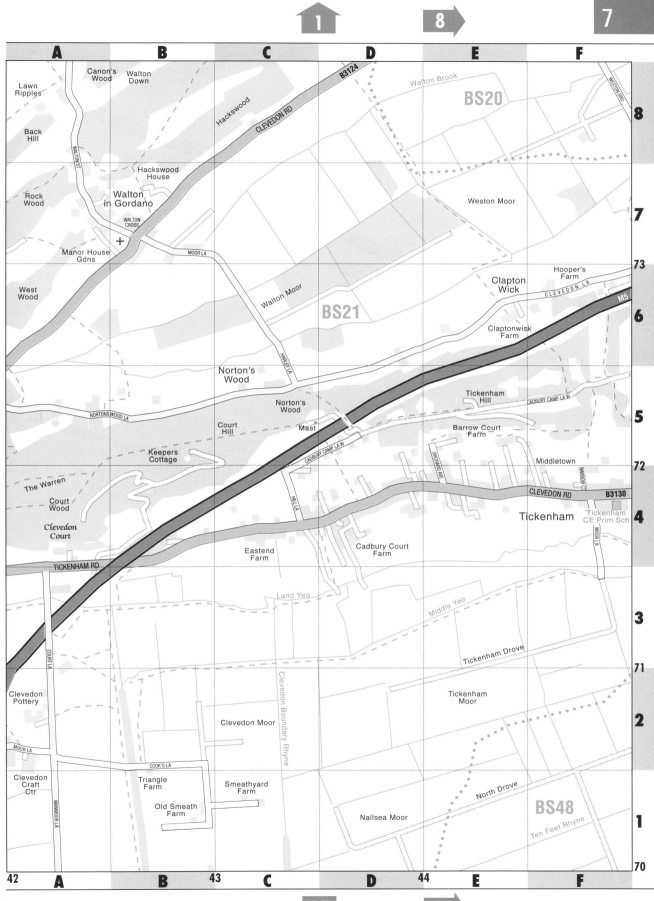
A
B
C
D
E
F
Canon's Wood
Walton Down
B3124
Walton Brook
BS20
Lawn Ripples
WESTON DRO
Hackswood
CLEVEDON RD
8
Back Hill
WALTON ST
Hackswood House
Rock Wood
Walton in Gordano
Weston Moor
WALTON CROSS
7
Manor House Gdns
MOOR LA
73
Clapton Wick
Hooper's Farm
West Wood
CLEVEDON LA
M5
Walton Moor
BS21
6
Claptonwick Farm
HARLEY LA
Norton's Wood
Tickenham Hill
CADBURY CAMP LA W
Norton's Wood
NORTONS WOOD LA
5
Court Hill
Mast
Barrow Court Farm
Keepers Cottage
CADBURY CAMP LA W
ORCHARD AVE
Middletown
72
BARROW CT
The Warren
CLEVEDON RD
B3130
Court Wood
HILL LA
Tickenham
Tickenham CE Prim Sch
4
Clevedon Court
MOOR LA
Eastend Farm
Cadbury Court Farm
TICKENHAM RD
Land Yeo
Middle Yeo
3
COURT LA
Tickenham Drove
71
Clevedon Pottery
Clevedon Boundary Rhyne
Tickenham Moor
Clevedon Moor
2
MOOR LA
COOK'S LA
Clevedon Craft Ctr
Triangle Farm
Smeathyard Farm
North Drove
MANMOOR LA
Old Smeath Farm
BS48
Nailsea Moor
1
Ten Feet Rhyne
70
42
43
44

17
8

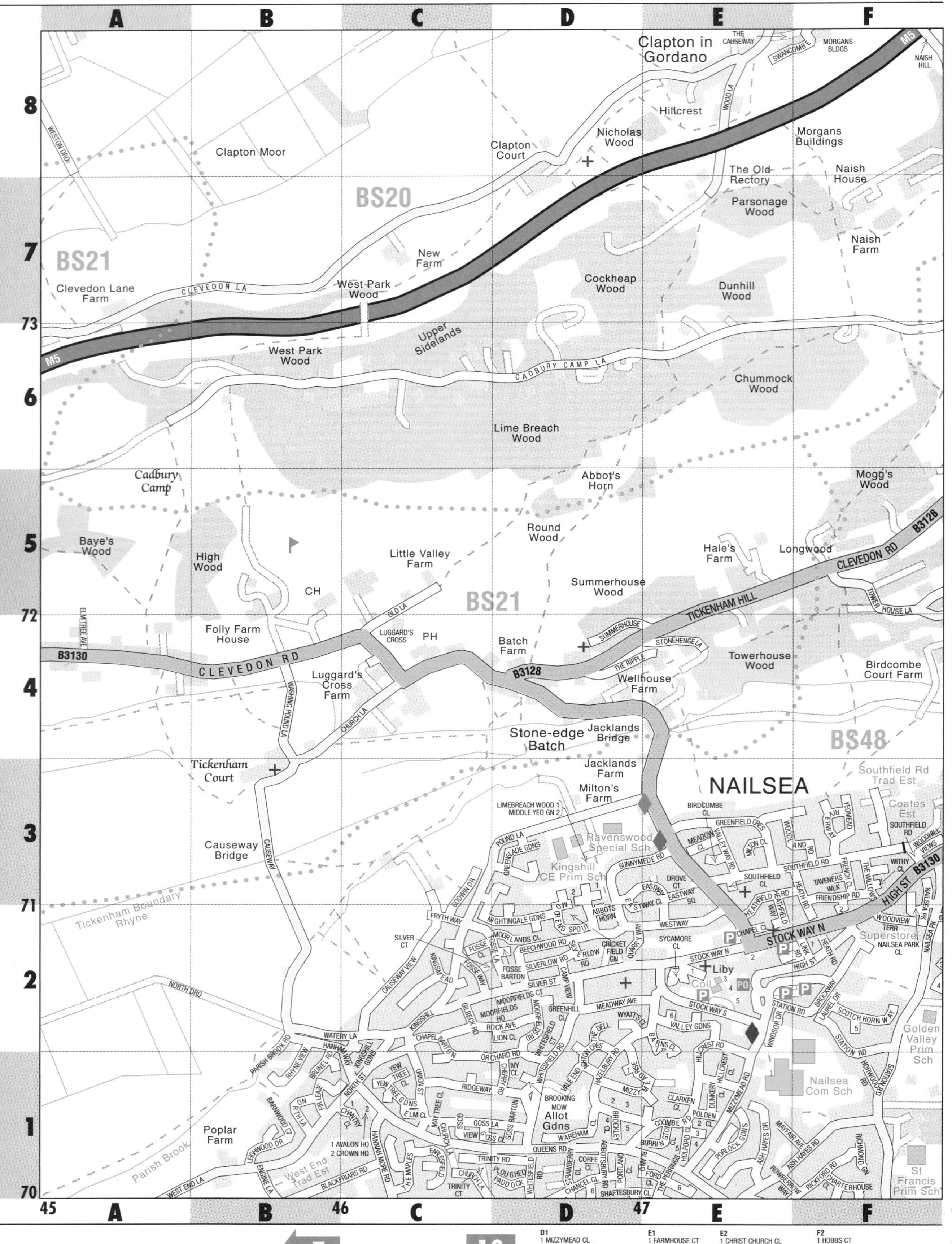

Map labels and grid references:

A B C D E F

8 7 73 6 5 72 4 3 71 2 1 70

45 A B 46 C D 47 E F

Clapton in Gordano

BS20
BS21
BS21
BS48

NAILSEA

Clapton Moor
West Lwd
Clevedon Lane Farm
Clevedon La
West Park Wood
New Farm
Upper Sidelands
Clapton Court
Nicholas Wood
Hillcrest
The Causeway
Swancombe
Morgans Bldgs
Naish Hill
M5
The Old Rectory
Parsonage Wood
Morgans Buildings
Naish House
Naish Farm
Cockheap Wood
Dunhill Wood
West Park Wood
Cadbury Camp La
Lime Breach Wood
Chummock Wood
Cadbury Camp
Abbot's Horn
Mogg's Wood
Baye's Wood
High Wood
CH
Little Valley Farm
Round Wood
Summerhouse Wood
Hale's Farm
Longwood
Clevedon Rd
B3128
Tower House La
Folly Farm House
OLD LA
Luggard's Cross
PH
Batch Farm
Summerhouse
Stonehenge La
The Ripple
Towerhouse Wood
Birdcombe Court Farm
B3130
Clevedon Rd
Washing Pound La
Luggard's Cross Farm
Church La
B3128
Wellhouse Farm
Stone-edge Batch
Jacklands Bridge
Jacklands Farm
Milton's Farm
BS48
Southfield Rd Trad Est
Tickenham Court
Causeway Bridge
Causeway
Tickenham Boundary Rhyne
North Dro
Tickenham Hill
Birdcombe Cl
Coates Est
Southfield Rd
Nailsea Com Sch
Golden Valley Prim Sch
St Francis Prim Sch
High St
B3130
Parish Brook
Poplar Farm
Watery La
West End Trad Est
West End La
Parish Brook
Nailsea Park Cl
Superstore
Woodview Terr

LIMEBREACH WOOD 1
MIDDLE YEO GN 2
Ravenswood Special Sch
Kingshill CE Prim Sch
Liby
Coll
PO
P

D1
1 MIZZYMEAD CL
2 BEAUFORT GDNS
3 AMBERLEY GDNS
4 CLAREMONT GDNS
5 DOWNLAND CL
6 DORCHESTER CL

E1
1 FARMHOUSE CT
2 BRENDON GDNS
3 MENDIP CL
4 SELWORTHY GDNS
5 DUNSTER GDNS
6 BIDDISHAM CL

E2
1 CHRIST CHURCH WLK
2 CLEVEDON WLK
3 SOMERSET SQ
4 COLLIERS WLK
5 CROWN GLASS PL
6 VALLEY CL
7 FARMHOUSE CL

F2
1 HOBBS CT
2 FRIENDSHIP GR
3 SCOTS PINE AVE
4 HAWTHORN WAY
5 SCOTCH HORN CL
6 BLACKTHORN WAY

3
10

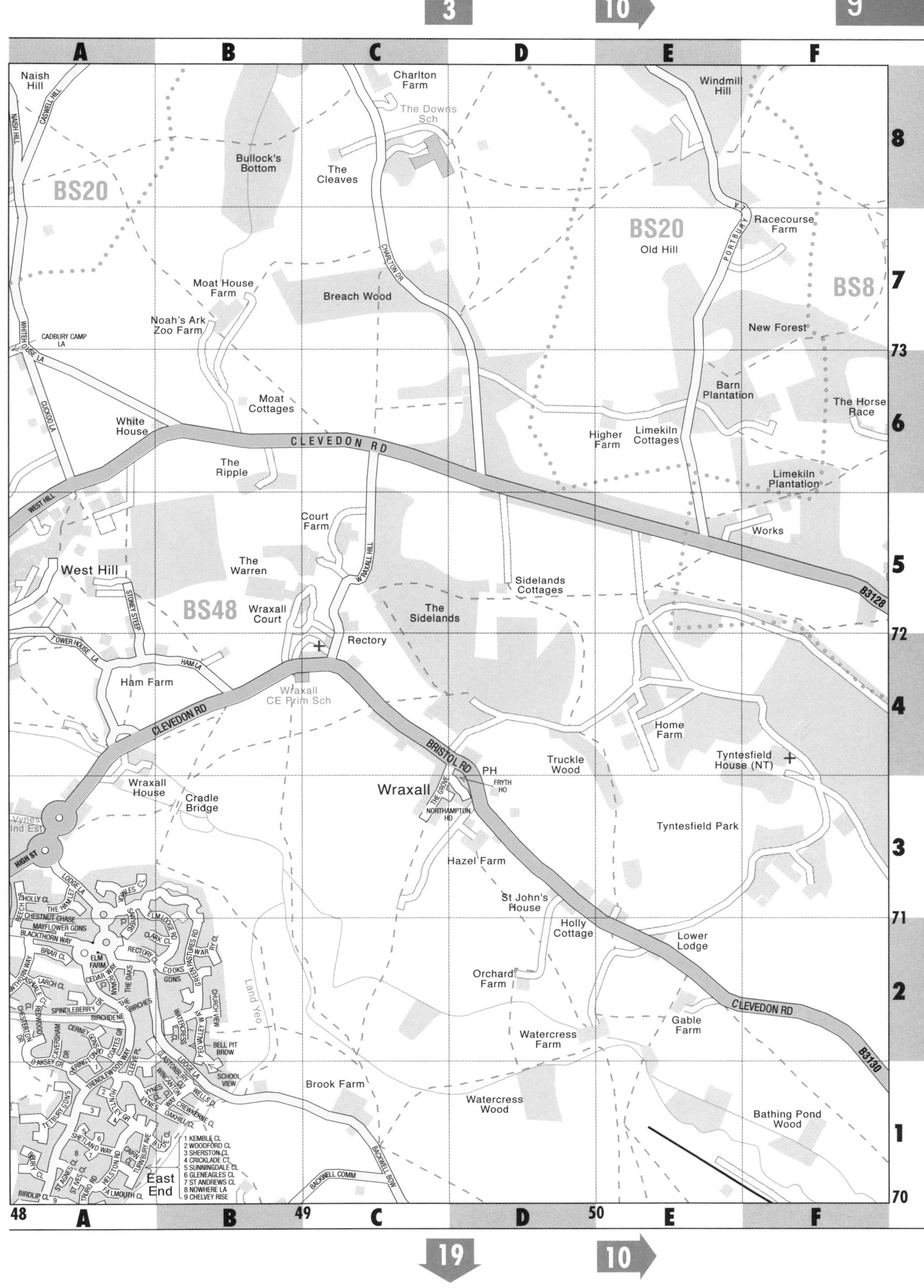
A
B
C
D
E
F
Naish Hill
Charlton Farm
The Downs Sch
Windmill Hill
Bullock's Bottom
The Cleaves
BS20
Racecourse Farm
BS20
Old Hill
BS8
Moat House Farm
Breach Wood
Noah's Ark Zoo Farm
New Forest
CADBURY CAMP LA
Barn Plantation
Moat Cottages
The Horse Race
White House
CLEVEDON RD
Higher Farm
Limekiln Cottages
The Ripple
Limekiln Plantation
Court Farm
Works
West Hill
The Warren
Sidelands Cottages
BS48
Wraxall Court
The Sidelands
B3128
Rectory
Ham Farm
Wraxall CE Prim Sch
CLEVEDON RD
BRISTOL RD
Home Farm
Truckle Wood
Tyntesfield House (NT)
PH
Wraxall House
Cradle Bridge
Wraxall
FRYTH HO
NORTHAMPTON HO
Vynes Ind Est
Tyntesfield Park
HIGH ST
Hazel Farm
St John's House
Holly Cottage
Lower Lodge
Orchard Farm
Land Yeo
CLEVEDON RD
Gable Farm
Watercress Farm
B3130
Brook Farm
Watercress Wood
Bathing Pond Wood
East End
1 KEMBLE CL
2 WOODFORD CL
3 SHERSTON CL
4 CRICKLADE CT
5 SUNNINGDALE CL
6 GLENEAGLES CL
7 ST ANDREWS CL
8 NOWHERE LA
9 CHELVEY RISE
BACKWELL COMM
BACKWELL BOW
8
7
73
6
5
72
4
3
71
2
1
70
48
49
50

19
10

A B C D E F

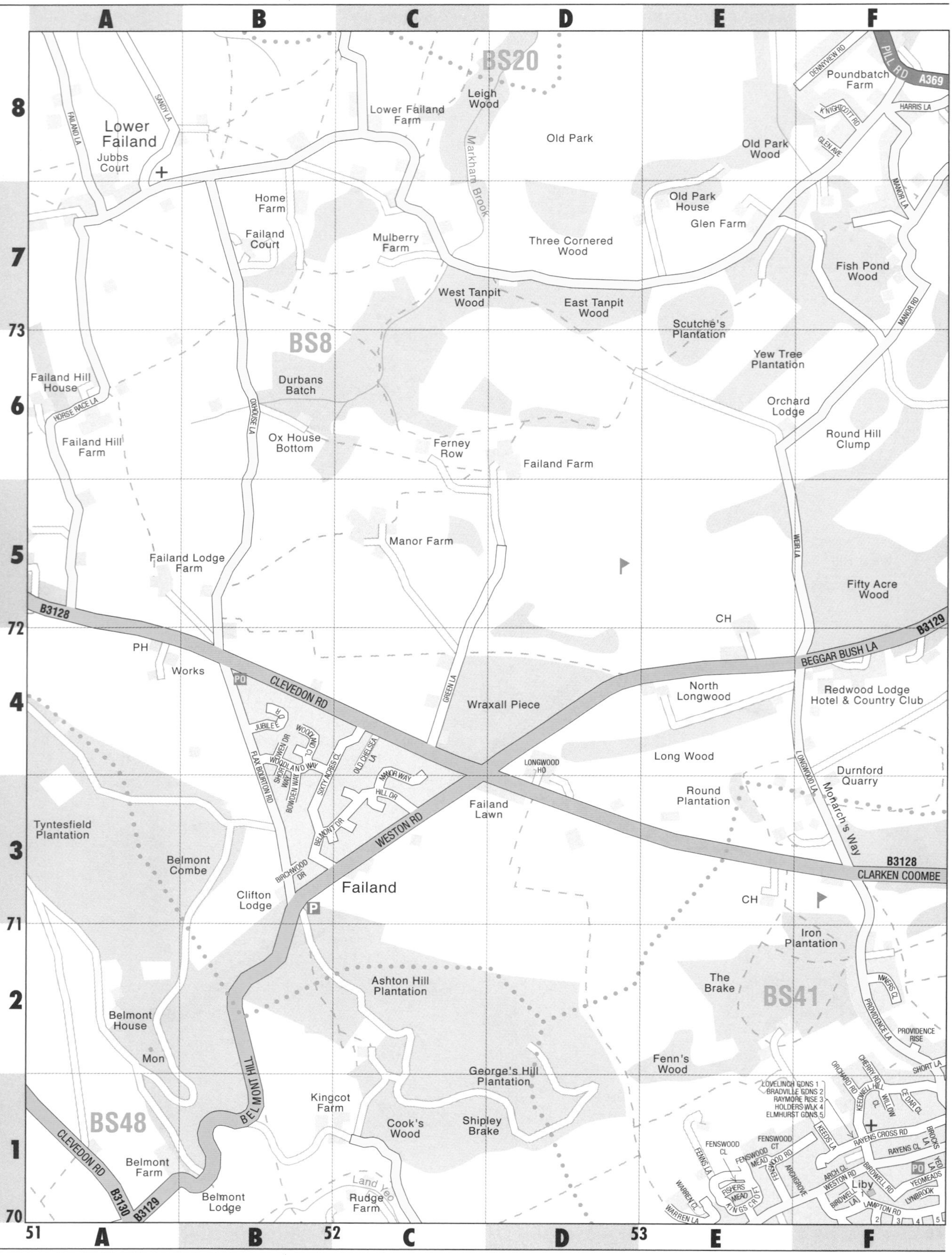

8

Lower
Failand

Jubbs
Court

Leigh
Wood

Lower Failand
Farm

Old Park

Old Park
Wood

Poundbatch
Farm

A369

Home
Farm

7

Failand
Court

Mulberry
Farm

Three Cornered
Wood

Old Park
House

Glen Farm

Fish Pond
Wood

73

BS8

West Tanpit
Wood

East Tanpit
Wood

Scutche's
Plantation

6

Failand Hill
House

Durbans
Batch

Yew Tree
Plantation

Failand Hill
Farm

Ox House
Bottom

Ferney
Row

Failand Farm

Orchard
Lodge

Round Hill
Clump

5

Failand Lodge
Farm

Manor Farm

Fifty Acre
Wood

72

B3128

CH

BEGGAR BUSH LA

B3129

PH

Works

CLEVEDON RD

Wraxall Piece

North
Longwood

Redwood Lodge
Hotel & Country Club

4

Tyntesfield
Plantation

Belmont
Combe

Long Wood

Durnford
Quarry

3

Clifton
Lodge

WESTON RD

Failand
Lawn

Failand

Round
Plantation

CH

B3128
CLARKEN COOMBE

71

Iron
Plantation

2

Belmont
House

Ashton Hill
Plantation

The
Brake

BS41

Mon

PROVIDENCE
RISE

SHORT LA

1

BS48

Kingcot
Farm

George's Hill
Plantation

Fenn's
Wood

LOVELINCH GDNS 1
BRADVILLE GDNS 2
RAYMORE RISE 3
HOLDERS WLK 4
ELMHURST GDNS 5

Belmont
Farm

Cook's
Wood

Shipley
Brake

RAVENS CROSS RD

70

CLEVEDON RD

B3130
B3129

Belmont
Lodge

Rudge
Farm

Land Yeo

Liby

LAMPTON RD

51 A 52 B C 53 D E F

F5
1 BRISTOL GATE
2 FARADAY RD
3 DOWRY PL
4 LITTLE CAROLINE PL
5 GRANVILLE CHAPEL
6 HUMPHRY DAVY WAY

F5
7 GRENVILLE PL
8 ASHMEAD WAY
9 CUMBERLAND RD
10 BRUNSWICK PL

F6
1 HABERFIELD HO
2 DAWES CT
3 CLEVE CT
4 BROWNE CT
5 ADAMS CT
6 CUMBERLAND PL

7 CARRICK HO
8 SOUTH GREEN ST
9 ALBERMARLE ROW
10 HOPECHAPEL HILL
11 NORTH GREEN ST
12 HINTON LA
13 WINDSOR CT

F6
14 VICTORIA TERR
15 THE POLYGON
16 GLENDALE
17 PRINCE'S BLDGS
18 WELLINGTON TERR
19 OXFORD PL

F7
1 CLIFTON CL
2 HARLEY MEWS
3 HARLEY CT
4 HARLEY PL
5 CLIFTON DOWN RD
6 GLOUCESTER ROW

7 BEAUFORT BLDGS
8 GLOUCESTER ST
9 WATERLOO ST
10 BEAUFORT MEWS

5

226

11

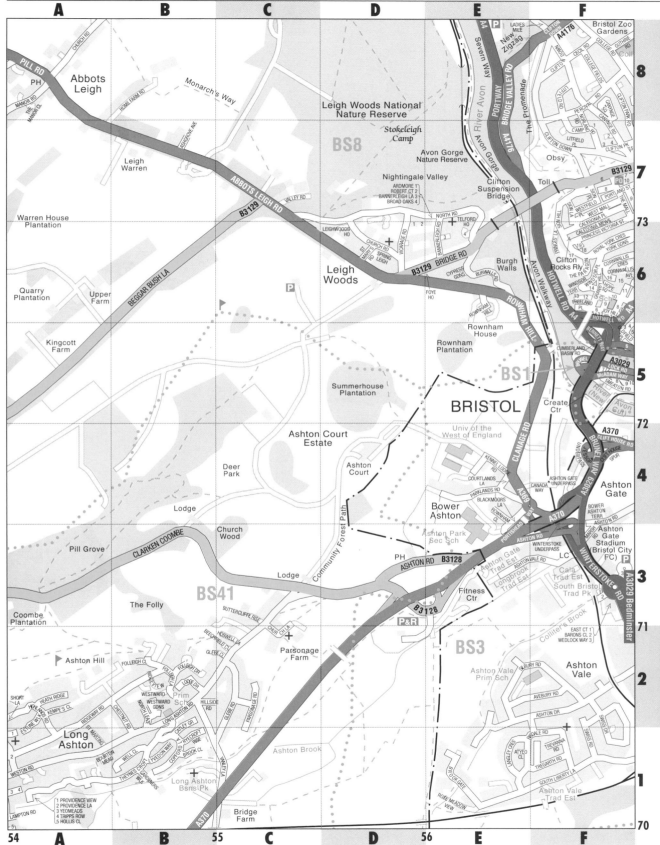

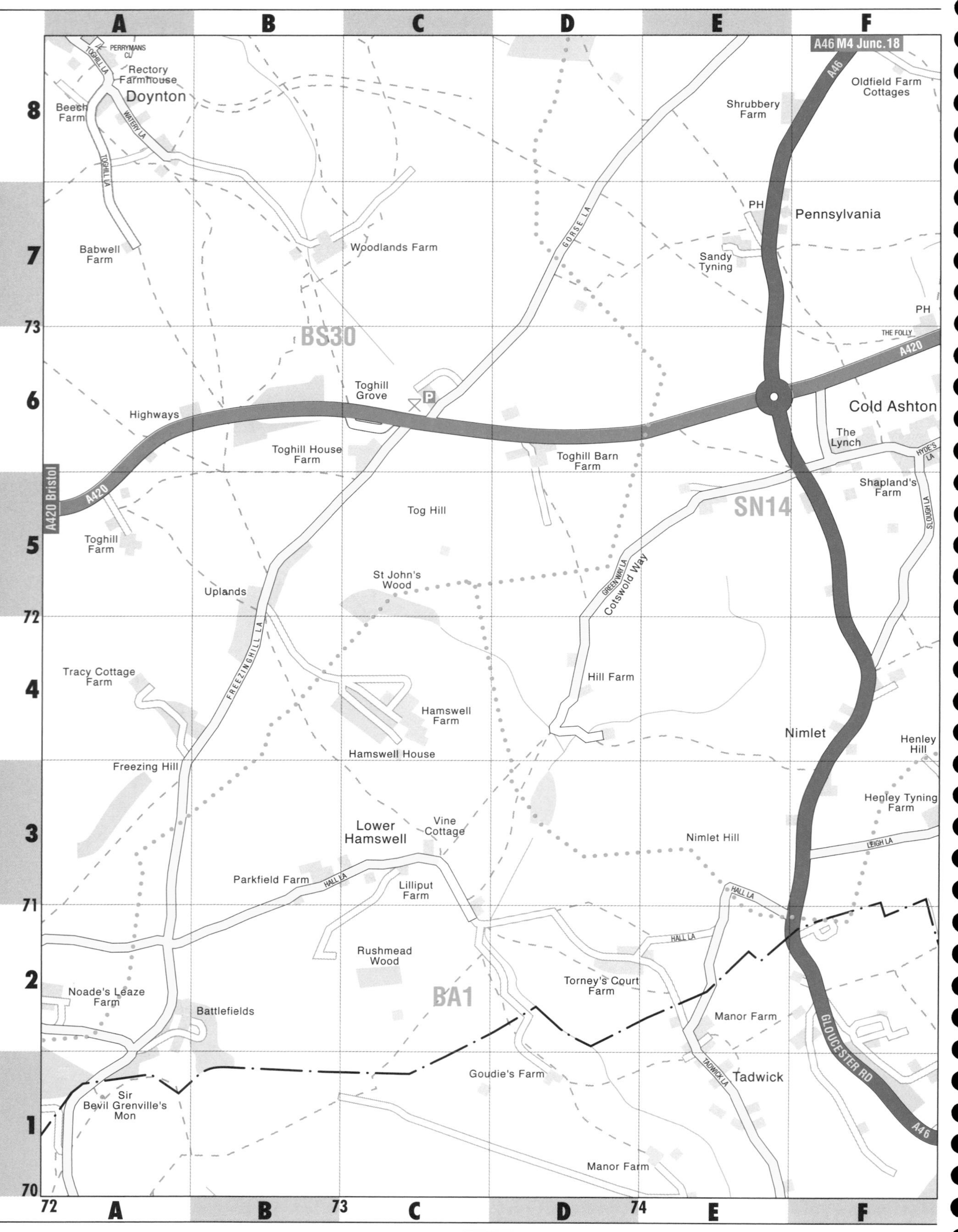
A
B
C
D
E
F
A46 M4 Junc.18
PERRYMANS CL
TOGHILL LA
Rectory Farmhouse
Doynton
Beech Farm
WATERY LA
Oldfield Farm Cottages
Shrubbery Farm
A46
8
7
6
5
4
3
2
1
73
72
71
70
PH
Pennsylvania
Babwell Farm
Woodlands Farm
GORSE LA
Sandy Tyning
PH
THE FOLLY
A420
BS30
Toghill Grove
P
Highways
Cold Ashton
The Lynch
HYDE'S LA
Toghill House Farm
Toghill Barn Farm
Shapland's Farm
A420 Bristol
A420
Tog Hill
SN14
SLOUGH LA
Toghill Farm
St John's Wood
GREEN WAY LA
Cotswold Way
Uplands
FREEZINGHILL LA
Tracy Cottage Farm
Hill Farm
Hamswell Farm
Hamswell House
Nimlet
Henley Hill
Freezing Hill
Henley Tyning Farm
Lower Hamswell
Vine Cottage
Nimlet Hill
LEIGH LA
Parkfield Farm
HALL LA
Lilliput Farm
HALL LA
HALL LA
Rushmead Wood
Noade's Leaze Farm
BA1
Torney's Court Farm
Battlefields
Manor Farm
GLOUCESTER RD
Goudie's Farm
TADWICK LA
Tadwick
Sir Bevil Grenville's Mon
A46
Manor Farm
72
73
74

27

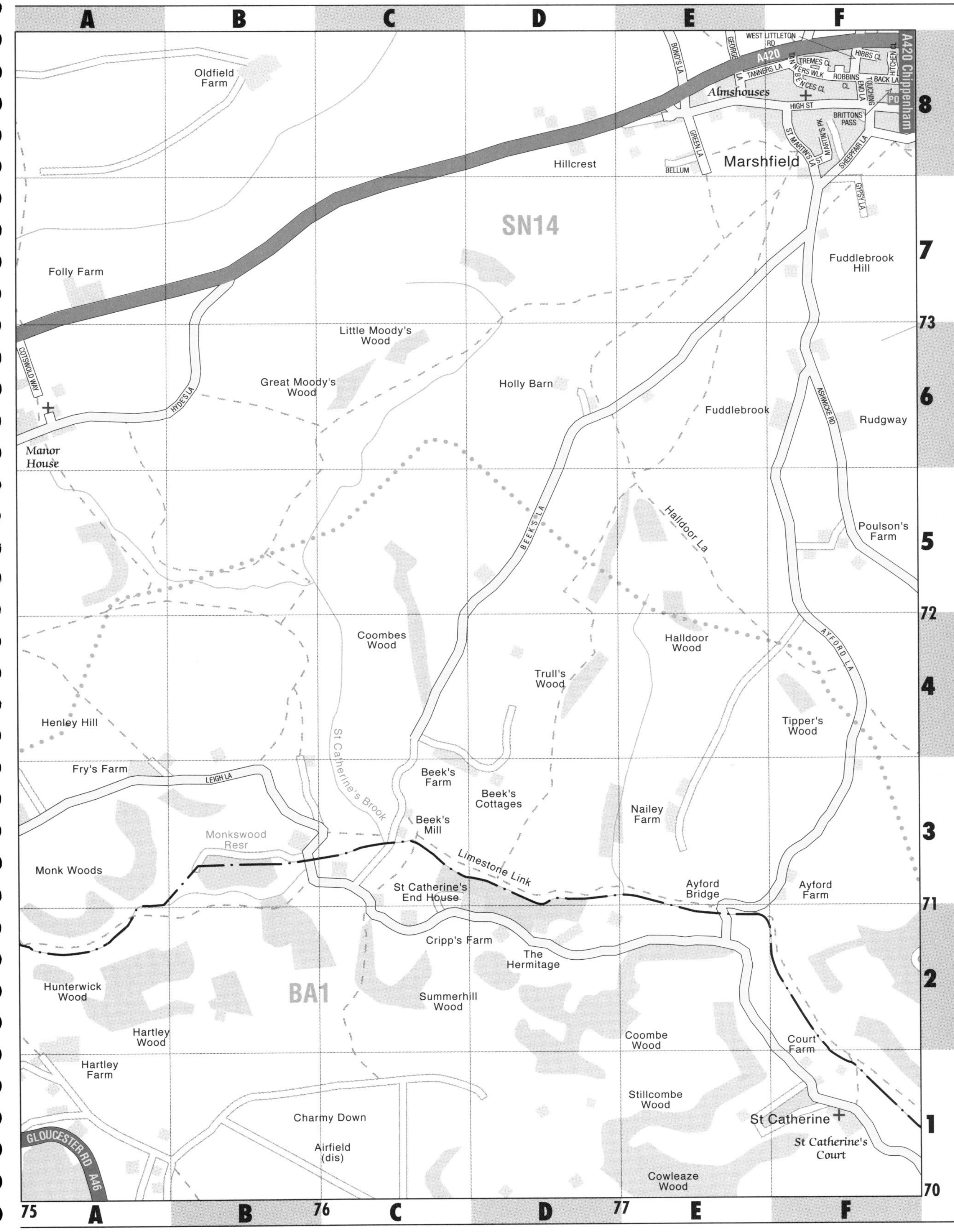
A
B
C
D
E
F
WEST LITTLETON RD
BOND'S LA
GEORGE LA
A420
TANNERS LA
TREMES CL
HIBBS CL
ROBBINS CL
BACK LA
TOUCHING END LA
Almshouses
HIGH ST
PO
A420 Chippenham
8
Oldfield Farm
GREEN LA
BRITTONS PASS
ST MARTIN'S LA
SHEEPFAIR LA
Hillcrest
BELLUM
Marshfield
GYPSY LA
SN14
7
Folly Farm
Fuddlebrook Hill
73
Little Moody's Wood
COTSWOLD WAY
Great Moody's Wood
HYDE'S LA
Holly Barn
ASHWICKE RD
6
Fuddlebrook
Rudgway
Manor House
BEEK'S LA
Halldoor La
Poulson's Farm
5
72
Coombes Wood
Halldoor Wood
AYFORD LA
Trull's Wood
4
Henley Hill
Tipper's Wood
St Catherine's Brook
Fry's Farm
LEIGH LA
Beek's Farm
Beek's Cottages
Nailey Farm
Beek's Mill
3
Monkswood Resr
Limestone Link
Monk Woods
St Catherine's End House
Ayford Bridge
Ayford Farm
71
Cripp's Farm
The Hermitage
Hunterwick Wood
BA1
Summerhill Wood
2
Hartley Wood
Coombe Wood
Court Farm
Hartley Farm
Stillcombe Wood
Charmy Down
St Catherine
1
GLOUCESTER RD A46
Airfield (dis)
St Catherine's Court
Cowleaze Wood
70
75
76
77

28

St Thomas's
Head

Piers

Woodspring Bay

Wick Warth

Middle Hope
(Nature Reserve)

BS22

River Banwell

WARTH LA

Twr
Woodspring
Priory

Woodspring
Farm

33   A   B   34   C   D   35   E   F

16

A
B
C
D
E
F
8
7
69
6
5
68
4
3
67
2
1
66
Dowlais Ditch
Kingston Pill
Hook's Ear
Seawall Farm
Treble House Farm
BACK LA
Sewage Works
Channel View Farm
BS21
MIDDLE LA
MIDDLE LA
Broadstone Rhyne
Broadstone Farm
BROADSTONE LA
Wharf Farm
New House Farm
HAM LA
Ham Farm
Pool Farm
Ham Rhyne
BS22
Sewage Works
Mendip View Farm
Yeo Bank Farm
YEO BANK LA
Mill Leaze Rhyne
MUDDY LA
BS22
36
37
38
A
B
C
D
E
F

32

16

6

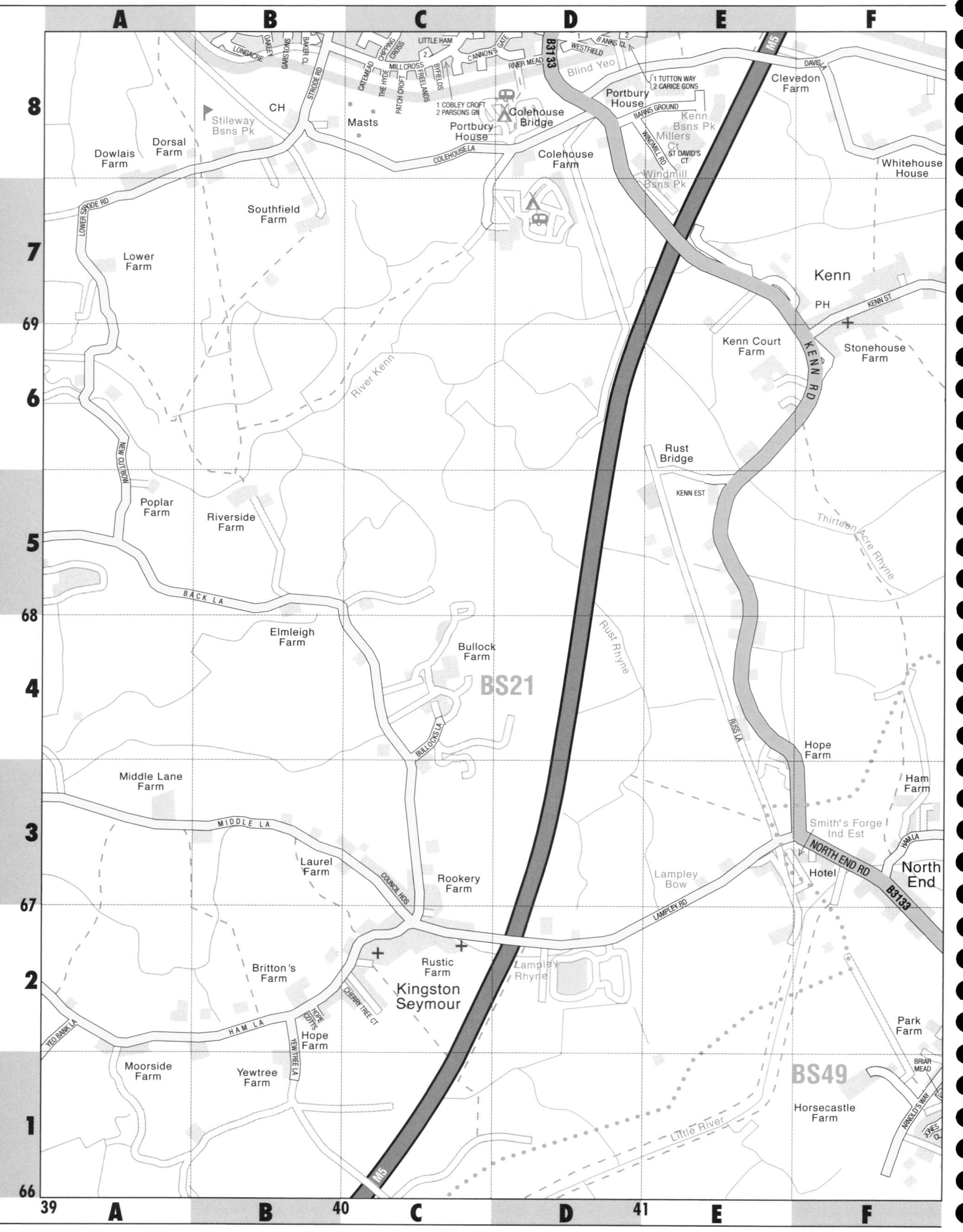

A
B
C
D
E
F
8
7
69
6
5
68
4
3
67
2
1
66
39
40
41
LONGACRE
OAKLEY
GARSTONS
BAKER CL
STRODE RD
CATEMEAD
THE HYDE
CHIPPING CROSS
MILLCROSS
PATCH CROFT
FREELANDS
BYFIELDS
LITTLE HAM
CANNON'S GATE
RIVER MEAD
B3133
WESTFIELD
BANKS CL
Blind Yeo
1 TUTTON WAY
2 CARICE GDNS
DAVIS LA
M5
Clevedon Farm
Portbury House
BARNS GROUND
Kenn Bsns Pk
Millers Ct
WINDMILL RD
ST DAVID'S CT
Windmill Bsns Pk
1 COBLEY CROFT
2 PARSONS GN
Colehouse Bridge
Portbury House
Masts
CH
Stileway Bsns Pk
Dorsal Farm
Dowlais Farm
COLEHOUSE LA
Colehouse Farm
Whitehouse House
LOWER STRODE RD
Southfield Farm
Lower Farm
Kenn
PH
KENN ST
Kenn Court Farm
KENN RD
Stonehouse Farm
River Kenn
NEW CUT BOW
Rust Bridge
KENN EST
Poplar Farm
Riverside Farm
Thirteen Acre Rhyne
BACK LA
Elmleigh Farm
Bullock Farm
Rust Rhyne
BS21
BULLOCKS LA
RUSS LA
Hope Farm
Middle Lane Farm
Ham Farm
MIDDLE LA
Smith's Forge Ind Est
HAM LA
NORTH END RD
North End
Laurel Farm
COUNCIL HOS
Rookery Farm
Lampley Bow
Hotel
B3133
LAMPLEY RD
Britton's Farm
Rustic Farm
Lampley Rhyne
CHERRY TREE CT
Kingston Seymour
YEO BANK LA
HAM LA
HOPE COTTS
Hope Farm
YEW TREE LA
Park Farm
Moorside Farm
Yewtree Farm
BRIAR MEAD
BS49
Horsecastle Farm
ARNOLD'S WAY
JONES CL
Little River

33

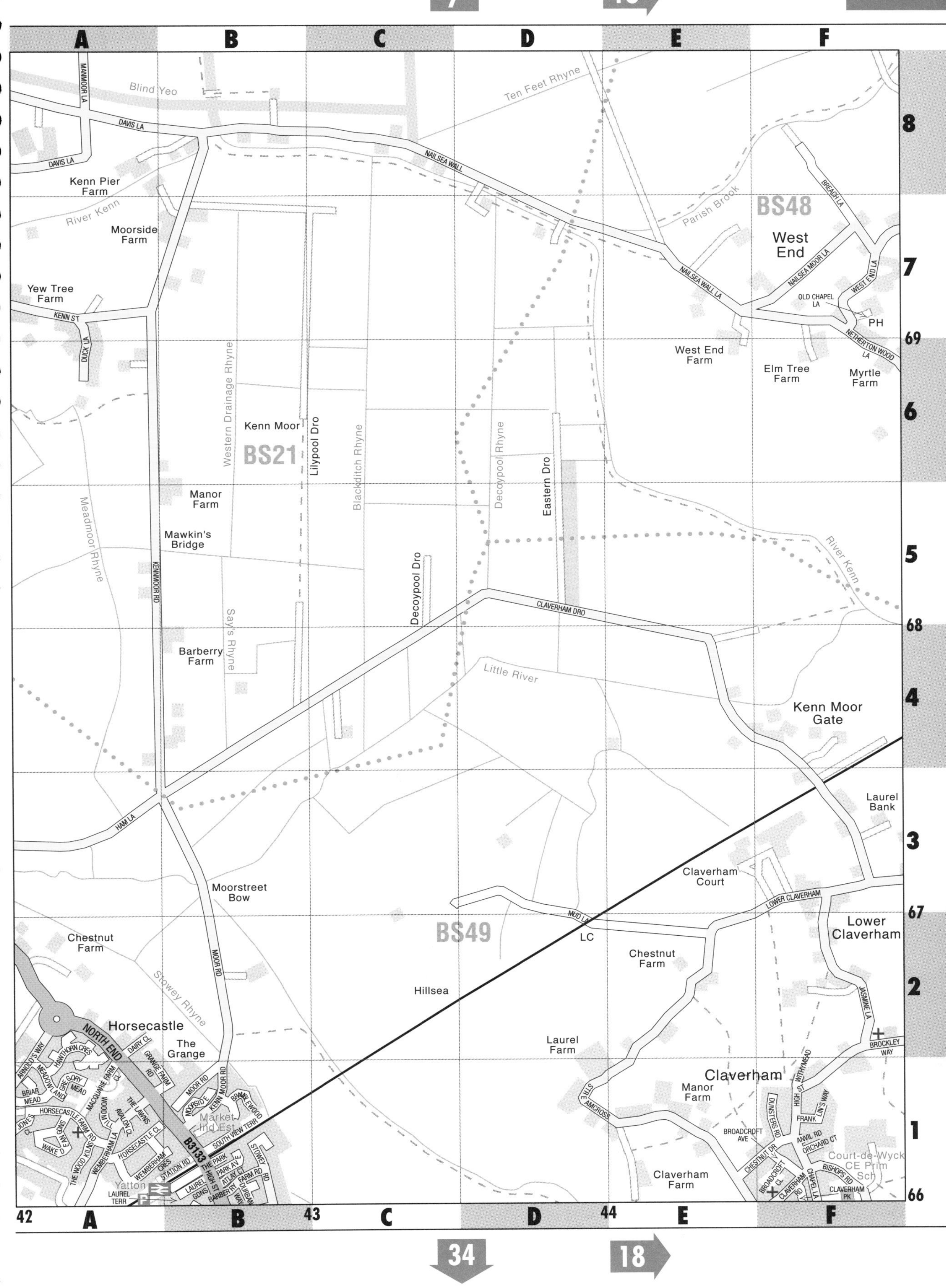
A
B
C
D
E
F
Blind Yeo
Ten Feet Rhyne
MANMOOR LA
DAVIS LA
NAILSEA WALL
Kenn Pier Farm
River Kenn
Moorside Farm
Parish Brook
BS48
West End
BREACH LA
NAILSEA WALL LA
NAILSEA MOOR LA
WEST END LA
OLD CHAPEL LA
PH
NETHERTON WOOD LA
Yew Tree Farm
KENN ST
DUCK LA
West End Farm
Elm Tree Farm
Myrtle Farm
Western Drainage Rhyne
Kenn Moor
Lilypool Dro
Blackditch Rhyne
BS21
Decoypool Rhyne
Eastern Dro
Manor Farm
Meadmoor Rhyne
Mawkin's Bridge
KENNMOOR RD
Decoypool Dro
River Kenn
CLAVERHAM DRO
Say's Rhyne
Barberry Farm
Little River
Kenn Moor Gate
Laurel Bank
HAM LA
Moorstreet Bow
Claverham Court
LOWER CLAVERHAM
MUD LA
LC
Lower Claverham
BS49
Chestnut Farm
Chestnut Farm
MOOR RD
Stowey Rhyne
Hillsea
JASMINE LA
Horsecastle
The Grange
Laurel Farm
BROCKLEY WAY
NORTH END
B3133
Market Ind Est
Claverham
Manor Farm
Claverham Farm
Court-de-Wyck CE Prim Sch
Yatton
HIGH ST
STATION RD
WITHYMEAD
DUNSTERS RD
FRANK
LIN'S WAY
ANVIL RD
ORCHARD CT
BROADCROFT AVE
CHESTNUT DR
BROADCROFT CL
CLAVERHAM RD
CHAPEL LA
BISHOPS RD
CLAVERHAM PK
STREAMCROSS
HORSECASTLE FARM RD
WEMBERHAM LA
WEMBERHAM CRES
HORSECASTLE CL
SOUTH VIEW TERR
STOWEY RD
PARK AVE
FARM RD
THE PARK
LAUREL TERR
LAUREL GDNS
8
7
69
6
5
68
4
3
67
2
1
66
42
43
44

17
8

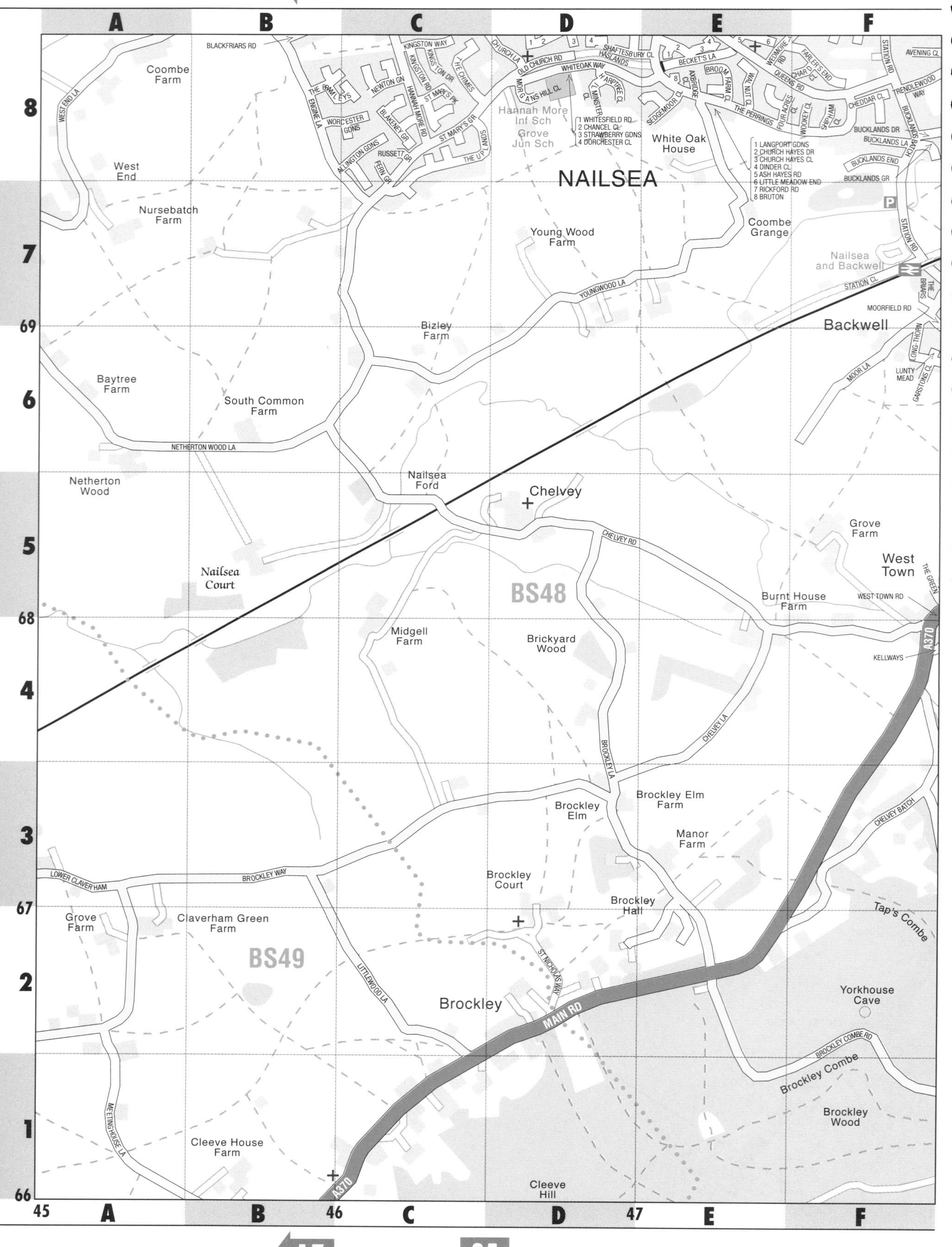
NAILSEA
Coombe Farm
West End
Nursebatch Farm
Baytree Farm
South Common Farm
Netherton Wood
Nailsea Court
Bizley Farm
Young Wood Farm
White Oak House
Coombe Grange
Nailsea and Backwell
Backwell
Hannah More Inf Sch
Grove Jun Sch
Nailsea Ford
Chelvey
BS48
Grove Farm
West Town
Burnt House Farm
Midgell Farm
Brickyard Wood
Brockley Elm Farm
Brockley Elm
Manor Farm
Brockley Court
Brockley Hall
Grove Farm
Claverham Green Farm
BS49
Brockley
Tap's Combe
Yorkhouse Cave
Brockley Combe
Brockley Wood
Cleeve House Farm
Cleeve Hill
BLACKFRIARS RD
WEST END LA
NETHERTON WOOD LA
YOUNGWOOD LA
STATION CL
MOORFIELD RD
MOOR LA
CHELVEY RD
WEST TOWN RD
KELLWAYS
CHELVEY LA
BROCKLEY LA
CHELVEY BATCH
LOWER CLAVER HAM
BROCKLEY WAY
LITTLEWOOD LA
ST NICHOLAS WAY
MAIN RD
A370
BROCKLEY COMBE RD
MEETING HOUSE LA
1 WHITESFIELD RD
2 CHANCEL CL
3 STRAWBERRY GDNS
4 DORCHESTER CL
1 LANGPORT GDNS
2 CHURCH HAYES DR
3 CHURCH HAYES CL
4 DINDER CL
5 ASH HAYES RD
6 LITTLE MEADOW END
7 RICKFORD RD
8 BRUTON
A B C D E F
8 7 69 6 5 68 4 3 67 2 1 66
45 46 47

17
35

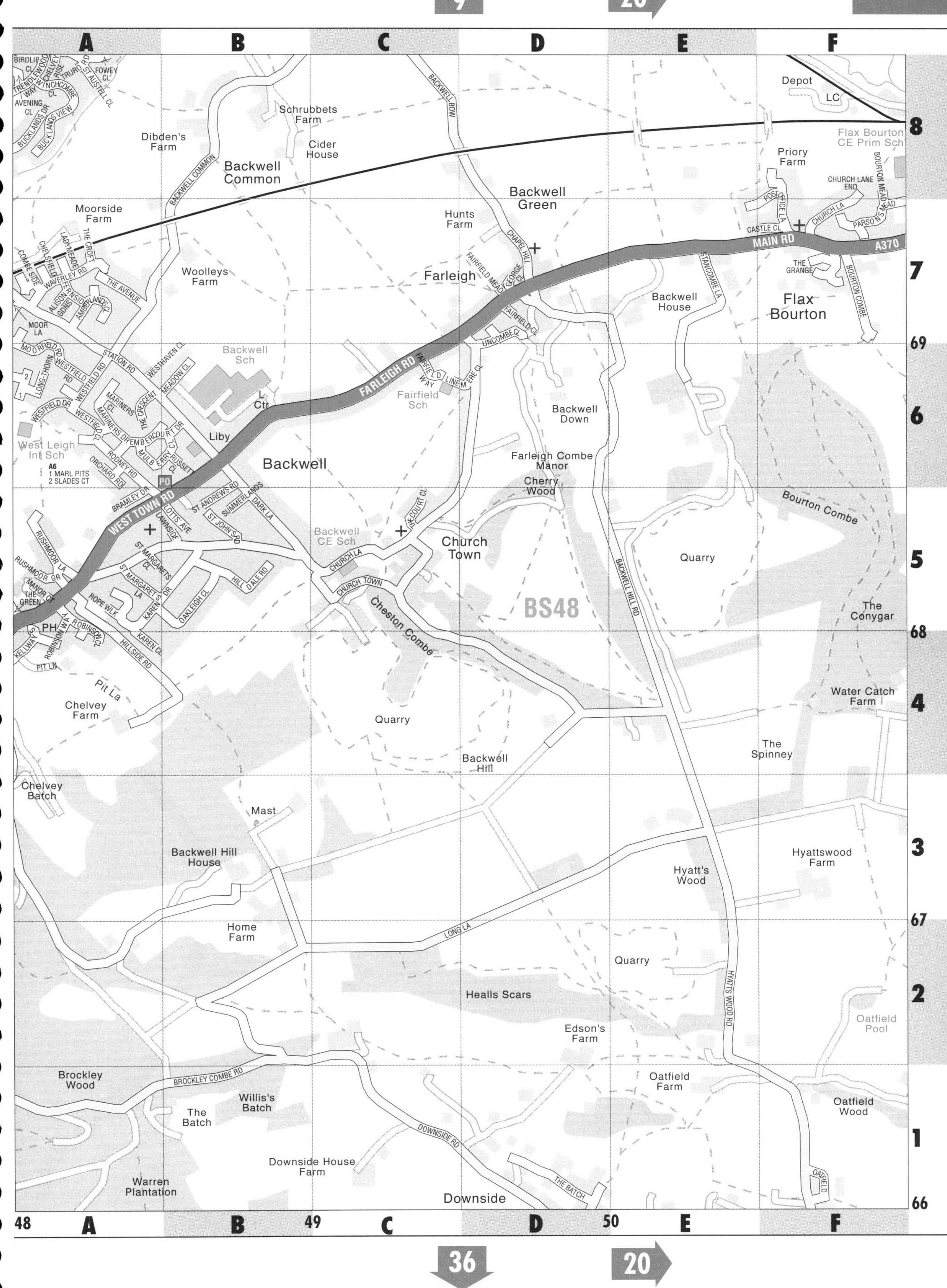
9
20
A
B
C
D
E
F
8
7
69
6
5
68
4
3
67
2
1
66
48
49
50
Depot
LC
Schrubbets Farm
Cider House
Dibden's Farm
Backwell Common
Flax Bourton CE Prim Sch
Priory Farm
Moorside Farm
Backwell Green
Hunts Farm
MAIN RD
A370
Woolleys Farm
Farleigh
Backwell House
Flax Bourton
Backwell Sch
L Ctr
FARLEIGH RD
Fairfield Sch
Backwell Down
West Leigh Inf Sch
Liby
Backwell
Farleigh Combe Manor
Cherry Wood
PO
WEST TOWN RD
Bourton Combe
Backwell CE Sch
Church Town
Quarry
BS48
The Conygar
Cheston Combe
PH
Pit La
Chelvey Farm
Water Catch Farm
Backwell Hill
The Spinney
Chelvey Batch
Mast
Backwell Hill House
Hyatt's Wood
Hyattswood Farm
Home Farm
LONG LA
Healls Scars
Edson's Farm
Oatfield Pool
Brockley Wood
BROCKLEY COMBE RD
Willis's Batch
The Batch
Oatfield Farm
Oatfield Wood
DOWNSIDE RD
Downside House Farm
Warren Plantation
Downside
THE BATCH
HYATTS WOOD RD
BACKWELL HILL RD
STANCOMBE LA
BACKWELL COMMON
BACKWELL BOW
A6
1 MARL PITS
2 SLADES CT

36
20

19
10

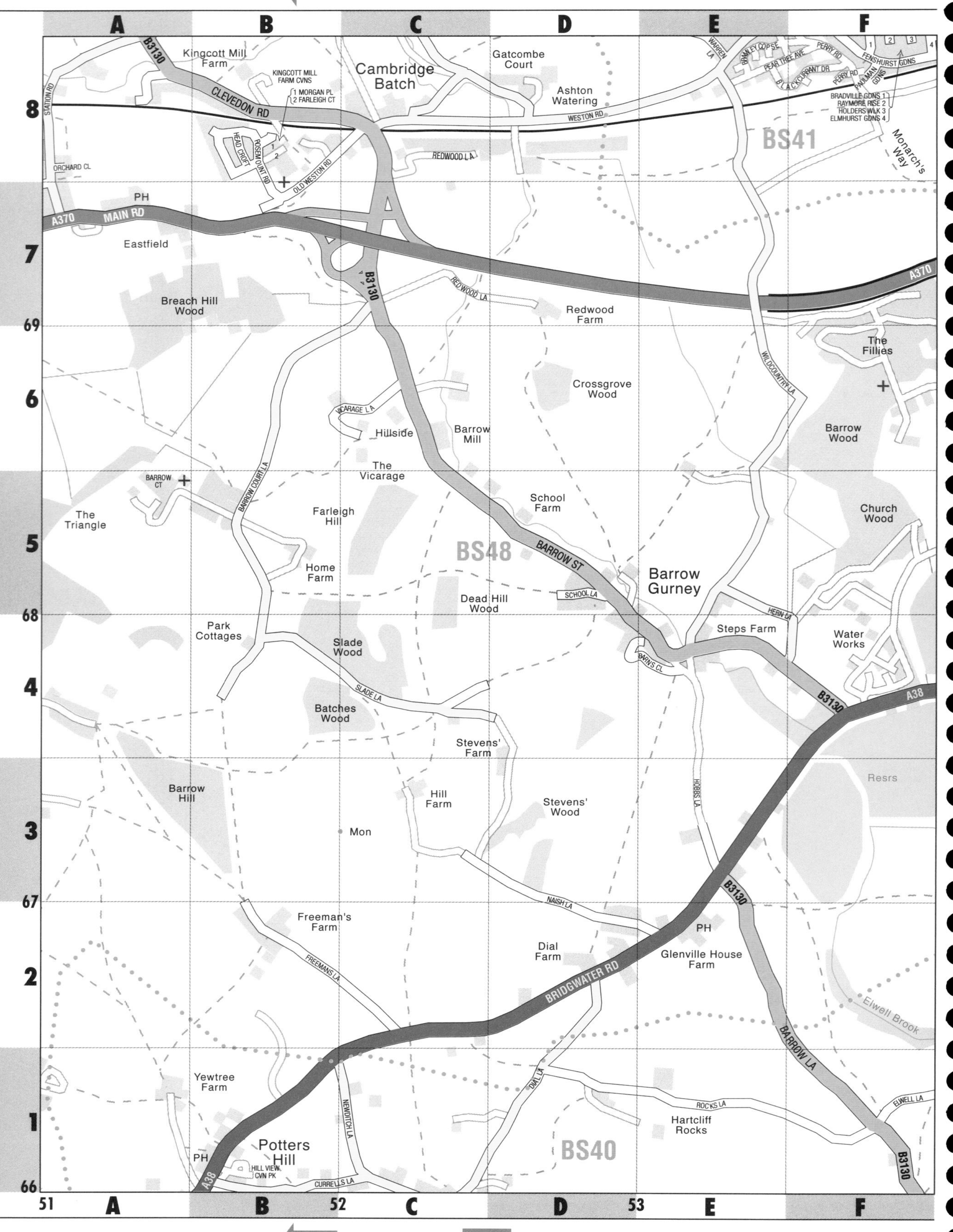
A
B
C
D
E
F
8
7
69
6
5
68
4
3
67
2
1
66
51
52
53
Kingcott Mill
Farm
KINGCOTT MILL
FARM CVNS
1 MORGAN PL
2 FARLEIGH CT
Cambridge
Batch
Gatcombe
Court
Ashton
Watering
WESTON RD
CLEVEDON RD
B3130
STATION RD
ORCHARD CL
HEAD CROFT
ROSEMOUNT RD
OLD WESTON RD
REDWOOD LA
WARREN LA
BRAMLEY COPSE
PEAR TREE AVE
PERRY RD
FENSHURST GDNS
BLACKCURRANT DR
PAULMAN GDNS
BRADVILLE GDNS 1
RAYMORE RISE 2
HOLDERS WLK 3
ELMHURST GDNS 4
BS41
Monarch's
Way
PH
A370
MAIN RD
Eastfield
Breach Hill
Wood
Redwood
Farm
The
Fillies
WILDCOUNTRY LA
Crossgrove
Wood
VICARAGE LA
Hillside
Barrow
Mill
Barrow
Wood
The
Vicarage
BARROW
CT
The
Triangle
BARROW COURT LA
Farleigh
Hill
School
Farm
Church
Wood
BS48
BARROW ST
Home
Farm
Barrow
Gurney
Dead Hill
Wood
SCHOOL LA
HERN LA
Park
Cottages
Slade
Wood
Steps Farm
Water
Works
BARN'S CL
SLADE LA
Batches
Wood
A38
Stevens'
Farm
Resrs
Barrow
Hill
Hill
Farm
Stevens'
Wood
Mon
HOBBS LA
NAISH LA
Freeman's
Farm
PH
Dial
Farm
Glenville House
Farm
FREEMANS LA
BRIDGWATER RD
Elwell Brook
BARROW LA
Yewtree
Farm
DIAL LA
ROCKS LA
ELWELL LA
Hartcliff
Rocks
NEWDITCH LA
PH
Potters
Hill
HILL VIEW
CVN PK
BS40
CURRELLS LA

19
37

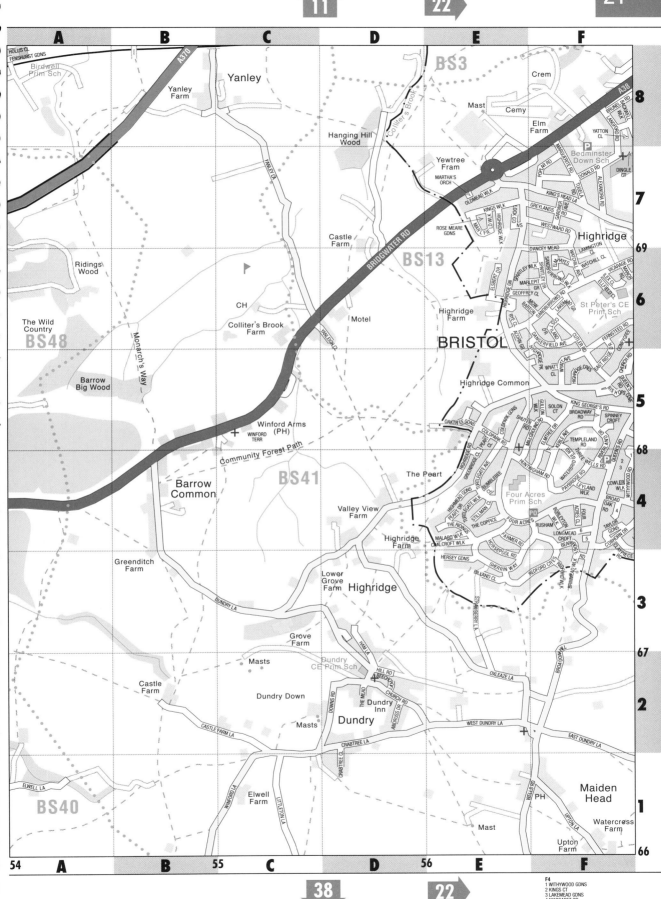

F4
1 WITHYWOOD GDNS
2 KINGS CT
3 LAKEMEAD GDNS
4 MARGARET RD
5 ROSSITER GRANGE
6 GRANGE LANE

21

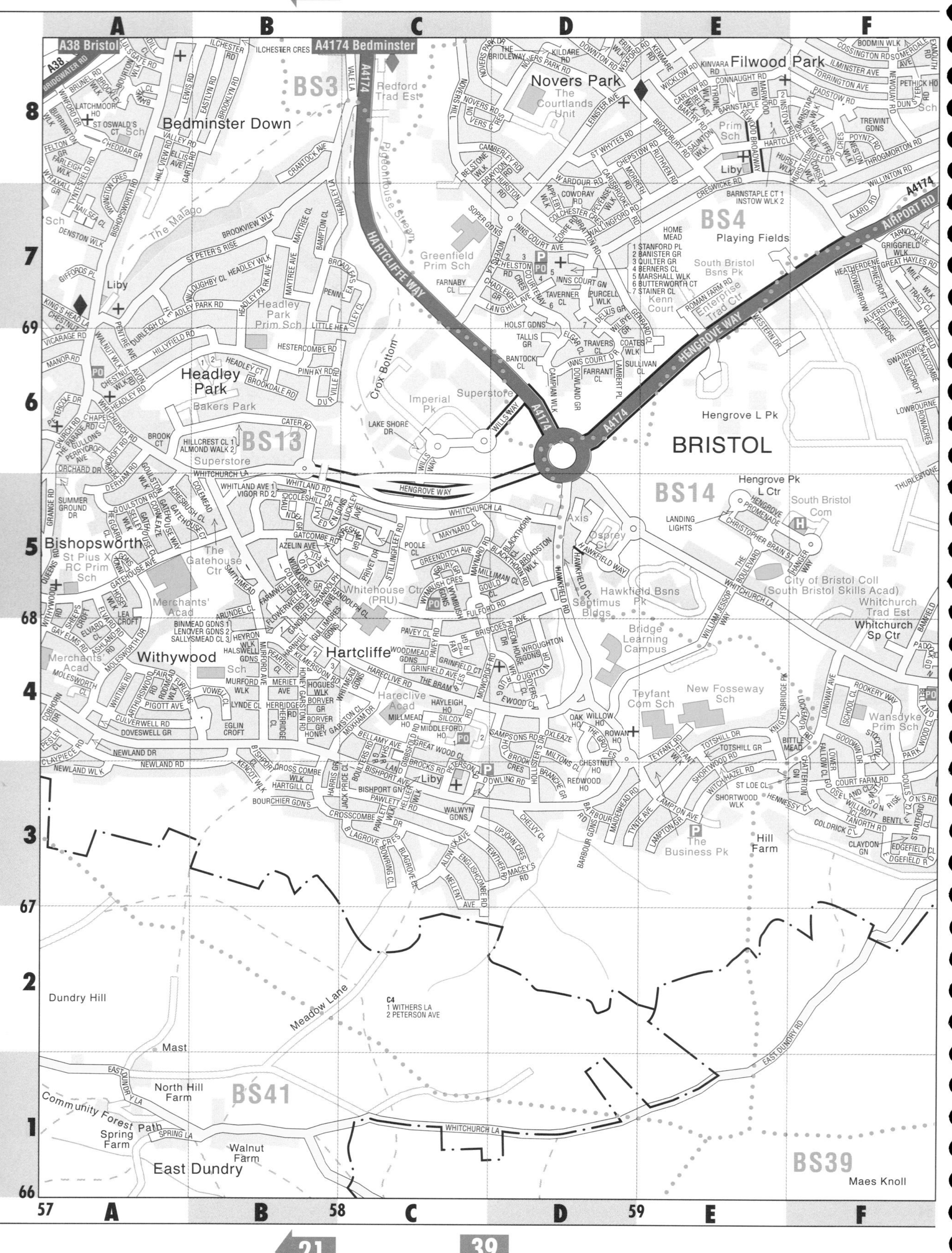

A B C D E F
8 7 69 6 5 68 4 3 67 2 1 66
57 58 59
A38 Bristol
A4174 Bedminster
BS3
BS4
BS13
BS14
BS41
BS39
Bedminster Down
Novers Park
Filwood Park
Headley Park
Bishopsworth
Withywood
Hartcliffe
BRISTOL
Redford Trad Est
The Courtlands Unit
Greenfield Prim Sch
Headley Park Prim Sch
Bakers Park
Superstore
Imperial Pk
Crox Bottom
Pigeonhouse Stream
HARTCLIFFE WAY
HENGROVE WAY
AIRPORT RD
A4174
The Malago
Playing Fields
South Bristol Bsns Pk
Enterprise Trad Ctr
Kenn Court
Hengrove L Pk
Hengrove Pk L Ctr
South Bristol Com
City of Bristol Coll (South Bristol Skills Acad)
Whitchurch Trad Est
Whitchurch Sp Ctr
Hawkfield Bsns Pk
Septimus Bldgs
Bridge Learning Campus
Teyfant Com Sch
New Fosseway Sch
Wansdyke Prim Sch
The Business Pk
Hill Farm
Whitehouse Ctr (PRU)
The Gatehouse Ctr
Merchants' Acad
St Pius X RC Prim Sch
Hareclive Acad
Liby
Dundry Hill
Mast
Meadow Lane
North Hill Farm
Community Forest Path
Spring Farm
Walnut Farm
East Dundry
Maes Knoll
WHITCHURCH LA
EAST DUNDRY RD
EAST DUNDRY LA
SPRING LA
C4
1 WITHERS LA
2 PETERSON AVE

21
39

24

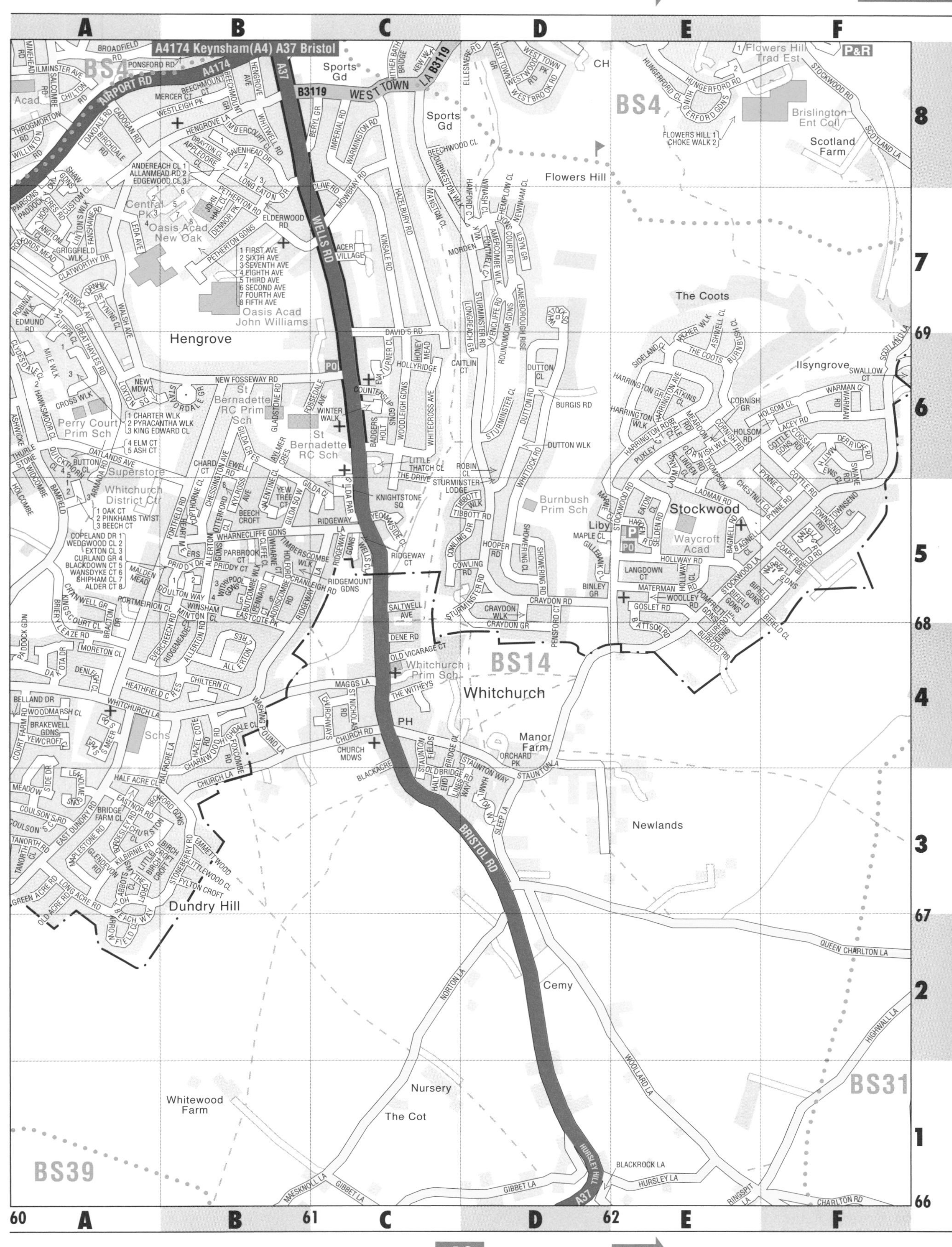
A4174 Keynsham(A4) A37 Bristol
BS4
AIRPORT RD
Sports Gd
B3119 WEST TOWN LA
Flowers Hill Trad Est
Brislington Ent Coll
Scotland Farm
Flowers Hill
Central Pk
Oasis Acad New Oak
WELLS RD
Oasis Acad John Williams
Hengrove
The Coots
Ilsyngrove
St Bernadette RC Prim Sch
St Bernadette RC Sch
Perry Court Prim Sch
Superstore
Whitchurch District Ctr
Burnbush Prim Sch
Stockwood
Waycroft Acad
Liby
Whitchurch Prim Sch
BS14
Whitchurch
Schs
Manor Farm
Newlands
BRISTOL RD
Dundry Hill
QUEEN CHARLTON LA
Cemy
BS31
Whitewood Farm
Nursery
The Cot
BS39
HURSLEY HILL
BLACKROCK LA
HURSLEY LA
GIBBET LA
MAESKNOLL LA
CHARLTON RD
A B C D E F
8 7 6 5 4 3 2 1
69 68 67 66
60 61 62

40

24

23

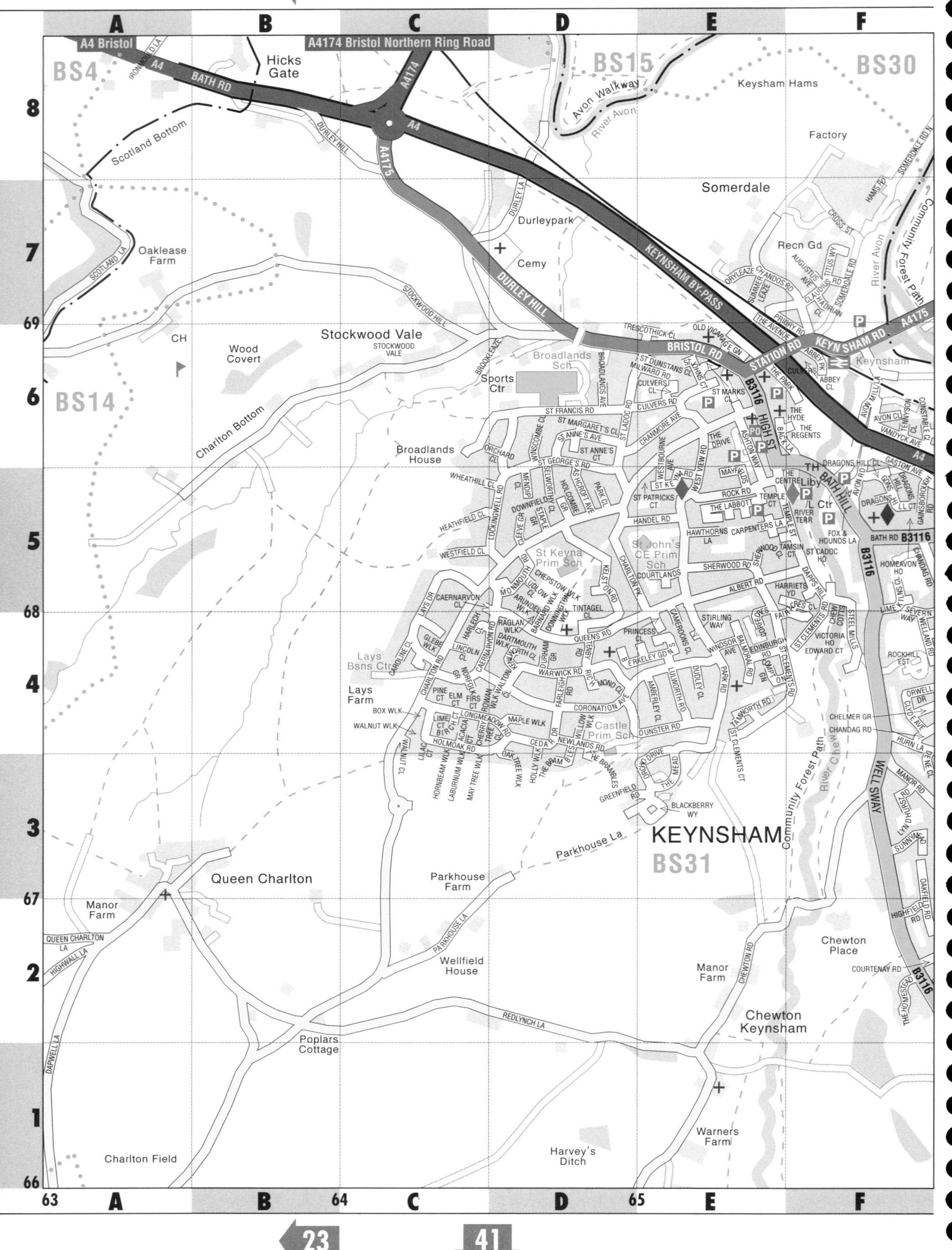

A B C D E F
A4 Bristol
A4174 Bristol Northern Ring Road
Hicks Gate
BS4
BS15
BS30
Keysham Hams
Scotland Bottom
Avon Walkway
River Avon
Factory
Somerdale
Durleypark
Cemy
Oaklease Farm
Recn Gd
Stockwood Vale
CH
Wood Covert
Broadlands Sch
Sports Ctr
BS14
Charlton Bottom
Broadlands House
KEYNSHAM BY-PASS
DURLEY HILL
BRISTOL RD
STATION RD
KEYNSHAM RD
HIGH ST
BATH HILL
St Keyna Prim Sch
St John's CE Prim Sch
Lays Bsns Ctr
Lays Farm
Castle Prim Sch
KEYNSHAM
BS31
Parkhouse La
Queen Charlton
Parkhouse Farm
Manor Farm
Wellfield House
Chewton Place
Chewton Keynsham
Poplars Cottage
Community Forest Path
River Chew
WELL SWAY
Warners Farm
Harvey's Ditch
Charlton Field
63 64 65
8 7 69 6 5 68 4 3 67 2 1 66

23
41

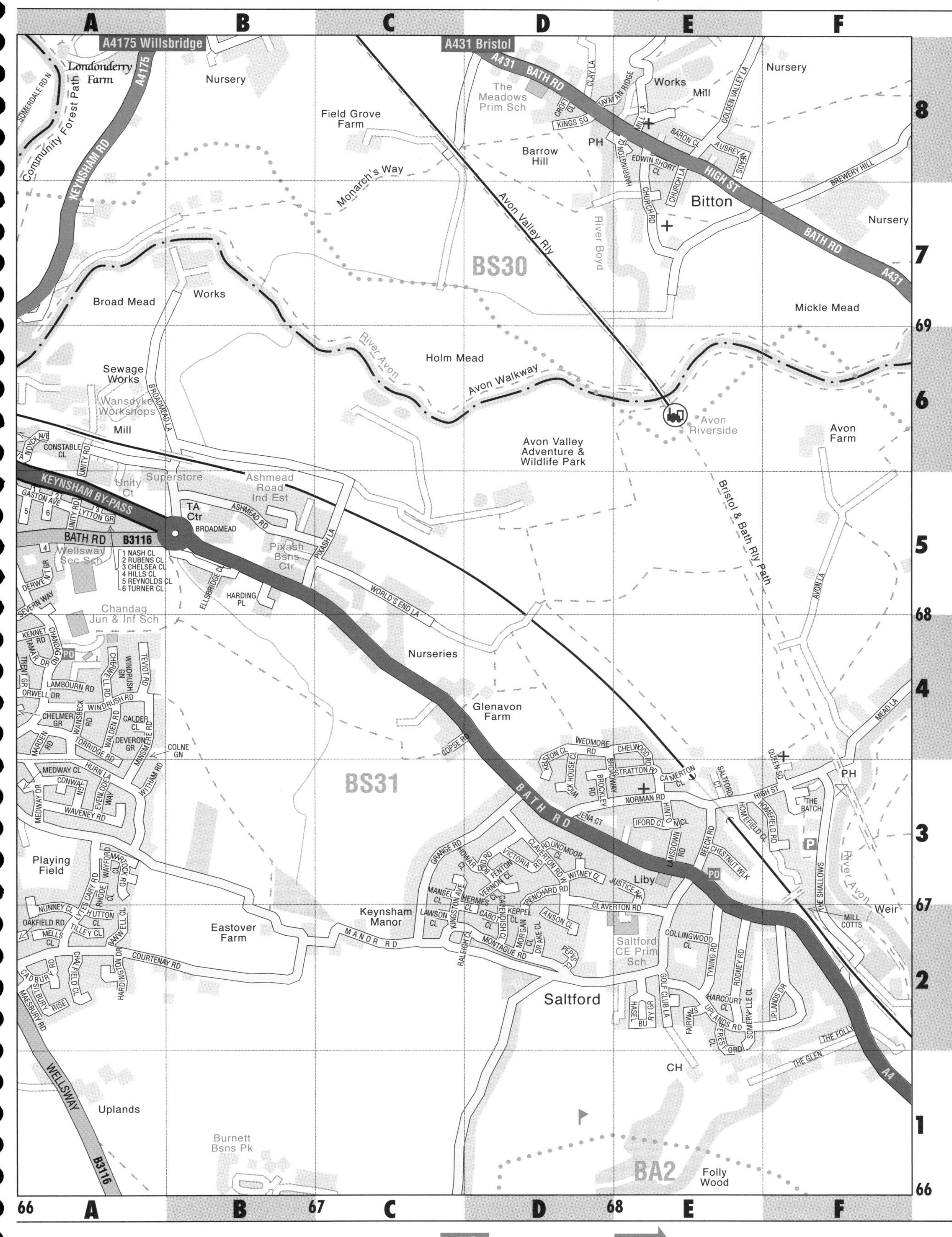

26

Map grid columns: A B C D E F

42 26

A4175 Willsbridge
A431 Bristol
A431
BATH RD

Londonderry Farm
SOMERDALE RD N
Community Forest Path
KEYNSHAM RD
Nursery
Field Grove Farm
Monarch's Way
The Meadows Prim Sch
KINGS SQ
BAYCLIFF RIDGE
CLAY LA
MILL LA
Works
Mill
GOLDEN VALLEY LA
Nursery
Nursery
HARBOURNE
GROVE RD
CATHERINE RD
AUBREY RD
BARON CL
EDWIN SHORT CL
CHURCH LA
PH
CHURCH RD
Bitton
HIGH ST
BREWERY HILL
BATH RD
A431
Nursery
BS30
Avon Valley Rly
River Boyd
Barrow Hill
Mickle Mead
69
Broad Mead
Works
River Avon
Holm Mead
Avon Walkway
Avon Riverside
Avon Farm
Avon Valley Adventure & Wildlife Park
Bristol & Bath Rly Path
6
Sewage Works
Wansdyke Workshops
BRADMEAD LA
Mill
CONSTABLE CL
LANDSEER AVE
UNITY RD
AVON LA
MEAD LA
Superstore
Ashmead Road Ind Est
ASHMEAD RD
PIXASH LA
TA Ctr
BROADMEAD
Unity Ct
KEYNSHAM BY-PASS
BATH RD
B3116
GASTON AVE
LYTTON GR
UNITY RD
DERWENT RD
Wellsway Sec Sch
1 NASH CL
2 RUBENS CL
3 CHELSEA CL
4 HILLS CL
5 REYNOLDS CL
6 TURNER CL
ELLSBRIDGE CL
Pixash Bsns Ctr
HARDING PL
WORLD'S END LA
5
SEVERN WAY
Chandag Jun & Inf Sch
PO
Nurseries
68
KENNET RD
CHANDAG RD
TRENT GR
TAMAR DR
LAMBOURN RD
ORWELL DR
CHERWELL RD
WINDRUSH GN
TEVIOT RD
WINDRUSH RD
CHELMER GR
WANSBECK RD
WALDEN RD
CALDER GR
DEVERONE GR
WINDSMERE RD
COLNE GN
Glenavon Farm
GOPSE RD
WEDMORE CL
CHELWOOD RD
GASTON CL
WICK HOUSE CL
BROOKLEY
BROADSTRATTON
STRATTON CL
CA MERTON CL
SALTFORD RD
QUEEN SQ
HIGH ST
HOMEFIELD CL
PH
THE BATCH
4
MARDEN RD
MEDWAY DR
HURN LA
TORRIDGE RD
WITHAM RD
CHELMER GR
CONWAY RD
WAVENEY RD
EVENLODE WAY
MEDWAY CL
NORMAN RD
JENA CT
IFORD CL
NICL
LANSDOWN
BEECH RD
CHESTNUT WLK
HOMEFIELD RD
P
River Avon
3
BS31
Playing Field
EMBACK WAY
BROE
WAYFORD CL
CRAY CL
HUTTON CL
NUNNEY CL
OAKFIELD RD
MELLS CL
TILLEY CL
Eastover Farm
COURTENAY RD
GRANGE RD
HOWARD
MANSEL CL
KINGSTON AVE
HERMES CL
VERNON CL
CLAVERTON RD
VICTORIA
FENTON
CL
WITNEY CL
LANDMOOR
CLAVERTON RD W
CABENDISH
KEPPEL
FRENCHARD
JUSTICE AVE
Liby
PO
Weir
MILL COTTS
THE SHALLOWS
67
Saltford CE Prim Sch
MANOR RD
Keynsham Manor
LAWSON CL
RALEIGH RD
MONTAGUE RD
MORGAN
DRAKE CL
ANSON CL
CLAVERTON RD
PEPYS
COLLINGWOOD CL
TYNING RD
RODNEY RD
SOMERVILLE CL
HARCOURT RD
UPLANDS DR
THE FOLLY
2
CHADBURY RD
MAESBURY RD
HARDINGTON DR
Saltford
GOLF CLUB LA
RY BR
BURY BR
HASEL
FAIRWAYS
TYNING
FORD
PRIESTFEST RD
A4
CH
1
WELLSWAY
B3116
Uplands
Burnett Bsns Pk
BA2
Folly Wood
66

8
7
5
4
3
1

25

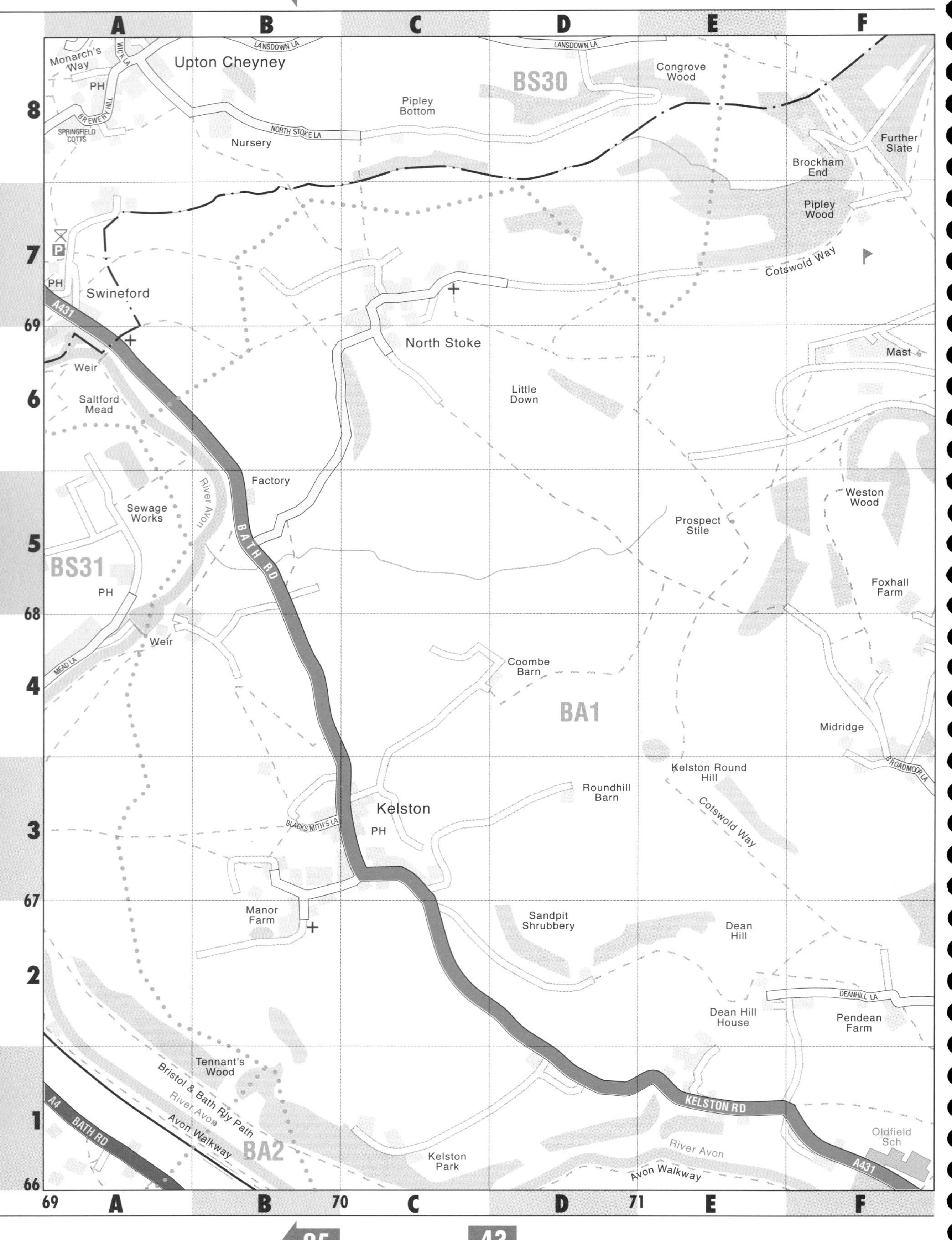
A
B
C
D
E
F
Monarch's Way
WICK LA
LANSDOWN LA
Upton Cheyney
LANSDOWN LA
Congrove Wood
BS30
PH
8
BREWERY HILL
SPRINGFIELD COTTS
Pipley Bottom
NORTH STOKE LA
Nursery
Further Slate
Brockham End
Pipley Wood
7
P
Cotswold Way
PH
Swineford
A431
69
North Stoke
Mast
Weir
Little Down
6
Saltford Mead
Factory
River Avon
Weston Wood
Sewage Works
Prospect Stile
5
BATH RD
BS31
PH
Foxhall Farm
68
Weir
Coombe Barn
MEAD LA
4
BA1
Midridge
BROADMOOR LA
Kelston Round Hill
Roundhill Barn
Kelston
Cotswold Way
3
BLACKSMITH'S LA
PH
67
Manor Farm
Sandpit Shrubbery
Dean Hill
2
DEANHILL LA
Dean Hill House
Pendean Farm
Tennant's Wood
Bristol & Bath Rly Path
River Avon
KELSTON RD
1
A4
BATH RD
Avon Walkway
BA2
Oldfield Sch
River Avon
Kelston Park
A431
Avon Walkway
66
69
70
71

25
43

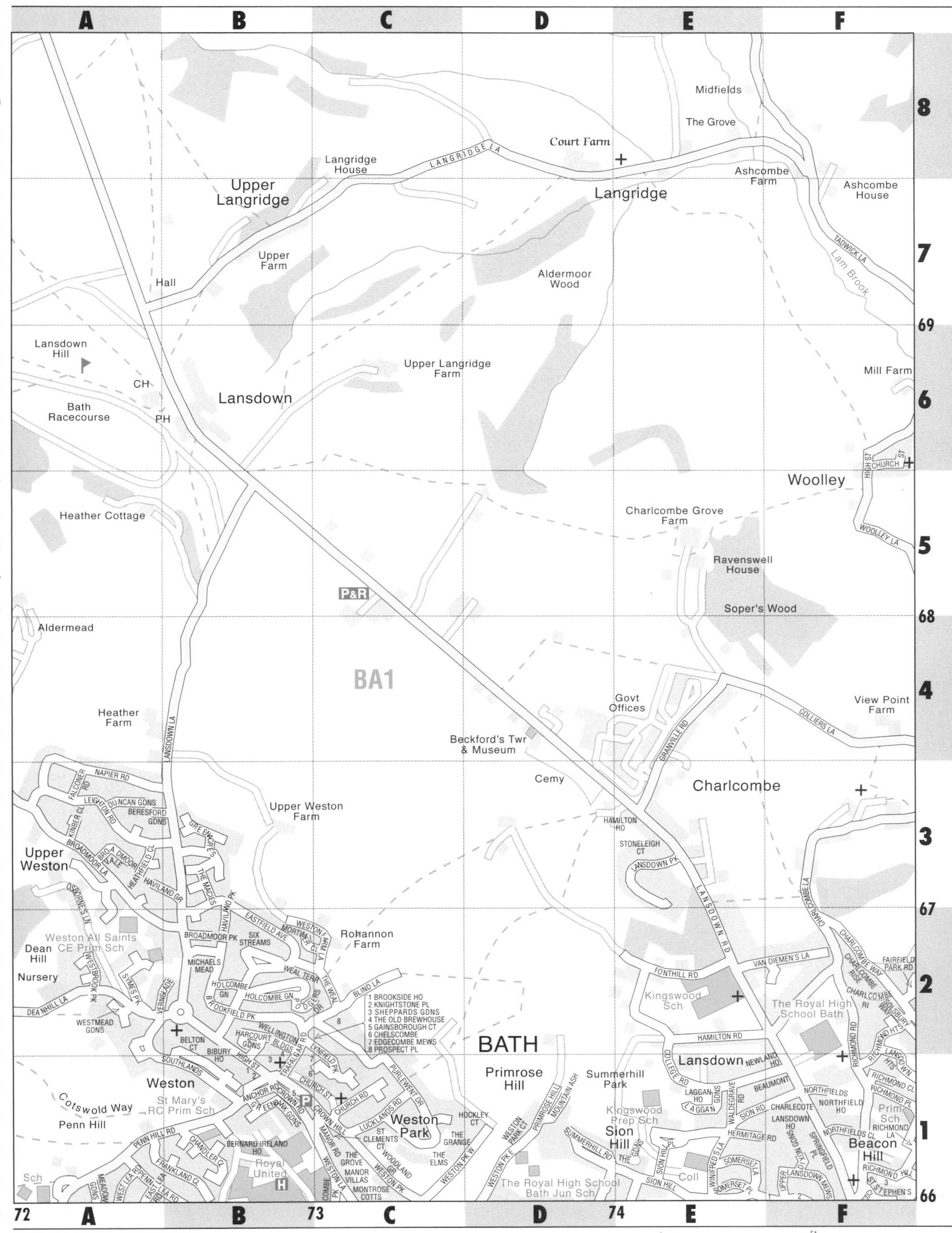

F1
1 LANSDOWN PL W
2 LANSDOWN CRES
3 MOUNT BEACON PL

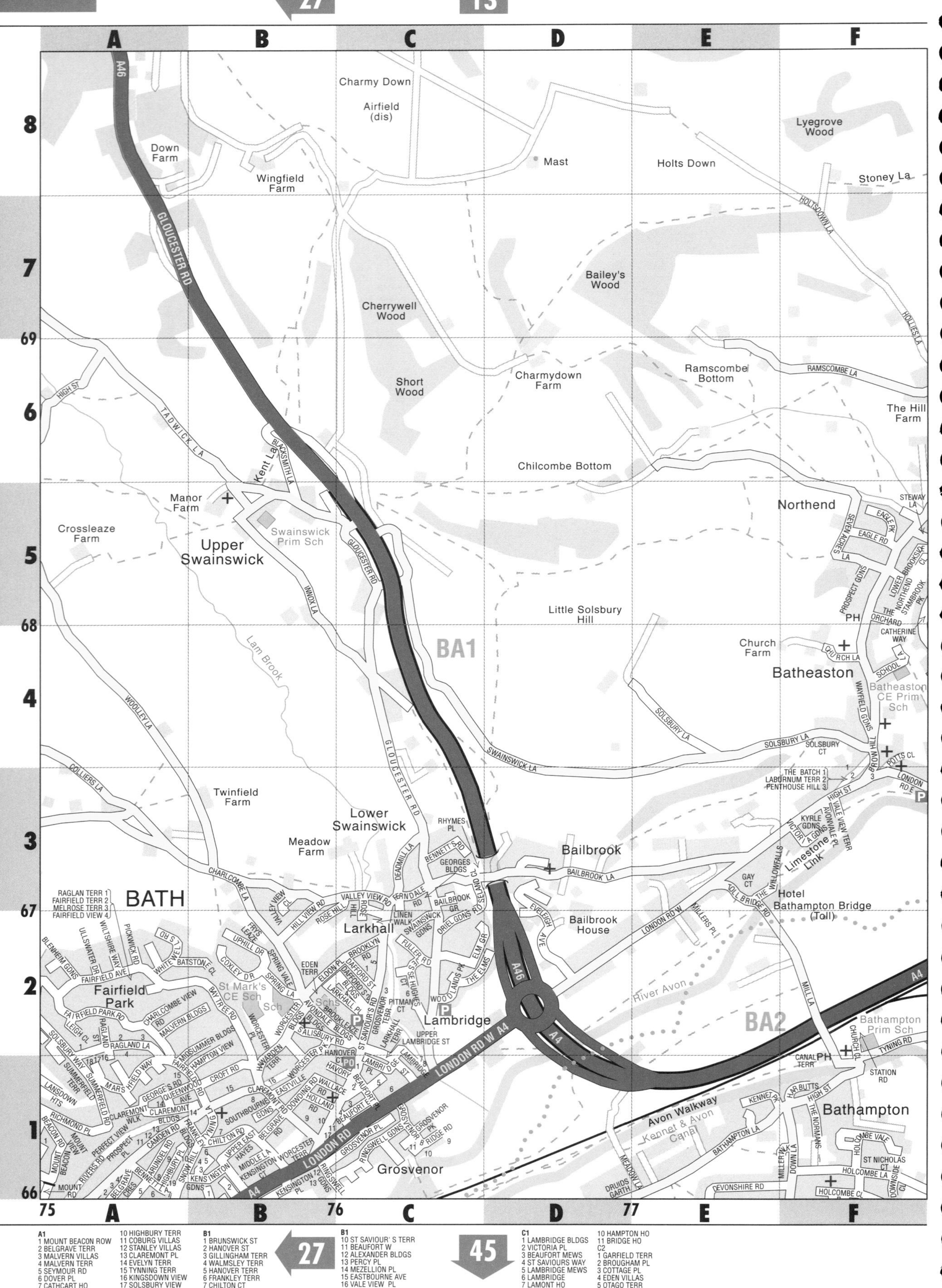

27   45

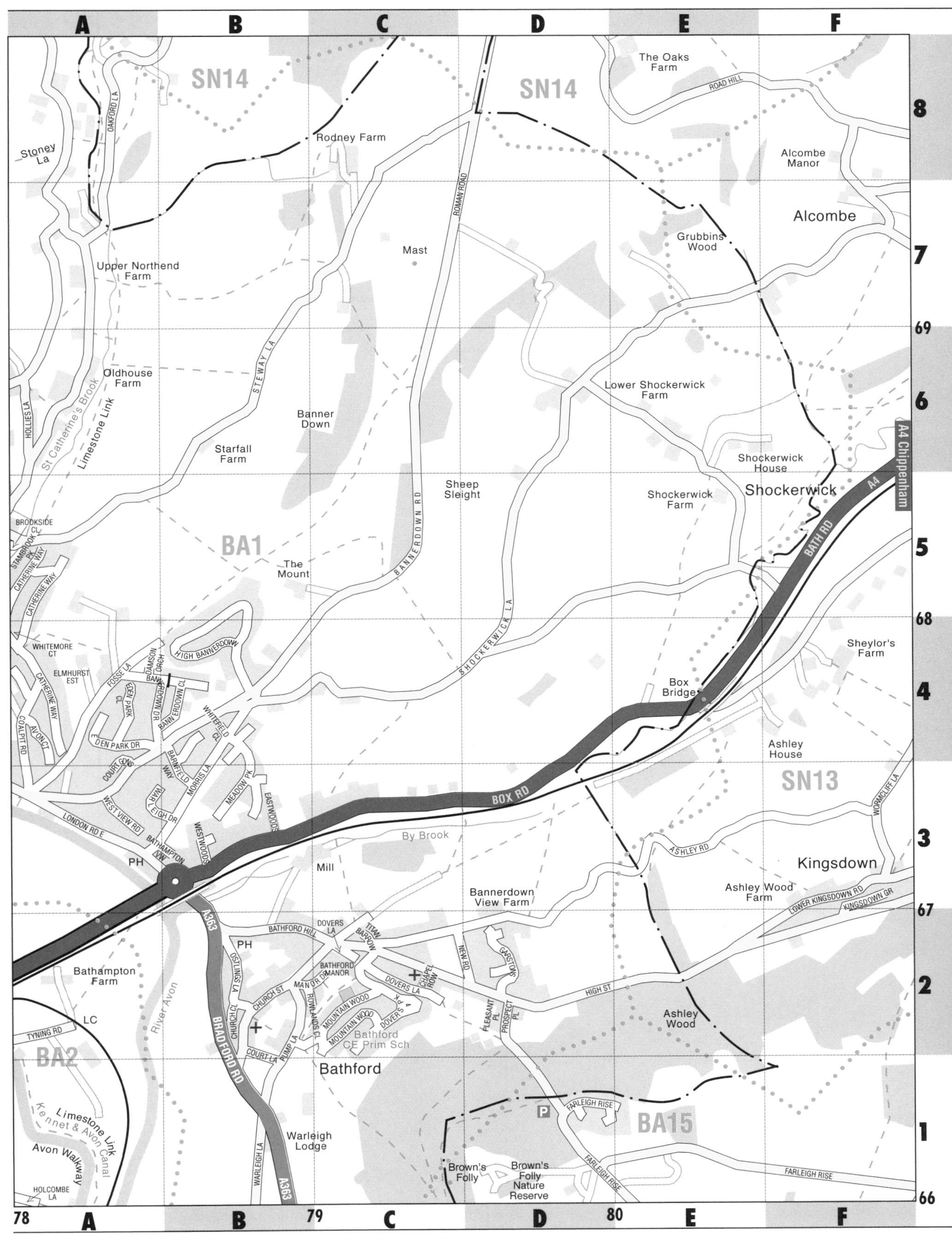
A
B
C
D
E
F
SN14
SN14
The Oaks Farm
ROAD HILL
8
Stoney La
OAKFORD LA
Rodney Farm
Alcombe Manor
ROMAN ROAD
Alcombe
Grubbins Wood
Mast
7
Upper Northend Farm
69
Oldhouse Farm
STEWAY LA
Lower Shockerwick Farm
6
HOLLIES LA
St Catherine's Brook
Limestone Link
Banner Down
A4 Chippenham
Starfall Farm
Shockerwick House
Sheep Sleight
Shockerwick Farm
Shockerwick
A4
BROOKSIDE CL
BANNERDOWN RD
BA1
5
STAMBROOK PK
The Mount
BATH RD
CATHERINE WAY
68
WHITEMORE CT
HIGH BANNERDOWN
SHOCKERWICK LA
Sheylor's Farm
ELMHURST EST
FOSSE LA
DAMSON ORCH
BANNERDOWN CL
Box Bridge
4
EDEN PARK CL
COALPIT RD
AVON CT
WHITEFIELD CL
EDEN PARK DR
COURT GDNS
BARNFIELD WAY
MORRIS LA
Ashley House
SN13
MEADOW PK
EASTWOODS
WEST VIEW RD
LEIGH DR
BOX RD
WORMCLIFF LA
LONDON RD E
WESTWOODS
By Brook
3
BATHAMPTON LA
ASHLEY RD
PH
Mill
Kingsdown
Bannerdown View Farm
Ashley Wood Farm
LOWER KINGSDOWN RD
KINGSDOWN GR
67
A363
BATHFORD HILL
DOVERS LA
TYAN BARROW
PH
NEW RD
GASSTONS
Bathampton Farm
OSTLINGS LA
BATHFORD MANOR
CHAPEL ROW
DOVERS LA
2
MANOR DR
HIGH ST
CHURCH ST
MOUNTAIN WOOD
DOVER'S PK
Ashley Wood
LC
PLEASANT PL
PROSPECT PL
River Avon
TYNING RD
CHURCH CL
ROWLANDS CL
BRADFORD RD
Bathford CE Prim Sch
BA2
COURT LA
PUMP LA
Bathford
P
FARLEIGH RISE
BA15
Limestone Link
Kennet & Avon Canal
Warleigh Lodge
1
Avon Walkway
WARLEIGH LA
Brown's Folly
Brown's Folly Nature Reserve
FARLEIGH RISE
FARLEIGH RISE
HOLCOMBE LA
A363
66
78
A
B
79
C
D
80
E
F

46

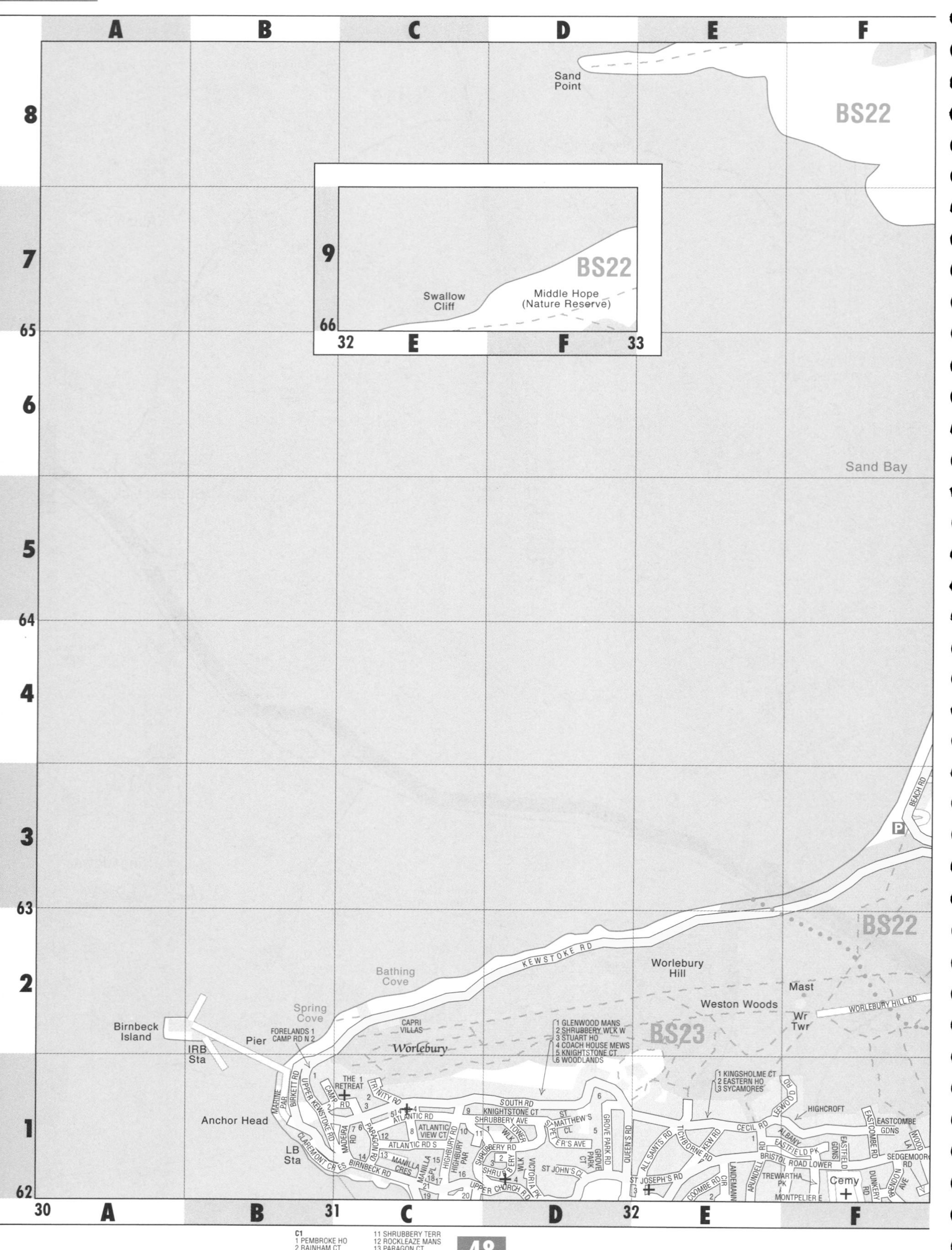

C1
1 PEMBROKE HO
2 RAINHAM CT
3 LEAWOOD CT
4 TRINITY PL
5 MORETON MANS
6 GOSFORD MANS
7 FRANKFORD MANS
8 HAMILTON RD
9 MAPLE CT
10 ROCKHALL HO
11 SHRUBBERY TERR
12 ROCKLEAZE MANS
13 PARAGON CT
14 ROZEL HO
15 HIGHBURY CT
16 VILLA ROSA
17 BADMINTON CT
18 CAIRO CT
19 GLENTWORTH CT
20 RAGLAN PL
21 MANILLA CRES

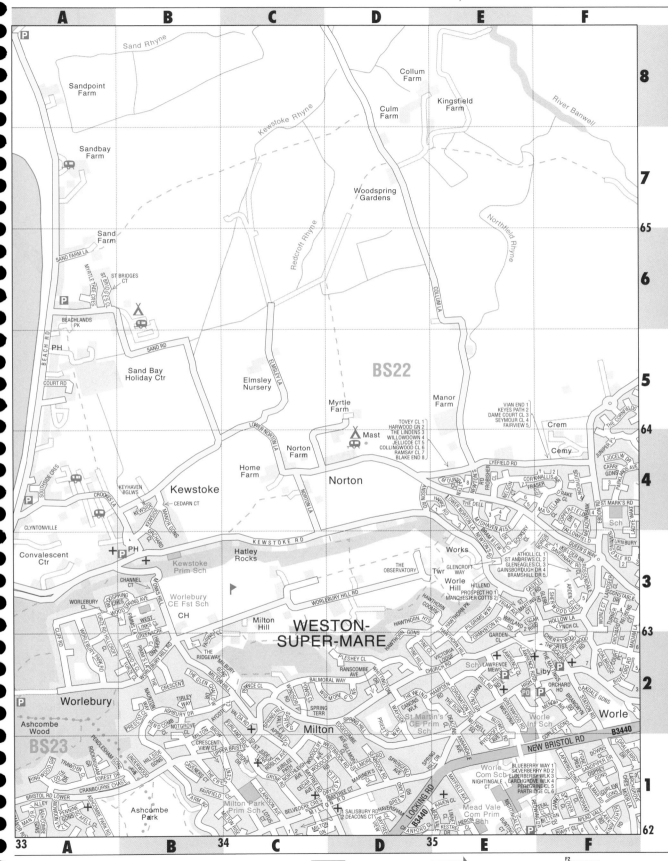

A B C D E F

8 7 65 6 5 64 4 3 63 2 1 62

Sandpoint Farm

Collum Farm

Sandbay Farm

Culm Farm

Kingsfield Farm

River Banwell

Sand Rhyne

Kewstoke Rhyne

Woodspring Gardens

Sand Farm

Redcroft Rhyne

Northfield Rhyne

SAND FARM LA

MYRTLE TREE CRES

ST BRIDGES CT

ST BRIDGES LA

COLLUM LA

BEACHLANDS PK

BEACH RD

PH

COURT RD

SAND RD

Sand Bay Holiday Ctr

Elmsley Nursery

ELMSLEY LA

Myrtle Farm

Manor Farm

BS22

VIAN END 1
KEYES PATH 2
DAME COURT CL 3
SEYMOUR CL 4
FAIRVIEW 5

Crem

Cemy

SOUTHSIDE CRES

LOWER NORTON LA

Norton Farm

Mast

TOVEY CL 1
HARWOOD GN 2
THE LINDENS 3
WILLOWDOWN 4
JELLICOE CT 5
COLLINGWOOD CL 6
RAMSAY CL 7
BLAKE END 8

LYEFIELD RD

THE CORNFIELDS

JUNIPER PL

JOCELIN DR

CARRE GDNS

PARKLANDS AVE

CROOKES LA

KEYHAVEN BGLWS

CEDARN CT

Kewstoke

Home Farm

NORTON LA

Norton

MOUNTBATTEN CL
NEWTON'S RD
FROBISHER
CL

CORNWALLIS AVE

FRASER

NELSON

MAGELLAN CL

DRAKE

COPPERFIELD DR

SOUTHORN

NEWTON CT

FALLOWFIELD

ST MARK'S RD

Sch

LADYE WAKE

EBDON RD

TURNBURY

GLENNGALE RD

CLYNTONVILLE

KEWSTOKE

MANOR GDNS

ORCHARD

PH

KEWSTOKE RD

Hatley Rocks

Works

Twr

ANSON RD

HAWKE RD

THE DELL

MIDHAVEN RISE

BRAM BLEW

ROOKERY

BORGIE

CASTLE

QUEEN'S WAY

KEWSTOKE RD RESSHOLE

OVERMAKE

ARDEN CL

SHERWOOD CL

TURNER

CONSTABLE DR

LANDSEER

Convalescent Ctr

Kewstoke Prim Sch

THE OBSERVATORY

Worle Hill

GLENCROFT WAY

HILLEND
PROSPECT HO 1
MANCHESTER COTTS 2

ATHOLL CL 1
ST ANDREWS CL 2
GLENEAGLES CL 3
GAINSBOROUGH DR 4
BRAMSHILL DR 5

HOLLOW LA

LYNCH CL

WORLE CT

ORCHARD RD

COPLEY RD

MADAM LA

Worlebury CE Fst Sch

CH

Milton Hill

WESTON-SUPER-MARE

WORLEBURY HILL RD

HAWTHORN COMB

HAWTHORN HTS

HAWTHORN GDNS

PILGRIMS WAY

WAYLAND RD

CHERRYWOOD RISE

THE SCAUSEWAY

CHERRYWOOD RD

BIDEFORD RD

BS23

CLIFF RD

FIRZE RD

WORLEBURY CL

WOOD SPRING AVE

GOSPRING CRES

HILL CROFT

WEST LINKS CL

GREENACRE

WORLEBURY PARK RD

ST DAVID'S CL

PINNS LA

MILTON HILL RD

FAIRWAY CL

THE RIDGEWAY

MILTON HILL

ASHBURY DR

PLESHEY CL

RANSCOMBE AVE

WHITMORE RD

CHURCH RD

VICTORIA LODGE

THE WEIND

HAMPDEN RD

CORONATION RD

NUTWELL RD

GREENWOOD RD

HIGH ST

Worle Inf Sch

ORCHARD HO

MENDIP AVE

STATION RD

Worle

B3440

Worlebury

Ashcombe Wood

Ashcombe Park

PENDLESHAM GDNS

ROCKINGHAM GRO

FOREST DR

CRANBOURNE CHASE

NAUNTON WAY

PRESCOT CL

TIRLEY WAY

RENDCOMBE CL

NOTGROVE

THE GLEN

MILTON BROW

CRESCENT VIEW CT

UPPER BRISTO

SPRING HILL

WINDSOR RD

POWIS CL

BALMORAL WAY

SPRING TERR

EDGECOMBE AVE

PRIEST

WAYSIDE

SPRING HILL GRO

THE ROW

DEACONS CL

ANNANDALE

NEW BRISTOL RD

Milton

St Martin's CE Prim Sch

CANONS RD

Sch

LAWRENCE MEWS

Liby

THE MAIDINGS

CASTLE GDNS

B3440

RINGWOOD GRO

LODGE

TRAWDEN GRO

MANOR

PENNINE

ASHCOMBE GDNS

BRISTOL RD LOWER

UNDERWOOD RD

HILLSIDE

JANE

FERLAND RD

ST JUDE'S

ROSLYN AVE

JUBILEE PATH

GROVE RD

CAVENERS RD

THE CRES

DRY'S

MILTON RISE

MILTON GN

CLARENCE AVE

LOTUS

BELVEDERE CRES

HAVERSHAM CL

MARINER'S CL

WESTBROOK RD

SPRINGFIELD AVE

SPRING HILL GRO

LOCKING RD

MAYFIELD AVE

MEAD VALE

HERON

RAVEN CL

BUNTING CT

KESTREL DR

CRANFORD CL

LINNET CL

NIGHTINGALE CT

Worle Com Sch

Mead Vale Com Prim Sch

BLUEBERRY WAY 1
SILVERBERRY RD 2
ELDERBERRY WLK 3
LARCHGROVE WLK 4
PEREGRINE CL 5
PARTRIDGE CL 6

CYGNET

DOWNS

SANDPIPER CT

LAPWING GDNS

CORMORANT

CURLEW

MEAD VALE

LAPWING GDNS

DIPPER

SWIFT CL

BITTERN

Milton Park Prim Sch

SALISBURY RD 1
DEACONS CT 2

Fairfield

BAYTREE CT

BAYTREE RD

F2
1 COTMAN WLK
2 WESTWOOD CL
3 BLACKMOOR
4 APPLEDORE
5 BAMPTON
6 KENNFORD
7 KNIGHTSTONE PL

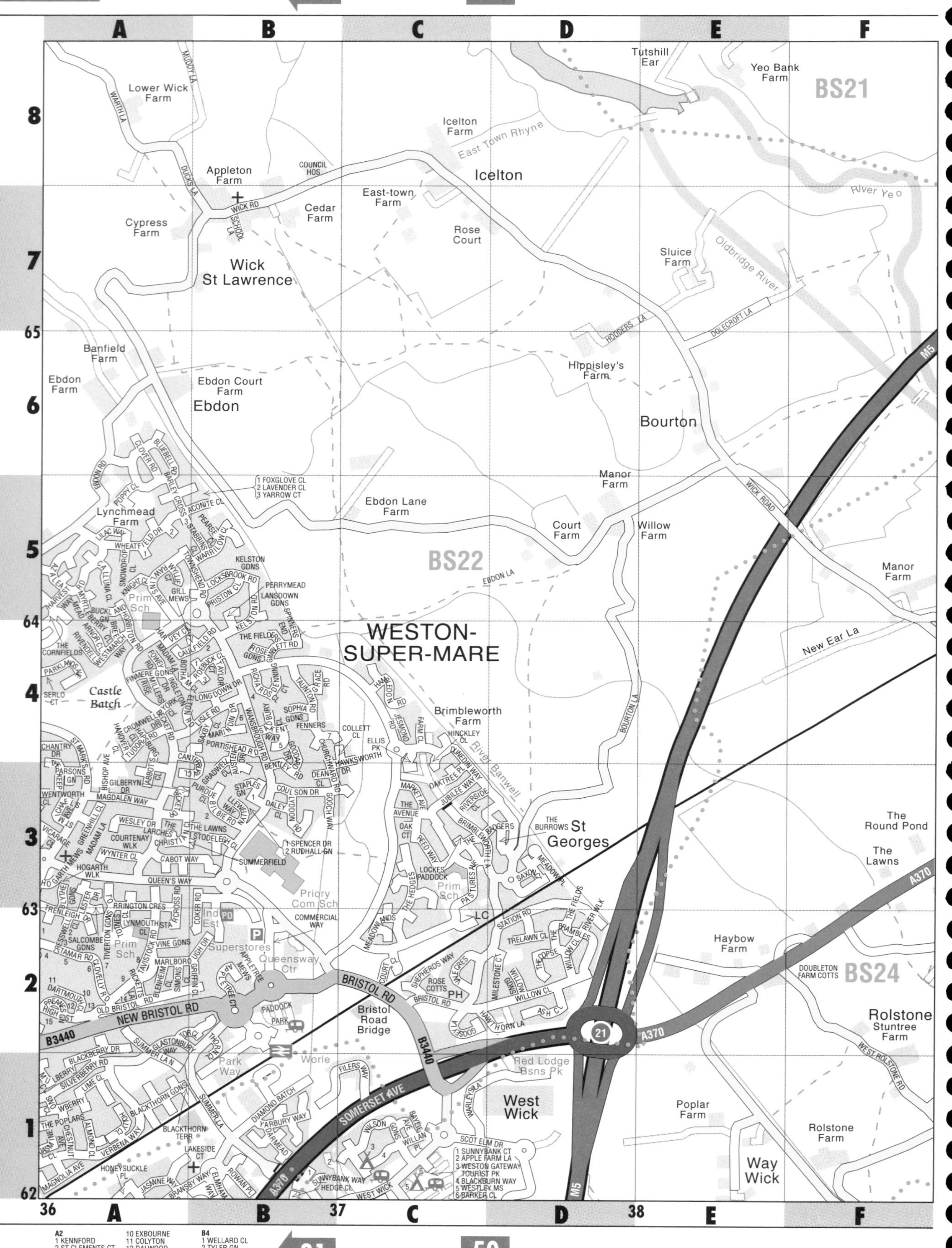

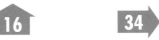
A B C D E F

BS21

BS22

BS49

8

Phipp's Bridge

Little River

Wemberham Cott

WEMBERHAM LA

Riverside Farm

7

River Yeo

Pilhay Farm

65

The Elms

Hewish Farm

East Hewish

New Rhyne

Pilhay Bridge

6

LC

The Oaks

Pool Farm

Heathgate Farm

Works

St Anne's CE Prim Sch

PH

Hewish

MOORLAND PK

A370 WESTON RD

5

West Hewish

The Grange Bsns Pk

Chestnut Farm

The Grange

Waterman's Bow

64

WICK ROAD

Willow Farm

4

PH PALMER'S ELM

Oldbridge River

BS24

DOLEMOOR LA

Balls Yeo Rhyne

Mayfield Farm

Old Bridges

May's Green

MAY'S GREEN LA

MAY'S LA

Puxton

Chestnut Barn Ind Est

Meer Wall Rhyne

BS49

3

Villa Farm

Grange Farm

Chestnut Farm

PUXTON LA

Puxton Park (Adventure Park)

COUNCIL HOUSES

63

Puxton Court Farm

Goose Acre Farm

Puxton Moor

COWSLIP LANE

PUXTON RD

2

BALLS BARN LA

Puxton Moor Farm

PUXTON MOOR LA

Rolstone Court

South Farm

The Laurels

Land Farm

BOX BUSH LA

Box Bush Farm

Blackstone's Rhyne

1

WEST ROLSTONE RD

East Rolstone

62

33 17

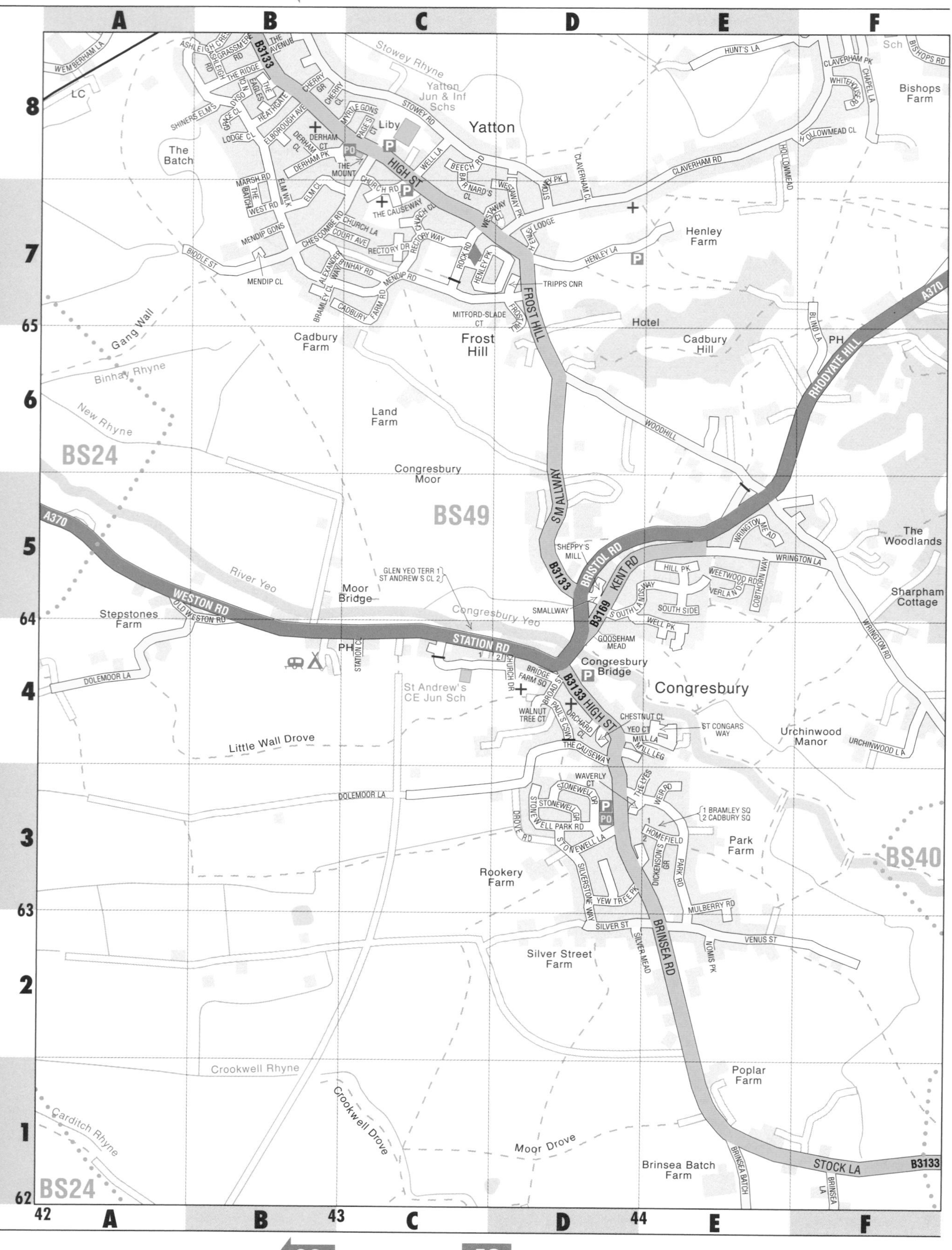

A B C D E F
8 7 65 6 5 64 4 3 63 2 1 62
42 43 44
Yatton
Yatton Jun & Inf Schs
Stowey Rhyne
Liby
HIGH ST
B3133
The Batch
Henley Farm
Bishops Farm
Sch
HUNT'S LA
CLAVERHAM RD
CLAVERHAM PK
CHAPEL LA
HOLLOWMEAD CL
HOLLOWMEAD
BISHOPS RD
WEMBERHAM LA
LC
Cadbury Farm
Frost Hill
FROST HILL
TRIPPS CNR
MITFORD-SLADE CT
Hotel
Cadbury Hill
PH
A370
RHODYATE HILL
BLIND LA
Gang Wall
Binhay Rhyne
New Rhyne
Land Farm
BS24
Congresbury Moor
BS49
WOODHILL
SMALLWAY
The Woodlands
WRINGTON LA
WRINGTON RD
Sharpham Cottage
River Yeo
Moor Bridge
Stepstones Farm
WESTON RD
OLD WESTON RD
Congresbury Yeo
STATION RD
BRISTOL RD
KENT RD
B3169
Congresbury Bridge
Congresbury
DOLEMOOR LA
St Andrew's CE Jun Sch
Little Wall Drove
Urchinwood Manor
URCHINWOOD LA
THE CAUSEWAY
Park Farm
BS40
Rookery Farm
SILVER ST
VENUS ST
BRINSEA RD
Silver Street Farm
Crookwell Rhyne
Crookwell Drove
Poplar Farm
Carditch Rhyne
Moor Drove
Brinsea Batch Farm
STOCK LA
BRINSEA BATCH
BRINSEA LA

33 52

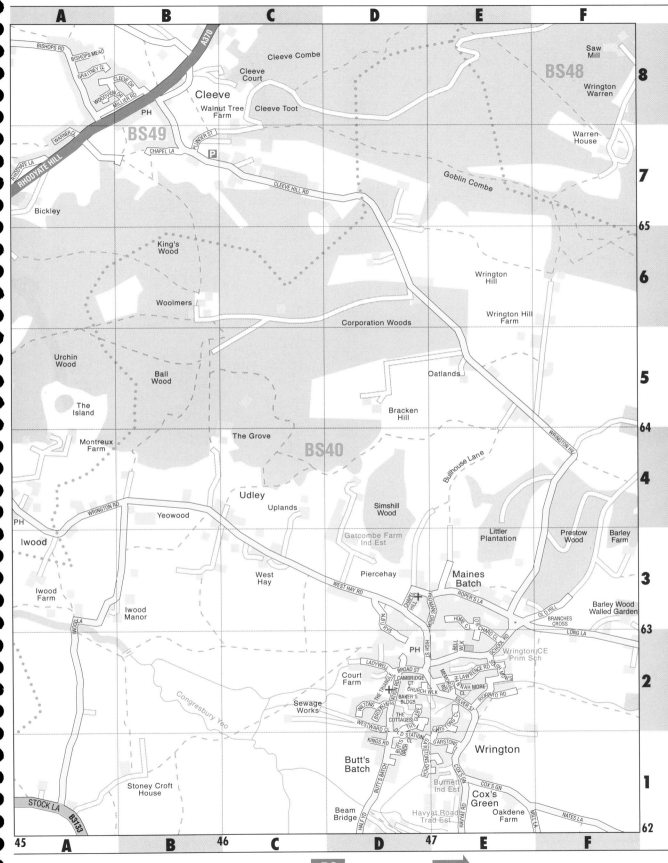

A B C D E F

Bishops Rd
Bishops Mead
Graitney Cl
Cleeve Dr
Woodview Dr
Millier Rd
A370
Cleeve Combe
Cleeve Court
Cleeve
PH
Walnut Tree Farm
Cleeve Toot
Saw Mill
BS48
Wrington Warren
8
Warner Cl
BS49
Plunder St
P
Chapel La
Rhodyate La
Rhodyate Hill
Warren House
Goblin Combe
7
Cleeve Hill Rd
Bickley
65
King's Wood
Wrington Hill
6
Woolmers
Corporation Woods
Wrington Hill Farm
Urchin Wood
Ball Wood
Oatlands
5
The Island
Bracken Hill
64
Montreux Farm
The Grove
BS40
Wrington Hill
Bullhouse Lane
4
Udley
Uplands
Simshill Wood
Wrington Rd
Yeowood
PH
Iwood
Gatcombe Farm Ind Est
Littler Plantation
Prestow Wood
Barley Farm
West Hay
Piercehay
Maines Batch
3
Iwood Farm
West Hay Rd
Chapel Hill
Yeomans Orch
Roper's La
Iwood Manor
Old Hill
Barley Wood Walled Garden
Iwood La
Alburys
Home Cl
Orchard Cl
Branches Cross
63
Long La
High St
Bell Wlk
School Rd
PH
Wrington CE Prim Sch
Ladywell
Broad St
Memorial Rd
Lawrence Rd
South Mdws
Court Farm
The Triangle
Station Rd
Cambridge Ct
Church Wlk
Hannah More Cl
2
Baker's Bldgs
Rickyard Rd
Silver St
Congresbury Yeo
Sewage Works
Wiltons
Brooklyn
The Cottages
The Glebe
Garstons Cl
Westward Cl
Old Station Cl
Kings Rd
Butts Orch
Garstons
Garstons Orch
Wrington
Butt's Batch
Butt's Batch
Cox's Gn
Burnett Ind Est
Cox's Gn
1
Stoney Croft House
Cox's Green
Stock La
B3133
Beam Bridge
Havyat Road Trad Est
Oakdene Farm
Mill La
Nates La
Half Yd
Havyat Rd
62

45 A B 46 C D 47 E F

53
36

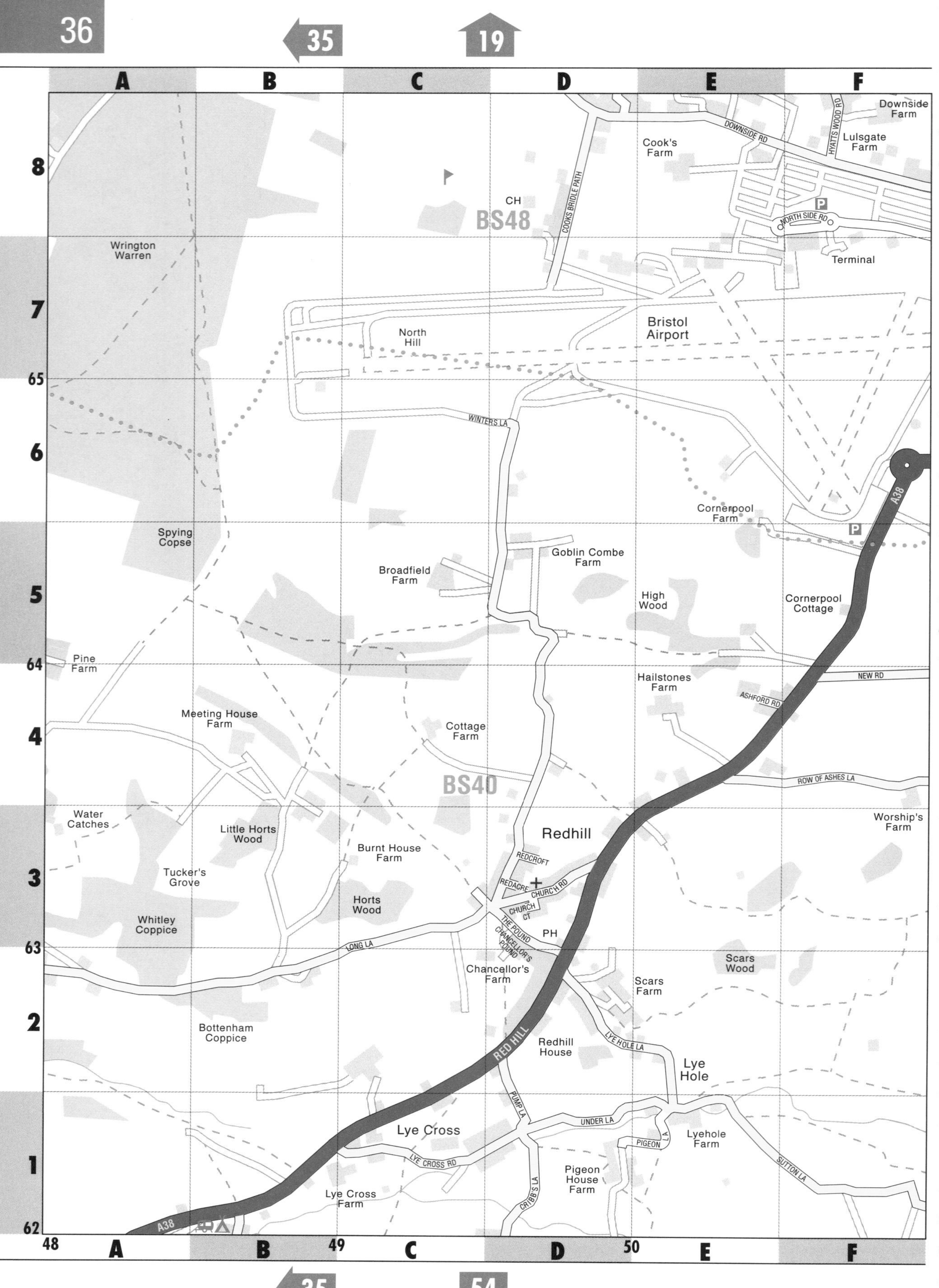

35
19

BS48

Wrington
Warren

CH

Cook's
Farm

Downside
Farm

DOWNSIDE RD

HYATTS WOOD RD

Lulsgate
Farm

P

NORTH SIDE RD

Terminal

North
Hill

Bristol
Airport

COOKS BRIDLE PATH

WINTERS LA

Spying
Copse

Cornerpool
Farm

P

A38

Broadfield
Farm

Goblin Combe
Farm

High
Wood

Cornerpool
Cottage

Pine
Farm

Meeting House
Farm

Hailstones
Farm

ASHFORD RD

NEW RD

Cottage
Farm

BS40

ROW OF ASHES LA

Water
Catches

Little Horts
Wood

Redhill

Worship's
Farm

Tucker's
Grove

Burnt House
Farm

REDCROFT

REDACRE

CHURCH CT

CHURCH RD

Whitley
Coppice

Horts
Wood

LONG LA

THE POUND
CHANCELLOR'S POUND

PH

Scars
Wood

Chancellor's
Farm

Scars
Farm

Bottenham
Coppice

RED HILL

Redhill
House

LYE HOLE LA

Lye
Hole

PUMP LA

UNDER LA

PIGEON LA

Lyehole
Farm

SUTTON LA

Lye Cross

LYE CROSS RD

CRIBBS LA

Pigeon
House
Farm

Lye Cross
Farm

A38

35
54

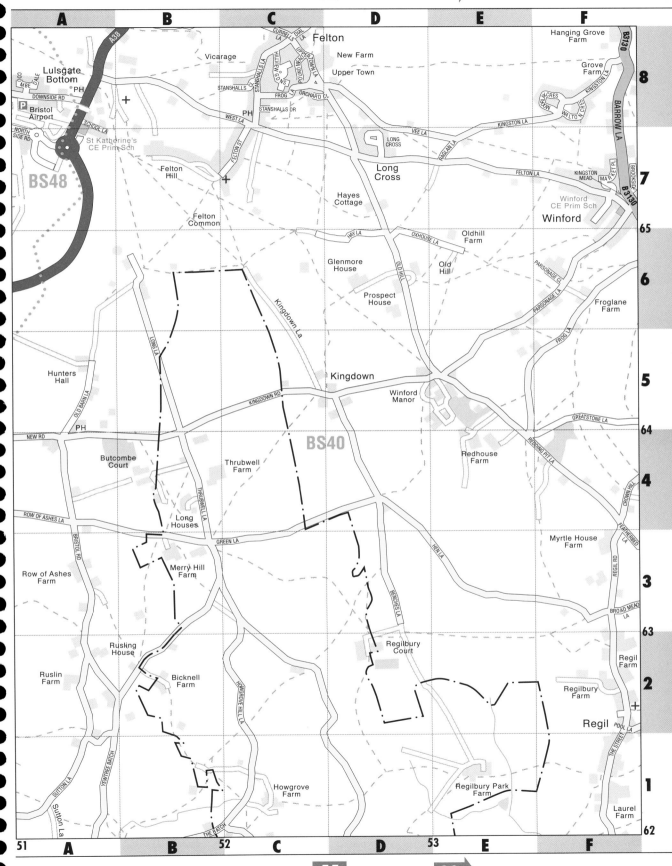
20
38

A
B
C
D
E
F
Felton
Hanging Grove Farm
Vicarage
New Farm
Grove Farm
Lulsgate Bottom
Upper Town
Bristol Airport
St Katherine's CE Prim Sch
BS48
Felton Hill
Long Cross
Hayes Cottage
Winford CE Prim Sch
Felton Common
Winford
Oldhill Farm
Glenmore House
Old Hill
Prospect House
Froglane Farm
Kingdown La
Hunters Hall
Kingdown
Winford Manor
BS40
Butcombe Court
Thrubwell Farm
Redhouse Farm
Long Houses
Myrtle House Farm
Merry Hill Farm
Row of Ashes Farm
Rusling House
Regilbury Court
Regil Farm
Ruslin Farm
Bicknell Farm
Regilbury Farm
Regil
Howgrove Farm
Regilbury Park Farm
Laurel Farm
Sutton La
A38
B3130
BARROW LA
DOWNSIDE RD
NORTH SIDE RD
SCHOOL LA
WEST LA
FELTON ST
STANSHALLS CL
STANSHALLS LA
STANSHALLS DR
FROG LA
ORCHARD CL
HILLVIEW GDNS
POUND MEAD
UPPER TOWN LA
CURRELLS LA
DIAL LA
VEE LA
LONG CROSS
RAGLAN LA
KINGSTON LA
FELTON LA
KINGSTON MEAD
MARKET PL
BROOKSIDE
WALTON CRES
HAY LA
OXHOUSE LA
OLD HILL
PARSONAGE CL
PARSONAGE LA
FROG LA
LONG LA
KINGDOWN RD
OLD BARN LA
NEW RD
PH
GREATSTONE LA
REDDING PIT LA
THRUBWELL LA
ROW OF ASHES LA
GREEN LA
BRISTOL RD
HEN LA
CROWN HILL
FEATHERBED LA
REGIL RD
BENCHES LA
BROAD MEAD LA
HOWGROVE HILL LA
POOL LA
THE STREET
YEWTREE BATCH
SUTTON LA
THE BATCH
8
7
65
6
5
64
4
3
63
2
1
62
51
52
53

37 21

A B C D E F

8 7 65 6 5 64 4 3 63 2 1 62

Barns Batch
BS41
WINFORD LA
UPTON COTTS
UPTON LA
WELLS RD
Elton Farm
DUNDRY LA
Monarch's Way
WILLIAM'S YARD
Meade Farm
LITTLETON LA
CHURCH RD
CHURCH RISE
HIGH ST
PO
CHAPEL CL
CHAPEL LA
RUSSELL
Kentshare Farm
Primrose Farm
Court Farm
Greenleigh Farm
B3130
FROG LA
KENTSHARE LA
F MEAD
THE RICKLANDS
Upper Littleton
Avon Livestock Centre
Littleton Court
REGIL LA
Inman's Batch
Powdermill Farm
Hazel Farm
Chew Hill
Lane-end Farm
Bitham's Wood
Malvern Lodge
CROWN HILL
GREATSTONE LA
Spring Farm
CHEW RD
Littleton
WATERY LA
LITTLETON LA
LIMEBURN HILL
Chewhill Farm
Limeburn House
PINCHAY LA
Mill
The Crown Inn (PH)
Leighdown Farm
BS40
Littleton Farm
Littleton
FEATHERBED LA
Chew Magna Resr
Ford
BROAD MEAD LA
Hounsley Batch
Hounsley Farm
Blackmoor
BROADCROFT
WINFORD RD
B3130
Chillyhill Farm
CHILLYHILL LA
B3114
PAGANS HILL
POOL LA
WHITLING ST
Pagans Hill
Chillyhouse Farm
COCK AND YEW TREE HILL
North Hill Farm
The Oaks
Tavern Scott
CHEW LA
SCOT LA
Pagans Hill Farm
Chew Valley Sch
Ledbury House
Nut Grove
SALWAY CL
BLIND LA
PILGRIMS WAY
B3114
BRISTOL RD

54 A B 55 C D 56 E F

37 56

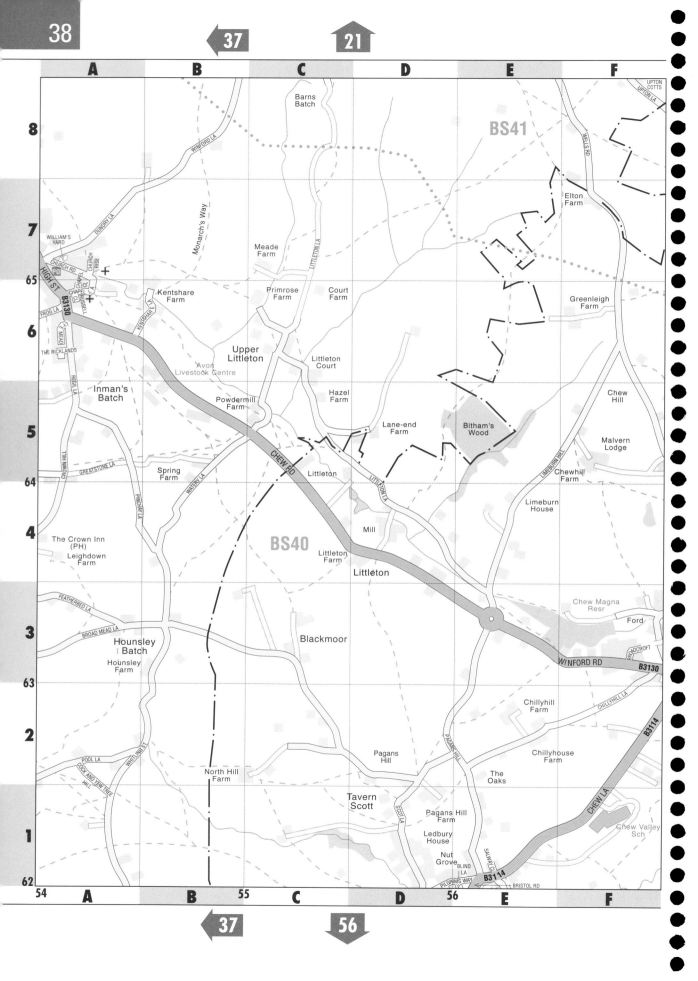

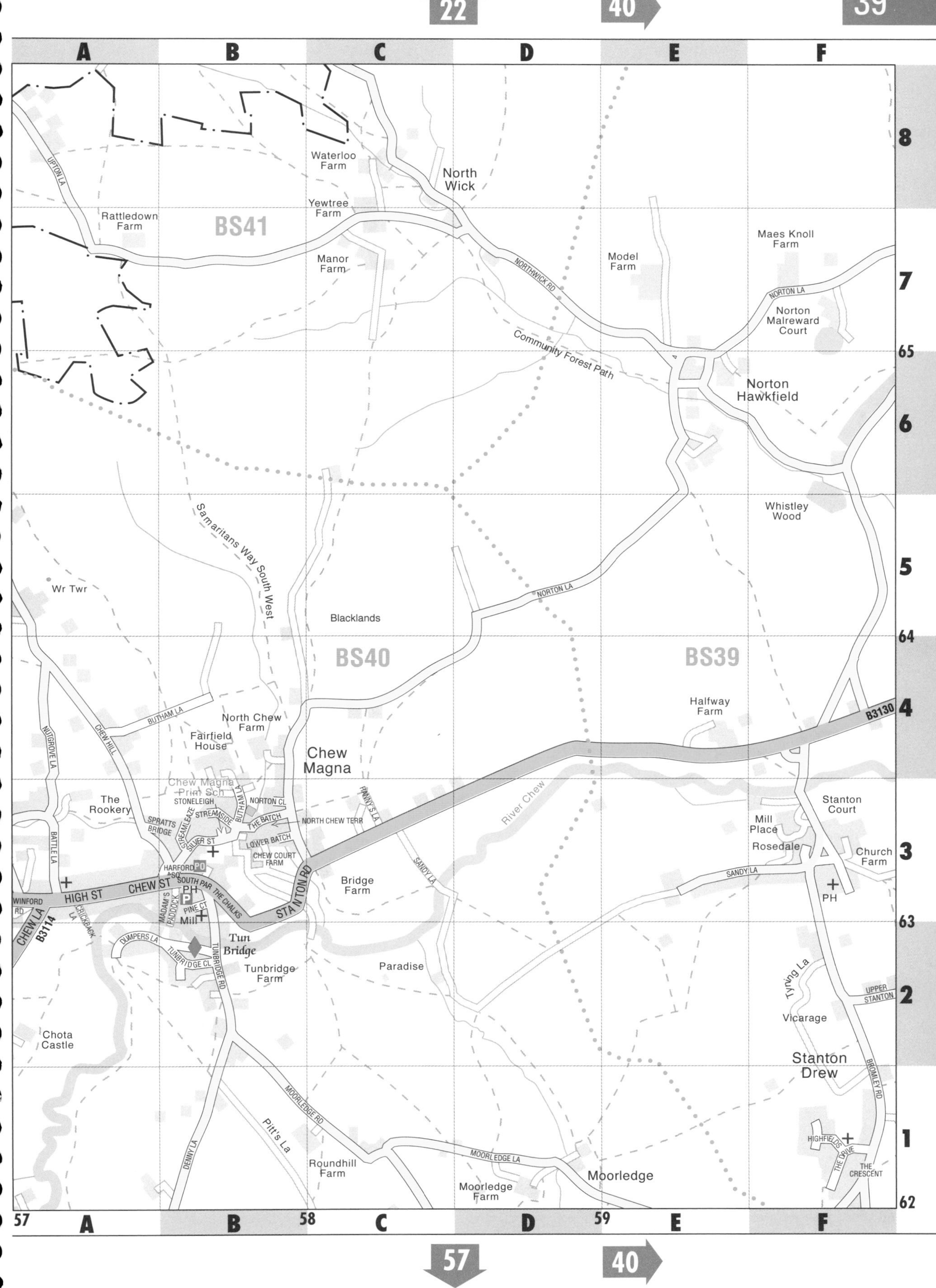

A B C D E F

8

Waterloo Farm

North Wick

Rattledown Farm

BS41

Yewtree Farm

Maes Knoll Farm

7

Manor Farm

NORTHWICK RD

Model Farm

NORTON LA

Norton Malreward Court

65

Community Forest Path

Norton Hawkfield

6

Samaritans Way South West

Whistley Wood

5

Wr Twr

Blacklands

NORTON LA

64

BS40

BS39

Halfway Farm

B3130

4

BUTHAM LA

North Chew Farm

Chew Magna

River Chew

Stanton Court

NUTGROVE LA

CHEW HILL

Fairfield House

Mill Place

The Rookery

Chew Magna Prim Sch

STONELEIGH

NORTON CL

Rosedale

Church Farm

3

STREAMSIDE

SCREAM EAZE

THE BATCH

FINNY'S LA

BATTLE LA

SPRATTS BRIDGE

SILVER ST

NORTH CHEW TERR

LOWER BATCH

PH

SANDY LA

SANDY LA

PH

HARFORD SQ

CHEW COURT FARM

WINFORD RD

HIGH ST

CHEW ST

SOUTH PAR

THE CHALKS

Bridge Farm

63

B3114

CRICKBACK LA

MADAM'S PADDOCK

PINE CT

STANTON RD

Mill

JUMPERS LA

Tun Bridge

TUNBRIDGE RD

TUNBRIDGE CL

Tunbridge Farm

Paradise

Tyning La

UPPER STANTON

2

CHEW LA

Chota Castle

Vicarage

Stanton Drew

BROMLEY RD

DENNY LA

Pitt's La

MOORLEDGE RD

HIGHFIELDS

THE DRIVE

THE CRESCENT

1

Roundhill Farm

MOORLEDGE LA

Moorledge

Moorledge Farm

62

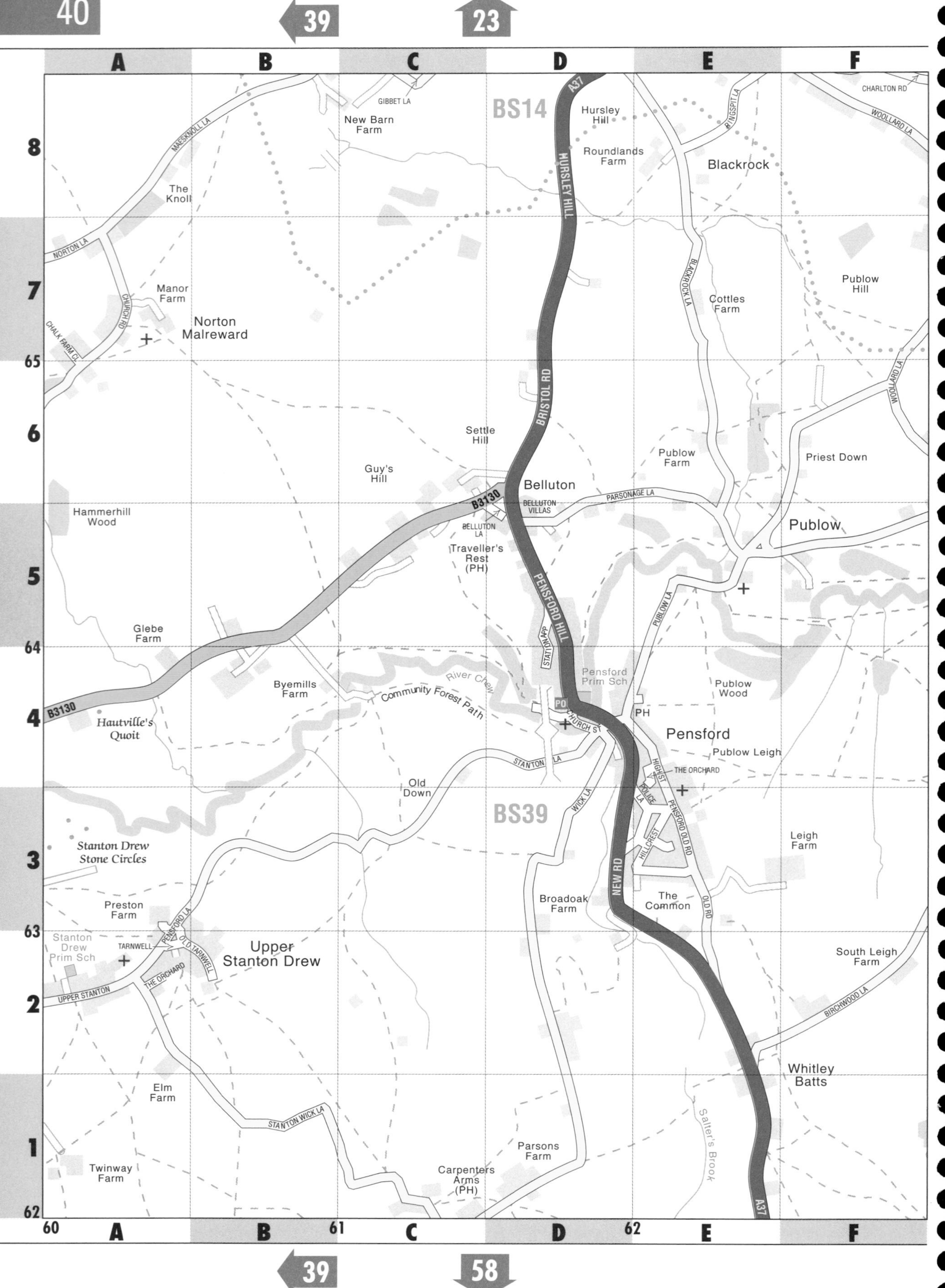

BS14

CHARLTON RD

WOOLLARD LA

Hursley Hill

Roundlands Farm

Blackrock

Publow Hill

New Barn Farm

GIBBET LA

A37

HURSLEY HILL

MAESKNOLL LA

The Knoll

NORTON LA

CHURCH RD

Manor Farm

Norton Malreward

CHALK FARM CL

Cottles Farm

BLACKROCK LA

RIGSPIT LA

WOOLLARD LA

Settle Hill

BRISTOL RD

Publow Farm

Priest Down

Guy's Hill

Belluton

PARSONAGE LA

Publow

Hammerhill Wood

B3130

BELLUTON VILLAS

BELLUTON LA

Traveller's Rest (PH)

PUBLOW LA

Glebe Farm

PENSFORD HILL

Byemills Farm

River Chew

Community Forest Path

STATION LA

Pensford Prim Sch

Publow Wood

B3130

Hautville's Quoit

PO

CHURCH ST

PH

Pensford

Publow Leigh

STANTON LA

Old Down

WICK LA

HIGH ST

THE ORCHARD

PENSFORD OLD RD

Leigh Farm

BS39

Stanton Drew Stone Circles

NEW RD

HILLCREST

BRIDGE LA

Broadoak Farm

The Common

OLD RD

Preston Farm

Stanton Drew Prim Sch

TARNWELL

PENSFORD LA

OLD TARNWELL

Upper Stanton Drew

South Leigh Farm

UPPER STANTON

THE ORCHARD

Elm Farm

STANTON WICK LA

BIRCHWOOD LA

Whitley Batts

Twinway Farm

Parsons Farm

Salter's Brook

Carpenters Arms (PH)

A37

24
42

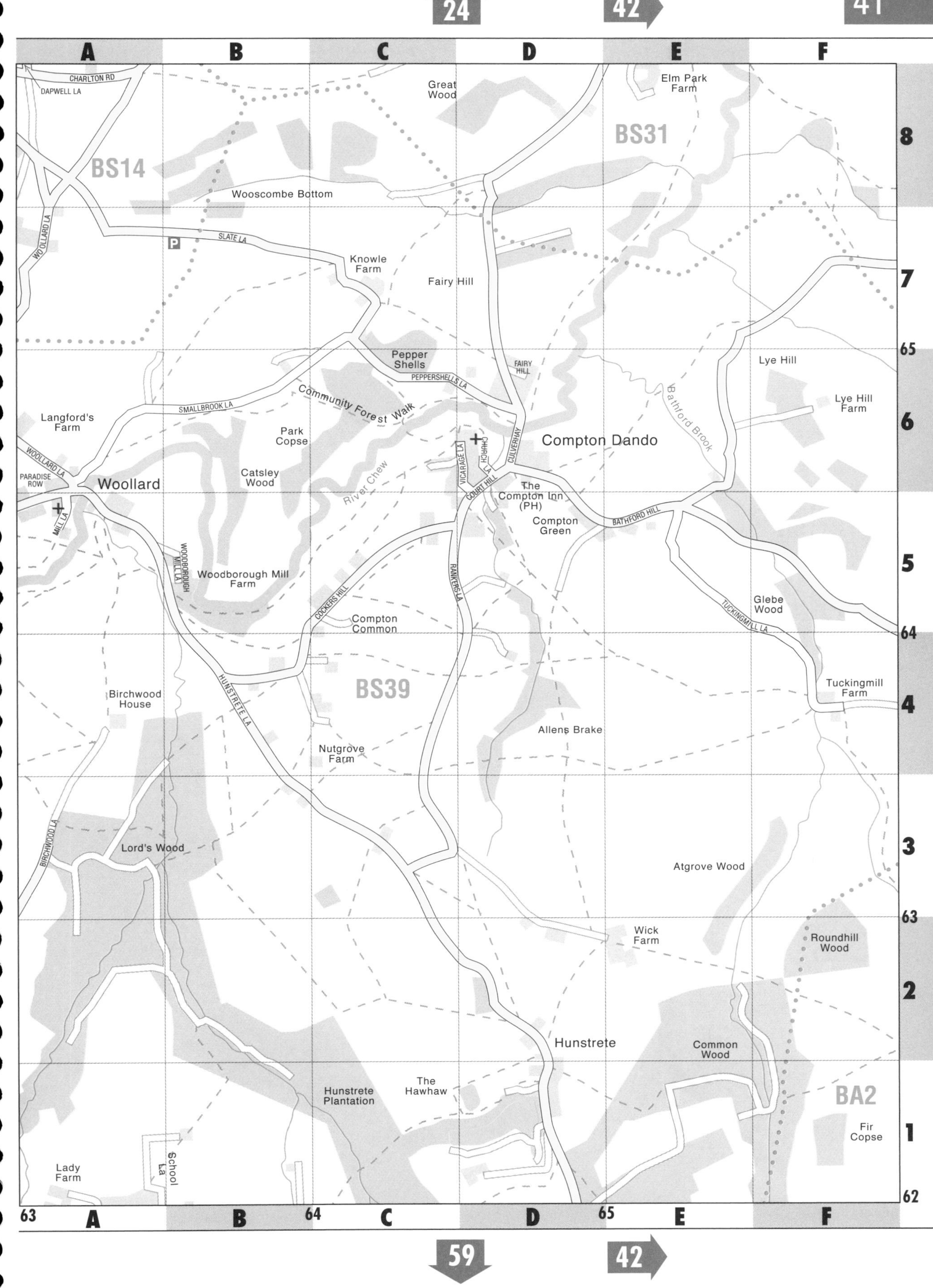
A
B
C
D
E
F
CHARLTON RD
DAPWELL LA
Great Wood
Elm Park Farm
BS31
BS14
8
Wooscombe Bottom
WOOLLARD LA
SLATE LA
P
Knowle Farm
Fairy Hill
7
Pepper Shells
FAIRY HILL
65
Lye Hill
PEPPERSHELLS LA
SMALLBROOK LA
Community Forest Walk
Bathford Brook
Lye Hill Farm
Langford's Farm
Park Copse
Compton Dando
6
WOOLLARD LA
VICARAGE LA
CHURCH LA
CULVERHAY
Catsley Wood
River Chew
PARADISE ROW
Woollard
COURT HILL
The Compton Inn (PH)
Compton Green
BATHFORD HILL
MILL LA
WOODBOROUGH MILL LA
5
Woodborough Mill Farm
RANKERS LA
COCKERS HILL
Glebe Wood
TUCKINGMILL LA
Compton Common
64
BS39
Tuckingmill Farm
Birchwood House
HUNSTRETE LA
4
Allens Brake
Nutgrove Farm
BIRCHWOOD LA
3
Lord's Wood
Atgrove Wood
63
Wick Farm
Roundhill Wood
2
Hunstrete
Common Wood
The Hawhaw
Hunstrete Plantation
BA2
1
Fir Copse
School La
Lady Farm
62
63
64
65

59
42

A   B   C   D   E   F

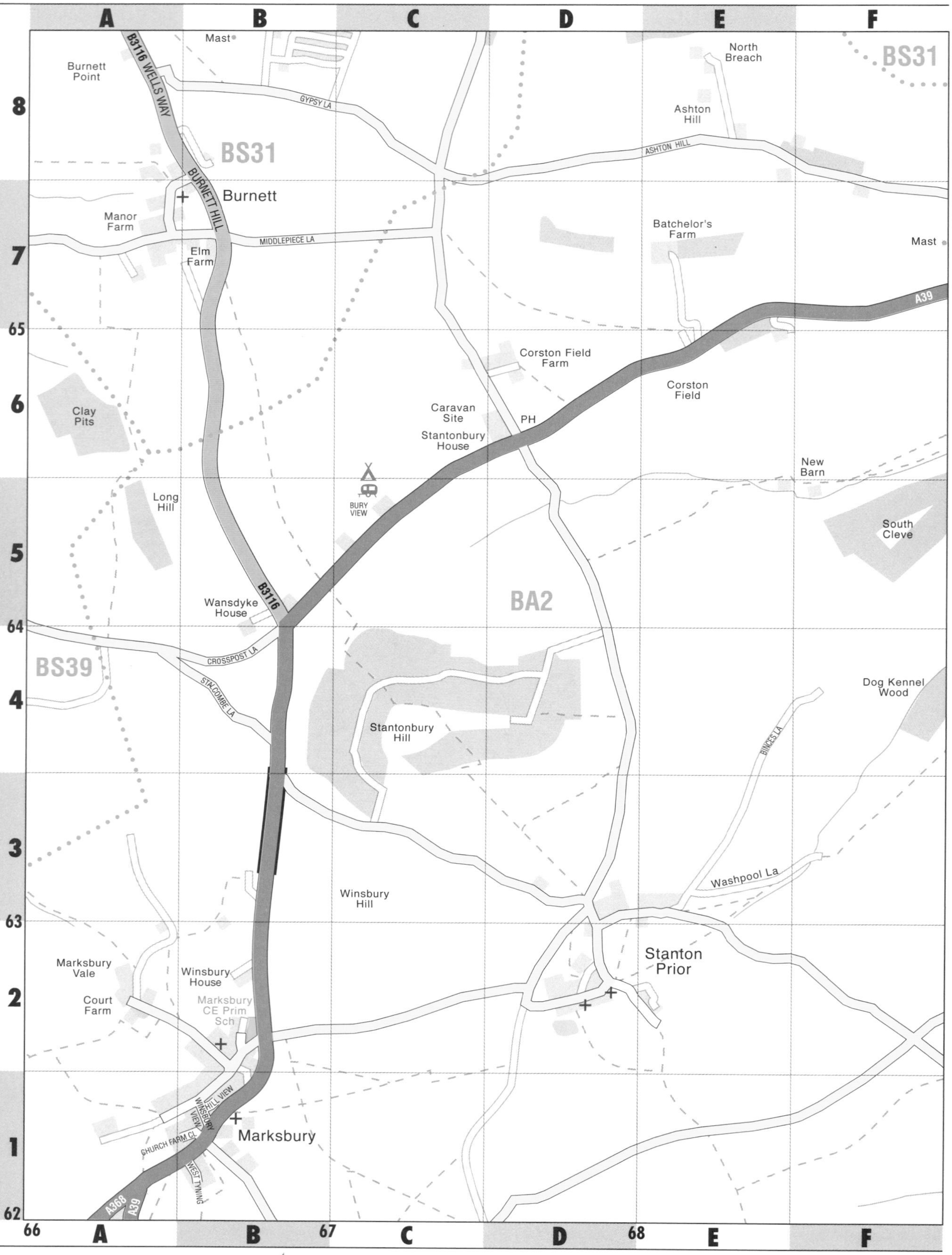

BS31

Mast

Burnett
Point

GYPSY LA

North
Breach

8

ASHTON HILL

Ashton
Hill

BS31

B3116 WELLS WAY

BURNETT HILL

Burnett

Manor
Farm

MIDDLEPIECE LA

Elm
Farm

7

Batchelor's
Farm

Mast

65

A39

Corston Field
Farm

6

Clay
Pits

Caravan
Site
Stantonbury
House

PH

Corston
Field

New
Barn

Long
Hill

BURY
VIEW

South
Cleve

5

BA2

64

Wansdyke
House

B3116

Dog Kennel
Wood

BS39

CROSSPOST LA

4

Stantonbury
Hill

STK COMBE LA

BUNCES LA

Washpool La

3

Winsbury
Hill

63

Marksbury
Vale

Winsbury
House

Marksbury
CE Prim
Sch

Stanton
Prior

2

Court
Farm

HILL VIEW

WINSBURY
VIEW

1

CHURCH FARM CL

Marksbury

WEST TYNING

62

A368
A39

66   A   B   67   C   D   68   E   F

26
44

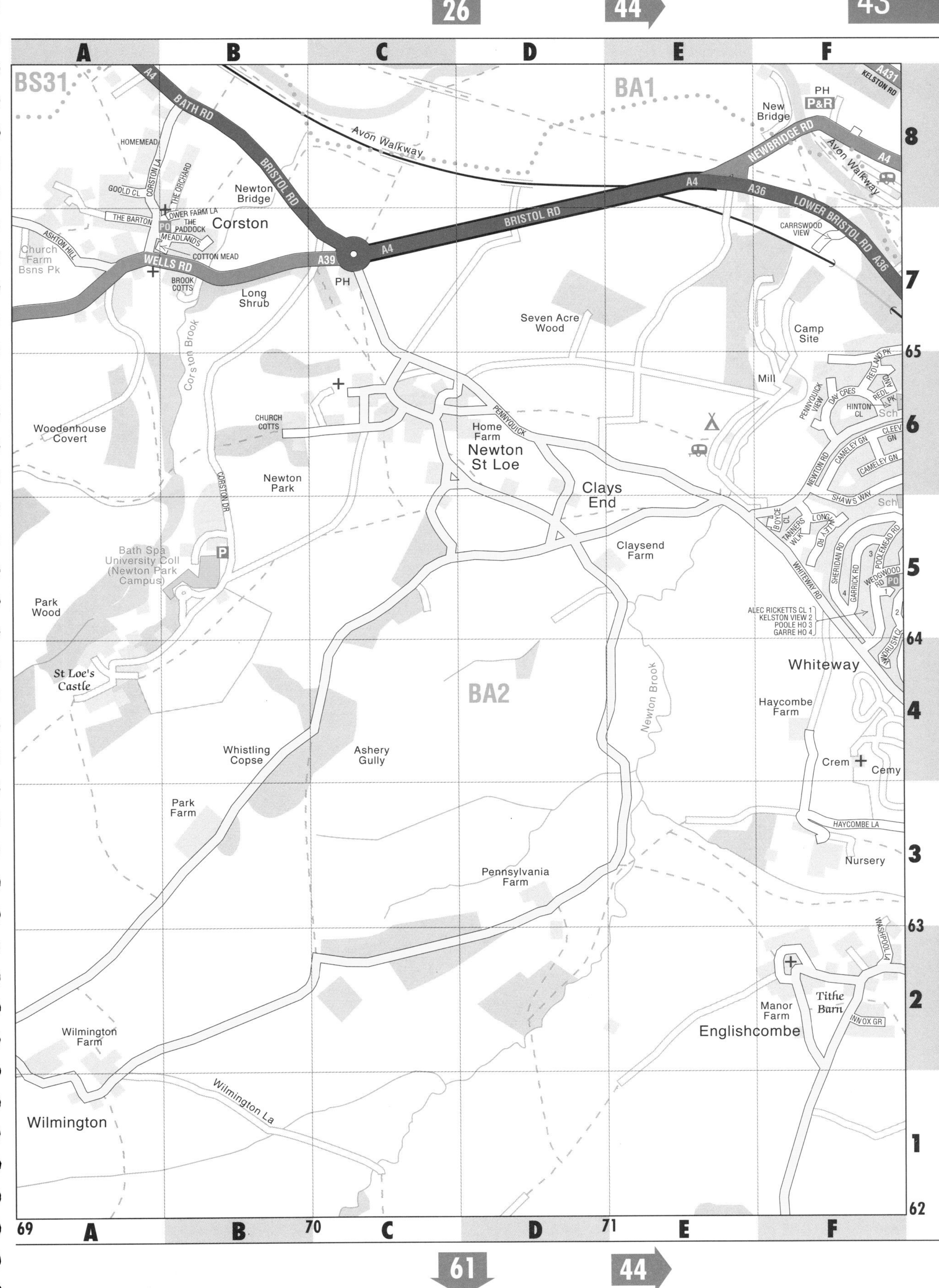
A
B
C
D
E
F
BS31
BA1
BA2
A4
BATH RD
BRISTOL RD
A39
WELLS RD
A431
KELSTON RD
Avon Walkway
NEWBRIDGE RD
A36
LOWER BRISTOL RD
HOMEMEAD
CORSTON LA
THE ORCHARD
GOOLD CL
THE BARTON
LOWER FARM LA
THE PADDOCK
MEADLANDS
COTTON MEAD
ASHTON HILL
BROOK COTTS
Corston
Newton Bridge
Church Farm Bsns Pk
Long Shrub
PH
New Bridge
P&R
CARRSWOOD VIEW
Seven Acre Wood
Camp Site
Mill
Corston Brook
Woodenhouse Covert
CHURCH COTTS
Home Farm
Newton St Loe
PENNYQUICK
Newton Park
CORSTON DR
Clays End
Claysend Farm
Bath Spa University Coll (Newton Park Campus)
Park Wood
St Loe's Castle
PENNYQUICK VIEW
DAY CRES
HINTON CL
REDLAND PK
Sch
NEWTON RD
CAMELEY GN
SHAWS WAY
BOYCE CL
TANNERS WLK
LONG VALLEY RD
SHERIDAN RD
GARRICK RD
POOLEMEAD RD
WEDGWOOD RD
WHITEWAY RD
ALEC RICKETTS CL 1
KELSTON VIEW 2
POOLE HO 3
GARRE HO 4
WINDRUSH CL
Whiteway
Haycombe Farm
Newton Brook
Whistling Copse
Ashery Gully
Crem
Cemy
Park Farm
HAYCOMBE LA
Nursery
Pennsylvania Farm
WASHPOOL LA
Tithe Barn
Manor Farm
Englishcombe
INNOX GR
Wilmington Farm
Wilmington La
Wilmington
8
7
65
6
5
64
4
3
63
2
1
62
69
70
71

61
44

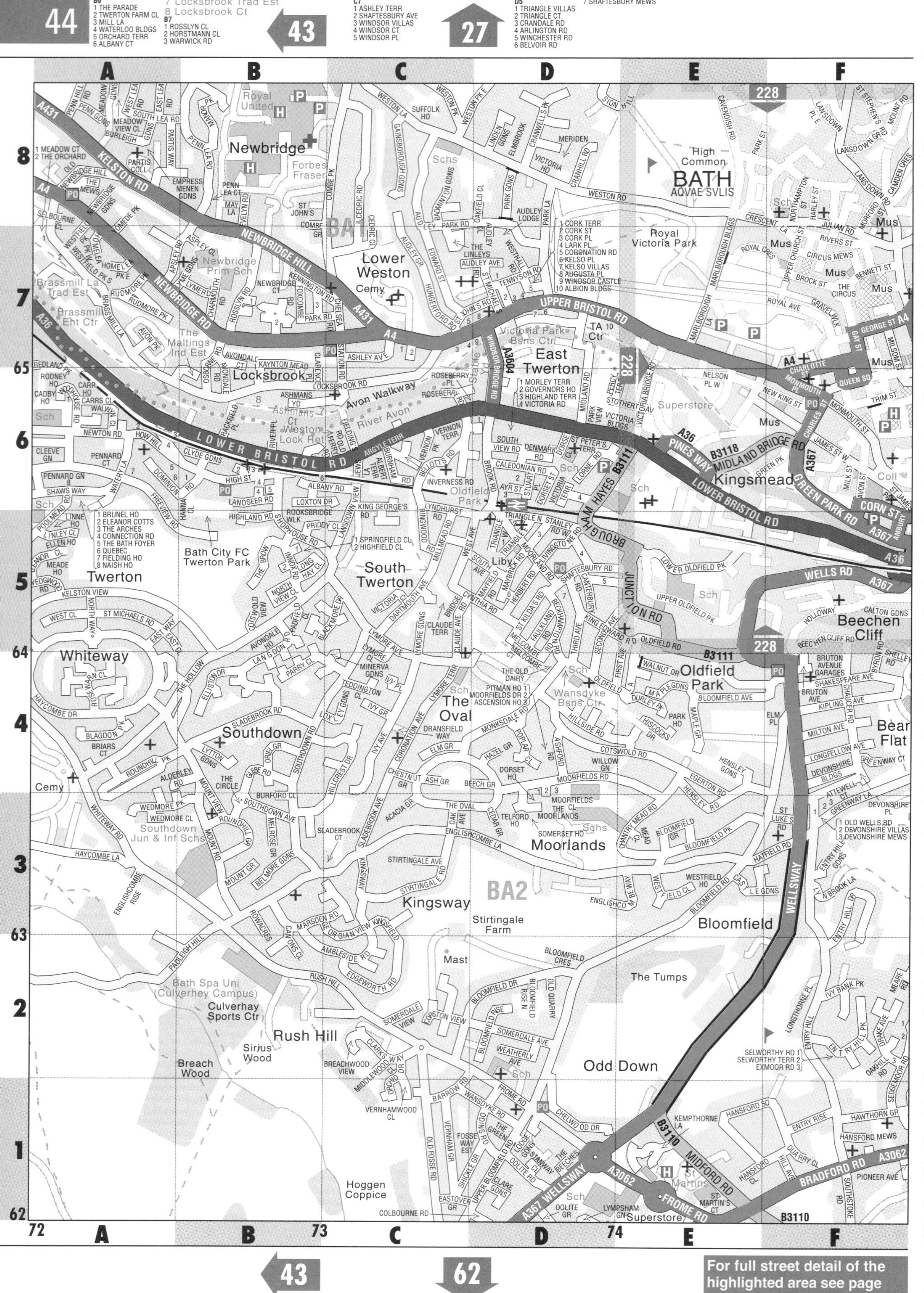

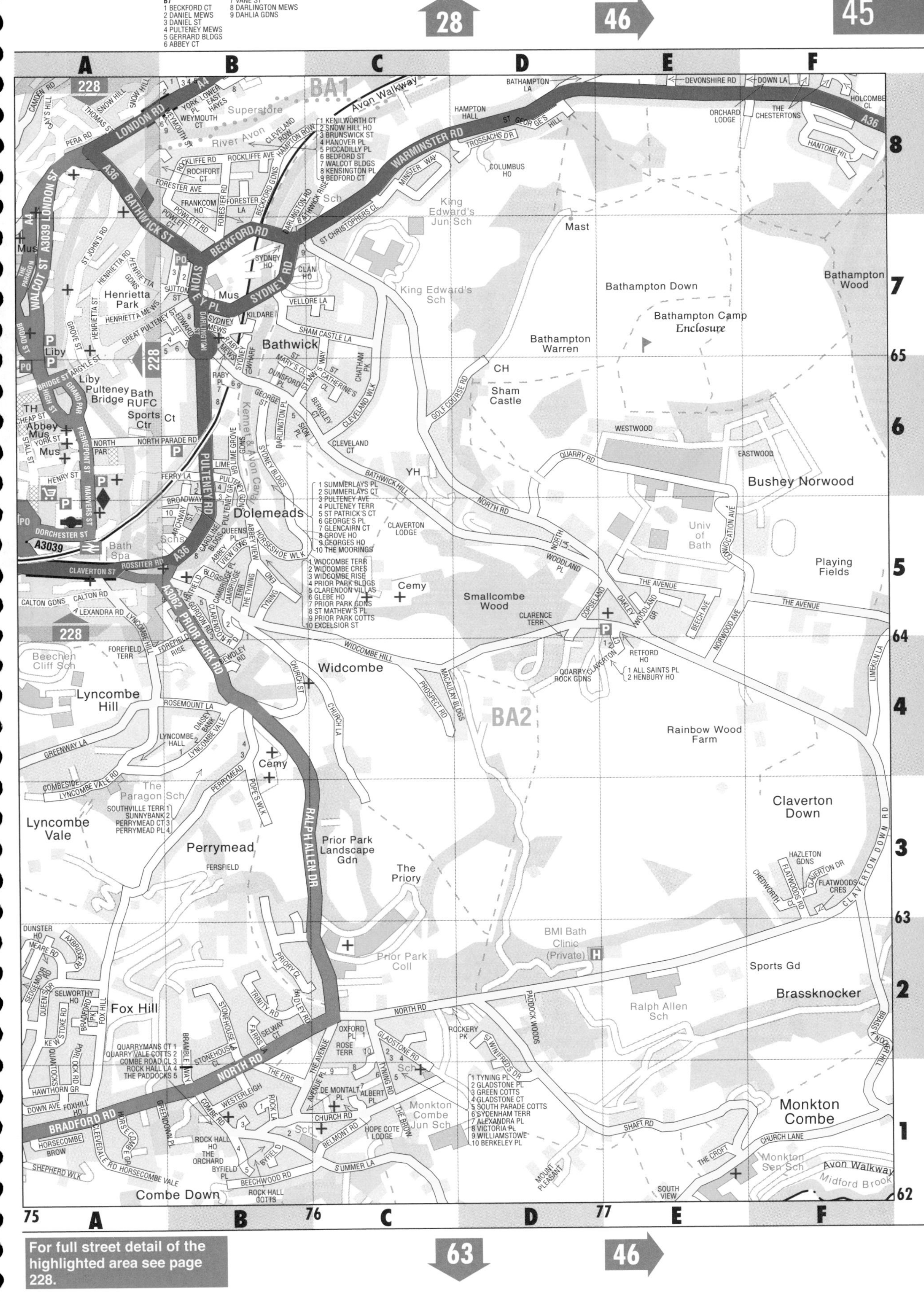

45
29

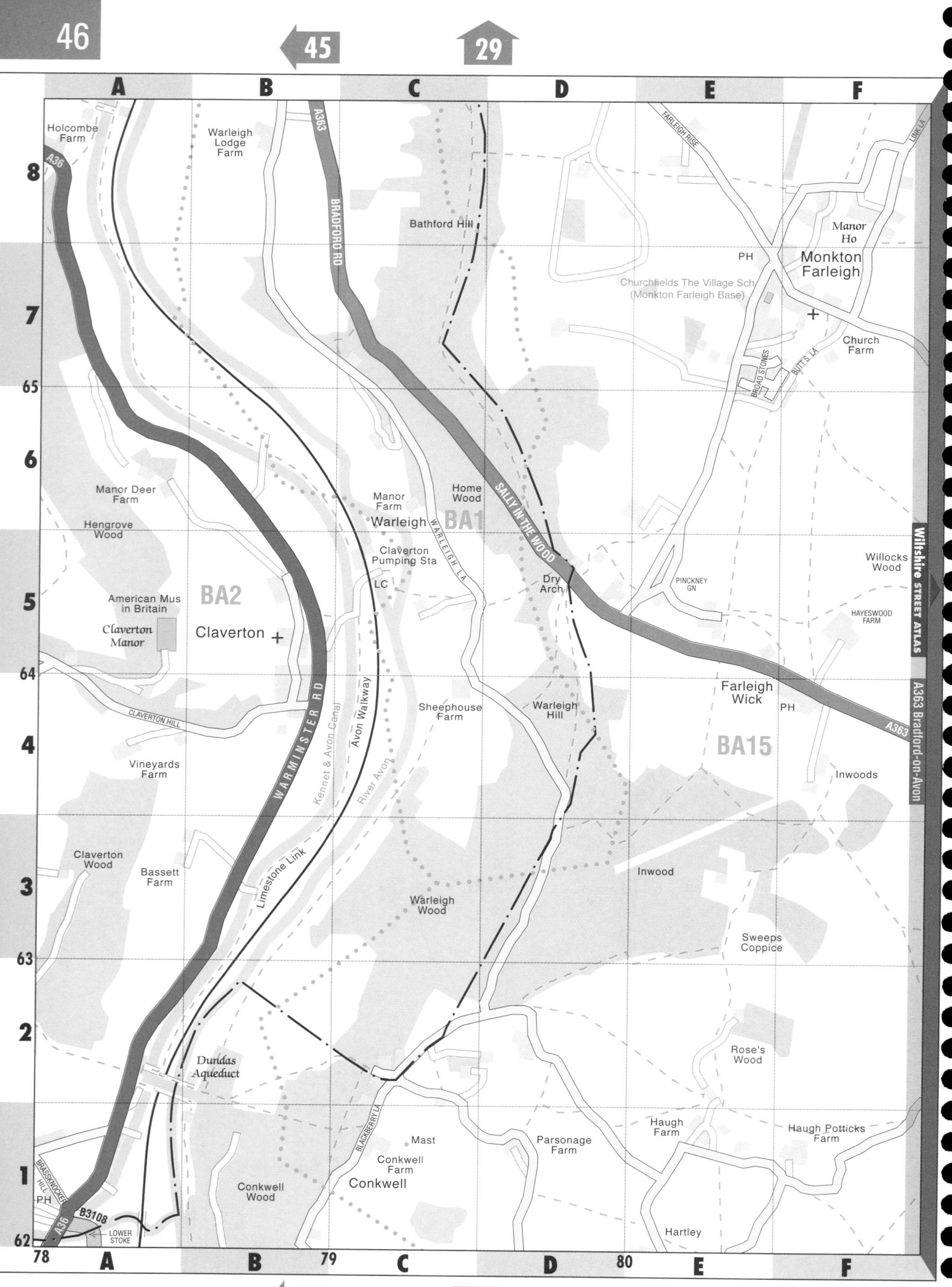
A
B
C
D
E
F
8
7
65
6
5
64
4
3
63
2
1
62
78
79
80
Holcombe Farm
Warleigh Lodge Farm
A36
A363
BRADFORD RD
Bathford Hill
FARLEIGH RISE
LINK LA
Manor Ho
PH
Monkton Farleigh
Churchfields The Village Sch (Monkton Farleigh Base)
Church Farm
BROAD STONES
BUTT'S LA
Manor Deer Farm
Hengrove Wood
Manor Farm
Home Wood
Warleigh
BA1
WARLEIGH LA
SALLY IN THE WOOD
Claverton Pumping Sta
LC
Dry Arch
PINCKNEY GN
Willocks Wood
HAYESWOOD FARM
American Mus in Britain
BA2
Claverton Manor
Claverton
CLAVERTON HILL
WARMINSTER RD
Kennet & Avon Canal
Avon Walkway
River Avon
Sheephouse Farm
Warleigh Hill
Farleigh Wick
PH
A363
BA15
Inwoods
Vineyards Farm
Claverton Wood
Bassett Farm
Limestone Link
Inwood
Warleigh Wood
Sweeps Coppice
Rose's Wood
Dundas Aqueduct
BLACKBERRY LA
Mast
Conkwell Farm
Conkwell
Parsonage Farm
Haugh Farm
Haugh Potticks Farm
BRASSKNOCKER HILL
PH
B3108
LOWER STOKE
Conkwell Wood
Hartley
Wiltshire STREET ATLAS
A363 Bradford-on-Avon

45
64

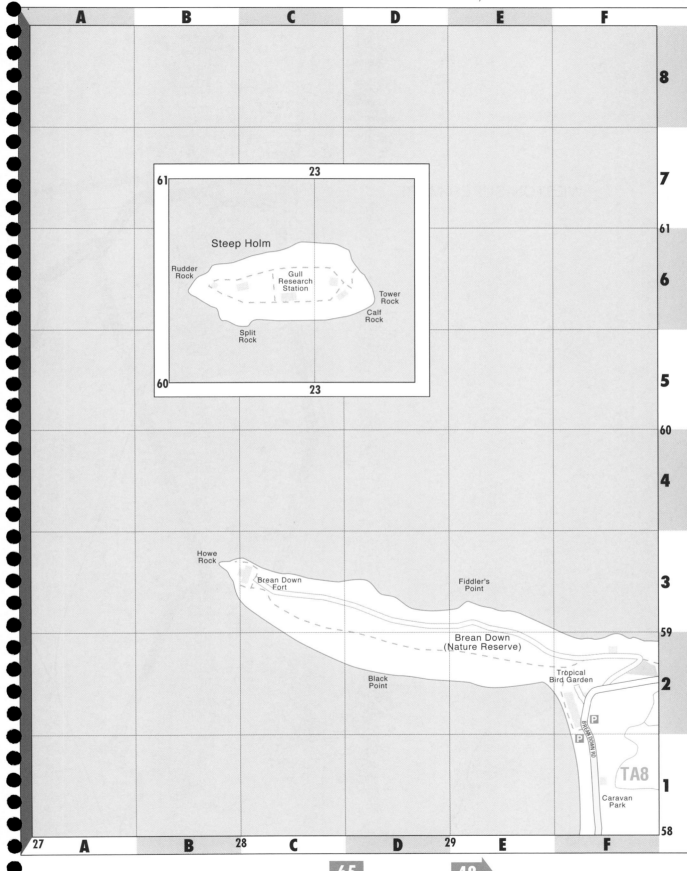

A   B   C   D   E   F

8

7

61

6

23

61
Steep Holm
Rudder
Rock
Gull
Research
Station
Tower
Rock
Calf
Rock
Split
Rock
60

23

5

60

4

Howe
Rock
Brean Down
Fort
Fiddler's
Point
3

59
Brean Down
(Nature Reserve)

Black
Point
Tropical
Bird Garden
2

P
BREAN DOWN RD
P

TA8

1

Caravan
Park

58

27 A   B 28 C   D 29 E   F

← 47   ↑ 30

WESTON-SUPER-MARE

BS23

BS24

TA8

← 47   66

31

50

D7
1 TEMPLARS CT
2 CLOVER CT
3 CHARLOCK CL
4 CAMPION CL

E8
1 MERLIN CL
2 KITE WLK
3 HARRIER PATH
4 THRUSH CL
5 LOMBARDY CL
6 GREENGAGE CL

7 MALLARD WLK
F8
1 SWEETGRASS RD
2 CASTLE VIEW
3 TRELISSICK GDNS
4 MONTACUTE CIR
5 THE INCLOSURES

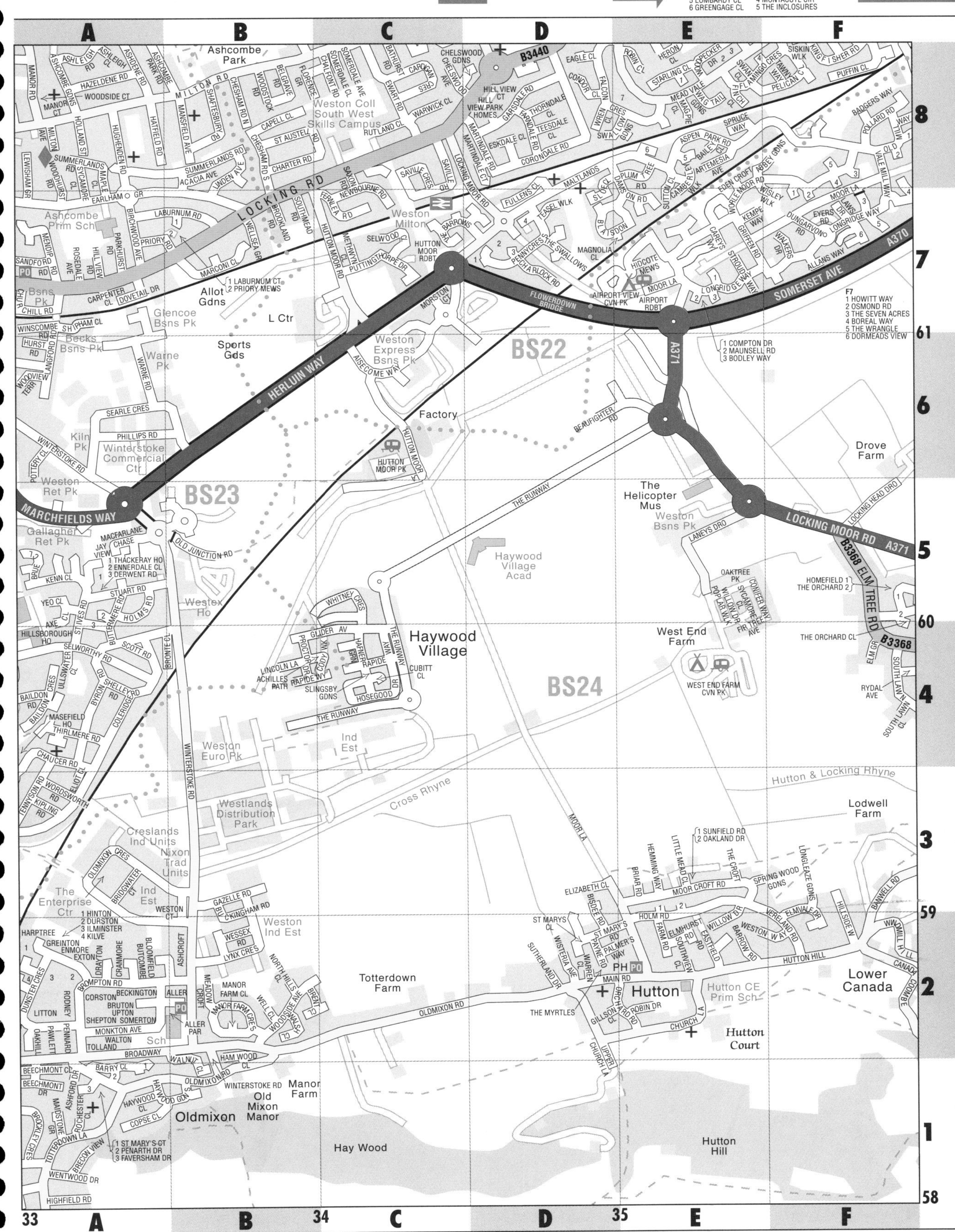

BS22

BS23

BS24

49
32

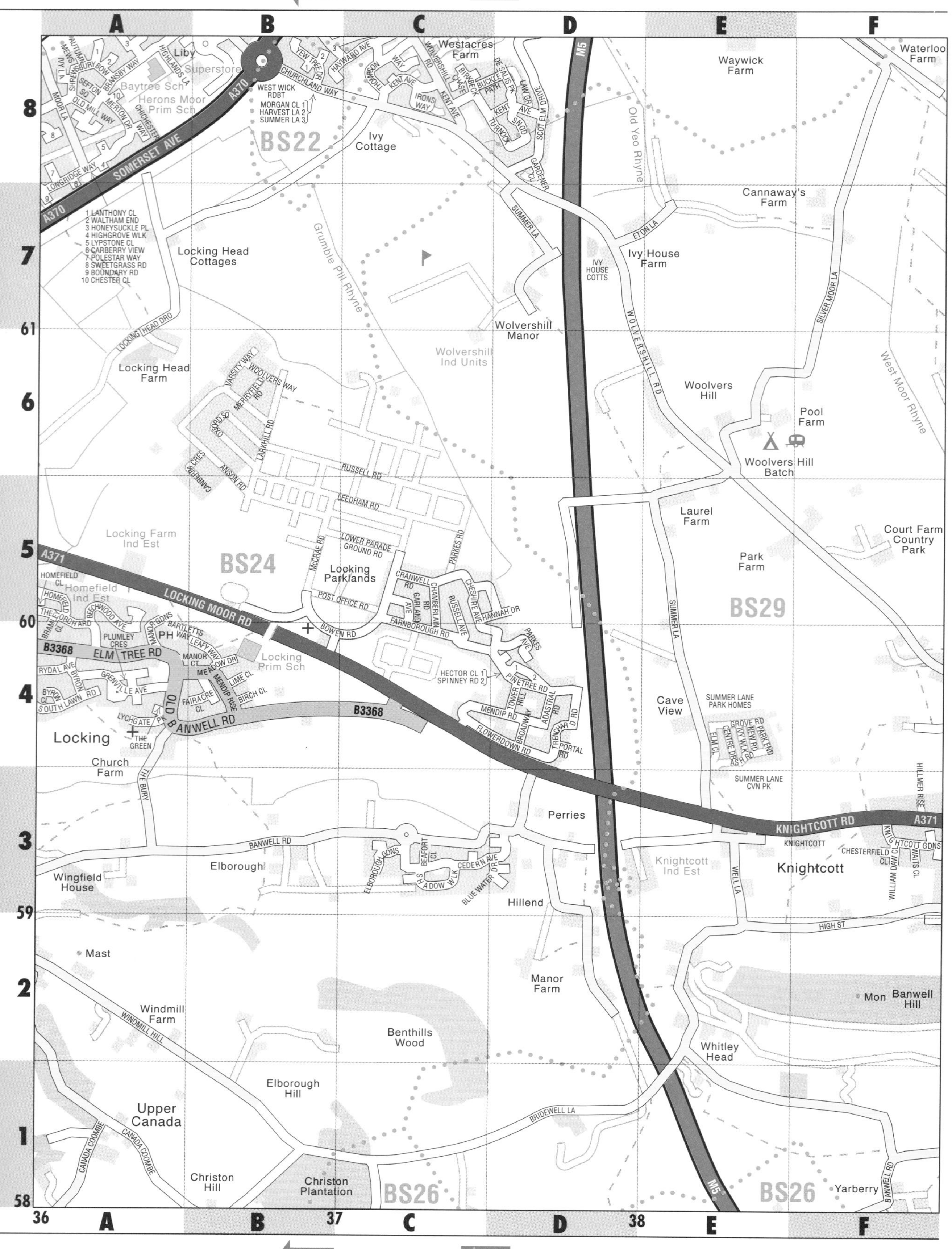
A
B
C
D
E
F
8
7
61
6
5
60
4
3
59
2
1
58
36
37
38
Liby Superstore
Baytree Sch
Herons Moor Prim Sch
WEST WICK RDBT
MORGAN CL 1
HARVEST LA 2
SUMMER LA 3
CHURCHLAND WAY
HAYWARD AVE
YEW TREE DR
Westacres Farm
KENT AVE
IRONS WAY
BUCKLE PATH
DE SALIS PK
SCOT ELM DRIVE
TURNOCK
KENT AVE
Ivy Cottage
BS22
SOMERSET AVE
A370
LONGRIDGE WAY
1 LANTHONY CL
2 WALTHAM END
3 HONEYSUCKLE PL
4 HIGHGROVE WLK
5 LYPSTONE CL
6 CARBERRY VIEW
7 POLESTAR WAY
8 SWEETGRASS RD
9 BOUNDARY RD
10 CHESTER CL
Locking Head Cottages
Grumble Pill Rhyne
Old Yeo Rhyne
GARDENER CL
SUMMER LA
IVY HOUSE COTTS
Waywick Farm
Waterloo Farm
Cannaway's Farm
ETON LA
Ivy House Farm
WOLVERSHILL RD
SILVER MOOR LA
Wolvershill Manor
Wolvershill Ind Units
LOCKING HEAD DRO
Locking Head Farm
VARSITY WAY
WOOLVERS WAY
MERRYFIELD RD
LARKHILL RD
ANSON RD
CANBERRA CRES
RUSSELL RD
LEEDHAM RD
Woolvers Hill
Pool Farm
West Moor Rhyne
Woolvers Hill Batch
Laurel Farm
Locking Farm Ind Est
LOWER PARADE GROUND RD
MCCRAE RD
PARKES RD
Locking Parklands
BS24
A371
HOMEFIELD CL
Homefield Ind Est
LOCKING MOOR RD
POST OFFICE RD
CRANWELL RD
CHAMBERLAIN RD
GARLAND AVE
CHESHIRE AVE
RUSSELL AVE
HANNAH DR
FARNBOROUGH RD
BOWEN RD
PARKES AVE
Park Farm
Court Farm Country Park
BS29
SUMMER LA
PLUMLEY CRES
PH
BARTLETTS WAY
LEAFY WAY
B3368
ELM TREE RD
MANOR CT
MEADOW DR
Locking Prim Sch
HECTOR CL 1
SPINNEY RD 2
PINETREE RD
RYDAL AVE
BYRON RD
GRENVILLE AVE
SOUTH LAWN RD
FAIRACRE CL
MENDIP RISE
LIME CL
BIRCH CL
OLD BANWELL RD
B3368
MENDIP RD
TOWER HILL
BROADWAY
ADASTRAL RD
TRENCHARD RD
PORTAL RD
FLOWERDOWN RD
Cave View
SUMMER LANE PARK HOMES
GROVE RD
ELM CL
CENTRE DR
IVY WLK
NEW RD
PARK END
ASH RD
SUMMER LANE CVN PK
Locking
LYCHGATE PK
THE GREEN
Church Farm
THE BURY
Perries
KNIGHTCOTT RD
A371
HILLMER RISE
KNIGHTCOTT
KNIGHTCOTT GDNS
CHESTERFIELD CL
WILLIAM DAW CL
WAITS CL
BANWELL RD
Elborough
ELBOROUGH GDNS
BEAFORT CL
SHADOW WLK
CEDERN AVE
BLUE WATER DR
Knightcott Ind Est
Knightcott
WELL LA
Wingfield House
Hillend
HIGH ST
Mast
Manor Farm
Mon
Banwell Hill
Windmill Farm
WINDMILL HILL
Benthills Wood
Whitley Head
Elborough Hill
BRIDEWELL LA
Upper Canada
CANADA COOMBE
Christon Hill
Christon Plantation
BS26
M5
BS26
Yarberry
BANWELL RD

49
68

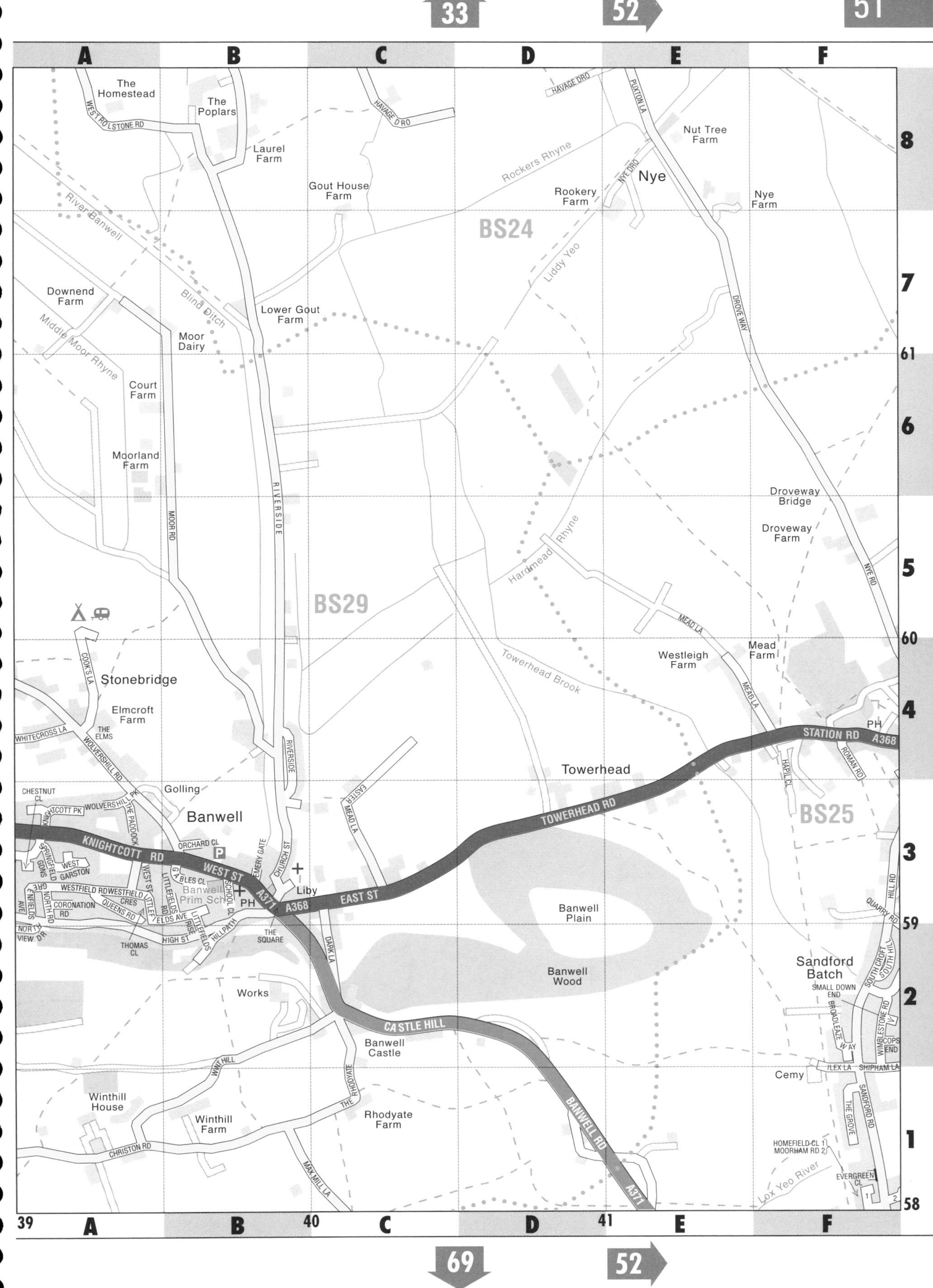
33
52
A
B
C
D
E
F
8
7
61
6
5
60
4
3
59
2
1
58
39
40
41
The Homestead
The Poplars
Laurel Farm
Gout House Farm
Rockers Rhyne
Nut Tree Farm
Rookery Farm
Nye
Nye Farm
BS24
River Banwell
Liddy Yeo
Downend Farm
Blind Ditch
Lower Gout Farm
Middle Moor Rhyne
Moor Dairy
Court Farm
Moorland Farm
RIVERSIDE
MOOR RD
DROVE WAY
Droveway Bridge
Droveway Farm
Hardmead Rhyne
NYE RD
BS29
MEAD LA
Mead Farm
Westleigh Farm
Towerhead Brook
Stonebridge
Elmcroft Farm
COOK'S LA
WHITECROSS LA
THE ELMS
WOLVERSHILL RD
STATION RD
A368
PH
ROMAN RD
HAPIL CL
Towerhead
Golling
Banwell
BS25
TOWERHEAD RD
KNIGHTCOTT RD
WEST ST
EAST ST
A371
Liby
Banwell Prim Sch
Banwell Plain
Banwell Wood
Sandford Batch
Works
CASTLE HILL
Banwell Castle
Cemy
Winthill House
Winthill Farm
Rhodyate Farm
CHRISTON RD
BANWELL RD
MAX MILL LA
Lox Yeo River
SHIPHAM LA
SANDFORD RD
THE GROVE
69
52

51
34

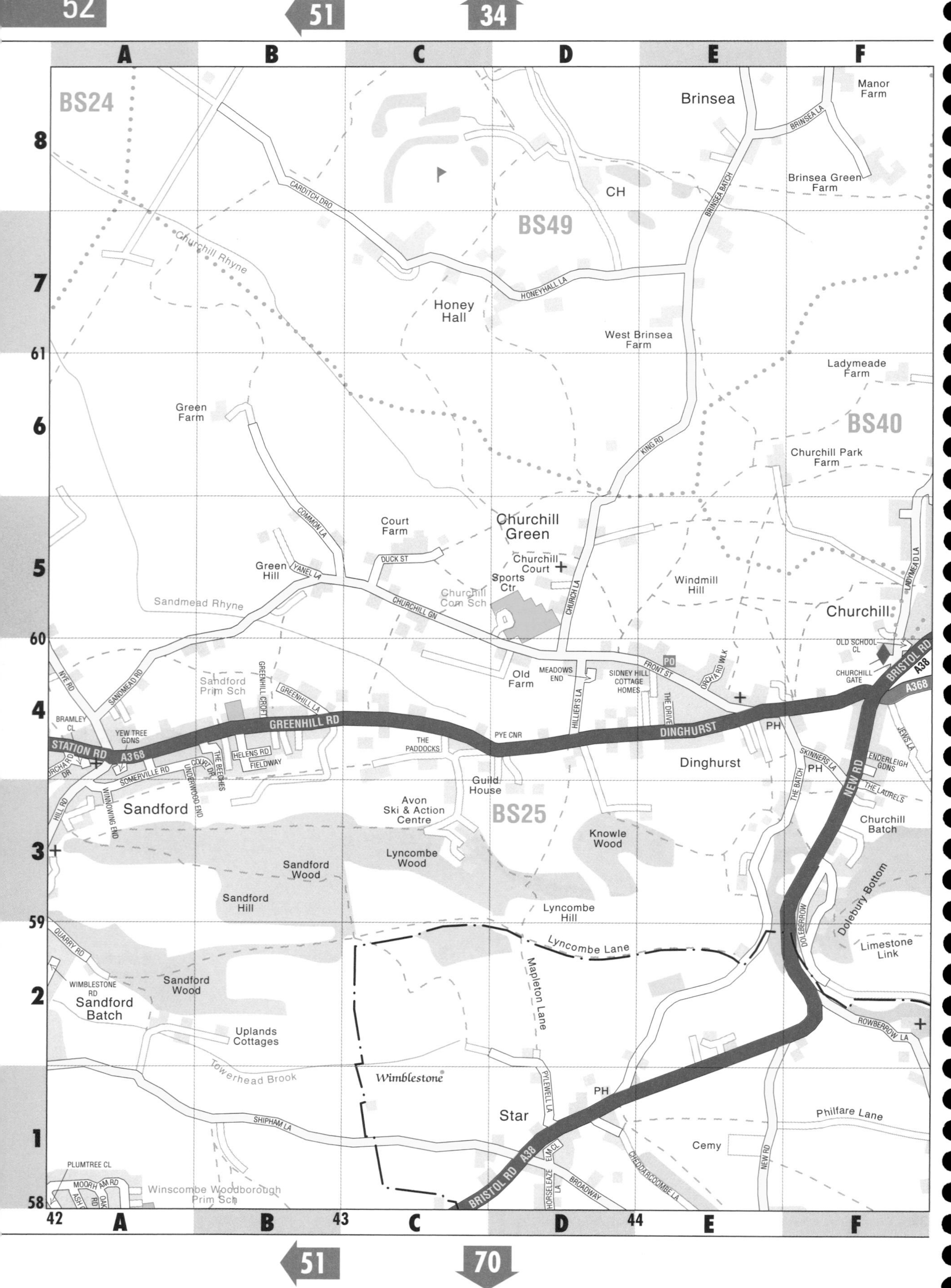
A
B
C
D
E
F
BS24
8
7
61
6
5
60
4
3
59
2
1
58
42
43
44
Brinsea
Manor Farm
BRINSEA LA
Brinsea Green Farm
CH
BRINSEA BATCH
CARDITCH DRO
BS49
Churchill Rhyne
HONEYHALL LA
Honey Hall
West Brinsea Farm
Ladymeade Farm
BS40
Green Farm
KING RD
Churchill Park Farm
COMMON LA
Court Farm
Churchill Green
DUCK ST
Churchill Court
Green Hill
YANEL LA
Sports Ctr
Windmill Hill
Sandmead Rhyne
Churchill Com Sch
CHURCHILL GN
CHURCH LA
LADYMEAD LA
Churchill
OLD SCHOOL CL
BRISTOL RD
A38
NYE RD
SANDMEAD RD
Sandford Prim Sch
GREENHILL CROFT
GREENHILL LA
Old Farm
MEADOWS END
SIDNEY HILL COTTAGE HOMES
FRONT ST
PO
ORCHARD WLK
CHURCHILL GATE
A368
BRAMLEY CL
YEW TREE GDNS
GREENHILL RD
HILLIER'S LA
THE DRIVE
DINGHURST
PH
JEWS LA
STATION RD
A368
HELENS RD
FIELDWAY
THE PADDOCKS
PYE CNR
SKINNERS LA
ENDERLEIGH GDNS
ORCHARD DR
SOMERVILLE RD
COURT DR
UNDERWOOD END
THE BEECHES
Dinghurst
THE BATCH
NEW RD
THE LAURELS
HILL RD
WINNOWING END
Sandford
Guild House
Avon Ski & Action Centre
BS25
Knowle Wood
Churchill Batch
Lyncombe Wood
Sandford Wood
Sandford Hill
Lyncombe Hill
DOLEBERROW
Dolebury Bottom
QUARRY RD
Lyncombe Lane
Limestone Link
WIMBLESTONE RD
Sandford Batch
Sandford Wood
Mapleton Lane
ROWBERROW LA
Uplands Cottages
Towerhead Brook
Wimblestone
PYLEWELL LA
Philfare Lane
SHIPHAM LA
Star
Cemy
ELM CL
NEW RD
PLUMTREE CL
MOORHAM RD
ASH
RD
OAK
Winscombe Woodborough Prim Sch
HORSELEAZE LA
BROADWAY
CHEDDARCOOMBE LA

51
70

35
54

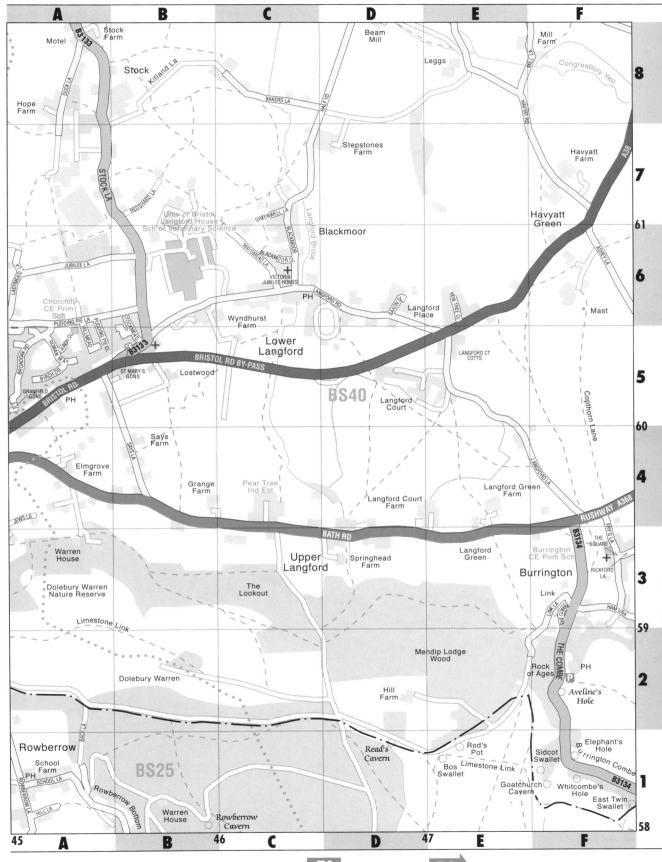
A
B
C
D
E
F
Motel
Stock Farm
B3133
Stock
Kitland La
Beam Mill
Leggs
Mill Farm
Congresbury Yeo
Hope Farm
DUCK LA
BAKERS LA
HALF YD
MILL LA
HAVYATT RD
Stepstones Farm
Havyatt Farm
A38
STOCK LA
REDSHARD LA
Univ of Bristol
Langford House
Sch of Veterinary Science
GREENWELL LA
Langford Brook
Blackmoor
Havyatt Green
BLACKMOOR
MAYSMEAD LA
BLACKMOOR CL
JUBILEE LA
LADYMEAD LA
VICTORIA JUBILEE HOMES
ASHEY LA
PH
LANGFORD RD
SAXON ST
YEW TREE CL
Churchill CE Prim Sch
Langford Place
Mast
PUDDING PIE LA
HILLMEAD
PUDDING PIE CL
STOCKMEAD
Wyndhurst Farm
BROADOAK RD
ROWAN WAY
ARCH CL
Lower Langford
LANGFORD CT COTTS
BIRCH DR
ST MARY'S GDNS
BRISTOL RD BY-PASS
Lostwood
GRANFIELD GDNS
BRISTOL RD
BS40
Langford Court
Copthorn Lane
Says Farm
SAYS LA
LANGFORD LA
Elmgrove Farm
Grange Farm
Pear Tree Ind Est
Langford Green Farm
Langford Court Farm
RUSHWAY A368
JEWS LA
BATH RD
B3134
FRY'S LA
THE SQUARE
Warren House
Upper Langford
Springhead Farm
Langford Green
Burrington CE Prim Sch
RICKFORD LA
Burrington
Dolebury Warren Nature Reserve
The Lookout
Link
LINK LA
THE COMBE
HAM LINK
Limestone Link
Mendip Lodge Wood
Rock of Ages
PH
Dolebury Warren
P
Aveline's Hole
Hill Farm
BACK LA
Rowberrow
Read's Cavern
Rod's Pot
Elephant's Hole
School Farm
Bos Swallet
Limestone Link
Sidcot Swallet
Burrington Combe
BS25
PH
SCHOOL LA
Goatchurch Cavern
Whitcombe's Hole
B3134
ROWBERROW LA
Rowberrow Bottom
East Twin Swallet
HILL LA
Warren House
Rowberrow Cavern
8
7
61
6
5
60
4
3
59
2
1
58
45
46
47

71
54

53 36

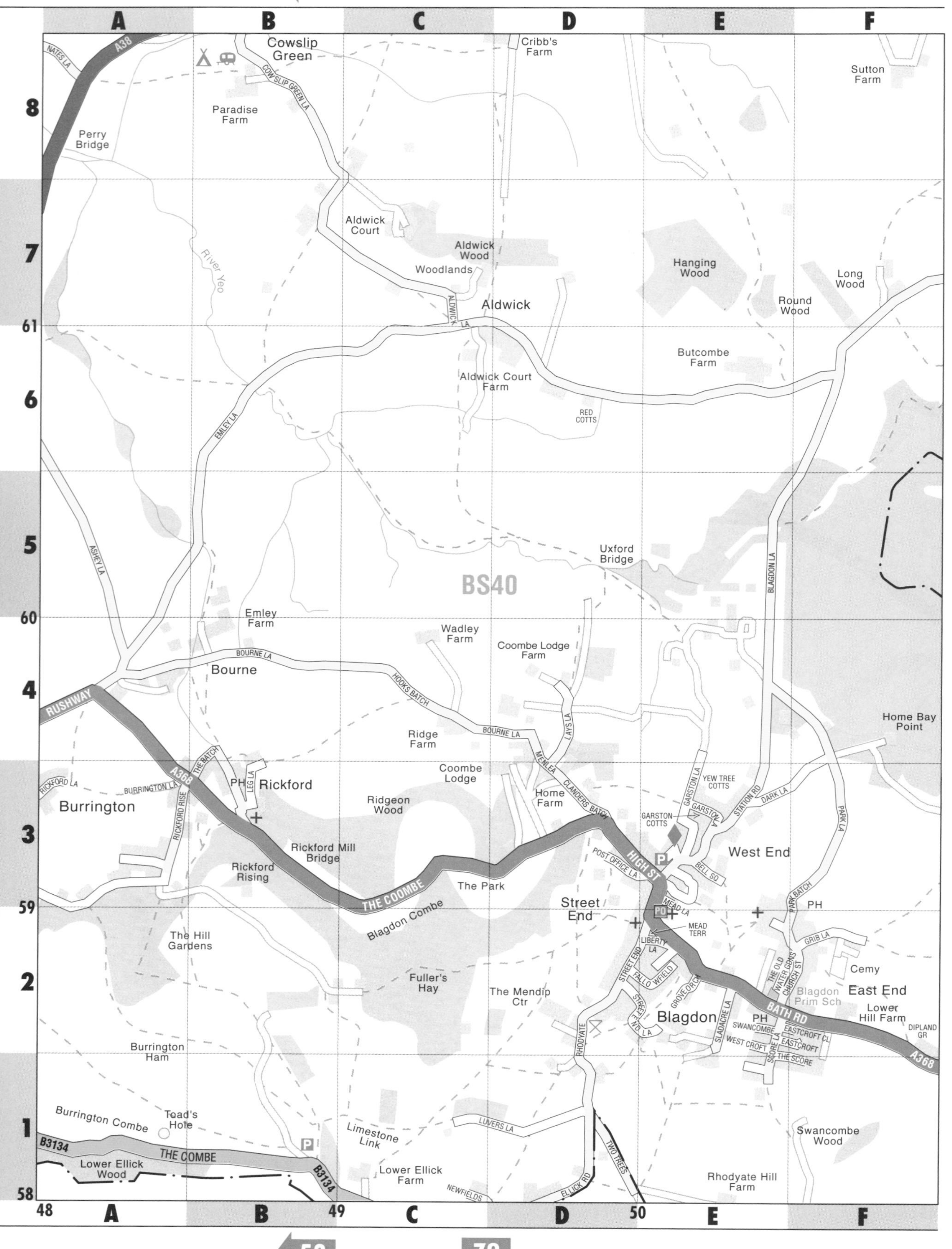

A B C D E F
8 7 61 6 5 60 4 3 59 2 1 58
48 49 50
Cowslip Green
Cribb's Farm
Sutton Farm
Paradise Farm
Perry Bridge
Aldwick Court
Aldwick Wood
Woodlands
Aldwick
Hanging Wood
Long Wood
Round Wood
Butcombe Farm
Aldwick Court Farm
RED COTTS
River Yeo
Uxford Bridge
BS40
Emley Farm
Wadley Farm
Coombe Lodge Farm
Bourne
Ridge Farm
Coombe Lodge
Home Farm
Home Bay Point
Rickford
Burrington
Ridgeon Wood
Rickford Mill Bridge
Rickford Rising
The Park
West End
Street End
Blagdon Combe
The Hill Gardens
Fuller's Hay
The Mendip Ctr
Blagdon
Blagdon Prim Sch
East End
Lower Hill Farm
Cemy
Burrington Ham
Burrington Combe
Toad's Hole
Limestone Link
Lower Ellick Wood
Lower Ellick Farm
Swancombe Wood
Rhodyate Hill Farm
A38
A368
B3134
RUSHWAY
THE COOMBE
HIGH ST
BATH RD
NATES LA
COWSLIP GREEN LA
ALDWICK LA
EMLEY LA
ASHEY LA
BOURNE LA
HOOKS BATCH
LAYS LA
MENLEA
CLANDERS BATCH
BLAGDON LA
PARK LA
STATION RD
DARK LA
GARSTON LA
YEW TREE COTTS
GARSTON COTTS
BELL SQ
POST OFFICE LA
MEAD LA
MEAD TERR
LIBERTY LA
STREET END
FALLOWFIELD
GROVE ORCH
SLADACRE LA
SWANCOMBE
WEST CROFT
EASTCROFT
EASTCROFT CL
SCORE LA
THE SCORE
THE OLD WATER GDNS
CHURCH ST
GRIB LA
PARK BATCH
DIPLAND GR
RHODYATE
LUVERS LA
TWO TREES
ELLICK RD
NEWFIELDS
RICKFORD LA
BURRINGTON LA
RICKFORD RISE
THE BATCH
LEG LA
PH
PO
P

53 72

A B C D E F

8
7
61
6
5
60
4
3
59
2
1
58

Pit Farm
THE BATCH
YEWTREE BATCH
Fairy Toot
Two Rivers Way
Walnut Tree Farm
Sutton La
Butcombe
THE COUNCIL HOUSES
MILL LA
UPPER GREEN LA
Upton Farm
LOWER STRODE
Wapsell
Phippens Farm
PH
Marlfield Cottage
GREEN LA
Yew Tree Farm
BLAGDON LA
Sage's Farm
LONG THORN LA
Strode
UPPER STRODE
Nempnett Farm
Strode Farm
Brook Farm
BUTCOMBE LA
GRAVEL HILL
West Town Farm
Plaster's Green
West Town
Highlands
Bellevue Farm
Street Farm
Church Farm
Belvedere Manor
PIT LA
BS40
Nempnett Thrubwell
Bellevue House
CHAPEL HILL
LAKESIDE CL
AWKWARD HILL
Grove Farm
Monarch's Way
East House
NEMPNETT ST
Dewdown Lodge
Blagdon Lake
PH
Rugmoor Farm
Breach Hill
Rainbow Point
Henmarsh Farm
Mast
Pixey Hall
Cook's Gully
Ubley Park House
Holt Farm
Ubley Hatchery
Holt Copse
Chy
Snatch Farm
Woodbridge Farm
Factory
Dipland Batch
Lag Farm
River Yeo
WALNUT TREE CL
STILEMEAD LA
Ubley CE Prim Sch
BATH RD
Dipland Grove Farm
FROG LA
Merecombe Farm
Ubley Farm
THE STREET
Park Farm
SQUIRE LA
INNICKS CL
Ubley
Rookery Farm
TUCKER'S LA
A368

51 A B 52 C D 53 E F

73
56

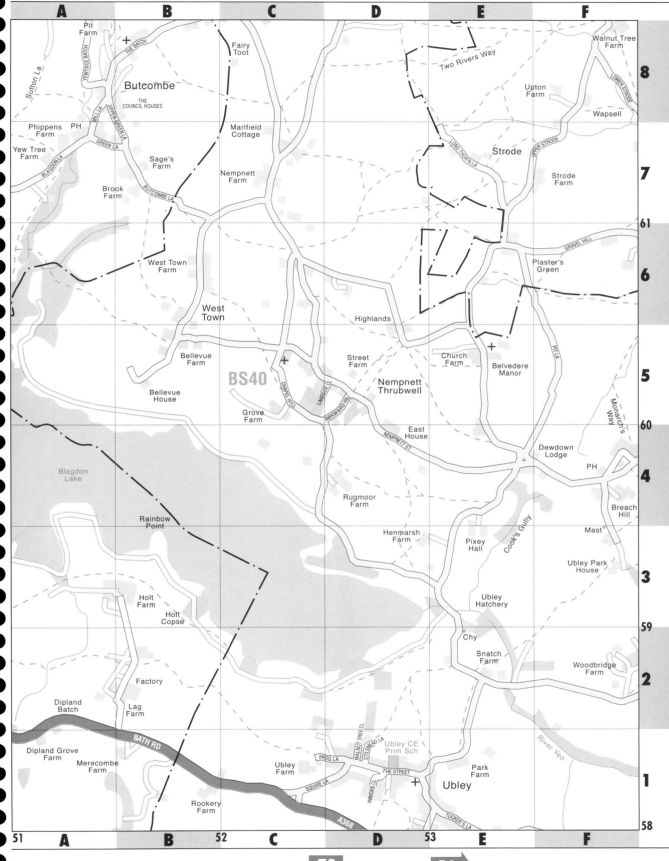

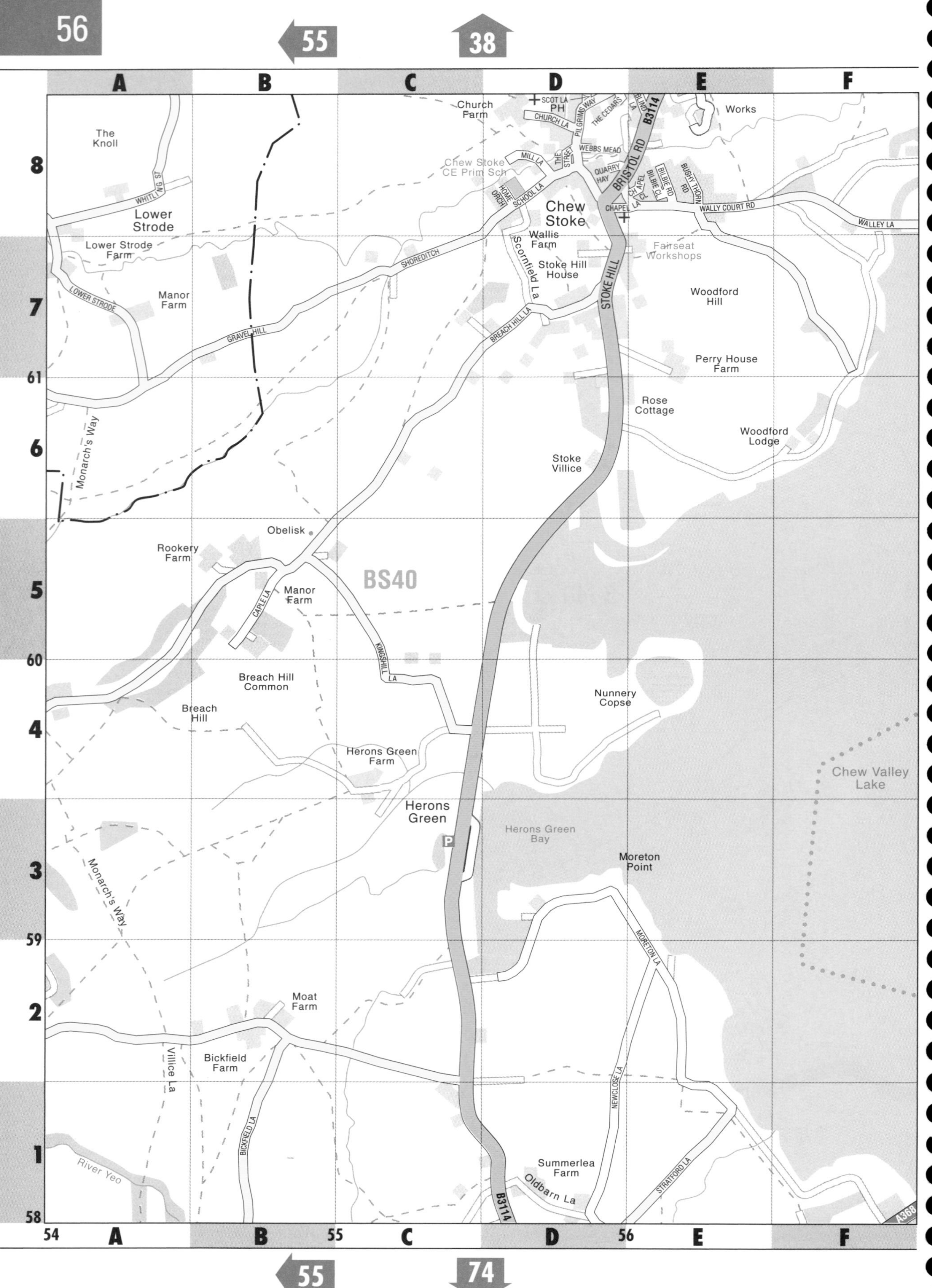
55
38
A B C D E F
8
7
61
6
5
60
4
3
59
2
1
58
54
55
56
The Knoll
Whitling St
Lower Strode
Lower Strode Farm
Lower Strode
Manor Farm
Gravel Hill
Shoreditch
Church Farm
Scot La
PH
Church La
Pilgrims Way
The Cedars
Blind La
B3114
Works
Mill La
The Street
Webbs Mead
Quarry Hay
Bristol Rd
Chew Stoke CE Prim Sch
Home Orch
School La
Chew Stoke
Chapel La
Chapel Cl
Bilbie Cl
Bilbie Rd
Bushy Thorn Rd
Wally Court Rd
Walley La
Wallis Farm
Scornfield La
Stoke Hill House
Fairseat Workshops
Stoke Hill
Woodford Hill
Breach Hill La
Perry House Farm
Rose Cottage
Woodford Lodge
Monarch's Way
Stoke Villice
Obelisk
Rookery Farm
BS40
Caple La
Manor Farm
Kingshill La
Breach Hill Common
Breach Hill
Nunnery Copse
Herons Green Farm
Chew Valley Lake
Herons Green
P
Herons Green Bay
Moreton Point
Monarch's Way
Moreton La
Moat Farm
Bickfield Farm
Villice La
Newclose La
Bickfield La
River Yeo
Summerlea Farm
Oldbarn La
B3114
Stratford La
A368

39
58

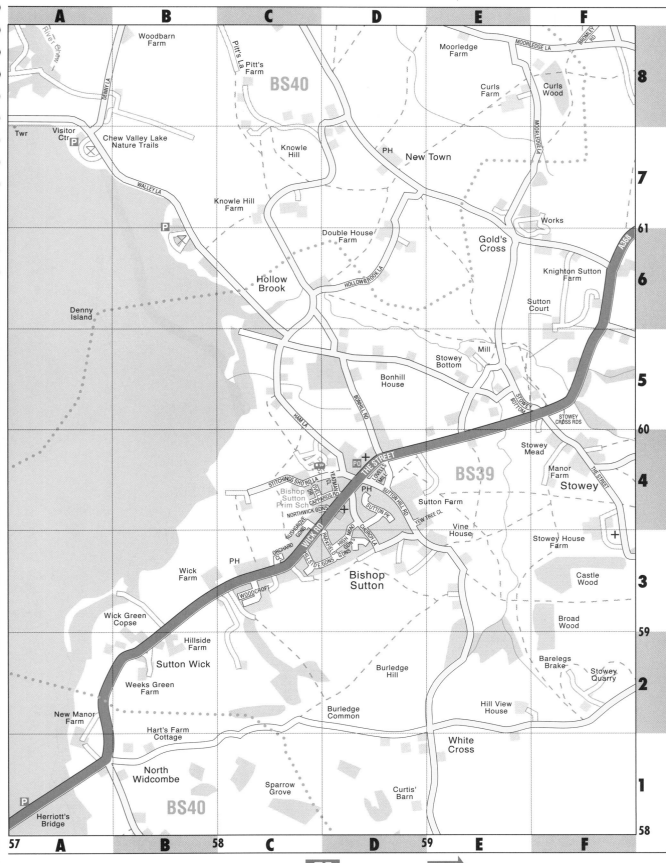
A B C D E F
8
7
61
6
5
60
4
3
59
2
1
58
57 A B 58 C D 59 E F
River Chew
Woodbarn Farm
DENNY LA
Pitt's La
Pitt's Farm
BS40
Moorledge Farm
MOORLEDGE LA
BROMLEY RD
Curls Farm
Curls Wood
MOORLEDGE LA
Twr
Visitor Ctr
Chew Valley Lake Nature Trails
Knowle Hill
PH
New Town
WALLEY LA
Knowle Hill Farm
Works
Double House Farm
Gold's Cross
A368
Hollow Brook
HOLLOWBROOK LA
Knighton Sutton Farm
Denny Island
Sutton Court
Mill
Stowey Bottom
Bonhill House
STOWEY BOTTOM
BONHILL RD
HAM LA
STOWEY CROSS RDS
Stowey Mead
THE STREET
PO
LOVELLS MILL
BS39
Manor Farm
Stowey
THE STREET
STITCHINGS SHORD LA
LOVELL DR
YEATMAN CL
CAPPARDS RD
Bishop Sutton Prim Sch
PH
SUTTON HILL RD
SUTTON PK
Sutton Farm
NORTHWICK GDNS
YEW TREE CL
RUSHGROVE GDNS
WICK RD
PARKFIELD
HIGH MEAD GDNS
CHURCH LA
Vine House
Stowey House Farm
ORCHARD CL
HILLSIDE GDNS
PH
Wick Farm
Bishop Sutton
Castle Wood
WOODCROFT
Wick Green Copse
Broad Wood
Hillside Farm
Sutton Wick
Burledge Hill
Barelegs Brake
Stowey Quarry
Weeks Green Farm
New Manor Farm
Burledge Common
Hill View House
Hart's Farm Cottage
White Cross
North Widcombe
Sparrow Grove
Curtis' Barn
BS40
Herriott's Bridge

75
58

57
40

A B C D E F

8
7
61
6
5
60
4
3
59
2
1
58

Stanton Wick La
Stanton Wick
Chelwood Rdbt
A37
A368
Bromley Farm
Curl's Farm
Utcombe Farm
Chelwood House Hotel
Stanton Wick Farm
Park Farm
Fry's Bottom
A368
Round Hill
Salter's Brook
Feathered La
Red Hill
Breach
Folly Wood
Honey Gaston
BS39
North End Farm
Folly Farm Nature Reserve
The Flat
North End
Dowling's Wood
King La
Taylor's Farm
Hill Farm
Lower Bristol Rd
Cinderlands Brake
Tynemoor Wood
Tynings Way
Tynings
Upper Bristol Rd
Rogers Cl
Warwick Gdns
Clutton Prim Sch
Broomhill La
Burchill Cl
Maypole Cl
Batch La
Warwick Arms (PH)
The Mead
Furnleaze
Greenridge
Greensbrook
Station Rd
PO
Moorsfield
Clutton Hill
Tynemore Farm
Clutton
Church La
Valley View
Maynard Terr
Venus La
Carlton Ct
Church Farm
Cholwell Farm
Kings Oak Mdw
Church Sq
Sleight Farm
Cholwell House
Bendalls Bridge
Cholwell
Willow Farm
New Cholwell Farm
Cholwell Cotts
Marsh La
Nanny Hurn's La
Limestone Link
Temple Cloud
The Square
Temple Inn La
Goldney Cl
Oaklands
Tiledown
Chardyke Dr
Goldney Way
Greyfield View
Paulwood Rd
PH
Meadway
Paul Wood
Paulmont Rise
Ashmead
Tiledown Cl
Fieldgardens Rd
Ham Cl
Fairview
Elm View
A37
Cameley CE Prim Sch

60 A B 61 C D 62 E F

57
76

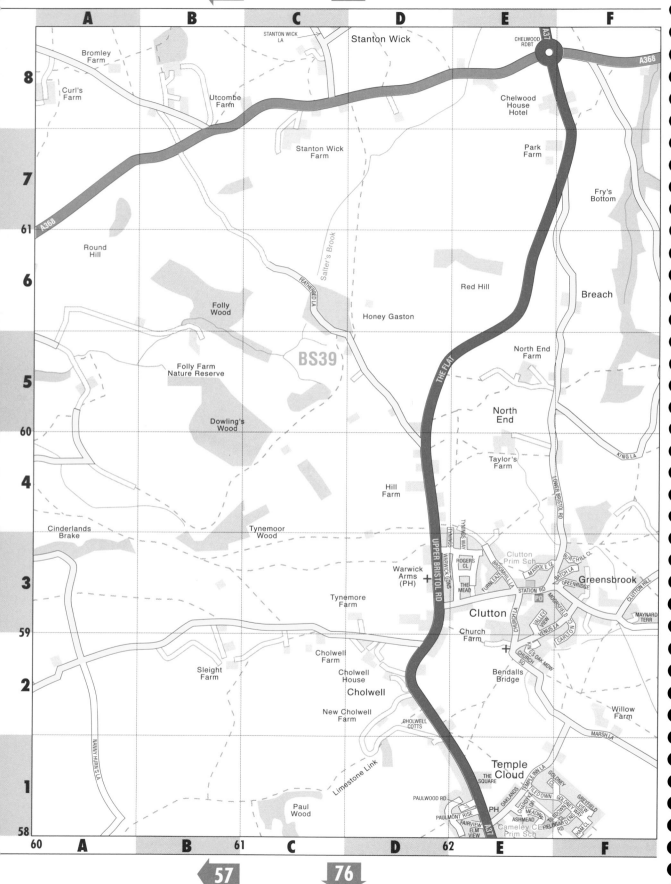

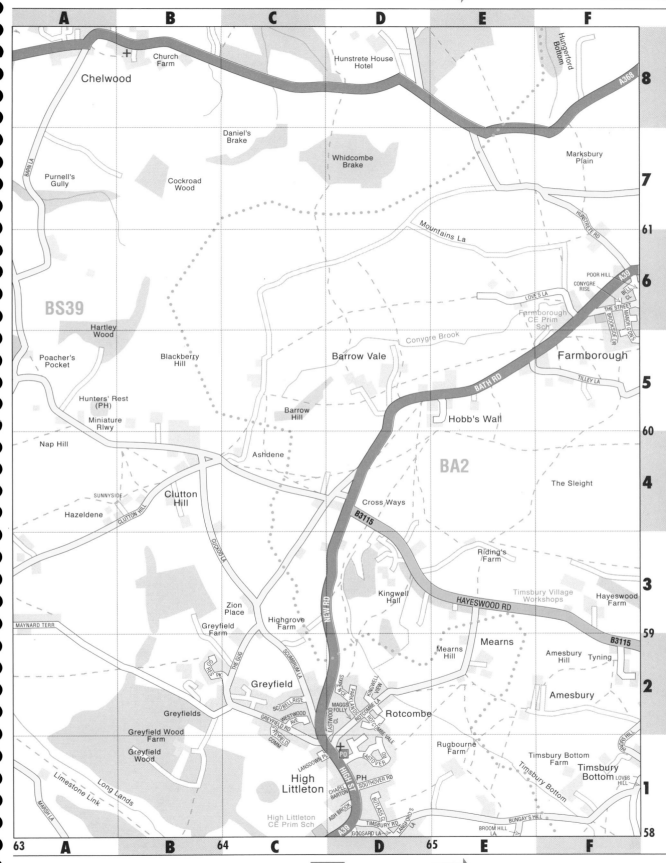

A · B · C · D · E · F

Chelwood

Church Farm

Daniel's Brake

Whidcombe Brake

Hunstrete House Hotel

Hungerford Bottom

A368

8

Marksbury Plain

7

Purnell's Gully

Cockroad Wood

Mountains La

61

BARN LA

BS39

Hartley Wood

Blackberry Hill

Barrow Vale

Conygre Brook

Love's La

POOR HILL

CONYGRE RISE

A39

Farmborough CE Prim Sch

THE STREET

MANOR GDNS

BELL CL

BROOKSIDE DR

6

Poacher's Pocket

Barrow Hill

Hobb's Wall

BATH RD

Farmborough

TILLEY LA

5

Hunters' Rest (PH)

Miniature Rlwy

60

Nap Hill

Ashdene

BA2

The Sleight

4

SUNNYSIDE

Hazeldene

Clutton Hill

CLUTTON HILL

Cross Ways

B3115

Riding's Farm

Timsbury Village Workshops

Hayeswood Farm

3

CUCKOO LA

Kingwell Hall

HAYESWOOD RD

B3115

59

Zion Place

Highgrove Farm

NEW RD

Mearns Hill

Mearns

Amesbury Hill

Tyning

MAYNARD TERR

Greyfield Farm

THE GUG

GS RES PK

SQUBRIM LA

Amesbury

2

Greyfield

SCOBELL RISE

WESTWOOD AVE

GREYFIELD RD

PEYFIELD

COMM

Greyfields

Rotcombe

SWPE N CE

PARK LANDS

KINGWELL VIEW

ROTCOMBE LA

MAGGS FOLLY

EASTWOOD CL

COMBE VALE

Rugbourne Farm

Timsbury Bottom Farm

Timsbury Bottom

Greyfield Wood Farm

Greyfield Wood

LANSDOWN PL

EASTOVER

PO

Timsbury Bottom

LOVES HILL

1

Limestone Link

Long Lands

High Littleton

HIGH ST

CHAPEL BARTON

PH

SOUTHOVER RD

BUTTASS CL

LANGFORD'S LA

BUNGAY'S HILL

MARSH LA

High Littleton CE Prim Sch

ASH BROOK

TIMSBURY RD

GOOSARD LA

A39

BROOM HILL LA

58

59 42

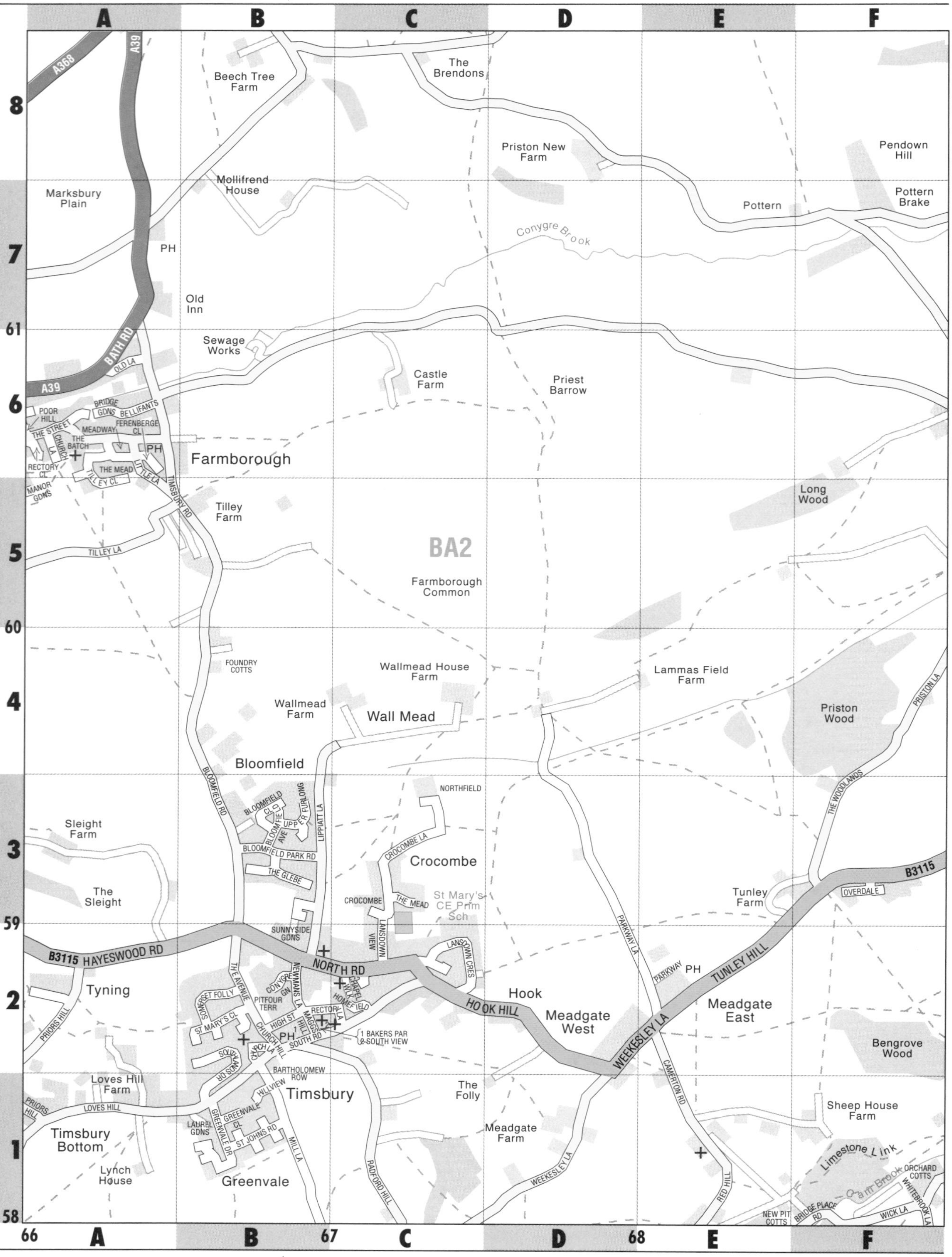

A B C D E F

8

Beech Tree Farm
The Brendons
Priston New Farm
Pendown Hill

Marksbury Plain
Mollifrend House
Pottern
Pottern Brake

7

A368
A39
PH
Conygre Brook

Old Inn

61

BATH RD
Sewage Works
A39
Castle Farm
Priest Barrow

6

Poor Hill
BRIDGE GDNS
BELLIFANTS
FERENBERGE CL
MEADWAY
THE STREET
CHURCH
THE BATCH
PH
RECTORY CL
THE MEAD
Farmborough
MANOR GDNS
TILLEY CL
LTTLE LA
TIMSBURY RD
OLD LA

Long Wood

Tilley Farm
BA2

5

TILLEY LA
Farmborough Common

60

FOUNDRY COTTS
Wallmead House Farm
Lammas Field Farm
Priston Wood

4

Wallmead Farm
Wall Mead
THE WOODLANDS
PRISTON LA

Bloomfield
Northfield
B3115

3

Sleight Farm
BLOOMFIELD RD
BLOOMFIELD CL
BLOOMFIELD AVE
UPPER FURLONG
LIPPIATT LA
Crocombe
CROCOMBE LA
Tunley Farm
OVERDALE

The Sleight
BLOOMFIELD PARK RD
THE GLEBE
CROCOMBE
THE MEAD
St Mary's CE Prim Sch

59

B3115 HAYESWOOD RD
SUNNYSIDE GDNS
LANSDOWN
VIEW
LANSDOWN
LAWN CRES
PARKWAY LA
PH
TUNLEY HILL

2

Tyning
THE AVENUE
NORTH RD
Hook
Meadgate East
PRIORS HILL
SOMERSET FOLLY
CONYGRE
NEWMANS LA
HIGH ST
MEADOW
RECTORY
HOME FIELD
HOOK HILL
Meadgate West
PARKWAY
WEEKESLEY LA
CAMERTON RD
Bengrove Wood

PITFOUR TERR
ST MARY'S CL
SOUTH RD
1 BAKERS PAR
2 SOUTH VIEW
PH
CHURCH
RD SQUARE
BARTHOLOMEW ROW
VIEW
Sheep House Farm

Loves Hill Farm
Timsbury
The Folly
Limestone Link

1

PRIORS HILL
LOVES HILL
LAUREL GDNS
GREENVALE CL
GREENVALE DR
ST JOHNS RD
MILL LA
RAFFORD HILL
Meadgate Farm
WEEKESLEY LA
RED HILL
ORCHARD COTTS
WHITEBROOK LA

Timsbury Bottom
Lynch House
Greenvale
NEW PIT COTTS
BRIDGE PLACE RD
WICK LA

58

66 A B 67 C D 68 E F
59 78

43
62

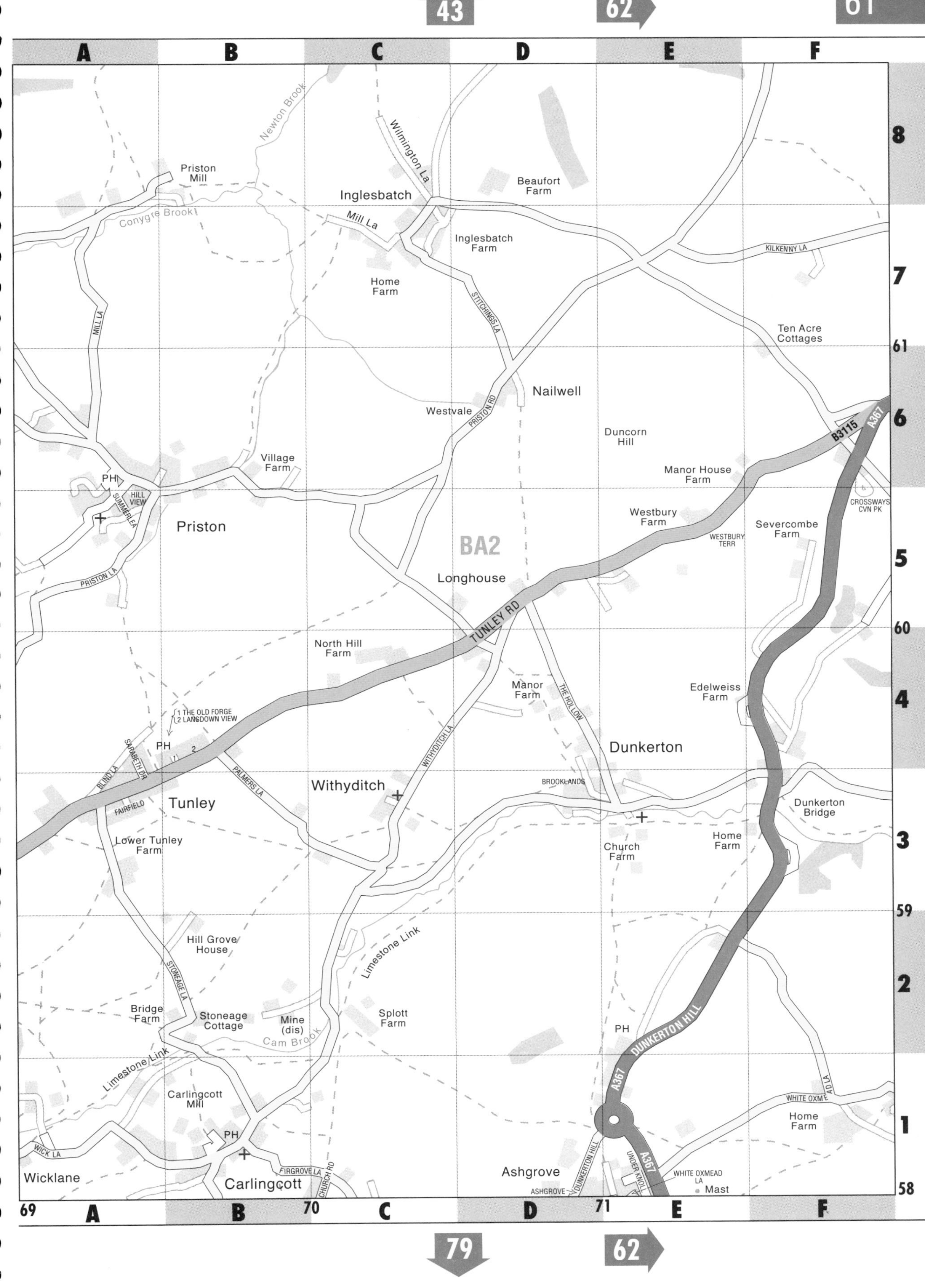
A
B
C
D
E
F
8
7
61
6
5
60
4
3
59
2
1
58
69
70
71
Priston Mill
Newton Brook
Wilmington La
Beaufort Farm
Inglesbatch
Conygre Brook
Mill La
Inglesbatch Farm
KILKENNY LA
Home Farm
MILL LA
STITCHINGS LA
Ten Acre Cottages
Nailwell
Westvale
PRISTON RD
Duncorn Hill
B3115
A367
Village Farm
Manor House Farm
PH
HILL VIEW
SUMMER LA
Priston
Westbury Farm
CROSSWAYS CVN PK
Severcombe Farm
WESTBURY TERR
BA2
PRISTON LA
Longhouse
TUNLEY RD
North Hill Farm
Manor Farm
THE HOLLOW
Edelweiss Farm
1 THE OLD FORGE
2 LANSDOWN VIEW
WITHYDITCH LA
Dunkerton
SARABETH DR
PH
BLIND LA
PALMERS LA
Withyditch
BROOKLANDS
Dunkerton Bridge
Tunley
FAIRFIELD
Lower Tunley Farm
Church Farm
Home Farm
Hill Grove House
Limestone Link
STONEAGE LA
Bridge Farm
Stoneage Cottage
Mine (dis)
Splott Farm
Cam Brook
PH
DUNKERTON HILL
Limestone Link
A367
Carlingcott Mill
WHITE OXMEAD LA
Home Farm
PH
WICK LA
FIRGROVE LA
CHURCH RD
Ashgrove
DUNKERTON HILL
UNDER KNOLL
A367
WHITE OXMEAD LA
Wicklane
Carlingcott
ASHGROVE
Mast

79
62

61
44

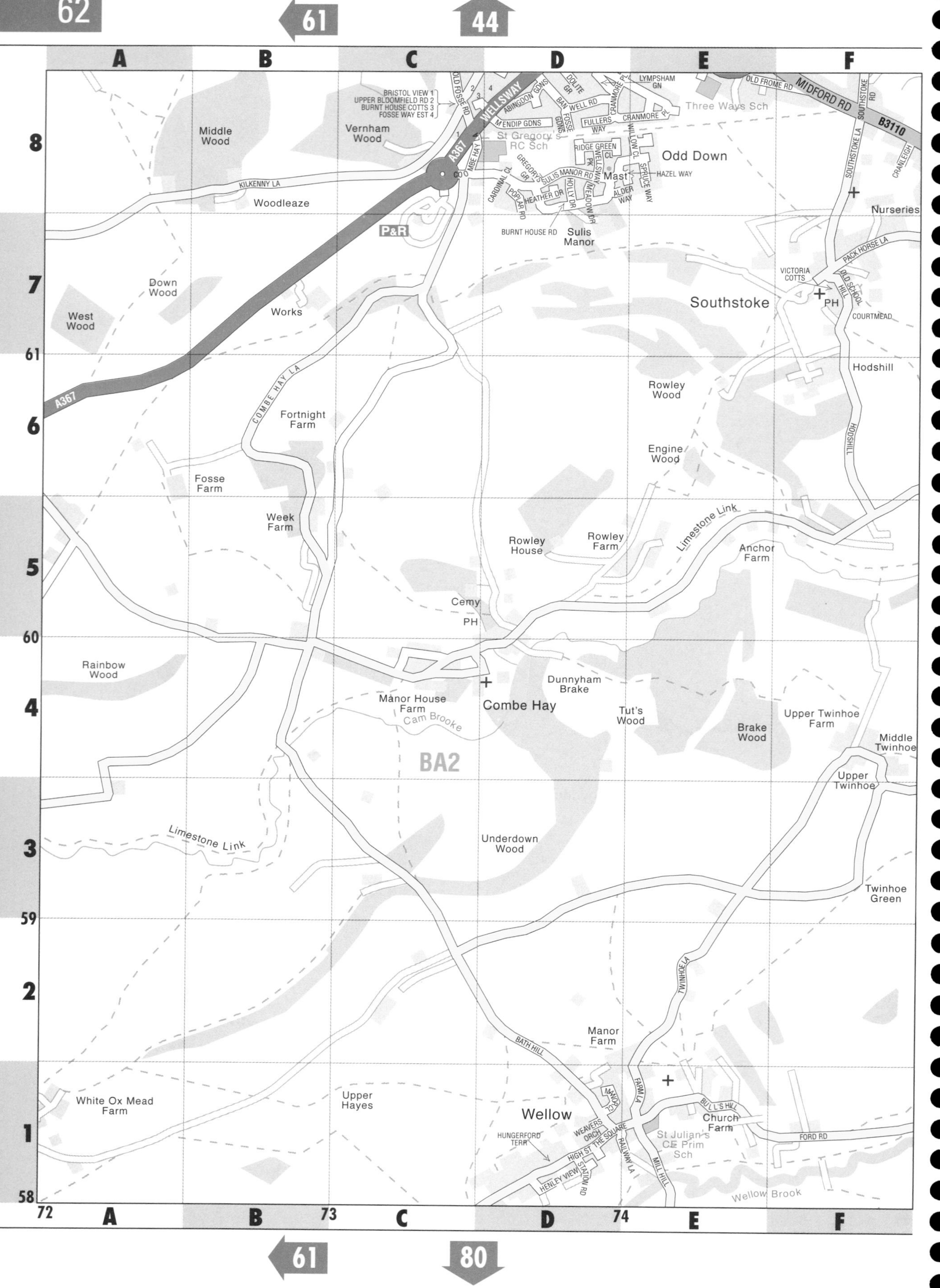
A
B
C
D
E
F
8
7
61
6
5
60
4
3
59
2
1
58
72
73
74
Middle Wood
Vernham Wood
BRISTOL VIEW 1
UPPER BLOOMFIELD RD 2
BURNT HOUSE COTTS 3
FOSSE WAY EST 4
OLD FOSSE RD
WELLSWAY
A367
ABINGDON GDNS
MENDIP GDNS
St Gregory's RC Sch
DOLITE GR
WELL RD
FOSSE GDNS
FULLERS WAY
CRANMORE PL
LYMPSHAM GN
Three Ways Sch
OLD FROME RD
MIDFORD RD
B3110
SOUTHSTOKE RD
SOUTHSTOKE LA
CRANLEIGH
Odd Down
RIDGE GREEN CL
SULIS MANOR RD
Mast
HAZEL WAY
SPRUCE WAY
ALDER WAY
GREGORYS GR
CARDINAL CL
POPLAR RD
HEATHER DR
HOLLY DR
MEADOW DR
KILKENNY LA
Woodleaze
P&R
BURNT HOUSE RD
Sulis Manor
Nurseries
PACK HORSE LA
VICTORIA COTTS
OLD SCHOOL HILL
Southstoke
PH
COURTMEAD
Down Wood
West Wood
Works
Hodshill
Rowley Wood
A367
COMBE HAY LA
Fortnight Farm
HODSHILL
Engine Wood
Fosse Farm
Week Farm
Limestone Link
Rowley House
Rowley Farm
Anchor Farm
Cemy
PH
Rainbow Wood
Manor House Farm
Combe Hay
Dunnyham Brake
Tut's Wood
Upper Twinhoe Farm
Brake Wood
Middle Twinhoe
Cam Brooke
BA2
Upper Twinhoe
Limestone Link
Underdown Wood
Twinhoe Green
TWINHOE LA
BATH HILL
Manor Farm
FARM LA
White Ox Mead Farm
Upper Hayes
Wellow
BULL'S HILL
Church Farm
St Julian's CE Prim Sch
FORD RD
HUNGERFORD TERR
WEAVERS ORCH
THE SQUARE
HIGH ST
HENLEY VIEW
STATION RD
RAILWAY LA
MILL HILL
Wellow Brook

61
80

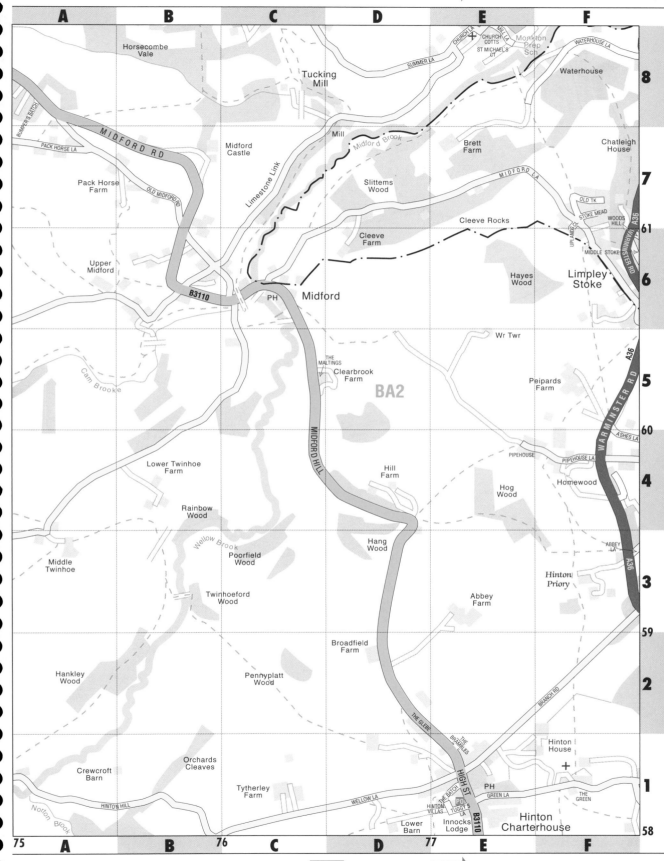

A B C D E F

Horsecombe Vale
Tucking Mill
SUMMER LA
CHURCH LA
MILL LA
CHURCH COTTS
ST MICHAEL'S CT
Monkton Prep Sch
WATERHOUSE LA
Waterhouse
8
BUMPER'S BATCH
MIDFORD RD
PACK HORSE LA
Midford Castle
Mill
Midford Brook
Brett Farm
Chatleigh House
Pack Horse Farm
OLD MIDFORD RD
Limestone Link
Slittems Wood
MIDFORD LA
7
OLD TK
STOKE MEAD
WOODS HILL
A36
Cleeve Rocks
Cleeve Farm
UPLANDS CL
61
MIDDLE STOKE
WARMINSTER RD
Upper Midford
Hayes Wood
Limpley Stoke
B3110
PH
Midford
6
Wr Twr
THE MALTINGS
Clearbrook Farm
Cam Brook
BA2
Peipards Farm
5
WARMINSTER RD
ASHES LA
60
MIDFORD HILL
Lower Twinhoe Farm
PIPEHOUSE
PIPEHOUSE LA
Hill Farm
Hog Wood
Homewood
4
Rainbow Wood
Wellow Brook
Hang Wood
Middle Twinhoe
Poorfield Wood
ABBEY LA
A36
Hinton Priory
3
Twinhoeford Wood
Abbey Farm
59
Broadfield Farm
Hankley Wood
Pennyplatt Wood
BRANCH RD
2
THE GLEBE
THE BRAMBLES
Hinton House
Orchards Cleaves
Crewcroft Barn
HIGH ST
Tytherley Farm
PH
THE BATCH
PO
GREEN LA
THE GREEN
1
HINTON HILL
WELLOW LA
HINTON VILLAS
TUGGY'S LA
Norton Brook
Lower Barn
Innocks Lodge
B3110
Hinton Charterhouse
58

75 A B 76 C D 77 E F

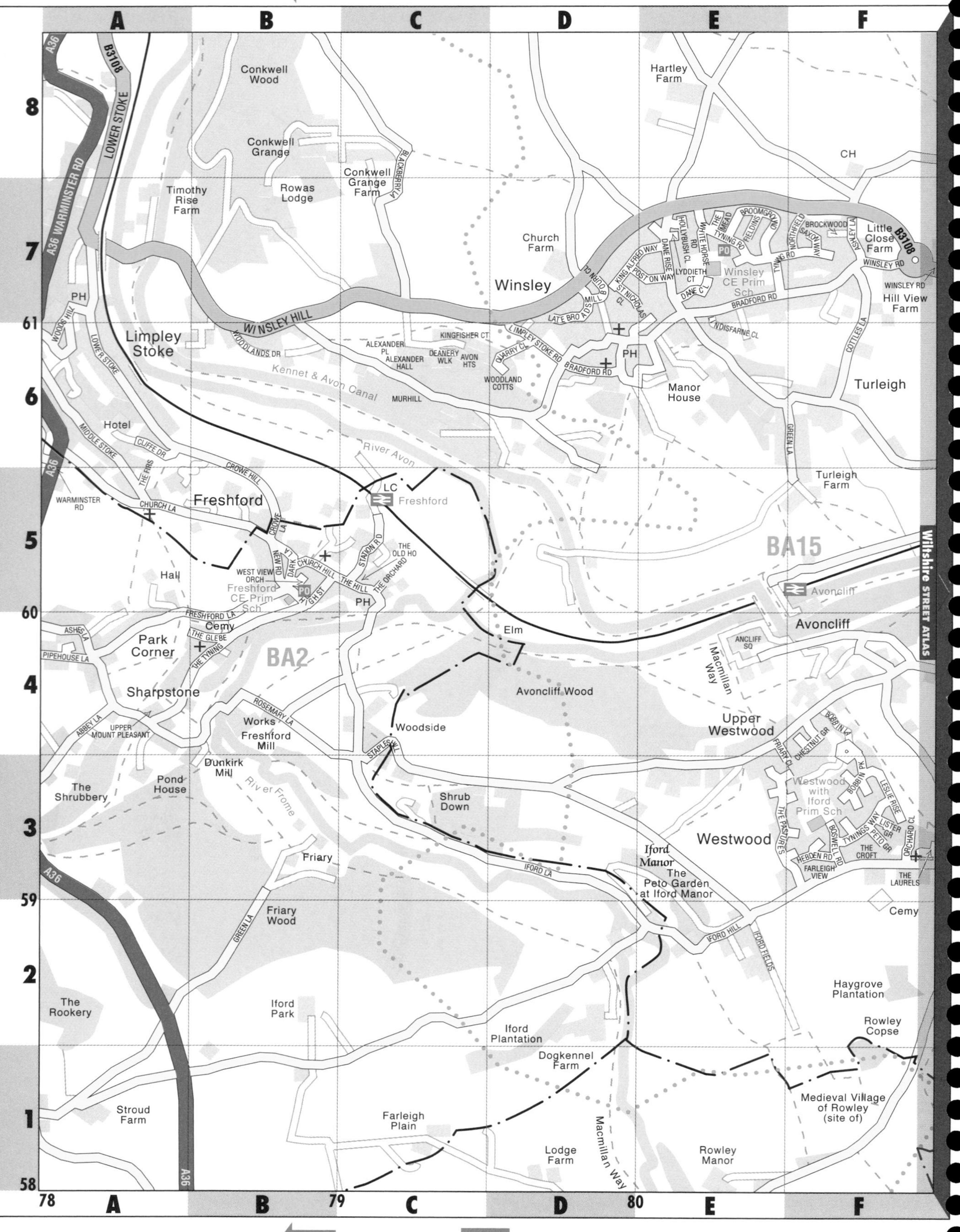

A   B   C   D   E   F

8

Conkwell Wood

Conkwell Grange

Rowas Lodge

Conkwell Grange Farm

BLACKBERRY LA

Hartley Farm

CH

7

Timothy Rise Farm

Church Farm

Winsley

HOLLYBUSH CL
THE LIMB
BROOMGROUND
WELDING
NORTHFIELD
BROCKWOOD
WHITE HORSE RD
KING ALFRED WAY
THE TYNING RD
TYNING RD
SAXON WAY
DANE RISE
POST ON WAY
PO
LYDDIETH CT
ST NICHOLAS CL
DANE CL
LINDISFARNE CL
Winsley CE Prim Sch
BRADFORD RD

B3108
Little Close Farm

WINSLEY RD

WINSLEY RD

Hill View Farm

61

Limpley Stoke

WINSLEY HILL

WOODLANDS DR

ALEXANDER PL
ALEXANDER HALL
DEANERY WLK
KINGFISHER CT
AVON HTS

LIMPLEY STOKE RD
MILL RD
LATE BRO
QUARRY CL
BRADFORD RD

PH

Manor House

GREEN LA

OTTLEYS LA

Turleigh

PH

Woods Hill

Lower B

6

Kennet & Avon Canal

MURHILL

WOODLAND COTTS

River Avon

Turleigh Farm

A36

MIDDLE STOKE

Hotel

CLIFFE DR

CROWE HILL

BA15

Avoncliff

5

WARMINSTER RD

THE FIRS

CHURCH LA

Freshford

LC

Freshford

ANCLIFF SQ

Macmillan Way

Avoncliff

Hall

CROWE LA

WEST VIEW ORCH
DARK LA
THE MAIN
CHURCH HILL
STATION RD
THE OLD HO
THE HILL
THE ORCHARD
Freshford CE Prim Sch
PO
HIGH ST
PH

Elm

Avoncliff Wood

Upper Westwood

60

ASHES

FRESHFORD LA
THE GLEBE
Cemy

BA2

BOBBIN LA
CHESTNUT GR
PRIORY CL
BOBBIN PK
LESLIE RISE
Westwood with Iford Prim Sch

Pipehouse La

Park Corner

THE TYNING

Westwood

4

Sharpstone

ROSEMARY LA

Works
Freshford Mill

STAPLES HILL

Woodside

THE PASTURES
TYNINGS WAY
HEBDEN RD
BOSWELL CL
FARLEIGH VIEW
PETO GR
LISTER GR
ORCHARD CL
THE CROFT
THE LAURELS

ABBEY LA
UPPER MOUNT PLEASANT

Dunkirk Mill

Pond House

River Frome

Shrub Down

Iford Manor
The Peto Garden at Iford Manor

Cemy

3

The Shrubbery

IFORD LA

FORD HILL
IFORD FIELDS

59

A36

Friary

GREEN LA

Friary Wood

Haygrove Plantation

Rowley Copse

2

The Rookery

Iford Park

Iford Plantation

Dogkennel Farm

Macmillan Way

Medieval Village of Rowley (site of)

1

Stroud Farm

Farleigh Plain

Lodge Farm

Rowley Manor

58

A36

78   A   B   79   C   D   80   E   F

Wiltshire STREET ATLAS

47
66

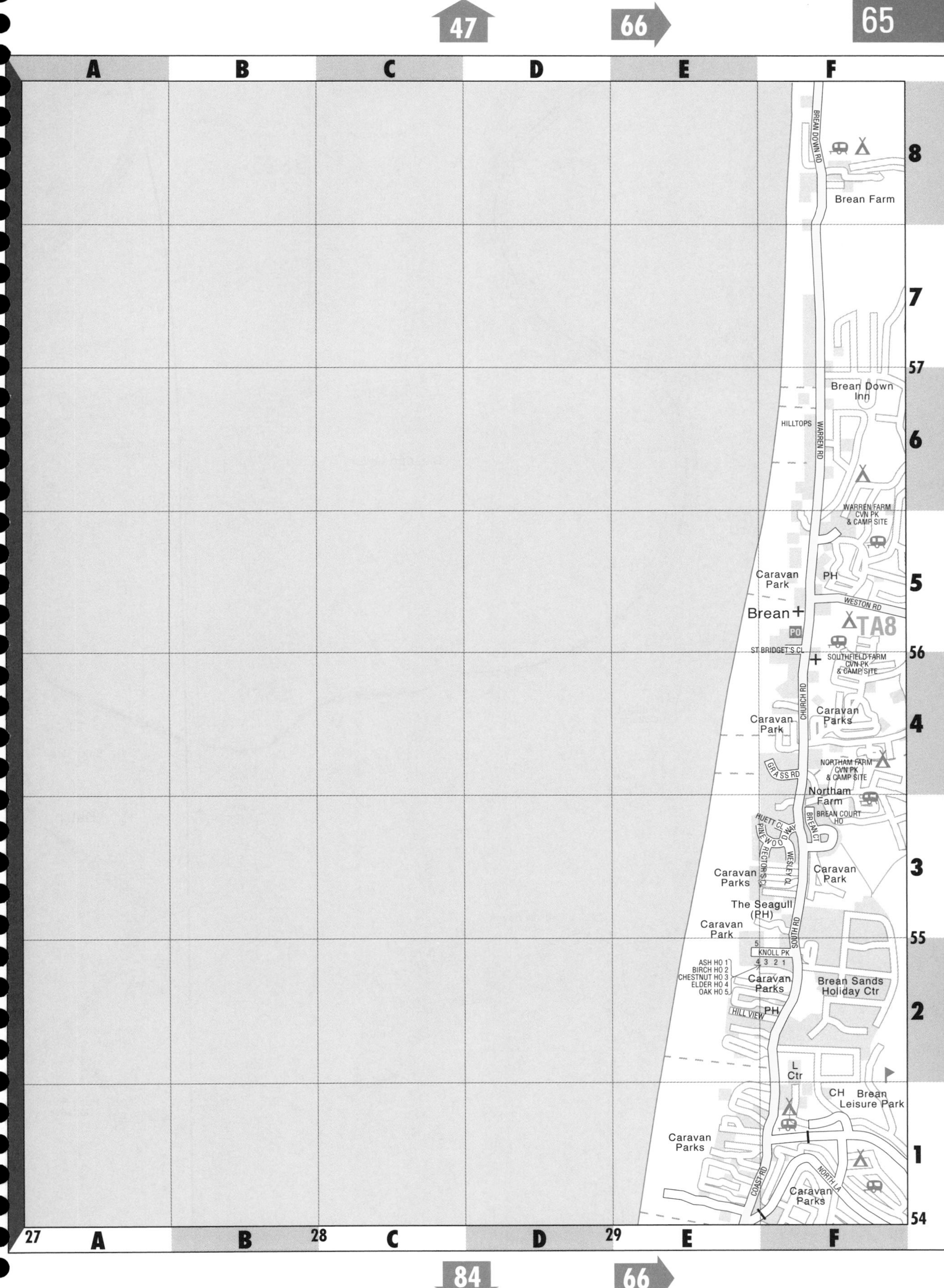
A
B
C
D
E
F
8
7
57
6
5
56
4
3
55
2
1
54
27
28
29
BREAN DOWN RD
Brean Farm
Brean Down Inn
HILLTOPS
WARREN RD
WARREN FARM CVN PK & CAMP SITE
Caravan Park
PH
WESTON RD
Brean
PO
TA8
ST BRIDGET'S CL
SOUTHFIELD FARM CVN PK & CAMP SITE
CHURCH RD
Caravan Park
Caravan Parks
NORTHAM FARM CVN PK & CAMP SITE
GRASS RD
Northam Farm
BREAN CT
BREAN COURT HO
HUETT CL
PINEWOOD WAY
RECTOR'S CL
WESLEY CL
Caravan Parks
Caravan Park
The Seagull (PH)
SOUTH RD
Caravan Park
KNOLL PK
ASH HO 1
BIRCH HO 2
CHESTNUT HO 3
ELDER HO 4
OAK HO 5
Caravan Parks
Brean Sands Holiday Ctr
HILL VIEW
PH
L Ctr
CH
Brean Leisure Park
Caravan Parks
COAST RD
NORTH LA
Caravan Parks

84
66

65
48

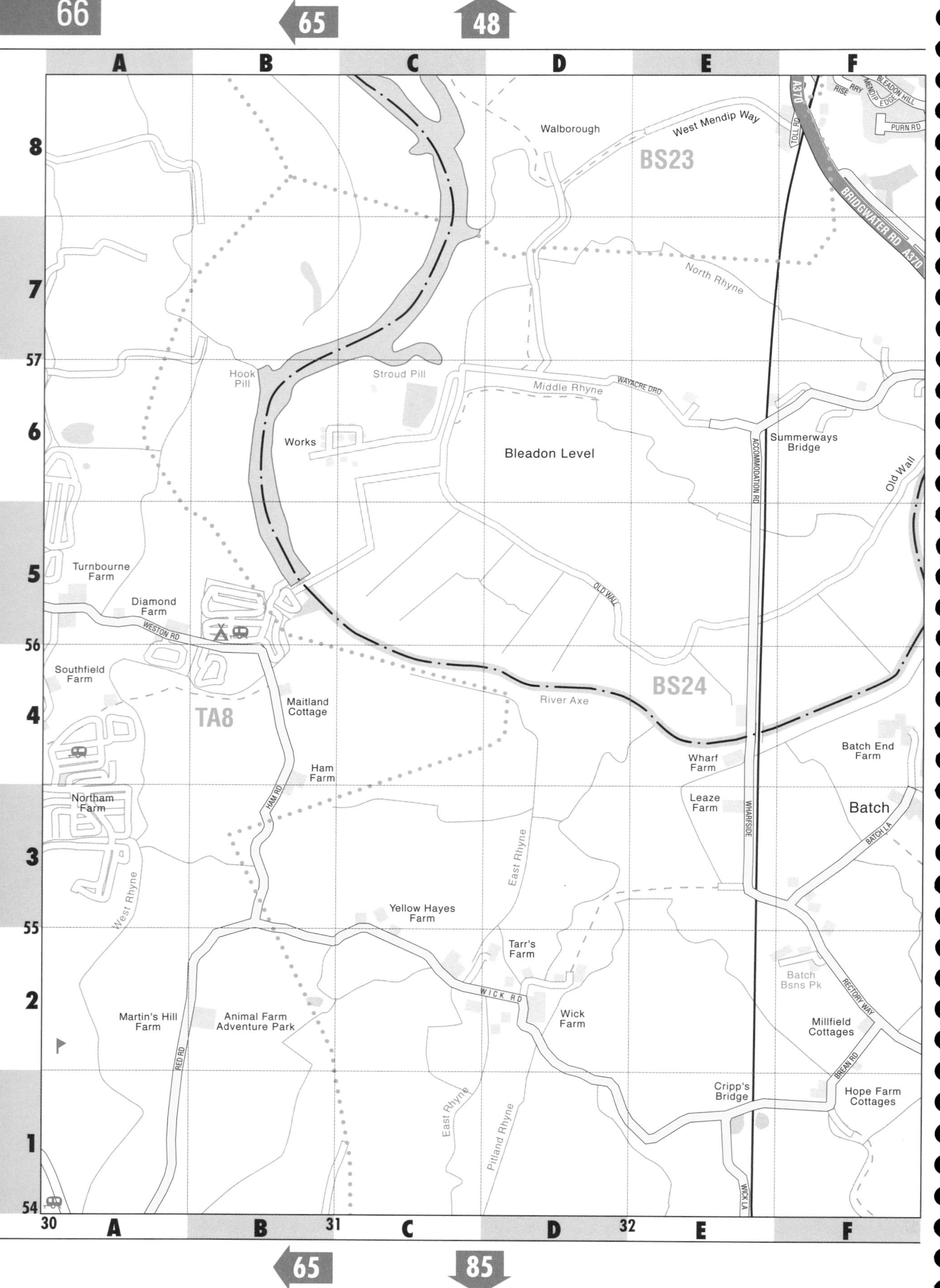
Walborough
West Mendip Way
BS23
A370
TOLL RD
BLEADON HILL
MENDIP EDGE
RISE
PURN RD
BRIDGWATER RD A370
North Rhyne
Hook Pill
Stroud Pill
Middle Rhyne
WAYACRE DRO
Works
Bleadon Level
Summerways Bridge
ACCOMMODATION RD
Old Wall
Turnbourne Farm
Diamond Farm
WESTON RD
OLD WALL
Southfield Farm
Maitland Cottage
TA8
River Axe
BS24
Batch End Farm
Wharf Farm
Ham Farm
HAM RD
Northam Farm
Leaze Farm
WHARFSIDE
Batch
BATCH LA
East Rhyne
West Rhyne
Yellow Hayes Farm
Tarr's Farm
Batch Bsns Pk
RECTORY WAY
WICK RD
Martin's Hill Farm
Animal Farm Adventure Park
Wick Farm
Millfield Cottages
RED RD
BREAN RD
Cripp's Bridge
Hope Farm Cottages
East Rhyne
Pitland Rhyne
WICK LA
8
7
57
6
5
56
4
3
55
2
1
54
30
31
32
A
B
C
D
E
F

65
85

49
68

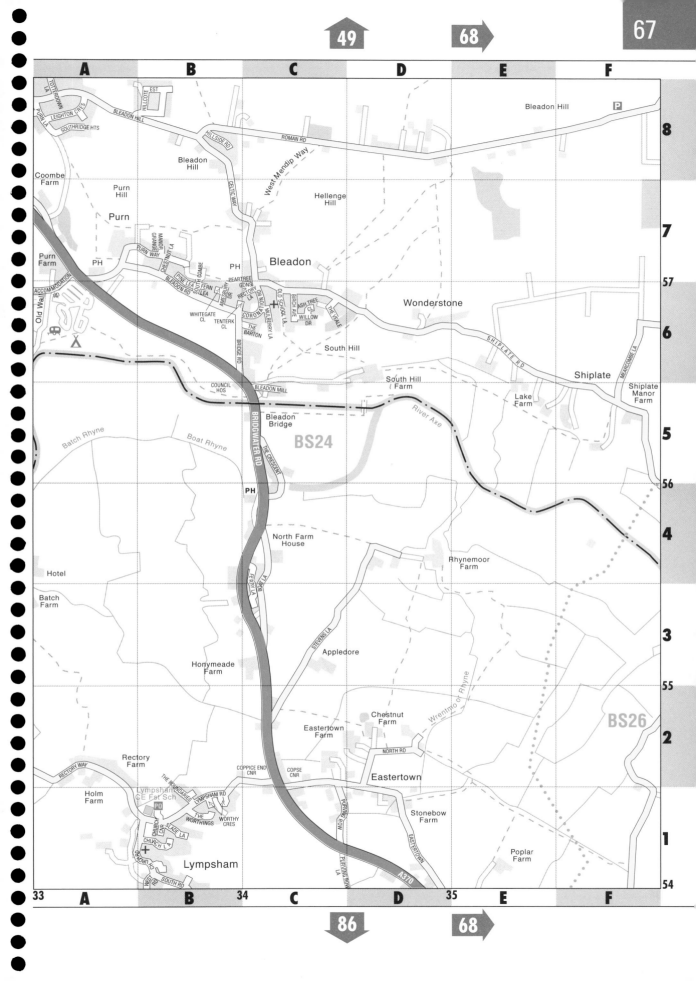
A
B
C
D
E
F
Bleadon Hill
Bleadon
Purn
Purn Hill
Coombe Farm
Purn Farm
Hellenge Hill
West Mendip Way
Wonderstone
South Hill
South Hill Farm
Shiplate
Shiplate Manor Farm
Lake Farm
Bleadon Bridge
River Axe
BS24
Batch Rhyne
Boat Rhyne
BRIDGWATER RD
North Farm House
Rhynemoor Farm
Hotel
Batch Farm
Appledore
Honymeade Farm
Chestnut Farm
Eastertown Farm
Wrentmoor Rhyne
BS26
Rectory Farm
Eastertown
Holm Farm
Stonebow Farm
Poplar Farm
Lympsham
Lympsham CE Fst Sch
ROMAN RD
SHIPLATE RD
MEARCOMBE LA
CELTIC WAY
HILLSIDE RD
BLEADON HILL
HILLCOTE EST
TOTTERDOWN LA
PURN LA
LEIGHTON CRES
SOUTHRIDGE HTS
ACCOMMODATION RD
Old Wall
PURN WAY
MANOR GRANGE
CHESTNUT LA
PINE LEA
SOUTH COMBE
FERN LEA
BLEADON RD
AMESBURY DR
PEARTREE GDNS
RECTORY LA
CORONATION RD
OLD SCHOOL LA
BIRCH AVE
ASH TREE CL
WILLOW DR
THE VEALE
WHITEGATE CL
TENTERK CL
THE BARTON
MULBERRY LA
BRIDGE RD
COUNCIL HOS
BLEADON MILL
THE CRESCENT
FERRY LA
BOAT LA
STEVENS LA
NORTH RD
COPPICE END CNR
COPSE CNR
RECTORY WAY
THE BOUNDARIES
LYMPSHAM RD
THE WORTHINGS
WORTHY CRES
CHURCH CNR
SLADE LA
CHURCH LA
ORCHARD CL
WEST RD
SOUTH RD
PURVING ROW
PURVING ROW LA
EASTERTOWN
A370
PH
8
7
57
6
5
56
4
3
55
2
1
54
33
34
35

86
68

67 50

A B C D E F

8

7

57

6

5

56

4

3

55

2

1

54

36 A B 37 C D 38 E F

67 87

CANADA COOMBE

BS29

Keeper's Cottage

Barleycombe Lodge

Yarberry Farm

Yarberry

WESTON LA

Manor Farm

FLAGSTAFF RD

BANWELL RD

M5

BS24

Shiplate Slait

Hamwood

Christon

Lox Yeo River

MEARCOOMBE LA

Loxton Hill

CHRISTON RD

Oakes Farm

BS25

West Mendip Way

Loxton Wood

BARTON RD

Long Acre

Shiplate Wood

The Paddock

West Mendip Way

SHIPLATE RD

BS26

HILL VIEW RD

The Lodge

Crook Peak

Shiplate House Farm

CHURCH LA

Loxton

Hotel

SEVIER RD

COWSLIP LA

Webbington

KENNEL LA

WEBBINGTON RD

White House Farm

Old Lox Yeo

WHITE HOUSE LA

HAMS LA

River Axe

M5

Poplar Farm

North Yeo Farm

Mark Yeo

Crab Hole

BOSSINGTON LA

Riverside Farm

Tile House Farm

M5

A B C D E F

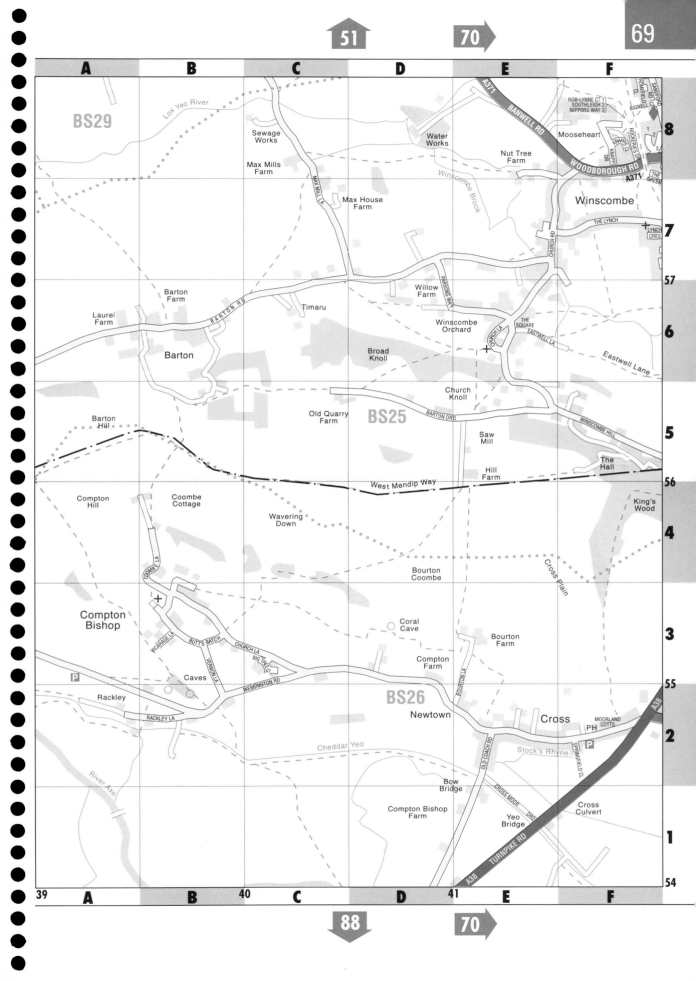
BS29
Lox Yeo River
Sewage Works
Max Mills Farm
MAX MILL LA
Max House Farm
Water Works
A371
BANWELL RD
Nut Tree Farm
Mooseheart
ROB-LYNNE CT 1
SOUTHLEIGH 2
NIPPORS WAY 3
HOMEFIELD CL
SANDFORD RD
BIGNELL CL
KNAPPS CL
KNAPPS DR
ROCKERIES DR
WOODBOROUGH RD
THE GREEN
Winscombe Brook
Winscombe
THE LYNCH
LYNCH CRES
CHURCH RD
Barton Farm
Laurel Farm
BARTON RD
Timaru
Willow Farm
PARSONS WAY
Winscombe Orchard
THE SQUARE
CHURCH LA
EASTWELL LA
Eastwell Lane
Barton
Broad Knoll
Church Knoll
Old Quarry Farm
BS25
BARTON DRO
WINSCOMBE HILL
Barton Hill
Saw Mill
The Hall
Hill Farm
West Mendip Way
Compton Hill
Coombe Cottage
Wavering Down
King's Wood
COOMBE LA
Bourton Coombe
Cross Plain
Compton Bishop
Coral Cave
Bourton Farm
VICARAGE LA
BUTT'S BATCH
CHURCH LA
BIG TREE CL
VERNON LA
Compton Farm
Caves
WEBBINGTON RD
BOURTON LA
Rackley
BS26
RACKLEY LA
Newtown
Cross
MOORLAND COTTS
PH
A38
Cheddar Yeo
Stock's Rhyne
SPRINGFIELD CL
OLD COACH RD
River Axe
Bow Bridge
CROSS MOOR DRO
Compton Bishop Farm
Yeo Bridge
Cross Culvert
TURNPIKE RD
8
7
57
6
5
56
4
3
55
2
1
54
39
40
41

A B C D E F

69 52

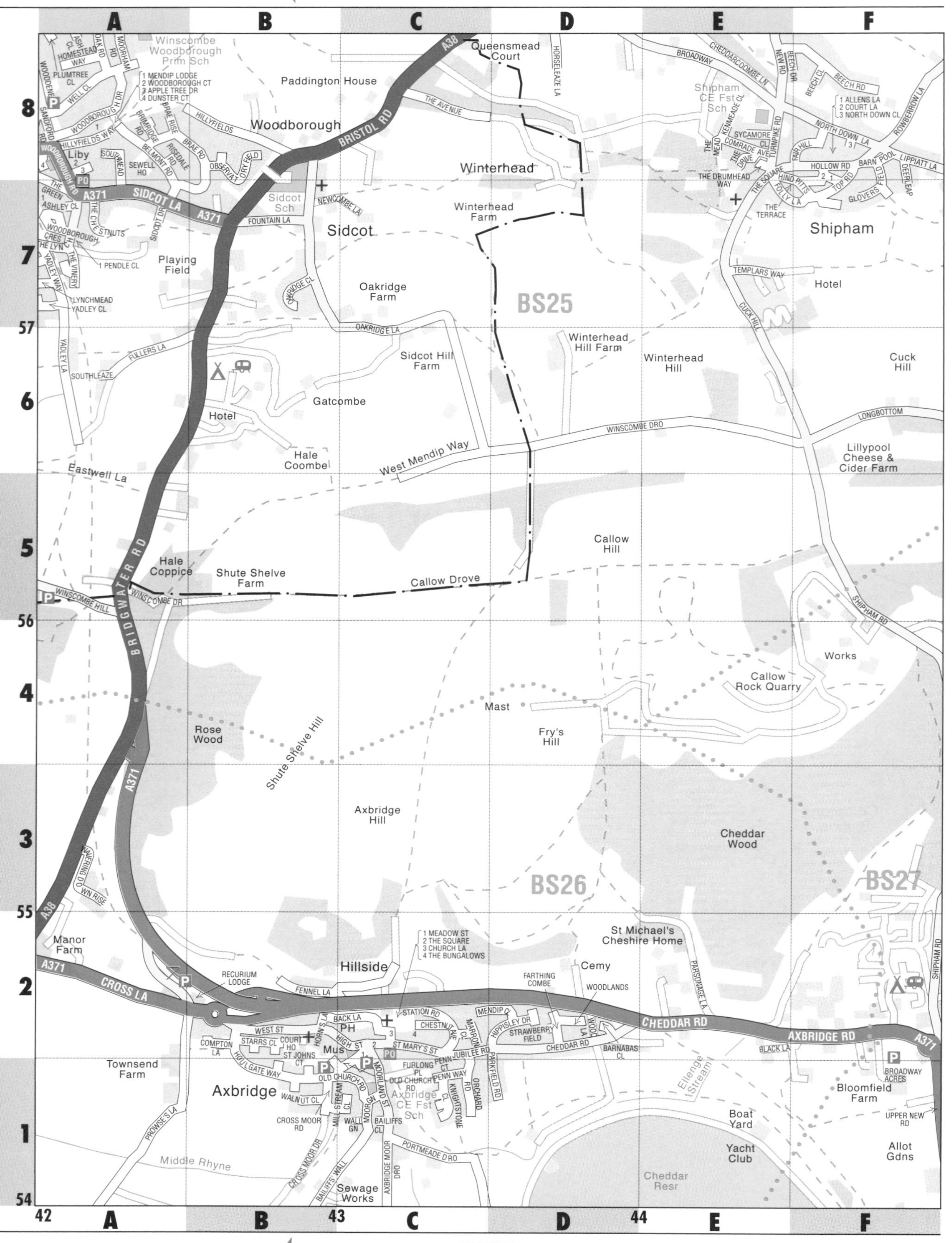

Woodborough
Liby
Sidcot
Winterhead
Winterhead Farm
Shipham
Oakridge Farm
Playing Field
BS25
Winterhead Hill Farm
Winterhead Hill
Cuck Hill
Sidcot Hill Farm
Gatcombe
Hotel
Hale Coombe
West Mendip Way
Lillypool Cheese & Cider Farm
Eastwell La
Callow Hill
Hale Coppice
Shute Shelve Farm
Callow Drove
Works
Callow Rock Quarry
Mast
Rose Wood
Fry's Hill
Shute Shelve Hill
Axbridge Hill
Cheddar Wood
BS26
BS27
Manor Farm
St Michael's Cheshire Home
Hillside
Cemy
CROSS LA
CHEDDAR RD
AXBRIDGE RD
Townsend Farm
Axbridge
Bloomfield Farm
Boat Yard
Yacht Club
Allot Gdns
Cheddar Resr
Middle Rhyne
Sewage Works
Paddington House
Queensmead Court
BRISTOL RD
BRIDGWATER RD

69 89

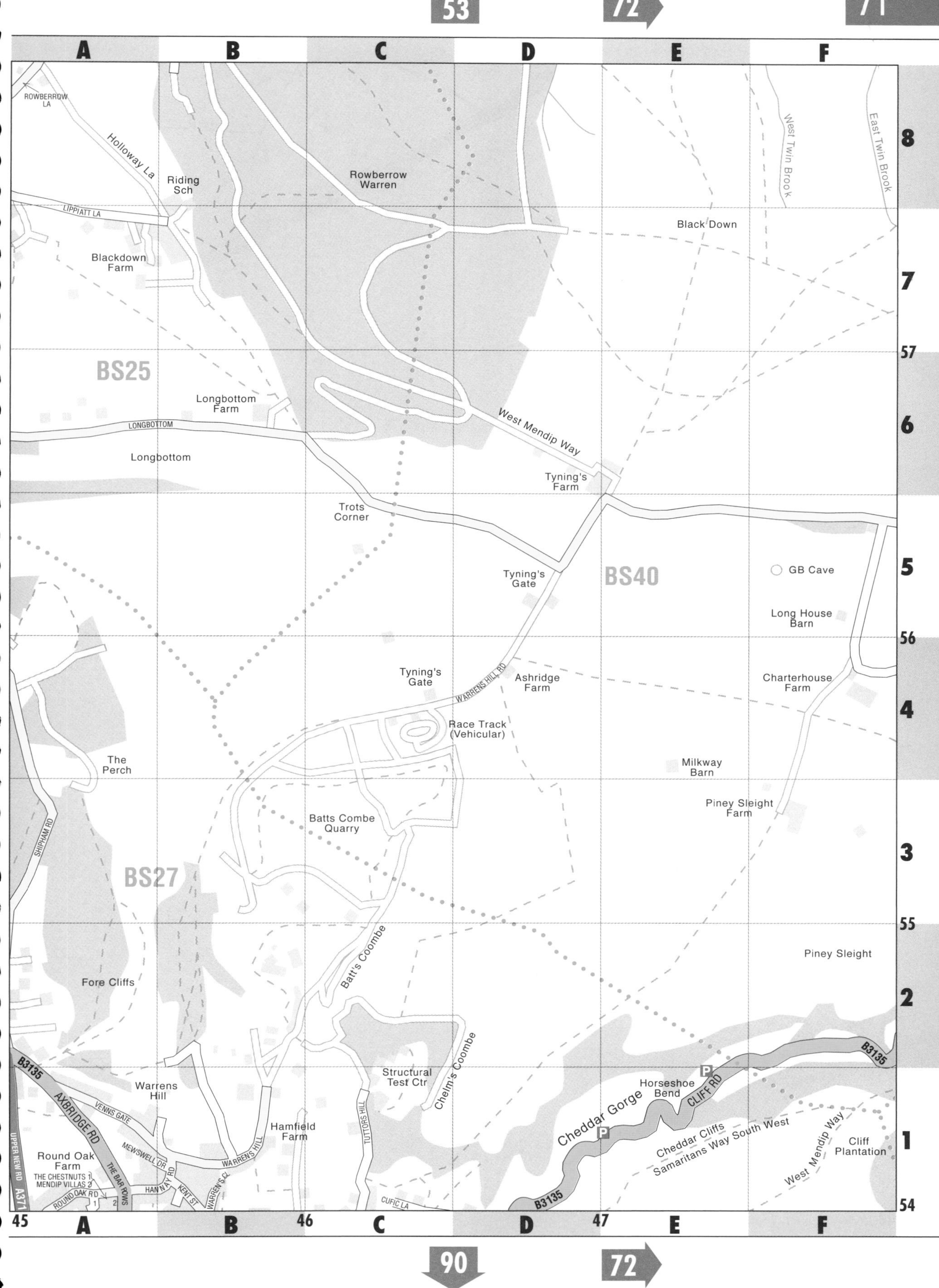

A B C D E F

ROWBERROW LA
Holloway La
Riding Sch
Rowberrow Warren
Black Down
West Twin Brook
East Twin Brook

8

LIPPIATT LA
Blackdown Farm

7

BS25

57

Longbottom Farm
West Mendip Way

6

LONGBOTTOM
Longbottom
Tyning's Farm
Trots Corner

Tyning's Gate
BS40
GB Cave

5

56

Tyning's Gate
WARRENS HILL RD
Ashridge Farm
Long House Barn
Charterhouse Farm

4

The Perch
Race Track (Vehicular)
Milkway Barn

BS27
Batts Combe Quarry
Piney Sleight Farm

3

55

SHIPHAM RD
Fore Cliffs
Batt's Coombe
Piney Sleight

2

B3135
AXBRIDGE RD
Warrens Hill
VENNS GATE
MEWSWELL DR
Hamfield Farm
Structural Test Ctr
TUTTORS HILL
Chelm's Coombe
Cheddar Gorge
Horseshoe Bend
CLIFF RD
Cheddar Cliffs
Samaritans Way South West
West Mendip Way
Cliff Plantation

1

UPPER NEW RD
A371
Round Oak Farm
THE CHESTNUTS 1
MENDIP VILLAS 2
ROUND OAK RD
WARREN'S HILL
THE BARROWS
HANNAY RD
KENT ST
WARREN'S CL
CUFIC LA
B3135

54

45
A
B
46
C
D
47
E
F

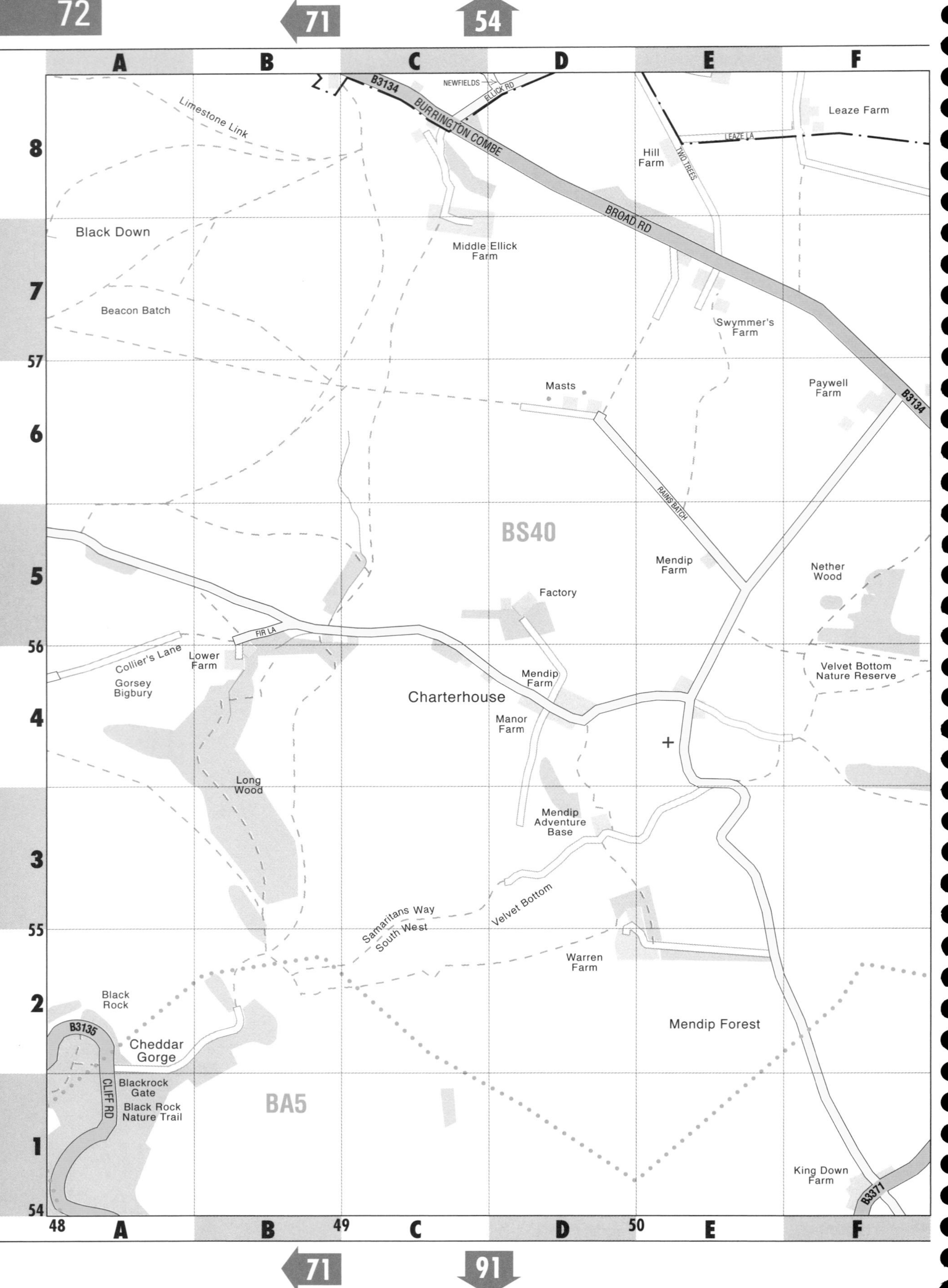

71
54

A   **B**   **C**   **D**   **E**   **F**

B3134

NEWFIELDS

ELLICK RD

Limestone Link

Leaze Farm

LEAZE LA

8

BURRINGTON COMBE

Hill Farm

TWO TREES

Black Down

Middle Ellick Farm

BROAD RD

7

Beacon Batch

Swymmer's Farm

57

Masts

Paywell Farm

B3134

6

RAINS BATCH

BS40

Mendip Farm

Nether Wood

5

Factory

FIR LA

56

Collier's Lane

Lower Farm

Mendip Farm

Velvet Bottom Nature Reserve

Gorsey Bigbury

Charterhouse

Manor Farm

4

Long Wood

Mendip Adventure Base

3

Velvet Bottom

55

Samaritans Way South West

Warren Farm

Black Rock

2

Mendip Forest

B3135

Cheddar Gorge

Blackrock Gate

BA5

Black Rock Nature Trail

CLIFF RD

1

King Down Farm

B3371

54

48   **A**   **B**   49   **C**   **D**   50   **E**   **F**

71
91

55
74

A B C D E F

Merecombe Wood
Ubley Wood
Saw Mill
A368
THE STREET
TUCKER'S LA
THE SIDELINGS
Ubley Sideling
Cleve Hill Farm
Wood House Farm
CLEEVE HILL
DURNHILL
MENDIP VILLAS
A368
THE STREET
Ubley Hill Farmhouse
GREEN LA
Ubley Hill Farm
UBLEY DRO
Limestone Link
Compton Wood
Well Plantation
Hazel Manor
Ubley Drove Farm
Green Lane
Hazel Farm
Browning's Tump
Compton Combe
Hillcroft Farm
Hazel Corner
Whitegate Lodge
Hazel Warren Farm
Home Farm
NORDRACH LA
Fairfield Wood
Butts Quarry Farm
Nordrach
BS40
Rabbit Warren
Starve Lark Farm
Parson's Piece
Long Wood
Fernhill Farm
Warren Lodge
Lord's Lot
Harptree Wood
Ubley Warren Farm
Fernhill Plantation
Whitestown Farm
B3371
Templedown Farm
Beech Farm
DANGER AREA
Yoxter Ranges
BA5
Yoxter Cadet Training Centre
Butts
Haydon Grange Farm
B3134
Pool Farm
Yoxter Farm

8 7 57 6 5 56 4 3 55 2 1 54

51 A B 52 C D 53 E F

92
74

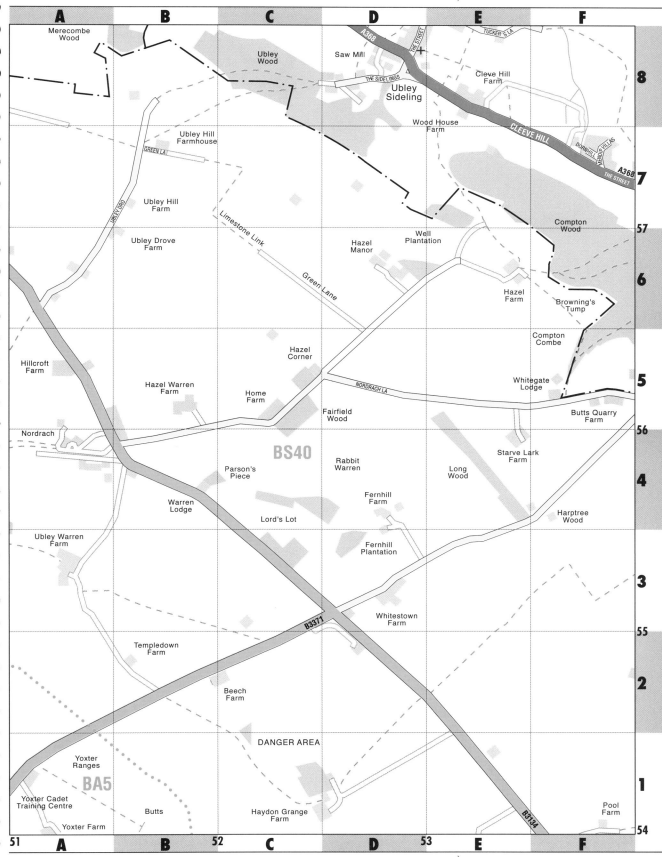

73
56

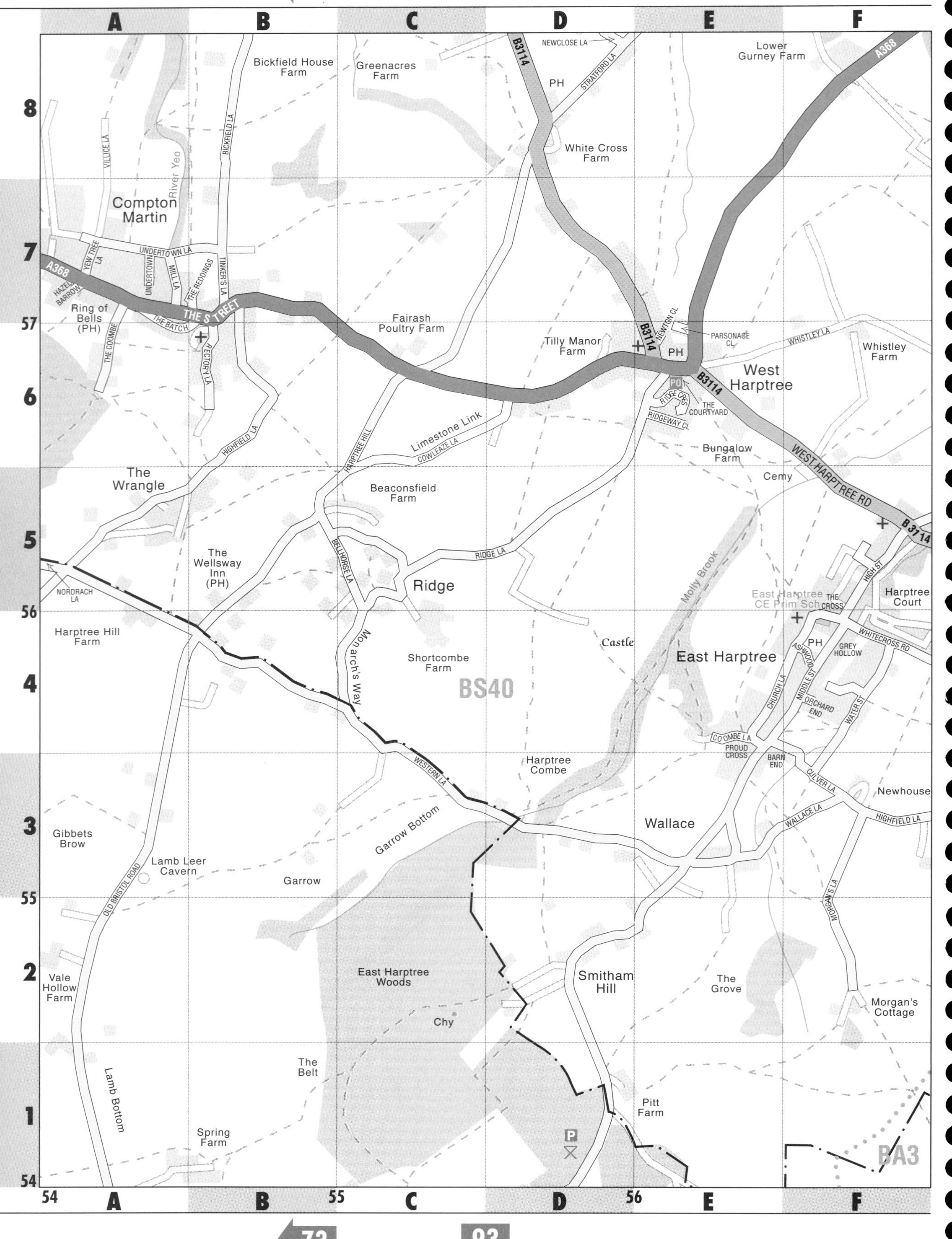
Bickfield House Farm
Greenacres Farm
Lower Gurney Farm
A368
B3114
NEWCLOSE LA
STRATFORD LA
PH
White Cross Farm
River Yeo
VILLICE LA
BICKFIELD LA
Compton Martin
UNDERTOWN LA
YEW TREE LA
UNDERTOWN
MILL LA
THE REDDINGS
TINKER'S LA
HAZEL BARROW
Ring of Bells (PH)
THE BATCH
THE STREET
THE COOMBE
RECTORY LA
Fairash Poultry Farm
Tilly Manor Farm
NEWTON CL
PARSONAGE CL
WHISTLEY LA
Whistley Farm
West Harptree
PO
RIDGE CRES
THE COURTYARD
RIDGEWAY CL
Limestone Link
COWLEAZE LA
HARPTREE HILL
HIGHFIELD LA
Bungalow Farm
WEST HARPTREE RD
Cemy
The Wrangle
Beaconsfield Farm
The Wellsway Inn (PH)
BELLHORSE LA
RIDGE LA
Ridge
Molly Brook
HIGH ST
Harptree Court
NORDRACH LA
East Harptree CE Prim Sch
THE CROSS
Harptree Hill Farm
Monarch's Way
Shortcombe Farm
Castle
East Harptree
WHITECROSS RD
ASHWOOD
GREY HOLLOW
BS40
CHURCH LA
MIDDLE ST
ORCHARD END
WATER ST
COOMBE LA
PROUD CROSS
BARN END
WESTERN LA
Harptree Combe
CULVER LA
Newhouse
Garrow Bottom
Wallace
WALLACE LA
HIGHFIELD LA
Gibbets Brow
Lamb Leer Cavern
OLD BRISTOL ROAD
Garrow
MORGAN'S LA
Vale Hollow Farm
East Harptree Woods
Smitham Hill
The Grove
Morgan's Cottage
Chy
The Belt
Lamb Bottom
Pitt Farm
Spring Farm
P
BA3
A B C D E F
8 7 6 5 4 3 2 1
57 56 55 54
54 55 56

73
93

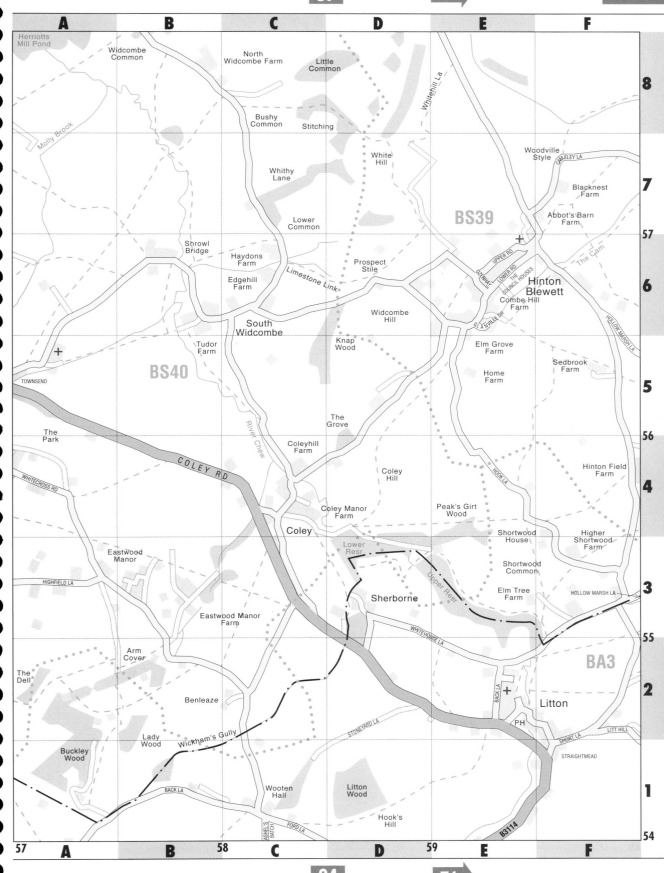

57
76

A B C D E F
8 7 6 5 4 3 2 1
57 56 55 54
57 58 59
Herriotts Mill Pond
Widcombe Common
North Widcombe Farm
Little Common
Whitehill La
Molly Brook
Bushy Common
Stitching
White Hill
Woodville Style
CAMELEY LA
Whithy Lane
Blacknest Farm
BS39
Abbot's Barn Farm
Lower Common
Shrowl Bridge
Haydons Farm
Prospect Stile
UPPER RD
The Cam
OZENHAY
LOWER RD
THE COUNCIL HOUSES
Hinton Blewett
Limestone Link
Edgehill Farm
Combe Hill Farm
Widcombe Hill
GLANVILLE DR
HOLLOW MARSH LA
South Widcombe
Tudor Farm
Knap Wood
Elm Grove Farm
Sedbrook Farm
BS40
Home Farm
TOWNSEND
The Grove
River Chew
The Park
Coleyhill Farm
COLEY RD
Coley Hill
Hinton Field Farm
WHITECROSS RD
HOOK LA
Peak's Girt Wood
Coley Manor Farm
Coley
Shortwood House
Higher Shortwood Farm
Lower Resr
Eastwood Manor
Shortwood Common
Upper Resr
HIGHFIELD LA
Elm Tree Farm
HOLLOW MARSH LA
Sherborne
Eastwood Manor Farm
WHITEHOUSE LA
Arm Cover
BA3
The Dell
BACK LA
Benleaze
Litton
PH
Lady Wood
Wickham's Gully
STONEYARD LA
LITT HILL
SHORT LA
STRAIGHTMEAD
Buckley Wood
Wooten Hall
Litton Wood
BACK LA
Hook's Hill
ASHEL'S BATCH
FORD LA
B3114

94
76

75
58

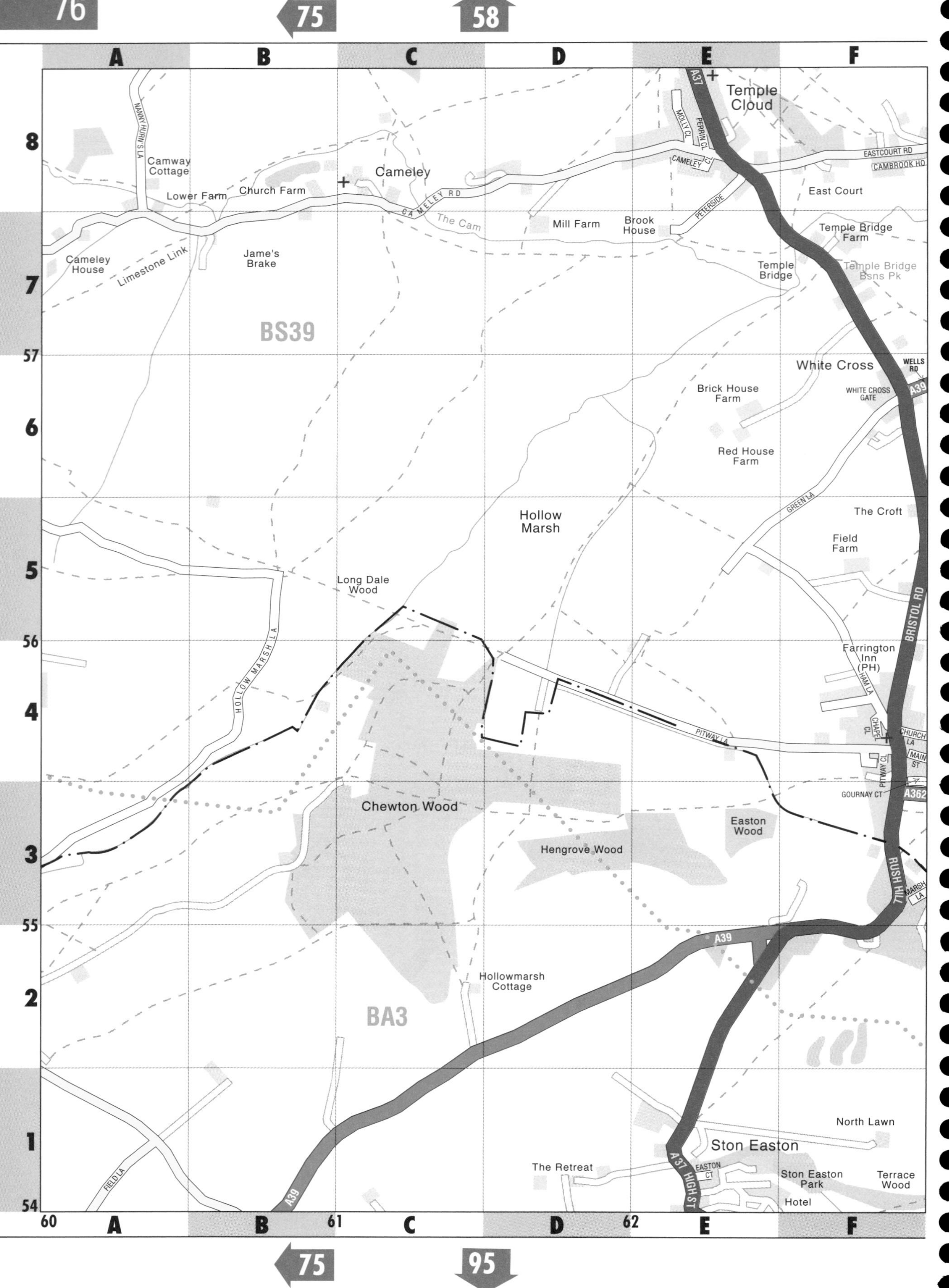
A
B
C
D
E
F
8
7
57
6
5
56
4
3
55
2
1
54
60
61
62
Temple Cloud
A37
MOLLY CL
PERRIN CL
CAMELEY CL
EASTCOURT RD
CAMBROOK HO
NANNY HURN'S LA
Camway Cottage
Cameley
Lower Farm
Church Farm
CAMELEY RD
The Cam
Mill Farm
Brook House
PETERSIDE
East Court
Temple Bridge Farm
Temple Bridge
Temple Bridge Bsns Pk
Cameley House
Limestone Link
James's Brake
BS39
White Cross
WELLS RD
WHITE CROSS GATE
A39
Brick House Farm
Red House Farm
GREEN LA
The Croft
Hollow Marsh
Field Farm
Long Dale Wood
BRISTOL RD
HOLLOW MARSH LA
Farrington Inn (PH)
HAM LA
CHAPEL CL
CHURCH LA
MAIN ST
PITWAY LA
PITWAY CL
GOURNAY CT
A362
Chewton Wood
Easton Wood
Hengrove Wood
RUSH HILL
MARSH LA
A39
Hollowmarsh Cottage
BA3
North Lawn
Ston Easton
The Retreat
A37 HIGH ST
EASTON CT
Ston Easton Park
Hotel
Terrace Wood
FIELD LA
A39
A
B
C
D
E
F

75
95

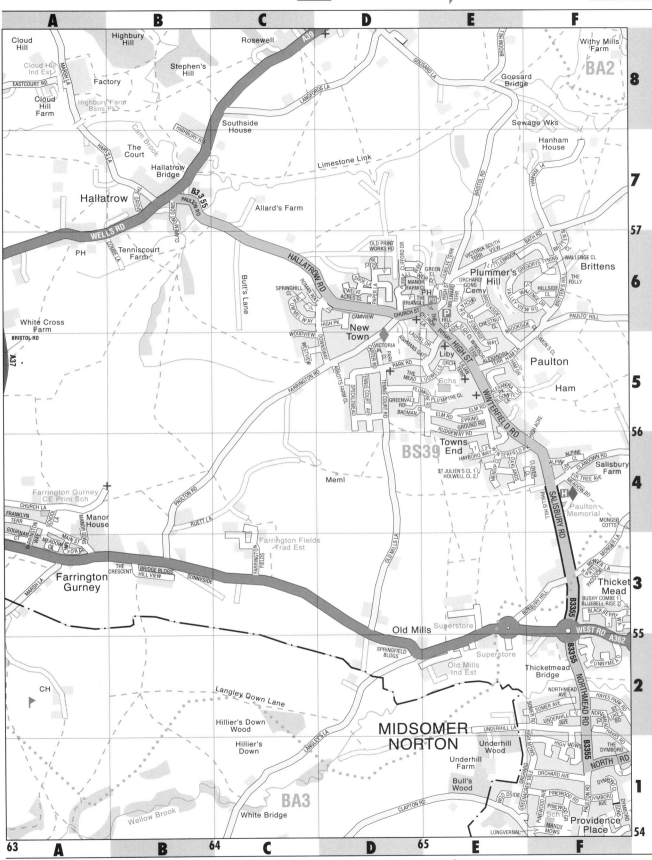
59
78

A B C D E F
8 7 57 6 5 56 4 3 55 2 1 54
63 64 65
Cloud Hill
Highbury Hill
Rosewell
Withy Mills Farm
BA2
Cloud Hill Ind Est
Stephen's Hill
Goosard Bridge
EASTCOURT RD
Factory
Cloud Hill Farm
Highbury Farm Bsns Pk
Southside House
Sewage Wks
Cam Brook
Hanham House
The Court
Limestone Link
Hallatrow Bridge
Hallatrow
Allard's Farm
WELLS RD
PH
Tenniscourt Farm
HALLATROW RD
Butt's Lane
Plummer's Hill
Brittens
New Town
Paulton
White Cross Farm
BRISTOL RD
A37
Liby
Schs
Ham
Towns End
BS39
Meml
Salisbury Farm
Paulton Memorial
Farrington Gurney CE Prim Sch
Manor House
Farrington Fields Trad Est
Farrington Gurney
Thicket Mead
Old Mills
Superstore
WEST RD
A362
Old Mills Ind Est
Thicketmead Bridge
CH
Langley Down Lane
MIDSOMER NORTON
Hillier's Down Wood
Hillier's Down
Underhill Wood
Underhill Farm
Bull's Wood
BA3
Wellow Brook
White Bridge
Providence Place
SALISBURY RD
NORTHMEAD RD
B3355
HIGH ST
WINTERFIELD RD
CLAPTON RD
LONGVERNAL

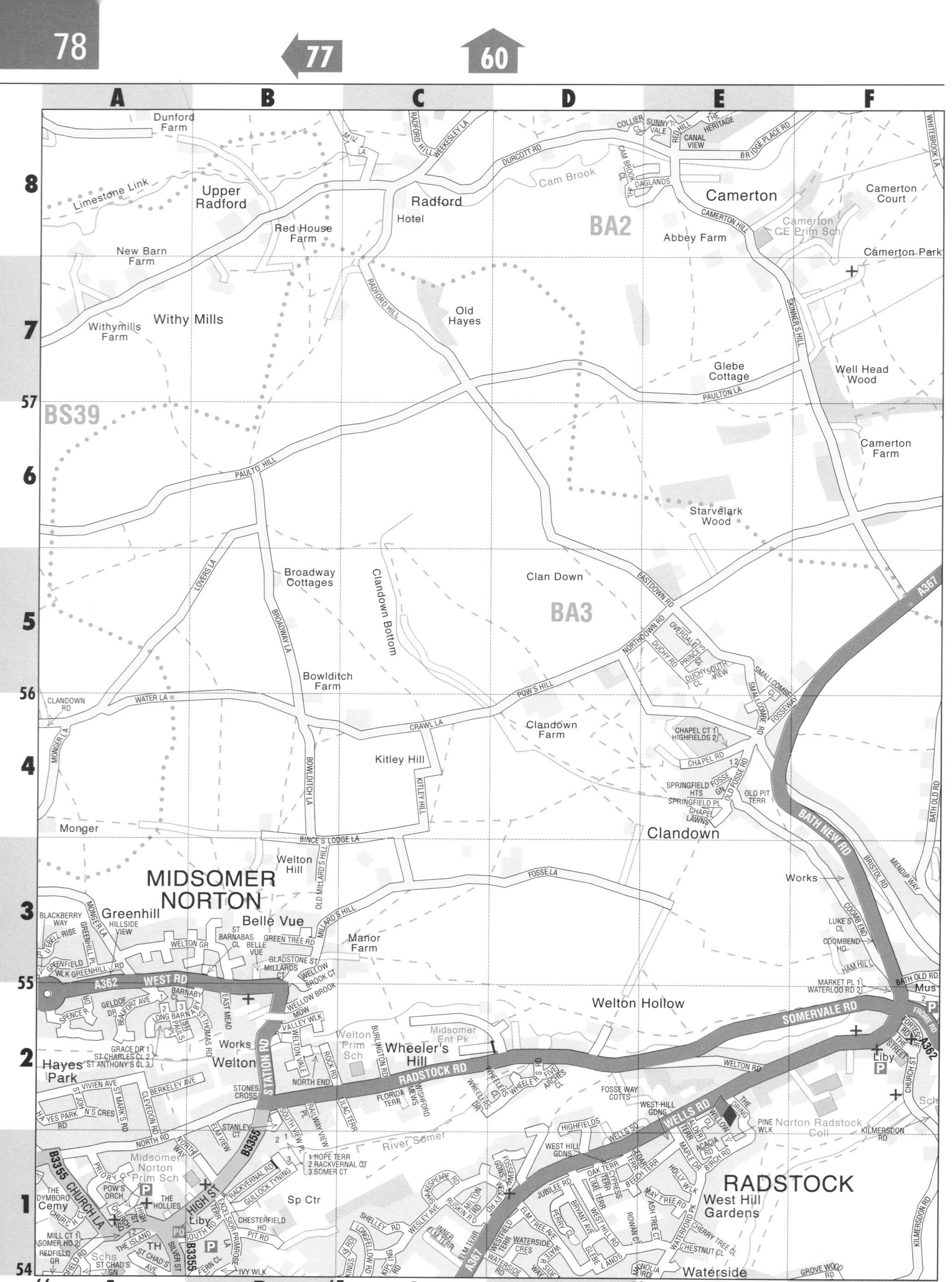
Dunford Farm
Upper Radford
Radford
Camerton
Camerton Court
Limestone Link
Red House Farm
Hotel
BA2
Abbey Farm
Camerton CE Prim Sch
Camerton Park
New Barn Farm
Withy Mills
Withymills Farm
Old Hayes
Glebe Cottage
Well Head Wood
BS39
Camerton Farm
Starvelark Wood
Broadway Cottages
Clan Down
Clandown Bottom
BA3
Bowlditch Farm
Clandown Farm
Kitley Hill
Monger
Clandown
Welton Hill
MIDSOMER NORTON
Works
Greenhill
Belle Vue
Manor Farm
Welton Hollow
Wheeler's Hill
Welton
Hayes Park
River Somer
Sp Ctr
RADSTOCK
West Hill Gardens
Waterside
Norton Radstock Coll
Cam Brook

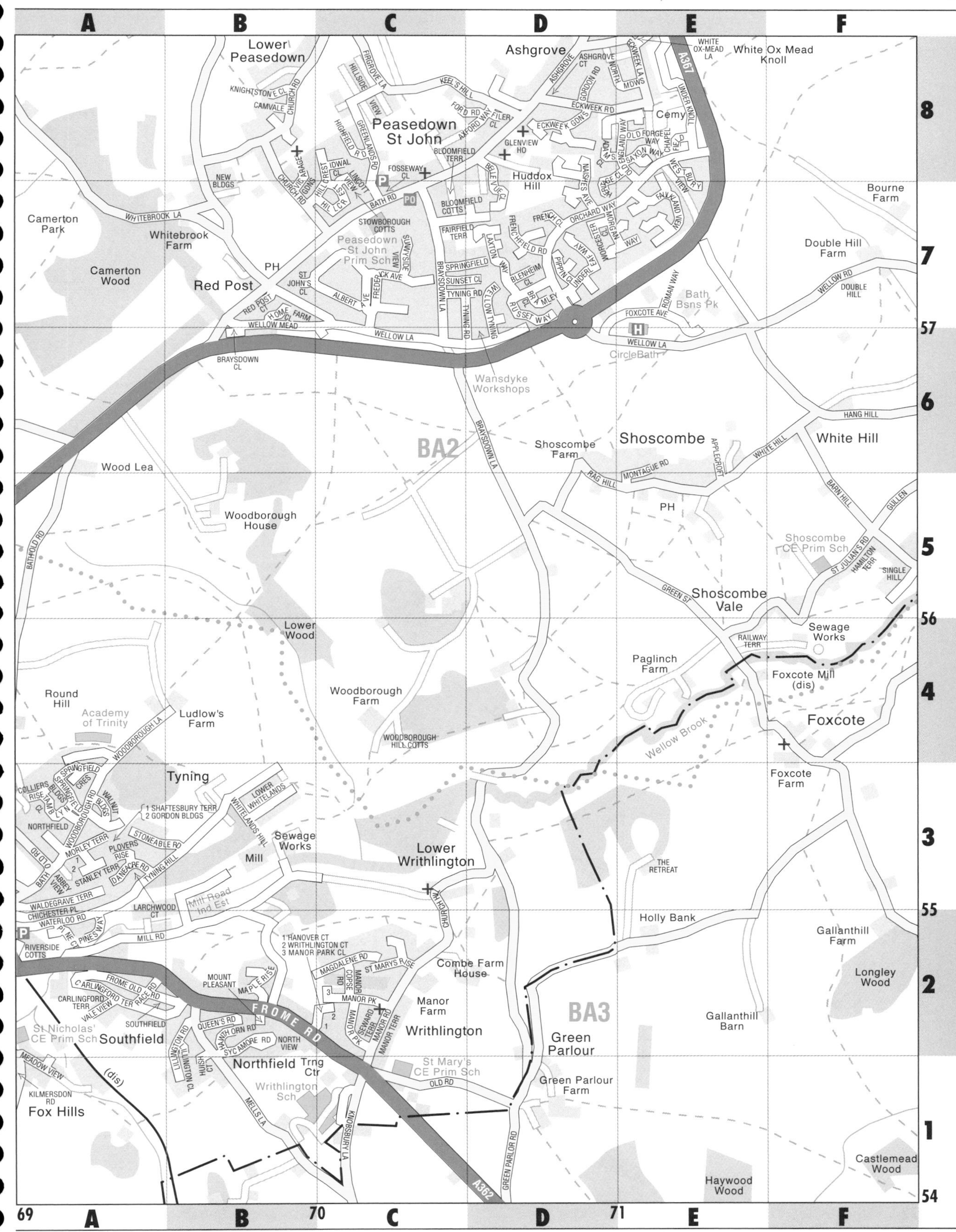
61
80
Lower Peasedown
Ashgrove
White Ox Mead Knoll
Peasedown St John
Huddox Hill
Cemy
Bourne Farm
Camerton Park
Whitebrook Farm
Camerton Wood
Red Post
PH
Stowborough Cotts
Peasedown St John Prim Sch
Double Hill Farm
Bath Bsns Pk
CircleBath
Wansdyke Workshops
BA2
Shoscombe Farm
Shoscombe
White Hill
Wood Lea
Woodborough House
Shoscombe CE Prim Sch
Shoscombe Vale
Lower Wood
Sewage Works
Paglinch Farm
Foxcote Mill (dis)
Round Hill
Academy of Trinity
Ludlow's Farm
Woodborough Farm
Foxcote
Woodborough Hill Cotts
Wellow Brook
Foxcote Farm
Tyning
Sewage Works
Mill
Lower Writhlington
The Retreat
Mill Road Ind Est
Holly Bank
Gallanthill Farm
Combe Farm House
Longley Wood
Manor Farm
BA3
Gallanthill Barn
St Nicholas' CE Prim Sch
Southfield
Writhlington
Green Parlour
Northfield
Trng Ctr
St Mary's CE Prim Sch
Green Parlour Farm
Writhlington Sch
Fox Hills
Castlemead Wood
Haywood Wood
FROME RD
A367
A362
A
B
C
D
E
F
8
7
57
6
5
56
4
3
55
2
1
54
69
70
71
98
80

79
62

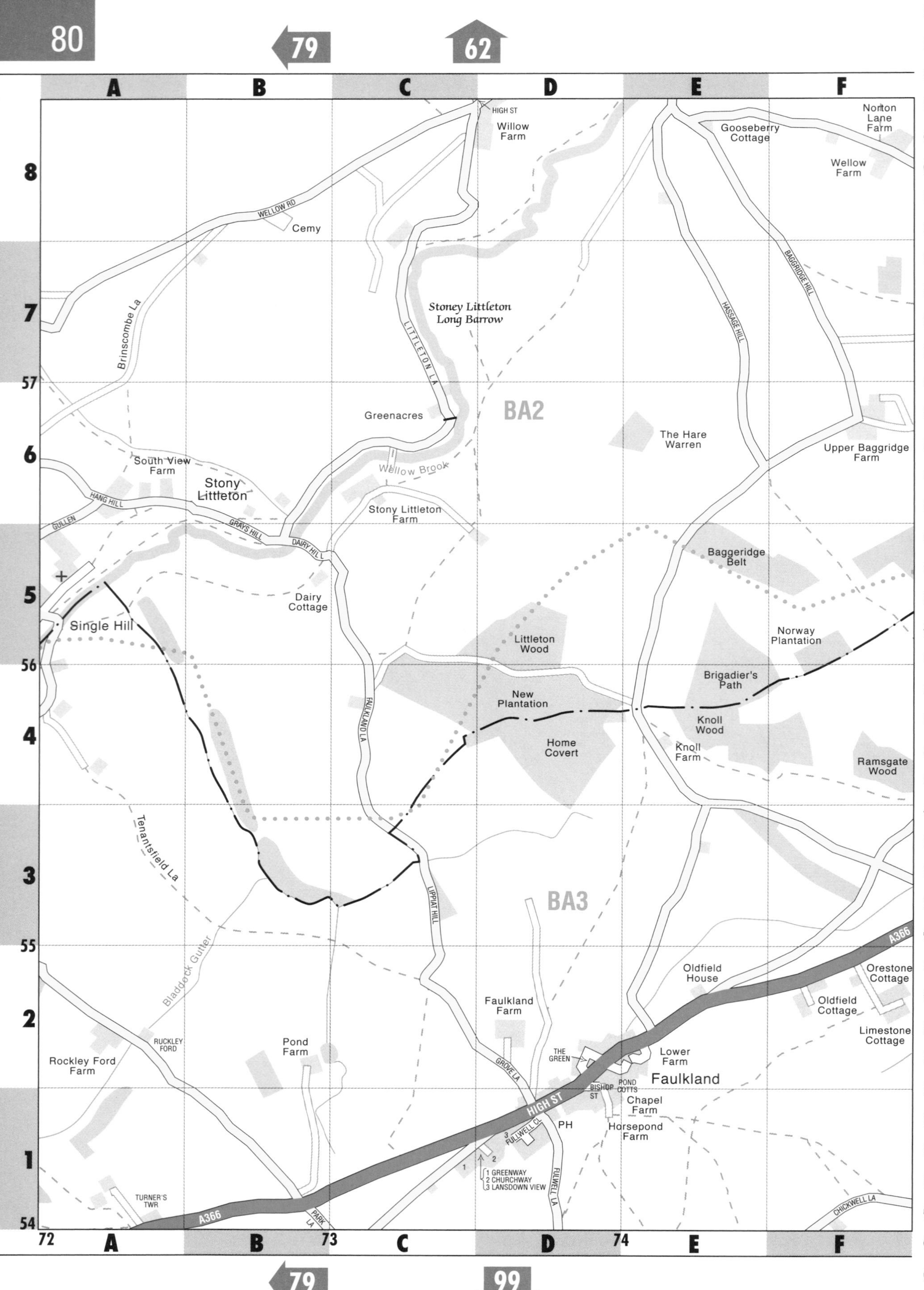
A
B
C
D
E
F
8
7
57
6
5
56
4
3
55
2
1
54
72
73
74
HIGH ST
Willow Farm
Gooseberry Cottage
Norton Lane Farm
Wellow Farm
WELLOW RD
Cemy
BAGGRIDGE HILL
HASSAGE HILL
Brinscombe La
Stoney Littleton Long Barrow
LITTLETON LA
Greenacres
BA2
The Hare Warren
Upper Baggridge Farm
South View Farm
Stony Littleton
Wellow Brook
HANG HILL
GULLEN
GRAYS HILL
DAIRY HILL
Stony Littleton Farm
Baggeridge Belt
Dairy Cottage
Single Hill
Littleton Wood
Norway Plantation
Brigadier's Path
New Plantation
FAULKLAND LA
Knoll Wood
Home Covert
Knoll Farm
Ramsgate Wood
Tenantsfield La
LIPPIAT HILL
BA3
A366
Bladdock Gutter
Oldfield House
Orestone Cottage
Oldfield Cottage
Faulkland Farm
Limestone Cottage
RUCKLEY FORD
Pond Farm
THE GREEN
Lower Farm
Rockley Ford Farm
GROVE LA
Faulkland
BISHOP ST
POND COTTS
Chapel Farm
HIGH ST
PH
Horsepond Farm
FULLWELL CL
1 GREENWAY
2 CHURCHWAY
3 LANSDOWN VIEW
FULWELL LA
TURNER'S TWR
A366
PARK LA
CHICKWELL LA

79
99

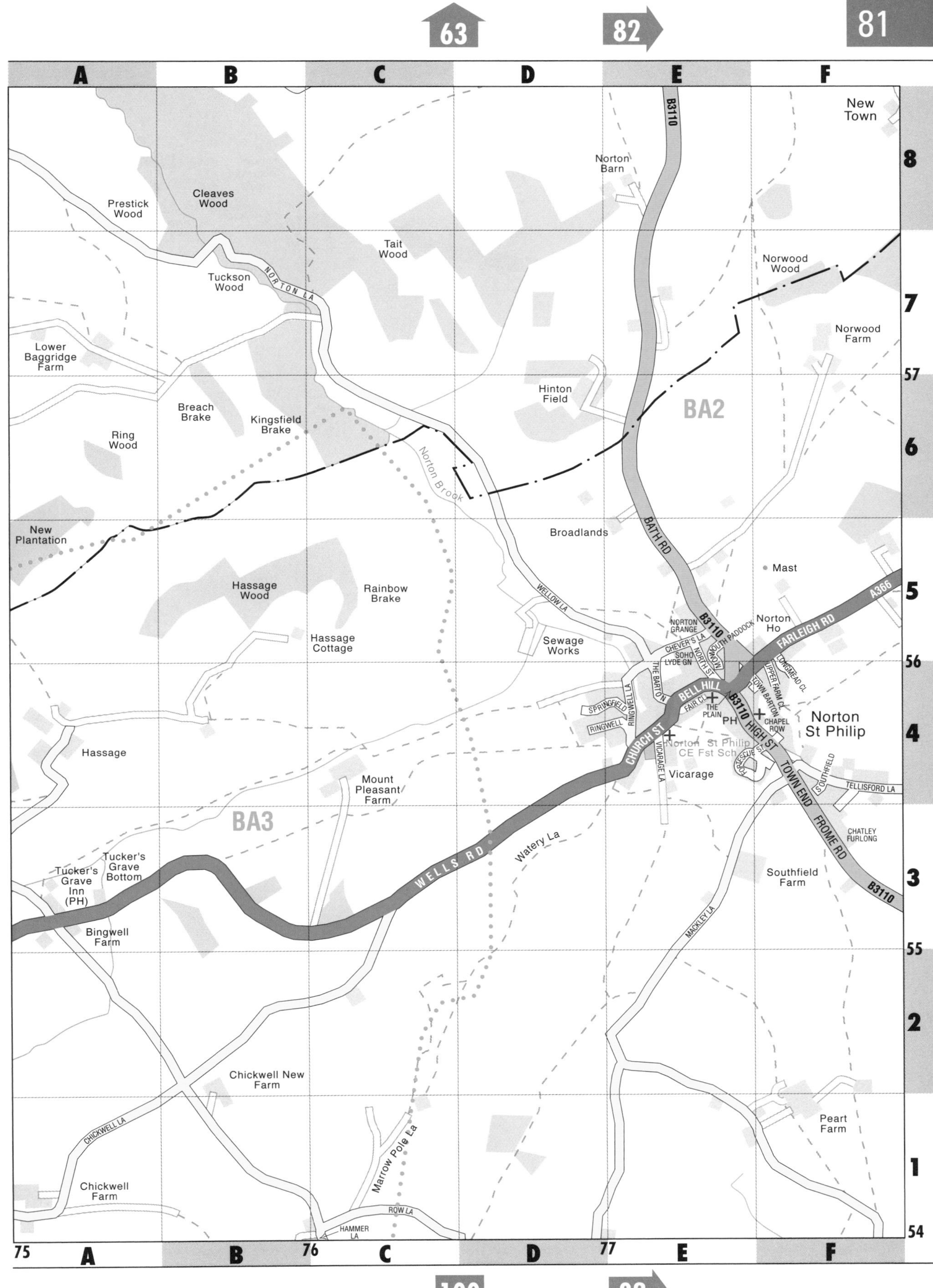

	A	B	C	D	E	F	

New Town

Prestick Wood

Cleaves Wood

Tait Wood

Norton Barn

8

B3110

Tuckson Wood

NORTON LA

Norwood Wood

7

Lower Baggridge Farm

Hinton Field

Norwood Farm

57

BA2

Breach Brake

Kingsfield Brake

Norton Brook

6

Ring Wood

New Plantation

Hassage Wood

Rainbow Brake

Broadlands

• Mast

BATH RD

WELLOW LA

B3110

A366

FARLEIGH RD

5

Hassage Cottage

Sewage Works

NORTON GRANGE

Norton Ho

56

CHEVER'S LA

SOHO

LYDE GN

NORTH ST

SOUTH PADDOCK

TIPPET FARM CL

LONGMEAD CL

Norton St Philip

THE BARTON

BELL HILL

FAIR CL

THE PLAIN

TOWN BARTON

TOWN END

CHAPEL ROW

Hassage

SPRINGFIELD LA

RINGWELL LA

PH

B3110 HIGH ST

4

RINGWELL

CHURCH ST

VICARAGE LA

Norton St Philip CE Fst School

SOUTHFIELD

TELLISFORD LA

Mount Pleasant Farm

Vicarage

FROME RD

CHATLEY FURLONG

BA3

Tucker's Grave Bottom

WELLS RD

Watery La

Southfield Farm

B3110

3

Tucker's Grave Inn (PH)

MACKLEY LA

Bingwell Farm

55

2

Chickwell New Farm

Peart Farm

CHICKWELL LA

MARROW POLE LA

1

Chickwell Farm

ROW LA

HAMMER LA

54

75	A	B	76	C	D	77	E	F	

81
64

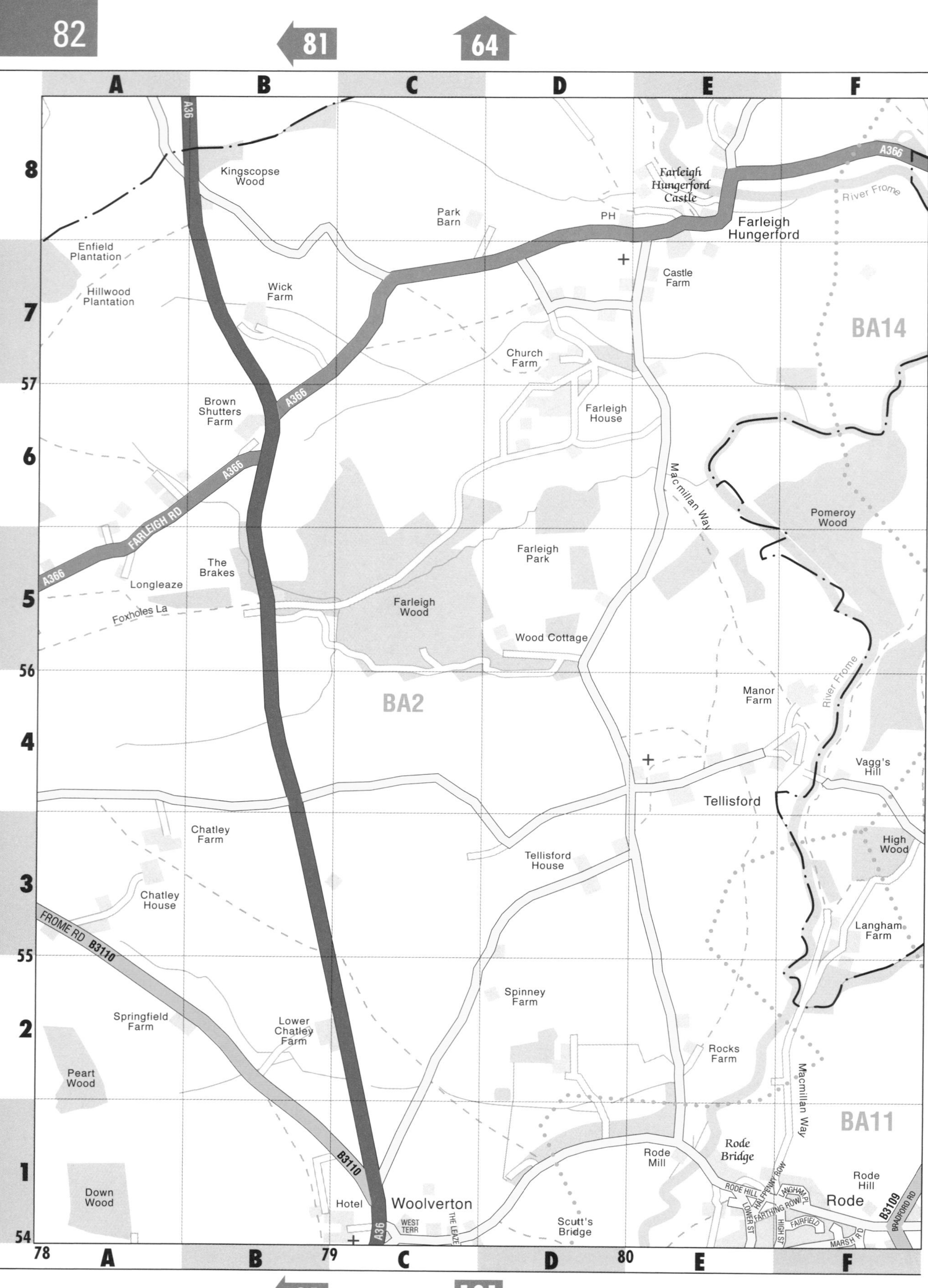
A
B
C
D
E
F
8
7
57
6
5
56
4
3
55
2
1
54
78
79
80
A36
A366
Kingscopse Wood
Farleigh Hungerford Castle
Farleigh Hungerford
PH
River Frome
Park Barn
Enfield Plantation
Hillwood Plantation
Wick Farm
Castle Farm
BA14
Church Farm
Brown Shutters Farm
Farleigh House
FARLEIGH RD
Macmillan Way
Pomeroy Wood
The Brakes
Farleigh Park
Longleaze
Foxholes La
Farleigh Wood
Wood Cottage
BA2
Manor Farm
Vagg's Hill
Tellisford
Chatley Farm
High Wood
Tellisford House
Chatley House
Langham Farm
FROME RD
B3110
Spinney Farm
Springfield Farm
Lower Chatley Farm
Rocks Farm
Peart Wood
BA11
Rode Mill
Rode Bridge
Rode Hill
Down Wood
Hotel
Woolverton
Rode
WEST TERR
THE LEAZE
Scutt's Bridge
RODE HILL
HALFPENNY ROW
LANGHAM PL
FARTHING ROW
LOWER ST
HIGH ST
FAIRFIELD
MARSH RD
B3109
BRADFORD RD

81
101

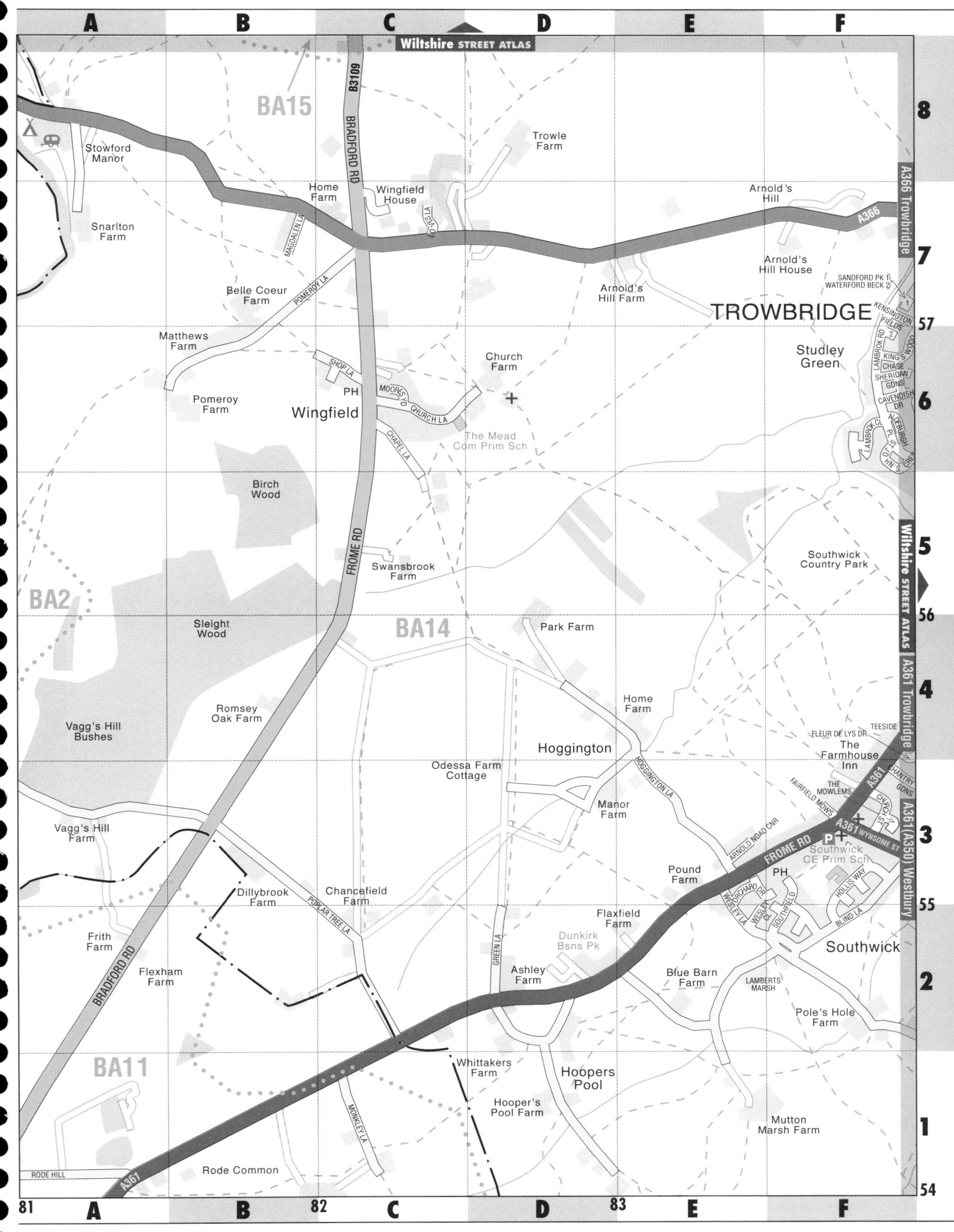

BA15

BA2

BA14

BA11

TROWBRIDGE

Studley Green

Southwick Country Park

Hoggington

Southwick

Stowford Manor

Snarlton Farm

Home Farm

Wingfield House

Trowle Farm

Arnold's Hill

Arnold's Hill House

Belle Coeur Farm

Arnold's Hill Farm

Matthews Farm

Church Farm

Pomeroy Farm

Wingfield

The Mead Com Prim Sch

Birch Wood

Swansbrook Farm

Sleight Wood

Park Farm

Vagg's Hill Bushes

Romsey Oak Farm

Home Farm

The Farmhouse Inn

Odessa Farm Cottage

Vagg's Hill Farm

Manor Farm

Pound Farm

Dillybrook Farm

Chancefield Farm

Flaxfield Farm

Southwick CE Prim Sch

Frith Farm

Dunkirk Bsns Pk

Blue Barn Farm

Flexham Farm

Ashley Farm

Pole's Hole Farm

Whittakers Farm

Hoopers Pool

Hooper's Pool Farm

Mutton Marsh Farm

Rode Common

Rode Hill

SANDFORD PK
WATERFORD BECK

KENSINGTON FIELDS
KING'S CHASE
SHERIDAN GDNS
CAVENDISH DR

FLEUR DE LYS DR
TEESIDE
THE MOWLEMS
FAIRFIELD MDWS

LAMBERTS MARSH

BRADFORD RD
B3109
MAGDALEN LA
SHOP LA
POMEROY LA
CHAPEL LA
CHURCH LA
MOORES YD
FROME RD
HOGGINGTON LA
POPLAR TREE LA
GREEN LA
MONKLEY LA
A367
A366 Trowbridge
A361 Trowbridge
A361 (A350) Westbury
FROME RD
ARNOLD ND AD CHR
WESLEY LA
ORCHARD DR
WEST PK RD
SOUTHFIELD
HOLLIS WAY
BLIND LA
WYNSOME ST
CHANTRY GDNS
CHURCH ST

PH

65

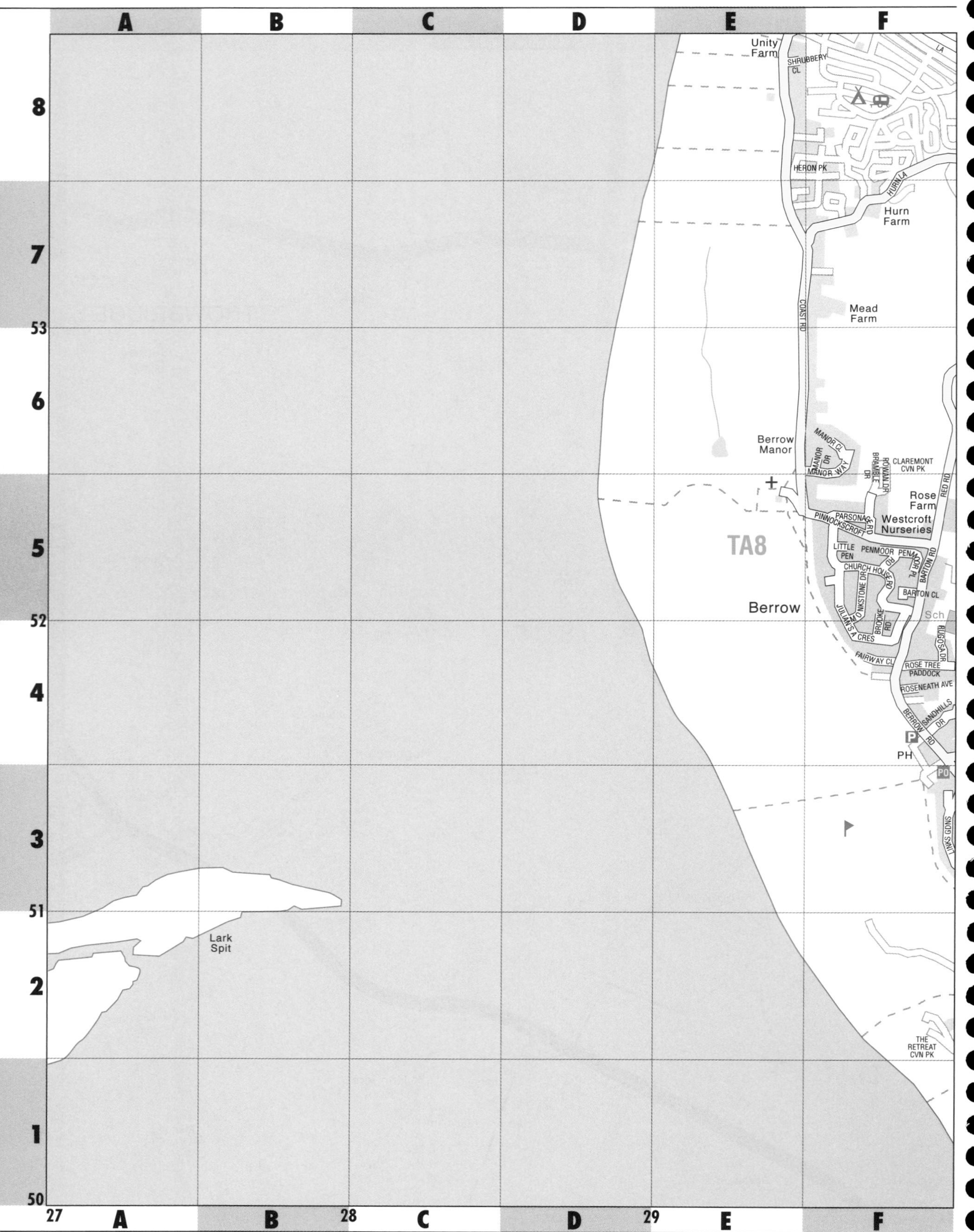
A
B
C
D
E
F
8
7
53
6
5
52
4
3
51
2
1
50
27
28
29
Unity Farm
SHRUBBERY CL
LA
HERON PK
HURN LA
Hurn Farm
COAST RD
Mead Farm
Berrow Manor
MANOR CL
MANOR DR
MANOR WAY
BRAMBLE DR
ROWAN DR
CLAREMONT CVN PK
RED RD
Rose Farm
PARSONAGE RD
PINNOCKSCROFT
Westcroft Nurseries
TA8
LITTLE PEN
PENMOOR RD
PENMOOR PL
BARTON RD
CHURCH HOUSE RD
MONKSTONE DR
BARTON CL
Berrow
JULIANS A CRES
BROOKE RD
Sch
RUGOSA DR
FAIRWAY CL
ROSE TREE PADDOCK
ROSENEATH AVE
BERROW RD
SANDHILLS DR
P
PH
PO
LINKS GDNS
Lark Spit
THE RETREAT CVN PK

103

66
86

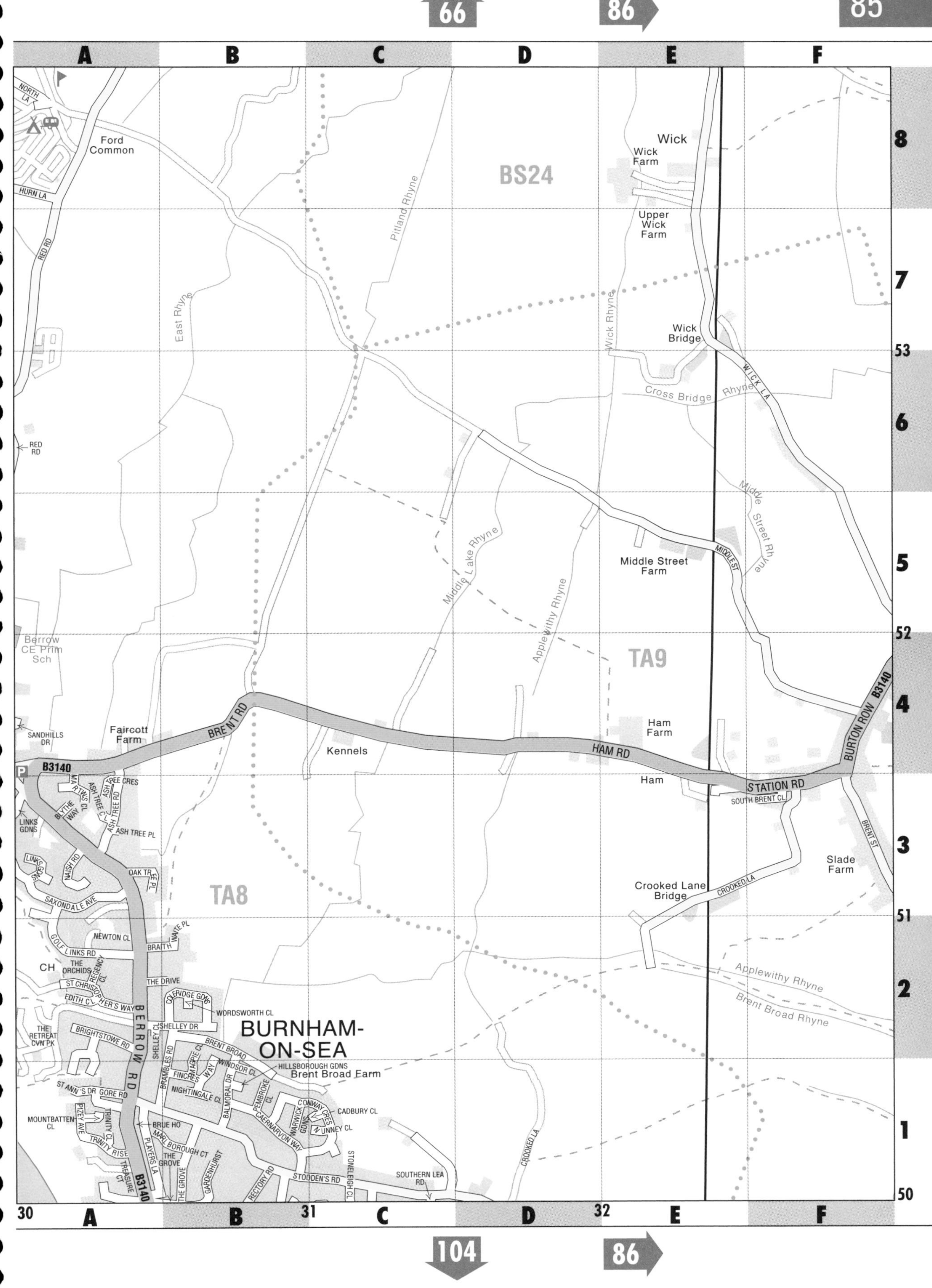
A
B
C
D
E
F
8
7
53
6
5
52
4
3
51
2
1
50
30
31
32
Ford Common
NORTH LA
HURN LA
RED RD
Wick
Wick Farm
BS24
Upper Wick Farm
Pitland Rhyne
East Rhyne
Wick Rhyne
Wick Bridge
WICK LA
Cross Bridge Rhyne
Middle Street Rhyne
Middle Lake Rhyne
Applewithy Rhyne
Middle Street Farm
MIDDLE ST
TA9
Berrow CE Prim Sch
SANDHILLS DR
Faircott Farm
BRENT RD
Kennels
HAM RD
Ham Farm
Ham
STATION RD
SOUTH BRENT CL
BURTON ROW
B3140
BRENT ST
Slade Farm
Crooked Lane Bridge
CROOKED LA
TA8
LINKS GDNS
MARTINS CL
BLYTHE WAY
ASH TREE CRES
ASH TREE CL
ASH TREE RD
ASH TREE PL
NAISH RD
OAK TREE PL
SAXONDALE AVE
NEWTON CL
WAITE PL
BRAITH
GOLF LINKS RD
CH
THE ORCHIDS
REGENCY CL
ST CHRISTOPHER'S WAY
EDITH CL
THE DRIVE
COLERIDGE GDNS
WORDSWORTH CL
SHELLEY DR
BERROW RD
THE RETREAT CVN PK
BRIGHTSTOWE RD
BURNHAM-ON-SEA
BRENT BROAD
HILLSBOROUGH GDNS
Brent Broad Farm
WINDSOR CL
FINCHES WAY
MAGPIE CL
BRAMBLES RD
NIGHTINGALE CL
BALMORAL DR
PEMBROKE CL
ST ANN'S DR
GORE RD
CONWAY CRES
CADBURY CL
WARWICK GDNS
CAERNARVON WAY
MOUNTBATTEN CL
PIZEY AVE
TRINITY CL
TRINITY RISE
BRUE HO
MARLBOROUGH CT
PLAYERS LA
THE GROVE
GARDENHURST
RECTORY RD
STODDEN'S RD
STONELEIGH CL
SOUTHERN LEA RD
CROOKED LA
TREASURE CT
Applewithy Rhyne
Brent Broad Rhyne

104
86

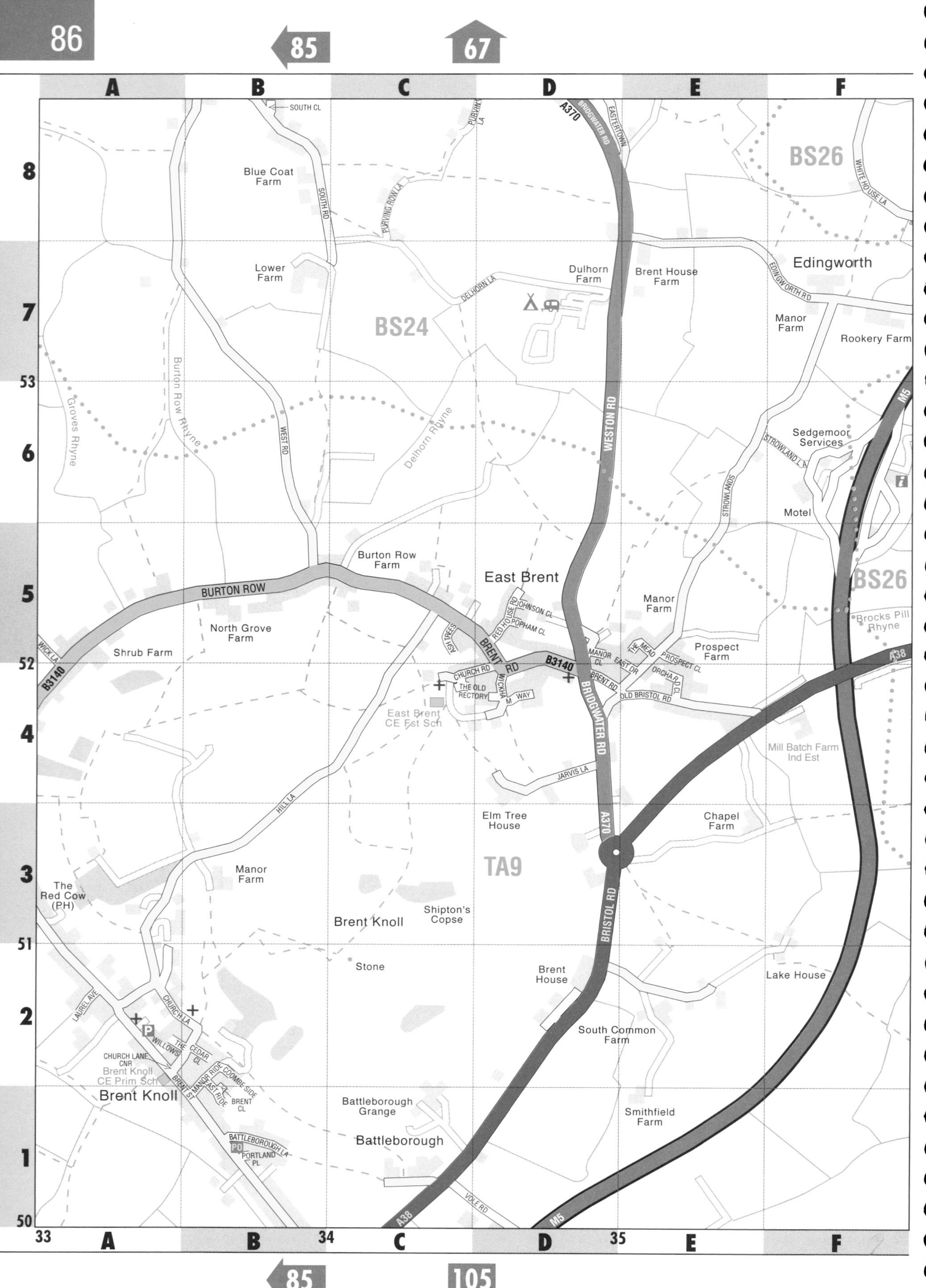

85 67

A B C D E F

8

BS26

White House La

Blue Coat
Farm

SOUTH CL

PURVING ROW LA

PURVING LA

A370

BRIDGWATER RD

EAST FIELD LA

Lower
Farm

Edingworth

Dulhorn
Farm

Brent House
Farm

EDINGWORTH RD

7

BS24

DELHORN LA

Manor
Farm

Rookery Farm

53

Groves Rhyne

Burton Row Rhyne

WEST RD

Delhorn Rhyne

WESTON RD

STROWLAND LA

Sedgemoor
Services

M5

6

Motel

i

STROWL MDS

Burton Row
Farm

Brocks Pill
Rhyne

BS26

5

BURTON ROW

East Brent

Manor
Farm

A38

WICK LA

B3140

North Grove
Farm

JOHNSON CL

POPHAM CL

Prospect
Farm

52

Shrub Farm

EAST TRES

RED HOUSE RD

BRENT

MANOR
CL

EAST DR

MEAD

PROSPECT CL

ORCHA.. CL

OLD BRISTOL RD

B3140

CHURCH RD

RD

WICKHA

THE OLD
RECTORY

BRENT.RD

ORCHA R D CL

4

THE RED COW (PH)

HILL LA

East Brent
CE Est Sch

M WAY

BRIDGWATER RD

Mill Batch Farm
Ind Est

JARVIS LA

Elm Tree
House

Chapel
Farm

3

The
Red Cow
(PH)

Manor
Farm

TA9

A370

51

Stone

Brent Knoll

Shipton's
Copse

Brent
House

Lake House

BRISTOL RD

2

LAUREL AVE

CHURCH LA

P

THE CEDAR CL

WILLOWS

COOMBE SIDE

BRENT ST

MANOR RIDE

EAST RIDE

BRENT
CL

South Common
Farm

CHURCH LANE
CNR
Brent Knoll
CE Prim Sch

Brent Knoll

Battleborough
Grange

Smithfield
Farm

1

PO

BATTLEBOROUGH LA

PO

PORTLAND
PL

Battleborough

VOLE RD

M5

50

33 A B 34 C D 35 E F

85 105

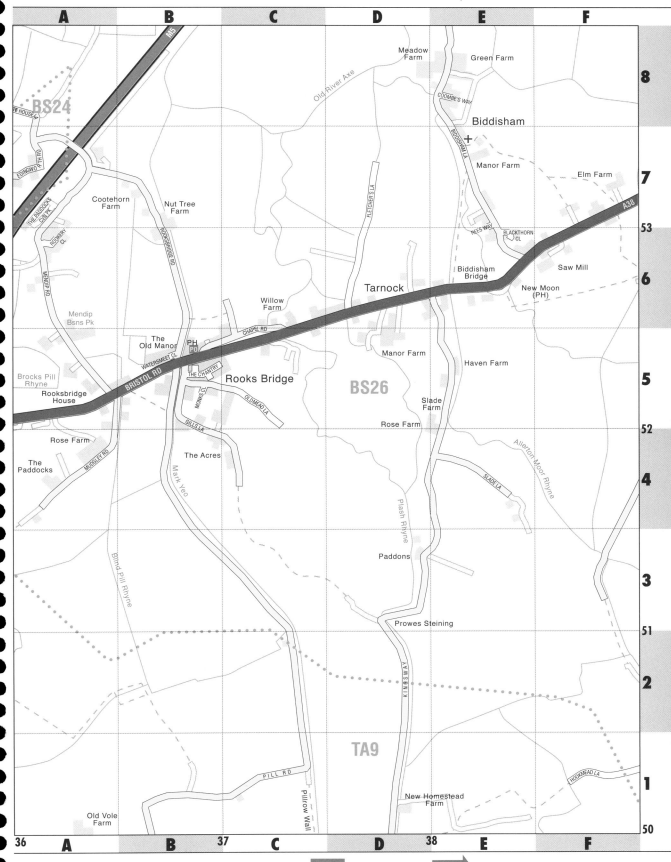

A B C D E F

8
7
53
6
5
52
4
3
51
2
1
50

BS24
TE HOUSE LA
EDINGWO
TH RD
M5
THE PADDOCKS CVN PK
ROOKERY CL
MENDIP RD
Cootehorn Farm
Nut Tree Farm
ROOKSBRIDGE RD
Mendip Bsns Pk
The Old Manor
PH
PO
WATERSMEET CL
BRISTOL RD
THE CHANTRY
Brocks Pill Rhyne
Rooksbridge House
MONKS CL
OLDMEAD LA
GILLS LA
Rose Farm
The Paddocks
MUDGLEY RD
The Acres
Mark Yeo
Rooks Bridge
Willow Farm
CHAPEL RD
Old River Axe
Meadow Farm
Green Farm
COOMBE'S WAY
Biddisham
BIDDISHAM LA
Manor Farm
Elm Farm
A38
FLETCHER'S LA
REES WAY
BLACKTHORN CL
Biddisham Bridge
Saw Mill
New Moon (PH)
Tarnock
Manor Farm
Haven Farm
BS26
Slade Farm
Rose Farm
Allerton Moor Rhyne
SLADE LA
Plash Rhyne
Paddons
Blind Pill Rhyne
Prowes Steining
KINGSWAY
TA9
HOOKMEAD LA
PILL RD
Pillrow Wall
New Homestead Farm
Old Vole Farm

36 A B 37 C D 38 E F

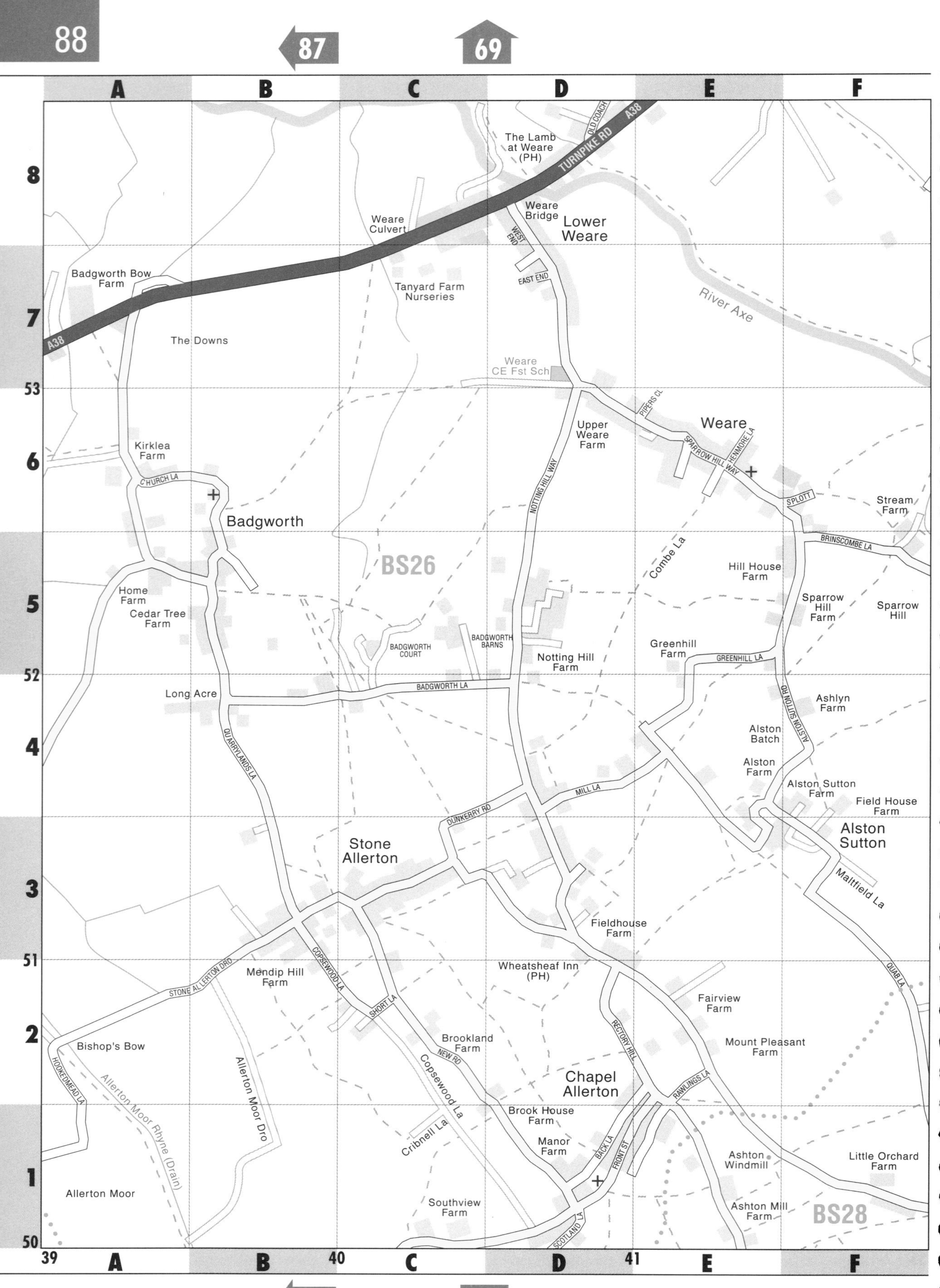

A B C D E F

8

Badgworth Bow
Farm

The Lamb
at Weare
(PH)

Weare
Culvert

TURNPIKE RD

A38

OLD COACH

Weare
Bridge

Lower
Weare

7

The Downs

A38

Tanyard Farm
Nurseries

WEST END

EAST END

River Axe

53

Weare
CE Fst Sch

6

Kirklea
Farm

CHURCH LA

Upper
Weare
Farm

PIPERS CL

SPARROW HILL WAY

HENMORE LA

Weare

SPLOTT

Stream
Farm

Badgworth

BS26

Combe La

Hill House
Farm

BRINSCOMBE LA

5

Home
Farm

Cedar Tree
Farm

Long Acre

BADGWORTH COURT

BADGWORTH
BARNS

BADGWORTH LA

Notting Hill
Farm

NOTTING HILL WAY

Greenhill
Farm

GREENHILL LA

Sparrow
Hill
Farm

ALSTON NOTTING LA

Sparrow
Hill

Ashlyn
Farm

52

QUABRANDS LA

Alston
Batch

Alston
Farm

Alston Sutton
Farm

Field House
Farm

4

MILL LA

DUNKERRY RD

Alston
Sutton

3

Stone
Allerton

Fieldhouse
Farm

Maltfield La

51

STONE ALLERTON DRO

Mendip Hill
Farm

COPSEWOOD LA

SHORT LA

Wheatsheaf Inn
(PH)

RECTORY HILL

Fairview
Farm

Mount Pleasant
Farm

QUAB LA

2

HOOKBRIDGE LA

Bishop's Bow

Allerton Moor Rhyne (Drain)

Allerton Moor Dro

NEW RD

Brookland
Farm

COPSEWOOD LA

CRIBNELL LA

Chapel
Allerton

Brook House
Farm

Manor
Farm

BACK LA

FRONT ST

RAWLINGS LA

Ashton
Windmill

Ashton Mill
Farm

Little Orchard
Farm

BS28

1

Allerton Moor

Southview
Farm

SCOTLAND LA

50

39 A B 40 C D 41 E F

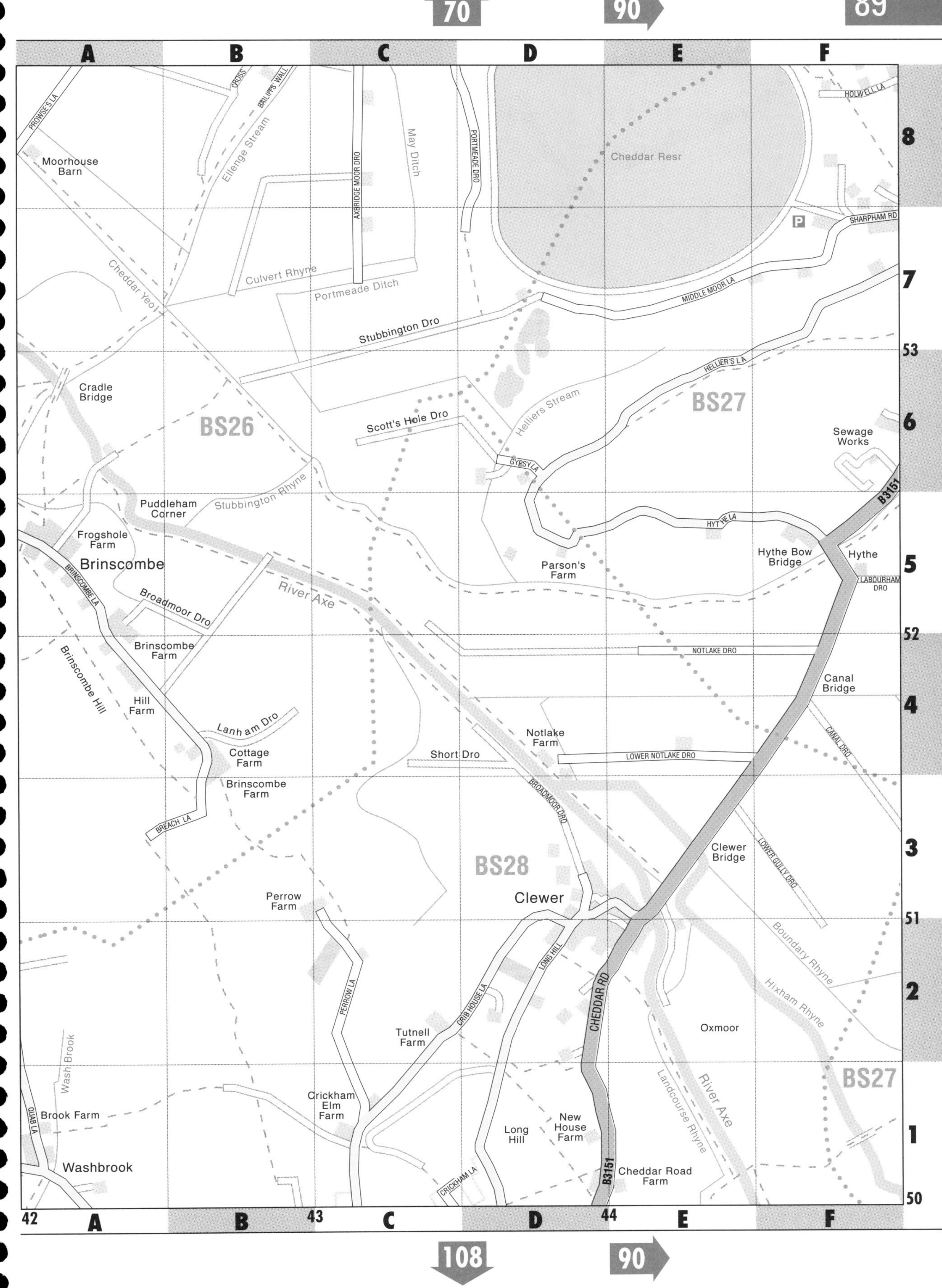

70
90
A
B
C
D
E
F
8
7
53
6
5
52
4
3
51
2
1
50
42
43
44
108
90
PROWSE'S LA
CROSS
BAILIFFS WALL
Moorhouse Barn
Ellenge Stream
AXBRIDGE MOOR DRO
May Ditch
PORTMEADE DRO
Cheddar Resr
HOLWELL LA
SHARPHAM RD
Culvert Rhyne
Portmeade Ditch
Cheddar Yeo
MIDDLE MOOR LA
Stubbington Dro
Cradle Bridge
HELLIER'S LA
BS27
Helliers Stream
BS26
Scott's Hole Dro
Sewage Works
GYPSY LA
Puddleham Corner
Stubbington Rhyne
B3151
HYTHE LA
Frogshole Farm
Brinscombe
Hythe Bow Bridge
Hythe
Parson's Farm
LABOURHAM DRO
BRINSCOMBE LA
Broadmoor Dro
River Axe
NOTLAKE DRO
Brinscombe Farm
Brinscombe Hill
Canal Bridge
Hill Farm
Lanham Dro
Notlake Farm
CANAL DRO
Cottage Farm
Short Dro
LOWER NOTLAKE DRO
Brinscombe Farm
BROADMOOR DRO
BREACH LA
Clewer Bridge
LOWER GULLY DRO
BS28
Perrow Farm
Clewer
Boundary Rhyne
LONG HILL
CHEDDAR RD
Hixham Rhyne
PERROW LA
CRIB HOUSE LA
Tutnell Farm
Oxmoor
Wash Brook
BS27
Landcourse Rhyne
River Axe
Crickham Elm Farm
QUAB LA
Brook Farm
New House Farm
Long Hill
Washbrook
CRICKHAM LA
B3151
Cheddar Road Farm

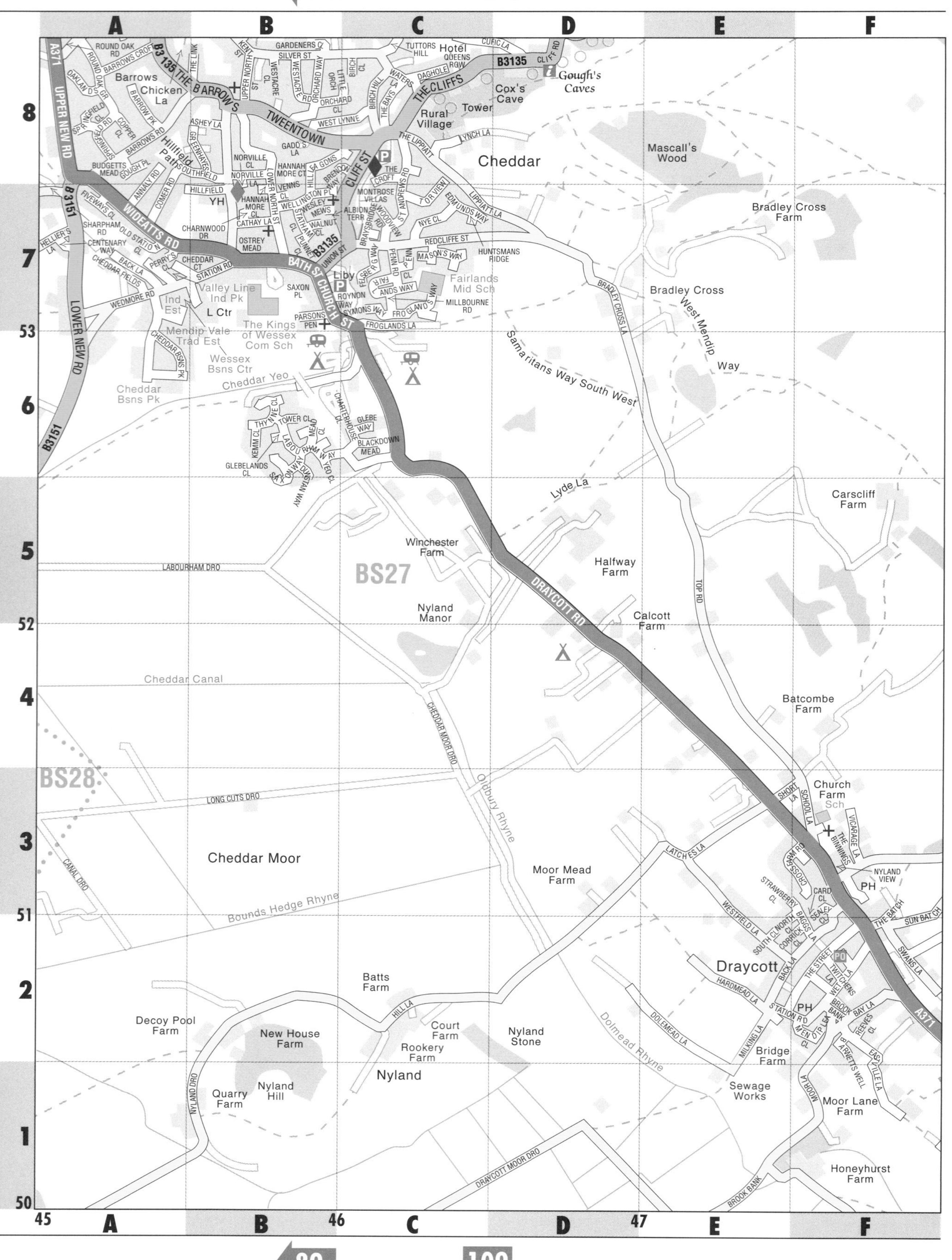
A
B
C
D
E
F
8
7
53
6
5
52
4
3
51
2
1
50
45
46
47
Barrows
Chicken La
Hillfield Paths
Cheddar
Gough's Caves
Cox's Cave
Tower
Rural Village
Hotel
Mascall's Wood
Bradley Cross Farm
Bradley Cross
West Mendip Way
Samaritans Way South West
Valley Line Ind Pk
Ind Est
L Ctr
The Kings of Wessex Com Sch
Mendip Vale Trad Est
Wessex Bsns Ctr
Cheddar Bsns Pk
Cheddar Yeo
Fairlands Mid Sch
Liby
YH
Carscliff Farm
Lyde La
Winchester Farm
Halfway Farm
BS27
Nyland Manor
Calcott Farm
Cheddar Canal
Batcombe Farm
BS28
Church Farm
Sch
Cheddar Moor
Moor Mead Farm
Bounds Hedge Rhyne
Oldbury Rhyne
Draycott
PH
Batts Farm
Decoy Pool Farm
New House Farm
Court Farm
Rookery Farm
Nyland Stone
Nyland
Quarry Farm
Nyland Hill
Bridge Farm
Sewage Works
Moor Lane Farm
Honeyhurst Farm
Dolmead Rhyne
UPPER NEW RD
LOWER NEW RD
WIDEATTS RD
DRAYCOTT RD
TWEENTOWN
THE BARROWS
THE CLIFFS
CLIFF ST
BATH ST
CHURCH ST
LABOURHAM DRO
LONG CUTS DRO
CHEDDAR MOOR DRO
TOP RD
BRADLEY CROSS LA
LATCHES LA
DRAYCOTT MOOR DRO
NYLAND DRO
HILL LA
BROOK BANK
MOOR LA
A371
B3151
B3135

72
92

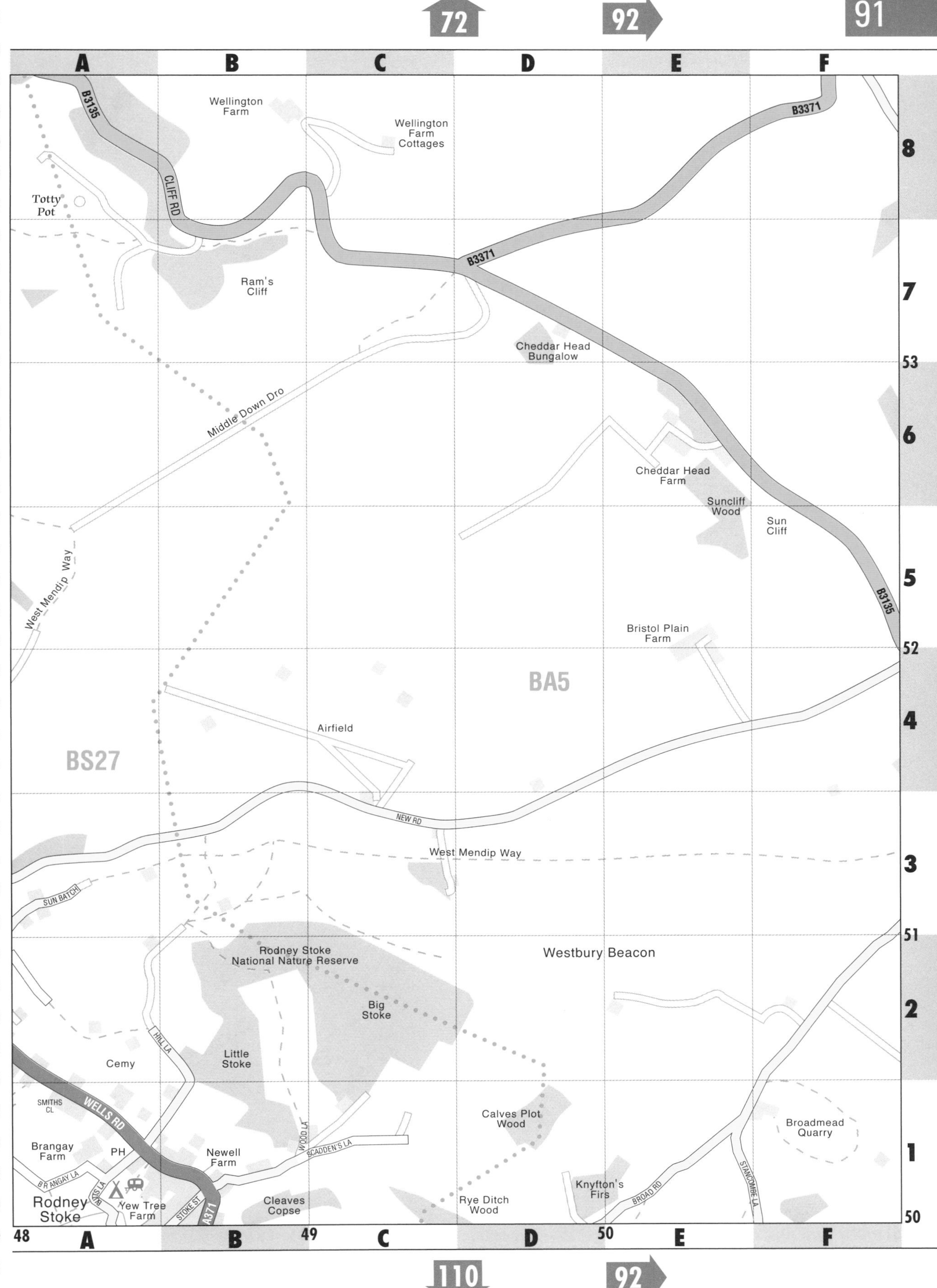
A
B
C
D
E
F
Wellington Farm
Wellington Farm Cottages
B3135
CLIFF RD
B3371
Totty Pot
Ram's Cliff
Cheddar Head Bungalow
Middle Down Dro
Cheddar Head Farm
Suncliff Wood
Sun Cliff
West Mendip Way
B3135
Bristol Plain Farm
BA5
Airfield
BS27
NEW RD
West Mendip Way
SUN BATCH
Rodney Stoke National Nature Reserve
Westbury Beacon
Big Stoke
Little Stoke
Cemy
HILL LA
SMITHS CL
WELLS RD
Calves Plot Wood
Broadmead Quarry
Brangay Farm
PH
Newell Farm
WOOD LA
SCADDEN'S LA
BRANGAY LA
Rodney Stoke
Yew Tree Farm
STOKE ST
A371
Cleaves Copse
Rye Ditch Wood
Knyfton's Firs
BROAD RD
STANCOMBE LA
8
7
53
6
5
52
4
3
51
2
1
50
48
49
50

110
92

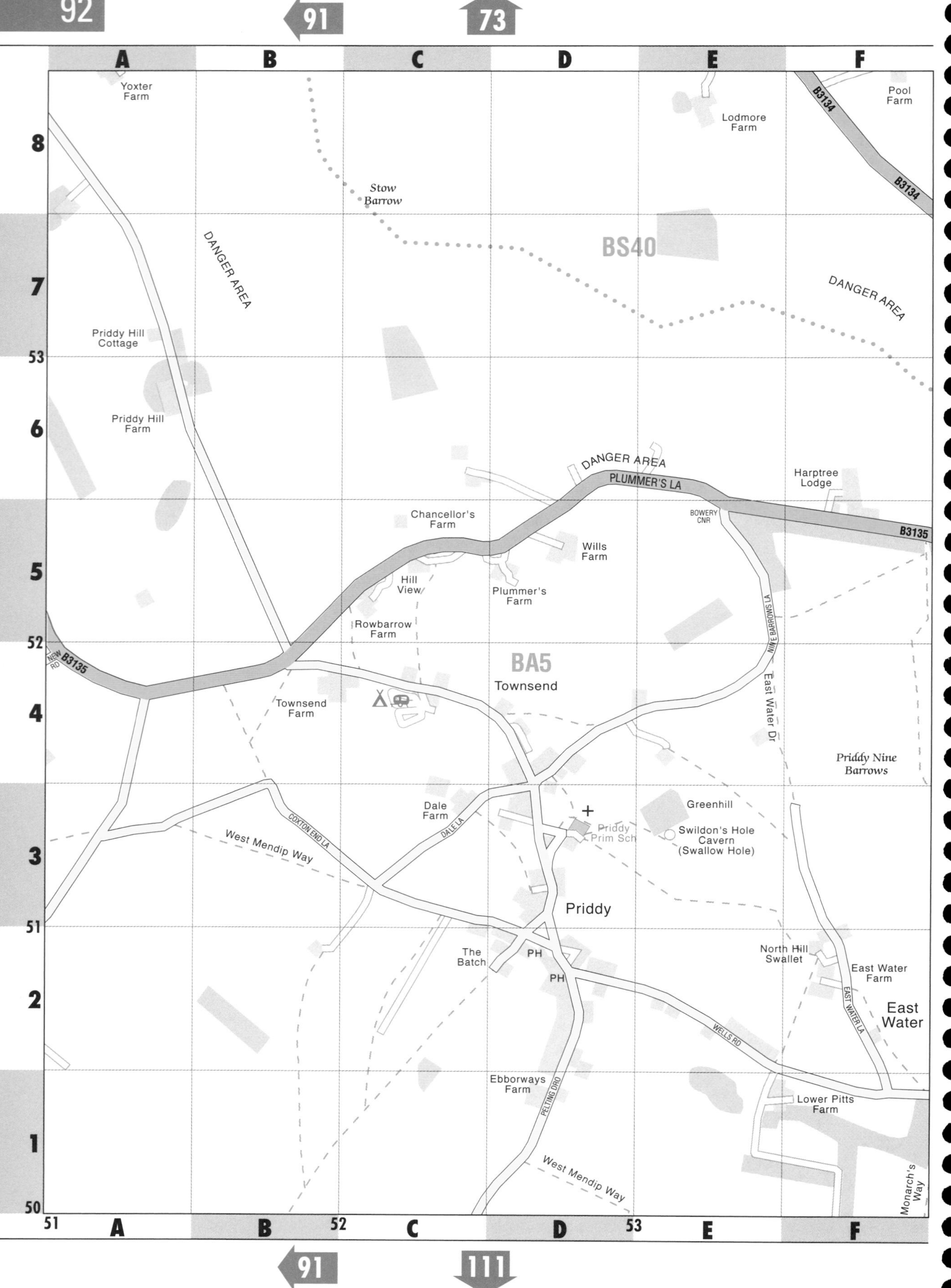

91

73

A B C D E F

8

91
7

53

6

5

52

4

3

51

2

1

50

91 111

Yoxter Farm

Stow Barrow

BS40

Lodmore Farm

Pool Farm

B3134

B3134

DANGER AREA

DANGER AREA

Priddy Hill Cottage

Priddy Hill Farm

DANGER AREA

PLUMMER'S LA

Harptree Lodge

B3135

Chancellor's Farm

Wills Farm

BOWERY CNR

Hill View

Plummer's Farm

Rowbarrow Farm

BA5

Townsend

MIN BARROWS LA

East Water Dr

NEW RD B3135

Townsend Farm

Priddy Nine Barrows

West Mendip Way

COXTON END LA

Dale Farm

DALE LA

Greenhill

Swildon's Hole Cavern (Swallow Hole)

Priddy Prim Sch

Priddy

North Hill Swallet

East Water Farm

The Batch

PH

PH

EAST WATER LA

East Water

Ebborways Farm

PELTING DRO

WELLS RD

Lower Pitts Farm

West Mendip Way

Monarch's Way

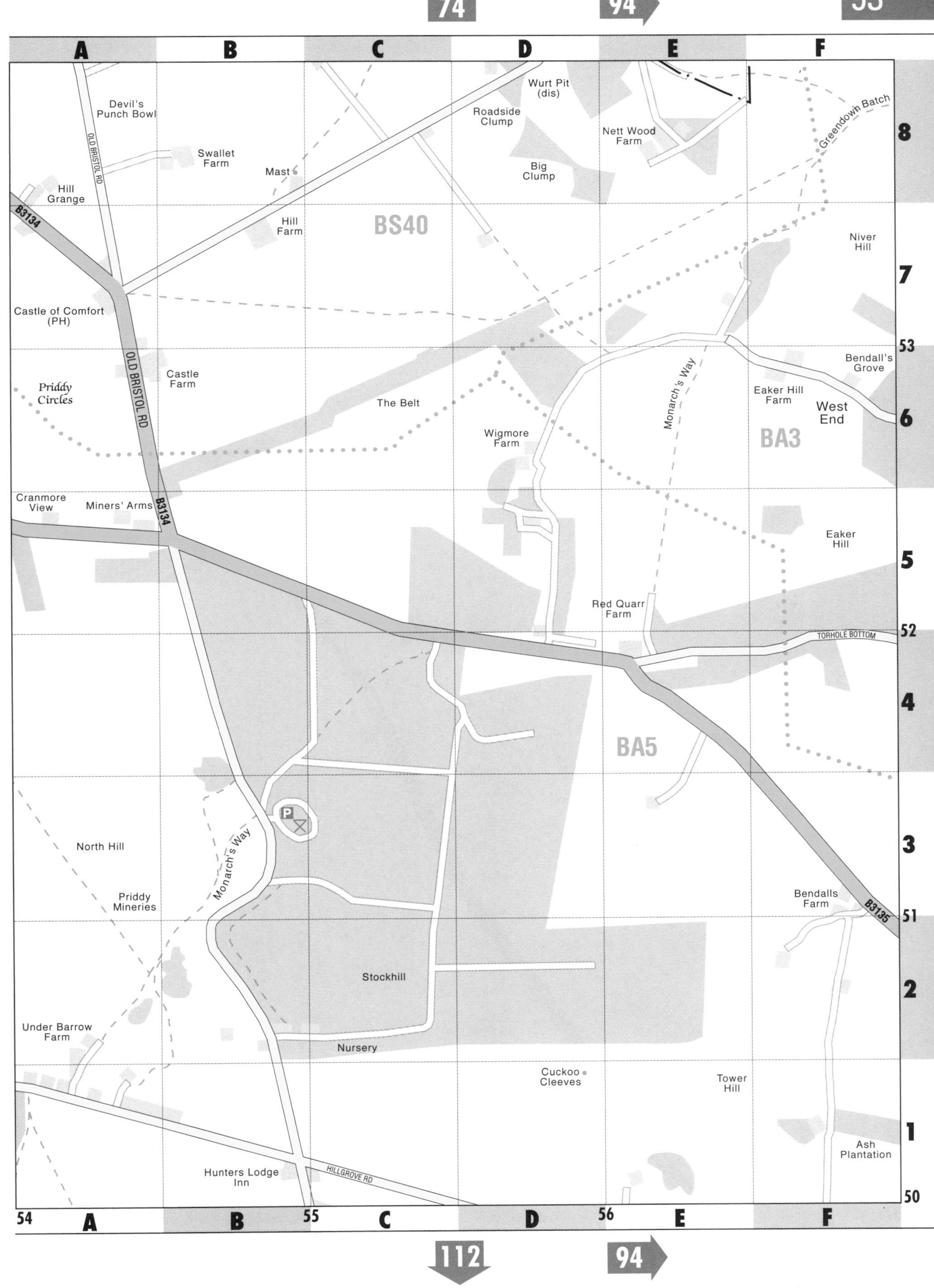

74
94

A B C D E F

8

Devil's Punch Bowl

Wurt Pit (dis)

Roadside Clump

Nett Wood Farm

Greendown Batch

Swallet Farm

Mast

Big Clump

Hill Grange

BS40

Niver Hill

Hill Farm

7

B3134

Castle of Comfort (PH)

53

Bendall's Grove

Priddy Circles

Castle Farm

Monarch's Way

Eaker Hill Farm

West End

6

The Belt

OLD BRISTOL RD

Wigmore Farm

BA3

Cranmore View

Miners' Arms

B3134

Eaker Hill

5

Red Quarr Farm

TORHOLE BOTTOM

52

4

BA5

3

North Hill

Monarch's Way

Bendalls Farm

51

B3135

Priddy Mineries

Stockhill

2

Under Barrow Farm

Nursery

Cuckoo Cleeves

Tower Hill

1

Ash Plantation

Hunters Lodge Inn

HILLGROVE RD

50

54 A B 55 C D 56 E F

112
94

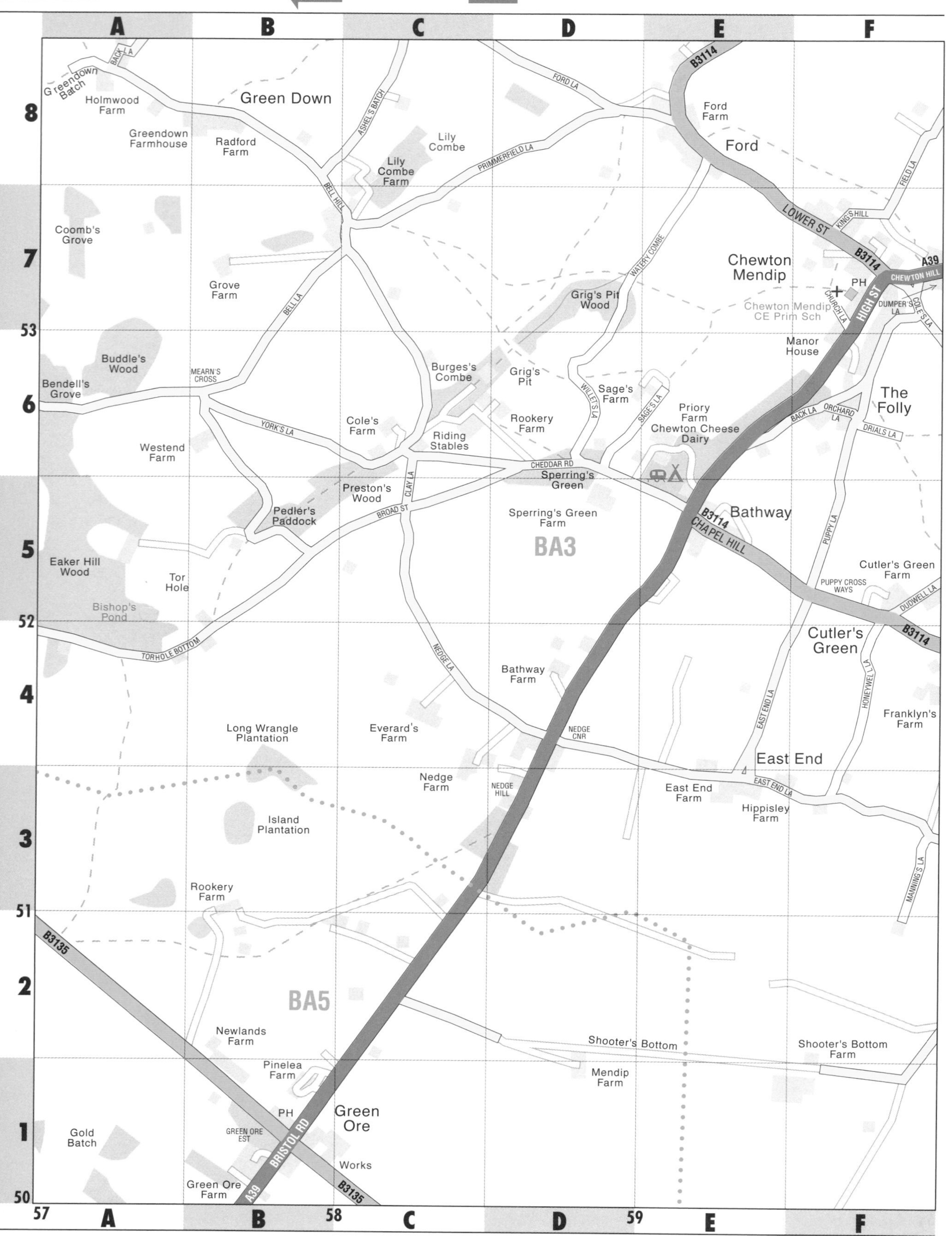

93 75

A B C D E F

8

7

53

6

5

52

4

3

51

2

1

50

57 A B 58 C D 59 E F

93 113

Greendown Batch
Holmwood Farm
Green Down
BACK LA
Greendown Farmhouse
Radford Farm
ASHEL'S BATCH
Lily Combe
Ford LA
Ford Farm
B3114
Ford

Coomb's Grove
Lily Combe Farm
PRIMMERFIELD LA
LOWER ST
B3114
KING'S HILL
FIELD LA
A39
CHEWTON HILL

BELL HILL
Grove Farm
Chewton Mendip
DUMPER'S LA
COLE'S LA

Buddle's Wood
BELLA
WATERY COMBE
Grig's Pit Wood
Chewton Mendip CE Prim Sch
CHURCH LA
PH
HIGH ST
KING'S HILL

MEARN'S CROSS
Burges's Combe
Grig's Pit
WILLET'S LA
Sage's Farm
SAGE'S LA
Manor House
The Folly

Bendell's Grove
YORK'S LA
Cole's Farm
Rookery Farm
Priory Farm
Chewton Cheese Dairy
BACK LA
ORCHARD LA
DRIALS LA

Westend Farm
Riding Stables
CHEDDAR RD
Sperring's Green
Bathway

Preston's Wood
CLAY LA
Sperring's Green Farm
B3114
CHAPEL HILL
PUPPY LA
Cutler's Green Farm

Pedler's Paddock
BROAD ST
BA3
PUPPY CROSS WAYS
DUDWELL LA
B3114

Eaker Hill Wood
Tor Hole
Cutler's Green

Bishop's Pond
NEDGE LA
Bathway Farm
EAST END LA
Franklyn's Farm

TORHOLE BOTTOM
Long Wrangle Plantation
Everard's Farm
NEDGE CNR
East End
HOMEWELL LA

Island Plantation
Nedge Farm
NEDGE HILL
East End Farm
Hippisley Farm
MANNING'S LA

Rookery Farm
BA5

B3135
Newlands Farm
Shooter's Bottom
Shooter's Bottom Farm

Pinelea Farm
Mendip Farm

PH
Green Ore
BRISTOL RD

Gold Batch
GREEN ORE EST
A39
Works
B3135
Green Ore Farm

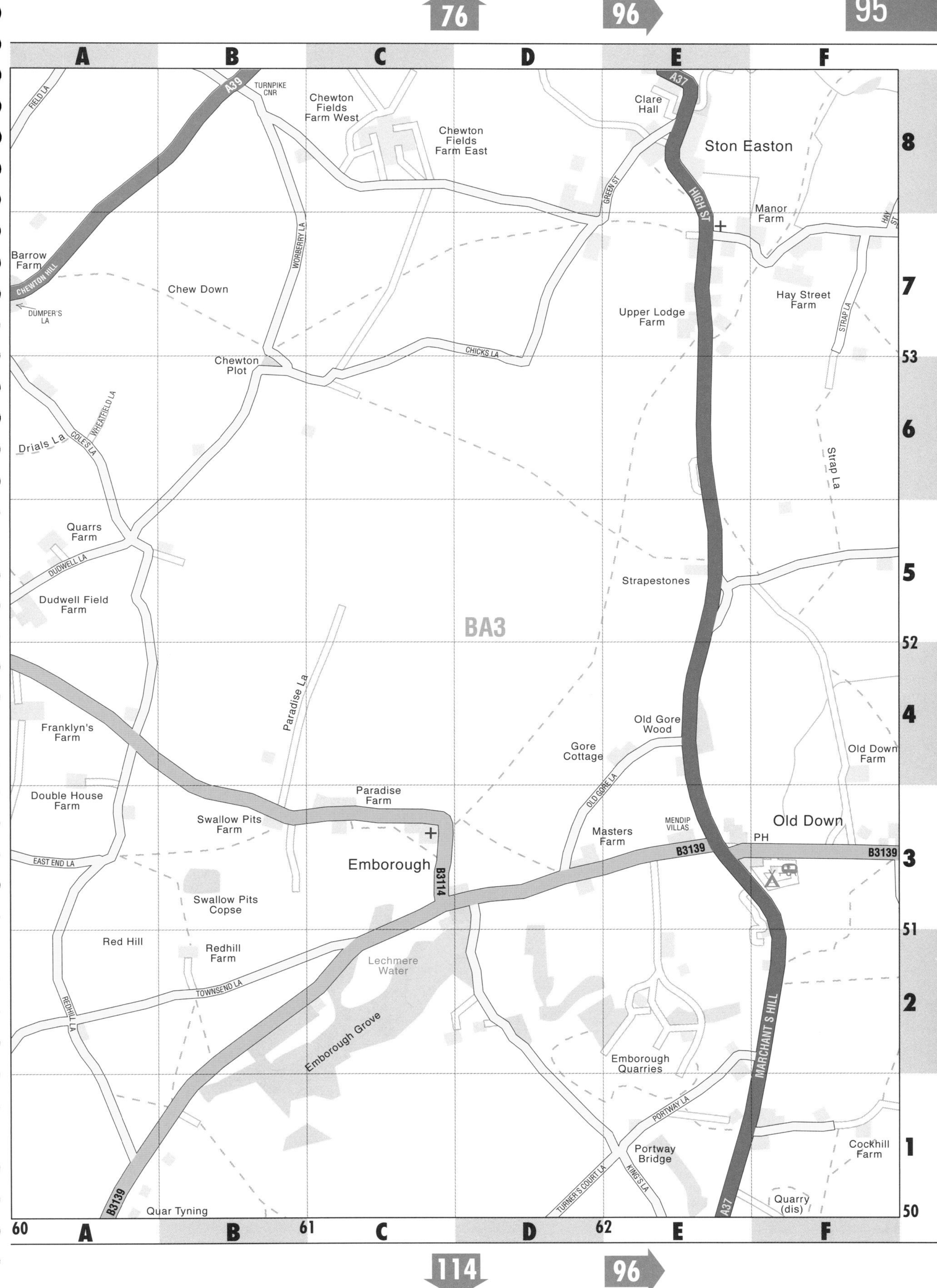
76
96
A
B
C
D
E
F
8
7
53
6
5
52
4
3
51
2
1
50
60
61
62
114
96
FIELD LA
A39
TURNPIKE CNR
Chewton Fields Farm West
Chewton Fields Farm East
A37
Clare Hall
Ston Easton
GREEN ST
HIGH ST
Manor Farm
HAY ST
Barrow Farm
CHEWTON HILL
DUMPER'S LA
Chew Down
WORBERRY LA
Upper Lodge Farm
Hay Street Farm
STRAP LA
CHICKS LA
Chewton Plot
WHEATFIELD LA
Drials La
COLE'S LA
Strap La
Quarrs Farm
DUDWELL LA
Dudwell Field Farm
Strapestones
BA3
Paradise La
Old Gore Wood
Franklyn's Farm
Gore Cottage
Old Down Farm
OLD GORE LA
Double House Farm
Paradise Farm
Swallow Pits Farm
MENDIP VILLAS
Masters Farm
Old Down
PH
B3139
EAST END LA
Emborough
B3114
Swallow Pits Copse
Red Hill
Redhill Farm
Lechmere Water
TOWNSEND LA
REDHILL LA
Emborough Grove
MARCHANT'S HILL
Emborough Quarries
PORTWAY LA
Portway Bridge
Cockhill Farm
TURNER'S COURT LA
KING'S LA
Quarry (dis)
Quar Tyning

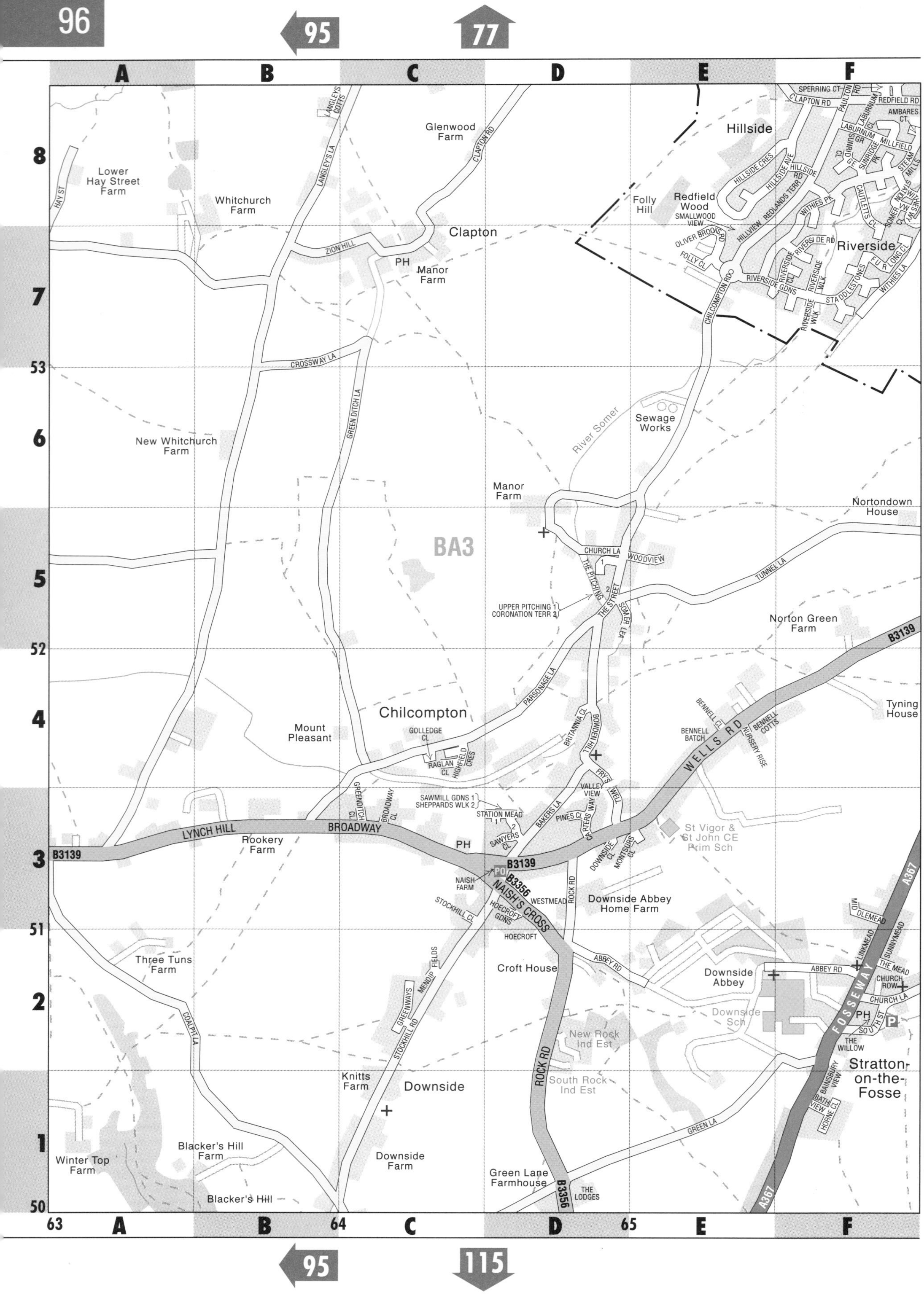

A B C D E F

8
7
53
6
5
52
4
3
51
2
1
50

Lower Hay Street Farm
HAY ST
Whitchurch Farm
LANGLEY'S LA
LANGLEY'S COTTS
Glenwood Farm
CLAPTON RD
ZION HILL
PH
Clapton
Manor Farm
CROSSWAY LA
GREEN DITCH LA
New Whitchurch Farm

Hillside
SPERRING CT
CLAPTON RD
REDFIELD RD
PAULTON RD
LABURNUM
MILLFIELD
AMBARES CT
Folly Hill
Redfield Wood
SMALLWOOD VIEW
HILLSIDE CRES
HILLSIDE AVE
HILLSIDE
REDLANDS TERR
WITHIES PK
OLIVER BROOKS
HILLVIEW
FOLLY CL
CHILCOMPTON RD
RIVERSIDE GDNS
RIVERSIDE DE RD
RIVERSIDE
RIVERSIDE WLK
STA
DOLL STONES
WITHIES LA
Riverside
RIVERSIDE WLK
R LONG CL

River Somer
Sewage Works
Nortondown House

BA3

Manor Farm
CHURCH LA
WOODVIEW
THE PITCHING
THE STREET
SOMER LA
TUNNEL LA
UPPER PITCHING
CORONATION TERR
Norton Green Farm
B3139
Tyning House

PARSONAGE LA
Chilcompton
GOLLEDGE CL
RAGLAN CL
HIGHFIELD CRES
BRITANNIA CL
BOWDEN HILL
FRY'S WELL
Mount Pleasant
WELLS RD
BENNELL CL
BENNELL BATCH
NURSERY RISE
BENNELL COTTS

GREENDITCH CL
BROADWAY CL
SAWMILL GDNS
SHEPPARDS WLK
STATION MEAD
VALLEY VIEW
BAKERS LA
PINES CL
CARTERS WAY
St Vigor & St John CE Prim Sch
LYNCH HILL
BROADWAY
PH
Rookery Farm
SAWYERS CL
DOWNSIDE CL
MONTSURS CL
B3139
B3139
NAISH FARM
PO
B3356
WESTMEAD
ROCK RD
Downside Abbey Home Farm
NAISH'S CROSS
STOCKHILL CL
HOECROFT GDNS
HOECROFT
A367

Three Tuns Farm
COALPIT LA
GREENWAYS
STOCKHILL RD
MENDIP FIELDS
Croft House
ABBEY RD
Downside Abbey
Downside Sch
MID DLEMEAD
LINKMEAD
SUNNYMEAD
ABBEY RD
THE MEAD
CHURCH ROW
CHURCH LA
FOSSEWAY
PH

Knitts Farm
Downside
New Rock Ind Est
ROCK RD
South Rock Ind Est
THE WILLOW
Stratton-on-the-Fosse
BANISBURY VIEW
BATH VIEW
HORNE CL
SOUTH ST

Winter Top Farm
Blacker's Hill Farm
Downside Farm
Green Lane Farmhouse
B3356
THE LODGES
GREEN LA
A367
Blacker's Hill

78
98

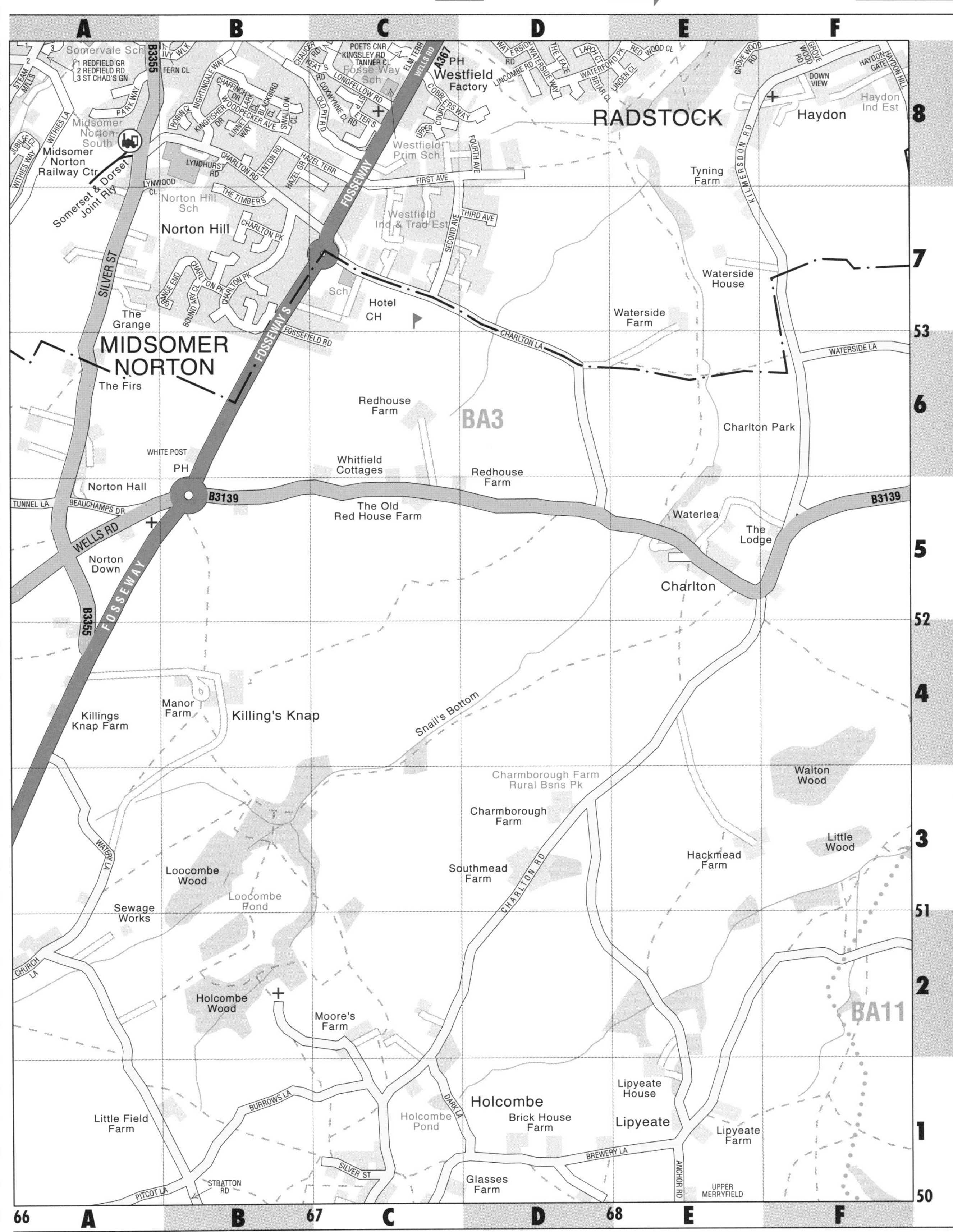
RADSTOCK
MIDSOMER NORTON
Westfield
Haydon
Haydon Ind Est
Tyning Farm
Waterside House
Waterside Farm
Charlton Park
Redhouse Farm
BA3
Whitfield Cottages
The Old Red House Farm
Waterlea
The Lodge
Charlton
Norton Hall
Norton Down
Norton Hill
The Grange
The Firs
Midsomer Norton Railway Ctr
Somerset & Dorset Joint Rly
Midsomer Norton South
Somervale Sch
Norton Hill Sch
Westfield Prim Sch
Westfield Ind & Trad Est
Fosse Way Sch
Factory
Hotel
CH
Sch
PH
WHITE POST
Killings Knap Farm
Manor Farm
Killing's Knap
Snail's Bottom
Charmborough Farm Rural Bsns Pk
Charmborough Farm
Walton Wood
Little Wood
Hackmead Farm
Southmead Farm
Loocombe Wood
Loocombe Pond
Sewage Works
Holcombe Wood
Moore's Farm
BA11
Holcombe
Holcombe Pond
Brick House Farm
Lipyeate House
Lipyeate
Lipyeate Farm
Little Field Farm
Glasses Farm
UPPER MERRYFIELD
FOSSEWAY
FOSSEWAY S
A367
WELLS RD
B3355
B3139
SILVER ST
CHARLTON LA
CHARLTON RD
WATERSIDE LA
KILMERSDON RD
BREWERY LA
ANCHOR RD
DARK LA
BURROWS LA
SILVER ST
PITCOT LA
STRATTON RD
CHURCH LA
WATERY LA
TUNNEL LA
BEAUCHAMPS DR
FOSSEFIELD RD
CHARLTON PK
BOUNDARY CL
GRANGE END
THE TIMBERS
LYNWOOD CL
LYNDHURST RD
HAZEL TERR
HAZEL GR
LYNTON RD
FIRST AVE
SECOND AVE
THIRD AVE
FOURTH AVE
COBBLERS WAY
UPPER COURTENAY
POETS CNR
KINGSLEY RD
TANNER CL
ELM TERR
LONGFELLOW RD
GOXWYNNE CL
OLD PIT RD
CHAUCER RD
KEATS RD
NIGHTINGALE WAY
CHAFFINCH DR
KINGFISHER DR
WOODPECKER AVE
LINNET WAY
LARK CL
BLACKBIRD WAY
SWALLOW CL
ROBIN CL
FERN CL
IVY WLK
PARK WAY
WITHIES LA
WITHIES WAY
JUBILEE CL
STEAM MILLS
1 REDFIELD GR
2 REDFIELD RD
3 ST CHAD'S GN
LINCOMBE RD
WATERSIDE RD
WATERSIDE WAY
THE LEAZE
LARCH CL
BRIAR CL
WATERFORD PK
LINDEN CL
RED WOOD CL
GROVE WOOD RD
DOWN VIEW
HAYDON GATE
HAYDON HILL
A B C D E F
8 7 6 5 4 3 2 1
53 52 51 50
66 67 68

116
98

97
79

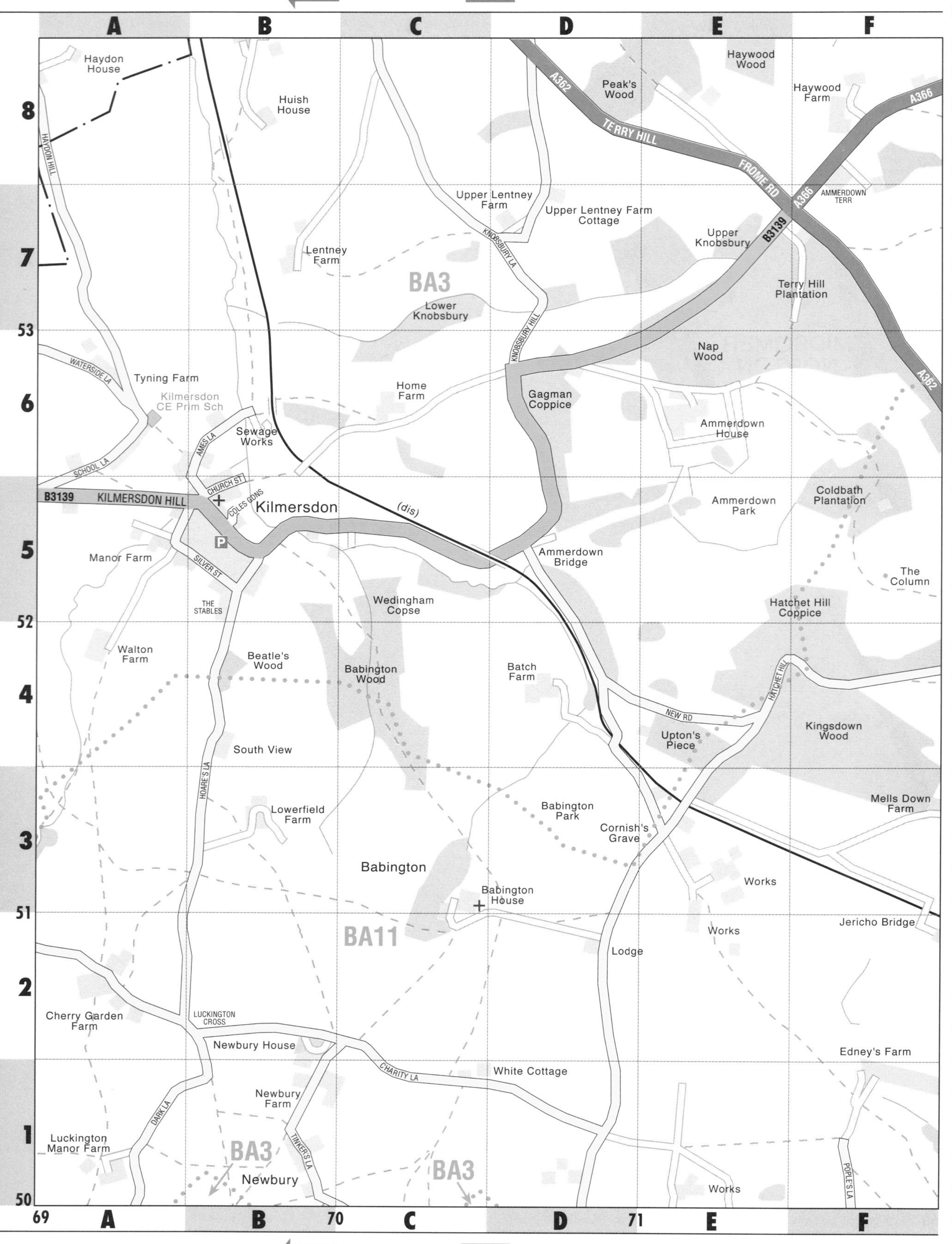
Haydon House
Huish House
Haywood Wood
Peak's Wood
Haywood Farm
A362
TERRY HILL
FROME RD
A366
AMMERDOWN TERR
HAYDON HILL
Upper Lentney Farm
Upper Lentney Farm Cottage
Upper Knobsbury
B3139
Lentney Farm
KNOBSBURY LA
BA3
Lower Knobsbury
Terry Hill Plantation
KNOBSBURY HILL
Nap Wood
WATERSIDE LA
Tyning Farm
Kilmersdon CE Prim Sch
Home Farm
Gagman Coppice
Ammerdown House
AMES LA
Sewage Works
SCHOOL LA
CHURCH ST
COLES GDNS
Kilmersdon
(dis)
Ammerdown Park
Coldbath Plantation
B3139
KILMERSDON HILL
P
Manor Farm
SILVER ST
Ammerdown Bridge
The Column
THE STABLES
Wedingham Copse
Hatchet Hill Coppice
Walton Farm
Beatle's Wood
Babington Wood
Batch Farm
HATCHET HILL
NEW RD
Upton's Piece
Kingsdown Wood
South View
HOARE'S LA
Lowerfield Farm
Babington Park
Mells Down Farm
Cornish's Grave
Babington
Works
Babington House
BA11
Jericho Bridge
Works
Lodge
Cherry Garden Farm
LUCKINGTON CROSS
Newbury House
CHARITY LA
White Cottage
Edney's Farm
Newbury Farm
DARK LA
Luckington Manor Farm
BA3
TINKER'S LA
Newbury
BA3
Works
POPLE'S LA
A B C D E F
8 7 6 5 4 3 2 1
53 52 51 50
69 70 71

97
117

80
100

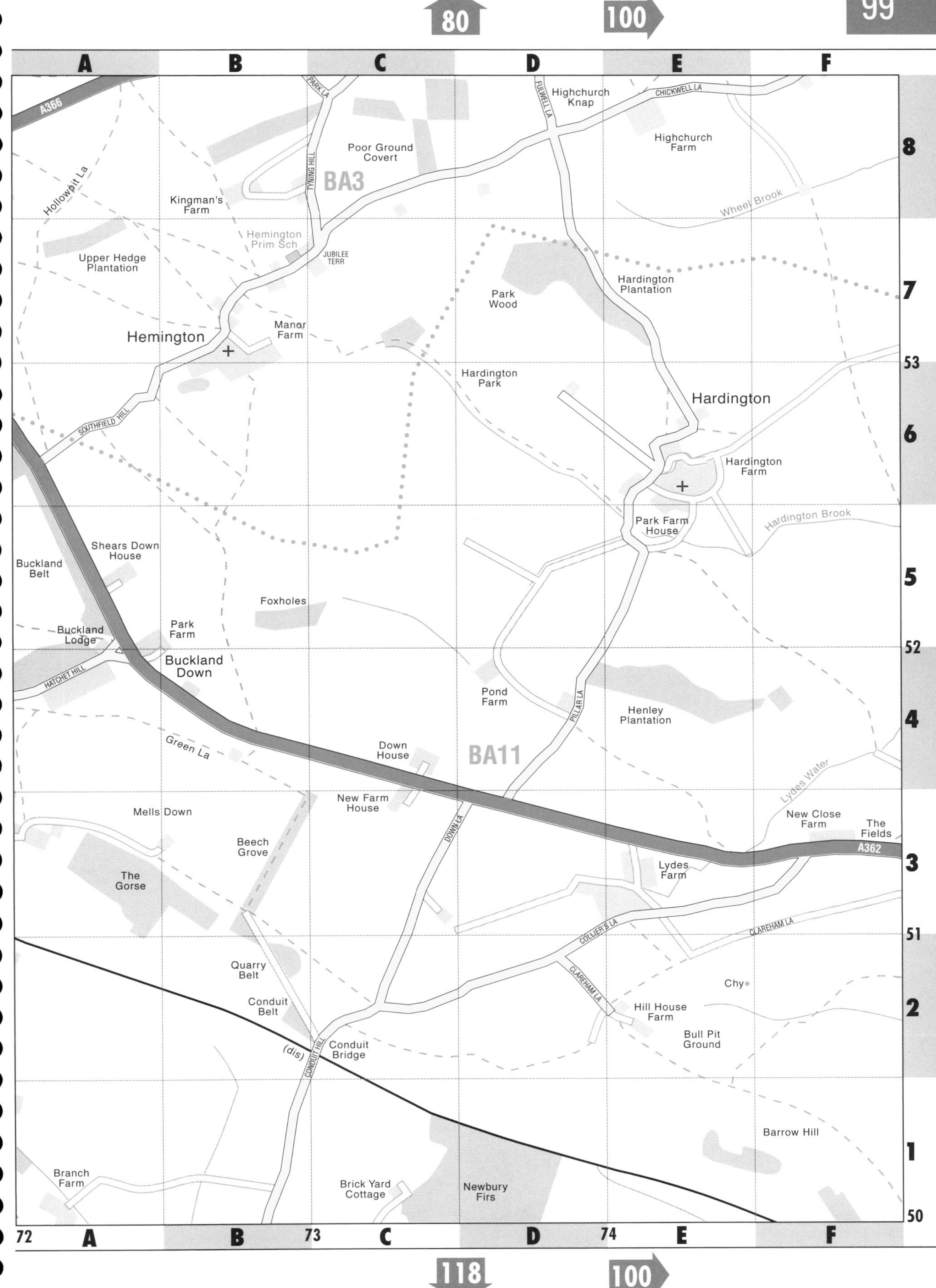
A B C D E F
8
7
53
6
5
52
4
3
51
2
1
50
72
73
74
A366
PARK LA
FULWELL LA
CHICKWELL LA
Highchurch Knap
Highchurch Farm
Poor Ground Covert
TYNING HILL
BA3
Wheel Brook
Hollowpit La
Kingman's Farm
Hemington Prim Sch
JUBILEE TERR
Upper Hedge Plantation
Park Wood
Hardington Plantation
Manor Farm
Hemington
Hardington Park
Hardington
SOUTHFIELD HILL
Hardington Farm
Park Farm House
Hardington Brook
Shears Down House
Buckland Belt
Foxholes
Buckland Lodge
Park Farm
HATCHET HILL
Buckland Down
Pond Farm
PILLAR LA
Henley Plantation
Green La
Down House
BA11
New Farm House
Lydes Water
Mells Down
New Close Farm
The Fields
DOWN LA
Beech Grove
A362
The Gorse
Lydes Farm
COLLIER'S LA
CLAREHAM LA
Quarry Belt
Chy
Conduit Belt
Hill House Farm
Bull Pit Ground
(dis)
CONDUIT HILL
Conduit Bridge
Barrow Hill
Branch Farm
Brick Yard Cottage
Newbury Firs

118
100

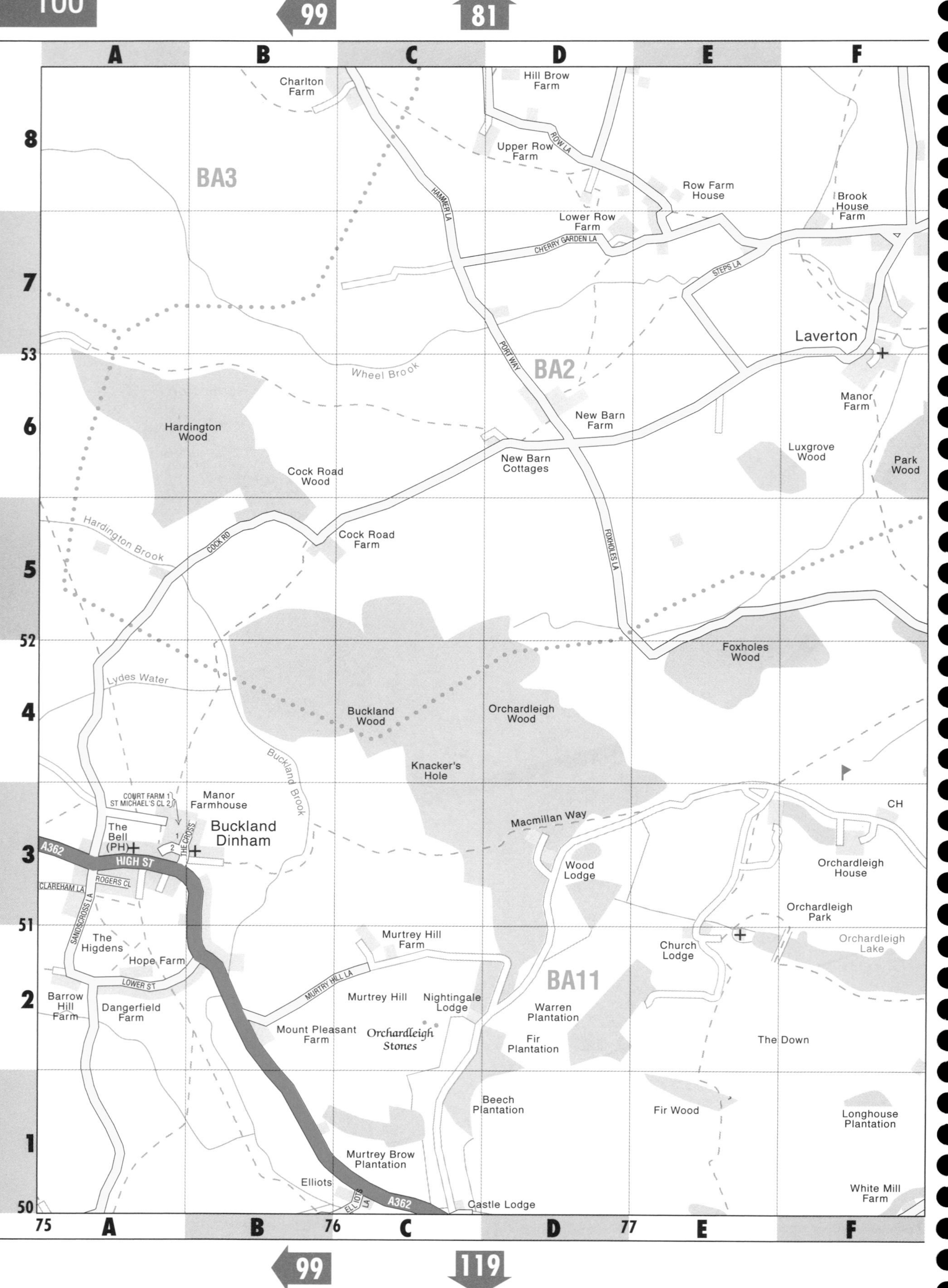

99
81

BA3

Charlton Farm

Hill Brow Farm

Upper Row Farm

Lower Row Farm

Row Farm House

Brook House Farm

ROW LA

HAMMER LA

CHERRY GARDEN LA

STEPS LA

Laverton

Wheel Brook

PORT WAY

BA2

Manor Farm

Hardington Wood

New Barn Farm

Luxgrove Wood

Park Wood

Cock Road Wood

New Barn Cottages

Hardington Brook

COCK RD

Cock Road Farm

FOXHOLES LA

Foxholes Wood

Lydes Water

Buckland Wood

Orchardleigh Wood

Knacker's Hole

Buckland Brook

COURT FARM 1
ST MICHAEL'S CL 2

Manor Farmhouse

Macmillan Way

CH

THE CROSS

The Bell (PH)

Buckland Dinham

Wood Lodge

Orchardleigh House

A362

HIGH ST

Orchardleigh Park

Orchardleigh Lake

ROGERS CL

CLAREHAM LA

SANDYSCROSS LA

The Higdens

Murtrey Hill Farm

Church Lodge

Hope Farm

MURTREY HILL LA

BA11

LOWER ST

Barrow Hill Farm

Dangerfield Farm

Murtrey Hill

Nightingale Lodge

Warren Plantation

The Down

Mount Pleasant Farm

Orchardleigh Stones

Fir Plantation

Beech Plantation

Fir Wood

Longhouse Plantation

Murtrey Brow Plantation

Elliots

ELLIOTS LA

A362

Castle Lodge

White Mill Farm

99
119

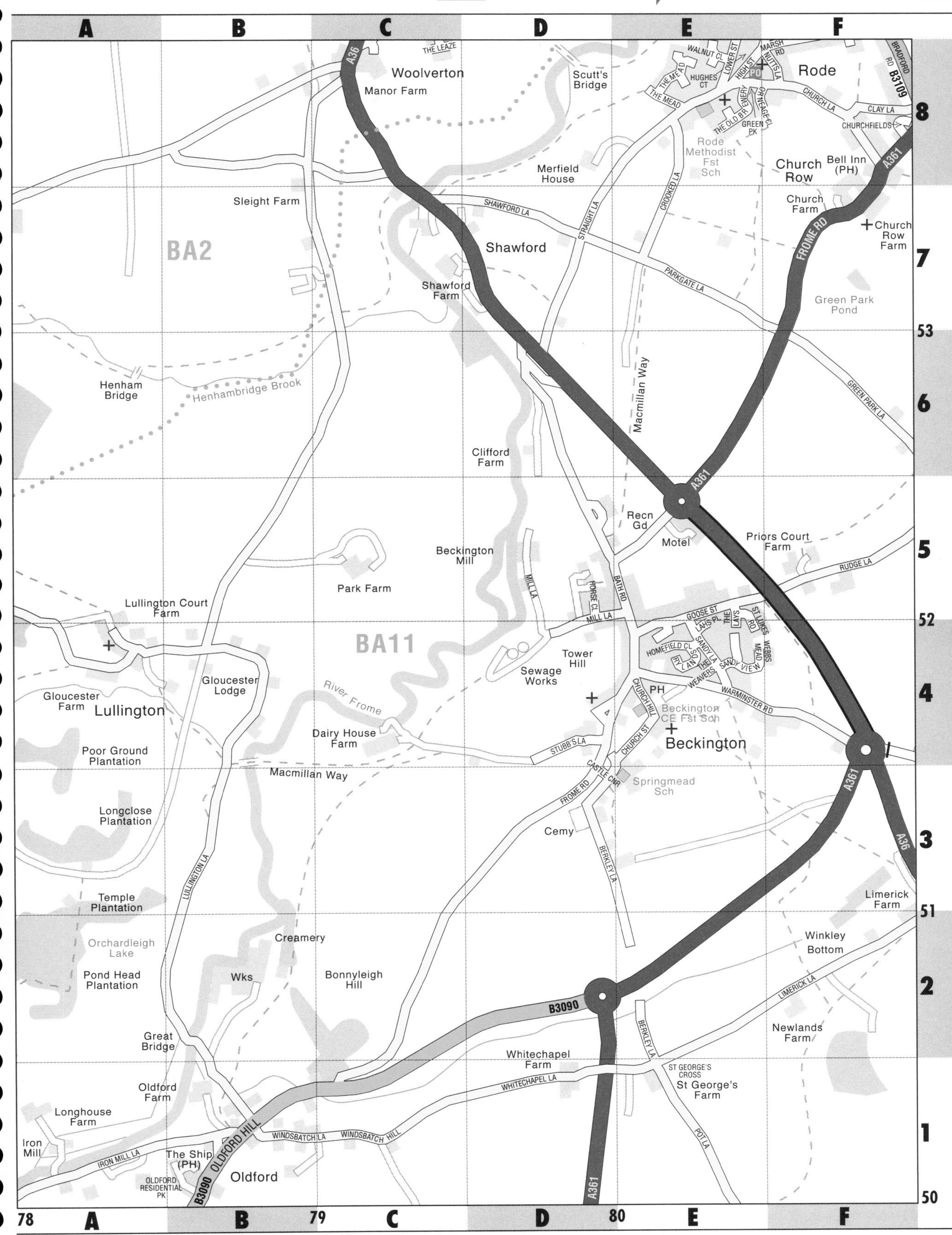

82
102
120
102

Woolverton
Manor Farm
THE LEAZE
Scutt's Bridge
WALNUT CT
LOWER ST
HIGH ST
MARSH RD
BUTTS LA
PO
Rode
BRADFORD RD
B3109
THE MEAD
HUGHES CT
THE OLD BREWERY
PACKGATE CL
GREEN PK
CHURCH LA
CLAY LA
CHURCHFIELDS
A361
Sleight Farm
Merfield House
SHAWFORD LA
CROOKED LA
Rode Methodist Fst Sch
Church Row
Bell Inn (PH)
8
BA2
Shawford
STRAIGHT LA
Church Farm
Church Row Farm
FROME RD
7
Shawford Farm
PARKGATE LA
53
Henham Bridge
Henhambridge Brook
Macmillan Way
Green Park Pond
6
Clifford Farm
A361
GREEN PARK LA
Park Farm
Beckington Mill
Recn Gd
Motel
Priors Court Farm
5
Lullington Court Farm
MILL LA
RUDGE LA
52
BA11
BATH RD
HORSE CL
MILL LA
GOOSE ST
LAMBS
THE LAYS
ST LUKES RD
WEBBS
Gloucester Lodge
Sewage Works
Tower Hill
HOMEFIELD CL
LADS LA
SANDY LA
THE WEAVERS
MEAD
SANDY VIEW
4
Gloucester Farm
Lullington
River Frome
PH
CHURCH ST
CHURCHILL
Beckington CE Fst Sch
WARMINSTER RD
Poor Ground Plantation
Dairy House Farm
Macmillan Way
STUBB'S LA
CHURCH ST
Beckington
Longclose Plantation
CASTLE CNR
FROME RD
Springmead Sch
A361
A36
3
Temple Plantation
Cemy
BERKLEY LA
Limerick Farm
51
Orchardleigh Lake
Creamery
Winkley Bottom
Pond Head Plantation
Bonnyleigh Hill
Wks
B3090
LIMERICK LA
2
Great Bridge
Whitechapel Farm
BERKLEY LA
Newlands Farm
Oldford Farm
WHITECHAPEL LA
ST GEORGE'S CROSS
St George's Farm
Longhouse Farm
OLDFORD HILL
WINDSBATCH LA
WINDSBATCH HILL
POT LA
1
Iron Mill
IRON MILL LA
The Ship (PH)
B3090
Oldford
A361
OLDFORD RESIDENTIAL PK
50

A **B** **C** **D** **E** **F**

A361
BRADFORD RD
B3109
A361

8
Parsonage Farm

Rode Farm

Monkley La

BA14

The Devil's Bed & Bolster

7
Mount Pleasant

Duck Pool La

53

6
Seymour's Court
RUDGE LA
DUCK POOL LA
Duck Pool Farm

Castley Farm
CASTLEY LA

Norris Hill Farm

Overcourt Farm

Silver Street Farm

Brokerswood Country Pk

Hazel Wood

Waterslade

Upper Castley Farm

FAIRWOOD RD

5
Church Farm

Round Wood

Lower Rudge Hill Farm

RUDGE HILL

Honeybridge Farm

Rudge

Brokerswood

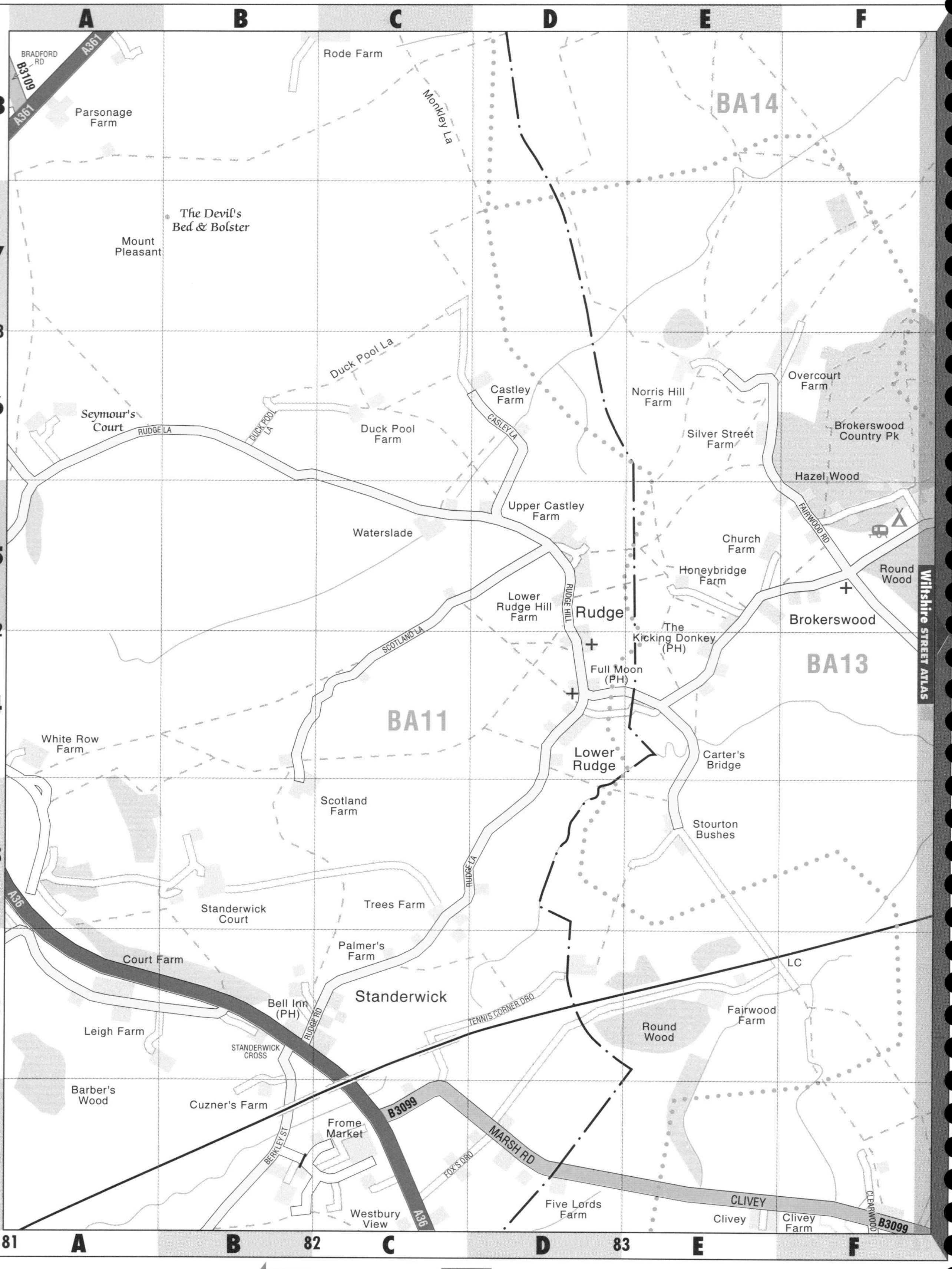

52
The Kicking Donkey (PH)

BA13

SCOTLAND LA

Full Moon (PH)

4
BA11

Lower Rudge

Carter's Bridge

Stourton Bushes

White Row Farm

Scotland Farm

3
A36

Standerwick Court

Trees Farm

HUBER LA

51
Court Farm

Palmer's Farm

LC

2
Bell Inn (PH)
RUDGE RD
Standerwick

Leigh Farm

STANDERWICK CROSS

TENNIS CORNER DRO

Round Wood

Fairwood Farm

Barber's Wood

Cuzner's Farm

B3099

MARSH RD

CLIVEY

1
BERKLEY ST
Frome Market

FOX'S DRO

50
A36
Westbury View

Five Lords Farm

Clivey

Clivey Farm

CLEARWOOD
B3099

Wiltshire STREET ATLAS

81 **A** **B** **82** **C** **D** **83** **E** **F**

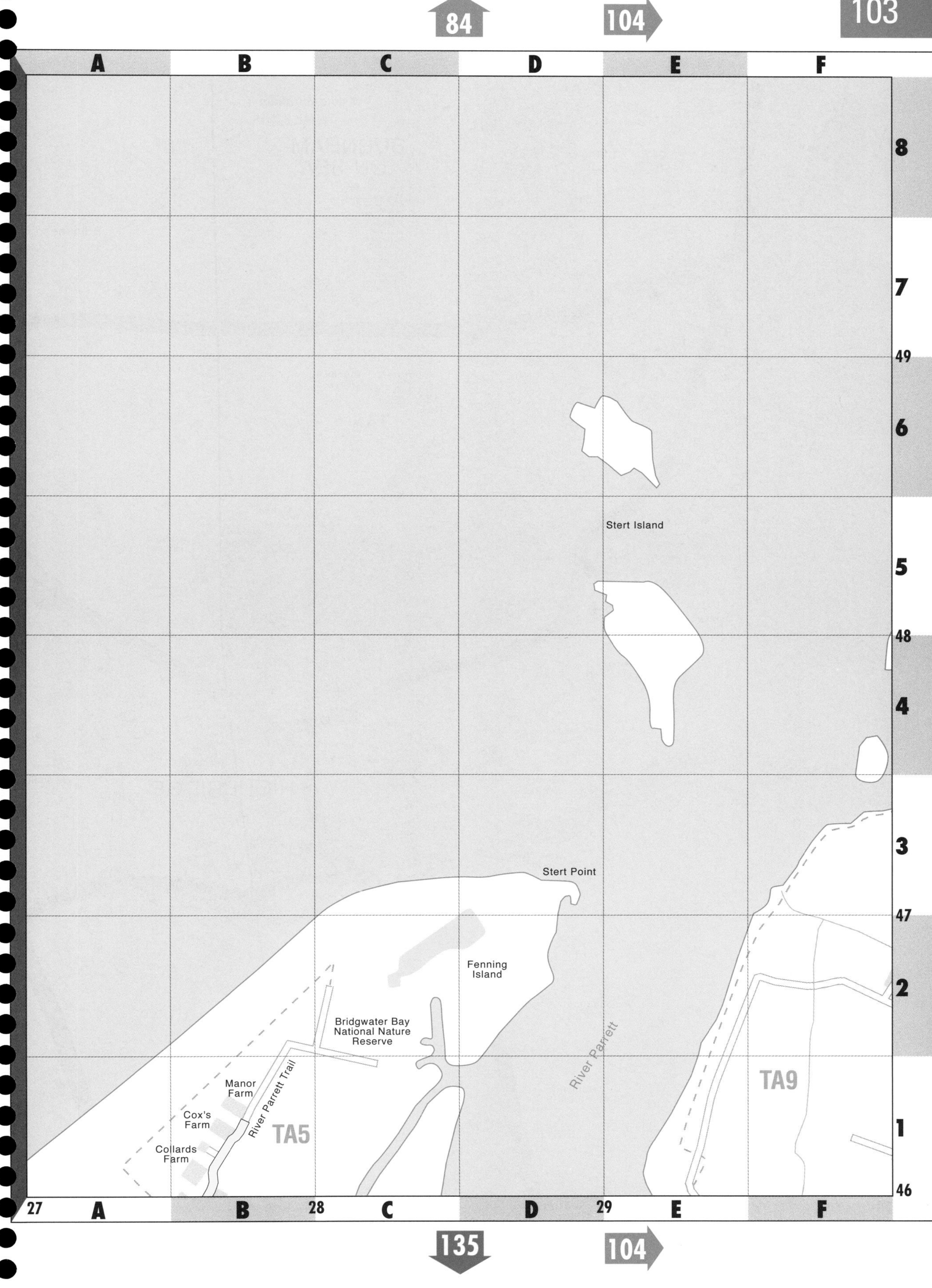

	A	B	C	D	E	F

8

7

49

6

Stert Island

5

48

4

3

47

Stert Point

Fenning
Island

Bridgwater Bay
National Nature
Reserve

2

River Parrett

TA9

Manor
Farm

River Parrett Trail

Cox's
Farm

TA5

1

Collards
Farm

46

27   A   B   28   C   D   29   E   F

103
85

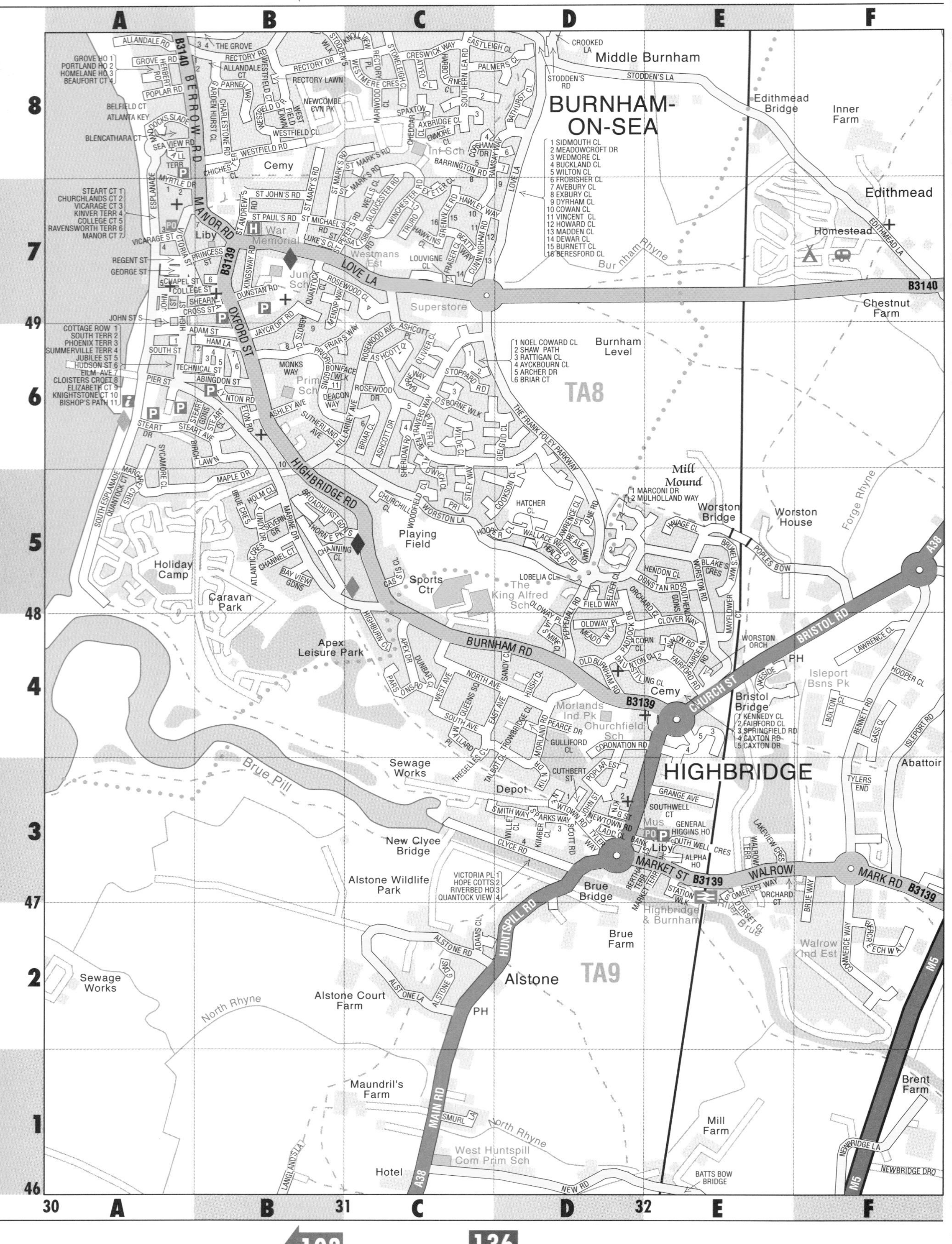
A
B
C
D
E
F
8
7
49
6
5
48
4
3
47
2
1
46
30
31
32
BURNHAM-
ON-SEA
Middle Burnham
HIGHBRIDGE
TA8
TA9
Edithmead
Edithmead Bridge
Inner Farm
Homestead
Chestnut Farm
Burnham Level
Mill Mound
Worston Bridge
Worston House
Forge Rhyne
Burnham Rhyne
Superstore
Westmans Est
War Memorial
Cemy
Liby
Playing Field
Sports Ctr
The King Alfred Sch
Holiday Camp
Caravan Park
Apex Leisure Park
Sewage Works
Brue Pill
Depot
Morlands Ind Pk
Churchfield Sch
Isleport Bsns Pk
Bristol Bridge
Abattoir
Walrow Ind Est
New Clyce Bridge
Alstone Wildlife Park
Brue Bridge
Brue Farm
Highbridge & Burnham
River Brue
Alstone
Alstone Court Farm
North Rhyne
Maundril's Farm
West Huntspill Com Prim Sch
Hotel
Mill Farm
Brent Farm
PH
Mus
B3140
B3139
A38
M5
BERROW RD
MANOR RD
OXFORD ST
HIGHBRIDGE RD
LOVE LA
BURNHAM RD
CHURCH ST
BRISTOL RD
MARKET ST
WALROW
MARK RD
HUNTSPILL RD
MAIN RD
STODDEN'S LA
CROOKED LA
EDITHMEAD LA
POPLES BOW
NEWBRIDGE LA
NEWBRIDGE DRO
NEW RD
BATTS BOW BRIDGE
1 SIDMOUTH CL
2 MEADOWCROFT DR
3 WEDMORE CL
4 BUCKLAND CL
5 WILTON CL
6 FROBISHER CL
7 AVEBURY CL
8 EXBURY CL
9 DYRHAM CL
10 COWAN CL
11 VINCENT CL
12 HOWARD CL
13 MADDEN CL
14 DEWAR CL
15 BURNETT CL
16 BERESFORD CL
1 NOEL COWARD CL
2 SHAW PATH
3 RATTIGAN CL
4 AYCKBOURN CL
5 ARCHER DR
6 BRIAR CT
1 MARCONI DR
2 MULHOLLAND WAY
1 KENNEDY CL
2 FAIRFORD CL
3 SPRINGFIELD RD
4 CAXTON RD
5 CAXTON DR
VICTORIA PL 1
HOPE COTTS 2
RIVERBED HO 3
QUANTOCK VIEW 4
GROVE HO 1
PORTLAND HO 2
HOMELANE HO 3
BEAUFORT CT 4
STEART CT 1
CHURCHLANDS CT 2
VICARAGE CT 3
KINVER TERR 4
COLLEGE CT 5
RAVENSWORTH TERR 6
MANOR CT 7
COTTAGE ROW 1
SOUTH TERR 2
PHOENIX TERR 3
SUMMERVILLE TERR 4
JUBILEE ST 5
HUDSON ST 6
ELIM AVE 7
CLOISTERS CROFT 8
ELIZABETH CT 9
KNIGHTSTONE CT 10
BISHOP'S PATH 11

103
136

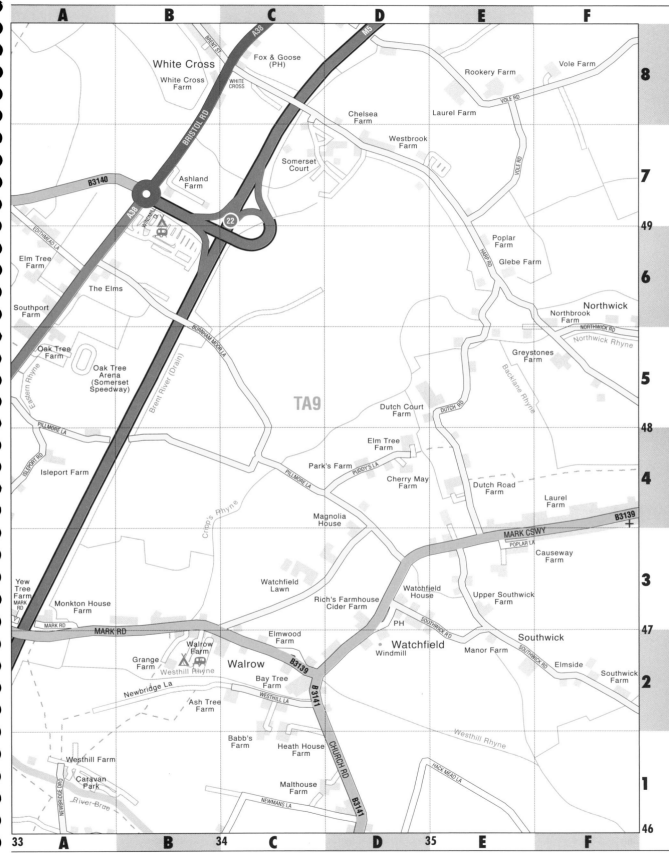

A B C D E F

8 7 49 6 5 48 4 3 47 2 1 46

White Cross
White Cross Farm
BRENT ST
A38
Fox & Goose (PH)
WHITE CROSS
M5
Rookery Farm
Vole Farm
VOLE RD
Laurel Farm
Chelsea Farm
BRISTOL RD
Westbrook Farm
Somerset Court
VOLE RD
B3140
Ashland Farm
A38
WINDMILL CL
22
EDITHMEAD LA
Poplar Farm
HARP RD
Glebe Farm
Elm Tree Farm
The Elms
Southport Farm
Northwick
Northbrook Farm
NORTHWICK RD
Northwick Rhyne
BURNHAM MOOR LA
Oak Tree Farm
Oak Tree Arena (Somerset Speedway)
Greystones Farm
Backlane Rhyne
Eastern Rhyne
Brent River (Drain)
TA9
Dutch Court Farm
DUTCH RD
PILLMORE LA
Elm Tree Farm
ISLEPORT RD
Isleport Farm
Park's Farm
PUDDY'S LA
PILLMORE LA
Cherry May Farm
Dutch Road Farm
Laurel Farm
Cripp's Rhyne
Magnolia House
B3139
MARK CSWY
POPLAR LA
Causeway Farm
Watchfield Lawn
Watchfield House
Upper Southwick Farm
Yew Tree Farm
MARK RD
Monkton House Farm
Rich's Farmhouse Cider Farm
PH
SOUTHWICK RD
MARK RD
MARK RD
Elmwood Farm
Southwick
Walrow Farm
Watchfield
Windmill
Manor Farm
SOUTHWICK RD
Grange Farm
Walrow
B3139
Elmside
Westhill Rhyne
Southwick Farm
Bay Tree Farm
Newbridge La
B3141
WESTHILL LA
Ash Tree Farm
Westhill Rhyne
Babb's Farm
Heath House Farm
CHURCH RD
Westhill Farm
HACK MEAD LA
Caravan Park
NEWBRIDGE DRO
Malthouse Farm
River Brue
NEWMANS LA
B3141

33 A B 34 C D 35 E F

105
87

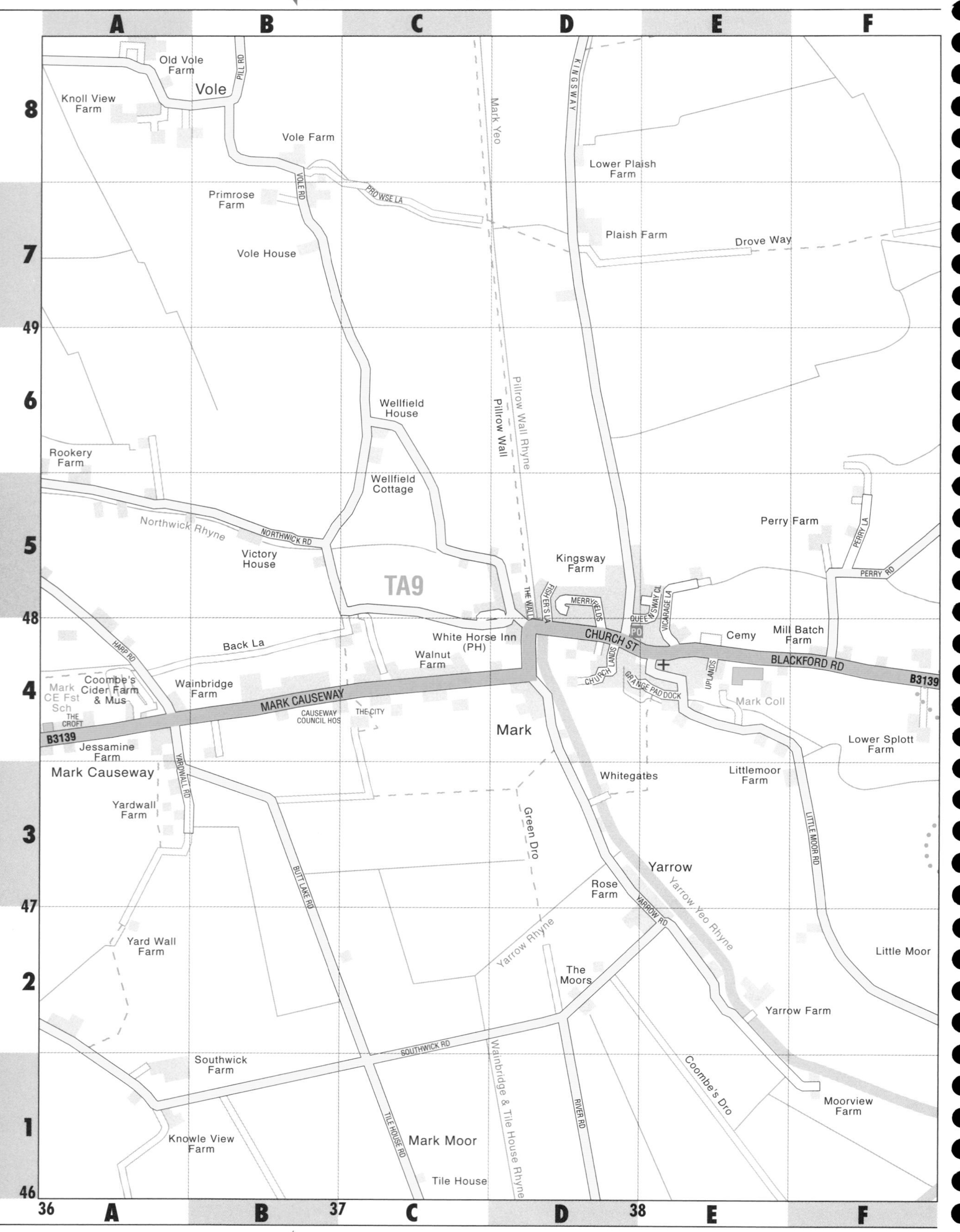
A
B
C
D
E
F
8
7
49
6
5
48
4
3
47
2
1
46
36
37
38
Old Vole Farm
Vole
Knoll View Farm
PILL RD
Vole Farm
Mark Yeo
KINGSWAY
Lower Plaish Farm
Primrose Farm
VOLE RD
PROWSE LA
Plaish Farm
Drove Way
Vole House
Wellfield House
Pillrow Wall
Pillrow Wall Rhyne
Rookery Farm
Wellfield Cottage
Perry Farm
PERRY LA
Northwick Rhyne
NORTHWICK RD
Victory House
Kingsway Farm
PERRY RD
TA9
THE WALL
FISHER'S LA
MERRYFIELDS
VICARAGE LA
PO
White Horse Inn (PH)
CHURCH ST
Cemy
Mill Batch Farm
Back La
Walnut Farm
BLACKFORD RD
HARP RD
Coombe's Cider Farm & Mus
Mark CE Fst Sch
Wainbridge Farm
MARK CAUSEWAY
CHURCH LANDS
GRANGE PADDOCK
UPLANDS
Mark Coll
B3139
THE CROFT
CAUSEWAY COUNCIL HOS
THE CITY
Mark
Lower Splott Farm
Jessamine Farm
Mark Causeway
YARDWALL RD
Whitegates
Littlemoor Farm
Yardwall Farm
Green Dro
LITTLE MOOR RD
BUTT LAKE RD
Yarrow
Rose Farm
YARROW RD
Yarrow Yeo Rhyne
Yard Wall Farm
Yarrow Rhyne
Little Moor
The Moors
Yarrow Farm
Southwick Farm
SOUTHWICK RD
Wainbridge & Tile House Rhyne
Coombe's Dro
Moorview Farm
RIVER RD
Knowle View Farm
TILE HOUSE RD
Mark Moor
Tile House

105
137

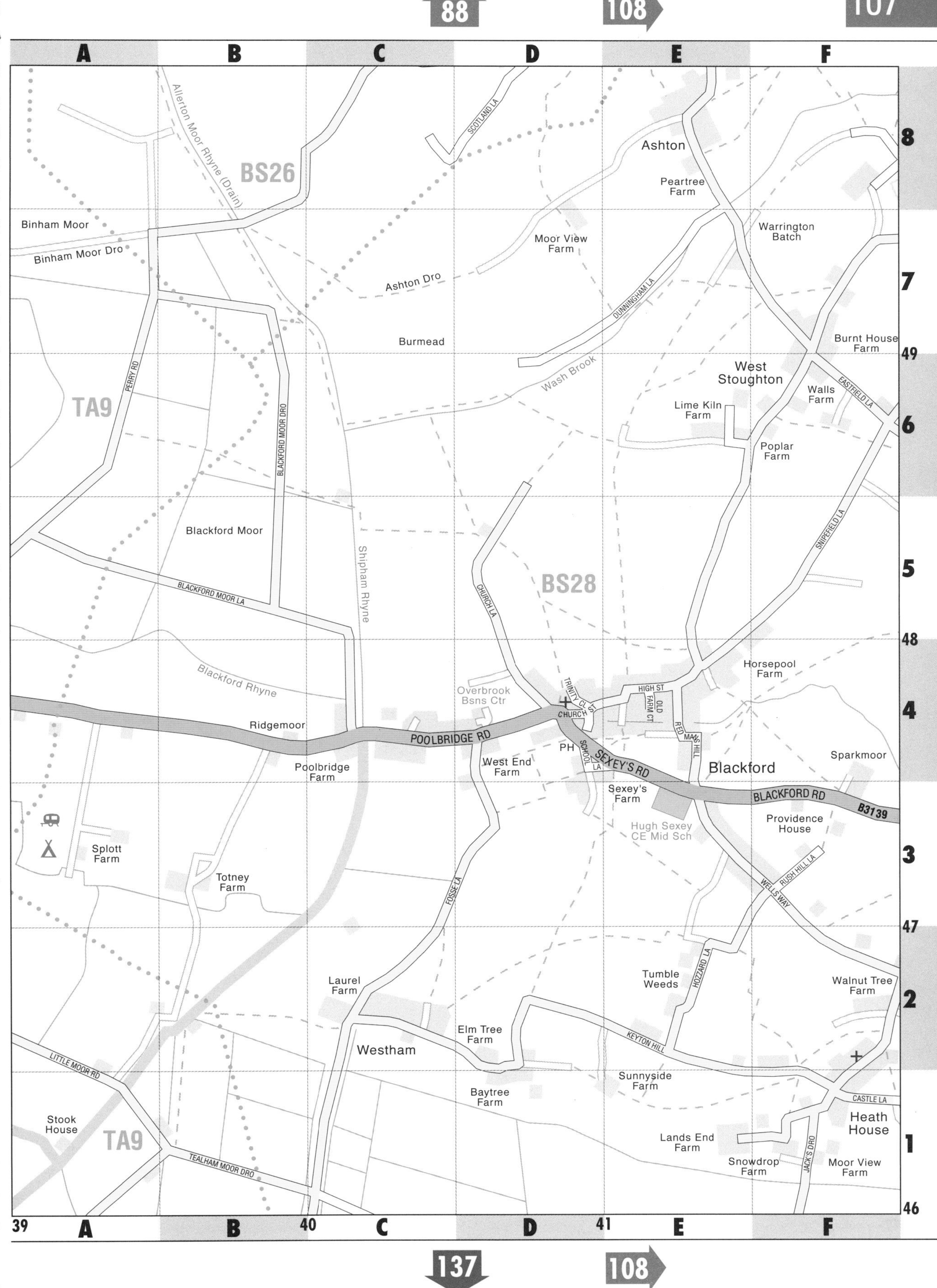

A B C D E F

8
7
49
6
5
48
4
3
47
2
1
46

Allerton Moor Rhyne (Drain)

BS26

Binham Moor
Binham Moor Dro

TA9

PERRY RD

BLACKFORD MOOR DRO

Blackford Moor

BLACKFORD MOOR LA

Shipham Rhyne

Blackford Rhyne

Ridgemoor

POOLBRIDGE RD

Poolbridge
Farm

West End
Farm

Splott
Farm

Totney
Farm

Laurel
Farm

FOSSE LA

Westham

Elm Tree
Farm

Baytree
Farm

LITTLE MOOR RD

Stook
House

TA9

TEALHAM MOOR DRO

Scotland La

Ashton Dro

Burmead

Wash Brook

CHURCH LA

BS28

Overbrook
Bsns Ctr

TRINITY CL
CHURCH ST

HIGH ST

OLD
FARM CT

RED
MAY HILL

SCHOOL LA

PH

SEXEY'S RD

Sexey's
Farm

Hugh Sexey
CE Mid Sch

Tumble
Weeds

HOZZARD LA

KEYTON HILL

Sunnyside
Farm

Lands End
Farm

Snowdrop
Farm

JACK'S DRO

Moor View
Farm

Ashton

Peartree
Farm

Moor View
Farm

DUNNINGHAM LA

West
Stoughton

Lime Kiln
Farm

Poplar
Farm

Horsepool
Farm

Blackford

BLACKFORD RD

Providence
House

WELLS WAY

RUSH HILL LA

Warrington
Batch

Burnt House
Farm

EASTFIELD LA

Walls
Farm

SNURFIELD LA

Sparkmoor

B3139

Walnut Tree
Farm

CASTLE LA

Heath
House

39 40 41

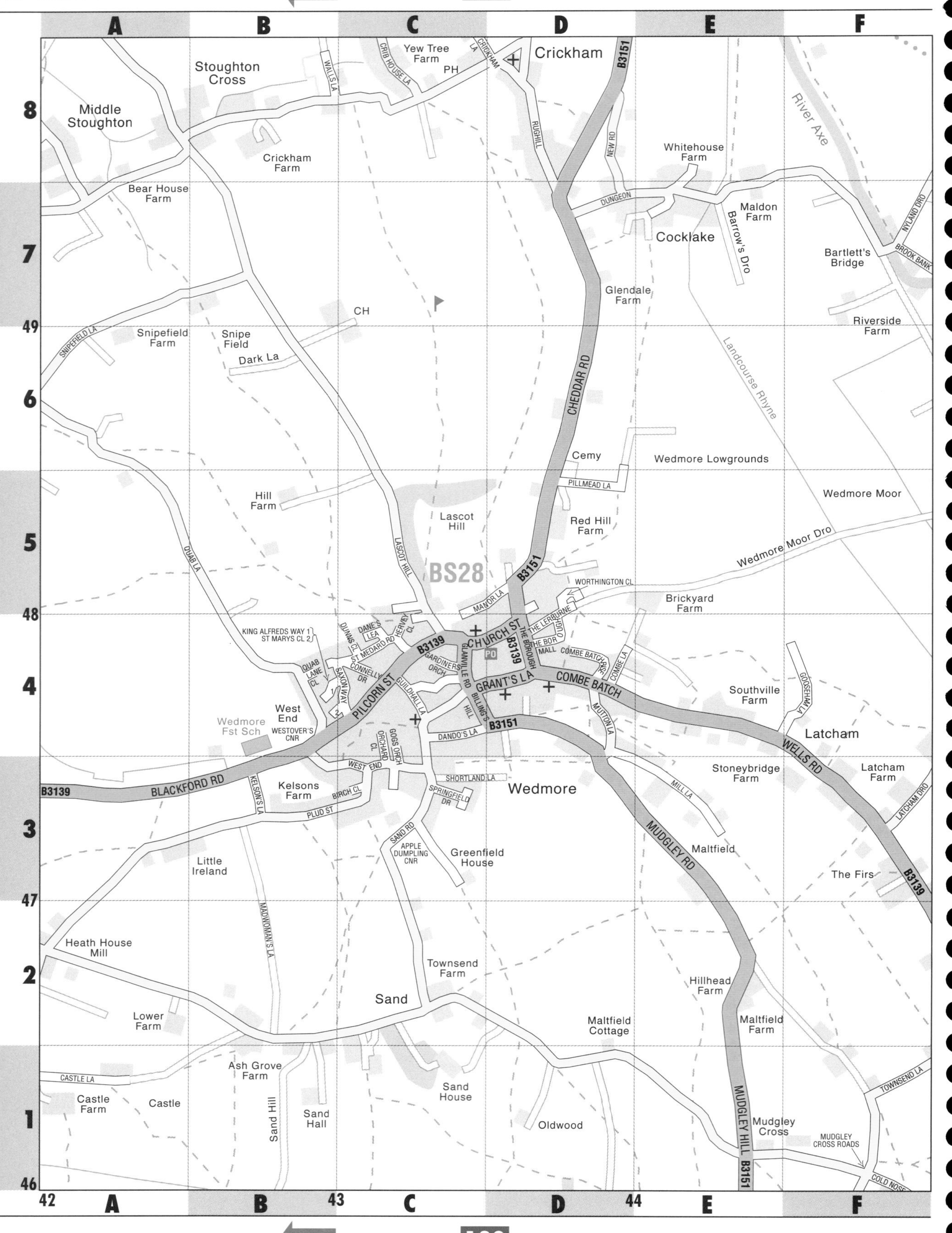

107
89

A   B   C   D   E   F

8

Middle
Stoughton

Stoughton
Cross

Crickham
Farm

Yew Tree
Farm
PH

Crickham

Whitehouse
Farm

Cocklake

Maldon
Farm

Barrow's Dro

Bartlett's
Bridge

Riverside
Farm

River Axe

Bear House
Farm

7

49

Snipefield La

Snipefield
Farm

Snipe
Field

Dark La

CH

Glendale
Farm

Cheddar Rd

B3151

New Rd

Rughill

Dungeon

Nyland Dro

Brook Bank

Landcourse Rhyne

6

Duab La

Hill
Farm

Lascot Hill

Lascot
Hill

Cemy

Red Hill
Farm

Wedmore Lowgrounds

Pillmead La

Wedmore Moor

Wedmore Moor Dro

5

BS28

B3151

Worthington Cl

Wedmore Moor Dro

48

King Alfreds Way 1
St Marys Cl 2

Dunns Cl

Dane's
Lea

St Medard Rd

Verney Rd

B3139

Gardiners
Orch

Manor La

Church St

The Borough

The Lerburne

The Bor

Mall

Brickyard
Farm

4

Quab
Lane
Cl

Connelly
Dr

Saxon Way

Pilcorn St

Guildhall La

Glanville Rd

Billings Hill

Grant's La

Combe Batch

Combe Batch

Combe La

Mutton La

Southville
Farm

Gooseham La

Latcham

Wells Rd

West
End

Wedmore
Fst Sch

Westover's
Cnr

Goss Dro

Orchard
Cl

West End

Dando's La

B3151

Stoneybridge
Farm

Latcham
Farm

Latcham Dro

3

B3139

Blackford Rd

Kelson's La

Kelsons
Farm

Birch Cl

Plud St

Shortland La

Springfield
Dr

Sand Rd

Apple
Dumpling
Cnr

Greenfield
House

Wedmore

Mudgley Rd

Maltfield

Mill La

Hillhead
Farm

The Firs

B3139

47

Little
Ireland

Heath House
Mill

Madoman's La

Townsend
Farm

Maltfield
Cottage

Maltfield
Farm

Townsend La

2

Sand

Lower
Farm

Ash Grove
Farm

Sand Hill

Sand
Hall

Sand
House

Oldwood

Mudgley
Cross

Mudgley Hill

B3151

Mudgley
Cross Roads

Cold Nose

1

Castle La

Castle
Farm

Castle

46

42   A   B   43   C   D   44   E   F

107
138

90
110

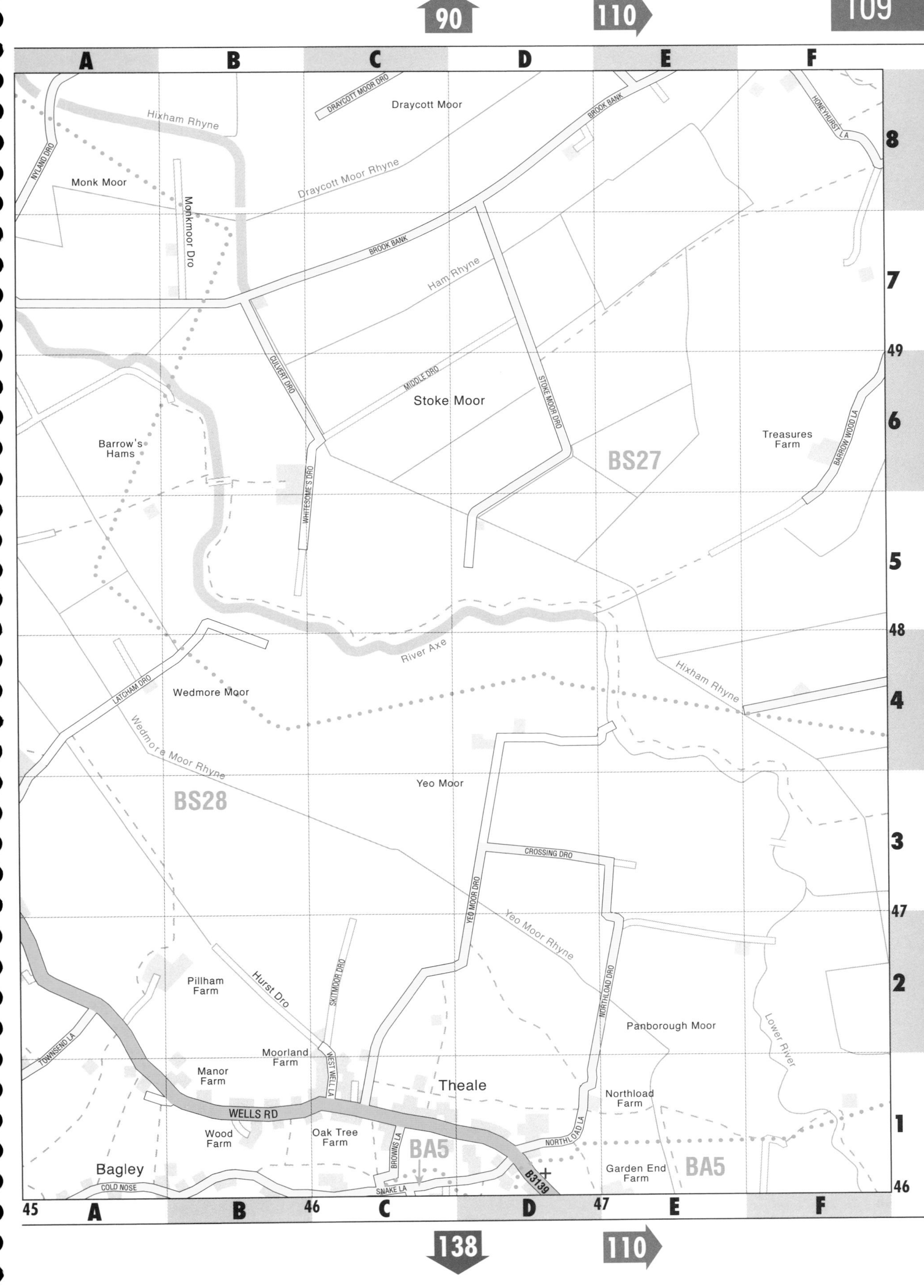
A
B
C
D
E
F
8
7
49
6
5
48
4
3
47
2
1
46
45
46
47
Draycott Moor
DRAYCOTT MOOR DRO
Hixham Rhyne
NYLAND DRO
Monk Moor
Monkmoor Dro
Draycott Moor Rhyne
BROOK BANK
HONEYHURST LA
Ham Rhyne
CULVERT DRO
MIDDLE DRO
Stoke Moor
STOKE MOOR DRO
BS27
Treasures Farm
BARROW WOOD LA
Barrow's Hams
WHITESOME'S DRO
River Axe
Hixham Rhyne
LATCHAM DRO
Wedmore Moor
Wedmore Moor Rhyne
BS28
Yeo Moor
CROSSING DRO
YEO MOOR DRO
Yeo Moor Rhyne
NORTHLOAD DRO
Pillham Farm
Hurst Dro
SKITMOOR DRO
Panborough Moor
Lower River
TOWNSEND LA
Moorland Farm
WEST WELL LA
Manor Farm
Theale
Northload Farm
WELLS RD
Wood Farm
Oak Tree Farm
BROWNS LA
BA5
NORTHLOAD LA
Bagley
Garden End Farm
BA5
B3139
COLD NOSE
SNAKE LA

138
110

109
91

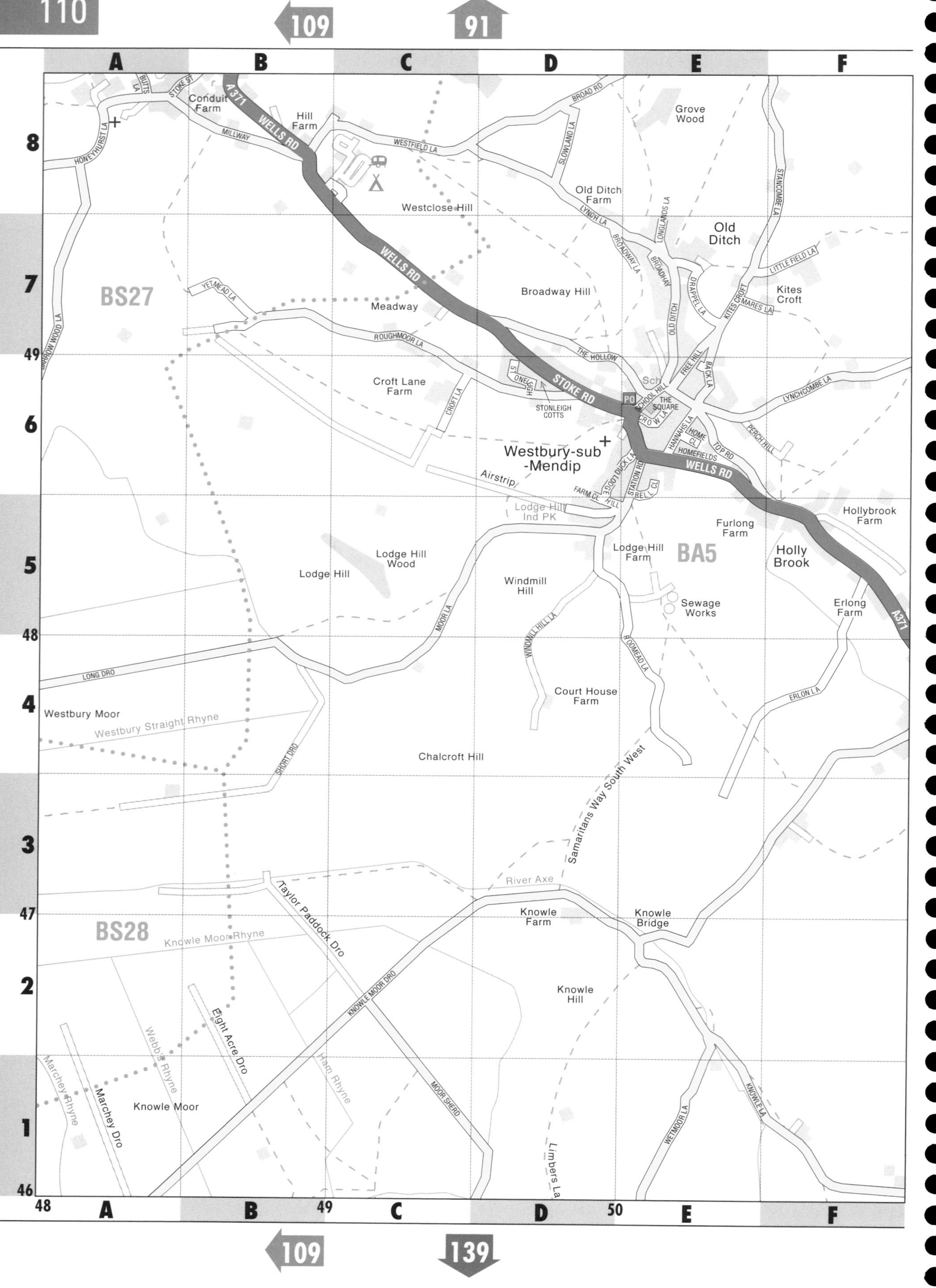
A
B
C
D
E
F
8
7
49
6
5
48
4
3
47
2
1
46
BUTTS LA
STOKE ST
Conduit Farm
A371
WELLS RD
Hill Farm
MILLWAY
HONEYHURST LA
WESTFIELD LA
BROAD RD
SLOWLAND LA
Grove Wood
STANCOMBE LA
Westclose Hill
Old Ditch Farm
LYNCH LA
LONGLANDS LA
Old Ditch
BROADWAY LA
BROADWAY
LITTLE FIELD LA
DRAPPEL LA
Kites Croft
KITES CROFT
MARES LA
OLD DITCH
Broadway Hill
BS27
YETMEAD LA
Meadway
BURROW WOOD LA
ROUGHMOOR LA
THE HOLLOW
FREE HILL
BACK LA
Sch
Croft Lane Farm
STONELEIGH
STOKE RD
PO
SCHOOL HILL
THE SQUARE
LYNCHCOMBE LA
CROFT LA
STONLEIGH COTTS
CROW LA
HANNAHS LA
HOME CL
HOMEFIELDS
TOP RD
PERCH HILL
Westbury-sub-Mendip
Airstrip
DUCK LA
STATION RD
BELL CL
FARM CL
LODGE HILL
Lodge Hill Ind PK
Hollybrook Farm
Furlong Farm
Lodge Hill Farm
BA5
Holly Brook
Lodge Hill Wood
Lodge Hill
Windmill Hill
Sewage Works
Erlong Farm
MOOR LA
WINDMILL HILL LA
RODMEAD LA
48
LONG DRO
Court House Farm
ERLON LA
Westbury Moor
Westbury Straight Rhyne
Chalcroft Hill
SHORT DRO
Samaritans Way South West
River Axe
Taylor Paddock Dro
Knowle Farm
Knowle Bridge
BS28
Knowle Moor Rhyne
KNOWLE MOOR DRO
Knowle Hill
Eight Acre Dro
Webb's Rhyne
Ham Rhyne
Marchey Rhyne
Marchey Dro
Knowle Moor
MOOR SHERD
WETMOOR LA
KNOWLE LA
Limbers La
48
49
50

109
139

92
112

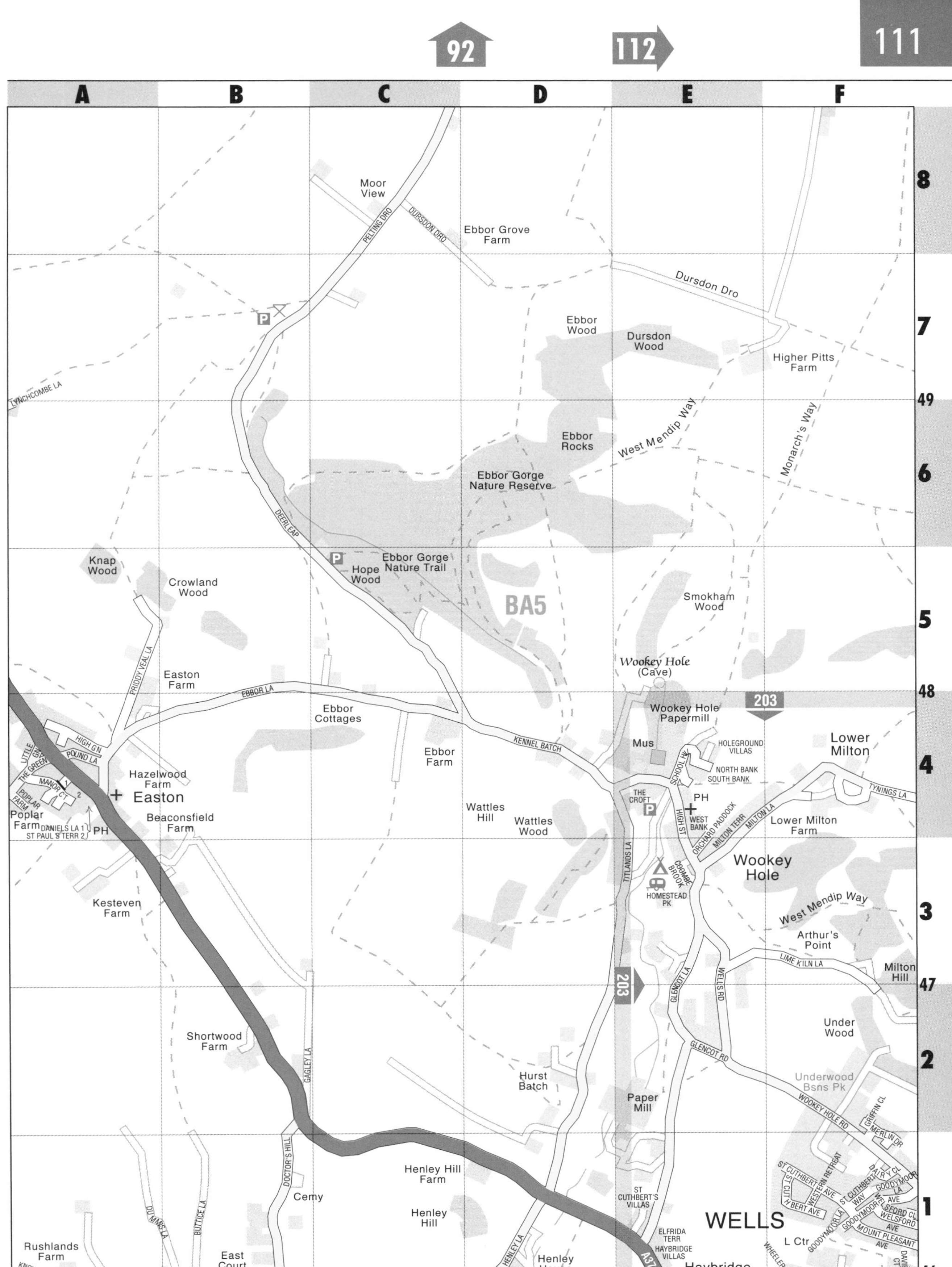
A
B
C
D
E
F
8
7
49
6
5
48
4
3
47
2
1
46
51
52
53
Moor View
PELTING DRO
DURSDON DRO
Ebbor Grove Farm
Dursdon Dro
Ebbor Wood
Dursdon Wood
Higher Pitts Farm
LYNCHCOMBE LA
West Mendip Way
Monarch's Way
Ebbor Rocks
Ebbor Gorge Nature Reserve
DEER LEAP
Knap Wood
Crowland Wood
Ebbor Gorge Nature Trail
Hope Wood
BA5
Smokham Wood
Wookey Hole (Cave)
PRIDDY VEAL LA
Easton Farm
EBBOR LA
Ebbor Cottages
Wookey Hole Papermill
203
Lower Milton
Mus
HOLEGROUND VILLAS
KENNEL BATCH
Ebbor Farm
SCHOOL HL
NORTH BANK
SOUTH BANK
HIGH GN
POUND LA
LITTLE GN
THE GREEN
MANOR CT
Hazelwood Farm
Easton
THE CROFT
PH
TYNINGS LA
Poplar Farm
POPLAR FARM
DANIELS LA 1
ST PAUL'S TERR 2
PH
Beaconsfield Farm
Wattles Hill
Wattles Wood
WEST BANK
HIGH ST
ORCHARD PADDOCK
MILTON TERR
MILTON LA
Lower Milton Farm
TITLANDS LA
COOMBE BROOK
HOMESTEAD PK
Wookey Hole
Kesteven Farm
West Mendip Way
Arthur's Point
LIME KILN LA
Milton Hill
203
GLENCOT LA
WELLS RD
Under Wood
Shortwood Farm
GLENCOT RD
Underwood Bsns Pk
GAGLEY LA
Hurst Batch
Paper Mill
WOOKEY HOLE RD
GRIFFIN CL
MERLIN DR
DOCTOR'S HILL
Henley Hill Farm
Cemy
Henley Hill
ST CUTHBERT'S VILLAS
WESTERN RETREAT
ST CUTHBERT'S AVE
DAIRY CL
GOODYMOOR LA
DU MARS LA
BUTTICE LA
WELLS
ELFRIDA TERR
HAYBRIDGE VILLAS
WELSFORD AVE
MOUNT PLEASANT AVE
Rushlands Farm
East Court
HENLEY LA
Henley House
A371
Haybridge
L Ctr
WHEELER GR
DAVIES CT
KNOWLE LA

139
112

111
93

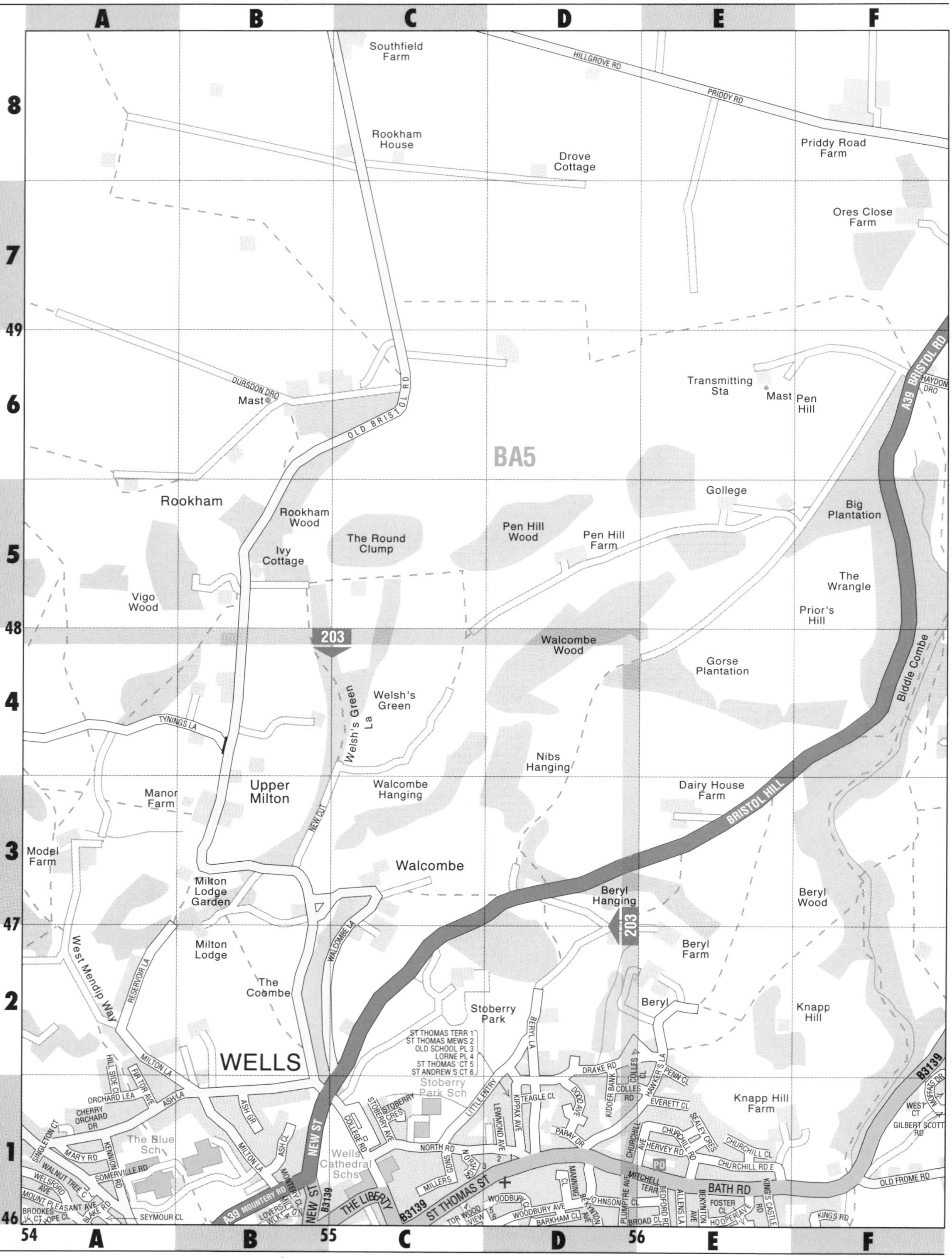

A B C D E F

8
7
49
6

5
48
4

3
47
2
1
46

54 A B 55 C D 56 E F

Southfield Farm
HILLGROVE RD
PRIDDY RD
Rookham House
Drove Cottage
Priddy Road Farm
Ores Close Farm

DURSDON DRO
Mast
OLD BRISTOL RD
BA5
Transmitting Sta
Mast Pen Hill
A39 BRISTOL RD
HAYDON DRO

Rookham
Rookham Wood
The Round Clump
Pen Hill Wood
Gollege
Big Plantation

Ivy Cottage
Pen Hill Farm
The Wrangle
Prior's Hill

Vigo Wood
Walcombe Wood
Gorse Plantation
Biddle Combe

203
Welsh's Green La
Welsh's Green
Nibs Hanging
Dairy House Farm

TYNINGS LA
Upper Milton
Walcombe Hanging
BRISTOL HILL

NEW CUT
Manor Farm
Model Farm
Walcombe
Beryl Hanging
Beryl Wood

Milton Lodge Garden
203
Beryl Farm

47
Milton Lodge
WALCOMBE LA
The Coombe
Beryl
Knapp Hill

West Mendip Way
RESERVOIR LA
MILTON LA
WELLS
Stoberry Park
Knapp Hill Farm

St Thomas Park Sch
St Thomas Terr 1
St Thomas Mews 2
Old School Pl 3
Lorne Pl 4
St Thomas Ct 5
St Andrew's Ct 6

B3139
HILL SIDE CL
FEL TOR AVE
ASH GR
ASH LA
ASH CL
MONTREY RD
NEW ST
STOBERRY CRES
STOBERRY AVE
COLLEGE RD
BERYL LA
KIDDER BANK
DRAKE RD
COLLES CL
HAWKER'S LA
PENN CL
EVERETT CL
CHURCHILL CL
CHURCHILL RD E
B3139

CHERRY ORCHARD DR
SINGLETON CT
MARY RD
The Blue Sch
MILTON CL
SOMERVILLE RD
LITTLE ENTRY
KIPPAX AVE
TEAGLE CL
LENNMOND AVE
DODD AVE
PARAY DR
SEALEY CRES
HERVEY RD
PO
WEST CT
GILBERT SCOTT RD

WALNUT TREE C
WELSFORD
LK CT
HOPE CL
Wells Cathedral Schs
NORTH RD
ST THOMAS ST
TOR WOOD VIEW
MANNING CL
JOHNSON RD
MITCHELL TERR
BATH RD
KING'S CASTLE RD
OLD FROME RD

MOUNT PLEASANT AVE
BROOKES CL
SEYMOUR CL
THE LIBERTY
B3139
MILLERS
WOODBURY AVE
BARKHAM CLI
BEKYNTON AVE
PLUMPTRE AVE
BEDFORD RD
ALLENS LA
HOOPER LANE
BROAD CL
FOSTER CL
KINGS RD

A39 MOUNTERY RD
LOVERS WLK

94
114

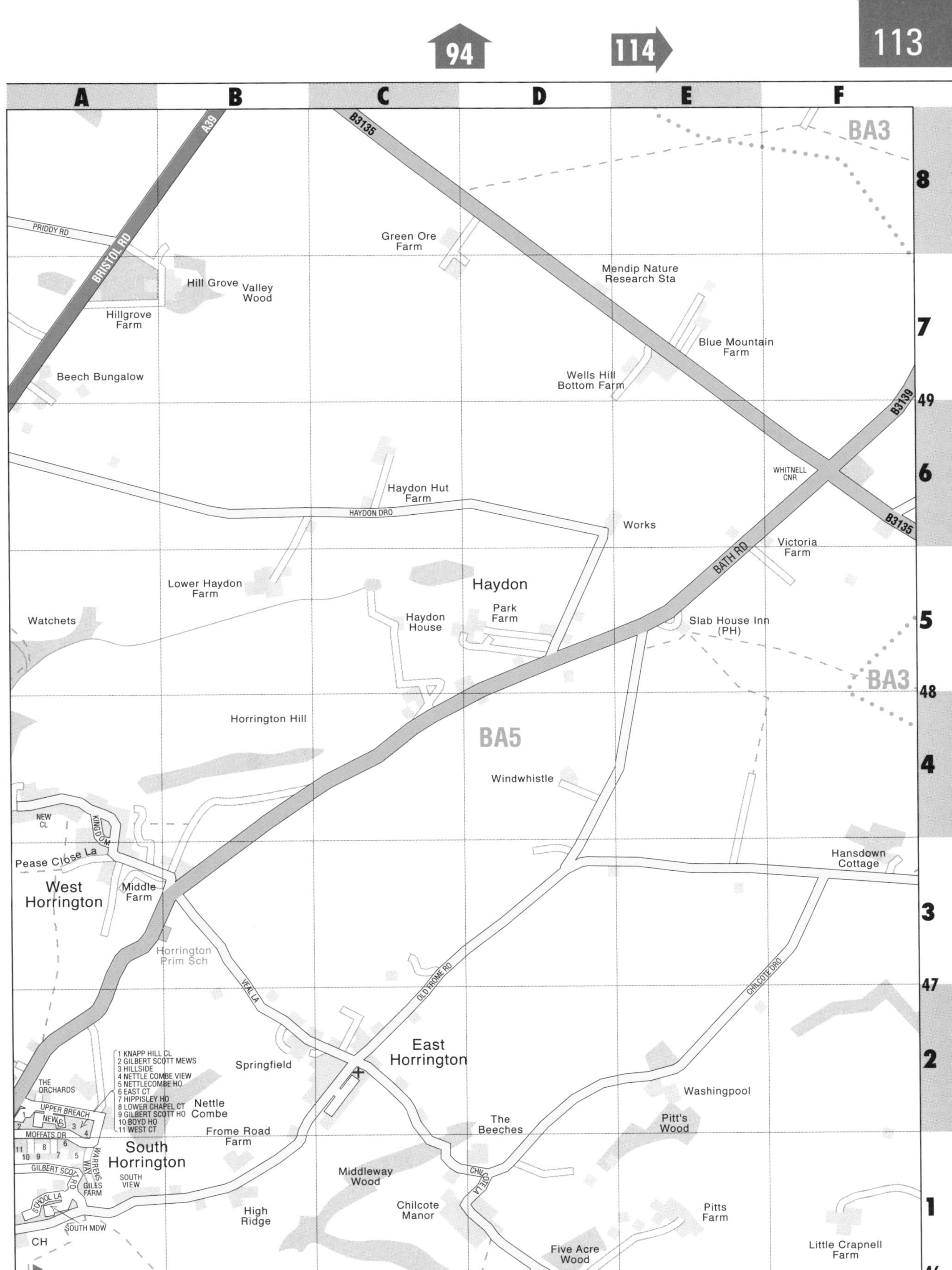
A
B
C
D
E
F
8
7
49
6
5
48
4
3
47
2
1
46
57
58
59
BA3
B3135
A39
PRIDDY RD
BRISTOL RD
Green Ore
Farm
Hill Grove
Valley
Wood
Mendip Nature
Research Sta
Hillgrove
Farm
Blue Mountain
Farm
Beech Bungalow
Wells Hill
Bottom Farm
B3139
WHITNELL
CNR
Haydon Hut
Farm
HAYDON DRO
Works
B3135
Victoria
Farm
BATH RD
Lower Haydon
Farm
Haydon
Park
Farm
Haydon
House
Watchets
Slab House Inn
(PH)
BA3
Horrington Hill
BA5
Windwhistle
NEW
CL
KINGDOM
Pease Close La
Hansdown
Cottage
West
Horrington
Middle
Farm
Horrington
Prim Sch
VEAL LA
OLD FROME RD
CHILCOTE DRO
East
Horrington
Springfield
1 KNAPP HILL CL
2 GILBERT SCOTT MEWS
3 HILLSIDE
4 NETTLE COMBE VIEW
5 NETTLECOMBE HO
6 EAST CT
7 HIPPISLEY HO
8 LOWER CHAPEL CT
9 GILBERT SCOTT HO
10 BOYD HO
11 WEST CT
THE
ORCHARDS
UPPER BREACH
NEWS
MOFFATS DR
Nettle
Combe
Washingpool
Frome Road
Farm
The
Beeches
Pitt's
Wood
South
Horrington
WARRENS WAY
GILBERT SCOTT RD
SOUTH
VIEW
GILES
FARM
Middleway
Wood
CHILCOTE LA
SCHOOL LA
SOUTH MDW
High
Ridge
Chilcote
Manor
Pitts
Farm
CH
Five Acre
Wood
Little Crapnell
Farm
LYATT LA

140
114

113
95

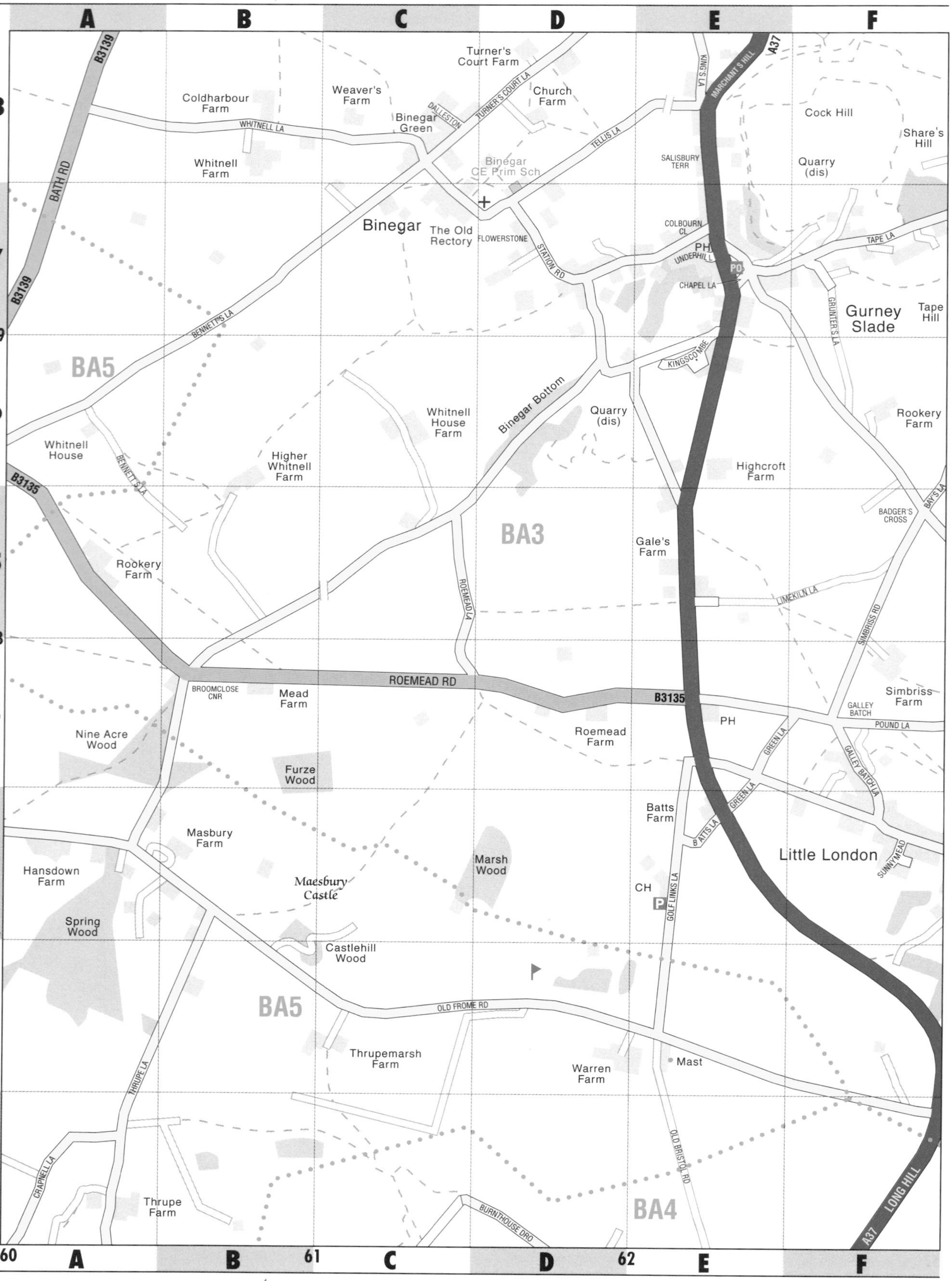

A B C D E F

8

B3139

Coldharbour Farm
Weaver's Farm
Turner's Court Farm
Church Farm
WHITNELL LA
DALLESTON
TURNER'S COURT LA
TELLIS LA
Cock Hill
Share's Hill
Whitnell Farm
Binegar Green
Binegar CE Prim Sch
SALISBURY TERR
Quarry (dis)

7

BATH RD
Binegar
The Old Rectory
FLOWERSTONE
STATION RD
COLBOURN CL
UNDERHILL
PH
PO
CHAPEL LA
TAPE LA

49

B3139
BENNETTS LA
KINGSCOMBE
Gurney Slade
GRUNTER'S LA
Tape Hill

6

BA5
Whitnell House Farm
Binegar Bottom
Quarry (dis)
Highcroft Farm
Rookery Farm
BAY'S LA

Whitnell House
BENNETT'S LA
Higher Whitnell Farm
BA3
Gale's Farm
BADGER'S CROSS

5

B3135
ROEMEAD LA
LIMEKILN LA
SIMBRISS RD

Rookery Farm
Simbriss Farm

48

ROEMEAD RD
B3135
GALLEY BATCH
POUND LA

4

BROOMCLOSE CNR
Mead Farm
Roemead Farm
PH
GREEN LA
GALLEY BATCH LA

Nine Acre Wood
Furze Wood
Batts Farm
Simbriss

3

Masbury Farm
Marsh Wood
B ATTS LA
GREEN LA
Little London
SUNNYMEAD

Hansdown Farm
Maesbury Castle
CH
P
GOLF LINKS LA

47

Spring Wood
Castlehill Wood

2

BA5
OLD FROME RD
Warren Farm
Mast
LONG HILL

THRUPE LA
Thrupemarsh Farm

1

CRAPNELL LA
Thrupe Farm
OLD BRISTOL RD
BURNTHOUSE DRO
BA4
A37

46

60 A B 61 C D 62 E F

96
116

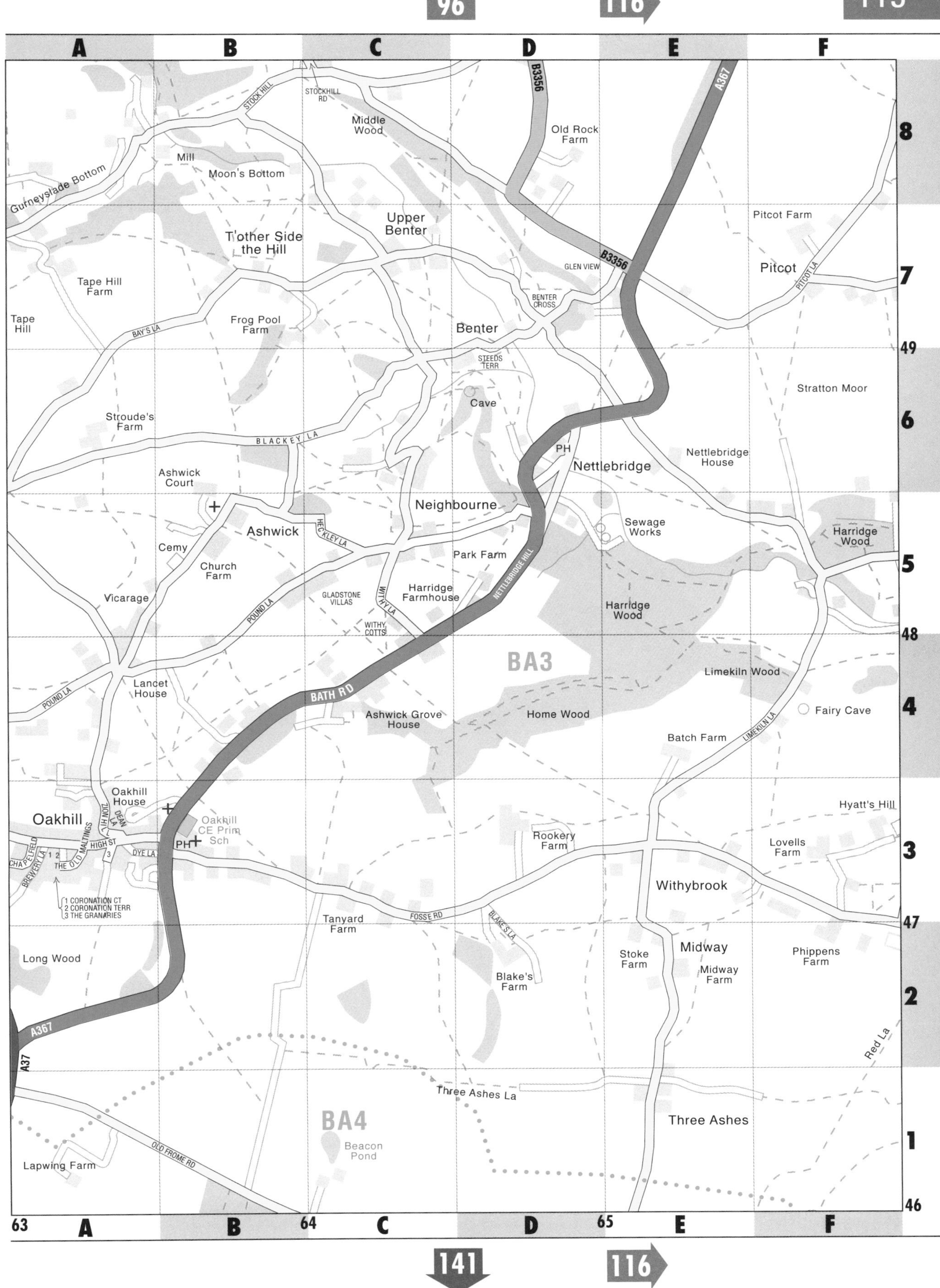

Stock Hill
Stockhill Rd
Middle Wood
Old Rock Farm
Mill
Moon's Bottom
Gurneyslade Bottom
Upper Benter
T'other Side the Hill
Pitcot Farm
Pitcot
Pitcot La
Glen View
Benter Cross
Tape Hill Farm
Tape Hill
Bay's La
Frog Pool Farm
Benter
Steeds Terr
Stratton Moor
Cave
Stroude's Farm
Blackey La
PH
Nettlebridge
Nettlebridge House
Ashwick Court
Neighbourne
Ashwick
Heckley La
Sewage Works
Harridge Wood
Cemy
Church Farm
Park Farm
Vicarage
Gladstone Villas
Withy La
Harridge Farmhouse
Nettlebridge Hill
Pound La
Withy Cotts
BA3
Limekiln Wood
Lancet House
Bath Rd
Ashwick Grove House
Home Wood
Fairy Cave
Limekiln La
Batch Farm
Oakhill House
Oakhill
Zion Hill
Dean La
Oakhill CE Prim Sch
Rookery Farm
Hyatt's Hill
Lovells Farm
The Old Maltings
High St
Dye La
Chapelfield
Brewery La
Withybrook
1 Coronation Ct
2 Coronation Terr
3 The Granaries
Tanyard Farm
Fosse Rd
Blake's La
Stoke Farm
Midway
Midway Farm
Phippens Farm
Long Wood
Blake's Farm
A367
A37
Red La
Three Ashes La
Three Ashes
BA4
Beacon Pond
Old Frome Rd
Lapwing Farm
63
64
65
46
47
48
49
A
B
C
D
E
F
1
2
3
4
5
6
7
8

141
116

115
97

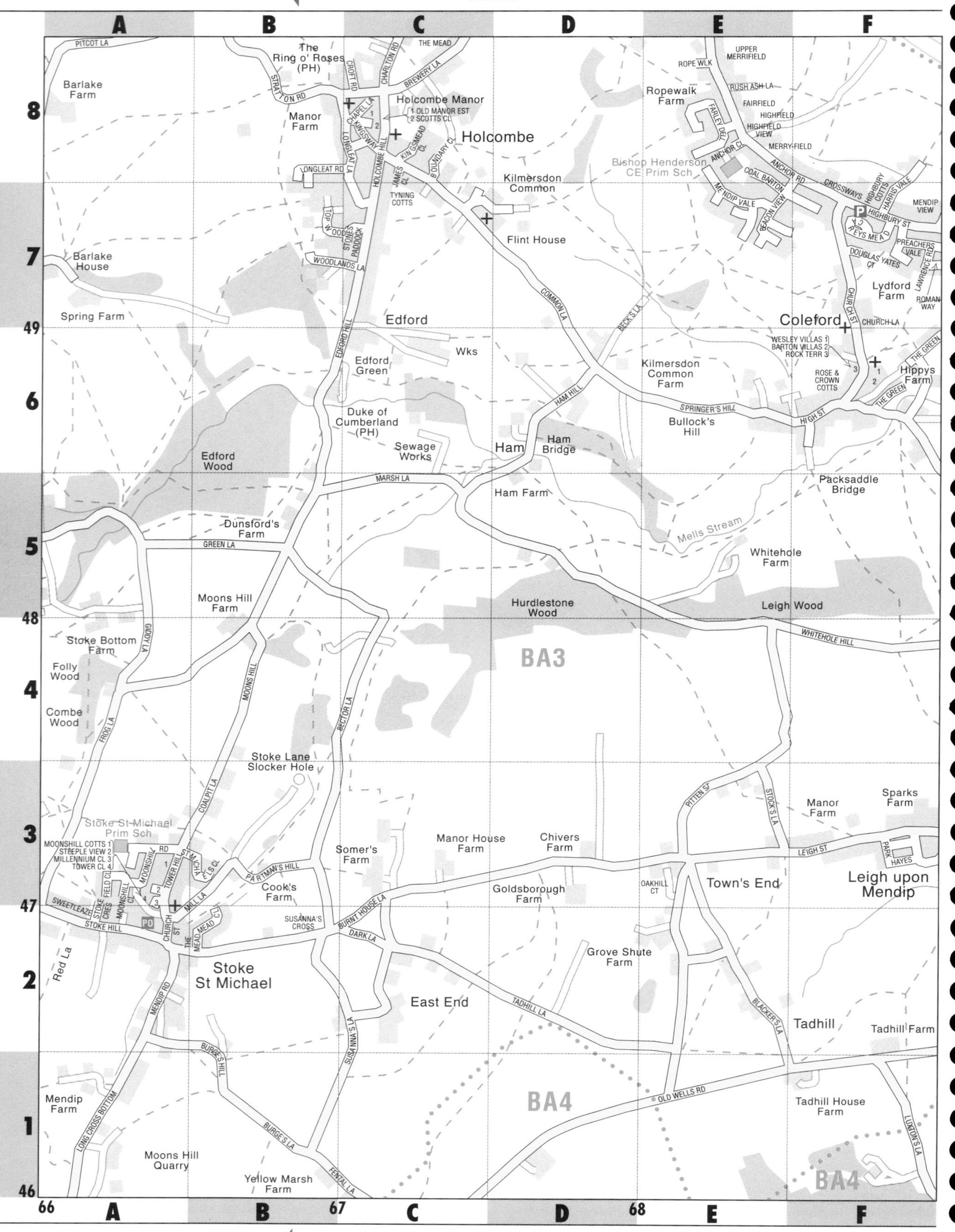

A B C D E F
8 7 49 6 5 48 4 3 47 2 1 46
66 67 68
Barlake Farm
The Ring o' Roses (PH)
Manor Farm
Holcombe Manor
1 OLD MANOR EST
2 SCOTTS CL
Holcombe
Kilmersdon Common
Flint House
Ropewalk Farm
Bishop Henderson CE Prim Sch
Barlake House
Spring Farm
Edford
Wks
Edford Green
Duke of Cumberland (PH)
Sewage Works
Ham
Ham Bridge
Ham Farm
Edford Wood
Kilmersdon Common Farm
Bullock's Hill
Coleford
Lydford Farm
Hippys Farm
Packsaddle Bridge
Mells Stream
Whitehole Farm
Leigh Wood
Dunsford's Farm
Moons Hill Farm
Hurdlestone Wood
BA3
Stoke Bottom Farm
Folly Wood
Combe Wood
Stoke Lane Slocker Hole
Stoke St Michael Prim Sch
Manor Farm
Sparks Farm
Somer's Farm
Manor House Farm
Chivers Farm
Cook's Farm
Goldsborough Farm
Town's End
Leigh upon Mendip
Stoke St Michael
Grove Shute Farm
East End
Tadhill
Tadhill Farm
Red La
Mendip Farm
BA4
Tadhill House Farm
Moons Hill Quarry
Yellow Marsh Farm
PITCOT LA
STRATTON RD
CROFT RD
CHARLTON RD
THE MEAD
BREWERY LA
CHAPEL LA
KINGSWAY
LONGLEAT LA
HOLCOMBE HILL
KINGSMEAD CL
BOUNDARY CL
JAMES CL
TYNING COTTS
LONGLEAT RD
TOP WOODS
STONES PADDOCK
WOODLANDS LA
COMMON LA
EDFORD HILL
MARSH LA
GREEN LA
HAM HILL
BECK'S LA
SPRINGER'S HILL
HIGH ST
ROPE WLK
UPPER MERRIFIELD
RUSH ASH LA
FAIRFIELD
HIGHFIELD
HIGHFIELD VIEW
MERRY-FIELD
FARLEY DELL
ANCHOR CL
ANCHOR RD
COAL BARTON
MENDIP VALE
BEACON VIEW
CROSSWAYS
HIGHBURY COTTS
HARRIS VALE
MENDIP VIEW
HIGHBURY ST
REYS MEAD
PREACHERS VALE
DOUGLAS YATES CT
LAWRENCE RD
ROMAN WAY
CHURCH ST
CHURCH LA
WESLEY VILLAS 1
BARTON VILLAS 2
ROCK TERR 3
ROSE & CROWN COTTS
THE GREEN
WHITEHOLE HILL
GIDDY LA
MOONS HILL
FROG LA
BECTOR LA
COALPIT LA
MOONSHILL COTTS 1
STEEPLE VIEW 2
MILLENNIUM CL 3
TOWER CL 4
MOONSHILL RD
TOWER HILL
ST MICHAEL'S CL
FIELD CL
STOKE CRES
SWEETLEAZE
STOKE HILL
CHURCH ST
MILL LA
THE MEAD
MEAD CL
PO
PARTMAN'S HILL
SUSANNA'S CROSS
BURNT HOUSE LA
DARK LA
PITTEN ST
STOCK'S LA
LEIGH ST
PARK
HAYES
OAKHILL CT
TADHILL LA
BLACKER'S LA
MENDIP RD
BURGE'S HILL
SUSANNA'S LA
OLD WELLS RD
LONG CROSS BOTTOM
BURGE'S LA
FENTAL LA
LUXTON'S LA

115
142

98
118

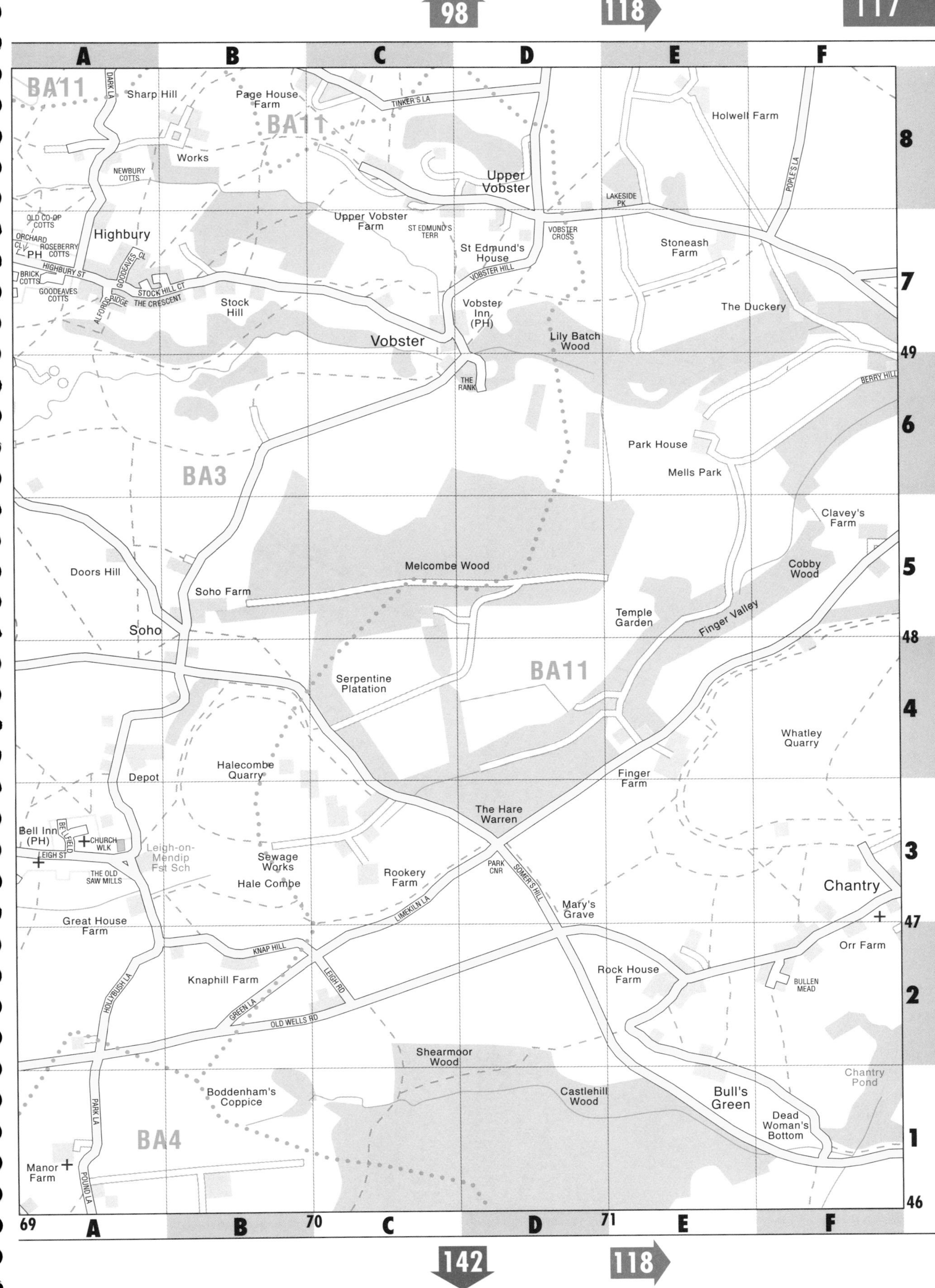
A
B
C
D
E
F
BA11
Sharp Hill
DARK LA
Page House Farm
TINKER'S LA
Holwell Farm
Works
NEWBURY COTTS
Upper Vobster
LAKESIDE PK
POPLE'S LA
OLD CO-OP COTTS
Highbury
ORCHARD CL
PH
ROSEBERRY COTTS
Upper Vobster Farm
ST EDMUND'S TERR
VOBSTER CROSS
Stoneash Farm
St Edmund's House
HIGHBURY ST
BRICK COTTS
GOODEAVES CL
STOCK HILL CT
VOBSTER HILL
GOODEAVES COTTS
ALFORDS RIDGE
THE CRESCENT
Stock Hill
Vobster Inn (PH)
The Duckery
Vobster
Lily Batch Wood
THE RANK
BERRY HILL
Park House
BA3
Mells Park
Clavey's Farm
Cobby Wood
Doors Hill
Melcombe Wood
Soho Farm
Temple Garden
Finger Valley
Soho
Serpentine Platation
Whatley Quarry
Halecombe Quarry
Depot
Finger Farm
The Hare Warren
Bell Inn (PH)
BELLFIELD
CHURCH WLK
LEIGH ST
Leigh-on-Mendip Fst Sch
Sewage Works
THE OLD SAW MILLS
Hale Combe
Rookery Farm
PARK CNR
SOMER'S HILL
Chantry
Mary's Grave
LIMEKILN LA
Great House Farm
Orr Farm
KNAP HILL
Rock House Farm
BULLEN MEAD
LEIGH RD
Knaphill Farm
HOLLYBUSH LA
GREEN LA
OLD WELLS RD
Shearmoor Wood
Chantry Pond
Boddenham's Coppice
Castlehill Wood
Bull's Green
Dead Woman's Bottom
PARK LA
BA4
Manor Farm
POUND LA
8
7
49
6
5
48
4
3
47
2
1
46
69
70
71

142
118

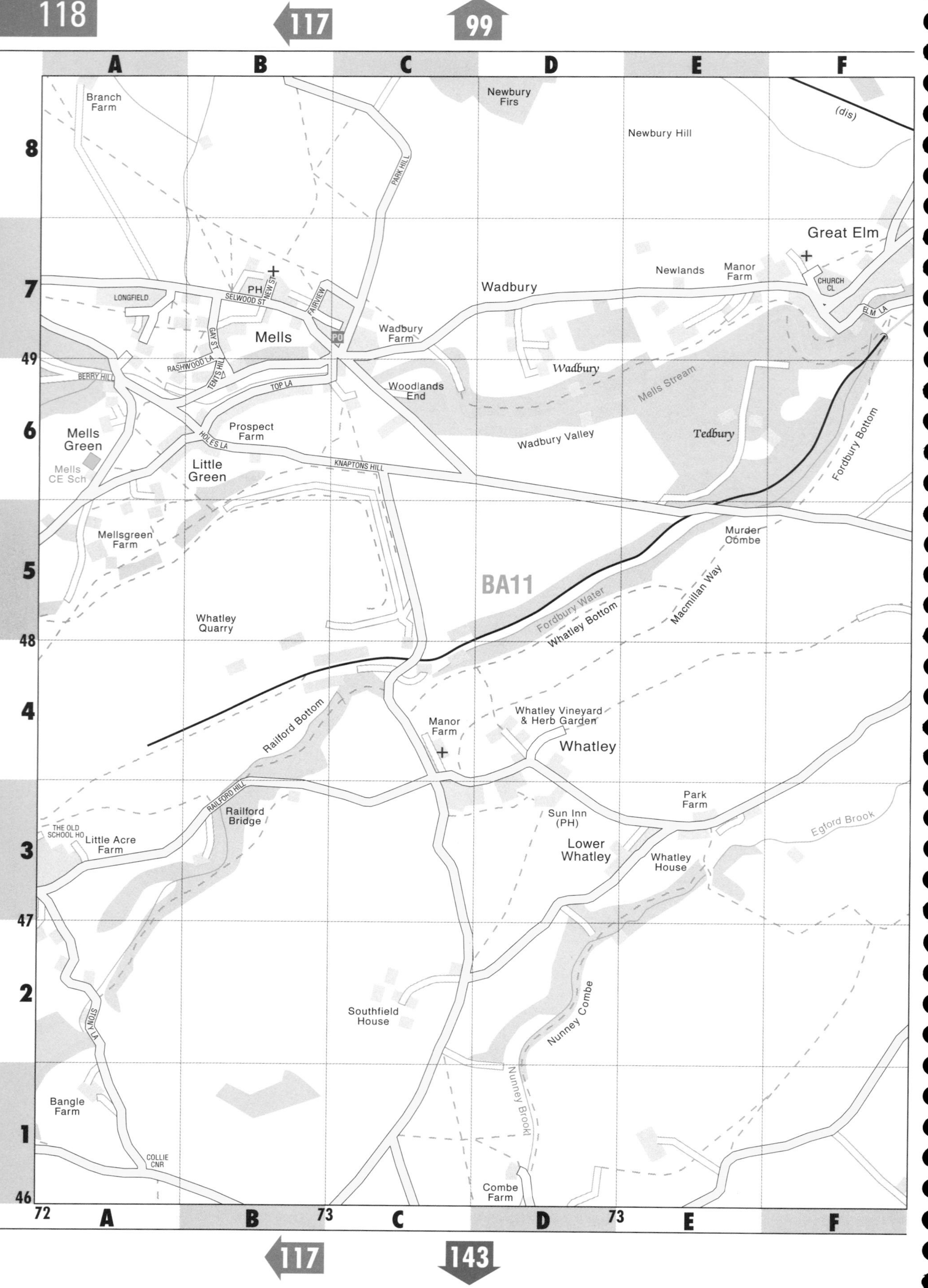

117
99

A　　B　　C　　D　　E　　F

8

Branch Farm

Newbury Firs

Newbury Hill

(dis)

7

Great Elm

Longfield

PH

SELWOOD ST

NEW ST

FAIRVIEW

Mells

Wadbury

Newlands

Manor Farm

CHURCH CL

ELM LA

49

GAY ST

TENTS HILL

RASHWOOD LA

TOP LA

PO

Wadbury Farm

Wadbury

BERRY HILL

HOLES LA

Prospect Farm

Woodlands End

6

Mells Green

Little Green

Wadbury Valley

Tedbury

Fordbury Bottom

Mells Stream

Mells CE Sch

KNAPTONS HILL

5

Mellsgreen Farm

Murder Combe

BA11

Macmillan Way

Whatley Quarry

Fordbury Water

Whatley Bottom

48

4

Railford Bottom

Manor Farm

Whatley Vineyard & Herb Garden

Whatley

RAILFORD HILL

3

THE OLD SCHOOL HO

Little Acre Farm

Railford Bridge

Sun Inn (PH)

Park Farm

Egford Brook

Lower Whatley

Whatley House

47

STONY LA

2

Southfield House

Nunney Combe

1

Bangle Farm

Nunney Brook

COLLIE CNR

46

Combe Farm

117
143

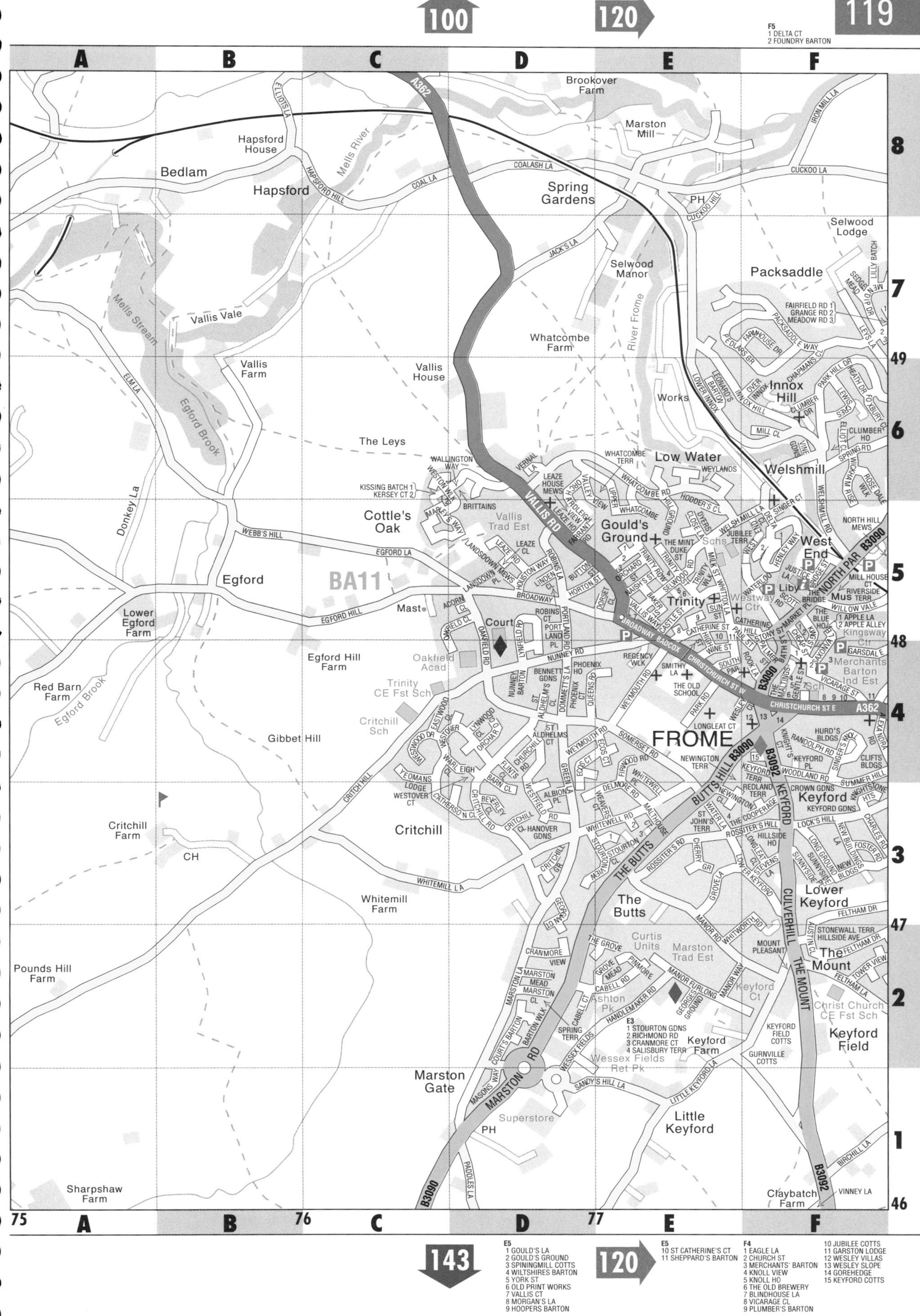
A
B
C
D
E
F
8
7
49
6
5
48
4
3
47
2
1
46
75
76
77
Brookover Farm
Marston Mill
Hapsford House
Bedlam
Hapsford
Mells River
HAPSFORD HILL
COAL LA
COALASH LA
Spring Gardens
CUCKOO LA
CUCKOO HILL
IRON MILL LA
ELLIOTS LA
A362
PH
Selwood Lodge
JACK'S LA
Selwood Manor
Packsaddle
Mells Stream
Vallis Vale
Whatcombe Farm
River Frome
FAIRFIELD RD 1
GRANGE RD 2
MEADOW RD 3
PACKSADDLE WAY
PEDLARS GR
FARMHOUSE DR
CHAPMANS CL
PARK HILL DR
Vallis Farm
Vallis House
ELM LA
Egford Brook
Works
LOWER INNOX
INNOX HILL
Innox Hill
CLUMBER DR
MILL CL
The Leys
WALLINGTON WAY
KISSING BATCH 1
KERSEY CT 2
VERNAL LA
WHATCOMBE TERR
Low Water
WEYLANDS
LEAZE HOUSE MEWS
WHATCOMBE RD
HODDER'S CL
Welshmill
CLUMBER HO
SPRING RD
WICKHAM RISE
ROSE DALE WLK
Donkey La
Cottle's Oak
BRITTAINS
Vallis Trad Est
VALLIS RD
UPPER WHATCOMBE
Gould's Ground
WELSH MILL LA
SINGER'S CT
WELSHMILL RD
NORTH HILL MEWS
WEBB'S HILL
EGFORD LA
LEAZE RD
LEAZE CL
ROBINS LA
BUTTON ST
THE MINT
DUKE ST
JUBILEE TERR
Schs
West End
NORTH PAR
B3090
MILL HOUSE CT
RIVERSIDE
Egford
BA11
LANSDOWN PL
HOUSTON WAY
HORTON ST
ORCHARD ST
TRINITY ROW
SELWOOD RD
MILK ST
WHITTOX LA
Westway Ctr
Liby
Mus
BRIDGE ST
MUS TERR
WILLOW VALE
1 APPLE LA
2 APPLE ALLEY
Kingsway Ctr
Lower Egford Farm
EGFORD HILL
Mast
ACORN CL
BROADWAY
Trinity
Court
OAKFIELD CL
OAKFIELD RD
LINFIELD RD
ROBINS CT
PORTLAND PL
PORTLAND RD
DORSET CL
BROADWAY BADCOX
CATHERINE ST
CATHERINE HILL
GARSDALE
Merchants Barton Ind Est
Egford Hill Farm
Oakfield Acad
NUNNEY RD
PHOENIX HO
REGENCY WLK
SMITHY LA
CHRISTCHURCH ST W
SOUTH PAR
VICARAGE ST
Red Barn Farm
Trinity CE Fst Sch
NUNNEY BARTON
BENNETT GDNS
ST ALDHELM'S CL
DOMMETT'S LA
PHOENIX CT
QUEENS RD
WEYMOUTH RD
THE OLD SCHOOL
PARK RD
CHRISTCHURCH ST E
A362
ALEXANDRA RD
Egford Brook
Critchill Sch
Gibbet Hill
EASTWOOD CL
WESTWOOD DR
WESTOVER CL
LYNWOOD CL
ST ALDHELMS CT
LONGLEAT CT
FROME
HURD'S BLDGS
RANDOLPH RD
KNIGHT'S CT
SINGER'S KNOLL
WARLEIGH CL
CHURCHILL RD
EDGS CT
SOMERSET RD
NEWINGTON TERR
BUTTS HILL
B3092
KEYFORD PL
CLIFTS BLDGS
YEOMANS LODGE
WESTOVER CT
CRITCH HILL
FLINTS BARN CL
GREEN LA
FIRWOOD RD
WHITEWELL PL
KEYFORD TERR
REDLAND TERR
WOODLAND RD
SUMMER HILL
CROWN GDNS
Keyford
KNIGHTSTONE HTS
KEYFORD GDNS
Critchill Farm
CATHERSON CL
BEVERLEY CL
CRITCHILL RD
ALBIONS PL
WESTFIELD RD
DELMORE RD
NEWINGTON CL
THE COOPERAGE
ST JOHN'S TERR
WATER LA
ROSSITER'S HILL
LOCK'S HILL
NEW BUILDINGS LA
CHARLES RD
CH
Critchill
HANOVER GDNS
WHITEWELL RD
MALTHOUSE
STOURTON CL
STOURTON VIEW
ROSSITER'S RD
CHERRY GR
HILLSIDE HO
LONG GROUND
FOSTER RD
WHITEMILL LA
CRITCHILL GR
THE BUTTS
GROVE LA
STEVENS LA
LOWER KEYFORD
SUNNYSIDE PL
Lower Keyford
Whitemill Farm
The Butts
GEORGE CL
MANOR RD
WHITWORTH RD
CULVERHILL
FELTHAM DR
STONEWALL TERR
HILLSIDE AVE
Curtis Units
Marston Trad Est
THE GROVE
MOUNT PLEASANT
The Mount
Pounds Hill Farm
CRANMORE VIEW
MARSTON LA
MARSTON MEAD
MARSTON CL
GROVE MEAD
PINMORE
CABELL RD
MANOR FURLONG
MANOR WAY
TOWER VIEW
FELTHAM LA
Ashton Pk
HANDLEMAKER RD
GEORGES GROUND
Keyford Ct
THE MOUNT
Christ Church CE Fst Sch
COURT'S BARTON
BARTON WLK
SPRING TERR
WESSEX FIELDS
E3
1 STOURTON GDNS
2 RICHMOND RD
3 CRANMORE CT
4 SALISBURY TERR
Keyford Farm
KEYFORD FIELD COTTS
GURNVILLE COTTS
Keyford Field
Wessex Fields Ret Pk
Marston Gate
MASONS WAY
MARSTON RD
SANDY'S HILL LA
LITTLE KEYFORD LA
Little Keyford
Superstore
PH
BIRCHILL LA
PADDLES LA
Sharpshaw Farm
B3090
Claybatch Farm
VINNEY LA
B3092

119
99

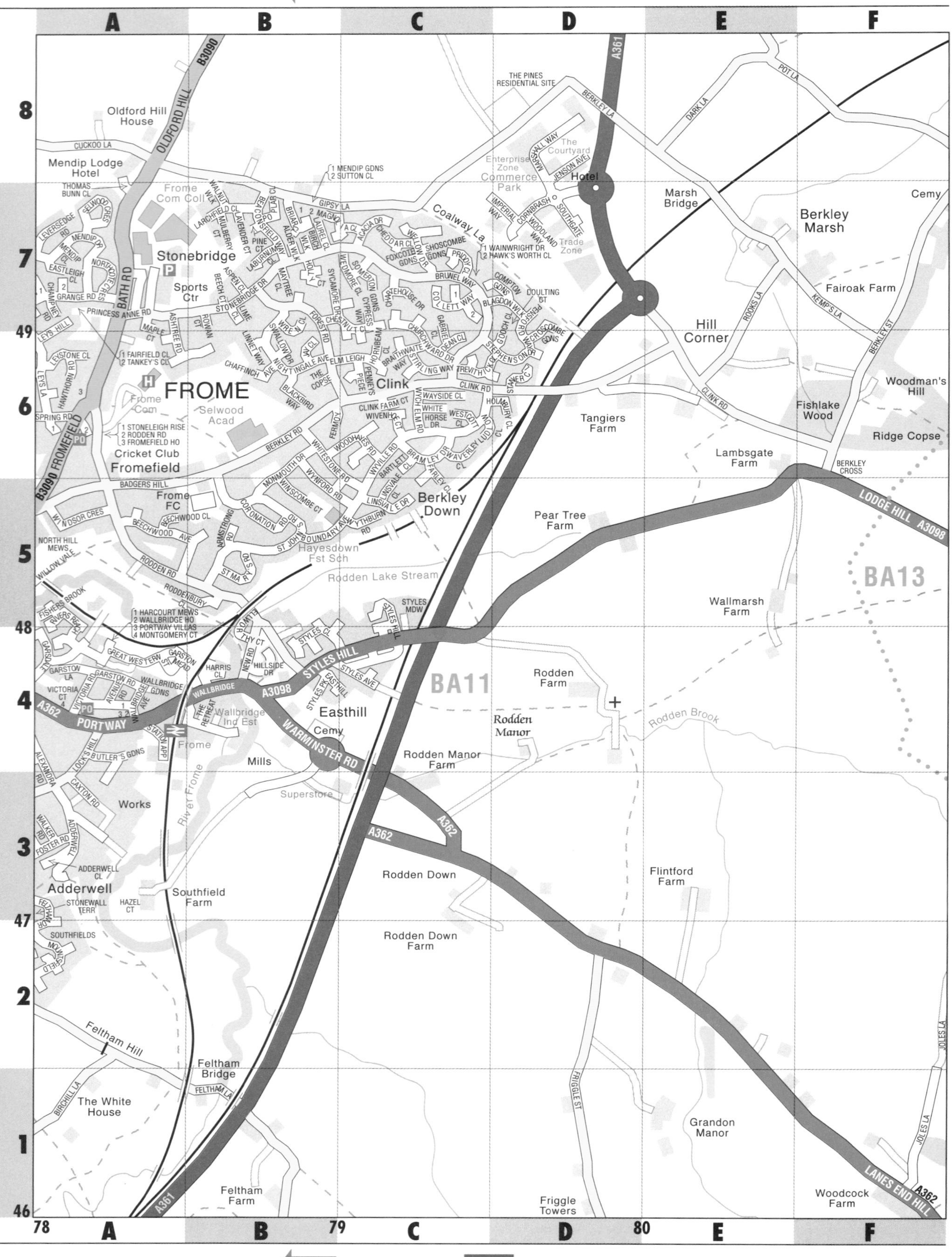
FROME
Oldford Hill House
Mendip Lodge Hotel
Frome Com Coll
Stonebridge
Sports Ctr
Clink
Selwood Acad
Cricket Club
Fromefield
Frome FC
Berkley Down
Hayesdown Fst Sch
Rodden Lake Stream
Enterprise Zone
Commerce Park
The Courtyard
Hotel
Trade Zone
The Pines Residential Site
Marsh Bridge
Berkley Marsh
Cemy
Fairoak Farm
Hill Corner
Woodman's Hill
Fishlake Wood
Ridge Copse
Tangiers Farm
Lambsgate Farm
Berkley Cross
Lodge Hill A3098
Pear Tree Farm
BA13
Wallmarsh Farm
BA11
Rodden Farm
Rodden Manor
Rodden Brook
Easthill
Cemy
Styles Hill
Wallbridge Ind Est
Frome
Mills
Superstore
Works
River Frome
Rodden Manor Farm
Rodden Down
Rodden Down Farm
Flintford Farm
Adderwell
Southfield Farm
Feltham Hill
Feltham Bridge
The White House
Feltham Farm
Friggle Towers
Grandon Manor
Woodcock Farm
Lanes End Hill
A361
A362
A3098
B3090
Oldford Hill
Bath Rd
Portway
Warminster Rd
Coalway La
Berkley La
Dark La
Pot La
Clink Rd
Berkley Rd
Berkley St
Rooks La
Kemp's La
Friggle St
Joles La
Birchill La
Feltham La
Cuckoo La
Gipsy La
A B C D E F
8 7 49 6 5 48 4 3 47 2 1 46
78 79 80

119
144

102

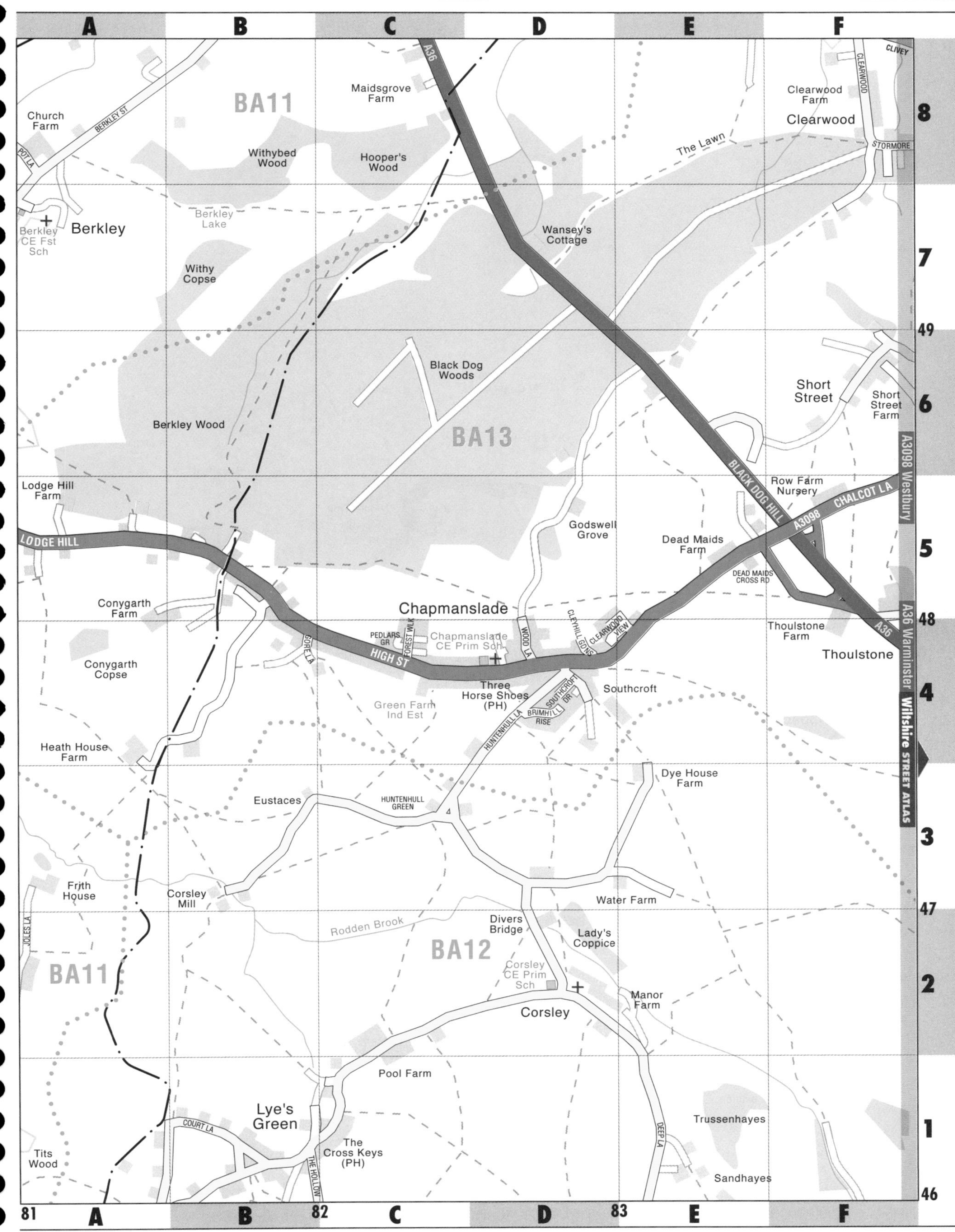

A
B
C
D
E
F
8
7
49
6
5
48
4
3
47
2
1
46
81
82
83
BA11
BA13
BA12
Church Farm
BERKLEY ST
POT LA
Maidsgrove Farm
A36
CLIVEY
CLEARWOOD
Clearwood Farm
Clearwood
Withybed Wood
Hooper's Wood
The Lawn
STORMORE
Berkley Lake
Berkley
Berkley CE Fst Sch
Wansey's Cottage
Withy Copse
Black Dog Woods
Short Street
Short Street Farm
Berkley Wood
A3098 Westbury
BLACK DOG HILL
Lodge Hill Farm
Row Farm Nursery
CHALCOT LA
A3098
LODGE HILL
Godswell Grove
Dead Maids Farm
DEAD MAIDS CROSS RD
Conygarth Farm
Chapmanslade
CLEYHILL GDNS
CLEARWOOD VIEW
WOOD LA
Thoulstone Farm
A36 Warminster
Thoulstone
PEDLARS GR
FOREST WLK
Chapmanslade CE Prim Sch
GORE LA
HIGH ST
Conygarth Copse
Three Horse Shoes (PH)
SOUTHCROFT DR
Southcroft
Green Farm Ind Est
BRIMHILL RISE
HUNTENHULL LA
Wiltshire STREET ATLAS
Heath House Farm
Dye House Farm
Eustaces
HUNTENHULL GREEN
Frith House
Corsley Mill
Water Farm
JOLES LA
Rodden Brook
Divers Bridge
Lady's Coppice
Corsley CE Prim Sch
Manor Farm
Corsley
Pool Farm
Lye's Green
COURT LA
Trussenhayes
DEEP LA
Tits Wood
The Cross Keys (PH)
THE HOLLOW
Sandhayes

141

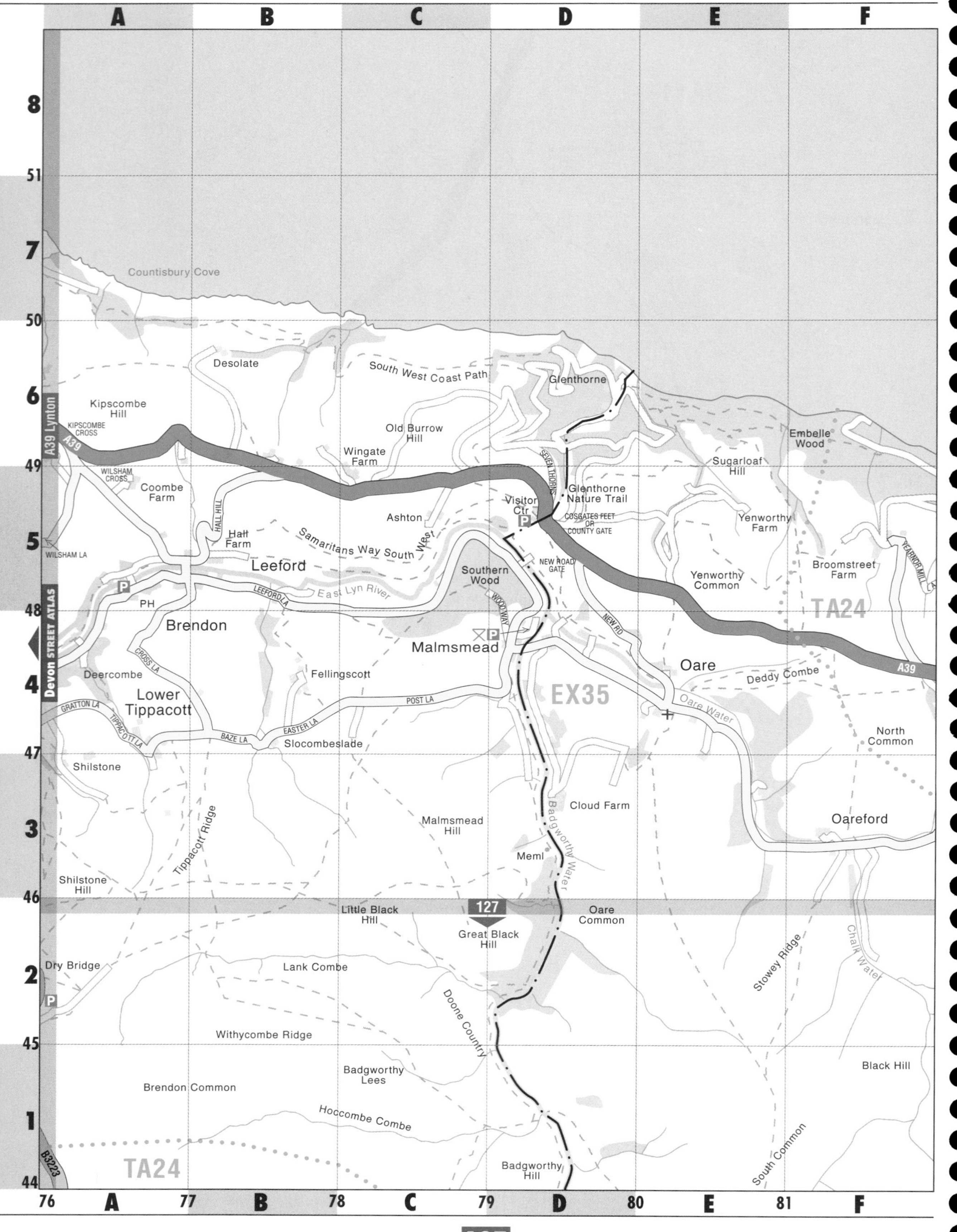

A   B   C   D   E   F

8

51

7

50

6

A39 Lynton   A39

49

5

48

Devon STREET ATLAS

4

47

3

46

2

45

1

44

76 A 77 B 78 C 79 D 80 E 81 F

Countisbury Cove

Desolate

Kipscombe Hill

KIPSCOMBE CROSS

WILSHAM CROSS

Coombe Farm

HALL HILL

WILSHAM LA

Half Farm

Leeford

Samaritans Way South West

Ashton

Old Burrow Hill

Wingate Farm

South West Coast Path

Glenthorne

SEVEN THORNS

Visitor Ctr

Glenthorne Nature Trail

COSGATES FEET OR COUNTY GATE

Embelle Wood

Sugarloaf Hill

Yenworthy Farm

TEARNOR MILL LA

Broomstreet Farm

TA24

A39

Yenworthy Common

Yenworthy Common

Oare

Deddy Combe

North Common

Oareford

East Lyn River

Southern Wood

WOODY WAY

NEW ROAD GATE

NEW RD

Malmsmead

EX35

Oare Water

PH

Brendon

LEEFORD LA

Deercombe

CROSS LA

Lower Tippacott

GRATTON LA

TIPPACOTT LA

BAZE LA

EASTER LA

Fellingscott

POST LA

Slocombeslade

Shilstone

Tippacott Ridge

Malmsmead Hill

Cloud Farm

Badgworthy Water

Meml

Shilstone Hill

Little Black Hill

127

Great Black Hill

Oare Common

Stowey Ridge

Chalk Water

Dry Bridge

Lank Combe

Doone Country

Withycombe Ridge

Badgworthy Lees

Hoccombe Combe

Brendon Common

Black Hill

South Common

B3223

TA24

Badgworthy Hill

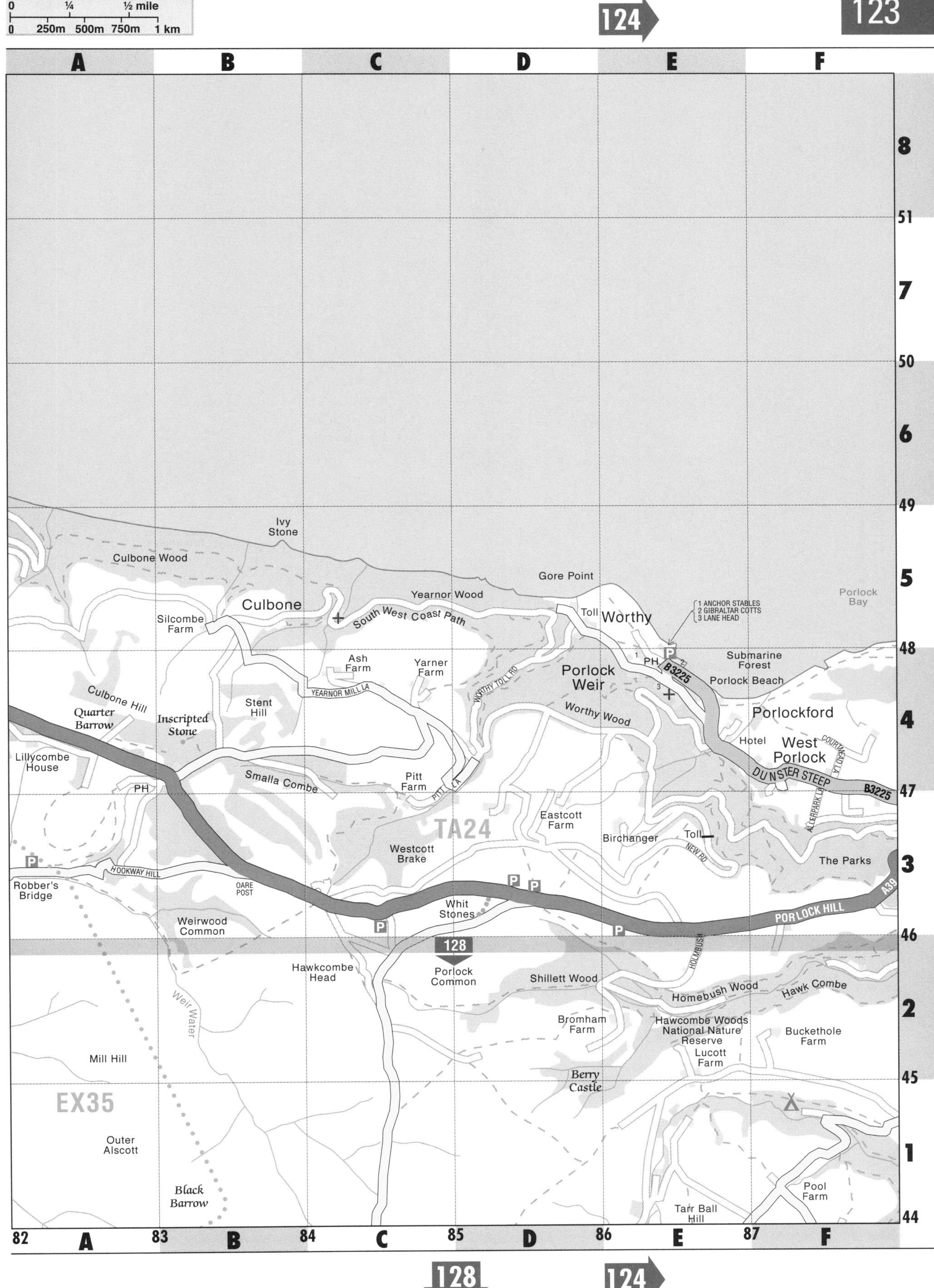

A   B   C   D   E   F

8

51

7

50

6

49

Ivy Stone

Culbone Wood

Yearnor Wood

Gore Point

Porlock Bay

5

Culbone

South West Coast Path

Toll

Worthy

1 ANCHOR STABLES
2 GIBRALTAR COTTS
3 LANE HEAD

48

Silcombe Farm

Ash Farm

Yarner Farm

PH

P

B3225

Submarine Forest

Porlock Beach

Culbone Hill

Stent Hill

YEARNOR MILL LA

WORTHY TOLL RD

Porlock Weir

3

Worthy Wood

Porlockford

4

Quarter Barrow

Inscripted Stone

Hotel

West Porlock

COURTWAY LA

Lillycombe House

Smalla Combe

Pitt Farm

PITT LA

DUNSTER STEEP

B3225

ALLERPARK LA

PH

TA24

Eastcott Farm

Birchanger

Toll

NEW RD

47

Westcott Brake

The Parks

A39

P

Robber's Bridge

HOOKWAY HILL

OARE POST

P P

Whit Stones

P

HOLMBUSH

POR LOCK HILL

3

Weirwood Common

P

128

Porlock Common

46

Hawkcombe Head

Shillett Wood

Homebush Wood

Hawk Combe

2

Weir Water

Bromham Farm

Hawcombe Woods National Nature Reserve

Buckethole Farm

Mill Hill

Berry Castle

Lucott Farm

45

EX35

Outer Alscott

1

Black Barrow

Tarr Ball Hill

Pool Farm

44

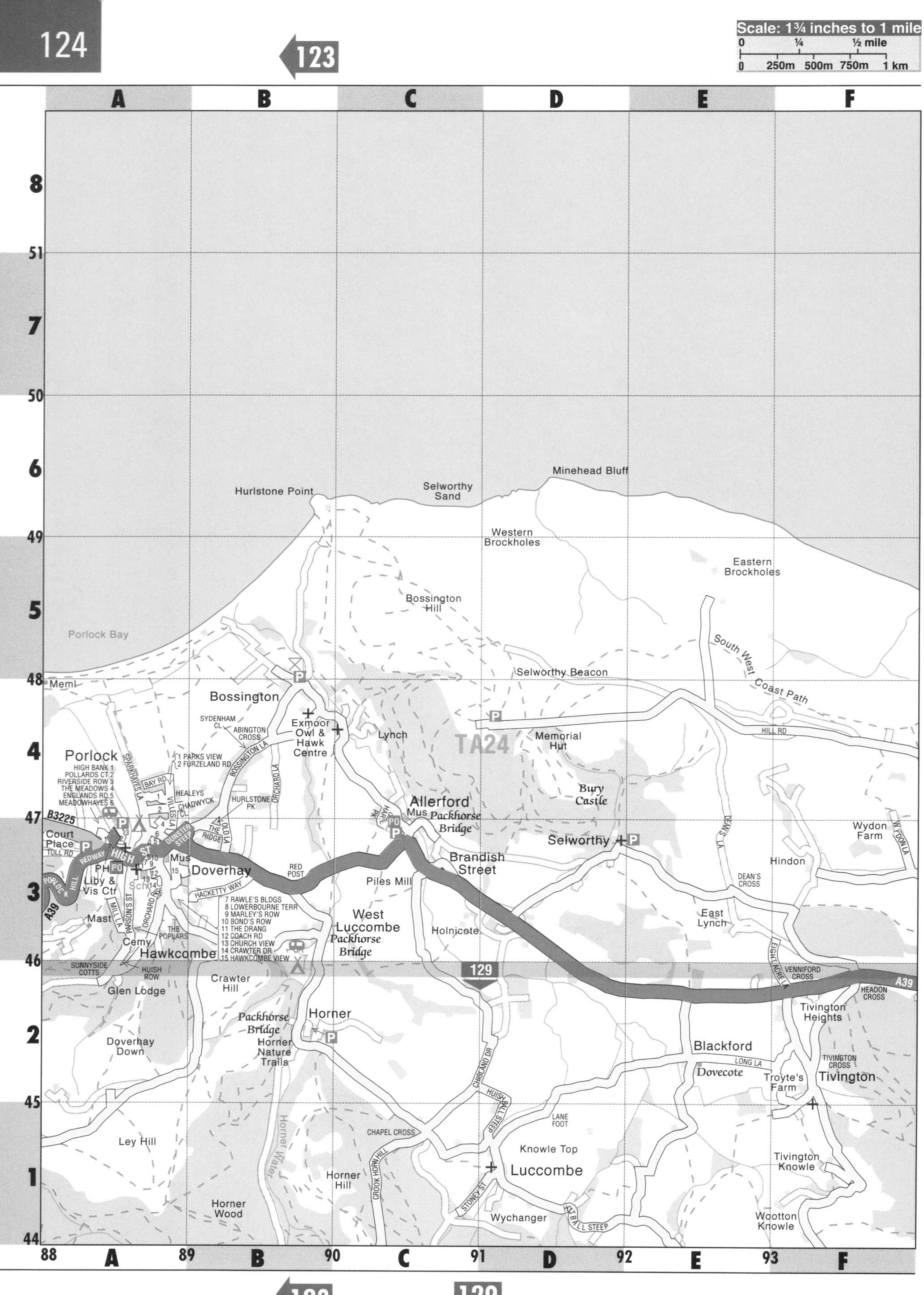

123

Scale: 1¾ inches to 1 mile

0   ¼   ½ mile
0   250m   500m   750m   1 km

A   B   C   D   E   F

8
51
7
50
6
49
5
48
4
47
3
46
2
45
1
44

Hurlstone Point

Selworthy Sand

Minehead Bluff

Western Brockholes

Eastern Brockholes

Bossington Hill

Porlock Bay

Selworthy Beacon

South West Coast Path

Meml

Bossington

SYDENHAM CL

ABINGTON CROSS

Exmoor Owl & Hawk Centre

Lynch

TA24

Memorial Hut

HILL RD

Porlock

HIGH BANK 1
POLLARDS CT 2
RIVERSIDE ROW 3
THE MEADOWS 4
ENGLANDS RD 5
MEADOWHAYES 6

1 PARKS VIEW
2 FURZELAND RD

HEALEYS

CHADWYCK

HURLSTONE PK

SPARKHAYES LA

BAY RD

VILLES LA

BOSSINGTON LA

LA CHURCH LA

Allerford
Mus

Packhorse Bridge

Bury Castle

Wydon Farm

B3225

Court Place
TOLL RD

HILL RD

PORLOCK

A39

Mast

Cemy

Hawkcombe

REDWAY

HIGH ST

PH PO

Liby & Vis Ctr

PARSONS ST

ORCHARD RD

DUNSTER STEEP

THE RIDGEWAY

Mus

Doverhay

HACKETTY WAY

7 RAWLE'S BLDGS
8 LOWERBOURNE TERR
9 MARLEY'S ROW
10 BOND'S ROW
11 THE DRANG
12 COACH RD
13 CHURCH VIEW
14 CRAWTER DR
15 HAWKCOMBE VIEW

THE POPLARS

RED POST

Piles Mill

West Luccombe
Packhorse Bridge

Holnicote

Brandish Street

Selworthy

East Lynch

DEAN'S CROSS

DEAN'S LA

EIGHT ACRE LA

WYDON LA

Hindon

SUNNYSIDE COTTS

HUISH ROW

Glen Lodge

Crawter Hill

Horner

Packhorse Bridge

Horner Nature Trails

129

Venniford Cross

HEADON CROSS

A39

Tivington Heights

Doverhay Down

CHURCHLAND DR

HUISH

WALL STEEP

Blackford

Dovecote

LONG LA

Troyte's Farm

TIVINGTON CROSS

Tivington

Ley Hill

Horner Water

CHAPEL CROSS

CROOK HORN HILL

LANE FOOT

Knowle Top

STONEY ST

Luccombe

Tivington Knowle

Horner Hill

Horner Wood

Wychanger

EAST BALL STEEP

Wootton Knowle

88   A   89   B   90   C   91   D   92   E   93   F

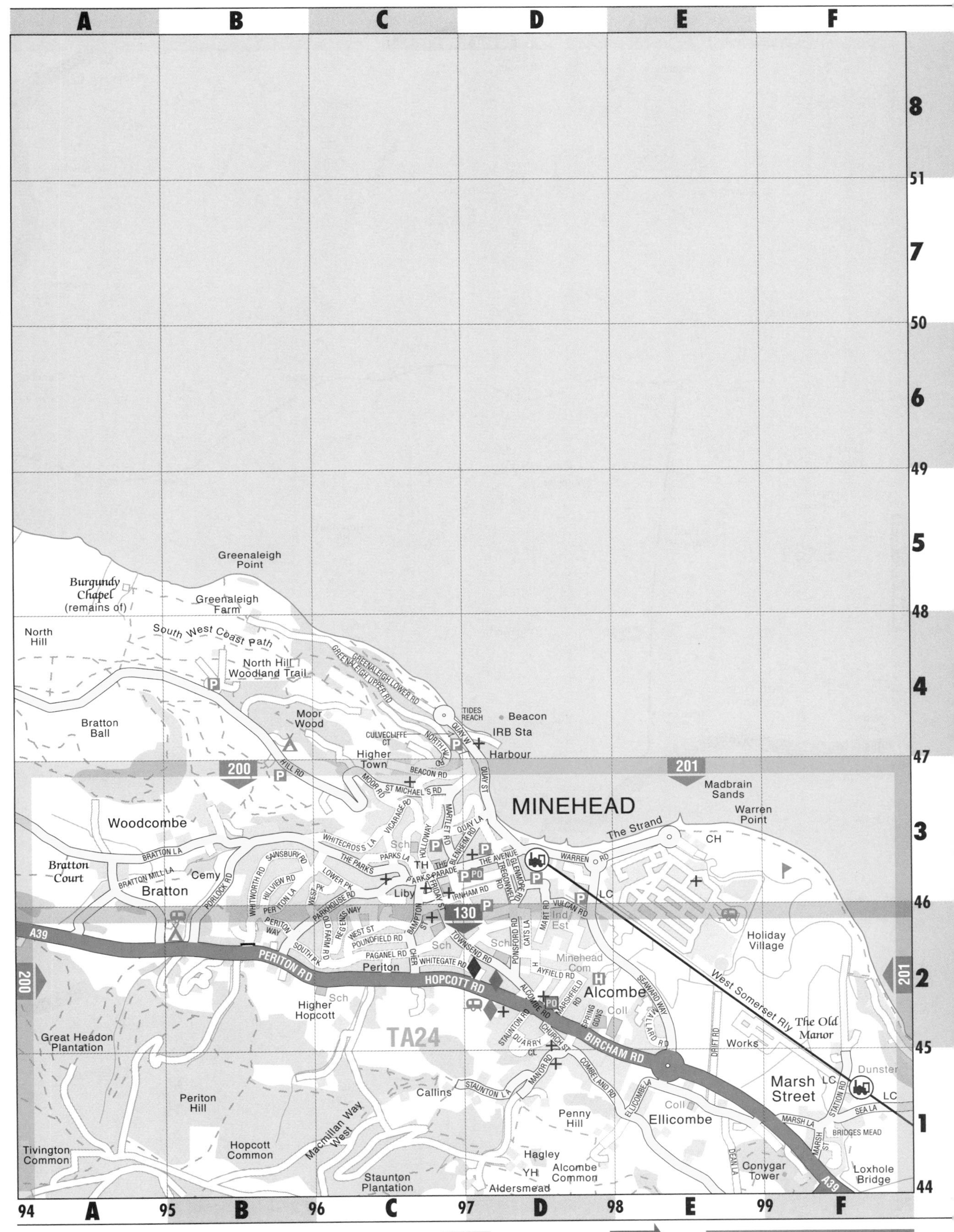

130

131

For full street detail of the highlighted areas see pages 200 and 201.

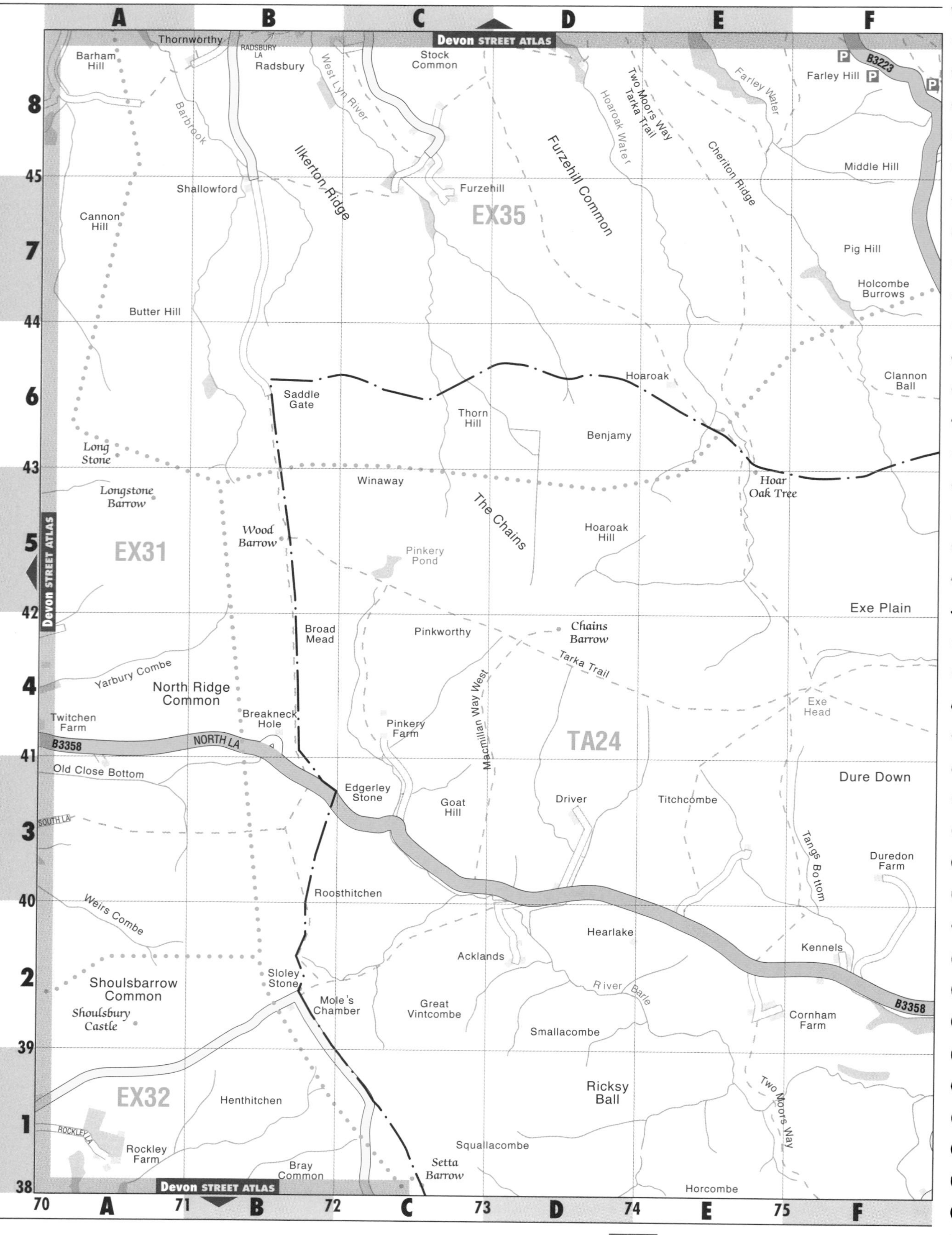

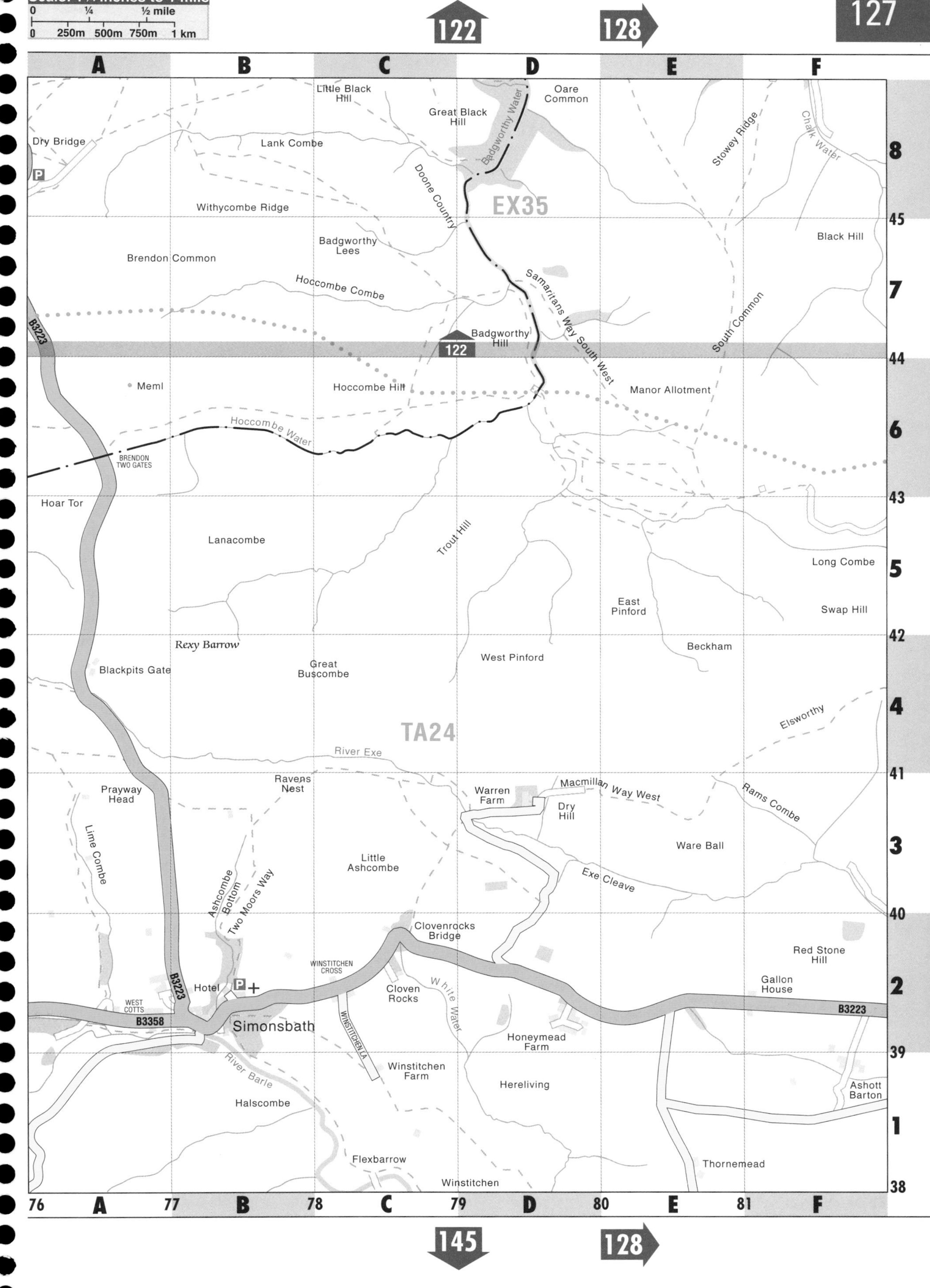
Scale: 1¾ inches to 1 mile
0 ¼ ½ mile
0 250m 500m 750m 1 km
122
128
A B C D E F
Little Black Hill
Great Black Hill
Oare Common
Badgworthy Water
Dry Bridge
Lank Combe
Stowey Ridge
Chalk Water
Doone Country
EX35
Withycombe Ridge
Black Hill
Badgworthy Lees
Brendon Common
Samaritans Way South West
Hoccombe Combe
B3223
South Common
Badgworthy Hill
Meml
Hoccombe Hill
Manor Allotment
Hoccombe Water
BRENDON TWO GATES
Hoar Tor
Lanacombe
Trout Hill
Long Combe
East Pinford
Swap Hill
Rexy Barrow
Beckham
West Pinford
Blackpits Gate
Great Buscombe
Elsworthy
TA24
River Exe
Prayway Head
Ravens Nest
Warren Farm
Macmillan Way West
Rams Combe
Dry Hill
Lime Combe
Ware Ball
Little Ashcombe
Ashcombe Bottom
Two Moors Way
Exe Cleave
Clovenrocks Bridge
Red Stone Hill
WINSTITCHEN CROSS
Gallon House
Hotel
Cloven Rocks
White Water
WEST COTTS
B3358
Simonsbath
Honeymead Farm
WINSTITCHEN LA
River Barle
Winstitchen Farm
Hereliving
Ashott Barton
Halscombe
Thornemead
Flexbarrow
Winstitchen
8 45 7 44 6 43 5 42 4 41 3 40 2 39 1 38
76 77 78 79 80 81
145
128

A   B   C   D   E   F

8

45

7

44   123

6

43

5

42

4

41

3

40

2

39

1

38

82   A   83   B   84   C   85   D   86   E   87   F

Weir Water

Mill Hill

EX35

Outer Alscott

Black Barrow

Meads

Madacombe

Larkbarrow (ruin)

Hawkcombe Head

Porlock Common

Shillett Wood

Homebush Wood

Hawk Combe

Bromham Farm

Hawcombe Woods National Nature Reserve

Berry Castle

Lucott Farm

Buckethole Farm

Tarr Ball Hill

Pool Farm

Wilmersham

Stoke Pero

Lucott Moor

Babe Hill

Nutscale Water

Nutscale Reservoir

Lucott Cross

Chetsford Water

Stoke Ridge

Lang Combe

Stoke Pero Common

Alderman's Barrow

Wilmersham Common

Almsworthy Common

Wellshead Allotment

TA24

Ember Combe

Rowbarrows

Greenlands

Macmillan Way West

Greenland Water

Allcombe Water

Exford Common

Hoar Moor

Codsend Moors

WELLSHEAD LA

Pitsworthy Farm

HILLHEAD CROSS

River Quarme

Hill Farm

Westermill Farm

Wellshead Farm

THE TUNNEL

BONNY LA

Riscombe

Downscombe

MILL LA

Samaritans Way South West

Kitnor Heath

Sharcott

Langdon's Way

B3224

Higher Riscombe Farm

B3223

River Exe

MUDDICOMBE CROSS

MUDDICOMBE LA

YEALSCOMBE LA

WHITE CROSS

Coombe Farm

STONE LA

Stone Cross

Larcombe Farm

Edgcott

Stone

WESTCOTT MEAD

Stetfold Rocks

B3224

Pennycombe Water

Newland

NEWLAND CROSS

Higher Thorne

North & South Ley

EDGCOTT RD

Kennels

TUDBALLS

CHAPEL STREET

Hotel

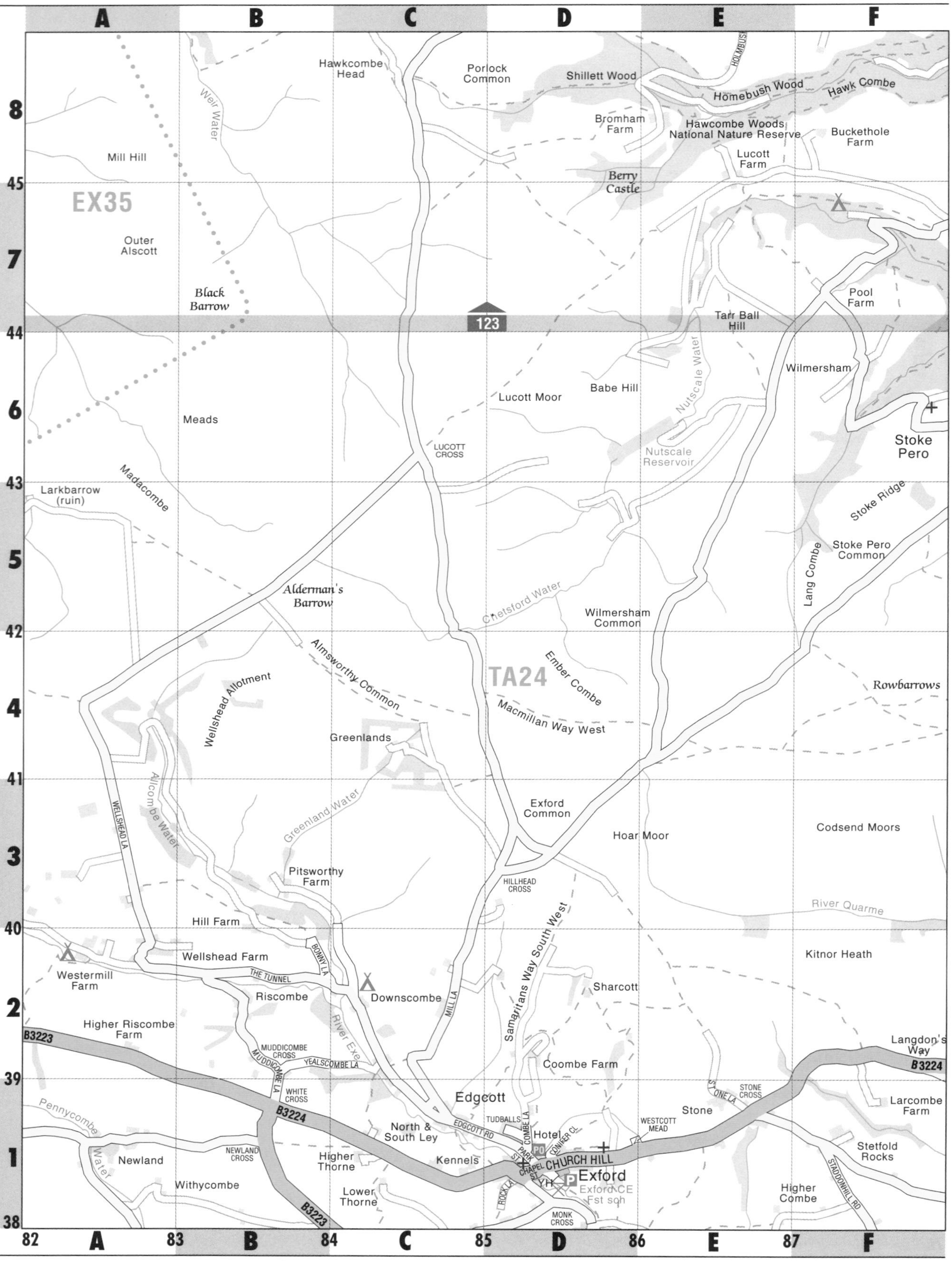

POUND LA

COMBE LA

CORNER CL

CHURCH HILL

Exford

ExfordCE Fst sch

Higher Combe

STADDONHILL RD

Withycombe

Lower Thorne

MONK CROSS

ROCK LA

YH

P

B3223

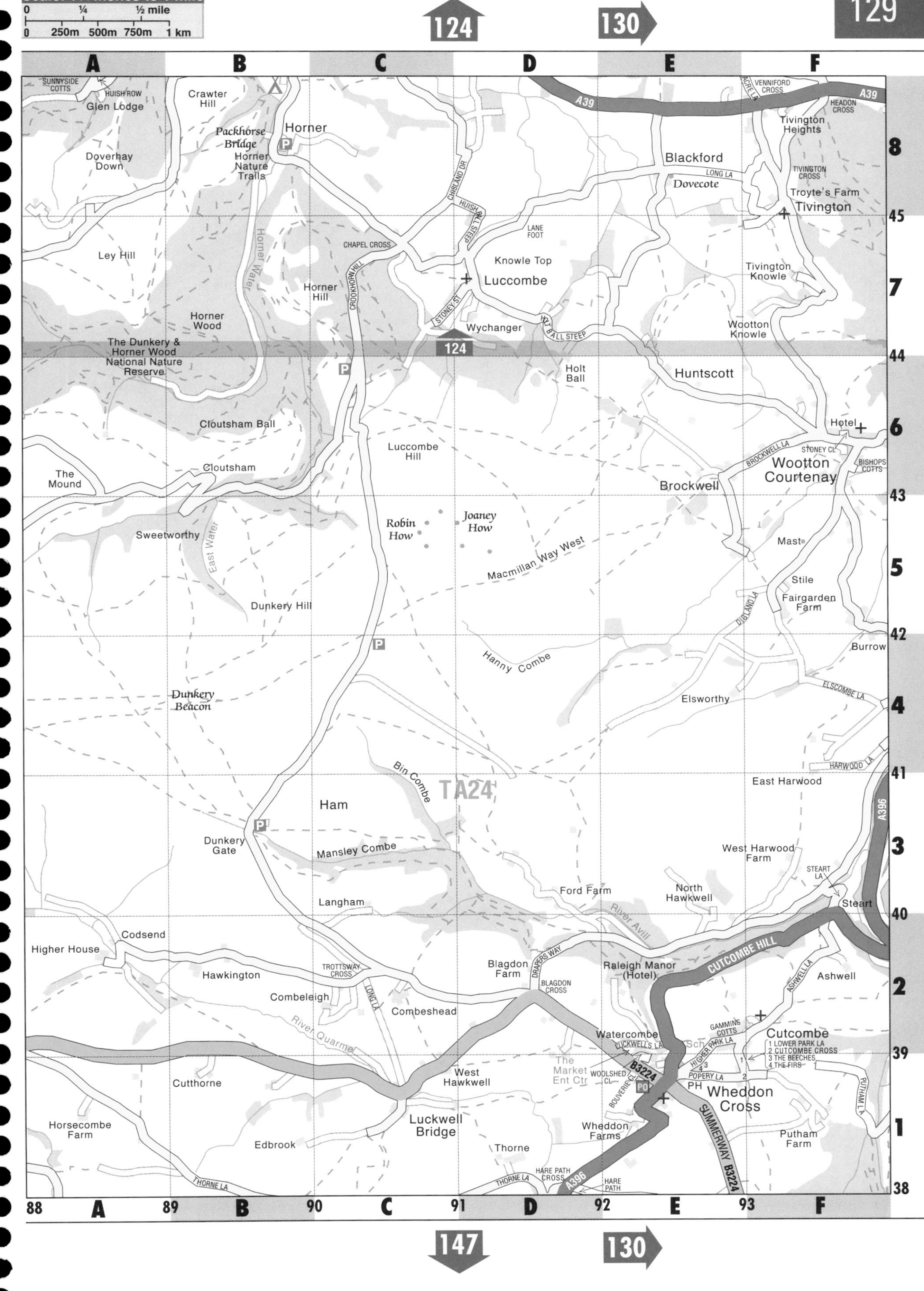
Scale: 1¾ inches to 1 mile
0 ¼ ½ mile
0 250m 500m 750m 1 km
124
130
A B C D E F
Sunnyside Cotts
Huish Row
Glen Lodge
Crawter Hill
Packhorse Bridge
Horner
Horner Nature Trails
Doverhay Down
Blackford
Dovecote
Long La
Venniford Cross
Headon Cross
A39
Tivington Heights
Tivington Cross
Troyte's Farm
Tivington
Chisland Dr
Huish Ball Steep
Lane Foot
Chapel Cross
Ley Hill
Horner Water
Knowle Top
Luccombe
Horner Hill
Crookhorn Hill
Tivington Knowle
Stoney St
Wychanger
Holt Ball Steep
Wootton Knowle
Horner Wood
The Dunkery & Horner Wood National Nature Reserve
Holt Ball
Huntscott
Cloutsham Ball
Luccombe Hill
Hotel
Brockwell La
Stoney Cl
Wootton Courtenay
Bishops Cotts
The Mound
Cloutsham
Brockwell
Robin How
Joaney How
Sweetworthy
East Water
Macmillan Way West
Mast
Stile
Fairgarden Farm
Dunkery Hill
Dibland La
Hanny Combe
Burrow
Elscombe La
Elsworthy
Dunkery Beacon
Harwood La
Bin Combe
TA24
East Harwood
Ham
A396
Dunkery Gate
Mansley Combe
West Harwood Farm
Steart La
Ford Farm
North Hawkwell
Langham
River Avill
Steart
Codsend
Higher House
Cutcombe Hill
Blagdon Farm
Drapers Way
Raleigh Manor (Hotel)
Ashwell
Trottsway Cross
Hawkington
Blagdon Cross
Ashwell La
Long La
Combeleigh
Combeshead
River Quarme
Watercombe
Lackwells La
Sch
Gammins Cotts
Higher Park La
Cutcombe
1 Lower Park La
2 Cutcombe Cross
3 The Beeches
4 The Firs
The Market Ent Ctr
Woolshed Cl
B3224
PO
Popery La
PH
Cutthorne
West Hawkwell
Bouverie Cl
Wheddon Cross
Putham La
Summerway B3224
Horsecombe Farm
Luckwell Bridge
Wheddon Farms
Putham Farm
Edbrook
Thorne
Thorne La
Hare Path Cross
Hare Path
8 45 7 44 6 43 5 42 4 41 3 40 2 39 1 38
88 89 90 91 92 93
147

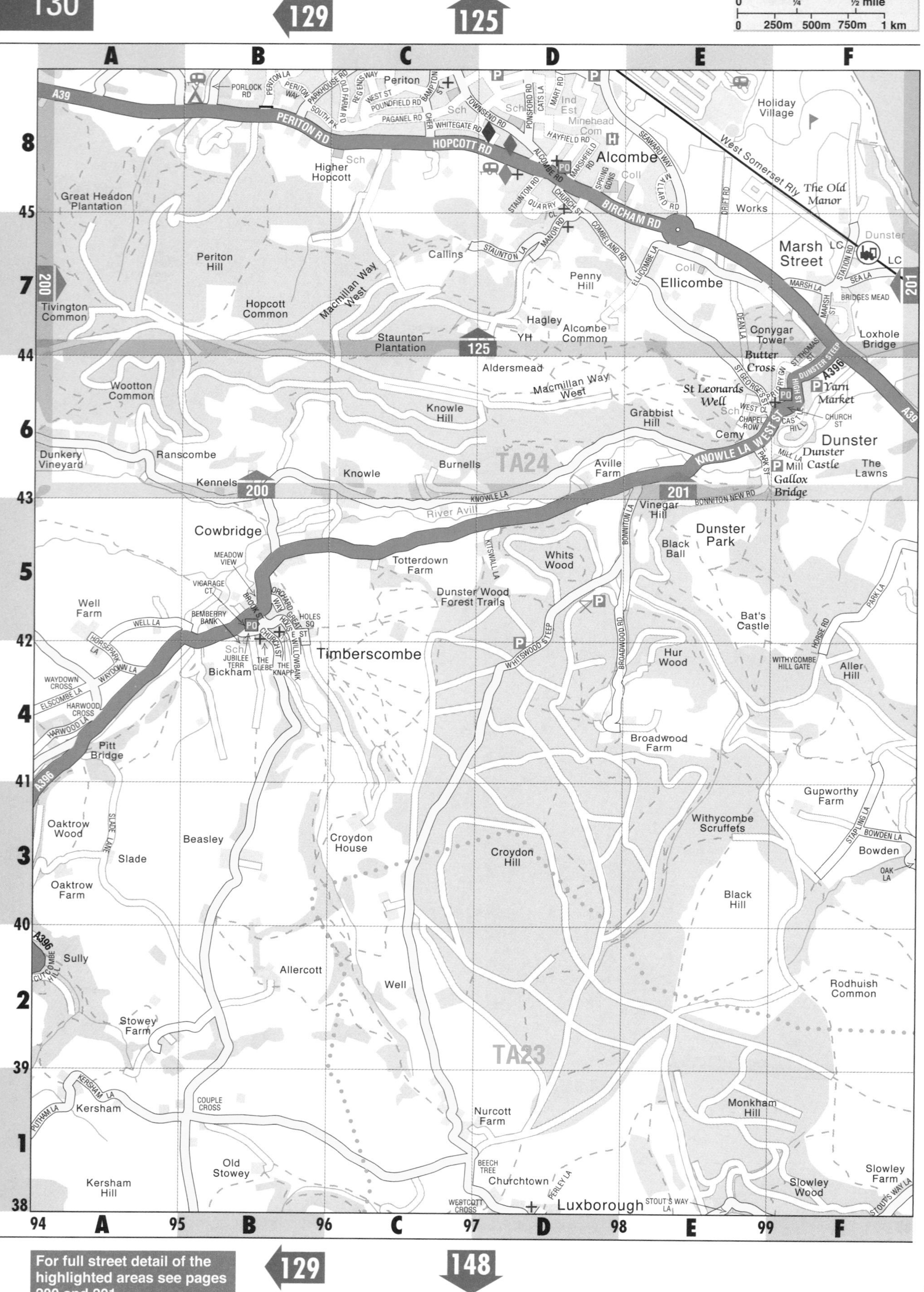

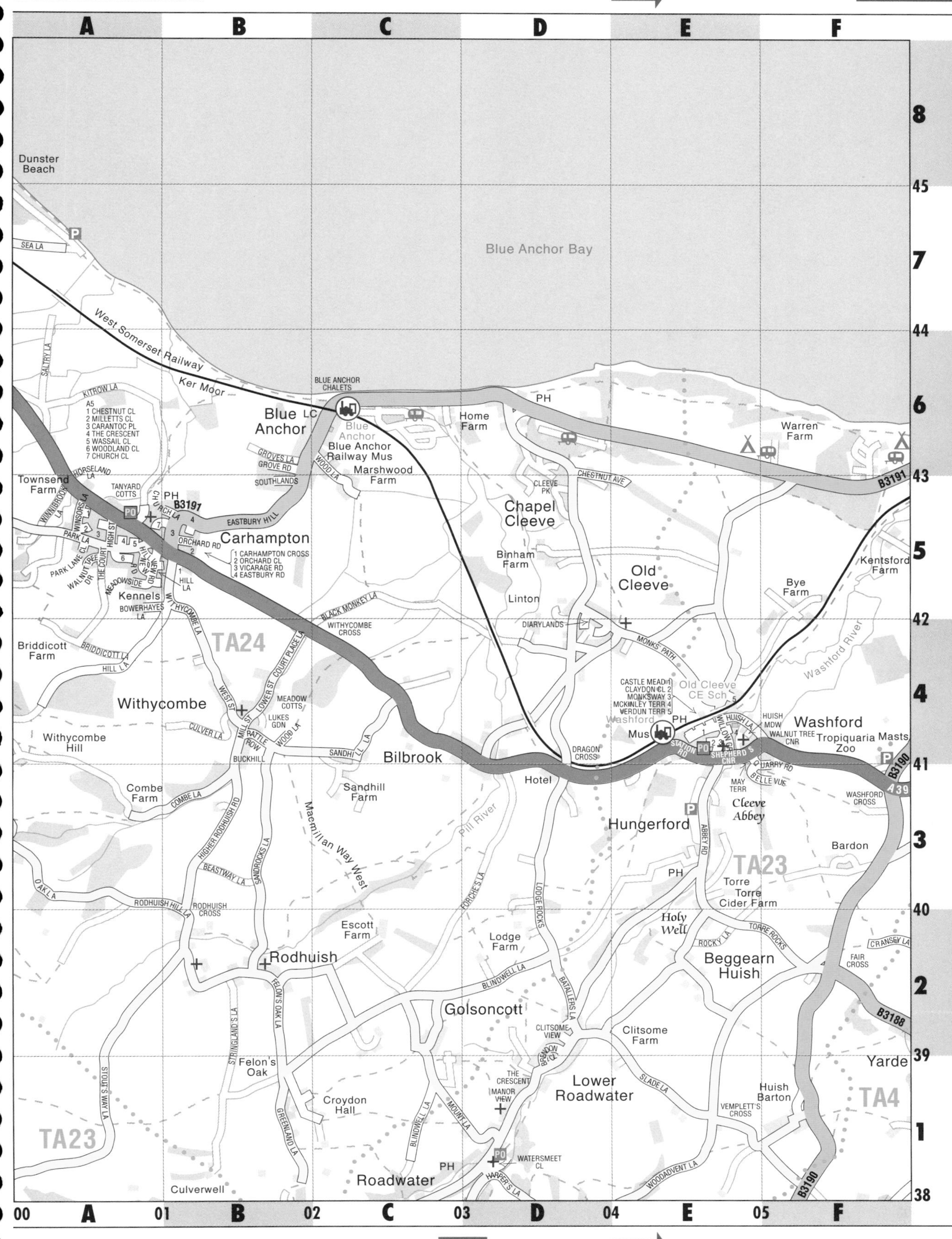

132
149   132

Scale: 1¾ inches to 1 mile
0   ¼   ½   mile
0   250m 500m 750m 1 km

A   B   C   D   E   F

8

45

Dunster
Beach

Blue Anchor Bay

7

44

West Somerset Railway

Ker Moor

6

BLUE ANCHOR
CHALETS

Blue
Anchor   LC

Blue
Anchor
Railway Mus

PH

Home
Farm

Warren
Farm

SALTRY LA

KITROW LA

A5
1 CHESTNUT CL
2 MILLETTS CL
3 CARANTOC PL
4 THE CRESCENT
5 WASSAIL CL
6 WOODLAND CL
7 CHURCH CL

GROVES LA
GROVE RD

SOUTHLANDS

WOOD LA

Marshwood
Farm

CLEEVE
PK

CHESTNUT AVE

B3191   43

Townsend
Farm

HORSELAND LA

TANYARD
COTTS

PH

B3191

PO

ORCHARD RD

Carhampton

1 CARHAMPTON CROSS
2 ORCHARD CL
3 VICARAGE RD
4 EASTBURY RD

EASTBURY HILL

Chapel
Cleeve

Old
Cleeve

Kentsford
Farm

5

WINDSORS LA

PARK LA

WALNUT TREE DR

THE COURT

HIGH ST

HILL WAY RD

MEADOWSIDE

HILL LA

Kennels

BOWERHAYES
LA

WHYCOMBE LA

BLACK MONKEY LA

WITHYCOMBE
CROSS

Binham
Farm

Linton

DIARYLANDS

MONKS PATH

Bye
Farm

42

Briddicott
Farm

BRIDDICOTT LA

HILL LA

TA24

Withycombe

WEST ST

MILL LA

LOWER ST

COURT PLACE LA

MEADOW
COTTS

LUKES
GDN

WOOD LA

SANDHILL LA

CASTLE MEAD 1
CLAYDON CL 2
MONKSWAY 3
MCKINLEY TERR 4
VERDUN TERR 5

Old Cleeve
CE Sch

HUISH
MDW

Washford

4

Withycombe
Hill

CULVER LA

BATTLE
ROW

BUCKHILL

Sandhill
Farm

Bilbrook

Hotel

DRAGON
CROSS

Washford
Mus

PH

STATION
RD

PO

WILTON CL

SHEPHERD'S
CNR

HUISH LA

WALNUT TREE
CNR

Washford

Tropiquaria
Zoo

Masts

P   B3190

41

Combe
Farm

COMBE LA

HIGHER RODHUISH RD

SANDROCKS LA

Macmillan Way West

Pill River

MAY
TERR

BELLE VUE

Cleeve
Abbey

QUARRY RD

WASHFORD
CROSS

A39

3

OAK LA

BEASTWAY LA

RODHUISH HILL LA

RODHUISH
CROSS

P

Hungerford

ABBEY RD

PH

TA23

Torre
Torre
Cider Farm

Bardon

40

FELON'S OAK LA

ST DECUMANS LA

Rodhuish

FORCHE'S LA

LODGE ROCKS

Lodge
Farm

Escott
Farm

BLINDWELL LA

BALKLERS LA

Holy
Well

ROCKY LA

TORRE ROCKS LA

CRANSEY LA

FAIR
CROSS

Beggearn
Huish

B3188

2

STOUT'S WAY LA

Felon's
Oak

GREENLAND LA

BLINDWELL LA

MOUNT LA

Golsoncott

CLITSOME
VIEW

MEADOW
RD

Clitsome
Farm

SLADE LA

Huish
Barton

Yarde

TA4

39

Croydon
Hall

THE
CRESCENT

MANOR
VIEW

Lower
Roadwater

VEMPLETT'S
CROSS

WOODADVENT LA

B3190

1

TA23

Culverwell

Roadwater

PH

HARPER'S LA

PO

WATERSMEET
CL

38

00   A   01   B   02   C   03   D   04   E   05   F

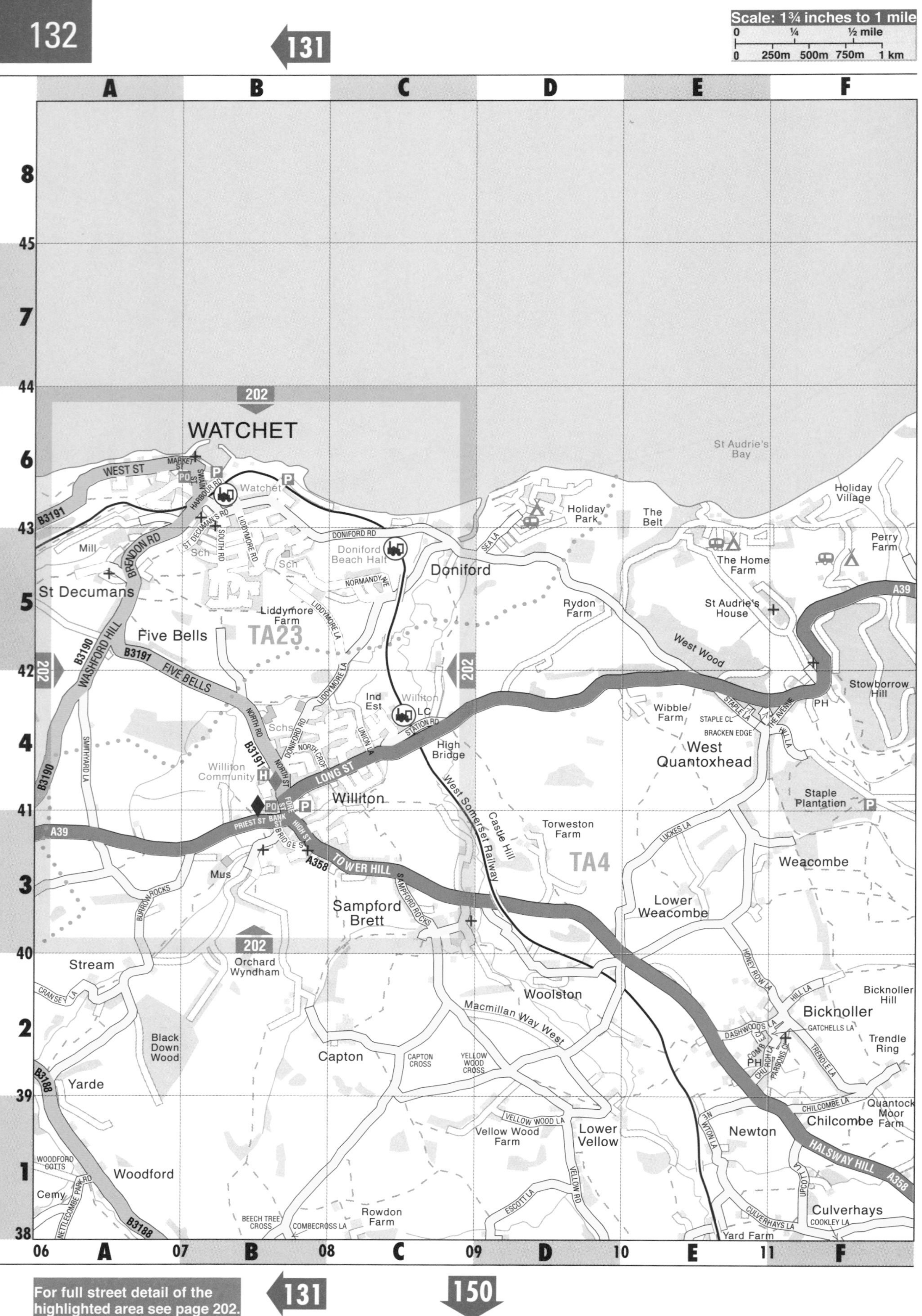

WATCHET

202

WEST ST

PO

P

Watchet

P

MARKET ST

SWAIN ST

HARBOUR RD

ST DECUMAN'S RD

SOUTH RD

LIDDYMORE RD

B3191

Mill

BRENDON RD

Sch

Sch

DONIFORD RD

Doniford Beach Halt

NORMANDY AVE

Doniford

St Decumans

B3190

WASHFORD HILL

B3191

FIVE BELLS

Five Bells

Liddymore Farm

LIDDYMORE LA

TA23

B3190

SMITHYARD LA

202

NORTH RD

B3191

Schs

DONIFORD RD

NORTH CROFT

UNION LA

Ind Est

STATION RD

Williton

LC

High Bridge

St Audrie's Bay

Holiday Park

SEA LA

The Belt

The Home Farm

Rydon Farm

St Audrie's House

West Wood

Holiday Village

Perry Farm

A39

Stowborrow Hill

PH

Wibble Farm

STAPLE LA

STAPLE CL

BRACKEN EDGE

THE AVENUE

HILL LA

West Quantoxhead

Staple Plantation

P

Williton Community

H

PO

P

LONG ST

Williton

West Somerset Railway

Castle Hill

Torweston Farm

TA4

LUCKES LA

Weacombe

A39

PRIEST ST

BANK ST

BRIDGE ST

HIGH ST

Mus

A358

TOWER HILL

SAMPFORD ROCKS

BURROW ROCKS

Sampford Brett

Lower Weacombe

HONEY ROW LA

202

Stream

Orchard Wyndham

Woolston

Macmillan Way West

Bicknoller Hill

HILL LA

DASHWOODS LA

Bicknoller

GATCHELLS LA

Trendle Ring

CRAN SEY LA

Black Down Wood

Capton

CAPTON CROSS

YELLOW WOOD CROSS

CHURCH LA

COMBE LA

PARSONS LA

TRENDLE LA

PH

CHILCOMBE LA

Quantock Moor Farm

Yarde

B3188

39

Woodford

WOODFORD COTTS

NETTLECOMBE PARK RD

Cemy

Vellow Wood Farm

ESCOTT LA

VELLOW RD

Lower Vellow

NEWTON LA

Newton

Chilcombe

HALSWAY HILL

A358

PT LOGAN

CULVERHAYS LA

COOKLEY LA

Culverhays

B3188

BEECH TREE CROSS

COMBECROSS LA

Rowdon Farm

Yard Farm

06   A   07   B   08   C   09   D   10   E   11   F

For full street detail of the highlighted area see page 202.

131

150

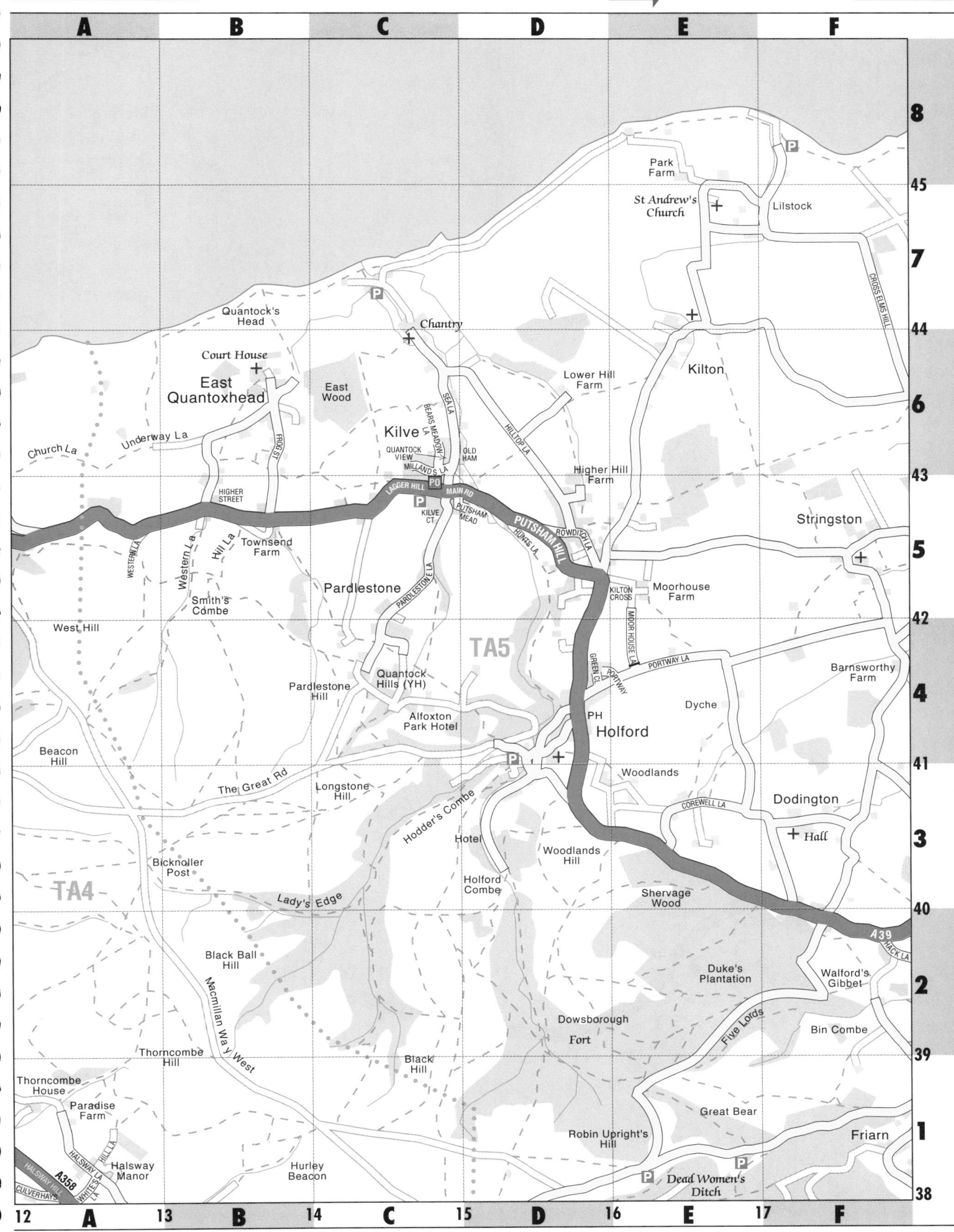

Scale: 1¾ inches to 1 mile

0   ¼   ½   mile
0   250m   500m   750m   1 km

134

A   B   C   D   E   F

8
45
7
44
6
43
5
42
4
41
3
40
2
39
1
38

Park Farm

St Andrew's Church

Lilstock

CROSS ELMS HILL

Kilton

Quantock's Head

Chantry

Lower Hill Farm

Court House

East Quantoxhead

East Wood

Kilve

SEA LA

BEARS MEADOW LA

OLD HAM

QUANTOCK VIEW

MILLANDS LA

HILLTOP LA

Higher Hill Farm

Stringston

Church La

Underway La

FROG ST

HIGHER STREET

LAGGER HILL

PO

MAIN RD

PUTSHAM MEAD

PUTSHAM HILL

ROWDITCH LA

KILVE CT

HONES LA

WESTERN LA

Western La

Hill La

Townsend Farm

Smith's Combe

Pardlestone

PARDLESTONE LA

KILTON CROSS

Moorhouse Farm

West Hill

MOORHOUSE LA

PORTWAY LA

Barnsworthy Farm

TA5

Pardlestone Hill

Quantock Hills (YH)

GREEN CL

PORTWAY

Dyche

Alfoxton Park Hotel

PH

Holford

Beacon Hill

The Great Rd

Longstone Hill

Hodder's Combe

Woodlands

CORWELL LA

Dodington

Hall

Bicknoller Post

Hotel

Woodlands Hill

Shervage Wood

A39

JACK LA

TA4

Lady's Edge

Holford Combe

Black Ball Hill

Macmillan Way West

Black Hill

Dowsborough Fort

Duke's Plantation

Walford's Gibbet

Five Lords

Bin Combe

Thorncombe Hill

Thorncombe House

Paradise Farm

Great Bear

Robin Upright's Hill

Friarn

HALSWAY LA

HILL LA

WHITES LA

A358

CULVER HAYS

HALSWAY HILL

Halsway Manor

Hurley Beacon

Dead Women's Ditch

12   A   13   B   14   C   15   D   16   E   17   F

151

134

133

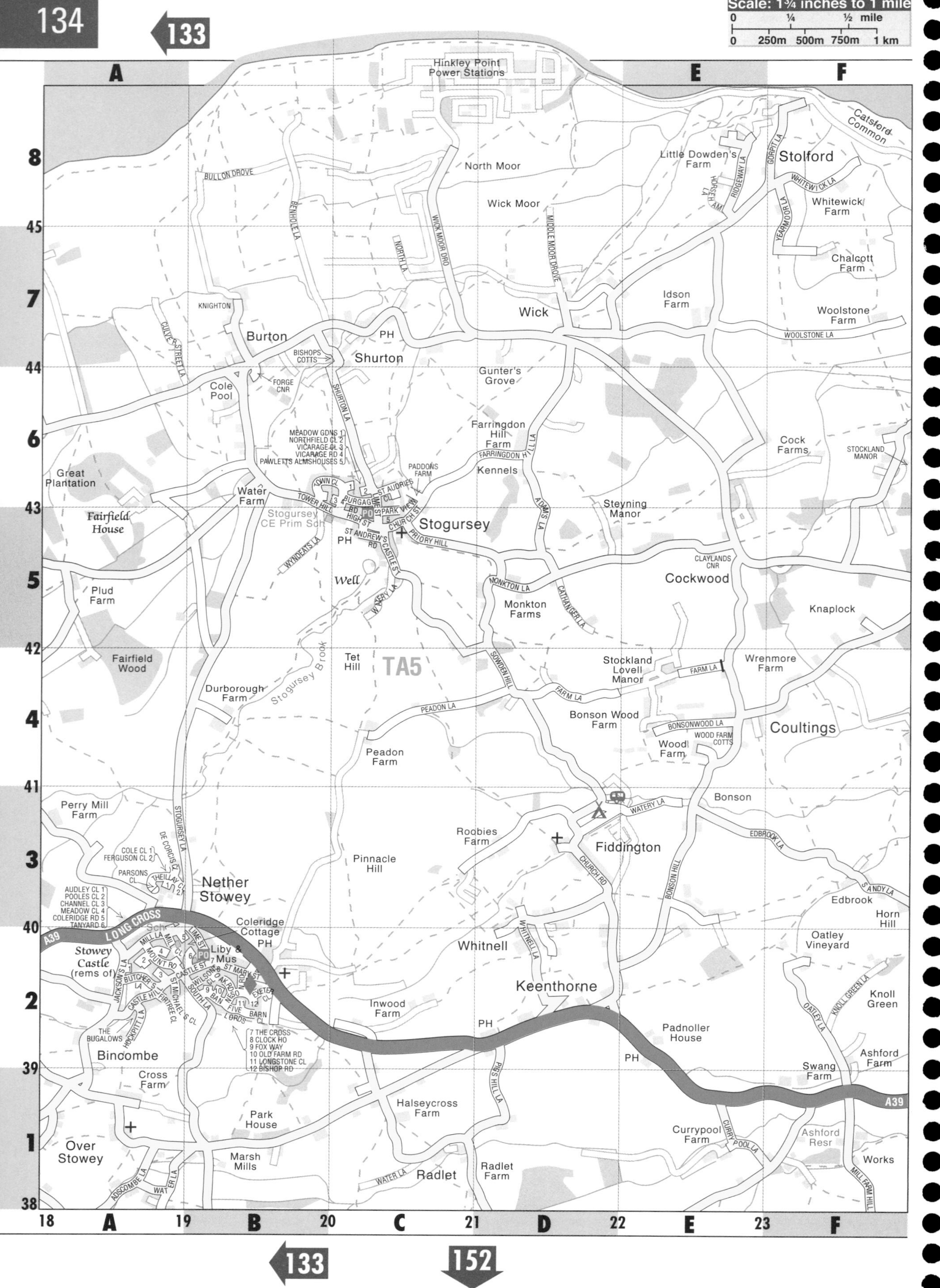
Scale: 1¾ inches to 1 mile
Hinkley Point Power Stations
North Moor
Wick Moor
Little Dowden's Farm
Stolford
Catsford Common
Whitewick Farm
Chalcott Farm
Idson Farm
Woolstone Farm
Wick
Burton
Shurton
Gunter's Grove
Cole Pool
Farringdon Hill Farm
Kennels
Cock Farms
Great Plantation
Water Farm
Fairfield House
Stogursey
Stogursey CE Prim Sch
Steyning Manor
Cockwood
Plud Farm
Monkton Farms
Knaplock
Fairfield Wood
Tet Hill
TA5
Stockland Lovell Manor
Wrenmore Farm
Durborough Farm
Bonson Wood Farm
Coultings
Wood Farm
Peadon Farm
Perry Mill Farm
Bonson
Roobies Farm
Fiddington
Pinnacle Hill
Nether Stowey
Edbrook
Horn Hill
Coleridge Cottage
Whitnell
Oatley Vineyard
Stowey Castle (rems of)
Keenthorne
Knoll Green
Inwood Farm
Padnoller House
Ashford Farm
Bincombe
Swang Farm
Cross Farm
Halseycross Farm
Park House
Currypool Farm
Ashford Resr
Over Stowey
Marsh Mills
Radlet
Radlet Farm
Works
A39
LONG CROSS

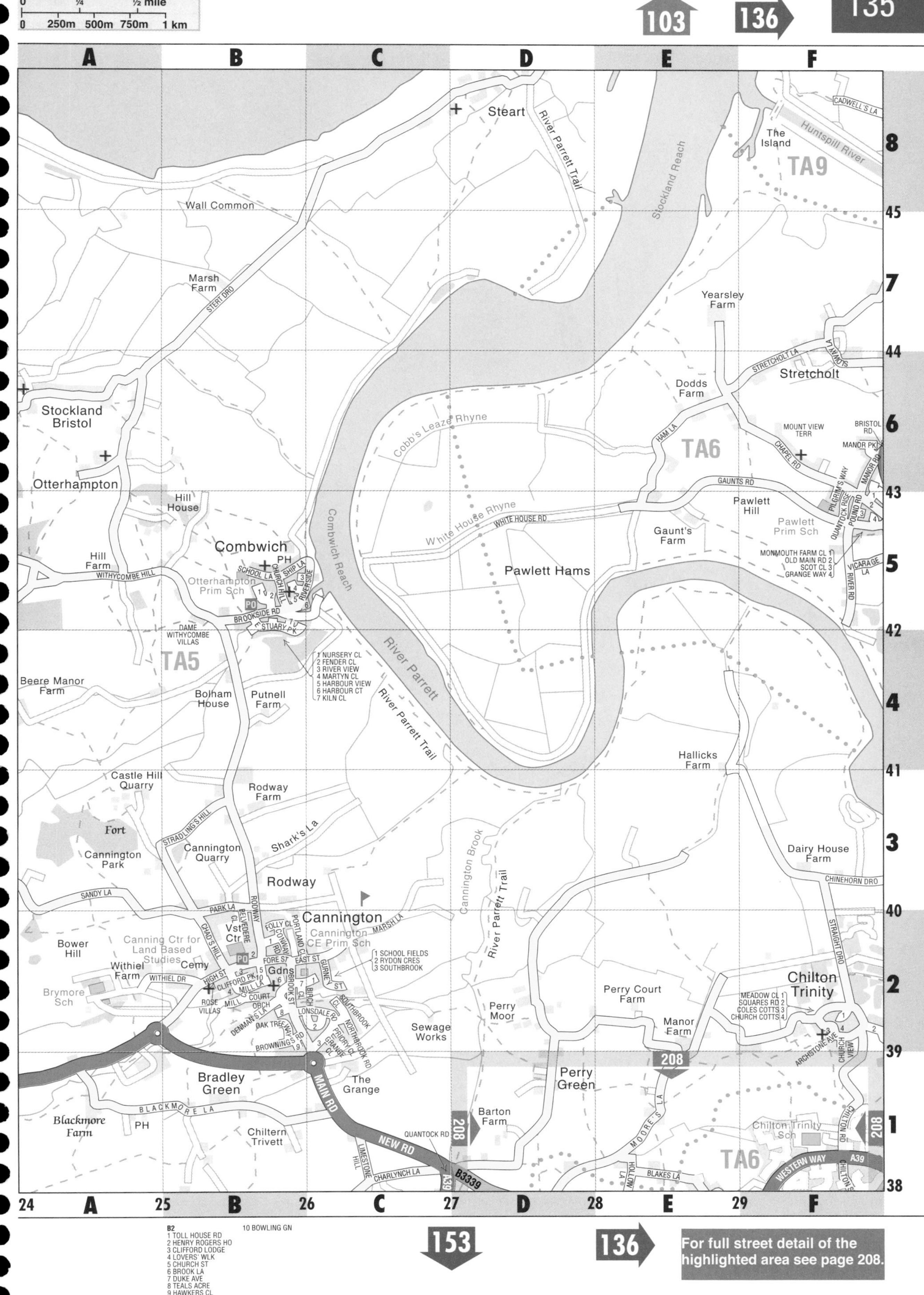

A   B   C   D   E   F

8
45
7
44
6
43
5
42
4
41
3
40
2
39
1
38

Steart

River Parrett Trail

Stockland Reach

Huntspill River

CADWELL'S LA

The Island

TA9

Wall Common

Marsh Farm

STEART DRO

Yearsley Farm

STRETCHOLT LA

SHAKL'Y

Stretcholt

Dodds Farm

Stockland Bristol

Cobb's Leaze Rhyne

HAM LA

TA6

MOUNT VIEW TERR

BRISTOL RD

MANOR PK

CHAPEL RD

Otterhampton

Hill House

White House Rhyne

WHITE HOUSE RD

GAUNTS RD

Pawlett Hill

Pawlett Prim Sch

PILGRIM'S WAY

QUANTOCK SIDE

POUND RD

Hill Farm

WITHYCOMBE HILL

Combwich

PH

SCHOOL LA
CHURCH RD
SHIP LA
PINKETSIDE

Otterhampton Prim Sch

PO

BROOKSIDE RD

Gaunt's Farm

Pawlett Hams

MONMOUTH FARM CL 1
OLD MAIN RD 2
SCOT CL 3
GRANGE WAY 4

VICARAGE LA

RIVER RD

TA5

DAME WITHYCOMBE VILLAS

1 NURSERY CL
2 FENDER CL
3 RIVER VIEW
4 MARTYN CL
5 HARBOUR VIEW
6 HARBOUR CT
7 KILN CL

Combwich Reach

River Parrett

Beere Manor Farm

Bolham House

Putnell Farm

River Parrett Trail

Hallicks Farm

Castle Hill Quarry

Rodway Farm

Fort

STRADLING'S HILL

Cannington Park

Cannington Quarry

Shark's La

Dairy House Farm

CHINEHORN DRO

SANDY LA

Rodway

Cannington Brook

River Parrett Trail

STRAIGHT DRO

PARK LA

RODWAY

Cannington

MARSH LA

Chilton Trinity

Canning Ctr for Land Based Studies

Vst Ctr

BELVEDERE RD

CHAD'S HILL

PO

Cemy

FOLLY CL
COTHAY
PORTLAND CL
FORE ST
EAST ST

Cannington CE Prim Sch

GURNEY ST

1 SCHOOL FIELDS
2 RYDON CRES
3 SOUTHBROOK

Perry Court Farm

MEADOW CL 1
SQUARES RD 2
COLES COTTS 3
CHURCH COTTS 4

Bower Hill

Withiel Farm

WITHIEL DR

HIGH ST

CLIFFORD PK

Gdns

BRIDGE

BRIDG

SOUTHBROOK

NORTHBROOK RD

Perry Moor

Manor Farm

ARCHSTONE AVE

CHURCH VIEW

Brymore Sch

ROSE VILLAS

CLIFFORD RD

MILL LA

COURT ORCH

DENMAN'S LA

OAK TREE WAY

LONSDALE RD

PRIORY RD

GRANGE CL

BROWNING'S RD

Sewage Works

208

Bradley Green

MAIN RD

The Grange

Blackmore Farm

PH

BLACKMORE LA

Chiltern Trivett

NEW RD

LIMESTONE HILL

CHARLYNCH RD

QUANTOCK RD

208

B3339

Barton Farm

Perry Green

MOORE'S LA

MOTLOH

BLAKES LA

Chilton Trinity Sch

TA6

208

WESTERN WAY

CHILTON

A39

24   A   25   B   26   C   27   D   28   E   29   F

B2
1 TOLL HOUSE RD
2 HENRY ROGERS HO
3 CLIFFORD LODGE
4 LOVERS' WLK
5 CHURCH ST
6 BROOK LA
7 DUKE AVE
8 TEALS ACRE
9 HAWKERS CL

10 BOWLING GN

Scale: 1¾ inches to 1 mile
0 ¼ ½ mile
0 250m 500m 750m 1 km

Huntspill

CADWELL'S LA
LABURNUM LODGES
SLOWAY LA
CHURCH RD
RANGE RD
MILL GREEN
SILVER ST
GROVE RD
SEALEY'S CL
SWELL RD
ILEX CL
RINGSTONE
MAIN RD
A38
OLD PAWLETT RD
PAWLETT RD
PURITON RD
A38

1 PLYMOR RD
2 CARAMIA PK
3 CHAPEL FORGE CL
4 SUNNY CL
5 GREENWOOD CL

NEWBRIDGE LA
NEW RD
CATHERINE ST

Secret World Wildlife Rescue

Hackness

East Huntspill Prim Sch
B3141
FACTORY LA
Brue Bsns Pk
HACK MEAD LA
Moor Row
MERRY LA
MEAD RD
ORCHARD CL
CHAPEL LA
COMBE TERR
CHURCH RD

1 NUT TREE CL
2 CHURCH CL

East Huntspill
Cote

Bleak Bridge

West Huntspill

STRAIGHT DRO
RUGG'S DRO
LC
HARDY MEAD DRO
WITHY GR
WITHY RD
WEST CORNMOOR DRO
Withy Grove Farm
CORNMOOR CRES
CORNMOOR DRO

TA9

PH
WHITE HOUSE LA
WILLOW LA
MILL LA
BURTLE RD
COTE CNR
Cornmoor Farm

Withy Farm
Huntspill River
Huntspill River National Nature Reserve

Huntspill Moor
GOLD CORNER DRO

Pawlett
OLD MAIN RD
PO
VICARAGE LA
North Farm
PAWLETT MEAD DRO
PURITON RD
LC
Landfill Site
Black Ditch
CAUSEWAY
PYDE DRO
Middle Moor Dro
MOORMEAD DRO
Middlemoor Water Park
Woolavington Level

PARSONAGE CT 1
PURITON MANOR 2
COURT GR 3
POOL CL 4
ROOKERY CL 5
PUREWELL 6
CULVERHAY CL 7
WALNUT CL 8

BATCH RD
NORTH MEAD DRO
Factory
Puriton Level

Walpole
Motte & Baileys
DOWNEND TERR
BANNOCK DRO
CHURCH FIELD
RYE
BATCH
RIVERTON RD
PO
WATERLOO
WOOLAVINGTON RD
WEST APPROACH RD
EAST APPROACH RD
Puriton
MORTIMER
HECTORS STONES
CAUSEWAY CL
CROCKERS
LOWER RD
CHERSEY
HIGHER RD
LOCKSWELL
CHILPITTS

1 THE DRIVE
2 THE SQUARE
3 CHURCH ST
3 VICARAGE RD

Down End
Dunball Ind Est
DOWN END RD
DOWNEND CRES
PURITON HILL
23
A39
Factory
Dunball
BRISTOL RD
STATION RD
WEBBERS WAY
Puriton Prim Sch

9 HILLSIDE DR
10 HILLSIDE CRES
11 ROWAN CL
12 BIRCH AVE
13 MAPLE CL
14 MANSE LA
15 SPRING RISE
16 ELM LEA CL

ROWLANDS RISE
CYPRESS DR
HILLSIDE DR

Woolavington Village Prim Sch
EDGEBURY
COMBE LA
KIDNER CL
BAWDEN
HIGHCROFT
Woolavington

5 CROSSMEAD
6 CLARK CL
7 BROADLAWN
8 MOUNT VIEW
9 HILLSBORO
10 ORCHARD WAY

TA7

TA6
CHINEH DRY DRO
River Parrett
TA5
Horsey Pill

FIELD WAY
GEMOOR RD
SEDGEMOOR RD
GRANCOMBE LA
TOR VIEW
Gardiners Bsns Pk
WALNUT LA
BROAD ERIP
BRENT RD
PARK CRES
LOCKS WAY
MILLMOOT RD
MIDDLE RD

MARTLAND CL 10
POLDEN WLK 11
WINDMILL CRES 12
BITHAM WLK 13
MILL WLK 14

MAPLE TREE CT 1
THE COPSE 2
MANOR CT 3
ST MARY'S CL

FAIRWAYS CVN PK
B3141
WOOLAVINGTON HILL
Cossington
Cossington Prim Sch
MANOR RD

Horsey Level
Woodlands Court Bsns Pk
KINGS RD
HORSEY LA

1 SEDGEMOUNT IND PK
2 THE WIREWORKS EST
3 KINGS DR
4 CLARENCE TER
5 IMPERIAL WAY
6 WESTMINSTER WAY
7 WHITEHALL DR
8 BALRAVIA DR
9 ROYAL DR
10 LANCASTER CL

Knowle Hall

Crandon Bridge
BATH RD
A39
PH
Little Wall La
NEW RD
CHURCH WLK
GREENFIELD
SOUTH VIEW
St Michaels CT
St Kingsmoor Prim Sch
King's Farm
EAST SIDE LA
Brook La
THISTLEDOO VINE
Knowle
Bawdrip
Bawdrip Level
STONE DRO

The Polden Bsns Ctr
Express Pk
SQUARES RD
MARSH LA
Horsey
209
BRADNEY LA
Peasey Farm

Sewage Works
Crypton Tech Bsns Pk
WYLDS RD
Acad
BRIDGWATER
Bradney
WEST END CT
PENDON Hill
WOOD LA

A39
A38
Works
H
BOWER LA
WHITLEY RD
CHED ZOY LA
SIDE LA
Slape Cross
209
209
A39
M5

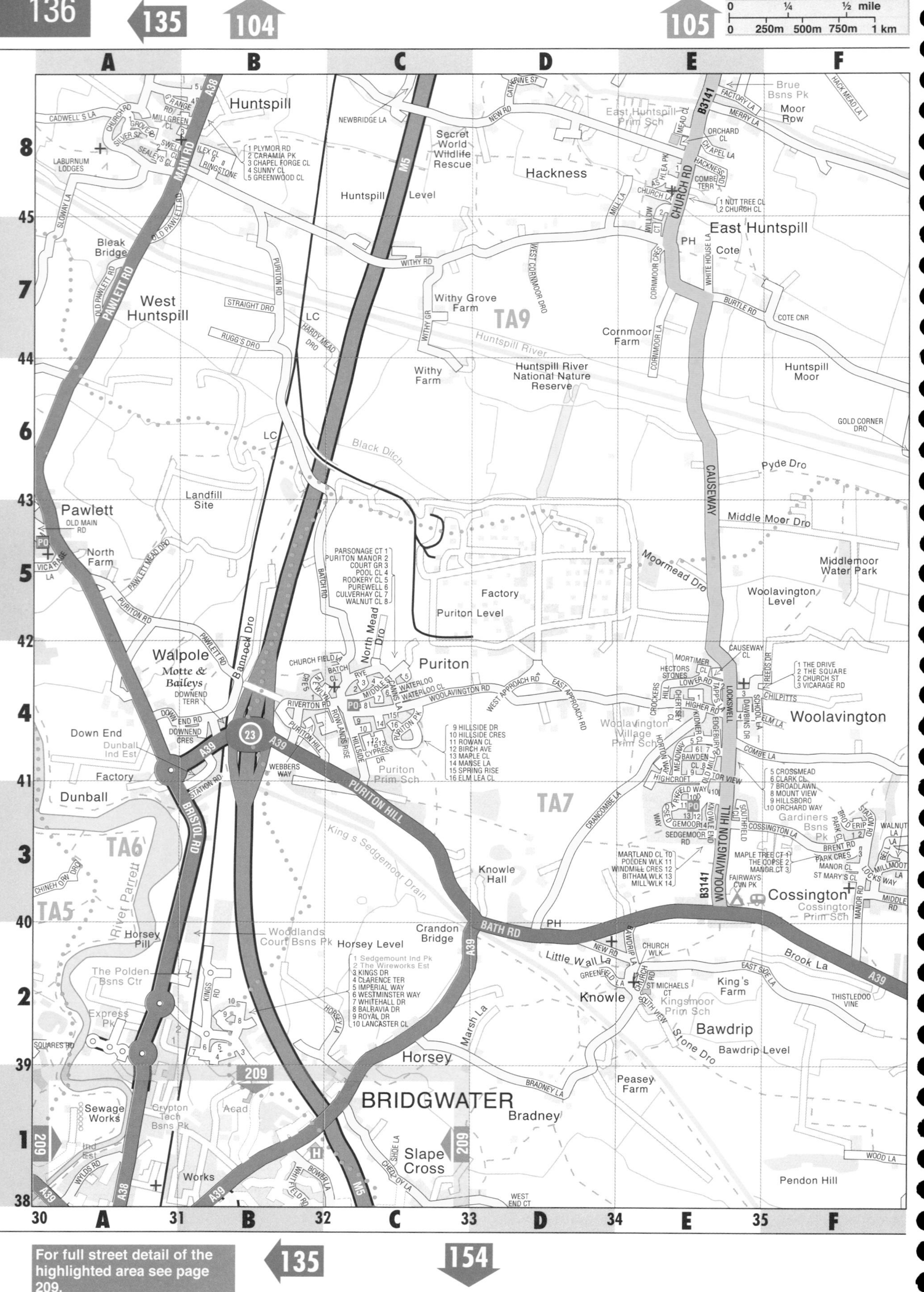

For full street detail of the highlighted area see page 209.

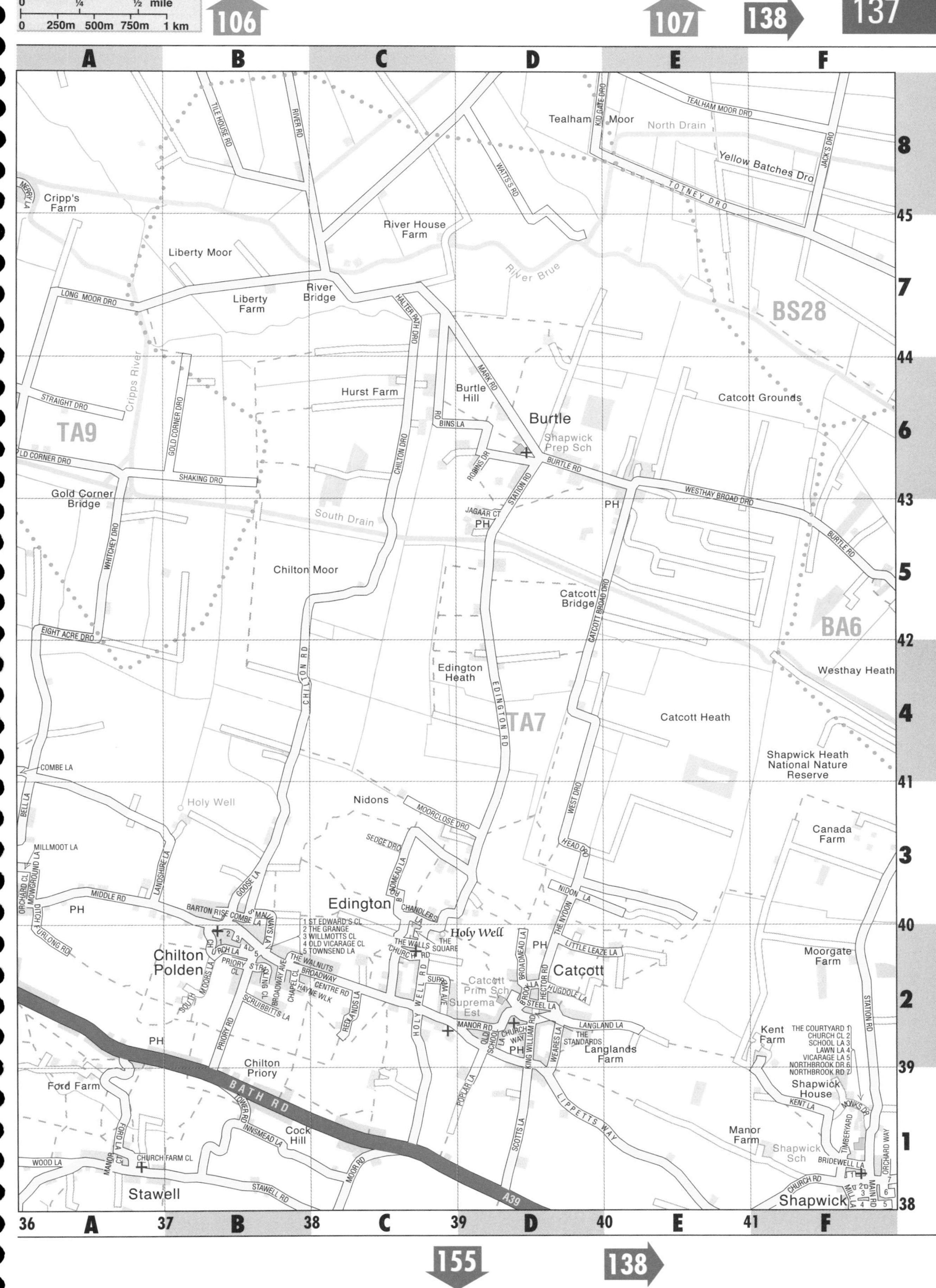
Scale: 1¾ inches to 1 mile
106
107
138
Tealham Moor
North Drain
Yellow Batches Dro
TOTNEY DRO
TEALHAM MOOR DRO
JACK'S DRO
KID GATE DRO
WATTS'S RD
TILE HOUSE RD
RIVER RD
Cripp's Farm
River House Farm
Liberty Moor
Liberty Farm
River Bridge
River Brue
LONG MOOR DRO
HALTER PATH DRO
BS28
Hurst Farm
Burtle Hill
MARK RD
Burtle
Shapwick Prep Sch
Catcott Grounds
STRAIGHT DRO
Cripps River
GOLD CORNER DRO
TA9
BINS LA
ROBINS DR
BURTLE RD
WESTHAY BROAD DRO
GOLD CORNER DRO
SHAKING DRO
Gold Corner Bridge
CHILTON DRO
South Drain
JAGAAR CT
STATION RD
PH
BURTLE RD
WHITCHEY DRO
Chilton Moor
Catcott Bridge
CATCOTT BROAD DRO
BA6
EIGHT ACRE DRO
Edington Heath
Westhay Heath
CHILTON RD
EDINGTON RD
TA7
Catcott Heath
Shapwick Heath National Nature Reserve
COMBE LA
Holy Well
Nidons
MOORCLOSE DRO
BELL LA
WEST DRO
Canada Farm
MILLMOOT LA
SEDGE DRO
HEAD DRO
MOWGROUND LA
ORCHARD CL
LANDSHIRE LA
GOOSE LA
MIDDLE RD
Edington
NIDON LA
DITCH FURLONG RD
BARTON RISE
COMBE LA
MAIN RD
CHANDLERS LA
Holy Well
1 ST EDWARD'S CL
2 THE GRANGE
3 WILLMOTTS CL
4 OLD VICARAGE CL
5 TOWNSEND LA
THE WALLS
THE SQUARE
CHURCH RD
BROADMEAD LA
THE NYDON
LITTLE LEAZE LA
Moorgate Farm
Chilton Polden
PRIORY CL
THE WALNUTS
BROADWAY
CENTRE RD
HAYNE WLK
Catcott
Catcott Prim Sch
Suprema Est
SUPREMA AVE
HECTOR RD
HUGDOLE LA
STEEL LA
STATION RD
SOUTH MOORS LA
SCRUIBBITTS LA
REDLANDS LA
HOLY WELL RD
MANOR RD
LANGLAND LA
THE STANDARDS
Langlands Farm
Kent Farm
THE COURTYARD 1
CHURCH CL 2
SCHOOL LA 3
LAWN LA 4
VICARAGE CL 5
NORTHBROOK DR 6
NORTHBROOK RD 7
PRIORY RD
Chilton Priory
BATH RD
OLD SCHOOL LA
CHURCH WAY
KING WILLIAM RD
WEARES LA
Shapwick House
Ford Farm
POPLAR LA
LIPPETTS WAY
KENT LA
MONKS DR
TOWER RD
INNSMEAD LA
Cock Hill
FORD LA
SCOTTS LA
Manor Farm
TIMBERYARD
WOOD WAY
Shapwick Sch
WOOD LA
MANOR CL
CHURCH FARM CL
MOOR RD
BRIDEWELL LA
ORCHARD CL
Stawell
STAWELL RD
A39
CHURCH RD
Shapwick
MILL LA
MAIN RD
36
37
38
39
40
41
155
138

137 108 109

Scale: 1¾ inches to 1 mile

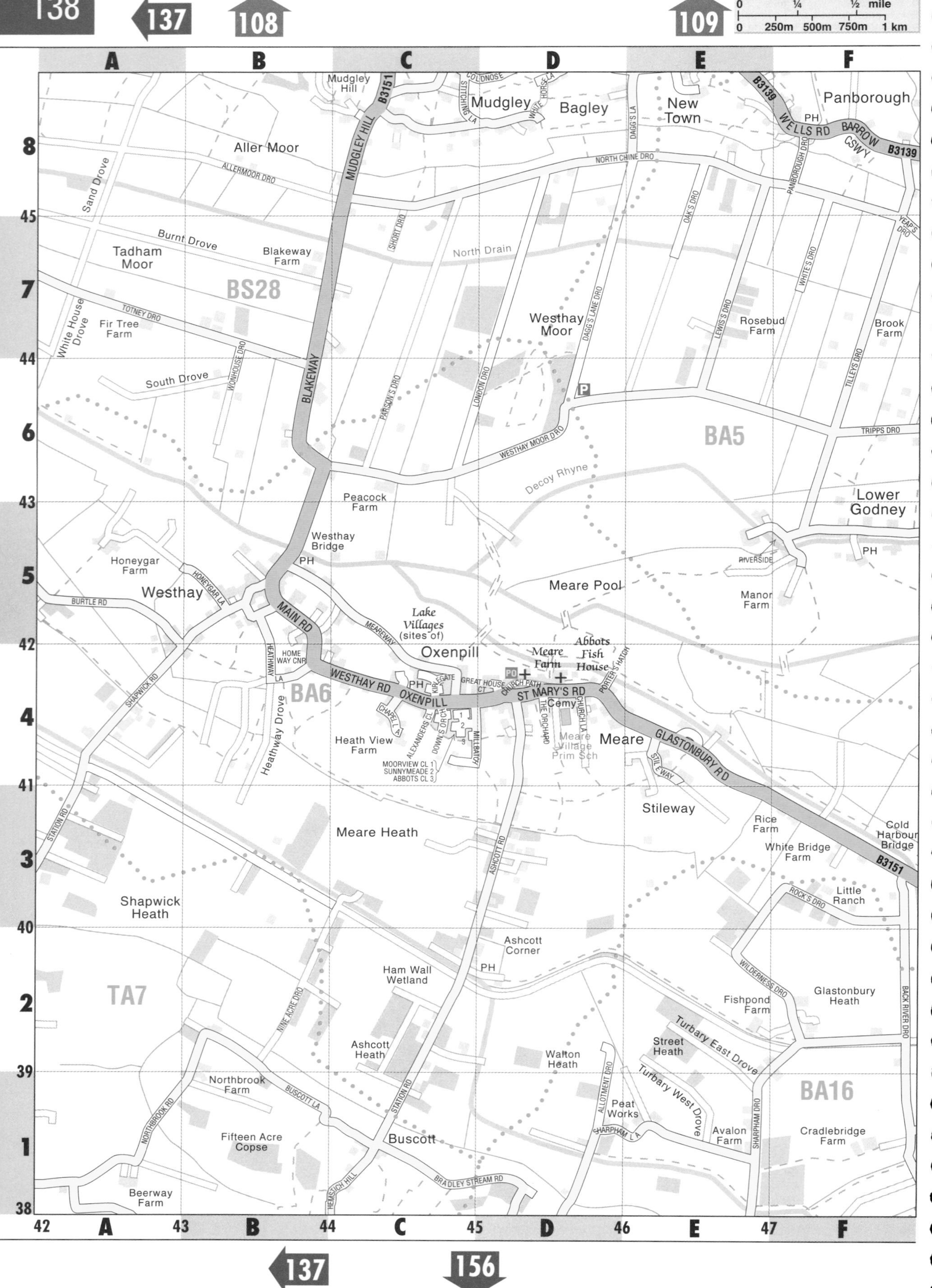

Mudgley Hill
Mudgley
Bagley
New Town
Panborough
Aller Moor
Tadham Moor
Blakeway Farm
BS28
Fir Tree Farm
Westhay Moor
Rosebud Farm
Brook Farm
BA5
Peacock Farm
Lower Godney
Westhay Bridge
Honeygar Farm
Westhay
Meare Pool
Manor Farm
Lake Villages (sites of)
Oxenpill
Meare Farm
Abbots Fish House
BA6
Heath View Farm
Meare
Stileway
Meare Heath
Rice Farm
White Bridge Farm
Cold Harbour Bridge
Shapwick Heath
Little Ranch
Ashcott Corner
Ham Wall Wetland
TA7
Fishpond Farm
Glastonbury Heath
Ashcott Heath
Walton Heath
Street Heath
Northbrook Farm
Peat Works
BA16
Fifteen Acre Copse
Buscott
Avalon Farm
Cradlebridge Farm
Beerway Farm
North Drain
Decoy Rhyne
Burnt Drove
South Drove
Sand Drove
White House Drove
Heathway Drove
Turbary East Drove
Turbary West Drove

137 156

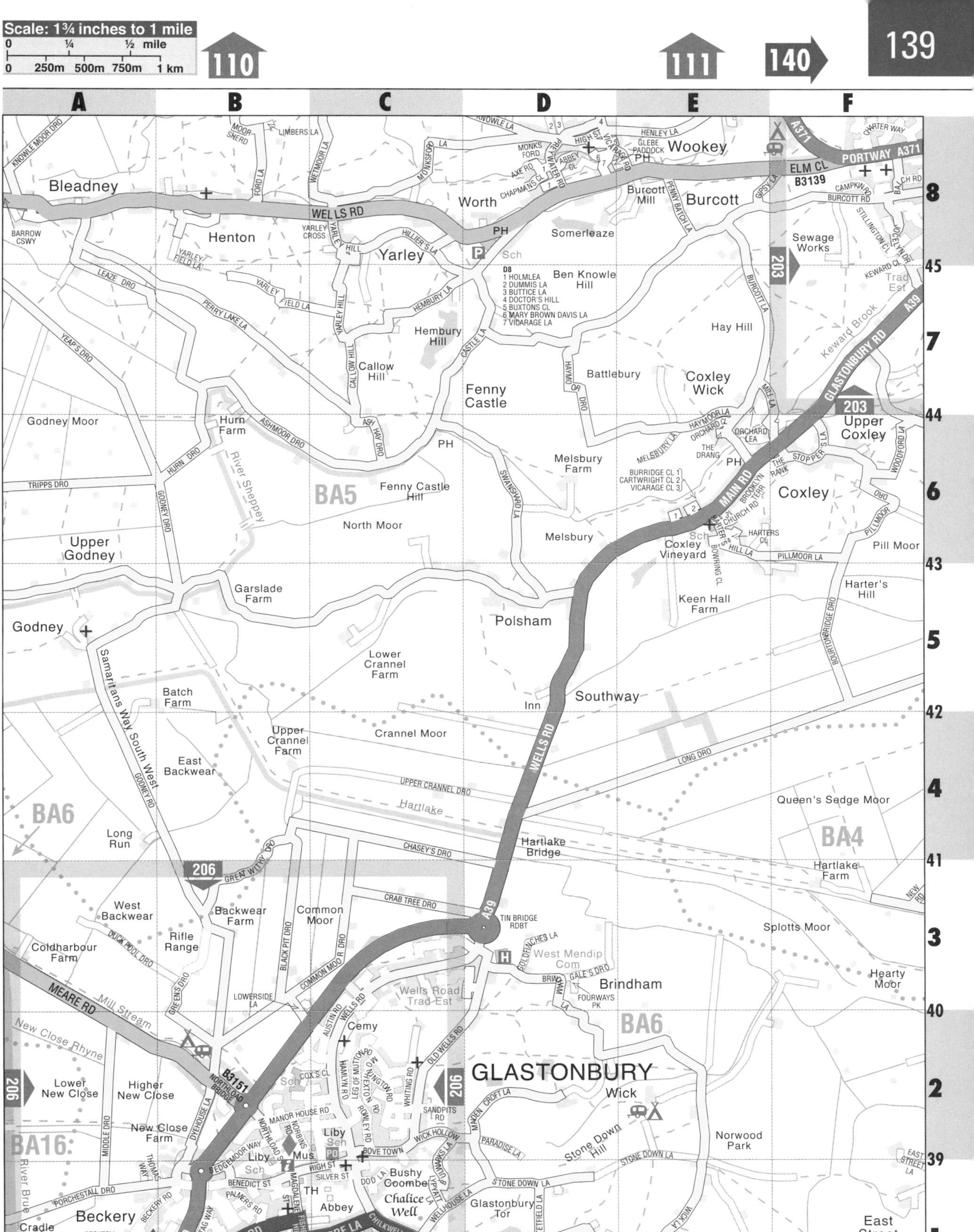

A   B   C   D   E   F

Knowle Moor Dro
MOOR SNERD
LIMBERS LA
KNOWLE LA
CHARTER WAY
PORTWAY A371
A371

Bleadney
Henton
MONKS FORD
Worth
Wookey
PH
Burcott Mill
Burcott
ELM CL
B3139
CAMPKIN RD
BURCOTT RD
BATCH RD

BARROW CSWY
WELLS RD
YARLEY CROSS
Yarley
P
Somerleaze
Sewage Works
203
8

45

Godney Moor
Hurn Farm
Hembury Hill
D8
1 HOLMLEA
2 DUMMIS LA
3 BUTTICE LA
4 DOCTOR'S HILL
5 BUXTONS CL
6 MARY BROWN DAVIS LA
7 VICARAGE LA
Ben Knowle Hill
Hay Hill
KEWARD CL
Trad Est
7

LEAZE DRO
PERRY LANE LA
Callow Hill
Fenny Castle
PH
Battlebury
Coxley Wick
Keward Brook
GLASTONBURY RD
A39
Upper Coxley
203
44

TEAP'S DRO
TRIPPS DRO
BA5
Fenny Castle Hill
North Moor
Melsbury Farm
Melsbury
THE DRANG
ORCHARD LEA
PH
THE RANK
Coxley
PILLMOOR
6

Upper Godney
River Sheppey
Garslade Farm
Lower Crannel Farm
Coxley Vineyard
Sch
HARTERS CL
Keen Hall Farm
Pill Moor
PILLMOOR LA
Harter's Hill
43

Godney
Batch Farm
Upper Crannel Farm
Crannel Moor
Polsham
BURTONBRIDGE DRO
5

Samaritans Way South West
East Backwear
UPPER CRANNEL DRO
Hartlake
Inn
Southway
Queen's Sedge Moor
BA4
42

BA6
Long Run
CHASEY'S DRO
Hartlake Bridge
LONG DRO
Hartlake Farm
4

206
GREAT WITHY DRO
CRAB TREE DRO
WELLS RD
A39
TIN BRIDGE RDBT
Splotts Moor
NEW RD
41

West Backwear
Backwear Farm
Common Moor
COLD EACHES LA
West Mendip Com
H
Brindham
FOURWAYS PK
Hearty Moor
3

Coldharbour Farm
MEARE RD
Mill Stream
LOWERSIDE LA
BLACK PIT DRO
COMMON MOOR DRO
Wells Road Trad Est
GALE'S DRO
40

New Close Rhyne
Lower New Close
Higher New Close
B3151
Cemy
OLD WELLS RD
206
GLASTONBURY
Wick
BA6
Norwood Park
2

206
New Close Farm
River Brue
MIDDLE DRO
PORCHESTALL DRO
NORTH RD
DYEHOUSE LA
Liby Sch
Mus
HIGH ST
BOVE TOWN
Stone Down Hill
STONE DOWN LA
EAST STREET LA
39

BA16
Beckery
BECKERY RD
THOMAS WAY
Liby
Sch
PO
SILVER ST
Bushy Coombe
Chalice Well
Glastonbury Tor
WICK LA
GIPSY LA
East Street
38

Cradle Bridge
Sewage Works
MORLAND RD
HILL RD
Northover
A39
WIRRAL PARK RDBT
STREET RD
BERE LA
Abbey
Mus
COURSING BATCH
EDGARLEY RD A361
Edgarley
A361
EDGARLEY RD

48   A   49   B   50   C   51   D   52   E   53   F

For full street detail of the highlighted areas see pages 203 and 206.

157   140

139
112
113

Scale: 1¾ inches to 1 mile

0   ¼   ½   mile
0   250m   500m   750m   1 km

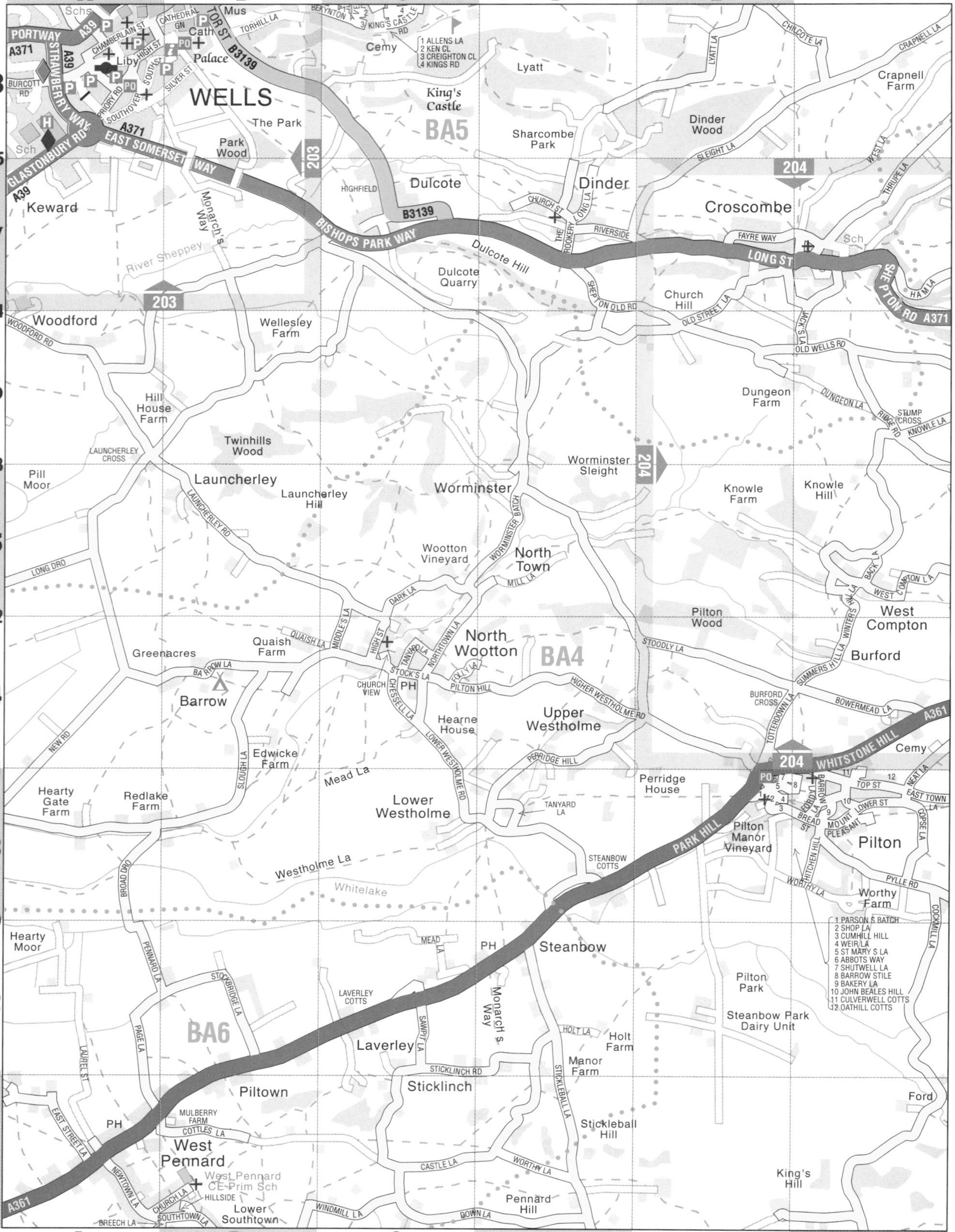

A   B   C   D   E   F

8

PORTWAY
A371
STRAWBERRY WAY
A39
BURCOTT RD
Schs
CHAMBERLAIN ST
CATHEDRAL GN
Cath
HIGH ST
Lib
PO
SILVER ST
SOUTHOVER
PRIORY RD
SOUTOUT ST
TOR ST
Mus
TORHILL LA
B3139
BEKYNTON
KING'S CASTLE
Cemy
1 ALLENS LA
2 KEN CL
3 CREIGHTON CL
4 KINGS RD
Lyatt
King's
Castle
BA5
CHINGOTE LA
Crapnell
Farm
CRAPNELL LA

WELLS
Palace
The Park
Park Wood
Sharcombe
Park
Dinder
Wood
WEST LA
THRUPE LA

45

Sch
H
A371
EAST SOMERSET   WAY
203
HIGHFIELD
Dulcote
B3139
Dinder
Croscombe
SLEIGHT LA
204

Keward
A39
Monarch's Way
BISHOPS PARK WAY
CHURCH ST
LONG LA
RIVERSIDE
FAYRE WAY
LONG ST
SHEPTON RD
A371
HAM LA

7

River Sheppey
Dulcote Hill
THE ROOKER
SHEPTON OLD RD
Church
Hill
OLD STREET LA

44

203
Woodford
WOODFORD RD
Wellesley
Farm
Dulcote
Quarry
OLD WELLS RD
JACK'S LA
Dungeon
Farm
DUNGEON LA
RIDGE RD
STUMP
CROSS
KNOWLE LA

6

Hill
House
Farm
Worminster
Sleight
204

43

Pill
Moor
LAUNCHERLEY
CROSS
Twinhills
Wood
Launcherley
Launcherley
Hill
Worminster
Knowle
Farm
Knowle
Hill

5

LONG DRO
LAUNCHERLEY RD
Wootton
Vineyard
North
Town
MILL LA
WORMINSTER BATCH
Pilton
Wood
SUMMERS HILL LA
WINTERS LA
BACK LA
COMPTON LA
WEST

42

Greenacres
QUAISH LA
Quaish
Farm
MIDDLES LA
HIGH ST
DARK LA
North
Wootton
BA4
STOODLY LA
West
Compton
Burford

4

NEW RD
BARROW LA
Barrow
STOCK'S LA
CHESSELL LA
TANYARD LA
PILTON LA
PILTON HILL
CHURCH
VIEW
PH
Hearne
House
Upper
Westholme
HIGHER WESTHOLME RD
BURFORD
CROSS
BOWERMEAD LA
A361

41

Hearty
Gate
Farm
Redlake
Farm
SLOUGH LA
Edwicke
Farm
Mead La
LOWER WESTHOLME RD
Lower
Westholme
PERRIDGE HILL
Perridge
House
TANYARD LA
TOTTERIDGE LA
204
WHITSTONE HILL
Cemy

3

BROAD DRO
Westholme La
Whitelake
STEANBOW
COTTS
PARK HILL
PO
Pilton
Manor
Vineyard
Pilton
MOUNT
PLEASANT
LOWER ST
TOP ST
EAST TOWN
LA
COPSE LA

40

Hearty
Moor
PENNARD LA
STOCKBRIDGE LA
PAGE LA
MEAD
PH
Steanbow
Pilton
Park
Steanbow Park
Dairy Unit
WORTHY LA
Worthy
Farm
COCKMILL LA
PYLLE RD

1 PARSON'S BATCH
2 SHOP LA
3 CUMHILL HILL
4 WEIR LA
5 ST MARY'S LA
6 ABBOTS WAY
7 SHUTWELL LA
8 BARROW STILE
9 BAKERY LA
10 JOHN BEALES HILL
11 CULVERWELL COTTS
12 OATHILL COTTS

2

BA6
LAVERLEY
COTTS
Monarch's
Way
Laverley
SAWPIT LA
STICKLINCH RD
Sticklinch
HOLT LA
Holt
Farm
Manor
Farm
STICKLEBALL LA

39

LAUREL ST
EAST STREET LA
Piltown
MULBERRY
FARM
COTTLES LA
NEWTOWN LA
Sticklinch
STICKLEBALL LA
Stickleball
Hill
Ford

1

PH
West
Pennard
West Pennard
CE Prim Sch
CHURCH LA
HILLSIDE
CASTLE LA
WORTHY LA
King's
Hill

38

A361
BREECH LA
SOUTHTOWN LA
Lower
Southtown
WINDMILL LA
DOWN LA
Pennard
Hill

54   A   55   B   56   C   57   D   58   E   59   F

139
158

For full street detail of the
highlighted area see
pages 203 and 204.

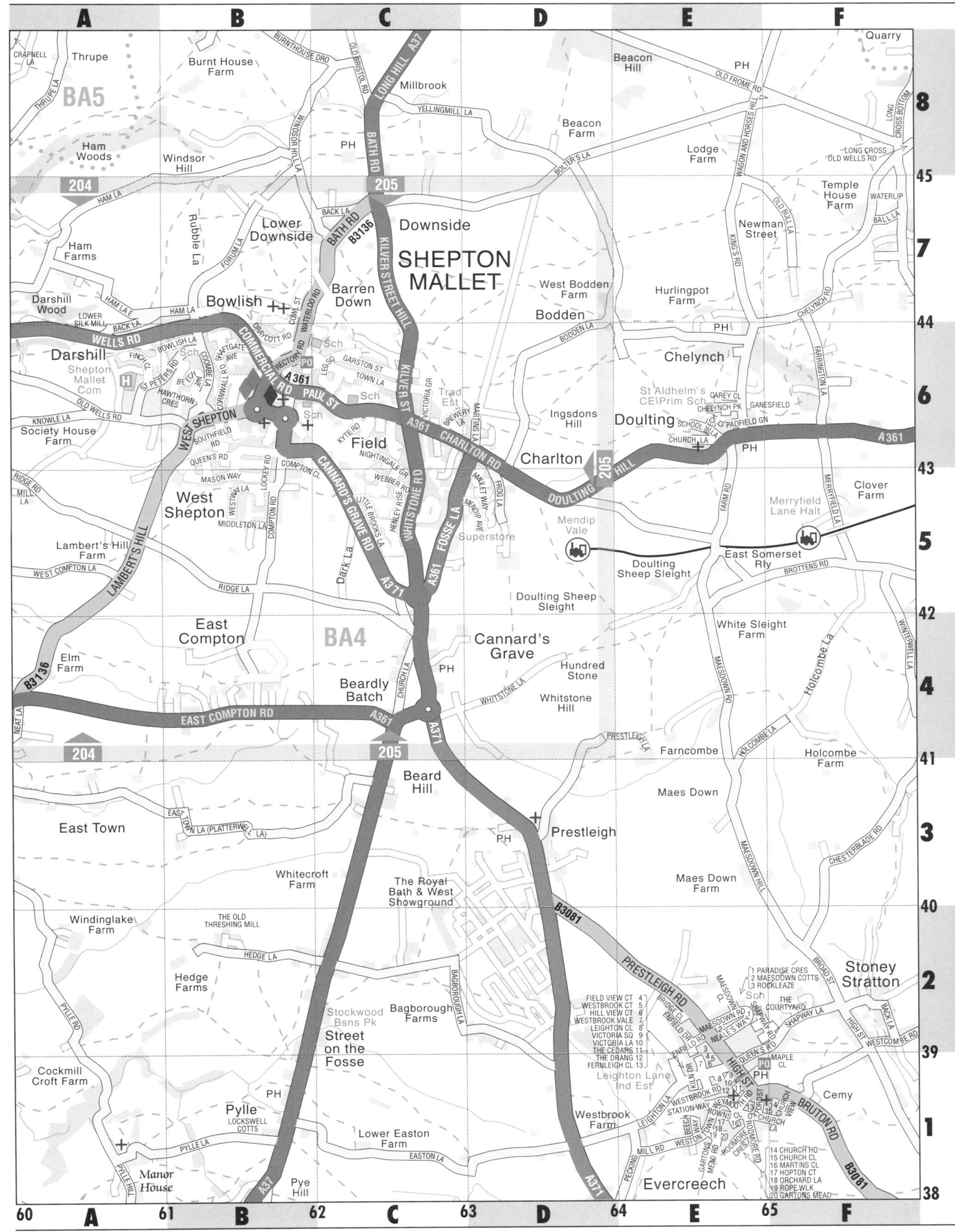

141 116 117

Scale: 1¾ inches to 1 mile

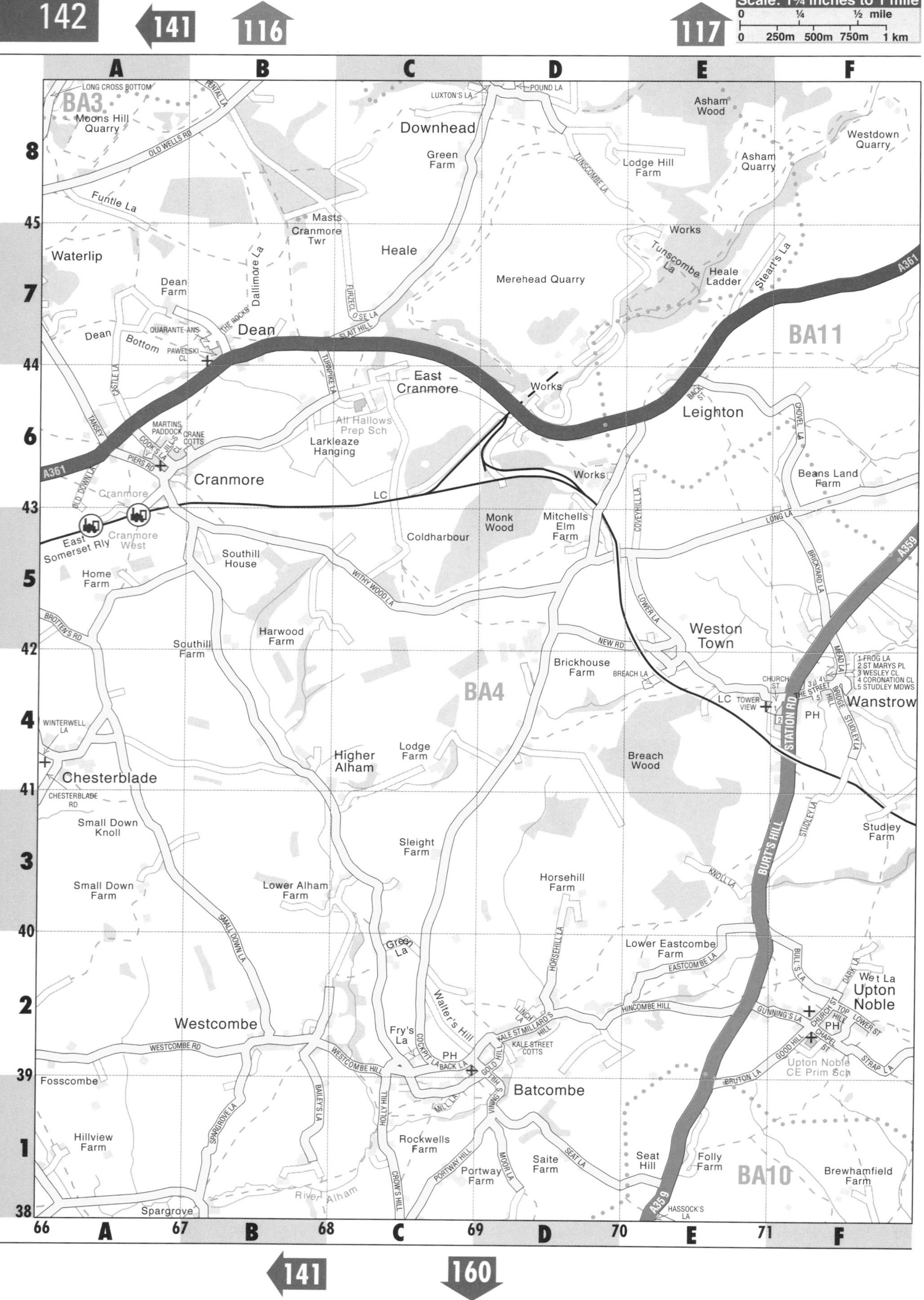
A
B
C
D
E
F
BA3
Moons Hill Quarry
LONG CROSS BOTTOM
OLD WELLS RD
Funtle La
Waterlip
Dean Farm
Dallimore La
THE ROCKS
Dean
Dean Bottom
QUARANTE-ANS
PAWELSKI CL
CASTLE LA
TANSEY
MARTINS PADDOCK
CRANE COTTS
COOK'S LA
HILL'S CL
PIERS RD
A361
OLD DOWN LA
Cranmore
Cranmore West
East Somerset Rly
Downhead
LUXTON'S LA
POUND LA
Green Farm
Masts
Cranmore Twr
Heale
FURZECLOSE LA
SLAIT HILL
TURNPIKE LA
East Cranmore
All Hallows Prep Sch
Larkleaze Hanging
LC
Coldharbour
Monk Wood
Mitchells Elm Farm
Works
Merehead Quarry
TUNSCOMBE LA
Lodge Hill Farm
Asham Wood
Asham Quarry
Westdown Quarry
Tunscombe La
Heale Ladder
Steart's La
BA11
Leighton
BACK ST
CHOVEL LA
Beans Land Farm
COVEHILL LA
LONG LA
BRICKYARD LA
A359
LOWER LA
Weston Town
NEW RD
Brickhouse Farm
BREACH LA
CHURCH ST
TOWER VIEW
THE STREET
BRIDGE HILL
MEAD LA
1 FROG LA
2 ST MARYS PL
3 WESLEY CL
4 CORONATION CL
5 STUDLEY MDWS
Wanstrow
PH
STATION RD
STUDLEY LA
Breach Wood
Studley Farm
Southill House
WITHY WOOD LA
Home Farm
BROTTEN'S RD
Southill Farm
Harwood Farm
BA4
WINTERWELL LA
Chesterblade
CHESTERBLADE RD
Higher Alham
Lodge Farm
Small Down Knoll
Sleight Farm
Small Down Farm
Lower Alham Farm
Horsehill Farm
KNOLL LA
BURT'S HILL
SMALL DOWN LA
Green La
Walter's Hill
HORSEHILL LA
Lower Eastcombe Farm
EASTCOMBE LA
BULL'S LA
DARK LA
Wet La
Upton Noble
Westcombe
WESTCOMBE RD
Fry's La
COCKPIT LA
BACK LA
LINCH LA
KALE ST
MILLARD'S HILL
HINCOMBE HILL
KALE STREET COTTS
GUNNING'S LA
CHURCH ST
TOP HILL
LOWER ST
CHAPEL ST
STRAP LA
GOOD HILL
Upton Noble CE Prim Sch
BRUTON LA
WESTCOMBE HILL
GOLD HILL
Fosscombe
BAILEY'S LA
HOLLY HILL
MILL LA
VINING'S HILL
Batcombe
SPARGROVE LA
Hillview Farm
Rockwells Farm
PORTWAY HILL
Portway Farm
MOOR LA
Saite Farm
SEAT LA
Seat Hill
Folly Farm
BA10
Brewhamfield Farm
CROW'S HILL
River Alham
Spargrove
HASSOCK'S LA
66
67
68
69
70
71
38
39
40
41
42
43
44
45

141 160

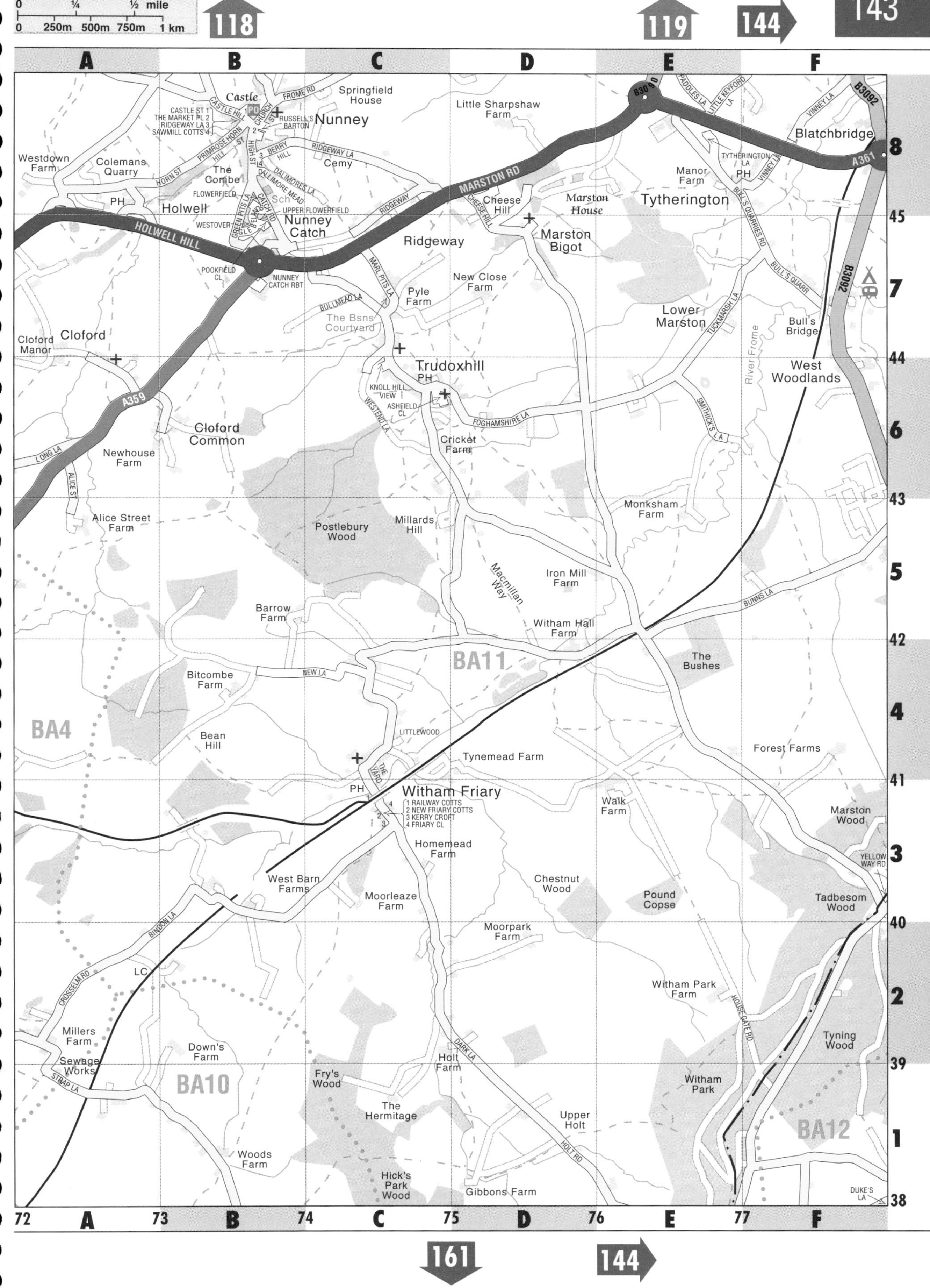
Scale: 1¾ inches to 1 mile
0 ¼ ½ mile
0 250m 500m 750m 1 km
118
119
144
A
B
C
D
E
F
Castle
Nunney
Springfield House
Little Sharpshaw Farm
Westdown Farm
Colemans Quarry
The Combe
Cemy
Holwell
Nunney Catch
Ridgeway
Cheese Hill
Marston House
Marston Bigot
Tytherington
Manor Farm
Blatchbridge
MARSTON RD
HOLWELL HILL
New Close Farm
Pyle Farm
The Bsns Courtyard
Lower Marston
Bull's Bridge
Cloford Manor
Cloford
Trudoxhill
West Woodlands
River Frome
A359
Cloford Common
Newhouse Farm
Cricket Farm
Monksham Farm
Alice Street Farm
Postlebury Wood
Millards Hill
Macmillan Way
Iron Mill Farm
Barrow Farm
Witham Hall Farm
BA11
The Bushes
Bitcombe Farm
BA4
Bean Hill
Tynemead Farm
Forest Farms
Witham Friary
1 RAILWAY COTTS
2 NEW FRIARY COTTS
3 KERRY CROFT
4 FRIARY CL
Walk Farm
Marston Wood
Homemead Farm
West Barn Farms
Moorleaze Farm
Chestnut Wood
Pound Copse
Tadbesom Wood
Moorpark Farm
Witham Park Farm
Millers Farm
Sewage Works
Down's Farm
Holt Farm
Tyning Wood
BA10
Fry's Wood
The Hermitage
Witham Park
Upper Holt
BA12
Woods Farm
Hick's Park Wood
Gibbons Farm
72
73
74
75
76
77
38
39
40
41
42
43
44
45
1
2
3
4
5
6
7
8

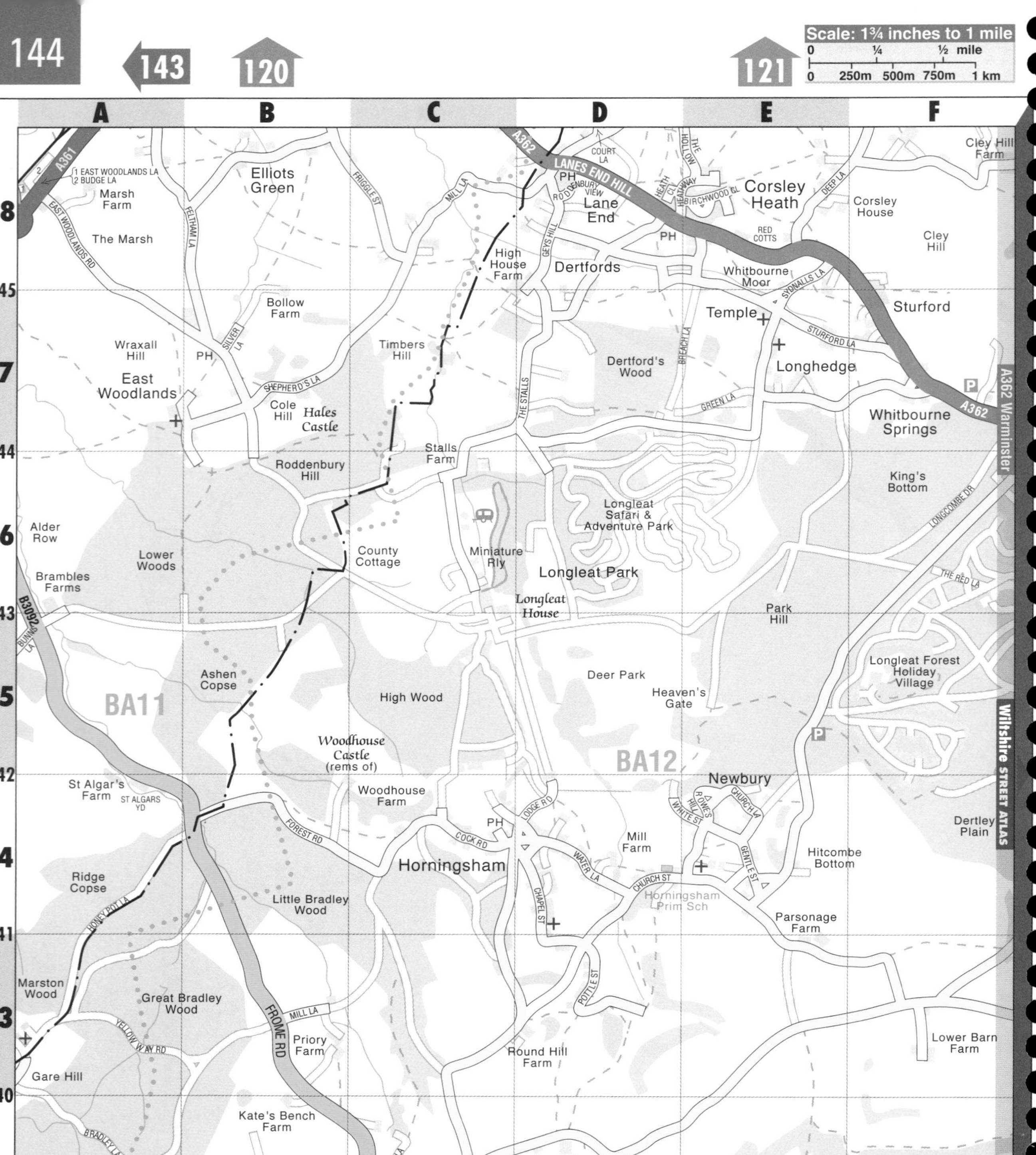

A | B | C | D | E | F

8
45
7
44
6
43
5
42
4
41
3
40
2
39
1
38

A361
1 EAST WOODLANDS LA
2 BUDGE LA
Marsh Farm
The Marsh
Elliots Green
FELTHAM LA
FRIGGLE ST
MILL LA
A362
COURT LA
THE HOLLOW
LANES END HILL
PH
Lane End
Corsley Heath
Cley Hill Farm
DEEP LA
Corsley House
Cley Hill
EAST WOODLANDS RD
Wraxall Hill
PH
SILVER LA
Bollow Farm
High House Farm
GEYS HILL
DENBURY VIEW RD
HEATH
HEADWAY
BIRCHWOOD LA
RED COTTS
Dertfords
PH
Whitbourne Moor
SIGNALLS LA
Sturford
East Woodlands
SHEPHERD'S LA
Cole Hill
Hales Castle
Timbers Hill
Temple
Longhedge
STURFORD LA
Whitbourne Springs
Roddenbury Hill
Stalls Farm
Dertford's Wood
BREACH LA
GREEN LA
King's Bottom
LONGCOMBE DR
Alder Row
Lower Woods
County Cottage
Miniature Rly
Longleat Safari & Adventure Park
Park Hill
THE RED LA
Brambles Farms
B3092
BUNN LA
Longleat Park
Longleat House
Deer Park
Heaven's Gate
P
Longleat Forest Holiday Village
BA11
Ashen Copse
High Wood
BA12
P
Newbury
Dertley Plain
St Algar's Farm
ST ALGARS YD
Woodhouse Castle (rems of)
Woodhouse Farm
PH
LODGE RD
CHURCH LA
ROWE'S WHITE ST
Mill Farm
GENTLE ST
Hitcombe Bottom
Ridge Copse
FOREST RD
COCK RD
Horningsham
WATER LA
CHURCH ST
Horningsham Prim Sch
Parsonage Farm
Little Bradley Wood
CHAPEL ST
POTTLE ST
Round Hill Farm
Lower Barn Farm
Marston Wood
HONEY POTT LA
YELLOW WAY RD
Great Bradley Wood
FROME RD
MILL LA
Priory Farm
Gare Hill
Kate's Bench Farm
Baycliffe Farm
Brimsdown Hill
Bidcombe Hill
Penstones Wood
BRADLEY LA
CROWN LA
FROME VIEW
HIGH ST
Perry Farm
1 THE RANK
2 THE SQUARE
3 CHESTNUT CL
Woodcombe Bottom
BARCROFT
BACK LA
Maiden Bradley
KINGSTON LA
Newmead Cottages
Whitecliff Down
Bushcombe Bottom
Manor Farm
Mapperton Hill
PH
CHURCH ST
Church Farm
Bradley House
B3092
Newmead Farm
DUKE'S LA

A362 Warminster   Wiltshire STREET ATLAS

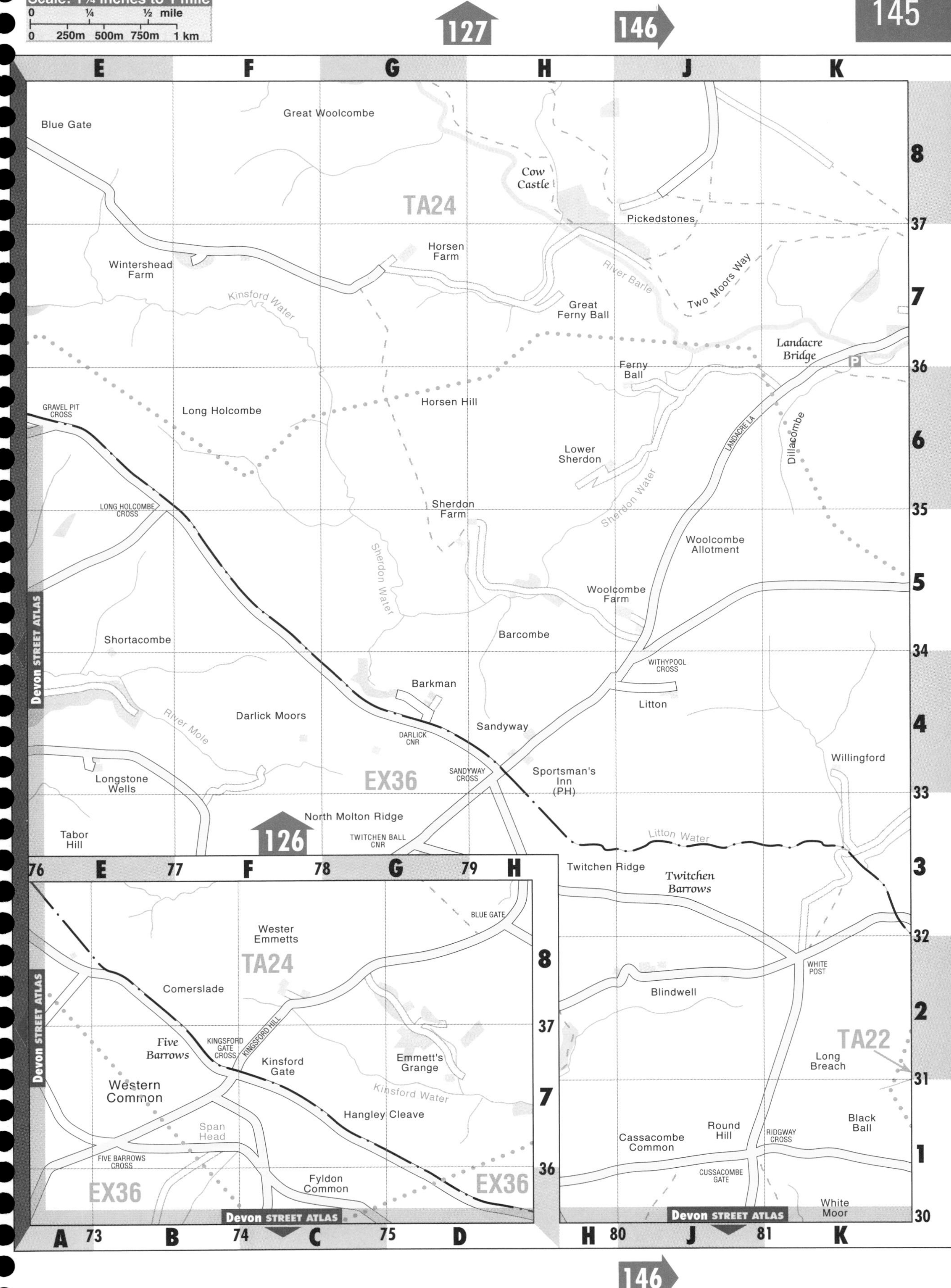

Scale: 1¾ inches to 1 mile

0   ¼   ½   mile

0   250m   500m   750m   1 km

127

146

E   F   G   H   J   K

Blue Gate

Great Woolcombe

Cow Castle

TA24

Pickedstones

Horsen Farm

River Barle

Two Moors Way

Wintershead Farm

Kinsford Water

Great Ferny Ball

Ferny Ball

Landacre Bridge

P

Gravel Pit Cross

Long Holcombe

Horsen Hill

Lower Sherdon

Landacre La

Dillacombe

Long Holcombe Cross

Sherdon Farm

Sherdon Water

Woolcombe Allotment

Shortacombe

Sherdon Water

Woolcombe Farm

Barcombe

Withypool Cross

Barkman

Litton

Darlick Moors

River Mole

Darlick Cnr

Sandyway

EX36

Sandyway Cross

Sportsman's Inn (PH)

Willingford

Longstone Wells

North Molton Ridge

Tabor Hill

126

Twitchen Ball Cnr

Litton Water

Twitchen Ridge

Twitchen Barrows

76   E   77   F   78   G   79   H

White Post

Blindwell

Blue Gate

TA24

Wester Emmetts

Comerslade

TA22

Kingsford Gate Cross

Kingsford Hill

Emmett's Grange

Long Breach

Five Barrows

Kinsford Gate

Kinsford Water

Western Common

Span Head

Hangley Cleave

Black Ball

Round Hill

Cassacombe Common

Ridgway Cross

Five Barrows Cross

Fyldon Common

EX36

EX36

Cussacombe Gate

White Moor

Devon STREET ATLAS

A   73   B   74   C   75   D

H   80   J   81   K

146

8

37

7

36

6

35

5

34

4

33

3

32

2

31

1

30

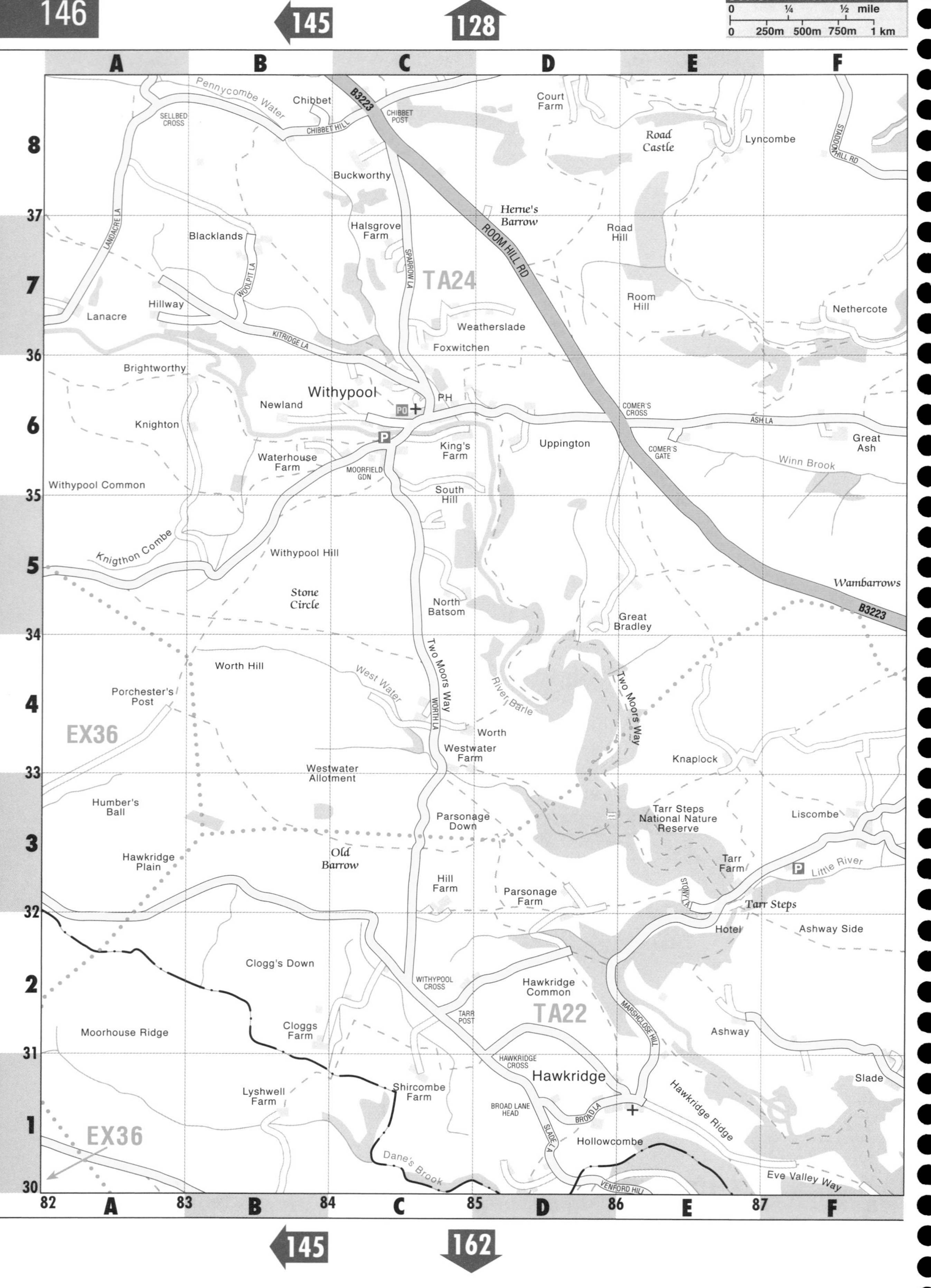

146

145

128

Scale: 1¾ inches to 1 mile
0   ¼   ½   mile
0   250m 500m 750m 1 km

A   B   C   D   E   F

Pennycombe Water
Chibbet
Chibbet Hill
B3223
CHIBBET POST
Court Farm
Road Castle
Lyncombe
SHADDON HILL RD

8

SELLBED CROSS
LANACRE LA
Buckworthy
Herne's Barrow
Road Hill

37

Blacklands
WOOLPIT LA
Halsgrove Farm
SPARROW LA
TA24
Room Hill
Nethercote

7

Lanacre
Hillway
KITRIDGE LA
Weatherslade
Foxwitchen

36

Brightworthy
Withypool
PH
COMER'S CROSS
ASH LA
Great Ash

6

Knighton
Newland
PO +
King's Farm
Uppington
COMER'S GATE
Winn Brook

Waterhouse Farm
P
MOORFIELD GDN

35

Withypool Common
South Hill

Knigthon Combe
Withypool Hill

5

Stone Circle
North Batsom
Great Bradley
Wambarrows
B3223

34

Worth Hill
West Water
Two Moors Way
WORTH LA
River Barle
Two Moors Way

4

EX36
Porchester's Post
Worth
Westwater Farm
Knaplock

33

Humber's Ball
Westwater Allotment
Parsonage Down
Tarr Steps National Nature Reserve
Liscombe

3

Hawkridge Plain
Old Barrow
Tarr Farm
P
Little River

Hill Farm
Parsonage Farm
STONX LA
Tarr Steps

32

Clogg's Down
Withypool Cross
Hawkridge Common
Hotel
Ashway Side

2

Moorhouse Ridge
Cloggs Farm
TARR POST
TA22
Ashway

31

Lyshwell Farm
Shircombe Farm
HAWKRIDGE CROSS
Hawkridge
MARSHCLOSE HILL
Hawkridge Ridge
Slade

1

EX36
BROAD LANE HEAD
SLADE LA
BROAD LA
+
Hollowcombe
Eve Valley Way

Dane's Brook
VENFORD HILL

30

82   A   83   B   84   C   85   D   86   E   87   F

Scale: 1¾ inches to 1 mile

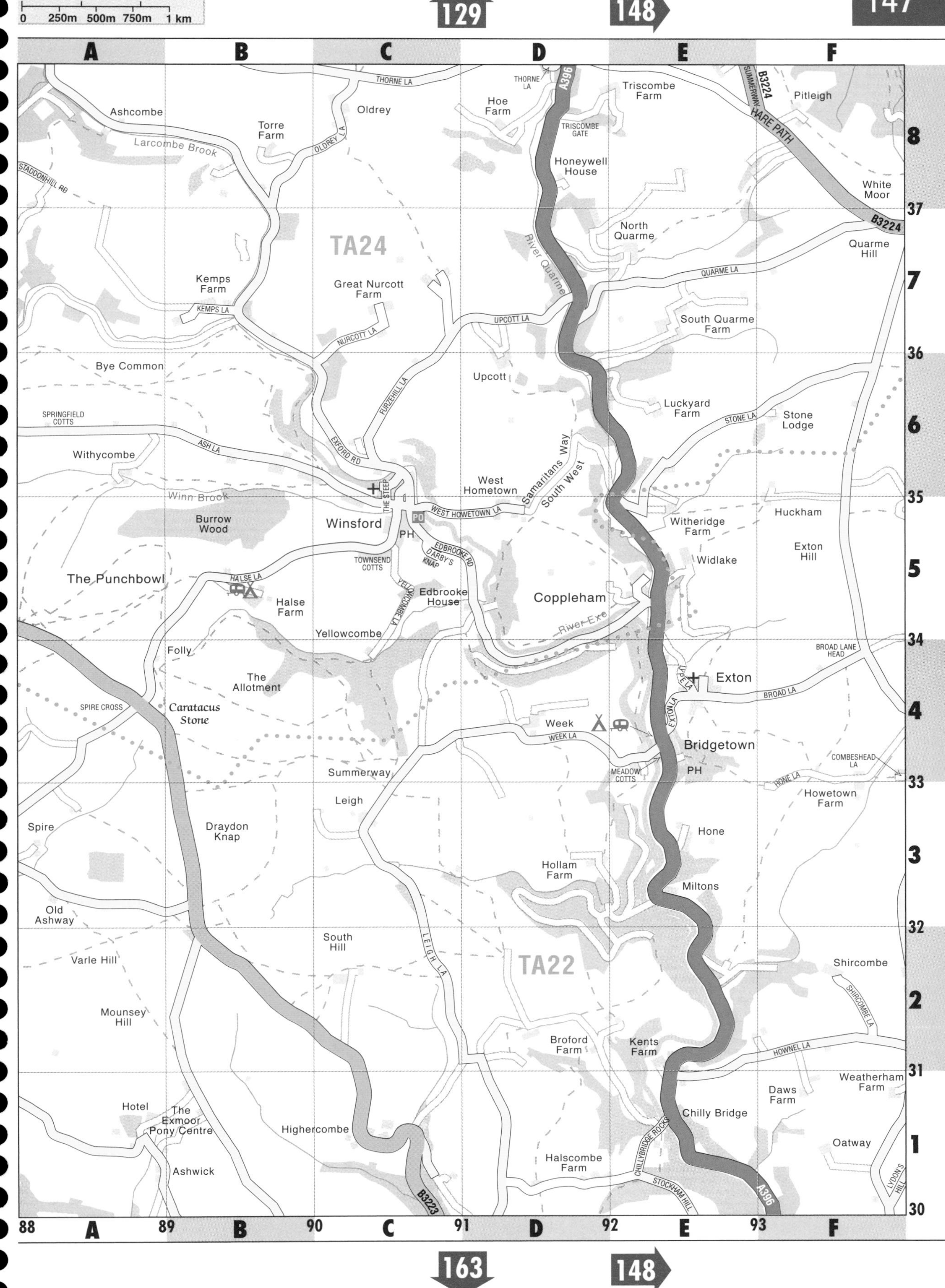

129
148
A
B
C
D
E
F
Ashcombe
Torre Farm
Oldrey
THORNE LA
Hoe Farm
Triscombe Farm
Pitleigh
Larcombe Brook
OLDREY LA
TRISCOMBE GATE
Honeywell House
HARE PATH
B3224
White Moor
STADDONHILL RD
TA24
North Quarme
Quarme Hill
Kemps Farm
KEMPS LA
Great Nurcott Farm
River Quarme
QUARME LA
South Quarme Farm
NURCOTT LA
UPCOTT LA
Bye Common
Upcott
FURZEHILL LA
Luckyard Farm
STONE LA
Stone Lodge
SPRINGFIELD COTTS
Withycombe
ASH LA
EXFORD RD
West Hometown
Samaritans Way
South West
Winn Brook
THE STEEP
WEST HOWETOWN LA
Huckham
Burrow Wood
Winsford
PO
PH
Witheridge Farm
TOWNSEND COTTS
EDBROOKE RD
DARBY'S KNAP
Widlake
Exton Hill
The Punchbowl
HALSE LA
Halse Farm
YELLOWCOMBE LA
Edbrooke House
Coppleham
Yellowcombe
River Exe
Folly
BROAD LANE HEAD
The Allotment
Exton
BROAD LA
SPIRE CROSS
Caratacus Stone
Week
WEEK LA
EXTON LA
Bridgetown
Summerway
MEADOW COTTS
PH
COMBESHEAD LA
HONE LA
Leigh
Howetown Farm
Spire
Draydon Knap
Hone
Hollam Farm
Miltons
Old Ashway
South Hill
LEIGH LA
TA22
Varle Hill
Shircombe
SHIRCOMBE LA
Mounsey Hill
Broford Farm
Kents Farm
HOWNEL LA
Weatherham Farm
Hotel
The Exmoor Pony Centre
Daws Farm
Chilly Bridge
Highercombe
CHILLYBRIDGE ROCKS
Oatway
Ashwick
Halscombe Farm
STOCKHAM HILL
B3223
A396
LYDON'S HILL
8
37
7
36
6
35
5
34
4
33
3
32
2
31
1
30
88
89
90
91
92
93
163
148

147
130

Scale: 1¾ inches to 1 mile

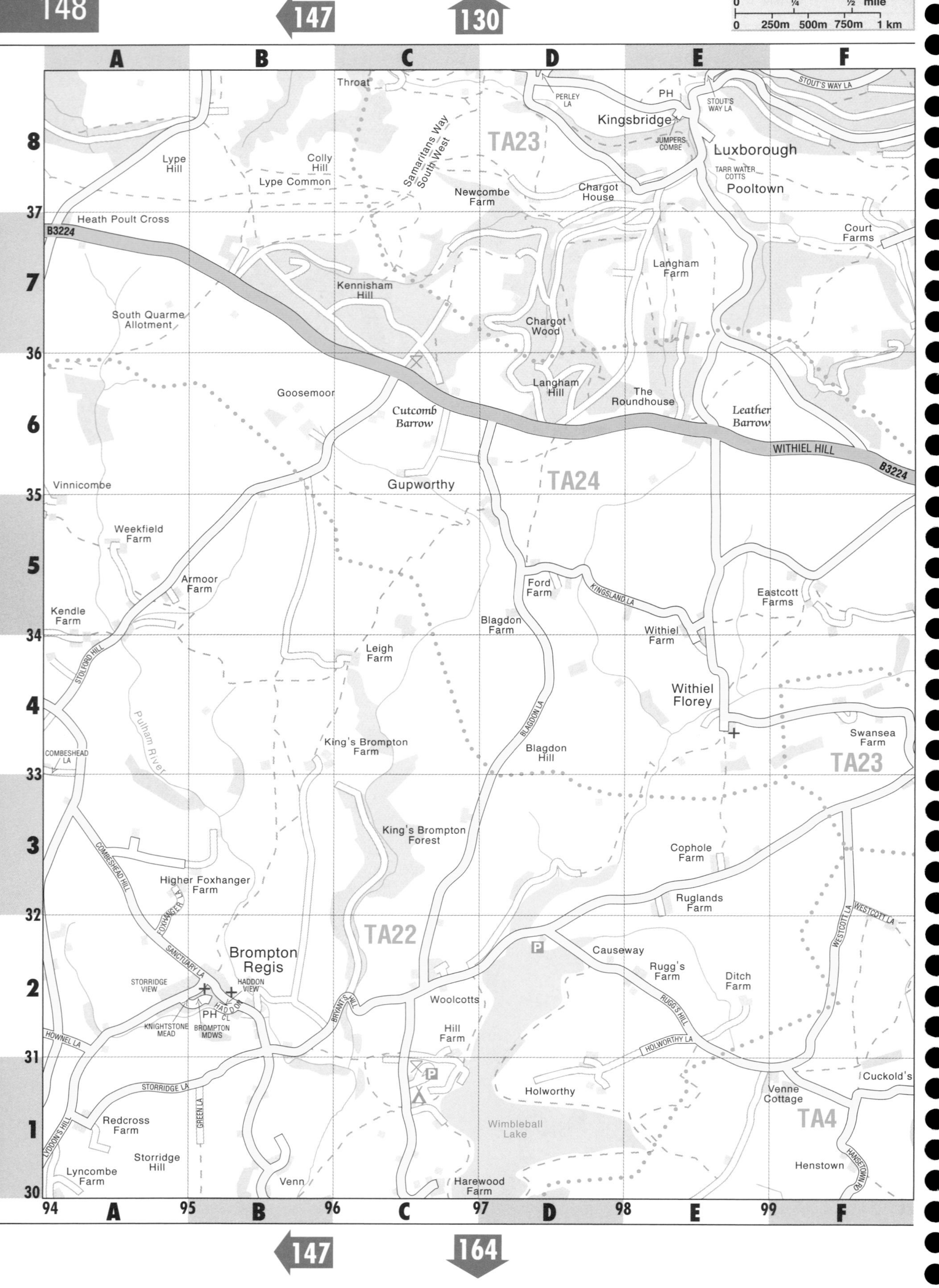
A
B
C
D
E
F
Throat
PERLEY LA
PH
STOUT'S WAY LA
Kingsbridge
JUMPERS COMBE
Luxborough
TARR WATER COTTS
Pooltown
TA23
Samaritans Way South West
Lype Hill
Colly Hill
Lype Common
Newcombe Farm
Chargot House
Heath Poult Cross
B3224
Court Farms
Langham Farm
Kennisham Hill
South Quarme Allotment
Chargot Wood
Goosemoor
Langham Hill
The Roundhouse
Cutcomb Barrow
Leather Barrow
WITHIEL HILL
Vinnicombe
Gupworthy
TA24
Weekfield Farm
Armoor Farm
Ford Farm
KINGSLAND LA
Eastcott Farms
Kendle Farm
Blagdon Farm
Withiel Farm
STOLFORD HILL
Leigh Farm
Withiel Florey
Pulham River
BLAGDON LA
Swansea Farm
COMBESHEAD LA
King's Brompton Farm
Blagdon Hill
King's Brompton Forest
COMBESHEAD HILL
Cophole Farm
Higher Foxhanger Farm
FOXHANGER LA
Ruglands Farm
WESTCOTT LA
TA22
Brompton Regis
SANCTUARY LA
Causeway
Rugg's Farm
Ditch Farm
STORRIDGE VIEW
HADDON VIEW
HADDON CL
PH
KNIGHTSTONE MEAD
BROMPTON MDWS
BRYANT'S HILL
Woolcotts
RUGG'S HILL
HOWNEL LA
Hill Farm
HOLWORTHY LA
Cuckold's
STORRIDGE LA
Holworthy
Venne Cottage
GREEN LA
Redcross Farm
Wimbleball Lake
TA4
LYDDON'S HILL
Storridge Hill
Henstown
HANSETOWN RD
Lyncombe Farm
Venn
Harewood Farm
37
8
7
36
6
35
5
34
4
33
3
32
2
31
1
30
94
95
96
97
98
99

147
164

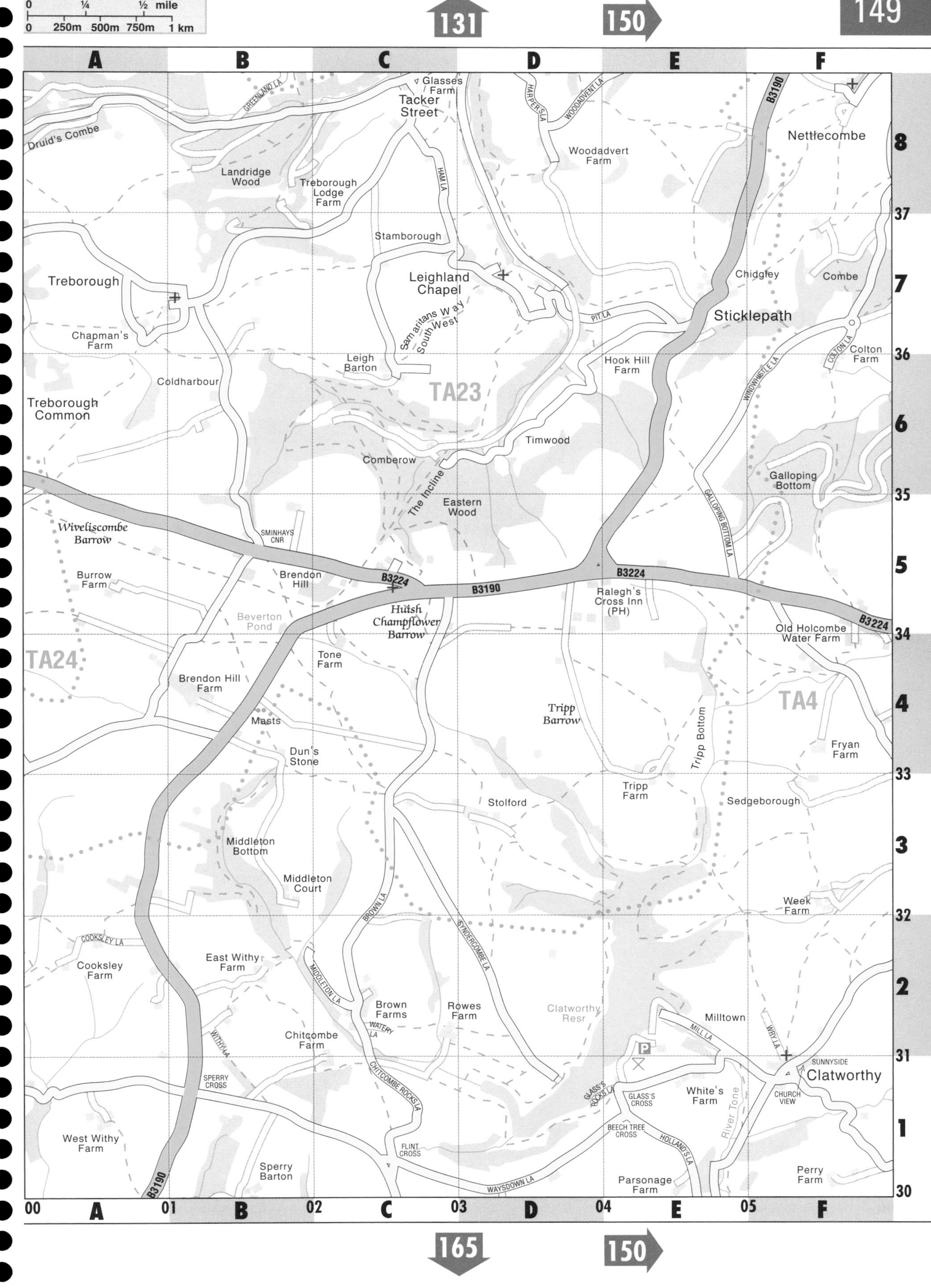
Scale: 1¾ inches to 1 mile
0 ¼ ½ mile
0 250m 500m 750m 1 km
131
150
A B C D E F
Glasses Farm
Tacker Street
Druid's Combe
Landridge Wood
Treborough Lodge Farm
Woodadvert Farm
Nettlecombe
Stamborough
Treborough
Leighland Chapel
Samaritans Way South West
Chidgley
Combe
Sticklepath
Chapman's Farm
Leigh Barton
Hook Hill Farm
Colton Farm
Coldharbour
Treborough Common
TA23
Timwood
Comberow
The Incline
Eastern Wood
Galloping Bottom
Wiveliscombe Barrow
SMINHAYS CNR
Brendon Hill
Burrow Farm
B3224
B3190
Ralegh's Cross Inn (PH)
Beverton Pond
Huish Champflower Barrow
Old Holcombe Water Farm
TA24
Tone Farm
Brendon Hill Farm
Tripp Barrow
TA4
Masts
Tripp Bottom
Fryan Farm
Dun's Stone
Tripp Farm
Stolford
Sedgeborough
Middleton Bottom
Middleton Court
Week Farm
COOKSLEY LA
Cooksley Farm
East Withy Farm
Brown Farms
Rowes Farm
Clatworthy Resr
Milltown
Chitcombe Farm
SPERRY CROSS
GLASS'S CROSS
White's Farm
Clatworthy
SUNNYSIDE
CHURCH VIEW
River Tone
BEECH TREE CROSS
FLINT CROSS
West Withy Farm
Sperry Barton
Parsonage Farm
Perry Farm
WAYSDOWN LA
8 37 7 36 6 35 5 34 4 33 3 32 2 31 1 30
00 01 02 03 04 05
165
150

Scale: 1¾ inches to 1 mile

0 ¼ ½ mile
0 250m 500m 750m 1 km

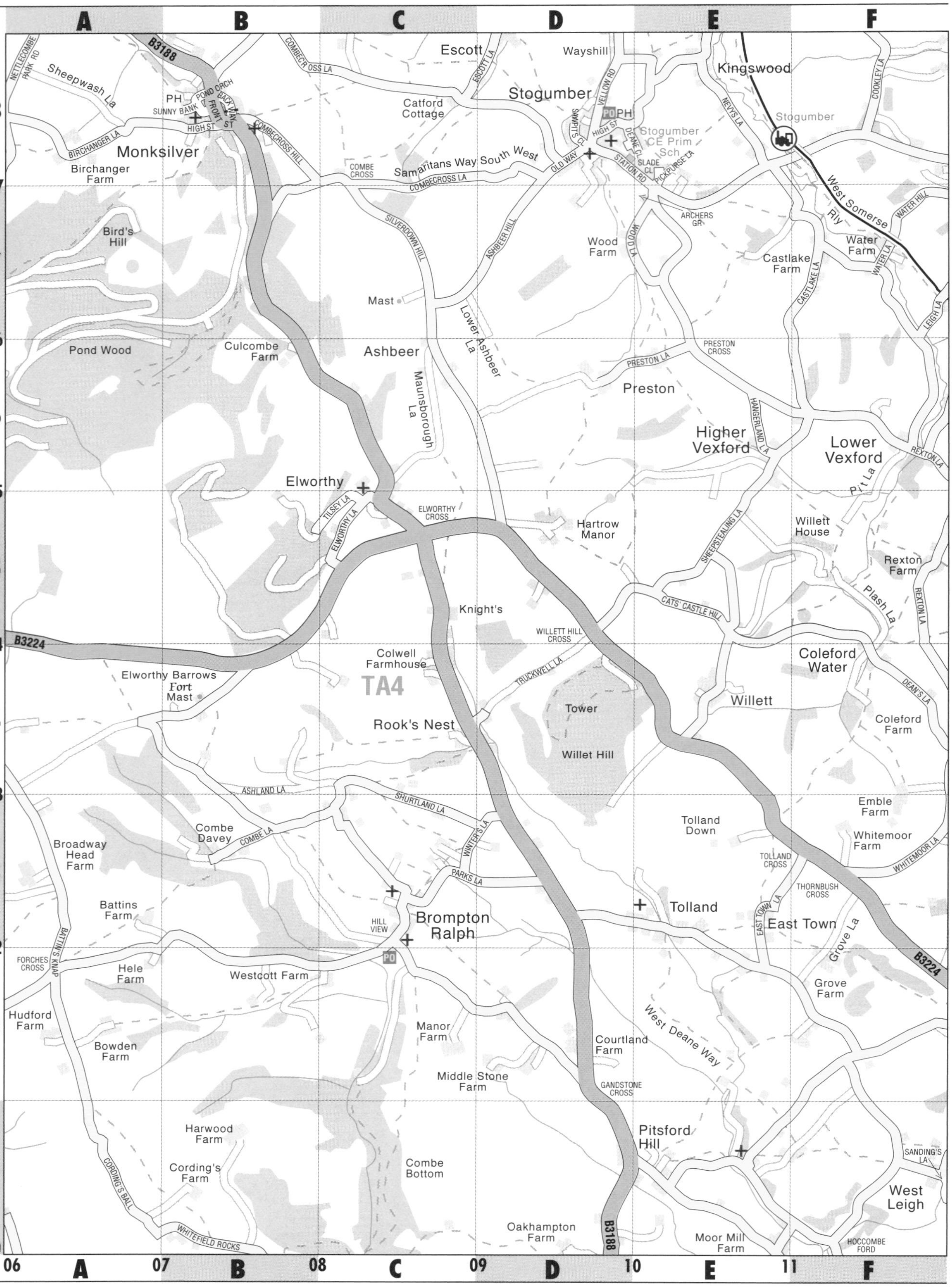

A B C D E F

8

NETTLECOMBE PARK RD
B3188
Sheepwash La
Birchanger La
PH
SUNNY BANK
POND ORCH
HIGH ST
FRONT ST
BACK LA
COMBECROSS HILL
Monksilver
Birchanger Farm

Escott
COMBE CROSS LA
Catford Cottage
Stogumber
Wayshill
Kingswood
Stogumber
NEVIS LA
COOKLEY LA

37
COMBE CROSS
Samaritans Way South West
COMBECROSS LA
ASHBEER HILL
OLD WAY
YELLOW RD
HIGH ST
STATION RD
DENE CL
SLADE CL
PICKPURSE LA
Stogumber CE Prim Sch
ARCHERS GR
West Somerset Rly
WATER HILL

7
Bird's Hill
SILVERTOWN HILL
Mast
Lower Ashbeer La
Wood Farm
WOOD LA
Castlake Farm
CASTLAKE LA
WATER LA
Water Farm
LEIGH LA

36
Pond Wood
Culcombe Farm
Ashbeer
Maunsborough La
PRESTON CROSS
PRESTON LA
Preston

6
Higher Vexford
HANGERLAND LA
Lower Vexford
REXTON LA

35
Elworthy
TILSEY LA
ELWORTHY LA
Elworthy Cross
Hartrow Manor
SHEEPSTEALING LA
Willett House

5
Knight's
CATS CASTLE HILL
Rexton Farm
PLASH LA
PIT LA
REXTON LA

34
B3224
Elworthy Barrows Fort Mast
Colwell Farmhouse
WILLETT HILL CROSS
TRUCKWELL LA
Tower
Willett
Coleford Water
DEAN'S LA

TA4

4
Rook's Nest
Willet Hill
Coleford Farm

33
ASHLAND LA
SHURTLAND LA
Combe Davey
COMBE LA
Tolland Down
Emble Farm
Whitemoor Farm
WHITEMOOR LA

3
Broadway Head Farm
Battins Farm
WINTERS LA
PARKS LA
HILL VIEW
PO
Brompton Ralph
Tolland
TOLLAND CROSS
EAST TOWN LA
THORNBUSH CROSS
East Town
GROVE LA
B3224

32
FORCHES CROSS
BATTIN'S KNAP
Hele Farm
Westcott Farm
PO
Grove Farm

2
Hudford Farm
Bowden Farm
Manor Farm
Middle Stone Farm
Courtland Farm
West Deane Way

31
Harwood Farm
GANDSTONE CROSS
Pitsford Hill
SANDING'S LA

1
CORDING'S BALL
Cording's Farm
Combe Bottom
West Leigh

30
WHITEFIELD ROCKS
Oakhampton Farm
B3188
Moor Mill Farm
HOCCOMBE FORD

06 A 07 B 08 C 09 D 10 E 11 F

Scale: 1¾ inches to 1 mile

133
152

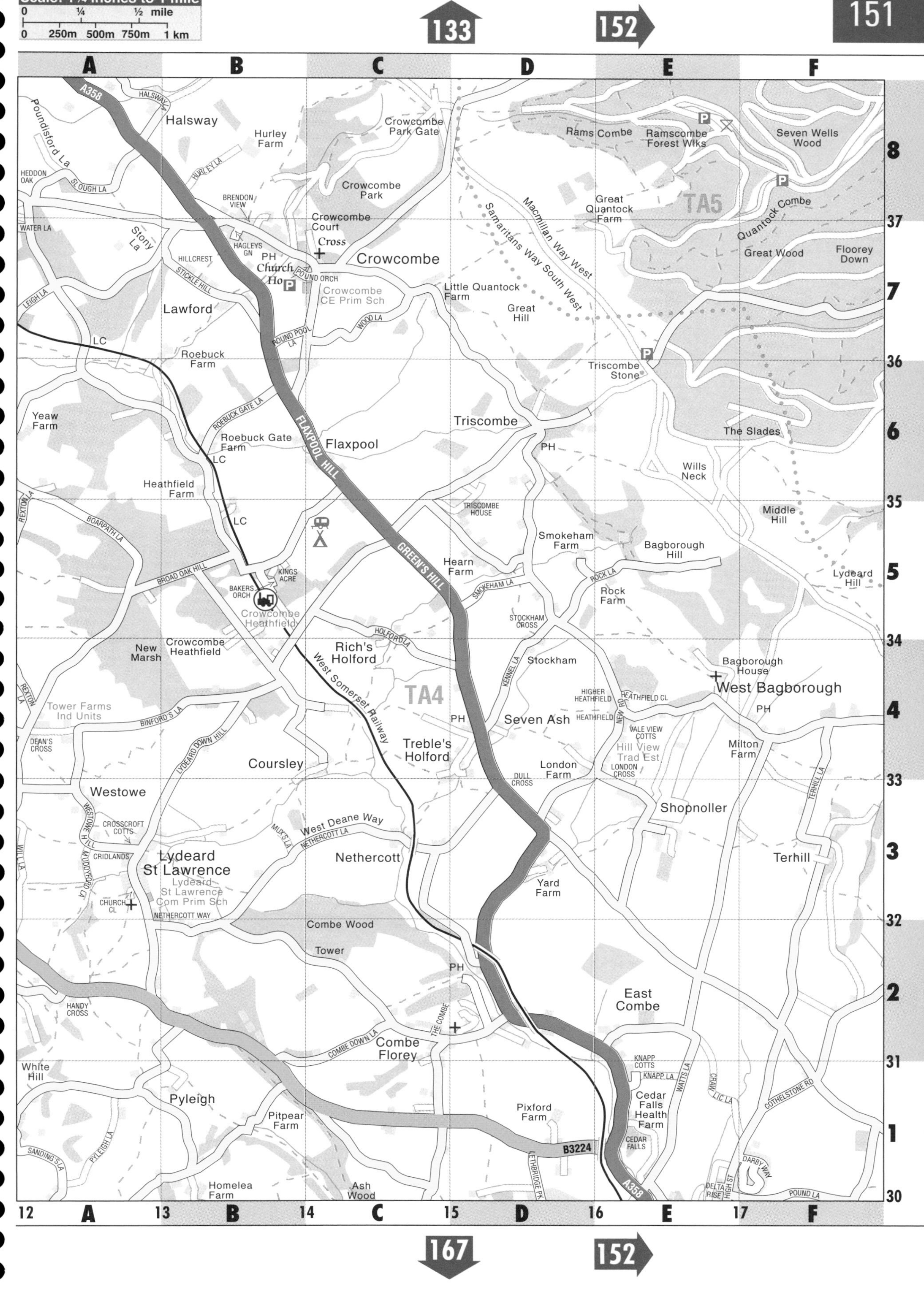
Halsway
Hurley Farm
Crowcombe Park Gate
Rams Combe
Ramscombe Forest Wlks
Seven Wells Wood
Crowcombe Park
Great Quantock Farm
TA5
Quantock Combe
Crowcombe Court
Cross
Crowcombe
Church Ho
Crowcombe CE Prim Sch
Great Wood
Floorey Down
Lawford
Little Quantock Farm
Great Hill
Samaritans Way South West
Macmillan Way West
Roebuck Farm
Triscombe Stone
Yeaw Farm
Triscombe
Roebuck Gate Farm
Flaxpool
The Slades
Wills Neck
Heathfield Farm
Middle Hill
Smokeham Farm
Bagborough Hill
Hearn Farm
Rock Farm
Lydeard Hill
Crowcombe Heathfield
New Marsh
Rich's Holford
Stockham
Bagborough House
West Bagborough
TA4
Tower Farms Ind Units
Seven Ash
Hill View Trad Est
Treble's Holford
Coursley
London Farm
Milton Farm
Westowe
Shopnoller
West Deane Way
Nethercott
Lydeard St Lawrence
Lydeard St Lawrence Com Prim Sch
Terhill
Yard Farm
Combe Wood
Tower
East Combe
Combe Florey
White Hill
Pyleigh
Cedar Falls Health Farm
Pitpear Farm
Pixford Farm
Homelea Farm
Ash Wood
West Somerset Railway
A358
B3224
FLAXPOOL HILL
GREEN'S HILL

167
152

151 134

Scale: 1¾ inches to 1 mile
0   ¼   ½   mile
0   250m   500m   750m   1 km

A   B   C   D   E   F

Adscombe
ADSCOMBE LA
ALEY
Quantock Lodge
Pepper Hill
Round Hill
Plainsfield
PARSONS LA
BROOMYLAND HILL
Aisholt Wood
Aisholt
Aisholt Common
Durborough Farm
Luxborough Farm
BEECH TREE HILL
Hawkridge Common
Lower Aisholt
GOOD'S LA
ELLIS'S LA
Good's Farm
Bishpool Farm
Lower Merridge
Merridge
Great Holwell
MERRIDGE HILL
Radlet Common
Rowdens Farm
TUT WELL LA
The Gables
Tuxwell Farm
Ebsley Farm
Hawkridge Resr
Hawkridge Farm
LAWYER'S HILL
PEARTWATER HILL
PEARTWATER RD
TWINELL LA
Bush
BUSH RD
VICTORIA WAY
Holwell Combe
PARISH LAND LA
NO PLACE LA
Tudball
Courtway
TA5
PH
THREE HORSE SHOES HILL
Gib Hill
SAMARITANS WAY SOUTH WEST
Park End
Kenley Bottom
BIRCHES CNR
Twenty Acre Plantation
Timbercombe
Merridge Hill
Cuckold's Row
Splatt
Spaxton
SPLATT LA
CHURCH RD
HIGH ST
Stephens Farm
Spaxton CE Prim Sch
FOUR FORKS LA
PIGHTLEY RD
Tutton's Farm
BUSH LA
Pightley
PIGHTLEY LA
Charlynch
CHARLYNCH HILL
CHARLYNCH RD
Four Forks
POD
Postridge Farm
PH
Holmes Farm
BARFORD CL
BARFORD RD
Durleigh Brook
Barford House
Enmore Castle
Enmore CE Prim Sch
ENMORE RD
BLAXHOLD LA
Smocombe House
Broomfield Hall
Higher Heathcombe Farm
WATERY LA
Wind Down
Ruborough Camp
Rockhouse Farm
LYDEARD CROSS
Lydeard Farm
Bolts
SHALLA LA
Broomfield Hill
Ducks' Pool
Westleigh Farm
Fyne Court Nat Res & Visitor Ctr
Fyne Court
Broomfield
Rose Hill
SHELTHORN HILL
ROSE HILL
Wort Wood
Owls Hill Farm
Raswell Farm
Row's Farm
BUNCOMBE HILL
Buncombe Wood
Ball Covert
MACMILLAN WAY WEST
BALL LA
CUSHUISH LA
Ivyton Farm
West Dean Way
Cushuish
Toulton
Middlebrooks
CUSHUISH LANE COTTS
FENNINGTON LA
TA2
Tetton House
Tetton Farm
Beech Copse
Tanyard
Cheddon Down
Kingston Beacon
Yards Barn
VOLIS CROSS
VOLIS HILL
LODES LA
Cothelstone Hill
TA4
COTHELSTONE RD
Badger Copse
Holy Well
Cothelstone
Cothelstone Farm

37   7   36   6   35   5   34   4   33   3   32   2   31   1   30

18   A   19   B   20   C   21   D   22   E   23   F

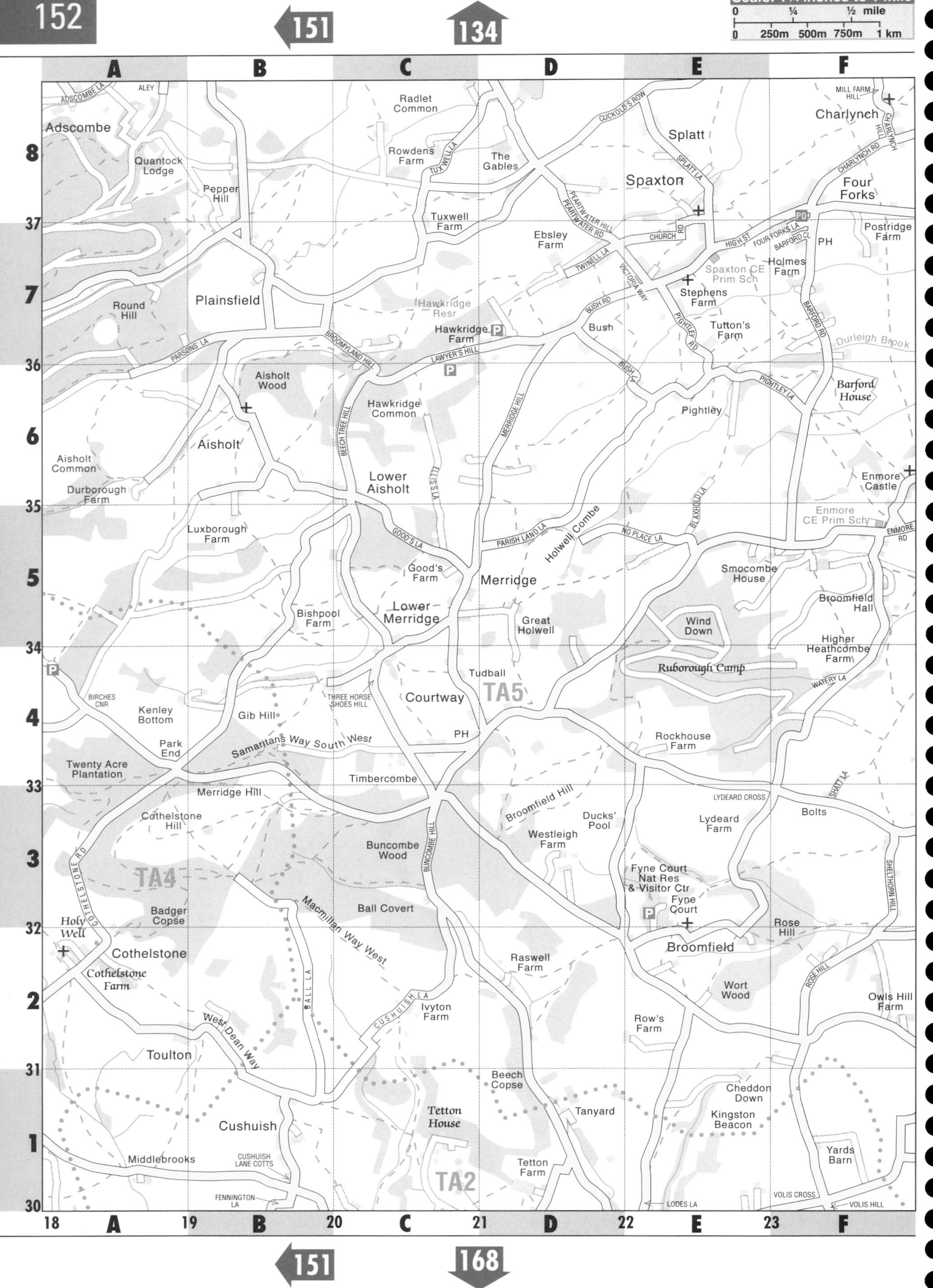

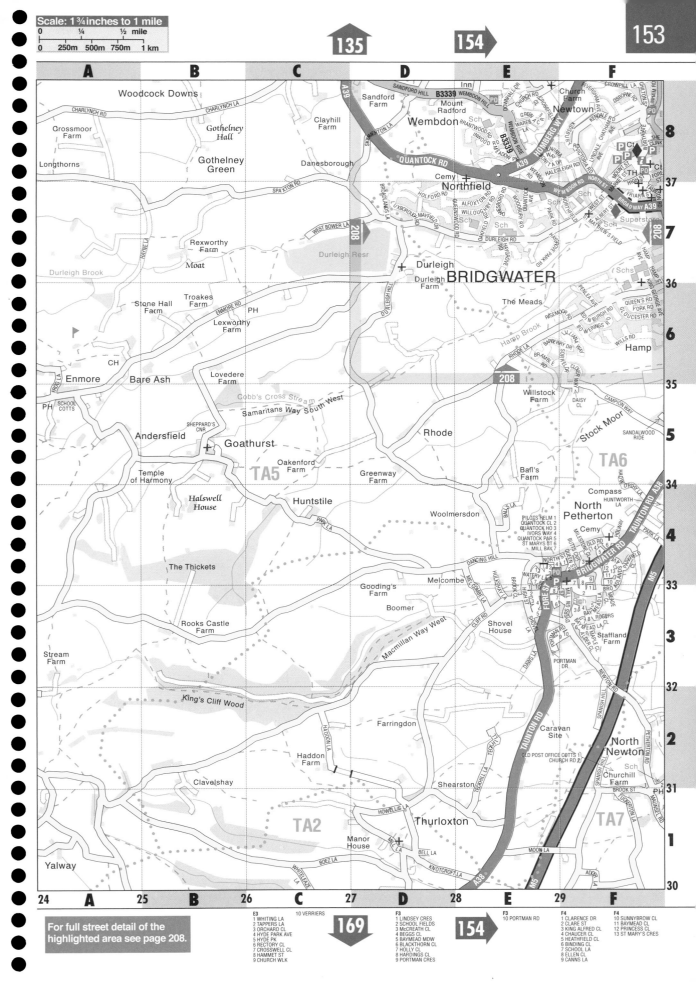

Scale: 1¾inches to 1 mile

0   ¼   ½   mile
0   250m   500m   750m   1 km

135   154

Map labels (A–F columns, 30–38 rows):

Woodcock Downs
CHARLYNCH RD
Crossmoor Farm
Longthorns
Gothelney Hall
Gothelney Green
CHARLYNCH LA
Clayhill Farm
Danesborough
SPAXTON RD
Sandford Hill
Sandford Farm
B3339
Mount Radford
Wembdon
Newtown
Church Farm
CROWPILL LA
QUANTOCK RD
A39
HOMBERG WY
B3339
Cemy
Northfield
BRIDGWATER
WEST BOWER LA
208
Durleigh Resr
Durleigh
Durleigh Farm
The Meads
Harp Brook
Hamp
Rexworthy Farm
Moat
HAYE LA
Durleigh Brook
Stone Hall Farm
Troakes Farm
ENMORE RD
PH
Lexworthy Farm
DURLEIGH HILL
RISEMOOR RD
RHODE LA
Queen's Park
CH
Enmore
Bare Ash
Lovedere Farm
Cobb's Cross Stream
Samaritans Way South West
Willstock Farm
Stock Moor
SANDALWOOD RIDE
CAMPION WAY
DAISY CL
FROG LA
PH
SCHOOL COTTS
SHEPPARD'S CNR
Andersfield
Goathurst
Oakenford Farm
Rhode
Ball's Farm
Compass
TA6
TA5
Temple of Harmony
Halswell House
Huntstile
Greenway Farm
Woolmersdon
North Petherton
HUNTWORTH LA
Cemy
PARK LA
The Thickets
Gooding's Farm
Boomer
Melcombe
DANCING HILL
MELCOMBE LA
Shovel House
BRIDGWATER RD
Staffland Farm
M5
Rooks Castle Farm
Macmillan Way West
CLIFF RD
FORE ST
PORTMAN DR
TAUNTON RD
PARK LA
Stream Farm
King's Cliff Wood
Farringdon
Caravan Site
North Newton
SPANISH HILL
PETHERTON RD
HADDON LA
Haddon Farm
Clavelshay
Shearston
TECH LA
Churchill Farm
PH
BROOK ST
TA7
TA2
Manor House
Thurloxton
BELL LA
MOON LA
Yalway
BOEZ LA
WHITELEAZE LA
KNOTCROFT LA
A38
M5
ADOR LA
MAUNSEL LA

For full street detail of the highlighted area see page 208.

169   154

E3
1 WHITING LA
2 TAPPERS LA
3 ORCHARD CL
4 HYDE PARK AVE
5 HYDE PK
6 RECTORY CL
7 CROSSWELL CL
8 HAMMET ST
9 CHURCH WLK

10 VERRIERS

F3
1 LINDSEY CRES
2 SCHOOL FIELDS
3 McCREATH CL
4 BEGGS CL
5 BAYMEAD MDW
6 BLACKTHORN CL
7 HOLLY CL
8 HARDINGS CL
9 PORTMAN CRES

F3
10 PORTMAN RD

F4
1 CLARENCE DR
2 CLARE ST
3 KING ALFRED CL
4 CHAUCER CL
5 HEATHFIELD CL
6 BINDING CL
7 SCHOOL LA
8 ELLEN CL
9 CANNS LA

F4
10 SUNNYBROW CL
11 BAYMEAD CL
12 PRINCESS CL
13 ST MARY'S CRES

153 136

Scale: 1¾ inches to 1 mile
0   ¼   ½ mile
0 250m 500m 750m 1 km

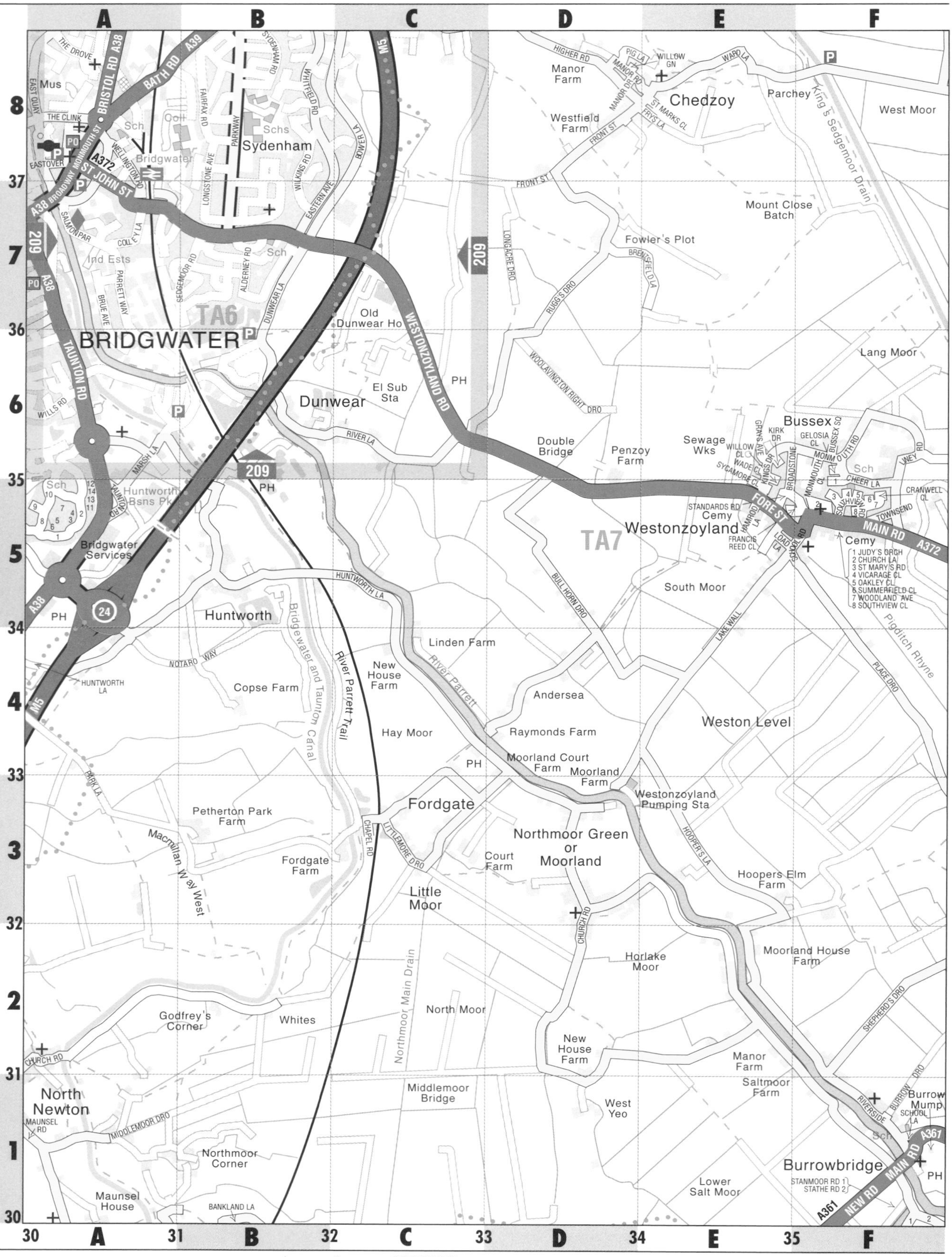

A B C D E F

THE DROVE
Mus
EAST QUAY
THE CLINK
EASTOVER
BROADWAY MONMOUTH ST
ST JOHN ST
BRISTOL RD A38
BATH RD A39
A39
WELLINGTON RD
FAIRFAX RD
WILKINS RD
PARKWAY
LONGSTONE AVE
SYDENHAM RD
WHITFIELD RD
HAVEN
EASTERN AVE

Sch
Coll
Bridgwater
Sydenham
Schs

A372
A38
209
P
PO

BRIDGWATER
TA6
Ind Ests
PARRETT WAY
BLUE LA
SEDGEMOOR RD
ALDERNEY RD
COLE LA
DUNWEAR LA
Sch

Old Dunwear Ho
Dunwear
El Sub Sta
PH
RIVER LA

209

MARSH LA
TAUNTON RD
WILLS RD

Sch
Huntworth Bsns Pk

Bridgwater Services
24
A38
M5
PH
HUNTWORTH LA
NOTARO WAY

Huntworth
Copse Farm
Bridgwater and Taunton Canal
River Parrett Trail
New House Farm
Hay Moor
Linden Farm

HUNTWORTH LA

Petherton Park Farm
Macmillan Way West
Fordgate Farm

CHAPEL RD
LITTLEMOOR DRO
Northmoor Main Drain

Fordgate
PH
Court Farm
Little Moor

PARK LA

Godfrey's Corner
Whites
North Moor

CHURCH RD
North Newton
MAUNSEL RD
MIDDLEMOOR DRO
Northmoor Corner
Maunsel House
BANKLAND LA
Middlemoor Bridge

WESTONZOYLAND RD
PH
Double Bridge
Penzoy Farm

HIGHER RD
PIG LA
WILLOW GN
MANOR DRO
WARD LA
KING'S SEDGEMOOR DRAIN
P
Manor Farm
ST MARKS CL
FRYS LA
FRONT ST
Chedzoy
Westfield Farm
Parchey
West Moor

FRONT ST
Mount Close Batch
Fowler's Plot
BRENSFIELD LA
LONGACRE DRO
RUGGS DRO
209
WOOLAVINGTON RIGHT DRO

Lang Moor

Bussex
KIRK CL
GRANS AVE
WILLOW CL
WADE CL
SYCAMORE CL
GELOSIA CL
BUSSEX SQ
MONM OUTH RD
BROADSTONE
CHEER LA
CRANWELL CL
Sch

Sewage Wks
STANDARDS RD
FRANCIS REED CL
FORE ST
LOAD DRO
Cemy
Westonzoyland
TA7
MAIN RD A372
Cemy
1 JUDY'S ORCH
2 CHURCH LA
3 ST MARY'S RD
4 VICARAGE CL
5 OAKLEY CL
6 SUMMERFIELD CL
7 WOODLAND AVE
8 SOUTHVIEW CL

South Moor
BULL HORN DRO
LAKE WALL

Andersea
Weston Level

Raymonds Farm
Moorland Court Farm
Moorland Farm
Westonzoyland Pumping Sta
HOOPER'S LA

Northmoor Green or Moorland
PLACE DRO
PIDITCH RHYNE
Hoopers Elm Farm

CHURCH RD
Horlake Moor
Moorland House Farm

New House Farm
West Yeo
Manor Farm
Saltmoor Farm
SHEPHERD'S DRO

RIVERSIDE
BURROW DRO
Burrow Mump
BURROW SCHOOL LA
Sch
NEW RD
MAIN RD
A361
Burrowbridge
STANMOOR RD 1
STATHE RD 2
PH

Lower Salt Moor
A361

8 7 37 7 36 6 35 5 34 4 33 3 32 2 31 1 30

30 A 31 B 32 C 33 D 34 E 35 F

For full street detail of the highlighted area see page 209

153 170

A5
1 MUSCOVY DR
2 ROMNEY RD
3 SAVANNAH DR
4 VIENNA WAY
5 TUNDRA WALK
6 CHEVIOT ST
7 MERINO WAY
8 CHAROLAIS DR
9 TEESWATER WAY
10 STOCKMOOR DR
11 CHAMBRAY RD
12 ANGUS WAY
13 SHIRE ST
14 CHILLINGHAM DRO

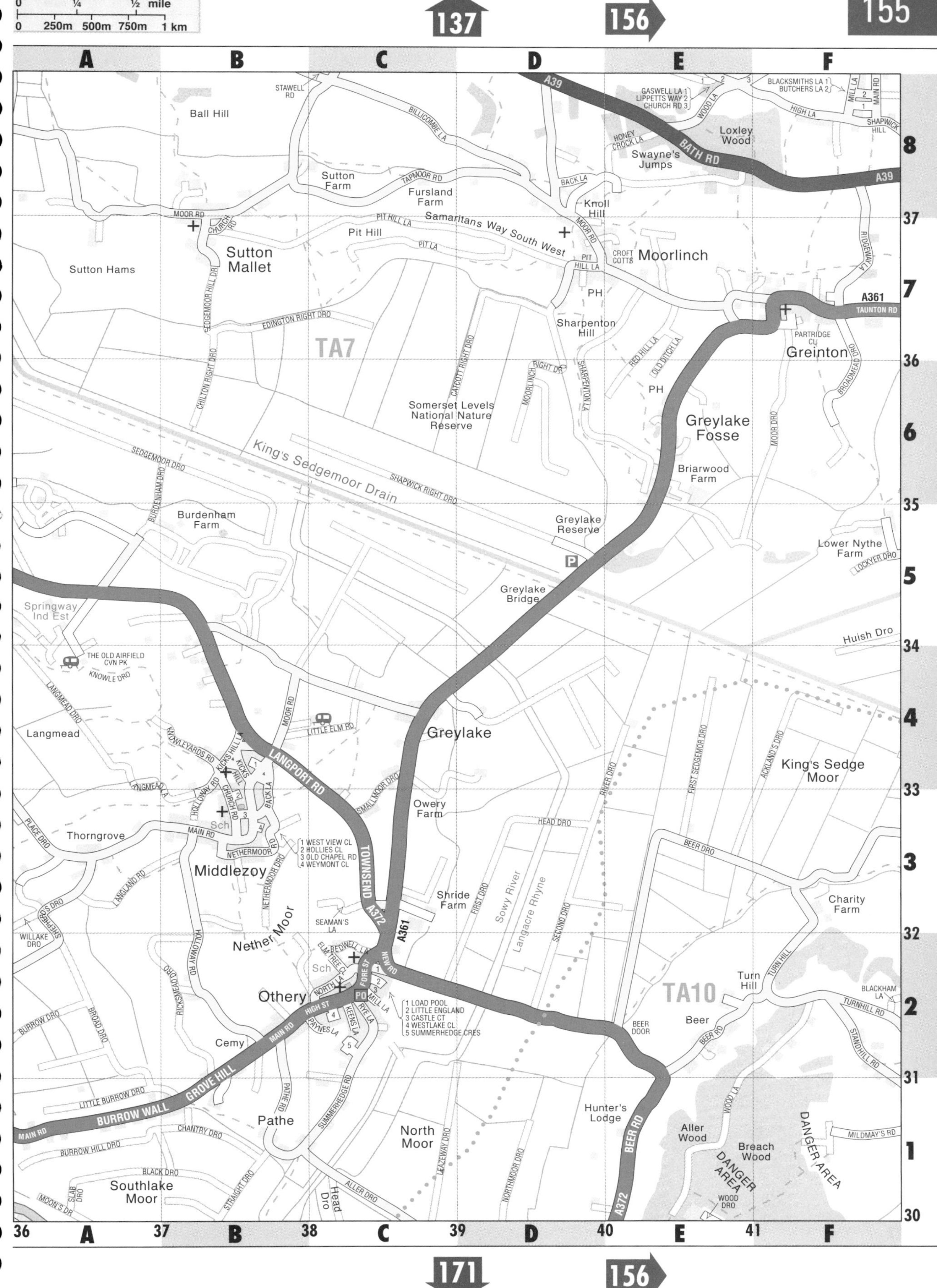
Scale: 1¾ inches to 1 mile
137
156
Ball Hill
Sutton Farm
Fursland Farm
Sutton Mallet
Sutton Hams
Pit Hill
Samaritans Way South West
Knoll Hill
Moorlinch
Loxley Wood
Swayne's Jumps
BATH RD
A39
Sharpenton Hill
Greinton
A361
TA7
Somerset Levels National Nature Reserve
Greylake Fosse
Briarwood Farm
King's Sedgemoor Drain
Burdenham Farm
Greylake Reserve
Lower Nythe Farm
Greylake Bridge
Springway Ind Est
THE OLD AIRFIELD CVN PK
Huish Dro
Langmead
Greylake
King's Sedge Moor
LANGPORT RD
Owery Farm
Thorngrove
Middlezoy
TOWNSEND
A372
Shride Farm
Sowy River
Langacre Rhyne
Charity Farm
Nether Moor
Othery
Turn Hill
TA10
Beer
Cemy
GROVE HILL
BURROW WALL
Pathe
North Moor
Hunter's Lodge
BEER RD
Aller Wood
Breach Wood
DANGER AREA
Southlake Moor
171
156

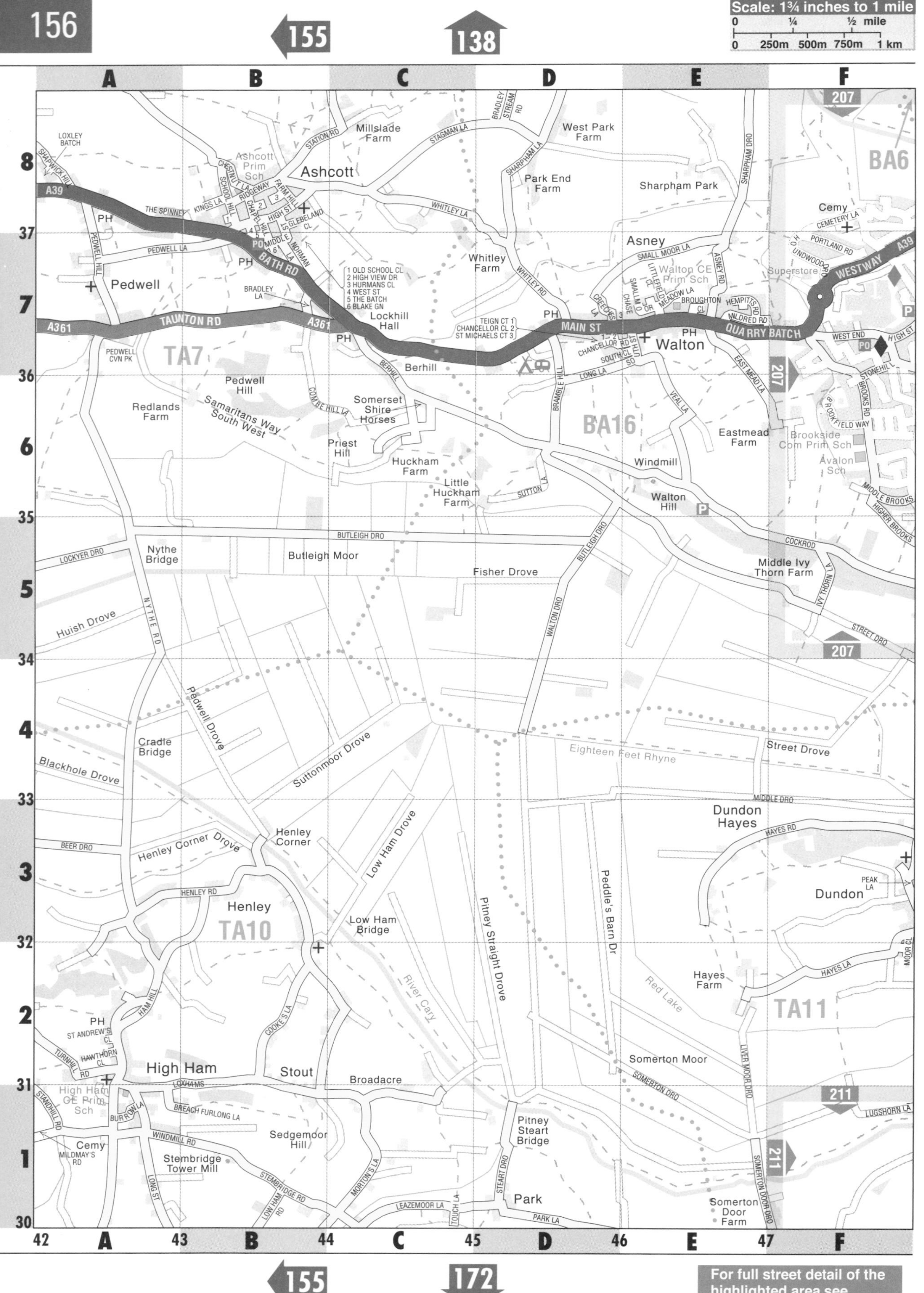

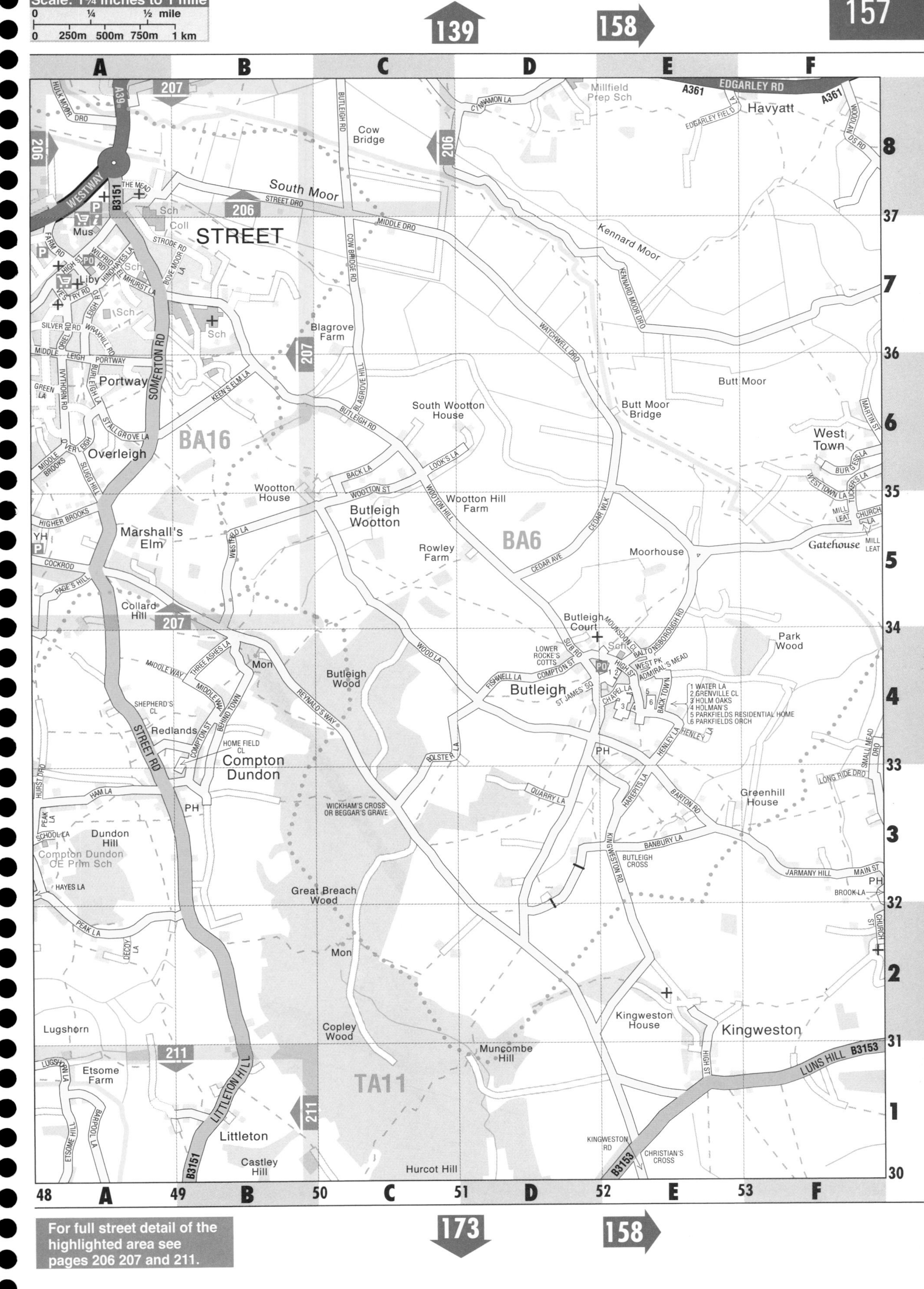

Scale: 1¾ inches to 1 mile

0   ¼   ½ mile
0 250m 500m 750m 1 km

139
158
206
207
206
207
206
211
211
173
158

A   B   C   D   E   F

8
37
7
36
6
35
5
34
4
33
3
32
2
31
1
30

EDGARLEY RD
A361
Millfield Prep Sch
Havyatt
A361
Edgarley Field
WOODLANDS RD
CYNAMON LA
Cow Bridge
BUTLEIGH RD
South Moor
STREET DRO
MIDDLE DRO
COW BRIDGE RD
Kennard Moor
KENNARD MOOR DRO
WATCHWELL DRO
Butt Moor
Butt Moor Bridge
Blagrove Farm
BLAGROVE DRO
West Town
WEST TOWN LA
TUCKERS LA
BURYES LA
MARTIN LA
MILL LEAT
CHURCH LA
Gatehouse
MILL LEAT
South Wootton House
BUTLEIGH RD
BACK LA
WOOTTON ST
LOOK'S LA
WOOTTON HILL
Wootton Hill Farm
CEDAR WLK
BA6
Moorhouse
Park Wood
Butleigh Wootton
Wootton House
Rowley Farm
CEDAR AVE
Butleigh Court
MONKSTON CL
BALTONSBOROUGH RD

STREET
THE MEAD
B3151
Sch
Coll
Mus
STREET DRO
STRODE RD
WILFRID'S LA
WINDMILL LA
Sch
BOVE MOOR RD
206
KEEN'S ELM LA
207
BA16
Portway
PORTWAY
Sch
HURST DRO
MIDDLE LEIGH
BURLEIGH
WRAXHILL RD
SOMERTON RD
STALLGROVE LA
Overleigh
SILVER RD
LEIGH RD
IVYTHORN RD
GREEN LA
MIDDLE BROOKS
HIGHER BROOKS
SLUGG HILL
OVER LEIGH
Liby
Marshall's Elm
OLD LA
WEST END
YH
COCKROD
PAGE'S HILL
Collard Hill
207
MIDDLE WAY
THREE ASHES LA
Mon
BEHIND TOWN
SHEPHERD'S CL
MIDDLE WAY
REYNALD'S WAY
Butleigh Wood
WOOD LA
Redlands
COMPTON ST
HOME FIELD CL
STREET RD
Compton Dundon
PH
BOLSTER LA
WICKHAM'S CROSS OR BEGGAR'S GRAVE
PEAK LA
SCHOOL LA
Dundon Hill
HAM LA
Compton Dundon CE Prim Sch
HAYES LA
Great Breach Wood
Mon
PEAK LA
ZOEY LA
Lugshorn
LUGS HILL LA
211
Etsome Farm
ETSOME HILL
BARPOOL LA
LITTLETON HILL
B3151
Littleton
Castley Hill
TA11
Copley Wood
Muncombe Hill
Hurcot Hill
QUARRY LA
HARPEYS LA
HENLEY LA
Butleigh
St JAMES SQ
HIGH ST
CHAPEL LA
BACK TOWN
WEST PK
Admiral's Mead
Lower Rocke's Cotts
FISHWELL LA
SUB RD
COMPTON ST
Henley
PH
BARTON RD
Greenhill House
KINGWESTON RD
Butleigh Cross
BANBURY LA
JARMANY HILL
MAIN ST
PH
BROOK LA
LONG RIDE DRO
SMALL MEAD
Kingweston House
Kingweston
HIGH ST
KINGWESTON RD
Christian's Cross
LUNS HILL
B3153
CHURCH ST
B3153

1 WATER LA
2 GRENVILLE CL
3 HOLM OAKS
4 HOLMAN'S
5 PARKFIELDS RESIDENTIAL HOME
6 PARKFIELDS ORCH

HULK MOOR DRO
FARM RD
A39
WESTWAY
B3151

48   49   50   51   52   53

For full street detail of the highlighted area see pages 206 207 and 211.

157
140

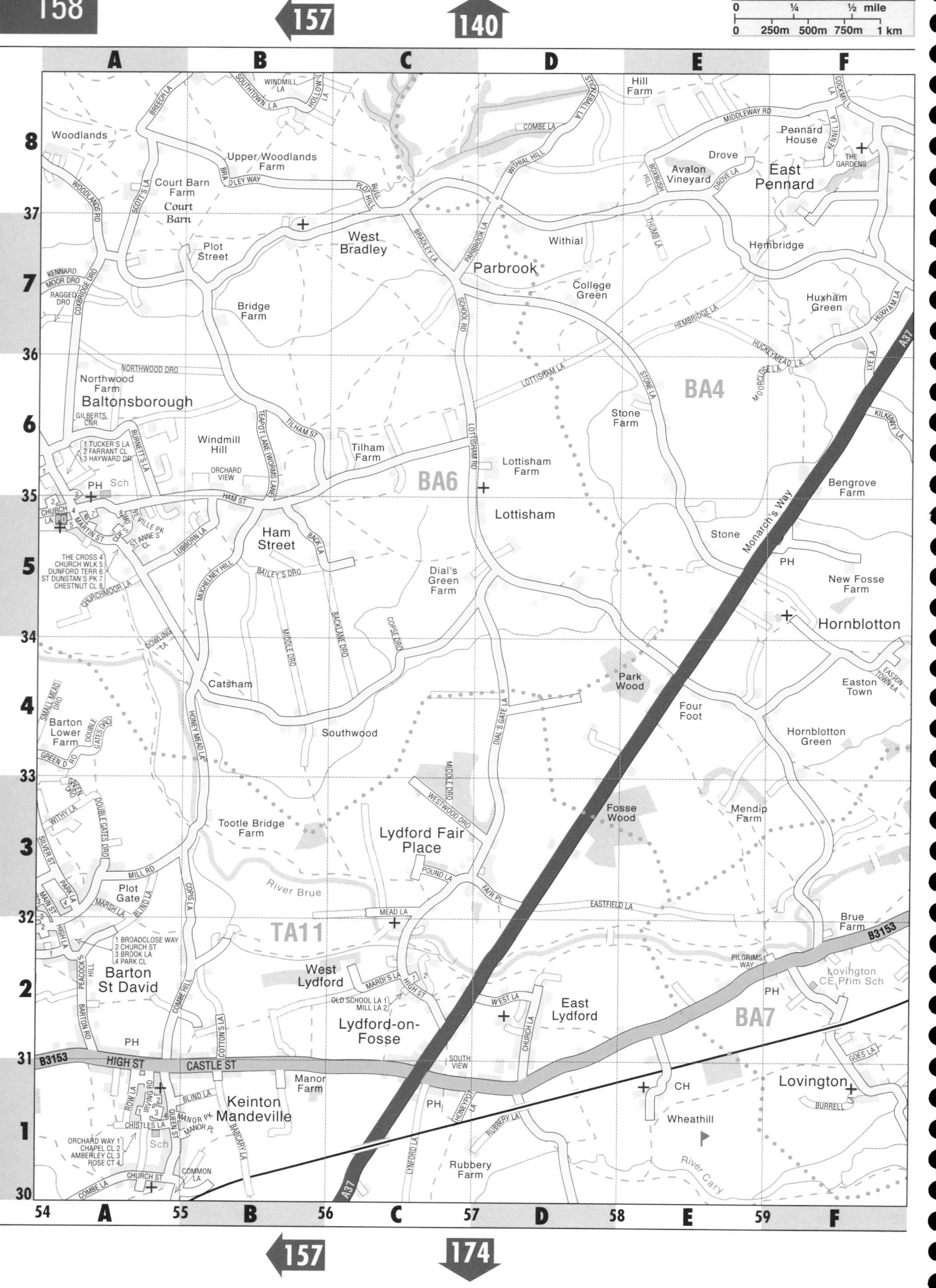
Scale: 1¾ inches to 1 mile
0 ¼ ½ mile
0 250m 500m 750m 1 km
Woodlands
Upper Woodlands Farm
Court Barn Farm
Court Barn
Plot Street
West Bradley
Parbrook
Withial
College Green
Hill Farm
Avalon Vineyard
Drove
Pennard House
East Pennard
Hembridge
Huxham Green
Bridge Farm
Northwood Farm
Baltonsborough
Windmill Hill
Tilham Farm
Lottisham Farm
Lottisham
Stone Farm
Stone
Bengrove Farm
New Fosse Farm
Hornblotton
Ham Street
Dial's Green Farm
Catsham
Southwood
Park Wood
Four Foot
Easton Town
Hornblotton Green
Barton Lower Farm
Tootle Bridge Farm
Lydford Fair Place
Fosse Wood
Mendip Farm
Plot Gate
River Brue
Brue Farm
West Lydford
Barton St David
Lydford-on-Fosse
East Lydford
Lovington CE Prim Sch
Keinton Mandeville
Manor Farm
Wheathill
Lovington
Rubbery Farm
River Cary
BA4
BA6
BA7
TA11
A37
B3153
Monarch's Way
HIGH ST
CASTLE ST
1 TUCKER'S LA
2 FARRANT CL
3 HAYWARD DR
THE CROSS 4
CHURCH WLK 5
DUNFORD TERR 6
ST DUNSTAN'S PK 7
CHESTNUT CL 8
1 BROADCLOSE WAY
2 CHURCH ST
3 BROOK LA
4 PARK CL
OLD SCHOOL LA 1
MILL LA 2
ORCHARD WAY 1
CHAPEL CL 2
AMBERLEY CL 3
ROSE CT 4

157
174

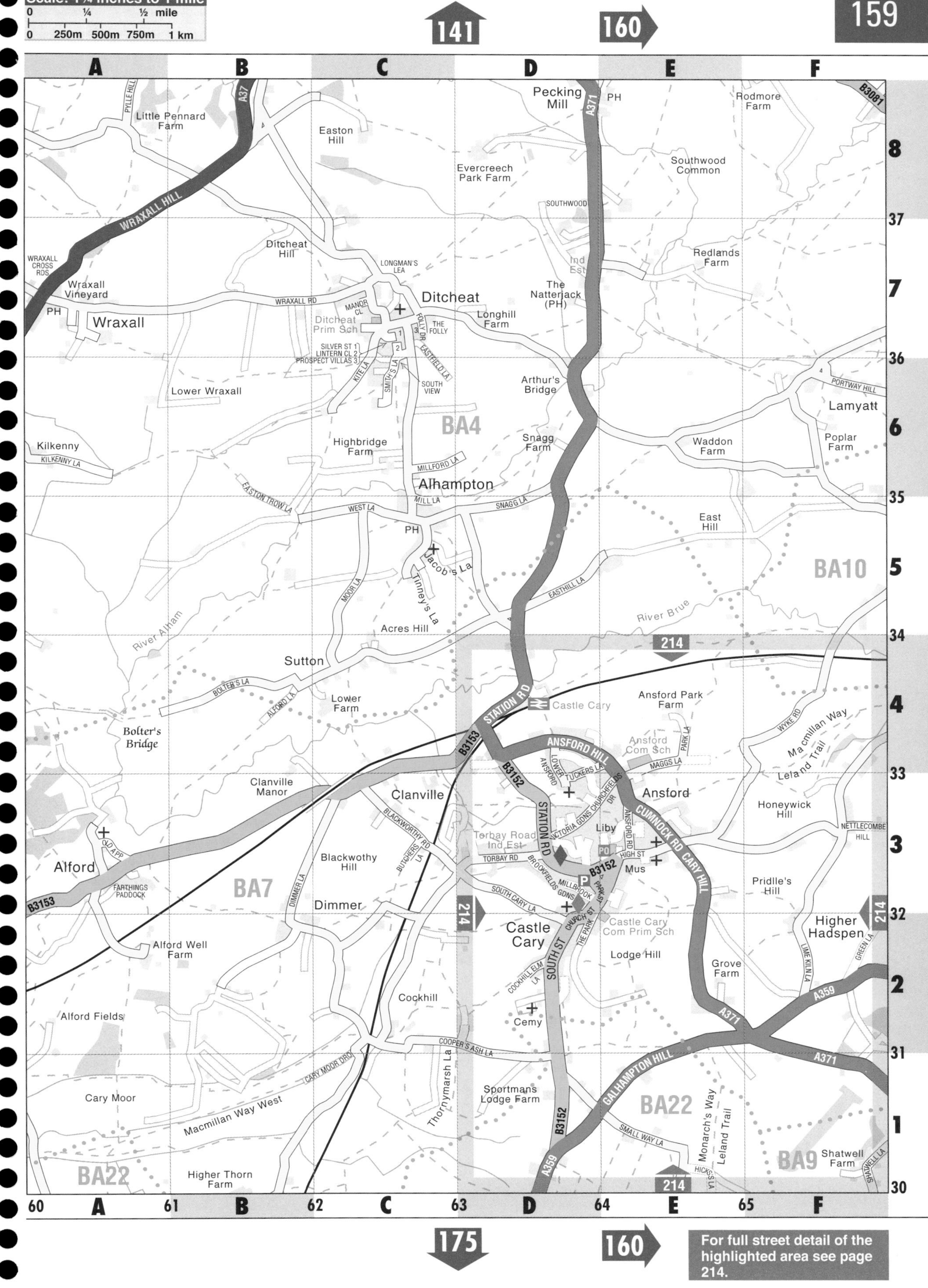

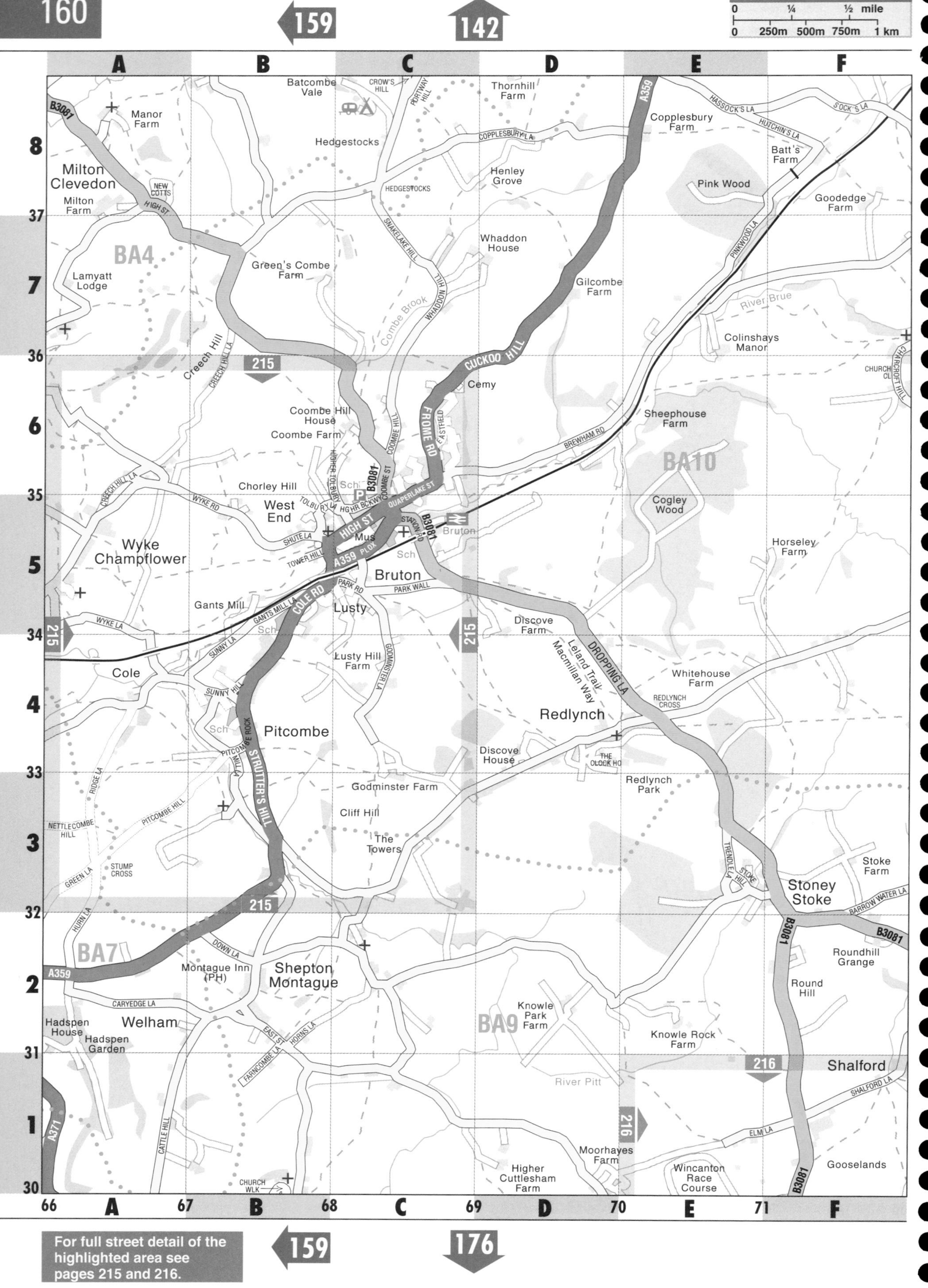

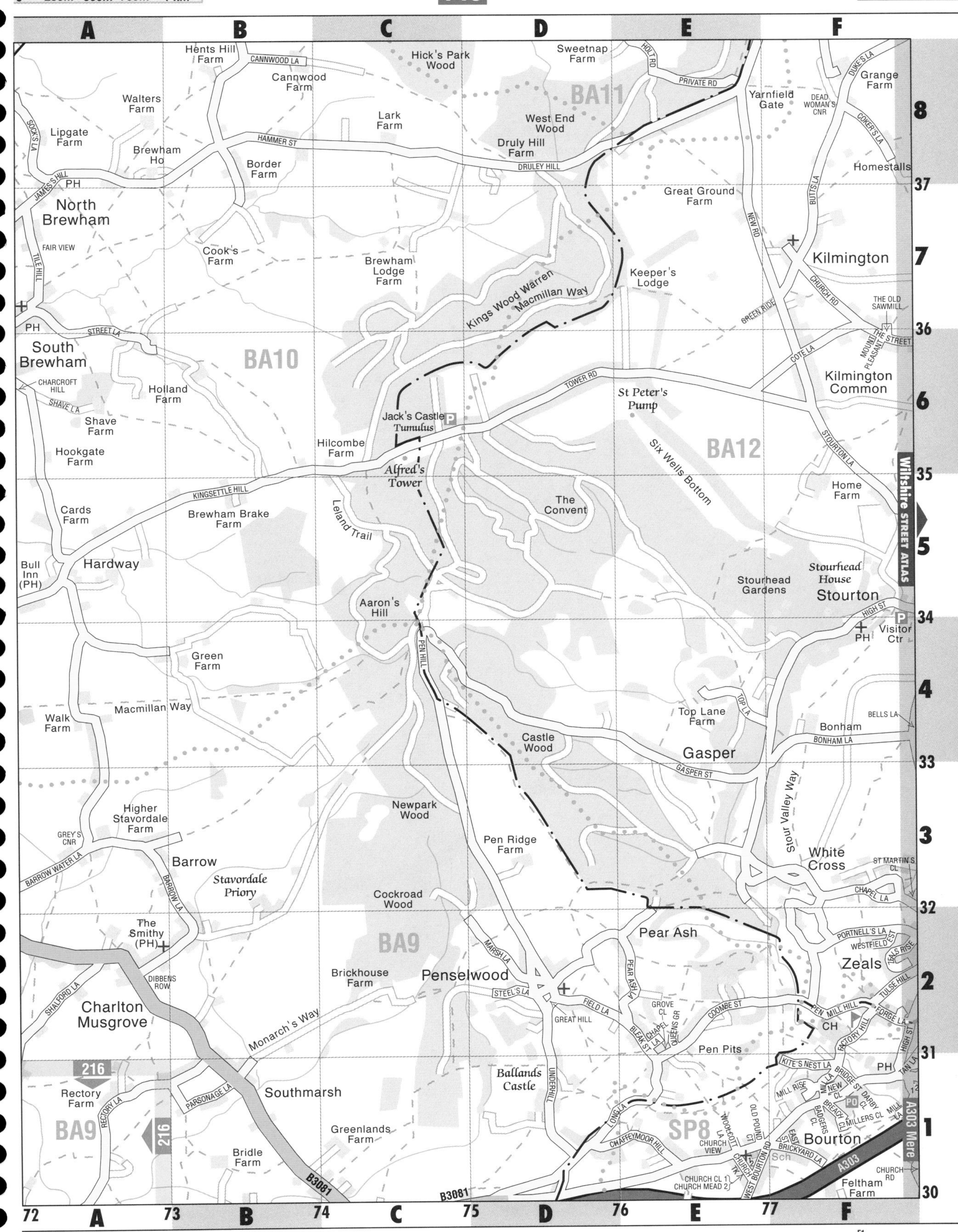

Scale: 1¾ inches to 1 mile

143

177

For full street detail of the highlighted area see page 216.

F1
1 SILTON RD
2 THE MEADOWS

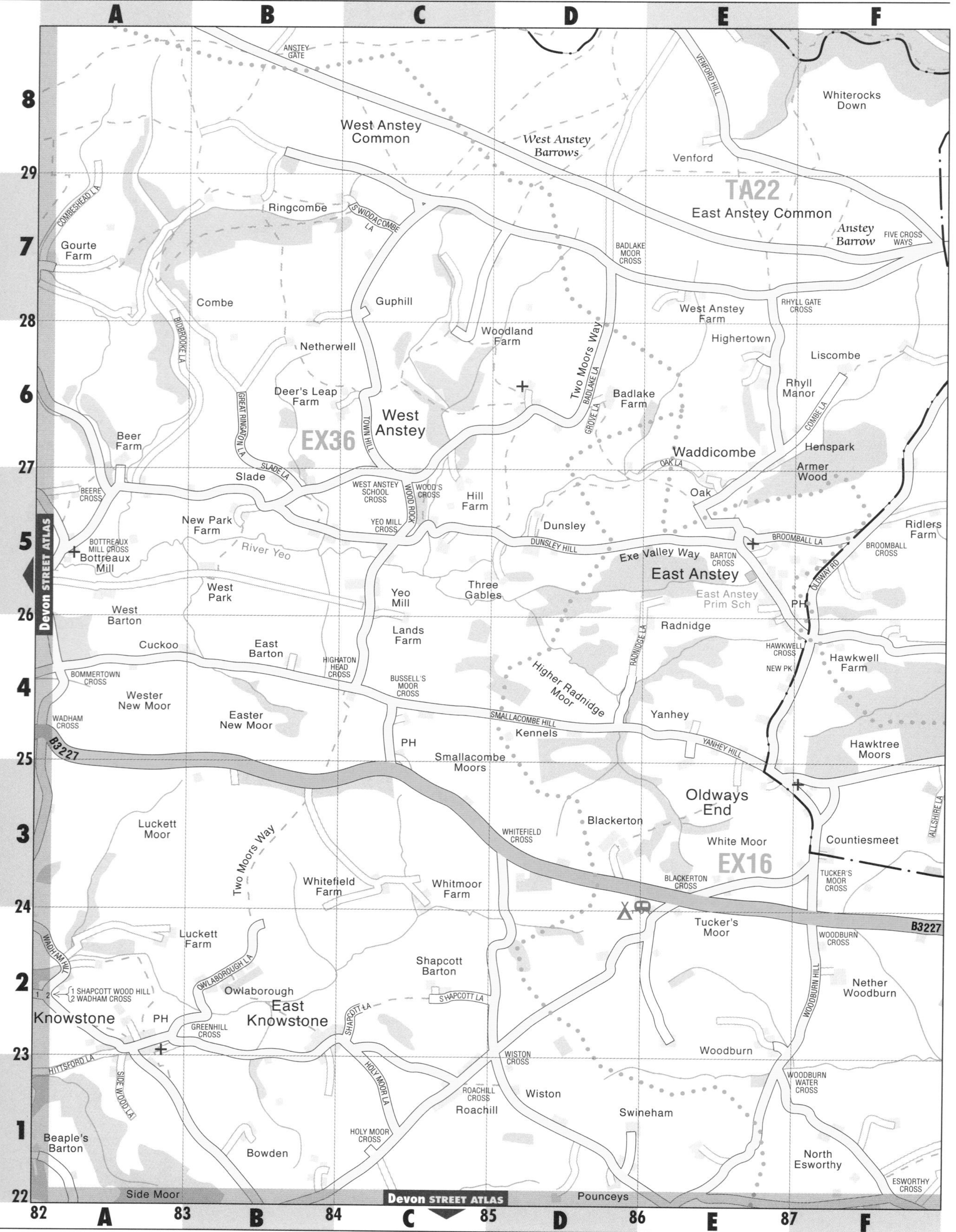

Scale: 1¾ inches to 1 mile

0 ¼ ½ mile
0 250m 500m 750m 1 km

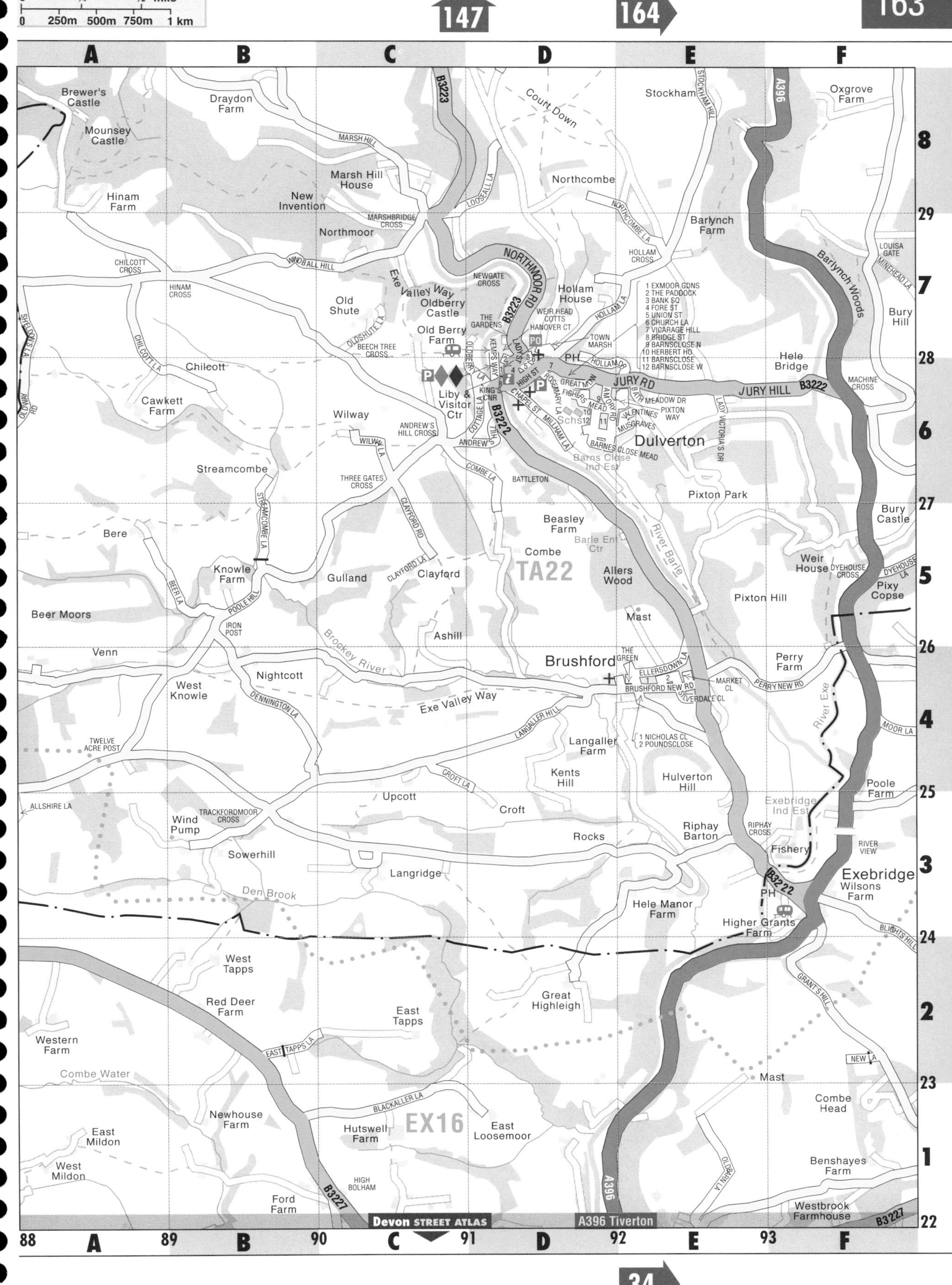
Scale: 1¾ inches to 1 mile
0 ¼ ½ mile
0 250m 500m 750m 1 km
147
164
A B C D E F
Brewer's Castle
Mounsey Castle
Draydon Farm
MARSH HILL
Marsh Hill House
New Invention
Hinam Farm
Northmoor
MARSHBRIDGE CROSS
LOOSEALL LA
Court Down
Stockham
STOCKHAM HILL
Oxgrove Farm
A396
B3223
Northcombe
NORTHCOMBE LA
Barlynch Farm
HOLLAM CROSS
NORTHMOOR RD
WINDBALL HILL
CHILCOTT CROSS
HINAM CROSS
Exe Valley Way
NEWGATE CROSS
Hollam House
Old Shute
Oldberry Castle
THE GARDENS
WEIR HEAD COTTS
HANOVER CT
HOLLAM LA
1 EXMOOR GDNS
2 THE PADDOCK
3 BANK SQ
4 FORE ST
5 UNION ST
6 CHURCH LA
7 VICARAGE HILL
8 BRIDGE ST
9 BARNSCLOSE N
10 HERBERT HO
11 BARNSCLOSE
12 BARNSCLOSE W
Barlynch Woods
LOUISA GATE
MINEHEAD LA
Bury Hill
Old Berry Farm
OLDSHUTE LA
BEECH TREE CROSS
TOWN MARSH
PO
PH
Hele Bridge
Chilcott
CHILCOTT LA
SHILLOWS LA
OLDWAY RD
JURY RD
JURY HILL
B3222
MACHINE CROSS
Liby & Visitor Ctr
KING'S CNR
HIGH ST
GREAT MDW
FISHERS MEAD
AMORY RD
BATH MEADOW DR
PIXTON WAY
VALENTINES
MUSGRAVES
LADY VICTORIA'S DR
Cawkett Farm
Wilway
ANDREW'S HILL CROSS
COTTAGE LA
CHAPEL ST
MILLHAM LA
ROSEMARY LA
Schs
Dulverton
BARNES CLOSE MEAD
Barns Close Ind Est
WILWAY LA
THREE GATES CROSS
ANDREW'S HILL
COMBE LA
BATTLETON
Streamcombe
STREAMCOMBE LA
Pixton Park
CLAYFORD RD
Beasley Farm
Bury Castle
Bere
Barle Ent Ctr
Combe
River Barle
Weir House
DYEHOUSE CROSS
DYEHOUSE LA
Knowle Farm
BEER LA
Gulland
CLAYFORD LA
Clayford
TA22
Allers Wood
Pixy Copse
Pixton Hill
POOLE HILL
IRON POST
Beer Moors
Mast
Brockey River
Ashill
Venn
THE GREEN
Brushford
ELLERSDOWN LA
Perry Farm
Nightcott
West Knowle
MARKET CL
PERRY NEW RD
BRUSHFORD NEW RD
SILVERDALE CL
DENNINGTON LA
Exe Valley Way
River Exe
LANGALLER HILL
1 NICHOLAS CL
2 POUNDSCLOSE
MOOR LA
TWELVE ACRE POST
Langaller Farm
Kents Hill
CROFT LA
Hulverton Hill
Poole Farm
ALLSHIRE LA
Upcott
Croft
Exebridge Ind Est
TRACKFORDMOOR CROSS
Wind Pump
Rocks
Riphay Barton
RIPHAY CROSS
Fishery
RIVER VIEW
Sowerhill
Langridge
Exebridge
Wilsons Farm
Den Brook
PH
Hele Manor Farm
Higher Grants Farm
BLIGHTS HILL
West Tapps
GRANT'S HILL
Great Highleigh
Red Deer Farm
East Tapps
Western Farm
EAST TAPPS LA
NEW LA
Combe Water
Mast
BLACKALLER LA
Combe Head
Newhouse Farm
East Mildon
Hutswell Farm
EX16
East Loosemoor
West Mildon
OLDWAYS LA
Benshayes Farm
HIGH BOLHAM
B3227
Ford Farm
Westbrook Farmhouse
Devon STREET ATLAS
A396 Tiverton
8 29 7 28 6 27 5 26 4 25 3 24 2 23 1 22
88 89 90 91 92 93
34

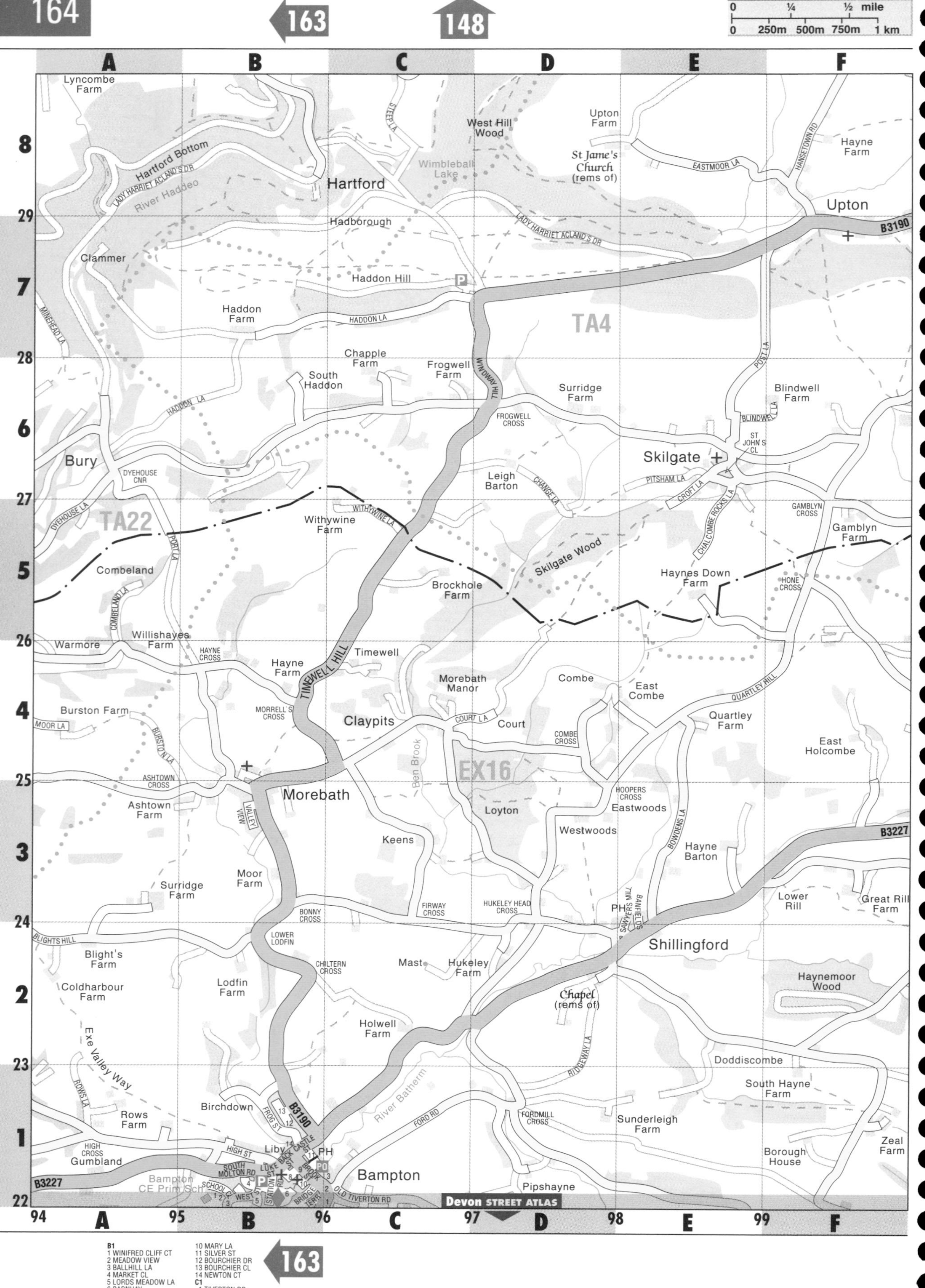

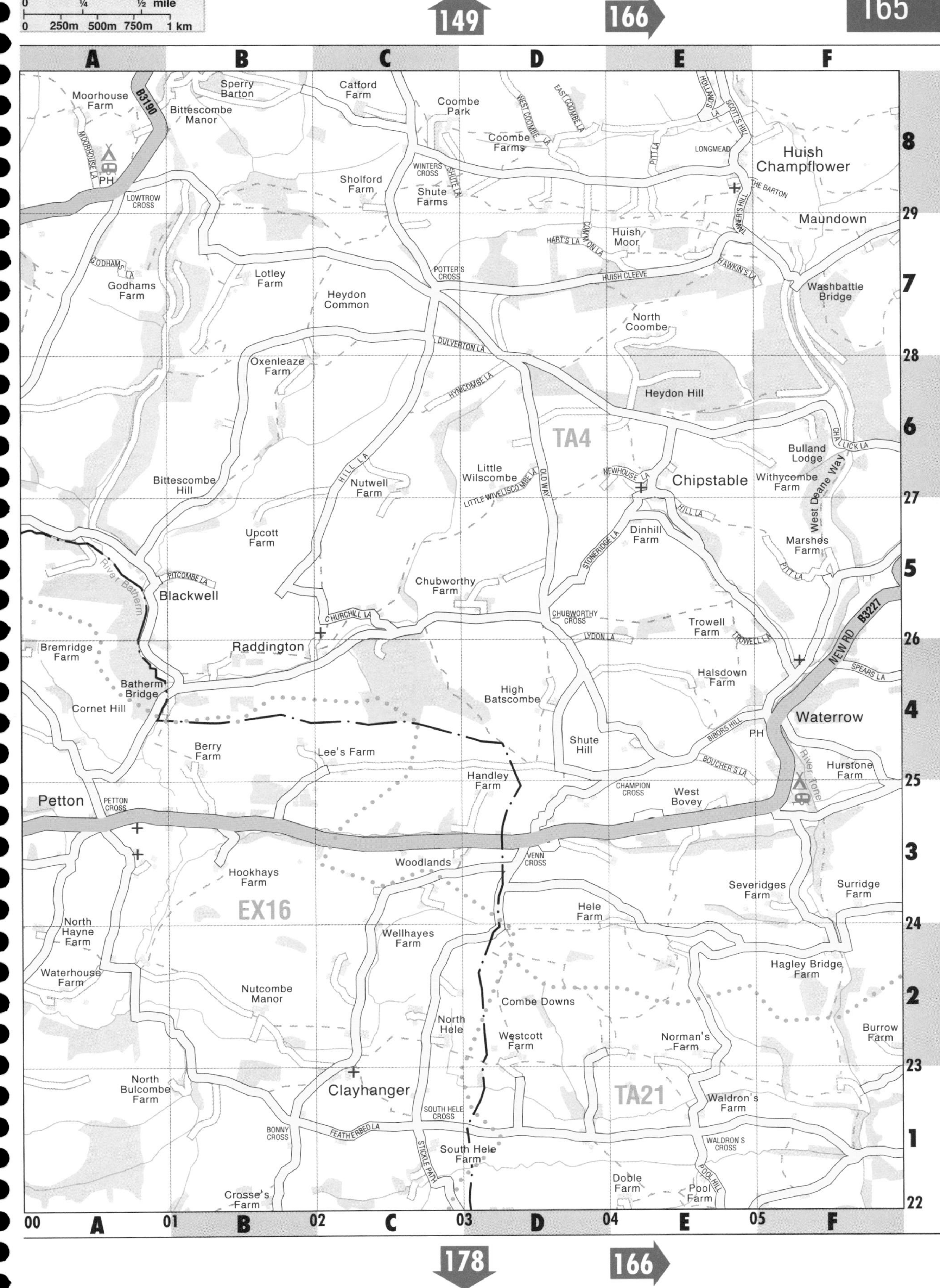

Scale: 1¾ inches to 1 mile

0   ¼   ½   mile
0   250m   500m   750m   1 km

149
166

A   B   C   D   E   F

Moorhouse Farm
B3190
Sperry Barton
Bittescombe Manor
Catford Farm
Coombe Park
Coombe Farms
WEST COOMBE LA
EAST COOMBE LA
HOLLAND LA
SCOTT'S HILL
Longmead
Huish Champflower
THE BARTON
8
PH
LOWTROW CROSS
MOORHOUSE LA
Sholford Farm
WINTERS CROSS
SHUTE LA
Shute Farms
PITT LA
THE SHENKS
Maundown
29
GODHAM LA
Godhams Farm
Lotley Farm
Heydon Common
POTTER'S CROSS
DULVERTON LA
HART'S LA
COMMON LA
Huish Moor
Huish Cleeve
HAWKIN'S LA
Washbattle Bridge
7
Oxenleaze Farm
HYNCOMBE LA
North Coombe
28
Bittescombe Hill
HILL LA
Nutwell Farm
Little Wilscombe
LITTLE WIVELISCOMBE LA
OLD WAY
TA4
Heydon Hill
Newhouse LA
NEWHOUSE LA
Chipstable
Bulland Lodge
CLICK LA
6
Upcott Farm
Withycombe Farm
West Deane Way
27
River Batherm
PITCOMBE LA
Blackwell
Chubworthy Farm
STONERIDGE LA
Dinhill Farm
HILL LA
Marshes Farm
PITT LA
5
Bremridge Farm
CHURCHILL LA
Raddington
CHUBWORTHY CROSS
LYDON LA
Trowell Farm
TROWELL LA
NEW RD
B3227
SPEARS LA
26
Batherm Bridge
High Batscombe
Halsdown Farm
Waterrow
4
Cornet Hill
Berry Farm
Lee's Farm
Handley Farm
Shute Hill
BIBORS HILL
BOUCHER'S LA
PH
River Tone
Hurstone Farm
25
Petton
PETTON CROSS
Champion Cross
West Bovey
3
Hookhays Farm
Woodlands
VENN CROSS
Hele Farm
Severidges Farm
Surridge Farm
EX16
North Hayne Farm
Wellhayes Farm
24
Waterhouse Farm
Nutcombe Manor
North Hele
Westcott Farm
Combe Downs
Hagley Bridge Farm
2
Norman's Farm
Burrow Farm
23
North Bulcombe Farm
Clayhanger
SOUTH HELE CROSS
TA21
Waldron's Farm
1
BONNY CROSS
FEATHERBED LA
STOKE PARK
South Hele Farm
WALDRON'S CROSS
Crosse's Farm
Doble Farm
Pool Farm
POOL HILL
22

00   A   01   B   02   C   03   D   04   E   05   F

178
166

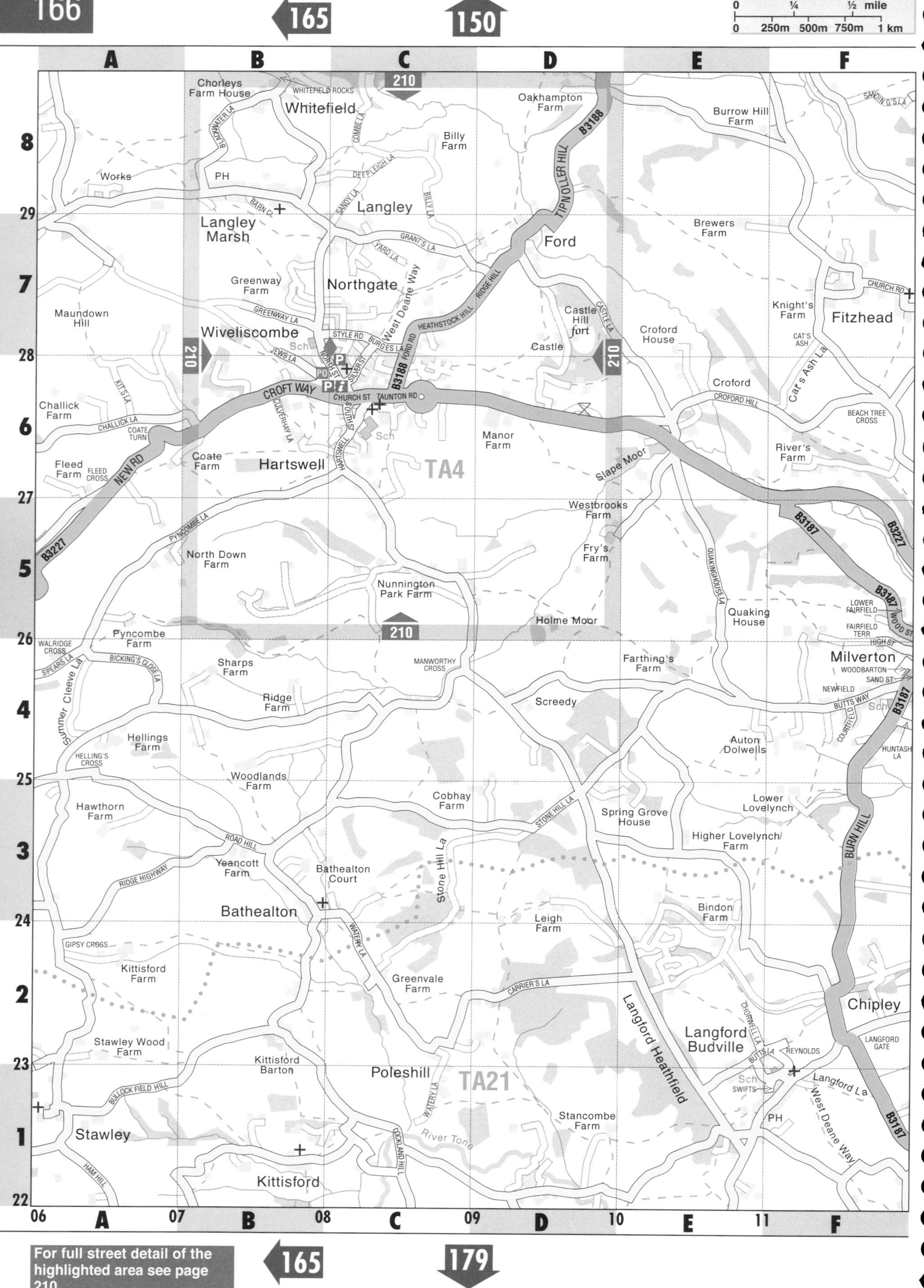

Scale: 1¾ inches to 1 mile
0   ¼   ½ mile
0 250m 500m 750m 1 km

165
150

A B C D E F

8
29
7
28
6
27
5
26
4
25
3
24
2
23
1
22

Chorleys Farm House
WHITEFIELD ROCKS
Whitefield
COMBE LA
Billy Farm
Oakhampton Farm
B3188
Burrow Hill Farm
SMOIN'G'S LA

BLACKWATER LA
PH
SANDY LA
Langley
DEEP LEIGH LA
T/PNOLLER HILL
Brewers Farm
CHURCH RD

Works
Langley Marsh
BARN CL
GRANT'S LA
Ford
Knight's Farm
Fitzhead
CAT'S ASH

Greenway Farm
YARD LA
Northgate
BILLY LA
Castle Hill fort
CASTLE LA
Croford House
CAT'S ASH LA

Maundown Hill
GREENWAY LA
West Dearle Way
HEATHSTOCK HILL
RIDGE HILL
Castle
210
Croford
BEACH TREE CROSS

Wiveliscombe
210
Sch
STYLE RD
SILVER ST
BURGES LA
B3188 FORD RD
CROFORD HILL
River's Farm

JEWS LA
P
PO&S
P i
CROFT WAY
CHURCH ST
TAUNTON RD
Slape Moor

Challick Farm
KITS LA
CHALLICK LA
COATE TURN
HARTSWELL LA
Sch
Manor Farm
B3187
B3227

Fleed Farm
FLEED CROSS
NEW RD
Coate Farm
Hartswell
TA4
Westbrooks Farm
B3187

PYNCOMBE LA
North Down Farm
Fry's Farm
QUAKINGHOUSE LA
LOWER FAIRFIELD
B3187

B3227
Nunnington Park Farm
210
Holme Moor
Quaking House
FAIRFIELD TERR
HIGH ST

WALRIDGE CROSS
Pyncombe Farm
MANWORTHY CROSS
Farthing's Farm
Milverton
WOODBARTON
SAND ST

SPEARS LA
BICKING'S CLOSE LA
Sharps Farm
Screedy
NEWFIELD
BUTTS WAY
Sch
B3187

Summer Cleeve La
Ridge Farm
Auton Dolwells
COURTFIELD LA
HUNTASH LA

Hellings Farm
Woodlands Farm
Cobhay Farm
Spring Grove House
Lower Lovelynch
BURN HILL

HELLING'S CROSS
ROAD HILL
STONE HILL LA
Higher Lovelynch Farm

Hawthorn Farm
Yeancott Farm
Stone Hill La
Leigh Farm
Bindon Farm
Chipley

RIDGE HIGHWAY
Bathealton Court
WATERY LA
LANGFORD GATE

GIPSY CROSS
Bathealton
Greenvale Farm
CARRIER'S LA
Langford Budville
CHURCHILL LA
REYNOLDS
LANGFORD LA

Kittisford Farm
Kittisford Barton
Poleshill
TA21
Langford Heathfield
BUTTS LA
Sch
PH
West Dearle Way
B3187

Stawley Wood Farm
WATERY LA
Stancombe Farm
SWIFTS

BULLOCK FIELD HILL
Stawley
River Tone
COCKLAND HILL
Kittisford
HAM HILL

06 A 07 B 08 C 09 D 10 E 11 F

165
179

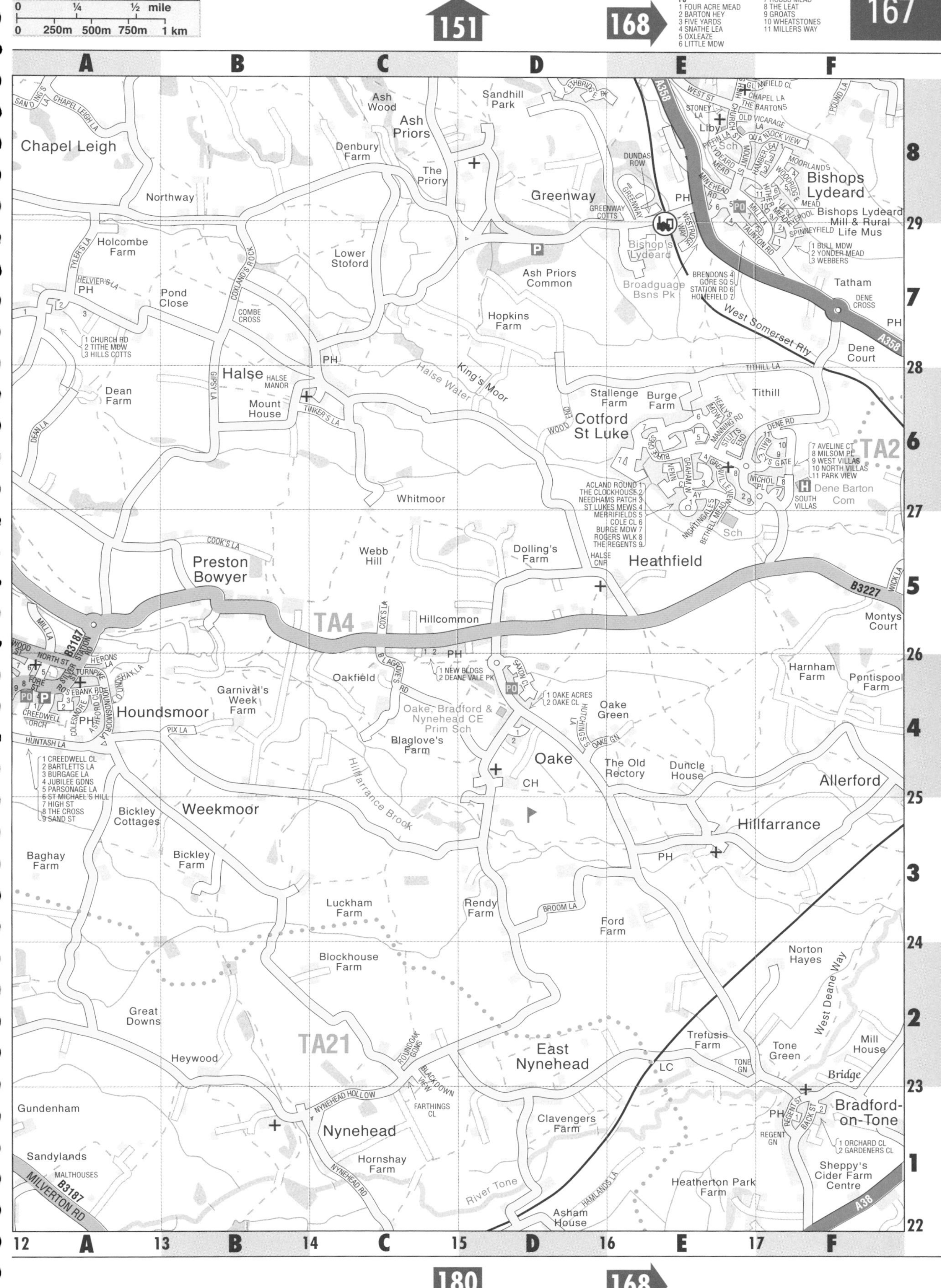

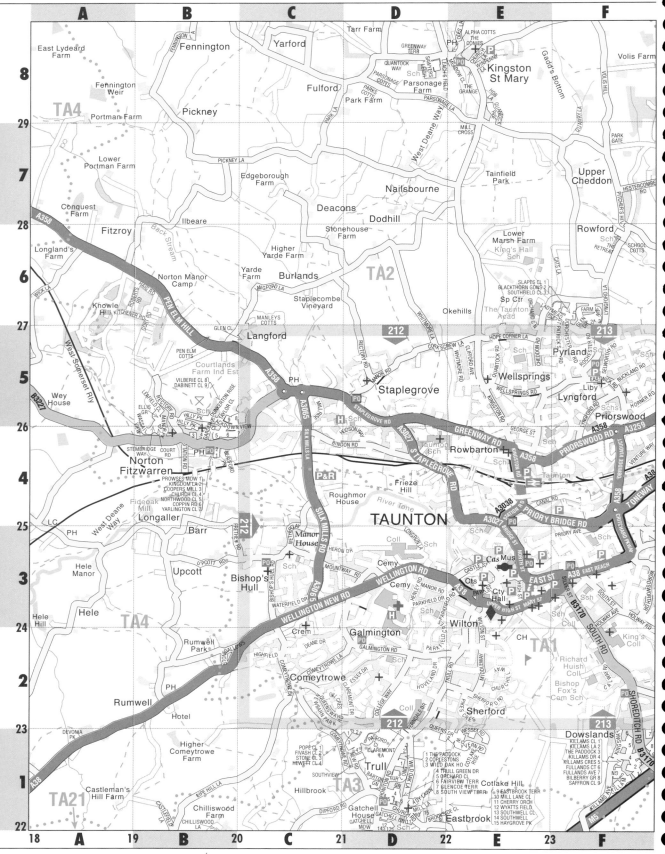

167
152

Scale: 1¾ inches to 1 mile

0 ¼ ½ mile
0 250m 500m 750m 1 km

A **B** **C** **D** **E** **F**

East Lydeard Farm
Tarr Farm
Yarford
GREENWAY TERR
Alpha Cotts THE CONIES
PH
P
Volis Farm

8

Fennington
Fulford
QUANTOCK WAY
PARSONAGE COTTS
Parsonage Farm
SAWYERS LEIGH
Sch
THE GRANGE
Kingston St Mary

TA4

Fennington Weir
Pickney
Park Farm
PARKS COTTS
PARSONAGE LA

29

Portman Farm
PICKNEY LA
Nailsbourne
Tainfield Park
MILL CROSS

7

Lower Portman Farm
Edgeborough Farm
Deacons
PARK GATE
Upper Cheddon
HESTERCOMBE RD

A358

Conquest Farm
Ilbeare
Dodhill
Stonehouse Farm
Lower Marsh Farm
King's Hall Sch
THE RETREAT
SCHOOL COTTS

28

Longland's Farm
Fitzroy
Higher Yarde Farm
TA2
Okehills
Sp Ctr
The Taunton Acad
Rowford

6

WICK LA
B3227
Norton Manor Camp
Yarde Farm
STAPLECOMBE Vineyard
MANLEYS COTTS
HOPE CORNER LA
Pyrland
213

27

West Somerset Rly
Khowle Hill
PEN ELM HILL
GLEN CL
Langford
212
Wellsprings
Lyngford
Liby
Priorswood

5

Wey House
PEN ELM COTTS
A358
PH
Staplegrove
GREENWAY RD
A358
A3259

26

Courtlands Farm Ind Est
Norton Fitzwarren
PH
P PO
PO
Staplegrove Sch
Rowbarton
PRIORSWOOD RD
VENTURE WAY

4

West Deane Way
Longaller
Barr
212
P&R
Roughmor House
Frieze Hill
River Tone
TAUNTON
A3027
PRIORY BRIDGE RD
A38

25

Hele Manor
Upcott
Manor House
Coll
Sch
PRIORY AVE

3

Hele Hill
Hele
TA4
Bishop's Hull
Sch
WELLINGTON RD
Cemy
Cemy
Cas Mus
EAST ST
A38 EAST REACH

24

Rumwell Park
WELLINGTON NEW RD
Crem
Galmington
H
Wilton
CH
TA1
King's Coll

2

Rumwell
Hotel
Comeytrowe
College Way
Sherford
Bishop Fox's Com Sch
SHOREDITCH RD

23

DEVONIA PK
Higher Comeytrowe Farm
Trull
212
Coll
QUEENS DR
Dowslands
213
B3170

1

A38
TA21
Castleman's Hill Farm
Chilliswood Farm
Hillbrook
TA3
Gatchell House
Eastbrook
M5

22

18 **A** 19 **B** 20 **C** 21 **D** 22 **E** 23 **F**

167
181

For full street detail of the highlighted area see pages 212 and 213.

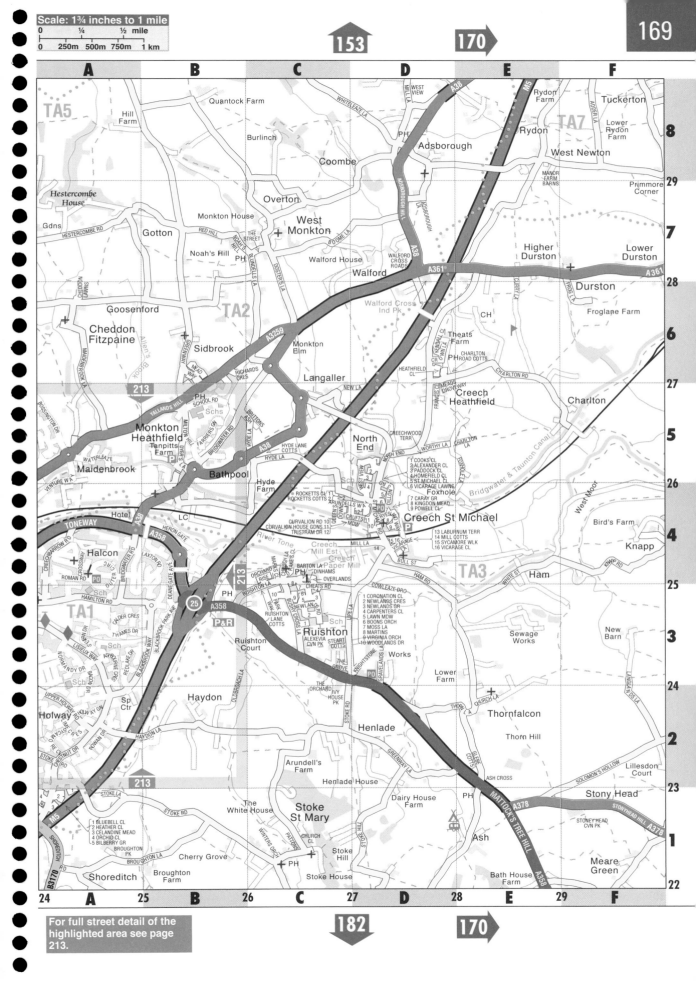

Scale: 1¾ inches to 1 mile

0   ¼   ½ mile
0 250m 500m 750m 1 km

A   B   C   D   E   F

TA5
Quantock Farm
Hill Farm
Burlinch
Coombe
WEST LEAZE LA
WEST VIEW
MILL LA
A38
Rydon Farm
TA7
Tuckerton
ALDER LA
Lower Rydon Farm
PH
Adsborough
Rydon
West Newton
MANOR FARM BARNS
8
29

Hestercombe House
Gdns
HESTERCOMBE RD
Gotton
Monkton House
Overton
WEST Monkton
RED HILL
NOAH'S LA
THE STREET
COOMBE LA
BLUNDELLS LA
DOSTERS LA
Walford House
WEST LEAZE LA
ADSBOROUGH HILL
ADSBOROUGH
A38
Walford
A361
Higher Durston
Lower Durston
A361
7
28

Noah's Hill
PH
Walford Cross Ind Pk
CURRY LA
CH
Durston
Froglane Farm
FROG LA
6

Goosenford
Cheddon Fitzpaine
TA2
Sidbrook
Allen's Brook
GREENWAY
MEAD WAY
A3259
RICHARDS CRES
Monkton Elm
Langaller
NEW LA
HEATHFIELD CL
HEATHFIELD CL
Theats Farm
PH
CHARLTON ROAD COTTS
MEAGS DROVEWAY
FRANCIS LA
CHARLTON RD
CHARLTON LA
Creech Heathfield
Charlton
27

213
YALLANDS HILL
PH
SCHOOL RD
Schs
MILTON HILL
DYERS CL
FARRERS GR
BRIDGWATER RD
BRITTONS LA
HYDE LA
ASH
A38
HYDE LA
HYDE LANE COTTS
CREECHWOOD TERR
WORTHY LA
CHARLTON LA
FOXHOLE
Bridgwater & Taunton Canal
West Moor
5
26

Monkton Heathfield
Tanpitts Farm
P
Maidenbrook
WATERLEAZE
VENTURE WAY
Bathpool
Hyde Farm
Sch
WEST VIEW
4
North End
QUEEN'S DOWNS
SMITHS CL
DILLONS
1 COOKS CL
2 ALEXANDER CL
3 PADDOCK CL
4 HOMEFIELD CL
5 ST MICHAEL CL
6 VICARAGE LAWNS
7 CARAY GR
8 KINGDON MEAD
9 POWELL CL
Bird's Farm
Knapp
KNAPP RD

Hotel
A38
TONEWAY
HERON GATE
LC
River Tone
ROCKETTS CL
ROCKETTS COTTS
CURVALION RD 10
CURVALION HOUSE GDNS 11
TRISTRAM DR 12
ARUNDELLS WK
CROFTS
MDW
Creech St Michael
13 LABURNUM TERR
14 MILL COTTS
15 SYCAMORE WLK
16 VICARAGE CL
4

Halcon
CREECH BARROW RD
CROSSWAY
Roman Rd
PO
HAMILTON RD
A358
BRIDGWATER RD
LAXTON CL
DEANE GATE AVE
BLACKBROOK PARK AVE
BLACKBROOK WAY
25
A358
P&R
213
ORCHARD RISE
PARK VIAW
RUISHTON LA
BUSHY CROSS LA
Creech Mill Est
Creech Paper Mill
BARTON LA
DINHAMS
OVERLANDS
CHEATS RD
MILL LA
BULL ST
HAM RD
TA3
WHITE ST
Ham
25

TA1
Sch
CALDER CRES
THAMES DR
NORMANDY DR
LISIEUX WAY
ASHBOURNE CRES
REDLAKE CR
BACON DR
Sch
Sp Ctr
Ruishton Court
RUISHTON LANE COTTS
NEWLAND
ALEXEVIA CVN PK
STEART COTTS
1 CORONATION CL
2 NEWLANDS CRES
3 NEWLANDS GR
4 CARPENTERS CL
5 LAWN MDW
6 BOONS ORCH
7 MOSS LA
8 MARTINS
9 VIRGINIA ORCH
10 WOODLANDS DR
Ruishton
Works
KNIGHTSTONE LA
GRAVELANDS LA
PO
UPLA LA
COWLEAZE DRO
Lower Farm
Sewage Works
New Barn
3

Holway
UPPER HOLWAY RD
HOLWAY GN
MERE LA
SYCAMORE
HOLWAY RD
Haydon
HAYDON LA
OLDBROACH LA
STOKE RD
THE ORCHARD
IVY HOUSE PK
Henlade
THE GROVE
THORN LA
CHURCH LA
Thornfalcon
Thorn Hill
24

M5
B3170
SKIMMERTON
STOKE LA
UPPER HOLWAY RD
NUT CHESTNUT DR
ROWAN DR
213
STOKE CHESTNUT DR
STOKE LA
STOKE RD
WINTERS ORCH
PATTONS
Arundell's Farm
Henlade House
GREENWAY LA
GLEBE COTTS
A378
MATTOCK'S TREE HILL
ASH CROSS
SOLOMON'S HOLLOW
Lillesdon Court
Stony Head
2
23

1 BLUEBELL CL
2 HEATHER CL
3 CELANDINE MEAD
4 ORCHID CL
5 BILBERRY GR
BROUGHTON PK
BROUGHTON LA
Shoreditch
Cherry Grove
Broughton Farm
The White House
Stoke St Mary
STOKE HILL
CHURCH CL
Stoke Hill
Stoke House
Dairy House Farm
PH
STONE HILL
Ash
A378
Bath House Farm
A358
STONEYHEAD HILL
A378
Stony Head
STONEY MEAD CVN PK
Meare Green
1
22

24 A 25 B 26 C 27 D 28 E 29 F

For full street detail of the highlighted area see page 213.

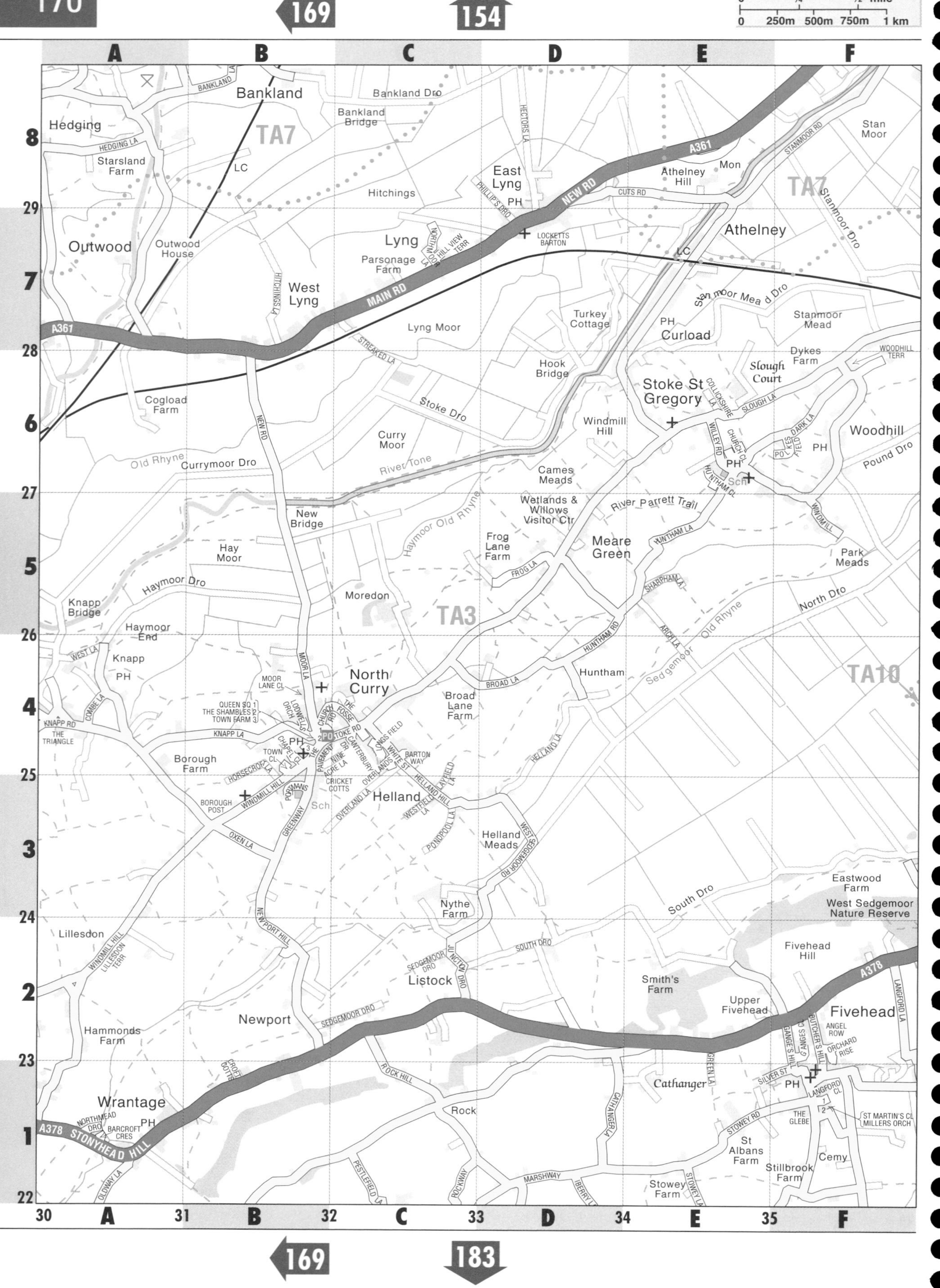

Scale: 1¾ inches to 1 mile

0   ¼   ½ mile
0 250m 500m 750m 1 km

8
Hedging
Starsland
Farm
Bankland
Bankland Dro
HEDGING LA
BANKLAND LA
Bankland
Bridge
TA7
LC
Stan
Moor
HECTORS LA
A361
NEW RD
Athelney
Hill
Mon
TA7
STANMOOR RD

29
Outwood
Outwood House
Hitchings
East
Lyng
PH
PHILLIP'S DRO
Athelney
CUTS RD
Athelney
LC
STANMOOR DRO

7
West
Lyng
Lyng
Parsonage
Farm
HITCHINGS LA
HILL VIEW TERR
WITHY RD
MAIN RD
Lyng Moor
Stanmoor Mead Dro
PH
Curload
Stanmoor
Mead
Dykes
Farm
WOODHILL
TERR

28
A361
Cogload
Farm
STREAKED LA
Hook
Bridge
Stoke Dro
Slough
Court
Stoke St
Gregory
COLLISCHIRE LA
SLOUGH LA
Woodhill

6
Old Rhyne
Currymoor Dro
NEW RD
Curry
Moor
Rivet Tone
Windmill
Hill
WILLEY RD
CHURCH
PH
PO
DARK LA
PH
Pound Dro
WINDMILL

27
New
Bridge
Haymoor Old Rhyne
Cames
Meads
Wetlands &
Willows
Visitor Ctr
HUNTHAM CL
Sch
River Parrett Trail

5
Hay
Moor
Haymoor Dro
Moredon
Frog
Lane
Farm
FROG LA
Meare
Green
HUNTHAM LA
SHARPHAM LA
North Dro
Old Rhyne
Park
Meads

26
Knapp
Bridge
WEST LA
Haymoor
End
Knapp
PH
MOOR LA
MOOR LANE CL
TA3
HUNTHAM RD
Huntham
ARG LA
Sedgemoor
TA10

4
KNAPP RD
COMBE LA
THE
TRIANGLE
QUEEN SQ 1
THE SHAMBLES 2
TOWN FARM 3
KNAPP LA
LUDWELLS
ORCH
CHURCH
North
Curry
STOKE RD
THE ROSE
Broad
Lane
Farm
BROAD LA
HELLAND LA

25
Borough
Farm
HORSECROFT
TOWN
CL
WINDMILL HILL
PH
GREENWAY
PANSERY
STOKE RD
CANTERBURY
WHITE ST
MOOR LA
KINGS FIELD
Barton
Way
Helland
OVERLANDS
WESTFIELD LA
HELLAND HILL

3
Borough
Post
Sch
OXEN LA
PO
Cricket
Cotts
PONDPOOL LA
Helland
Meads
WEST
GREENWAY RD
HOOKWAY RD

24
Lillesdon
WINDMILL HILL
LILLESDON TERR
NEWPORT HILL
Nythe
Farm
SEDGEMOOR DRO
JUNCTION DRO
SOUTH DRO
South Dro
West Sedgemoor
Nature Reserve
Eastwood
Farm

2
Hammonds
Farm
Newport
SEDGEMOOR DRO
Listock
Smith's
Farm
Upper
Fivehead
Fivehead
Hill
A378
LANGFORD LA
Fivehead
Angel
Row

23
Wrantage
NORTHMEAD
DRO
BARCROFT
CRES
PH
CROFT BOTTOM
ROCK HILL
Rock
GREEN LA
CATHANGRA
Cathanger
STOWEY RD
PH
BUTCHERS HILL
ORANGE'S HILL
SILVER ST
LANGFORD CL
ORCHARD RISE
THE
GLEBE
ST MARTIN'S CL
MILLERS ORCH

1
A378
STONYHEAD HILL
OLD WAY LA
PESTLEFIELD LA
ROCKWAY
MARSHWAY
BERRY LA
Stowey
Farm
STOWEY LA
St Albans
Farm
Cemy
Stillbrook
Farm

22

30   A   31   B   32   C   33   D   34   E   35   F

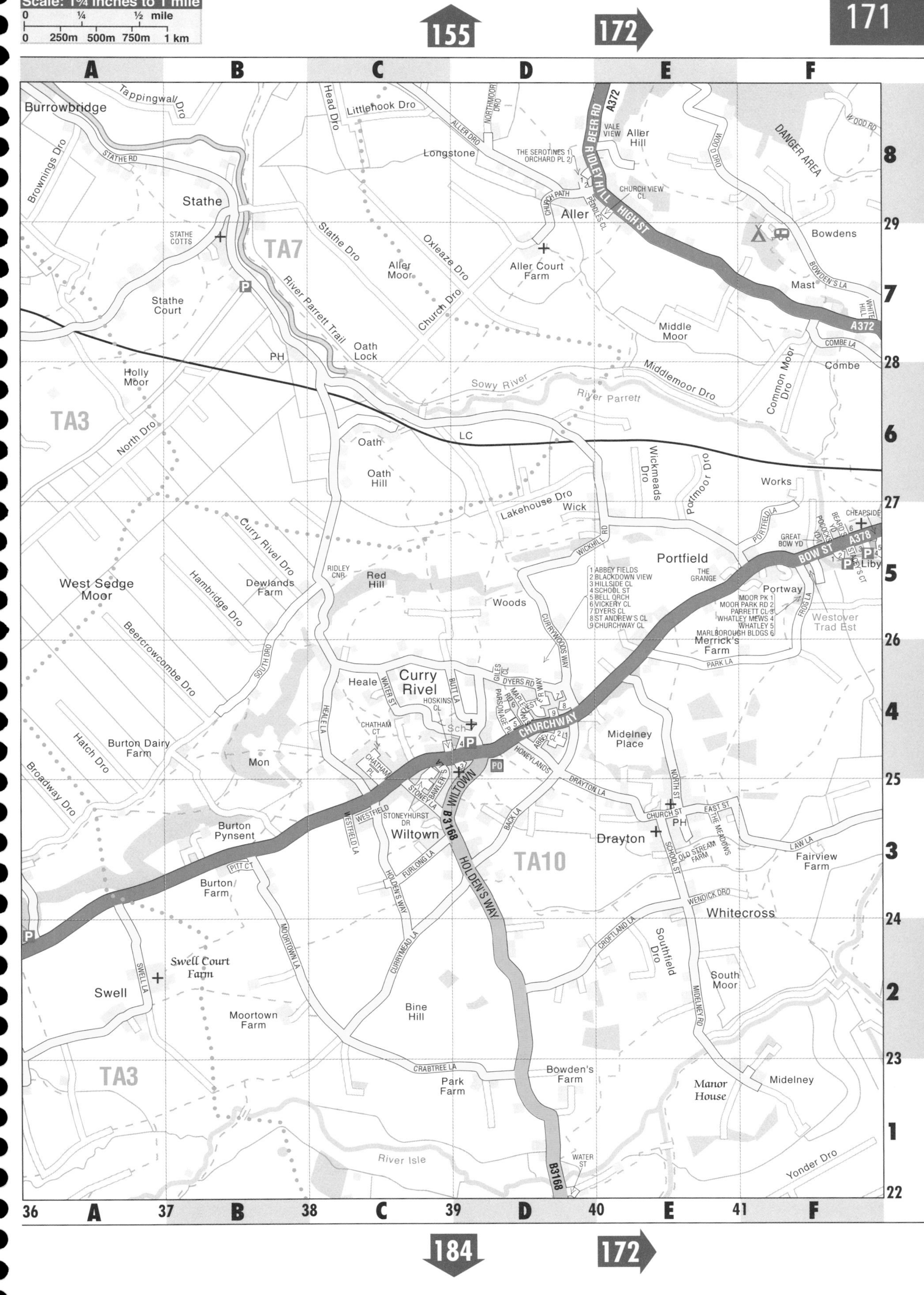
Scale: 1¾ inches to 1 mile
155
172
184
172
Burrowbridge
Stathe
Stathe Court
TA7
TA3
TA10
Aller
Aller Court Farm
Longstone
Aller Moor
Oath Lock
Oath
Oath Hill
Holly Moor
West Sedge Moor
Dewlands Farm
Red Hill
Woods
Curry Rivel
Heale
Wiltown
Burton Pynsent
Burton Farm
Burton Dairy Farm
Swell
Swell Court Farm
Moortown Farm
Bine Hill
Park Farm
Bowden's Farm
Drayton
Midelney Place
Whitecross
South Moor
Manor House
Midelney
Fairview Farm
Portfield
Portway
Merrick's Farm
Westover Trad Est
Wick
Combe
Middle Moor
Bowdens
Mast
Works
Langport
Sowy River
River Parrett
River Isle
1 ABBEY FIELDS
2 BLACKDOWN VIEW
3 HILLSIDE CL
4 SCHOOL ST
5 BELL ORCH
6 VICKERY CL
7 DYERS CL
8 ST ANDREW'S CL
9 CHURCHWAY CL
MOOR PK 1
MOOR PARK RD 2
PARRETT CL 3
WHATLEY MEWS 4
WHATLEY 5
MARLBOROUGH BLDGS 6

171
156

Scale: 1¾ inches to 1 mile
0 ¼ ½ mile
0 250m 500m 750m 1 km

A B C D E F

WOOD RD
LOW HAM RD
MORTON'S LA
Pitney Wood
Park Farm
SOMERTON DOOR DRO
Bradley Hill

8

+ Bramwell
West Wood
UNDERWOOD LA
Woodbirds Hill
Whiscombe Hill
Bancombe Hill
PARK LA
BRADLEY HILL LA

FIELD RD
LONG ST
Low Ham +
LAZENWOOD LA
Bsns Pk

29
NEW WAY
PAR HILL LA
Hext Hill
WOODBIRDS HILL LA
MIDDLEGATE RD
WESTERN GATE
MIDDLE GATE
SOMERTONFIELD RD
Westcombe
SOMERTONFIELD RD
BANCOMBE RD

7
Paradise
Wearne
ONE ELM
CULVER HILL
GORE LA
CHURCH HILL
Pitney House
STONEY RD
MARSH LA
211
LANGPORT RD B3153
TA11

A372
28
SPARKS HILL
COMBE LA
WALNUT RD
MAPLE RD
Pict's Hill
FURJPITS LA
Rectory Hill
Pitney
PH
HERMITAGE RD
Somerton Hill
SOMERTON HILL
RICKSEY LA

A378
6
NEWTON RD
SOMERTON RD
WILLOW
BROOKLAND RD
B3153
Hamdown Farm
HAMDOWN CT
WAGG DRO
Tengore Farm
UNION DRO
LONGMARSH LA
B3165
WINDYRIDGE LA
211
SUTTON RD

KENNEL LA
MOOR PL
GARDEN CITY
BARRYMORE CL
THE LEECHES

27
PO
NORTH ST
PORT FALLS RD
EASTOVER
Acad
PORTLAND RD
TENGORE LA
DOWNSIDE LA
ROWMARSH LA
LIMEPITS LA
LONG FURLONG LA
Burnt House La
MONCK'S COURT LA
HARDING'S HILL

5
The Hill
Sch
ST GILDES CT 7
BONDS POOL 8
ORCHARD VALE 9
WHATLEY LA 10
WHATLEY 11
BUSH PL 12
ST GILDA'S CL 13
COUNSELL LA
COURT FIELD
DUCKS HILL
WINDMILL LA
LEVEL VIEW
Wagg
Rose Cottage Farm
Upton
Manor House Farm
LANGPORT RD
STEPHEN'S HILL
B3165

Huish Episcopi
LANGPORT
Pibsbury
GAINSBOROUGH LA
BATT'S LA
ARLAKE LA
VEGO DRO
WEST VIEW
Long Sutton

26
Bicknell's Bridge
Horsey Farm
TANYARD LA
SNAPS LA
HORSEY LA
Muchelney Level
TA10
Ablake
HELE LA
LITTLE FIELD LA
CROUD'S LA
ORCHARD CL
PARSONS CL
SHUTE LA
KNIGHTLANDS LA
Sch
B3165
A372

4
River Parrett Trail
Macmillan Way Link
River Parrett
HAYMOOR LA
LANDMOOR LA
Macmillan Way West
River Yeo
Hay Moor
NEW ST
WITTMOOR DRO
PO
MARTOCK RD
PH
CROSS LA
GLEBE LA
KNOLE CSWY

25
Priest's House
LAW LA
Muchelney Abbey
SUTTON CROSS
CHESTER LA
Lame Hill
SUTTON RD

3
Westover Farm
THORNEYMOOR LA
Muchelney
THE ROW
POUND WAY
SILVER LA
Whit Moor
Wet Moor
CH
King's Moor
SUTTON HILL

24
Thorney Moor
Little Load
MILTON LEAZE

2
Muchelney Ham
WETMOOR LA
CHURCH LA
Load Bridge
SUTTON VIEW
Crown Inn (PH)
Long Load
Witcombe Bottom

23
Muchelney Pottery & The John Leach Gallery
Thorney
COLLEGE CL
TEMPLARS CT
MEADOW VIEW

1
River Parrett Trail
River Parrett
COOMBE LA
TA12
Stapleton Mead Farm
TOWN TREE LA
TA12
WITCOMBE LA 1
THORNHILL DRO 2
WITCOMBE DRO
New Witcombe Farm

22

42 A 43 B 44 C 45 D 46 E 47 F

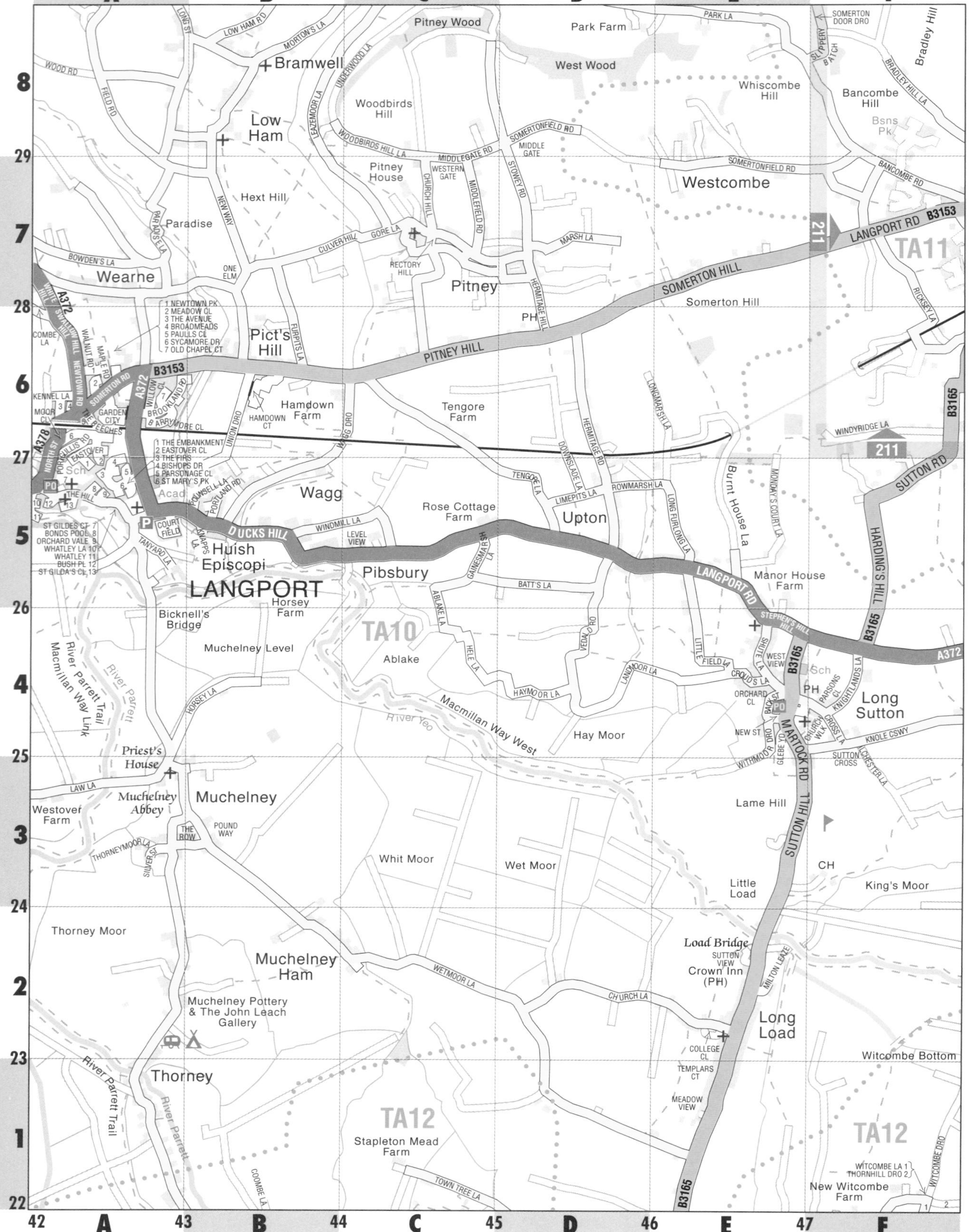

171
185

For full street detail of the highlighted area see page 211.

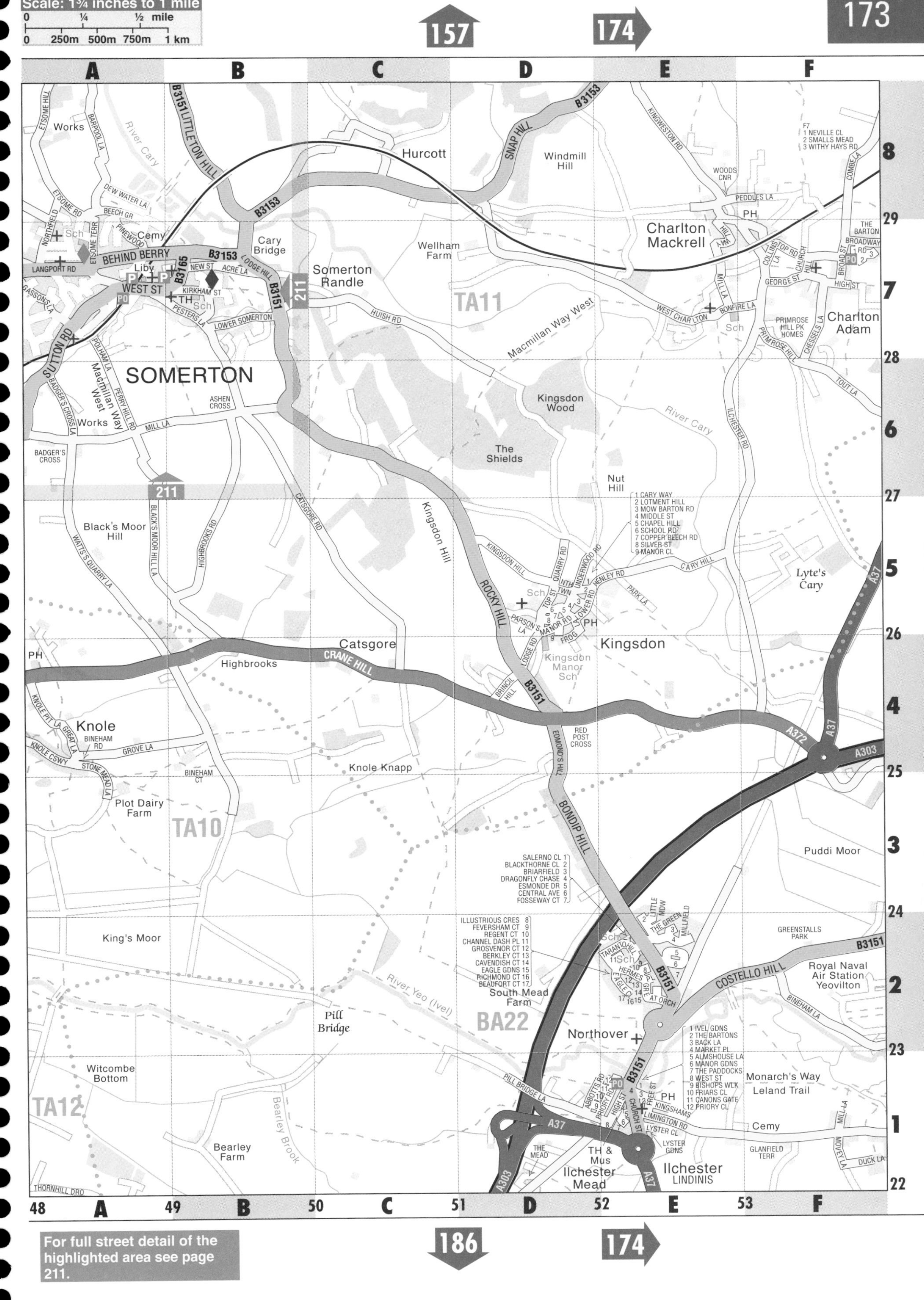

173
158

Scale: 1¾ inches to 1 mile

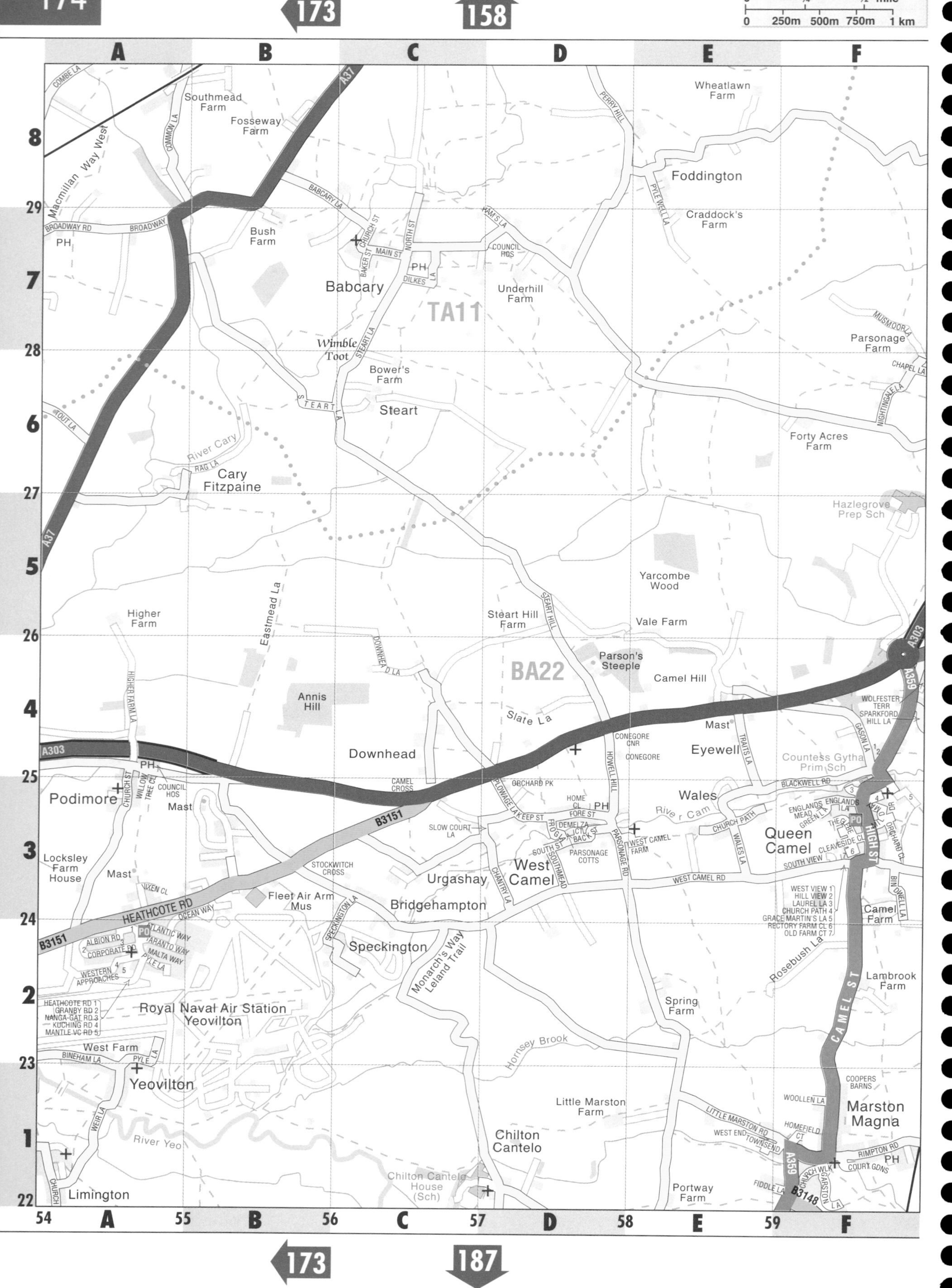

Southmead Farm
Fosseway Farm
Macmillan Way West
Bush Farm
Babcary
Wimble Toot
Bower's Farm
Steart
Foddington
Craddock's Farm
Wheatlawn Farm
Underhill Farm
TA11
Parsonage Farm
Forty Acres Farm
Hazlegrove Prep Sch
River Cary
Cary Fitzpaine
Yarcombe Wood
Higher Farm
Eastmead La
Steart Hill Farm
Vale Farm
Parson's Steeple
BA22
Camel Hill
Annis Hill
Slate La
Downhead
Mast
Eyewell
Countess Gytha Prim Sch
Podimore
Wales
River Cam
Queen Camel
Locksley Farm House
Urgashay
West Camel
Fleet Air Arm Mus
Bridgehampton
Speckington
Monarch's Way Leland Trail
Camel Farm
Rosebush La
Lambrook Farm
Royal Naval Air Station Yeovilton
Spring Farm
West Farm
Hornsey Brook
Yeovilton
Little Marston Farm
Marston Magna
Chilton Cantelo
River Yeo
Chilton Cantelo House (Sch)
Portway Farm
Limington
A37
A303
A359
B3151
B3148
HEATHCOTE RD
CAMEL ST
HIGH ST
HEATHCOTE RD 1
GRANBY RD 2
NANGA-GAT RD 3
KUCHING RD 4
MANTLE VC RD 5
WEST VIEW 1
HILL VIEW 2
LAUREL LA 3
CHURCH PATH 4
GRACE MARTIN'S LA 5
RECTORY FARM CL 6
OLD FARM CT 7

173
187

Scale: 1¾ inches to 1 mile

159
176

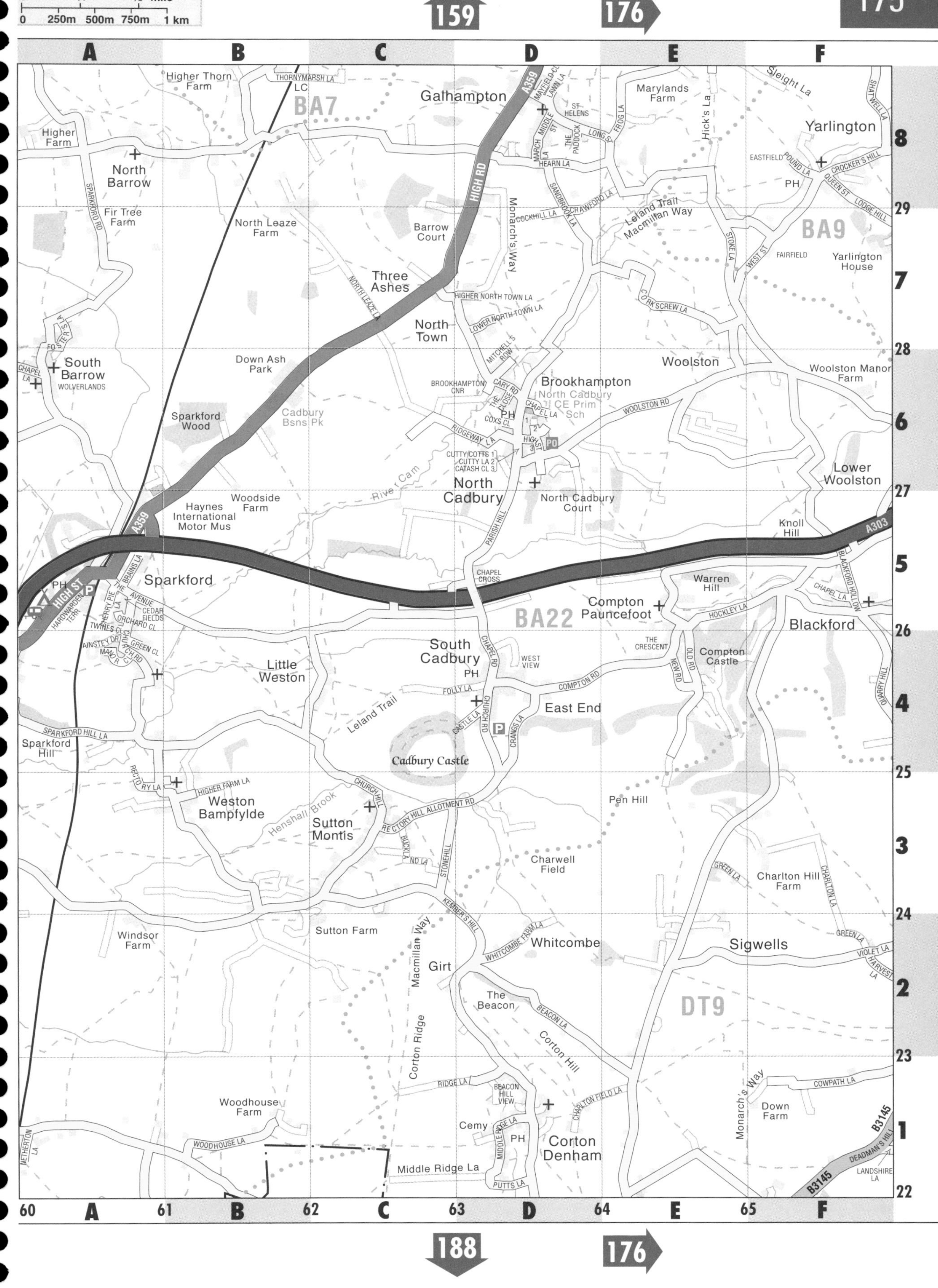
Higher Thorn Farm
Galhampton
Marylands Farm
Yarlington
Higher Farm
North Barrow
Fir Tree Farm
North Leaze Farm
Barrow Court
Yarlington House
Three Ashes
North Town
South Barrow
Down Ash Park
Brookhampton
North Cadbury CE Prim Sch
Woolston
Woolston Manor Farm
Sparkford Wood
Cadbury Bsns Pk
North Cadbury
North Cadbury Court
Lower Woolston
Haynes International Motor Mus
Woodside Farm
Knoll Hill
Sparkford
Warren Hill
Compton Pauncefoot
Blackford
South Cadbury
Little Weston
Compton Castle
East End
Sparkford Hill
Cadbury Castle
Weston Bampfylde
Sutton Montis
Pen Hill
Charwell Field
Charlton Hill Farm
Windsor Farm
Sutton Farm
Whitcombe
Sigwells
Girt
The Beacon
Corton Ridge
Corton Hill
Woodhouse Farm
Cemy
Corton Denham
Down Farm
Middle Ridge La
Leland Trail
Macmillan Way
Monarch's Way
River Cam
Henshall Brook
BA7
BA9
BA22
DT9
A359
A303
B3145

188
176

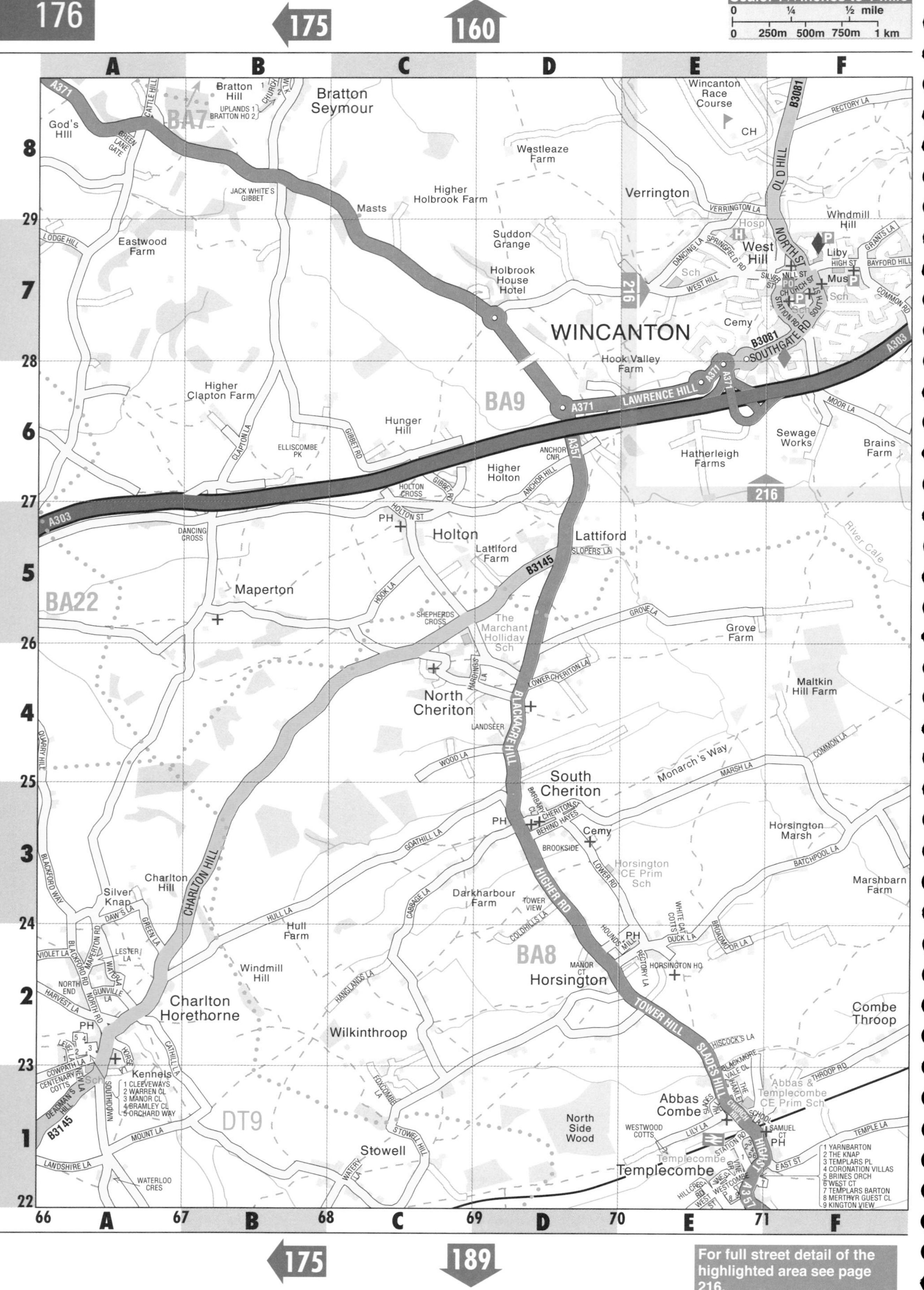

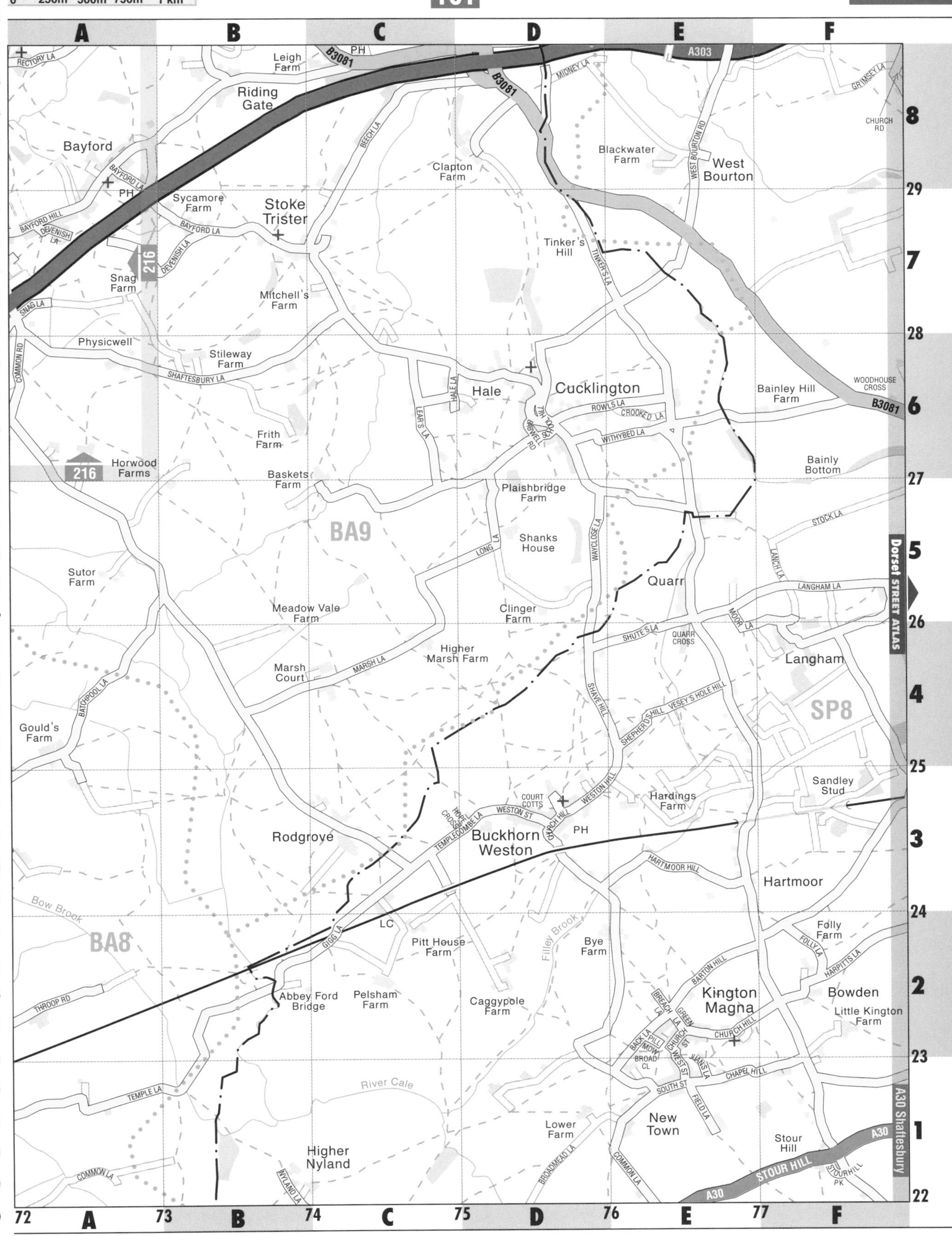

161

Scale: 1¾ inches to 1 mile

0   ¼   ½   mile
0   250m 500m 750m 1 km

A B C D E F

Dorset STREET ATLAS

RECTORY LA

Bayford

PH
BAYFORD HILL
DEVENISH LA
BAYFORD LA
SNAG LA
COMMON RD

Snag
Farm

Physicwell

216

Horwood
Farms

Sutor
Farm

Gould's
Farm

BATIPOOL LA

THROOP RD

BA8

TEMPLE LA

COMMON LA

Riding
Gate

Leigh
Farm

B3081

PH

BEECH LA

Sycamore
Farm

Stoke
Trister

Mitchell's
Farm

SHAFTESBURY LA

Stileway
Farm

Frith
Farm

Baskets
Farm

Meadow Vale
Farm

Marsh
Court

MARSH LA

Rodgrove

GIGG LA

LC

Abbey Ford
Bridge

NYLAND LA

Higher
Nyland

Clapton
Farm

B3081

LEAR'S LA
HALE LA

Hale

LONG LA

BA9

Higher
Marsh Farm

Pitt House
Farm

Pelsham
Farm

Bow Brook

River Cale

MIDNEY LA

A303

B3081

Blackwater
Farm

TINKER'S LA

Tinker's
Hill

Cucklington

ROWLS LA
CROOKED LA

WITHYBED LA

Plaishbridge
Farm

Shanks
House

WAYCLOSE LA

Clinger
Farm

Quarr

SHUTE'S LA

SHIVE HILL

SHEPHER'S HILL
VESEY'S HOLE HILL

HIGHER CROSSCOMBE LA
TEMPLECOMBE LA

Court
Cotts

WESTON ST

Buckhorn
Weston

RIGEOT HILL
PH

WESTON HILL

Hardings
Farm

HARTMOOR HILL

Caggypole
Farm

Filley Brook

Bye
Farm

BARTON HILL

BROADMEAD LA

Lower
Farm

New
Town

COMMON LA

WEST BOURTON RD

West
Bourton

Bainley Hill
Farm

WOODHOUSE
CROSS

B3081

Bainly
Bottom

STOCK LA

LANGH LA

LANGHAM LA

MOOR LA

QUARR
CROSS

SP8

Langham

Sandley
Stud

Hartmoor

Folly
Farm

FOLLY LA
HARPITTS LA

Bowden

Little Kington
Farm

Kington
Magna

BREACH
GREEN
BACK LA
MILL PILL
BROAD CL
C WEST ST
W WEST ST
HANS LA
SOUTH ST
FIELD LA
CHURCH HILL
CHAPEL HILL
CHURCH

Stour
Hill
STOURHILL
PK

A30 Shaftesbury

A30

STOUR HILL

GRIMSEY LA

CHURCH
RD

8

29

7

28

6

27

5

26

4

25

3

24

2

23

1

22

72 73 74 75 76 77

190

For full street detail of the
highlighted area see page
216.

216

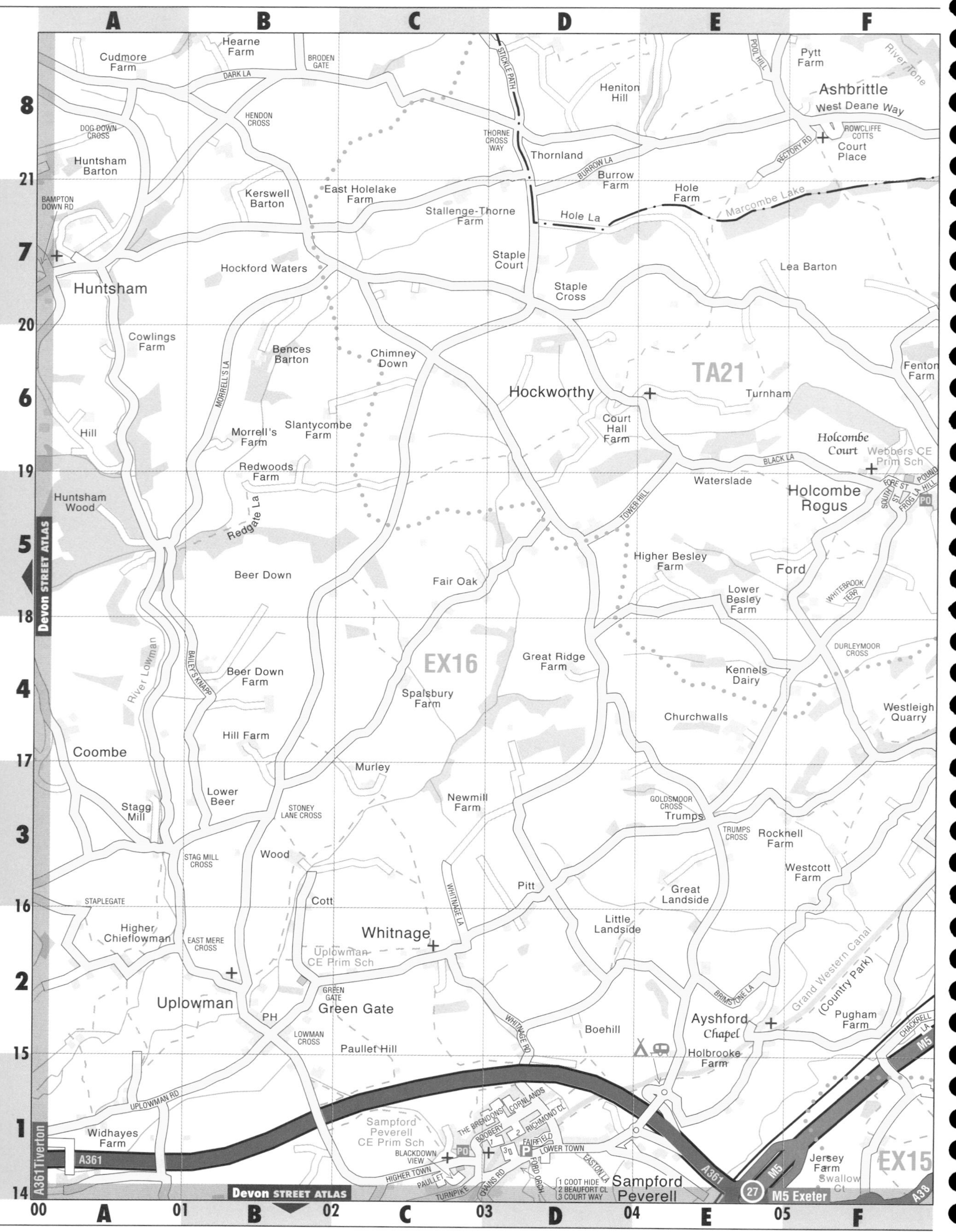

Scale: 1¾ inches to 1 mile

0   ¼   ½ mile
0 250m 500m 750m 1 km

8

Cudmore Farm

Hearne Farm

BRODEN GATE

DARK LA

Heniton Hill

Pytt Farm

Ashbrittle

West Deane Way

HENDON CROSS

DOG DOWN CROSS

21

Huntsham Barton

BAMPTON DOWN RD

Kerswell Barton

East Holelake Farm

Thornland

ROWCLIFFE COTTS

Court Place

RECTORY RD

POOL HILL

River Tone

THORNE CROSS WAY

BURROW LA

Burrow Farm

Hole Farm

7

Huntsham

Hockford Waters

Stallenge-Thorne Farm

Hole La

Marcombe Lake

STICKLE PATH

Staple Court

Lea Barton

20

Cowlings Farm

Bences Barton

Chimney Down

Staple Cross

MORRELL'S LA

Hockworthy

Turnham

TA21

Fenton Farm

6

Hill

Morrell's Farm

Slantycombe Farm

Court Hall Farm

Holcombe Court

Webbers CE Prim Sch

19

Redwoods Farm

Redgate La

Waterslade

BLACK LA

Holcombe Rogus

SOUTH ST
SHORE ST
FROG LA
FROG LA HILL
PO

Huntsham Wood

Higher Besley Farm

Ford

WHITSBROOK TERR

5

Beer Down

Fair Oak

Lower Besley Farm

18

River Lowman

BAILEY'S STAMPP

Great Ridge Farm

Kennels Dairy

DURLEYMOOR CROSS

4

Beer Down Farm

Spalsbury Farm

Churchwalls

Westleigh Quarry

Coombe

Hill Farm

17

Stagg Mill

Lower Beer

Murley

Newmill Farm

GOLDSMOOR CROSS

Trumps

3

STONEY LANE CROSS

STAG MILL CROSS

Wood

TRUMPS CROSS

Rocknell Farm

Westcott Farm

STAPLEGATE

Pitt

Great Landside

16

Higher Chieflowman

EAST MERE CROSS

Cott

Whitnage

WHITNAGE LA

Little Landside

2

Uplowman
CE Prim Sch

Green Gate

GREEN GATE

Boehill

Ayshford Chapel

BRIMSTONE LA

Grand Western Canal (Country Park)

Pugham Farm

CHACKRELL LA

M5

Uplowman

PH

LOWMAN CROSS

Paullet Hill

WHITNAGE RD

Holbrooke Farm

15

Widhayes Farm

UPLOWMAN RD

Sampford Peverell CE Prim Sch

BLACKDOWN VIEW

THE BROADWAY
CORNLANDS
BOOBERY
RICHMOND CL
LOWER TOWN CL

EASTON LA

Jersey Farm

Swallow Ct

EX15

1

A361 Tiverton

A361

HIGHER TOWN

PAULLET
TURNPIKE

PO

CHANS RD

FORD ORCH

FAIRFIELD

Lower Town

1 COOT HIDE
2 BEAUFORT CL
3 COURT WAY

Sampford Peverell

A361

M5

27

M5 Exeter

A38

14

Devon STREET ATLAS

00 **A** **01** **B** **02** **C** **03** **D** **04** **E** **05** **F**

Scale: 1¾ inches to 1 mile

166
180

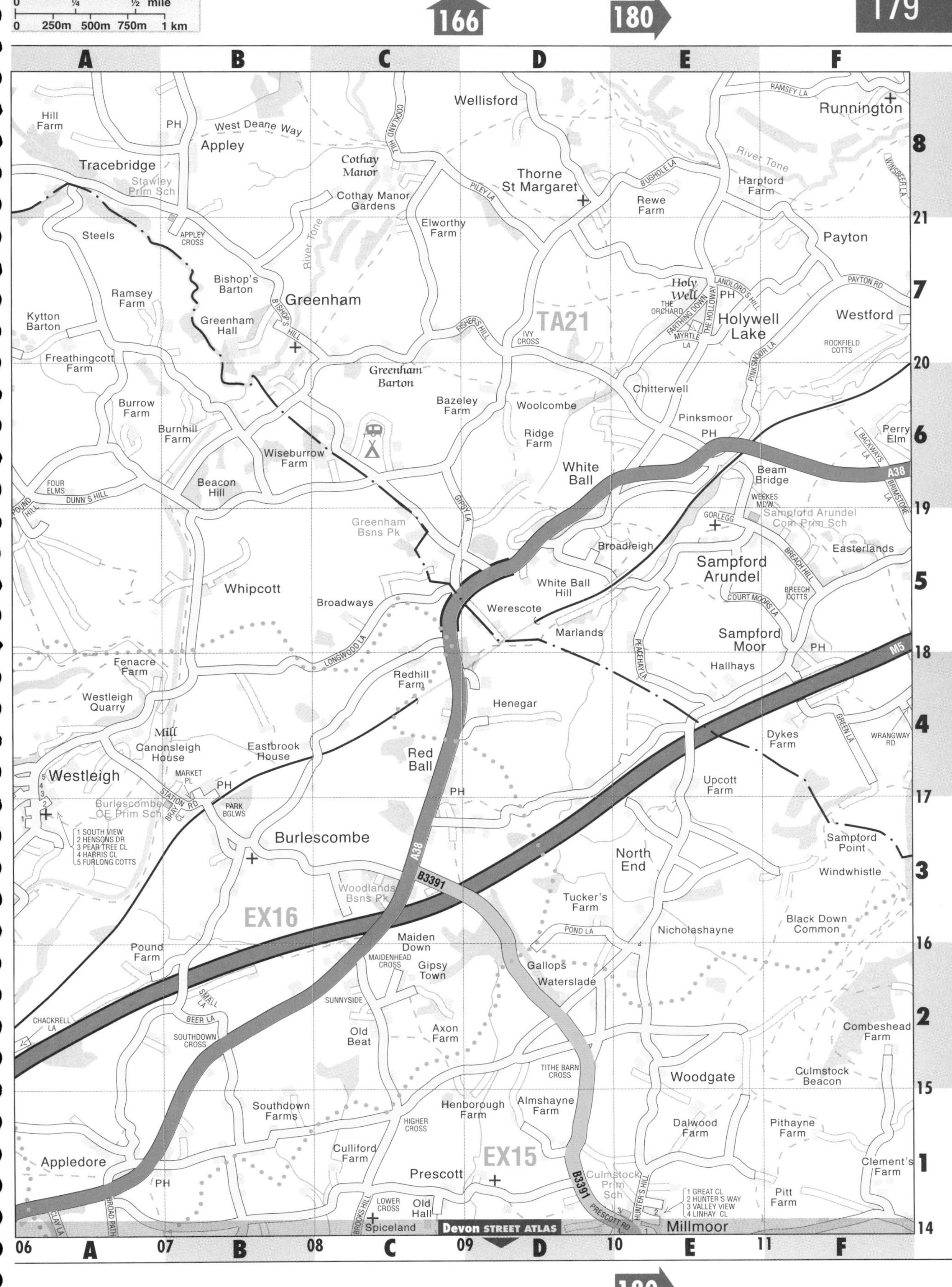
Wellisford
Runnington
Hill Farm
PH
West Deane Way
Appley
Tracebridge
Stawley Prim Sch
Cothay Manor
Cothay Manor Gardens
Thorne St Margaret
Rewe Farm
Harpford Farm
River Tone
Steels
Appley Cross
Elworthy Farm
Payton
Bishop's Barton
Greenham
Holy Well
Holywell Lake
Westford
Ramsey Farm
Kytton Barton
Greenham Hall
TA21
Ivy Cross
Rockfield Cotts
Freathingcott Farm
Greenham Barton
Chitterwell
Bazeley Farm
Woolcombe
Pinksmoor
Burrow Farm
Burnhill Farm
Ridge Farm
Perry Elm
Wiseburrow Farm
White Ball
Beam Bridge
A38
Beacon Hill
Four Elms
Dunn's Hill
Greenham Bsns Pk
Sampford Arundel Com Prim Sch
Broadleigh
Easterlands
Sampford Arundel
White Ball Hill
Whipcott
Broadways
Werescote
Marlands
Sampford Moor
Hallhays
M5
Fenacre Farm
Redhill Farm
Westleigh Quarry
Henegar
Mill
Canonsleigh House
Eastbrook House
Red Ball
Dykes Farm
Westleigh
Upcott Farm
Burlescombe CE Prim Sch
Burlescombe
North End
Sampford Point
Windwhistle
1 South View
2 Hensons Dr
3 Pear Tree Cl
4 Harris Cl
5 Furlong Cotts
B3391
Woodlands Bsns Pk
EX16
Tucker's Farm
Black Down Common
Nicholashayne
Pound Farm
Maiden Down
Maidenhead Cross
Gipsy Town
Gallops
Waterslade
Sunnyside
Combeshead Farm
Old Beat
Axon Farm
Southdown Cross
Tithe Barn Cross
Woodgate
Culmstock Beacon
Southdown Farms
Henborough Farm
Almshayne Farm
Higher Cross
Dalwood Farm
Pithayne Farm
Appledore
Culliford Farm
EX15
Prescott
Culmstock Prim Sch
Clement's Farm
1 Great Cl
2 Hunter's Way
3 Valley View
4 Linhay Cl
Pitt Farm
Lower Cross
Old Hall
Spiceland
Millmoor
Devon Street Atlas

180

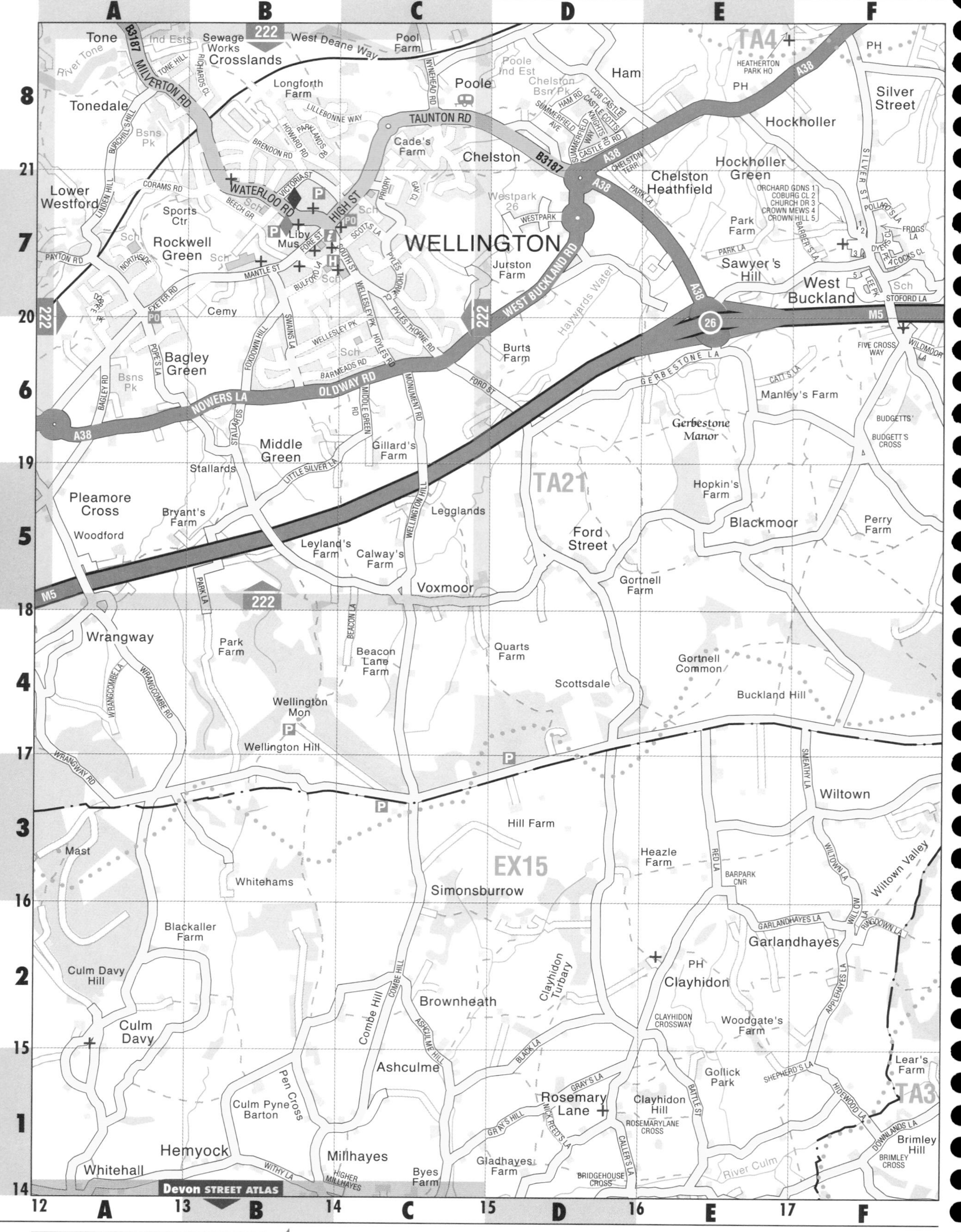

180

179

167

Scale: 1¾ inches to 1 mile
0   ¼   ½   mile
0   250m 500m 750m 1 km

For full street detail of the
highlighted area see page
222.

179

191

Devon STREET ATLAS

Scale: 1¾ inches to 1 mile

168
182

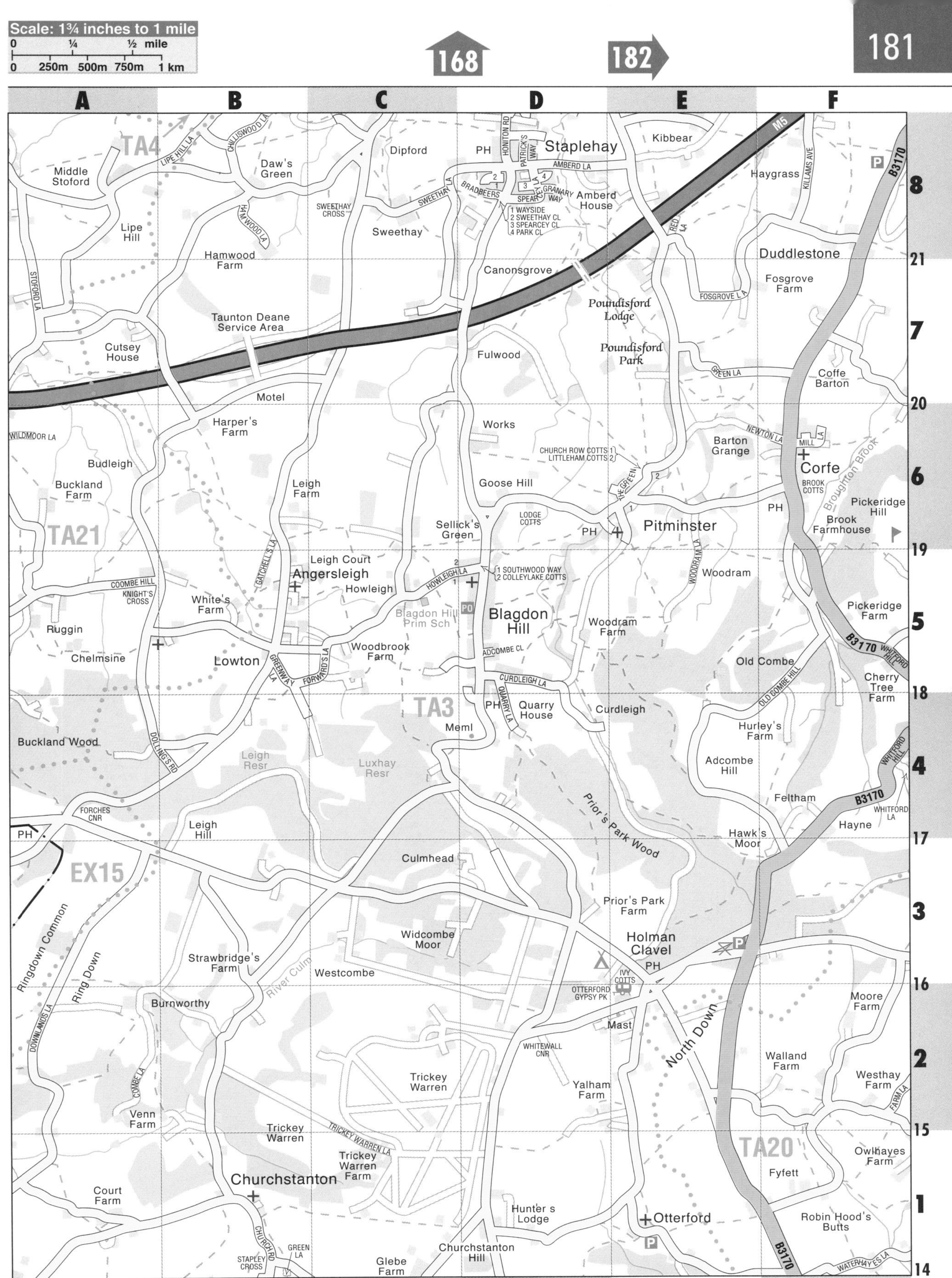

Staplehay
Kibbear
Dipford
Daw's Green
Middle Stoford
Lipe Hill
Hamwood Farm
Sweethay
Amberd House
Haygrass
Duddlestone
Fosgrove Farm
Canonsgrove
Poundisford Lodge
Poundisford Park
Taunton Deane Service Area
Cutsey House
Fulwood
Coffe Barton
Motel
Harper's Farm
Works
Barton Grange
Corfe
Budleigh
Buckland Farm
Leigh Farm
Goose Hill
Pitminster
Pickeridge Hill
Brook Farmhouse
Sellick's Green
Leigh Court
Angersleigh
Howleigh
Woodram
White's Farm
Ruggin
Blagdon Hill
Blagdon Hill Prim Sch
Woodram Farm
Pickeridge Farm
Chelmsine
Lowton
Woodbrook Farm
Old Combe
Cherry Tree Farm
Quarry House
Curdleigh
Buckland Wood
Meml
Hurley's Farm
Adcombe Hill
Leigh Resr
Luxhay Resr
Feltham
Leigh Hill
Prior's Park Wood
Hawk's Moor
Hayne
Culmhead
Prior's Park Farm
Widcombe Moor
Holman Clavel
Strawbridge's Farm
Westcombe
Ringdown Common
Ring Down
Burnworthy
River Culm
North Down
Moore Farm
Mast
Walland Farm
Trickey Warren
Yalham Farm
Westhay Farm
Venn Farm
Trickey Warren Farm
Owlhayes Farm
Fyfett
Churchstanton
Court Farm
Hunter's Lodge
Otterford
Robin Hood's Butts
Churchstanton Hill
Glebe Farm
TA4
TA21
TA3
EX15
TA20
M5
B3170

191
192
182

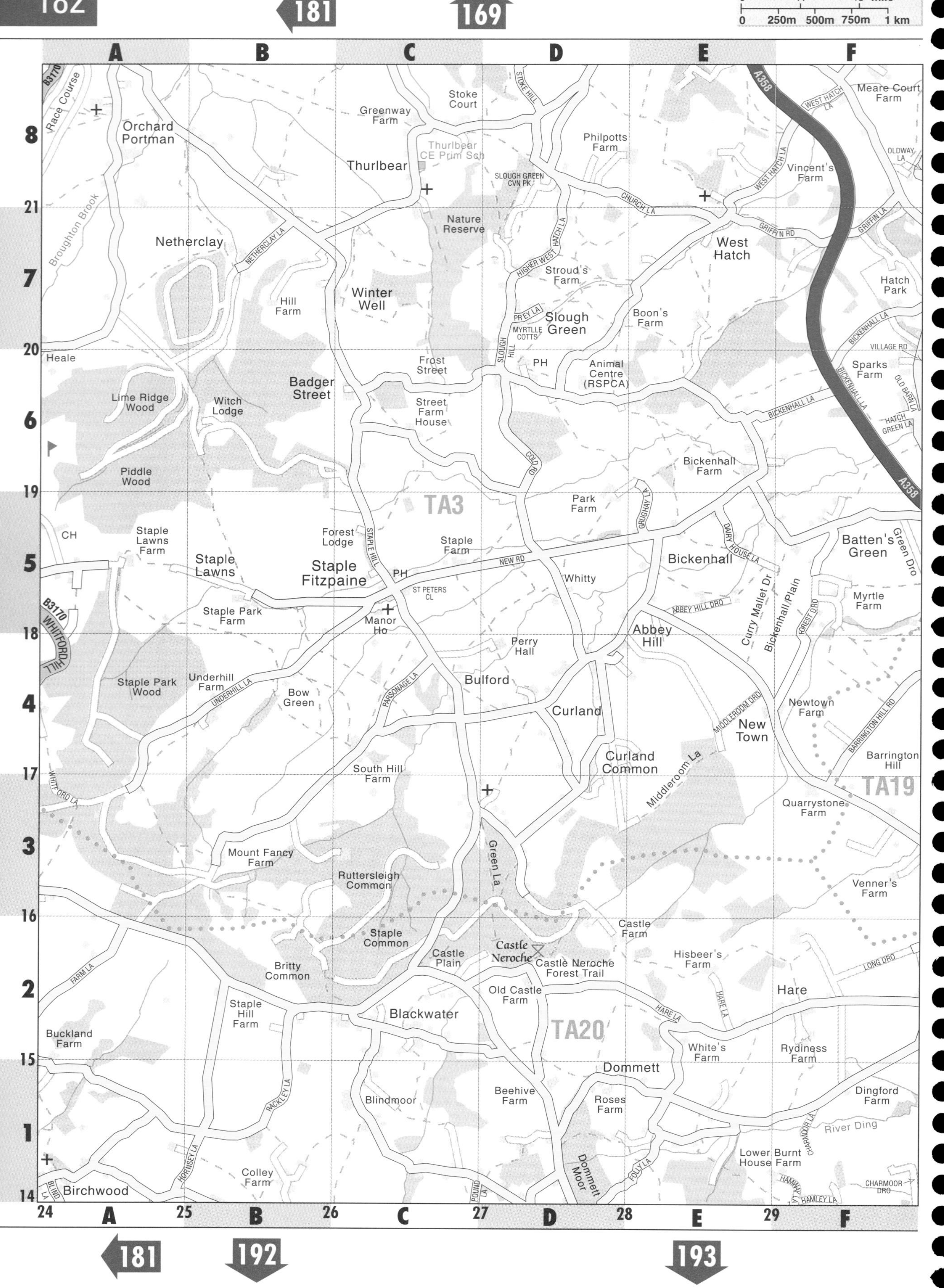

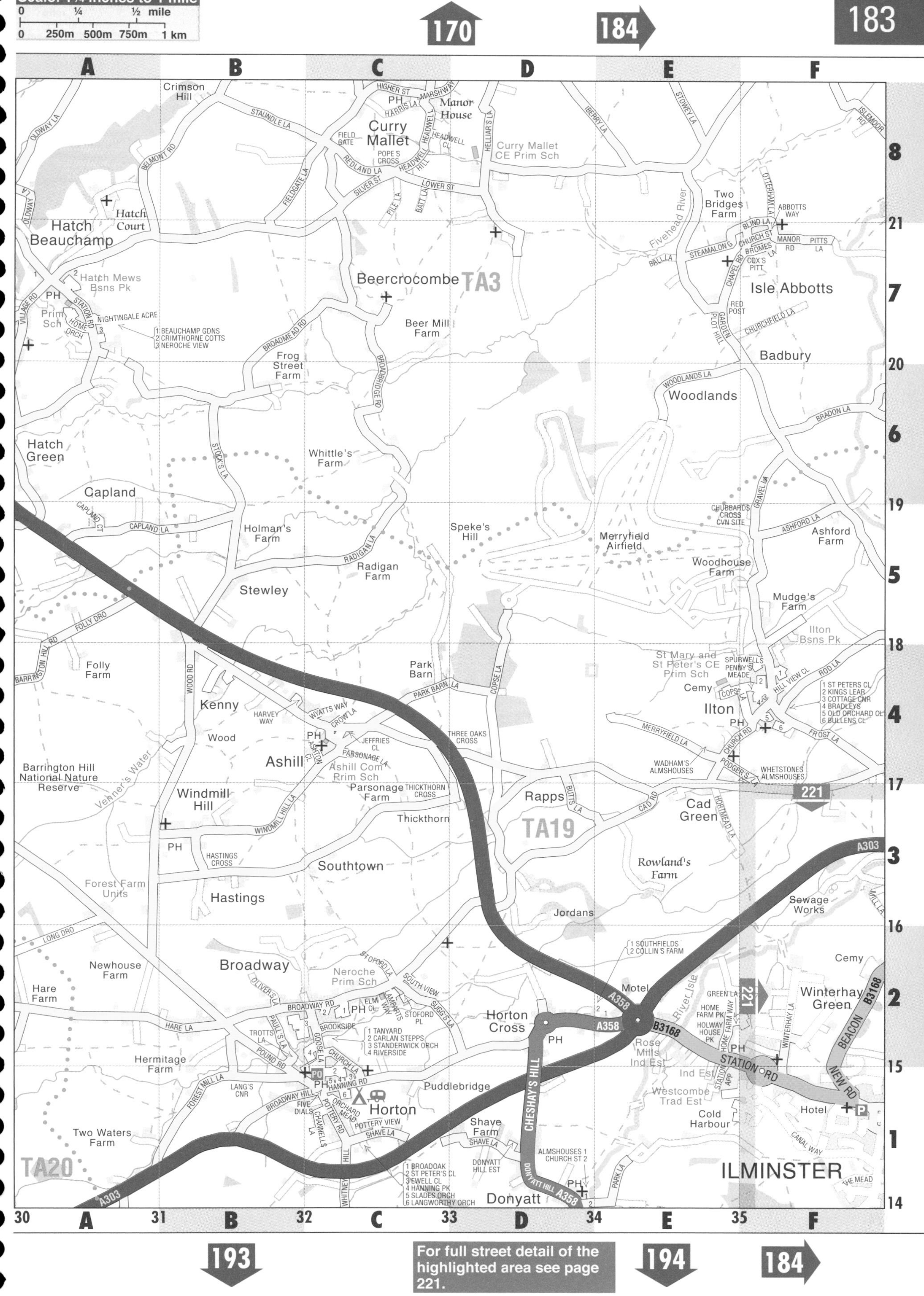

Scale: 1¾ inches to 1 mile

0   ¼   ½   mile
0   250m 500m 750m 1 km

170

184

183

A B C D E F

Crimson Hill

HIGHER ST
MARSHWAY
PH
MANOR HOUSE
STAUNDLE LA
Curry Mallet
FIELD GATE
POPE'S CROSS
HEADWELL CL
HELLIAR'S LA
Curry Mallet CE Prim Sch

STOREY LA
IBERLI LA

Two Bridges Farm
ABBOTTS WAY

8

21

Hatch Court
Hatch Beauchamp

OLDWAY LA
BELMONT RD
REDLAND LA
SILVER ST
PILE LA
BATT LA
LOWER ST

Fivehead River
BALL LA
STEAMALON G'S
CHAPEL LA
BROMES
COX'S PITT
CHURCH ST
MANOR RD
PITTS LA
OTTERHAM LA
BLIND LA

Isle Abbotts

7

Hatch Mews Bsns Pk
VILLAGE RD
STATION RD
PH
Prim Sch
HOME ORCH
NIGHTINGALE ACRE
1 BEAUCHAMP GDNS
2 CRIMTHORNE COTTS
3 NEROCHE VIEW

Beercrocombe TA3

Beer Mill Farm

RED POST
GARDEN HILL
PLOT HILL
CHURCHFIELD LA

Badbury

20

Frog Street Farm
BROADMEAD RD
BROADRIDGE DRO

WOODLANDS LA

Woodlands

BRADON LA

6

Hatch Green

Whittle's Farm

GRAVEL LA

19

Capland
CAPLAND CT
CAPLAND LA

STOCK'S LA

Speke's Hill

Merryfield Airfield

Woodhouse Farm

CHUBBARDS CROSS CVN SITE
ASHFORD LA
Ashford Farm

5

Holman's Farm
RADIGAN LA
Radigan Farm
Stewley

Mudge's Farm

Ilton Bsns Pk

18

FOLLY DRO
Folly Farm
BARRINGTON HILL RD

WOOD RD

Park Barn
COPSE LA
PARK BARN LA

St Mary and St Peter's CE Prim Sch
SPURWELLS
PENNY S MEADE
COPSE
Cemy
HILL VIEW RD
ROD LA
1 ST PETERS CL
2 KINGS LEAR
3 COTTAGE CNR
4 BRADLEYS
5 OLD ORCHARD CL
6 BULLENS CL

4

Kenny
HARVEY WAY
WYATTS WAY
CROWL LA
JEFFRIES CL
PH
PARSONAGE
Ashill
Wood

THREE OAKS CROSS
Ashill Com Prim Sch
THICKTHORN CROSS
Parsonage Farm

MERRYFIELD LA
WADHAM'S ALMSHOUSES
CHURCH RD
PODGER'S LA
Ilton
PH
WHETSTONES ALMSHOUSES
FROST LA

Barrington Hill National Nature Reserve
VERNEL'S WATER
Windmill Hill
WINDMILL HILL LA
PH
HASTINGS CROSS
Thickthorn

Rapps
BUTTS LA
CAD RD

TA19

Cad Green

221

17

Forest Farm Units
LONG DRO
Southtown
WINDMILL HILL RD

Rowland's Farm

A303

3

Hastings

Jordans

Sewage Works
MALL LA

16

Hare Farm
Newhouse Farm
HARE LA
Broadway
OLIVER'S LA
Neroche Prim Sch
STOFORD LA
SOUTH VIEW
STOFORD PL
SUGG'S LA
1 SOUTHFIELDS
2 COLLIN'S FARM

Motel
A358
A358
River Isle
STATION RD APP
221
GREEN LA
HOME FARM PK
HOLWAY HOUSE LA

Cemy

Winterhay Green
B3168

2

BROADWAY RD
PH
ELM CL
AMOR'S WAY
TANYARD
2 CARLAN STEPPS
3 STANDERWICK ORCH
4 RIVERSIDE
Horton Cross

B3168
Rose Mills Ind Est
Ind Est
STATION RD
WINTERHAY LA
PH

BEACON
NEW RD

15

Hermitage Farm
TROTTS LA
PAUL'S LA
POUND RD
FOREST MILL LA
LANG'S CNR
BROADWAY HILL
ORCHARD MEAD
FIVE DIALS
GOOSE LA
CHURCH LA
PO
PH
HANNING RD
POTTERY VIEW
Horton
X
POTTERY RD
Puddlebridge
CHESHAY'S HILL
Westcombe Trad Est
Cold Harbour
Hotel
P
CANAL WAY

Two Waters Farm
TA20
HARE LA

WHITNEY LA
TITH
SHAVE LA
Shave Farm
SHAVE LA
DONYATT HILL EST
DONYATT HILL
1 BROADOAK
2 ST PETER'S CL
3 EWELL CL
4 HANNING PK
5 SLADES ORCH
6 LANGWORTHY ORCH

ALMSHOUSES 1
CHURCH ST 2
PARK LA
PH
Donyatt
A358

ILMINSTER
THE MEAD

1

14

A303

30 A 31 B 32 C 33 D 34 E 35 F

193

For full street detail of the highlighted area see page 221.

194

184

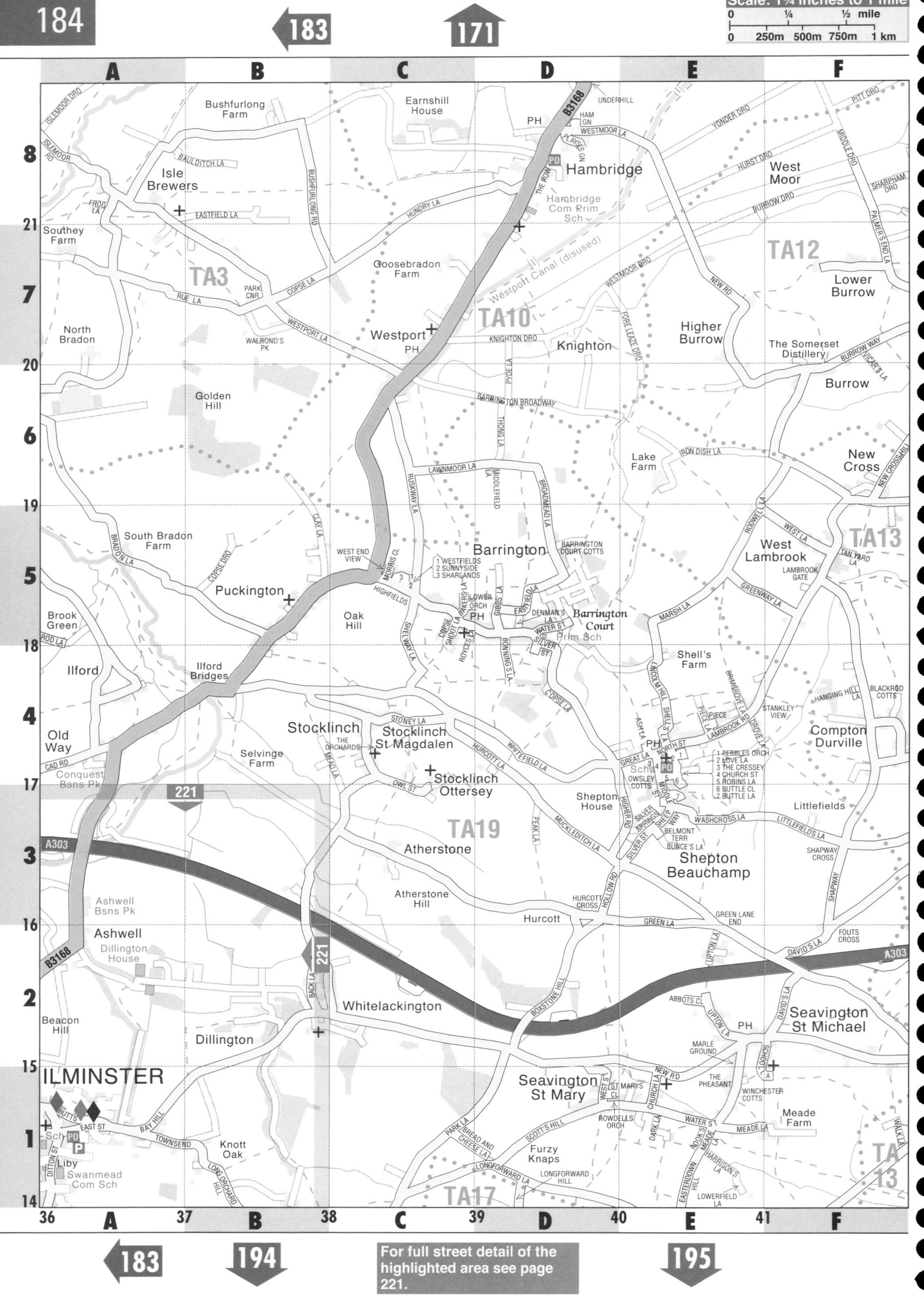

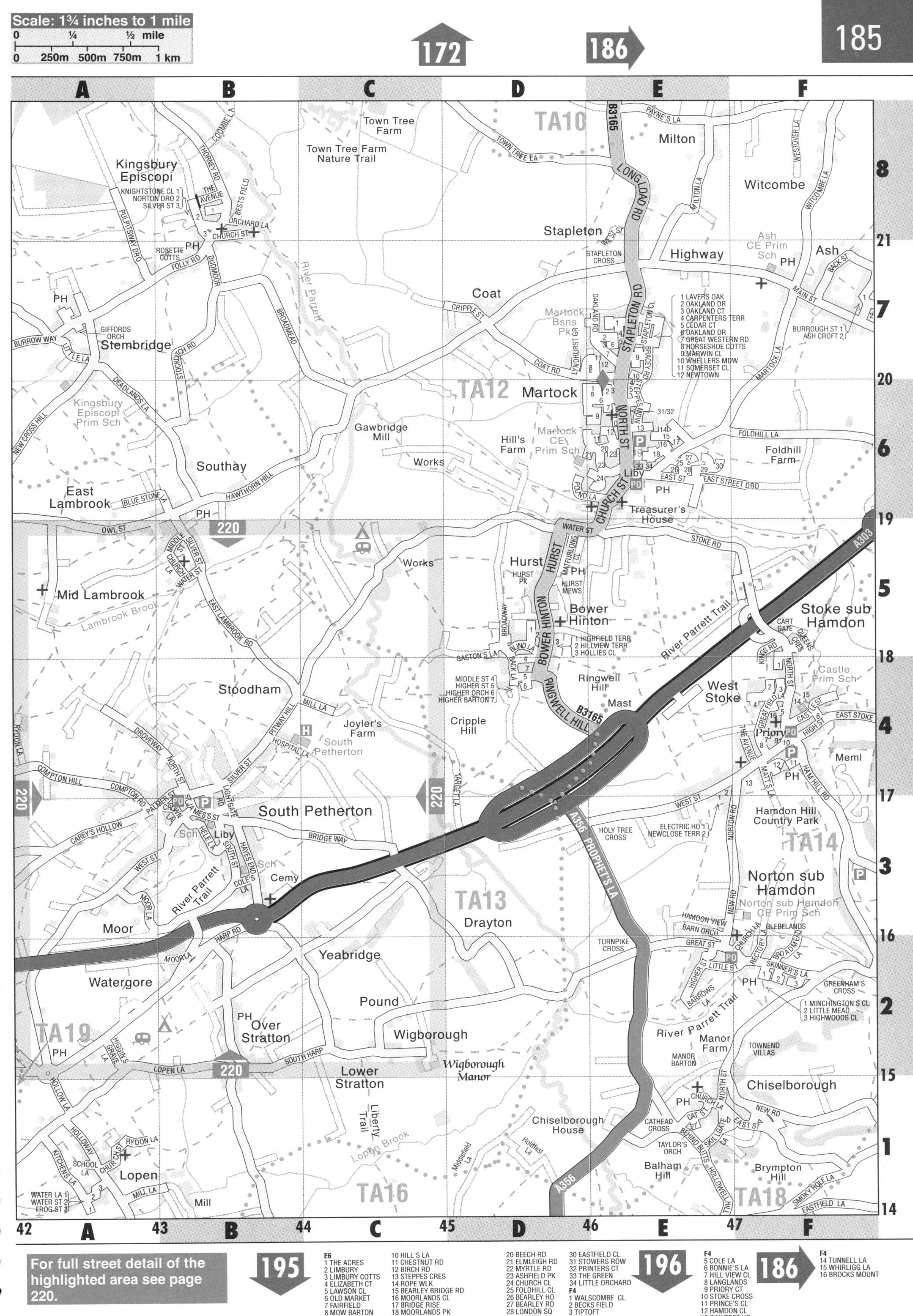

Scale: 1¾ inches to 1 mile

0 ¼ ½ mile
0 250m 500m 750m 1 km

172 186

For full street detail of the highlighted area see page 220.

195 196 186

E6
1 THE ACRES
2 LIMBURY
3 LIMBURY COTTS
4 ELIZABETH CT
5 LAWSON CL
6 OLD MARKET
7 FAIRFIELD
8 MOW BARTON
9 HILLS ORCH
10 HILL'S LA
11 CHESTNUT RD
12 BIRCH RD
13 STEPPES CRES
14 ROPE WLK
15 BEARLEY BRIDGE RD
16 MOORLANDS CL
17 BRIDGE RISE
18 MOORLANDS PK
19 Moorlands Pk Sh Ctr

20 BEECH RD
21 ELMLEIGH RD
22 MYRTLE RD
23 ASHFIELD PK
24 CHURCH CL
25 FOLDHILL CL
26 BEARLEY HO
27 BEARLEY RD
28 LONDON SQ
29 EASTFIELD

30 EASTFIELD CL
31 STOWERS ROW
32 PRINTERS CT
33 THE GREEN
34 LITTLE ORCHARD

F4
1 WALSCOMBE CL
2 BECKS FIELD
3 TIPTOFT
4 GLOVERS CL

F4
5 COLE LA
6 BONNIE'S LA
7 HILL VIEW CL
8 LANGLANDS
9 PRIORY CT
10 STOKE CROSS
11 PRINCE'S CL
12 HAMDON CL
13 OAK TREE HO

F4
14 TUNNELL LA
15 WHIRLIGG LA
16 BROCKS MOUNT

185 173

A B C D E F

8
21
7
20
6
19
5
18
4
17
3
16
2
15
1
14

Ash Dro
Ash
BACK ST
LAVERS CT
MIDDLE LEAZE DRO
TA12
Durnfield
FOLDHILL LA
Halfway House Farm
Caravan Pk
Wellham's Mill
East Stoke
MULBERRY LA
WINDSOR LA
STONEHILL
EAST STOKE
Hedgecock Hill
Ham Hill Ctry Pk
TA14
Monarch's Way
Little Norton
Liberty Trail
Bagnell Farm
EASTFIELD LA
Eastfield
TA18
Chiselborough Hill

Bearley Brook
BURLINGHAM'S LA
Burlingham's Farm
STONE LA
BEARLEY LA
Broadleaze Farm
Stonecroft Manor Farm
QUEEN ST
LITTLE TRUMPS
Tintinhull Garden
FARM ST
Tintinhull House
CHURCH ST
VICARAGE
St Margaret's Sch
PH
HALLETS ORCH
SCHOOL CL
HEAD ST
YEOVIL RD
Tintinhull
THURLOCKS
MONTACUTE RD
Perren's Hill Farm
COLE CROSS
Wellham's Brook
MARSH LA
Windmill Farm
WINDMILL COTTS
Stanchester Sports Com Sch
LOWER HYDE RD
HYDE LA
LOWER TOWN
MASON LA
MONTACUTE RD
St Michael's Hill
SMITH'S ROW
Montacute House
Twr
WASH LA
Montacute
TA15
HOLLOW LA
MIDDLE ST
THE BOROUGH
SOUTH ST
STONE LA
All Saints CE Prim Sch
Woodhouse Farm
PARK LA
Gaundle Farm
BALL'S HILL
Leland Trail
FIVE ASHES
DRAY RD
HAM HILL RD
Higher Odcombe
STREET LA
GORS
CHERRY LA
DONNE LA
LONG RUN
WESTBURY
LANDSHIRE LA
GREEN LA
East Chinnock Hill
Lower Odcombe
PH
Odcombe
HOLLY TERR
ORCHARD CL
BROADWAY
CORYATE CL
CHURCH TERR
CHAPEL HILL
REX RD
Cloverleaf Farm
Pye Corner Farm
NEW RD
High Leaze Farm
DIBBLES LA
CAMP RD
Camp Hill

Sock Dennis Farm
A303
A37
Higher Oakley Farm
Oakley Brook
Rushley Farm
Oakley Farms
OAKLEY LA
Shortland Farm
KINGS HILL
HALFWAY
PH
ILCHESTER RD
Sock Farm
CHILTHORNE LA
MAIN ST
FORT'S
FORT'S ORCH
Chilthorne Domer CE Sch
Chilthorne Domer
Little Sammons
PH
BA21
Vagg
VAGG HILL
TINTINHULL RD
Vagg Farm
Vagg Pk
Axesclose Farm
BA22
Thorne Coffin
218
THORNE LA
LARKHILL RD
WESSEX RD
Cambian Lufton Coll
HIGSON CL
Lufton
COPSE RD
Huish Park
Trad Est
MEMORIAL
ARTILLERY RD
Houndstone
BOUNDARY WAY
WESTERN AVE
POPLAR DR
ARLINGTON
STOURTON WAY
ST ACRE DR
Prim Sch
MONKS DALE
WHITE MEAD
Tithe Barn
Preston Sch
PRESTON RD
LUFTON WAY
ROE AVE
BLUEBELL RD
Cfem
BUNFORD LA
ALVINGTON
Preston Plucknett
218
Alvington
A3088
Yeovil Airfield
BUNFORD LA
WATERCOMBE LA
BRYMPTON
Brympton House
Brympton D'Evercy
BA20
Broadleaze Farm
LABURNUM WAY
RUSSET WAY
LYSANDER RD
A3088
Trad Est
WATERCOMBE LA
A3088
Feebarrow
GOOSEACRE LA
WEST COKER RD A30
HELENA RD
NASH LA
218

A 48 B 49 C 50 D 51 E 52 F 53

185 196 197 For full street detail of the highlighted area see page 218.

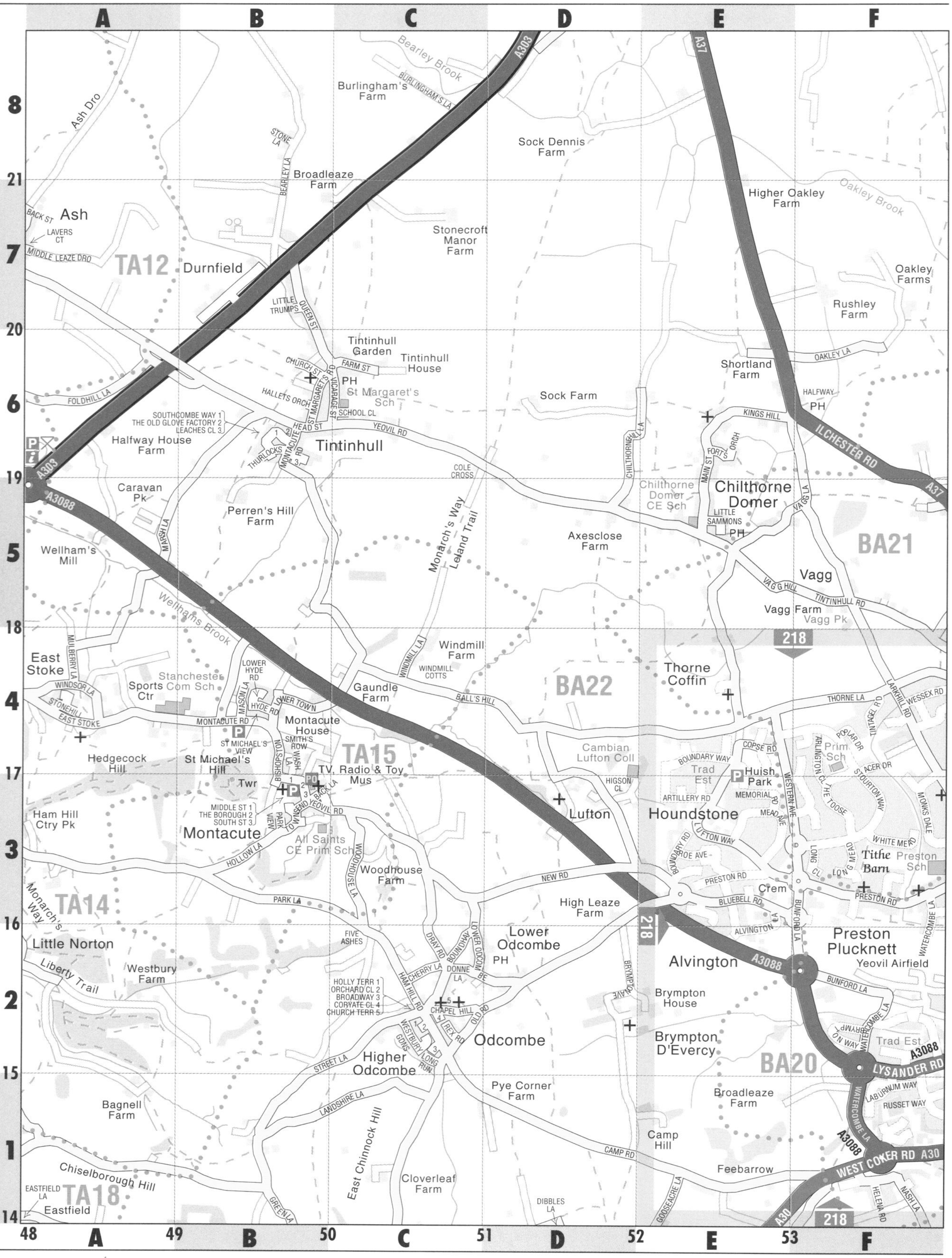

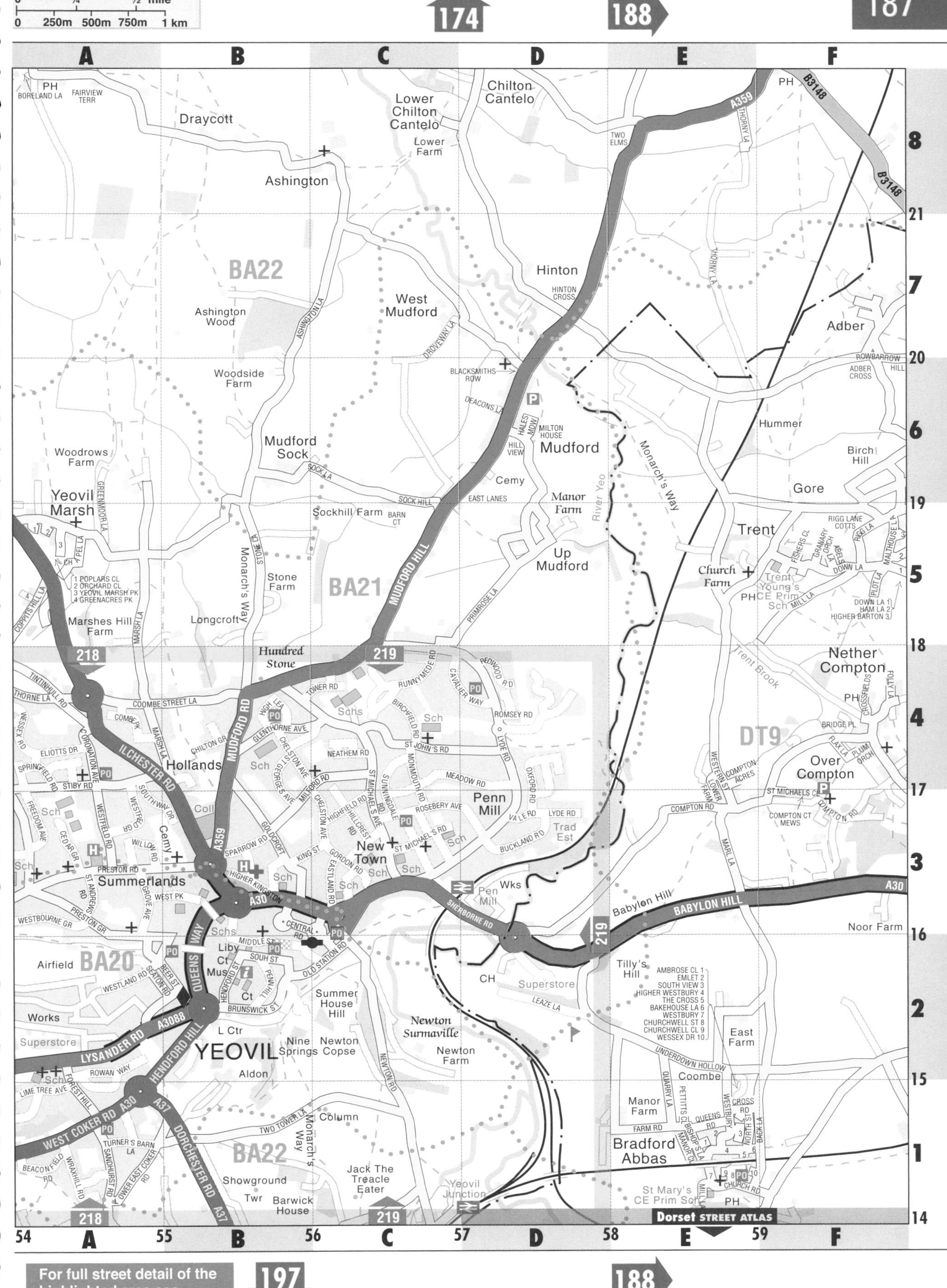

Scale: 1¾ inches to 1 mile
0   ¼   ½ mile
0   250m   500m   750m   1 km

174

188

A | **B** | **C** | **D** | **E** | **F**

PH BORELAND LA
FAIRVIEW TERR
Draycott
Ashington
Lower Chilton Cantelo
Lower Farm
Chilton Cantelo
PH
TWO ELMS
A359
THORNY LA
B3148

BA22
Ashington Wood
West Mudford
DROVENAY LA
Hinton
HINTON CROSS
THORNY LA
Adber
B3148

Woodside Farm
BLACKSMITHS ROW
DEACONS LA
P
HALES MDW
MILTON HOUSE
HILL VIEW
Mudford
Monarch's Way
ROWBARROW
ADBER CROSS
HILL

Woodrows Farm
Mudford Sock
SOCA LA
Cemy
EAST LANES
Hummer
Gore
Birch Hill

Yeovil Marsh
GREENMOOR LA
SOCK HILL
Sockhill Farm
BARN CT
Manor Farm
River Yeo
Trent
FISHERS CL
RIGG LANE COTTS
GRANARY LOFT
ABBEL A
MALTHOUSE LA

1 POPLARS CL
2 ORCHARD CL
3 YEOVIL MARSH PK
4 GREENACRES PK
Marshes Hill Farm
Monarch's Way
Longcroft
Stone Farm
BA21
Up Mudford
MUDFORD HILL
PRIMROSE LA
Church Farm
Trent Young's PHCE Prim Sch
MILL LA
DOWN LA
DOWN LA 1
HAM LA 2
HIGHER BARTON 3

218
Hundred Stone
219
TOWER RD
RUNNY MEDE RD
REDWOOD RD
CAVALIER WAY
ROMSEY RD
Trent Brook
Nether Compton
PH
CROSSFIELDS LA
FOTLA

COPPITS HILL LA
TINTINHULL RD
THORNE LA
COOMBE STREET LA
HIGH LEA
P
BIRCHFIELD RD
Sch
St JOHN'S RD
LYDE RD
BRIDGE PL
DT9
Over Compton
FLAXLA
PLUM ORCH

WESSEX RD
ELIOTTS DR
SPRINGFIELD
STIBY RD
ILCHESTER RD
COMBE
MARSH LA
CHILTON GR
GLENTHORNE AVE
CHELSTON AVE
St GEORGES AVE
NEATHEM RD
Sch
HIGHFIELD FOREST RD
MONMOUTH RD
MEADOW RD
ROSEBERY AVE
OXFORD RD
VALE RD
Penn Mill
COMPTON RD
COMPTON ACRES
St Michaels C
COMPTON CT MEWS

Hollands
Sch
Sch
CHELSTON AVE
MILFORD RD
CHELSTON AVE
St MICHAELS AVE
KING ST
St MICHAEL'S RD
BUCKLAND RD
Trad Est
WESTBY
LOWER RD
MARL LA

Sch
FREEDOM AVE
CEDAR GR
WILLOW RD
SOUTHVIEW RD
A359
SPARROW RD
HIGHER KINGSTON
New Town
St MICHAEL'S RD
Sch
LYDE RD
Wks
Babylon Hill
BABYLON HILL
A30
Noor Farm

Sch
ST ANDREWS RD
PRESTON RD
GROVE AVE
WEST PK
H
H
Sch
EASTLAND RD
Sch
Pen Mill
SHERBORNE RD
219
Tilly's Hill

Summerlands
WESTBOURNE GR
PRESTON GR
A30
Schs
CENTRAL RD
MIDDLE ST
P
CH
Superstore
LEAZE LA
AMBROSE CL 1
EMLET 2
SOUTH VIEW 3
HIGHER WESTBURY 4
THE CROSS 5
BAKEHOUSE LA 6
WESTBURY 7
CHURCHWELL ST 8
CHURCHWELL CL 9
WESSEX DR 10

Airfield
BA20
PO
QUEENS WAY
Liby
Ct Mus
SOUH ST
PENN HILL
Ct
BRUNSWICK ST

Works
Superstore
LYSANDER RD
A3088
HENFORD HILL
L Ctr
Nine Springs
Summer House Hill
Newton Surmaville
Newton Copse
Newton Farm
UNDERDOWN HOLLOW
Coombe
East Farm

YEOVIL
Aldon
NEWTON RD
Manor Farm
QUARRY LA
FARM RD
PETTITS CL
BISHOP'S CL
QUEENS RD
WORTH LA
BACK LA
CROSS

LIME TREE AVE
FORREST HILL
WEST COKER RD
A30
A37
DORCHESTER HILL
PO
Column
TWO TOWER LA
Monarch's Way
Bradford Abbas
CHURCH RD

BEACONFIELD RD
WRAXHILL RD
SANDHURST RD
OVER EAST COKER RD
TURNER'S BARN LA
BA22
Showground
Barwick House
Jack The Treacle Eater Twr
Yeovil Junction
219
St Mary's CE Prim Sch
PH

54 | 55 | 56 | 57 | 58 | 59

197

188

For full street detail of the highlighted area see pages 218 and 219.

A B C D E F

8

21

7

20

6

19

5

18

4

17

3

16

2

15

1

14

B3145

Rimpton
BA22
Heaven's Door

HOME FARM LA DAISYFIELD MIDD ST CHURCH LA BACK LA MILL ST HIGH ST
Weathergrove Farm
PINK KNOLL HOLLOW

Windmill Hill

PUTT'S LA Wheat Sheaf Hill

Seven Wells Down

Milborne Down

B3148
HILTON
PH White Post
PITFIEL L CNR
ROE LA
SLADE LA
GREAT PIT LA
PENMORE RD

Sandford Orcas Manor House
DARK LA
SHILLER'S LA
FARM ORCH
PH

Stafford's Green

Poyntington Down

Poyntington Hill

ROWBARROW HILL
MIDDLE FIELD LA
MOOR WAY LA
SPRING LA
Sandford Orcas

Higher Sandford

PH
Holway Hill
Holway

WINTER LA
MACMILLAN WAY

THE BUNGALOWS
THE RIDGE
Washingpool

Poyntington
Red Post

THE RIDGE

HAM LA
DOWN LA
LOWSOME LA
Monarch's Way
Trent Barrow

Charlock Hill

PATSON HILL LA
Patson Hill

COOMBE LA

Coombe Farm

Higher Clatcombe Farm
CH
CLATCOMBE LA
WHITEPOST GATE

225
Ambrose Hill

SANDFORD ORCAS RD
REDHOLE LA

LOWER BOYSTON LA

Oborne

A30
BARGERS

CHECCOMBE LA

TUCKER'S CROSS
GUINEAGORE LA
KITTON LA
RAPH'S LA
RATLE CTL LA

MARSTON RD
COOMBE
TRENT PATH LA
SHEEP LANDS LA

SHERBORNE

225

DT9

B3148

YEOVIL RD
A352
Stallen
Hotel
BRADFORD RD
RIDGEWAY
LOW'S HILL LA
Halfway House Farm
Lenthay Dairy House
WESTBRIDGE PK
STH AVE
LENTHAP RD
HORSECASTLES LA
RICHMOND RD
Cemy

BRISTOL RD
B3145
ST ALDHELM'S RD
CASTLE TOWN WAY
GRANVILLE WAY
Sch
CASTLE RD
Blackmarsh Farm

KINGS RD
COLD HARBOUR
Sch
GREENHILL
CHEAP ST
NEWLAND
LONG ST
TINNEYS LA
OBORNE RD
B3145
225
Sch
P INFORD LA
Sherborne Lake

DIGBY RD
H
Sch
Mus
Abbey
SOUTH ST
Liby
Sherborne Old Castle
Sherborne Castle
NEW RD
Sherborne

P
LC
Home Farm

QUARR LA
CASTLE RD
QUARR LA

WESTBURY
HORSECASTLES

B3145 NEW RD
Dancing Hill
GAINSBOROUGH HILL
The Kennels

Stallen

Bedmill Farm
Silverlake Farm
SILVERLAKE COTTS
Lenthay Common
LC
Sch
Sewage Works
WEST MILL LA
Limekiln Farm
225

SHERBORNE HILL
MACMILLAN WAY

LC Wyke Farm
Honeycombe Farm
Court House Dairy
Honeycombe Wood

A30

A3030
A3030
Westhill Lodge
A352
A3030
GREEN LA
WEST LA
CLOTTURLONG LA
North Wootton
PH

A352 Dorchester

For full street detail of the highlighted area see page 225.

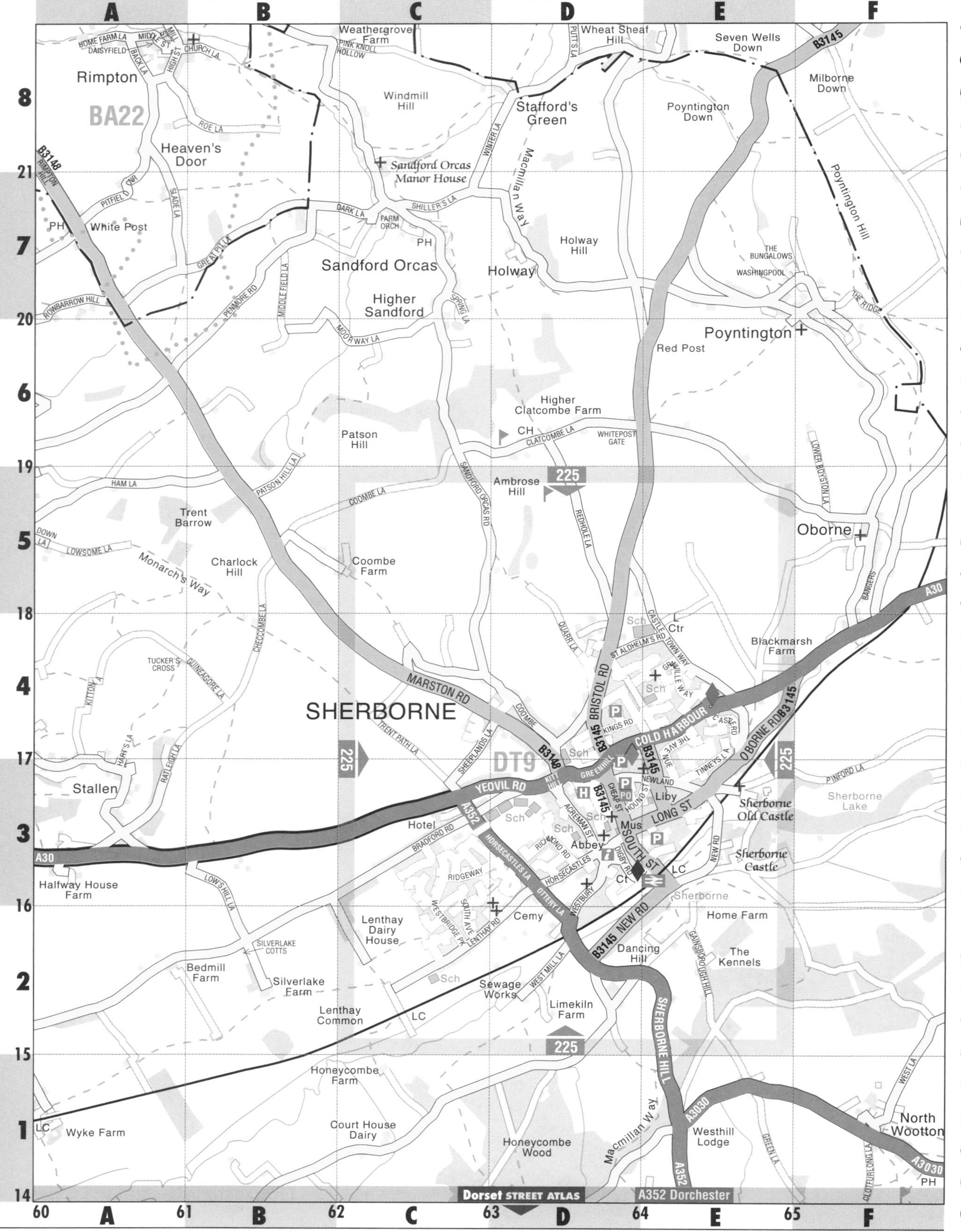

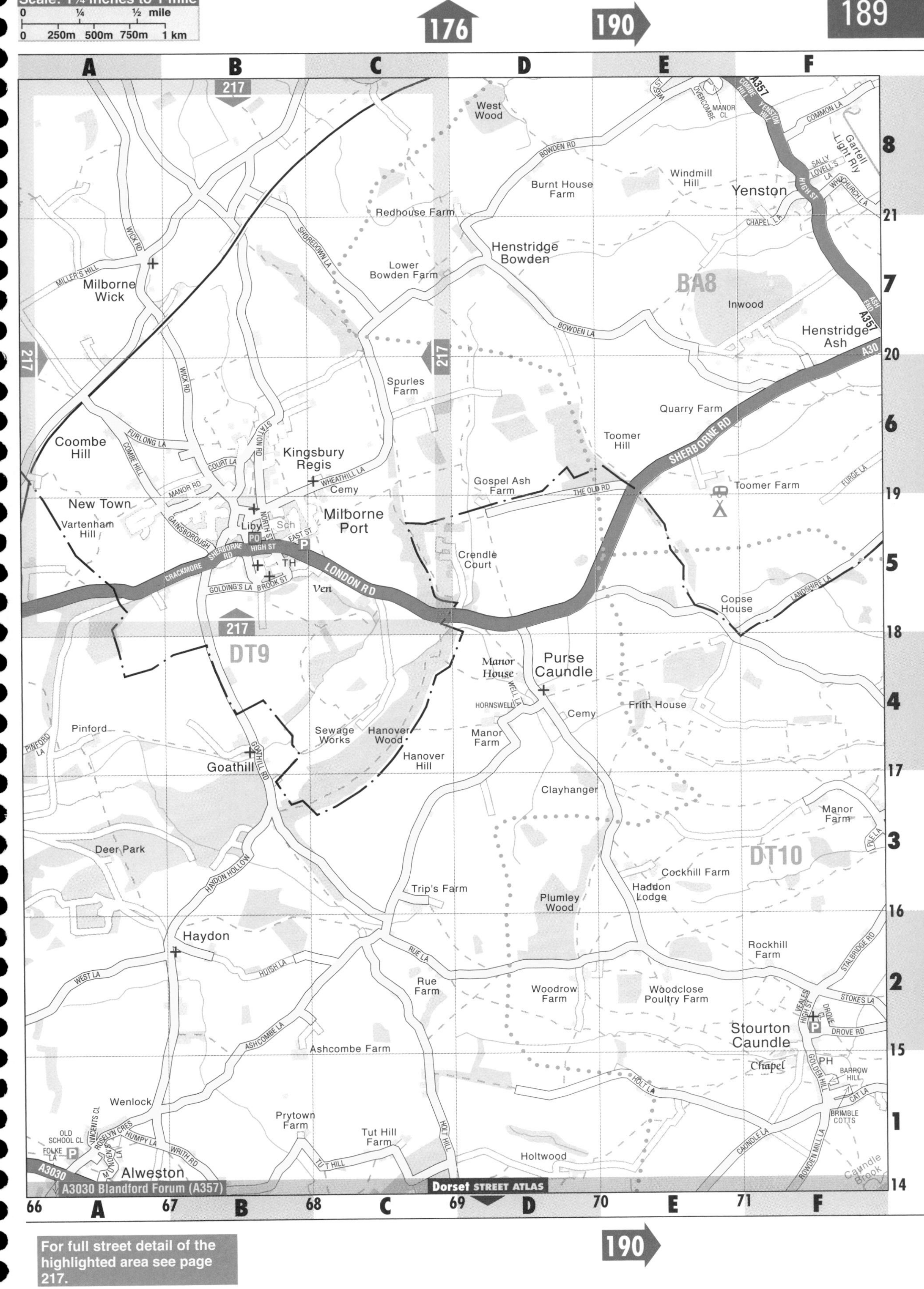

Scale: 1¾ inches to 1 mile

0   ¼   ½   mile

0   250m   500m   750m   1 km

176
190

A   B   C   D   E   F

8

21

7

6

20

19

5

18

4

17

3

16

2

15

1

14

West Wood

Bowden Rd

Burnt House Farm

Windmill Hill

Yenston

MANOR CL

COMBE LA

OVERCOMBE

A357

YENSTON

SALLY LOVELL'S LA

COMMON LA

Garrett Light Rly

HIGH ST

WINCHURCH LA

CHAPEL LA

BA8

Inwood

Henstridge Ash

A357

ASH LA

A30

Redhouse Farm

Lower Bowden Farm

Henstridge Bowden

Bowden La

Miller's Hill

Milborne Wick

217

WICK RD

WICK RD

FURLONG LA

COMBE HILL

COURT LA

STATION RD

SHREDDOWN LA

217

Spurles Farm

Quarry Farm

Toomer Hill

Gospel Ash Farm

THE OLD RD

SHERBORNE RD

Toomer Farm

TURGE LA

Coombe Hill

MANOR RD

Kingsbury Regis

WHEATHILL LA

Cemy

New Town

NORTH ST

EAST ST

Sch

Libry

PO

HIGH ST

Milborne Port

Crendle Court

LANDSHIRE LA

Copse House

Vartenham Hill

GAINSBOROUGH

SHERBORNE RD

CRACKMORE

TH

GOLDING'S LA

BROOK ST

Ven

LONDON RD

217

DT9

Manor House

WELL LA

Purse Caundle

Cemy

Frith House

HORNSWELL LA

Pinford

PINFORD LA

Sewage Works

Hanover Wood

Manor Farm

Hanover Hill

Clayhanger

Manor Farm

PILE LA

Goathill

GOATHILL RD

DT10

Deer Park

HADDON HOLLOW

Cockhill Farm

Haddon Lodge

Rockhill Farm

STALBRIDGE RD

Trip's Farm

Plumley Wood

Haydon

WEST LA

HUISH LA

RUE LA

Rue Farm

Woodrow Farm

Woodclose Poultry Farm

Stourton Caundle

LYDFALLS

HIGH ST

STOKES LA

DROVE RD

P

Chapel

GOLDEN HILL

PH

BARROW HILL

CAT LA

ASHCOMBE LA

Ashcombe Farm

HOLT LA

BRIMBLE COTTS

Wenlock

VINCENTS CL

ROSELYN CRES

HUMPY LA

WRITH RD

Prytown Farm

TUT HILL

Tut Hill Farm

HOLT HILL

Holtwood

CAUNDLE LA

BOWDEN MILL LA

Candle Brook

OLD SCHOOL CL

FOLKE LA

P

Alweston

A3030

A3030 Blandford Forum (A357)

For full street detail of the highlighted area see page 217.

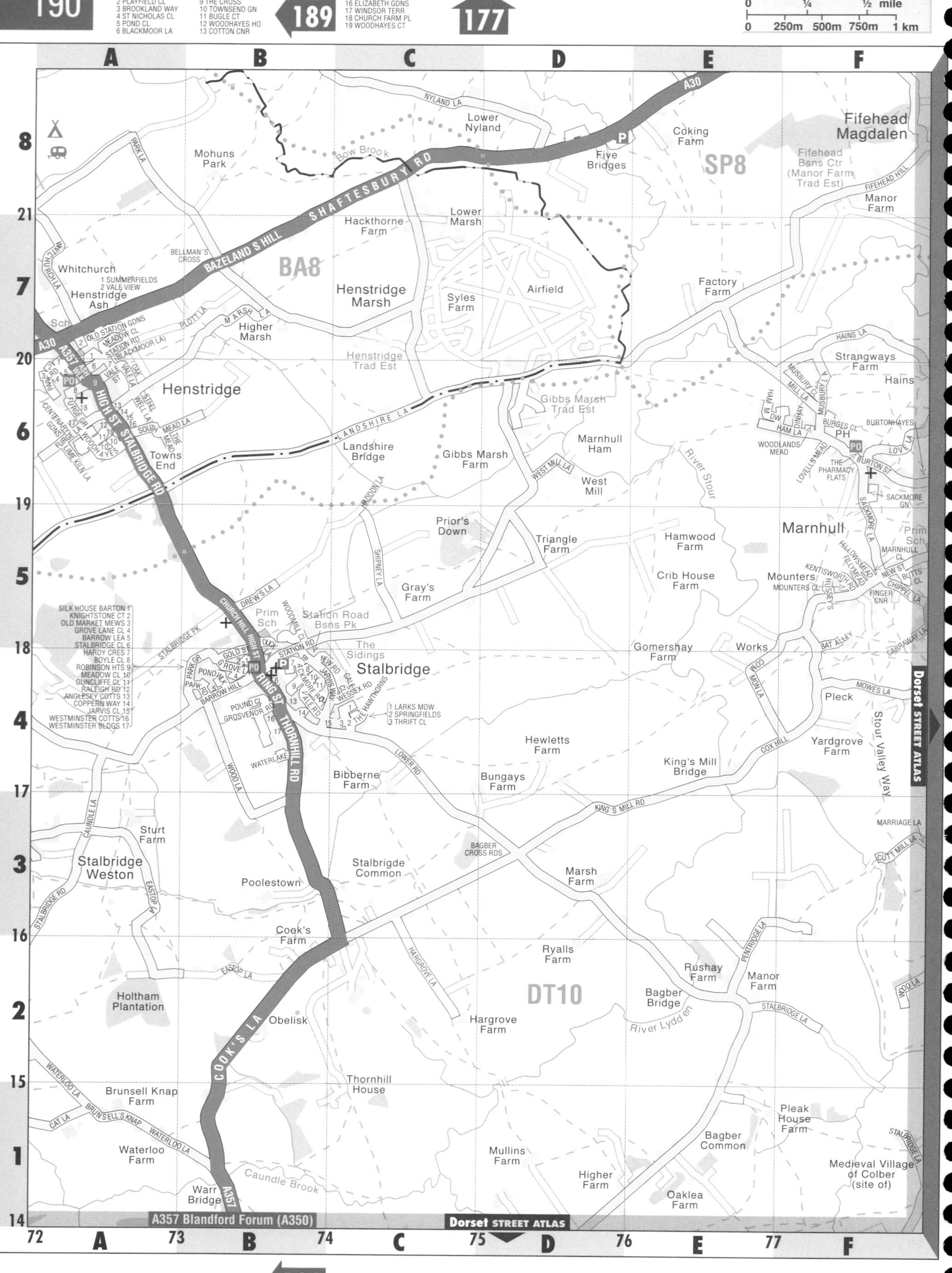

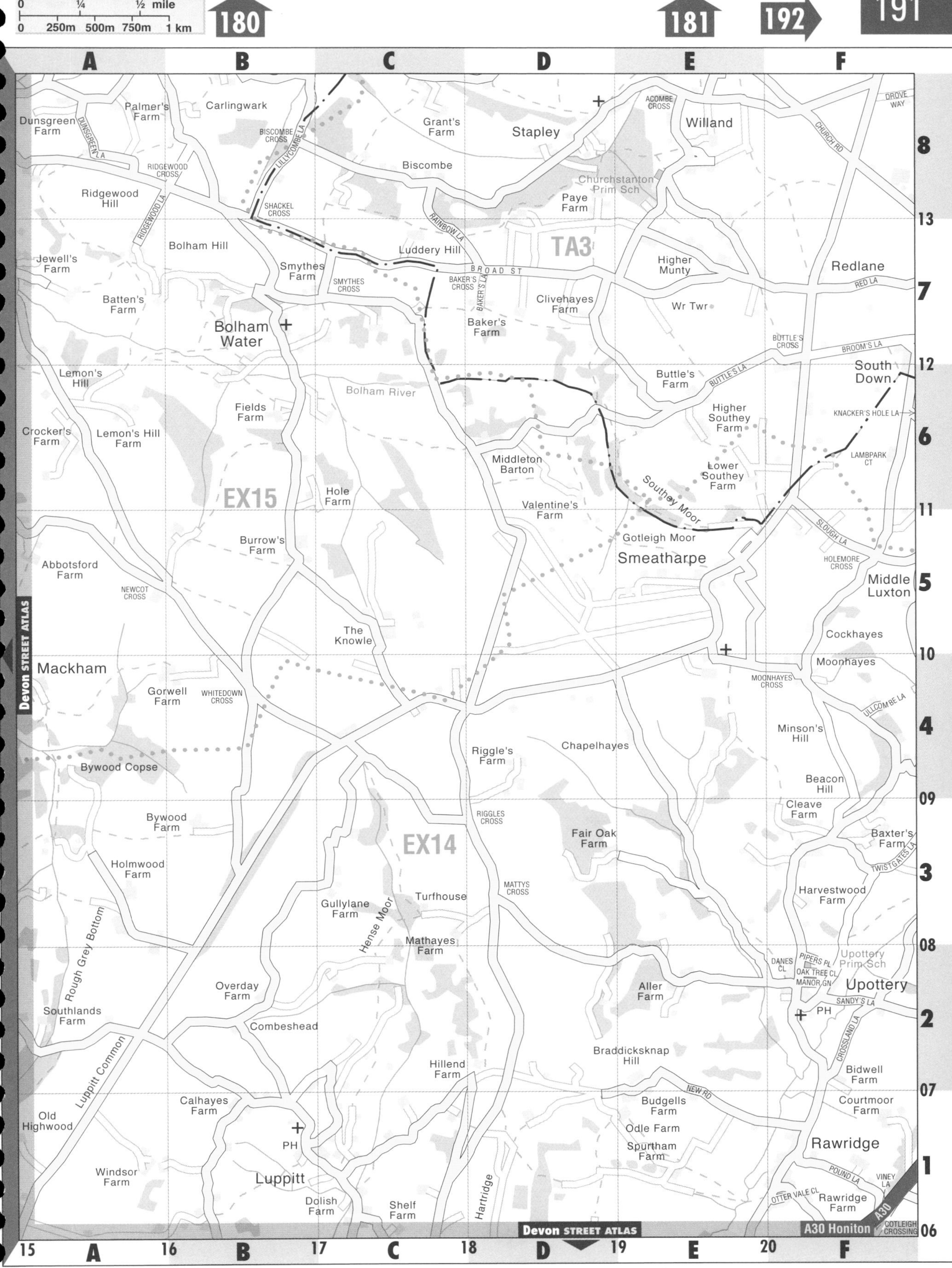

Scale: 1¾ inches to 1 mile

0   ¼   ½   mile
0   250m   500m   750m   1 km

180

181

192

191

Dunsgreen Farm
Palmer's Farm
Carlingwark
Grant's Farm
Stapley
ACOMBE CROSS
Willand
DROVE WAY

Ridgewood Hill
RIDGEWOOD CROSS
BISCOMBE CROSS
SHACKEL CROSS
Biscombe
Churchstanton Prim Sch

Jewell's Farm
Bolham Hill
Smythes Farm
RAINBOW LA
Luddery Hill
Paye Farm
TA3
CHURCH RD
Redlane
RED LA

Batten's Farm
SMYTHES CROSS
BROAD ST
BAKER'S CROSS
Higher Munty
Wr Twr

Bolham Water
Baker's Farm
Clivehayes Farm
BAKER'S LA

BUTTLE'S CROSS
BROOM'S LA

Lemon's Hill
Fields Farm
Bolham River
Buttle's Farm
South Down
BUTTLE'S LA

Crocker's Farm
Lemon's Hill Farm
Middleton Barton
Higher Southey Farm
KNACKER'S HOLE LA
LAMBPARK CT

EX15
Hole Farm
Valentine's Farm
Lower Southey Farm
Southey Moor
SLOUGH LA

Abbotsford Farm
Burrow's Farm
Gotleigh Moor
Smeatharpe
HOLEMORE CROSS

NEWCOT CROSS
Middle Luxton

Mackham
The Knowle
Cockhayes
Moonhayes

Gorwell Farm
WHITEDOWN CROSS
MOONHAYES CROSS
ULLCOMBE LA

Bywood Copse
Riggle's Farm
Chapelhayes
Minson's Hill

Bywood Farm
RIGGLES CROSS
Beacon Hill

Holmwood Farm
EX14
Fair Oak Farm
Cleave Farm
Baxter's Farm

Gullylane Farm
Turfhouse
MATTYS CROSS
Harvestwood Farm
TWISTGATES LA

Rough Grey Bottom
Hense Moor
Mathayes Farm
DANES CL
PIPERS PL
OAK TREE CL
Upottery Prim Sch

Overday Farm
Aller Farm
MANOR GN
Upottery

Southlands Farm
Combeshead
Hillend Farm
SANDY'S LA
PH

Luppitt Common
Calhayes Farm
PH
Braddicksknap Hill
NEW RD
Bidwell Farm
CROSSLAND LA

Old Highwood
Luppitt
Budgells Farm
Odle Farm
Courtmoor Farm

Windsor Farm
Dolish Farm
Shelf Farm
Hattridge
Spurtham Farm
Rawridge
POUND LA
VINEY LA

Devon STREET ATLAS
A30 Honiton
OTTER VALE CL
Rawridge Cross
GOTLEIGH CROSSING
A30

Devon STREET ATLAS

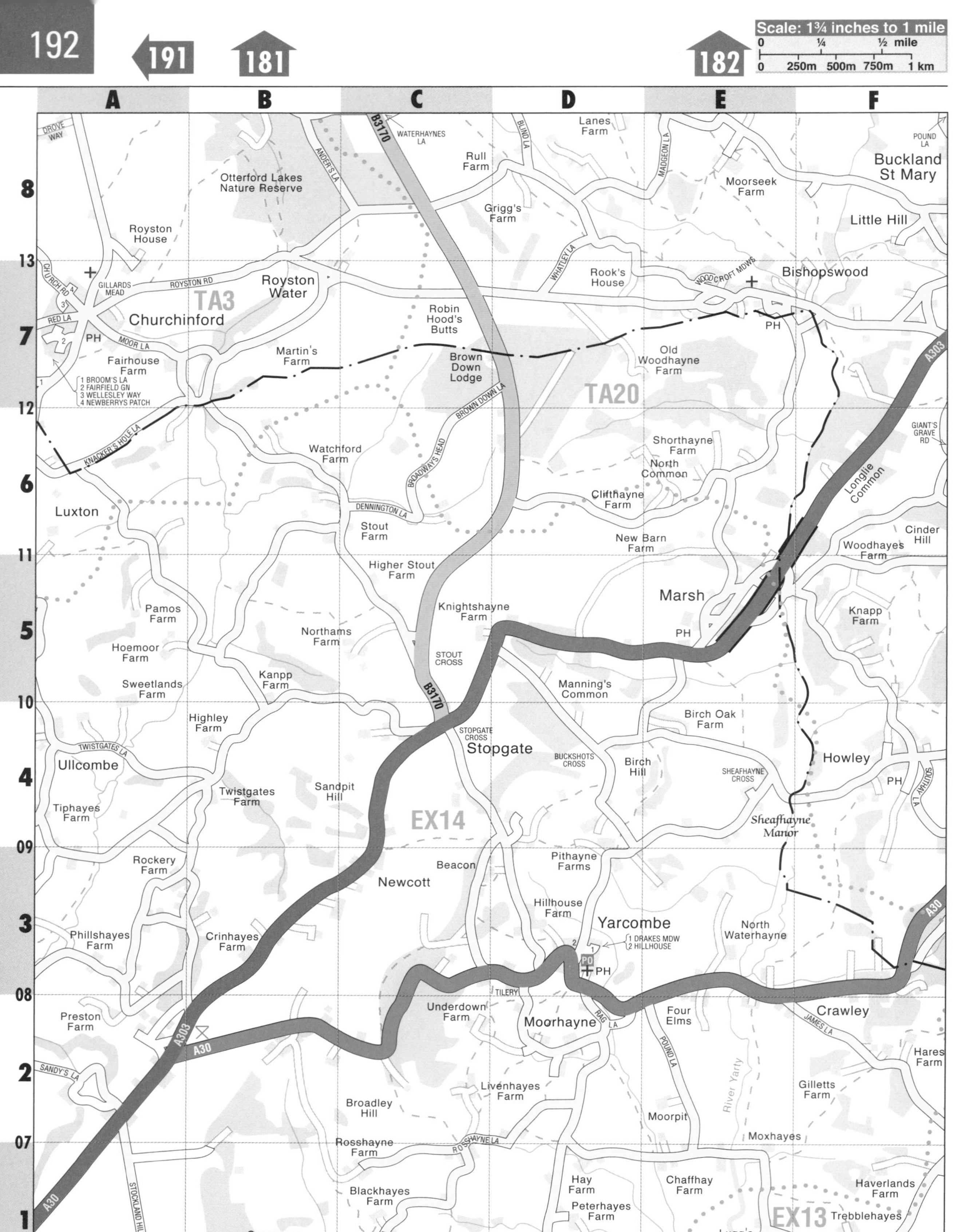

191
181
182
191

Scale: 1¾ inches to 1 mile

0 ¼ ½ mile
0 250m 500m 750m 1 km

A B C D E F

8

13

7

12

6

11

5

10

4

09

3

08

2

07

1

06

21 A 22 B 23 C 24 D 25 E 26 F

DROVE WAY
Otterford Lakes Nature Reserve
Royston House
CHURCH RD
GILLARDS MEAD
RED LA
PH
TA3
Royston Water
Churchinford
ROYSTON RD
MOOR LA
Fairhouse Farm
1 BROOM'S LA
2 FAIRFIELD GN
3 WELLESLEY WAY
4 NEWBERRYS PATCH
Martin's Farm
KNACKER'S HOLE LA
Luxton
Watchford Farm
DENNINGTON LA
Stout Farm
Higher Stout Farm
BROADWAY'S HEAD
Pamos Farm
Hoemoor Farm
Northams Farm
Sweetlands Farm
Kanpp Farm
Knightshayne Farm
STOUT CROSS
Highley Farm
B3170
TWISTGATES LA
Ullcombe
Twistgates Farm
Sandpit Hill
STOPGATE CROSS
Stopgate
Tiphayes Farm
EX14
Newcott
Beacon
Rockery Farm
Phillshayes Farm
Crinhayes Farm
A303
A30
Preston Farm
SANDY'S LA
STOCKLAND HILL
A30
Broadley Hill
Rosshayne Farm
ROSSHAYNE LA
Corrymoor Farm
BLACK HAYES LA
Blackhayes Farm
Rower Hill
Ley Farm
Underdown Farm
TILERY
Moorhayne
Hay Farm
Peterhayes Farm
Livenhayes Farm
Hillhouse Farm
Pithayne Farms
Yarcombe
1 DRAKES MDW
2 HILLHOUSE
PH
BAG LA
POUND LA
Four Elms
Moorpit
River Yarty
Chaffhay Farm
Lugg's Farm
Manning's Common
Buckshots Cross
Birch Hill
Birch Oak Farm
SHEAFHAYNE CROSS
Sheafhayne Manor
North Waterhayne
JAMES LA
Crawley
Moxhayes
Gilletts Farm
Hares Farm
EX13
Haverlands Farm
Trebblehayes
Grays Farm
WATERHAYNES LA
B3170
Rull Farm
Grigg's Farm
BLIND LA
Lanes Farm
Robin Hood's Butts
Brown Down Lodge
BROWN DOWN LA
WHATLEY LA
Rook's House
MADGEON LA
Moorseek Farm
WOODCROFT MDWS
Bishopswood
PH
TA20
Old Woodhayne Farm
Shorthayne Farm
North Common
Clifthayne Farm
New Barn Farm
Marsh
PH
Buckland St Mary
POUND LA
Little Hill
A303
GIANT'S GRAVE RD
Longlie Common
Woodhayes Farm
Cinder Hill
Knapp Farm
Howley
PH
VT AWLING
A30

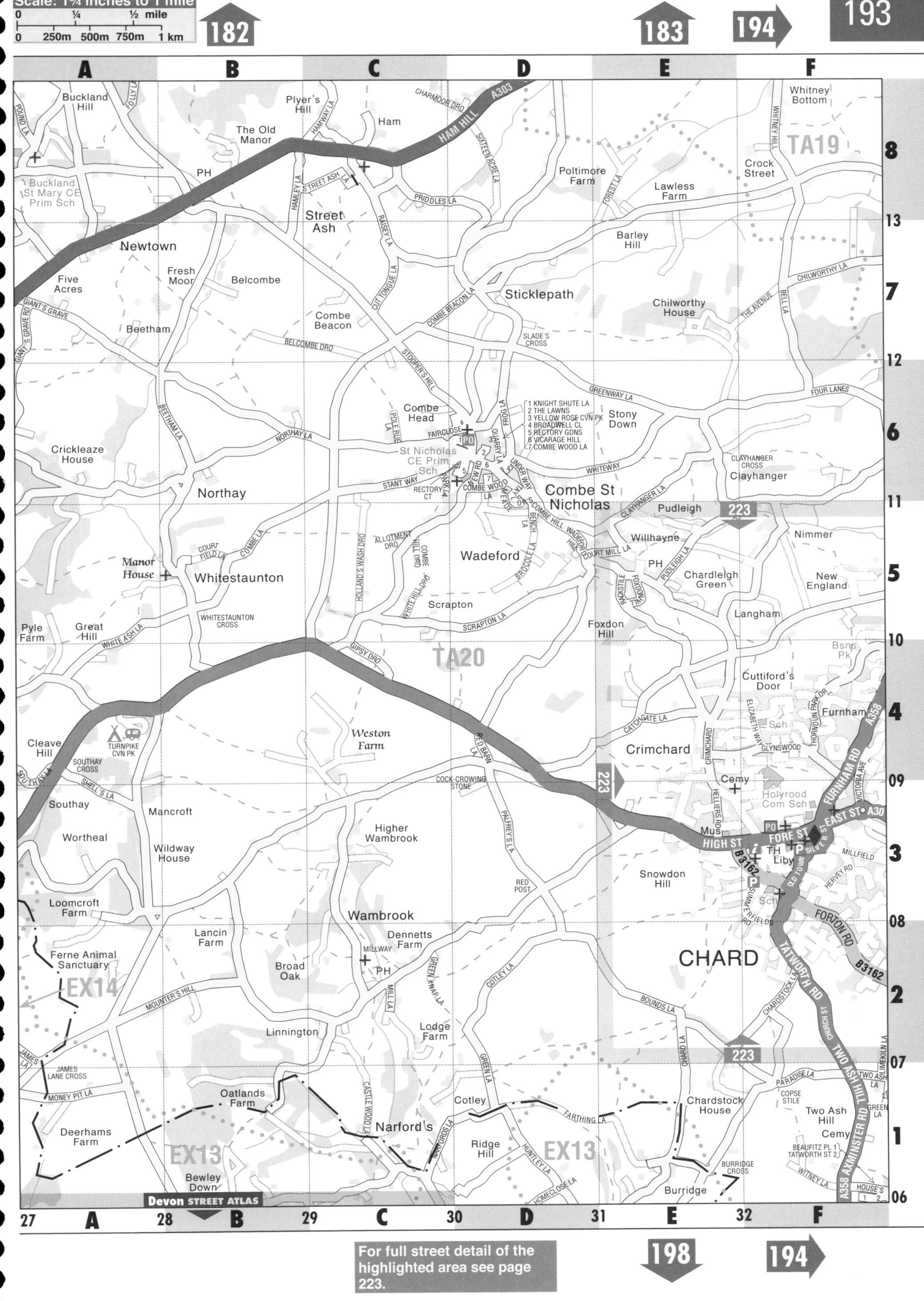

A   B   C   D   E   F

8
13
7
12
6
11
5
10
4
09
3
08
2
07
1
06

Buckland Hill
Pound La
Giant's Grave Rd
Buckland St Mary CE Prim Sch
PH
Newtown
Five Acres
Giant's Grave
Beetham
Crickleaze House
Plyer's Hill
The Old Manor
Ham
Hamley La
Street Ash
Priddles La
Raisey La
Belcombe
Fresh Moor
Combe Beacon
Belcombe Dro
Cut Tongue La
Combe Beacon La

CHARMOOR DRO   A303
HAM HILL
Sixteen Acre La
Poltimore Farm
Sticklepath
Slade's Cross
Stony Down
Whitney Bottom
TA19
Crock Street
Lawless Farm
Barley Hill
Chilworthy House
Chilworthy La
The Avenue
Bell La
Four Lanes
Greenway La

Northay La
Beetham La
Combe Head
Fairclose
St Nicholas CE Prim Sch
Combe Wood La
Stant Way
Rectory Ct
Combe La
Court Field La
Whitestaunton
Whitestaunton Cross
White Ash La
Manor House
Stoppers Hill
Pole Rue
New La
Quarry La
Union Way
Bouchers
1 KNIGHT SHUTE LA
2 THE LAWNS
3 YELLOW ROSE CVN PK
4 BROADWELL CL
5 RECTORY GDNS
6 VICARAGE HILL
7 COMBE WOOD LA
Combe St Nicholas
Whiteway
Clayhanger Cross
Clayhanger
Pudleigh   223
Willhayne
PH
Pudleigh La
Chardleigh Green
Nimmer
New England
Langham
Wadeford
Brodcull La
Combe Hill
Waldron La
Court Mill La
Backstile
Foxdon Hill
Foxdon

Pyle Farm
Great Hill
Allotment Dro
Holland's Wash Dro
Scrapton
White Hill Dro
Scrapton La
Gipsy Dro
TA20
Weston Farm
Red Barn La
Cock-Crowing Stone
Cuttiford's Door
Catgate La
Crimchard
Bsns Pk
Furnham
A358
Furnham Rd
Thordon Park Dr
Elizabeth Way
Glynswood
Sch
Crimchard
Victoria Ave
Cemy
Holyrood Com Sch
223
Hellers Rd
Mus
HIGH ST
East St   A30
PO
Fore St
TH   P
Liby
Silver St
B3162
Snowdon Hill
Snowdon Hill
Millfield
Hervey Rd
Old Town
CHARD
P
Summerfields
Sch
Tatworth Rd
Church St
Forton Rd
B3162

Cleave Hill
Southay La
Southay Cross
Shell's La
TURNPIKE CVN PK
Southay
Mancroft
Wortheal
Wildway House
Loomcroft Farm
Ferne Animal Sanctuary
EX14
Mounter's Hill
Lancin Farm
Broad Oak
Millway
PH
Wambrook
Dennetts Farm
Green Anna La
Mill La
Red Post
Palfrey's La
Cotley La
Higher Wambrook
Bounds La
Chard La
223
Chardstock House
Paradise La
Copse Stile
Two Ash Hill
Beaufitz Pl 1
Tatworth St 2
Cemy
Green La
Limekiln La
Two Ash
House 1
A358 Axminster Rd   TH
Witney La
House La 1 2

James La
James Lane Cross
Money Pit La
Deerhams Farm
EX13
Oatlands Farm
Castle Wood La
Narford's
Bewley Down
Ridge Hill
Cotley
Green La
Huntley La
EX13
Farthing La
Burridge Cross
Burridge
Lodge Farm
Linnington
Home Close La

For full street detail of the highlighted area see page 223.

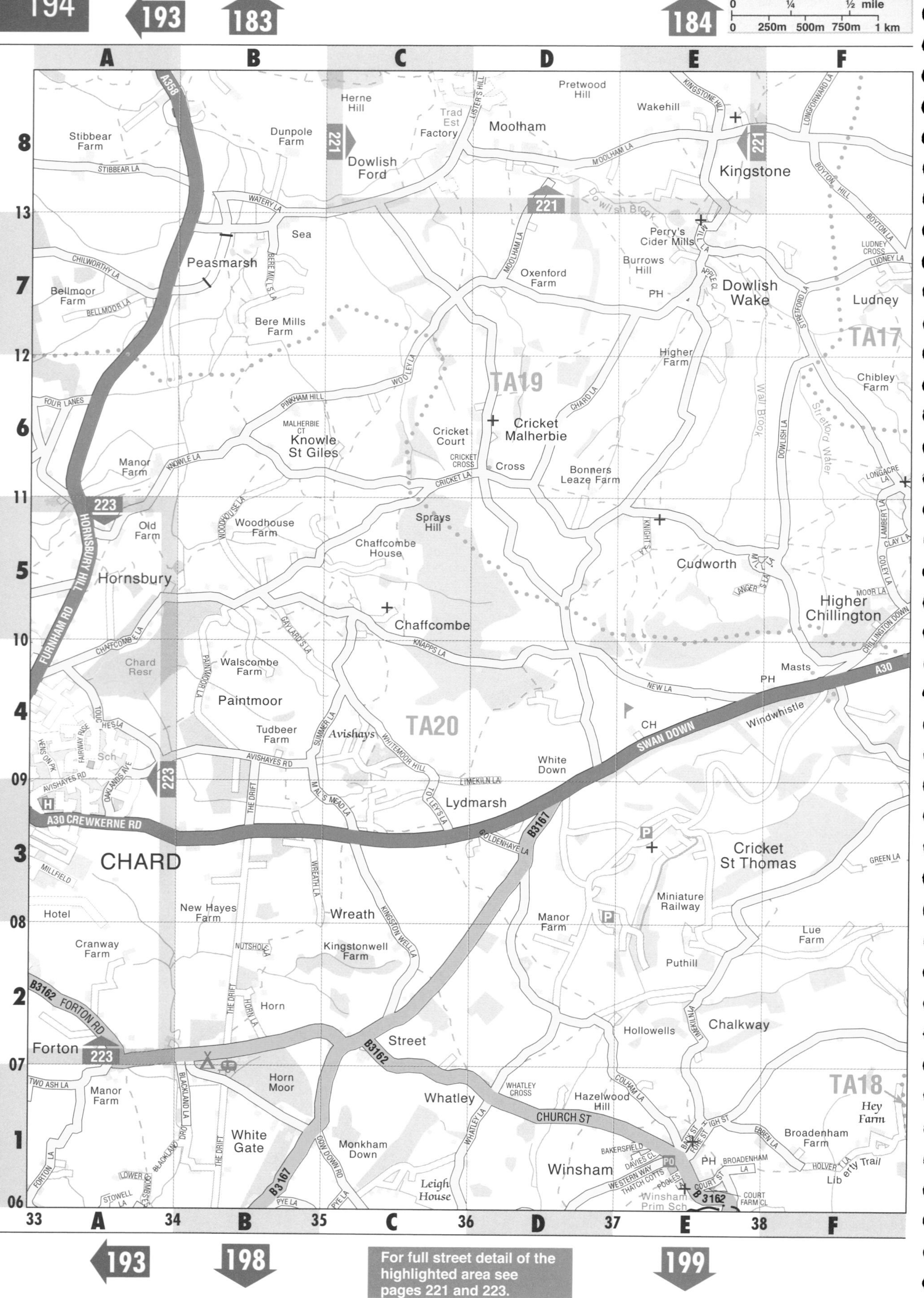

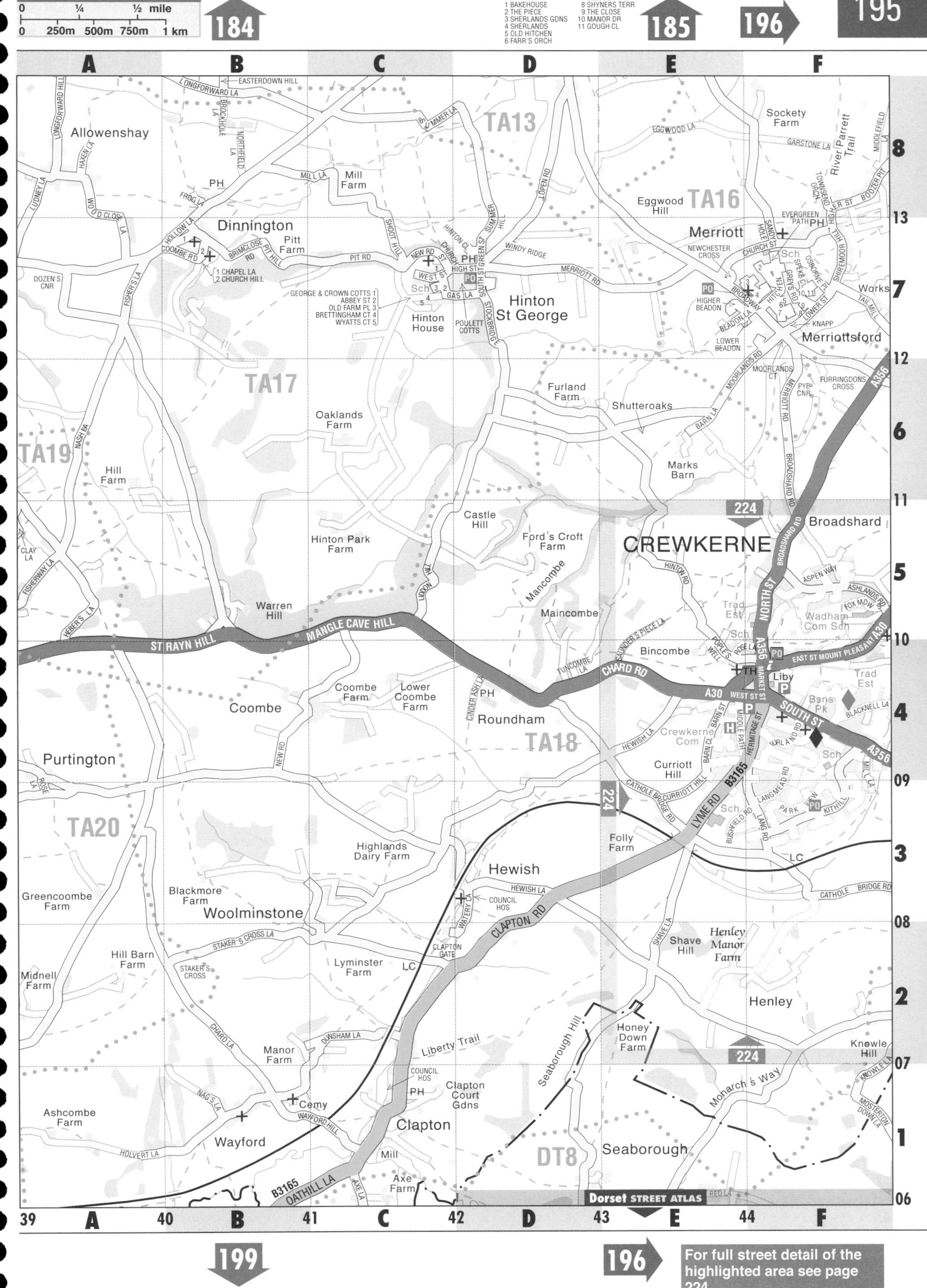

195 185 186

Scale: 1¾ inches to 1 mile

0   ¼   ½ mile
0   250m   500m   750m   1 km

A B C D E F

MIDDLEFIELD LA
WALL DITCH LA
TABBOTT LA
HUT GATE
Bow Barn Farm
BOW GATE
BOOZER PIT
TA16
TAIL MILL
A356
A30
Cemy

West Chinnock
West Chinnock CE Prim Sch
HOLLOWELL LA
LEAZE LA
POOP HILL
1 HAUNTS
2 SMITHS HILL
POOP HILL LA
Broadway La
EASTFIELD LA

East Chinnock
GREEN LA
CHINNOCK HOLLOW
COLLARWAY LA
WEST COKER HILL
BRIDGE COTTS
Mast
RIDGE LA
A30

Middle Chinnock
Chinnock Brook
WEST WAYS
OLD LA
SCOTTS WAY
LAYNE TERR
HIGHER LA
NEW COTTS
DUCKPOOL LA
EAST LA
Monarch's Way
ORCHARD CL 1
WESTON CL 2
BARROWS CT 3
SPRINGFIELD
WESTON ST
LEIGH RD
FORDHAY HIGH ST
FORGE LA
CARTERS LA
PH
4 BACK LA
5 ODCOMBE HOLLOW
FORDHAY TERR
ST MARY'S VIEW

Snails Hill
West Chinnock Hill
HIGHFIELD 1
RIDGWAY 1
HILL VIEW CL 3
RICKHAY RISE 4
CHURCH CL 5
LONG
BROADSTONE LA
FOXWELL LA
North Down Farm
Barrows Hill
ELLIOTT'S HILL
BROAD LA
BROAD HILL
Cott Farm
PARTWAY LA
WIMBO ROUGH LA

Rushy Wood Farm
GLOBE ORCH
NEW LA
DOWNEY
FIELD LA
Broad Hill Farm
Broad River
BA22
HILL CROSS
Hill End
BROADSTONE LA
BARRY LA
COLD HARBOUR LA

Lower Severalls Gdn
Lower Severalls Farm
PH
Haselbury Bridge
224
A3066
ORCHARD VIEW
NORTH ST
Haselbury Plucknett
PH
FROG LA
GIFFORDS
BRAMBLE LA
CLAY CASTLE LA
Sch
CHURCH LA
SWAN HILL
East Lease Farm
New Plantation
Hewingbere Farm
Bridge Close Farm
NEW RD
Monarch's Way
COMMON LA

Manor Farm
PUDDLE TOWN
STONESFIELD
EAST LA
WINTERFIELD
Liberty Trail
River Parrett Trail
Lower Easthams Farm
HIGHER EASTHAMS LA
YEOVIL RD
A30

1 PEGGY'S LA
2 CASTLETON
STONAGE LA
PETVINS CT
CLAY CAST LE
TA18

COMMON LA
Cowcroft Farm
Hardington Marsh
Marsh Farm
SHORTMARSH LA

WILLIS'S LA
NEW ST
TRINDLEWELL LA
NORTH PERROTT RD
MANOR BLDGS
Perrott Hill Sch
CHURCH LA
North Perrott
MIDDLE ST
HILL HEAD LA
1 SYMES CL
2 EAST ST
EASTHILL LA
PH
NEW BLDGS
DOWNCLOSE LA

CREWKERNE
Hellings Farm
224
STATION RD
A356
PH
Crewkerne
Misterton
PO
MIDDLE ST
MILL LA
ROSE LA
PARK VIEW
SILVER ST
SCHOOL LA
1 PACKERS WAY
2 TURNPIKE CL
3 TURNPIKE GN
Grey Abbey Farm
Downclose Farm
Haselbury Park Farm
Kingswood Farm
Ashland Hill
Whitevine Farm
Cemy
Sch
PH Cemy
Well Spring Farm
TURNPIKE CROSS
PIPPLEPEN LA
Pipplepen Farm
Knowle Hill
WOOD LA
River Parrett

KNOWLE LA
Knowle Farm
Works
DT8
Cheddington Woods
Wyke Farm

224
Bluntsmoor Farm
MOSTERTON DOWN LA
A3066
LEGHER LA
PH
SCHOOL HILL
Sockety
CH
HOLT LA
Chapel Court Farm
Mohun Castle
MANOR CL
PARRETT MEAD
PICKET LA
Orchard Farm
South Perrott
Manor Farm
Crook Hill
Winyard's Gap
DT12
A356
A3066 Beaminster
Dorset STREET ATLAS
A356 Dorchester (A37)

45 46 47 48 49 50

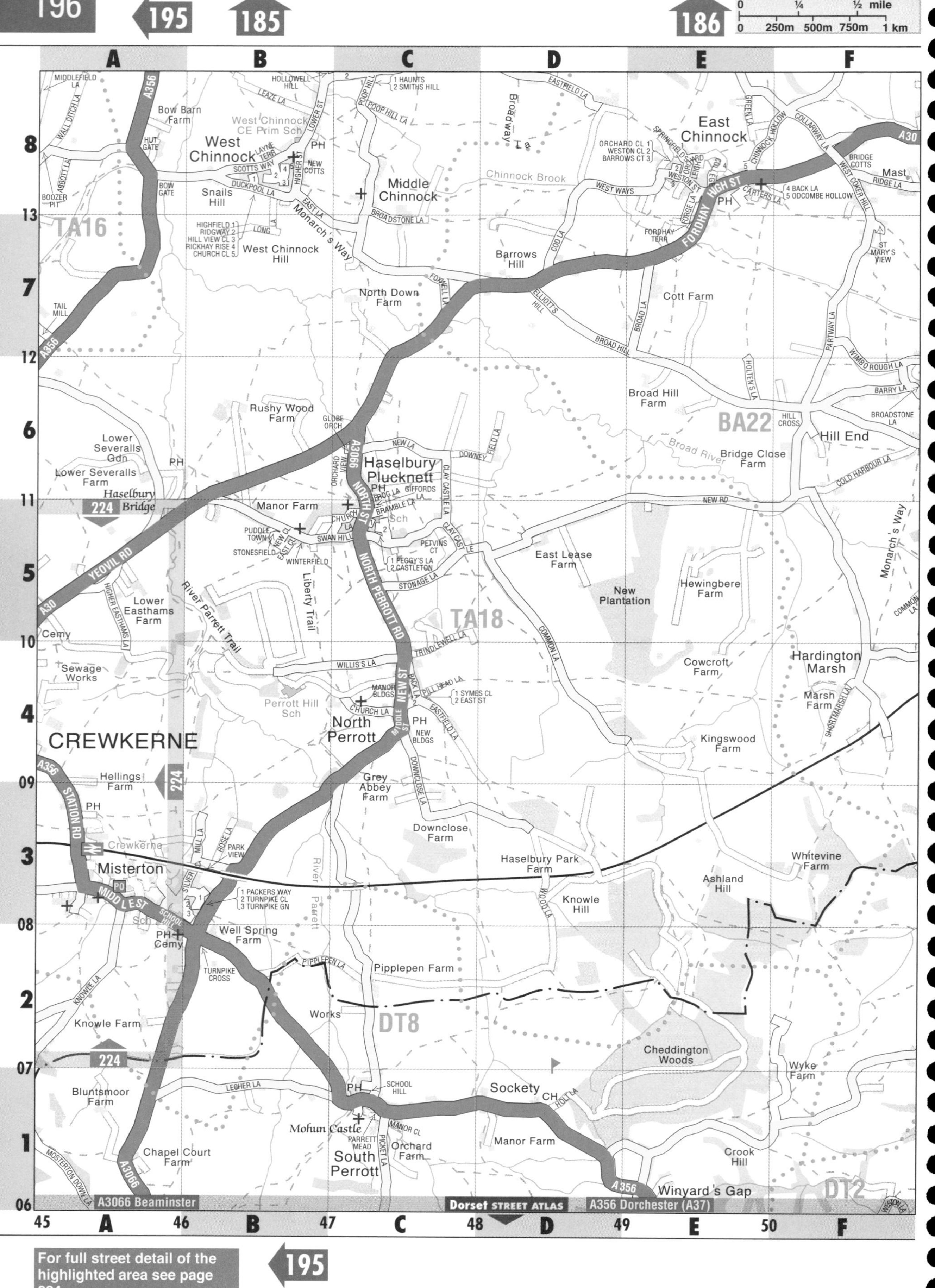

For full street detail of the highlighted area see page 224. 195

F8
1 HILLSIDE VIEW
2 YEO VALLEY
3 FIVE ACRES
4 MEADOW VIEW
5 HAMPTON CL
6 COURT ACRES
7 COURT LA
8 THE GREEN
9 CLIFTON VIEW
10 WHITCROSS
11 MOWLEAZE
12 SOUTH VIEW
13 SCHOOL COTTS

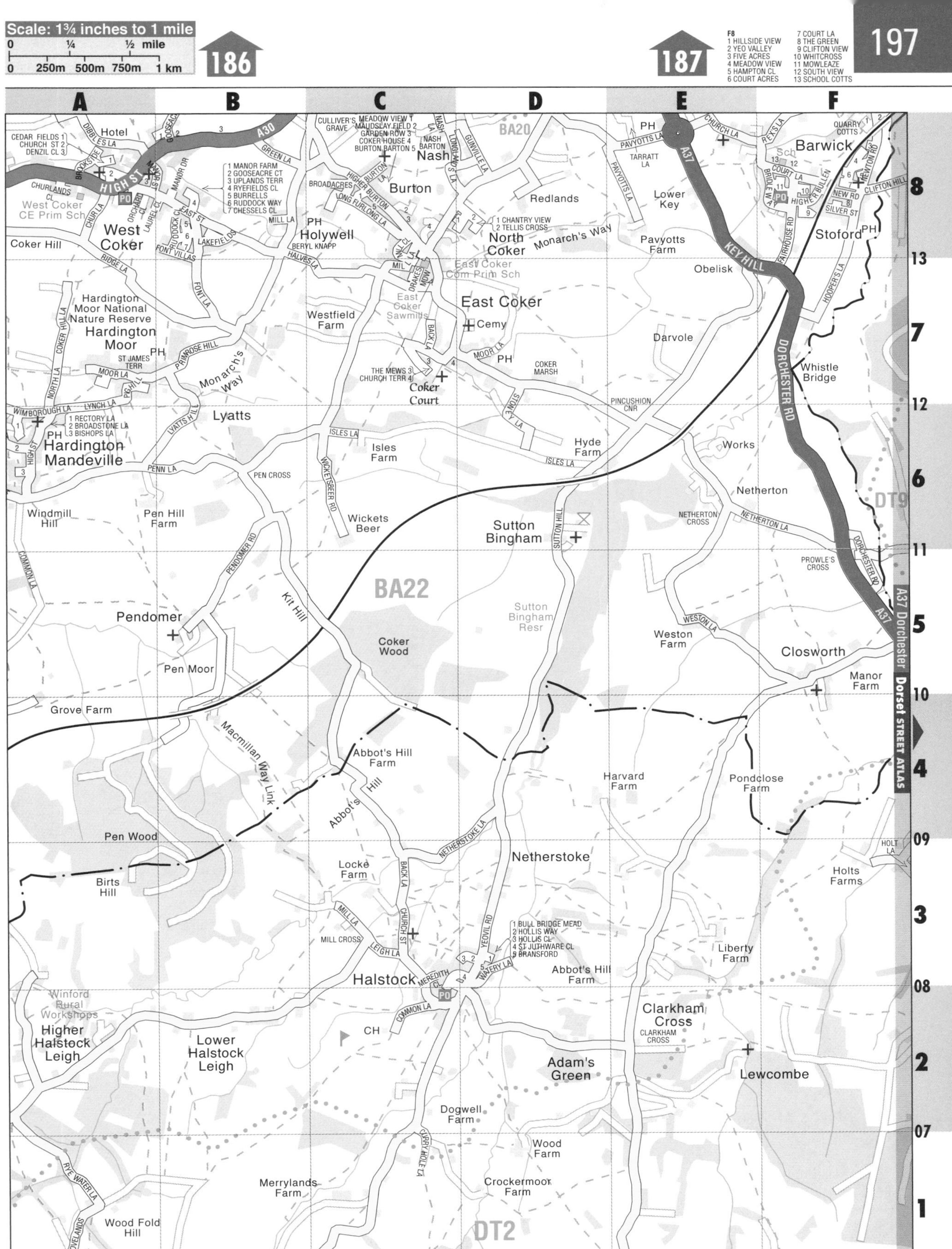

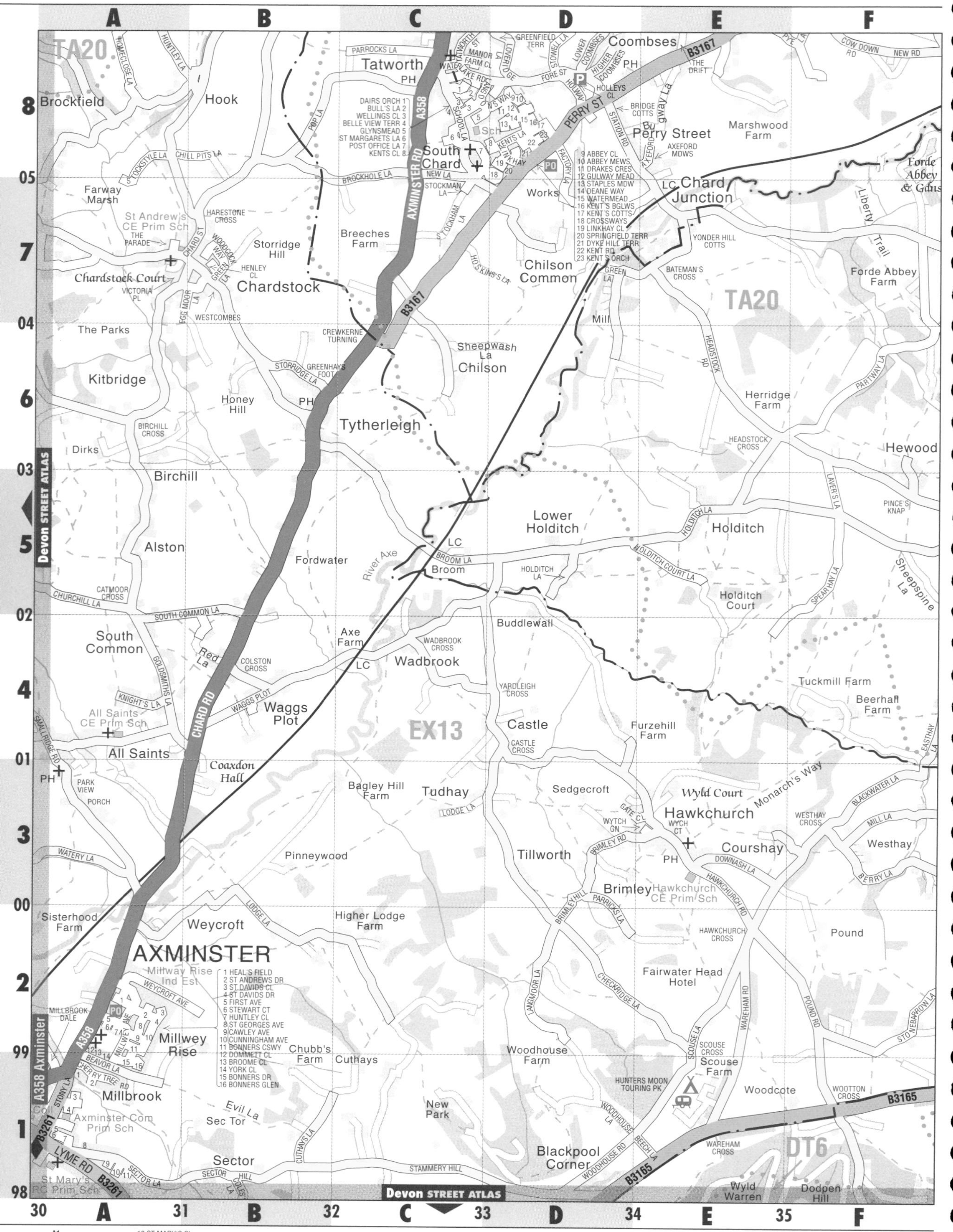

Scale: 1¾ inches to 1 mile
0   ¼   ½ mile
0   250m 500m 750m   1 km

TA20

8 Brockfield   Hook
                                                    Tatworth
                                                         PH
                        DAIRS ORCH 1
                        BULL'S LA 2
                        WELLINGS CL 3   South
                        BELLE VIEW TERR 4   Chard
                        ST MARGARETS LA 6
                        POST OFFICE LA 7
                        KENTS CL 8

05 Farway
     Marsh   Harestone
                    Cross
     St Andrew's   Works
     CE Prim Sch
     THE   Breeches
     PARADE   Farm   Chilson
7   Storridge   Common
     Chardstock   Hill
     Court   Henley
                       CL
     VICTORIA   Chardstock
     PL
04   Crewkerne
     The Parks   Turning
                                             Sheepwash
                     Storridge   La
     Kitbridge   Greenhays   Chilson
                     Foot
     Honey   Mill
6   Hill
                     Tytherleigh
     Dirks
     Birchill
                                            Lower
03   Holditch   Holditch
                                                                              Hewood
     Alston   River Axe   Buddlewall
                     Fordwater   Broom
5   LC BROOM LA
                                     Broom   HOLDITCH
                                                    LA   Holditch
02   Court
     South   Axe
     Common   Red   Farm
                     La   COLSTON   Wadbrook
                          CROSS   LC
4   WAGGS PLOT
     All Saints   Waggs   Castle
     CE Prim Sch   Plot   Furzehill
                                               CASTLE   Farm
01   CROSS
     All Saints   Wyld Court
     PH   Coaxdon   Hawkchurch
           Hall   Bagley Hill Tudhay   Courshay
3   Farm
                                                    Sedgecroft
                    Pinneywood   Brimley
     Sisterhood   Higher Lodge   Hawkchurch
     Farm   Weycroft   Farm   CE Prim Sch
00
                                                                    Pound
2   AXMINSTER
                    1 HEAL'S FIELD
                    2 ST ANDREWS DR   Fairwater Head
                    3 ST DAVIDS CL   Hotel
                    4 ST DAVIDS DR
                    5 FIRST AVE
                    6 STEWART CT
                    7 HUNTLEY CL
99   Axminster   8 ST GEORGES AVE
                    9 CAWLEY AVE   Chubb's   Woodhouse
                    10 CUNNINGHAM AVE Farm   Farm   Scouse
                    11 BONNERS CSWY   Cuthays   Farm
     Millbrook   12 DOMMET CL
                    13 BROOME CL   Woodcote
                    14 YORK CL
                    15 BONNERS DR   New
1   Axminster Com 16 BONNERS GLEN   Park
     Prim Sch   Evil La
                    Sector   Blackpool   DT6
                    Sector Tor   Corner
                                                        Wyld   Dodpen
98   St Mary's   Warren   Hill
     RC Prim Sch

30   A   31   B   32   C   33   D   34   E   35   F

A1
1 MILLBROOK CROSS   10 ST MARY'S CL
2 CATNIP CL   11 SALWAY GDNS
3 JEFFS WAY
4 NEWBERY CL
5 LORETTO GDNS
6 MONKSTONE GDNS
7 CRIDLAKE
8 VALLEY VIEW
9 PRESTOR

Devon STREET ATLAS

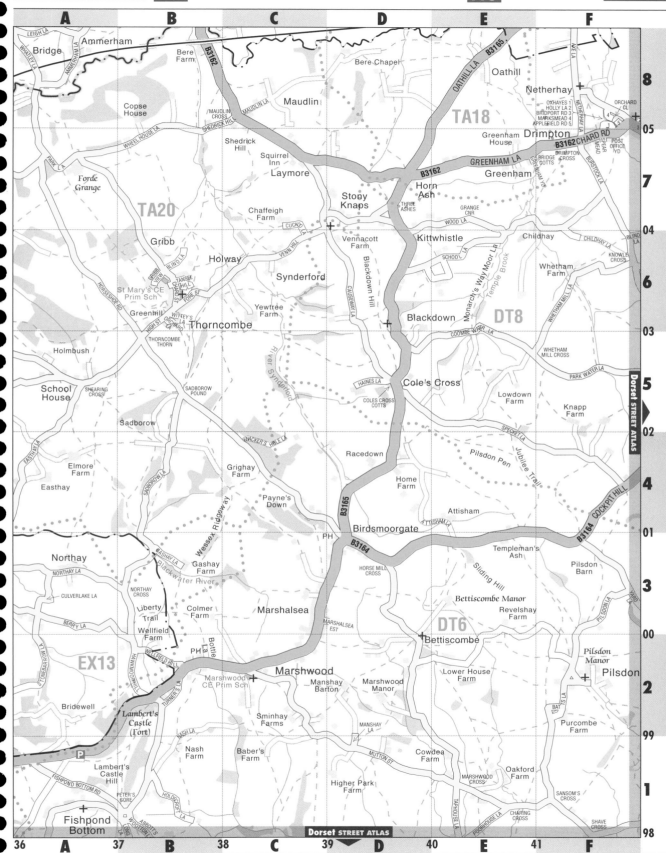

Leigh La
Ammerham
Bridge
Whatley La
Amberham La
Copse House
Wheel House La
Park La
Forde Grange
TA20
Gribb
Gribb View
Blind La
Tansey Hill
St Mary's CE Prim Sch
Foye St
Greenhill
High St
Witter's Orchard
Thorncombe
Thorncombe Thorn
Holmbush

B3162
Bere Farm
Maudlin La
Maudlin Cross
Shedrick Hill
Shedrick Hill
Squirrel Inn
Laymore
Chaffeigh Farm
Holway
Venn Hill
Synderford
Yewtree Farm
River Synderford
Cuck La

Bere Chapel
Maudlin
Stony Knaps
Vennacott Farm
Three Ashes
Blackdown Hill
Causeway La
Haines La
Coles Cross Cotts

B3165
Oathill La
Oathill
Netherhay
TA18
Greenham House
Drimpton
B3162
Horn Ash
Greenham La
Greenham
Grange Cnr
Wood La
Kittwhistle
School La
Blackdown
Monarch's Way
Moor La
Temple Brook
Coombe Water La
Cole's Cross
Coles Cross
Lowdown Farm

Axe La
Spear Mead
Netherhay La
Oxhayes 1
Holly La 2
Bridport Rd 3
Marksmead 4
Applefield Rd 5
Orchard Cl
Chard Rd
05
Post Office Yd
B3162
Bridge Cotts
Drimpton Cross
Greenham Vd
Burstock La
Blind La
Childhay
Childhay La
Knowle Cross
Wheltham Farm
Whetham Mill La
DT8
Whetham Mill Cross
Park Water La
Knapp Farm

School House
Shearing Cross
Sadborow
Elmore Farm
Easthay
Easthay La
Sadborow La
Sadborow Pound
Grighay Farm
Wessex Ridgeway
Payne's Down
Racedown
Home Farm
Knacker's Hole La
Pilsdon Pen
Jubilee Trail
Specket La

Northay
Northay La
Culverlake La
Berry La
Northay Cross
Gashay La
Blackwater River
Liberty Trail
Wellfield Farm
Gashay Farm
Colmer Farm
Marshalsea
Birdsmoorgate
PH
B3164
Horse Mill Cross
B3165
Attisham
Attisham La
Templeman's Ash
Sliding Hill
Bettiscombe Manor
Revelshay Farm
DT6
Bettiscombe
Lower House Farm
Cockpit Hill
B3164
Pilsdon Barn
Pilsdon La
Pilsdon Manor
Pilsdon

EX13
Stonebarrow La
Bridewell
Fishpond Bottom Rd
Peter's Gore
Fishpond Bottom
Lambert's Castle (Fort)
P
Lambert's Castle Hill
Hawkmoor Hill
Wellfield Hill
Turner's La
PH
Bottle La
Holdsport La
Woodyton La
Abbots La
Nash La
Nash Farm
Marshwood CE Prim Sch
Sminhay Farms
Baber's Farm
Marshwood
Manshay Barton
Manshay La
Higher Park Farm
Mutton St
Marshwood Manor
Cowdea Farm
Poorhouse La
Taphouse La
Marshwood Cross
Charing Cross
Bat's La
Purcombe Farm
Oakford Farm
Sansom's Cross
Shave Cross

Dorset STREET ATLAS

8
05
7
04
6
03
5
02
4
01
3
00
2
99
1
98

124 125

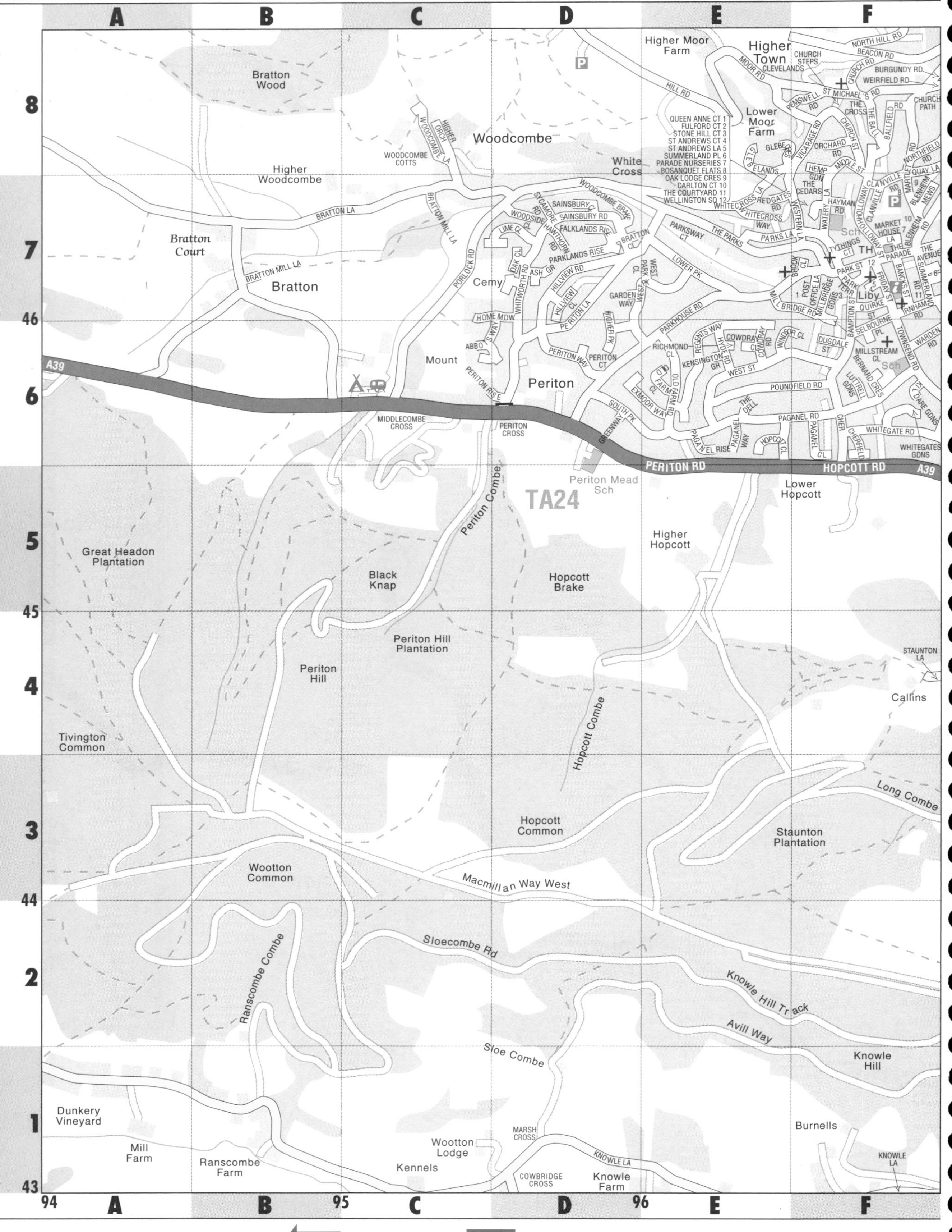

A B C D E F
8 7 46 6 5 45 4 3 44 2 1 43
94 95 96
Bratton Wood
Higher Moor Farm
Higher Town
Woodcombe
Higher Woodcombe
Lower Moor Farm
White Cross
Bratton Court
Bratton
Cemy
Mount
Periton
TA24
Periton Mead Sch
Lower Hopcott
Higher Hopcott
Great Headon Plantation
Black Knap
Hopcott Brake
Periton Hill Plantation
Periton Hill
Periton Combe
Hopcott Combe
Tivington Common
Callins
Long Combe
Hopcott Common
Staunton Plantation
Wootton Common
Macmillan Way West
Sloecombe Rd
Ranscombe Combe
Knowle Hill Track
Avill Way
Sloe Combe
Knowle Hill
Dunkery Vineyard
Burnells
Mill Farm
Ranscombe Farm
Wootton Lodge
Kennels
Knowle Farm
MARSH CROSS
COWBRIDGE CROSS
KNOWLE LA
STAUNTON LA
A39
PERITON RD
HOPCOTT RD
MIDDLECOMBE CROSS
PERITON CROSS
BRATTON LA
BRATTON MILL LA
PORLOCK RD
HILL RD
MOOR RD
WOODCOMBE COTTS
QUEEN ANNE CT 1
FULFORD CT 2
STONE HILL CT 3
ST ANDREWS CT 4
ST ANDREWS LA 5
SUMMERLAND PL 6
PARADE NURSERIES 7
BOSANQUET FLATS 8
OAK LODGE CRES 9
CARLTON CT 10
THE COURTYARD 11
WELLINGTON SQ 12

129 130

125
131

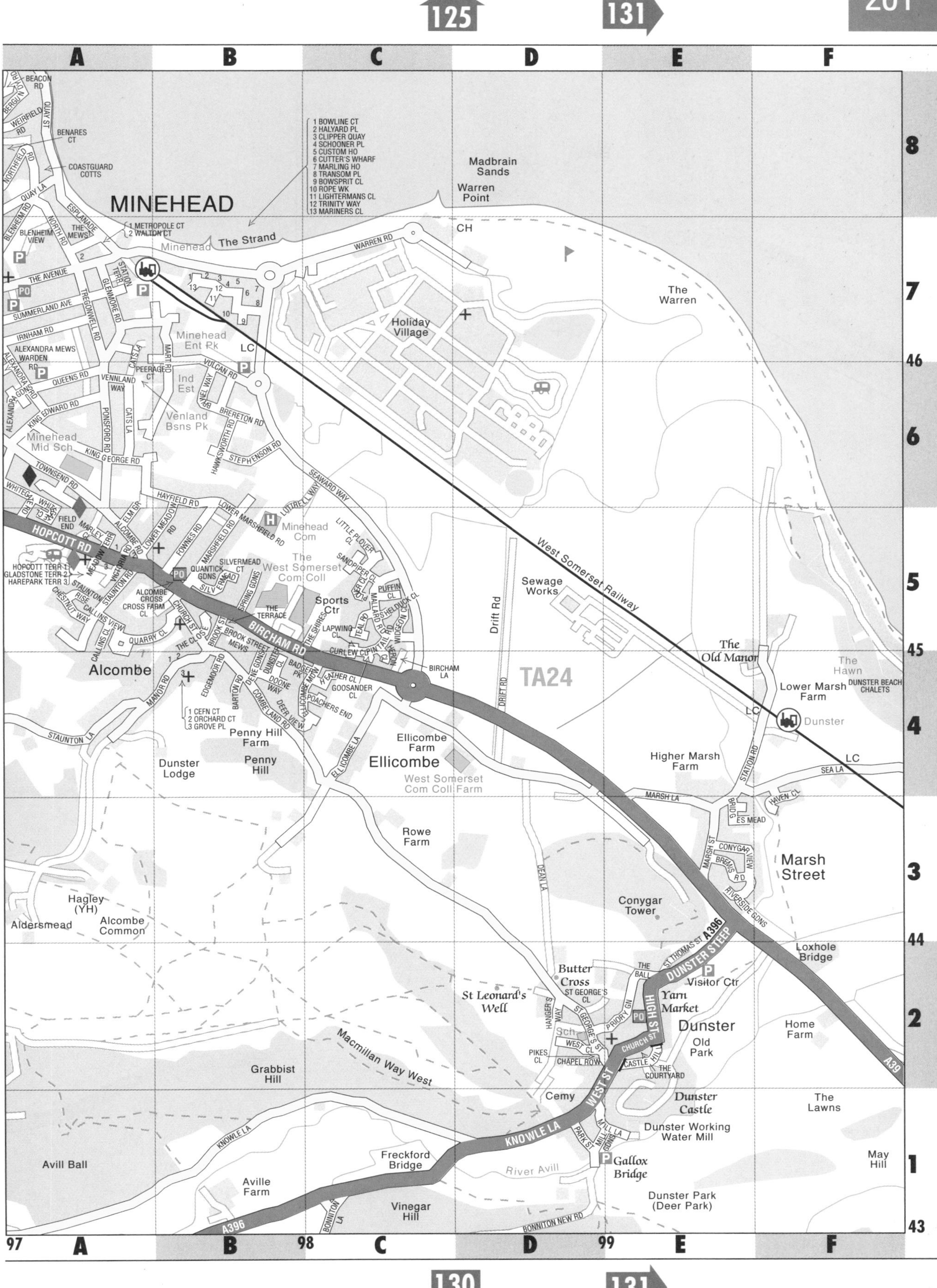
MINEHEAD
The Strand
Madbrain Sands
Warren Point
The Warren
Holiday Village
Minehead Ent Pk
Ind Est
Venland Bsns Pk
Minehead Mid Sch
Minehead Com
The West Somerset Com Coll
Sports Ctr
West Somerset Railway
Sewage Works
Drift Rd
TA24
The Old Manor
The Hawn
Lower Marsh Farm
DUNSTER BEACH CHALETS
Dunster
Higher Marsh Farm
Alcombe
Penny Hill Farm
Penny Hill
Dunster Lodge
Ellicombe Farm
Ellicombe
West Somerset Com Coll Farm
Rowe Farm
Marsh Street
Conygar Tower
Hagley (YH)
Aldersmead
Alcombe Common
Loxhole Bridge
Butter Cross
St Leonard's Well
Yarn Market
Visitor Ctr
Dunster
Old Park
Home Farm
Macmillan Way West
Grabbist Hill
Cemy
Dunster Castle
The Lawns
Dunster Working Water Mill
Avill Ball
Freckford Bridge
Aville Farm
River Avill
Gallox Bridge
May Hill
Vinegar Hill
Dunster Park (Deer Park)
BIRCHAM RD
HOPCOTT RD
KNOWLE LA
WEST ST
HIGH ST
DUNSTER STEEP
A396
A39
1 BOWLINE CT
2 HALYARD PL
3 CLIPPER QUAY
4 SCHOONER PL
5 CUSTOM HO
6 CUTTER'S WHARF
7 MARLING HO
8 TRANSOM PL
9 BOWSPRIT CL
10 ROPE WK
11 LIGHTERMANS CL
12 TRINITY WAY
13 MARINERS CL
1 METROPOLE CT
2 WALTON CT
1 CEFN CT
2 ORCHARD CT
3 GROVE PL
HOPCOTT TERR 1
GLADSTONE TERR 2
HAREPARK TERR 3
A B C D E F
8 7 46 6 5 45 4 3 44 2 1 43
97 98 99

130
131

131
132

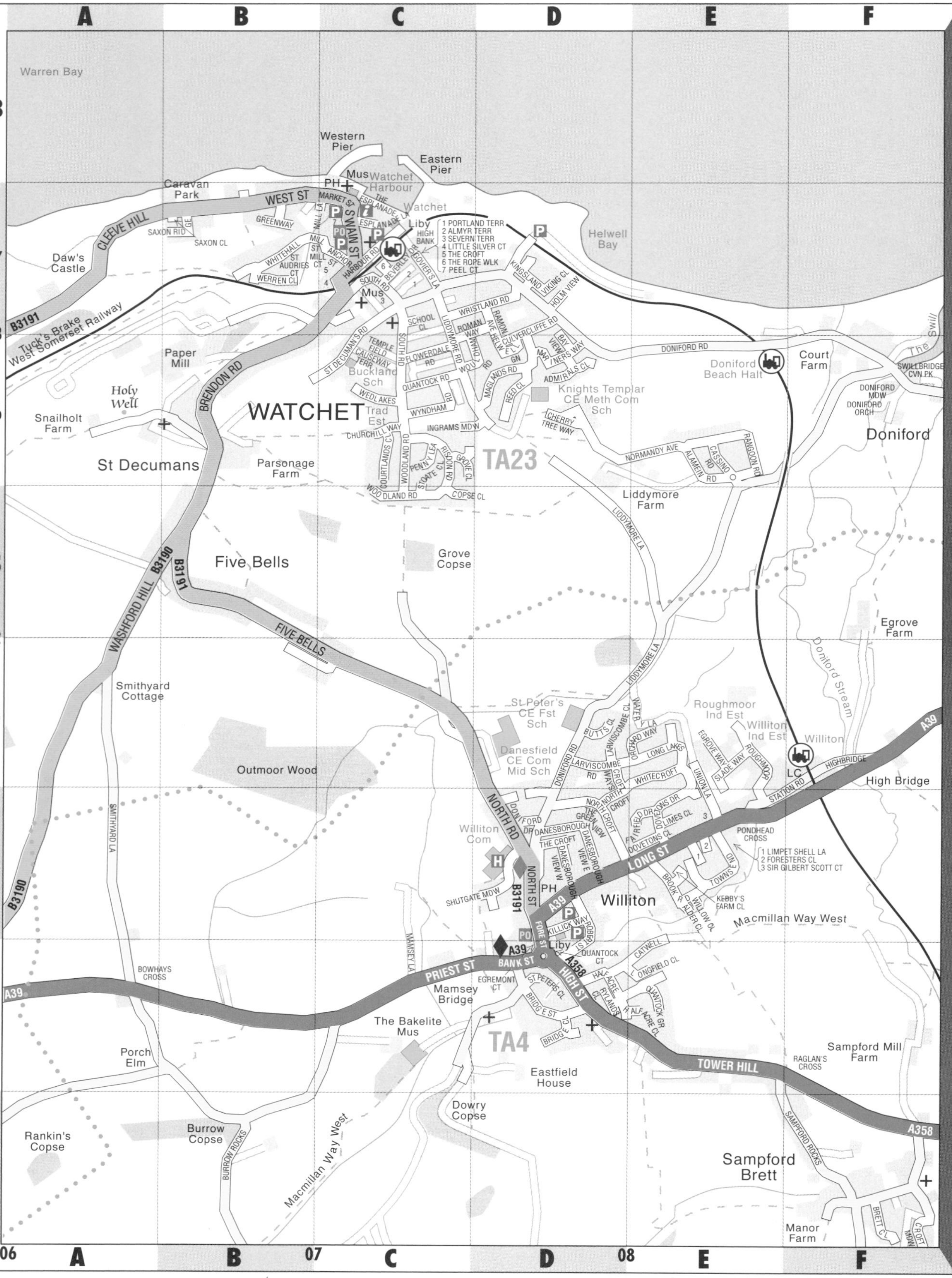

A   B   C   D   E   F

8

Warren Bay

Western Pier

Eastern Pier

Caravan Park

Mus
Watchet Harbour
Watchet

Daw's Castle

Cleeve Hill

WEST ST   SWAIN ST
MARKET ST
GREENWAY
Saxon Rd
GE
Saxon Cl

PH
P
PO
P
P
Liby
HIGH
Bank
THE ESPLANADE

7

1 PORTLAND TERR
2 ALMYR TERR
3 SEVERN TERR
4 LITTLE SILVER CT
5 THE CROFT
6 THE ROPE WLK
7 PEEL CT

P

Helwell Bay

B3191
Tuck's Brake
West Somerset Railway

43

Paper Mill

BRENDON RD

WHITEHALL
ST
AUDRIES
CL
MILL
ST
MILL
CT
WERREN CL

South BEVERLEY TERR
ANCHOR ST
HARBOUR RD
Mus

DONIFORD RD

Doniford Beach Halt

Court Farm

THE SWILL
SWILLBRIDGE
CVN PK
DONIFORD
MDW
DONIFORD
ORCH

Holy Well

ST DECUMANS RD
CAUSEWAY
TEMPLE
FIELD
Buckland
Sch
WEDLAKES
WYNDHAM

SCHOOL
CL
ROMAN
FLOWERDALE RD
QUANTOCK RD
BARNON
AVE VIEW N
MAGNOLIA
REED CL
WRISTLAND RD
MND ST
CULVERCLIFFE RD
M2
VIKING CL
HOLM VIEW
KINGSLAND
VIEW W
VIEW WAY
ADMIRALS CL
CHERRY
TREE WAY

Knights Templar CE Meth Com Sch

6

WATCHET

Snailholt Farm

St Decumans

Parsonage Farm

TA23

INGRAMS MDW

NORMANDY AVE
ALMEIN
RD
CASSINO
RD
RANGOON RD

Doniford

CHURCHILL WAY
COURTLANDS
WOODLAND RD
WOODLAND
STATE CL
BEGIN RD
GORE CL
PENN TCE
COPSE CL

Liddymore Farm

Washford Hill
B3190
B3191

Five Bells

Grove Copse

Liddymore La

Doniford Stream

Egrove Farm

5

Five Bells
FIVE BELLS

Smithyard Cottage

42

Outmoor Wood

SMITHYARD LA

St Peter's CE Fst Sch

Danesfield CE Com Mid Sch

DONIFORD RD
LARVISCOMBE
RD
BUTTS CL
BRISCOMBE LA
WATER
OXFORD WAY
LONG LANE
WHITECROFT
Roughmoor Ind Est
Williton Ind Est

EGROVE PARK
GLADE WAY
ROUGHMOOR
UNION LA

A39

Williton

LC
HIGHBRIDGE
STATION RD

High Bridge

4

B3190

B3191

NORTH RD

Williton Com

H

SHUTGATE MDW
NORTH ST
B3191

DANESBOROUGH RD
DONIFORD
DR
THE CROFT
DANESBOROUGH
DANESBOROUGH
VIEW E
VIEW W
GREEN
VIEW
FYRFRED
DRAONS DR
LIMES CL
OOVETONS CL
TOWNS

PONDHEAD CROSS

Macmillan Way West

1 LIMPET SHELL LA
2 FORESTERS CL
3 SIR GILBERT SCOTT CT

3

B3190

MAMSEY LA

PH
A39
P
KILLICK WAY
PO
PUNE ST

Williton

BROOK CL
WILLOW CL
KERBY'S
FARM CL

41

A39
PRIEST ST
BANK ST
Mamsey Bridge
EGREMONT
CT

HIGH ST
A39
A358
Liby
P
QUANTOCK
CT
CATWELL
HALF ACRE
LONGFIELD CL
HALF ACRE
RYLANDS
QUANTOCK GR

Macmillan Way West

BOWHAYS CROSS

2

A39

The Bakelite Mus

TA4

ST PETERS CL
BRIDG E ST
BRIDG E
Eastfield House

Dowry Copse

TOWER HILL

RAGLAN'S CROSS

Sampford Mill Farm

Porch Elm

Burrow Copse

BURROW ROCKS

Macmillan Way West

1

Rankin's Copse

A358
SAMPFORD ROCKS

Sampford Brett

Manor Farm

BRETT CL
CROFT
MDW

40

06   A   B   07   C   D   08   E   F

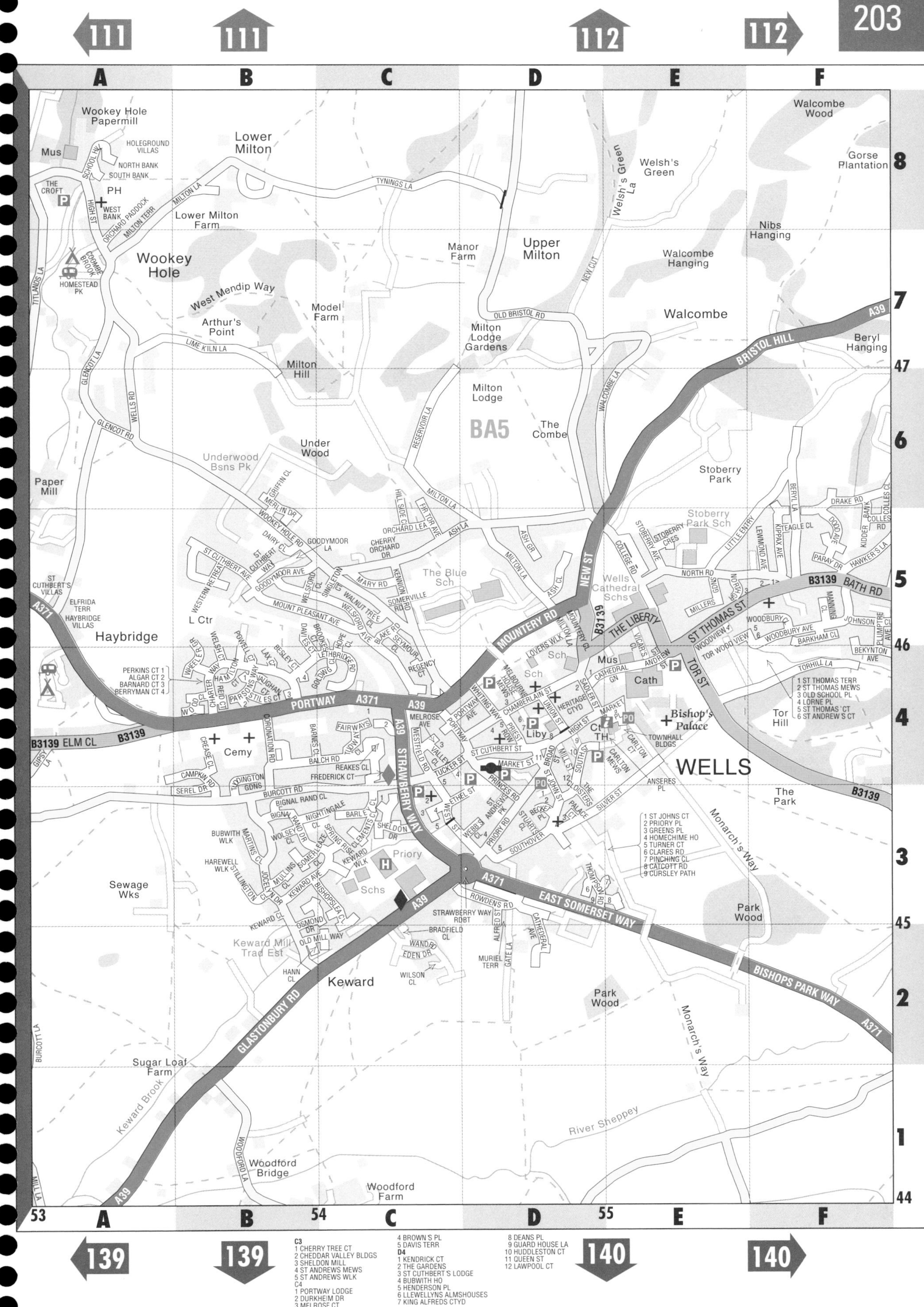

111
111
112
112
139
139
140
140

A B C D E F

8 7 47 6 5 46 4 3 45 2 1 44

53 54 55

C3
1 CHERRY TREE CT
2 CHEDDAR VALLEY BLDGS
3 SHELDON MILL
4 ST ANDREWS MEWS
5 ST ANDREWS WLK
C4
1 PORTWAY LODGE
2 DURKHEIM DR
3 MELROSE CT

4 BROWN'S PL
5 DAVIS TERR
D4
1 KENDRICK CT
2 THE GARDENS
3 ST CUTHBERT'S LODGE
4 BUBWITH HO
5 HENDERSON PL
6 LLEWELLYNS ALMSHOUSES
7 KING ALFREDS CTYD

8 DEANS PL
9 GUARD HOUSE LA
10 HUDDLESTON CT
11 QUEEN ST
12 LAWPOOL CT

Wookey Hole Papermill
Mus
HOLEGROUND VILLAS
Lower Milton
NORTH BANK
SOUTH BANK
THE CROFT
WEST BANK
PH
Wookey Hole
Lower Milton Farm
Welsh's Green
Welsh's La
Walcombe Wood
Gorse Plantation
TYNINGS LA
Manor Farm
Upper Milton
Nibs Hanging
West Mendip Way
Model Farm
Walcombe Hanging
Arthur's Point
OLD BRISTOL RD
Walcombe
A39
Milton Hill
Milton Lodge Gardens
BA5
BRISTOL HILL
Beryl Hanging
Under Wood
Milton Lodge
The Combe
Underwood Bsns Pk
Stoberry Park
B3139 BATH RD
Paper Mill
Stoberry Park Sch
DRAKE RD
St Cuthbert's Villas
ELFRIDA TERR
HAYBRIDGE VILLAS
Haybridge
Wells Cathedral Schs
St Thomas Terr
NEW ST
MOUNTERY RD
THE LIBERTY
ST THOMAS ST
The Blue Sch
Cath
Mus
Tor Hill
PORTWAY A371
A39
Liby
Bishop's Palace
WELLS
Cemy
TH
B3139 ELM CL B3139
PO
Townhall Bldgs
The Park
B3139
STRAWBERRY WAY
Market St
Priory
H
Schs
Sewage Wks
EAST SOMERSET WAY
Park Wood
A39
GLASTONBURY RD
Keward Mill Trad Est
Strawberry Way Robt
Park Wood
Keward
BISHOPS PARK WAY
A371
Sugar Loaf Farm
Monarch's Way
Keward Brook
River Sheppey
Woodford Bridge
Woodford Farm

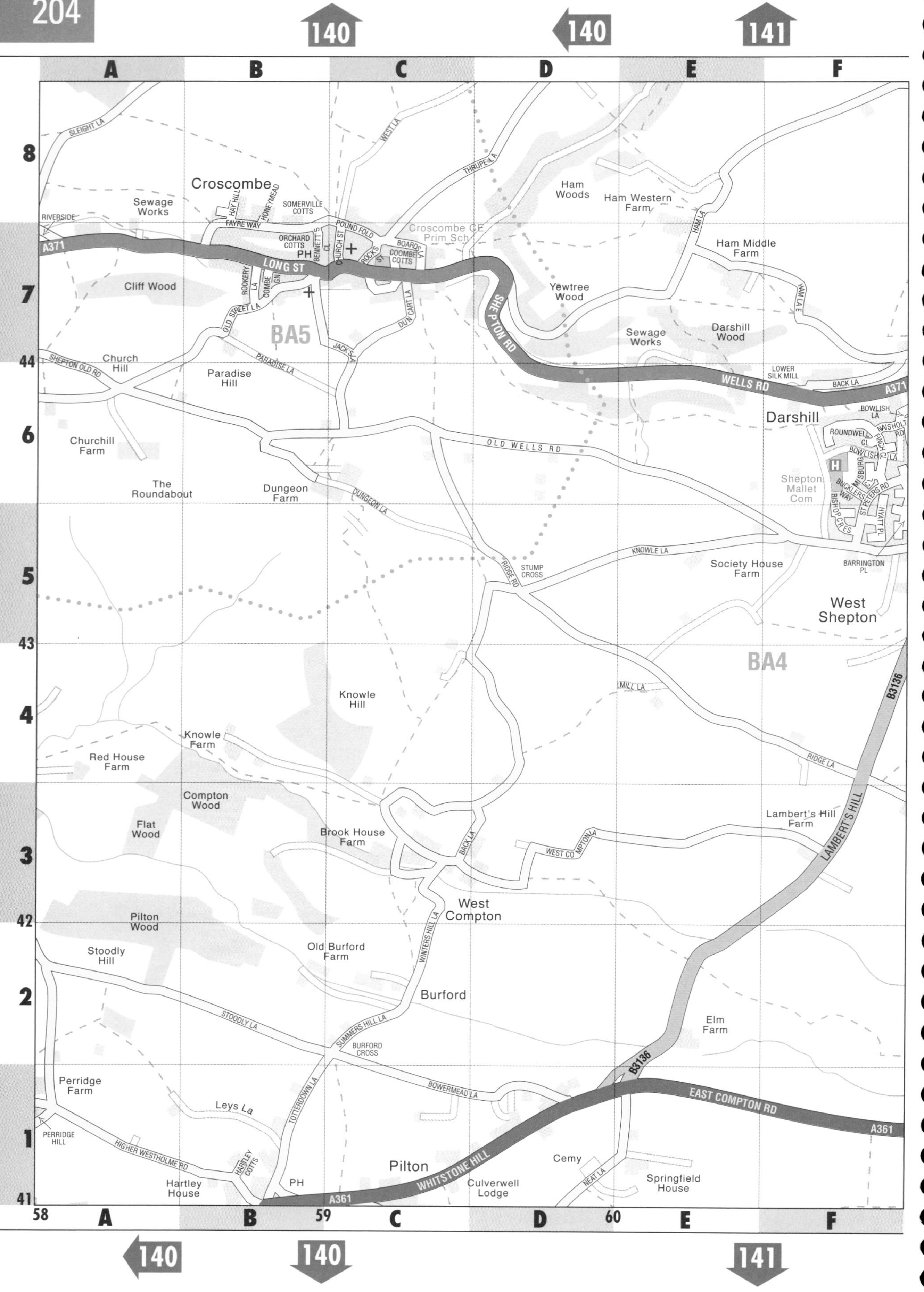

A   B   C   D   E   F

8

Croscombe

SLEIGHT LA

RIVERSIDE

Sewage Works

HAY HILL
HONEYMEAD
FAYRE WAY
ORCHARD COTTS
PH
SOMERVILLE COTTS
BENNETT'S CL
POUND FOLD
CHURCH ST
WEST LA
THRUPE LA
Ham Woods
Ham Western Farm
HAM LA

Ham Middle Farm

7

A371

LONG ST

Cliff Wood

ROOKERY LA
COMBE GN
OLD STREET LA
JACKS LA
DUN CART LA
ROCKS
BOARD LA
COOMBE COTTS

Croscombe CE Prim Sch

SHEPTON RD

Yewtree Wood

Sewage Works

Darshill Wood

HAM LA

BA5

44   Church Hill

SHEPTON OLD RD
PARADISE LA
Paradise Hill

WELLS RD

LOWER SILK MILL

BACK LA

A371

Darshill

BOWLISH LA
WASHOLT RD
ROUNDWELL CL
FINCH PL
BOWLISH LA

6   Churchill Farm

The Roundabout

Dungeon Farm

DUNGEON LA

OLD WELLS RD

Shepton Mallet Com

H

BUCALERS RD
ST PETERS RD
MISSBURG WAY
BISHOP CRES
HYATT PL

5

RIDGE RD

STUMP CROSS

KNOWLE LA

Society House Farm

BARRINGTON PL

West Shepton

43

BA4

B3136

4

Knowle Hill

MILL LA

Red House Farm

Knowle Farm

Compton Wood

RIDGE LA

Lambert's Hill Farm

LAMBERT'S HILL

3

Flat Wood

Brook House Farm

BACK LA

WEST COMPTON LA

West Compton

42   Pilton Wood

Old Burford Farm

WINTERS HILL LA

Elm Farm

2   Stoodly Hill

STOODLY LA

SUMMERS HILL LA

Burford

BURFORD CROSS

B3136

Perridge Farm

Leys La

TOTTERDOWN LA

BOWERMEAD LA

EAST COMPTON RD

A361

1   PERRIDGE HILL

HIGHER WESTHOLME RD
HARTLEY COTTS

PH

Pilton

WHITSTONE HILL

Culverwell Lodge

Cemy

NEAT LA

Springfield House

Hartley House

A361

41

58   A   59   B   C   60   D   E   F

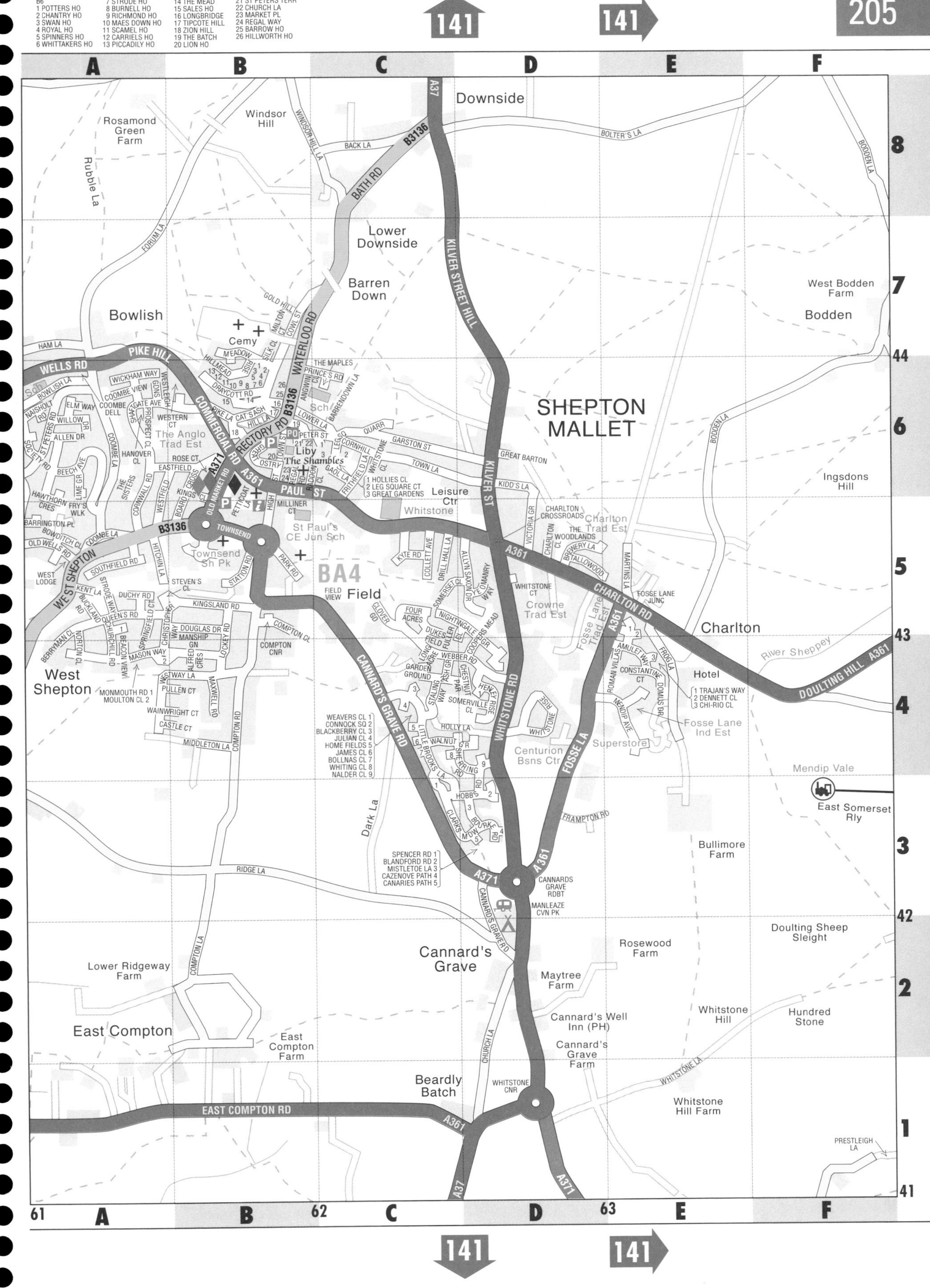
B6
1 POTTERS HO
2 CHANTRY HO
3 SWAN HO
4 ROYAL HO
5 SPINNERS HO
6 WHITTAKERS HO
7 STRODE HO
8 BURNELL HO
9 RICHMOND HO
10 MAES DOWN HO
11 SCAMEL HO
12 CARRIELS HO
13 PICCADILY HO
14 THE MEAD
15 SALES HO
16 LONGBRIDGE
17 TIPCOTE HILL
18 ZION HILL
19 THE BATCH
20 LION HO
21 ST PETERS TERR
22 CHURCH LA
23 MARKET PL
24 REGAL WAY
25 BARROW HO
26 HILLWORTH HO
141
141
A
B
C
D
E
F
8
7
44
6
5
43
4
3
42
2
1
41
61
62
63
Downside
Windsor Hill
Rosamond Green Farm
Rubble La
BACK LA
BOLTER'S LA
BODDEN LA
BATH RD
B3136
A37
Lower Downside
Barren Down
KILVER STREET HILL
West Bodden Farm
Bodden
Bowlish
Cemy
HAM LA
WELLS RD
PIKE HILL
WATERLOO RD
THE MAPLES
SHEPTON MALLET
COMMERCIAL RD
RECTORY RD
The Anglo Trad Est
Liby
The Shambles
GARSTON ST
GREAT BARTON
TOWN LA
KIDD'S LA
Ingsdons Hill
1 HOLLIES CL
2 LEG SQUARE CT
3 GREAT GARDENS
Leisure Ctr
Whitstone
PAUL ST
A361
A371
KILVER ST
CHARLTON CROSSROADS
Charlton Trad Est
St Paul's CE Jun Sch
Townsend Sh Pk
TOWNSEND
B3136
WEST SHEPTON
BA4
Field
Crowne Trad Est
Fosse Lane Trad Est
CHARLTON RD
Charlton
River Sheppey
DOULTING HILL
A361
Hotel
1 TRAJAN'S WAY
2 DENNETT CL
3 CHI-RIO CL
West Shepton
MONMOUTH RD 1
MOULTON CL 2
WEAVERS CL 1
CONNOCK SQ 2
BLACKBERRY CL 3
JULIAN CL 4
HOME FIELDS 5
JAMES CL 6
BOLLNAS CL 7
WHITING CL 8
NALDER CL 9
CANNARD'S GRAVE RD
WHITSTONE RD
FOSSE LA
Fosse Lane Ind Est
Superstore
Centurion Bsns Ctr
Mendip Vale
East Somerset Rly
COMPTON CNR
MIDDLETON LA
Dark La
FRAMPTON RD
SPENCER RD 1
BLANDFORD RD 2
MISTLETOE LA 3
CAZENOVE PATH 4
CANARIES PATH 5
Bullimore Farm
RIDGE LA
CANNARDS GRAVE RDBT
MANLEAZE CVN PK
Doulting Sheep Sleight
Rosewood Farm
Cannard's Grave
Lower Ridgeway Farm
COMPTON LA
Maytree Farm
Cannard's Well Inn (PH)
Whitstone Hill
Hundred Stone
East Compton
East Compton Farm
Cannard's Grave Farm
WHITSTONE LA
Beardly Batch
WHITSTONE CNR
Whitstone Hill Farm
EAST COMPTON RD
CHURCH LA
PRESTLEIGH LA
A37
A371

138 139 139

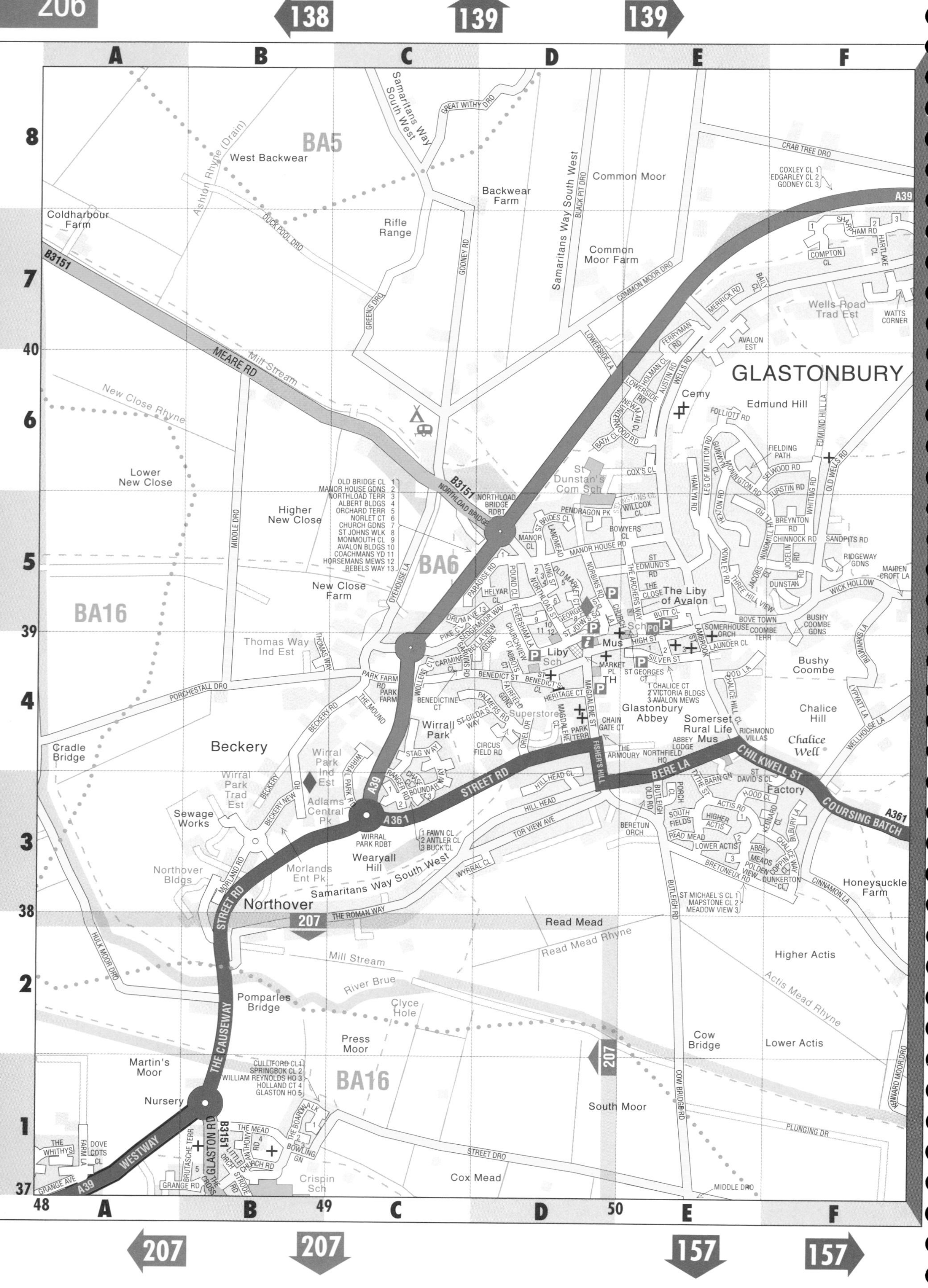
GLASTONBURY
BA5
BA6
BA16
West Backwear
Coldharbour Farm
Rifle Range
Backwear Farm
Common Moor
Common Moor Farm
Lower New Close
Higher New Close
New Close Farm
Thomas Way Ind Est
Beckery
Cradle Bridge
Wirral Park Trad Est
Sewage Works
Northover Bldgs
Morlands Ent Pk
Wearyall Hill
Northover
Read Mead
Mill Stream
River Brue
Pomparles Bridge
Clyce Hole
Press Moor
Martin's Moor
Nursery
Crispin Sch
Cox Mead
South Moor
Cow Bridge
Lower Actis
Higher Actis
Honeysuckle Farm
Chalice Hill
Chalice Well
Bushy Coombe
Edmund Hill
Wells Road Trad Est
The Liby of Avalon
Glastonbury Abbey
Somerset Rural Life Mus
Superstore
Wirrall Park
Adlams Central Pk
Wirral Park Ind Est
St Dunstan's Com Sch
Cemy
Factory
A39
A361
B3151
MEARE RD
STREET RD
BERE LA
CHILKWELL ST
COURSING BATCH
THE CAUSEWAY
WESTWAY
GLASTON RD
Samaritans Way South West
OLD BRIDGE CL 1
MANOR HOUSE GDNS 2
NORTHLOAD TERR 3
ALBERT BLDGS 4
ORCHARD TERR 5
NORLET CT 6
CHURCH GDNS 7
ST JOHNS WLK 8
MONMOUTH CL 9
AVALON BLDGS 10
COACHMANS YD 11
HORSEMANS MEWS 12
REBELS WAY 13
COXLEY CL 1
EDGARLEY CL 2
GODNEY CL 3
1 CHALICE CT
2 VICTORIA BLDGS
3 AVALON MEWS
1 FAWN CL
2 ANTLER CL
3 BUCK CL
ST MICHAEL'S CL 1
MAPSTONE CL 2
MEADOW VIEW 3
CULLIFORD CL 1
SPRINGBOK CL 2
WILLIAM REYNOLDS HO 3
HOLLAND CT 4
GLASTON HO 5
8
7
6
5
4
3
2
1
40
39
38
37
48
49
50
A
B
C
D
E
F

207 207 157 157

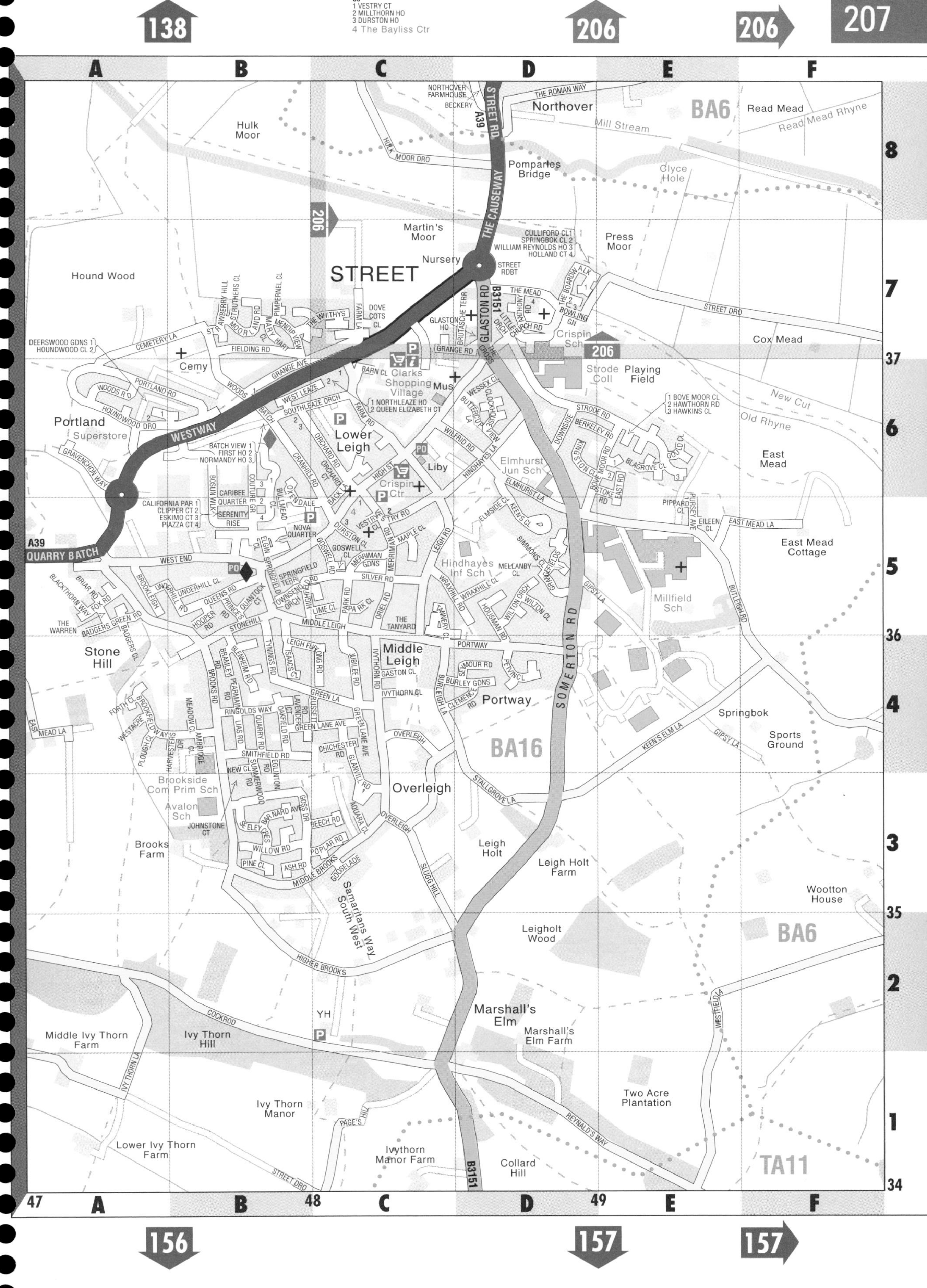

138

206

206

C5
1 VESTRY CT
2 MILLTHORN HO
3 DURSTON HO
4 The Bayliss Ctr

A B C D E F

NORTHOVER
FARMHOUSE
BECKERY
Northover
THE ROMAN WAY
BA6
Read Mead
Read Mead Rhyne
Mill Stream

Hulk
Moor
HULK MOOR DRO
Pomparles
Bridge
Clyce
Hole

206
Martin's
Moor
CULLIFORD CLT
SPRINGBOK CL 2
WILLIAM REYNOLDS HO 3
HOLLAND CT 4
Press
Moor
STREET DRO

Hound Wood
Nursery
STREET
STREET
RDBT
THE MEAD
Cox Mead

DEERSWOOD GDNS 1
HOUNDWOOD CL 2
CEMETERY LA
FIELDING RD
THE WHITHYS
DOVE
COTS
CL
GLASTON
HO
GRANGE RD
BRUNASCHE TERR
LITTLE
BOWLING
GN
Crispin
Sch
206
37

Portland
Superstore
Cemy
GRANGE AVE
WEST LEAZE
BARN CL
Clarks
Shopping
Village
Mus
Strode
Coll
Playing
Field
New Cut
1 BOVE MOOR CL
2 HAWTHORN RD
3 HAWKINS CL
Old Rhyne
East
Mead

WOODS RD
PORTLAND RD
HOUNDWOOD DRO
WESTWAY
BATCH
SOUTHLEAZE ORCH
1 NORTHLEAZE HO
2 QUEEN ELIZABETH CT
Lower
Leigh
Liby
WILFRID RD
STRODE RD
BERKELEY RD
BLAGROVE
RD
East Mead
Cottage

GRAVENCHON WAY
BATCH VIEW 1
FIRST HO 2
NORMANDY HO 3
CRAMPILL RD
ORCHARD RD
HIGH ST
Crispin
Ctr
Elmhurst
Jun Sch
ELMHURST LA
PIPPARD
CL
EILEEN
CL
EAST MEAD LA

A39
QUARRY BATCH
CARIBEE
QUARTER
COUTURE
GR
BOSUN WLK
BULLMEAD
NOVA
Quarter
DURSTON RD
VESTRY
RD
TRY RD
LEGFIELD
SIMMONS CL
GIPSY LA
Millfield
Sch
East Mead
Cottage

CALIFORNIA PAR 1
CLIPPER CT 2
ESKIMO CT 3
PIAZZA CT 4
SERENITY
RISE
GOSWELL RD
MERRIMAN
GDNS
Hindhayes
Inf Sch
WAXHILL RD
WILTON ORCH
WILTON CL
5

WEST END
UNDERHILL CL
SPRINGFIELD
TERR
SILVER RD
ORIEL RD
PORTWAY
36

BRIAR RD
FOX RD
BADGERS GREEN CL
QUEENS RD
PRINCES RD
QUANTOCK
STONEHILL
LIME RD
MIDDLE LEIGH
PARK RD
THE
TANYARD
LANNER CT
Middle Leigh
Portway

THE
WARREN
HOOPER
RD
THINGS RD
ISAACS CL
JUBILEE RD
IVYTHORN CL
ARMOUR RD
BURLEY GDNS
BA16

Stone
Hill
FORTH CL
BROOME RD
MEADOW
CL
CAMBRIDGE
RINGOLDS WAY
LEIGH FURLONG RD
GREEN LA
CHICHESTER
GREEN LANE AVE
OVERLEIGH
CLEMENTS
RD
BURLEIGH LA
Overleigh
STALLGROVE LA
Leigh
Holt
4

BLACKTHORN WAY
WESTON CL
PLOUGH CL
HARVESTERS
LAS
OAKFIELD
SMITHFIELD RD
QUARRY CL
GLANVILL
AUDREY
CL
ADNAM
CL
SOMERTON RD
Leigh Holt
Farm
Springbok
Sports
Ground

Brookside
Com Prim Sch
NEW CL
SUMMERWOOD
BROOKS
BEECH RD
GOSELADE
Samaritans Way
South West
3
Wootton
House

Avalon
Sch
JOHNSTONE
CT
BARNARD AVE
ST ELEYS
CRES
WILLOW RD
POPLAR RD
Leigholt
Wood
BA6
35

Brooks
Farm
PINE CL
ASH RD
MIDDLE BROOKS
SLUNG HILL
HIGHER BROOKS
2

Middle Ivy Thorn
Farm
COCKROD
Ivy Thorn
Hill
YH
P
Marshall's
Elm
WESTFIELD LA

Ivy Thorn
Manor
STREET DRO
PAGE'S
Ivythorn
Manor Farm
Collard
Hill
B3151
Marshall's
Elm Farm
Two Acre
Plantation
REYNALD'S WAY
TA11
1

Lower Ivy Thorn
Farm
IVY THORN LA
34

47 A B 48 C D 49 E F

156

157

157

135 135

BRIDGWATER

TA5
TA6

Places and features:
Perrycroft, Perry Green, Perry Green Farm, Barton Farm, Sandford Farm, Perrymoor Brook, Manor Lodge, Grabhams Cottage, Grabhams Farm, Blakes Farm, Moores, Wembdon Farm, Wembdon, Inn, Mount Radford, Cokerhurst Farm, Greenway Farm, Wembdon St George's CE Prim Sch, Church Farm Newtown, Chilton Trinity Sch, Sports Ctr, Chilton Pk, Western Way, River Parrett Trail, Homberg Way, Marina Dock, Hinkley Point Visitor Ctr, York Ct, Queenswood Farm, Cemy, Northfield, St Mary's CE Prim Sch, Haygrove Sch, St Joseph's RC Prim Sch, Westover Green Com Sch, Durleigh, Durleigh Elms, Durleigh Brook Farm, Durleigh Farm, Durleigh Reservoir, Haygrove House, Haygrove Farm, Robert Blake Science Coll, Hamp Inf Sch, Hamp Com Jun Sch, Hamp, Elmwood Sch, The Meads, Hamp Brook, Samaritans Way South West, Poultry Farm, Shortlands Farm

Roads: B3339, A39, Sandford Hill, Wembdon Hill, Wembdon Rise, Wembdon Rd, North St, Broadway, Superstore, Charter

153 153

E7
1 DUCHESS CL
2 POSITANO CT
3 FLORENCE CL
4 TURIN PATH

SOUTHBOURNE HO 1
WEST BOW HO 2
WESTFIELD HO 3
ALBERT CT 4
ELEVEN CT 5

FORSYTHIA WAY 1
LAVENDER WALK 2
KORRESIA WALK 3
PRIMROSE WALK 4
BUGLE WALK 5
CORNFLOWER CL 6
CRISTATA WAY 7

SNOWBERRY CL 1
OCTAVIA CL 2

1 SPILLERS CL
2 WOLMER CL

1 PENNYCRESS WAY
2 FOXGLOVE WALK
3 BLUEBELL DR
4 TANSEY COURT

ASHLEIGH AVE 1
ASHLEIGH TERR 2
GREENFIELDS 3

SHELLTHORN GR 1
BAGBOROUGH DR 2

F4
1 ST MARY'S CT
2 BLAKE ST
3 OLD TAUNTON RD
4 GREEN DRAGON CT

F5
1 CHALICE MEWS
2 HOMECASTLE HO
3 THE AVENUE
4 CHURCH PASS
5 COURT ST
6 Angel Place Sh Ctr
7 Bridgwater Ent Ctr
8 MARKET CT

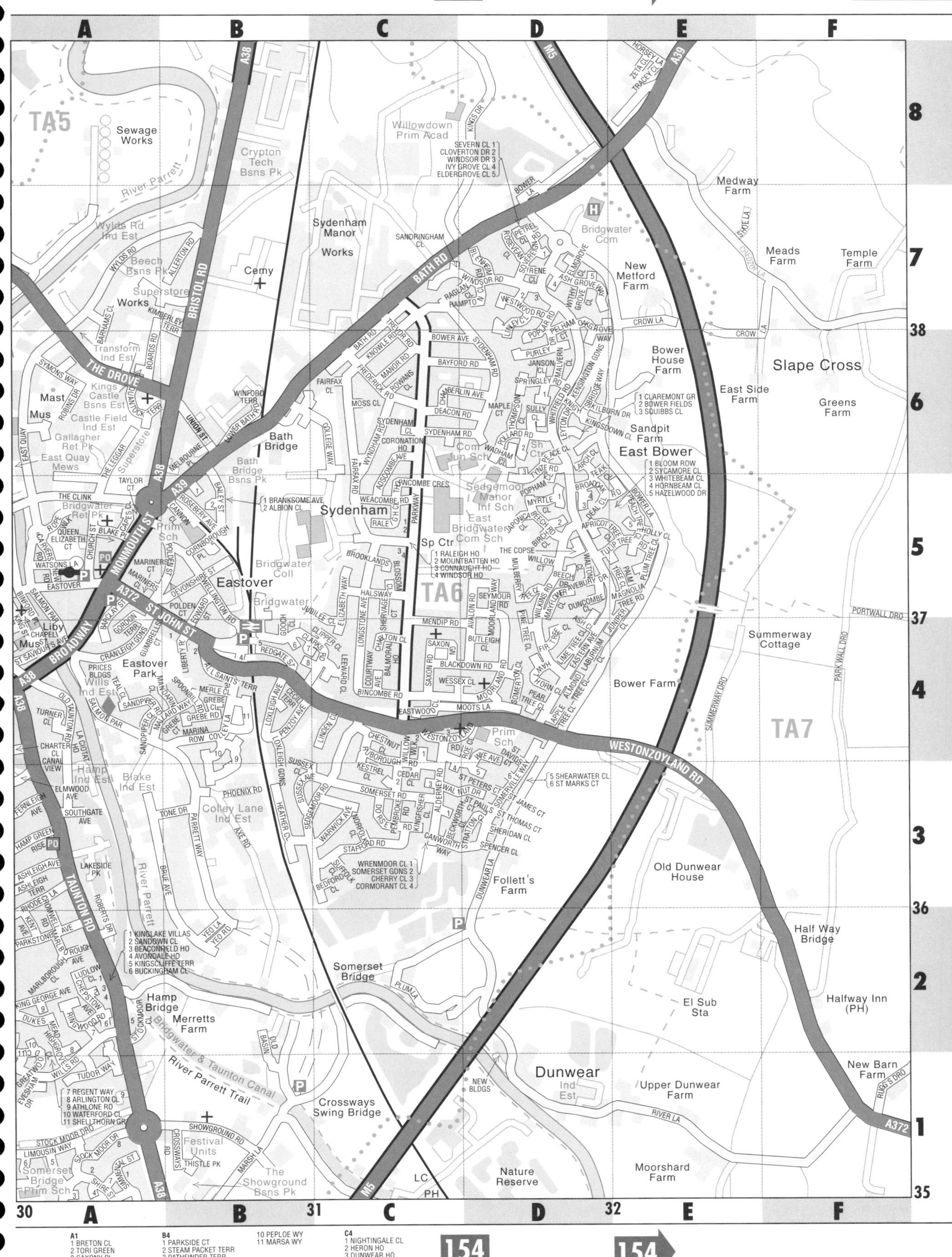

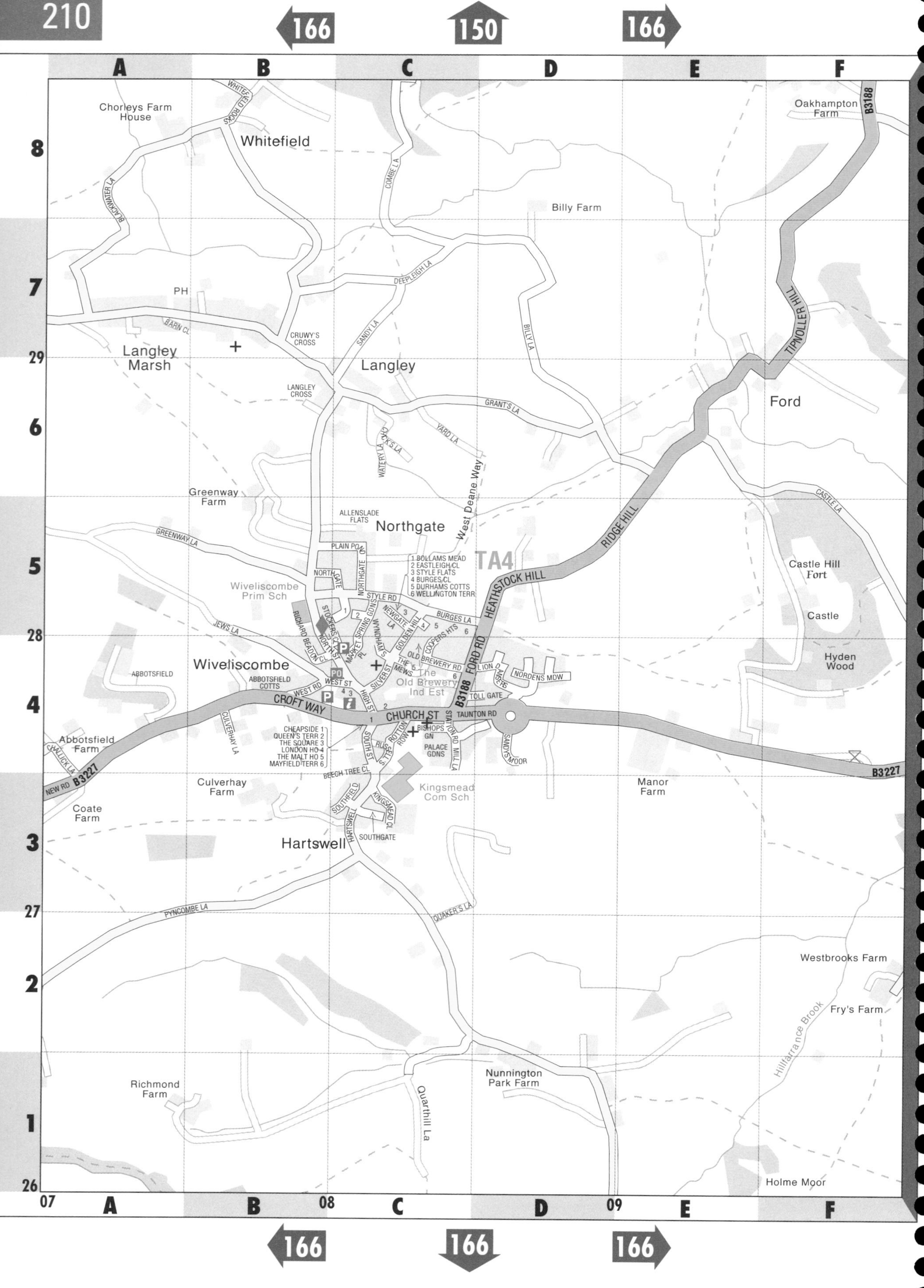
166
150
166
Chorleys Farm House
Whitefield
Oakhampton Farm
Billy Farm
PH
Langley Marsh
Langley
Ford
Greenway Farm
Northgate
TA4
Wiveliscombe Prim Sch
Castle Hill Fort
Castle
Hyden Wood
Wiveliscombe
The Old Brewery Ind Est
Abbotsfield Farm
Culverhay Farm
Coate Farm
Kingsmead Com Sch
Manor Farm
Hartswell
Westbrooks Farm
Fry's Farm
Richmond Farm
Nunnington Park Farm
Quarthill La
Holme Moor
West Deane Way
Hillfarrance Brook
HEATHSTOCK HILL
RIDGE HILL
TIPNOLLER HILL
CROFT WAY
CHURCH ST
B3227
B3188
1 BOLLAMS MEAD
2 EASTLEIGH CL
3 STYLE FLATS
4 BURGES CL
5 DURHAMS COTTS
6 WELLINGTON TERR
CHEAPSIDE 1
QUEEN'S TERR 2
THE SQUARE 3
LONDON HO 4
THE MALT HO 5
MAYFIELD TERR 6
166
166
166

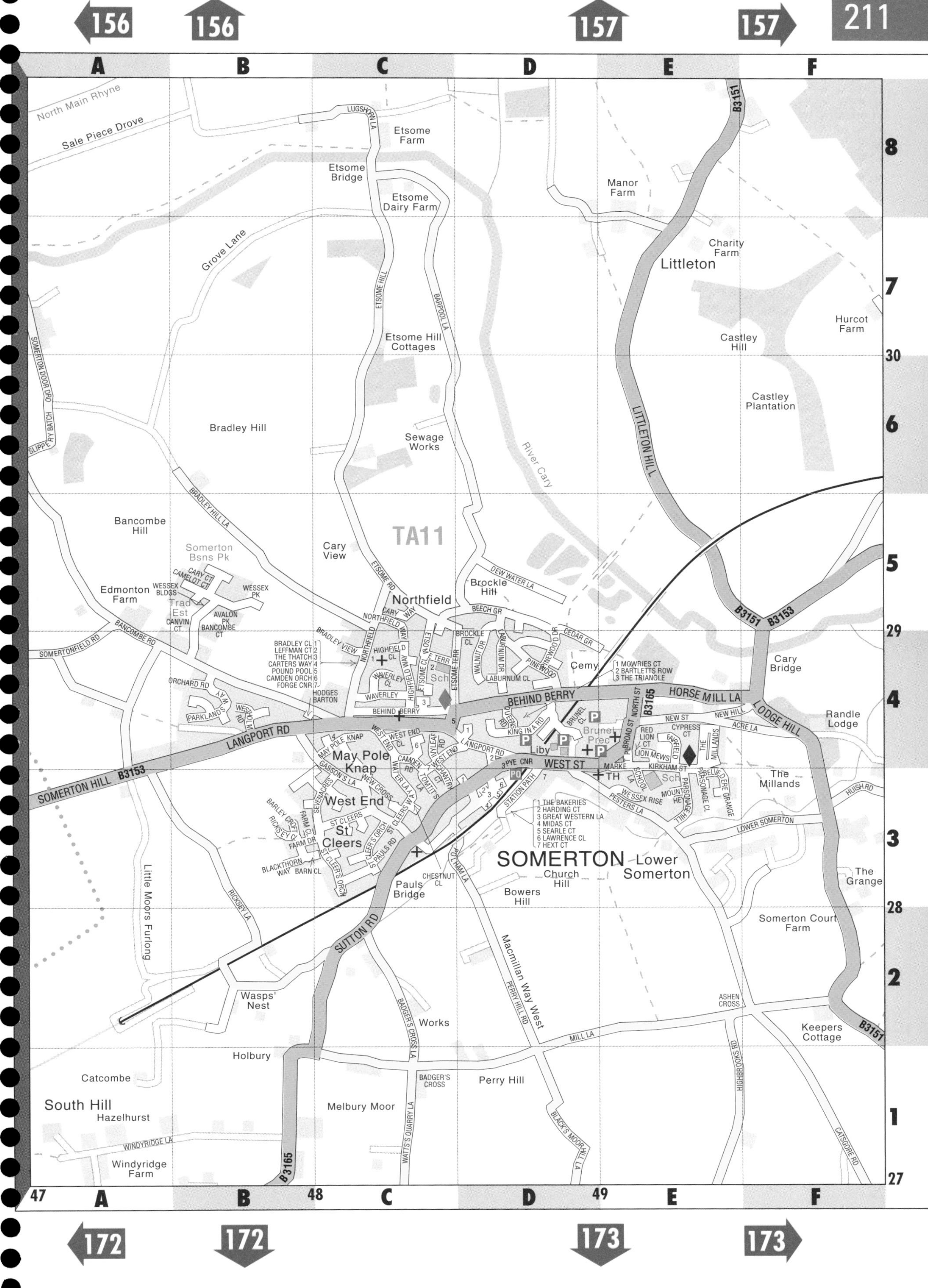
156
156
157
157
A B C D E F
8
7
30
6
5
29
4
3
28
2
1
27
North Main Rhyne
Sale Piece Drove
Etsome Farm
Etsome Bridge
Etsome Dairy Farm
Manor Farm
Charity Farm
Littleton
Grove Lane
Castley Hill
Hurcot Farm
Etsome Hill Cottages
Castley Plantation
Bradley Hill
Sewage Works
River Cary
LITTLETON HILL
Bancombe Hill
Somerton Bsns Pk
Cary View
TA11
Edmonton Farm
Northfield
Brockle Hill
Trad Est
Cemy
Cary Bridge
Randle Lodge
LANGPORT RD
May Pole Knap
West End
St Cleers
SOMERTON
Lower Somerton
Church Hill
The Millands
The Grange
Pauls Bridge
Bowers Hill
Somerton Court Farm
Little Moors Furlong
SUTTON RD
Macmillan Way West
Wasps' Nest
Works
Keepers Cottage
Holbury
Catcombe
Perry Hill
South Hill
Hazelhurst
Melbury Moor
Windyridge Farm
SOMERTON HILL B3153
BEHIND BERRY
HORSE MILL LA
LODGE HILL
WEST ST
B3151
B3153
B3165
47 48 49
172
172
173
173

168
168

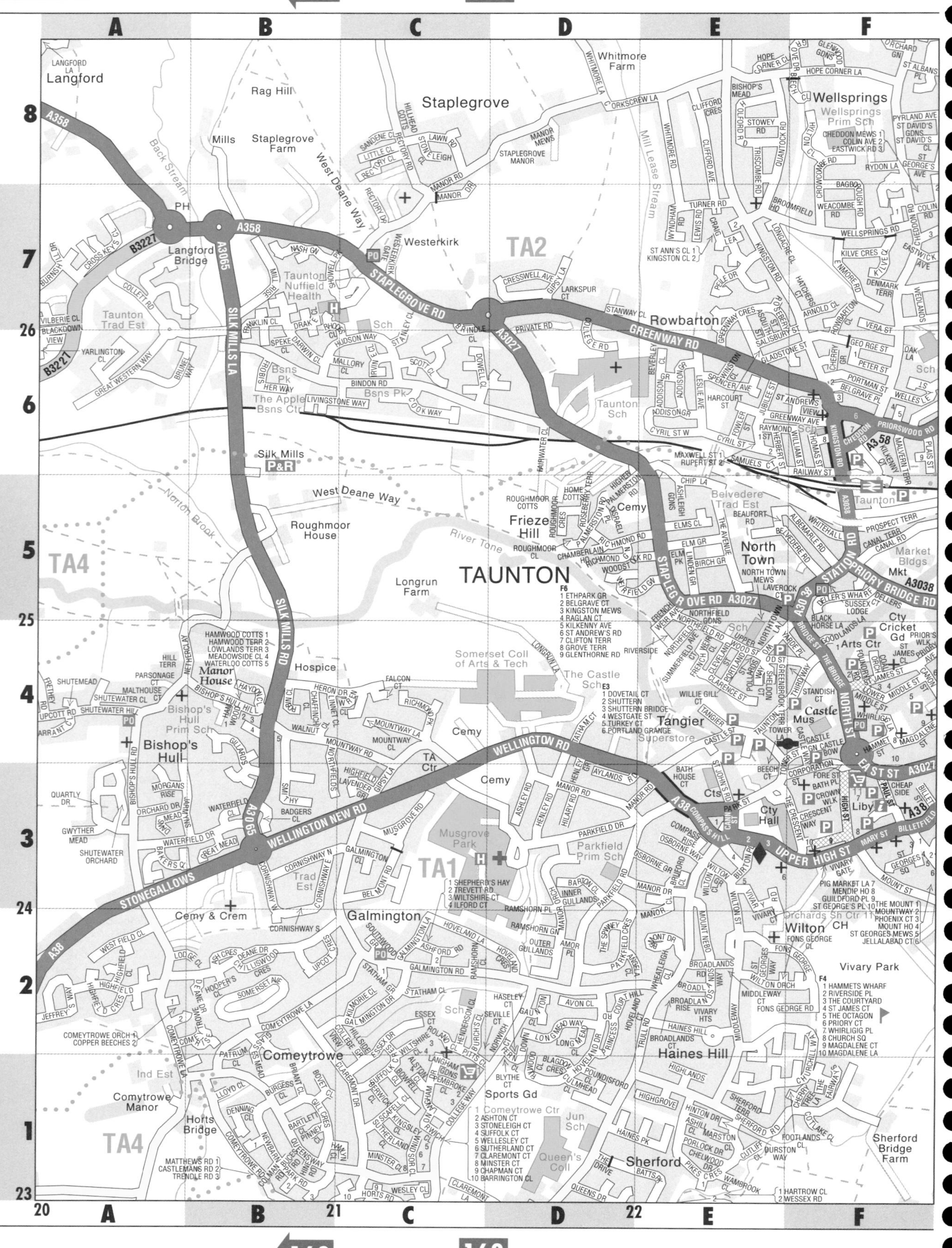
A
B
C
D
E
F
8
7
26
6
5
25
4
3
24
2
1
23
20
21
22
Langford
Rag Hill
Staplegrove
Whitmore Farm
Wellsprings
Wellsprings Prim Sch
Mills
Staplegrove Farm
PH
Langford Bridge
Westerkirk
TA2
Taunton Nuffield Health
Taunton Trad Est
Rowbarton
Bsns Pk
The Apple Bsns Ctr
Taunton Sch
Silk Mills
West Deane Way
Roughmoor House
Frieze Hill
Cemy
Belvedere Trad Est
Taunton
TA4
River Tone
Longrun Farm
TAUNTON
North Town
Market Bldgs
Mkt
Cty Cricket Gd
Arts Ctr
Somerset Coll of Arts & Tech
The Castle Sch
Hospice
Manor House
Bishop's Hull Prim Sch
Bishop's Hull
Tangier
Superstore
Castle
Mus
Cemy
TA Ctr
Musgrove Park
Parkfield Prim Sch
Cts
Cty Hall
Liby
TA1
Trad Est
Cemy & Crem
Galmington
Wilton
Orchards Sh Ctr
Vivary Park
Comeytrowe
Ind Est
Haines Hill
Sports Gd
Comytrowe Manor
Horts Bridge
TA4
Jun Sch
Queen's Coll
Sherford
Sherford Bridge Farm
A358
A3065
A3027
A38
A3038
B3227
SILK MILLS LA
SILK MILLS RD
STAPLEGROVE RD
GREENWAY RD
WELLINGTON RD
WELLINGTON NEW RD
STONEGALLOWS
UPPER HIGH ST
PRIORY BRIDGE RD
STATION RD
NORTH ST
EAST ST
F6
1 ETHPARK GR
2 BELGRAVE CT
3 KINGSTON MEWS
4 RAGLAN CT
5 KILKENNY AVE
6 ST ANDREW'S RD
7 CLIFTON TERR
8 GROVE TERR
9 GLENTHORNE RD
E3
1 DOVETAIL CT
2 SHUTTERN
3 SHUTTERN BRIDGE
4 WESTGATE ST
5 TURKEY CT
6 PORTLAND GRANGE
1 SHEPHERD'S HAY
2 TREVETT RD
3 WILTSHIRE CT
4 ILFORD CT
F4
1 HAMMETS WHARF
2 RIVERSIDE PL
3 THE COURTYARD
4 ST JAMES CT
5 THE OCTAGON
6 PRIORY CT
7 WHIRLIGIG PL
8 CHURCH SQ
9 MAGDALENE CT
10 MAGDALENE LA
PIG MARKET LA 7
MENDIP HO 8
GUILDFORD PL 9
ST GEORGE'S PL 10
THE MOUNT 1
MOUNTWAY 2
PHOENIX CT 3
MOUNT HO 4
ST GEORGES MEWS 5
JELLALABAD CT 6
1 Comeytrowe Ctr
2 ASHTON CT
3 STONELEIGH CT
4 SUFFOLK CT
5 WELLESLEY CT
6 SUTHERLAND CT
7 CLAREMONT CT
8 MINSTER CT
9 CHAPMAN CT
10 BARRINGTON CL
HAMWOOD COTTS 1
HAMWOOD TERR 2
LOWLANDS TERR 3
MEADOWSIDE CL 4
WATERLOO COTTS 5
MATTHEWS RD 1
CASTLEMANS RD 2
TRENDLE RD 3
COMEYTROWE ORCH 1
COPPER BEECHES 2
1 HARTROW CL
2 WESSEX RD
CHEDDON MEWS 1
COLIN AVE 2
EASTWICK RD 3
ST ANN'S CL 1
KINGSTON CL 2
MAXWELL ST 1
RUPERT ST 2

168
168

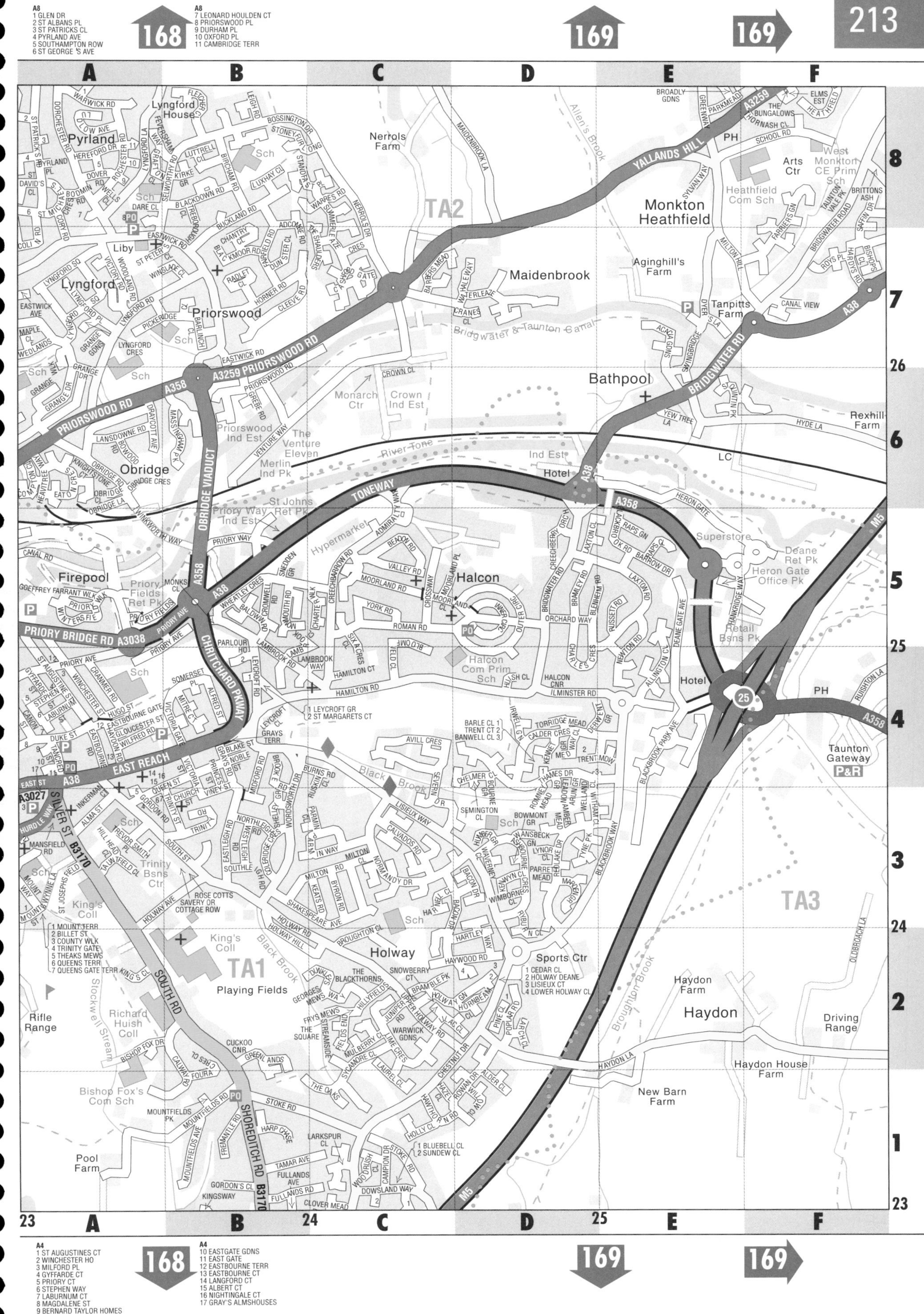

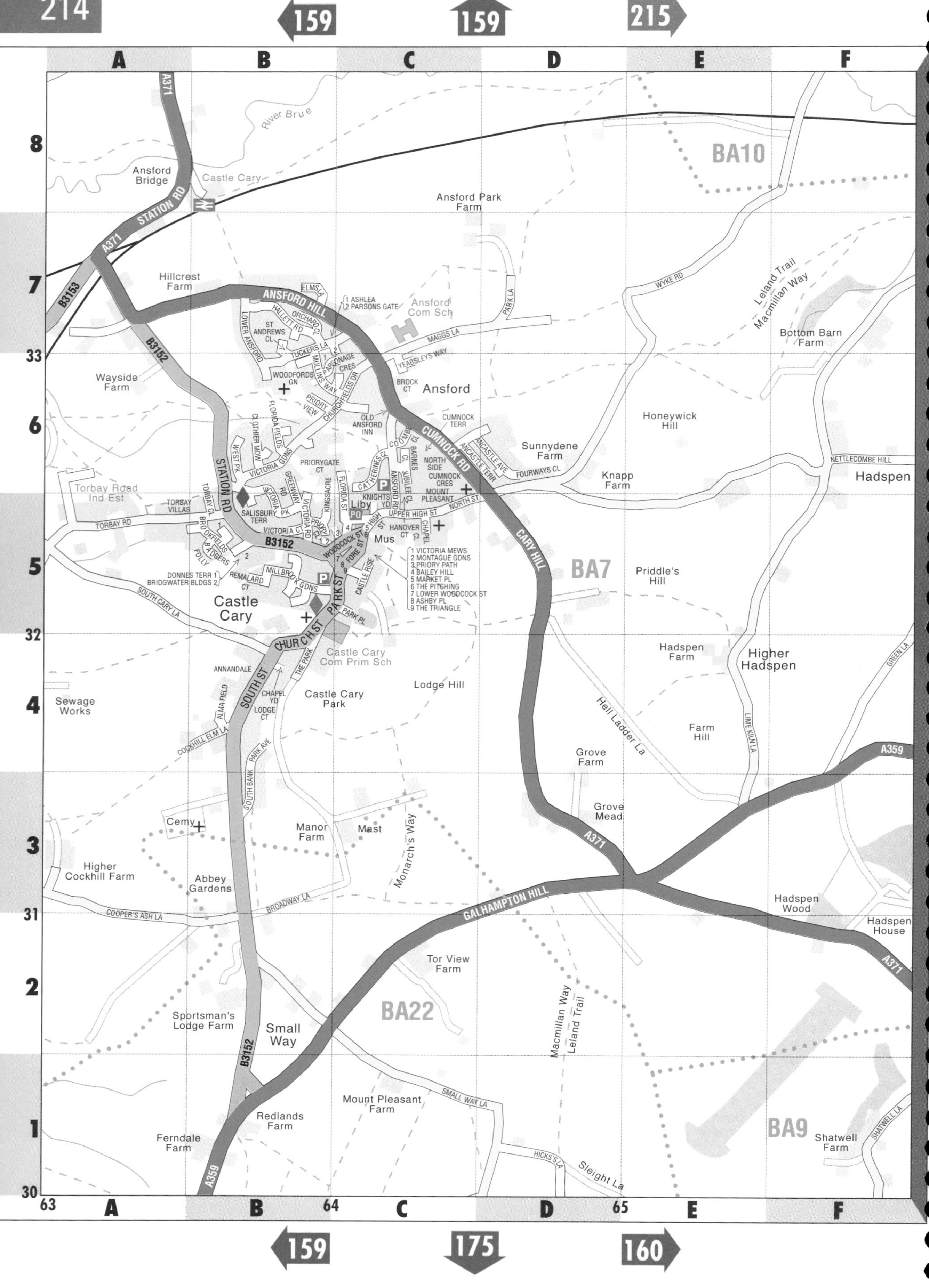
159
159
215
A
B
C
D
E
F
8
7
33
6
5
32
4
3
31
2
1
30
63
64
65
A
B
C
D
E
F
159
175
160
River Brue
Ansford Bridge
Castle Cary
A371
STATION RD
A371
B3153
BA10
Ansford Park Farm
Hillcrest Farm
ANSFORD HILL
B3152
Ansford Com Sch
MAGGS LA
PARK LA
WYKE RD
Leland Trail
Macmillan Way
Bottom Barn Farm
Wayside Farm
Ansford
Honeywick Hill
Sunnydene Farm
Knapp Farm
NETTLECOMBE HILL
Hadspen
FOURWAYS CL
CUMNOCK RD
Torbay Road Ind Est
TORBAY RD
STATION RD
B3152
Liby
PO
Mus
CARY HILL
BA7
Priddle's Hill
1 VICTORIA MEWS
2 MONTAGUE GDNS
3 PRIORY PATH
4 BAILEY HILL
5 MARKET PL
6 THE PITCHING
7 LOWER WOODCOCK ST
8 ASHBY PL
9 THE TRIANGLE
Castle Cary
SOUTH CARY LA
CHURCH ST
PARK ST
PARK PL
Castle Cary Com Prim Sch
Hadspen Farm
Higher Hadspen
GREEN LA
Sewage Works
SOUTH ST
Castle Cary Park
Lodge Hill
Hell Ladder La
Farm Hill
LIME KILN LA
Grove Farm
A359
Grove Mead
Cemy
Manor Farm
Mast
Monarch's Way
A371
Higher Cockhill Farm
Abbey Gardens
COOPER'S ASH LA
BROADWAY LA
GALHAMPTON HILL
Hadspen Wood
Hadspen House
A371
Tor View Farm
BA22
Macmillan Way
Leland Trail
Sportsman's Lodge Farm
Small Way
B3152
SMALL WAY LA
Mount Pleasant Farm
Redlands Farm
BA9
Shatwell Farm
SHATWELL LA
Ferndale Farm
A359
HICKS'S LA
Sleight La

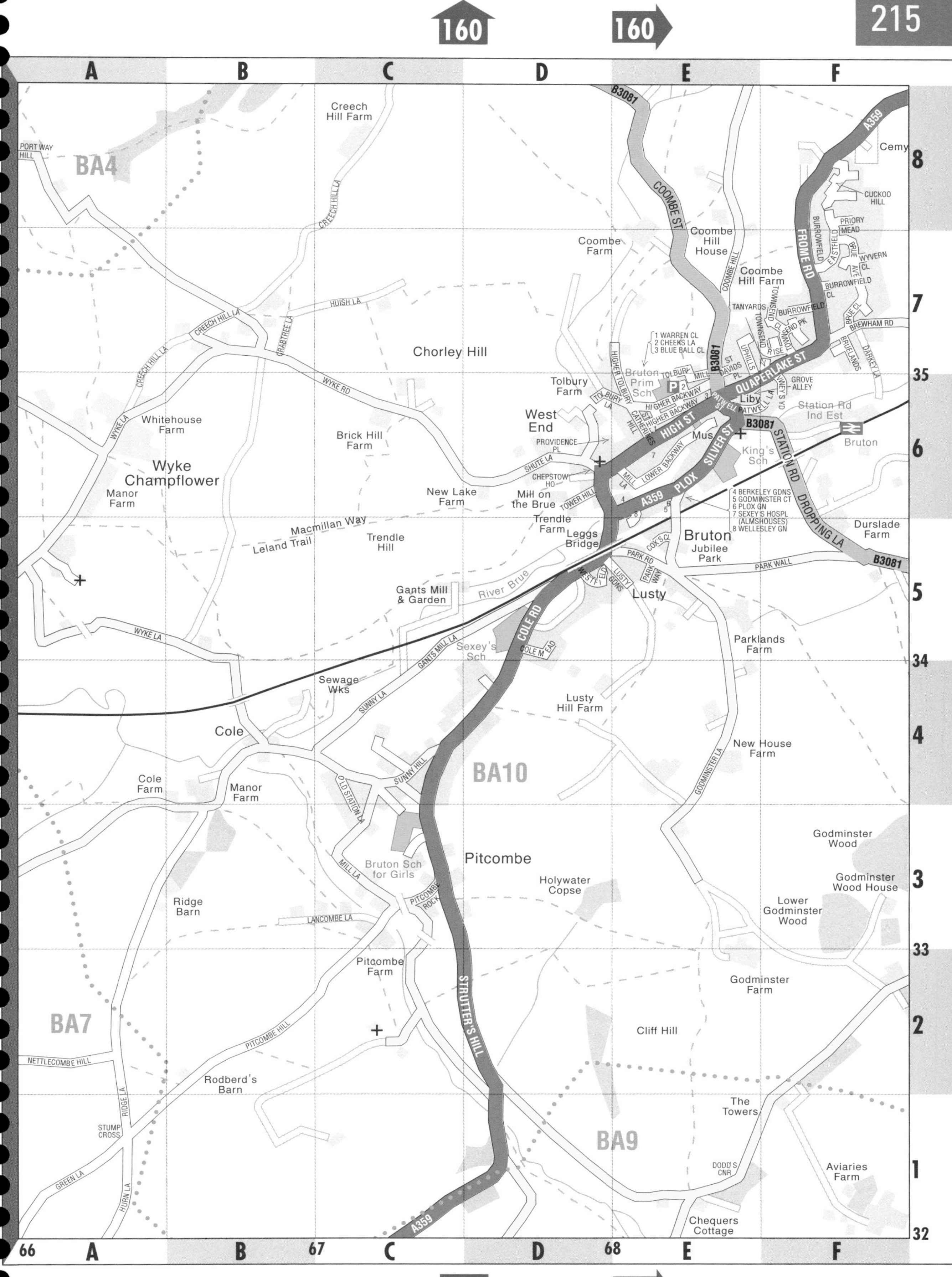
160
160
A
B
C
D
E
F
BA4
Creech Hill Farm
PORT WAY HILL
CREECH HILL LA
Coombe Farm
Coombe Hill House
COOMBE ST
B3081
A359
Cemy
CUCKOO HILL
PRIORY MEAD
FROME RD
BURROWFIELD
EASTFIELD
BRUE AVE
WYVERN CL
BURROWFIELD CL
Coombe Hill Farm
COOMBE HILL
TANYARDS
TOWNSEND
BURROWFIELD
BREWHAM RD
HUISH LA
CRABTREE LA
Chorley Hill
1 WARREN CL
2 CHEEKS LA
3 BLUE BALL CL
BRUELANDS
DARKEY LA
HIGHER TOLBURY
Bruton Prim Sch
ST DAVIDS PL
UPHILLS
QUAPERLAKE ST
GROVE ALLEY
WYKE RD
Tolbury Farm
TOLBURY LA
HIGHER BACKWAY
Liby
PATWELL LA
Station Rd Ind Est
Whitehouse Farm
West End
HIGH ST
B3081
Bruton
Brick Hill Farm
PROVIDENCE PL
Mus
SILVER ST
STATION RD
King's Sch
WYKE LA
Wyke Champflower
SHUTE LA
LOWER BACKWAY
Manor Farm
CHEPSTOW HO
New Lake Farm
Mill on the Brue
TOWER HILL
MILL LA
PLOX
A359
4 BERKELEY GDNS
5 GODMINSTER CT
6 PLOX GN
7 SEXEY'S HOSPL (ALMSHOUSES)
8 WELLESLEY GN
DROPPING LA
Durslade Farm
Macmillan Way
Leland Trail
Trendle Hill
Trendle Farm
Leggs Bridge
COX'S CL
Bruton
Jubilee Park
PARK RD
B3081
PARK WALL
Gants Mill & Garden
River Brue
WESTFIELD GDNS
LUSTY
PARK WAY
Lusty
COLE RD
WYKE LA
GANTS MILL LA
Sexey's Sch
COLE MEAD
Parklands Farm
Sewage Wks
SUNNY LA
Lusty Hill Farm
Cole
New House Farm
Cole Farm
Manor Farm
SUNNY HILL
OLD STATION LA
BA10
GODMINSTER LA
Godminster Wood
Pitcombe
Bruton Sch for Girls
MILL LA
Holywater Copse
Godminster Wood House
Ridge Barn
PITCOMBE ROCK
LANCOMBE LA
Lower Godminster Wood
Pitcombe Farm
Godminster Farm
STRUTTER'S HILL
BA7
Cliff Hill
PITCOMBE HILL
NETTLECOMBE HILL
Rodberd's Barn
RIDGE LA
The Towers
STUMP CROSS
BA9
GREEN LA
HURN LA
DODD'S CNR
Aviaries Farm
A359
Chequers Cottage
66
67
68
8
7
35
6
5
34
4
3
33
2
1
32
160
160

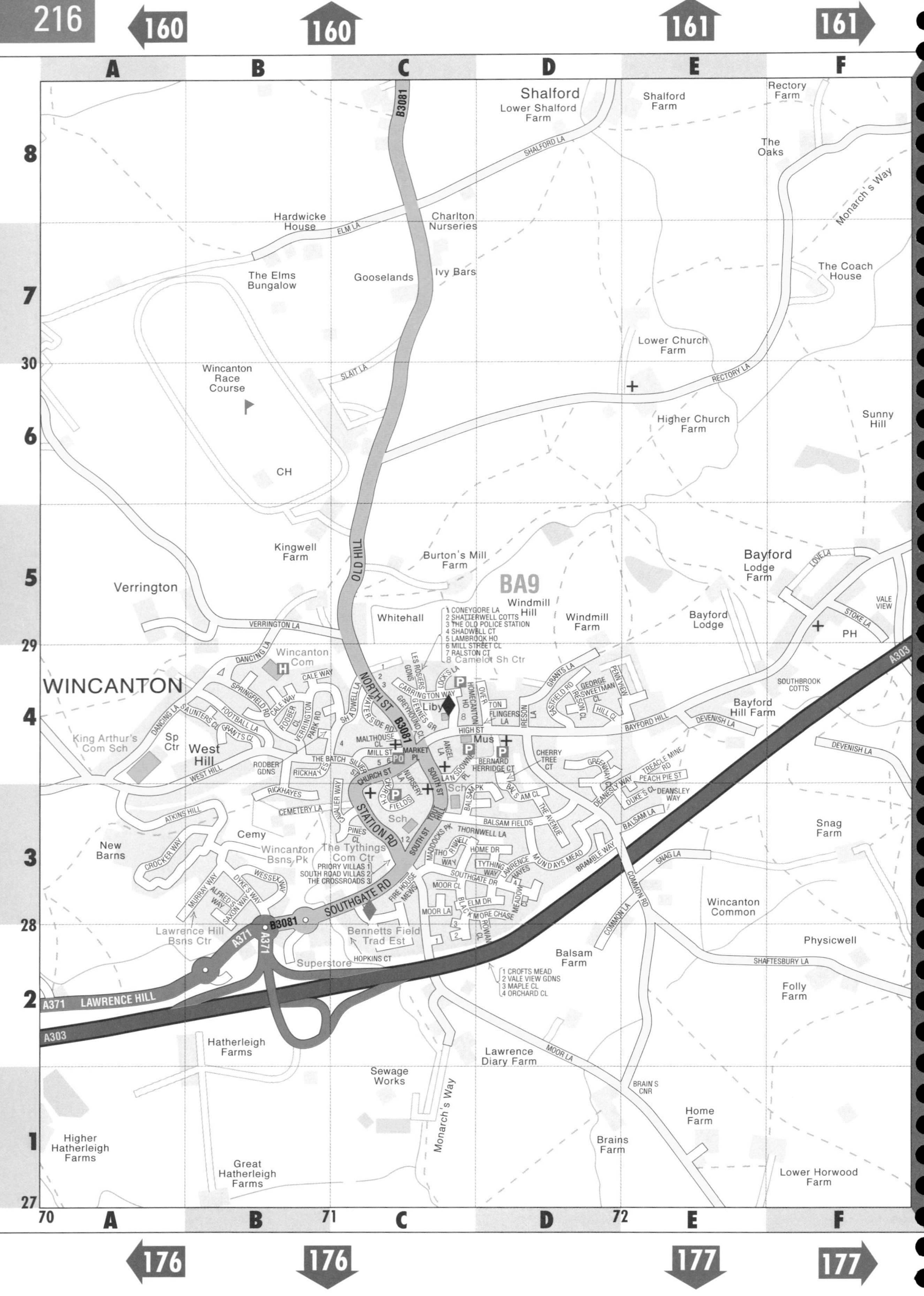

A   B   C   D   E   F

8

7

30

6

5

29

4

3

28

2

1

27

Shalford
Lower Shalford Farm
Shalford Farm
Rectory Farm
The Oaks

Hardwicke House
ELM LA
Charlton Nurseries
The Coach House
Monarch's Way

The Elms Bungalow
Gooselands
Ivy Bars
SHALFORD LA

SLAIT LA
Lower Church Farm
RECTORY LA
Sunny Hill

Wincanton Race Course
Higher Church Farm

CH
Kingwell Farm
Burton's Mill Farm
BA9
Windmill Hill
Windmill Farm
Bayford Lodge Farm
LOVE LA
VALE VIEW
STOKE LA

Verrington
Whitehall
1 CONEYGORE LA
2 SHATTERWELL COTTS
3 THE OLD POLICE STATION
4 SHADWELL CT
5 LAMBROOK HO
6 MILL STREET CL
7 RALSTON CT
8 CAMELOT Sh Ctr
Bayford Lodge
Bayford Hill Farm
PH

VERRINGTON LA
Wincanton Com
DANCING LA
CALE WAY
LES ROGERS GDNS
DENNING GR
LOCK'S LA
GRANTS LA
GEORGE SWEETMAN
PENNY YEN
SOUTHBROOK COTTS

WINCANTON
H
SPRINGFIELD RD
CALE WAY
FOOTBALL LA
VERRINGTON PARK RD
SHADWELL
WATERSIDE RD
NORTH ST
CARRINGTON WAY
GREYHOUND RD
HIGH ST
OVER
HOMEGARTON
TON
FLINGERS LA
RESON
EASFIELD RD
HILL CL
Bayford Hill Farm
DEVENISH LA

Sp Ctr
Liby
King Arthur's Com Sch
SAUNTERS CL
GRANTS CL
MALTHOUSE CL
SILVER
PO
MARKET
ANGEL LA
Mus
P
GREENWAY
DEANSLEY WAY
TREACLE MINE RD
PEACH PIE ST
DEVENISH LA

West Hill
RODBER
CALE WAY
THE BATCH
CHURCH ST
SOUTH ST
BERNARD HERRIDGE CT
DUKE'S CL
DEANSLEY WAY
Snag Farm

WEST HILL
RODBER GDNS
RICKHAYES
QUAKER WAY
SILVER
CHURCH
FIELDS
Sch
BALSAM
SAM CL
CHERRY TREE CT
BALSAM LA

New Barns
ATKINS HILL
Cemy
RICKHAYES
CEMETERY LA
PINES CL
NURSERY
SOUTH ST SCH HILL
MADDOCKS PK
THORNWELL LA
BALSAM FIELDS
THE AVENUE

CROCKER WAY
Wincanton Bsns Pk
The Tythings Com Ctr
PRIORY VILLAS 1
SOUTH ROAD VILLAS 2
THE CROSSROADS 3
WELL
WAY
HOME DR
TYTHING WAY
LAWRENCE HAYES
WAIN DAY'S MEAD
BRAMBLE WAY
Wincanton Common

MURRAY WAY
ALFRED'S CL
DYKE'S WAY
SAXON WAY
WESSEX VW
B3081
SOUTHGATE RD
FIRE HOUSE MEWS
SOUTHGATE DR
MEADOW
MOOR LA
SNAG LA
COMMON RD
Physicwell

Lawrence Hill Bsns Ctr
A371
Bennetts Field Trad Est
MOOR LA
BLACK MORE CHASE
ROWAN CL
1 CROFTS MEAD
2 VALE VIEW GDNS
3 MAPLE CL
4 ORCHARD CL
SHAFTESBURY LA
Folly Farm

Superstore
HOPKINS CT
Balsam Farm
BRAIN'S CNR

A371   LAWRENCE HILL
A303
Hatherleigh Farms
Sewage Works
MOOR LA
Lawrence Diary Farm
Home Farm
Lower Horwood Farm

Higher Hatherleigh Farms
Great Hatherleigh Farms
Monarch's Way
Brains Farm

70   A   B   71   C   D   72   E   F

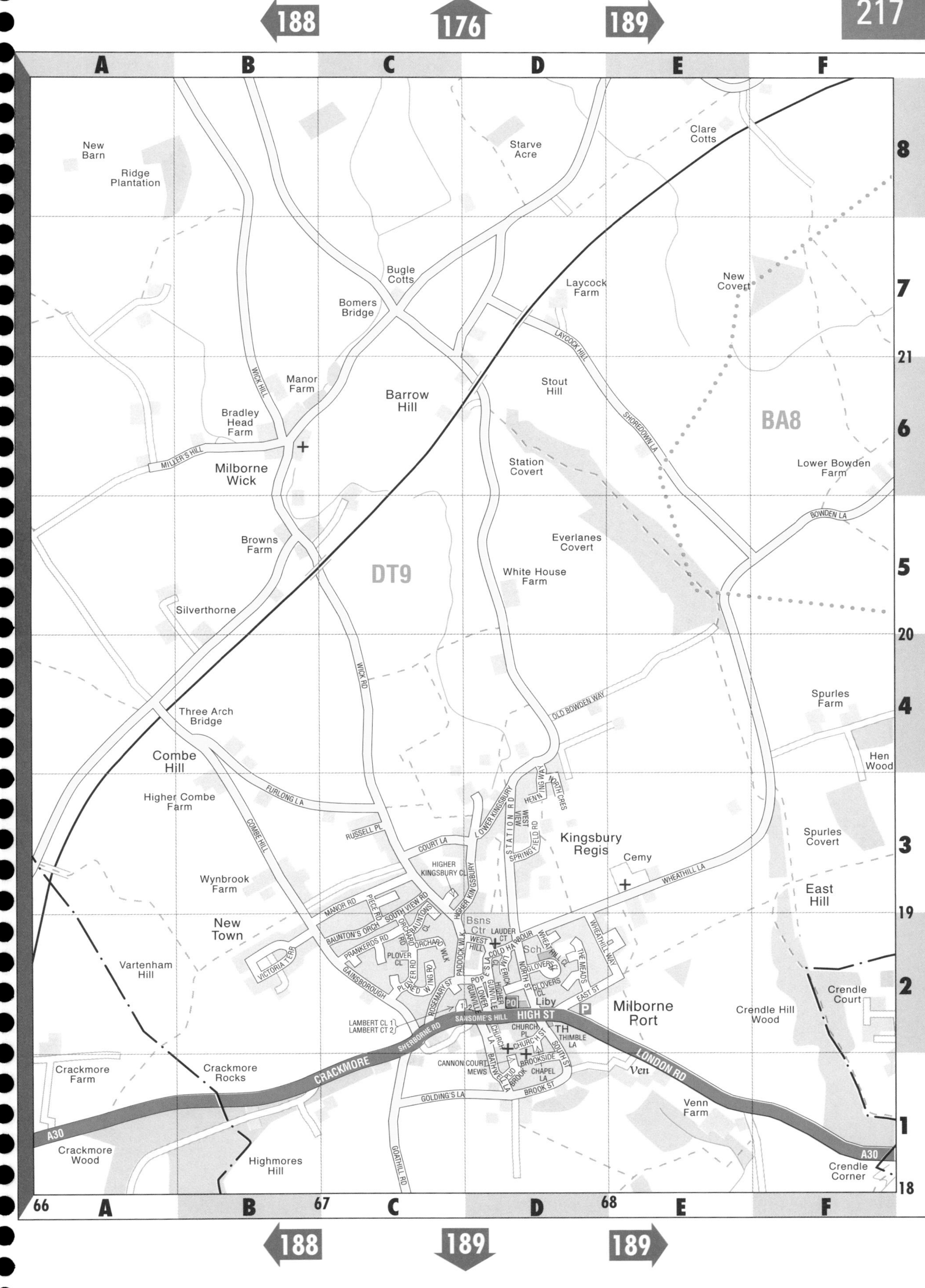
188
176
189
A
B
C
D
E
F
8
7
21
6
5
20
4
3
19
2
1
18
66
67
68
New Barn
Ridge Plantation
Starve Acre
Clare Cotts
Bugle Cotts
Bomers Bridge
Laycock Farm
New Covert
LAYCOCK HILL
WICK HILL
Manor Farm
Barrow Hill
Stout Hill
Bradley Head Farm
SHOREDOWN LA
BA8
MILLER'S HILL
Milborne Wick
Station Covert
Lower Bowden Farm
BOWDEN LA
Browns Farm
Everlanes Covert
DT9
White House Farm
Silverthorne
WICK RD
OLD BOWDEN WAY
Spurles Farm
Three Arch Bridge
Combe Hill
Hen Wood
FURLONG LA
Higher Combe Farm
LOWER KINGSBURY
STATION RD
WEST VIEW
SPRINGFIELD RD
NORTH CRES
RUSSELL PL
COURT LA
Kingsbury Regis
Spurles Covert
COMBE HILL
HIGHER KINGSBURY CL
HIGHER KINGSBURY
Cemy
WHEATHILL LA
Wynbrook Farm
East Hill
MANOR RD
PIECE RD
SOUTH VIEW RD
Bsns Ctr
LAUDER CT
New Town
BAUNTON'S ORCH
ORCHARD RD
BAUNTONS CL
ORCHARD WLK
PADDOCK WLK
WEST HILL
COLD HARBOUR
WHEATHILL CL
Sch
THE MEADS
WHEATHILL WAY
PRANKERDS RD
PLOVER CL
GLOVERS CL
Vartenham Hill
VICTORIA TERR
NORTH ST
GAINSBOROUGH
PLOVER RD
WING RD
ROSEMARY ST
POP
GUNVILLE LA
EAST ST
Crendle Court
PO
Liby
P
HIGH ST
Milborne Port
Crendle Hill Wood
LAMBERT CL 1
LAMBERT CT 2
SANSOME'S HILL
CHURCH PL
TH
THIMBLE LA
SHERBORNE RD
CHURCH LA
CHURCH ST
SOUTH ST
Crackmore Farm
Crackmore Rocks
CANNON COURT MEWS
BROOKSIDE
LONDON RD
CRACKMORE
BATHWELL LA
CHAPEL LA
Ven
BROOK ST
GOLDING'S LA
Venn Farm
A30
Crackmore Wood
Highmores Hill
GOATHILL RD
Crendle Corner

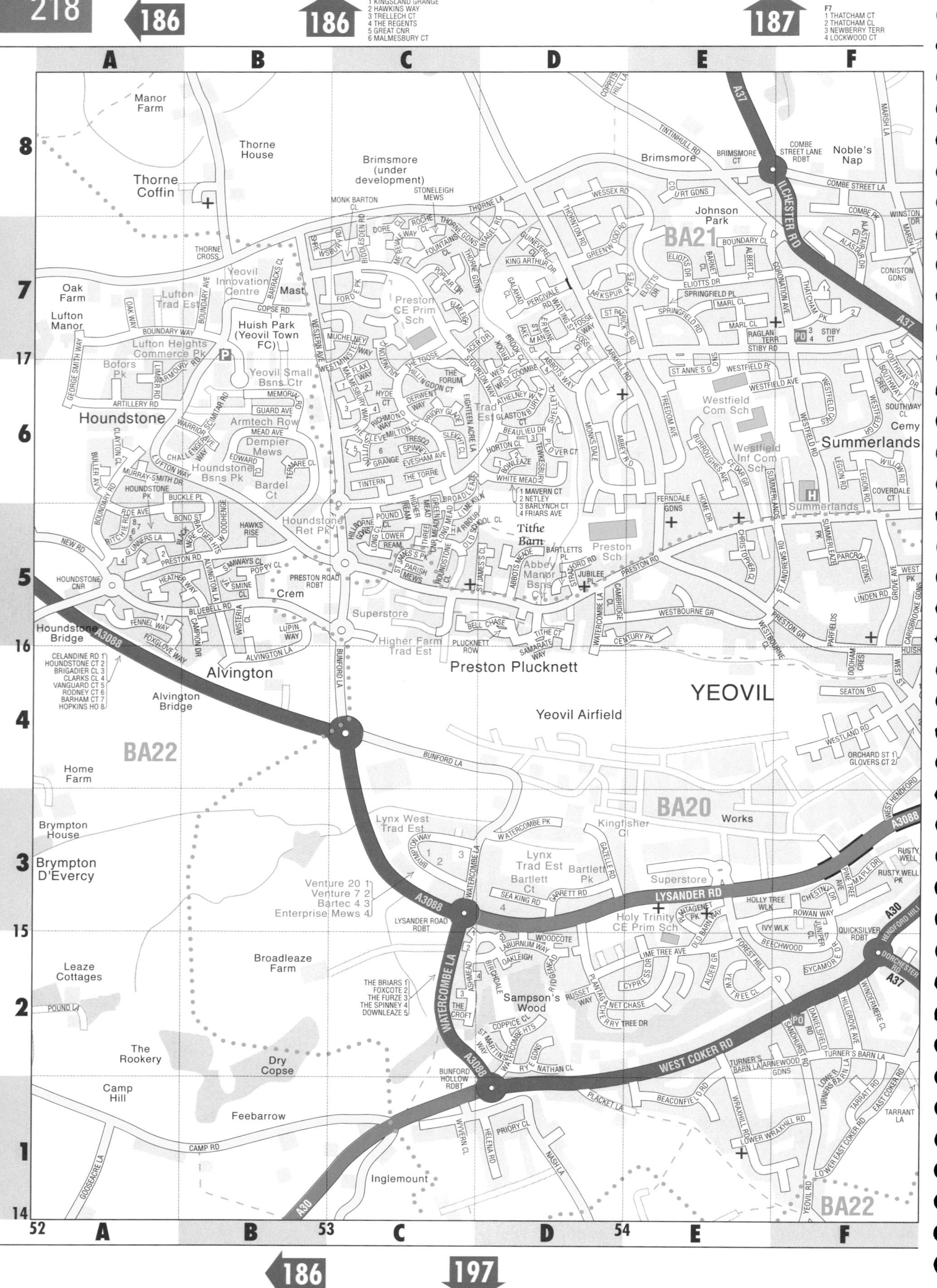

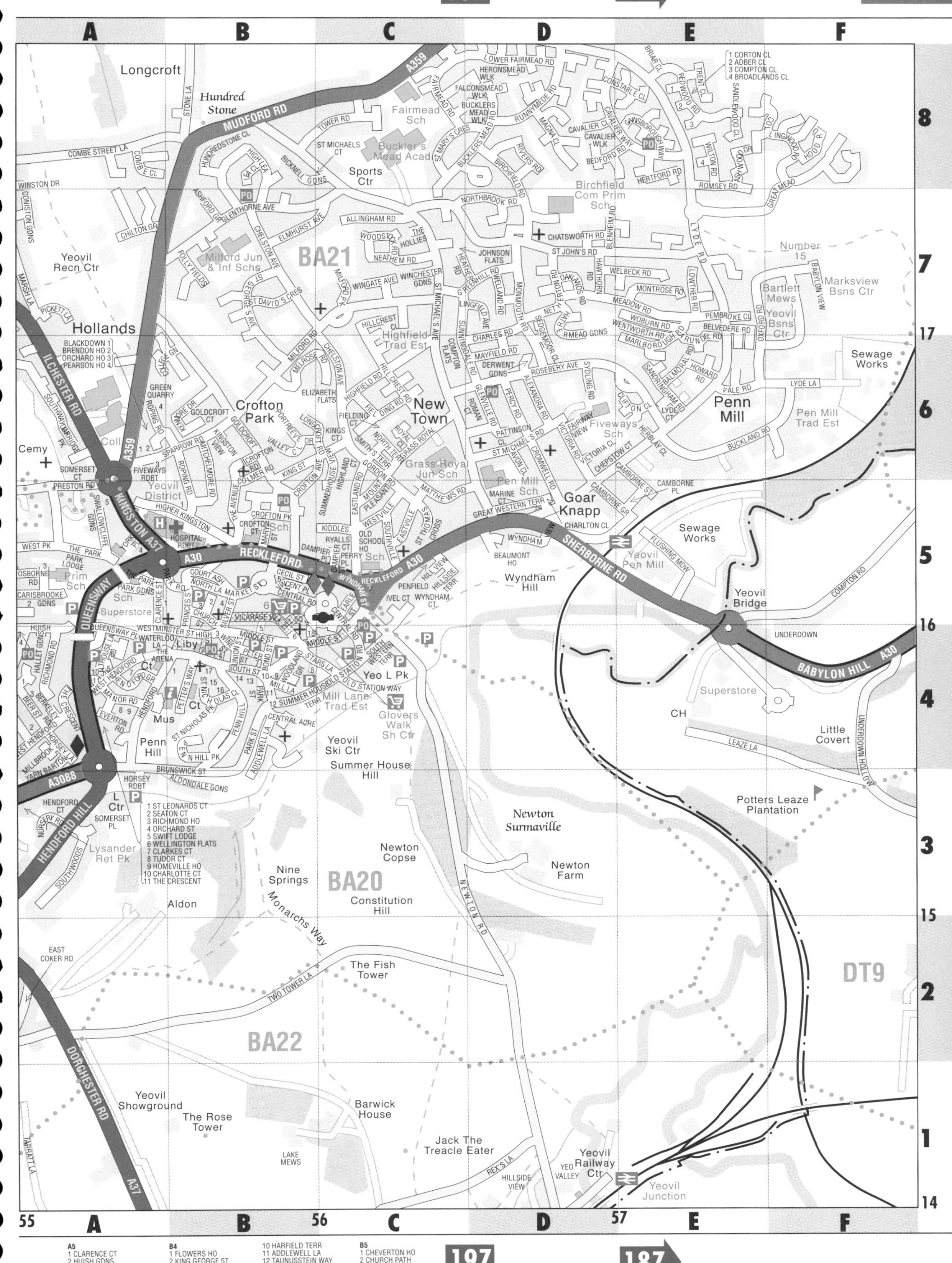

A5
1 CLARENCE CT
2 HUISH GDNS
3 SANDOWN CL
4 YORK LODGE
5 SWALLOWCLIFFE CT

B4
1 FLOWERS HO
2 KING GEORGE ST
3 THE BOROUGH
4 TABERNACLE LA
5 FREDRICK PL
6 VICARAGE ST
7 YEOVIL TRINITY FOYER
8 CLARENCE TERR
9 BROAD OAK
10 HARFIELD TERR
11 ADDLEWELL LA
12 TAUNUSSTEIN WAY
13 TRINITY CT
14 BELMONT HO
15 TOWNRISE
16 MARSH POTTINSON HO
17 PEGASUS CT
18 GLOVERS WLK

B5
1 CHEVERTON HO
2 CHURCH PATH
3 ST JOHNS HO
4 CHURCH TERR
5 VINCENT ST
6 QUEDAM SH CTR

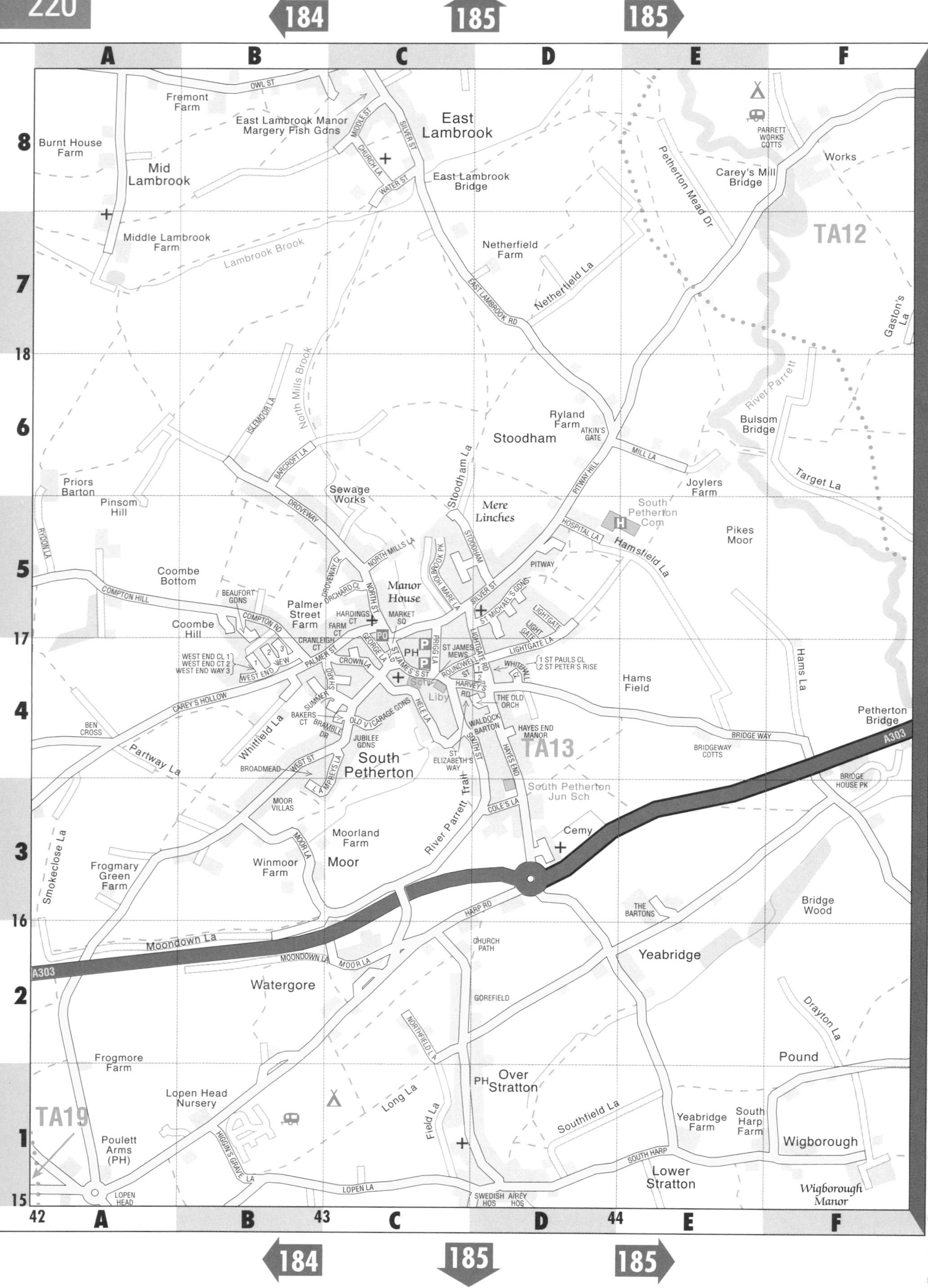
184
185
185
East Lambrook
Mid Lambrook
Burnt House Farm
Fremont Farm
East Lambrook Manor Margery Fish Gdns
East Lambrook Bridge
Middle Lambrook Farm
Lambrook Brook
Netherfield Farm
Netherfield La
Petherton Mead Dr
Carey's Mill Bridge
Works
TA12
Stoodham
Ryland Farm
Bulsom Bridge
Joylers Farm
Target La
Priors Barton
Pinsom Hill
Sewage Works
Mere Linches
South Petherton Com
Hamsfield La
Pikes Moor
Coombe Bottom
Coombe Hill
Palmer Street Farm
Manor House
Hams Field
Hams La
Petherton Bridge
South Petherton
TA13
Whitfield La
Partway La
South Petherton Jun Sch
River Parrett Trail
Moorland Farm
Moor
Winmoor Farm
Frogmary Green Farm
Smokeclose La
Cemy
Bridge Wood
Yeabridge
Moondown La
A303
Watergore
Frogmore Farm
Lopen Head Nursery
Poulett Arms (PH)
TA19
Long La
Field La
Over Stratton
Southfield La
Yeabridge Farm
South Harp Farm
Pound
Drayton La
Wigborough
Lower Stratton
Wigborough Manor
Gaston's La
River Parrett
Stoodham La
184
185
185

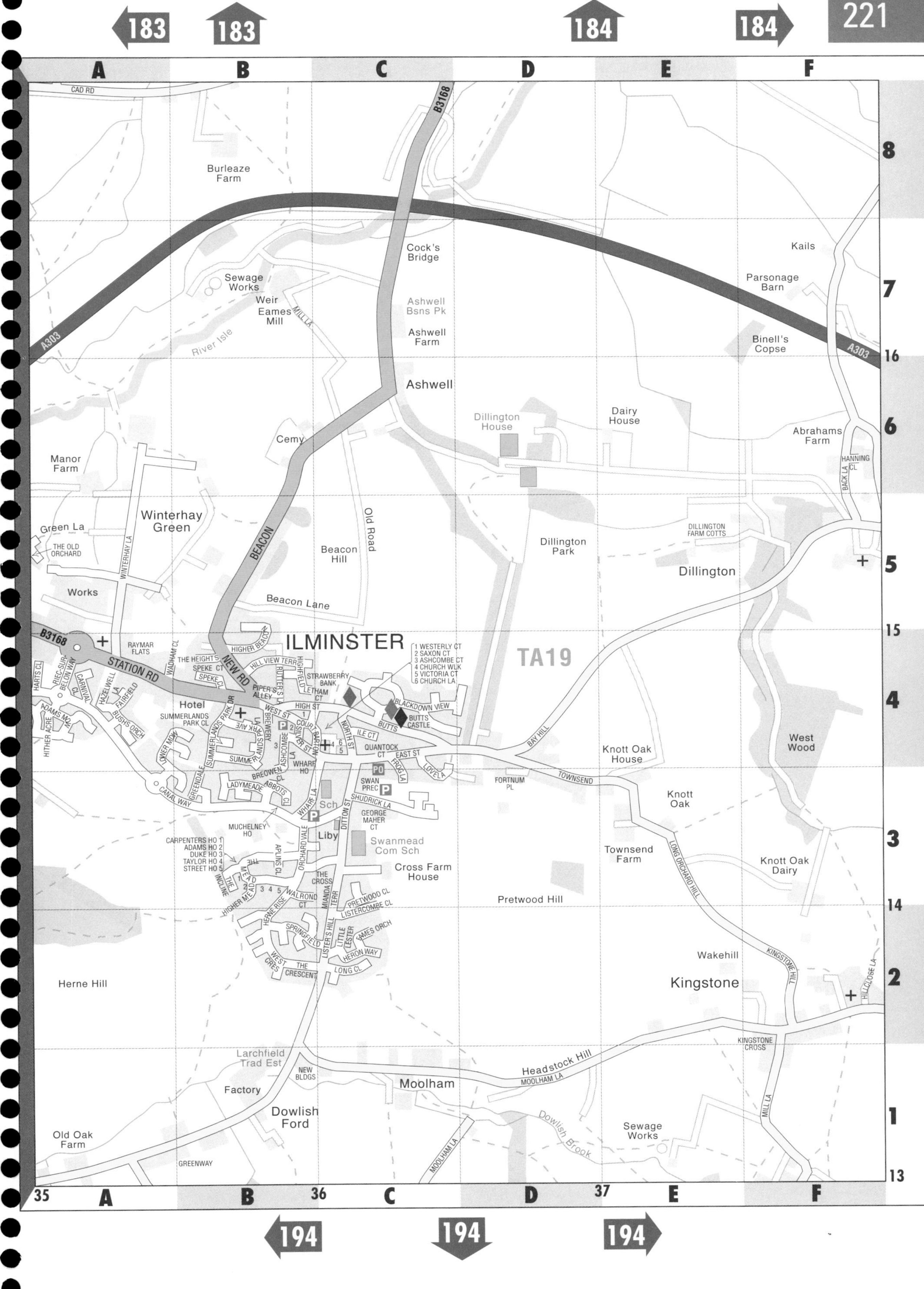

183 183 184 184

A B C D E F

8
7
16
6
15
5
4
3
14
2
1
13

CAD RD

Burleaze Farm

Sewage Works

Weir Eames Mill

River Isle

A303

B3168

Cock's Bridge

Ashwell Bsns Pk

Ashwell Farm

Ashwell

Kails

Parsonage Barn

Binell's Copse

A303

Dillington House

Dairy House

Abrahams Farm

HANNING CL

BACK LA

Manor Farm

Green La

THE OLD ORCHARD

Winterhay Green

WINTERHAY LA

Cemy

BEACON

Old Road

Beacon Hill

Dillington Park

Dillington

DILLINGTON FARM COTTS

Works

Beacon Lane

B3168

STATION RD

RAYMAR FLATS

WADHAM CL

HIGHER BEACON

HILL VIEW TERR

RUTTER'S LA

HIGHFIELD

PIPER'S ALLEY

THE HEIGHTS

SPEKE CT

SPEKE

NEW RD

ILMINSTER

STRAWBERRY BANK

LETHAM CT

1 WESTERLY CT
2 SAXON CT
3 ASHCOMBE CT
4 CHURCH WLK
5 VICTORIA CT
6 CHURCH LA

TA19

HARTS CL

REC GDN

BELOW WAY

CARNIVAL

HAZELWELL

FAIRFIELD

ADAMS MD

HITHER ACRE

BUSHS ORCH

LOWER MDW

GRENDALE

SUMMERLANDS

SUMMER

Hotel

SUMMERLANDS PARK CL

PARK AVE

PARK DR

BREWERY

WEST ST

COURT BARTON

ASHCOMBE

HIGH ST

NORTH ST

ILE CT

BUTTS

BLACKDOWN VIEW

Castle

QUANTOCK

EAST ST

FROG LA

LOVE LA

BAY HILL

TOWNSEND

Knott Oak House

West Wood

CANAL WAY

LADYMEAD

ABBOTS

WHARF LA

BREOWEN

DITTON ST

SWAN PREC

GEORGE MAHER CT

SHUDRICK LA

FORTNUM PL

Knott Oak

MUCHELNEY HO

Sch

Liby

Swanmead Com Sch

Cross Farm House

Pretwood Hill

Townsend Farm

LONG ORCHARD HILL

Knott Oak Dairy

CARPENTERS HO 1
ADAMS HO 2
DUKE HO 3
TAYLOR HO 4
STREET HO 5

APLINS CL

ORCHARDVALE

THE CROSS

MIRANDA

THE MEAD

HIGHER MILL

INCLINE

HERNE RISE

WALROND CT

LISTER'S HILL

LITTLE LESTER

PRETWOOD CL

LISTERCOMBE CL

JAMES ORCH

SPRINGFIELD

LESTER

HERON WAY

Wakehill

KINGSTONE HILL

CHILLYDONE LA

Herne Hill

WEST CRES

THE CRESCENT

LONG CL

Kingstone

Larchfield Trad Est

NEW BLDGS

Factory

Dowlish Ford

GREENWAY

Old Oak Farm

Moolham

MOOLHAM LA

Headstock Hill

MOOLHAM LA

Dowlish Brook

Sewage Works

KINGSTONE CROSS

MILL LA

194 194 194

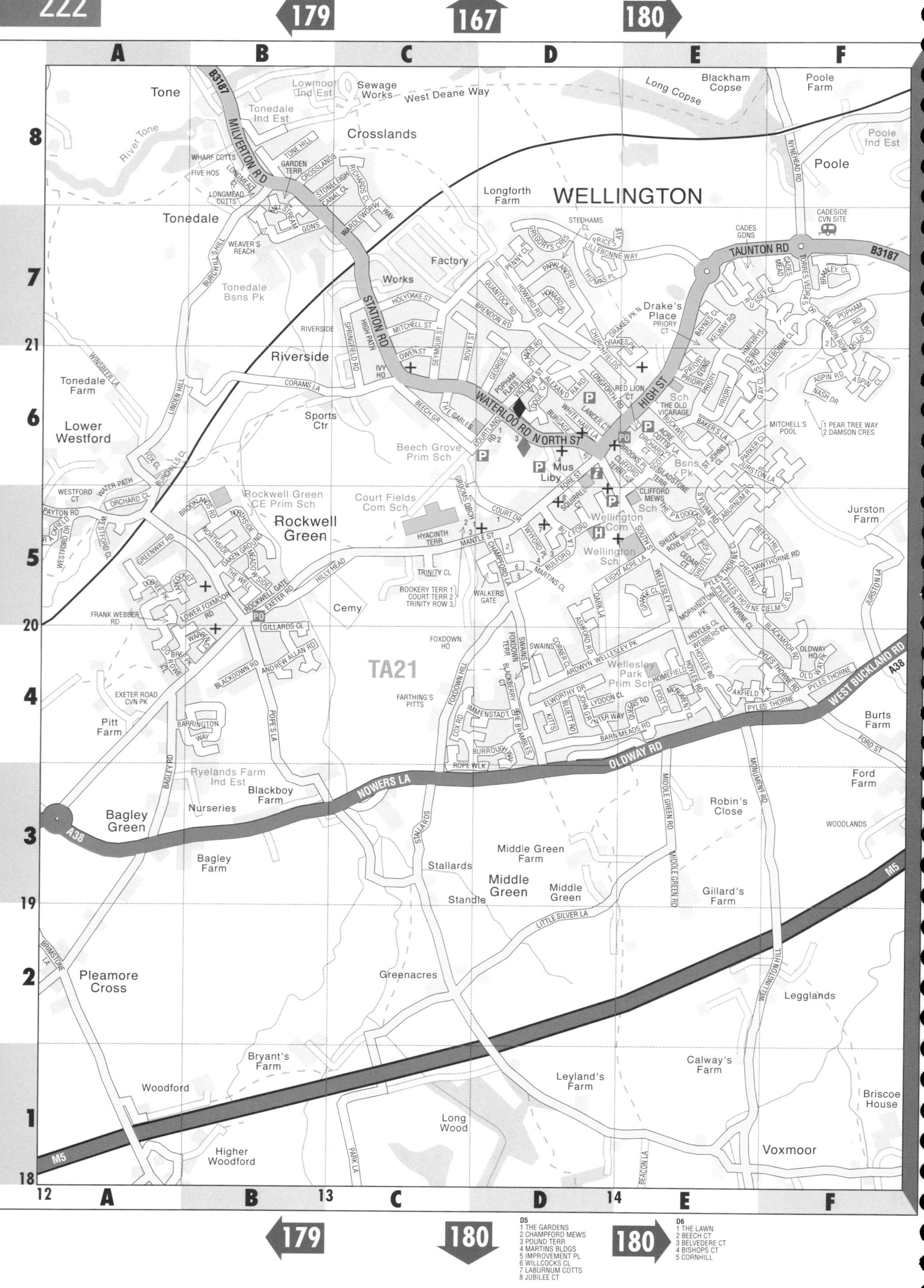

D5
1 THE GARDENS
2 CHAMPFORD MEWS
3 POUND TERR
4 MARTINS BLDGS
5 IMPROVEMENT PL
6 WILLCOCKS CL
7 LABURNUM COTTS
8 JUBILEE CT

D6
1 THE LAWN
2 BEECH CT
3 BELVEDERE CT
4 BISHOPS CT
5 CORNHILL

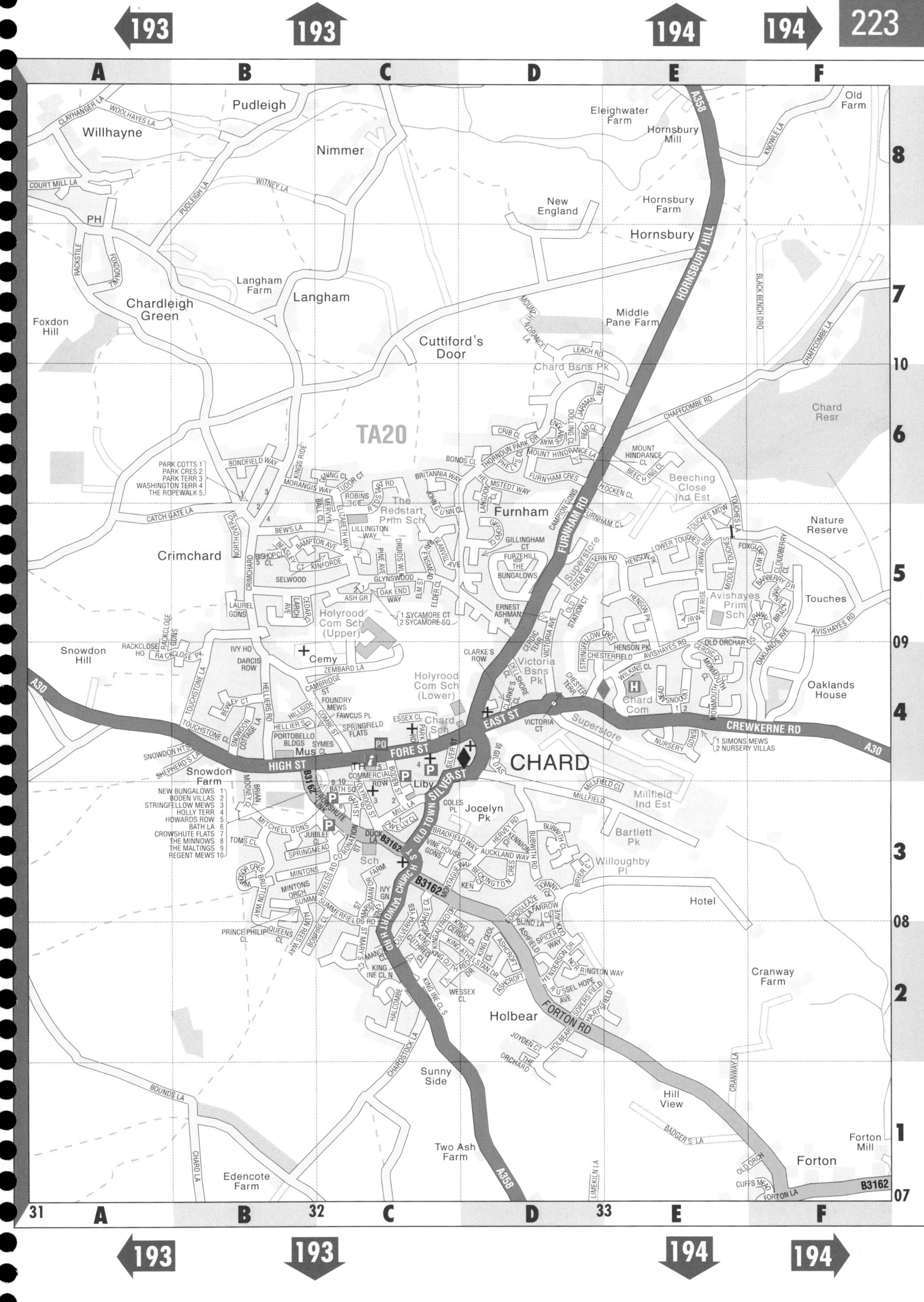

193
193
194
194
A
B
C
D
E
F
8
7
10
6
5
09
4
3
08
2
1
07
31
32
33
Pudleigh
Willhayne
Nimmer
CLAYHANGER LA
WOOLHAYES LA
COURT MILL LA
WITNEY LA
PUDLEIGH LA
PH
RACKSTILE
FOXDOWN
Chardleigh Green
Langham Farm
Langham
Foxdon Hill
Cuttiford's Door
Eleighwater Farm
Hornsbury Mill
Old Farm
KNOWLE LA
New England
Hornsbury Farm
Hornsbury
HORNSBURY HILL
A358
Middle Pane Farm
BLACK BENCH DRO
CHAFFCOMBE LA
MOUNT HINDRANCE LA
LEACH RD
Chard Bsns Pk
JARMAN WAY
Chard Resr
CHAFFCOMBE RD
TA20
PARK COTTS 1
PARK CRES 2
PARK TERR 3
WASHINGTON TERR 4
THE ROPEWALK 5
BONDFIELD WAY
KINGS RIDE
CATCH GATE LA
MORANGIS WAY
TUDOR CT
ROBINS CT
The Redstart Prim Sch
BRITANNIA WAY
BONDS CL
CRIB CL
THORNDUN PARK DR
MOUNT HINDRANCE CL
BEECH CL
Beeching Close Ind Est
HOCKEN CL
FURNHAM CRES
HELMSTEDT WAY
Furnham
FURNHAM RD
FURNHAM CL
TOUCHES LA
Nature Reserve
Crimchard
NORTHOVER
BEWS LA
BAMPTON AVE
LILLINGTON WAY
KINFORDE
SELWOOD
BISHOP CL
CRIMCHARD
GLYNSWOOD
PINE AVE
DRUIDS WAY
GLANVILL AVE
ELM ST
ELDER CL
GILLINGHAM CT
FURZEHILL
THE BUNGALOWS
Superstore
GREAT WESTERN RD
HENSON PK
LOWER TOUCHES
FAIRWAY RISE
MIDDLE TOUCHES
FOXGLOVE WAY
CLOUDBERRY
BARBERRY DR
Avishayes Prim Sch
Touches
AVISHAYES RD
OAKLANDS AVE
ASH GR
OAK END WAY
CEDAR CT
LARCH AVE
LAUREL GDNS
Holyrood Com Sch (Upper)
1 SYCAMORE CT
2 SYCAMORE SQ
ERNEST ASHMAN PL
OLD STATION CT
VICTORIA AVE
CERDIC TERR
Victoria Bsns Pk
STRINGFELLOW CRES
CHESTERFIELD
OLD ORCHARD
HENSON PK
WILKINS CL
MONMOUTH CT
Snowdon Hill
RACKCLOSE HO
RACKCLOSE PK
RACKCLOSE GDNS
IVY HO
DARCIS ROW
Cemy
ZEMBARD LA
CLARKE'S ROW
Holyrood Com Sch (Lower)
Chard Com
Oaklands House
A30
TOUCHSTONE LA
BEWLEY CT
HELLIERS RD
CAMBRIDGE ST
FOUNDRY MEWS
FAWCUS PL
SPRINGFIELD FLATS
HILLSIDE
COMBE ST
HELLIER'S CL
PORTOBELLO BLDGS
SYMES CL
ESSEX CL
PARK RD
Chard Sch
EAST ST
VICTORIA CT
Superstore
NURSERY GDNS
CREWKERNE RD
1 SIMONS MEWS
2 NURSERY VILLAS
TOUCHSTONE CL
SNOWDON COTTAGE LA
SNOWDON HTS
SHEPHERD'S LA
PO
Mus
FORE ST
HIGH ST
SILVER ST
CHARD
Snowdon Farm
TH
COMMERCIAL ROW
BATH SQ
BODEN ST
HOLYROOD ST
Liby
OLD TOWN
MILLFIELD CL
MILLFIELD
Millfield Ind Est
NEW BUNGALOWS 1
BODEN VILLAS 2
STRINGFELLOW MEWS 3
HOLLY TERR 4
HOWARDS ROW 5
BATH LA 6
CROWSHUTE FLATS 7
THE MINNOWS 8
THE MALTINGS 9
REGENT MEWS 10
B3162
CROWSHUTE LINK
MILL LA
COLES PL
Jocelyn Pk
HERVEY RD
KENNION CL
BUBWITH RD
Bartlett Pk
MITCHELL GDNS
TOMS CL
JUBILEE CL
SPRINGMEAD
CORONATION
DUCK LA
Sch
BRADFIELD WAY
VINE HOUSE GDNS
AUCKLAND WAY
MONTAGUE WAY
BECKINGTON CRES
Willoughby Pl
MINTONS
MINTONS ORCH
BRUTON WAY
SUMMERFIELDS RD
FARM
IVY GN
CHURCH ST
TATWORTH RD
KEN
LORDSLEAZE LA
FARROW CL
BLIND LA
Hotel
PRINCE PHILIP CL
QUEENS CL
ALLIN REES WAY
BONFIRE CL
ST MARY'S CL
CULVERHAYES
KINGFRED RD
KING CERDIC CL
KING ATHELSTAN DR
KING CEOL CL
ASHCROFT
ASHFIELD
SPICER WAY
HENDERSON DR
HARRINGTON WAY
RUSSEL HOPE AVE
SOPERS FIELD
HARTSFIELD
KING INE CL N
MANOR
WESSEX CL
KING INE CL S
Cranway Farm
HALCOMBE
Holbear
FORTON RD
JOYDEN CT
HOLBEAR
THE ORCHARD
CHARDSTOCK LA
Sunny Side
CRANWAY LA
Hill View
BOUNDS LA
BADGER'S LA
CHARD LA
Two Ash Farm
Forton Mill
Forton
Edencote Farm
LIMEKILN LA
OLD ORCH
CUFFS MEAD
FORTON LA
B3162

195 195 196 196

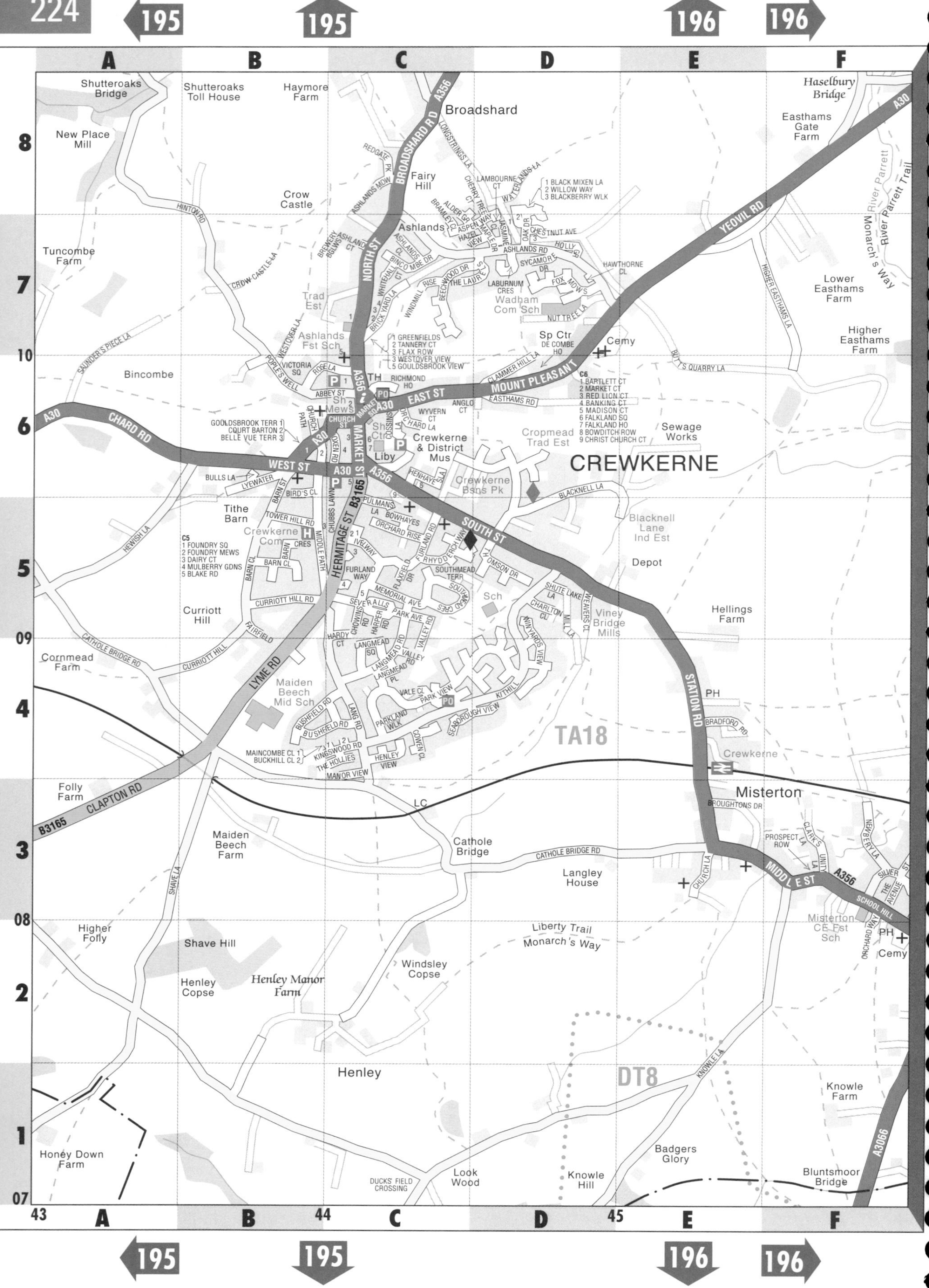

CREWKERNE
Broadshard
Fairy Hill
Ashlands
Crow Castle
Tuncombe Farm
New Place Mill
Shutteroaks Bridge
Shutteroaks Toll House
Haymore Farm
Haselbury Bridge
Easthams Gate Farm
Lower Easthams Farm
Higher Easthams Farm
Bincombe
Tithe Barn
Curriott Hill
Cornmead Farm
Maiden Beech Mid Sch
Folly Farm
Maiden Beech Farm
Cathole Bridge
Langley House
Misterton
Hellings Farm
Sewage Works
Blacknell Lane Ind Est
Depot
Viney Bridge Mills
Cropmead Trad Est
Crewkerne & District Mus
Crewkerne Bsns Pk
Wadham Com Sch
Ashlands Fst Sch
Trad Est
Crewkerne Com
TA18
DT8
Higher Folly
Shave Hill
Henley Copse
Henley Manor Farm
Windsley Copse
Henley
Liberty Trail
Monarch's Way
Knowle Farm
Badgers Glory
Knowle Hill
Look Wood
Honey Down Farm
Bluntsmoor Bridge
Ducks' Field Crossing
Misterton CE Fst Sch
River Parrett
River Parrett Trail
A30
A356
B3165
A3066
YEOVIL RD
CHARD RD
WEST ST
EAST ST
MOUNT PLEASANT
SOUTH ST
STATION RD
LYME RD
CLAPTON RD
MIDDLE ST
SCHOOL HILL
HERMITAGE ST
MARKET ST
NORTH ST
BROADSHARD RD
CATHOLE BRIDGE RD
BUTTS QUARRY LA
1 BLACK MIXEN LA
2 WILLOW WAY
3 BLACKBERRY WLK
1 GREENFIELDS
2 TANNERY CT
3 FLAX ROW
3 WESTOVER VIEW
5 GOULDSBROOK VIEW
C6
1 BARTLETT CT
2 MARKET CT
3 RED LION CT
4 BANKING CT
5 MADISON CT
6 FALKLAND SQ
7 FALKLAND HO
8 BOWDITCH ROW
9 CHRIST CHURCH CT
C5
1 FOUNDRY SQ
2 FOUNDRY MEWS
3 DAIRY CT
4 MULBERRY GDNS
5 BLAKE RD
GOULDSBROOK TERR 1
COURT BARTON 2
BELLE VUE TERR 3
MAINCOMBE CL 1
BUCKHILL CL 2
A B C D E F
8 7 6 5 4 3 2 1
10 09 08 07
43 44 45

195 195 196 196

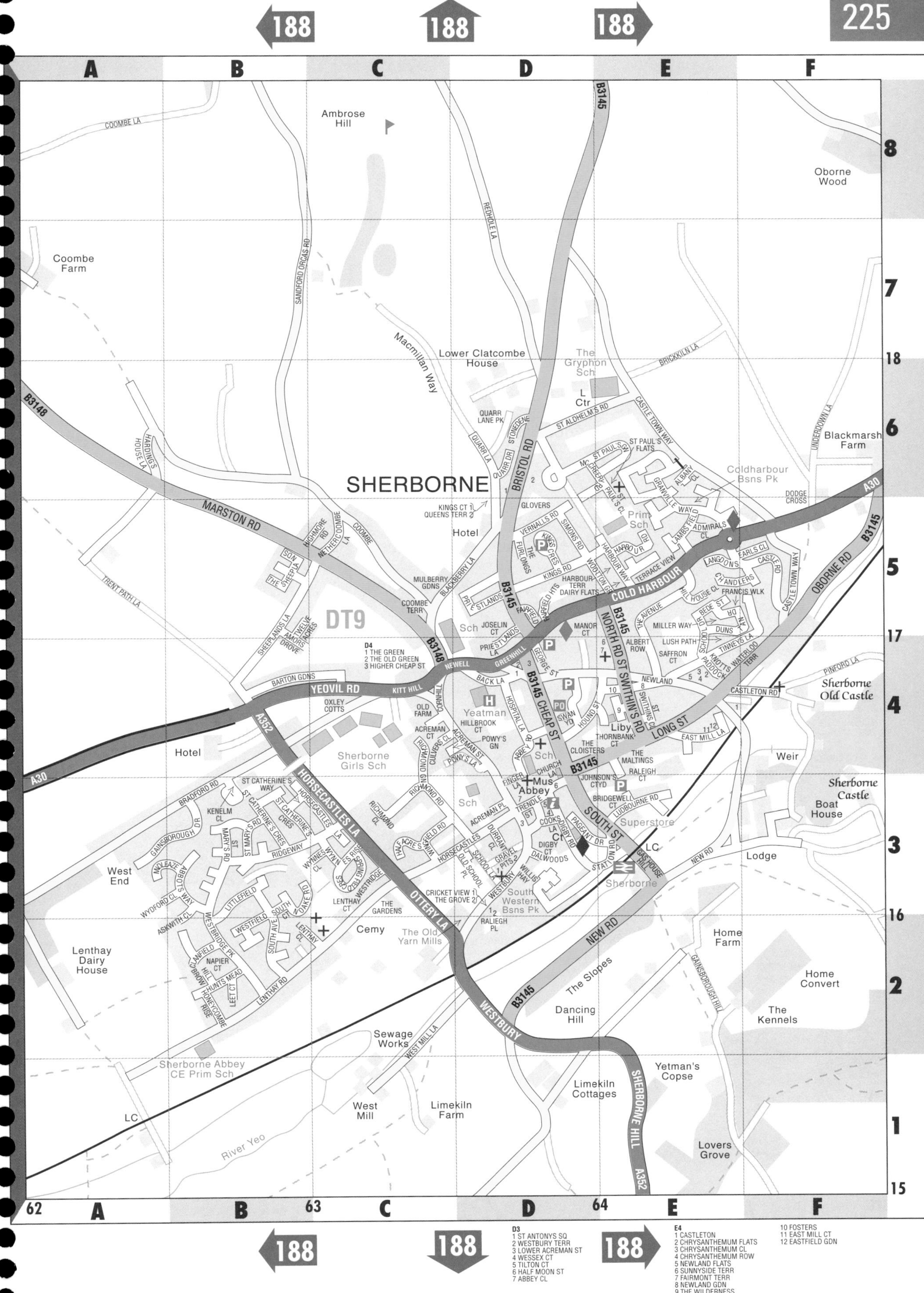

188
188
188

A   B   C   D   E   F

8

Oborne
Wood

Ambrose
Hill

COOMBE LA

Coombe
Farm

7

18

Lower Clatcombe
House

The
Gryphon
Sch

Macmillan Way

BRICKKILN LA

L
Ctr

6

B3148

Blackmarsh
Farm

HARDINGS
HOUSE LA

MARSTON RD

SHERBORNE

QUARR
LANE PK

ST ALDHELM'S RD

CASTLE TOWN WAY

St PAUL'S
FLATS

Coldharbour
Bsns Pk

DODGE
CROSS

A30

B3145

OBORNE RD

NETHER COOMBE
LA
COOMBE LA

QUARR LA

STONEGENE

ST PAUL'S RD

MC CREERY RD
ST PAUL'S

Prim
Sch

ADMIRALS
WK

UNDERDOWN LA

DT9

HIGHMORE
RD

KINGS CT 1
QUEENS TERR 2

GLOVERS

VERNALLS RD

GRANVILLE
WAY

AMBS YEL

EARLS CL

CASTLE TOWN WAY

5

Hotel

THE
SHEPPA

COOMBE
TERR

MULBERRY
GDNS

BLACKBERRY LA

KINGS RD

THE
FURLONGS

SIMONS RD

WORTTON RD

HARBOUR
WAY

HARBOUR
TERR
DAIRY FLATS

COLD HARBOUR

LANGDON'S

MILLER WAY

CHANDLEYS

HOUSE CL

FRANCIS WLK

AVENUE

DUNS

KNOTTS LA

TINNEYS LA

WATERLOO
TERR

17

TRENT PATH LA

SHEEPLANDS LA

SOM
PL

TWELVE
ACRES
DROVE

B3148

ST LANDS

PRIESTLANDS
LA

FAIRFIELD

NEWELL

GREENHILL

Sch

JOSELIN
CT

GEORGE'S RD

MANOR
CT

NORTH RD

ALBERT
ROW

NEWLAND

ST
SWITHIN'S

SAFFRON
CT

LUSH PATH

PADDOCK

WATERLOO

CASTLETON RD

PINFORD LA

Sherborne
Old Castle

4

BARTON GDNS

YEOVIL RD

KITT HILL

OXLEY
COTTS

OLD
FARM

BACK LA

H
Yeatman

HILLBROOK
CT

POWY'S
GN

HOSPITAL LA

B3145 CHEAP ST

SWAN

PO

Liby

10

NEWLAND

ST
SWITHIN'S RD

LONG ST

EAST MILL LA

1½

A352

A30

Hotel

Sherborne
Girls Sch

ACREMAN
CT

CULVERS CL

RICHMOND RD

ACREMAN ST

POWY'S LA

Sch

ST
SWITHIN'S

THORNBANK

THE
CLOISTERS

THE
MALTINGS

RALEIGH

JOHNSON'S
CTYD

Sherborne
Castle
Boat
House

Weir

3

West
End

BRADFORD RD

ST CATHERINE'S
WAY

KENELM
CL

ST MARY'S RD

ST CATHERINE'S
CRES

ST CATHERINE'S

RIDGEWAY

HORSECASTLES LA

RICHMOND
RD

FIELD RD

HORSECASTLES

OLD SCHOOL LA

GRAVEL
PITS

DURRANT RD

FINGER
LA

Mus
Abbey

ACREMAN PL

TRENDLE ST

COOKS
LA

DALWOODS

BRIDGEWELL

LUDBOURNE RD

SOUTH ST

B3145

PAGEANT DR

Superstore

LC

NEW RD

Lodge

16

GAINSBOROUGH RD

MOLEAZE

ABBOTS CL

LITTLEFIELD

WYNNE'S
CL

WYNNE'S
RISE

SPRING
RD

WESTRIDGE

WESTBRIDGE PK

Sherborne
Girls Sch

THE
GARDENS

CRICKET VIEW 1
THE GROVE 2

WESTBURY
RD

South
Western
Bsns Pk

RALEIGH
PL

St
Sherborne

NEW RD

Home
Farm

2

Lenthay
Dairy
House

WYDFORD CT

WESTFIELD

KIM RD

SOUTH AVE

DYKE RD

LENTHAY
CT

LENTHAY RD

Cemy

The Old
Yarn Mills

OTTERY LA

WESTBURY

B3145

The Slopes

Dancing
Hill

GAINSBOROUGH HILL

Home
Convert

The
Kennels

ASKWITH RD

CANFIELD

NAPIER
CT

HUNTS MEAD

LEFT CT

BROOK CL

HONEYCOMBE
RISE

Sewage
Works

WEST MILL LA

WEST MILL LA

Limekiln
Cottages

SHERBORNE HILL

Yetman's
Copse

1

15

LC

Sherborne Abbey
CE Prim Sch

West
Mill

Limekiln
Farm

A352

Lovers
Grove

River Yeo

62   A   B   63   C   D   64   E   F

188
188
188

D4
1 THE GREEN
2 THE OLD GREEN
3 HIGHER CHEAP ST

D3
1 ST ANTONYS SQ
2 WESTBURY TERR
3 LOWER ACREMAN ST
4 WESSEX CT
5 TILTON CT
6 HALF MOON ST
7 ABBEY CL

E4
1 CASTLETON
2 CHRYSANTHEMUM FLATS
3 CHRYSANTHEMUM CL
4 CHRYSANTHEMUM ROW
5 NEWLAND FLATS
6 SUNNYSIDE TERR
7 FAIRMONT TERR
8 NEWLAND GDN
9 THE WILDERNESS

10 FOSTERS
11 EAST MILL CT
12 EASTFIELD GDN

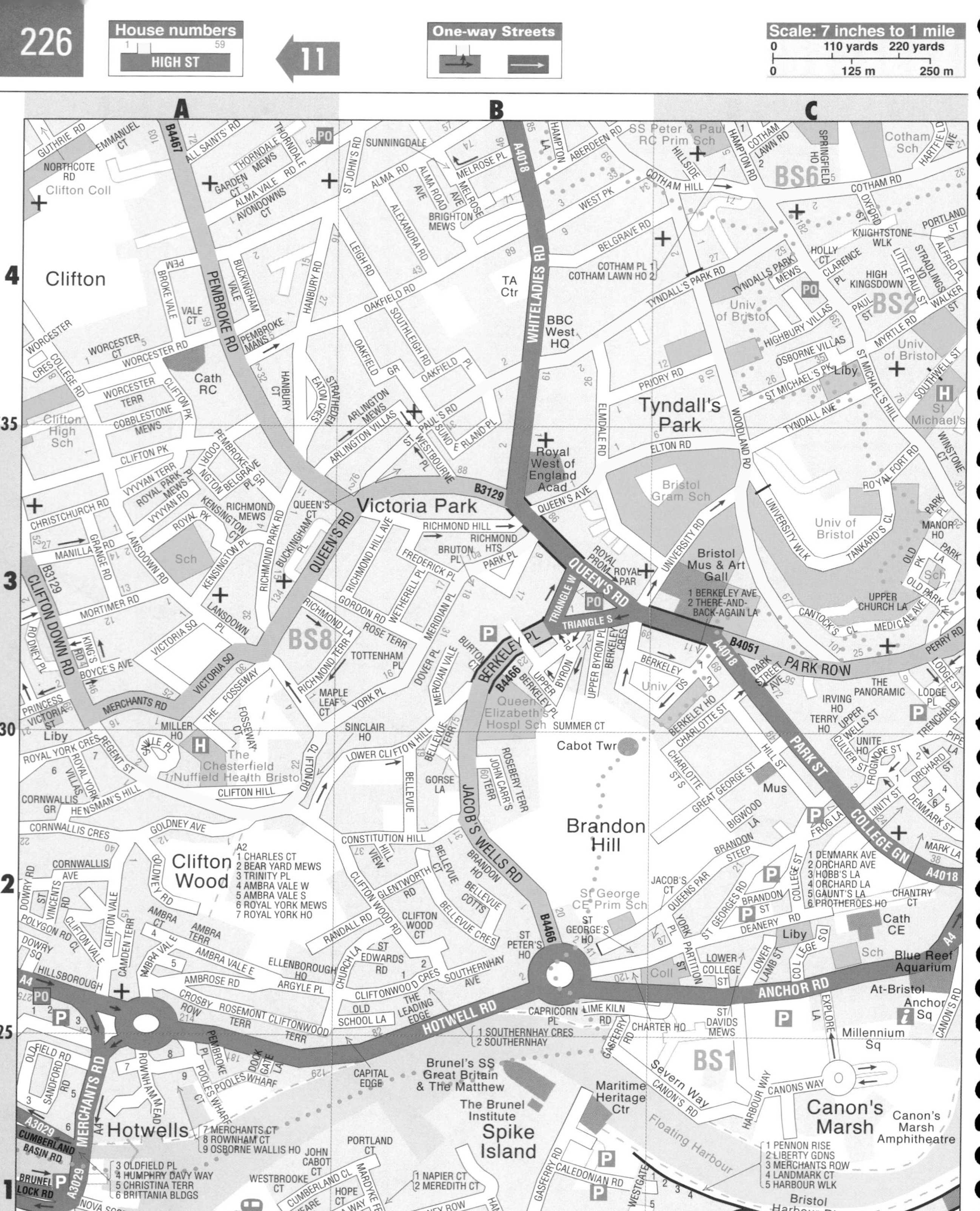

One-way Streets

A   B   C

4   Clifton

735

3

Victoria Park

Tyndall's Park

BS6

BS2

H
St Michael's

BS8

730

The Chesterfield
Nuffield Health Bristol

Cabot Twr

Brandon Hill

2   Clifton Wood

BS1

725   Hotwells

Canon's Marsh

Spike Island

1   BRUNEL LOCK RD

720

570   A   575   B   580   C

11

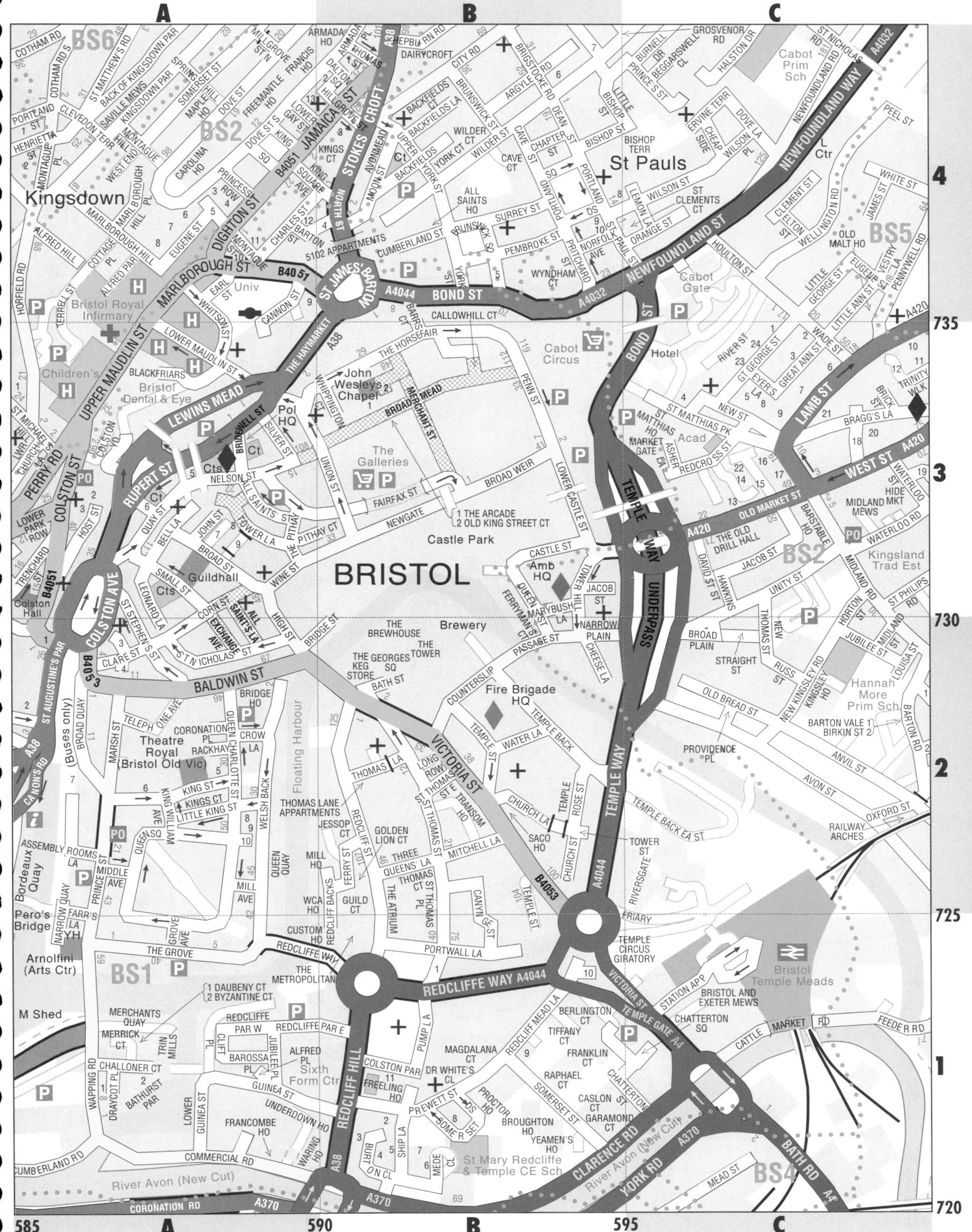

A3
1 COLSTON'S ALMSHOUSES
2 CHRISTMAS STEPS
3 FOSTER'S ALMSHOUSES
4 ST JOHN'S BRIDGE
5 NELSON HO

6 CHRISTMAS ST
7 TAILOR'S CT
8 FITZHARDING HO
9 NEWMARKET AVE

One-way streets

B4
1 HENDERSON HO
2 PHILIPS HO
3 RON JONES HO
4 CHERRY LA
5 GLOUCESTER ST

House numbers
1 ——— 59
HIGH ST

B4
6 CHESTERTON HO
7 BRIGHTON ST
8 PORTLAND LOFTS
9 PORTLAND MANS
10 NORFOLK HTS

A2
1 ST AUGUSTINE'S PL
2 HANOVER ST
3 ST STEPHEN'S AVE
4 MARSH ST
5 ST NICHOLAS ALMSHOUSES
6 MERCHANTS ALMSHOUSES
7 KING GEORGE V PL

8 THE GRANARY
9 THE GRAIN STORE
10 QUEEN SQUARE AVE
A4
1 KNIGHTSTONE HO
2 COLSTON FORT
3 DIGHTON CT
4 MONTAGUE CT

5 MONTAGUE HILL S
6 MONTAGUE FLATS
7 EUGENE FLATS
8 MARLBOROUGH FLATS
9 HAYMARKET WLK
10 BLENHEIM CT
11 HAMILTON CT
12 CHERRY CT

13 HATHAWAY HO
B1
1 PHIPPEN ST
2 CANYNGE HO
3 PLIMSOLL HO
4 ASTON HO
5 CHATTERTON HO
6 SPENCER HO

7 NORTON HO
8 PATTERSON HO
9 CORINTHIAN CT
10 PORTWALL LA E
11 FRYS HOUSE OF MERCY
C3
1 WHITSON HO
2 ELTON HO

3 ELBRIDGE HO
4 NEW STREET FLATS
5 JOHN COZENS HO
6 HAVILAND HO
7 CHARLETON HO
8 LANGTON HO
9 ALBION PL
10 WESSEX HO

11 GLOUCESTER HO
12 SOMERSET HO
13 STEEVENS HO (ALMSHOUSES)
14 REDCROSS MEWS
15 TRINITY NEWS
16 ALBION PL
17 LAWFORDS GATE HO
18 GLOUCESTER LA

19 WATERLOO PL
20 THE OLD TANNERY
21 ST JUDES HO
22 PERRETT HO
23 ROPE WALK HO
24 FIELD MARSHAL SLIM CT

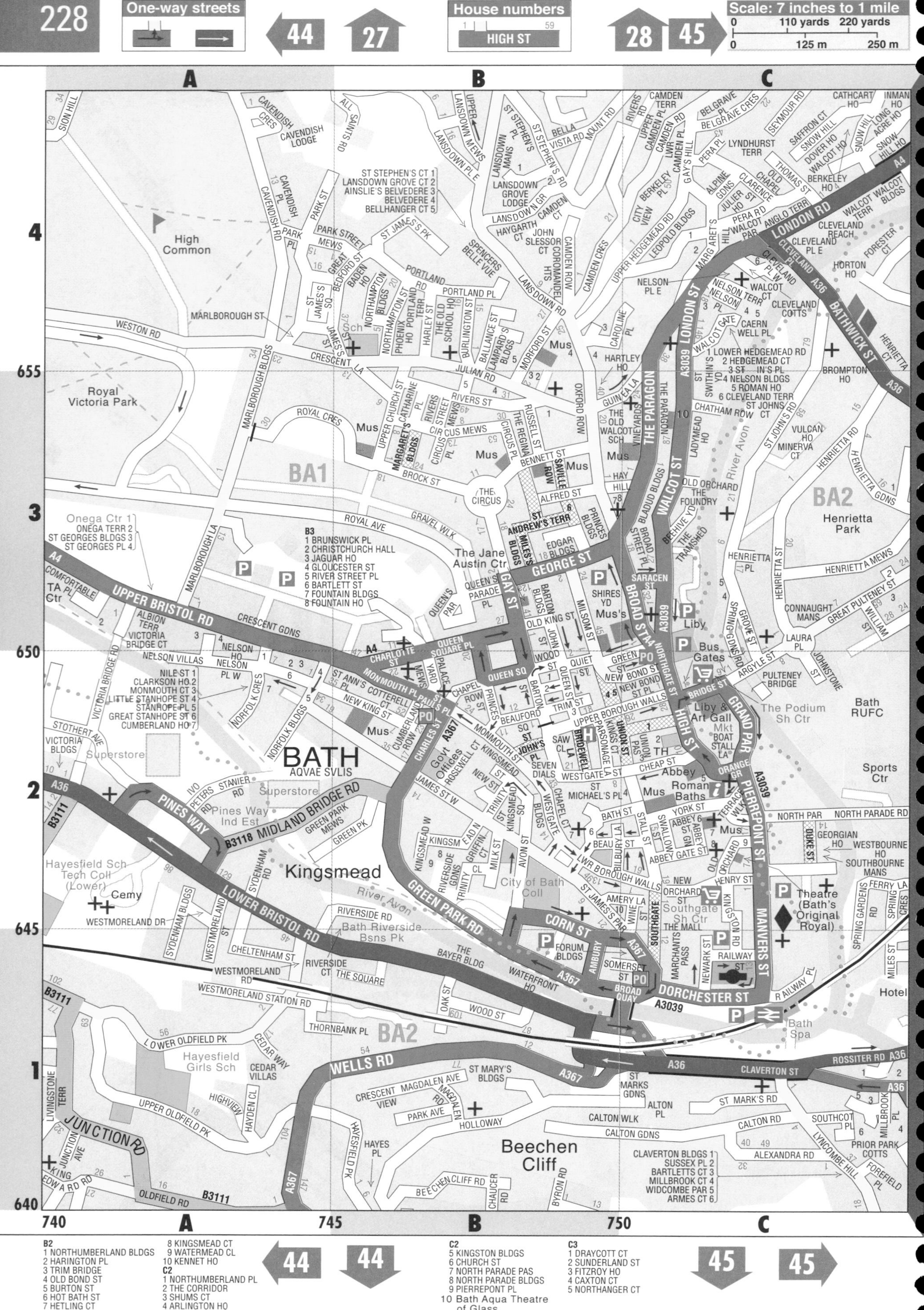

Place name May be abbreviated on the map → **Church Rd** [6] Beckenham BR2..........**53** C6

Location number Present when a number indicates the place's position in a crowded area of mapping

Locality, town or village Shown when more than one place has the same name

Postcode district District for the indexed place

Page and grid square Page number and grid reference for the standard mapping

Cities, towns and villages are listed in CAPITAL LETTERS

Public and commercial buildings are highlighted in magenta **Places of interest** are highlighted in blue with a star★

Abbreviations used in the index

Acad	**Academy**	Comm	**Common**	Gd	**Ground**	L	**Leisure**	Prom	**Promenade**
App	**Approach**	Cott	**Cottage**	Gdn	**Garden**	La	**Lane**	Rd	**Road**
Arc	**Arcade**	Cres	**Crescent**	Gn	**Green**	Liby	**Library**	Recn	**Recreation**
Ave	**Avenue**	Cswy	**Causeway**	Gr	**Grove**	Mdw	**Meadow**	Ret	**Retail**
Bglw	**Bungalow**	Ct	**Court**	H	**Hall**	Meml	**Memorial**	Sh	**Shopping**
Bldg	**Building**	Ctr	**Centre**	Ho	**House**	Mkt	**Market**	Sq	**Square**
Bsns, Bus	**Business**	Ctry	**Country**	Hospl	**Hospital**	Mus	**Museum**	St	**Street**
Bvd	**Boulevard**	Cty	**County**	HQ	**Headquarters**	Orch	**Orchard**	Sta	**Station**
Cath	**Cathedral**	Dr	**Drive**	Hts	**Heights**	Pal	**Palace**	Terr	**Terrace**
Cir	**Circus**	Dro	**Drove**	Ind	**Industrial**	Par	**Parade**	TH	**Town Hall**
Cl	**Close**	Ed	**Education**	Inst	**Institute**	Pas	**Passage**	Univ	**University**
Cnr	**Corner**	Emb	**Embankment**	Int	**International**	Pk	**Park**	Wk, Wlk	**Walk**
Coll	**College**	Est	**Estate**	Intc	**Interchange**	Pl	**Place**	Wr	**Water**
Com	**Community**	Ex	**Exhibition**	Junc	**Junction**	Prec	**Precinct**	Yd	**Yard**

Index of towns, villages, streets, hospitals, industrial estates, railway stations, schools, shopping centres, universities and places of interest

5102 Apartments BS1 . . . **227** B4

A

ABBAS COMBE **176** E1
Abbas & Templecombe CE Prim Sch BA8 . . . . **176** E1
Abbey Cl
Curry Rivel TA10 . . . . **171** D4
Keynsham BS31 . . . . **24** F6
[7] Sherborne DT9 . . . . **225** D3
Tatworth TA20 . . . . **198** D8
Wookey BA5 . . . . **139** D8
Abbey Ct [6] BA2 . . . . **45** B7
Abbey Fields TA10 . . . . . . **171** D4
Abbey Gate BS9 . . . . **5** E5
Abbey Gate St BA1 . . . . . . **228** C2
Abbey Gdns BS22 . . . . **49** E8
Abbey Gn BA1 . . . . **228** C2
ABBEY HILL **182** E5
Abbey Hill Dro TA3 . . . . . . **182** E5
Abbey La BA3 . . . . **64** A4
Abbey Lodge BA6 . . . . **206** E4
Abbey Manor Bsns Ctr BA21 . . . . **218** D5
Abbey Meads BA6 . . . . **206** E3
Abbey Mews TA20 . . . . **198** D8
Abbey Pk BS31 . . . . **24** F6
Abbey Rd
Bristol BS9 . . . . **5** F7
Chilcompton BA3 . . . . **96** D2
Sherborne DT9 . . . . **225** D4
Stratton-on-t F BA3 . . . . **96** F2
Washford TA23 . . . . **131** E3
Yeovil BA21 . . . . **218** D6
Abbey St
Bath BA1 . . . . **228** C2
Crewkerne TA18 . . . . **224** C6
Hinton St George TA17 . . . . **195** C7
Abbey Trad Est BA21 . . . . **218** D6
Abbey View
Bath BA2 . . . . **45** B5
Radstock BA3 . . . . **79** A3
Abbey View Gdns BA2 . . . . **45** B5
Abbeywood Dr BS9 . . . . **5** C5
Abbotsbury Rd BS48 . . . . . . **8** D1
Abbots Cl
Bristol BS14 . . . . **23** A3
Burnham-on-S TA8 . . . . **104** B6
Ilminster TA19 . . . . **221** B3
Oxenpill BA6 . . . . **138** C4
Abbots Cl *continued*
Seavington St Michael TA19 . . . . **184** E2
Abbot's Cl BS22 . . . . **32** A3
Abbots Ct BA6 . . . . **206** D4
Abbotsfield TA4 . . . . **210** A4
Abbotsfield Cotts TA4 . . . **210** B4
Abbots Fish House★ BA6 . . . . **138** D4
Abbots Horn BS48 . . . . **8** D2
ABBOTS LEIGH **11** A8
Abbots Leigh Rd BS8 . . . . . **11** C7
Abbots Meade BA21 . . . . . **218** D5
Abbots Way
Minehead TA24 . . . . **200** C6
Pilton BA4 . . . . **140** E3
Sherborne DT9 . . . . **225** B3
Yeovil BA21 . . . . **218** D6
Abbott La TA16 . . . . **196** A8
Abbotts Farm Cl BS39 . . . . **77** D5
Abbotts Rd BA22 . . . . **173** D1
Abbotts Way TA3 . . . . **183** F7
Abbott's Wootton La DT6 . . . . **199** B1
Abels La DT9 . . . . **187** F5
Aberdeen Rd BS6 . . . . **226** B4
Abingdon Gdns BA2 . . . . . . **62** D8
Abingdon St TA8 . . . . **104** B6
Abington Cross TA24 . . . . . **124** B4
Ablake La TA10 . . . . **172** C5
Ableton Wlk BS9 . . . . **5** C5
Abon Ho BS9 . . . . **5** C4
Acacia Ave BS23 . . . . **49** B8
Acacia Ct BS31 . . . . **24** C4
Acacia Dr BA11 . . . . **120** C7
Acacia Gdns TA2 . . . . **213** E7
Acacia Gr BA2 . . . . **44** C3
Acacia Rd BA3 . . . . **78** E1
Academy of Trinity BA3 . . . **79** A4
Accommodation Rd BS24 . **66** E6
Acer Dr BA21 . . . . **218** C7
Acer Village BS14 . . . . **23** C7
Achilles Path BS23 . . . . **49** B4
Ackland's Dro TA10 . . . . . **155** F4
Acland Round TA4 . . . . . . **167** E6
Acombe Cross TA3 . . . . . . **191** E8
Aconite Cl BS22 . . . . **32** B5
Acorn Cl
Frome BA11 . . . . **119** D5
Highbridge TA9 . . . . **104** D4
Acorn Gr BS13 . . . . **21** E6
Acre Cotts TA21 . . . . **222** E6
Acre La TA11 . . . . **211** F4
Acreman Ct DT9 . . . . **225** C4
Acreman Pl DT9 . . . . **225** D3
Acreman St DT9 . . . . **225** D4
Acresbush Cl BS13 . . . . **22** A5
Acres Ct BA22 . . . . **197** F8
Acres The [1] TA12 . . . . . . **185** E6
Acretree Cl TA6 . . . . **208** E3
Actis Rd BA6 . . . . **206** E3
Adams Cl
Highbridge TA9 . . . . **104** C2
Peasedown St John BA2 . . . **79** D8
Adams Ct [5] BS8 . . . . **11** F6
ADAM'S GREEN **197** D2
Adams Ho TA19 . . . . **221** B3
Adam's La TA5 . . . . **134** D6
Adams Mdw TA19 . . . . **221** A4
Adam St TA8 . . . . **104** B6
Adastral Rd BS24 . . . . **50** D4
ADBER **187** F7
Adber Cl BA21 . . . . **219** E8
Adber Cross DT9 . . . . **187** F6
Adcombe Cl TA3 . . . . **181** D5
Adcombe Rd TA2 . . . . **213** B8
Adder La TA7 . . . . **169** F8
ADDERWELL **120** A3
Adderwell BA11 . . . . **120** A3
Adderwell Cl BA11 . . . . . . **120** A3
Addicott Rd BS23 . . . . **48** E6
Addiscombe Rd
Bristol BS14 . . . . **23** B5
Weston-super-Mare BS23 . . **48** E4
Addison Gr TA2 . . . . **212** E6
Addlewell La [11] BA20 . . . **219** B4
Adlams Central Pk BA6 . **206** B3
Admirals Cl
Sherborne DT9 . . . . **225** E5
Watchet TA23 . . . . **202** D6
Admirals Ct TA6 . . . . **208** F5
Admiral's Mead BA6 . . . . . **157** E4
Admiral's Wlk BS20 . . . . **2** B5
Admiralty Way TA1 . . . . . . **213** C5
ADSBOROUGH **169** D8
Adsborough Hill TA2 . . . . . **169** D7
Adsborough La TA2 . . . . . . **169** D7
ADSCOMBE **152** A8
Adscombe Ave TA6 . . . . . . **209** C6
Adscombe La TA5 . . . . **134** A1
Aelfric Mdw BS20 . . . . **2** F4
Ainslie's Belvedere BA1 . . **228** B4
Ainstey Dr BA22 . . . . **175** A4
Airey Hos TA13 . . . . **220** D1
Airport Rd BS14 . . . . **23** A8
Airport Rdbt BS24 . . . . **49** E7
Airport View Cvn Pk BS24 **49** D7
Aisecome Way BS22 . . . . . . **49** C6
AISHOLT **152** B6
Akeman Cl BA21 . . . . **218** D7
Akeman Way BS11 . . . . **4** C8
Alamein Rd TA23 . . . . **202** E6
Alard Rd BS4 . . . . **22** F7
Alastair Cl BA21 . . . . **218** F7
Alastair Dr BA21 . . . . **218** F7
Albany BS23 . . . . **30** F1
Albany Cl DT9 . . . . **225** E6
Albany Ct [6] BA1 . . . . **44** B6
Albany Rd BA2 . . . . **44** C6
Albemarle Rd TA1 . . . . **212** F5
Albermarle Row [9] BS8 . . . **11** F6
Albert Ave
Peasedown St John BA2 . . . **79** C7
Weston-super-Mare BS23 . . **48** E6
Albert Bldgs BA6 . . . . **206** D5
Albert Cl BA21 . . . . **218** E7
Albert Ct
Bridgwater TA6 . . . . **208** E4
[15] Taunton TA1 . . . . **213** A4
Weston-super-Mare BS23 . . **48** E6
Albert Pl
Bath BA2 . . . . **45** C1
Portishead BS20 . . . . **2** D4
Albert Quadrant BS23 . . . . . **48** E8
Albert Rd
Clevedon BS21 . . . . **6** C3
Keynsham BS31 . . . . **24** E5
Portishead BS20 . . . . **2** D5
Weston-super-Mare BS23 . . **48** E6
Albert Row DT9 . . . . **225** E4
Albert St TA6 . . . . **208** E4
Albert Terr BA2 . . . . **44** C6
Albion Bldgs BA1 . . . . **44** D7
Albion Cl TA6 . . . . **209** B5
Albion Pl
[16] Bristol BS2 . . . . **227** C3
Frome BA11 . . . . **119** D3
Albion Rd BA22 . . . . **174** A2
Albion Terr
Bath BA1 . . . . **228** A3
Cheddar BS27 . . . . **90** B7
Alburys BS40 . . . . **35** D3
ALCOMBE
Kingsdown **29** F7
Minehead **201** A4
Alcombe Cross TA24 . . . . . **201** B5
Alcombe Rd TA24 . . . . **201** A5
Aldeburgh Pl BA14 . . . . **83** F6
Alder Cl
North Petherton TA6 . . . . . **153** F3
Taunton TA1 . . . . **213** D1
Williton TA4 . . . . **202** E3
Aldercombe Rd BS9 . . . . **5** C8
Alder Ct BS14 . . . . **23** B5
Alderdown Cl BS11 . . . . **5** A8
Alder Gr
Crewkerne TA18 . . . . **224** C7
Yeovil BA20 . . . . **218** E2
Alderley Rd BA2 . . . . **44** B4
Alderney Rd TA6 . . . . **209** C3
Alder Terr BA3 . . . . **78** E2
Alder Way BA2 . . . . **62** D8
Alder Wlk BA11 . . . . **120** B7
Aldondale Gdns BA20 . . . . **219** B3
ALDWICK **54** D7
Aldwick Ave BS13 . . . . **22** C3
Aldwick La BS40 . . . . **54** C7
Aldwych Cl TA8 . . . . **104** C6
Alec Ricketts Cl BA2 . . . . . . **43** F5
Alexander Bldgs [12] BA1 . . **28** B1
Alexander Cl TA3 . . . . **169** D5
Alexander Hall BA3 . . . . **64** C6
Alexander Ho [5] BS23 . . . . **48** F4
Alexander Mews [5] BS23 . . **48** E7
Alexander Pl BA3 . . . . **64** C6
Alexanders Cl BA6 . . . . **138** C4
Alexander Way BS49 . . . . . . **34** B7
Alexandra Ct BS21 . . . . **6** C4
Alexandra Gdns TA24 . . . . **201** A6
Alexandra Mews TA24 . . . . **201** A7
Alexandra Par BS23 . . . . . . **48** E7
Alexandra Pk BS39 . . . . **77** E5
Alexandra Pl BA2 . . . . **45** C1
Alexandra Rd
Bath BA2 . . . . **228** C1
Bridgwater TA6 . . . . **208** E5
Bristol BS8 . . . . **226** B4
Bristol, Highridge BS13 . . . . **21** F7
Clevedon BS21 . . . . **6** C4
Frome BA11 . . . . **119** F4
Minehead TA24 . . . . **201** A6
Wellington TA21 . . . . **222** D6
Yeovil BA21 . . . . **219** D6
Alexandra Terr BS39 . . . . . . **77** E5
Alexevia Cvn Pk TA3 . . . . **169** C3
Aley TA5 . . . . **152** A8
ALFORD **159** A3
Alford La BA4, BA7 . . . . . . **159** B4

Alfords Ridge BA3 . . . . . . 117 A7
Alfoxton Rd TA6 . . . . 208 C4
Alfred Cres BA4. . . . . 205 B4
Alfred Ct 4 BS23 . . . . 48 E7
Alfred Hill BS2. . . . . 227 A4
Alfred Par BS2. . . . . 227 A4
Alfred Pl
Bristol BS2. . . . . 226 C4
BS1 . . . . 227 A1
Alfred St
Bath BA1 . . . . 228 B3
Taunton TA1. . . . . 213 B4
Wells BA5 . . . . 203 D3
Weston-super-Mare BS23 . . 48 E8
Alfred's Twr* BA10 . . . . . 161 C6
Alfred's Way BA9 . . . . . . 216 B3
Algar Ct BA5. . . . . 203 B4
ALHAMPTON. 159 C6
Alice St BA11 . . . . 143 A6
Alison Gdns BS48 . . . . 19 A7
Allandale Ct TA8. . . . . 104 B8
Allandale Rd TA8 . . . . 104 A8
Allanmead Rd BS14 . . . . . . 23 B8
Allans Way BS24. . . . . 49 F7
Allen Dr BA4. . . . . 205 A6
Allen Rd TA6 . . . . 208 F1
Allens La
Shipham BS25 . . . . 70 F8
Wells BA5 . . . . 112 E1
Allenslade Flats TA4 . . . . 210 C5
ALLER 171 D8
Aller BS24. . . . . 49 B2
Aller Dro
Aller TA10 . . . . 171 D8
Othery TA7. . . . . 155 C1
ALLERFORD
Porlock. 124 C4
Taunton 167 F4
Allermoor Dro BS28. . . . . 138 B8
Aller Par BS24. . . . . 49 B2
Allerpark La TA24 . . . . 123 F3
Allerton Cres BS14. . . . . . . 23 B4
Allerton Gdns BS14 . . . . . . 23 B5
Allerton Rd
Bridgwater TA6 . . . . 209 B7
Bristol BS14. . . . . 23 B4
All Hallows Prep Sch
BA4. . . . . 142 C6
Allingham Rd BA21. . . . . . 219 C7
Allington Cl TA1 . . . . 213 E4
Allington Gdns BS48 . . . . . 18 C8
Allington Rd BS3. . . . . 226 C1
Allotment Dro
Combe St Nicholas TA20 . . 193 C5
Glastonbury BA16 . . . . 138 D1
Allotment Rd BA22 . . . . . . 175 C3
ALLOWENSHAY 195 A8
ALL SAINTS. 198 A4
All Saints CE Prim Sch
Axminster EX13. . . . . 198 A4
Dulverton TA22 . . . . 163 D6
Montacute TA15. . . . . 186 B3
All Saints East Clevedon CE
Prim Sch BS21. . . . . 6 F4
All Saints Ho BS2 . . . . 227 B4
All Saints La BS21. . . . . 6 F4
All Saints' La BS1 . . . . 227 A2
All Saints Pl BA2. . . . . 45 E4
All Saints Rd BA1 . . . . 228 B4
All Saints' Rd
Bristol BS8. . . . . 226 A4
Weston-super-Mare BS23 . . 30 E1
All Saints' St BS1 . . . . 227 A3
All Saints' Terr TA6 . . . . . 209 B4
Allshire La EX16 . . . . 162 F3
Allyn Saxon Dr BA4 . . . . . 205 D5
Alma Field BA7 . . . . 214 B4
Alma Rd BS8 . . . . 226 B4
Alma Road Ave BS8 . . . . . 226 B4
Alma St
Taunton TA1. . . . . 213 A3
Weston-super-Mare BS23 . . 48 E7
Alma Vale Rd BS8. . . . . 226 A4
Almond Cl BS22. . . . . 32 A1
Almond Tree Cl TA6. . . . . 209 D4
Almond Wlk BS13. . . . . 22 B6
Almshouse La BA22 . . . . . 173 E1
Almshouses
Donyatt TA19 . . . . 183 D1
Marshfield SN14 . . . . 13 E8
Almyr Terr TA23 . . . . 202 C7
Alpha Cotts TA2 . . . . 168 E8
Alpha Ho TA9. . . . . 104 E3
Alpine Cl BS39. . . . . 77 F4
Alpine Gdns BA1. . . . . 228 C4
Alpine Rd BS39 . . . . 77 F4
ALSTON. 198 A5
Alston Cl TA1 . . . . 212 C1
Alstone Gdns TA9. . . . . . . 104 C2
Alstone La TA9 . . . . 104 C2
Alstone Rd TA9 . . . . 104 C2
Alstone Wildlife Pk*
TA9. . . . . 104 C3
ALSTON SUTTON 88 F3
Alston Sutton Rd BS26 . . . 88 F4
Alton Pl BA2. . . . . 228 C1
Alun Rees Way TA20 . . . . 223 B3
Alverstoke BS14 . . . . 22 F7
Alveston Wlk BS9. . . . . 5 B7
ALVINGTON. 218 B4
Alvington La BA22 . . . . . . 218 B5
ALWESTON 189 A1
Alweston DT9. . . . . 189 A1
Ambares Ct BA3 . . . . 96 F8
Amberd La TA3 . . . . 181 D8
Amberey Rd BS23. . . . . 48 F5
Amberlands Cl BS48 . . . . . 19 A7
Amberley Cl
Keinton Mandeville TA11 . . 158 A1
Keynsham BS31. . . . . 24 E4
Amberley Gdns 3 BS48 . . . 8 D1
Amber Mead TA1 . . . . 213 D3
Ambleside Rd BA2 . . . . 44 C2
Ambra Ct BS8 . . . . 226 A2
Ambra Terr BS8 . . . . 226 A2
Ambra Vale BS8 . . . . 226 A2
Ambra Vale E BS8. . . . . . . 226 A2
Ambra Vale S 5 BS8 . . . . 226 A2
Ambra Vale W 4 BS8 . . . . 226 A2
Ambridge Cl BA16 . . . . . . 207 B4
Ambrose Cl DT9 . . . . 187 E1
Ambrose Rd BS8. . . . . 226 A2
Ambury BA1 . . . . 228 B1
Amercombe Wlk BS14. . . . 23 D7
American Mus in Britain*
BA2. . . . . 46 A5
Amery La BA1 . . . . 228 C2
AMESBURY 59 F2
Amesbury Dr BS24 . . . . 67 B6
Ames La BA3 . . . . 98 B6
Ammerdown Terr BA3 . . . 98 F7
AMMERHAM 199 A8
Ammerham La TA20. . . . . 199 A8
Amor Pl TA1. . . . . 212 D2
Amors Dro DT9 . . . . 225 B4
Amory Rd TA22 . . . . 163 D6
Amulet Way BA4 . . . . 205 E4
Ancastle Ave BA7 . . . . 214 D6
Ancastle Terr BA7 . . . . . . 214 C6
Anchorage The BS20. . . . . . 2 E6
Anchor Cl BA3 . . . . 116 E8
Anchor Cnr BA9 . . . . 176 D6
Anchor Hill BA9. . . . . 176 D6
Anchor Rd
Bath BA1 . . . . 27 B1
Bristol BS1. . . . . 226 C2
Coleford BA3 . . . . 116 E8
Anchor Sq BS1. . . . . 226 C2
Anchor St TA23 . . . . 202 C7
Anchor Stables TA24 . . . . 123 E4
Anchor Way BS20. . . . . 4 D4
Ancliff Sq BA15 . . . . 64 E4
Andalusia Acad BS2. . . . . . 227 C3
Andereach Cl BS14. . . . . . . 23 B8
ANDERSFIELD. 153 B5
Andersfield Cl TA6 . . . . . . 208 A4
Ander's La TA3 . . . . 192 B8
Andrew Allan Rd TA21. . . 222 B4
Andrew's Hill TA22. . . . . . 163 D6
Andrew's Hill Cross
TA22 . . . . 163 C6
Andruss Dr BS41. . . . . 21 D2
Angela Cl TA1 . . . . 212 D2
Angel Cres TA6 . . . . 208 F5
Angelica Dr TA6 . . . . 208 E1
Angel La BA9 . . . . 216 C4
Angel Place Sh Ctr 6
TA6 . . . . 208 F5
Angel Row TA3 . . . . 170 F2
ANGERSLEIGH 181 C5
Anglesey Cotts DT10 . . . . 190 B4
Anglo Ct TA18 . . . . 224 C6
Anglo Terr BA1 . . . . 228 C4
Anglo Trad Est The BA4. . 205 B6
Angus Way 12 TA6 . . . . . . 154 A5
Angwin Cl BA4. . . . . 205 B6
Animal Farm Adventure
Park* TA8. . . . . 66 B2
Annaly Rd BS27. . . . . 90 A7
Annandale BA7 . . . . 214 B4
Annandale Ave BS22 . . . . . 31 E1
Anseres Pl BA5 . . . . 203 E4
ANSFORD 214 C6
Ansford Com Sch BA7. . . 214 C7
Ansford Hill BA7 . . . . 214 B7
Ansford Rd BA7. . . . . 214 C6
Anson Cl BS31 . . . . 25 D2
Anson Rd
Locking BS24 . . . . 50 B6
Weston-super-Mare BS22 . . 31 D4
Anson Way TA6. . . . . 208 F5
Anstey Gate TA22 . . . . 162 B8
Anthony Rd BA16 . . . . 207 D7
Antler Cl BA6 . . . . 206 C3
Antona Ct BS11 . . . . 4 D7
Antona Dr BS11. . . . . 4 D7
Anvil Rd BS49. . . . . 17 F1
Anvil St BS2 . . . . 227 C2
Apex Dr TA9. . . . . 104 C4
Aplins Cl TA19 . . . . 221 B3
Apple Alley BA11. . . . . 119 F5
Apple Bsns Ctr The TA2. . 212 B6
Appleby Wlk BS4 . . . . 22 D7
Apple Cl TA19 . . . . 194 E7
Applecroft BA2 . . . . 79 E6
APPLEDORE 179 A1
Appledore 4 BS22. . . . . 31 F2
Appledore Cl BS14. . . . . . . 23 B8
Appledore Dr 9 TA6 . . . . 209 B4
Apple Dumpling Cnr
BS28 . . . . 108 C3
Apple Farm La BS24. . . . . . 32 B1
Applefield Rd DT8 . . . . . . 199 F8
Applehayes La EX15. . . . . 180 F2
Applehayes Rise BS20. . . . . 4 B3
Apple La BA11 . . . . 119 F5
Apple Tree Cl TA6 . . . . . . 209 D4
Appletree Ct BS22 . . . . 32 B2
Apple Tree Dr BS25 . . . . . . 70 A8
Appletree Mews BS22. . . . . 32 B2
APPLEY 179 B8
Appley Cross TA21 . . . . . . 179 B7
Appsley Cl BS22 . . . . 31 C1
Apricot Tree Cl TA6 . . . . . 209 D5
Apsley Rd BA1. . . . . 44 A7
Aquara Cl BA16 . . . . 207 C3
Arbutus Dr BS9. . . . . 5 C8
Arcade The BS1. . . . . 227 B3
Archbishop Cranmer CE Com
Prim Sch TA1 . . . . 213 A4
Arch Cl BS41 . . . . 10 F1
Archer Ct BS21 . . . . 6 D4
Archer Dr TA8 . . . . 104 C6
Archers Grove TA4. . . . . . 150 E7
Archers Way The BA6 . . . 206 E5
Archer Wlk BS14. . . . . 23 E6
Arches The BA2. . . . . 44 A6
Archgrove BS41. . . . . 10 F1
Arch La TA3 . . . . 170 E4
Archstone Ave TA5. . . . . . 135 F2
Archway St BA2. . . . . 45 B5
Arden Cl BS22 . . . . 31 F3
Ardern Cl BS9 . . . . 5 B8
Ardmore BS8 . . . . 11 D7
Ardwyn TA21 . . . . 222 D4
Arena The BA20. . . . . 219 A4
Argentia Pl BS20. . . . . 2 F7
Argyle Ave BS23 . . . . 48 F4
Argyle Pl BS8. . . . . 226 A2
Argyle Rd
Bristol BS2. . . . . 227 B4
Clevedon BS21. . . . . 6 D6
Argyle St BA2. . . . . 228 C2
Argyle Terr BA2. . . . . 44 C6
Arlington Cl
Bridgwater TA6 . . . . 209 A2
Yeovil BA21 . . . . 218 C7
Arlington Ho 4 BA1 . . . . . 228 C2
Arlington Mans BS8. . . . . 226 B4
Arlington Rd 4 BA2. . . . . . 44 D5
Arlington Villas BS8. . . . . 226 B3
Armada Ho BS2. . . . . 227 A4
Armada Pl BS1 . . . . 227 B4
Armada Rd BS14. . . . . 23 A6
Armes Ct BA2. . . . . 228 C1
Armoury Rd BA22 . . . . 218 A6
Armoury The BA6. . . . . . . 206 D4
Armstrong Rd BA11 . . . . . 120 B5
Armtech Row BA22 . . . . . . 218 B6
Arnewood Gdns BA20 . . . 218 F2
Arnold Cl TA2. . . . . 212 F7
Arnold Noad Cnr BA14 . . . 83 E3
Arnold's Way BS49. . . . . . . 17 A2
Arnolfini (Arts Ctr)*
BS1. . . . . 227 A1
Arnor Cl BS22. . . . . 32 A4
Arrowfield Cl BS14. . . . . . . 23 A2
Artemesia Ave BS22. . . . . . 49 E8
Arthurswood Rd BS13 . . . . 22 A4
Artillery Rd BA22 . . . . 218 A6
Arundel Cl BS13 . . . . 22 B5
Arundell Ct BS23. . . . . 48 E8
Arundell Rd BS23 . . . . 30 E1
Arundells Way TA3. . . . . . 169 D4
Arundel Rd
Bath BA1 . . . . 28 A1
Clevedon BS21. . . . . 6 D3
Yeovil BA21 . . . . 219 E6
Arundel Wlk BS31. . . . . 24 D5
Arun Gr TA1 . . . . 213 D4
Ascension Ho BA2 . . . . 44 D4
ASH
Martock 185 F7
Taunton 169 E1
ASHBEER. 150 C6
Ashbeer Hill TA4. . . . . 150 D7
Ashbourne Cres TA1 . . . . 213 D3
ASHBRITTLE 178 F8
Ash Brook BS39. . . . . 59 D1
Ashbrooke House Sch
BS23 . . . . 48 D6
Ashbury Dr BS22. . . . . 31 B2
Ashby Pl BA7 . . . . 214 C5
Ash CE Prim Sch TA12. . . 185 F7
Ash Cl
Bridgwater TA6 . . . . 209 D4
Wells BA5 . . . . 203 D5
Weston-super-Mare BS22 . . 32 D2
Winscombe BS25. . . . . 52 A1
Ashcombe Ct
Ilminster TA19. . . . . 221 B4
1 Weston-super-Mare
BS23 . . . . 48 F7
Ashcombe Gdns BS23 . . . . 49 A8
Ashcombe La
Alweston DT9 . . . . 189 B2
Ilminster TA19. . . . . 221 B4
Ashcombe Park Rd BS23 . 31 A1
Ashcombe Pl 4 BS23 . . . . 48 F7
Ashcombe Prim Sch BS23 49 A7
Ashcombe Rd BS23 . . . . . . 48 F7
ASHCOTT. 156 B8
Ashcott BS14 . . . . 22 F7
Ashcott Cl TA8. . . . . 104 C6
Ashcott Dr TA8 . . . . 104 C6
Ashcott Pl TA8. . . . . 104 C6
Ashcott Prim Sch TA7 . . . 156 B8
Ashcott Rd BA6. . . . . 138 D3
Ash Cres TA1 . . . . 212 B2
Ashcroft
Chard TA20. . . . . 223 D2
Weston-super-Mare BS24 . . 49 B2
Ash Croft TA12. . . . . 185 F7
Ashcroft Ave BS31 . . . . 24 D5
Ashcroft Rd BS9 . . . . 5 C7
Ash Cross TA3 . . . . 169 E2
Ash Ct BS14 . . . . 23 A6
ASHCULME 180 C1
Ashculme Hill EX15 . . . . . 180 C2
Ashdene Rd BS23 . . . . 49 A8
Ashdown Ct BS9 . . . . 5 F8
Ashdown Rd BS20. . . . . 2 A6
Ashel's Batch BA3 . . . . 94 C8
Ashen Cross TA11. . . . . . . 211 E2
Ash End BA8. . . . . 189 F7
Asher La BS2 . . . . 227 C3
Ashes La BA3 . . . . 64 A4
Ashey La
Burrington BS40 . . . . 54 A5
Cheddar BS27 . . . . 90 B8
Ashfield TA20. . . . . 223 D2
Ashfield Cl BA11 . . . . 143 C6
Ashfield Pk 23 TA12 . . . . . 185 E6
Ashford Cl
Bridgwater TA6 . . . . 208 E2
Milverton TA4. . . . . 167 A4
Ashford Dr BS24 . . . . 49 A1
Ashford Gr BA21 . . . . 219 B7
Ashford La TA19 . . . . 183 F5
Ashford Rd
Bath BA2 . . . . 44 D4
Redhill BS40 . . . . 36 E4
Taunton TA1 . . . . 212 C2
Wellington TA21. . . . . 222 D4
Ash Gr
Bath BA2 . . . . 44 C4
Chard TA20. . . . . 223 C5
Clevedon BS21. . . . . 6 E4
Minehead TA24 . . . . 200 D7
Shepton Mallet BA4. . . . . . 205 C4
Wells BA5 . . . . 203 D5
Weston-super-Mare BS23 . . 48 E2
ASHGROVE 79 D8
Ashgrove BA2 . . . . 79 D8
Ashgrove Ave BS8 . . . . 11 B7
Ashgrove Ct BA2. . . . . 79 D8
Ash Grove Way TA6 . . . . . 209 D7
Ash Hay Dro BA5. . . . . 139 C6
Ash Hayes Dr BS48. . . . . 8 E1
Ash Hayes Rd BS48. . . . . 8 F1
Ash Ho TA8. . . . . 65 F2
ASHILL. 183 B4
Ashill Cl TA1. . . . . 212 E1
Ashill Com Prim Sch
TA19 . . . . 183 C4
ASHINGTON 187 B8
Ashington La BA21. . . . . . . 187 B7
Ash La
Shepton Beauchamp
TA19 . . . . 184 E4
Wells BA5 . . . . 203 C5
Winsford TA24 . . . . 147 B6
Ashland Ct TA18 . . . . 224 C7
Ashland La TA4 . . . . 150 B4
Ashland Rd BS13. . . . . 22 A4
Ashlands Cl TA18 . . . . 224 C7
Ashlands Fst Sch TA18 . . 224 C7
Ashlands Mdw TA18. . . . . 224 C8
Ashlands Rd TA18. . . . . . . 224 D7
Ashlea BA7 . . . . 214 B6
Ashlea Pk TA9 . . . . 136 E8
Ashleigh Ave TA6 . . . . 209 A3
Ashleigh Cl
Paulton BS39. . . . . 77 E6
Weston-super-Mare BS23 . . 49 A8
Ashleigh Cres BS49 . . . . . . 34 B8
Ashleigh Gdns TA1. . . . . . 212 E5
Ashleigh Rd
Weston-super-Mare BS23 . . 49 A8
Yatton BS49. . . . . 34 B8
Ashleigh Terr TA6 . . . . . . 209 A3
Ashley Ave
Bath BA1 . . . . 44 C7
Burnham-on-S TA8. . . . . . . 104 B6
Ashley Cl BS25. . . . . 70 A7
Ashley La BA15 . . . . 64 F7
Ashley Rd
Bathford BA1. . . . . 29 E3
Clevedon BS21. . . . . 6 B1
Taunton TA1 . . . . 212 D3
Ashley Terr 1 BA1. . . . . . . 44 C7
Ashmans Ct BA1 . . . . 44 B6
Ashmans Gate BS39. . . . . . 77 E5
Ashmans Yd BA1. . . . . 44 B6
Ashman Way TA6 . . . . 208 D4
Ashmead
Temple Cloud BS39 . . . . 58 E1
Yeovil BA20 . . . . 218 C2
Ashmead Rd BS31. . . . . 25 B5
Ashmead Road Ind Est
BS31. . . . . 25 B5
Ashmead Way 8 BS1 . . . . 11 F5
Ashmoor Dro BA5. . . . . . . 139 C6
ASH PRIORS 167 C8
Ash Rd
Banwell BS29. . . . . 50 E4
Street BA16. . . . . 207 B3
ASHTON. 107 E8
Ashton Ave BS1. . . . . 226 A1
Ashton Cl
Ashill TA19 . . . . 183 C4
Clevedon BS21. . . . . 6 B1
Ashton Court Estate*
BS41. . . . . 11 C4
Ashton Cres BS48. . . . . 8 D1
Ashton Ct TA1 . . . . 212 C1
Ashton Dr BS3. . . . . 11 F2
ASHTON GATE 11 F4
Ashton Gate Stadium (Bristol
City FC)* BS3 . . . . 11 F3
Ashton Gate Trad Est BS3. 11 E3
Ashton Gate Underpass
BS3 . . . . 11 F3
Ashton Hill
Burnett BA2. . . . . 42 E8
Corston BA2. . . . . 43 A7
Ashton Park Sec Sch BS3 11 E3
Ashton Pk BA11. . . . . 119 E2
Ashton Rd
Bridgwater TA6 . . . . 208 F2
Bristol, Ashton Gate BS3. . . 11 F4
Bristol, Bower Ashton BS3 . 11 D3
ASHTON VALE 11 F2
Ashton Vale Prim Sch
BS3. . . . . 11 F2
Ashton Vale Rd BS3. . . . . . 11 E3
Ashton Vale Trad Est BS3 . 11 F1
Ashton Way BS31. . . . . 24 E6
Ashton Windmill* BS28. . . 88 E1
Ashtown Cross EX16 . . . . 164 A3
Ash Tree Cl
Bleadon BS24 . . . . 67 C6
Burnham-on-S TA8 . . . . 85 A3
Ash Tree Cres TA8 . . . . 85 A3
Ash Tree Ct BA3 . . . . 78 E1
Ash Tree Pl TA8. . . . . 85 A3
Ashtree Rd BA11. . . . . 120 A6
Ash Tree Rd TA8 . . . . 85 A3
Ash Trees TA9 . . . . 86 C5
Ashvale Cl BS48. . . . . 9 A2
ASHWELL 221 C6
Ashwell Bsns Pk TA19 . . . 221 C7
Ashwell Cl BS14 . . . . 23 E6
Ashwell La
Glastonbury BA6 . . . . 139 D1
Wheddon Cross TA24. . . . . 129 F2
ASHWICK. 115 B5
Ashwicke BS14 . . . . 23 A6
Ash Wlk BA8. . . . . 190 A6
Ashwood BS40. . . . . 74 F4
Ashwood Dr BA21. . . . . . . 219 E8
Askwith Cl DT9 . . . . 225 B3
ASNEY 156 E7
Asney Rd BA16. . . . . 156 E7
Aspen Cl BA11 . . . . 120 B7
Aspen Ct TA6 . . . . 208 E4
Aspen Park Rd BS22 . . . . . 49 E8
Aspen Way TA18 . . . . 224 D7
Aspin Cl TA21. . . . . 222 F6
Aspin Rd TA21 . . . . 222 F6
Aspley Cl BA1. . . . . 44 B7
Asquith St TA2. . . . . 212 E6
Assembly Rooms La BS1 227 A2
Aston Ho 4 BS1 . . . . 227 B1
At-Bristol* BS1 . . . . 226 C1
Athelney Way BA21 . . . . . 218 D6
ATHERSTONE 184 C3
Athlone Rd TA6. . . . . 209 A2
Atholl Cl BS22 . . . . 31 F3
Atkins Cl BS14 . . . . 23 E6
Atkin's Gate TA13 . . . . 220 D6
Atkins Hill BA9 . . . . 216 A3
Atlanta Key TA8. . . . . 104 A8
Atlantic Cres TA8 . . . . 104 B5
Atlantic Rd
Bristol BS11. . . . . 4 C8
Weston-super-Mare BS23 . . 30 C1
Atlantic Rd S BS23 . . . . 30 C1
Atlantic View Ct BS23 . . . . 30 C1
Atlantic Way BA22 . . . . . . 174 A2
Atlay Ct BS49 . . . . 17 B1
Atrium The BS1. . . . . 227 B2
Attewell Ct BA2. . . . . 44 F4
Attisham La DT6 . . . . 199 D4
Atyeo Cl
Bristol BS3. . . . . 11 E1
Burnham-on-S TA8. . . . . . . 104 C8
Aubrey Meads BS30. . . . . . . 25 E8
Auckland Cl BS23 . . . . 48 F3
Auckland Way TA20 . . . . . 223 D3
Audley Ave BA1. . . . . 44 D7
Audley Cl
Bath BA1 . . . . 44 D7
Nether Stowey TA5 . . . . . . 134 A2
Audley Gr BA1 . . . . 44 C7
Audley Lodge BA1 . . . . 44 D7
Audley Park Rd BA1. . . . . . 44 C7
Augusta Pl BA1 . . . . 44 D7
Augustine's Cl BS20. . . . . 1 E4
Augustus Ave BS31. . . . . . . 24 F7
Austen Dr BS22 . . . . 32 B4
Austen Pl BS11 . . . . 4 E7
Austin Cl BA11. . . . . 119 F2
Austin Rd BA6 . . . . 206 E3
Autumn Mews BS24. . . . . . . 50 A8
Avalon Bldgs BA6 . . . . 206 D5
Avalon Cl BS49 . . . . 17 A1
Avalon Est BA6 . . . . 206 E7
Avalon Ho BS48. . . . . 8 C1
Avalon Mews BA6. . . . . . . 206 E4
Avalon Pk TA11 . . . . 211 B5
Avalon Rd
Bridgwater TA6 . . . . 209 D5
Highbridge TA9 . . . . 104 E4
Avalon Sch BA16. . . . . 207 B3
Avalon Vineyard BA4 . . . . 158 E8
Avebury Cl TA8 . . . . 104 D8
Avebury Dr TA6. . . . . 209 D5
Avebury Rd BS3. . . . . 11 F2
Aveline Ct TA4 . . . . 167 F6
Avening Cl BS48 . . . . 19 A8
Avenue Pl BA2. . . . . 45 B1
Avenue Rd BA11 . . . . 120 A4
Avenue The
Backwell BS48. . . . . 19 A7
Bath, Bushey Norwood BA2 45 E5
Bath, Combe Down BA2. . . . 45 C1
Bicknoller TA4 . . . . 132 F4
3 Bridgwater TA6. . . . . 208 F5
Bristol, Sneyd Park BS9. . . . . 5 E3
Chard TA20. . . . . 193 F7
Clevedon BS21. . . . . 6 E6
Keynsham BS31. . . . . 24 E6
Kingsbury Episcopi TA12 . . 185 B8
Langport TA10 . . . . 172 A6
Minehead TA24 . . . . 201 A7

Avenue The *continued*
Misterton TA18 224 F3
Sherborne DT9 225 E5
Sparkford BA22 175 A5
Stoke sub Hamdon TA14 185 F4
Taunton TA1 212 E5
Timsbury BA2 60 B2
Weston-super-Mare BS22 32 C3
Wincanton BA9 216 D3
Winscombe BS25 70 C8
Yatton BS49 34 B8
Yeovil BA21 219 B5
Averill Ct BS21 6 D4
Avill Cres TA1 213 C4
Avishayes Prim Sch TA20 223 E5
Avishayes Rd TA20 223 E4
Avonbank Ind Est BS11 4 B7
Avonbridge Trad Est BS11 4 C8
Avon Cl
Keynsham BS31 24 F6
Taunton TA1 212 D2
Weston-super-Mare BS23 48 F2
Yeovil BA21 219 D6
AVONCLIFF 64 F4
Avoncliff Halt BA15 64 F5
Avon Cres BS1 226 A1
Avon Ct BA1 29 A4
Avondale Bldgs BA1 28 B2
Avondale Ct
Bath BA1 44 B7
Bristol, Sneyd Park BS9 5 D3
Avondale Ho
Bath BA2 44 B5
Bridgwater TA6 209 A2
Avondale Rd BA1 44 B6
Avondowns Ct BS8 226 A4
Avon Gorge Ind Est BS11 4 C7
Avon Gorge Nature Reserve★ BS8 11 E7
Avon Gr BS9 5 D2
Avon Hts BA3 64 C6
Avon La BS31 25 F5
Avonleaze BS9 5 B5
Avon Livestock Ctr BS40 38 B6
Avonmead BS2 227 B4
Avon Mill La BS31 24 F6
AVONMOUTH 4 B8
Avonmouth CE Prim Sch BS11 4 C8
Avonmouth Dock BS11 4 A8
Avonmouth Rd BS11 4 C8
Avon Pk BA1 44 A7
Avon Prim Sch BS11 4 D8
Avon Rd
Bristol BS13 22 A6
Keynsham BS31 24 F5
Pill BS20 4 C5
Avon Riverside Est BS11 4 B7
Avon Riverside Sta★ BS30 25 E6
Avon Ski & Action Centre★ BS25 52 C3
Avon & Somerset Pol HQ BS20 1 F3
Avon St
Bath BA1 228 B2
Bristol BS2 227 C2
Avon Vale BS9 5 D4
Avonvale Pl BA1 28 F3
Avon Valley Adventure & Wildlife Pk★ BS31 25 D6
Avon Valley Rly★ BS30 25 D7
Avon Way
Bristol, Sneyd Park BS9 5 C4
Portishead BS20 2 C5
Avonwood Cl BS11 4 E6
Awkward Hill BS40 55 D5
AXBRIDGE 70 B1
Axbridge CE Fst Sch BS26 70 C1
Axbridge Cl
Burnham-on-S TA8 104 C8
Nailsea BS48 18 E8
Axbridge & District Mus★ BS26 70 C2
Axbridge Moor Dro BS26 70 C1
Axbridge Rd
Bath BA2 45 A2
Cheddar BS27 70 F2
Axe Cl BS23 49 A5
Axeford TA20 198 E8
Axeford Mdws TA20 198 E8
Axe La
Clapton DT8 195 C1
Drimpton DT8 199 F8
Axe Rd
Bridgwater TA6 209 B3
Wookey BA5 139 D8
Axe Valley Com Coll The EX13 198 A1
Axford Way BA2 79 D8
Axis BS14 22 D5
AXMINSTER 198 B2
Axminster Com Prim Sch EX13 198 A1
Axminster Rd TA20 198 C7
Ayckbourn Cl TA8 104 C6
Aycote Cl BS22 31 C2
Ayford La SN14 13 F4
Aylands Rd TA1 212 D3
Aylmer Cres BS14 23 B6
Ayr St BA2 44 D6
AYSHFORD 178 E2
Azalea Rd BS22 32 A5
Azelin Ave BS13 22 B5

B

BABCARY 174 C7
Babcary La BA22 174 B8
Babwell Rd BA9 177 D6
Babylon Hill
Sherborne DT9 188 A3
Yeovil BA21 219 F4
Babylon View BA21 219 F7
Backfields BS2 227 B4
Backfields Ct BS2 227 B4
Backfields La BS2 227 B4
Back La
Axbridge BS26 70 C2
Baltonsborough BA6 158 B5
Batcombe BA4 142 C2
Bradford Abbas DT9 187 F1
Chapel Allerton BS26 88 D1
Cheddar BS27 90 A7
Chewton Mendip BA3 75 B1
Curry Rivel TA10 171 D3
Draycott BS27 90 F2
East Chinnock BA22 196 E8
East Coker BA22 197 C7
Halstock BA22 197 C3
Ilchester BA22 173 E1
Keynsham BS31 24 E6
Kingston Seymour BS21 16 A5
Kington Magna SP8 177 E2
Litton BA3 75 E2
Maiden Bradley BA12 144 C2
Marshfield SN14 13 F8
Martock TA12 185 D4
Middlezoy TA7 155 B3
Montacute TA15 186 B3
Moorlinch TA7 155 D8
North Perrott TA18 196 C4
Pill BS20 4 C5
Pilton BA4 204 D3
Rimpton BA22 188 A8
Rowberrow BS25 53 A1
Shepton Mallet, Darshill BA4 204 F6
Shepton Mallet, Downside BA4 205 C8
Sherborne DT9 225 D4
Stoney Stratton BA4 141 F2
Street BA16 207 C6
Street, Butleigh Wootton BA6 157 C6
Westbury-sub-Mendip BA5 110 E6
Whitelackington TA19 221 F6
Backlane Dro BA6 158 C5
Back Of Kingsdown Par BS6 227 A4
Back River Dro BA16 138 F2
Back St
Ash TA12 186 A7
Bampton EX16 164 B1
Bradford On Tone TA4 167 F1
Leighton BA11 142 E6
Long Sutton TA10 172 E4
Martock TA12 185 F7
West Camel BA22 174 D3
Weston-super-Mare BS23 48 E7
Winsham TA20 194 E1
Back Stoke La BS9 5 F6
Back Town BA6 157 E4
Back Way TA4 150 B8
Backways La TA21 179 F6
BACKWELL 19 B6
Backwell Bow BS48 9 C1
Backwell CE Jun Sch BS48 19 C5
Backwell Comm BS48 19 B8
BACKWELL COMMON 19 D8
BACKWELL GREEN 19 D8
Backwell Hill Rd BS48 19 E5
Backwell Sch BS48 19 B6
Backwell Wlk BS13 21 F8
Bacon Dr TA1 213 D3
BADBURY 183 F7
Badcox BA11 119 E4
Badenham Gr BS11 4 F8
Baden Ho BA1 228 B4
Badger Hts BA22 218 B5
Badger Pk TA24 201 C4
Badger Rise BS20 1 F3
Badgers Cl
Bourton SP8 161 F1
Street BA16 207 A5
Taunton TA1 212 B3
Badger's Cross
Oakhill BA3 114 F5
Somerton TA11 211 C1
Badger's Cross La TA11 211 C2
Badgers Folly BA7 214 B5
Badgers Green Rd BA16 207 A5
Badgers Hill BA11 120 A5
Badgers Holt BS14 23 C6
Badgers' La TA20 223 E1
Badgers The BS22 32 D3
BADGER STREET 182 B6
Badgers Way BS24 49 F8
Badgers Wlk BS20 4 B4
BADGWORTH 88 B6
Badgworth Barns BS26 88 D5
Badgworth Ct BS26 88 C5
Badgworth La BS26 88 C4
Badlake La EX36 162 D6
Badlake Moor Cross TA22 162 D7
Badman Cl BS39 77 D5
Badminton Ct 17 BS23 30 C1
Badminton Gdns BA1 44 C8
Bagber Cross Rds DT10 190 D3
Bagborough Dr TA6 208 F2
Bagborough La BA4 141 C2
Bagborough Rd TA2 212 F7
Baggridge Hill BA2 80 F7
Baggs La BS27 90 F2
BAGLEY 109 A1
BAGLEY GREEN 222 A3
Bagley Rd TA21 222 A3
Bagnell Cl BS14 23 E5
Bagnell Rd BS14 23 E5
BAILBROOK 28 D3
Bailbrook Gr BA1 28 C3
Bailbrook La BA1 28 D3
Baildon Cres BS23 49 A4
Baildon Ct 2 BS23 48 F4
Baildon Rd BS23 49 A4
Bailey Cl BS22 49 E8
Bailey Ct BS20 2 F6
Bailey Hill BA7 214 C5
Bailey's Dro BA6 158 B5
Baileys Gate TA4 167 F6
Bailey's Knapp EX16 178 B4
Bailey's La BA4 142 B1
Bailey St TA6 209 B5
Bailiffs Cl BS26 70 C1
Bailiffs' Wall BS26 70 B1
Baily Cl BA6 206 E7
Bainsbury View BA3 96 F1
Bakehouse 1 TA16 195 F7
Bakehouse La DT9 187 E1
Bakelite Mus The★ TA4 202 C2
Baker Cl 8 BS21 6 B1
Bakeries The TA11 211 D3
Baker's Bldgs BS40 35 D2
Bakers Cl TA1 212 A3
Baker's Cross TA3 191 D7
Bakers Ct TA13 220 C4
Bakersfield TA20 194 E1
Bakers La
Barrington TA19 184 C5
Chilcompton BA3 96 D3
Lower Langford BS40 53 C8
Baker's La
Churchinford TA3 191 D7
Wellington TA21 222 E6
Bakers Orch TA4 151 B5
Bakers Par BA2 60 B2
Bakers Pk BS13 22 B6
Baker St
Babcary TA11 174 C7
Frome BA11 119 E5
Weston-super-Mare BS23 48 E8
Bakery La BA4 140 F3
Balch Rd BA5 203 C4
Baldwin Rd TA1 213 B5
Baldwin St BS1 227 A2
Ballance St BA1 228 B4
Ballfield Rd TA24 200 F8
Ballhill La EX16 164 B1
Ball La
Doulting BA4 141 F7
Isle Abbotts TA3 183 E7
Spaxton TA2 & TA5 152 B2
Balls Barn La BS24 33 A2
Ball's Hill BA22, TA15 186 C4
Ball's La TA5 153 E4
Ball The
Dunster TA24 201 E2
Minehead TA24 200 F8
Balmoral Dr TA8 85 B1
Balmoral Ho TA6 209 C4
Balmoral Rd
Keynsham BS31 24 E4
Yeovil BA21 219 E6
Balmoral Way BS22 31 D2
Balsam Cl BA9 216 D3
Balsam Fields BA9 216 D3
Balsam La BA9 216 E3
Balsam Pk BA9 216 C3
Baltic Pl BS20 4 D4
BALTONSBOROUGH 158 A6
Baltonsborough CE Prim Sch BA6 158 A6
Baltonsborough Rd BA6 157 E4
Balustrade 17 BA1 28 B1
Bamfield BS14 23 A6
BAMPTON 164 C1
Bampton 5 BS22 31 F2
Bampton Ave TA20 223 B5
Bampton Cl BS13 22 B7
Bampton Down Rd EX16 178 A7
Bampton Prim Sch EX16 164 B1
Bampton St TA24 200 F6
Banbury La BA6 157 E3
Bancks St TA24 200 F7
Bancombe Ct TA11 211 B5
Bancombe Rd TA11 211 A4
Banfield Cl BS11 5 A8
Bangers DT9 188 F5
Bangrove Wlk BS11 4 E8
Banister Gr BS4 22 D7
Banking Ct 4 TA18 224 C6
Bankland La TA7 154 B1
Bank Pl BS20 4 D4
Banks Cl BS21 16 D8
Bank Sq TA22 163 D6
Bank St
Highbridge TA9 104 D3
Williton TA4 202 D2
Bannerdown Cl BA1 29 B4
Bannerdown Dr BA1 29 A4
Bannerdown Rd BA1 29 C5
Bannerleigh La BS8 11 E6
Bannerleigh Rd BS8 11 E6
Banneson Rd TA5 134 B2
Bantock Cl BS4 22 D6
Bantry Rd BS4 22 E8
BANWELL 51 B3
Banwell Cl
Bristol BS13 22 A8
Keynsham BS31 25 A2
Taunton TA1 213 D4
Banwell Prim Sch BS29 51 B3
Banwell Rd
Banwell BS26, BS29 68 E8
Bath BA2 62 D8
Locking BS24 50 B3
Winscombe BS25, BS29 69 E8
Banyard Rd BS20 3 E5
Barbary Cl BA8 176 D3
Barberry Dr
Bridgwater TA6 208 D1
Chard TA20 223 F5
Barberry Farm Rd BS49 17 B1
Barber's La TA21 180 F7
Barbers Mead TA2 213 C7
Barbour Gdns BS13 22 D3
Barbour Rd BS13 22 D3
Barclay St TA6 209 A5
Barcroft BA12 144 B2
Barcroft Cres TA3 170 A1
Barcroft La TA13 220 B6
Bardel Ct BA22 218 B6
BARE ASH 153 B6
Barford Cl TA5 152 F7
Barford Rd TA5 152 F7
Barham Ct BA22 218 A5
Barhams Cl TA6 209 A7
Barker Cl BS24 32 C1
Barkham Cl BA5 203 F5
Barle Cl TA1 213 D4
Barle Ent Ctr TA22 163 D5
Barley Cl BA5 203 C3
Barley Croft
Bristol BS9 5 F5
Somerton TA11 211 B3
Barley Cross BS22 32 A5
Barley Wood Walled Garden★ BS40 35 F3
Barlinch Cl TA2 213 B7
Barlynch Ct BA21 218 D6
Barnabas Cl BS26 70 D2
Barnaby Cl BA3 78 B2
Barnard Ave BA16 207 B3
Barnard Ct BA5 203 B4
Barnard's Cl BS49 34 C7
Barnard Wlk BS31 24 D4
Barn Cl
Crewkerne TA18 224 B5
Frome BA11 119 D3
Nether Stowey TA5 134 B2
Somerton TA11 211 B3
Street BA16 207 C6
Wiveliscombe TA4 210 A7
Barn Cres TA18 224 B5
Barn Ct BA21 187 C5
Barn End BS40 74 E3
Barnes Cl
Castle Cary BA7 214 C6
Wells BA5 203 B4
Barnes Close Mead TA22 163 D6
Barnet Cl BA21 218 E7
Barnetts Well BS27 90 F2
Barnfield Way BA1 29 B3
Barn Gn BA6 206 E3
Barnhay 6 EX16 164 B1
Barn Hill BA2 79 F5
Barn La
Clutton BS39 59 A7
Crewkerne TA18 195 E6
Barn Meads Rd TA21 222 E4
Barn Orchard TA14 185 E3
Barn Pool BS25 70 F8
Barns Cl
Barrow Gurney BS48 20 E4
Nailsea BS48 8 E2
Barnsclose TA22 163 D6
Barns Close Ind Est TA22 163 D6
Barnsclose N TA22 163 D6
Barnsclose W TA22 163 D6
Barns Gd BS21 16 E8
Barn St TA18 224 B6
Barnstaple Ct BS4 22 E8
Barnstaple Rd BS4 22 E8
Barnstaple Wlk BS4 22 F8
Barnwood Ct BS48 8 B1
Baron Cl BS30 25 E8
Barons Cl BS3 11 F3
Barossa Pl BS1 227 A1
Barpark Cnr EX15 180 E3
Barpool La TA11 211 D6
BARR 168 B3
Barracks Cl BA22 218 B7
Barrack's La BS11 4 D8
BARREN DOWN 205 C7
Barrendown La BA4 205 C6
Barrie Way TA8 104 C6
BARRINGTON 184 D5
Barrington Broadway TA10 184 D6
Barrington Cl TA1 212 C1
Barrington Court★ TA19 184 D5
Barrington Court Cotts TA19 184 D5
Barrington Hill National Nature Reserve★ TA19 183 A4
Barrington Hill Rd TA19 182 F4
Barrington Pl BA4 204 F5
Barrington Rd TA8 104 C8
Barrington Wy TA21 222 B4
BARROW
Wells 140 B4
Wincanton 161 B3
BARROW COMMON 21 B4
Barrow Court La BS19 20 B5
Barrow Cswy BA5 138 F8
Barrow Ct
Barrow Gurney BS48 20 A5
Tickenham BS21 7 F4
Barrow Dr TA1 213 E5
BARROW GURNEY 20 E5
Barrow Hill
Stalbridge DT10 190 B4
Stourton Caundle DT10 189 F1
Barrow Hill Cres BS11 4 C7
Barrow Hill Rd BS11 4 D6
Barrow Ho 25 BA4 205 B6
Barrow La
Charlton Musgrove BA9 161 B3
North Wootton BA4 140 B4
Pilton BA4 140 F3
Winford BS40 20 F1
Barrow Lea DT10 190 B4
Barrowmead Dr BS11 4 F7
Barrow Pk BS27 90 A8
Barrow Rd
Bath BA2 44 C1
Hutton BS24 49 E2
Barrows Cl TA6 208 E2
Barrows Croft BS27 90 A8
Barrows Ct BA22 196 E8
Barrows La TA14 185 E2
Barrows Rd BS27 90 A8
Barrows St BS48 20 D5
Barrows The
Cheddar BS27 90 A8
Weston-super-Mare BS22 49 C7
Barrow Stile BA4 140 F3
BARROW VALE 59 D5
Barrow Water La BA9 161 A3
Barrow Wood La BS27 110 A7
Barrs Ct BS1 227 B3
Barry Cl BS24 49 A1
Barry La BA22 196 F6
Barrymore Cl TA10 172 A6
Barstable Ho BS2 227 C3
Bartec 4 BA20 218 C3
Bartholomew Row BA2 60 B2
Bartlett Cl
Frome BA11 120 C6
Taunton TA1 212 B1
Bartlett Ct 1 TA18 224 C6
Bartlett Ct BA20 218 D3
Bartlett Mews BA21 219 F7
Bartlett Pk
Chard TA20 223 E3
Yeovil BA20 218 D3
Bartletts Ct BA2 228 C1
Bartletts La TA4 167 A4
Bartletts Pl BA21 218 D5
Bartletts Row TA11 211 D4
Bartlett St 6 BA1 228 B3
Bartletts Way BS24 50 A4
BARTON 69 B6
Barton Bldgs BA1 228 B3
Barton Cl
Berrow TA8 84 F5
Taunton TA1 212 D3
Barton Cross EX16 162 E5
Barton Dro BS25 69 D5
Barton Gdns DT9 225 B4
Barton Gn TA3 168 D1
Barton Hey 2 TA4 167 F8
Barton Hill SP8 177 E2
Barton La TA3 169 C4
Barton Rd
Barton St David TA11 158 A2
Berrow TA8 84 F4
Bristol BS2 227 C2
Butleigh BA6 157 E3
Minehead TA24 201 B4
Winscombe BS26 69 C6
Barton Rise TA7 137 B3
BARTON ST DAVID 158 A2
Barton St
Bath BA1 228 B2
Bristol BS1 227 A4
Bartons The
Bishops Lydeard TA4 167 E8
Ilchester BA22 173 E1
South Petherton TA13 220 E3
Barton The
Bleadon BS24 67 C6
Charlton Adam TA11 173 F7
Corston BA2 43 A7
Huish Champflower TA4 165 E8
Norton St Philip BA2 81 E4
Barton Vale BS2 227 C2
Barton Villas BA3 116 F6
Barton Way TA3 170 C4
Barton Wlk BA11 119 D2
BARWICK 197 F8
Barwick Ho BS11 4 E7
Barwick & Stoford Com Prim Sch BA22 197 F8
Basketfield La BA6 139 D1
Batallers La TA23 131 D2
Bat Alley DT10 190 F5
BATCH 66 F3
Batch Bsns Pk BS24 66 F2
Batch Cl TA7 136 C4
Batch La
Clutton BS39 58 F3
Lympsham BS24 66 F3
Batchpool La BA8 176 F3
Batch Rd TA7 136 B5
Batch The
Ashcott TA7 156 B7
Backwell BS48 19 D1

Batch The continued
Batheaston BA1 . . . . **28** F3
Burrington BS40 . . . . **54** B3
Butcombe BS40 . . . . **55** B8
Chew Magna BS40 . . . . . . **39** B3
Churchill BS25 . . . . **52** F4
Draycott BS27 . . . . **90** F2
Farmborough BA2 . . . . **60** A6
Hinton Charterhouse BA2 . . **63** E1
Saltford BS31 . . . . **25** F3
19 Shepton Mallet BA4 . . **205** B6
Wincanton BA9 . . . . **216** B4
Yatton BS49 . . . . **34** B7
Batch View BA16 . . . . **207** B6
BATCOMBE **142** D1
Bateman's Cross TA20 . . **198** E7
BATH **228** A2
Bath Abbey★ BA1 . . . . . . **228** C2
BATHAMPTON **28** F1
Bathampton La BA2 . . . . . **28** E1
Bathampton Prim Sch
BA2 . . . . **28** F2
Bathampton View BA1 . . **29** B3
Bath Aqua Theatre of Glass★
10 . . . . **228** C3
Bath Bridge Bsns Pk
TA6 . . . . **209** B6
Bath Bsns Pk BA2 . . . . . . **79** E7
Bath City FC Twerton Park
. . . . **44** B5
Bath Cl BA6 . . . . **206** D6
BATHEALTON **166** B3
BATHEASTON **28** F4
Batheaston CE Prim Sch
BA1 . . . . **28** F4
BATHFORD **29** C1
Bathford CE Prim Sch
BA1 . . . . **29** C2
Bathford Hill
Bathford BA1 . . . . **29** B2
Compton Dando BS39 . . . . **41** E5
Bathford Manor BA1 . . . . **29** C2
Bath Foyer The BA2 . . . . **44** A6
Bath Hill
Keynsham BS31 . . . . **24** F5
Wellow BA2 . . . . **62** D2
Bath House Ct TA1 . . . . . **212** E3
Bath La TA20 . . . . **223** C3
Bath Meadow Dr TA22 . . **163** E6
Bath New Rd BA3 . . . . **78** F4
Bath Old Rd BA3 . . . . **78** F4
Bath Pl TA1 . . . . **212** E3
BATHPOOL **213** E6
Bath Postal Mus★ BA1 . **228** C3
Bath Racecourse★ BA1 . . **27** A6
Bath Rd
Ashcott TA7 . . . . **156** B7
Bawdrip TA7 . . . . **136** D2
Beckington BA11 . . . . **101** D5
Bitton BS30 . . . . **25** D8
Blagdon BS40 . . . . **55** B1
Bridgwater TA6 . . . . **209** C7
Bristol BS2 . . . . **227** C1
Farmborough BA2 . . . . **59** E5
Frome BA11 . . . . **120** A7
Horrington BA3, BA5 . . . . . **113** D5
Kelston BA1, BS30 . . . . **26** B6
Kingsdown SN13 . . . . **29** F5
Moorlinch TA7 . . . . **155** E8
Norton St Philip BA2 . . . . . **81** E5
Oakhill BA3 . . . . **115** B3
Paulton BS39 . . . . **77** F6
Peasedown St John BA2 . . **79** C7
Saltford BS31 . . . . **25** D3
Shepton Mallet BA4 . . . . . **141** C8
Stawell TA7 . . . . **137** B1
Upper Langford BS40 . . . . **53** D3
Wells BA5 . . . . **112** E1
Bath Riverside Bsns Pk
BA2 . . . . **228** B1
Bath's Original Theatre Royal
& Masonic Mus★ BA1 . **228** C2
Bath Spa Sta BA1 . . . . . . **228** C1
Bath Spa Univ Coll BA1 . . **27** E1
Bath Spa University Coll
(Newton Pk Campus)
BA2 . . . . **43** B5
Bath Spa University
(Culverhey Campus)
BA2 . . . . **44** B2
Bath Sq TA20 . . . . **223** C3
Bath St
Bath BA1 . . . . **228** C2
Bristol BS1 . . . . **227** B2
Chard TA20 . . . . **223** C3
Cheddar BS27 . . . . **90** B7
Frome BA11 . . . . **119** D4
Bathurst Ct TA8 . . . . **104** D8
Bathurst Par BS1 . . . . . . **227** A1
Bathurst Rd BS22 . . . . . . **49** C8
Bath View BA3 . . . . **96** F1
BATHWAY **94** E5
Bathwell La DT9 . . . . **217** D1
BATHWICK **45** B7
Bathwick Hill BA2 . . . . . . **45** C6
Bathwick Rise BA2 . . . . . . **45** B7
Bathwick St BA1, BA2 . . . **228** C4
Batstone Cl BA1 . . . . **28** B2
BATTEN'S GREEN **182** F5
Battery La BS20 . . . . **2** D7
Battery Rd BS20 . . . . **2** D6
Battin's Knap TA4 . . . . . . **150** A3
Batt La TA3 . . . . **183** C8
BATTLEBOROUGH **86** C1
Battleborough La TA9 . . . . **86** B1

Battle La BS40 . . . . **39** A3
Battle St EX15 . . . . **180** E1
Battleton TA22 . . . . **163** D6
Batts Bow Bridge TA9 . . **104** E1
Batts La
Oakhill BA3 . . . . **114** E3
Pilsdon DT6 . . . . **199** F2
Batt's La TA10 . . . . **172** D5
Battson Rd BS14 . . . . **23** E4
Batts Pk TA1 . . . . **212** E1
Baulditch La TA3 . . . . **184** B8
Bauntons Cl DT9 . . . . **217** C2
Baunton's Orch DT9 . . . . . **217** C2
Bawden Cl TA7 . . . . **136** E4
BAWDRIP **136** E2
Bawdrip La TA7 . . . . **136** E2
Bawler's La TA10 . . . . **171** C3
Bayer Bldg The BA2 . . . . **228** B1
BAYFORD **216** F5
Bayford Hill BA9 . . . . **216** E4
Bayford La BA9 . . . . **177** B7
Bayford Rd TA6 . . . . **209** C6
Bay Hill TA19 . . . . **221** D4
Baylie Ave BS24 . . . . **32** C1
Bayliss Ctr The **4** BA16 . **207** C5
Baymead Cl **11** TA6 . . . . . **153** F4
Baymead La TA6 . . . . **153** F3
Baymead Mdw **5** TA6 . . **153** F3
Baynes Cl TA21 . . . . **222** E7
Bay Rd
Clevedon BS21 . . . . **6** D6
Porlock TA24 . . . . **124** A4
Bay's La BA3 . . . . **115** A7
Bays The BS27 . . . . **90** C8
Baytree Ct BS22 . . . . **31** D1
Baytree Rd BS22 . . . . **31** C1
Bay Tree Rd
Bath BA1 . . . . **28** B2
Clevedon BS21 . . . . **6** E1
Baytree Sch BS24 . . . . **50** A8
Baytree View BS22 . . . . . . **31** D1
Bay Tree View BS22 . . . . . **31** D1
Bay View TA23 . . . . **202** D6
Bay View Gdns TA8 . . . . **104** B5
Baze La EX35 . . . . **122** B4
Bazelands Hill BA8 . . . . . **190** B7
Beach Ave BS21 . . . . **6** C2
Beach Ct BS23 . . . . **48** D6
Beach End Rd BS23 . . . . . . **48** C2
Beach Hill BS20 . . . . **2** C6
Beachlands Pk BS22 . . . . . **31** A6
Beachley Wlk BS11 . . . . **4** D7
Beach Mews BS21 . . . . **6** C4
Beach Rd
Weston-super-Mare BS23 . . **48** D6
Weston-super-Mare, Kewstoke
BS22 . . . . **31** A5
Beach Rd E BS20 . . . . **2** D6
Beach Rd W BS20 . . . . **2** C6
Beach Tree Cross TA4 . . **166** E6
Beacon TA19 . . . . **221** B5
Beaconsfield Ho TA6 . . . . **209** A2
Beaconfield Rd BA20 . . . . **218** E1
BEACON HILL **27** F1
Beacon Hill View DT9 . . **175** D1
Beacon La
Corton Denham DT9 . . . . . **175** D2
Wellington TA21 . . . . **180** C4
Beacon Rd
Bath BA1 . . . . **28** A1
Minehead TA24 . . . . **200** F8
Beaconsfield Rd
Clevedon BS21 . . . . **6** D4
Weston-super-Mare BS23 . . **48** E7
Beaconsfield Way BA1 . . **120** B7
Beacon View
Coleford BA3 . . . . **116** E7
Shepton Mallet BA4 . . . . . **205** A4
Beadon La TA16 . . . . **195** F7
Beadon Rd TA1 . . . . **213** C5
Beafort Cl BS24 . . . . **50** C3
Beale Cl BS14 . . . . **23** E6
Beale Way TA8 . . . . **104** D5
Bean Acre The BS11 . . . . . . **4** D8
Bearbridge Rd BS13 . . . . . **21** F4
BEARD HILL **141** C3
BEARDLY BATCH **205** C1
Beard's Yd TA10 . . . . **171** F5
BEAR FLAT **44** F4
Bearley Bridge Rd **15**
TA12 . . . . **185** E6
Bearley Ho **28** TA12 . . . . . **185** E6
Bearley La BA22 . . . . **186** B7
Bearley Rd **27** TA12 . . . . . **185** E6
Bears Meadow La TA5 . . **133** B3
Bear Yard Mews **2** BS8 . **226** A2
Beasley Ct TA20 . . . . **223** B5
Beastway La TA24 . . . . . . **131** B3
Beatty Way TA8 . . . . **104** C7
Beauchamp Gdns TA3 . . **183** A7
Beauchamps Dr BA3 . . . . **97** A5
Beaufighter Rd BS24 . . . . **49** D6
Beaufitz Pl TA20 . . . . **193** F1
Beauford Pk TA2 . . . . **168** B4
Beauford Sq BA1 . . . . **228** B2
Beaufort Ave BA3 . . . . **78** A2
Beaufort Bldgs **7** BS8 . . **11** F7
Beaufort Ct
Clevedon BS21 . . . . **6** C5
Ilchester BA22 . . . . **173** E2
Beaufort E BA1 . . . . **28** C1
Beaufort Gdns
2 Nailsea BS48 . . . . **8** D1
South Petherton TA13 . . . . **220** B5

Beaufort Mews
3 Bath BA1 . . . . **28** C1
10 Bristol BS8 . . . . **11** F7
Beaufort Pl BA1 . . . . **28** C1
Beaufort Rd
Taunton TA1 . . . . **212** E5
Weston-super-Mare BS23 . . **48** F7
Beaufort Villas **8** BA1 . . . **28** B1
Beaufort W **11** BA1 . . . . . . **28** B1
Beauley Rd BS3 . . . . **226** B1
Beaulieu Dr BA21 . . . . **218** D6
Beaumont BA1 . . . . **27** F1
Beaumont Cl BS23 . . . . **48** F4
Beaumont Ho BA21 . . . . . **219** D5
Beau St BA1 . . . . **228** B2
Beavor La EX13 . . . . **198** A1
BECKERY **206** B4
Beckery Rd BA6 . . . . **206** B3
Beckery New Rd BA6 . . . . **206** B3
Beckery Rd BA6 . . . . **206** B4
Becket Dr BS22 . . . . **32** A3
Becket Pl BA5 . . . . **203** D3
Becket Prim Sch BS22 . . . **32** A2
Becket Rd BS22 . . . . **32** A4
Becket's La BS48 . . . . **18** E8
Beckford Ct **1** BA2 . . . . . **45** B7
Beckford Gdns
Bath BA2 . . . . **45** B8
Bristol BS14 . . . . **23** A3
Beckford Rd BA2 . . . . **45** B7
Beckford's Twr & Mus★
BA1 . . . . **27** D4
Beckhampton Rd BA2 . . . . **44** D5
BECKINGTON **101** E4
Beckington BS24 . . . . **49** A2
Beckington CE Fst Sch
BA11 . . . . **101** E4
Beckington Cres TA20 . . **223** D3
Becks Bsns Pk BS23 . . . . . **49** A7
Becks Field **2** TA14 . . . . **185** F4
Beck's La BA11 . . . . **116** D6
Beckworth Cl TA6 . . . . . . **209** C3
Bector La BA3 . . . . **116** C4
Bede St DT9 . . . . **225** E5
Bedford Cl TA6 . . . . **209** C3
Bedford Ct BA1 . . . . **45** B8
Bedford Rd
Wells BA5 . . . . **112** E1
Weston-super-Mare BS23 . . **48** E4
Yeovil BA21 . . . . **219** D8
Bedford St BA1 . . . . **45** B8
BEDLAM **119** B8
BEDMINSTER DOWN **22** B8
Bedminster Down Sch
BS13 . . . . **21** F7
Bedwell La TA7 . . . . **155** C2
Bedwin Cl BS20 . . . . **1** F4
Beech Ave
Bath BA2 . . . . **45** E5
Shepton Mallet BA4 . . . . . **205** A6
Beech Bsns Pk TA6 . . . . . **209** A7
Beech Cl
Doulting BA4 . . . . **141** E6
Shipham BS25 . . . . **70** E8
Taunton TA2 . . . . **212** F8
Beechcroft BS41 . . . . **21** D2
Beech Croft BS14 . . . . **23** B5
Beech Ct
Bristol BS14 . . . . **23** A5
Frome BA11 . . . . **120** B7
Taunton TA1 . . . . **212** E3
2 Wellington TA21 . . . . **222** D6
Beech Dr
Bridgwater TA6 . . . . **209** D5
Nailsea BS48 . . . . **9** A3
Shipham BS25 . . . . **70** E8
BEECHEN CLIFF **228** B1
Beechen Cliff Rd BA2 . . . **228** B1
Beechen Cliff Sch BA2 . . . **45** A4
Beeches The
Bath BA2 . . . . **44** D1
Langport TA10 . . . . **172** A6
Sandford BS25 . . . . **52** B4
Wheddon Cross TA24 . . . . **129** E1
Beechfield Cl BS41 . . . . . . **11** C2
Beechfield Gr BS9 . . . . **5** C8
Beech Gr
Bath BA2 . . . . **44** D4
Somerton TA11 . . . . **211** D5
Wellington TA21 . . . . **222** C6
Beech Grove Prim Sch
TA21 . . . . **222** C6
Beech Hill TA21 . . . . **222** F5
Beeching Cl TA20 . . . . . . **223** E6
Beeching Close Ind Est
TA20 . . . . **223** E6
Beech La
Axminster EX13 . . . . **198** E1
Stoke Trister BA9 . . . . **177** C8
Beechmont Dr BS24 . . . . . **49** A1
Beechmount Cl BS24 . . . . **48** F1
Beechmount Ct BS14 . . . . **23** B8
Beechmount Gr BS14 . . . . **23** B8
Beech Rd
Bridgwater TA6 . . . . **209** D5
20 Martock TA12 . . . . . **185** E6
Saltford BS31 . . . . **25** E3
Shipham BS25 . . . . **70** F8
Street BA16 . . . . **207** C3
Yatton BS49 . . . . **34** C8
Beech Terr BA3 . . . . **78** C1
Beech Tree BS33 . . . . **130** C1
Beech Tree Cl TA4 . . . . . . **210** C4
Beech Tree Cross
Clatworthy TA4 . . . . **149** E1
Dulverton TA22 . . . . **163** C7
Monksilver TA4 . . . . **132** B1
Beech Tree Hill TA5 . . . . **152** C6

Beech Way BA4 . . . . **141** E1
Beechwood
Frome BA11 . . . . **120** A5
Locking BS24 . . . . **50** A5
Beechwood Ave
Bristol BS14 . . . . **23** C8
Frome BA11 . . . . **120** A5
Beechwood Cl
Crewkerne TA18 . . . . **224** C7
Portishead BS20 . . . . **1** E5
Beechwood Dr
Portishead BS20 . . . . **1** E5
Beechwood Rd
Bath BA2 . . . . **45** B1
Easton-in-G BS20 . . . . **4** A4
Nailsea BS48 . . . . **8** D2
Portishead BS20 . . . . **1** E5
Beehive Yd BA1 . . . . **228** C3
Beek's La SN14, BA1 . . . . . **13** D5
Beer Door TA10 . . . . **155** E2
Beer Dro TA10 . . . . **155** E3
Beere Cross EX36 . . . . . . **162** A5
Beer La
Burlescombe EX16 . . . . . . **179** B2
Dulverton TA22 . . . . **163** B5
Beer Rd TA10 . . . . **155** E1
Beer St
Curry Mallet TA3 . . . . **183** C7
Yeovil BA20 . . . . **219** A4
Bees Ho BS21 . . . . **6** C2
Beetham La TA20 . . . . **193** B6
Beggar Bush La BS8 . . . . . **11** B6
Beggarswell Cl BS2 . . . . . **227** C4
BEGGEARN HUISH **131** E2
Beggs Cl **4** TA6 . . . . **153** F3
Behind Berry TA11 . . . . . . **211** D4
Behind Butts TA14 . . . . . . **185** E1
Behind Hayes BA8 . . . . . . **176** D3
Behind Town TA11 . . . . . . **157** B4
Bekynton Ave BA5 . . . . . **203** F4
Belcombe Dro TA20 . . . . **193** B7
Belfast Wlk BS4 . . . . **22** E8
Belfield Ct TA8 . . . . **104** A8
Belgrave Cres BA1 . . . . . **228** C4
Belgrave Ct **2** TA2 . . . . . **212** F6
Belgrave Pl
Bath BA1 . . . . **228** C4
Bristol BS8 . . . . **226** A3
Taunton TA2 . . . . **212** F6
Belgrave Rd
Bath BA1 . . . . **28** B1
Bristol BS8 . . . . **226** A4
Weston-super-Mare BS22 . . **49** B8
Belgrave Terr **2** BA1 . . . . **28** A1
Belgravia Rd TA6 . . . . . . **136** B2
Bellamy Ave BS13 . . . . . . **22** C4
Belland Dr BS14 . . . . **22** F4
Bella View Gdns BA6 . . . **206** D4
Bella Vista Rd BA1 . . . . . **228** B4
Bell Barn Rd BS9 . . . . **5** D6
Bell Chase BA20 . . . . **218** D5
Bell Cl
Bridgwater TA6 . . . . **208** F6
Farmborough BA2 . . . . **59** F6
Westbury-sub-Mendip BA5 **110** E6
Belle View Terr TA20 . . . **198** C8
BELLE VUE **78** B3
Bellevue BS8 . . . . **226** B2
Belle Vue
Midsomer Norton BA3 . . . . **78** B3
Washford TA23 . . . . **131** E3
Belle Vue Cl BA2 . . . . **79** D7
Bellevue Cotts BS8 . . . . . **226** B2
Bellevue Cres BS8 . . . . . . **226** B2
Bellevue Ct
Bristol BS8 . . . . **226** B2
Clevedon BS21 . . . . **6** D4
Bellevue Mans BS21 . . . . . . **6** D4
Bellevue Rd BS21 . . . . **6** D4
Bellevue Rd BS8 . . . . **226** B2
Belle Vue Terr TA18 . . . . **224** B6
Bellfield BA3 . . . . **117** A3
Bellhanger Ct BA1 . . . . . . **228** B4
Bell Hill
Chewton Mendip BA3 . . . . **94** B7
Norton St Philip BA2 . . . . . **81** E4
Bellhorse La BS40 . . . . **74** C5
Bellifants BA2 . . . . **60** A6
Bell La
Bristol BS1 . . . . **227** A3
Chard TA19, TA20 . . . . . . **193** F7
Chewton Mendip BA3 . . . . **94** B7
Cossington TA7 . . . . **137** A3
Thurloxton TA2 . . . . **153** D1
Bell Language Sch The
BA1 . . . . **44** C8
Bellman's Cross BA8 . . . . **190** B7
Bellmoor La TA19 . . . . . . **194** A7
Bell Orch TA10 . . . . **171** D4
Bellotts Rd BA2 . . . . **44** C6
Bell Sq BS40 . . . . **54** E3
Bellum SN14 . . . . **13** E8
BELLUTON **40** D6
Belluton La BS39 . . . . **40** D5
Belluton Villas BS39 . . . . . **40** D5
Bell Wlk BS40 . . . . **35** E2
Belmont Cl TA6 . . . . **208** B4
Belmont Dr
Failand BS8 . . . . **10** B3
Taunton TA1 . . . . **212** E2
Belmont Hill BS48 . . . . **10** B1
Belmont Ho **14** BA20 . . . . **219** B4
Belmont Rd
Bath BA2 . . . . **45** C1
Hatch Beauchamp TA3 . . . **183** A8
Taunton TA1 . . . . **212** C3

Belmont Rd continued
Winscombe BS25 . . . . **70** A8
Belmont Terr TA19 . . . . . **184** E1
Belmont The BS21 . . . . **6** D3
Belmore Gdns BA2 . . . . . . **44** B3
Belstone Wlk BS4 . . . . **22** C8
Belton Ct BA1 . . . . **27** B2
Belton Rd BS20 . . . . **2** A6
Belvedere BA1 . . . . **228** B4
Belvedere Cl TA5 . . . . **135** B2
Belvedere Cres BS22 . . . . **31** C1
Belvedere Ct **3** TA21 . . . **222** D6
Belvedere Grange TA11 . **211** E3
Belvedere Rd
Taunton TA1 . . . . **212** F5
Yeovil BA21 . . . . **219** E7
Belvedere Trad Est TA1 . **212** E5
Belvoir Rd **6** BA2 . . . . **44** D5
Bemberry Bank TA24 . . . **130** B5
Benares Ct TA24 . . . . **201** A8
Bences Cl SN14 . . . . **13** F8
Benches La BS40 . . . . **37** D3
Bench La TA20 . . . . **193** D5
Ben Cross TA13 . . . . **220** A4
Benedictine Cl BA6 . . . . . **206** C4
Benedict St BA6 . . . . **206** D4
Benhole La TA5 . . . . **134** B8
Bennell Batch BA3 . . . . . . **96** E4
Bennell Cl BA3 . . . . **96** E4
Bennell Cotts BA3 . . . . . . **96** E4
Bennett Gdns BA11 . . . . . **119** D4
Bennett La BA1 . . . . **28** A1
Bennett Rd TA9 . . . . **104** F4
Bennett's Cl BA5 . . . . **204** B7
Bennetts Field Trad Est
BA9 . . . . **216** C2
Bennett's La BA3, BA5 . . . **114** B7
Bennett's Rd BA1 . . . . **28** C3
Bennett St BA1 . . . . **228** B3
Bennetts Way BS21 . . . . . . **6** E5
Bennett Way BS1, BS8 . . . . **11** F5
BENTER **115** C7
Benter Cross BA3 . . . . . . **115** D7
Bentley Cl BS14 . . . . **22** F3
Bentley Rd BS22 . . . . **32** B3
Ben Travers Way TA4 . . . **104** C6
Benville Ave BS9 . . . . **5** C8
Bere La BA6 . . . . **206** E4
Bere Mills La TA19 . . . . . **194** B7
Beresford Cl
Burnham-on-S TA8 . . . . . . **104** C7
Saltford BS31 . . . . **25** E2
Beresford Gdns BA1 . . . . . **27** A3
Beretun Orch BA6 . . . . . . **206** E3
Berhill TA7 . . . . **156** C7
Berkeley Ave
Bristol BS8 . . . . **226** C3
Midsomer Norton BA3 . . . . **78** A2
Berkeley Cres
Bristol BS8 . . . . **226** B3
Weston-super-Mare BS23 . . **48** C2
Berkeley Ct BA2 . . . . **45** C6
Berkeley Gdns
Bruton BA10 . . . . **215** E6
Keynsham BS31 . . . . **24** E4
Berkeley Ho
Bath BA1 . . . . **228** C4
Bristol BS1 . . . . **226** C3
Berkeley Pl
Bath BA1 . . . . **228** C4
Bristol BS8 . . . . **226** B3
Berkeley Rd
Street BA16 . . . . **207** E6
Yeovil BA20 . . . . **219** A4
Berkeley Sq BS8 . . . . **226** B3
BERKLEY **121** A7
Berkley Ave BS8 . . . . **226** B3
Berkley CE Fst Sch BA11 **121** A7
Berkley Cross BA11 . . . . . **120** F6
Berkley Ct BA22 . . . . **173** E2
BERKLEY DOWN **120** C5
Berkley La
Beckington BA11 . . . . **101** D3
Frome BA11 . . . . **120** D8
BERKLEY MARSH **120** F7
Berkley Rd BA11 . . . . **120** B6
Berkley St BA11 . . . . **121** A8
Berlington Ct BS1 . . . . . . **227** B1
Bernard Cres TA24 . . . . . **200** F6
Bernard Herridge Ct
BA9 . . . . **216** D4
Bernard Ireland Ho BA1 . . **27** B1
Bernard Taylor Homes **9**
TA1 . . . . **213** A4
Berners Cl BS4 . . . . **22** D7
BERROW **84** E5
Berrow CE Prim Sch TA8 . **84** F4
Berrow Lodge **7** BS23 . . . **48** E5
Berrow Rd TA8 . . . . **85** A2
Berry Cl TA6 . . . . **208** E2
Berrydale Ave TA6 . . . . . **208** F6
Berry Hill
Mells BA11 . . . . **118** A6
Nunney BA11 . . . . **143** B8
Berry La EX13 . . . . **198** F3
Berryman Cl BA4 . . . . **205** A5
Berryman Ct BA5 . . . . **203** B4
Bertha Terr TA9 . . . . **104** D3
Berwick Cl TA1 . . . . **212** C1
Beryl Gr BS14 . . . . **23** C8
Beryl Knapp BA22 . . . . . . **197** B8
Beryl La BA5 . . . . **203** F6
Besley Ct BA5 . . . . **203** B4
Bests Field TA12 . . . . **185** B8
Bethell Mead TA4 . . . . . . **167** C6
BETTISCOMBE **199** E2
Beverley Cl
Frome BA11 . . . . **119** D3

Beverley Cl *continued*
  Taunton TA2............212 E6
Beverley Dr TA23......202 C7
Beverley Gdns BS9.......5 D7
Bewdley Rd BA2.........45 B4
Bews La TA3............223 B5
Bibors Hill TA4........165 E4
Bibury Cl BS48..........9 A1
Bibury Ho BA1..........27 B2
BICKENHALL............182 E5
Bickenhall La TA3......182 F6
Bickfield La BS40......74 B8
Bicking's Close La TA4..166 A4
Bicknell Gdns BA21.....219 B8
BICKNOLLER............132 F2
Bidbrooke La EX36......162 A6
Biddiscombe Cl TA6.....208 E1
BIDDISHAM..............87 E8
Biddisham Cl 6 BS48.....8 E1
Biddisham La BS26......87 E7
Biddlesden Rd BA21.....218 C2
Biddle St BS49.........34 B7
Bideford Cres BS4......22 F8
Bideford Rd BS22.......31 F2
Bifield Cl BS14........23 F5
Bifield Gdns BS14......23 E5
Bifield Rd BS14........23 F5
Bignal Rand Cl BA5.....203 B3
Bignal Rand Dr BA5.....203 B3
Bignell Cl BS25........69 F8
Big Tree Cl BS26.......69 C3
Bigwood La BS1........226 C2
Bilberry Cl BS9.........5 C8
Bilberry Gr TA1.......168 F1
Bilbie Cl BS40.........56 E8
Bilbie Rd
  Chew Stoke BS40.......56 E8
  Weston-super-Mare BS22..32 A5
BILBROOK.............131 C4
Bilbury La
  Bath BA1.............228 B2
  Glastonbury BA6......206 F3
Billand Cl BS13........21 E3
Billetfield TA1.......212 F3
Billet St TA1.........212 F4
Billicombe La TA7.....155 C8
Billing's Hill BS28...108 C4
Billy La TA4..........210 D7
Binces La BS22.........42 E3
Bince's Lodge La BA3....78 B3
BINCOMBE.............134 A2
Bincombe Dr TA18......224 C7
Bincombe Rd TA6.......209 C4
Binding Cl 6 TA6......153 F4
Bindon La BA11........143 B2
Bindon Rd TA2.........212 C6
Bindwell La BA22......174 F3
BINEGAR...............114 C2
Binegar CE Prim Sch
  BA3.................114 D8
Bineham Ct TA10.......173 B4
Bineham La
  Ilchester BA22.......173 F2
  Yeovilton BA22.......174 A2
Bineham Rd TA10.......173 B4
Binford Pl TA6........209 A5
Binford's La TA4......151 A4
Binhay Rd BS49.........34 C7
Binley Gr BS14.........23 D5
Binmead Gdns BS13......22 B4
Binnings The BS27......90 F3
Birbeck Chase BS24.....50 C8
Birbeck Rd BS9..........5 E5
Bircham Cl TA6.......208 C4
Bircham La TA24.......201 C4
Bircham Rd
  Minehead TA24.......201 B5
  Taunton TA2..........213 B8
Birchanger La TA4.....150 A8
Birch Ave
  Bleadon BS24..........67 C6
  Clevedon BS21..........6 E4
  Puriton TA7..........136 C4
Birch Cl
  Bridgwater TA6.......209 D5
  Cannington TA5......135 B2
  Cheddar BS27..........90 C8
  Locking BS24..........50 B4
  Wedmore BS28........108 C3
Birch Croft BS14.......23 A3
Birch Ct BS31..........24 C4
Birchdale BA20........218 D2
Birchdale Rd BS14......23 A8
Birchdene BS48..........9 A2
Birch Dr BS40..........53 A5
Birches Cnr TA4.......152 A4
Birches The BS48.......9 A2
Birchfield Com Prim Sch
  BA21................219 D7
Birchfield Rd BA21....219 D8
Birch Gr
  Portishead BS20........2 C4
  Taunton TA1.........212 E5
Birch Hill BS27........90 C8
Birch Ho TA8..........65 F2
BIRCHILL.............198 A5
Birchill Cross EX13...198 A6
Birchill La BA11......120 A1
Birch Lawn TA8.......104 B6
Birch Rd
  12 Martock TA12......185 E6
  Radstock BA3..........78 E1
  Wellington TA21......222 E5
Birch Wlk BA11.......120 B7
BIRCHWOOD...........182 A1
Birchwood Ave BS23....49 A7
Birchwood Cl BA12....144 E8

Birchwood Dr BS8.......10 B3
Birchwood La BS39......40 F2
Birdcombe Cl BS48.......8 E3
Birdlip Cl BS48.........9 A1
Bird's Cl TA18........224 B6
BIRDSMOORGATE........199 D4
Birdwell La BS41.......10 F1
Birdwell Prim Sch BS41..21 A8
Birdwell Rd BS41.......10 F1
Birkbeck Ct BS23.......48 D7
Birkett Rd BS23........30 B1
Birkin St BS2.........227 C2
Birnbeck Rd BS23.......30 C1
Biscay Dr BS20.........2 F7
Biscombe Cross TA3....191 B8
Bisdee Rd BS24.........49 D2
Bishop Ave BS22........32 A3
Bishop Cres BA4.......204 F5
Bishop Fox Dr TA1.....213 A2
Bishop Fox's Com Sch
  TA1.................213 A1
Bishop Henderson CE Prim
 Sch
  Coleford BA3.........116 E8
  Taunton TA1.........212 C2
Bishop Rd TA5.........134 B2
Bishops Cl
  Bristol BS9...........5 E3
  Taunton TA3.........213 F7
Bishops Cotts
  Stogursey TA5.......134 B7
  Wootton Courtenay TA24..129 F6
Bishops Cove BS13......21 F5
Bishops Ct 4 TA21....222 D6
Bishops Dr TA10.......172 A5
Bishops Gn TA4.......210 A4
Bishop's Hill TA21....179 B7
BISHOP'S HULL........212 A4
Bishop's Hull Hill TA1..212 B4
Bishop's Hull Prim Sch
  TA1.................212 B4
Bishop's Hull Rd TA1..212 A3
Bishops Knoll BS9......5 C3
Bishops La BA22.......197 A6
Bishop's La DT9.......187 E1
Bishopslea Cl BA5.....203 C3
BISHOPS LYDEARD......167 F8
Bishops Lydeard CE Prim Sch
  TA4.................167 E8
Bishops Lydeard Mill & Rural
 Life Mus TA4.........167 E8
Bishops Lydeard Mill & Rural
 Life Mus* TA4........167 F8
Bishop's Lydeard Sta
  TA4.................167 E7
Bishops Mead TA10.....173 D1
Bishop's Mead 1 TA12..212 E8
Bishops Park Way BA5..203 F2
Bishop's Palace* BA5..203 E4
Bishop's Path TA6.....104 B6
Bishops Rd BS49........35 A8
Bishop St
  Bristol BS2..........227 B4
  Faulkland BA3.........80 D2
Bishopston TA15.......186 B4
BISHOP SUTTON.........57 D3
Bishop Sutton Prim Sch
  BS39................57 D4
Bishops Wlk BA22.....173 D1
BISHOPSWOOD..........192 E7
BISHOPSWORTH..........22 A5
Bishopsworth Rd BS13...22 A7
Bishop Terr BS2......227 C4
Bishport Ave BS13......22 C3
Bishport Cl BS13.......22 B4
Bishport Gn BS13.......22 C3
Bitham Wlk TA7.......136 E3
Bittern Ave BS20.......2 F7
Bittern Cl BS22........31 F1
Bittlemead BS13........22 F4
BITTON................25 E7
Blackacre BS14.........23 C4
Blackacre Hill BA8....176 D4
Blackaller La EX16....163 C1
Black Bench Dro TA20..223 F7
Blackberry Cl BA4.....205 C4
Blackberry Ct TA21....222 D4
Blackberry Dr BS22.....32 A2
Blackberry La
  Portishead BS20........1 F2
  Sherborne DT9.......225 D5
  Winsley BA3, BA15.....64 C8
Blackberry Way BA3.....77 F3
Blackberry Wlk TA18..224 D7
Blackberry Wy BS31....24 E3
Blackbird Cl BA3.......97 B8
Blackbird Way BA11....120 B6
Blackbrook Park Ave
  TA1.................213 E4
Blackbrook Prim Sch
  TA1.................213 D3
Blackbrook Rd TA1....213 E5
Blackbrook Way TA1...213 E3
Blackburn Wy BS24.....32 C1
Blackcurrant Dr BS41...20 E8
Black Dog Hill BA13...121 E6
BLACKDOWN............199 D6
Blackdown BA21.......219 A6
Blackdown Bsns Pk
  TA21................222 E6
Blackdown Ct TA3......23 B5
Blackdown Mead BS27...90 C6
Blackdown Rd
  Bridgwater TA6.......209 D4
  Portishead BS20.......2 B5
  Rockwell Green TA21..222 B4
  Taunton TA2.........213 B8

Blackdown View
  Curry Rivel TA10.....171 D4
  Ilminster TA19.......221 C4
  Norton Fitzwarren TA2..168 B5
  Nynehead TA21.......167 C2
  Sampford Peverell EX16..178 C1
Black Dro TA7........155 A1
Blacker's La BA3.....116 E2
Blackerton Cross EX16..162 B7
Blackey La BA3.......115 B6
BLACKFORD
  Minehead............129 E8
  Wedmore.............107 E4
  Wincanton...........175 F5
Blackford Hollow BA22..175 F5
Blackford Moor Dro BS26,
  BS28................107 B6
Blackford Moor La TA9,
  BS28................107 B5
Blackford Rd
  Charlton Horethorne
    DT9...............176 A2
  Mark TA9............106 F4
  Wedmore BS28.......108 A3
Blackford Way DT9....176 A3
Blackfriars BS1......227 A3
Blackfriars Rd BS48.....8 B1
Blackham La TA10.....155 F2
Blackhayes La EX14...192 C1
Black Horse La TA1...212 F5
Black La
  Axbridge BS26.........70 E2
  Hemyock EX15........180 D2
  Holcombe Rogus TA21..178 E6
Blackland Dro TA20...194 A1
Blackland La TA20....194 B1
Blacklands TA6.......208 F5
Black Mere BA22......218 B5
Black Mixen La TA18..224 C7
Black Monkey La TA24..131 C5
BLACKMOOR
  Chew Stoke...........38 C3
  Churchill.............53 D6
  Wellington...........180 E5
Blackmoor
  Clevedon BS21..........6 C1
  Lower Langford BS40....53 C6
  3 Weston-super-Mare
    BS22..............31 F2
Blackmoor Cl BS40.....53 C6
Blackmoor La 6 BA8...190 A6
Blackmoor Rd
  Abbots Leigh BS8.......4 E2
  Taunton TA2.........213 B7
  Wellington TA21......222 F4
Blackmoors La BS3.....11 E4
Blackmore Chase BA9..216 D3
Blackmore Dr BA2......44 C5
Blackmore La TA5.....135 B1
Blackmore Rd DT10....190 B4
Blackmore Vale Cl BA8..176 E1
Blacknell La TA18....224 C6
Blacknell Lane Ind Est
  TA18................224 E5
Black Nore Point BS20...1 F5
Black Pit Dro BA6....206 D8
BLACKPOOL CORNER....198 D1
BLACKROCK.............40 E8
Blackrock La BS39......40 E7
Black Rock Nature Trail*
  BA5.................72 A1
Blackrock Villas BS20...2 B1
Blackrod Cotts TA13..184 F4
Blacksmith La TA11.....28 B6
Blacksmith's La TA7...155 F8
Blacksmith's La BA1....26 B3
Blacksmiths Row BA21.187 D6
Black's Moor Hill La
  TA11................173 A5
Blackthorn Cl
  Biddisham BS26........87 E6
  Bristol BS13..........22 D5
  6 North Petherton TA6..153 F3
Blackthorn Dr BS20.....2 E5
Blackthorne Cl BA22..173 E2
Blackthorn Gdns
  Taunton TA2.........168 F6
  Weston-super-Mare BS22..32 A1
Blackthorn Rd BS13....22 D5
Blackthorn Sq BS21.....6 D1
Blackthorns The TA1..213 C2
Blackthorn Terr BS22..32 A1
Blackthorn Way
  Nailsea BS48..........9 A2
  Somerton TA11.......211 B3
  Street BA16.........207 A5
BLACKWATER..........182 C2
Blackwater La
  Axminster EX13......198 F3
  Wiveliscombe TA4....210 A8
BLACKWELL............165 B5
Blackwell Rd BA22....174 F3
Blackworthy Rd BA7...159 C3
Bladen Cl BS20.........2 E4
Bladud Bldgs BA1.....228 C3
BLAGDON...............54 E2
Blagdon Cl BS24.......48 F1
Blagdon Cres TA1.....212 D1
Blagdon Cross TA24...129 D2
BLAGDON HILL.........181 D5
Blagdon Hill Prim Sch
  TA3.................181 C5
Blagdon La
  Blagdon BS40.........54 F6
  Brompton Regis TA22,
    TA24.............148 D4
Blagdon Pk BA2........44 A4
Blagdon Prim Sch BS40..54 F2

Blagdon Wlk BA11.....120 D7
Blagrove Cl
  Bristol BS13..........22 C3
  Street BA16.........207 E6
Blagrove Cres BS13....22 C3
Blagrove Hill BA6....157 C6
Blagrove's Rd TA4....167 C4
Blaisdon BS22.........49 D7
Blaise Wlk BS9..........5 C6
Blake End BS22........31 E4
Blake Gn TA7.........156 B7
Blake Ind Est 5 TA6..209 A3
Blake Mus The* TA6...209 A4
Blakeney La BS48......18 C8
Blake Pl TA6.........209 A5
Blake Rd
  5 Crewkerne TA18...224 C5
  Wells BA5...........203 C5
Blake's Cres TA9.....104 E5
Blakes La TA5, TA6....208 C7
Blake's La BA3.......115 D2
Blakes Rd TA6........208 D6
Blake St
  2 Bridgwater TA6....208 F4
  Taunton TA1.........213 B4
Blakeway BS28........138 B6
Blandford Cl BS48......8 E1
Blandford Rd BA4.....205 D3
BLATCHBRIDGE........143 F8
Blaxhold La TA5......152 E5
BLEADNEY............139 A8
BLEADON..............67 C8
Bleadon Hill BS23, BS24..67 A8
Bleadon Mill BS24......67 C5
Bleadon Rd BS24.......67 B7
Bleak St BA9.........161 E2
Blencathara Ct TA8...104 A8
Blenheim Cl
  Peasedown St John BA2..79 D7
  Weston-super-Mare BS22..32 A2
Blenheim Ct 10 BS1...227 A4
Blenheim Gdns BA1.....28 A2
Blenheim Mews TA24..200 F7
Blenheim Rd
  Bridgwater TA6.......209 D7
  Minehead TA24.......201 A7
  Street BA16.........207 B4
  Taunton TA1.........213 D5
  Yeovil BA21.........219 D7
Blenheim View TA24...201 A7
Blenheim Way BS20......2 E5
Blights Hill EX16, TA22..163 F3
Blindhouse La 7 BA11..119 F4
Blind La
  Barton St David TA11..158 A2
  Bath BA1.............27 C2
  Buckland St Mary TA20..182 A1
  Chard TA20..........223 D2
  Chew Stoke BS40......56 E8
  Congresbury BS49.....34 F6
  Drimpton DT8........199 F6
  Isle Abbotts TA3.....183 F8
  Keinton Mandeville TA11..158 B1
  Martock TA12........185 D5
  Southwick BA14.......83 F2
  Thorncombe TA20.....199 B6
  Tunley BA2...........61 A4
Blindwell La
  Golsoncott TA23, TA24..131 C1
  Skilgate TA4........164 E6
BLOOMFIELD
  Bath................44 E3
  Timsbury............60 B4
Bloomfield Cl BS39....49 A2
Bloomfield Ave
  Bath BA2.............44 E4
  Timsbury BA2.........60 B3
Bloomfield Cl
  Taunton TA1.........213 C5
  Timsbury BA2.........60 B3
Bloomfield Cotts BA2..79 C7
Bloomfield Cres BA2....44 D2
Bloomfield Dr BA2......44 D2
Bloomfield Gr BA2......44 E3
Bloomfield La BS39....77 E5
Bloomfield Park Rd BA2..60 B3
Bloomfield Pk BA2.....44 E3
Bloomfield Rd
  Bath BA2.............44 E3
  Timsbury BA2.........60 B3
Bloomfield Rise BA2....44 D2
Bloomfield Rise N BA2..44 D2
Bloomfield Terr BA2....79 C7
Bloom Row TA6.......209 D5
Blossom Cl TA6.......209 C5
BLUE ANCHOR.........131 B6
Blue Anchor Chalets
  TA24................131 C6
Blue Anchor Railway Mus*
  TA24................131 C6
Blue Anchor Sta TA24..131 C6
Blue Ball Cl BA10....215 E6
Bluebell Cl
  Bristol BS9...........5 B6
  Taunton TA1.........213 C1
Bluebell Dr TA6......208 E1
Bluebell Rd
  Weston-super-Mare BS22..32 A6
  Yeovil BA22.........218 B5
Bluebell Rise BA3......77 F3
Blueberry Way BS22....31 F1
Blue Gate TA24.......145 D8
Blue Ho The BA11.....119 F5
Blue Reef Aquarium*
  BS1.................226 C2
Blue Sch The BA5.....203 C5
Blue Stone La TA13...185 B6
Bluett Rd TA21.......222 D4

Blue Water Dr BS24....50 D3
Blundells La TA2.....169 C7
Blythe Ct TA1........212 D1
Blythe Gdns BS22......32 A3
Blythe Way TA8........85 A3
BMI Bath Clinic Private Hospl
  BA2.................45 D2
Board Cross BA4......205 B6
Boards La BA5........204 C7
Boards Rd TA6........209 A6
Boardwalk The BA16..207 D7
Boarpath La TA4......151 A5
Boat La BA5...........67 C3
Boat Stall La BA2....228 C2
Bobbin La BA15........64 F4
Bobbin Pk BA15........64 F3
BODDEN...............205 F7
Bodden La BA4........205 E6
Boden St TA20........223 C3
Boden Villas TA20....223 C3
Bodley Way BS24......49 E7
Bodmin Rd TA2........213 A8
Bodmin Wlk BS4.......22 F8
Boez La TA2..........153 D1
Bofors Pk BA22.......218 A6
BOLHAM WATER........191 B7
Bollams Mead TA4....210 C5
Bollnas Cl BA4.......205 C4
Bolster La BA6.......157 C4
Bolter's La
  Alhampton BA4, BA7...159 B4
  Shepton Mallet BA4...141 D8
Bolton Cl TA9........104 F4
Bommertown Cross
  EX36................162 A4
Bondfield Way TA20...223 B6
Bondip Hill BA22, TA11..173 D3
Bonds Cl TA20........223 D6
Bond's La SN14........13 E8
Bonds Pool TA10......172 A5
Bond's Row TA24......124 A3
Bond St
  Bridgwater TA6......208 F5
  Bristol BS1.........227 B3
  Yeovil BA20.........219 B4
  Yeovil, Houndstone BA22..218 B5
Bonfire Cl TA20......223 C2
Bonfire La TA11......173 E7
Bonham La BA12......161 F4
Bonhill Rd BS39.......57 D5
Boniface Wlk TA8.....104 B6
Bonita Dr TA6.......208 D5
Bonners Cswy EX13...198 A2
Bonners Dr EX13.....198 A1
Bonners Glen EX13...198 A1
Bonnie's La 6 TA14..185 F4
Bonning's La TA19...184 D4
Bonniton La TA24....130 E5
Bonniton New Rd TA24..201 D1
Bonny Cross
  Clayhanger EX16.....165 B1
  Morebath EX16.......164 B3
Bonny La TA24........128 B2
Bonson Hill TA5.....134 E3
Bonsonwood La TA5...134 E4
Boobery EX16........178 D1
Book Cl BS39.........77 D6
Boome La TA2........169 C7
Boons Orch TA3......169 C3
Boon Villas BS11.......4 E7
Booth Way TA6.......208 D5
Boozer Pit TA16......195 F8
Borden Gate EX16....178 B8
Bordesley Rd BS14....23 A3
Boreal Way 4 BS24....49 F7
Boreland La BA22....187 A8
Borgie Pl BS22.......31 F3
Borleyton Wlk BS13....21 F4
Borough Mall The BS28..108 D4
Borough Post TA3....170 B3
Borough The
  Montacute TA15......186 B3
  Wedmore BS28.......108 D4
  3 Yeovil BA20........219 B4
Borver Gr BS13........22 B4
Bosanquet Flats TA24..200 F7
BOSSINGTON..........124 B4
Bossington Dr TA2....213 B8
Bossington La TA24...124 B4
Bosun Wlk BA16......207 B6
Boswell Rd BA15......64 F3
Botham Cl BS22.......32 A4
Bottreaux Mill Cross
  EX36................162 A5
Boucher's La TA4.....165 E4
Boulevard BS23........48 E8
Boulevard The BS14....22 E5
Boulters Rd BS13......22 C4
Boundaries The BS24...67 B1
Boundary Ave
  Frome BA11..........120 B5
  Yeovil BA22.........218 B7
Boundary Cl
  Holcombe BA3........116 C8
  Midsomer Norton BA3...97 B7
  Weston-super-Mare BS23..48 E3
  Yeovil BA22.........218 E7
Boundary Rd
  Weston-super-Mare BS24..50 A7
  Yeovil BA22.........218 A5
Boundary Way
  Glastonbury BA6.....206 C3
  Yeovil BA22.........218 A7
Boundhay BA22.......186 C2
Bounds La TA20.......223 A1

Bourchier Cl **13** EX16.... **164** B1
Bourchier Dr **12** EX16.... **164** B1
Bourchier Gdns BS13.... **22** B3
Bourke Rd BA4 .... **205** D3
BOURNE **54** B4
Bourne Gr TA1.......... **213** D4
Bourne La
　Blagdon BS40 .... **54** C4
　Burrington BS40 ...... **54** B4
Bournville Prim Sch BS23 **48** F5
Bournville Rd BS23...... **48** F4
BOURTON
　Gillingham **161** F1
　Weston-super-Mare..... **32** E6
Bourtonbridge Dro BA5 . **139** F5
Bourton Combe BS48 .... **19** F7
Bourton La
　Cross BS26 .... **69** E3
　Weston-super-Mare BS22 . **32** D4
Bourton Mead
　Flax Bourton BS48...... **19** F8
　Long Ashton BS41 ...... **11** A1
Bourton Wlk BS13 ...... **22** A8
Bouverie Cl TA24 ...... **129** E1
Bouverie Rd TA6........ **208** D5
Bove Moor Cl BA16..... **207** E6
Bove Moor Rd BA16..... **207** E6
Bovet Cl TA1............ **212** B1
Bove Town BA6......... **206** E5
Bovet St TA21.......... **222** C6
Bow Cotts BS20......... **4** C4
BOWDEN **177** F2
Bowden Cl BS9 .... **5** C8
Bowden Hill BA3....... **96** B4
Bowden La
　Milborne Port BA8...... **217** F5
　Rodhuish TA24.......... **130** F3
　Yenston BA8 .... **189** D7
Bowden Rd BA8......... **189** D8
Bowdens La EX16 ...... **164** E3
Bowden's La TA10 ..... **171** F5
Bowden Way BS8 .... **10** B3
Bowditch Cl BA4....... **205** A5
Bowditch Row **8** TA18 . **224** C6
Bowen Rd BS24......... **50** C5
BOWER ASHTON **11** E4
Bower Ashton Terr BS3 . . **11** F4
Bower Ave TA6......... **209** C6
Bower Fields TA6...... **209** D6
Bowerhayes La TA24 ... **131** A5
BOWER HINTON **185** D5
Bower Hinton TA12..... **185** D5
Bowerings Rd TA6..... **208** E2
Bower La TA6.......... **209** E6
Bowerleaze BS9 .... **5** C5
Bower Manor Sh Ctr
　TA6................... **209** D6
Bowermead La BA4..... **204** C1
Bowery Cnr BA5....... **92** E5
Bowfell Cl TA1........ **212** C1
Bow Gate TA18........ **196** A8
Bowhayes TA18 .... **224** C5
Bowhays Cross TA4.... **202** A2
Bowlditch La BA3...... **78** B4
Bowleaze BA21........ **218** D6
Bowline Cl TA6........ **208** E7
Bowline Ct TA24....... **201** B7
Bowling Gn
　10 Cannington TA5 ..... **135** B2
　Street BA16........... **207** D7
BOWLISH................ **205** A7
Bowlish Inf Sch BA4 ... **205** A6
Bowlish La BA4........ **205** A6
Bowmont Gr TA1....... **213** D3
Bowns Cl BA4.......... **141** E1
Bowood Rd TA2........ **213** A6
Bowring Cl
　Bristol BS13........... **22** C3
　Coxley BA5............ **139** E6
Bowsprit Cl TA24 ..... **201** B7
Bow St TA10........... **171** F5
Bowyers Cl BA6........ **206** E5
Boxbury Hill BS39..... **77** F3
Boxbush Hill BA4 ..... **158** E8
Box Bush La BS24...... **33** C1
Box Rd BA1............ **29** C3
Boxstone Hill TA19..... **184** D2
Box Wlk BS31.......... **24** C4
Boyce Cl BA2.......... **43** F5
Boyce's Ave BS8 ...... **226** A3
Boyd Ho BA5.......... **113** A1
Boyd Rd BS31.......... **25** D3
Boyle Cl DT10......... **190** B4
Boyton Hill TA19...... **194** F8
Boyton La TA19....... **194** F7
Bracey Rd TA12....... **185** E7
Bracken Edge TA4..... **132** E4
Bracken Way TA20..... **223** F5
Brackenwood Gdns★ BS20 .1 F5
Brackenwood Rd BS21 .... **6** E6
Bracton Dr BS14...... **23** A5
Bradbeers TA3........ **181** D8
Bradfield Cl
　Bridgwater TA6....... **208** E1
　Wells BA5............ **203** C2
Bradfield Way TA20... **223** C3
BRADFORD ABBAS **187** E1
Bradford Cl
　Clevedon BS21........ **6** C1
　Taunton TA1......... **168** D1
BRADFORD ON TONE .. **167** F1
Bradford Pk BA2...... **45** A2
Bradford Rd
　Bath BA2............. **45** A1
　Bathford BA1......... **29** B2

Bradford Rd *continued*
　Misterton TA18 .... **224** E4
　Rode BA11, BA14...... **83** A2
　Sherborne DT9 .... **225** B3
　Wingfield BA14, BA15.. **83** C8
　Winsley BA15......... **64** D6
　Winsley BA15......... **64** E7
Bradley Ave BS11 .... **4** E6
Bradley Cl TA11......... **211** C4
Bradley Cres BS11 .... **4** E6
Bradley Cross La BS27 ... **90** D7
BRADLEY GREEN **135** B1
Bradley Hill La TA11... **211** B5
Bradley La
　Ashcott TA7 .... **156** B7
　Maiden Bradley BA11,
　　BA12................ **144** B2
　Parbrook BA6 .... **158** C2
Bradley Rd BS20 .... **3** E5
Bradleys TA19 .... **183** F4
Bradley Stream Rd BA16,
　TA7................. **138** C1
Bradley View TA11 .... **211** C4
Bradley Way BA6 ..... **158** B8
BRADNEY **136** D1
Bradney La TA7....... **136** D1
Bradon La
　Isle Abbotts TA3 ..... **183** F6
　Stocklinch TA19 ..... **184** A5
Bradville Gdns BS41... **20** F8
Brae Rd BS25 .... **70** B8
Brae Rise BS25 .... **70** A8
Bragg's La BS2 .... **227** C3
Braikenridge Cl BS21 . . **6** C1
Brain's Cnr BA9....... **216** E1
Brainsfield BS9........ **5** F6
Brains La BA22........ **175** A5
Braithwaite Pl TA8..... **85** A2
Braithwaite Way BA11.. **120** C6
Brakewell Gdns BS14... **23** A4
Bramble Dr
　Berrow TA8 .... **84** F5
　Bristol BS9............ **5** D3
　South Petherton TA13 . **220** C4
Bramble Hill BA16 ... **156** D6
Bramble La
　Bristol BS9............ **5** C3
　Haselbury Plucknett TA18 . **196** C5
Bramble Pk TA1....... **213** C2
Bramble Rd TA6....... **208** D1
Brambles Rd TA8 ..... **85** B1
Brambles The
　Bristol BS13........... **22** C4
　Hinton Charterhouse BA2 . **63** E1
　Keynsham BS31....... **24** D3
　Wellington TA21....... **222** D4
　Weston-super-Mare BS22 . **32** D2
Bramble Way BA2..... **45** B1
Bramblewood BS49 ... **17** B1
Bramblewood Rd BS22 . **31** E3
Bramley Cl
　Charlton Horethorne
　　DT9................ **176** A2
　Crewkerne TA18...... **224** C7
　Locking BS24.......... **50** A5
　Peasedown St John BA2 . **79** D7
　Pill BS20.............. **4** C4
　Sandford BS25........ **52** A4
　Wellington TA21....... **222** F7
　Yatton BS49.......... **34** B7
Bramley Copse BS41... **20** E8
Bramley Dr
　Backwell BS48........ **19** A5
　Frome BA11........... **120** C6
Bramley Rd
　Street BA16........... **207** B4
　Taunton TA1.......... **213** D5
Bramley Sq BS49...... **34** E3
Bramleys The
　Nailsea BS48 .... **18** B8
　Portishead BS20 .... **2** F5
Brampton Ho BS20..... **2** E4
Brampton Way BS20 .... **2** E4
Bramshill Dr BS22 .... **31** F3
BRAMWELL **172** B8
Branche Gr BS13...... **22** D3
Branches Cross BS40... **35** E3
Branch Rd BA2 .... **63** F2
BRANDISH STREET **124** C3
BRANDON HILL........ **226** B2
Brandon Ho BS8 ..... **226** B2
Brandon St BS1....... **226** C2
Brandon Steep BS1 ... **226** C2
Brangay La BS27...... **91** A1
Brangwyn Sq BS22.... **31** F2
Branksome Ave TA6... **209** B5
Bransby Way BS24.... **50** A8
Branscombe Rd BS9 .... **5** C4
Branscombe Wlk BS20 .. **1** F3
Bransford BA22....... **197** D3
Brantwood Rd TA6.... **208** C5
BRASSKNOCKER **45** F2
Brassknocker Hill BA2 . **45** F2
Brassmill Ent Ctr BA1 .. **44** A7
Brassmill La BA1..... **44** A7
Brassmill Lane Trad Est
　BA1................. **44** A7
BRATTON **200** B7
Bratton Cl TA24...... **200** D7
Bratton Ho BA9...... **176** B8
Bratton La TA24...... **200** B7
Bratton Mill La
　Minehead, Bratton TA24 . **200** B7
　Minehead, Woodcombe
　　TA24............... **200** C7
Bratton Rd BS4...... **22** D7
BRATTON SEYMOUR .. **176** C8
Bray Cl EX16......... **179** B3

Braysbridge BS27 .... **90** C7
Braysdown Cl BA2 ..... **79** B6
Braysdown La BA2..... **79** C7
BREACH **58** F6
Breach Cl SP8 .... **161** F1
Breaches The BS20 ...... **4** B5
Breach Furlong La TA10 . **156** A1
Breach Hill TA21...... **179** F5
Breach Hill La BS40 ... **56** C6
Breach La
　Brinscombe BS26 ..... **89** B3
　Corsley Heath BA12 ... **144** E7
　Kington Magna SP8 ... **177** E2
　Nailsea BS48 .... **17** F7
　Weston Town BA4 .... **142** E4
Breachwood View BA2.. **44** C2
Bread And Cheese La
　TA19................ **184** C1
Bread St BA4 .... **140** F3
BREAN **65** F5
Brean Court Ho TA8.... **65** F3
Brean Ct TA8 .... **65** F3
Brean Down Ave BS23.. **48** E4
Brean Down Rd TA8... **47** F1
Brean Leisure Pk★ TA8 . . **65** F1
Brean Rd BS24........ **66** F1
Brecon View BS24 .... **49** A1
Breech Cotts TA21 ... **179** F5
Breech La BA6........ **158** A8
Bree Cl BS22 .... **32** A4
Bremis Rd TA24...... **201** E3
BRENDON **122** A4
Brendon Ave BS23 ... **48** F8
Brendon Cl TA23...... **131** D2
Brendon Gdns **2** BS48 ... **8** E1
Brendon Ho BA21..... **219** A6
Brendon Rd
　Bridgwater TA6....... **208** F6
　Portishead BS20 .... **2** A5
　Watchet TA23........ **202** B6
　Wellington TA21....... **222** D7
Brendons TA4........ **167** E8
Brendons The TA6 ... **178** D1
Brendon Two Gates
　TA24................ **127** A6
Brendon View TA4.... **151** B7
Brendon Way
　Bridgwater TA6....... **208** F6
　Cheddar BS27......... **90** C8
Brent Broad TA8...... **85** B2
Brent Cl
　Brent Knoll TA9....... **86** B1
　Weston-super-Mare BS24 . **49** B2
BRENT KNOLL......... **86** A1
Brent Knoll CE Prim Sch
　TA9................. **86** A2
Brent Rd
　Burnham-on-S TA8, TA9 . **85** B4
　Cossington TA7 ...... **136** F3
　East Brent TA9....... **86** C5
Brentsfield La TA7 ... **154** E7
Brent St TA9.......... **86** A2
Breowen Cl TA19 .... **221** B3
Brereton Rd TA24..... **201** B6
Breton Cl **1** TA9....... **209** A1
Bretoneux Rd BA6.... **206** E3
Brett Cl TA1.......... **202** F1
Brettingham Ct TA17.. **195** C7
Brewery Bglws TA18 .. **224** C7
Brewery Hill BS30..... **25** F7
Brewery La
　Holcombe BA3 .... **97** D1
　Ilminster TA19....... **221** B4
　Oakhill BA3........... **115** A3
　Shepton Mallet BA4... **205** D5
Brewham Rd BA10 ... **160** D6
Brewhouse The BS1... **227** B2
Brewhouse Theatre & Arts
　Ctr★ TA1............ **212** F4
Breynton Rd BA6..... **206** F5
Brian Mooney Cl TA20.. **223** B3
Briant Cl TA1......... **212** B1
Briar Cl
　Burnham-on-S TA8.... **104** C6
　Frome BA11.......... **120** B7
　Nailsea BS48......... **9** A2
　Radstock BA3........ **97** D8
　Yeovil BA21.......... **219** E8
Briar Ct
　Bridgwater TA6....... **208** E5
　Burnham-on-S TA8.... **104** C6
　Pill BS20............. **4** C4
Briarfield BA22....... **173** E2
Briar Mead BS49 ..... **17** A1
Briar Rd
　Hutton BS24.......... **49** E3
　Street BA16.......... **207** A5
Briars Ct BA2 .... **44** A4
Briars The
　Backwell BS48........ **18** F7
　Yeovil BA20 .... **218** C2
Briarwood BS9........ **5** F6
Briary Rd BS20....... **2** C5
Brick Cotts BA3...... **117** A7
Brickkiln La DT9 ..... **225** E7
Brick St BS2 .... **227** C3
Brickyard La
　Bourton SP8......... **161** F1
　Wanstrow BA4........ **142** F5
Brick Yard La TA18.... **224** C7
Briddicott La TA24.... **131** A4
Bridewell La
　Bath BA1............ **228** B2
　Hutton BS24, BS26, BS29 . **50** D1
　Shapwick TA7........ **137** F1
Bridewell St BS1..... **227** A3
BRIDGE **199** A8
Bridge Bldgs BS39 .... **77** B3

Bridge Cl
　Evercreech BA4....... **141** E2
　Whitchurch BS14...... **23** C4
　Williton TA4......... **202** D2
Bridge Cotts
　Chard Junction TA20 .. **198** D8
　Drimpton DT8 .... **199** F7
　East Chinnock BA22... **196** F8
Bridge Farm Cl BS14... **23** A3
Bridge Farm Inf Sch BS14 **23** A4
Bridge Farm Jun Sch
　BS14................ **23** A4
Bridge Farm Sq BS49.. **34** D4
Bridge Gdns BA2...... **60** A6
BRIDGEHAMPTON **174** C3
Bridge Hill BA4 ...... **142** F4
Bridge Ho
　11 Bath BA1.......... **28** C1
　Bristol BS1........... **227** A2
　9 Clevedon BS21...... **6** C2
　Weston-super-Mare BS23 . **48** E6
Bridgehouse Cross EX15 **180** D1
Bridge House Pk TA13 .. **220** F4
Bridge Learning Campus
　BS13................ **22** D4
Bridge Pl DT9 .... **187** F4
Bridge Place Rd BA2... **78** E8
Bridge Rd
　Bath BA2............. **44** C5
　Bleadon BS24........ **67** B6
　Leigh Woods BS8..... **11** E6
　Weston-super-Mare BS23 . **48** F6
Bridge Rise **17** TA12... **185** E6
Bridges Mead TA24 .. **201** E3
Bridge St
　Bath BA2............. **228** C2
　Bourton SP8.......... **161** F1
　Bristol BS1........... **227** A2
　Dulverton TA22...... **163** D6
　Frome BA11.......... **119** F5
　Taunton TA1......... **212** F4
　Williton TA4......... **202** D2
Bridge Terr EX16..... **164** B1
Bridge The
　Frome BA11.......... **119** F5
　Taunton TA1......... **212** F4
BRIDGETOWN **147** E4
Bridge Valley Rd BS8... **11** E8
Bridge Way TA13..... **220** E4
Bridgeway Cotts TA13.. **220** E4
Bridgewell Ct DT9 ... **225** E3
BRIDGWATER **208** E3
Bridgwater TA6...... **208** F4
Bridgwater Bay National
　Nature Reserve★ TA5 . **103** C2
Bridgwater Bldgs BA7.. **214** B5
Bridgwater Coll TA6... **209** B5
Bridgwater Com Hospl
　TA6................. **209** D7
Bridgwater Ct BS24 ... **49** A3
Bridgwater Ent Ctr **7**
　TA6................. **208** F5
Bridgwater Rd
　Dundry BS41, BS13, BS48 . **21** D6
　East Brent TA9....... **86** D4
　Lympsham BS24....... **67** C5
　North Petherton TA6 . **153** F4
　Taunton, Bathpool TA2 . **213** F7
　Taunton TA1......... **213** D5
　Weston-super-Mare BS23,
　　BS24............... **48** F2
　Winscombe BS25...... **70** A5
Bridgwater Ret Pk TA6.. **209** A5
Bridgwater Sta TA6 .. **209** B4
Bridle Way TA6...... **197** F8
Bridleway The BS4.... **22** D8
Bridport Rd DT8 ..... **199** F8
Briercliffe Rd BS9..... **5** D7
Briery Leaze Rd BS14 .. **23** A4
Brigadier Cl BA22..... **218** A5
Brigg Cl TA6.......... **208** E7
Brighton Mews BS8 ... **226** B4
Brighton Rd BS23..... **48** E6
Brighton St **7** BS2..... **227** B4
Brightstowe Rd TA8... **85** A2
Brigstocke Rd BS2.... **227** B4
Brimble Cotts DT10 .. **189** F1
Brimbleworth La BS22 . **32** C3
Brimclose Rd TA17.... **195** B7
Brimgrove La TA19.... **184** E4
Brimhill Rise BA13.... **121** D4
BRIMLEY **198** D3
Brimley Cross TA3.... **180** F1
Brimley Hill EX13 .... **198** D2
Brimley Rd EX13 .... **198** D3
Brimridge Rd BS25.... **70** A8
Brimsmore Ct BA21... **218** E8
Brimstone La
　Rockwell Green TA21... **222** A2
　Sampford Arundel TA21... **179** F6
　Sampford Peverell EX16 . **178** E2
Brincil Hill TA11..... **173** D4
BRINDHAM **139** D3
Brindham La BA6..... **139** D3
Brindle Cl TA2....... **212** C7
Brines Orch BA8 ..... **176** E1
Brinmead Wlk BS13... **21** F3
BRINSCOMBE.......... **89** A5
Brinscombe La BS26... **89** A5
BRINSEA **52** E8
Brinsea Batch BS49... **52** E8
Brinsea La BS49 ..... **52** F8
Brinsea Rd BS49 ..... **34** E2
Brinsmead Cres BS20 . **4** D4
Briscoes Ave BS13 ... **22** D4
Brislington Ent Coll BS4.. **23** F8
BRISTOL **227** B3

Bristol and Exeter Mews
　BS1 .... **227** C1
Bristol Cathedral Sch
　BS1................. **226** C2
Bristol Dental Hospl
　BS1................. **227** A3
Bristol Eye Hospl BS1.. **227** A3
Bristol Gate **1** BS8 .... **11** F5
Bristol Gram Sch BS8.. **226** C3
Bristol Harbour Rly★
　BS1................. **226** C1
Bristol Hill BA5 ..... **112** E4
Bristol Airport BS48... **36** E7
Bristol Museum &
　Art Gallery★ BS8 ... **226** C3
Bristol Rd
　Bridgwater TA6....... **209** B7
　Chew Stoke BS40..... **56** E8
　Chewton Mendip BA5 . **113** A8
　Churchill BS25........ **53** A5
　Congresbury BS49..... **34** B5
　Farrington Gurney BS39 . **76** F5
　Highbridge TA9....... **104** F4
　Horrington BA5....... **112** F6
　Keynsham BS31....... **24** E6
　Newton St Loe BA2... **43** D7
　Paulton BS39......... **77** E7
　Pensford BS39........ **40** D6
　Portishead BS20...... **2** E4
　Radstock BA3........ **78** F3
　Redhill BS40......... **37** A3
　Rooks Bridge BS26, TA9 . **87** B5
　Sherborne DT9....... **225** D5
　Walpole TA6......... **136** B3
　Weston-super-Mare BS22 . **32** C2
　Whitchurch BS14..... **23** D3
　Winscombe BS25..... **70** C8
　Wraxall BS48........ **9** D4
Bristol Rd By-pass BS40.. **53** C5
Bristol Rd Lower BS23.. **30** F1
Bristol Road Lower BS23 . **30** E1
Bristol Royal Hospl for
　Children BS2........ **227** A3
Bristol Royal
　Infirmary BS2........ **227** A4
Bristol Temple Meads
　Station BS1.......... **227** C1
Bristol View BA2...... **62** C8
Bristol Zoo Gdns★ BS8.. **5** F1
Britannia Cl BA3..... **96** D4
Britannia Way
　Chard TA20........... **223** C6
　Clevedon BS21........ **6** C1
Briton St **2** EX16..... **164** C1
Brittains BA11........ **119** D6
Brittania Bldgs BS8 .. **226** A1
Brittan Pl BS20....... **3** E3
BRITTENS **77** F6
Britten's Cl BS39..... **77** F6
Britten's Hill BS39.... **77** F6
Brittons Ash TA2..... **213** E8
Brittons Pass SN14.... **13** F8
Broadacres BA22 .... **197** C8
Broadbridge Rd TA3... **183** C6
Broadbury Rd BS4.... **22** E8
Broad Cl
　Kington Magna SP8... **177** E1
　Wells BA5............ **112** E1
Broadclose Way TA11.. **158** A2
Broadcroft BS40..... **38** F3
Broadcroft Ave BS49.. **17** F1
Broadcroft Cl BS49... **17** F1
Broad Dro
　Burrowbridge TA7.... **155** A2
　North Wootton BA4... **140** A3
Broadenham La TA20 . **194** E1
Broadfield Rd BS4.... **23** A8
Broadgauge Bsns Pk
　TA4................. **167** E7
Broadhay BA5........ **110** E7
Broad Hill BA22...... **196** D7
Broadhurst Gdns TA8.. **104** B5
Broad La
　East Chinnock BA22.... **196** E7
　Hawkridge TA22...... **146** D1
　North Curry TA3...... **170** D4
　Winsford TA22....... **147** F4
Broadlands BS21...... **6** F3
Broadlands Ave
　Keynsham BS31....... **24** D6
　North Petherton TA6 . **153** F4
Broadlands Cl BA21... **219** E8
Broadlands Ct TA1.... **212** E2
Broadlands Dr BS11.... **5** A8
Broadlands La TA5.... **208** A4
Broadlands Rd TA1 ... **212** E2
Broadlands Rise TA1.. **212** E2
Broadlands Sch BS31.. **24** D6
Broadlands Way TA1.. **212** E2
Broad Lane Head
　Hawkridge TA22...... **146** D1
　Winsford TA22....... **147** F4
Broadlawn TA7...... **136** E4
Broadleas BS13...... **22** C7
Broadleaze
　Bristol BS11.......... **4** E7
　Yeovil BA21.......... **218** C6
Broadleaze Way BS25 . **51** F2
Broadly Gdns TA2.... **213** E8
Broadmead
　Bristol BS1.......... **227** B3
　Keynsham BS31....... **25** B5
　Kingsbury Episcopi TA12 . **185** B7
　South Petherton TA13 . **220** B4
Broadmead Dro TA7... **155** F6
Broadmead La
　Barrington TA19...... **184** D6
　Catcott TA7.......... **137** D2

Broadmead La *continued*
Edington TA7 137 C3
Keynsham BS31 25 A6
Kington Magna SP8 177 D1
Norton Sub Hamdon TA14 185 F2
Broad Mead La BS40 38 A3
Broadmead Rd TA3 183 B7
Broadmeads TA10 172 A6
Broadmoor Dro BS28 89 D3
Broadmoor La
Bath BA1 27 A3
Horsington BA8 176 E2
Broadmoor Pk BA1 27 B2
Broadmoor Vale BA1 27 A3
Broadoak TA19 183 C1
Broad Oak 9 BA20 219 B4
Broadoak Hill BS41 21 F2
Broad Oak Hill TA4 151 B5
Broadoak Mathematics & Computing Coll BS23 48 E3
Broadoak Rd
Bridgwater TA6 209 D5
Churchill BS40 53 A5
Weston-super-Mare BS23 48 D3
Broad Oak Rd BS13 21 F4
Broad Oaks BS8 11 E6
Broad Path EX15 179 A1
Broad Plain BS2 227 C2
Broad Quay
Bath BA1 228 C1
Bristol BS1 227 A2
Broad Rd
Blagdon BS40 72 D8
Rodney Stoke BA5 91 E1
Broadshard Rd TA18 224 C8
Broad St
Bath BA1 228 C3
Bristol BS1 227 A3
Charlton Adam TA11 173 F7
Chewton Mendip BA3 94 C5
Churchinford TA3 191 D7
Congresbury BS49 34 D4
Somerton TA11 211 E4
Stoney Stratton BA4 141 F2
Wells BA5 203 D4
Wrington BS40 35 D2
Broadstone TA7 154 E6
Broadstone La
Hardington Mandeville BA22 197 A6
Kingston Seymour BS21 15 F3
West Chinnock TA18 196 C7
Broad Stones BA15 46 E7
Broadstone Wlk BS13 22 D5
Broad Street Pl BA1 228 C3
BROADWAY 183 B2
Broadway
Bath BA2 45 B6
Bridgwater TA6 208 F4
Charlton Adam TA11 174 A7
Chilcompton BA3 96 C3
Chilton Polden TA7 137 B2
Frome BA11 119 D5
Locking BS24 50 D4
Merriott TA16 195 F7
Odcombe BA22 186 C2
Saltford BS31 25 D3
Shipham BS25 70 E8
Weston-super-Mare BS24 49 A2
Broad Way TA12 185 D5
Broadway Acres BS27 70 F1
Broadway Ave TA7 137 B2
Broadway Cl BA3 96 C3
Broadway Hill TA19 183 B1
Broadway La
Castle Cary BA22 214 B3
Midsomer Norton BA3 78 B5
Westbury-sub-Mendip BA5 110 D7
Broadway Rd
Bristol, Bishopsworth BS13 21 F5
Charlton Adam TA11 173 F7
Horton TA19 183 C2
Broadways Head EX14, TA20 192 C6
Broad Weir BS1 227 B3
Broadwell Cl TA20 193 D6
Broadwood Rd TA24 130 D4
Brock Ct BA7 214 C6
Brock End BS20 1 F3
BROCKFIELD 198 A8
Brockhole La
Dinnington TA17 195 B8
Tatworth EX13, TA20 198 B7
Brockle Cl TA11 211 D4
BROCKLEY 18 C2
Brockley Cl
Nailsea BS48 8 D1
Weston-super-Mare BS24 48 F1
Brockley Combe Rd BS48 19 B1
Brockley Cres BS24 48 F1
Brockley La BS48 18 D4
Brockley Rd BS31 25 D3
Brockley Way BS49 18 B3
Brockley Wlk BS13 22 A8
Brocks La BS41 10 F1
Brocks Mount 16 TA14 185 F4
Brocks Rd BS13 22 C3
Brock St BA1 228 B3
Brockway BS48 8 F2
BROCKWELL 129 E6
Brockwell La TA24 129 F6
Brockwood BA15 64 F7
Brocole La TA20 193 D5
Broderip TA7 136 F3
BROKERSWOOD 102 F5
Brokerswood Country Pk BA13 102 F6
Bromes La TA3 183 F7
Bromley Rd BS39 39 F1
Brompton Ho BA2 228 C4
Brompton Mdws TA22 148 B2
BROMPTON RALPH 150 C3
Brompton Rd BS24 49 A2
BROMPTON REGIS 148 B2
Bronte Cl BS23 49 B4
Brook Bank
Draycott BS27 90 F2
Rodney Stoke BS27 109 C7
Brook Cl
Long Ashton BS41 11 B1
Minehead TA24 200 F7
North Petherton TA6 153 E3
Yeovil BA21 218 D7
Brook Cotts
Corfe TA3 181 F6
Corston BA2 43 B7
Brook Ct BS13 22 A6
Brookdale Rd BS13 22 B6
Brooke Rd
Berrow TA8 84 F4
Taunton TA1 213 B4
Brookes Ct BA5 203 C5
Brookfield Pk BA1 27 B2
Brookfields BA7 214 B5
Brookfield Way BA16 207 A4
Brookfield Wlk BS21 6 F3
Brook Gate BS3 11 E1
BROOKHAMPTON 175 D6
Brookhampton Cnr BA22 175 D6
Brooking Mdw BS48 8 D1
Brook La
Barton St David BA6 157 F3
6 Cannington TA5 135 B2
Catcott TA7 137 D2
7 Henstridge BA8 190 A6
Brookland Rd
Langport TA10 172 A6
Weston-super-Mare BS22 49 B7
Brooklands
Bridgwater TA6 209 C5
Dunkerton BA2 61 D3
Brooklands Rd TA21 222 B5
Brookland Way 3 BA8 190 A6
Brookleaze
Bristol BS9 5 C5
Keynsham BS31 24 D6
Brookleaze Bldgs BA1 28 B2
Brookleigh BA16 207 A5
Brooklyn BS40 35 D2
Brooklyn Rd
Bath BA1 28 C2
Bristol BS13 22 B8
Brooklyn Terr BA5 139 E6
Brook Rd
Bath BA2 44 D6
Williton TA4 202 E3
Brook's Hill EX15 179 C1
Brookside
Broadway TA19 183 C2
Milborne Port DT9 217 D1
Paulton BS39 77 E6
Pill BS20 4 D3
South Cheriton BA8 176 D3
West Coker BA22 197 A8
Brookside Cl
Batheaston BA1 28 F5
Paulton BS39 77 E6
Taunton TA3 168 D1
Brookside Com Prim Sch BA16 207 B4
Brookside Dr BA2 59 F6
Brookside Ho BA1 27 B1
Brookside Rd TA5 135 B5
Brooks Pl TA21 222 E6
Brooks Rd BA16 207 B4
Brook St
Bampton EX16 164 B1
Cannington TA5 135 B2
Milborne Port DT9 217 D1
Minehead TA24 201 B5
North Newton TA7 153 F1
Timberscombe TA24 130 B5
Brook Street Mews TA24 201 B5
Brookview Wlk BS13 22 B7
Broomball Cross TA22 162 F5
Broomball La EX16 162 E5
Broomclose Cnr BA3 114 B4
Broome Cl EX13 198 A1
Broom Farm Cl BS48 18 E8
BROOMFIELD 152 E2
Broomfield Ho TA2 212 E7
Broomground BA15 64 E7
Broomhill La BS39 58 E3
Broom Hill La BS39 77 E8
Broom La
Chardstock EX13 198 C5
Oake TA4 167 D3
Broom's La TA3 191 F7
Broomyland Hill TA5 152 C7
Brottens Rd
Cranmore BA4 142 A5
Doulting BA4 141 F5
Brougham Hayes BA2 44 D6
Brougham Pl 2 BA1 28 C2
Broughton Cl
Taunton TA1 213 C2
Walton BA16 156 E7
Broughton Ho BS1 227 B1
Broughton La TA3 169 B1
Broughton Pk TA3 169 A1
Broughtons Dr TA18 224 E3
Brow Hill BA2 28 F4
Brown Down La TA20 192 C7
Browne Ct 4 BS8 11 F6
BROWNHEATH 180 C2
Brownings Rd TA5 135 B2
Brown La TA4, TA23 149 C3
Brownlow Rd BS23 48 E4
Browns Ct BS23 48 E6
Brown's Folly Nature Reserve BA15 29 D1
Browns La BS28 109 C1
Brown's Pl 4 BA5 203 C4
Brow The
Bath BA2 44 B5
Bath, Combe Down BA2 45 C1
Broxholme Wlk BS11 4 F8
Brue Ave
Bridgwater TA6 209 B3
Bruton BA10 215 F7
Brue Bsns Pk TA9 136 E8
Brue Cl
Bruton BA10 215 F7
Weston-super-Mare BS23 49 A5
Brue Cres TA8 104 B5
Brue Ho TA8 85 A1
Bruelands BA10 215 F7
Brue Way TA9 104 F3
Bruford Cl TA1 212 E3
Brummel Way BS39 77 C6
Brunel Cl
Somerton TA11 211 D4
Weston-super-Mare BS24 48 F1
Brunel Ct
Bridgwater TA6 208 F6
Portishead BS20 2 D6
Brunel Ho BA2 44 A6
Brunel Institute The BS3 226 B1
Brunel Lock Rd BS1 11 F5
Brunel Prec TA11 211 D4
Brunel Rd
Bristol BS13 22 A8
Nailsea BS48 8 B1
Brunel's SS Great Britain & The Matthew BS1 226 B1
Brunel's Way TA9 104 E5
Brunel Way
Bristol BS1, BS3 11 F4
Frome BA11 120 C7
Minehead TA24 201 B6
Taunton TA2 212 A6
Brunsell's Knap DT10 190 A1
Brunswick Pl
1 Bath BA1 228 B3
10 Bristol BS1 11 F5
Brunswick Sq BS2 227 B4
Brunswick St
1 Bath BA1 28 B1
Bristol BS2 227 B4
Yeovil BA20 219 A4
BRUSHFORD 163 D4
Brushford New Rd TA22 163 E4
Brutasche Terr BA16 207 D7
BRUTON 215 E5
Bruton BS24 49 A2
Bruton Ave
Bath BA2 44 F4
Portishead BS20 2 A5
Bruton Avenue Garages BA2 44 F4
Bruton Cl BS48 18 E8
Bruton La BA4 142 F2
Bruton Mus BA10 215 E6
Bruton Pl BS8 226 B3
Bruton Prim Sch BA10 215 E6
Bruton Rd BA4 141 F1
Bruton Sch for Girls BA10 215 C3
Bruton Sta BA10 215 F6
Brutton Way TA20 223 B3
Bryant Ave BA3 78 D1
Bryant Gdns BS21 6 C1
Bryant's Hill TA22 148 C2
Bryer Cl
Bridgwater TA6 208 E1
Chard TA20 223 D3
Brymore Cl TA6 208 D5
Brymore Sch TA5 135 A2
Brympton Ave BA22 186 D2
BRYMPTON D'EVERCY 218 A3
Brympton Way BA20 218 C3
Bsns Courtyard The BA11 143 C7
Bubwith Cl TA20 223 D3
Bubwith Ho 4 BA5 203 D4
Bubwith Rd TA20 223 D3
Bubwith Wlk BA5 203 B3
Buces Rd TA1 212 B1
Buck Cl BA6 206 C3
Buckhill TA24 131 B4
Buckhill Cl TA18 224 C4
BUCKHORN WESTON 177 D3
Buckingham Cl TA6 209 A2
Buckingham Pl BS8 226 A3
Buckingham Rd BS24 49 B2
Buckingham Vale BS8 226 A4
Buckland Cl TA8 104 C8
BUCKLAND DINHAM 100 A3
BUCKLAND DOWN 99 B4
Buckland Gn BS22 32 A5
Buckland La BA22 175 C3
Buckland Rd
Shepton Mallet BA4 205 A5
Taunton TA2 213 B8
Yeovil BA21 219 E6
BUCKLAND ST MARY 192 F8
Buckland St Mary CE Prim Sch TA20 193 A8
Bucklands Batch BS48 18 F8
Buckland Sch TA23 202 C6
Bucklands Dr BS48 19 A8
Bucklands End BS48 18 F8
Bucklands Gr BS48 18 F8
Bucklands La BS48 18 F8
Bucklands View BS48 19 A8
Buckle Path BS24 50 C8
Buckle Pl BA22 218 B6
Buckler's Mead Acad BA21 219 C8
Bucklers Mead Rd BA21 219 D8
Bucklers Mead Wlk BA21 219 D8
Bucklers Way BA4 204 F6
Bucklewell Cl BS11 4 F6
Buckshots Cross EX14 192 D4
Buckwell TA21 222 E6
Bude Cl BS48 9 B1
Budge La BA11 144 A8
Budgetts TA21 180 F6
Budgett's Cross TA21 180 F6
Bughole La TA21 179 E8
Bugle Ct 11 BA8 190 A6
Bugle Wlk TA6 208 D1
Building of Bath Mus BA1 228 C3
BULFORD 182 C4
Bulford TA21 222 D5
Bulford La TA21 222 D5
Bull Bridge Mead BA22 197 D3
Bullen Mead BA11 117 F2
Bullens Cl TA19 183 F4
Buller Ave BA22 218 A6
Bull Horn Dro TA7 154 D5
Bull La BS20 4 C4
Bull Mdw TA4 167 F7
Bullmead Cl BA16 207 B5
Bullmead La BA11 143 C7
Bullock Field Hill TA21 166 B2
Bullocks La BS21 16 C4
Bullon Drove TA5 134 B7
Bull Plot Hill BA6 158 C8
BULL'S GREEN 117 E1
Bull's Hill BA2 62 E1
Bulls La TA18 224 B6
Bull's La
Tatworth TA20 198 C8
Upton Noble BA4 142 F2
Bull's Quarr BA11 143 E8
Bull's Quarries Rd BA11 143 F7
Bull St TA3 169 D4
Bulwarks La BA6 206 F4
Bumblebee Cl BS13 21 E4
Bumper's Batch BA2 63 A8
Bunce's La TA19 184 E3
Buncombe Hill TA5 152 C3
Bune Villas TA6 208 E7
Bunford Hollow Rdbt BA20 218 D1
Bunford La BA20, BA21 218 C4
Bungalows The
Axbridge BS26 70 C2
Chard TA20 223 D5
Monkton Heathfield TA2 213 F8
Nether Stowey TA5 134 A2
Poyntington DT9 188 E7
Bungay's Hill BA2, BS39 59 E1
Bunker Military Mus The TA9 104 D3
Bunns La
Horningsham BA11 144 A5
Witham Friary BA11 143 F5
Bunting Ct BS22 31 E1
Bunting La BS20 3 A6
Burchill Cl BS39 58 F3
Burchills Cl TA21 222 A6
Burchill's Hill TA21 222 B7
Burch's Cl TA1 212 C2
BURCOTT 139 E8
Burcott La
Coxley BA5 139 E7
Wells BA5 203 A3
Burcott Mill BA5 139 E8
Burcott Rd BA5 203 B3
Burdenham Dro TA7 155 A6
Burfoote Gdns BS14 23 E4
Burfoot Rd BS14 23 E4
BURFORD 204 C2
Burford Cl
Bath BA2 44 B3
Portishead BS20 2 E4
Burford Cross BA4 204 C2
Burford Gr BS11 4 F5
Burgage TA21 222 D6
Burgage La TA4 167 A4
Burgage Rd TA5 134 C6
Burge Cres TA4 167 E6
Burge Mdw TA4 167 E6
Burges Cl
Marnhull DT10 190 F6
Wiveliscombe TA4 210 C5
Burge's Hill BA3 116 B1
Burges La TA4 210 C5
Burge's La BA3 116 B1
Burgess Cl TA1 212 B1
Burgess La BA6 157 F6
Burgis Rd BS14 23 D6
Burgundy Rd TA24 201 A8
BURLANDS 168 C6
Burleigh Gdns BA1 44 A8
Burleigh La BA16 207 C4
BURLESCOMBE 179 B3
Burlescombe CE Prim Sch EX16 179 B3
Burley Gdns BA16 207 D4
Burlingham's La BA22 186 C8
Burlington Ct BS20 2 E6
Burlington Rd
Midsomer Norton BA3 78 C2
Portishead BS20 2 E7
Burlington St
Bath BA1 228 B4
15 Weston-super-Mare BS23 48 E8
Burnbush Cl BS14 23 E6
Burnbush Prim Sch BS14 23 D5
Burnell Dr BS2 227 C4
Burnell Ho 8 BA4 205 B6
BURNETT 42 B7
Burnett Bsns Pk BS31 25 B1
Burnett Cl TA8 104 C7
Burnett Hill BS31 42 B8
Burnett Ind Est BS40 35 E1
Burnett's La BA6 158 A6
Burnham Cl BS24 48 F1
Burnham Dr BS24 48 F1
Burnham Moor La TA9 105 B5
BURNHAM-ON-SEA 104 D8
Burnham-on-Sea Inf Sch TA8 104 C8
Burnham Rd
Bath BA2 44 C6
Bristol BS11 4 D6
Highbridge TA9 104 D4
Burn Hill TA4, TA21 166 F3
Burnshill Dr TA2 212 A7
Burns Rd TA1 213 C4
Burnt House Cotts BA2 62 C8
Burnthouse Dro BA5 141 B8
Burnt House La BA3 116 C2
Burnt House Rd BA2 62 D8
Burrell La BA7 158 F1
Burrells BA22 197 B8
Burridge Cl BA5 139 E6
Burridge Cross TA20 193 E1
BURRINGTON 53 F3
Burrington Ave BS24 48 F1
Burrington CE Prim Sch BS40 53 F3
Burrington Cl
Nailsea BS48 8 E1
Weston-super-Mare BS24 48 F1
Burrington Combe BS40 72 C8
Burrington Coombe BS40 54 A1
Burrington La BS40 54 A3
Burrington Wlk BS13 22 A8
Burroughes Ave BA21 218 E6
Burrough St TA12 185 F7
Burrough Way TA21 222 D4
BURROW 184 F6
BURROWBRIDGE 154 F1
Burrowbridge CE Sch TA7 154 F1
Burrow Dro
Burrowbridge TA7 154 F1
Hambridge TA12 184 F8
Burrowfield BA10 215 F7
Burrowfield Cl BA10 215 F7
Burrow Hill Dro TA7 155 A1
Burrow La
Ashbrittle TA21 178 D8
High Ham TA10 156 A1
Burrow Mump TA7 154 F1
Burrow Rocks TA4 202 B1
Burrows La BA3 97 B1
Burrows The BS22 32 D3
Burrow Wall TA7 155 A1
Burrow Way
Hambridge TA12 184 F7
Kingsbury Episcopi TA12 185 A7
Burstock La DT8 199 F7
Burston La EX16 164 A4
BURTLE 137 D6
Burtle Rd
Burtle TA7 137 D6
East Huntspill TA9 136 E7
Westhay BA6 138 A5
BURTON
Stogursey 134 B7
Yeovil 197 C8
Burton Barton BA22 197 C8
Burton Cl BS1 227 B1
Burton Ct BS8 226 B3
Burtonhayes DT10 190 F6
Burton La BA22 197 C8
Burton Pl TA1 212 E3
Burton Row TA9 86 A5
Burton St
5 Bath BA1 228 B2
Marnhull DT10 190 F6
Burt's Hill BA4 142 F3
Burwalls Rd BS8 11 E6
BURY 164 A6
Bury The BS24 50 A3
Bury View BA2 42 C5
BUSCOTT 138 C1
Buscott La TA7 138 B1
BUSHEY NORWOOD 45 F6
Bushfield Rd TA18 224 B4
Bushfurlong Rd TA3 184 B8
Bush La TA5 152 E6
Bush Pl TA10 172 A5
Bush Rd TA5 152 D7
Bushs Orch TA19 221 A4
Bushy Combe BA3 77 F3
Bushy Coombe Gdns BA6 206 F5
Bushy Cross La TA3 169 C3
Bushy Thorn Rd BS40 56 E8
Business Pk The BS13 22 E3
Bussell's Moor Cross EX36 162 C4
BUSSEX 154 F6
Bussex Sq TA7 154 F6

- Butcher's Hill TA3 170 F2
- Butchers La
  - Castle Cary BA7 159 C3
  - Shapwick TA7 155 F8
- Butcher's La TA5 134 A2
- BUTCOMBE 55 B8
- Butcombe BS24 49 A2
- Butcombe La BS40 55 B7
- Butcombe Wlk BS14 23 B5
- Butham La
  - Chew Magna BS40 39 A4
  - Chew Magna BS40 39 B3
- Butlass Cl BS39 59 D1
- BUTLEIGH 157 D4
- Butleigh CE Prim Sch BA6 157 E4
- Butleigh Cl TA6 209 D4
- Butleigh Cross BA6 157 E3
- Butleigh Dro
  - Ashcott TA7, BA16 156 C5
  - Walton BA16 156 D6
- Butleigh Old Rd BA6 206 E3
- Butleigh Rd
  - Glastonbury BA6 206 E3
  - Street BA16 207 E5
- BUTLEIGH WOTTON 157 C5
- Butler's Gdns BA11 120 A4
- Butt Cl BA6 206 E5
- Buttercliffe Rise BS41 11 C3
- Buttercup La BA16 207 D6
- Butterfield Pk BS21 6 C1
- Buttermere Rd BS23 49 A5
- Butterworth Ct BS4 22 D7
- Buttice La BA5 111 B1
- Butt La TA10 171 D4
- Butt Lake Rd TA9 106 B3
- Buttle Cl TA19 184 E4
- Buttle La TA19 184 E3
- Buttle's Cross TA3 191 F7
- Buttle's La TA3 191 E6
- Button Cl BS14 23 A6
- Button St BA11 119 D5
- Butts TA19 221 C4
- BUTT'S BATCH 35 D1
- Butts Batch BS26 69 B3
- Butt's Batch BS40 35 D1
- Butts Castle TA19 221 C4
- Butts Cl
  - Marnhull DT10 190 F5
  - Williton TA4 202 D4
- Butts Cnr TA6 153 F4
- Butts Hill BA11 119 E3
- Butts La
  - Ilton TA19 183 D3
  - Kilmington BA12 161 F7
  - Langford Budville TA21 166 F2
  - Rodney Stoke BS27 91 A1
- Butts Orch BS40 35 D1
- Butts Quarry La TA18 224 E6
- BUTTS THE 119 E3
- Butts The BA11 119 E3
- Butts Way TA4 166 F4
- Buxtons Cl 5 BA5 139 D8
- Byfield BA2 45 B1
- Byfield Pl BA2 45 B1
- Byfields BS21 16 C8
- Byron Cl BS24 50 A4
- Byron Ct BS23 48 F8
- Byron Pl BS8 226 B3
- Byron Rd
  - Bath BA2 44 F4
  - Locking BS24 50 A4
  - Taunton TA1 213 C3
  - Weston-super-Mare BS23 49 A4
- Byways Cvn Pk BS21 6 C1
- Byzantine Ct BS1 227 A1

C

- Cabbage La BA8 176 C3
- Cabell Ct BA11 119 D2
- Cabell Rd BA11 119 E2
- Cabot Circus Sh Ctr BS1 227 B3
- Cabot Cl BS31 25 D2
- Cabot Gate BS2 227 C4
- Cabot Prim Sch BS2 227 C4
- Cabot Rise BS20 2 A5
- Cabot Twr★ BS8 226 B2
- Cabot Way
  - Bristol BS8 11 F5
  - Pill BS20 4 D3
  - Weston-super-Mare BS22 32 A3
- Cabstand BS20 2 D6
- Cadbury Bsns Pk BA22 175 B6
- Cadbury Camp La BS20 8 D6
- Cadbury Camp La W BS21 7 C5
- Cadbury Castle★ BA22 175 C4
- Cadbury Cl TA8 85 C1
- Cadbury Farm Rd BS49 34 C7
- Cadbury Halt BS20 1 F1
- Cadbury Ho BS20 2 E4
- Cadbury La BS20 1 F1
- Cadbury Rd
  - Keynsham BS31 25 A2
  - Portishead BS20 2 E4
- Cadbury Sq BS49 34 E3
- Cadby Ho BA2 44 A6
- Cades Gdns TA21 222 E7
- Cadeside Cvn Site TA21 222 F7
- Cades Mead TA21 222 F7
- CAD GREEN 183 E3
- Cadogan Rd BS14 23 A8
- Cad Rd
  - Ilminster TA19 221 A8
- Cad Rd *continued*
  - Ilton TA19 183 E3
- Cadwell's La TA9 136 A8
- Caernarvon Cl BS31 24 C5
- Caernarvon Rd BS31 24 C4
- Caernarvon Way TA8 85 B1
- Caern Well Pl BA1 228 C4
- Cairn Cl BS48 9 A1
- Cairo Ct 18 BS23 30 C1
- Caitlin Ct BS14 23 D6
- Cala Trad Est BS3 11 F3
- Calder Cl BS31 25 A4
- Calder Cres TA1 213 D4
- Cale Cl DT10 190 C4
- Caledonia Mews BS8 11 F6
- Caledonian Rd
  - Bath BA2 44 D6
  - Bristol BS1 226 B1
- Caledonia Pl BS8 11 F7
- Cale Way BA9 216 B4
- California Par BA16 207 B6
- Caller's La EX15 180 D1
- Callins Cl TA24 201 A5
- Callins View TA24 201 A5
- Callow Hill BA5 139 C7
- Callowhill Ct BS1 227 B3
- Calluna Cl BS22 32 A5
- Calton Gdns BA2 228 C1
- Calton Rd BA2 228 C1
- Calton Wlk BA2 228 B1
- Calvados Rd TA1 213 C3
- Calway Rd TA1 213 B2
- Camberley Rd BS4 22 D8
- Camberley Wlk BS22 49 E8
- Cambrian Lufton Coll BA22 186 D4
- Camborne Gr BA21 219 E5
- Camborne Pl BA21 219 E5
- Camborne St BA21 219 E5
- CAMBRIDGE BATCH 20 C8
- Cambridge Cl BA20 218 D5
- Cambridge Ct BS40 35 D2
- Cambridge Gr BS21 6 D5
- Cambridge Pl
  - Bath BA2 45 B5
  - Weston-super-Mare BS23 48 D8
- Cambridge Rd BS21 6 D5
- Cambridge St TA20 223 C4
- Cambridge Terr
  - Bath BA2 45 B5
  - 11 Taunton TA2 213 A8
- Cam Brook Cl BA2 78 D8
- Cambrook Ho BS39 76 F8
- Camden Cres BA1 228 B4
- Camden Ct
  - Bath BA1 228 B4
  - Bridgwater TA6 208 E5
- Camden Orch TA11 211 C4
- Camden Pl TA6 208 E5
- Camden Rd
  - Bath BA1 28 A1
  - Bridgwater TA6 208 E5
  - Bristol BS3 226 B1
  - Somerton TA11 211 C4
- Camden Row BA1 228 B4
- Camden Terr
  - Bath BA1 228 C4
  - Bristol BS8 226 A2
  - Weston-super-Mare BS23 48 E7
- Camel Cross BA22 174 C3
- CAMELEY 76 C8
- Cameley CE Prim Sch BS39 58 E1
- Cameley Cl BS39 76 E8
- Cameley Gn BA2 43 F6
- Cameley La BS39 75 F7
- Cameley Rd BS39 76 C8
- Camelot Ct TA11 211 B5
- Camelot Sh Ctr BA9 216 C4
- Camel St BA22 174 F2
- Cameroons Cl BS31 24 E4
- CAMERTON 78 E8
- Camerton CE Prim Sch BA2 78 E8
- Camerton Cl BS31 25 E3
- Camerton Hill BA2 78 E8
- Camerton Rd BA2 60 E1
- Camomile Wlk BS20 2 F5
- Campian Wlk BS4 22 D6
- Campion Cl 4 BS22 49 D7
- Campion Dr
  - Taunton TA1 213 C1
  - Yeovil BA22 218 B5
- Campion Gdns TA20 223 D5
- Campion Way TA6 208 E1
- Campkin Rd BA5 203 B4
- Camplins BS21 6 C1
- Camp Rd
  - Bristol BS8 11 F7
  - Weston-super-Mare BS23 30 C1
  - Yeovil BA22 186 D1
- Camp Rd N BS23 30 B1
- Camp View BS48 8 D2
- Camvale BA2 79 B8
- Camview BS39 77 D6
- Canada Coombe BS24 50 A1
- Canada Way BS1 226 B1
- Canada Wy BS3 11 F4
- Canal Cl TA21 222 B8
- Canal Dro BS27, BS28 90 A3
- Canal Rd TA1 212 F5
- Canal Terr
  - Bathampton BA2 28 F1
  - Taunton TA1 212 F5
- Canal View
  - Bridgwater TA6 209 A4
  - Taunton TA2 213 F7
- Canal Way TA19 221 A3
- Canaries Path BA4 205 D3
- Canberra Cres BS24 50 B6
- Canberra Rd BS23 48 F3
- Canford La BS9 5 E8
- Canford Rd BS9 5 F8
- CANNARD'S GRAVE 205 D2
- Cannard's Grave Rd BA4 205 C4
- Cannards Grave Rdbt BA4 205 D3
- Canning Ctr for Land Based Studies TA5 135 B2
- CANNINGTON 135 C2
- Cannington CE Prim Sch TA5 135 C2
- Cannington College Gdns★ TA5 135 B2
- Cannington Countryside Vst Ctr★ TA5 135 B2
- Cannon Cl TA6 209 B5
- Cannon Court Mews DT9 217 D1
- Cannons Gate BS21 16 C8
- CANNON'S MARSH 226 C1
- Cannon St BS1 227 A4
- Canns La
  - 9 North Petherton TA6 153 F4
  - Puriton TA7 136 C4
- Cann St TA1 212 E3
- Cannwood La BA10 161 B8
- Canons Cl BA2 44 B2
- Canons Gate BA22 173 E1
- Canon's Marsh Amphitheatre★ BS1 226 C1
- Canons Rd BS1 226 C2
- Canon's Rd
  - Bristol BS1 226 C1
  - Canon's Marsh BS1 226 C2
- Canon St TA1 213 A4
- Canons Way BS1 226 C1
- Canons Wlk BS22 31 D2
- Cantell Gr BS14 23 F5
- Canterbury Cl BS22 32 B3
- Canterbury Dr TA3 170 C4
- Canterbury Rd BA2 44 D5
- Cantock's Cl BS8 226 C3
- Canvin Ct TA11 211 B5
- Canworth Way TA6 209 C3
- Canynge Ho 2 BS1 227 B1
- Canynge Rd BS8 11 F8
- Canynge Sq BS8 11 F8
- Canynge St BS1 227 B2
- Capell Cl BS22 49 B8
- Capenor Cl BS20 2 C4
- Capes Cl TA6 209 A5
- Capital Edge BS8 226 B1
- CAPLAND 183 A6
- Capland Ct TA3 183 A5
- Capland La TA3 183 A5
- Caple La BS40 56 B5
- Cappards Rd BS39 57 D4
- Capricorn Pl BS8 226 B2
- Capri Villas BS23 30 C2
- CAPTON 132 C2
- Capton TA4 132 C2
- Capton Cross TA4 132 C2
- Caradon Pl TA6 208 F7
- Caramia Pk TA9 136 A8
- Carantoc Pl 3 TA24 131 A5
- Caraway Cl TA20 223 F5
- Caray Gr TA3 169 D4
- Carberry View BS24 50 A8
- Card Cl BS27 90 F3
- Cardigan Cres BS22 49 C8
- Cardill Cl BS13 22 A8
- Cardinal Cl BA2 62 D8
- Carditch Dro BS49 52 B8
- Carey Cl BA4 141 E6
- Carey Developments 1 BS21 6 C1
- Carey's Cl BS21 6 F4
- Carey's Hollow TA13 220 B4
- Careys Mead BA3 116 F7
- Careys Way BS24 49 E7
- CARHAMPTON 131 B5
- Carhampton Cross TA24 131 B5
- Caribee Quarter BA16 207 B5
- Carice Gdns BS21 16 D8
- Carisbrooke Gdns BA20 218 F5
- Carisbrooke Rd BS4 22 D7
- Carlan Stepps TA19 183 C2
- CARLINGCOTT 61 B1
- Carlingford Terr BA3 79 A2
- Carlingford Terrace Rd BA3 79 A2
- Carlow Rd BS4 22 E8
- Carlton Cl BS39 58 F3
- Carlton Ct
  - Minehead TA24 200 F7
  - Wells BA5 203 E4
- Carlton Dr TA6 208 F7
- Carlton Mans BS23 48 D7
- Carlton Mews BA5 203 E4
- Carlton St BS23 48 D7
- Carmine Cl BA6 206 C4
- Carnival Cl TA19 221 A4
- Carolina Ho BS2 227 A4
- Caroline Bldgs BA2 45 B5
- Caroline Cl BS31 24 C4
- Caroline Pl BA1 228 B4
- Carpenter Cl BS23 49 A7
- Carpenters Cl TA3 169 C3
- Carpenters Ho TA19 221 B3
- Carpenters La BS31 24 E5
- Carpenters Terr TA12 185 E7
- Carraway La DT10 190 F5
- Carre Gdns BS22 31 F4
- Carr Ho BA2 44 A6
- Carrick Ho 7 BS8 11 F6
- Carriels Ho 12 BA4 205 B6
- Carrier's La TA21 166 C2
- Carrington Way BA9 216 C4
- Carrs Cl BA2 44 A6
- Carrswood Vw BA2 43 F7
- Carstons Cl BS48 18 F6
- Carter Rd BS39 77 D5
- Carters La BA22 196 E8
- Carters Way
  - Chilcompton BA3 96 D3
  - Somerton TA11 211 C4
- Cart Gate TA14 185 F5
- Cartwright Cl BA5 139 E6
- Carver Cl TA6 208 D5
- Carvers Rd TA6 209 A5
- Cary Ct TA11 211 B5
- Caryedge La BA7 160 A2
- CARY FITZPAINE 174 B6
- Cary Hill
  - Castle Cary BA7 214 D5
  - Kingsdon TA11 173 E5
- Cary Moor Dro BA7 159 C1
- Cary Rd BA22 175 D6
- Cary Way
  - Kingsdon TA11 173 D5
  - Somerton TA11 211 C5
- Cashford Gate TA2 213 C7
- Casion Ct BS1 227 B1
- Casley La BA11 102 D6
- Cassino Rd TA23 202 E6
- Cassis Cl TA8 104 C5
- Castlake La TA4 150 F7
- CASTLE 198 D4
- Castle Batch Prim Sch BS22 32 A5
- Castle Bow TA1 212 F4
- CASTLE CARY 214 B5
- Castle Cary Com Prim Sch BA7 214 C4
- Castle Cary Mus★ BA7 214 C5
- Castle Cary Sta BA7 214 B8
- Castle Cl BS48 19 F7
- Castle Cnr BA11 101 D3
- Castle Cotts TA21 180 D8
- Castle Cross EX13 198 D4
- Castle Ct
  - Othery TA7 155 C2
  - Shepton Mallet BA4 205 A4
- Castle Farm La BS41 21 B2
- Castle Field Ind Est TA6 209 A6
- Castlefield La TA4 168 B1
- Castle Gdns BA2 44 E3
- Castle Gn TA1 212 F4
- Castle Hill
  - Banwell BS29 51 C2
  - Dunster TA24 201 E2
  - Nether Stowey TA5 134 A2
  - Nunney BA11 143 B8
- Castle La
  - Cranmore BA4 142 A6
  - South Cadbury BA22 175 D4
  - Wedmore BS28 108 A1
  - West Pennard BA6 140 C1
  - Wiveliscombe TA4 210 F6
  - Yarley BA5 139 D7
- Castlemans Rd TA1 212 B1
- Castle Mead TA23 131 E4
- Castle Moat TA6 208 F5
- Castle Neroche Forest Trail★ TA20 182 D2
- Castle Prim Sch BS31 24 D4
- Castle Rd
  - Clevedon BS21 6 E6
  - Sherborne DT9 225 F5
  - Wellington TA21 180 D8
  - Weston-super-Mare BS22 31 E3
- Castle Rise BA7 214 C5
- Castle Sch The TA1 212 D4
- Castle St
  - Bampton EX16 164 B1
  - Bridgwater TA6 208 F5
  - Bristol BS1 227 B3
  - Frome BA11 119 E5
  - Keinton Mandeville TA11 158 B1
  - Nether Stowey TA5 134 B2
  - Nunney BA11 143 B8
  - Stogursey TA5 134 C5
  - Stoke sub Hamdon TA14 185 F4
  - Taunton TA1 212 E4
- Castleton
  - Haselbury Plucknett TA18 196 C5
  - 1 Sherborne DT9 225 E4
- Castleton Rd DT9 225 F4
- Castle Town Way DT9 225 E6
- Castle View 2 BS24 49 F8
- Castle View Rd BS21 6 D5
- Castle Way TA1 212 F4
- Castlewood Cl BS21 6 D4
- Castle Wood La EX13, TA20 193 C1
- Caswell Hill BS20 3 B1
- Caswell La BS20 3 B2
- Catash Cl BA22 175 D6
- Catch Gate La TA20 223 A5
- Catch Rd BA11 143 B7
- CATCOTT 137 D2
- Catcott Broad Dro TA7 137 D5
- Catcott Prim Sch TA7 137 D2
- Catcott Rd BA5 203 E3
- Catcott Right Dro TA7 155 D6
- Catemead BS21 16 C8
- Cater Rd BS13 22 B6
- Cathanger La
  - Fivehead TA3 170 D1
  - Stogursey TA5 134 D5
- Catharine Pl BA1 228 B3
- Cathay La BS27 90 B7
- Cathcart Ho 7 BA1 28 A1
- Cathead Cross TA14 185 E1
- Cathederal Ave BA5 203 D2
- Cathedral Church of The Holy & Undivided Trinity★ BS1 226 C2
- Cathedral Gn BA5 203 E4
- Catherine Hill BA11 119 F5
- Catherines Cl BA7 214 C6
- Catherine St
  - Avonmouth BS11 4 C8
  - East Huntspill TA9 136 D8
  - Frome BA11 119 E5
- Catherine Way BA1 29 A5
- Catherson Cl BA11 119 D3
- Cathill La DT9 176 A2
- Cathole Bridge Rd TA18 224 A4
- Cat La
  - Stalbridge DT10 190 A1
  - Stourton Caundle DT10 189 F1
- Catley Gr BS41 11 B2
- Catmoor Cross EX13 198 A5
- Catnip Cl 2 EX13 198 A1
- Cat's Ash
  - Fitzhead TA4 166 F7
  - Shepton Mallet BA4 205 B6
- Cats' Castle Hill TA4 150 E5
- CATSGORE 173 C4
- Catsgore Rd TA11 173 C5
- Cats La
  - Minehead TA24 201 A6
  - Taunton TA2 168 F6
- Cat St TA14 185 E1
- Cattle Hill
  - Bratton Seymour BA9 176 A8
  - Welham BA7 160 A1
- Cattle Market Rd BS1 227 C1
- Catt's La TA21 180 E6
- Catwell TA4 202 E2
- Caulfield Rd BS22 32 B4
- Caundle La
  - Stalbridge Weston DT10 190 A3
  - Stourton Caundle DT10 189 F1
- Causeway
  - Nailsea BS48 8 B3
  - Woolavington TA7, TA9 136 E6
- Causeway Cl TA7 136 E4
- Causeway Council Hos TA9 106 B4
- Causeway La DT8 199 D6
- Causeway Terr TA23 202 C6
- Causeway The
  - Congresbury BS49 34 D4
  - Nailsea BS20 8 F8
  - Street BA16 207 D8
  - Yatton BS49 34 C7
- Causeway View BS48 8 C2
- Caultetts Cl BA3 96 F8
- Cavalier Cl BA21 219 D8
- Cavalier Way
  - Wincanton BA9 216 C3
  - Yeovil BA21 219 E8
- Cavalier Wlk BA21 219 D8
- Cave Ct BS2 227 B4
- Cavell Ct BS21 6 C1
- Cavendish Cl BS31 25 D2
- Cavendish Cres BA1 228 A4
- Cavendish Ct BA22 173 E2
- Cavendish Dr BA14 83 F6
- Cavendish Gdns BS9 5 C4
- Cavendish Lodge BA1 228 A4
- Cavendish Pl BA1 228 A4
- Cavendish Rd BA1 228 A4
- Caveners Ct BS22 31 B1
- Caversham Dr BS48 9 A2
- Cave St BS2 227 B4
- Cawley Ave EX13 198 A2
- Caxton Ct 4 BA2 228 C3
- Caxton Dr 5 TA9 104 E4
- Caxton Rd
  - Frome BA11 120 A3
  - 4 Highbridge TA9 104 E4
- Cazenove Path BA4 205 D3
- Cecil Rd
  - Bristol, Clifton BS8 11 F8
  - Weston-super-Mare BS23 30 E1
- Cecil St BA20 219 B5
- Cecil Terr TA6 209 B4
- Cedar Ave
  - Butleigh BA6 157 D5
  - Weston-super-Mare BS22 31 C1
- Cedar Cl
  - Brent Knoll TA9 86 B2
  - Bridgwater TA6 209 C3
  - Chard TA20 223 B5
  - Long Ashton BS41 10 F1
  - Taunton TA1 213 D2
- Cedar Ct
  - Bristol, Combe Dingle BS9 5 D7
  - Bristol, Sneyd Park BS9 5 C4
  - Bristol, Westbury on T BS9 5 F8
  - Martock TA12 185 E7
  - Wellington TA21 222 E5
- Cedar Dr BS31 24 D4
- Cedar Falls TA4 151 E1
- Cedar Fields
  - Sparkford BA22 175 A5
  - West Coker BA22 197 A8
- Cedar Gr
  - Bath BA2 44 D3
  - Bristol BS9 5 D5
  - Somerton TA11 211 D4
  - Yeovil BA21 218 E6
- Cedarhurst Rd BS20 1 E4
- Cedarn Ct BS22 31 B4
- Cedar Pk BS9 5 D5
- Cedar Row BS11 4 F6

Cedars The
Chew Stoke BS40 56 D8
Evercreech BA4 141 E1
Minehead TA24 200 F7
Cedar Terr BA3 78 D1
Cedar Villas BA2 228 A1
Cedar Way
Bath BA2 228 A1
Nailsea BS48 9 A2
Portishead BS20 2 C4
Cedar Wlk BA6 157 E5
Cedern Ave BS24 50 C3
Cedric Cl BA1 44 C7
Cedric Rd BA1 44 C8
Cefn Ct TA24 201 B4
Celandine Mead TA1 169 A1
Celandine Rd BA22 218 A5
Celtic Way BS24 67 B7
Cemetery La
Street BA16 207 A7
Wincanton BA9 216 B3
Centenary Cotts DT9 176 A1
Centenary Gdns BA8 190 A6
Centenary Way BS27 90 A7
Central Acre BA20 219 B4
Central Ave BA22 173 E2
Central Pk BS14 23 B7
Central Rd BA20 219 B5
Central Way BS21 6 E1
Centre Dr BS29 50 E4
Centre Quay BS20 2 E7
Centre Rd TA7 137 C2
Centre The
Keynsham BS31 24 F5
10 Weston-super-Mare BS23 48 E7
Centurion Bsns Ctr BA4 205 D4
Century Pk BA20 218 E5
Cerdic Cl TA20 223 E4
Cerdic Terr TA20 223 D4
Cerney Gdns BS48 9 A2
Cerney La BS11 4 E5
Chackrell La EX16 178 F2
Chadleigh Gr BS4 22 D7
Chad's Hill TA5 135 B2
Chadwyck Cl TA24 124 A4
CHAFFCOMBE 194 C5
Chaffcombe La TA20 194 B5
Chaffcombe Rd TA20 223 E6
Chaffeymoor Hill SP8 161 E1
Chaffinch Ave BA11 120 B6
Chaffinch Cl TA1 212 B4
Chaffinch Dr BA3 97 B8
Chaffins The BS21 6 E2
Chain Gate Ct BA6 206 D4
Chains Rd EX16 178 D1
Chalcombe Rocks La TA4 164 E5
Chalcot La BA13 121 F5
Chalcroft Wlk BS13 21 E4
Chalfield Cl BS31 25 A2
Chalfont Rd BS22 49 C8
Chalice Ct BA6 206 E4
Chalice Hill Cl BA6 206 E4
Chalice Mews 1 TA6 208 F5
Chalice Way BA6 206 F3
Chalice Well* BA6 206 F4
Chalk Farm Cl BS39 40 A7
Chalks The BS40 39 B3
CHALKWAY 194 E2
Challenger Way BA22 218 B6
Challick La TA4 166 A6
Challoner Ct BS1 227 A1
Challow Dr BS22 31 B2
Chamberlain Ho TA1 212 D5
Chamberlain Rd BS24 50 C5
Chamberlain St BA5 203 D4
Chamberlin Ave TA6 209 C6
Chambray Rd 11 TA6 154 A5
Champford La TA21 222 D5
Champford Mews 2 TA21 222 D5
Champion Cross TA4 165 E3
Champney Rd BA11 120 A7
Chancel Cl
Bristol BS9 5 D3
Nailsea BS48 8 D1
Chancellor Cl BA16 156 D7
Chancellor Rd BA16 156 D7
Chancellor's Pound BS40 36 D3
Chandag Inf Sch BS31 25 A4
Chandag Jun Sch BS31 25 A4
Chandag Rd BS31 25 A4
Chandler Cl BA1 27 B1
Chandlers DT9 225 E5
Chandlers La TA7 137 C3
Chandos Ct BS23 48 D6
Chandos Rd BS31 24 E7
Chandos St TA6 208 F5
Change La TA4 164 D6
Channel Cl TA5 134 A2
Channel Ct
Burnham-on-S TA8 104 B5
Weston-super-Mare BS22 31 B3
Channel Dash Pl BA22 173 E2
Channel Hts BS24 48 F1
Channells La TA19 183 C1
Channel Rd BS21 6 E5
Channel View Cres BS20 2 B5
Channel View Rd BS20 2 B5
Channing Cl TA8 104 B5
CHANTRY 117 F3
Chantry Cl
Nailsea BS48 8 C1
Taunton TA2 213 B7
Chantry Ct
Bristol BS1 226 C2
Somerton TA11 211 C3
Chantry Dr BS22 32 A4
Chantry Dro TA7 155 B1
Chantry Gdns BA14 83 F3
Chantry Ho 2 BA4 205 B6
Chantry La BA22 174 D3
Chantry Mead Rd BA2 44 E3
Chantry The BS26 87 B5
Chantry View BA22 197 D8
CHAPEL ALLERTON 88 D2
Chapel Barton
High Littleton BS39 59 D1
Nailsea BS48 8 C2
Chapel Cl
Castle Cary BA7 214 C5
Chew Stoke BS40 56 E8
Chilton Polden TA7 137 B2
Farrington Gurney BS39 76 F4
Keinton Mandeville TA11 158 A1
Nailsea BS48 8 E2
North Curry TA3 170 B4
Winford BS40 38 A6
CHAPEL CLEEVE 131 D5
Chapel Cross
North Cadbury BA22 175 D5
Porlock TA24 129 C7
Chapel Ct
Bath BA1 228 B2
Clandown BA3 78 E4
Clevedon BS21 6 D3
Chapelfield BA3 115 A3
Chapel Field BA2 79 E8
Chapel Forge Cl TA9 136 B8
Chapel Hill
Ashcott TA7 156 B8
Backwell BS48 19 D7
Chewton Mendip BA3 94 E5
Clevedon BS21 6 D3
Kingsdon TA11 173 D5
Kington Magna SP8 177 E1
Odcombe BA22 186 C2
Ubley BS40 55 C5
Wrington BS40 35 D3
Chapel La
Bishops Lydeard TA4 167 E8
Butleigh BA6 157 E4
Chew Stoke BS40 56 D8
Claverham BS49 34 F8
Cleeve BS49 35 B7
Dinnington TA17 195 B7
East Huntspill TA9 136 E8
Gurney Slade BA3 114 E7
Holcombe BA3 116 C8
Milborne Port DT9 217 D2
North Cadbury BA22 175 D6
Oxenpill BA6 138 C4
Penselwood BA9 161 E2
South Cadbury BA22 175 E5
Sparkford BA22 175 A6
Winford BS40 38 A6
Wingfield BA14 83 C6
Yenston BA8 189 F7
Yeovil Marsh BA21 187 A5
Zeals BA12 161 F3
Chapel Lawns BA3 78 E4
CHAPEL LEIGH 167 A8
Chapel Leigh La TA4 167 A8
Chapel Pill La BS20 4 E4
Chapel Rd
Bristol, Bishopsworth BS13 22 A6
Clandown BA3 78 E4
Fordgate TA7 154 C3
Isle Abbotts TA3 183 E7
Pawlett TA6 135 F6
Rooks Bridge BS26 87 C5
South Cadbury BA22 175 D4
Chapel Row
Bath BA1 228 B2
Bathford BA1 29 C2
Dunster TA24 201 D2
Norton St Philip BA2 81 F4
Pill BS20 4 C4
Chapel St
Bridgwater TA6 209 A5
Burnham-on-S TA8 104 A7
Dulverton TA22 163 D6
Exford TA24 128 D1
Horningsham BA12 144 D4
Upton Noble BA4 142 F2
Chapel Wlk BA2 60 C2
Chapel Yd BA7 214 B4
Chaplains Wood BS20 1 E5
Chapman Ct TA1 212 C1
Chapmans Cl
Frome BA11 119 F6
Wookey BA5 139 D8
CHAPMANSLADE 121 C5
Chapmanslade CE Prim Sch BA13 121 D4
Chapter St BS2 227 B4
Charbury Wlk BS11 4 E5
Charcroft Hill BA10 160 F6
CHARD 223 D4
Chard Bsns Pk TA20 223 D6
Chard Cl BS48 18 F8
Chard Com Hospl TA20 223 E4
Chard Ct BS14 23 B6
CHARD JUNCTION 198 E7
Chard La
Chard TA20 223 B1
Drimpton DT8 199 F8
Ilminster TA19 194 D6
Tatworth EX13, TA20 193 E1
Woolminstone TA18, TA20 195 B2
CHARDLEIGH GREEN 223 A7
Chard Mus* TA20 223 B4
Chard Rd
Axminster EX13 198 B4
Chard Rd *continued*
Clevedon BS21 6 E1
Crewkerne TA18 224 A6
Drimpton DT8 199 F7
Chard Sch TA20 223 C4
Chard St
Chardstock EX13 198 B7
Thorncombe TA20 199 B6
CHARDSTOCK 198 B7
Chardstock Ave BS9 5 D8
Chardstock La TA20 223 C2
Chardyke Dr BS39 58 E1
Charing Cross DT6 199 E1
Charity La BA11 98 C1
CHARLCOMBE 27 E3
Charlcombe La BA1 27 F3
Charlcombe Pk BS20 1 D3
Charlcombe Rise BA1 27 F2
Charlcombe View Rd BA1 28 A2
Charlcombe Way BA1 27 F2
Charlcome Rise BS20 1 D3
Charlecombe Ct BS9 5 F6
Charlecombe Rd BS9 5 F6
Charlecote BA1 27 F1
Charles Cres TA1 213 D4
Charles Ct 1 BS8 226 A2
Charles Pl BS8 226 A2
Charles Rd
Frome BA11 119 F3
Yeovil BA21 219 D6
Charles St
Bath BA1 228 B2
Bristol BS1 227 A4
Charlestone Rd TA8 104 B8
Charleton Ho 8 BS2 227 C3
Charlock Cl 3 BS22 49 D7
Charlock Rd BS22 49 D7
Charlotte Ct BA20 219 A4
Charlotte St S BS1 226 C2
Charlotte St
Bath BA1 228 B2
Bristol, Brandon Hill BS1 226 C3
CHARLTON
Creech St Michael 169 F5
Radstock 97 E5
Shepton Mallet 205 E5
CHARLTON ADAM 173 F7
Charlton Ave BS23 48 D4
Charlton Cl
Bridgwater TA6 209 C4
Crewkerne TA18 224 D5
Shepton Mallet BA4 205 D5
Yeovil BA21 219 D5
Charlton Crossroads BA4 205 D5
Charlton Dr BS48 9 C7
Charlton Field La DT9 175 D1
Charlton Hill DT9, BA8 176 B3
CHARLTON HORETHORNE 176 B2
Charlton Horethorne CE Prim Sch DT9 176 A1
Charlton La
Creech St Michael TA3 169 E5
Radstock BA3 97 D6
Sparkford DT9 175 F3
CHARLTON MACKRELL 173 E7
Charlton Mackrell CE Prim Sch TA11 173 E7
CHARLTON MUSGROVE 161 A2
Charlton Pk
Keynsham BS31 24 D5
Midsomer Norton BA3 97 B7
Charlton Rd
Creech St Michael TA3 169 E6
Holcombe BA3 97 D3
Keynsham BS31, BS14 24 C3
Midsomer Norton BA3 97 B8
Shepton Mallet BA4 205 D5
Weston-super-Mare BS23 48 D4
Charlton Road Cotts TA3 169 D6
Charlton Trad Est BA4 205 E5
Charlton View BS20 2 C5
CHARLYNCH 152 F8
Charlynch Hill TA5 152 F8
Charlynch La TA5 153 B8
Charlynch Rd TA5 153 A8
Charmborough Farm Rural Bsns Pk BA3 97 D3
Charmoor Dro TA20 182 F1
Charmoor La TA20 182 F1
Charmouth Rd BA1 44 B7
Charnwood Cl TA6 208 F7
Charnwood Dr BS27 90 B7
Charnwood Rd BS14 23 B4
Charolais Dr 8 TA6 154 A5
Charter Cl TA6 209 A4
Charter Ho BS1 226 B2
CHARTERHOUSE 72 C4
Charterhouse Cl
Cheddar BS27 90 C6
Nailsea BS48 8 F1
Charterhouse Dr BA11 120 C7
Charter Rd BS22 49 B8
Charter Way BA5 203 B4
Charter Wlk
Bristol BS14 23 A6
Taunton TA1 213 C5
Chartley BS9 5 D2
Chase Cl BA6 206 C3
Chasey's Dro BA6 139 C4
Chatham Ave TA6 208 E6
Chatham Ct TA10 171 C4
Chatham Pk BA2 45 C6
Chatham Pl TA10 171 C4
Chatham Row BA1 228 C3
Chatley Furlong BA2 81 F3
Chatsworth Rd BA21 219 D7
Chattenden Ho BS9 5 F3
Chatterton Gn BS14 22 F3
Chatterton Ho 5 BS1 227 B1
Chatterton Sq BS1 227 C1
Chatterton St BS1 227 C1
Chaucer Cl 4 TA6 153 F4
Chaucer Rd
Bath BA2 44 F4
Midsomer Norton BA3 97 B8
Weston-super-Mare BS23 49 A4
Chaundey Gr BS13 22 B5
Cheapside
Bristol BS2 227 C4
Langport TA10 171 F5
Taunton TA1 212 F3
Wiveliscombe TA4 210 C4
Cheap St
Bath BA1 228 C2
Frome BA11 119 F5
Sherborne DT9 225 D4
Cheats Rd TA3 169 C3
Checcombe La DT9 188 B4
Checkridge La EX13 198 D2
CHEDDAR 90 D8
Cheddar Bsns Pk BS27 90 A6
Cheddar Bsns Pk BS27 90 A6
Cheddar Cl
Burnham-on-S TA8 104 C8
Frome BA11 120 C7
Nailsea BS48 18 F8
Cheddarcoombe La BS25 70 E8
Cheddar Ct BS27 90 B7
Cheddar Fields BS27 90 A7
Cheddar Gorge* BS27 71 E1
Cheddar Gorge Rural Village* BS27 90 C8
Cheddar Gr BS13 22 A8
Cheddar Grove Prim Sch BS13 22 A8
Cheddar Moor Dro BS27 90 C4
Cheddar Rd
Axbridge BS26 70 E2
Chewton Mendip BA3 94 D6
Clewer BS28 89 D2
Wedmore BS28 108 D6
Cheddar Valley Bldgs 2 BA5 203 C3
CHEDDON FITZPAINE 169 A6
Cheddon Fitzpaine CE Prim Sch TA2 168 F6
Cheddon Lawns TA2 169 A6
Cheddon Mews TA2 212 F7
Cheddon Rd TA2 212 F7
Chedworth Cl BA2 45 F3
CHEDZOY 154 E8
Chedzoy La TA7 209 E7
Cheeks La BA10 215 E6
Cheer La TA7 154 F5
Cheese Hill BA11 143 D8
Cheese La BS2 227 B2
Chelmer Ct TA1 213 D4
Chelmer Gr BS31 24 F4
Chelscombe BA1 27 B1
Chelsea Cl BS31 25 A5
Chelsea Rd BA1 44 C7
Chelsfield BS48 19 A7
CHELSTON 180 D8
Chelston Ave BA21 219 B7
Chelston Bsn Pk TA21 180 D8
CHELSTON HEATHFIELD 180 E7
Chelston Rd BS4 22 D7
Chelston Terr TA21 180 D8
Chelswood Ave BS22 49 C8
Chelswood Gdns BS22 49 D8
Cheltenham St BA2 228 A1
CHELVEY 18 D5
Chelvey Batch BS48 18 F3
Chelvey La BS48 18 E4
Chelvey Rd BS48 18 D5
Chelvey Rise BS48 9 A1
Chelvy Cl BS13 22 D3
CHELWOOD 59 A8
Chelwood BS23 48 F8
Chelwood Dr
Bath BA2 44 D1
Taunton TA1 212 E1
Chelwood Rd
Bristol BS11 4 D7
Saltford BS31 25 E4
Chelwood Rdbt BS39 58 E8
CHELYNCH 141 E6
Chelynch Pk BA4 141 E6
Chelynch Rd BA4 141 F7
Chepstow Ave TA6 209 A2
Chepstow Ct BA21 219 D6
Chepstow Ho BA10 215 D6
Chepstow Rd BS4 22 D8
Chepstow Wlk BS31 24 D5
Cher TA24 200 F6
Cherfield TA24 200 F6
Cherington Rd BS48 9 A2
Cheriton St BA8 176 D3
Cherry Ave BS21 6 E2
Cherry Cl
Bridgwater TA6 209 C3
Yatton BS49 34 B8
Cherry Ct 12 BS1 227 A4
Cherry Garden La BA2 100 D7
Cherry Gr
Frome BA11 119 E3
Taunton TA2 212 F6
Yatton BS49 34 B8
Cherry Hay BS21 6 D1
Cherry La
4 Bristol BS1 227 B4
Odcombe BA22 186 C2
Cherry Orch TA3 168 D1
Cherry Orchard Dr BA5 203 C5
Cherry Pie La BA22 175 A5
Cherry Rd
Long Ashton BS41 10 F1
Nailsea BS48 8 D1
Cherry Tree Cl
Keynsham BS31 24 C4
Radstock BA3 78 E1
Cherry Tree Ct
Crewkerne TA18 224 D8
Kingston Seymour BS21 16 C2
1 Wells BA5 203 C3
Wincanton BA9 216 D4
Cherry Tree Dr BA20 218 D2
Cherry Tree La TA1 212 F1
Cherry Tree Rd EX13 198 A1
Cherry Tree Way TA23 202 D6
Cherrywood Rd BS22 31 F2
Cherrywood Rise BS22 31 F2
Chertsey Cl TA7 136 E4
Cherwell Rd BS31 25 A4
Chescombe Rd BS49 34 B7
Chesham Rd N BS22 49 B8
Chesham Rd S BS22 49 B8
Cheshay's Hill TA19 183 D1
Cheshire Ave BS24 50 C5
Chesle Cl BS20 1 E3
Cheslefield BS20 1 E3
Chesle Way BS20 1 E3
Chessell La BA4 140 C4
Chessels Cl BA22 197 B8
Chessels La TA11 173 F7
Chessington Ave BS14 23 B5
CHESTERBLADE 142 A4
Chesterblade Rd
Chesterblade BA4 142 A4
Evercreech BA4 141 F3
Chester Cl BS24 50 A8
Chester Cres BS13 22 B8
Chesterfield TA20 223 D4
Chesterfield Cl BS29 50 F3
Chesterfield Ho BA3 78 B1
Chesterfield Nuffield Health Bristol Hospl The BS8 226 A2
Chester Terr TA20 223 D4
Chesterton Dr BS48 9 A2
Chesterton Ho 6 BS2 227 B4
Chestertons The BA2 45 F8
Chestnut Ave
Axbridge BS26 70 C2
Chapel Cleeve TA24 131 D5
Crewkerne TA18 224 D7
Weston-super-Mare BS22 32 A1
Chestnut Barn Ind Est BS24 33 D3
Chestnut Chase BS48 9 A3
Chestnut Cl
Baltonsborough BA6 158 A5
Banwell BS29 51 A3
Bridgwater TA6 209 C4
Bristol BS14 23 F5
1 Carhampton TA24 131 A5
Congresbury BS49 34 D4
Frome BA11 120 C7
Maiden Bradley BA12 144 C2
Paulton BS39 77 E6
Radstock BA3 78 E1
Somerton TA11 211 C3
Wellington TA21 222 E5
Chestnut Ct BS13 22 A7
Chestnut Dr
Claverham BS49 17 F1
Taunton TA1 213 C1
Yeovil BA20 218 F3
Chestnut Gr
Bath BA2 44 C4
Clevedon BS21 6 E4
Westwood BA15 64 F4
Chestnut Ho
Brean TA8 65 F2
Bristol BS13 22 D3
Chestnut La
Ashcott TA7 156 B8
Bleadon BS24 67 B7
Chestnut Par BA4 205 D4
Chestnut Rd
Long Ashton BS41 11 B2
11 Martock TA12 185 E6
Chestnuts The
Cheddar BS27 71 A1
Winscombe BS25 70 A7
Chestnut Way TA24 201 A5
Chestnut Wlk
Bristol BS13 22 A6
Saltford BS31 25 E3
Chever's La BA2 81 E5
Cheverton Ho 1 BA21 219 B5
Cheviot Mdw BS20 2 F4
Cheviot St 6 TA6 154 A5
Chew Cotts BS31 24 F5
Chew Court Farm BS40 39 B3
Chew Hill BS40 39 A4
Chew La BS40 38 F1
CHEW MAGNA 39 C4
Chew Magna Prim Sch BS40 39 B3
Chew Rd BS40 38 C5
Chew St BS40 39 A3
CHEW STOKE 56 D8
Chew Stoke CE Prim Sch BS40 56 D8
Chewton Cheese Dairy* BA3 94 E6
Chewton Hill BA3 95 A7

CHEWTON KEYNSHAM 24 E2
CHEWTON MENDIP 94 E7
Chewton Mendip CE Prim
  Sch BA3. . . . . 94 F7
Chewton Rd BS31. . . . . 24 F2
Chew Valley Lake Nature
  Trails ★ BS39 . . . . 57 B7
Chew Valley Sch BS40 . . . . 38 F1
Cheyne Rd BS9 . . . . 5 D6
Chibbet Hill TA24 . . . . . . 146 B8
Chibbet Post TA24 . . . . . . 146 C8
Chichester Cl TA8. . . . . . . 104 B8
Chichester Pl BA3 . . . . 79 A2
Chichester Rd BA16 . . . . . 207 C4
Chichester Way BS24 . . . . 50 A8
Chicks La BA3 . . . . 95 D7
Chick's La TA4 . . . . 210 C6
Chickwell La BA3 . . . . 81 A1
Chidgey Cl TA6 . . . . 208 F5
CHILCOMBE 132 F1
Chilcombe La TA4 . . . . 132 F1
CHILCOMPTON 96 C4
Chilcompton Rd BA3 . . . . . 96 E7
Chilcote Dro BA5 . . . . 113 E2
Chilcote La BA5. . . . . 113 D1
Chilcott Cross TA22 . . . . . 163 A7
Chilcott La TA22 . . . . 163 A7
Childhay La DT8 . . . . 199 F6
Chilkwell St BA6. . . . . 206 E4
Chillingham Dro 14 TA7 . 154 A5
Chillington Down TA19,
  TA20 . . . . 194 F4
Chilliswood Cres TA1 . . . . 212 B2
Chilliswood La
  Staplehay TA3 . . . . 181 B8
  Taunton TA3 . . . . 168 B1
Chill Pits La EX13 . . . . 198 B8
Chillybridge Rocks TA22 147 E1
Chillyhill La BS40 . . . . 38 F2
Chilpitts TA7 . . . . 136 F4
CHILSON 198 C6
CHILSON COMMON 198 D7
Chiltern Cl BS14 . . . . 23 B4
Chiltern Cross EX16 . . . . . 164 B2
CHILTHORNE DOMER 186 E5
Chilthorne Domer CE Sch
  BA22 . . . . 186 E5
Chilthornehill La BA22 . . 186 D6
CHILTON CANTELO 174 D1
Chilton Cantelo House (Sch)
  BA22 . . . . 174 C1
Chilton Cl TA6 . . . . 208 F7
Chilton Ct 7 BA1 . . . . 28 B1
Chilton Dro TA7 . . . . 137 C6
Chilton Gr BA21. . . . . 219 A7
Chilton Pk TA6. . . . . 208 F7
CHILTON POLDEN 137 B2
Chilton Rd
  Bath BA1 . . . . 28 B1
  Bridgwater TA5, TA6 . . . 208 F8
  Bristol BS4. . . . . 23 A8
  Chilton Polden TA7. . . . . 137 B2
Chilton Right Dro TA7. . . 155 B6
Chilton St TA6 . . . . 208 F7
CHILTON TRINITY 135 F2
Chilton Trinity Sch TA6 . . 208 F7
Chilworthy La TA19, TA20 193 F7
Chimes The BS48 . . . . 18 C8
Chinehorn Dro TA5 . . . . . 135 F3
Chinnock Hollow BA22 . . 196 E8
Chinnock Rd BA6 . . . . 206 F5
Chip La TA1 . . . . 212 E5
CHIPLEY 166 F2
Chippel La DT10 . . . . 190 F5
Chipping Cross BS21. . . . . 16 C8
CHIPSTABLE 165 E6
Chi-Rio Cl BA4 . . . . 205 E4
CHISELBOROUGH. 185 F1
Chisland Dr TA24 . . . . 129 C8
Chistles La TA11 . . . . 158 A1
Chitcombe Rocks La
  TA4 . . . . 149 C1
Choke Wlk BS4 . . . . 23 E8
CHOLWELL 58 D2
Cholwell Cotts BS39. . . . . . 58 D2
Chorwell La TA21 . . . . 166 E2
Chovel La BA11. . . . . 142 F6
Chowins Rd TA18 . . . . 224 C6
Christ Church CE Fst Sch
  BA11. . . . . 119 F2
Christ Church CE Prim Sch
  Bristol BS8. . . . . 226 A3
  Weston-super-Mare BS23 . . 48 E8
Christ Church Cl 1 BS48 . .8 E2
Christ Church Ct 9
  TA18 . . . . 224 C6
Christchurch Hall 2
  BA1 . . . . 228 B3
Christ Church Path S 12
  BS23 . . . . 48 E8
Christchurch Rd BS8. . . . 226 A3
Christchurch St E BA11. . 119 F4
Christchurch St W BA11. 119 E4
Christian Cl BS22 . . . . 32 A3
Christian's Cross BA6. . . . 157 E1
Christina Terr BS8 . . . . . . 226 A1
Christmas St 6 BS1. . . . . . 227 A3
Christmas Steps 2 BS1. 227 A3
CHRISTON. 68 D7
Christon Rd
  Banwell BS29. . . . . 51 A1
  Loxton BS26. . . . . 68 C6
Christon Terr BS23. . . . . . . 48 F2
Christopher Brain St
  BS14 . . . . 22 E5

Christopher Cl BA20 . . . . 218 E5
Christopher Way BA4 . . . 205 A5
Chritchard Parkway TA1 213 B4
Chrysanthemum Cl 3
  DT9 . . . . 225 E4
Chrysanthemum Flats 2
  DT9 . . . . 225 E4
Chrysanthemum Row 4
  DT9 . . . . 225 E4
Chubbards Cross Cvn Site
  TA19 . . . . 183 E5
Chubbs Lawn TA18. . . . . . 224 C5
Chubworthy Cross TA4 . . 165 D5
Church Ave BS9 . . . . 5 E4
Church Cl
  Bathampton BA2 . . . . 28 F2
  Bathford BA1. . . . . 29 B2
  Bourton SP8. . . . . 161 E1
  7 Carhampton TA24. . . . 131 A5
  Clevedon BS21. . . . . 6 A2
  East Huntspill TA9 . . . . . 136 E8
  Evercreech BA4. . . . . 141 E1
  Great Elm BA11. . . . . 118 F7
  Lydeard St Lawrence TA4 . 151 A3
  24 Martock TA12 . . . . . . 185 E6
  Norton Fitzwarren TA2. . 168 B4
  Portishead BS20 . . . . 2 D5
  Shapwick TA7. . . . . 137 F1
  South Brewham BA10 . . . 160 F6
  Stoke St Gregory TA3. . . 170 E6
  Stoke St Mary TA3 . . . . . 169 C1
  West Chinnock TA18 . . . 196 B8
  Yatton BS49. . . . . 34 C7
Church Cnr 67 B1
Church Cotts
  Chilton Trinity TA5 . . . . . 135 F2
  Monkton Combe BA2. . . . 63 E8
  Newton St Loe BA2 . . . . . 43 B6
Church Ct
  Midsomer Norton BA3. . . 78 A1
  Redhill BS40 . . . . 36 D3
Churchdown Wlk BS11 . . . .4 E5
Church Dr
  Congresbury BS49. . . . . . 34 D4
  West Buckland TA21 . . . . 180 F7
Church Farm Bsns Pk
  BA2. . . . . 43 A7
Church Farm Cl
  Marksbury BA2 . . . . 42 B1
  Stawell TA7 . . . . 137 A1
Church Farm Pl 18 BA8. . 190 A6
Churchfield La TA3 . . . . . 183 F7
Church Field La TA7 . . . . 136 C4
Churchfields
  Rode BA11. . . . . 101 F8
  Wellington TA21. . . . . . . 222 D7
Church Fields
  Wellington TA21. . . . . . . 222 E6
  Wincanton BA9 . . . . 216 C3
Churchfield Sch TA9 . . . . 104 D4
Churchfields Dr BA7 . . . . 214 C6
Churchfields The Village Sch
  (Monkton Farleigh Base)
  BA15. . . . . 46 E7
Church Gdns BA6 . . . . 206 D5
Church Hayes Cl BS48. . . . 18 E8
Church Hayes Dr BS48. . . 18 E8
Church Hill
  Beckington BA11. . . . . . . 101 E4
  Buckhorn Weston SP8. . . 177 D3
  Charlton Adam TA11 . . . 173 F7
  Combwich TA5 . . . . 135 B5
  Dinnington TA17. . . . . . . 195 B7
  Exford TA24 . . . . 128 D1
  Freshford BA3. . . . . 64 B5
  Kington Magna SP8. . . . . 177 E2
  Pitney TA10 . . . . 172 C7
  Radstock BA3 . . . . 79 C3
  South Cadbury BA22 . . . 175 C3
  Stalbridge DT10. . . . . . . 190 B5
  Templecombe BA8. . . . . . 176 E1
  Timsbury BA2 . . . . 60 B2
Church Ho BA4 . . . . 141 F1
Church House Rd TA8. . . . 84 F5
CHURCHILL. 52 F5
Churchill Ave
  Clevedon BS21. . . . . 6 C2
  Wells BA5 . . . . 112 E1
Churchill Bsns Pk BS23 . . 49 A7
Churchill CE Prim Sch
  BS40 . . . . 53 A5
Churchill Cl
  Burnham-on-S TA8 . . . . . 104 C5
  5 Clevedon BS21. . . . . 6 C2
  Wells BA5 . . . . 112 E1
Churchill Com Sch BS25. .52 D5
Churchill Dr BS9. . . . . 5 D7
Churchill Gate BS25. . . . . 52 F4
Churchill Gn BS25 . . . . . . 52 C5
CHURCHILL GREEN 52 D5
Churchill La
  Axminster EX13 . . . . 198 A5
  Chipstable TA4. . . . . 165 C5
Churchill Rd
  Frome BA11. . . . . 119 D4
  Shepton Mallet BA4. . . . 205 A5
  Wells BA5 . . . . 112 E1
  Weston-super-Mare BS23 . 49 A7
Churchill Rd E BA5. . . . . . 112 E1
Churchill Way
  Taunton TA1. . . . . 212 F1
  Watchet TA23. . . . . 202 C6
CHURCHINFORD 192 A7
Church La
  Axbridge BS26. . . . . 70 C2
  Backwell BS48. . . . . 19 C5
  Badgworth BS26 . . . . 88 A6
  Baltonsborough BA6 . . . 158 A5

Church La continued
  Bath BA2 . . . . 45 C4
  Batheaston BA1. . . . . 28 F4
  Bicknoller TA4 . . . . 132 F2
  Bishop Sutton BS39. . . . . 57 D4
  Bitton BS30 . . . . 25 E7
  Blackford BS28 . . . . 107 D5
  Brent Knoll TA9 . . . . 86 A2
  Bristol BS1. . . . . 227 B2
  Bristol, Clifton Wood BS8 . 226 B2
  Bristol, Dundry Hill BS14. . 23 B3
  Carhampton TA24. . . . . . 131 B5
  Chew Stoke BS40 . . . . 56 D8
  Chewton Mendip BA3 . . . 94 F7
  Chilcompton BA3 . . . . . . 96 D5
  Chilton Polden TA7. . . . . 137 B2
  Churchill BS25 . . . . 52 D5
  Clutton BS39 . . . . 58 E3
  Coleford BA3 . . . . 116 F7
  Compton Bishop BS26. . . 69 B3
  Compton Dando BS39. . . 41 D6
  Doulting BA4 . . . . 141 E6
  Dulverton TA22 . . . . 163 D6
  East Coker BA22 . . . . 197 E8
  East Harptree BS40. . . . . 74 E4
  East Huntspill TA9 . . . . . 136 E8
  East Lambrook TA13 . . . 220 C8
  Evercreech BA4. . . . . 141 E1
  Farmborough BA2 . . . . . . 60 A6
  Farrington Gurney BS39 . 77 A4
  Flax Bourton BS48. . . . . . 19 F7
  Glastonbury BA6. . . . . . . 206 D5
  Haselbury Plucknett TA18 . 196 C5
  Hatch Beauchamp TA3. . 182 E8
  Horningsham BA12 . . . . 144 E4
  Horton TA19. . . . . 183 C2
  Hutton BS24 . . . . 49 E2
  Ilminster TA19 . . . . 221 C4
  Kingston St Mary TA2 . . 168 E8
  Limpley Stoke BA3. . . . . . 64 A5
  Long Ashton BS41 . . . . . . 11 C2
  Long Sutton TA10. . . . . . 172 D2
  Loxton BS26. . . . . 68 D4
  Lympsham BS24. . . . . 67 B1
  Lynford-on-F TA11 . . . . . 158 D2
  Meare BA6. . . . . 138 D4
  Midsomer Norton BA3. . . 78 A1
  Milborne Port DT9. . . . . . 217 D2
  Misterton TA18 . . . . 224 E3
  Monkton Combe BA2. . . . 45 F1
  Nailsea BS21. . . . . 8 C4
  Nailsea BS48. . . . . 8 C1
  North Perrott TA18 . . . . . 196 C4
  Norton Sub Hamdon,
    Chiselborough TA14 . . 185 E1
  Norton Sub Hamdon TA14 . 185 F2
  Paulton BS39. . . . . 77 E6
  Portbury BS20 . . . . 3 E3
  Rimpton BA22 . . . . 188 B8
  Rode BA11. . . . . 101 F8
  Ruishton TA3 . . . . 169 C4
  Ruishton, Thornfalcon TA3 . 169 E2
  Seavington St Mary TA19. 184 E1
  22 Shepton Mallet BA4 . . 205 B6
  Shepton Mallet, Cannards Grave
    BA4. . . . . 205 D2
  Sherborne DT9 . . . . 225 D4
  Stratton-on-t F BA3. . . . . 96 F2
  Timsbury BA2 . . . . 60 B2
  Westonzoyland TA7. . . . . 154 F5
  West Pennard BA6 . . . . . 140 B1
  Wingfield BA14 . . . . 83 C6
  Winscombe BS25. . . . . . . 69 E6
  Yatton BS49. . . . . 34 C7
Churchlands TA9 . . . . 106 D4
Churchlands Ct TA8. . . . . 104 A7
Churchland Way BS22. . . . 50 B8
Church Lane Cnr TA9 . . . . 86 A2
Church Lane End BS48. . . 19 F8
Church Leaze BS11 . . . . . . 4 D6
Church Mdw TA6 . . . . 208 E6
Church Mdws BS14. . . . . . 23 C4
Church Mead 8 . . . . 161 E1
Churchmoor La BA6. . . . . 158 A5
Church Pass 4 TA6. . . . . . 208 F5
Church Path
  Aller TA10 . . . . 171 D8
  Bridgwater TA6 . . . . 208 E5
  Crewkerne TA18. . . . . . . 224 B6
  Meare BA6. . . . . 138 D4
  Minehead TA24 . . . . 200 F8
  Queen Camel BA22 . . . . . 174 F3
  South Petherton TA13 . . 220 C2
  2 Yeovil BA20. . . . . 219 B5
Church Path Rd BS20 . . . . 4 C4
Church Pl
  Milborne Port DT9. . . . . . 217 D2
  Pill BS20 . . . . 4 C4
Church Rd
  Abbots Leigh BS8. . . . . . . 11 A8
  Bath, Combe Down BA2. . 45 C1
  Bath, Weston Park BA1. . . 27 C1
  Bawdrip TA7. . . . . 136 E2
  Bitton BS30 . . . . 25 E7
  Bourton SP8. . . . . 177 F8
  Bradford Abbas DT9 . . . . 187 E1
  Brean TA8 . . . . 65 F4
  Bristol, Bishopsworth BS13. 22 A6
  Bristol, Sneyd Park BS9. . . 5 D3
  Chapel Leigh TA4 . . . . . . 167 A7
  Churchinford TA3 . . . . . . 191 F8
  Churchstanton TA3. . . . . 181 B1
  Coxley BA5. . . . . 139 E6
  Dundry BA5. . . . . 21 D2
  East Brent TA9 . . . . 86 C4
  Easton-in-G BS20. . . . . 4 A4
  Edington TA7 . . . . 137 C2
  Fitzhead TA4 . . . . 166 F7

Church Rd continued
  Fordgate TA7 . . . . 154 D3
  Huntspill TA9 . . . . 136 A8
  Ilton TA19 . . . . 183 E4
  Keenthorne TA5 . . . . 134 D3
  Kilmington BA12 . . . . 161 F7
  Leigh Woods BS8. . . . . . . 11 D6
  Lympsham BS24. . . . . 67 B1
  Middlezoy TA7 . . . . 155 B3
  Minehead TA24 . . . . 200 F8
  North Curry TA3. . . . . . . 170 B4
  North Newton TA7 . . . . . 154 A2
  Peasedown St John BA2. . 79 B8
  Pensford BS39. . . . . 40 A7
  Redhill BS40 . . . . 36 D3
  Shapwick TA7. . . . . 137 F1
  South Cadbury BA22 . . . 175 D4
  Sparkford BA22 . . . . 175 A4
  Spaxton TA5. . . . . 152 E7
  Street BA16. . . . . 207 D7
  Sutton Mallet TA7 . . . . . 155 B7
  Taunton TA3 . . . . 168 D1
  Wembdon TA6. . . . . 208 D6
  Weston-super-Mare BS22. . 31 E2
  Whitchurch BS14. . . . . . . 23 C4
  Winford BS40 . . . . 38 A7
  Winscombe BS25. . . . . . . 69 E7
  Yatton BS49. . . . . 34 C7
Church Rd N BS20 . . . . 2 D5
Church Rd S BS20. . . . . 2 D4
Church Rise BS40 . . . . 38 A7
CHURCH ROW. 101 F8
Church Row BA3. . . . . 96 F2
Church Row Cotts TA3 . . 181 E6
Church Sq
  Clutton BS39 . . . . 58 E2
  Midsomer Norton BA3. . . 78 A1
  8 Taunton TA1 . . . . 212 F4
Church St
  Babcary TA11. . . . . 174 C7
  Banwell BS29. . . . . 51 B3
  Barton St David BA6 . . . 157 F2
  6 Bath BA1 . . . . 228 C2
  Bathford BA1. . . . . 29 B2
  Bath, Weston park BA1. . . 27 B1
  Bath, Widcombe BA2. . . . 45 B4
  Beckington BA11. . . . . . . 101 E4
  Bishops Lydeard TA4. . . . 167 E8
  Blackford BS28 . . . . 107 D4
  Blagdon BS40 . . . . 54 F2
  Bridgwater TA6 . . . . 209 A5
  Bristol BS1. . . . . 227 B2
  5 Cannington TA5. . . . . . 135 B2
  Castle Cary BA7. . . . . 214 B4
  Chard TA20. . . . . 223 C3
  Cheddar BS27 . . . . 90 B7
  Coleford BA3 . . . . 116 F7
  Crewkerne TA18. . . . . . . 224 C6
  Croscombe BA5 . . . . 204 C7
  Dinder BA5 . . . . 140 D7
  Donyatt TA19 . . . . 183 D1
  Drayton TA10 . . . . 171 E3
  Dunster TA24 . . . . 201 E2
  2 Frome BA11. . . . . 119 F4
  Halstock BA22 . . . . 197 C3
  8 Henstridge BA8 . . . . . . 190 A6
  Highbridge TA9 . . . . 104 E4
  Hinton St George TA17 . . 195 C7
  Horningsham BA12 . . . . 144 D4
  Ilchester BA22. . . . . 173 E1
  Isle Abbotts TA3 . . . . 183 F7
  Keinton Mandeville TA11. 158 A1
  Kilmersdon BA3. . . . . 98 B5
  Kingsbury Episcopi TA12 . 185 B8
  Kington Magna SP8. . . . . 177 E2
  Lopen TA13 . . . . 185 A1
  Maiden Bradley BA12 . . . 144 C1
  Mark TA9 . . . . 106 D4
  Martock TA12. . . . . 185 E6
  Merriott TA16. . . . . 195 F7
  Milborne Port DT9. . . . . . 217 D2
  Minehead, Alcombe TA24. 201 B5
  Minehead TA24 . . . . 200 F8
  Norton St Philip BA2 . . . . 81 E4
  Nunney BA11. . . . . 143 B8
  Paulton BS39. . . . . 77 D6
  Pensford BS39. . . . . 40 D4
  Podimore BA22 . . . . 174 A3
  Radstock BA3 . . . . 78 F2
  Shepton Beauchamp TA19. 184 E4
  Southwick BA14. . . . . 83 F3
  Stogursey TA5 . . . . 134 C5
  Stoke St Michael BA3 . . . 116 A2
  Taunton TA1. . . . . 213 B3
  Timberscombe TA24 . . . 130 B5
  Tintinhull BA22 . . . . 186 B6
  Upton Noble BA4. . . . . . . 142 F2
  Wanstrow BA4. . . . . 142 F4
  Wedmore BS28 . . . . 108 D4
  West Coker BA22 . . . . . . 197 A8
  Wincanton BA9 . . . . 216 C4
  Winsham TA20. . . . . 194 E1
  Wiveliscombe TA4 . . . . . 210 C4
  Woolavington TA7. . . . . . 136 E4
  Woolley BA1 . . . . 27 F6
  Yeovil BA20 . . . . 219 B5
  Yeovilton BA22. . . . . 174 A1
CHURCHSTANTON. 181 B1
Churchstanton Prim Sch
  TA3 . . . . 191 B8
Church Steps TA24. . . . . . 200 F8
Church Terr
  7 Bampton EX16 . . . . . . 164 B1
  East Coker BA22 . . . . 197 C7
  Odcombe BA22 . . . . 186 C2
  4 Yeovil BA20. . . . . 219 B5
Church Tk SP8. . . . . 161 E1
CHURCH TOWN 19 C5

Church Town BS48. . . . . . . 19 C5
Church View
  Bourton SP8. . . . . 161 E1
  Chilton Trinity TA5 . . . . . 135 F2
  Clatworthy TA4. . . . . 149 F1
  Evercreech BA4. . . . . 141 E1
  North Wootton BA4 . . . . 140 C4
  Porlock TA24 . . . . 124 A3
  Wraxall BS48. . . . . 9 B2
Church View Cl TA10. . . . 171 E8
Churchview Ct BA6 . . . . . 206 D4
Churchward Dr BA11. . . . 120 C6
Churchward Rd BS22. . . . 32 B3
Churchway
  Curry Rivel TA10 . . . . 171 D4
  Faulkland BA3 . . . . 80 D1
Church Way TA7. . . . . 137 D2
Churchway Cl TA10 . . . . . 171 D4
Churchways BS14. . . . . . . 23 C4
Churchwell Cl DT9 . . . . . . 187 E1
Churchwell St DT9 . . . . . . 187 E1
Church Wlk
  Baltonsborough BA6 . . . 158 A5
  Bawdrip TA7. . . . . 136 E2
  Bratton Seymour BA9 . . . 176 B8
  Ilminster TA19 . . . . 221 C4
  Leigh u M BA3 . . . . 117 A3
  Long Sutton TA10. . . . . . 172 F4
  Marston Magna BA22 . . . 174 F1
  9 North Petherton TA6 . . 153 E3
  Pill BS20 . . . . 4 C4
  Wrington BS40 . . . . 35 D2
Chur La BA22 . . . . 197 A8
Churlands Cl BA22 . . . . . . 197 A8
Churston Cl BS14 . . . . 23 A3
Cinder Ash La TA18 . . . . . 195 D4
Cinnamon La BA6. . . . . . . 206 F3
CircleBath Hospl BA2 . . . . 79 E6
Circle The BA2. . . . . 44 B3
Circular Rd BS9. . . . . 5 E2
Circus Field Rd BA6. . . . . 206 D4
Circus Mews BA1 . . . . 228 B3
Circus Pl BA1. . . . . 228 B3
Circus The BA1. . . . . 228 B3
City of Bath Coll BA1. . . . 228 B2
City of Bristol Coll BS1. . 226 C2
City of Bristol Coll (South
  Bristol Skills Acad)
  BA11. . . . . 22 E5
City Rd BS2. . . . . 227 B4
City The TA9. . . . . 106 C4
City View BA1 . . . . 228 C4
Clammer Hill La TA18 . . . 224 D6
Clanage Rd BS3. . . . . 11 E4
Clanders Batch BS40. . . . . 54 D3
CLANDOWN 78 E4
Clandown Rd BS39. . . . . . . 77 F4
Clanfield DT9. . . . . 225 B2
Clan Ho BA2. . . . . 45 C7
CLANVILLE 159 C3
Clanville TA24 . . . . 200 F7
Clanville Rd TA24 . . . . . . 200 F7
CLAPTON
  Crewkerne. 195 C1
  Midsomer Norton 96 C7
Clapton Court Gdns ★
  TA18 . . . . 195 D1
Clapton Dro BS20. . . . . 2 D1
Clapton Gate TA18. . . . . . 195 C2
CLAPTON IN GORDANO. . . .2 E1
Clapton La
  Holton BA9. . . . . 176 B6
  Portishead BS20 . . . . 2 E2
Clapton Rd
  Hewish TA18 . . . . 195 D2
  Midsomer Norton BA3. . . 77 D1
CLAPTON WICK 7 E6
Clapton Wlk BS9. . . . . 5 C5
Clare Gdns BA2. . . . . 44 D1
Clareham La
  Buckland Dinham BA11. . 99 D2
  Buckland Dinham BA11. . 99 F3
Claremont Bldgs BA1 . . . . 28 A1
Claremont Cres BS23. . . . 30 B1
Claremont Ct TA1 . . . . . . 212 C1
Claremont Cvn Pk TA8 . . 84 F6
Claremont Dr TA1. . . . . . 212 C1
Claremont Gdns
  Clevedon BS21. . . . . 6 E1
  Hallatrow BS39 . . . . 77 B7
  4 Nailsea BS48. . . . . 8 D1
Claremont Gr TA6. . . . . . . 209 D6
Claremont Hall BS21 . . . . .6 E4
Claremont La TA1. . . . . . . 212 C1
Claremont Pl 13 BA1 . . . . 28 A1
Claremont Rd BA1 . . . . . . 28 B1
Claremont Wlk BA1 . . . . . 28 A1
Clarence Ct 1 BA20 . . . . . 219 A5
Clarence Dr 1 TA6 . . . . . . 153 F4
Clarence Grove Rd BS23. . 48 E5
Clarence Pl
  Bath BA1. . . . . 44 B6
  Bristol BS2. . . . . 226 C4
Clarence Rd BS1. . . . . 227 B1
Clarence Rd E BS23. . . . . . 48 E5
Clarence Rd N BS23. . . . . 48 D5
Clarence Rd S BS23 . . . . . 48 D5
Clarence St
  Bath BA1. . . . . 228 C4
  Taunton TA1. . . . . 212 E4
  Yeovil BA20. . . . . 219 A4
Clarence Ter TA6 . . . . 136 B2
Clarence Terr
  Bath BA2 . . . . 45 D5
  6 Yeovil BA20. . . . . 219 B4
Clarendon Rd
  Bath BA2 . . . . 45 B5
  Weston-super-Mare BS23 . 48 F8

Clarendon Villas BA2 45 B5
Clares Rd BA5 203 D3
Clare St
Bridgwater TA6 208 F5
Bristol BS1 227 A2
2 North Petherton TA6 153 F4
Clark Cl
Woolavington TA7 136 E4
Wraxall BS48 9 B2
Clarken Cl BS48 8 E1
Clarken Coombe BS41 11 B3
Clarke's Cl TA20 223 D4
Clarkes Ct BA20 219 A4
Clarke's Row TA20 223 D4
CLARKHAM CROSS 197 E2
Clarkham Cross BA22 197 E2
Clarks Cl BA22 218 A5
Clark's La TA18 224 F3
Clarks Meadow BA4 205 C3
Clarkson Ave BS22 31 C1
Clarkson Ho BA1 228 A2
Clarks Rd TA6 209 C4
Clarks Shopping Village BA16 207 C6
Clarks Way BA2 44 C2
Classic Bldgs TA6 208 F4
Clatcombe La DT9 188 D6
CLATWORTHY 149 F1
Clatworthy Dr BS14 23 A7
Clatworthy Resr★ TA4 149 D2
Claude Ave BA2 44 C5
Claude Terr BA2 44 C5
Claudius Rd BS31 24 F7
CLAVERHAM 17 E1
Claverham Cl BS49 34 D7
Claverham Dro BS49 17 D5
Claverham Pk BS49 34 F8
Claverham Rd BS49 34 E8
CLAVERTON 46 B5
Claverton Bldgs BA2 228 C1
Claverton Ct BA2 45 E4
CLAVERTON DOWN 45 F3
Claverton Down Rd BA2 45 F3
Claverton Dr BA2 45 F3
Claverton Hill BA2 46 A4
Claverton Lodge BA2 45 C5
Claverton Pumping Sta★ BA2 46 C5
Claverton Rd BS31 25 E2
Claverton Rd W BS31 25 D3
Claverton St BA2 228 C1
Clay Castle TA18 196 C5
Clay Castle La TA18 196 C6
Claydon Cl TA23 131 E4
Claydon Gn BS14 22 F3
Clayford La TA22 163 C5
Clayford Rd TA22 163 C5
CLAYHANGER 165 C1
Clayhanger Cross TA20 193 E6
Clayhanger La
Chard TA20 223 A8
Combe St Nicholas TA20 193 E6
CLAYHIDON 180 E2
Clayhidon Crossway EX15 180 E2
Clay La
Barrington TA19 184 B5
Bitton BS30 25 D8
Chewton Mendip BA3 94 C5
Higher Chillington TA19 194 F5
Millmoor EX15 179 A1
Rode BA11 101 F8
Claylands Cnr TA5 134 E5
Claypiece Rd BS13 22 A4
CLAYPITS 164 C4
CLAYS END 43 D6
Clayton Cl
Portishead BS20 2 E4
Yeovil BA22 218 A6
CLEARWOOD 121 F8
Clearwood BA13 121 F8
Clearwood View BA13 121 E4
Cleaveside Cl BA22 174 F3
CLEEVE 35 B8
Cleeve Abbey★ TA23 131 E3
Cleevedale Rd BA2 45 A1
Cleeve Dr BS49 35 B8
Cleeve Gn BA2 44 A6
Cleeve Gr BS31 24 D5
Cleeve Hill
Ubley BS40 73 E8
Watchet TA23 202 A7
Cleeve Hill Rd BS40 35 C7
Cleeve Pk TA24 131 D5
Cleeve Pl BS48 9 A1
Cleeve Rd TA2 213 B7
Cleeveways DT9 176 A2
Clemence Rd BA16 207 D4
Clements Cl BA5 203 C3
Clement St BS2 227 C4
Cleve Ct 3 BS8 11 F6
CLEVEDON 6 B3
Clevedon Com Hospl BS21 6 E3
Clevedon Com Sch BS21 6 F5
Clevedon Court★ BS21 7 A4
Clevedon Craft Ctr★ BS21 7 A1
Clevedon La BS21 8 B7
Clevedon Min Rly★ BS21 6 B3
Clevedon Pier★ BS21 6 C4
Clevedon Rd
Flax Bourton BS48 9 F2
Midsomer Norton BA3 78 A2
Nailsea BS21 8 B4
Portishead BS20 1 E1
Portishead BS20 2 D3
Walton In Gordano BS21 7 C8
Weston-super-Mare BS23 48 E6
Wraxall BS48 9 B4
Clevedon Rd *continued*
Wraxall BS48 9 D6
Clevedon Terr BS6 227 A4
Clevedon Wlk 2 BS48 8 E2
Cleveland Cotts BA1 228 C4
Cleveland Ct BA2 45 C6
Cleveland Pl BA1 228 C4
Cleveland Pl E BA1 228 C4
Cleveland Pl W BA1 228 C4
Cleveland Reach BA1 228 C4
Cleveland Row BA1 45 B8
Clevelands TA24 200 F8
Cleveland St TA1 212 E4
Cleveland Terr BA1 228 C4
Cleveland Wlk BA2 45 C6
Cleve The BA21 218 C6
CLEWER 89 D3
Clewson Rise BS14 22 F3
Cleyhill Gdns BA13 121 D4
Cliffe Dr BA3 64 A6
Clifford Ave TA2 212 E8
Clifford Cres TA2 212 E8
Clifford Dr BS39 77 D6
Clifford Gdns BS11 4 E6
Clifford Ho BS23 48 D6
Clifford Lodge 3 TA5 135 B2
Clifford Mews TA21 222 E6
Clifford Pk TA5 135 B2
Clifford Terr TA21 222 E6
Cliff Rd
Cheddar BS27 71 E1
North Petherton TA6 153 E3
Weston-super-Mare BS22 31 A2
Cliff St BS27 90 C8
Cliffs The BS27 90 C8
Clift House Rd BS3 11 F4
Clift House Spur BS3 11 F4
CLIFTON 226 A4
Clifton Ave BS23 48 E5
Clifton Cl
1 Bristol BS8 11 F7
Yeovil BA21 219 E6
Clifton Coll BS8 226 A4
Clifton College Prep Sch BS8 5 F1
Clifton Ct 10 BS21 6 C2
Clifton Down BS8 11 F7
Clifton Down Rd BS8 226 A3
Clifton High Gr BS9 5 E5
Clifton High Sch BS8 226 A4
Clifton Hill
Barwick BA22 197 F8
Bristol BS8 226 A2
Clifton Park Rd BS8 11 F8
Clifton Pk BS8 226 A3
Clifton Rd
Bristol BS8 226 A2
Weston-super-Mare BS23 48 E5
Clifton Rocks Railway★ BS8 11 F6
Clifton St BS20 2 C2
Clifton Suspension Bridge★ BS8 11 E7
Clifton Terr 7 TA2 212 F6
Clifton Vale BS8 226 A2
Clifton Vale Cl BS8 226 A2
Clifton View 9 BA22 197 F8
CLIFTON WOOD 226 A2
Cliftonwood Cres BS8 226 B2
Clifton Wood Ct BS8 226 B2
Clifton Wood Rd BS8 226 B2
Cliftonwood Terr BS8 226 A2
Clift Pl BS1 227 A1
Clifts Bldgs BA11 119 F4
CLINK 120 C6
Clink Farm Ct BA11 120 C6
Clink Rd BA11 120 D6
Clink The TA6 209 A5
Clipper Cl TA6 209 C4
Clipper Ct BA16 207 B5
Clipper Quay TA24 201 B7
Clitsome View TA23 131 D2
Clive Rd BS14 23 C8
Clivey BA13 102 E1
Clock Ho TA5 134 B2
Clock Ho The BA10 160 D4
Clockhouse Mews BS20 2 D6
Clockhouse The TA4 167 E6
Clockhouse View BA16 207 D6
CLOFORD 143 A7
CLOFORD COMMON 143 B6
Cloisters Croft TA8 104 B6
Cloisters The BA5 203 D3
Cloister The DT9 225 D4
Closemead BS21 6 D1
Close The
Glastonbury BA6 206 E5
9 Merriott TA16 195 F7
Minehead TA24 201 B5
North Cadbury BA22 175 D6
Portishead BS20 1 F1
CLOSWORTH 197 F5
Clotfurlong La DT9 188 F1
Clothier Mdw BA7 214 B6
Cloudberry Cl TA20 223 F5
Cloud Hill Ind Est BS39 77 A8
Clovelly Rd BS22 32 A2
Clover Cl
Clevedon BS21 6 F3
Paulton BS39 77 E4
Clover Ct 2 BS22 49 D7
Clover Gd BA4 205 C5
Clover Mead TA1 213 C1
Clover Rd BS22 32 A6
Cloverton Dr TA6 209 D7
Clover Way
Bridgwater TA6 208 E1
Highbridge TA9 104 E4
Clumber Dr BA11 119 F6
Clumber Ho BA11 119 F6
CLUTTON 58 E3
CLUTTON HILL 59 B4
Clutton Hill BS39 59 B4
Clutton Prim Sch BS39 58 E3
Clyce Rd TA9 104 D3
Clyde Ave BS31 24 F4
Clyde Gdns BA2 44 B6
Clydesdale Cl BS14 23 A6
Clynder Gr BS21 6 E6
Clyntonville BS22 31 A4
Coach House Mews BS23 30 D1
Coachmans Yd BA6 206 D5
Coach Rd TA24 124 A3
Coalash La BA11 119 D8
Coal Barton BA3 116 E8
Coalbridge Cl BS22 31 F2
Coaley Rd BS11 4 D5
Coal La BA11 119 C8
Coal Orch TA1 212 F4
Coalpit La
Chilcompton BA3 96 A2
Stoke St Michael BA3 116 B3
Coalpit Rd BA1 29 A4
Coape Rd BS14 23 F5
Coast Cvn Pk BS21 1 B1
Coastguard Cotts TA24 201 A8
Coast Rd TA8 84 F7
COAT 185 D7
Coates Est BS48 8 F3
Coates Gr BS48 9 A2
Coates Wlk BS4 22 D6
Coate Turn TA4 166 A6
Coat Rd TA12 185 D7
Cobblers Way BA3 97 C8
Cobblestone Mews BS8 226 A4
Cob Castle TA21 180 D8
Cobhorn Dr BS13 21 F4
Cobley Croft BS21 16 C8
Cobthorn Way BS49 34 E5
Coburg Cl TA21 180 F7
Coburg Villas 11 BA1 28 A1
Cock And Yew Tree Hill BS40 38 A2
Cock-Crowing Stone TA20 193 D4
Cockers Hill BS39 41 C5
Cockhill Elm La BA7 214 B4
Cockhill La BA22 175 D7
COCKLAKE 108 E7
Cockland Hill TA21 166 C1
Cockmill La BA4 140 F1
Cockpit Hill DT6, DT8 199 F4
Cockpit La BA4 142 C2
Cock Rd
Buckland Dinham BA2, BA11 100 B5
Horningsham BA12 144 C4
Cockrod BA16 207 B2
COCKWOOD 134 E5
Cod La BA22 196 D7
Codrington Pl BS8 226 A3
Cogsall Rd BS14 23 F6
Coity Pl BS21 6 C4
Coker Hill BA22 196 F8
Coker Hill La BA22 197 A7
Coker Ho BA22 197 C8
Coker Marsh BA22 197 D7
Coker Rd BS22 32 B2
Coker's La BA12 161 F8
Colbourn Cl BA3 114 E7
Colbourne Rd BA2 44 D1
Colchester Cres BS4 22 D7
COLD ASHTON 12 F6
Cold Harbour
Milborne Port DT9 217 D2
Sherborne DT9 225 E5
Coldharbour Bsns Pk DT9 225 E6
Coldharbour La BS23 48 D3
Cold Harbour La BA22 196 F6
Coldhills La BA8 176 D2
Cold Nose BS28 138 D8
Coldpark Gdns BS13 21 E5
Coldpark Rd BS13 21 E5
Cold Rd TA3 182 D6
Coldrick Cl BS14 22 F3
Cole Cl
Cotford St Luke TA4 167 E6
Nether Stowey TA5 134 A3
Cole Cross BA22 186 C6
COLEFORD 116 F7
COLEFORD WATER 150 F4
Colehouse La BS21 16 C8
Cole La 5 TA14 185 F4
Colemead BS13 22 B5
Cole Mead BA10 215 D5
Cole Rd BA10 215 D5
Coleridge Cottage★ TA5 134 B2
Coleridge Cres TA1 213 B3
Coleridge Gdns TA8 85 B2
Coleridge Gn TA6 208 E5
Coleridge Rd
Bridgwater TA6 208 E6
Clevedon BS21 6 C3
Nether Stowey TA5 134 A2
Weston-super-Mare BS23 49 A4
Coleridge Sq TA6 208 E6
Coleridge Vale Rd E 1 BS21 6 D2
Coleridge Vale Rd N BS21 6 C2
Coleridge Vale Rd S BS21 6 D2
Coleridge Vale Rd W 2 BS21 6 C2
Coles Cotts TA5 135 F2
COLE'S CROSS 199 D5
Coles Cross Cotts DT8 199 D5
Coles Gdns BA3 98 B5
Coleshill Dr BS13 22 B5
Cole's La
Chewton Mendip BA3 95 A6
South Petherton TA13 220 D3
Colesmore TA4 167 A4
Coles Place TA20 223 C3
Coles's La EX13 198 B1
COLEY 75 C4
Coley La TA19 194 F5
Coley Rd BS40 75 B4
Colham La TA20 194 E1
Colin Ave TA2 212 F7
Colin Rd TA2 213 A7
Collarway La BA22 196 F8
College BA22 196 E8
College Cl TA10 172 E2
College Ct TA8 104 A7
College Fields BS8 11 F8
College Gn
Bristol BS1 226 C2
Yeovil BA21 219 B6
College Rd
Bath BA1 27 E1
Bristol, Clifton BS8 11 F8
Taunton TA2 212 D6
Wells BA5 203 E5
College Sq BS1 226 C2
College St
Bristol BS1 226 C2
Burnham-on-S TA8 104 A7
College View
18 Bath BA1 28 A1
Taunton TA1 212 C2
College Way
Bridgwater TA6 209 C6
Taunton TA1 212 C1
Colles Cl BA5 203 F5
Colles Rd BA5 203 F5
Collett Ave BA4 205 C5
Collett Cl BS22 32 C4
Collett Rd TA2 212 A7
Collett Way BA11 120 C7
Colley La TA6 209 B4
Colleylake Cotts TA3 181 C5
Colley Lane Ind Est TA6 209 B3
Collickshire La TA3 170 E6
Collie Cnr BA11 118 A1
Collier Cl BA2 78 D8
Colliers La BA1 27 F4
Collier's La BA11 99 D2
Colliers Rise BA3 79 A3
Colliers Wlk 4 BS48 8 E2
Collingwood Cl
Saltford BS31 25 E2
Weston-super-Mare BS22 31 E4
Collingwood Ct TA6 208 F5
Collingwood Rd BA21 219 F8
Collin's Farm TA19 183 E2
Collins' La TA11 173 F7
Collinson Rd BS13 22 B5
Collins St BS11 4 B8
Collum La BS22 31 E6
Colman Rd TA1 212 B1
Colmer Rd
Bridgwater TA6 208 F7
Yeovil BA21 219 B6
Colne Gn BS31 25 A4
Colombo Cres BS23 48 E3
Colston Ave BS1 227 A2
Colston Cross EX13 198 B4
Colston Fort 2 BS2 227 A4
Colston Par BS1 227 B1
Colston's Almshouses 1 BS1 227 A3
Colston St BS1 227 A3
Colston Yd BS1 227 A3
Colton La TA4 149 F7
Columbus Ho BA2 45 D8
Colyton 11 BS22 32 A2
Combe Ave BS20 2 C6
Combe Batch BS28 108 D4
Combe Batch Rise BS28 108 D4
Combe Beacon La TA20 193 C7
Combe Cl
Bicknoller TA4 132 E2
Yeovil BA21 219 A8
Combe Cross
Halse TA4 167 B7
Monksilver TA4 150 C8
Shillingford EX16 164 D4
Combecross Hill TA4 150 B8
Combecross La
Monksilver TA4 150 B8
Stogumber TA4 150 C8
COMBE DOWN 45 B1
Combe Down CE Prim Sch BA2 45 B1
Combe Down La TA4 151 C2
Combe Fields BS20 2 C6
COMBE FLOREY 151 C2
Combe Gn BA5 204 B7
Combe Gr BA1 44 B8
COMBE HAY 62 D4
Combe Hay La BA2 62 B6
COMBE HILL 217 A4
Combe Hill
Barton St David TA11 158 A2
Combe St Nicholas TA20 193 D5
Hemyock EX15 180 C2
Milborne Port DT9 217 B3
Templecombe BA8 176 E1
Yenston BA8 189 F8
Combe Hill Dro TA20 193 C5
Combe Hill La TA7 156 B7
Combe La
Brompton Ralph TA4 150 B3
Charlton Adam TA11 173 F8
Combe La *continued*
Chilton Polden TA7 137 B3
Churchstanton TA3 181 A2
Combe St Nicholas TA20 193 B5
Dulverton TA22 163 D6
East Anstey TA22 162 F6
Exford TA24 128 D1
Hallatrow BS39 77 B6
Langport TA10 171 F7
North Curry TA3 170 A4
Parbrook BA4 158 D8
Rodhuish TA24 131 B3
Wedmore BS28 108 D4
Wiveliscombe TA4 210 C8
Woolavington TA7 136 F4
Combeland La TA22 164 A5
Combeland Rd TA24 201 B4
Combe Pk
Bath BA1 44 C8
Yeovil BA21 218 F8
Combe Rd
Bath BA2 45 B1
Portishead BS20 2 D5
Combe Road Cl BA2 45 B1
COMBE ST NICHOLAS 193 D6
Combeshead Hill TA22 148 A3
Combeshead La
Brompton Regis TA22 148 A4
West Anstey EX36 162 A7
Combeside BA2 45 A3
Combe Side BS48 19 A7
Combe St TA20 223 C4
Combe Street La BA21 219 A8
Combe Street Lane Rdbt BA21 218 F8
Combe Terr TA9 136 E8
Combe The
Burrington BS40 53 F2
Lydeard St Lawrence TA4 151 C2
COMBE THROOP 176 F2
COMBWICH 135 B5
Comer Rd BS27 90 A7
Comer's Cross TA24 146 E6
Comer's Gate TA24 146 E6
COMEYTROWE 212 B1
Comeytrowe Ctr TA1 212 C1
Comeytrowe La TA1, TA4 212 A2
Comeytrowe Orch TA1 212 A2
Comeytrowe Rd TA1 212 B1
Comeytrowe Rise TA1 212 B2
Comfortable Pl BA1 228 A3
Commerce Pk BA11 120 D8
Commerce Way TA9 104 F2
Commercial Rd
Bristol BS1 227 A1
Shepton Mallet BA4 205 B6
Commercial Row TA20 223 C4
Commercial Way BS22 32 B2
Common La
Charlton Adam TA11 174 A8
Churchill Green BS25 52 B5
Easton-in-G BS20 4 B2
Halstock BA22 197 C2
Hardington Mandeville BA22 197 A5
Holcombe BA3 116 D7
Huish Champflower TA4 165 D7
Kington Magna SP8 177 E1
Marnhull DT10 190 E4
North Perrott TA18 196 D4
South Cheriton BA8 176 F4
Templecombe BA8 177 A1
Wincanton BA9 216 D3
Yenston BA8 189 F8
Common Moor Dro BA6 206 E7
Common Rd BA9 216 E3
Como Ct BS20 2 C6
Compass Hill TA1 212 E3
Compass Rise TA1 212 E3
Compton Acres DT9 187 E4
COMPTON BISHOP 69 A3
Compton Cl
Glastonbury BA6 206 F7
Shepton Mallet BA4 205 B5
Taunton TA2 213 A6
Yeovil BA21 219 E8
Compton Cnr BA4 205 B5
Compton Ct Mews DT9 187 F3
COMPTON DANDO 41 D6
Compton Dr
Bristol BS9 5 C7
Weston-super-Mare BS24 49 E7
COMPTON DUNDON 157 B4
Compton Dundon CE Prim Sch TA11 157 A3
COMPTON DURVILLE 184 F4
Compton Flats BA21 219 C6
Compton Gdns BA11 120 D7
Compton Gn BS31 24 E4
Compton Hill TA13 220 A5
Compton La
Axbridge BS26 70 B1
Shepton Mallet BA4 205 B2
COMPTON MARTIN 74 A7
COMPTON PAUNCEFOOT 175 E5
Compton Rd
Shepton Mallet BA4 205 B4
South Cadbury BA22 175 D4
South Petherton TA13 220 B5
Yeovil BA21 187 E3
Compton St
Butleigh BA6 157 D4
Compton Dundon TA11 157 B4
Comrade Ave BS25 70 E8

Concorde Dr BS21 ... 6 B1
Condell Cl TA6 ... 208 F7
Condor Cl BS22 ... 49 D8
Conduit Hill BA11 ... 99 B1
Conegore BA22 ... 174 D4
Conegore Cnr BA22 ... 174 D4
Coneygree BS13 ... 21 F6
Conference Ave BS20 ... 2 F5
Conference Cl BS20 ... 2 F4
CONGRESBURY ... 34 E4
Conies The TA2 ... 168 E8
Conifer Cl TA24 ... 128 D1
Conifer Way BS24 ... 49 E5
Coniston Ave BS9 ... 5 E6
Coniston Cres BS23 ... 48 F4
Coniston Gdns BA21 ... 219 A7
CONKWELL ... 46 C1
Connaught Ho TA6 ... 209 C5
Connaught Mans BA2 ... 228 C3
Connaught Pl BS23 ... 48 D8
Connaught Rd BS4 ... 22 E8
Connection Rd BA2 ... 44 A6
Connelly Dr BS28 ... 108 C4
Connock Sq BA4 ... 205 C4
Conquest Bsns Pk TA19 ... 184 A4
Constable Cl
Keynsham BS31 ... 24 F6
Yeovil BA21 ... 219 E8
Constable Dr BS22 ... 31 F3
Constantine Ct BA4 ... 205 E4
Constitution Hill BS8 ... 226 B2
Convocation Ave BA2 ... 45 E5
Conway Cres TA8 ... 85 C1
Conway Gn BS31 ... 25 A3
Conway Rd TA5 ... 135 B2
Conygar Cl BS21 ... 6 F5
Conygar View TA24 ... 201 E3
Conygre Gn BA2 ... 60 B2
Conygre Rise BA2 ... 59 F6
Cook Ave TA20 ... 223 D3
Cooke's La TA10 ... 156 B2
Cookley La TA4 ... 150 F8
Cooks Bridle Path BS48 ... 36 D8
Cooks Cl TA3 ... 169 D5
Cook's Folly Rd BS9 ... 5 D3
Cooks Gdns BS48 ... 9 A2
Cooks La DT9 ... 225 D3
Cook's La
Banwell BS29 ... 51 A4
Clevedon BS21 ... 7 B2
Cranmore BA4 ... 142 A6
Milverton TA4 ... 167 B5
Stalbridge DT10 ... 190 B2
Cooksley La TA4 ... 149 A2
Cookson Cl TA8 ... 104 D5
Cook St BS11 ... 4 C8
Cook Way TA2 ... 212 C6
COOMBE
Crewkerne ... 195 B4
Sampford Peverell ... 178 A4
Taunton ... 169 C8
Coombe DT9 ... 225 C5
Coombe Bridge Ave BS9 ... 5 D6
Coombe Brook BA5 ... 203 A7
Coombe Cl BA7 ... 214 C6
Coombe Cotts BA5 ... 204 C7
Coombe Dale
Backwell BS48 ... 37 A8
Bristol BS9 ... 5 C6
Coombe Dell BA4 ... 205 A6
COOMBE DINGLE ... 5 C8
Coombe Gdns BS9 ... 5 E6
Coombe Hill
Blagdon Hill TA21 ... 181 A5
Bruton BA10 ... 215 E7
Coombe La
Bristol BS9 ... 5 E6
Compton Bishop BS26 ... 69 B4
East Harptree BS40 ... 74 E4
Easton-in-G BS8 ... 4 A2
Kingsbury Episcopi TA12 ... 185 B8
Shepton Mallet BA4 ... 205 A6
Coomb End BA3 ... 78 F3
Coombend Ho BA3 ... 78 F3
Coombe Rd
Dinnington TA17 ... 195 B7
Nailsea BS48 ... 8 E1
Weston-super-Mare BS23 ... 30 E1
Coombe's Cider Farm & Mus★ TA9 ... 106 A4
Coombe Side TA9 ... 86 B2
Coombe St
Bruton BA10 ... 215 E7
Penselwood BA9 ... 161 E2
Coombe's Way BS26 ... 87 E8
Coombe Terr
Glastonbury BA6 ... 206 E5
Sherborne DT9 ... 225 C5
Coombe The
Blagdon BS40 ... 54 C3
Compton Martin BS40 ... 74 A6
Coombe View BA4 ... 205 A6
Coombe Water La DT8 ... 199 E5
Coomb Rocke BS9 ... 5 D6
Cooperage La BS3 ... 226 B1
Cooperage The BA11 ... 119 F3
Cooper Rd BS9 ... 5 F7
Cooper's Ash La BA7, BA22 ... 214 A2
Coopers Barns BA22 ... 174 F1
Coopers Hts TA4 ... 210 C4
Coopers Mead BA4 ... 205 D4
Coopers Mill TA2 ... 168 B4
Coot Hide EX16 ... 178 D1
Coots The BS14 ... 23 E6
Copeland Dr BS14 ... 23 B5
Copford La BS41 ... 11 B1
Copis La TA11 ... 158 B3
Coplestons TA3 ... 168 D1
Copley Gdns BS22 ... 31 F2
Coppack Ho 6 BS21 ... 6 C2
Copper Beeches TA1 ... 212 A2
Copper Beech Rd TA11 ... 173 D5
Copper Cl BS27 ... 90 A8
Copperfield Dr BS22 ... 31 F4
Coppern Way DT10 ... 190 B4
Coppice Cl BA20 ... 218 D2
Coppice End Cnr BS24 ... 67 C2
Coppice Mews BS21 ... 6 C4
Coppice The BS13 ... 21 E4
Coppin Cl BA6 ... 206 F3
Coppin Rd TA2 ... 168 B4
Coppits Hill La
Yeovil BA21 ... 218 D8
Yeovil Marsh BA21 ... 187 A5
COPPLEHAM ... 147 D5
Copplesbury La BA4, BA10 ... 160 D8
Copse Cl
Watchet TA23 ... 202 C5
Weston-super-Mare BS24 ... 49 A1
Copse Cnr BS24 ... 67 C2
Copse Dro
Baltonsborough BA6 ... 158 C5
Barrington TA19 ... 184 B5
Copse End BS25 ... 51 F2
Copse La
Ashill TA19 ... 183 D4
Barrington TA19 ... 184 D4
Hambridge TA3 ... 184 B7
Ilton TA19 ... 183 F4
Pilton BA4 ... 140 F3
Copseland BA2 ... 45 D5
Copse Rd
Clevedon BS21 ... 6 C4
Keynsham BS31 ... 25 C4
Yeovil BA22 ... 218 B7
Copse Shoot La TA19 ... 184 C5
Copse Stile TA20 ... 193 F1
Copse The
Bridgwater TA6 ... 209 D5
Cossington TA7 ... 136 F3
Frome BA11 ... 120 B6
Weston-super-Mare BS22 ... 32 D2
Copsewood La BS26 ... 88 B2
Copthorne Cl BS14 ... 23 B5
Coralberry Dr BS22 ... 31 F1
Corams La TA21 ... 222 B6
Cording's Ball TA4 ... 150 A1
Corewell La TA5 ... 133 E3
CORFE ... 181 F6
Corfe Cl BS48 ... 8 D1
Corfe Cres BS31 ... 24 E4
Corfe Rd BS4 ... 22 D7
Corinthian Ct 9 BS1 ... 227 B1
Cork Pl BA1 ... 44 D7
Corkscrew La
North Cadbury BA22 ... 175 E7
Staplegrove TA2 ... 212 D8
Cork St
Bath BA1 ... 44 D7
Frome BA11 ... 119 F5
Cork Terr BA1 ... 44 D7
Cormorant Cl
Bridgwater TA6 ... 209 C3
Weston-super-Mare BS22 ... 31 F1
Cornborough Pl TA6 ... 209 B5
Cornbrash BA11 ... 120 D7
Corner Cl TA21 ... 222 D4
Corner Croft BS21 ... 6 D1
Cornfields The BS22 ... 31 F5
Cornflower Cl TA6 ... 208 D1
Cornhill
Bridgwater TA6 ... 208 F5
Shepton Mallet BA4 ... 205 C6
Sherborne DT9 ... 225 C4
5 Wellington TA21 ... 222 D6
Cornhill Dr BS14 ... 23 A7
Cornish Gr BS14 ... 23 E6
Cornish Rd BS14 ... 23 E6
Cornishway E TA1 ... 212 B3
Cornishway N TA1 ... 212 B3
Cornishway S TA1 ... 212 B2
Cornishway W TA1 ... 212 B3
Cornish Wlk BS14 ... 23 E6
Cornlands EX16 ... 178 D1
Cornleaze BS13 ... 22 A5
Cornmoor Cres TA9 ... 136 E7
Cornmoor La TA9 ... 136 E7
Corn St
Bath BA1 ... 228 B2
Bristol BS1 ... 227 A3
Cornwallis Ave
Bristol BS8 ... 226 A2
Weston-super-Mare BS22 ... 31 F4
Cornwallis Cres BS8 ... 11 F6
Cornwallis Gr BS8 ... 226 A2
Cornwall Rd BA4 ... 205 A6
Coromandel Hts BA1 ... 228 B4
Coronation Ave
Bath BA2 ... 44 C4
Keynsham BS31 ... 24 D4
Yeovil BA21 ... 218 F7
Coronation Cl
Ruishton TA3 ... 169 C3
Wanstrow BA4 ... 142 F4
Coronation Ct BA3 ... 115 A3
Coronation Est BS23 ... 48 F3
Coronation Ho TA6 ... 209 C6
Coronation Pl BS1 ... 227 A2
Coronation Rd
Banwell BS29 ... 51 A3
Bath BA1 ... 44 D7
Coronation Rd *continued*
Bleadon BS24 ... 67 C6
Bridgwater TA6 ... 208 E5
Bristol BS3 ... 226 B1
Frome BA11 ... 120 B5
Highbridge TA9 ... 104 D4
Wells BA5 ... 203 B4
Weston-super-Mare BS22 ... 31 E2
Coronation St TA20 ... 223 C3
Coronation Terr
Chilcompton BA3 ... 96 D5
Oakhill BA3 ... 115 A3
Coronation Villas BA8 ... 176 E1
Corondale Rd BS22 ... 49 D8
Corporate Rd BA22 ... 174 A2
Corporation St TA1 ... 212 F3
Corpus Christi RC Prim Sch BS23 ... 48 D6
Corrick Cl BS27 ... 90 F2
Corridor The 2 BA1 ... 228 C2
Corsham Dr TA8 ... 104 C8
CORSLEY ... 121 D2
Corsley CE Prim Sch BA12 ... 121 D2
CORSLEY HEATH ... 144 E8
Corsley Wlk BS4 ... 22 F8
CORSTON ... 43 B7
Corston BS24 ... 49 A2
Corston Dr BA2 ... 43 B6
Corston La BA2 ... 43 A8
Corston View BA2 ... 44 C2
Corston Wlk BS11 ... 4 D7
Corton Cl BS21 ... 219 E8
CORTON DENHAM ... 175 D1
Coryate Cl BA22 ... 186 C2
Cory Rd TA2 ... 213 A8
Cosgates Feet or County Gate EX35 ... 122 D5
COSSINGTON ... 136 F3
Cossington La TA7 ... 136 E3
Cossington Prim Sch TA7 ... 136 F3
Cossington Rd BS4 ... 22 F8
Cossins La TA18 ... 224 C6
Costello Hill BA22 ... 173 F2
Costiland Dr BS13 ... 21 F6
Cote Cnr TA9 ... 136 F7
Cote House La BS9 ... 5 F5
Cote La BA12 ... 161 F6
Cote Paddock BS9 ... 5 F4
Cote Pk BS9 ... 5 E6
COTFORD ST LUKE ... 167 E6
Cotford St Luke Prim Sch TA4 ... 167 E5
Cotham Hill BS6 ... 226 C4
Cotham Lawn Ho BS6 ... 226 C4
Cotham Lawn Rd BS6 ... 226 C4
Cotham Pl BS6 ... 226 C4
Cotham Rd BS6 ... 226 C4
Cotham Rd S BS6 ... 227 A4
Cotham Sch BS6 ... 226 C4
Cothay Manor Gardens★ TA21 ... 179 C8
COTHELSTONE ... 152 A2
Cothelstone Cl TA6 ... 208 B4
Cothelstone Rd TA4 ... 151 F1
Cotlake Cl TA1 ... 212 F1
Cotlake Rise TA1 ... 168 E1
Cotleigh Crossing EX14 ... 191 F1
Cotley La TA20 ... 193 D2
Cotman Wlk 1 BS22 ... 31 F2
Cotswold Cl BS20 ... 2 E4
Cotswold Rd BA2 ... 44 E4
Cotswold View BA2 ... 44 B5
Cotswold Way SN14 ... 13 A6
Cottage Cnr TA19 ... 183 F4
Cottage La TA22 ... 163 D6
Cottage Pl
3 Bath BA1 ... 28 C2
Bristol BS2 ... 227 A4
Cottage Row TA8 ... 104 A6
Cottages The BS40 ... 35 D2
Cotterell Ct BA1 ... 228 B2
Cottle Gdns BS14 ... 23 F6
Cottle Rd BS14 ... 23 F6
Cottles La
West Pennard BA6 ... 140 B1
Winsley BA15 ... 64 F6
COTTLE'S OAK ... 119 C5
Cotton Cnr 13 BA8 ... 190 A6
Cotton Mead BA2 ... 43 B7
Cotton Patch Wlk 6 TA6 ... 209 A1
Cotton's La TA11 ... 158 B2
Cottonwick Cl BS11 ... 4 D5
Coulson Dr BS22 ... 32 B3
Coulson's Cl BS14 ... 23 A3
Coulson's Rd BS14 ... 23 A3
COULTINGS ... 134 F4
Council Hos
Babcary TA11 ... 174 D7
Bleadon BS24 ... 67 B5
Clapton TA18 ... 195 C1
Hewish TA18 ... 195 D3
Kingston Seymour BS21 ... 16 C3
Podimore BA22 ... 174 A4
Wick St Lawrence BS22 ... 32 B8
Council Houses BS24 ... 33 C3
Council Houses The
Butcombe BS40 ... 55 B8
Hinton Blewett BS39 ... 75 E6
Counterslip BS1 ... 227 B2
Counterslip Gdns BS14 ... 23 C6
Countess Ave TA6 ... 208 E7
Countess Gytha Prim Sch BA22 ... 174 F3
County Wlk TA1 ... 213 A3
Couple Cross TA24 ... 130 B1
COURSHAY ... 198 E3
Coursing Batch BA6 ... 206 F3
COURSLEY ... 151 B4
Court Acres 6 BA22 ... 197 F8
Court Ash BA20 ... 219 B5
Court Ave BS49 ... 34 C7
Court Barton
Crewkerne TA18 ... 224 B6
Ilminster TA19 ... 221 C4
Court Cl
Portishead BS20 ... 2 D4
Weston-super-Mare BS22 ... 32 C2
Court Cl The BS48 ... 19 C5
Court Cotts SP8 ... 177 D3
Court-de-Wyck CE Prim Sch BS49 ... 17 F1
Court Dr
Sandford BS25 ... 52 B4
Wellington TA21 ... 222 D5
Courtenay Cres BS4 ... 22 D7
Courtenay Rd BS31 ... 25 B2
Courtenay Wlk BS22 ... 32 A3
Court Farm BA11 ... 100 A3
Court Farm Cl TA20 ... 194 E1
Court Farm Country Park★
Banwell BS29 ... 50 F5
Weston-super-Mare BS24 ... 50 F5
Court Farm Rd BS14 ... 22 F3
Courtfield
Langport TA10 ... 172 A5
Milverton TA4 ... 166 F4
Court Field La TA20 ... 193 B5
Court Fields Com Sch TA21 ... 222 C5
Court Gdns
Batheaston BA1 ... 29 A4
Marston Magna BA22 ... 174 F1
Yeovil BA21 ... 218 E8
Court Gr TA7 ... 136 C4
Court Hay BS20 ... 4 A4
Court Hill
Compton Dando BS39 ... 41 D5
Taunton TA1 ... 212 D2
Court Ho BS26 ... 70 B2
Court La
7 Barwick BA22 ... 197 F8
Bathford BA1 ... 29 B2
Clevedon BS21 ... 7 A3
Lye's Green BA12 ... 121 B1
Milborne Port DT9 ... 217 C3
Morebath EX16 ... 164 D4
Shipham BS25 ... 70 F8
Courtland Rd TA21 ... 222 D6
Courtlands BS31 ... 24 E5
Courtlands Cl TA23 ... 202 C6
Courtlands Farm Ind Est TA2 ... 168 B5
Courtlands La BS3 ... 11 E4
Courtlands Unit BS4 ... 22 D8
Courtmead BA2 ... 62 F7
Courtmead La TA24 ... 123 F4
Court Mill La TA20 ... 223 A8
Court Moors La TA21 ... 179 E5
Court Orch TA5 ... 135 B2
Court Pl BS22 ... 31 F2
Court Place La TA24 ... 131 B4
Court Rd
Norton Fitzwarren TA2 ... 168 B4
Weston-super-Mare BS22 ... 31 A5
Court's Barton BA11 ... 119 D2
Court St
5 Bridgwater TA6 ... 208 F5
Winsham TA20 ... 194 E1
Court Terr TA21 ... 222 C5
Court The TA24 ... 131 A5
COURTWAY ... 152 C4
Court Way EX16 ... 178 D1
Courtway Ave TA6 ... 209 C4
Courtyard The
Dunster TA24 ... 201 E2
Evercreech BA4 ... 141 F2
Minehead TA24 ... 200 F7
Shapwick TA7 ... 137 F1
3 Taunton TA1 ... 212 F4
West Harptree BS40 ... 74 E6
Couture Gr BA16 ... 207 B6
Coverdale Ct BA21 ... 218 F6
Coveyhill La BA4 ... 142 E5
Cowan Cl TA8 ... 104 C7
COWBRIDGE ... 130 B5
Cowbridge Cross TA24 ... 200 D1
Cow Bridge Rd BA6 ... 157 C7
Cow Down Rd TA20 ... 194 C1
Cowdray Cl TA24 ... 200 E6
Cowdray Rd
Bristol BS4 ... 22 D7
Minehead TA24 ... 200 E6
Cowen Cl TA18 ... 224 C4
Cowleaze Dro TA3 ... 169 D3
Cowleaze La BS40 ... 74 C6
Cowler Wlk BS13 ... 21 F4
Cowling Dr BS14 ... 23 C5
Cowling Rd BS14 ... 23 D5
Cowl St BA4 ... 205 B7
Cowpath La DT9 ... 176 A1
COWSLIP GREEN ... 54 B8
Cowslip Green La BS40 ... 54 B8
Cowslip La
East Rolstone BS22 ... 33 A2
Loxton BS26 ... 68 D3
Cowslip Wlk TA6 ... 208 E1
Coxbridge Dro BA6 ... 158 A6
Cox Hill DT10 ... 190 E4
Coxland's Rock TA4 ... 167 B7
COXLEY ... 139 F6
Coxley Cl BA6 ... 206 F7
Coxley Dr BA1 ... 28 B2
Coxley Prim Sch BA5 ... 139 E6
COXLEY WICK ... 139 E7
Cox Rd TA21 ... 222 C4
Coxs Cl BA22 ... 175 D6
Cox's Cl
Bruton BA10 ... 215 E5
Glastonbury BA6 ... 206 E6
Cox's Dr BA6 ... 158 A5
Cox's Gn BS40 ... 35 E1
COX'S GREEN ... 35 E1
Cox's La TA4 ... 167 C5
Coxton End La BA5 ... 92 B3
Coxway BS21 ... 6 F2
Coxwithy La BA6 ... 139 D1
Coxwynne Cl BA3 ... 97 C8
Crabtree Cl BS41 ... 21 D1
Crab Tree Dro BA6 ... 206 F8
Crabtree La
Curry Rivel TA10 ... 171 C1
Dundry BS41 ... 21 D2
Wyke Champflower BA10 ... 215 B7
Crackmore DT9 ... 217 C1
Craig Lea TA2 ... 212 E7
Cranberry Wlk BS9 ... 5 C8
Cranbourne Chase BS23 ... 31 A1
Cranbourne Cl TA6 ... 208 F6
Crancombe La TA7 ... 136 D3
Crandale Rd 3 BA2 ... 44 D5
Crane Cotts BA4 ... 142 B6
Crane Hill TA10, TA11 ... 173 C4
Cranes Cl TA2 ... 213 D7
Cranford Cl BS22 ... 31 D1
Crangs La BA22 ... 175 D4
Cranhill Rd
Bath BA1 ... 44 D8
Street BA16 ... 207 B6
Cranleigh BA2 ... 62 F8
Cranleigh Ct TA13 ... 220 B4
Cranleigh Gdns
Bridgwater TA6 ... 209 A4
Bristol BS9 ... 5 E4
Cranleigh Rd BS14 ... 23 B5
Cranmer Rd TA1 ... 213 A4
CRANMORE ... 142 B6
Cranmore BS24 ... 49 A2
Cranmore Ave BS31 ... 24 E6
Cranmore Ct 3 BA11 ... 119 E3
Cranmore Pl BA2 ... 62 E8
Cranmore Sta★ BA4 ... 142 A5
Cranmore View BA11 ... 119 D2
Cranmore West Sta★ BA4 ... 142 A5
Cransey La
Washford TA4, TA23 ... 131 F2
Williton TA4 ... 132 A2
Crantock Ave BS13 ... 22 B8
Cranway La TA20 ... 223 F2
Cranwell Cl TA7 ... 154 F5
Cranwell Gr BS14 ... 23 A5
Cranwell Rd BS24 ... 50 C5
Cranwells Pk BA1 ... 44 D8
Crapnell La BA5 ... 140 F8
Crawford Cl 1 BS21 ... 6 B1
Crawford La BA22 ... 175 D7
CRAWLEY ... 192 F2
Crawlic La TA4 ... 151 E1
Crawl La BA3 ... 78 C4
Crawter Dr TA24 ... 124 A3
Craydon Gr BS14 ... 23 D4
Craydon Rd BS14 ... 23 D5
Craydon Wlk BS14 ... 23 D5
Crease Cl BA5 ... 203 B4
Create Ctr★ BS1 ... 11 F5
Crediton 5 BS22 ... 32 A2
Creechbarrow Rd TA1 ... 213 C5
Creechberry Orch TA1 ... 213 D5
Creeches La BA16 ... 156 D7
CREECH HEATHFIELD ... 169 E5
Creech Hill La BA10 ... 215 B7
Creech Mill Est TA3 ... 169 C4
Creech Paper Mill TA3 ... 169 C4
CREECH ST MICHAEL ... 169 D4
Creech St Michael CE Prim Sch TA3 ... 169 D4
Creechwood Terr TA3 ... 169 D5
Creedwell Cl TA4 ... 167 A4
Creedwell Orch TA4 ... 167 A4
Creighton Cl BA5 ... 140 C8
Crescent Gdns BA1 ... 228 A3
Crescent La BA1 ... 228 B4
Crescent The
Backwell BS48 ... 19 A6
Bristol, Sea Mills BS9 ... 5 C6
4 Carhampton TA24 ... 131 A5
Coleford BA3 ... 117 A7
Farrington Gurney BS39 ... 77 B3
Golsoncott TA23 ... 131 D1
Ilminster TA19 ... 221 B2
Lympsham BS24 ... 67 C5
South Cadbury BA22 ... 175 E4
Stanton Drew BS39 ... 39 F1
Taunton TA1 ... 212 F3
Weston-super-Mare BS22 ... 31 B1
Yeovil BA20 ... 219 A4
Crescent View BA2 ... 228 B1
Crescent View Ct BS22 ... 31 B1
Crescent Way TA1 ... 212 F3
Creslands Ind Units BS24 ... 49 A3
Cressey The TA19 ... 184 E4
Cresswell Ave TA2 ... 212 D7
Cresswell Cl BS22 ... 32 A2
Crestfield Ave TA6 ... 208 F7
Crest Heights BS20 ... 1 E4
Creswicke Rd BS4 ... 22 E7
Creswick Way TA8 ... 104 C8
CREWKERNE ... 224 D6
Crewkerne Bsns Pk TA18 ... 224 D6
Crewkerne Cl BS48 ... 9 B1

Crewkerne Com Hospl TA18 . . . . 224 B5
Crewkerne & District Mus★ TA18 . . . . 224 C6
Crewkerne Rd TA20 . . . . . 223 E4
Crewkerne Sta TA18 . . . . . 224 C6
Crewkerne Turning EX13 . . . . 198 C6
Cribb's La BS40 . . . . 36 D1
Crib Cl TA20 . . . . 223 D6
Crib House La BS28 . . . . . . 89 C1
Crickback La BS40 . . . . 39 A3
Cricket Cotts TA3 . . . . 170 B3
Cricket Cross TA19 . . . . . . 194 C6
Cricket Field Gn BS48 . . . . . 8 D2
Cricket La TA19, TA20 . . . . 194 C6
CRICKET MALHERBIE 194 E3
CRICKET ST THOMAS 194 E3
Cricket St Thomas Miniature Rly★ TA20 . . . . 194 E3
Cricket View DT9 . . . . 225 D3
CRICKHAM 108 D8
Crickham La BS28 . . . . 108 D8
Cricklade Ct BS48 . . . . 9 A1
Cridlake **7** EX13 . . . . 198 A1
Cridlands Mdw TA6 . . . . . . 208 E6
CRIMCHARD 223 B5
Crimchard TA20 . . . . 223 B5
Crimthorne Cotts TA3 . . . . 183 A7
Cripple St TA12 . . . . 185 D7
Crispin Ctr BA16 . . . . 207 C6
Crispin Sch BA16 . . . . 207 D7
Cristata Wy TA6 . . . . 208 D1
Critch Hill BA11 . . . . 119 C3
CRITCHILL 119 C3
Critchill Cl BA11 . . . . 119 D3
Critchill Gr BA11 . . . . 119 D3
Critchill Rd BA11 . . . . 119 D3
Critchill Sch BA11 . . . . . . 119 C4
Crockerne CE Prim Sch BS20 . . . . 4 C4
Crockerne Dr BS20 . . . . 4 C3
Crockerne Ho BS20 . . . . 4 D4
Crockers Hill TA7 . . . . 136 C4
Crocker's Hill TA4 . . . . . . 175 F8
Crocker Wy BA9 . . . . 216 A3
CROCOMBE 60 C3
Crocombe BA2 . . . . 60 C3
Crocombe La BA2 . . . . 60 C3
Croford Hill TA4 . . . . 166 E6
Croft Cl BS30 . . . . 25 D8
Croft Cotts Moorlinch TA7 . . . . 155 E7 Wrantage TA3 . . . . 170 B1
Croft La Brushford TA22 . . . . 163 C4 Skilgate TA4 . . . . 164 E6 Westbury-sub-Mendip BA5 110 C6
Croftland La TA10 . . . . 171 E2
Croft Mdw TA4 . . . . 202 F1
Crofton Ave TA21 . . . . 219 B6
Crofton Ct BA21 . . . . 219 B5
CROFTON PARK 219 B6
Crofton Pk BA21 . . . . 219 B5
Crofton Rd BA21 . . . . 219 B6
Croft Rd Bath BA1 . . . . 28 B1 Holcombe BA3 . . . . 116 C8
Crofts Mead BA9 . . . . 216 C2
Croft The Backwell BS48 . . . . 19 A7 Cheddar BS27 . . . . 90 C8 Clevedon BS21 . . . . 6 F4 Hutton BS24 . . . . 49 E3 Mark TA9 . . . . 106 A4 Monkton Combe BA2 . . . . 45 E1 Watchet TA23 . . . . 202 C7 Westwood BA15 . . . . 64 F3 Williton TA4 . . . . 202 D3 Wookey Hole BA5 . . . . . . 203 A8 Yeovil BA20 . . . . 218 C2
Croft Way TA4 . . . . 210 C4
Croftways TA4 . . . . 202 D4
Cromer Ct BS21 . . . . 6 D5
Cromer Rd BS23 . . . . 48 E5
Cromwell Dr BS22 . . . . 32 A4
Cromwell Rd Bridgwater TA6 . . . . 209 A2 Taunton TA1 . . . . 213 B5 Yeovil BA21 . . . . 219 D6
Crooked La Brent Knoll TA9 . . . . 85 E3 Burnham-on-S TA8 . . . . . . 85 D1 Cucklington SP8 . . . . 177 E6 Rode BA11 . . . . 101 E7
Crookes La BS22 . . . . 31 A4
Crookhorn Hill TA24 . . . . . 129 C7
Cropmead Trad Est TA18 . . . . 224 D6
Crosby Row BS8 . . . . 226 A2
CROSCOMBE 204 B8
Croscombe CE Prim Sch BA5 . . . . 204 C7
Croscombe Gdns BA11 . . . 120 D6
CROSS 69 E2
Crossacre TA6 . . . . 208 D6
Crosscombe Dr BS13 . . . . . 22 C3
Cross Combe Wlk BS13 . . . 22 B3
Crosscroft Cotts TA4 . . . . 151 A3
Crosselm Rd BA4 . . . . 143 A2
Cross Elms Hill TA5 . . . . . 133 F7
Cross Elms La BS9 . . . . 5 E5
Cross Farm Ct TA24 . . . . . 201 A5
Cross Farm Rd BS27 . . . . . 90 F3
Crossfield Cl TA6 . . . . 208 D6
Crossfields DT9 . . . . 187 F4
Crossing Dro BS28 . . . . . . 109 D3
Cross Keys Cl TA2 . . . . 212 A7

Cross La Axbridge BS26 . . . . 70 A2 Brendon EX35 . . . . 122 A4 Long Sutton TA10 . . . . . 172 F4
Crossland La EX14 . . . . . . 191 F2
CROSSLANDS 222 C8
Crosslands TA21 . . . . 222 B8
Cross Lanes BS20 . . . . 4 C4
Crossman Wlk BS21 . . . . . . 6 F2
Crossmead TA7 . . . . 136 E4
Cross Moor Dr BS26 . . . . . 70 B1
Cross Moor Dro BS26 . . . . 69 E1
Cross Moor Rd BS26 . . . . . 70 B1
Crosspost La BA2 . . . . 42 B4
Cross Rd DT9 . . . . 187 B1
Crossroads The BA9 . . . . . 216 C3
Cross St Burnham-on-S TA8 . . . . . 104 A7 Keynsham BS31 . . . . 24 F7 **3** Weston-super-Mare BS23 . . . . 48 E7
Cross The Baltonsborough BA6 . . . . 158 A5 Bradford Abbas DT9 . . . . 187 E1 Buckland Dinham BA11 . . 100 A3 East Harptree BS40 . . . . . 74 F3 **9** Henstridge BA8 . . . . 190 A6 Ilminster TA19 . . . . 221 C3 Milverton TA4 . . . . 167 A4 Minehead TA24 . . . . 200 F8 Nether Stowey TA5 . . . . 134 B2 Street BA16 . . . . 207 D7
Cross View Rise TA6 . . . . . 208 D6
Crossway TA1 . . . . 213 C5
Cross Way DT9 . . . . 187 B1
Crossway La BA3 . . . . 96 B7
Crossways Coleford BA3 . . . . 116 F7 Tatworth TA20 . . . . 198 D8
Crossways Cvn Pk BA2 . . . . 61 F5
Crossways Rd TA6 . . . . . . 209 B1
Crosswell Cl **7** TA6 . . . . . 153 E3
Cross Wlk BS14 . . . . 23 A6
Crouds La TA10 . . . . 172 E4
Crow Castle La TA18 . . . . . 224 B7
CROWCOMBE 151 C7
Crowcombe CE Com Prim Sch TA4 . . . . 151 C7
Crowcombe Heathfield Sta★ TA4 . . . . 151 B5
Crowcombe Rd TA2 . . . . . 212 F8
Crowcombe Wlk TA6 . . . . 208 C4
Crowe Hill BA3 . . . . 64 B5
Crowe La BA3 . . . . 64 B5
Crow La Ashill TA19 . . . . 183 C4 Bridgwater TA7 . . . . 209 E7 Bristol BS1 . . . . 227 A2 Broadway TA19 . . . . 194 A8 Slape Cross TA7 . . . . 209 E6 Westbury-sub-Mendip BA5 110 C6
Crown Cl TA2 . . . . 213 C6
Crowne Trad Est BA4 . . . . 205 D5
Crown Gdns BA11 . . . . . . 119 F3
Crown Glass Pl **5** BS48 . . . . 8 E2
Crown Hill Bath BA1 . . . . 27 C1 West Buckland TA21 . . . . 180 F7 Winford BS40 . . . . 38 A5
Crown Ho BS48 . . . . 8 C1
Crown Ind Est TA2 . . . . . . 213 C6
Crown La Creech St Michael TA3 . . . 169 D6 South Petherton TA13 . . . 220 C4
Crown Mews TA21 . . . . . . 180 F7
Crown Rd BA1 . . . . 27 B1
Crown Wlk TA1 . . . . 212 F3
Crowpill Cotts TA6 . . . . . . 208 F6
Crowpill La TA6 . . . . 208 F6
Crow's Hill BA4 . . . . 142 C1
Crowshute Flats TA20 . . . 223 C3
Crowshute Link TA20 . . . . 223 C3
Crufts Mdw TA3 . . . . 169 D4
Crusader Cl TA6 . . . . 208 E6
Crusty La BS20 . . . . 4 C5
Cruwy's Cross TA4 . . . . . . 210 B7
Crypton Tech Bsns Pk TA6 . . . . 209 B8
Cubitt Cl BS24 . . . . 49 C4
Cuck Hill BS25 . . . . 70 E7
CUCKLINGTON 177 D6
Cuckold's Row TA5 . . . . . . 152 E8
Cuckoo Cnr TA1 . . . . 213 B2
Cuckoo Hill Bruton BA10 . . . . 160 D6 Bruton BA10 . . . . 215 F8 Frome BA11 . . . . 119 E8
Cuckoo La Frome BA11 . . . . 119 F8 High Littleton BS39 . . . . . 59 B3 Thorncombe TA20 . . . . . 199 C7 Wraxall BS48 . . . . 9 A6
CUDWORTH 194 E5
Cuffs Mead TA20 . . . . 223 F1
Cufic La BS27 . . . . 90 C8
CULBONE 123 B5
Culliford Cl BA16 . . . . 207 D7
Culliver's Grave BA22 . . . . 197 C8
CULM DAVY 180 A2
Culmhead Cl TA1 . . . . 212 D1
Culmstock Prim Sch EX15 . . . . 179 E1
Culvercliffe Ct TA4 . . . . . . 125 C4
Culvercliffe Rd TA23 . . . . 202 D7
Culverhay BS39 . . . . 41 D6
Culverhayes TA20 . . . . . . 223 C2
Culverhay La TA4 . . . . 210 B4

CULVERHAYS 132 F1
Culverhays La TA4 . . . . . . 132 F1
Culverhill BA11 . . . . 119 F3
Culver Hill TA10 . . . . 172 B7
Culver La Carhampton TA24 . . . . . 131 B4 East Harptree BS40 . . . . . 74 F3
Culverlake La EX13 . . . . . . 199 A3
Culvers Cl Keynsham BS31 . . . . 24 E6 Sherborne DT9 . . . . 225 C4
Culvers Rd BS31 . . . . 24 E6
Culver St BS1 . . . . 226 C2
Culver Street La TA4 . . . . . 134 A7
Culvert Dro BS27 . . . . 109 B6
Culverwell Cotts BA4 . . . . 140 F3
Culverwell Rd BS13 . . . . . . 22 A4
Cumberland Basin Rd BS8 . . . . 11 F5
Cumberland Cl BS1 . . . . . . 226 A1
Cumberland Ho BA1 . . . . . 228 B2
Cumberland Pl **6** BS8 . . . . 11 F6
Cumberland Rd BS1 . . . . . 226 B1
Cumberland Row BA1 . . . . 228 B2
Cumberland St BS2 . . . . . 227 B4
Cumhill Hill BA4 . . . . 140 E3
Cumnock Cres BA7 . . . . . . 214 C6
Cumnock Rd BA7 . . . . 214 C6
Cumnock Terr BA7 . . . . . . 214 C6
Cunningham Ave EX13 . . . 198 A2
Cunningham Rd TA8 . . . . . 104 C7
Curdleigh La TA3 . . . . 181 D5
CURLAND 182 C8
CURLAND COMMON 182 D4
Curland Gr BS14 . . . . 23 B5
Curlew Cl TA24 . . . . 201 C4
Curlew Gdns BS22 . . . . 31 F1
Curlew Pl BS20 . . . . 2 F6
CURLOAD 170 E7
Currells La BS40 . . . . 20 B1
Curriott Hill TA18 . . . . . . 224 B4
Curriott Hill Rd TA18 . . . . 224 B5
Curry Hole La BA22 . . . . . 197 C2
Curry La TA3 . . . . 169 E6
CURRY MALLET 183 C8
Curry Mallet CE Prim Sch TA3 . . . . 183 D8
Currymead La TA10 . . . . . 171 C2
Currypool La TA5 . . . . 134 E1
CURRY RIVEL 171 C4
Curry Rivel CE Prim Sch TA10 . . . . 171 D4
Currywoods Way TA10 . . . 171 D4
Cursley Path BA5 . . . . 203 D3
Curtis Units BA11 . . . . . . 119 E2
Curvalion House Gdns TA3 . . . . 169 D4
Curvalion Rd TA3 . . . . 169 D4
CUSHUISH 152 B1
Cushuish La TA2 & TA5 . . . 152 C2
Cushuish Lane Cotts TA2 . . . . 152 B1
Cussacombe Gate EX36 . . 145 J1
Custom Cl BS14 . . . . 23 A7
Custom Ho Bristol BS1 . . . . 227 A1 Minehead TA24 . . . . 201 B7
CUTCOMBE 129 F2
Cutcombe CE Fst Sch TA24 . . . . 129 E1
Cutcombe Cross TA24 . . . . 129 E1
Cutcombe Hill TA24 . . . . . 129 F2
Cuthays La EX13 . . . . 198 B1
Cuthbert St TA9 . . . . 104 D3
Cutler Rd BS13 . . . . 21 F6
CUTLER'S GREEN 94 F4
Cutliff Cl TA1 . . . . 212 E1
Cutter's Wharf TA24 . . . . 201 B7
CUTTIFORD'S DOOR 223 C7
Cutt Mill La DT9 . . . . 190 F3
Cut Tongue La TA20 . . . . . 193 C2
Cutty Cotts BA22 . . . . 175 D6
Cutty La BA22 . . . . 175 D6
Cygnet Cres BS22 . . . . 31 F1
Cynthia Rd BA2 . . . . 44 D5
Cypress Ct Bristol BS9 . . . . 5 D3 Somerton TA11 . . . . 211 E4
Cypress Dr Puriton TA7 . . . . 136 C4 Yeovil BA20 . . . . 218 E2
Cypress Gdns BS8 . . . . 11 E6
Cypress Terr BA3 . . . . 78 D1
Cypress Way BA11 . . . . . . 120 C7
Cyril St W TA2 . . . . 212 E6
Cyril St TA2 . . . . 212 E6

D

Dabinett Cl TA2 . . . . 168 B5
Dafford's Bldgs BA1 . . . . . . 28 C2
Dafford St BA1 . . . . 28 C2
Dagg's La BS28 . . . . 138 E8
Dagg's Lane Dro BA5, BS28 . . . . 138 D7
Daghole BS27 . . . . 90 C8
Daglands The BA2 . . . . 78 E8
Dahlia Gdns **9** BA2 . . . . . . 45 B7
Dairs Orch TA20 . . . . 198 C8
Dairy Cl Horsecastle BS49 . . . . . . 17 A2 Wells BA5 . . . . 203 B5
Dairycroft BS2 . . . . 227 B4
Dairy Ct **3** TA18 . . . . 224 C6
Dairy Flats DT9 . . . . 225 E5
Dairy Hill BA2 . . . . 80 B5

Dairy House La TA3 . . . . . 182 E5
Dairylands TA24 . . . . 131 D4
Daisey Bank BA2 . . . . 45 B4
Daisy Cl TA6 . . . . 153 F5
Daisyfield BA22 . . . . 188 A8
Dakota Dr BS14 . . . . 23 A4
Dale La BS 92 C3
Daley Cl BS22 . . . . 32 B3
Dalimores La BA11 . . . . . . 143 B8
Dalleston BA3 . . . . 114 C8
Dallimore Mead BA11 . . . . 143 B8
Dalton Sq BS2 . . . . 227 B4
Dalwood **12** BS22 . . . . 32 A2
Dalwoods DT9 . . . . 225 D3
Dame Court Cl BS22 . . . . . 31 F4
Dame Withycombe Villas TA5 . . . . 135 B5
Dampier Pl BA11 . . . . 219 C5
Dampier St BA21 . . . . 219 C5
Dampiet St TA6 . . . . 208 F4
Damson Cres TA21 . . . . . . 222 F7
Damson Orch BA1 . . . . 29 A4
Damson Rd BS22 . . . . 49 E7
Damson Row TA21 . . . . . . 222 F7
Dancey Mead BS13 . . . . . . 21 F6
Dancing Cross BA9 . . . . . . 176 B5
Dancing Hill TA6 . . . . 153 E4
Dancing La BA9 . . . . 216 A4
DandO's La BS28 . . . . 108 C4
Dandy's Mdw BS20 . . . . 2 E4
Daneacre Rd BA3 . . . . 79 A3
Dane Cl BA15 . . . . 64 E7
Dane Rise BA15 . . . . 64 E7
Danesboro Rd TA6 . . . . . . 208 C4
Danesborough View TA4 . . . . 202 D3
Danesborough View E TA4 . . . . 202 D3
Danesborough View W TA4 . . . . 202 D3
Danes Cl EX14 . . . . 191 F2
Danesfield CE Com Mid Sch TA4 . . . . 202 D4
Dane's Lea BS28 . . . . 108 C4
Dangerfield Ave BS13 . . . . 21 F6
Daniel Cl BS21 . . . . 6 F3
Daniel Mews **2** BA2 . . . . . 45 B7
Danielsfield Rd BA20 . . . . 218 F2
Daniels La BA5 . . . . 111 A4
Daniel St **3** BA2 . . . . 45 B7
Dapps Hill BS31 . . . . 24 F5
Dapwell La BS14, BS31 . . . 24 A1
Darby Cl SP8 . . . . 161 F1
Darby's Knap TA24 . . . . . . 147 C5
Darby Way TA4 . . . . 151 F1
Darcis Row TA20 . . . . 223 B4
Dare Cl TA2 . . . . 213 A8
Darkey La BA10 . . . . 215 F7
Darkfield Way TA7 . . . . . . 136 E3
Dark La Backwell BS48 . . . . 19 B5 Banwell BS29 . . . . 51 C2 Berkley BA11 . . . . 120 E8 Blagdon BS40 . . . . 54 E3 Chew Magna BS40 . . . . . . 38 F3 Freshford BA3 . . . . 64 B5 Hockworthy EX16 . . . . . 178 B8 Holcombe BA3 . . . . 97 C1 Kilmersdon BA11 . . . . . . 98 A1 North Wootton BA4 . . . . 140 C5 Sandford Orcas DT9 . . . . 188 C7 Seavington St Mary TA19 . 184 E1 Stoke St Gregory TA3 . . . 170 F6 Stoke St Michael BA3 . . . 116 C2 Upton Noble BA4 . . . . . . 142 F2 Wellington TA21 . . . . . . 222 D5 Witham Friary BA11 . . . . 143 D2
Darlick Cnr EX36 . . . . 145 G4
Darlington Mews **8** BA2 . . 45 B7
Darlington Pl BA2 . . . . 45 B6
Darlington Rd BA2 . . . . . . 45 B8
Darlington St BA2 . . . . 45 B7
Darmead BS24 . . . . 32 B1
DARSHILL 204 F6
Dartmouth Ave BA2 . . . . . 44 C5
Dartmouth Cl BS22 . . . . . . 32 A2
Dartmouth Wlk BS31 . . . . 24 D4
Dart Rd BS21 . . . . 6 D1
Darwin Cl TA2 . . . . 212 B6
Dashwoods La TA4 . . . . . . 132 E2
Daubeny Ct BS1 . . . . 227 A1
Daunton Cl TA9 . . . . 104 D4
David's La TA19 . . . . 184 F2
David's Rd BS14 . . . . 23 C6
David St BS2 . . . . 227 C3
Davies Cl Bridgwater TA6 . . . . 208 F2 Winsham TA20 . . . . 194 E1
Davies Ct BA5 . . . . 203 B4
Davin Cres BS20 . . . . 4 C3
Davis La BS21 . . . . 16 F8
Davis St BS11 . . . . 4 B8
Davis Terr **5** BA5 . . . . . . 203 C4
Dawbins Dr TA7 . . . . 136 E4
Dawes Cl BS21 . . . . 6 D1
Dawes Ct **2** BS8 . . . . 11 F6
Daws Cl TA6 . . . . 208 E2
Daws La TA6 . . . . 153 E3
Daw's La DT9 . . . . 176 A3
Daws Mead TA1 . . . . 212 A3
Day Cres BA2 . . . . 43 F6
Deacon Rd TA6 . . . . 209 C6
DEACONS 168 C7
Deacons Cl BS22 . . . . 31 C2
Deacons Ct BS22 . . . . 31 C1
Deacons La BA21 . . . . 187 D6
Deacon Way TA8 . . . . 104 B6
Deadlands La TA12, TA13 . 185 A6

Dead Maids Cross Rd BA13 . . . . 121 E5
Deadman's Hill DT9 . . . . . 176 A1
Deadmill La BA1 . . . . 28 C3
Dead Woman's Cnr BA12 161 F8
Deal Cl TA6 . . . . 209 D5
DEAN 142 B7
Dean Cl Frome BA11 . . . . 120 C6 Weston-super-Mare BS22 . . 32 B3
Deane Cl TA4 . . . . 150 D8
Deane Dr TA1 . . . . 212 B2
Deane Gate Ave TA1 . . . . . 213 E5
Deane Ret Pk TA1 . . . . 213 F5
Deanery Rd BS1 . . . . 226 C2
Deanery Wlk BA9 . . . . 64 C6
Deanesly Way BA9 . . . . . . 216 D3
Deane Way TA20 . . . . 198 D8
Deanhill La BA1 . . . . 27 A2
Dean La Dunster TA24 . . . . 201 D3 Milverton TA4 . . . . 167 A6 Oakhill BA3 . . . . 115 A3
Dean's Cross Allerford TA24 . . . . 124 E3 Lydeard St Lawrence TA4 . 151 A4
Dean's La Allerford TA24 . . . . 124 E3 Brompton Ralph TA4 . . . . 150 F4
Deansley Way BA9 . . . . . . 216 E3
Deans Mead BS11 . . . . 5 A8
Deans Pl **8** BA5 . . . . 203 D4
Dean St BS2 . . . . 227 B4
Deans The BS20 . . . . 2 B4
Dean Vale Pk TA4 . . . . 167 C4
Debecca's La BS20 . . . . 4 B4
De Combe Ho TA18 . . . . . 224 D6
De Corcis Cl TA5 . . . . 134 A3
Decoy La TA11 . . . . 157 A2
Deep La BA12 . . . . 121 E1
Deepleigh La TA4 . . . . 210 C7
Deerleap Easton BA5 . . . . 111 B6 Shipham BS25 . . . . 70 F8
Deer Mead BS21 . . . . 6 B1
Deerswood Gdns BA16 . . . 207 A6
Deer View TA4 . . . . 201 C4
Delapre Rd BS23 . . . . 48 D3
Delhorn La BS24 . . . . 86 C7
Delius Gr BS4 . . . . 22 D7
Dellers Ct TA1 . . . . 212 F5
Deller's Wharf TA1 . . . . . . 212 F5
Dellshore Cl TA20 . . . . . . 223 D4
Dell The Bristol, Westbury on T BS9 . . 5 F5 Minehead TA24 . . . . 200 E6 Nailsea BS48 . . . . 8 D2 Weston-super-Mare BS22 . 31 E4
Delmore Rd BA11 . . . . 119 E5
Delta Cl BA11 . . . . 119 F5
Delta Ct **1** BA11 . . . . 119 F5
Delta Rise TA4 . . . . 151 E1
Demelza Ct BA22 . . . . 174 D3
De Montalt Pl BA2 . . . . . . 45 B1
Dempier Mews BA2 . . . . . 218 B6
Dene Barton Com Hospl TA4 . . . . 167 F6
Dene Cl BS31 . . . . 24 F3
Dene Cross TA4 . . . . 167 F7
Dene Gdns TA24 . . . . 201 B4
Dene Rd Cotford St Luke TA4 . . . . 167 F6 Whitchurch BS14 . . . . . . 23 C4
Dening Cl TA20 . . . . 223 C6
Denleigh Cl BS14 . . . . 23 A4
Denman's La Barrington TA19 . . . . . . 184 D5 Cannington TA5 . . . . 135 B2
Denmark Ave BS1 . . . . . . 226 C2
Denmark Rd BA2 . . . . 44 D6
Denmark St BS1 . . . . 226 C2
Denmark Terr TA2 . . . . . . 212 F7
Dennett Cl BA4 . . . . 205 E4
Denning Cl TA1 . . . . 212 B1
Denning Ct BS22 . . . . 32 B4
Dennington La Churchinford EX14 . . . . . 192 C6 Dulverton TA22 . . . . 163 B4
Dennor Pk BS14 . . . . 23 B7
Denny Cl BS20 . . . . 2 A5
Denny La BS40 . . . . 39 B1
Denny View BS20 . . . . 2 A5
Dennyview Rd BS8 . . . . . . 10 F8
Denston Dr BS20 . . . . 2 E4
Denston Wlk BS13 . . . . . . 22 A7
Dentwood Gr BS9 . . . . 5 B8
Denzil Cl BA22 . . . . 197 A8
Derham Cl BS49 . . . . 34 B8
Derham Ct BS49 . . . . 34 B8
Derham Pk BS49 . . . . 34 B8
Derham Rd BS13 . . . . 22 A5
Derricke Rd BS14 . . . . 23 F6
DERTFORDS 144 D8
Dertfords BA12 . . . . 144 D8
Derwent Gdns BA21 . . . . . 219 D6
Derwent Gr Keynsham BS31 . . . . 25 A5 Taunton TA1 . . . . 213 E4
Derwent Rd BS23 . . . . 49 A5
Derwent Way BA21 . . . . . 218 C6
De Salis Pk BS24 . . . . 50 D8
Devenish La BA9 . . . . 216 F4
Deveron Gr BS31 . . . . 25 A4
Devonia Pk TA4 . . . . 168 A1
Devonshire Bldgs BA2 . . . . 44 F4

Devonshire Ct BS23 48 E4
Devonshire Dr BS20 1 F5
Devonshire Mews BA2 44 F3
Devonshire Pl BA2 44 F4
Devonshire Rd
Bathampton BA2 28 E1
Weston-super-Mare BS23 48 E4
Devonshire St TA6 209 B5
Devonshire Villas BA2 44 F3
Dewar Cl TA8 104 C7
Dewberry Ave TA6 208 E1
Dew Water La TA11 211 D5
Dexter Wlk 8 TA6 209 A1
Dial Hill Rd BS21 6 D4
Dial La BS40 20 D1
Dial's Gate La BA6, TA11 158 D4
Diamond Batch BS24 32 B1
Dibbens Row BA9 161 A2
Dibbles La BA22 197 A8
Dickenson Rd BS23 48 E6
Dickenson's Gr BS49 34 E3
Digby Ct DT9 225 D3
Digby Rd DT9 225 D3
Dighton Ct 3 BS2 227 A4
Dighton St BS2 227 A4
Digland La TA24 129 F5
Dilkes La TA11 174 C7
DILLINGTON 221 E5
Dillington Farm Cotts
TA19 221 E5
Dillington House TA19 221 D6
Dillons Rd TA3 169 D4
DIMMER 159 C3
Dimmer La BA7 159 B2
DINDER 140 D7
Dinder Cl BS48 18 E8
DINGHURST 52 E4
Dinghurst Rd BS25 52 E4
Dingle Cl BS9 5 C6
Dingle Ct BS13 21 F7
Dingle Rd BS9 5 D7
Dingle The BS9 5 D7
Dingle View BS9 5 C7
Dinglewood Cl BS9 5 D7
Dinhams TA3 169 C4
Dinhay DT10 190 F6
DINNINGTON 195 B7
Dipford Rd TA3 168 D1
Dipland Gr BS40 54 F2
Disraeli Pl TA1 212 D5
DITCHEAT 159 C7
Ditcheat Prim Sch BA4 159 C7
Ditch Furlong Rd TA7 137 A2
Ditton St TA19 221 C3
Dixon Gdns BA1 27 F1
Dobree Pk TA21 222 A4
Dock Gate La BS8 226 A1
Doctor's Hill BA5 111 B1
Dodd Ave BA5 203 F5
Dodd's Cnr BA9 215 E1
Dodge Cross DT9 225 F5
Dodham Cres BA20 218 F4
DODHILL 168 D7
DODINGTON 133 F3
Dod La BA6 206 E4
Dog Down Cross EX16 178 A8
Doleberrow BS25 52 F3
Dolebury Warren Nature
Reserve★ BS40 53 A3
Dolecroft La BS22 32 E7
Dolemead La BS27 90 E2
DOLEMEADS 45 B5
Dolemoor La
Congresbury BS49 34 A4
Congresbury BS49 34 C3
Dolling Cl TA20 223 D6
Dolling's Rd TA3 181 B4
Dolphin Sq BS23 48 D7
Dominion Rd BA2 44 A6
Dominy Cl TA20 223 D3
DOMMETT 182 D1
Dommett Cl EX13 198 A2
Dommett's La BA11 119 D4
Domus Dr BA4 205 E4
Donald Rd BS13 21 F7
DONIFORD 202 F6
Doniford Beach Halt
TA23 202 E6
Doniford Dr TA4 202 D3
Doniford Mdw TA23 202 F6
Doniford Orch TA23 202 F6
Doniford Rd
Watchet TA23 202 E6
Williton TA4 202 D4
Donne La BA22 186 C2
Donnes Terr BA7 214 B5
Donnington Wlk BS31 24 D4
Donstan Rd TA9 104 E5
DONYATT 183 D1
Donyatt Hill TA19 183 D1
Donyatt Hill Est TA19 183 D1
Doone Way TA24 201 B4
Dorchester Cl 6 BS48 8 D1
Dorchester Rd
Barwick BA22 197 F7
East Coker BA22 197 F5
Taunton TA2 213 A8
Yeovil BA22 219 A1
Dorchester St BA1 228 C1
Dore Cl BA21 218 C7
Dormeads View 6 BS24 49 F7
Dorset Cl
Bath BA2 44 D6
Frome BA11 119 E5
Highbridge TA9 104 E2
Dorset Ho BA2 44 D3
Dorset Rd TA6 209 C3
Dorset St BA2 44 D6
Doster's La TA2 169 C6
Double Gates Dro TA11 158 A3
Double Hill BA2 79 F7
Douglas Ct 3 BS23 48 F5
Douglas Dr BA4 205 B5
Douglas Rd BS23 48 F5
Douglas Yates Ct BA3 116 F7
DOULTING 141 E6
Doulting Ct BA11 120 D7
Doulting Hill BA4 205 F4
Doulton Way BS14 23 B5
Dovai Dr TA6 208 E7
Dove Cots Cl BA16 207 C7
Dove La BS2 227 C4
DOVERHAY 124 B3
Dover Ho BA1 228 C4
Dover Pl
6 Bath BA1 28 A1
Bristol BS8 226 B3
Dover Rd TA2 213 A8
Dovers La BA1 29 C2
Dovers Pk BA1 29 C2
Dovery Manor Mus★
TA24 124 A3
Dove St S BS2 227 A4
Dove St BS2 227 A4
Doveswell Gr BS13 22 A4
Dovetail Ct 1 TA1 212 E3
Dovetail Dr BS23 49 A7
Dovetons Cl TA4 202 E3
Dovetons Dr TA4 202 E3
Dowding Rd BA1 28 B1
Dowell Cl TA2 212 C6
Dowland 13 BS22 32 A2
Dowland Gr BS4 22 D6
Dowling La BA6 158 A5
Dowling Rd BS13 22 D3
DOWLISH FORD 221 B1
Dowlish La TA19 194 F5
DOWLISH WAKE 194 E7
Downash La EX13 198 E3
Down Ave BA2 45 A1
Down Cl BS20 1 F4
Downclose La TA18 196 C3
Downend Cres TA6 136 B4
Downend Rd TA6 136 B4
Downend Terr TA6 136 B4
Downey Field La TA18 196 D6
Downfield
Bristol BS9 5 C7
Keynsham BS31 24 D5
Downhall Dr TA6 208 D6
DOWNHEAD
Stoke St Michael 142 C8
Yeovilton 174 C4
Downhead La BA22 174 C5
Down La
Bathampton BA2 28 F1
Buckland Dinham BA11 99 C3
Shepton Montague BA9 160 B2
Sherborne DT9 188 A5
Trent DT9 187 F5
West Pennard BA4, BA6 140 C1
Downland Cl 5 BS48 8 D1
Downlands La EX15, TA3 181 A2
Downleaze
Bristol, Stoke Bishop BS9 5 F3
Portishead BS20 2 A5
Yeovil BA20 218 D2
Downleaze Rd BS9 5 F3
Down Rd BS20 1 F4
Downs Cl BS22 31 F1
Downs Cote Ave BS9 5 F6
Downs Cote Dr BS9 5 F6
DOWNSIDE
Chilcompton 96 C1
Felton 19 D1
Shepton Mallet 205 D8
Downside
Portishead BS20 2 C5
Street BA16 207 D6
Downside Abbey★ BA3 96 E2
Downside Cl
Bathampton BA2 28 F1
Chilcompton BA3 96 D3
Downside Rd
Backwell BS48 36 E8
Weston-super-Mare BS23 48 F4
Downside Sch BA3 96 E2
Downslade La TA10 172 D5
Down's Orch BA6 138 C4
Downs Rd BS41 21 D2
Downs Sch The BS48 9 C8
Downs The BS20 2 B4
Downsway BS39 77 D6
Downton Rd BS13 22 D8
Down View BA3 97 F8
Dowry Pl 3 BS8 11 F5
Dowry Rd BS8 226 A2
Dowry Sq BS8 226 A2
DOWSLANDS 168 F1
Dowsland Way TA1 213 C1
DOYNTON 12 A8
Dozen's Cnr TA17 195 A7
Dragon Cross TA24 131 D3
Dragonfly Chase BA22 173 E2
Dragons Hill Cl BS31 24 F5
Dragons Hill Ct BS31 24 F5
Dragons Hill Gdns BS31 24 F5
Drake Ave BA2 44 F2
Drake Cl
Saltford BS31 25 D2
Staplegrove TA2 212 B7
Weston-super-Mare BS22 31 F4
Drake Rd BA5 203 F6
Drakes Cl TA6 208 F5
Drake's Cl TA3 169 C4
Drakes Cres TA20 198 D8
Drakes Mdw
East Coker BA22 197 C7
Yarcombe EX14 192 D3
Drakes Pk TA21 222 D7
Drakes Pk N TA21 222 D7
Drakes Way BS20 2 B5
Drang The
Coxley BA5 139 E6
Evercreech BA4 141 E1
Porlock TA24 124 A3
Dransfield Way BA2 44 C4
Drapers Way TA24 129 D2
Drappel La BA5 110 E7
Draycot Pl BS1 227 A1
DRAYCOTT
Cheddar 90 E2
Yeovil 187 B8
Draycott Ave TA2 213 A6
Draycott Ct 1 BA2 228 C3
Draycott Moor Dro BS27 90 D1
Draycott Rd
Cheddar BS27 90 D5
Shepton Mallet BA4 205 B6
Draycott & Rodney Stoke CE
Fst Sch BS27 90 F3
Draydon Rd BS4 22 D8
Dray Rd BA22 186 C2
DRAYTON
Curry Rival 171 E3
Southerton 185 D3
Drayton BS24 49 A2
Drayton Cl BS14 23 B8
Drayton La TA10 171 D3
Drayton Rd BS9 5 C8
Drew's La DT10 190 B5
Drials La BA3 94 F6
Drift Rd TA24 201 D4
Drift The
Chard Junction TA20 198 E8
Chard TA20 194 B3
Drill Hall La BA4 205 C5
DRIMPTON 199 F7
Drimpton Cross DT8 199 F7
Dring The BA3 78 E2
Drive The
Bristol BS14 23 C6
Burnham-on-S TA8 85 A2
Churchill BS25 52 E4
Keynsham BS31 24 E6
Shipham BS25 70 E8
Stanton Drew BS39 39 F1
Taunton TA1 212 D1
Weston-super-Mare BS23 48 F8
Woolavington TA7 136 E4
Dropping La BA10 160 D5
Drove Cl DT10 189 F2
Drove Ct BS48 8 E3
Drove La
East Pennard BA4 158 E8
Shepton Beauchamp TA19 184 E4
Drove Rd
Congresbury BS49 34 D3
Stourton Caundle DT10 189 F2
Weston-super-Mare BS23 48 F5
Drove The
Bridgwater TA6 209 A6
Portbury BS20 3 D6
Droveway TA13 220 B5
Drove Way
Churchinford TA3 191 F8
Sandford BS24, BS25 51 E7
Droveway Cl TA13 220 C5
Droveway La BA21 187 C7
Druid Cl BS9 5 E5
Druid Hill BS9 5 E5
Druid Rd BS9 5 D4
Druids Garth BA2 28 D1
Druid Stoke Ave BS9 5 D5
Druids Wlk TA20 223 C5
Druid Woods BS9 5 C5
Druley Hill BA10 161 D8
Drum Ave BA6 206 C5
Drumhead Way The BS25 70 E8
Dr White's Cl BS1 227 B1
DRY HILL 2 C6
Dryleaze BS31 24 E7
Drysdale Cl BS22 31 D1
Duchess Cl 1 TA6 208 E7
Duchy Cl BA3 78 E5
Duchy Rd
Clandown BA3 78 E5
Shepton Mallet BA4 205 A5
Duck La
Chard TA20 223 C3
Churchill BS40 53 A8
Horsington BA8 176 E2
Ilchester BA22 173 F1
Kenn BS21 17 A6
Stalbridge DT10 190 B5
Westbury-sub-Mendip BA5 110 E6
Duck Pool Dro BA6 206 B7
Duckpool La TA18 196 B8
Duck Pool La BA11 102 B6
Ducks' Field Crossing
TA18 224 C1
Ducks Hill TA10 172 B5
Ducks La BS22 32 A8
Duck St BS25 52 C5
DUDDLESTONE 181 F8
Dudley Cl BS31 24 E4
Dudmoor TA12 185 B7
Dudwell La BA3 95 A5
Dugdale St TA24 200 F6
Duke Ave 7 TA5 135 B2
Duke Ho TA19 221 B3
Duke's Cl BA9 216 E3
Dukes Field BA4 205 C5
Duke's La
Horningsham BA12 144 A1
Kilmington BA12 161 F8
Dukes Mead TA6 209 A2
Duke St
Bath BA2 228 C2
Bridgwater TA6 208 E7
Frome BA11 119 E5
Taunton TA1 213 A4
DULCOTE 140 C7
Dull Cross TA4 151 D3
DULVERTON 163 E6
Dulverton La TA4 165 D7
Dulverton Mid & Com Sch
TA22 163 D6
Dumfries Pl BS23 48 E5
Dummis La BA5 111 A1
Dumpers La BS40 39 B2
Dumper's La BA3 94 F7
DUNBALL 136 A3
Dunball Ind Est TA6 136 B4
Dunbar Cl TA9 104 C4
Duncan Gdns BA1 27 A3
Duncart La BA5 204 C7
Duncliffe Cl DT10 190 B4
Duncombe Cl TA6 209 D5
Dundas Row TA4 167 E8
DUNDON 156 F3
DUNDON HAYES 156 E3
DUNDRY 21 D2
Dundry CE Prim Sch
BS41 21 D2
DUNDRY HILL 23 B3
Dundry La
Dundry BS41 21 C3
Winford BS40 38 A7
Dunedin Way BS22 32 C4
Dunford Terr BA6 158 A5
Dungarvon Rd BS24 49 F7
Dungeon BS28 108 D7
Dungeon La BA5 204 C6
Dunkerry Rd BS26 88 C4
DUNKERTON 61 E4
Dunkerton Cl BA6 206 F3
Dunkerton Hill BA2 61 E2
Dunkerton Rise TA2 168 B5
Dunkery Cl BS48 8 E1
Dunkery & Horner Wood
National Nature Reserve
The★ TA24 129 A7
Dunkery Rd
Bridgwater TA6 208 D4
Weston-super-Mare BS23 30 F1
Dunkery Vineyard★
TA24 200 A1
Dunkirk Bsns Pk BA14 83 D2
Dunkleys Way TA1 213 C2
Dunlin Dr 1 BS20 2 F6
Dunningham La BS28 107 E7
Dunns Cl BS28 108 C4
Dunn's Hill TA21 179 A6
Dunsford Pl BA2 45 B6
Dunsgreen La EX15 191 A8
Dunsham La TA18 195 C2
Dunsley Hill EX16, EX36 162 D5
Dunstan Dr DT9 225 E5
Dunstan Rd
Burnham-on-S TA8 104 B7
Glastonbury BA6 206 F5
Dunstan Way BS27 90 B6
DUNSTER 201 E2
Dunster Beach Chalets
TA24 201 F4
Dunster Castle★ TA24 201 E1
Dunster Cl
Minehead TA24 201 B4
Taunton TA2 213 B7
Dunster Cres BS24 49 A2
Dunster Ct BS25 70 A8
Dunster Fst Sch TA24 201 D2
Dunster Gdns 5 BS48 8 E1
Dunster Ho BA2 45 A2
Dunster Rd
Bristol BS4 22 F8
Keynsham BS31 24 E4
Dunsters Rd BS49 17 F1
Dunster Sta★ TA24 201 F4
Dunster Steep
Dunster TA24 201 E2
Porlock, Doverhay TA24 124 A3
Porlock, West Porlock
TA24 123 F4
Dunster Visitor Ctr★
TA24 201 E2
Dunster Wood Forest Trails★
TA24 130 D5
Dunster Working Water
Mill★ TA24 201 E1
DUNWEAR 209 D1
Dunwear Ho 3 TA6 209 C4
Dunwear La TA6 209 D3
Durban Way BS49 17 B1
Durbin Park Rd BS21 6 D5
Durcott Rd BA2 78 D8
Durham Gr BS31 24 D4
Durham Pl 9 TA2 213 A8
Durhams Cotts TA4 210 C5
Durkheim Dr 2 BA5 203 C4
DURLEIGH 208 B3
Durleigh Cl
Bridgwater TA6 208 D3
Bristol BS13 22 A7
Durleigh Hill TA5 208 A2
Durleigh Rd TA6 208 C3
Durley Hill BS31 24 C7
Durley La BS31 24 D7
Durleymoor Cross EX16 178 F4
Durley Pk BA2 44 E4
DURNFIELD 186 B7
Durnhill BS40 73 F7
Durrant Cl DT9 225 D3
Dursdon Dro
Priddy BA5 111 C8
Wells BA5 112 B6
Dursley Rd BS11 4 E5
DURSTON 169 F6
Durston BS24 49 A2
Durston Cl BA16 207 C5
Durston Ho 3 BA16 207 C5
Durston Way TA1 212 E1
Durville Rd BS13 22 B6
Durweston Wlk BS14 23 C8
Dutch Rd TA9 105 E5
Dutton Cl BS14 23 D6
Dutton Rd BS14 23 D6
Dutton Wlk BS14 23 D6
Dwelly Cl TA20 223 C3
Dyehouse Cnr TA22 164 A6
Dyehouse Cross TA22 163 F5
Dyehouse La
Bury TA22 164 A5
Glastonbury BA6 206 C5
Dye La BA3 115 A3
Dyers Cl
Bristol BS13 22 D4
Curry Rivel TA10 171 D4
West Buckland TA21 180 F7
Dyers' Close La BA11 119 E5
Dyers Gn TA6 153 F3
Dyer's La TA2 213 E7
Dyers Rd TA10 171 D4
Dyke Hill Terr TA20 198 D8
Dyke's Way BA9 216 B3
Dymboro Ave BA3 77 F1
Dymboro Cl BA3 77 F1
Dymboro Gdns BA3 77 F1
Dymboro The BA3 77 F1
Dyrham Cl TA8 104 D7
Dyson Cl BS49 34 B8

E

Eagle Cl
Ilchester BA22 173 E2
Weston-super-Mare BS22 49 D8
Eagle Gdns BA22 173 E2
Eagle La 1 BA11 119 F4
Eagle Pk BA1 28 F5
Eagle Rd BA1 28 F5
Eagles The BS49 34 B8
Eames Orch TA19 221 C2
Earlesfield BS48 8 C1
Earle St BA20 219 C5
Earlham Gr BS23 49 A7
Earls Cl
Bridgwater TA6 208 E7
Sherborne DT9 225 F5
Earl St BS1 227 A4
EAST ANSTEY 162 E5
East Anstey Prim Sch
EX16 162 E5
East Approach Rd TA7 136 D4
East Ave TA9 104 C4
Eastbourne Ave 15 BA1 28 B1
Eastbourne Ct 13 TA1 213 A4
Eastbourne Gate TA1 213 A4
Eastbourne Rd TA1 213 A4
Eastbourne Terr 12 TA1 213 A4
EAST BOWER 209 E6
EAST BRENT 86 D5
East Brent CE Fst Sch
TA9 86 C4
East Bridgwater Com Sch
TA6 209 C5
EASTBROOK 168 E1
Eastbrook Terr TA3 168 D1
Eastbury Hill TA24 131 B5
Eastbury Rd TA24 131 B5
EAST CHINNOCK 196 E8
East Cl
Bath BA2 44 A5
Haselbury Plucknett TA18 196 B5
EAST CLEVEDON 6 F3
East Clevedon Triangle
BS21 6 F3
Eastcliff BS20 2 E7
EAST COKER 197 D7
East Coker Com Prim Sch
BA22 197 C7
East Coker Rd BA20 218 F2
East Coker Sawmills
BA22 197 C7
EAST COMBE 151 E2
Eastcombe Gdns BS23 30 F1
Eastcombe La BA4 142 E2
Eastcombe Rd BS23 30 F1
EAST COMPTON 205 A2
East Compton Rd
Pilton BA4 204 E1
Shepton Mallet BA4 205 B1
East Coombe La TA4 165 D8
Eastcote Pk BS14 23 B5
Eastcourt Rd BS39 76 F8
EAST CRANMORE 142 C6
Eastcroft BS40 54 E2
Eastcroft Cl BS40 54 E2
East Ct BS3 11 F3
East Ct BA5 113 A1
Eastdown Rd BA3 78 D5
East Dr TA9 86 E4
EAST DUNDRY 22 A1
East Dundry La BS41 22 A1

East Dundry Rd BS13, BS14 22 F2
EAST END
Blagdon 54 F2
Chewton Mendip 94 E4
Nailsea 9 A1
South Cadbury 175 D4
Stoke St Michael 116 C2
East End BS26 88 D7
East End La BA3 94 E4
Easterdown Hill
Dinnington TA17 195 B8
Seavington St Mary TA19 184 E1
Easter La EX35 122 B4
Eastermead La BS29 51 C3
Eastern Ave TA6 209 D4
Eastern Ho BS23 30 E1
EASTERTOWN 67 D2
Eastertown BS24 67 D1
Eastfield
Bruton BA10 215 F7
29 Martock TA12 185 E6
Shepton Mallet BA4 205 B6
Yarlington BA9 175 F8
Eastfield Ave BA1 27 B2
Eastfield Cl 30 TA12 185 E6
Eastfield Gdn 12 DT9 225 E4
Eastfield Gdns BS23 30 F1
Eastfield La
Barrington TA19 184 D5
Blackford BS28 107 F6
Ditcheat BA4 159 C7
East Chinnock BA22 196 D8
Hambridge TA3 184 B8
Lydford Fair Place TA11 158 D3
North Perrott TA18 196 C4
Norton Sub Hamdon BA22 185 F1
Eastfield Pk BS23 30 F1
Eastfield Rd
Hutton BS24 49 E2
Wincanton BA9 216 D4
East Gate 11 TA1 213 A4
Eastgate Gdns 10 TA1 213 A4
Easthams Rd TA18 224 D6
EAST HARPTREE 74 E4
East Harptree CE Prim Sch BS40 74 F4
Easthay La TA20 199 A4
EAST HEWISH 33 B6
EASTHILL 120 B4
Easthill BA11 120 B4
Easthill La BA7 159 D5
EAST HUNTSPILL 136 E7
East Huntspill Prim Sch TA9 136 E8
EAST KNOWSTONE 162 B2
East La TA18 196 B7
EAST LAMBROOK 220 C8
East Lambrook Manor Gdns* TA13 220 C8
East Lambrook Rd TA13 220 D7
Eastland Rd BA21 219 C5
East Lanes BA21 187 D6
Eastlea BS21 6 B1
East Lea Rd BA1 44 A8
Eastleigh Cl
Burnham-on-S TA8 104 C8
Frome BA11 120 A7
Wiveliscombe TA4 210 C5
Eastleigh Rd TA1 213 B3
EAST LYDFORD 158 D2
EAST LYNG 170 D8
Eastlyn Rd BS13 22 B8
East Mead BA3 78 B2
Eastmead Ct BS9 5 E4
Eastmead La BS9 5 E4
East Mead La
Street BA16 207 F5
Walton BA16 156 E6
East Mere Cross EX16 178 B2
East Mill Ct 11 DT9 225 E4
East Mill La DT9 225 E4
Eastmoor La TA4 164 E8
Eastnor Rd BS14 23 A3
EAST NYNEHEAD 167 D2
EASTON 111 A4
Easton Ct BA3 76 E1
Easton Ho 9 BA1 28 C1
EASTON-IN-GORDANO 4 A4
Easton La
Pylle BA4 141 C1
Sampford Peverell EX16 178 D1
Easton Rd BS20 4 C4
Easton Town La BA4 158 F4
Easton Trow La BA4 159 B5
Eastop La DT10 190 A3
EASTOVER 209 B5
Eastover
Bridgwater TA6 209 A5
Langport TA10 172 A6
Eastover Cl TA10 172 A5
Eastover Com Prim Sch TA6 209 B5
Eastover Gr BA2 44 C1
Eastover Rd BS39 59 D1
East Par BS9 5 C6
EAST PENNARD 158 F8
EAST QUANTOXHEAD 133 B6
East Quay TA6 209 A6
East Quay Mews TA6 209 A6
East Rd BA16 207 E6
East Reach TA1 213 A4
East Ride TA9 86 B1
East Ridge Dr BS13 21 F5
EAST ROLSTONE 33 B1
East Side La TA7 136 F2
East Somerset Railway* BA4 205 F3
East Somerset Way BA5 203 D3
East St
Banwell BS29 51 C3
Bourton SP8 161 F1
Cannington TA5 135 C2
Chard TA20 223 D4
Crewkerne TA18 224 C6
Drayton TA10 171 E3
East Coker BA22 197 B8
Ilminster TA19 221 C4
Martock TA12 185 E6
Milborne Port DT9 217 D2
North Perrott TA18 196 C4
Norton Sub Hamdon TA14 185 F1
Shepton Montague BA9 160 B2
Taunton TA1 212 F3
Templecombe BA8 176 F1
EAST STOKE 186 A4
East Stoke TA14 185 F4
EAST STREET 139 F1
East Street Dro TA12 185 E6
East Street La BA6 140 A1
East Tapps La EX16 163 B2
EAST TOWN
Lydeard St Lawrence 150 E3
Shepton Mallet 141 A3
East Town La TA4 150 E3
East Town La (Platterwell La) BA4 141 B3
EAST TWERTON 44 D7
Eastville
Bath BA1 28 B1
Yeovil BA21 219 C5
Eastville La BS27 90 F1
EAST WATER 92 F2
East Water La BA5 92 F2
Eastway BS48 8 E3
East Way BA2 44 A5
Eastway Cl BS48 8 D2
Eastway Sq BS48 8 E3
Eastwell La BS25 69 E6
Eastwick Ave TA2 212 F7
Eastwick Rd TA2 213 B7
Eastwood BA2 45 F6
Eastwood Cl
Bridgwater TA6 209 C4
Frome BA11 119 C4
High Littleton BS39 59 C1
EAST WOODLANDS 144 A7
East Woodlands Rd BA11 144 A7
East Wood Pl BS20 2 E7
Eastwoods BA1 29 B3
Eaton Cl BS14 23 E5
Eaton Cres
Bristol BS8 226 A4
Taunton TA2 213 A6
Ebben La TA20 194 F1
Ebbor Gorge Nature Reserve* BA5 111 D6
Ebbor Gorge Nature Trail* BA5 111 C5
Ebbor La BA5 111 B5
Ebden Lo 15 BS22 32 A2
EBDON 32 B6
Ebdon La BS22 32 C5
Ebdon Rd BS22 31 F4
Ebenezer La BS9 5 E5
Eckweek Gdns BA2 79 D8
Eckweek La BA2 79 E8
Eckweek Rd BA2 79 D8
Ecos Ct BA11 119 D4
Edbrooke Rd TA24 147 C5
Edbrook La TA5 134 F3
Eddington Ct BS23 48 D7
Eden Croft BS22 49 E8
Eden Dr BA5 203 C2
Eden Park Cl BA1 29 A4
Eden Park Dr BA1 29 A4
Eden Terr BA1 28 B2
Eden Villas 4 BA1 28 C2
EDFORD 116 C7
Edford Hill BA3 116 C6
Edgar Bldgs BA1 228 B3
EDGARLEY 139 E1
Edgarley Cl BA6 206 F7
Edgarley Ct BS21 6 C5
Edgarley Field La BA6 157 E8
Edgarley Rd
Glastonbury BA6 139 D1
West Pennard BA6 139 F1
EDGCOTT 128 C1
Edgcott Rd TA24 128 C1
Edgebury TA7 136 E4
Edgecombe Ave BS22 31 D2
Edgecombe Mews BA1 27 B1
Edgefield Cl BS14 22 F3
Edgefield Rd BS14 22 F3
Edgehill Rd BS21 6 D6
Edgemoor Rd TA24 201 B4
Edgewood Cl BS14 23 B8
Edgeworth Rd BA2 44 C2
Edinburgh Pl 1 BS23 48 E8
Edinburgh Rd
Bridgwater TA6 208 E2
Keynsham BS31 24 E4
EDINGTON 137 C3
Edington Rd TA7 137 D4
Edington Right Dro TA7 155 B7
EDINGWORTH 86 F7
Edingworth Rd BS24 86 F7
Edith Cl TA8 85 A2
EDITHMEAD 104 F7
Edithmead La TA9 105 A6
Edmond's Hill TA11 173 D4
Edmund Hill La BA6 206 F6
Edmund Rd BS14 23 A7
Edmunds Way BS27 90 C7
Edward Cl BA22 218 B6
Edward Ct BS31 24 F4
Edward Rd BS21 6 E5
Edward Rd S BS21 6 E5
Edward Rd W BS21 6 E6
Edward St
Bath, Bathwick BA2 45 B7
Bath, Lower Weston BA1 44 C7
Bridgwater TA6 209 B5
Edwin Short Cl BS30 25 E8
Egerton Rd BA2 44 E4
EGFORD 119 B5
Egford Hill BA11 119 C5
Egford La BA11 119 C5
Egg Moor La EX13 198 A7
Eggwood La TA13, TA16 195 E8
Eglin Croft BS13 22 B4
Eglinton Rd BA16 207 B4
Egremont Ct TA4 202 D2
Egrove Way TA4 202 E4
Eight Acre Dro TA7, TA9 137 A5
Eight Acre La
Wellington TA21 222 E5
Wootton Courtenay TA24 129 F8
Eighteen Arce La BA21 218 C6
Eighth Ave BS14 23 A7
Eileen Cl BA16 207 E5
Eirene Terr BS20 4 D4
Elberton Rd BS9 5 B7
Elborough Ave BS49 34 B8
Elborough Gdns BS24 50 C3
Elbridge Ho 3 BS2 227 C3
Elderberry Wlk BS22 31 F1
Elder Cl
Chard TA20 223 C5
Highbridge TA9 104 D5
Eldergrove Cl TA6 209 D7
Elder Ho TA8 65 E2
Elderwood Rd BS14 23 B7
Eldon Pl BA1 28 B2
Eldred Cl BS9 5 D5
Eleanor Cl BA2 44 A5
Eleanor Cotts BA2 44 A6
Electric Ho TA14 185 E3
Eleven Ct TA6 208 E4
Elfrida Terr BA5 203 A5
Elgar Cl
Bristol BS4 22 D6
Clevedon BS21 6 E1
Elgin Cl BA16 207 B5
Eliot Cl BS23 49 A3
Eliotts Dr BA21 218 E7
Elizabeth Cl BS24 49 D3
Elizabeth Ct
Burnham-on-S TA8 104 B6
4 Martock TA12 185 E6
Elizabeth Flats BA21 219 C6
Elizabeth Gdns 16 BA8 190 A6
Elizabeth Way
Bridgwater TA6 209 C5
Chard TA20 223 C5
Ellbridge Cl BS9 5 D5
Ellenborough Cres BS23 48 E6
Ellenborough Ct BS23 48 E6
Ellenborough Ho BS8 226 A2
Ellenborough Park Rd BS23 48 E6
Ellenborough Pk N BS23 48 D6
Ellenborough Pk S BS23 48 D6
Ellen Cl 8 TA6 153 F4
Ellen Ho BA2 44 A5
Ellersdown La TA22 163 E4
Ellesmere Rd
Bristol BS4 23 D8
Weston-super-Mare BS23 48 D2
Ellfield Cl BS13 21 F6
Ellick Rd BS40 54 D1
ELLICOMBE 201 C4
Ellicombe La TA24 201 C4
Ellicombe Mdw TA24 201 C4
Elliot Cl BA11 119 F6
ELLIOTS GREEN 144 B8
Elliots La BA11 119 B8
Elliott's Hill BA22 196 D7
Ellis Ave BS13 22 A8
Elliscombe Pk BA9 176 B6
Ellis Gr TA2 168 B5
Ellis Pk BS22 32 C4
Ellis's La TA5 152 C6
Elliston Dr BA2 44 B4
Ellsbridge Cl BS31 25 B5
Ellworthy Ct BA11 120 B4
Elm Ave TA8 104 B6
Elmbrook BA1 44 D8
Elm Cl
Banwell BS29 50 E4
Broadway TA19 183 C2
Nailsea BS48 8 C1
Star BS25 52 D1
Wells BA5 203 A4
Yatton BS49 34 B7
Elm Ct
Bristol BS14 23 A6
Keynsham BS31 24 C4
Elmdale Rd BS8 226 B3
Elm Dr BA9 216 C3
Elm Farm BS48 9 A2
Elm Gr
Bath, Larkhill BA1 28 C2
Bath, The Oval BA2 44 C4
Locking BS24 49 F4
Minehead TA24 201 A5
Taunton TA1 212 E5
Elmgrove Cl TA6 209 D7
Elmham Way BS24 32 B1
Elm Hayes BS13 21 F6
Elmhurst Ave BA21 219 B7
Elmhurst Est BA1 29 A4
Elmhurst Gdns BS41 20 F8
Elmhurst Jun Sch BA16 207 D6
Elmhurst La BA16 207 D6
Elmhurst Rd BS24 49 E2
Elmhyrst Rd BS23 48 F8
Elm La
Great Elm BA11 119 A6
Shalford BA9 216 B7
Woolavington TA7 136 F4
Elmlea Ave BS9 5 F5
Elm Lea Cl TA7 136 C4
Elmlea Jun & Inf Schs BS9 5 F5
Elmleigh BA21 218 C7
Elm Leigh BA11 120 C6
Elmleigh Rd 21 TA12 185 E6
Elm Lodge Rd BS48 9 B2
Elm Pk TA1 212 E5
Elm Pl BA2 44 F4
Elm Rd BS39 77 E5
Elms Cl TA1 212 E5
Elms Est TA2 213 F8
Elmside Cl BA16 207 D5
Elmside Ho TA6 208 F2
Elmside Rd TA6 208 E2
Elms La BA7 214 B7
Elmsleigh Rd BS23 48 E4
Elmsley La BS22 31 C5
Elms Rd TA21 222 F5
Elm St TA20 223 C5
Elms The
Banwell BS29 51 A4
Bath, Lambridge BA1 28 C2
Bath, Weston Park BA1 27 C1
Elmswood BS23 48 F8
Elm Terr BA3 97 C8
Elm Tree Ave
Nailsea BS21 8 A4
Radstock BA3 78 D1
Elm Tree Cl TA7 155 C2
Elmtree Dr BS13 21 F5
Elm Tree Pk BS20 3 D3
Elm Tree Rd
Clevedon BS21 6 D2
Locking BS24 50 A4
Elmvale Dr BS24 49 F3
Elm View
Midsomer Norton BA3 78 B1
Temple Cloud BS39 58 E1
Elm Way BA4 205 A6
Elm Wlk
Portishead BS20 2 C4
Yatton BS49 34 B7
Elmwood Ave TA6 208 F3
Elmwood Sch TA6 208 F3
Elsbert Dr BS13 21 E6
Elscombe La
Timberscombe TA24 130 A4
Wootton Courtenay TA24 129 F4
Elton Ho 2 BS2 227 C3
Elton Rd
Bristol BS8 226 C3
Clevedon BS21 6 C3
Weston-super-Mare BS22 32 A4
Elton St BS2 227 C4
Elvard Cl BS13 22 A4
Elvard Rd BS13 22 A4
Elwell La BS40, BS41 21 A1
ELWORTHY 150 C6
Elworthy Cross TA4 150 C5
Elworthy Dr TA21 222 D4
Elworthy La TA4 150 C5
Ely Gr BS9 5 B7
Embankment The TA10 172 A5
Embden Walk 4 TA6 209 A1
Embercourt Dr BS48 19 A6
EMBOROUGH 95 C3
Emery Gate BS29 51 B3
Emlet DT9 187 E1
Emley La BS40 54 B6
Emlyn Cl 6 BS22 32 B4
Emmanuel Ct BS8 226 A4
Emmett Wood BS14 23 B3
Empress Menen Gdns BA1 44 A8
Enderleigh Gdns BS25 52 F4
Enfield Dr BA4 141 E2
Enfield Rd BA4 141 E2
Engine La BS48 18 B8
Englands La BA22 174 F3
Englands Mead BA22 174 F3
Englands Rd TA24 124 A3
Englands Way TA20 223 D6
ENGLISHCOMBE 43 F2
Englishcombe La BA2 44 D3
Englishcombe Rd BS13 22 C3
Englishcombe Rise BA2 44 A3
Englishcombe Tithe Barn* BA2 43 F2
Englishcombe Way BA2 44 E3
ENMORE 153 A6
Enmore BS24 49 A2
Enmore CE Prim Sch TA5 152 F5
Enmore Cl TA8 104 C8
Enmore Rd
Bridgwater TA5 153 B6
Taunton TA2 212 F7
Ennerdale Cl BS23 49 A5
Enterprise Ctr The BS24 49 A3
Enterprise Mews BA20 218 D3
Enterprise Trade Ctr BS4 22 E7
Entry Hill BA2 44 F2
Entry Hill Dr BA2 44 F3
Entry Hill Gdns BA2 44 F3
Entry Hill Pk BA2 44 F2
Entry Rise BA2 44 F1
Erin Wlk BS4 22 D8
Erlon La BA5 110 F4
Ermine St BA21 218 D7
Ermine Way BS11 4 C7
Ernest Ashman Pl TA20 223 D5
Ervine Terr BS2 227 C4
ESCOTT 150 C8
Escott Ct TA6 208 F6
Escott La TA4 132 D1
Esgar Rise BS22 31 E3
Eskdale Cl BS22 49 D8
Eskimo Ct BA16 207 B5
Esmonde Dr BA22 173 E2
Esmond Gr BS21 6 D4
Esplanade
Burnham-on-S TA8 104 A7
Minehead TA24 201 A7
Esplanade La TA23 202 C7
Esplanade Rd BS20 2 C7
Esplanade The TA23 202 C7
Essex Cl TA20 223 C4
Essex Ct TA1 212 C2
Essex Dr TA1 212 C2
Estuary Ho BS20 2 E7
Estuary Pk TA5 135 B5
Estune Wlk BS41 11 A2
Esworthy Cross EX16 162 F1
Ethel St BA5 203 C3
Ethpark Gr 1 TA2 212 F6
Etonhurst BS23 48 D6
Eton La BS29 50 E7
Eton Rd TA8 104 B6
Etsome Cl TA11 211 C4
Etsome Hill TA11 211 C7
Etsome Rd TA11 211 C5
Etsome Terr TA11 211 C4
Ettlingen Way BS21 6 F2
Eugene Flats 7 BS2 227 A4
Eugene St
Bristol, Kingsdown BS2 227 A4
Bristol, St Pauls BS2, BS5 227 C4
Eva Turner Cl BS14 23 C6
Eveleigh Ave BA1 28 D2
Evelyn Rd BA1 44 B8
Evelyn Terr 14 BA1 28 A1
Evenlode Gdns BS11 4 F5
Evenlode Way BS31 25 A3
EVERCREECH 141 E1
Evercreech CE Prim Sch BA4 141 E2
Evercreech Rd BS14 23 B4
Evercreech Way TA9 104 F2
Everett Cl BA5 112 E1
Evergreen Cl BS25 51 F1
Evergreen Path TA16 195 F7
Everton Rd BA20 219 A4
Evesham Ave BA21 218 C6
Evesham Dr TA6 209 A1
Ewart Rd BS22 49 C8
Ewell Cl TA19 183 C1
Exbourne 10 BS22 32 A2
Exbury Cl TA8 104 C7
Excelsior St BA2 45 B5
Excelsior Terr BA3 78 B1
Exchange Ave BS1 227 A2
EXEBRIDGE 163 F3
Exebridge Ind Est TA22 163 F3
Exeter Cl
Burnham-on-S TA8 104 C7
Nether Stowey TA5 134 B2
Exeter Rd
Portishead BS20 2 E4
Rockwell Green TA21 222 B5
Weston-super-Mare BS23 48 E5
Exeter Road Cvn Pk TA21 222 A4
EXFORD 128 D1
Exford CE Fst sch TA24 128 D1
Exford Cl BS23 48 F2
Exford Rd TA24 147 C6
Exmoor Gdns TA22 163 D6
Exmoor Owl & Hawk Centre* TA24 124 B4
Exmoor Pony Centre The* TA22 147 A1
Exmoor Rd BA2 44 F2
Exmoor Way TA24 200 E6
Exmouth Rd BS4 22 F8
Explore La BS1 226 C2
Express Pk TA6 136 A2
EXTON 147 E4
Exton BS24 49 A2
Exton Cl BS14 23 B5
Exton La TA22 147 E4
Eyer's La BS2 227 C3
Eyers Rd BS24 49 F7
EYEWELL 174 E4

F

Faber Gr BS13 22 C4
Factory Hill SP8 161 F2
Factory La
East Huntspill TA9 136 E8
Tatworth TA20 198 D8
FAILAND 10 C3
Failand Cres BS9 5 C5
Failand La
Easton-in-G BS8 4 A1
Portbury BS20 3 F2
Failand Wlk BS9 5 C6
Fairacre Cl BS24 50 B4
Fairacres Cl BS31 24 F5
Fair Cl BA2 81 E4
Fairclose TA20 193 D6
Fair Cross TA23 131 F2

Fairdean Rd TA9 104 E4
Fairfax Cl TA6 209 C6
Fairfax Rd TA6 209 C5
Fairfax St BS1 227 B3
Fairfield
Coleford BA3 116 E8
Crewkerne TA18 224 B5
Ilminster TA19 221 A4
7 Martock TA12 185 E6
Rode BA11 82 F1
Sampford Peverell EX16 178 D1
Sherborne DT9 225 D5
Somerton TA11 211 E4
Tunley BA2 61 A3
Yarlington BA9 175 F7
Fairfield Ave BA1 28 A2
Fairfield Cl
Backwell BS48 19 D7
Frome BA11 120 A7
Marshfield SN14 13 F8
Weston-super-Mare BS22 31 B1
Fairfield Dr TA4 202 E3
Fairfield Gdns BA6 206 D4
Fairfield Gn TA3 192 A7
Fairfield Hts DT9 225 D5
Fairfield Mdws BA14 83 F3
Fairfield Mead BS48 19 D7
FAIRFIELD PARK 28 A2
Fairfield Park Rd BA1 28 A2
Fairfield Rd
Bath BA1 28 B1
Taunton TA2 213 B7
Fairfield Sch BS48 19 C6
Fairfield Terr
Bath BA1 28 A1
Fitzhead TA4 166 F5
Peasedown St John BA2 79 C7
Fairfield View BA1 28 A2
Fairfield Way BS48 19 C6
Fairford Cl TA9 104 E4
Fairford Rd
Bristol BS11 4 D7
Highbridge TA9 104 E4
Fair Furlong BS13 22 A4
Fair Furlong Prim Sch BS13 22 B4
Fair Hill BS25 70 F8
Fairhouse Rd BA22 197 F8
Fairlands Mid Sch BS27 90 C7
Fairlands Way BS27 90 C7
Fairmead Rd BA21 219 C8
Fairmead Sch BA21 219 C8
Fairmont Terr 7 DT9 225 E4
Fair Pl TA11 158 D3
Fairseat Workshops BS40 56 E7
Fairview
Mells BA11 118 B7
Weston-super-Mare BS22 31 F4
Fair View BA10 161 A7
Fairview Ho BS9 5 F8
Fairview Terr
Taunton TA3 168 D1
Yeovilton BA22 187 A8
Fairwater Cl TA2 212 D6
Fairway BS4 23 D8
Fairway Cl
Berrow TA8 84 F4
Weston-super-Mare BS22 31 B2
Fairway Rise TA20 223 E5
Fairways
Saltford BS31 25 E2
Wells BA5 203 C4
Fairways Cvn Pk TA7 136 E3
Fairways The TA1 212 F1
Fairway View BA21 219 D6
Fairwood Rd BA13 102 F5
Fairy Hill BS39 41 D6
Falcon Cl
Bristol, Westbury on T BS9 5 F8
Portishead BS20 2 D4
Falcon Cres BS22 49 D8
Falcon Ct TA1 212 C4
Falcondale Rd BS9 5 F7
Falconer Rd BA1 27 A3
Falconsmead Wlk BA21 219 D8
Falkland Ho 7 TA18 224 C6
Falkland Sq 6 TA18 224 C6
Falklands Rise TA24 200 D7
Fallowfield
Blagdon BS40 54 E2
Weston-super-Mare BS22 31 F3
Falmouth Cl BS48 9 A1
Fanshawe Rd BS14 23 A7
Faraday Rd 2 BS8 11 F5
FARLEIGH 19 D7
Farleigh Ct BS48 20 B8
FARLEIGH HUNGERFORD 82 E8
Farleigh Hungerford Castle* BA2 82 E8
Farleigh Rd
Backwell BS48 19 C6
Clevedon BS21 6 B1
Keynsham BS31 24 D4
Norton St Philip BA2 81 F5
Farleigh Rise
Monkton Farleigh BA15 29 E1
Monkton Farleigh BA15 46 E8
Farleigh View BA15 64 F3
FARLEIGH WICK 46 E4
Farleigh Wlk BS13 22 A8
Farler's End BS48 18 F8
FARLEY 1 B1
Farley Cl BA11 120 C6
Farley Dell BA3 116 E8
FARMBOROUGH 60 B6
Farmborough CE Prim Sch BA2 59 F6
Farm Cl
Somerton TA11 211 B3
Westbury-sub-Mendip BA5 110 D6
Weston-super-Mare BS22 32 C4
Farm Ct TA13 220 C5
Farm Dr TA11 211 B3
Farmer Rd BS13 21 E4
Farm Hill TA7 156 B8
Farmhouse Cl 7 BS48 8 E2
Farmhouse Ct 1 BS48 8 E1
Farmhouse Dr BA11 119 F7
Farm La
Buckland St Mary TA20 182 A2
Coultings TA5 134 E4
Stogursey TA5 134 D4
Street BA16 207 C7
Wellow BA2 62 E1
Farm Orch DT9 188 C7
Farm Rd
Bradford Abbas DT9 187 E1
Doulting BA4 141 E5
Hutton BS24 49 E2
Street BA16 207 C6
Weston-super-Mare BS22 31 B1
Farm St BA22 186 C6
Farm View TA2 168 F6
Farmwell Cl BS13 22 B5
Farnaby Cl BS4 22 C7
Farnborough Rd BS24 50 C4
Farncombe La BA9 160 B1
Farndale Rd BS22 49 D8
Farrant Cl
Baltonsborough BA6 158 A5
Bristol BS4 22 D6
Taunton TA1 212 A4
Farrant Rd BA11 119 D5
Farriers Gn TA2 213 F7
Farringdon Hill La TA5 134 D6
Farrington Fields BS39 77 C3
Farrington Fields Trad Est BS39 77 C3
FARRINGTON GURNEY 77 A3
Farrington Gurney CE Prim Sch BS39 77 A4
Farrington La BA4 141 F6
Farrington Rd BS39 77 C5
Farrington Way BS39 77 A3
Farrow Cl TA20 223 D3
Farrs La BA2 45 B2
Farr's La BS1 227 A2
Farr's Orch 6 TA16 195 F7
Farr St BS11 4 B8
Farthing Combe BS26 70 D2
Farthing Down TA21 179 E7
Farthing La EX13 193 D1
Farthing Rd TA6 208 E1
Farthing Row BA11 82 E1
Farthings Cl TA21 167 C2
Farthings Paddock BA7 159 A3
Farthing's Pitts TA21 222 C4
Fashion Mus* BA1 228 B3
FAULKLAND 80 E2
Faulkland La BA2, BA3 80 C4
Faulkland Rd BA2 44 D5
Faulkland View BA2 79 E7
Faversham Dr BS24 49 A1
Fawcus Pl TA20 223 C4
Fawn Cl BA6 206 C3
Fayre Way BA5 204 B7
Fearnville Est BS21 6 C2
Featherbed La
Chew Stoke BS40 38 A3
Clayhanger EX16 165 C1
Clutton BS39 58 C6
Fedden Village BS21 1 F5
Feeder Rd BS2 227 C1
Fellowsmead DT10 190 F5
Felon's Oak La TA24 131 B2
Felsberg Way BS27 90 C7
Feltham Dr BA11 120 A3
Feltham La BA11 144 B8
FELTON 37 C8
Felton Gr BS13 22 A8
Felton La BS40 37 E7
Felton St BS40 37 C7
Fender Cl TA5 135 B5
Feniton 6 BS22 32 A2
Fennel La BS26 70 B2
Fennel Rd BS20 3 A5
Fennel Way BA22 218 A5
Fenners BS22 32 B4
FENNINGTON 168 B8
Fennington La TA2 168 B8
Fenns La BS41 10 E1
FENNY CASTLE 139 D7
Fenshurst Gdns BS41 20 F8
Fenswood Cl BS41 10 F1
Fenswood Ct BS41 10 E1
Fenswood Mead BS41 10 E1
Fenswood Rd BS41 10 E1
Fental La BA3 116 C1
Fenton Cl BS31 25 D3
Ferenberge Cl BA2 60 A6
Ferguson Cl TA5 134 A3
Fermoy BA11 120 B6
Fern Cl BA3 78 B1
Ferndale Dr TA1 168 D1
Ferndale Gdns BA21 218 E6
Ferndale Rd
Bath BA1 28 C3
Portishead BS20 2 D6
Ferndown Cl
Bristol BS11 5 A7
Taunton TA1 212 D1
Ferne Animal Sanctuary* TA20 193 A2
Fern Gr BS48 18 C8
Fern Lea BS24 67 B6
Fernlea Gdns BS20 4 B4
Fernlea Rd BS22 49 C7
Fernleigh Ave TA6 209 A3
Fernleigh Cl BA4 141 E1
Fern Lodge BS23 48 D6
Fernside BS48 19 A7
Fernsteed Rd BS13 21 F6
Ferry Ct BA2 45 B6
Ferry La
Bath BA2 45 B6
Lympsham BS24 67 C3
Ferryman Rd BA6 206 E7
Ferryman's Ct BS2 227 B2
Ferry St BS1 227 B2
Fersfield BA2 45 B3
Festival Units TA6 209 B1
Feversham Ave TA6 208 E6
Feversham Ct BA22 173 E2
Feversham La BA6 206 D5
Feversham Way TA2 213 A8
FIDDINGTON 134 D3
Fiddle La BA22 174 F1
Fideoak Mill TA4 168 B4
FIELD 205 C5
Field Cl BA3 116 A3
Field End
Axminster EX13 198 A1
Minehead TA24 201 A5
Fielders The BS22 32 B4
Fieldfare Ave BS20 3 A6
Fieldgardens Rd BS39 58 F1
Field Gate TA3 183 C8
Fieldgate La TA3 183 B8
Fielding Ct BA21 219 C6
Fielding Ho BA2 44 A6
Fielding Path BA6 206 E6
Fielding Rd
Street BA16 207 B7
Yeovil BA21 219 C6
Fielding's Rd BA2 44 C6
Fieldins BA15 64 E7
Field La
Chewton Mendip BA3 94 F8
Kington Magna SP8 177 E1
Penselwood BA9 161 D2
Field Marshal Slim Ct 24 BS2 227 C3
Field Rd TA10 156 A1
Fields End TA1 213 C2
Fields The BS22 32 D2
Field View BA4 205 C5
Field View Ct BA4 141 E1
Fieldway BS25 52 B4
Field Way TA9 104 D5
Fifehead Bsns Ctr (Manor Farm Trad Est) BA8 190 F8
Fifehead Hill BA8 190 F8
FIFEHEAD MAGDALEN 190 F8
Fifth Ave BS14 23 B7
Filer Cl BA2 79 D8
Filers Wy BS24 32 C1
Fillymead DT10 190 F5
Filwood Broadway BS4 22 E8
FILWOOD PARK 22 E8
Finch Cl
Shepton Mallet BA4 204 F6
Weston-super-Mare BS22 49 E8
Finches The
4 Portishead BS20 2 F6
Portishead BS20 3 A6
Finches Way TA8 85 B1
Finger Cnr DT10 190 F5
Finger La DT9 225 D3
Finisterre Parade BS20 2 F6
Finmere Gdns BS22 32 A4
Fircliff Pk BS20 2 D7
Fire House Mews BA9 216 C3
FIREPOOL 213 A5
Firgrove La BA2 61 B1
Fir La BS40 72 B5
Fir Leaze BS48 8 B1
Firs Ct BS31 24 C4
First Ave
Axminster EX13 198 A2
Bath BA2 44 E4
Bristol BS14 23 A7
Portbury BS20 3 E5
Radstock BA3 97 C8
First Dro TA7 155 D3
Firs The
Bath BA2 45 B1
Langport TA10 172 A5
Limpley Stoke BA3 64 A5
Wheddon Cross TA24 129 E1
First Ho BA16 207 B6
First Sedgemoor Dro TA10 155 E4
Fir Tor Ave BA5 203 C5
Fir Tree Ave
Paulton BS39 77 F4
Weston-super-Mare BS24 49 E4
Firtree Cl TA5 134 A2
Fir Tree Cl TA6 209 D4
Firway Cross EX16 164 C3
Firwood Rd BA11 119 E4
Fishers Brook BA11 120 A5
Fishers Cl DT9 187 F5
Fisher's Hill
Glastonbury BA6 206 D4
Holywell Lake TA21 179 D7
Fisher's La
Dinnington TA17 195 A7
Mark TA9 106 D5
Fishers Mead TA22 163 D6
Fisherway La TA19 195 A5
FISHPOND BOTTOM 199 A1
Fishpond Bottom Rd DT6 199 A1
Fishwell La BA6 157 D4
Fitzharding Ho 8 BS1 227 A3
Fitzharding Rd BS20 4 E3
FITZHEAD 166 F7
FITZROY 168 A6
Fitzroy Circ BS20 2 F6
Fitzroy Ho 3 BA2 228 C3
Fivash Cl TA1 168 D1
Five Acres 3 BA22 197 F8
Five Arches Cl BA3 78 D2
Five Ashes BA22 186 C2
Five Barrows Cross EX36 145 B7
FIVE BELLS 202 B5
Five Bells TA23 202 B5
Five C Bsns Ctr BS21 6 B1
Five Cross Way TA21 180 F6
Five Cross Ways TA22 162 F7
Five Dials TA19 183 C1
FIVEHEAD 170 F2
Five Hos TA21 222 B8
Five Lords TA5 134 B2
Fiveways Cl BS27 90 A7
Fiveways Rdbt BA21 219 A6
Fiveways Sch BA21 219 D6
Five Yards 3 TA4 167 F8
Flagstaff Rd BS26 68 D7
Flamingo Cres BS22 49 E8
Flat The BS39 58 D5
Flatwoods Cres BA2 45 F3
Flatwoods Rd BA2 45 F3
FLAX BOURTON 19 F7
Flax Bourton CE Prim Sch BS48 19 F8
Flax Bourton Rd BS8 10 B3
Flaxfield Dr TA18 224 C5
Flax La DT9 187 F4
FLAXPOOL 151 C6
Flaxpool Hill TA4 151 C6
Flax Row TA18 224 C7
Flax Way BA21 218 C6
Fleed Cross TA4 166 A6
Fleet Air Arm Mus* BA22 174 B3
Fletcher Cl TA2 213 B8
Fletcher's La BS26 87 D6
Fleur De Lys Dr BA14 83 F4
Flingers La BA9 216 D4
Flint Cross TA4 149 C1
Flints Cl BA11 119 D4
Florence Cl 3 TA6 208 E7
Florence Gr BS22 49 B8
Florida Fields BA7 214 B6
Florida St BA7 214 C5
Florida Terr BA3 78 C2
Flowerdale Rd TA23 202 C6
Flowerdown Bridge BS22 49 D7
Flowerdown Rd BS24 50 D4
Flowerfield BA11 143 B8
Flowers Hill BS4 23 E8
Flowers Ho 1 BA20 219 B4
Flowerstone BA3 114 D7
Flowerwell Rd BS13 22 B5
Flushing Mdw BA21 219 E5
FODDINGTON 174 E8
Foghamshire La BA11 143 D6
Foldhill Cl 25 TA12 185 E6
Foldhill La
Ash BA22 186 A6
Martock TA12 185 F6
Folke La DT9 189 A1
Folleigh Cl BS41 11 B2
Folleigh Dr BS41 11 B2
Folleigh La BS41 11 B2
Folliott Rd BA6 206 E6
Folly Cl
Cannington TA5 135 B2
Midsomer Norton BA3 96 E7
Folly Dr BA4 159 C7
Folly Dro TA19 183 A5
Folly Farm Nature Reserve* BS39 58 B5
Folly Fields BA21 219 B7
Folly La
Buckland St Mary TA20 182 E1
Kington Magna SP8 177 F2
Nether Compton DT9 187 F4
North Wootton BA4 140 C4
Shipham BS25 70 E7
South Cadbury BA22 175 D4
Weston-super-Mare BS23 48 E1
Folly Rd TA12 185 B7
FOLLY THE 94 F6
Folly The
Cold Ashton SN14 12 F6
Ditcheat BA4 159 C7
Paulton BS39 77 F6
Saltford BS31 25 F2
Fons George TA1 212 F2
Fons George Cl TA1 212 E2
Fons George Rd TA1 212 F2
Fonthill Rd BA1 27 E2
Font La BA22 197 B7
Fontmell Ct BS14 23 D7
Font Villas BA22 197 B8
Football La BA9 216 B4
Footlands Cl TA1 212 F1
Forbes Fraser Hospl BA1 44 B8
Forches Cnr EX15 181 A4
Forche's La TA24 131 D3
FORD
Chewton Mendip 94 E8
Holcombe Rogus 178 F5
Wiveliscombe 210 F6
Forde Abbey & Gardens* TA20 198 F8
Forde Pk BA21 218 C7
FORDGATE 154 C3
Fordhay BA22 196 E7
Fordhay Terr BA22 196 E7
Ford La
Chewton Mendip BA3 94 D8
Pilton BA4 140 F3
Stawell TA7 137 A1
Yarley BA5 139 B8
Fordmill Cross EX16 164 D1
Ford Orch EX16 178 D1
Ford Rd
Bampton EX16 164 C1
Peasedown St John BA2 79 D8
Wellow BA2 62 F1
Wiveliscombe TA4 210 C4
Ford St TA21 222 F4
FORD STREET 180 D5
Forefield Pl BA2 228 C1
Forefield Rise BA2 45 B4
Forefield Terr BA2 45 A4
Forelands BS23 30 B1
Fore Leaze Dro TA12 184 E7
Fore St
9 Bampton EX16 164 B1
Bridgwater TA6 208 F5
Cannington TA5 135 B2
Castle Cary BA7 214 C5
Chard TA20 223 C4
Dulverton TA22 163 D6
Holcombe Rogus TA21 178 F5
Milverton TA4 167 A4
North Petherton TA6 153 E3
Othery TA7 155 C2
Tatworth TA20 198 D8
Taunton TA1 212 F3
Thorncombe TA20 199 B6
Wellington TA21 222 D6
West Camel BA22 174 D3
Westonzoyland TA7 154 E5
Williton TA4 202 D3
Winsham TA20 194 E1
Forest Dr BS23 31 A1
Forest Dro TA3 182 F5
Forester Ave BA2 45 B8
Forester Cl TA6 208 D5
Forester Ct BA2 228 C4
Forester La BA2 45 B8
Forester Rd
Bath BA2 45 B8
Portishead BS20 2 D4
Foresters Cl TA4 202 E3
Forest Farm Units TA19 183 A3
Forest Hill BA20 218 E2
Forest La TA20 193 E8
Forest Mill La TA19 183 B1
Forest Rd
Frome BA11 120 B7
Horningsham BA11, BA12 144 B4
Forest Wlk BA13 121 C4
Forge Cnr
Somerton TA11 211 C4
Stogursey TA5 134 B6
Forge End BS20 3 E3
Forge La
East Chinnock BA22 196 E8
Zeals SP8, BA12 161 F2
Forsythia Wy TA6 208 D1
Fortescue Rd BA3 78 F2
Fortescue St BA2 81 E4
Fortfield Rd BS14 23 B5
Forth Ave BS20 2 F6
Forth Cl BA16 207 A4
Fortnum Pl TA19 221 D3
FORTON 223 F1
Forton La
Chard TA20 223 F1
Tatworth TA20 194 A1
Forton Rd TA20 223 D2
Forts Orch BA22 186 E6
Forum Bldgs BA1 228 C1
Forum La BA4 205 A7
Forum The BA21 218 C6
Forward's La TA3 181 C5
Fosgrove La TA3 181 E7
Fosse Barton BS48 8 D2
Fosse Cl
Nailsea BS48 8 C2
Yeovil BA21 218 D7
Fossedale Ave BS14 23 C6
Fossefield Rd BA3 97 B6
Fosse Gdns BA2 62 D8
Fosse Gn BA3 78 E4
Fosse La
Batheaston BA1 29 A4
Blackford BS28 107 C3
Clandown BA3 78 D3
Nailsea BS48 8 D2
Shepton Mallet BA4 205 D4
Fosse Lane Ind Est BA4 205 E4
Fosse Lane Junc BA4 205 E5
Fosse Lane Trad Est BA4 205 D5
Fosse Rd BA3 115 C3
Fosse The TA3 170 C4
Fosseway
Clandown BA3 78 E4
Clevedon BS21 6 C2
Midsomer Norton BA3 97 A5
Radstock BA3 97 C8
Fosse Way
Nailsea BS48 8 C2
Yeovil BA21 218 D7
Fosseway Cl BA2 79 C7
Fosse Way Cotts BA3 78 D2
Fosseway Ct
Bristol BS8 226 A2
Ilchester BA22 173 E2
Fosse Way Est BA2 44 D1

Fosseway Gdns BA3 78 D1
Fosseway S BA3 97 B7
Fosse Way Sch BA3 97 C8
Fosseway The BS8 226 A3
Foster Cl BA5 112 E1
Foster Rd BA11 120 A3
Fosters 10 DT9 225 E4
Foster's Almshouses 3 BS1 227 A3
Foster's La BA22 175 A7
Foundry Barton 2 BA11 119 F5
Foundry Cotts BA2 60 B4
Foundry Mews
Chard TA20 223 C4
2 Crewkerne TA18 224 C5
Foundry Rd TA1 212 F4
Foundry Sq 1 TA18 224 C5
Foundry The BA1 228 C3
Fountain Bldgs 7 BA1 228 B3
Fountain Ho 8 BA1 228 B3
Fountain La BS25 70 B7
Fountains Cl BA21 218 C7
Four Acre Mdw TA6 208 E6
Four Acre Mead 1 TA4 167 F8
Four Acres
Bristol BS13 21 E4
Shepton Mallet BA4 205 C5
Fouracres Cl TA1 213 B1
Four Acres Cl
Bristol BS13 21 F4
Nailsea BS48 18 E8
Four Acres Prim Sch BS13 21 E4
Four Elms TA21 179 A6
FOUR FORKS 152 F8
Four Forks La TA5 152 F7
Four Lanes TA20 193 F6
Fourth Ave
Bristol BS14 23 B7
Radstock BA3 97 D8
Fourways Cl BA7 214 D6
Fourways Pk BA6 139 D3
Fouts Cross TA19 184 F2
Fowey Cl BS48 19 A8
Fowey Rd BS22 32 A4
Fowler St TA2 212 E6
Fownes Rd TA24 201 B5
Foxbury Cl BA11 119 F6
Fox Cl TA21 222 A6
Foxcombe La DT9 176 C1
Foxcombe Rd
Bath BA1 44 B7
Bristol BS14 23 B4
FOXCOTE 79 F4
Foxcote BA20 218 C2
Foxcote Ave BA2 79 E7
Foxcote Gdns BA11 120 C7
Foxdon Hill TA20 223 A7
Foxdown Hill TA21 222 C4
Foxdown Ho TA21 222 C4
Foxdown Terr TA21 222 D4
Foxglove Cl BS22 32 A5
Foxglove Way
Chard TA20 223 F5
Yeovil BA22 218 A5
Foxglove Wlk TA6 208 E1
Foxhanger La TA22 148 A2
FOX HILL 45 A2
Fox Hill BA2 45 A2
Foxhill Ho BA2 45 A1
FOX HILLS 79 A1
Foxhole La TA3 169 E5
Foxholes La BA2, BA11 100 D5
Fox & Hounds La BS31 24 F5
Fox Mdws TA18 224 D7
Fox Rd BA16 207 A5
Fox's Dro BA11 102 C1
Fox Way TA5 134 B2
Foxwell La BA22 196 C7
Foye Ho BS8 11 E6
Frampton Rd
Bridgwater TA6 208 F2
Shepton Mallet BA4 205 D3
Francis Cl TA3 169 D5
Francis Fox Rd 7 BS23 48 E7
Francis Ho BS2 227 A4
Francis Reed Cl TA7 154 F5
Francis Wlk BA11 225 E5
Francombe Ho BS1 227 A1
Frankcom Ho BA2 45 B7
Frank Foley Parkway The TA8 104 D6
Frankford Mans 7 BS23 30 C1
Frankland Cl BA1 27 B1
Frankley Bldgs BA1 28 B1
Frankley Terr 6 BA1 28 B1
Franklin Cl TA2 212 B7
Franklin Ct BS1 227 B1
Franklin's Way BS49 17 F1
Franklyn Terr BS39 77 A4
Frank Webber Rd TA21 222 A5
Fraser Cl
Burnham-on-S TA8 104 C7
Weston-super-Mare BS22 31 F4
Frederick Ave BA2 79 C7
Frederick Ct BA5 203 C4
Frederick Pl BS8 226 B3
Frederick Rd TA6 209 C6
Fredrick Pl 5 BA20 219 B4
Freedom Ave BA21 218 E6
Free Hill BA5 110 E6
Freeland Pl BS8 11 F6
Freelands BS21 16 C8
Freeling Ho BS1 227 B1
Freemans La BS48 20 B2
Freemantle Ho BS2 227 A4
Free St BA22 173 E1
Freeview Rd BA2 44 A5
Freezinghill La BS30 12 B4
Fremantle Rd TA1 213 B1
Frenchay Rd BS23 48 E4
French Cl
Nailsea BS48 8 F3
Peasedown St John BA2 79 D7
Frenchfield Rd BA2 79 D7
French Weir Ave TA1 212 E5
French Weir Cl TA1 212 E4
FRESHFORD 64 B5
Freshford CE Prim Sch BA3 64 B5
Freshford La BA3 64 A4
Freshford Sta BA3 64 C5
Freshmoor 6 BS21 6 F3
Frethey Rd TA1, TA4 168 B3
Friar Ave BS22 31 E3
FRIARN 133 F1
Friarn Ave TA6 208 F4
Friarn Lawn TA6 208 F4
Friarn St TA6 208 F4
Friars Ave BA21 218 D6
Friars Cl BA22 173 D1
Friars Way TA8 104 B6
Friary BS1 227 C1
Friary Cl
Clevedon BS21 6 C5
Westwood BA15 64 E4
Witham Friary BA11 143 C3
Friary Rd BS20 2 B5
Friday St TA24 200 F7
Friendly Row BS20 4 C5
Friendship Gr 2 BS48 8 F2
Friendship Rd BS48 8 F3
FRIEZE HILL 212 D5
Friggle St BA11 120 D1
Frithfield La BA4 205 C6
Frobisher Ave BS20 2 B5
Frobisher Cl
Burnham-on-S TA8 104 D8
Portishead BS20 2 A5
Weston-super-Mare BS22 31 E4
Frobisher Way TA2 212 B6
Frog La
Bristol BS1 226 C2
Combe St Nicholas TA20 193 D6
Creech St Michael TA3 169 F6
Dinnington TA17 195 B8
Enmore TA5 153 A6
Felton BS40 37 C8
Galhampton BA22 175 E8
Haselbury Plucknett TA18 196 C6
Holcombe Rogus TA21 178 F5
Ilminster TA19 221 C4
Isle Brewers TA3 184 A8
Kingsdon TA11 173 D5
Langport TA10 171 F5
North Curry TA3 170 D5
Shepton Mallet BA4 205 E4
Stoke St Michael BA3 116 A4
Ubley BS40 55 D1
Wanstrow BA4 142 F4
West Camel BA22 174 D3
Winford BS40 37 F5
Froglands La BS27 90 C7
Froglands Way BS27 90 C7
Frogmore St BS1 226 C2
Frogs La TA21 180 F7
Frog St
Bampton EX16 164 B1
East Quantoxhead TA5 133 B6
Lopen TA13 185 A1
Frogwell Cross TA4 164 D6
FROME 119 E4
Frome Com Coll BA11 120 A7
Frome Com Hospl BA11 120 A6
FROMEFIELD 120 A6
Fromefield BA11 120 A6
Fromefield Ho BA11 120 A6
Frome Mus* BA11 119 F5
Frome Old Rd BA3 79 A2
Frome Rd
Bath BA2 44 D1
Beckington BA11 101 D3
Bruton BA10 215 F7
Maiden Bradley BA12 144 B3
Norton St Philip BA2 81 F3
Nunney BA11 143 B8
Radstock BA3 79 B2
Rode BA11 101 F7
Southwick BA14 83 F3
Wingfield BA14 83 C5
Frome Sta BA11 120 A4
Frome View BA12 144 C2
Front St
Chapel Allerton BS26 88 D1
Chedzoy TA7 154 D8
Churchill BS25 52 E4
Monksilver TA4 150 B8
FROST HILL 34 C6
Frost Hill BS49 34 D7
Frost La TA19 183 F4
Frys House of Mercy 11 BS1 227 B1
Frys La TA7 154 E8
Fry's La BS40 53 F3
Frys Leaze BA1 28 B2
Frys Mews TA1 213 C2
Fry's Well BA3 96 D3
Fry's Wlk BA4 205 A5
Fryth Ho BS48 9 D3
Fryth Way BS48 8 C2
FULFORD 168 C8
Fulford Ct TA24 200 F7
Fulford Rd BS13 22 C5
Fulford Wlk BS13 22 B5
Fullands Ave TA1 168 F1
Fullands Ct TA1 168 F1
Fullands Rd TA1 213 B1
Fullens Cl BS22 49 D7
Fuller Cl BA4 205 D5
Fuller Rd BA1 28 C2
Fullers La BS25 70 A6
Fullers Way BA2 62 D8
Fullwell Cl BA3 80 D1
Fulmar Rd BS22 31 F1
Fulwell La BA3 80 D1
Fulwood Cl TA1 212 D1
Furge Gr BA8 190 A6
Furge La BA8 190 A6
Furland Rd
Crewkerne TA18 224 C5
Weston-super-Mare BS22 31 C2
Furland Way TA18 224 C5
Furlong Cl BA3 96 F7
Furlong Cotts EX16 179 A4
Furlong Gn TA3 168 D1
Furlong La
Curry Rivel TA10 171 C3
Milborne Port DT9 217 B3
Furlong Pl BS26 70 C1
Furlongs Ave TA6 208 E2
Furlongs The DT9 225 D5
FURNHAM 223 D5
Furnham Cl TA20 223 D5
Furnham Cres TA20 223 D6
Furnham Rd TA20 223 D5
Furnleaze BS39 58 E3
Furpits La TA10 172 B6
Furringdons Cross TA18 195 F6
Furze Cl
Bridgwater TA6 208 D4
Weston-super-Mare BS22 31 B2
Furzeclose La BA4 142 C7
Furzehill TA20 223 D5
Furzehill La TA24 147 C6
Furzeland Rd TA24 124 A4
Furze Rd BS22 31 A3
Furze The BA20 218 C2
Fylton Croft BS14 23 B3
Fyne Court Nat Res & Visitor Ctr* TA5 152 E3

G

Gables Cl BS29 51 B3
Gables The TA21 222 C6
Gabriel Cl BA11 120 C6
Gadd's La BS27 90 B8
Gagley La BA5 111 B2
Gainesmarsh La TA10 172 C5
Gainsborough DT9 217 C2
Gainsborough Ct BA1 27 B1
Gainsborough Dr
Sherborne DT9 225 B3
Weston-super-Mare BS22 31 F3
Gainsborough Gdns BA1 44 C8
Gainsborough Hill DT9 225 E2
Gainsborough Rd BS31 24 F5
Gainsborough Way BA21 219 E8
Galahad Cl BA21 218 D7
Gale's Dro BA6 139 D3
GALHAMPTON 175 D8
Galhampton Hill BA7, BA22 214 C2
Galingale Way BS20 2 F5
Gallagher Ret Pk
TA6 209 A6
Weston-super-Mare BS23 49 A5
Galleries The BS1 227 B3
Galley Batch BA3 114 F4
Galley Batch La BA3 114 F4
Galloping Bottom La TA23 149 E5
GALMINGTON 212 C2
Galmington Cl TA1 212 C3
Galmington Dr TA1 212 C2
Galmington La TA1 212 C2
Galmington Rd TA1 212 C2
Galmington Trad Est TA1 212 B3
Gamblyn Cross TA4 164 F5
Gammins Cotts TA24 129 E2
Gander Cl BS13 22 B5
Gandstone Cross TA4 150 D2
Ganesfield BA4 141 E6
Ganges Cl TA3 170 F2
Gange's Hill TA3 170 F2
Gannet Rd BS22 31 F1
Gants Mill & Gdn* BA10 215 C5
Gants Mill La BA10 215 D5
Gaol La BA4 205 C6
Garamond Ct BS1 227 B1
Garden City TA10 172 A6
Garden Cl
Bristol BS9 5 C5
Norton Fitzwarren TA2 168 B4
Weston-super-Mare BS22 31 E2
Garden Ct BS8 226 A4
Gardener Cl BS29 50 D8
Gardeners Cl
Bradford On Tone TA4 167 F1
Cheddar BS27 90 B8
Gardeners Wlk BS41 11 B1
Garden Ground BA4 205 C4
Gardenhurst TA8 85 B1
Garden Hurst Cl TA8 104 B8
Garden Plot Hill TA3 183 E7
Gardens Rd BS21 6 C4
Gardens The
Bath BA1 27 E1
Dulverton TA22 163 D7
East Pennard BA4 158 F8
Sherborne DT9 225 C3
1 Wellington TA21 222 D5
Gardens The continued
2 Wells BA5 203 D4
Garden Terr TA21 222 B7
Garden Way TA24 200 D7
Garden Wlk TA6 208 E2
Gardiners Bsns Pk TA7 136 F3
Gardiners Orch BS28 108 C4
Gardner Ave BS13 21 F7
Gardner Rd BS20 2 D6
Garfield Terr 1 BA1 28 C2
Garland Ave BS24 50 C5
GARLANDHAYES 180 F2
Garlandhayes La EX15 180 E2
Garland Ho 7 BS21 6 C2
Garner Ct 4 BS22 32 B4
Garonor Way BS20 3 F5
Garre Ho BA2 43 F5
Garrett Rd BA20 218 D3
Garrick Rd BA2 43 F5
Garsdale BA11 120 A4
Garsdale Rd BS22 49 D8
Garston Cotts BS40 54 E3
Garstone La TA16 195 F8
Garston La
Blagdon BS40 54 E3
Frome BA11 120 A4
Marston Magna BA22 174 F1
Garston Lodge 11 BA11 119 F4
Garston Mead BA11 120 A4
Garston Rd BA11 120 A4
Garstons
Bathford BA1 29 D2
7 Clevedon BS21 6 B1
Wrington BS40 35 E1
Garstons Cl
Backwell BS48 18 F6
Wrington BS40 35 E2
Garstons Orch BS40 35 D1
Garston St BA4 205 C6
Garstons The BS20 2 D4
Garth Rd BS13 22 A8
Gartons Mead BA4 141 E1
Gartons Mead Rd BA4 141 E1
Garvins Rd BA6 206 C4
Gasferry Rd BS1 226 B1
Gashay La EX13 199 B3
Gas La TA17 195 D7
Gason La BA22 174 F4
GASPER 161 E4
Gasper St BA12 161 E3
Gass Cl TA9 104 F4
Gasson's La TA11 211 C3
Gaston Ave BS31 24 F6
Gaston Cl BA16 207 C4
Gaston's La TA12 185 D5
Gastons The BS11 5 A8
Gaswell La TA7 155 E8
Gatchell Gn TA3 168 D1
Gatchell Mdw TA3 168 D1
Gatchells La TA4 132 F2
Gatchell's La TA3 181 B5
Gatcombe Farm Ind Est BS40 35 D3
Gatcombe Rd BS13 22 B5
Gate Cl EX13 198 E3
Gatehouse Ave BS13 22 A5
Gatehouse Cl BS13 22 A5
Gatehouse Ct BS13 22 B5
Gatehouse Ctr The BS13 22 B5
Gatehouse Way BS13 22 A5
Gate La BA5 203 D2
Gaunton Cl TA1 212 D2
Gaunts Cl BS20 1 F4
Gaunt's La BS1 226 C2
Gaunts Rd TA6 135 E6
Gay Cl TA21 222 E6
Gay Ct BA1 28 E3
Gay Elms Rd BS13 22 A4
Gaylard's La TA20 194 B5
Gay's Hill BA1 228 C4
Gay St
Bath BA1 228 B3
Mells BA11 118 B7
Wellington TA21 222 E6
Gazelle Rd
Weston-super-Mare BS24 49 B3
Yeovil BA20 218 D3
Gefle Cl BS1 226 B1
Geldof Dr BA3 78 A2
Gelosia Cl TA7 154 F6
General Higgins Ho TA9 104 E3
Gennes Gr BA9 216 C4
Gentle St
Frome BA11 119 F4
Horningsham BA12 144 E4
Geoffrey Cl BS13 21 E6
George Cl BS48 19 D7
George & Crown Cotts TA17 195 C7
George La
Marshfield SN14 13 E8
South Petherton TA13 220 C4
George Maher Ct TA19 221 C3
Georges Bldgs BA1 28 C3
Georges Ground BA11 119 E2
George Sh Ctr The TA18 224 C6
Georges Ho BA2 45 B6
Georges Mews TA1 213 C2
George Smith Way BA22 218 A6
George's Pl BA2 45 B6
George's Rd BA1 28 A1
Georges Sq BS1 227 B2
George St
Bath BA1 228 B3
Bath, Bathwick BA2 45 B6
Bridgwater TA6 208 F5
Burnham-on-S TA8 104 A7
Charlton Adam TA11 173 F7
George St continued
Glastonbury BA6 206 D5
Portishead BS20 2 C2
Sherborne DT9 225 D4
Taunton TA2 212 F6
Wellington TA21 222 D6
Weston-super-Mare BS23 48 E7
George Sweetman Cl BA9 216 D4
George William Ct TA6 208 F4
Georgian Ct BA11 119 D3
Georgian Ho BA2 228 C2
Georgian House (Mus)* BS1 226 C2
Georgian View BA2 44 C2
Gerard Rd BS23 48 F8
Gerbestone La TA21 180 E6
Gerrard Bldgs 5 BA2 45 B7
Gerrard Cl BS4 22 D7
Geys Hill BA12 144 D8
Giant's Grave TA20 193 A7
Giant's Grave Rd TA20 193 A7
Gibbet La BS14 23 D1
Gibbet Rd BA9 176 B6
Gibbsfold Rd BS13 22 C4
Gibbs' La TA19 184 D5
Gibbs Marsh Trad Est DT10 190 D6
Gibraltar Cotts TA24 123 E4
Giddy La BA3 116 A4
Gielgud Cl TA8 104 D6
Gifford Cl TA20 223 D5
Giffords La TA18 196 C5
Giffords Orch TA12 185 A7
Giffords Pl BS13 22 A7
Gigg La SP8 177 C2
Gilbeck Rd BS48 8 C2
Gilberts Cnr BA6 158 A6
Gilbert Scott Ho BA5 113 A1
Gilbert Scott Mews BA5 113 A2
Gilbert Scott Rd BA5 113 A1
Gilberyn Dr BS22 32 A3
Gilda Cl BS14 23 C5
Gilda Cres BS14 23 B6
Gilda Par BS14 23 C5
Gilda Sq W BS14 23 B5
Giles Cl TA10 171 D4
Giles Farm BA5 113 A1
Gillards TA1 212 B4
Gillards Cl TA21 222 B4
Gillards Mead TA3 192 A7
Gill Cres TA1 212 B1
Gillebank Cl BS14 23 D5
Gillingham Ct TA20 223 D5
Gillingham Terr 3 BA1 28 B1
Gill Mews BS22 32 B4
Gillmore Cl BS22 31 D1
Gillmore Rd BS22 31 D1
Gills La BS26 87 B5
Gillson Cl BS24 49 D2
Gimblett Rd BS22 32 B4
Gipsy Cross TA4 166 A2
Gipsy Dro TA20 193 C4
Gipsy La
Burcott BA5 139 E8
Frome BA11 120 B7
Glastonbury BA6 139 D1
Halse TA4 167 B6
Sampford Arundel TA21 179 D5
Staplegrove TA2 212 D7
Street BA16 207 E4
Taunton TA1 212 C3
Wells BA5 203 A4
GIRT 175 C2
Gladstone Ct BA2 45 C2
Gladstone Pl BA2 45 C2
Gladstone Rd
Bath BA2 45 C2
Bristol BS14 23 B6
Gladstone St
Midsomer Norton BA3 78 B3
Taunton TA2 212 E6
Gladstone Terr
Minehead TA24 201 A5
Wellington TA21 222 E6
Gladstone Villas BA3 115 C5
Glanfield Cl TA4 167 E8
Glanfield Terr BA22 173 F1
Glanvill Ave TA20 223 C5
Glanville Dr BS39 75 E6
Glanville Rd BS28 108 C4
Glanvill Rd BA16 207 C3
Glasses Mead TA1 212 B2
Glass House Hill DT9 225 E3
Glass's Cross TA4 149 E1
Glass's Rocks La TA4 149 D1
GLASTONBURY 206 F6
Glastonbury Abbey* BA6 206 E4
Glastonbury Cl BS48 9 B1
Glastonbury Ct BA21 218 D6
Glastonbury Rd
Meare BA6 138 E4
Wells BA5 203 B2
Glastonbury Tor* BA6 139 D1
Glastonbury Way BS22 32 A2
Glaston Ho BA16 207 D7
Glaston Rd BA16 207 D7
Glebe Ave BS20 2 E4
Glebe Cl BS41 11 C2
Glebe Cotts TA3 169 E2
Glebe Cres TA24 200 E8
Glebe Ho
Bath BA2 45 B5
Portishead BS20 2 E4

Glebe Ho *continued*
Weston-super-Mare BS22 31 F3
Glebeland Cl TA7 156 B8
Glebelands
7 Merriott TA16 195 F7
Minehead TA24 200 E8
Norton Sub Hamdon TA14 185 F3
Nunney BA11 143 B7
Radstock BA3 78 D1
Glebelands Cl BS27 90 B6
Glebe Paddock BA5 139 E8
Glebe Rd
Bath BA2 44 B4
Clevedon BS21 6 C2
Long Ashton BS41 11 C2
Portishead BS20 2 E4
Weston-super-Mare BS23 48 E8
Glebe The
Fivehead TA3 170 F1
Freshford BA3 64 B4
Hinton Charterhouse BA2 63 D2
Queen Camel BA22 174 F3
Timberscombe TA24 130 B4
Timsbury BA2 60 B3
Wrington BS40 35 D2
Glebe Way BS27 90 C6
Glebe Wlk BS31 24 C4
Glebe Yd TA10 172 E4
Glen Ave BS8 10 F8
Glenavon Pk BS9 5 C4
Glen Brook BS9 5 D4
Glencairn Ct BA2 45 B6
Glen Cl TA2 168 B5
Glencoe Bsns Pk BS23 49 A7
Glencoe Terr TA3 168 D1
Glencot La BA5 203 A7
Glencot Rd BA5 203 A6
Glencroft Way BS22 31 E3
Glendale 16 BS8 11 F6
Glendevon Rd BS14 23 A3
Glen Dr
Bristol BS9 5 D5
Taunton TA2 168 F6
Gleneagles Cl
Nailsea BS48 9 A1
Weston-super-Mare BS22 31 F3
Glenmore Rd TA24 201 A7
Glen The
Saltford BS31 25 F1
Weston-super-Mare BS22 31 B2
Glenthorne Ave BA21 219 B7
Glenthorne Nature Trail Gate★ EX35 122 D5
Glenthorne Rd 9 TA2 212 F6
Glentworth Ct 19 BS23 30 C1
Glentworth Rd BS8 226 B2
Glen View BA3 115 E7
Glenview Ho BA2 79 D8
Glenville Rd BA21 219 D6
Glenwood Gdns TA2 212 F8
Glenwood Mans BS23 30 D1
Glenwood Rise BS20 1 F5
Glen Yeo Terr BS49 34 C4
Glider Ave BS24 49 B4
Globe Orch TA18 196 C6
Gloucester Ho 11 BS2 227 C3
Gloucester La 18 BS2 227 C3
Gloucester Rd
Bath BA1 28 C3
Bridgwater TA6 208 F2
Burnham-on-S TA8 104 C7
Upper Swainswick BA1 28 A7
Gloucester Row 6 BS8 11 F7
Gloucester St
4 Bath BA1 228 B3
5 Bristol BS2 227 B4
8 Bristol, Clifton BS8 11 F7
Taunton TA1 213 A4
Weston-super-Mare BS23 48 D7
Glovers DT9 225 D5
Glovers Cl
Milborne Port DT9 217 D2
4 Stoke sub Hamdon TA14 185 F4
Glovers Ct BA20 218 F4
Glovers Field BS25 70 F7
Glovers Wlk 18 BA20 219 B4
Glovers Wlk Sh Ctr BA20 219 B5
Glynsmead TA20 198 C8
Glynswood TA20 223 C5
GOAR KNAPP 219 D5
GOATHILL 189 B4
Goathill La BA8 176 C3
Goathill Rd DT9 189 B4
GOATHURST 153 B5
Godhams La TA4 165 A7
Godminster Ct BA10 215 E6
Godminster La BA10 215 E4
GODNEY 139 A5
Godney Cl BA6 206 F7
Godney Dro BA5 139 B6
Godney Rd BA5, BA6 139 A4
Godwin Dr BS48 8 C3
Goeffrey Farrant Wlk TA1 213 A5
Goes La BA7 158 F2
Gogs Orch BS28 108 C3
Gold Corner Dro TA9 137 A6
Goldcrest Way BS20 2 F6
Goldcroft BA21 219 B6
Goldcroft Ct BA21 219 B6
Goldenhaye La TA20 194 D3
Golden Hill
Stourton Caundle DT10 189 F1
Wiveliscombe TA4 210 C5
Golden Lion Ct BS1 227 B2
Golden Valley La BS30 25 E8
Golden Valley Prim Sch BS48 8 F2
Goldfinches La BA6 139 D3
Gold Hill
Batcombe BA4 142 D2
Shepton Mallet BA4 205 B7
Golding Cl BA5 203 C4
Golding's La DT9 217 C1
Goldney Ave BS8 226 A2
Goldney Cl BS39 58 F1
Goldney Rd BS8 226 A2
Goldney Way BS39 58 F1
GOLD'S CROSS 57 E6
Goldsmiths La EX13 198 A4
Goldsmoor Cross EX16 178 E3
Gold St DT10 190 B4
Golf Club La BS31 25 E2
Golf Course Rd BA2 45 D6
Golf Links La BA3 114 E3
Golf Links Rd TA8 85 A2
Golledge Cl BA3 96 C4
GOLSONCOTT 131 D2
Gooch Cl
Bridgwater TA6 209 B4
Frome BA11 120 D6
Gooch Way BS22 32 B3
Goodard Dr BS22 32 B4
Goodeaves Cl BA3 117 A7
Goodeaves Cotts BA3 117 A7
Goodeve Pk BS9 5 D3
Goodeve Rd BS9 5 D3
Good Hill BA4 142 E2
Goodlands La TA1 212 F4
Good's La TA5 152 C5
Goodwin Dr BS14 22 F4
Goodymoor Ave BA5 203 B5
Goodymoor La BA5 203 B5
Goold Cl BA2 43 A8
Goosander Cl TA24 201 C4
Goosard La BS39 77 E8
Gooseacre Ct BA22 197 B8
Gooseacre La
East Coker BA22 197 B8
Yeovil BA22 218 A1
Gooseham La BS28 108 F4
Gooseham Mead BS49 34 D4
Goose La
Chilton Polden TA7 137 B3
Horton TA19 183 C2
Gooselade BA16 207 C3
Gooseland Cl BS14 22 F3
GOOSENFORD 169 A6
Goose St BA11 101 E5
Goosey La BS22 32 C2
Gordano Bsns Pk BS20 2 E5
Gordano Gdns BS20 4 B4
Gordano Rd BS20 3 D7
Gordano Sch BS20 2 D3
Gordano View BS20 2 C5
Gordano Way BS20 3 F5
Gordon Bldgs BA3 79 A3
Gordon Rd
Bath BA2 45 B5
Bristol BS8 226 B3
Peasedown St John BA2 79 D8
Taunton TA1 213 A3
Weston-super-Mare BS23 48 F7
Yeovil BA21 219 C6
Gordon's Cl TA1 213 B1
Gordon Terr TA6 209 A5
GORE 187 F6
Gorefield TA13 220 D2
Gore Hedge 14 BA11 119 F4
Gore La
Chapmanslade BA13 121 B4
Pitney TA10 172 C7
Gore Rd TA8 85 A1
Gores Pk BS39 59 B2
Gore Sq TA4 167 E8
Gorlangton Cl BS14 23 A7
Gorlegg TA21 179 E5
Gorpit La TA5 134 F8
Gorse La
Bristol BS8 226 B2
Cold Ashton BS30, SN14 12 D7
Gort Rd TA2 168 B6
Gosford Mans 6 BS23 30 C1
Goshawk Dr 8 BS20 2 F6
Goslet Rd BS14 23 E5
Goss Barton BS48 8 D1
Goss Cl BS48 8 C1
Goss Dr BA16 207 B3
Goss La BS48 8 C1
Goss View BS48 8 C1
Goswell Cl BA16 207 C5
Goswell Rd BA16 207 C5
GOTHELNEY GREEN 153 B8
GOTTON 169 B7
Gough Cl 11 TA16 195 F7
Gough Pl BS27 90 A8
Gough's Caves★ BS27 90 D8
Gould Cl
Bristol BS13 22 C5
Street BA16 207 E6
Gouldsbrook Terr TA18 224 B6
Gouldsbrook View TA18 224 C7
GOULD'S GROUND 119 E5
Gould's Ground 2 BA11 119 E5
Gould's La 1 BA11 119 E5
Goulston Rd BS13 22 A5
Goulston Wlk BS13 22 A5
Gournay Ct BS39 77 A3
Governors Ho BA2 44 D6
Govier's La TA23 202 C7
Grace Cl BS49 34 B8
Grace Dr BA3 78 A2
Grace Martin's La BA22 174 F3
Grace Rd BS22 32 B4
Gradwell Cl BS22 32 B3
Grafton Cl TA2 213 A8
Graham Rd BS23 48 E7
Graham Way TA4 167 E6
Grainger Ct BS11 4 E7
Grain Store The 9 BS1 227 A2
Graitney Cl BS49 35 A8
Granaries The BA3 115 A3
Granary Orch DT9 187 F5
Granary The 8 BS1 227 A2
Granary Way TA3 181 D8
Granby Hill BS8 11 F6
Granby Rd BA22 174 A2
Grand Par BA2 228 C2
Grand Pier★ BS23 48 D7
Grand Western Canal (Country Pk)★ EX16 178 F2
Granfield Gdns BS40 53 A5
Grange Ave
Highbridge TA9 104 E3
Street BA16 207 B6
Grange Bsns Pk The BS24 33 A5
Grange Cl
Cannington TA5 135 C2
Wellington TA21 222 E5
Weston-super-Mare BS23 48 E1
Grange Cnr DT8 199 E7
Grange Dr
Bridgwater TA6 208 D4
Taunton TA2 213 A6
Grange End BA3 97 B7
Grange Farm Rd BS49 17 A1
Grangefields BA16 207 D5
Grange Gdns TA2 213 A7
Grange La 6 BS13 21 F4
Grange Paddock TA9 106 E4
Grange Rd
Bristol, Bishopsworth BS13 22 A5
Bristol BS8 226 A3
Frome BA11 120 A7
Huntspill TA9 136 A8
Saltford BS31 25 C3
Street BA16 207 D7
Weston-super-Mare BS23 48 E1
Grange The
Bath BA1 27 C1
Bristol BS9 5 D7
Chilton Polden TA7 137 B2
Flax Bourton BS48 19 F7
Kingston St Mary TA2 168 E8
Langport TA10 171 E5
Grange Way TA6 135 F5
Grange Wlk TA2 213 A6
Grants Cl BA9 216 B4
Grant's Hill EX16, TA22 163 F2
Grants La BA9 216 D4
Grant's La
Wedmore BS28 108 D4
Wiveliscombe TA4 210 D6
Granville Chapel 5 BS8 11 F5
Granville Rd BA1 27 E4
Granville Way DT9 225 E6
Grasmere TA6 208 C5
Grasmere Dr BS23 48 F4
Grass Meers Dr BS14 23 A4
Grassmere Rd BS49 34 B8
Grass Rd TA8 65 F4
Grass Royal BA21 219 C6
Grass Royal Jun Sch BA21 219 C6
Gratton La EX35 122 A4
Gravelands La TA3 169 D3
Gravel Hill BS40 56 B7
Gravel La TA3, TA19 183 F6
Gravel Pit Cross EX36 145 E6
Gravel Pits DT9 225 D3
Gravel Wlk BA1 228 B3
Gravenchon Way BA16 207 A6
Graves Cl 7 TA6 209 B4
Gray Hollow BS40 74 F4
Grayling Ho BS9 5 F7
Gray's Almshouses 17 TA1 213 A4
Grays Ave TA7 154 E6
Grays Hill BA2 80 B5
Gray's Hill EX15 180 D1
Gray's La EX15 180 D1
Grays Rd TA1 213 B4
Grays Terr TA1 213 B4
Great Ann St BS2 227 C3
Great Barton BA4 205 D6
Great Bedford St BA1 228 B4
Great Bow Yd TA10 171 F5
Great Brockeridge BS9 5 F6
Great Cl EX15 179 E1
Great Cnr 5 BA21 218 C6
GREAT ELM 118 F7
Great Field La TA14 185 F4
Great Gardens BA4 205 C6
Great George St
Bristol, Brandon Hill BS1 226 C2
Bristol, St Pauls BS2 227 C3
Great Hayles Rd BS14 23 A6
Great Hill BA9 161 D2
Great House Ct BA6 138 D4
Great House St TA24 130 B5
Great La
Knole TA10 173 A4
Shepton Beauchamp TA19 184 E4
Great Mdw TA22 163 D6
Great Mead
Taunton TA1 212 B3
Yeovil BA21 219 F7
Great Orch BA22 173 E2
Great Ostry BA4 205 B6
Great Pit La BA22, DT9 188 B7
Great Pulteney St BA2 228 C3
Great Ringaton La EX36 162 B6
Great St TA14 185 E2
Great Stanhope St BA1 228 A2
Greatstone La BS40 37 F5
Great Western La TA11 211 D3
Great Western Rd
Chard TA20 223 D5
Clevedon BS21 6 D2
Martock TA12 185 E7
Great Western St BA11 120 A4
Great Western Terr BA21 219 D5
Great Western Way TA2 212 A6
Great Withy Dro BA5 206 C8
Greatwood Cl TA6 209 A2
Great Wood Cl BS13 22 C4
Grebe Cl TA6 209 B4
Grebe Ct TA6 209 B4
Grebe Rd
Bridgwater TA6 209 B4
Taunton TA2 213 B6
Greenacre
Wembdon TA6 208 D6
Weston-super-Mare BS22 31 B2
Green Acre Rd BS14 23 A3
Greenacres
Bath BA1 27 B3
Bristol BS9 5 E7
Midsomer Norton BA3 77 E1
Greenacres Pk BA21 187 A5
Greenaleigh Lower Rd TA24 125 C4
Greenaleigh Upper Rd TA24 125 C4
Greenbank Gdns BA1 27 B1
Greenbrook Terr TA1 212 E4
Green Cl
Holford TA5 133 D4
Paulton BS39 77 E6
Sparkford BA22 175 A4
Green Cotts BA2 45 C2
Greendale TA19 221 B3
Greenditch Ave BS13 22 C5
Greenditch Cl BA3 96 C3
Green Ditch La BA3 96 B6
GREEN DOWN 94 B8
Greendown Pl BA2 45 A1
Green Dragon Ct 4 TA6 208 F4
Green Dro TA11 158 A4
Green Farm Ind Est BA13 121 C4
Greenfield Cres BS48 8 E3
Greenfield La TA7 136 D2
Greenfield Pk BS20 2 C3
Greenfield Pl BS23 48 C8
Greenfield Prim Sch BS4 22 C7
Greenfield Rd BS31 24 D3
Greenfields
Bridgwater TA6 208 F3
Crewkerne TA18 224 C7
Greenfields Ave BS29 51 A3
Greenfield Terr TA20 198 D8
Greenfield Wlk BA3 78 A3
Greenfylde CE First Sch TA19 221 C3
Greengage Cl 6 BS22 49 E8
GREEN GATE 178 B2
Green Gate EX16 178 B2
GREENHAM
Drimpton 199 E7
Wellington 179 B7
Greenham Bsns Pk TA21 179 C5
Greenham La TA18 199 E7
Greenham's Cross TA14 185 F2
Greenham Yd TA18 199 E7
Greenhayes BS27 90 B8
Greenhays Foot EX13 198 B6
GREENHILL 78 A3
Greenhill DT9 225 D4
Greenhill Cl
Nailsea BS48 8 D2
Weston-super-Mare BS22 32 A3
Greenhill Croft BS25 52 B4
Greenhill Cross EX36 162 B2
Greenhill La
Alston Sutton BS26 88 E5
Sandford BS25 52 B4
Greenhill Pl BA3 78 A3
Greenhill Rd
Midsomer Norton BA3 78 A3
Sandford BS25 52 B4
Yeovil BA21 219 D7
Green Knap La TA20 193 C2
Green La
Bristol BS11 4 B8
Brompton Regis TA22 148 B1
Butcombe BS40 55 A7
Castle Cary BA7 214 F4
Chard Junction TA20 198 D7
Chardstock EX13 198 B7
Chard TA20 193 F1
Charlton Horethorne DT9 176 A2
Charlton Horethorne, Sigwells DT9 175 F2
Corfe TA3 181 E7
Corsley Heath BA12 144 E7
Cricket St Thomas TA20 194 F3
East Chinnock BA22 196 E8
East Coker BA22 197 B8
Failand BS8 10 C4
Farrington Gurney BS39 76 F6
Felton BS40 37 C3
Fivehead TA3 170 E2
Freshford BA3 64 B2
Frome BA11 119 D4
Hinton Charterhouse BA2 63 E1
Green La *continued*
Ilminster TA19 183 E2
Kington Magna SP8 177 E2
Leigh u M BA3, BA11 117 B2
Marshfield SN14 13 E8
Oakhill BA3 114 E4
Pitcombe BA7 215 A1
Priddy BS40 73 B7
Queen Camel BA22 174 F3
Sampford Arundel TA21 179 F4
Shepton Beauchamp TA19 184 E3
Sherborne DT9 188 E1
Southwick BA14 83 D2
Stoke St Michael BA3 116 B5
Stratton-on-t F BA3 96 E1
Street BA16 207 C4
Tatworth TA20 193 D1
Winsley BA15 64 F6
Greenland La TA24 131 B1
Greenland Rd BS22 31 D1
Greenlands TA1 213 B2
Greenlands Rd BA2 79 C8
Green Lane Ave BA16 207 C4
Green Lane End TA19 184 E3
Green Lane Gate BA9 176 A8
Green Mead BA21 218 C5
Greenmoor La BA21 187 A5
GREEN ORE 94 C1
Green Ore Est BA5 94 B1
Green Park La BA11 101 F6
Green Park Mews BA1 228 A2
Green Park Rd BA1 228 B2
Green Parlor Rd BA3 79 D1
GREEN PARLOUR 79 D2
Green Pastures Rd BS48 9 B2
Green Pits La BA11 143 B7
Green Pk
Bath BA1 228 B2
Rode BA11 101 E8
Green Quarry BA21 219 A6
Green Ride BA12 161 F7
Greenridge BS39 58 F3
Greenridge Cl BS13 21 E4
GREENSBROOK 58 F3
Green's Dro BA6 206 C7
Green's Hill TA4 151 C5
Greenslade Gdns BS48 8 D3
Greens Pl BA5 203 D3
Green St
Bath BA1 228 C2
Hinton St George TA17 195 D7
Shoscombe BA2 79 E5
Ston Easton BA3 95 E8
Greenstalls Pk BA22 173 F2
Green The
Backwell BS48 19 A5
8 Barwick BA22 197 F8
Bath BA2 44 D1
Bridgwater TA6 208 E2
Brushford TA22 163 E4
Coleford BA3 116 F6
Easton BA5 111 A4
Faulkland BA3 80 D2
Hinton Charterhouse BA2 63 F1
Ilchester BA22 173 E2
Locking BS24 50 A4
33 Martock TA12 185 E6
Pill BS20 4 D4
Pitminster TA3 181 E6
1 Sherborne DT9 225 D4
Williton TA4 202 D3
Winscombe BS25 70 A7
Green Tree Rd BA3 78 B3
GREENVALE 60 B1
Greenvale Cl BA2 60 B1
Greenvale Dr BA2 60 B1
Greenvale Rd BS39 77 D5
GREENWAY 167 D8
Greenway
Bishops Lydeard TA4 167 E8
Faulkland BA3 80 C1
Ilminster TA19 221 B1
Minehead TA24 200 D6
Monkton Heathfield TA2 169 B6
North Curry TA3 170 B3
Watchet TA23 202 B7
Greenway Ave TA2 212 E6
Greenway Cl BA9 216 D4
Greenway Cotts TA4 167 E8
Greenway Cres TA2 212 E7
Greenway Ct BA2 44 F4
Greenway La
Barrington TA13 184 E5
Bath BA2 45 A4
Blagdon Hill TA3 181 B5
Cold Ashton SN14 12 D5
Combe St Nicholas TA20 193 E6
Stoke St Mary TA3 169 D2
Wiveliscombe TA4 210 A5
Greenway Pk 3 BS21 6 F3
Greenway Rd
Castle Cary BA7 214 B6
Rockwell Green TA21 222 A5
Taunton TA2 212 E6
Greenways BA3 96 C2
Greenway Terr TA2 168 D8
Greenwell La BS40 53 C7
Greenwood Cl TA9 136 B8
Greenwood Rd
Weston-super-Mare BS22 31 E2
Yeovil BA21 218 D7
Gregory Mead BS49 17 A1
Gregorys Cres TA21 222 D7
Gregorys Gr BA2 62 D8
Gregorys Tyning BS39 77 F6
GREINTON 155 F7
Greinton BS24 49 A2
Grenville Ave BS24 50 A4

Grenville Cl BA6 . . . . 157 E4
Grenville Ho TA6 . . . . 208 F2
Grenville Pl **7** BS1 . . . . . 11 F5
Grenville Rd TA8 . . . . 104 C7
Grenville View TA4 . . . . . . 167 E6
GREYFIELD 59 C2
Greyfield Comm BS39 . . . . 59 C2
Greyfield Rd BS39 . . . . . . 59 C2
Greyfield View BS39 . . . . . 58 F1
Greyhound Cl BA9 . . . . . . 216 C4
GREYLAKE 155 C4
GREYLAKE FOSSE 155 C5
Greylake Reserve★ TA7 . 155 D5
Greylands BS13 . . . . 21 F7
Grey's Cnr BA9 . . . . 161 A3
Greys Rd TA16 . . . . 195 F7
Greystoke Bsns Ctr BS20 . . 2 D4
GRIBB 199 B6
Gribb View TA20 . . . . 199 B6
Grib La BS40 . . . . 54 F2
Griffen Cl TA6 . . . . 208 E6
Griffen Rd BS24 . . . . 49 E7
Griffin Cl
  Wells BA5 . . . . 203 B6
  Weston-super-Mare BS22 . . 32 B2
Griffin Ct BA1 . . . . 228 B2
Griffin La TA3 . . . . 182 F7
Griffin Rd
  Clevedon BS21 . . . . 6 E3
  Hatch Beauchamp TA3 . . 182 F7
Griggfield Wlk BS14 . . . . . 23 A7
Grimsey La SP8 . . . . 177 F8
Grinfield Ave BS13 . . . . . . 22 C4
Grinfield Ct BS13 . . . . 22 C4
Groats **9** TA4 . . . . 167 F8
Grooms Orch TA21 . . . . . 222 C5
GROSVENOR 28 C1
Grosvenor Bridge Rd BA1 28 C1
Grosvenor Ct BA22 . . . . . 173 E2
Grosvenor Pk BA1 . . . . . . 28 C1
Grosvenor Pl BA1 . . . . . . 28 C1
Grosvenor Rd
  Bristol BS2 . . . . 227 C4
  Stalbridge DT10 . . . . . . 190 B4
Grosvenor Terr BA1 . . . . . 28 C2
Grosvenor Villas **9** BA1 . 28 B1
Grove Alley BA10 . . . . . . 215 E6
Grove Ave
  Bristol BS1 . . . . 227 A1
  Bristol, Coombe Dingle BS9 . 5 D7
  Yeovil BA20 . . . . 218 F5
Grove Cl
  Penselwood BA9 . . . . . . 161 E2
  Watchet TA23 . . . . 202 C6
Grove Ct BS9 . . . . 5 E5
Grove Dr
  Taunton TA2 . . . . 212 F8
  Weston-super-Mare BS22 . . 31 C1
Grove Hill TA7 . . . . 155 B1
Grove Ho
  Bath BA2 . . . . 45 B6
  Burnham-on-S TA8 . . . . 104 A8
Grove Jun Sch BS48 . . . . . 18 D8
Grove La
  Faulkland BA3 . . . . 80 D2
  Frome BA11 . . . . 119 E3
  Knole TA10 . . . . 173 A4
  North Cheriton BA8 . . . . 176 E5
  Stalbridge DT10 . . . . . . 190 B4
  West Anstey EX36 . . . . . 162 D6
  Weston-super-Mare BS23 . . 48 D8
Grove Lane CI DT10 . . . . 190 B4
Grove Leaze BS11 . . . . 4 D6
Grove Mead BA11 . . . . . . 119 E2
Grove Orch BS40 . . . . 54 E2
Grove Park Ct BS23 . . . . . 30 D1
Grove Park Rd BS23 . . . . . 30 D1
Grove Pl TA24 . . . . 201 B4
Grove Rd
  Banwell BS29 . . . . 50 E4
  Blue Anchor TA24 . . . . . 131 B6
  Bristol, Coombe Dingle BS9 . 5 D8
  Burnham-on-S TA8 . . . . 104 A8
  Huntspill TA9 . . . . 136 A8
  Weston-super-Mare BS23 . . 48 D8
  Weston-super-Mare, Milton
    BS22 . . . . 31 C1
Groves La TA24 . . . . 131 B6
Grove St BA2 . . . . 228 C3
Groves The BS13 . . . . 22 D4
Grove Terr **8** TA2 . . . . 212 F6
Grove The
  Bath BA1 . . . . 27 C1
  Bristol BS1 . . . . 227 A1
  Burnham-on-S TA8 . . . . . 85 B1
  Frome BA11 . . . . 119 E2
  Hallatrow BS39 . . . . 77 B7
  Ruishton TA3 . . . . 169 C3
  Sherborne DT9 . . . . . . 225 D3
  Winscombe BS25 . . . . . . 51 F1
  Wraxall BS48 . . . . 9 C3
Grove Wood Rd BA3 . . . . . 78 F1
Grughay La TA3 . . . . 182 E5
Grunter's La BA3 . . . . 114 F7
Gryphon Sch The DT9 . . . 225 D4
Guard Ave BA22 . . . . 218 B6
Guard House La **9** BA5 . 203 D4
Gug The BS39 . . . . 59 C2
Guild Ct BS1 . . . . 227 B2
Guildford Pl TA1 . . . . . . 212 F3
Guildhall La BS28 . . . . . . 108 C4
Guillemot Rd **9** BS20 . . . 2 F6
Guineagore La DT9 . . . . . 188 B4
Guinea La BA1 . . . . 228 C3
Guinea St BS1 . . . . 227 A1
Guinevere Cl BA21 . . . . . 218 D7
Gullen BA2 . . . . 80 A6
Gulliford Cl TA9 . . . . 104 D4

Gulliford's Bank BS21 . . . . 6 F2
Gullimores Gdns BS13 . . . 22 B4
Gullock Tyning BA3 . . . . . 78 B1
Gullons Cl BS13 . . . . 22 A6
Gullon Wlk BS13 . . . . 21 F5
Gulway Mead TA20 . . . . . 198 D8
Gumbrells Ct TA6 . . . . . . 209 A4
Gunners La BA22 . . . . . . 218 A5
Gunning's La BA4 . . . . . . 142 F2
Gunville La
  Charlton Horethorne
    DT9 . . . . 176 A2
  East Coker BA22 . . . . . 197 D8
Gunwyn Cl BA6 . . . . 206 E6
GUPWORTHY 148 C6
GURNEY SLADE 114 F7
Gurney St TA5 . . . . 135 C2
Gurnville Cotts BA11 . . . . 119 F2
Guthrie Rd BS8 . . . . 226 A4
Gwynne La TA1 . . . . 213 A3
Gwyther Mead TA1 . . . . . 212 A3
Gyffarde Ct **4** TA1 . . . 213 A4
Gyffarde St TA1 . . . . 213 A4
Gypsy La
  Cheddar BS28 . . . . 89 D6
  Keynsham BS31 . . . . 42 B8
  Marshfield SN14 . . . . . . 13 F7

H

Haberfield Hill BS8 . . . . . . 4 E2
Haberfield Ho **1** BS8 . . 11 F6
Hacketty Way TA24 . . . . . 124 B3
Hack La
  Holford TA5 . . . . 133 F2
  Nether Stowey TA5 . . . . 134 A2
Hack Mead La TA9 . . . . . 105 L1
HACKNESS 136 D8
Hackness Rd TA9 . . . . . . 136 E8
Haddon Cl TA22 . . . . 148 B2
Haddon La
  Hartford TA4 . . . . 164 C7
  North Petherton TA6 . . . 153 C2
  Stalbridge DT10 . . . . . 190 C5
Haddon View TA22 . . . . . 148 B2
Hadley Rd BA2 . . . . 45 B2
Hadrian Cl
  Bristol BS9 . . . . 5 C4
  Keynsham BS31 . . . . . . 24 F7
HADSPEN 214 F6
Hadspen Garden★ BA7 . 160 A2
Hadworthy La TA6 . . . . . 153 F4
Hafner Gn BS24 . . . . 49 C4
Hagget Cl TA6 . . . . 208 F1
Hagleys Gn TA4 . . . . 151 B7
Haig Cl BS9 . . . . 5 B7
Haig Rd TA2 . . . . 168 B6
HAINES HILL 212 E2
Haines Hill TA1 . . . . 212 E2
Haines La DT8 . . . . 199 D5
Haines Pk TA1 . . . . 212 E1
Hains La DT10 . . . . 190 F7
Halcombe TA20 . . . . 223 C2
HALCON 213 D5
Halcon Cnr TA1 . . . . 213 D4
Halcon Com Prim Sch
  TA1 . . . . 213 D4
HALE 177 D6
Hale La BA9 . . . . 177 C6
Halesleigh Rd TA6 . . . . . 208 E5
Hales Mdw BA21 . . . . . . 187 D6
Hale Way TA2 . . . . 213 D7
Half Acre TA4 . . . . 202 D2
Half Acre Cl
  Bristol BS14 . . . . 23 A3
  Williton TA4 . . . . 202 D2
Halfacre La BS14 . . . . . . 23 B4
Half Acres DT9 . . . . 225 C3
Half Moon St **6** DT9 . . 225 D3
Halfpenny Row BA11 . . . . 82 E1
Halfway TA6 . . . . 208 E2
Half Yd BS40 . . . . 53 D8
Hallam Ct BS21 . . . . 6 C4
Hallam Rd BS21 . . . . 6 C4
Hallards Cl BS11 . . . . 4 F8
Hallatrow Rd BS39 . . . . . 77 C6
Hallen Dr BS9 . . . . 5 C7
Hallet Gdns BA20 . . . . . 219 A4
Hallets Orch BA22 . . . . . 186 B6
Hallett Rd BA7 . . . . 214 B7
Halletts Way
  Axminster EX13 . . . . . 198 A1
  Portishead BS20 . . . . . . 2 D5
Hall Hill EX35 . . . . 122 B5
Halliwell Rd BS20 . . . . . . 1 D4
Hall La 12 B3
Hall Terr TA8 . . . . 104 A8
HALSE 167 B6
Halse Cnr TA4 . . . . 167 D5
Halse La TA24 . . . . 147 B6
Halse Manor TA4 . . . . . . 167 B6
HALSTOCK 197 C3
Halston Dr BS2 . . . . 227 C4
HALSWAY 151 B8
Halsway TA6 . . . . 209 C5
Halsway Hill TA4 . . . . . . 132 F1
Halsway La
  Bicknoller TA4 . . . . . . 133 A1
  Crowcombe TA4 . . . . . 151 A8
Halswell Cl TA6 . . . . 208 E4
Halswell Gdns BS13 . . . . . 22 B4
Halswell Rd BS21 . . . . 6 D1
Halt End BS14 . . . . 23 C3
Halter Path Dro TA7 . . . . 137 C7
Halves La BA22 . . . . 197 D5
Halwyn Cl BS9 . . . . 5 D5

Halyard Dr TA6 . . . . 208 E7
Halyard Pl TA24 . . . . 201 B7
Halyard Wy BS20 . . . . 2 F7
HAM
  Creech St Michael 169 E4
  Holcombe 116 D6
  Paulton 77 F5
  Wellington 180 D8
Hamber Lea TA4 . . . . . . 167 F8
Hambledon Rd BS22 . . . . . 32 C4
HAMBRIDGE 184 D8
Hambridge Com Prim Sch
  TA10 . . . . 184 D8
Ham Cl TA3 . . . . 58 F1
Hamdon Cl **12** TA14 . . . 185 F4
Hamdon Hill Country Pk★
  TA14 . . . . 185 F3
Hamdon View TA14 . . . . 185 E3
Hamdown Ct TA10 . . . . . 172 B6
Ham Gn
  Hambridge TA10 . . . . . 184 D8
  Pill BS20 . . . . 4 D3
Ham Gr BS39 . . . . 77 E5
HAM GREEN 4 E4
Ham Hill
  Coleford BA3 . . . . 116 D6
  Combe St Nicholas TA20 . 193 D8
  High Ham TA10 . . . . . . 156 A2
  Langford Budville TA21 . . 166 A1
  Radstock BA3 . . . . 78 F3
Ham Hill Ctry Pk★ TA14 . 186 A3
Ham Hill Rd
  Odcombe BA22 . . . . . . 186 C2
  Stoke sub Hamdon TA14 . 185 F4
Hamilton Ct
  11 Bristol BS1 . . . . . 227 A4
  Taunton TA1 . . . . 213 C4
  Wells BA5 . . . . 203 B4
Hamilton Ho BA1 . . . . . . 27 E3
Hamilton Rd
  Bath BA1 . . . . 27 E2
  Taunton TA1 . . . . 213 C4
  8 Weston-super-Mare
    BS23 . . . . 30 C1
Hamilton Terr BA2 . . . . . 79 F5
Hamilton Wy BS14 . . . . . 23 D3
Ham La
  Bishop Sutton BS39 . . . . 57 C5
  Burnham-on-S TA8 . . . . 104 B6
  Compton Dundon TA11 . . 157 A3
  Croscombe BA4, BA5 . . . 204 E7
  Dundry BS41 . . . . 21 D3
  Farrington Gurney BS39 . . 76 F5
  Kingston Seymour BS21 . . 16 B2
  Marnhull DT10 . . . . . . 190 F6
  North End BS49 . . . . . . 17 A3
  Paulton BS39 . . . . 77 E5
  Pawlett TA6 . . . . 135 E6
  Rodhuish TA23 . . . . . . 149 C8
  Shepton Mallet BA4 . . . 205 A7
  Sherborne DT9 . . . . . . 188 A3
  Trent DT9 . . . . 187 F5
  Wraxall BS48 . . . . 9 B4
  Yatton BS49 . . . . 17 A3
Ham La E BA2 . . . . 204 F7
Hamlands La TA21 . . . . . 167 D1
Hamlet The
  Nailsea BS48 . . . . 9 A3
  Templecombe BA8 . . . . 176 E1
Hamley La
  Buckland St Mary TA20 . . 193 B8
  Combe St Nicholas TA20 . 193 B8
Ham Link BS40 . . . . 53 F3
Hamlyn Cl TA1 . . . . 212 C1
Hamlyn Rd BA6 . . . . 206 E6
Ham Mdw DT10 . . . . . . 190 E6
Hammer La BA2, BA3 . . . 100 C8
Hammer St BA10 . . . . . . 161 B8
Hammet St
  8 North Petherton TA6 . 153 E3
  Taunton TA1 . . . . 213 A3
Hammets Wharf **1** TA1 . 212 F4
Hammond Gdns BS9 . . . . . 5 E7
HAMP 208 F3
Hamp Ave TA6 . . . . 208 F3
Hamp Brook Way TA6 . . . 208 E2
Hamp Com Jun Sch TA6 . 208 F3
Hampden Rd BS22 . . . . . . 31 E2
Hamp Green Rise TA6 . . . 209 A3
Hamp Ind Est TA6 . . . . . 209 A3
Hamp Inf Sch TA6 . . . . . 208 F3
Hamp St TA6 . . . . 208 F3
Hampton Cl
  5 Barwick BA22 . . . . 197 F8
  Bridgwater TA6 . . . . . . 209 D7
Hampton Cnr BS11 . . . . . . 4 E6
Hampton H BA2 . . . . 45 D8
Hampton Ho **10** BA1 . . . 28 C1
Hampton La BS8 . . . . . . 226 B4
Hampton Rd BS6 . . . . . . 226 C4
Hampton Row BA2 . . . . . 45 B8
Hampton View BA1 . . . . . 28 B1
Ham Rd
  Brean BS24, TA8 . . . . . . 66 B3
  Burnham-on-S TA9 . . . . . 85 E4
  Creech St Michael TA3 . . 169 D4
  Wellington TA21 . . . . . 180 D8
Hamrod La TA4 . . . . 154 C5
Hams La BS26 . . . . 68 C3
Ham's La TA11 . . . . 174 D7
Hams Rd BS31 . . . . 24 F7
Ham St BA6 . . . . 158 B5
HAM STREET 158 B5
Ham Wall Wetland★
  BA6 . . . . 138 C2
Hamway La TA20 . . . . . . 193 C8
HAMWOOD 68 C7
Hamwood TA1 . . . . 212 B4

Ham Wood Cl BS24 . . . . . 49 B2
Hamwood Cotts TA1 . . . . 212 B4
Hamwood La TA3 . . . . . . 181 B8
Hamwood Terr TA1 . . . . 212 B4
Hanbury Cl BS8 . . . . 226 A4
Hanbury Rd BS8 . . . . . . 226 A4
Handel Rd BS31 . . . . 24 E5
Handlemaker Rd BA11 . . 119 C2
Handy Cross TA4 . . . . . . 151 A2
Hanford Ct BS14 . . . . 23 D7
Hanger's Way TA24 . . . . 201 D2
Hanger Wy BS14 . . . . 22 F5
Hang Hill BA2 . . . . 80 A6
Hanging Hill La TA13 . . . 184 F4
Hanglands La BA8 . . . . . 176 C2
Hanham La BS39 . . . . 77 F7
Hanham Way BS48 . . . . . . 8 B2
Hankridge Way TA1 . . . . 213 E5
Hanna Cl BA2 . . . . 44 B6
Hannah Dr BS22 . . . . 50 C5
Hannah More Cl
  Cheddar BS27 . . . . 90 B7
  Wrington BS40 . . . . 35 C2
Hannah More Inf Sch
  BS48 . . . . 18 D8
Hannah More Prim Sch
  BS1 . . . . 227 C2
Hannah More Rd BS48 . . . 18 C8
Hannahs La BA5 . . . . . . 110 E6
Hannay Rd BS27 . . . . 71 B1
Hann Cl BA5 . . . . 203 B2
Hanning Cl TA19 . . . . . . 221 F6
Hanning Pk TA19 . . . . . . 183 C1
Hanning Rd TA19 . . . . . . 183 C1
Hanny's La BS40 . . . . 39 C3
Hanover Cl
  Shepton Mallet BA4 . . . 205 A6
  Weston-super-Mare BS22 . . 32 A4
Hanover Ct
  Bath BA1 . . . . 28 B2
  Castle Cary BA7 . . . . . 214 C5
  Dulverton TA22 . . . . . 163 D7
  Radstock BA3 . . . . 79 C2
Hanover Gdns BA11 . . . . 119 D3
Hanover Ho BS20 . . . . 2 B5
Hanover Pl
  Bath BA1 . . . . 45 B8
  Bristol BS1 . . . . 226 B1
Hanover St
  2 Bath BA1 . . . . . . 28 B1
  2 Bristol BS1 . . . . . 227 A2
Hanover Terr **5** BA1 . . . 28 B1
Hansetown Rd TA4 . . . . . 148 F1
Hansford Cl BA2 . . . . 44 F1
Hansford Mews BA2 . . . . 44 F1
Hansford Sq BA2 . . . . . . 44 F1
Hanson's Way **1** BS21 . . 6 C2
Hans Price Acad BS23 . . . 48 F5
Hans Price Cl **18** BS23 . . 48 E8
Hans Price Ho **13** BS23 . . 48 E8
Hantone Hill BA2 . . . . . . 45 F8
Hapil Cl BS25 . . . . 51 F4
Happerton La BS20 . . . . . . 4 D2
Hapsburg Cl BS22 . . . . . . 32 A4
HAPSFORD 119 B8
Hapsford Hill BA11 . . . . 119 C8
Harbour BA21 . . . . 218 C5
Harbour Cres BS20 . . . . . . 2 E5
Harbour Ct TA5 . . . . 135 B5
Harbourne Cl TA8 . . . . . 104 C8
Harbour Rd
  Portishead BS20 . . . . . . 2 D6
  Sherborne DT9 . . . . . . 225 E5
  Watchet TA23 . . . . . . 202 C7
Harbour Road Trad Est
  BS20 . . . . 2 F6
Harbour Terr DT9 . . . . . 225 E5
Harbour View TA5 . . . . . 135 B5
Harbour Wall BS9 . . . . . . 5 B4
Harbour Way
  Bristol BS1 . . . . 226 C1
  Sherborne DT9 . . . . . . 225 E5
Harbour Wlk BS1 . . . . . . 226 C1
Harbutts BA2 . . . . 28 F1
Harcourt Cl BS31 . . . . . . 25 E2
Harcourt Gdns BA1 . . . . . 27 B2
Harcourt Mews BA11 . . . 120 A4
Harcourt St TA2 . . . . . . 212 E6
Harden Rd BS14 . . . . 23 E5
Harding Ct TA11 . . . . . . 211 D3
Harding Pl BS31 . . . . 25 B5
Hardings Cl **8** TA6 . . . . 153 F3
Hardings Ct TA13 . . . . . . 220 C5
Harding's Hill TA10, TA11 172 F5
Harding's House La DT9 . 225 A6
Harding's La BA8 . . . . . . 176 D4
HARDINGTON 99 E6
Hardington Dr BS31 . . . . 25 A2
HARDINGTON
  MANDEVILLE 197 A6
HARDINGTON MARSH . . . 196 F4
HARDINGTON MOOR 197 A7
Hardington Moor National
  Nature Reserve★ BA22 197 A7
Hardmead La BS27 . . . . . 90 C2
Hardwarden Terr BA22 . . 175 A5
HARDWAY 161 A5
Hardwick Rd BS20 . . . . . . 4 C5
Hardy Cres DT10 . . . . . . 190 B4
Hardy Ct TA18 . . . . 224 C5
Hardy Mead Dro TA9 . . . 136 B7
Hardys Rd TA2 . . . . 213 C4
HARE 182 F2
Hareclive Acad BS13 . . . . 22 C4
Hareclive Rd BS13 . . . . . . 22 C4
Hare La TA20 . . . . 182 E2
Harepark Terr TA24 . . . . 201 A5

Hare Path TA24 . . . . 147 F8
Hare Path Cross TA24 . . . 129 E1
Harepits La BA6 . . . . 157 E3
Hare Pk TA24 . . . . 124 C4
Harestone Cross EX13 . . . 198 B7
Harewell Wlk BA5 . . . . . 203 B3
Harfield Terr **10** BA20 . . 219 B4
Harford Cl BS9 . . . . 5 C7
Harford Sq BS40 . . . . 39 B3
Hargrove La DT10 . . . . . 190 C2
Harington Pl **2** BA1 . . . 228 B2
Harlech Cl BS31 . . . . 24 C4
Harley Ct **3** BS8 . . . . . 11 F7
Harley La BS21 . . . . 7 C6
Harley Mews **2** BS8 . . . 11 F7
Harley Pl **4** BS8 . . . . . 11 F7
Harley St BA1 . . . . 228 B4
Harmony Dr BS20 . . . . . . 1 F4
Harnell Cl TA1 . . . . 213 C3
Harnhill Cl BS13 . . . . 22 B4
Harp Chase TA1 . . . . . . 213 B1
Harper Rd TA18 . . . . . . 224 C5
Harper's La TA23 . . . . . . 131 D1
Harpitts La SP8 . . . . 177 F2
Harp Rd
  Brent Knoll TA9 . . . . . 105 E6
  South Petherton TA13 . . 220 C3
Harptree BS24 . . . . 49 A2
Harptree Cl BS48 . . . . . . 18 D8
Harptree Hill BS40 . . . . . 74 B5
Harrier Path **3** BS22 . . . 49 E8
Harriets Yd BS31 . . . . . . 24 F5
Harrington Ave BS14 . . . . 23 E6
Harrington Cl BS30 . . . . . 25 E8
Harrington Gr BS14 . . . . . 23 E6
Harrington Rd BS14 . . . . . 23 E6
Harrington Wlk BS14 . . . . 23 E6
Harris Cl
  Frome BA11 . . . . 120 B4
  Westleigh EX16 . . . . . 179 A4
Harris Gr BS13 . . . . 22 B3
Harris La
  Abbots Leigh BS8 . . . . . 10 F8
  Curry Mallet TA3 . . . . 183 C8
Harrison's La TA19 . . . . . 184 E1
Harris Vale BA3 . . . . . . 116 F7
Hart Cl BS20 . . . . 4 E4
HARTCLIFFE 22 C4
Hartcliffe Rd BS4 . . . . . . 22 E8
Hartcliffe Way BS3, BS4,
  BS13 . . . . 22 C7
Hartcliffe Wlk BS4 . . . . . 22 F8
Harters Cl BA5 . . . . 139 E6
Harter's Hill La BA5 . . . . 139 E6
Hartfield Ave BS6 . . . . . 226 C4
HARTFORD 164 C6
Hartgill Cl BS13 . . . . 22 B3
Hartlake Cl
  Glastonbury BA6 . . . . . 206 F7
  Glastonbury BA6 . . . . . 206 F7
Hartland **14** BS22 . . . . . 32 A2
Hartley Cotts BA4 . . . . . 204 B1
Hartley Ho BA1 . . . . 228 B3
Hartley Way TA1 . . . . . . 213 D2
HARTMOOR 177 F3
Hartmoor Hill SP8 . . . . . 177 E3
Hartrow Cl TA1 . . . . 212 E1
Harts Cl TA19 . . . . 221 A4
Hartsfield TA20 . . . . 223 D2
Hart's La
  Hallatrow BS39 . . . . . . 77 B7
  Huish Champflower TA4 . 165 D7
  Sherborne DT9 . . . . . . 188 A3
Harts Paddock BA3 . . . . . 77 F3
HARTSWELL 210 B3
Hartswell TA4 . . . . 210 C3
Harvesters Dr BA16 . . . . 207 B4
Harvest La
  Charlton Horethorne
    DT9 . . . . 176 A2
  Weston-super-Mare BS22 . . 50 B8
Harvest Way BS22 . . . . . . 32 A5
Harvey Cl BS22 . . . . 32 A4
Harvey's Rd TA13 . . . . . 220 C4
Harvey Way TA1 . . . . . . 183 B4
Harwood Cross TA24 . . . 130 A4
Harwood Gn BS22 . . . . . . 31 E4
Harwood La
  Timberscombe TA24 . . . 130 A4
  Wootton Courtenay TA24 . 129 F4
Haselbury Gr BS31 . . . . . 25 E2
HASELBURY
  PLUCKNETT 196 C6
Haselbury Plucknett CE Fst
  Sch TA18 . . . . 196 C5
Haseley Ct TA1 . . . . 212 D2
Haslands BS48 . . . . 18 D8
Hassage Hill BA2 . . . . . . 80 E7
Hassock's La BA10 . . . . . 160 E8
HASTINGS 183 B3
Hastings Cross TA19 . . . . 183 B3
HATCH BEAUCHAMP 183 A7
Hatch Beauchamp CE Prim
  Sch TA3 . . . . 183 A7
Hatch Court★ TA3 . . . . . 183 A8
Hatcher Cl TA8 . . . . 104 D5
Hatchers Ct TA2 . . . . . . 212 F7
Hatchet Hill BA3, BA11 . . . 98 E4
HATCH GREEN 183 A6
Hatch Green La TA3 . . . . 182 F6
Hatch Mews Bsns Pk
  TA3 . . . . 183 A7
Hatfield Bldgs BA2 . . . . . 45 B5
Hatfield Rd
  Bath BA2 . . . . 44 F3

Hatfield Rd *continued*
Weston-super-Mare BS23 . . **49** A8
Hathaway Ho 13 BS2 . . . . **227** A4
Hathermead Gdns BA21 **219** D7
Haunts TA18 . . . . **196** C8
Havage Cl TA9 . . . . **104** E5
Havage Dro BS24 . . . . . . **51** D8
Haven Cl TA24 . . . . **201** F3
Haven View BS20 . . . . **2** E5
Haversham Cl BS22 . . . . **31** D1
Haviland Gr BA1 . . . . . . **27** B3
Haviland Ho 7 BS2 . . . . **227** C3
Haviland Pk BA1 . . . . . . **27** B2
Havory BA1 . . . . **28** C1
Havyat Rd BS40 . . . . **53** E8
Havyat Road Trad Est
BS40 . . . . **35** E1
HAVYATT **157** F8
HAVYATT GREEN **53** F7
Hawarden Terr BA1 . . . . **28** B1
Hawcombe View TA24 . . **124** A3
Hawcombe Woods National
Nature Reserve★ TA24 . **123** F1
HAWKCHURCH **198** E3
Hawkchurch CE Prim Sch
EX13 . . . . **198** E3
Hawkchurch Cross EX13 . **198** E2
Hawkchurch Rd EX13 . . . **198** E3
HAWKCOMBE **124** A3
Hawke Rd BS22 . . . . **31** E4
Hawkers Cl 9 TA5 . . . . **135** B2
Hawker's La BA5 . . . . . . **112** E1
Hawkfield Bsns Pk BS14 . . **22** D5
Hawkfield Cl BS14 . . . . . **22** D5
Hawkfield Rd BS13 . . . . . **22** D5
Hawkfield Way BS14 . . . **22** D5
Hawkins Cl
Burnham-on-S TA8 . . . . . **104** C7
Street BA16 . . . . **207** D4
Hawkin's La TA4 . . . . . . **165** E7
Hawkins St BS2 . . . . **227** C3
Hawkins Way 2 BA21 . . **218** C6
Hawkmoor Hill DT6, EX13 **199** B2
HAWKRIDGE **146** D1
Hawkridge Cross TA22 . . **146** D1
Hawkridge Rd TA6 . . . . . **208** B4
Hawksmoor Cl BS14 . . . . **23** A6
Hawks Rise BA22 . . . . . . **218** B5
Hawk's Worth Cl BA11 . . **120** C7
Hawksworth Dr BS22 . . . **32** A3
Hawksworth Rd TA24 . . **201** B6
Hawkwell Cross EX16 . . **162** F4
Hawley Way TA8 . . . . . . **104** C7
Hawthorn Cl
Bridgwater TA6 . . . . **209** D4
High Ham TA10 . . . . **156** A2
Portishead BS20 . . . . **1** F5
Hawthorn Coombe BS22 . **31** E3
Hawthorn Cres
Shepton Mallet BA4 . . . . **205** A6
Yatton BS49 . . . . **17** A2
Hawthorne Cl TA18 . . . . **224** D7
Hawthorne Rd TA21 . . . . **222** F5
Hawthorn Gdns BS22 . . . **31** D2
Hawthorn Gr BA2 . . . . . . **45** A1
Hawthorn Hill
Kingsbury Episcopi TA13 . **185** B6
Weston-super-Mare BS22 . . **31** E2
Hawthorn Hts BS22 . . . . **31** D3
Hawthorn La BS22 . . . . . **32** C2
Hawthorn Pk BS22 . . . . . **31** E3
Hawthorn Rd
Frome BA11 . . . . **120** A6
Minehead TA24 . . . . **200** D7
Radstock BA3 . . . . **79** B2
Street BA16 . . . . **207** E6
Taunton TA1 . . . . **213** C1
Yeovil BA21 . . . . **219** D7
Hawthorns La BS31 . . . . **24** E5
Hawthorns The
Clevedon BS21 . . . . **6** C3
Stalbridge DT10 . . . . **190** C4
Hawthorn Way BS48 . . . . **9** A2
Haxen La TA17 . . . . **195** A8
Hayboro Way BS39 . . . . **77** E4
HAYBRIDGE **203** B5
Haybridge Villas BA5 . . **203** A5
Haycombe BS14 . . . . **22** F6
Haycombe Dr BA2 . . . . . **44** A4
Haycombe La BA2 . . . . . **44** A3
Hayden Cl BA2 . . . . **228** A1
HAYDON
Milborne Port **189** B2
Radstock **97** F8
Taunton **213** D5
Wells **113** D5
Haydon Cl TA1 . . . . **212** B4
Haydon Dro BA5 . . . . . . **113** C6
Haydon Gate BA3 . . . . . **97** F8
Haydon Hill BA3 . . . . . . **98** A8
Haydon Hollow DT9 . . . **189** B3
Haydon Ind Est BA3 . . . . **97** F8
Haydon La TA1, TA3 . . . . **213** E2
Haydon Rd TA1 . . . . **213** A4
Hayesdown Fst Sch
BA11 . . . . **120** B5
Hayes End TA13 . . . . . . **220** D4
Hayes End Manor TA13 . **220** D4
Hayesfield Girls Sch
BA2 . . . . **228** A1
Hayesfield Pk BA2 . . . . . **228** B1
Hayesfield Sch Tech Coll
BA2 . . . . **44** D6
Hayes La TA11 . . . . **156** F2
HAYES PARK **78** A2

Hayes Park Rd BA3 . . . . . **77** F2
Hayes Pl BA2 . . . . **228** B1
Hayes Rd
Compton Dundon TA11 . . **156** F3
Midsomer Norton BA3 . . . **77** F1
Hayes The BS27 . . . . **90** B8
Hayeswood Farm BA15 . . **46** F5
Hayeswood Rd BA2 . . . . **59** E3
Hayfield Rd TA24 . . . . . **201** B6
Haygarth Ct BA1 . . . . . . **228** B4
Haygrove La TA6 . . . . . . **208** C3
Haygrove Pk TA3 . . . . . **168** D1
Haygrove Pk Rd TA6 . . . **208** D3
Haygrove Rd TA6 . . . . . . **208** C3
Haygrove Sch TA6 . . . . . **208** C4
Hay Hill
Bath BA1 . . . . **228** B3
Croscombe BA5 . . . . **204** B8
Hay La BS40 . . . . **37** D6
Hayleigh Ho BS13 . . . . . **22** C4
Hayman Rd TA24 . . . . . **200** F7
Haymarket The BS1 . . . . **227** B3
Haymoor Dro BA5 . . . . . **139** D7
Haymoor La
Coxley BA5 . . . . **139** E6
Long Sutton TA10 . . . . . **172** D4
Hayne Cross EX16 . . . . . **164** B4
Hayne La TA5 . . . . **153** B7
Haynes International Motor
Mus★ BA22 . . . . **175** A4
Hayne Wlk TA7 . . . . . . **137** B2
Hay St BA3 . . . . **96** A8
Haytor Pk BS9 . . . . **5** D6
Hayward Ave BS24 . . . . **50** C8
Hayward Cl BS21 . . . . **6** C1
Hayward Dr BA6 . . . . . . **158** A6
Haywood Cl BS24 . . . . . **49** A1
Haywood Gdns BS24 . . . **49** B1
Haywood Rd TA1 . . . . . . **213** D4
HAYWOOD VILLAGE **49** C4
Haywood Village Acad
BS24 . . . . **49** D5
Hazel Barrow BS40 . . . . **74** A7
Hazelbury Rd
Bristol BS14 . . . . **23** C7
Nailsea BS48 . . . . **8** D1
Hazel Cl TA1 . . . . **213** C1
Hazel Cote Rd BS14 . . . . **23** B4
Hazel Ct BA11 . . . . **120** A3
Hazeldene Rd BS23 . . . . **49** A8
Hazel Gr
Bath BA2 . . . . **44** D4
Midsomer Norton BA3 . . . **97** B8
Hazell Cl BS21 . . . . **6** C1
Hazel Terr BA3 . . . . **97** C8
Hazel View TA18 . . . . . . **224** D7
Hazel Way BA2 . . . . **62** D8
Hazelwell La TA19 . . . . **221** A4
Hazelwood Ct BS9 . . . . . . **5** E3
Hazelwood Dr TA6 . . . . **209** E5
Hazelwood Rd BS9 . . . . . **5** D3
Hazlegrove Prep Sch
BA22 . . . . **174** F5
Hazleton Gdns BA2 . . . . **45** F3
Head Croft BS48 . . . . . . **20** B8
Head Dro
Catcott TA7 . . . . **137** D3
Othery TA7 . . . . **155** D3
Headley Cl BS13 . . . . . . **22** B6
Headley La BS13 . . . . . . **22** B7
HEADLEY PARK **22** B6
Headley Park Ave BS13 . . **22** B7
Headley Park Prim Sch
BS13 . . . . **22** B6
Headley Park Rd BS13 . . . **22** A7
Headley Rd BS13 . . . . . . **22** A6
Headley Wlk BS13 . . . . . **22** B7
Headon Cross TA24 . . . . **129** F8
Head St BA22 . . . . **186** B6
Headstock Cross TA20 . . **198** E6
Headstock Rd TA20 . . . . **198** E7
Headwell TA3 . . . . **183** C8
Headwell Cl TA3 . . . . . . **183** C8
Headwell Hill TA3 . . . . . **183** C8
Heal Cl TA8 . . . . **104** D5
HEALE **142** C7
Heale La TA10 . . . . **171** C4
Healeys TA24 . . . . **124** A4
Heal's Field EX13 . . . . . **198** A2
Healys Mdw TA4 . . . . . . **167** E4
Hearn La BA22 . . . . **175** D8
Heart Meers BS14 . . . . . **23** B5
Heath Cl BA12 . . . . **144** D8
Heathcombe Rd TA6 . . . **208** B4
Heathcote Rd BA22 . . . . **174** A2
Heath Dr BA11 . . . . **119** F6
Heather Cl
Bridgwater TA6 . . . . **209** B3
Minehead TA24 . . . . **201** C4
Taunton TA1 . . . . **169** A1
Heatherdene BS14 . . . . . **22** F7
Heather Dr BA21 . . . . . . **62** D8
Heather Rd BA21 . . . . . . **219** D7
Heatherton Park Ho TA4 **180** E8
Heather Way BA22 . . . . **218** A5
HEATHFIELD **167** E5
Heathfield TA4 . . . . **151** E4
Heathfield Cl
Bath BA1 . . . . **27** A3
Creech St Michael TA3 . . **169** D6
Keynsham BS31 . . . . **24** C5
5 North Petherton TA6 . **153** F4
West Bagborough TA4 . . **151** A4
Heathfield Com Sch Tech A . . **213** F8
Heathfield Cres BS14 . . . **23** B4
Heathfield Dr TA2 . . . . . **213** F8
Heathfield Rd BS48 . . . . . **8** E3

Heathfield Way BS48 . . . . **8** E2
Heathgate BS49 . . . . **34** B8
Heathgates BS23 . . . . . . **48** D4
HEATH HOUSE **107** F1
Heath Rd BS48 . . . . **8** F3
Heath Ridge BS41 . . . . . **11** A2
Heathstock Hill TA4 . . . **210** D5
Heathway BA12 . . . . . . **144** D8
Heathy La BA6 . . . . **138** B4
HEAVEN'S DOOR **188** A8
Heavitree Way TA2 . . . . **213** A6
Hebden Rd BA15 . . . . . . **64** F3
Heber's La TA19 . . . . . . **195** A5
Heckley La BA3 . . . . **115** B5
Hector Cl BS24 . . . . **50** D4
Hector Rd TA7 . . . . **137** D2
Hectors La TA3 . . . . **170** D8
Hectors Stones TA7 . . . **136** E4
Heddon Oak TA4 . . . . . . **151** A8
Hedge La BA4 . . . . **141** B2
Hedgemead Ct BA1 . . . . **228** C4
Hedges Cl 3 BS21 . . . . . . **6** B1
Hedges The BS22 . . . . . . **32** C3
Hedgestocks BA4 . . . . . **160** C8
HEDGING **170** A8
Hedging La TA7 . . . . . . **170** A8
Heggard Cl BS13 . . . . . . **22** A5
Heights The TA19 . . . . . **221** B4
HELE **168** A3
Hele La
Langport TA10 . . . . **172** C4
South Petherton TA13 . . **220** C4
Helena Rd BA20 . . . . . . **218** D1
Helens Rd BS25 . . . . **52** B4
Helicopter Mus The★
BS24 . . . . **49** E5
HELLAND **170** C3
Helland Hill TA3 . . . . . . **170** C3
Helland La TA3 . . . . **170** C4
Helliar's La
Curry Mallet TA3 . . . . . **183** D8
Fivehead TA3 . . . . **170** C1
Hellier's Cl TA20 . . . . . **223** B4
Hellier's La BS27 . . . . . . **89** E6
Helliers Rd TA20 . . . . . . **223** B4
Hellier Wlk BS13 . . . . . . **22** C3
Helling's Cross TA4 . . . **166** A4
Helmstedt Way TA20 . . **223** D6
Helston Rd BS48 . . . . **9** A1
Helvier's La TA4 . . . . . . **167** A7
Helwell Gn TA23 . . . . . . **202** C6
Helyar Cl BA6 . . . . **206** D5
Hembridge La BA4 . . . . **158** E7
Hembury La BA5 . . . . . . **139** C7
HEMINGTON **99** B7
Hemington Prim Sch BA3 **99** B7
Hemming Way BS24 . . . . **49** E3
Hemp Gdn TA24 . . . . . . **200** F8
Hempitts Rd BA6 . . . . . **156** E7
Hemplow Cl BS14 . . . . . **23** D7
Hemstich Hill TA7 . . . . . **138** C1
HEMYOCK **180** B1
Henacre Rd BS11 . . . . **4** F8
Henbury Hill BS9 . . . . **5** F8
Henbury Ho BA2 . . . . **45** E4
Henbury Rd BS9 . . . . **5** F8
Hencliffe Rd BS14 . . . . . **23** D7
Henderson Cl TA1 . . . . . **212** C2
Henderson Dr TA20 . . . . **223** D2
Henderson Ho 1 BS2 . . . **227** B4
Henderson Pl 5 BA5 . . . **203** D4
Hendford BA20 . . . . **219** A4
Hendford Cl BA20 . . . . . **219** A3
Hendford Gr BA20 . . . . . **219** A4
Hendford Hill BA20 . . . . **219** A3
Hendon Cl TA9 . . . . **104** E5
Hendon Cross EX16 . . . . **178** B8
HENGROVE **23** B6
Hengrove Ave BS14 . . . . **23** B8
Hengrove La BS14 . . . . . **23** B8
Hengrove Pk L Ctr BS14 . . **22** E5
Hengrove Prom BS14 . . . **22** E5
Hengrove Way BS14 . . . . **22** D6
Henhayes La TA18 . . . . . **224** C6
Hen La BS40 . . . . **37** E3
HENLADE **169** D2
HENLEY **156** B3
Henley Cl EX13 . . . . **198** B7
Henley Gr TA1 . . . . **212** D4
Henley La
Butleigh BA6 . . . . **157** E4
Wookey BA5 . . . . **139** E8
Yatton BS49 . . . . **34** D7
Henley Lodge BS49 . . . . **34** D7
Henley Pk BS49 . . . . **34** C7
Henley Rd
High Ham TA10 . . . . **156** B3
Kingsdon TA11 . . . . **173** E5
Taunton TA1 . . . . **212** D3
Henley Rise BA4 . . . . . . **205** D4
Henley View
Crewkerne TA18 . . . . . . **224** C4
Wellow BA2 . . . . **62** D1
Henley Way BA11 . . . . . **119** F5
Henmore La BS26 . . . . . . **88** E6
Hennessy Cl BS14 . . . . . **22** F3
Henning Way DT9 . . . . . **217** D3
Henrietta Ct BA2 . . . . . **228** C4
Henrietta Gdns BA2 . . . **228** C3
Henrietta Mews BA2 . . . **228** C3
Henrietta Pl BA2 . . . . . . **228** C3
Henrietta Rd BA2 . . . . . **228** C3
Henrietta St
Bath BA2 . . . . **228** C3
Bristol BS2 . . . . **227** A4
Henry Butt Ho 11 BS23 . **48** E8
Henry Rogers Ho 2 TA5 **135** B2
Henry St BA1 . . . . **228** C2

Hensley Gdns BA2 . . . . . **44** E4
Hensley Rd BA2 . . . . **44** E3
Hensman's Hill BS8 . . . . **226** A2
Henson Pk TA20 . . . . . . **223** E5
Hensons Dr EX16 . . . . . **179** A3
HENSTRIDGE **190** A6
HENSTRIDGE ASH **189** F7
HENSTRIDGE BOWDEN . . **189** D7
HENSTRIDGE MARSH . . . **190** C7
Henstridge Trad Est BA8 **190** C7
HENTON **139** B8
Hepburn Rd BS2 . . . . . . **227** B4
Herald Cl BS9 . . . . **5** D5
Herbert Ho TA22 . . . . . . **163** D6
Herbert Rd
Bath BA2 . . . . **44** D5
Burnham-on-S TA8 . . . . . **104** A8
Clevedon BS21 . . . . **6** C4
Herbert St TA2 . . . . **212** E6
Herblay Cl BA21 . . . . . . **219** E6
Hereford Dr TA2 . . . . . . **213** A8
Heritage Cl BA2 . . . . **79** D8
Heritage Ct BA6 . . . . . . **206** D4
Heritage Ctyd BA5 . . . . **203** D4
Heritage The BA2 . . . . . . **78** E8
Herluin Way BS22, BS23 . **49** B6
Hermes Cl BS31 . . . . **25** D2
Hermes Pl BA22 . . . . . . **173** E2
Hermitage Cl BS11 . . . . . . **4** E7
Hermitage Hill TA10 . . . **172** D6
Hermitage Rd
Bath BA1 . . . . **27** E1
Langport TA10 . . . . **172** D6
Hermitage St TA18 . . . . **224** C5
Herne Rise TA19 . . . . . . **221** B2
Hern La BS48 . . . . **20** E5
Heron Cl
Minehead TA24 . . . . **201** C4
Weston-super-Mare BS22 . **49** E8
Heron Ct BS21 . . . . **6** C2
Heron Dr TA1 . . . . **212** B4
Heron Gate TA1 . . . . . . **213** E6
Heron Gate Office Pk
TA1 . . . . **213** E5
Heron Gdns BS20 . . . . **2** E4
Heron Ho 2 TA6 . . . . . . **209** C4
Heron Pk TA8 . . . . **84** E8
HERONS GREEN **56** C3
Herons La TA4 . . . . **167** A4
Heronsmead Wlk BA21 . **219** D8
Herons Moor Prim Sch
BS24 . . . . **50** A8
Heron Way TA19 . . . . . . **221** C2
Herridge Cl BS13 . . . . . . **22** B4
Herridge Rd BS13 . . . . . **22** B4
Herschel Museum of
Astronomy★ BA1 . . . . **228** B2
Hersey Gdns BS13 . . . . . **21** E3
Hertford Rd BA21 . . . . . **219** E8
Hervey Cl BS28 . . . . **108** C4
Hervey Rd
Chard TA20 . . . . **223** D3
Wells BA5 . . . . **112** E1
Hestercombe Cl TA6 . . . **208** B4
Hestercombe House Gdns★
TA2 . . . . **169** A7
Hestercombe Rd
Bristol BS13 . . . . **22** B6
Taunton TA2 . . . . **169** A7
Hetling Ct 7 BA1 . . . . . **228** B2
Hewett Cl TA3 . . . . **168** D1
HEWISH
Crewkerne **195** D3
Weston-super-Mare **33** C3
Hewish Ct BS23 . . . . **48** E8
Hewish La
Crewkerne TA18 . . . . . . **224** A5
Hewish TA18 . . . . **195** D3
Hext Ct TA1 . . . . **211** D3
Hexton Rd BA6 . . . . **206** E5
Heyron Wlk BS13 . . . . . . **22** B4
Heywood Rd BS20 . . . . . . **4** C4
Heywood Terr BS20 . . . . . **4** C4
Hibbs Cl SN14 . . . . **13** F8
HICKS GATE **24** B8
Hicks's La BA22 . . . . **214** D1
Hidcote Mews BS24 . . . . **49** E7
Hide Mkt BS2 . . . . **227** C3
Hidewood La EX15 . . . . **180** F1
Higgin's Grave La TA13 . **220** B1
High Acre BS39 . . . . **77** F4
Highaton Head Cross
EX36 . . . . **162** C4
High Bank
Porlock TA24 . . . . **124** A3
Watchet TA23 . . . . **202** C7
High Bannerdown BA1 . . **29** B4
High Bolham EX16 . . . . . **163** C1
HIGHBRIDGE **104** E3
Highbridge TA4 . . . . . . **202** F4
Highbridge & Burnham Sta
TA9 . . . . **104** D3
Highbridge Rd TA8 . . . . **104** B5
Highbrooks Rd TA11 . . . **173** B5
Highburn Cl TA8 . . . . . . **104** C4
HIGHBURY **117** A7
Highbury Cotts
8 Bath BA1 . . . . **28** A1
Coleford BA3 . . . . **116** F7
Highbury Cl 15 BS23 . . . **30** C1
Highbury Farm Bsns Pk
BS39 . . . . **77** A8
Highbury Par BS23 . . . . . **30** C1
Highbury Pl BA1 . . . . . . **28** A1
Highbury Rd
Hallatrow BS39 . . . . **77** B7
Weston-super-Mare BS23 . **30** C1
Highbury St BA3 . . . . . . **117** A7

Highbury Terr 10 BA1 . . . **28** A1
Highbury Villas
9 Bath BA1 . . . . **28** A1
Bristol BS2 . . . . **226** C4
Highcroft
Weston-super-Mare BS23 . **30** F1
Woolavington TA7 . . . . . **136** E4
High Cross EX16 . . . . . . **164** A1
Highdale Ave BS21 . . . . . . **6** E3
Highdale Cl BS14 . . . . . . **23** B4
Highdale Rd BS21 . . . . . . **6** E3
High Down Jun & Inf Schs
BS20 . . . . **2** A4
Higher Actis BA6 . . . . . . **206** E3
HIGHER ALHAM **142** C4
Higher Backway BA10 . . **215** E6
Higher Barton
Martock TA12 . . . . **185** D4
Trent DT9 . . . . **187** F5
Higher Beacon TA19 . . . **221** B4
Higher Beadon TA16 . . . **195** F7
Higher Brooks BA16 . . . **207** C2
Higher Bullen BA22 . . . . **197** F8
HIGHER BURROW **184** E7
Higher Burton BA22 . . . **197** C8
Higher Cheap St 3 DT9 . **225** D4
HIGHER CHILLINGTON . . **194** F5
Higher Coombses TA20 . **198** D4
Higher Cross EX15 . . . . **179** C1
HIGHER DURSTON **169** E7
Higher Easthams La
TA18 . . . . **224** F7
Higher Farm La
Podimore BA22 . . . . **174** A4
Sparkford BA22 . . . . **175** B3
Higher Farm Trad Est
BA20 . . . . **218** C5
Higher Gunville DT9 . . . **217** D2
HIGHER HADSPEN **214** E4
HIGHER HALSTOCK
LEIGH **197** A2
Higher Heathfield TA4 . . **151** E4
Higher Kingsbury DT9 . . **217** D2
Higher Kingsbury Cl
DT9 . . . . **217** C3
Higher Kingston BA21 . . **219** B5
Higher Mead TA19 . . . . **221** B3
Higher Millhayes EX15 . **180** B1
Higher North Town La
BA22 . . . . **175** D7
HIGHER NYLAND **177** C1
HIGHER ODCOMBE **186** C2
Higher Orch
Martock TA12 . . . . **185** D4
Minehead TA24 . . . . **200** C8
Higher Palmerston Rd
TA2 . . . . **212** D6
Higher Park La TA24 . . . **129** E2
Higher Pk TA24 . . . . **200** D6
Higher Rd
Chedzoy TA7 . . . . **154** D8
Horsington BA8 . . . . **176** D3
Shepton Beauchamp TA19 **184** E1
Woolavington TA7 . . . . . **136** E4
Higher Ream BA21 . . . . . **218** C6
Higher Rodhuish Rd
TA24 . . . . **131** B3
HIGHER SANDFORD **188** C7
Higher St
Curry Mallet TA3 . . . . . **183** D8
Martock TA12 . . . . **185** D4
Merriott TA16 . . . . **195** F8
Norton Sub Hamdon TA14 **185** E2
West Chinnock TA18 . . . **196** B8
Higher Street TA5 . . . . . **133** B5
Higher Tolbury BA10 . . . **215** E6
HIGHER TOWN **200** E8
Higher Town EX16 . . . . **178** C1
HIGHER VEXFORD **150** E6
Higher Westbury DT9 . . **187** E1
Higher West Hatch La
TA3 . . . . **182** D7
Higher Westholme Rd
North Wootton BA4 . . . . **140** D4
Pilton BA4 . . . . **204** A1
Highfield
Coleford BA3 . . . . **116** E8
Ilminster TA19 . . . . **221** B4
Taunton TA1 . . . . **212** A2
Taunton TA1 . . . . **212** C3
Wells BA5 . . . . **140** C7
West Chinnock TA18 . . . **196** B8
Highfield Cl
Bath BA2 . . . . **44** B5
Somerton TA11 . . . . **211** C5
Taunton TA1 . . . . **212** A2
Highfield Cres
Chilcompton BA3 . . . . . . **96** C4
Taunton TA1 . . . . **212** A2
Highfield Dr BS20 . . . . . . **1** E3
Highfield La
Compton Martin BS40 . . . **74** B6
East Harptree BS40 . . . . . **75** A3
Highfield Rd
Keynsham BS31 . . . . **24** F2
Peasedown St John BA2 . . **79** C8
Street BA16 . . . . **207** B5
Weston-super-Mare BS24 . **49** A1
Yeovil BA21 . . . . **219** C6
Highfields
Barrington TA19 . . . . . . **184** C5
Clandown BA3 . . . . **78** E4
Midsomer Norton BA3 . . . **78** D2
Stanton Drew BS39 . . . . . **39** F1
Highfield Terr TA12 . . . . **185** D5
Highfield Trad Est BA21 . **219** C6
Highfield View BA3 . . . . **116** E8
Highfield Way TA11 . . . **211** C4

High Gn BA5 . . . . . 111 A4
High Gr BS9 . . . . . 5 B7
Highgrove TA1 . . . . . 212 E1
Highgrove Cl TA6 . . . . . 209 A2
Highgrove Wlk BS24 . . . . . 50 A8
HIGH HAM 156 A2
High Ham CE Prim Sch TA10 . . . . . 156 A1
High Kingsdown BS2 . . . . . 226 C4
High La
Barton St David TA11 . . . . . 158 A2
Shapwick TA7 . . . . . 155 F8
Highland Cl BS22 . . . . . 31 B2
Highland Ct BA21 . . . . . 219 C6
Highland Rd BA2 . . . . . 44 B5
Highlands TA1 . . . . . 212 E1
Highlands La BS24 . . . . . 50 A8
Highlands Rd
Long Ashton BS41 . . . . . 11 A2
Portishead BS20 . . . . . 2 B5
Highland Terr BA2 . . . . . 44 D6
High Lea BA21 . . . . . 219 B8
HIGH LITTLETON 59 C1
High Littleton CE Prim Sch BS39 . . . . . 59 C1
High Mdws BA3 . . . . . 77 F1
Highmead Gdns BS13 . . . . . 21 E4
High Mead Gdns BS39 . . . . . 57 D3
Highmore Rd DT9 . . . . . 225 C5
High Path TA21 . . . . . 222 C7
High Pk BS39 . . . . . 77 D6
High Rd BA22 . . . . . 175 D8
HIGHRIDGE
Bristol 21 F7
Dundry 21 D3
Highridge Cres BS13 . . . . . 21 F5
Highridge Gn BS13 . . . . . 21 E6
Highridge Pk BS13 . . . . . 21 F6
Highridge Rd BS13, BS41 . . 21 E4
Highridge Wlk BS13 . . . . . 21 E7
High St
Aller TA10 . . . . . 171 E8
Ashcott TA7 . . . . . 156 B8
Axbridge BS26 . . . . . 70 B2
Bampton EX16 . . . . . 164 B1
Banwell BS29 . . . . . 51 A2
Bathampton BA2 . . . . . 28 F1
Bath BA1 . . . . . 228 C2
Batheaston BA1 . . . . . 28 F3
Bathford BA1 . . . . . 29 D2
Bath, Twerton BA2 . . . . . 44 B6
Bath, Weston BA1 . . . . . 27 B1
Bishops Lydeard TA4 . . . . . 167 E8
Bitton BS30 . . . . . 25 E8
Blackford BS28 . . . . . 107 E4
Blagdon BS40 . . . . . 54 E3
Bourton SP8 . . . . . 161 F2
Bridgwater TA6 . . . . . 208 F5
Bristol BS1 . . . . . 227 A2
Bristol, Shirehampton BS11 . . 4 E6
Bruton BA10 . . . . . 215 E6
Buckland Dinham BA11 . . . 100 A3
Burnham-on-S TA8 . . . . . 104 A6
Butleigh BA6 . . . . . 157 E4
Cannington TA5 . . . . . 135 B2
Carhampton TA24 . . . . . 131 A5
Castle Cary BA7 . . . . . 214 C5
Chapmanslade BA13 . . . . . 121 C4
Chard TA20 . . . . . 223 B4
Charlton Adam TA11 . . . . . 173 F7
Chew Magna BS40 . . . . . 39 A3
Chewton Mendip BA3 . . . . . 94 F7
Claverham BS49 . . . . . 17 F1
Coleford BA3 . . . . . 116 F6
Congresbury BS49 . . . . . 34 D4
Dulverton TA22 . . . . . 163 D6
Dunster TA24 . . . . . 201 E2
East Chinnock BA22 . . . . . 196 E8
East Harptree BS40 . . . . . 74 F5
Evercreech BA4 . . . . . 141 E1
Faulkland BA3 . . . . . 80 D1
Freshford BA3 . . . . . 64 B5
Frome BA11 . . . . . 119 E5
Glastonbury BA6 . . . . . 206 E4
Hardington Mandeville BA22 . . . . . 197 A6
Henstridge BA8 . . . . . 190 A6
High Littleton BS39 . . . . . 59 D1
Hinton Charterhouse BA2 . . 63 E1
Hinton St George TA17 . . . 195 D7
Ilchester BA22 . . . . . 173 E1
Ilminster TA19 . . . . . 221 B4
Keinton Mandeville TA11 . . 158 A1
Keynsham BS31 . . . . . 24 E6
Kingweston BA6 . . . . . 157 E1
Lynford-on-F TA11 . . . . . 158 C2
Maiden Bradley BA12 . . . . . 144 C2
Marshfield SN14 . . . . . 13 F8
Midsomer Norton BA3 . . . . . 78 B1
Milborne Port DT9 . . . . . 217 D2
Milton Clevedon BA4 . . . . . 160 A8
Milverton TA4 . . . . . 166 F5
Monksilver TA4 . . . . . 150 B8
Nailsea BS48 . . . . . 8 F3
North Cadbury BA22 . . . . . 175 D6
North Petherton TA6 . . . . . 153 E4
North Wootton BA4 . . . . . 140 C4
Norton St Philip BA2 . . . . . 81 E4
Nunney BA11 . . . . . 143 B8
Oakhill BA3 . . . . . 115 A3
Othery TA7 . . . . . 155 C2
Paulton BS39 . . . . . 77 E5
Paulton, Plummer's Hill BS39 . . . . . 77 E6
Pensford BS39 . . . . . 40 E4
Porlock TA24 . . . . . 124 A3
Portbury BS20 . . . . . 3 E3
Portishead BS20 . . . . . 2 D5
High St *continued*
Queen Camel BA22 . . . . . 174 F3
Rimpton BA22 . . . . . 188 A8
Rode BA11 . . . . . 101 E8
Saltford BS31 . . . . . 25 F3
Shepton Mallet BA4 . . . . . 205 B5
Sparkford BA22 . . . . . 175 A5
Spaxton TA5 . . . . . 152 E7
Stalbridge DT10 . . . . . 190 B5
Stogumber TA4 . . . . . 150 D8
Stogursey TA5 . . . . . 134 C5
Stoke sub Hamdon TA14 . . 185 F4
Ston Easton BA3 . . . . . 95 E8
Stoney Stratton BA4 . . . . . 141 F2
Stourton BA12 . . . . . 161 F5
Stourton Caundle DT10 . . . 189 F2
Street BA16 . . . . . 207 C6
Taunton TA1 . . . . . 212 F3
Templecombe BA8 . . . . . 176 E1
Thorncombe TA20 . . . . . 199 B6
Timsbury BA2 . . . . . 60 B2
Wellington TA21 . . . . . 222 E6
Wellow BA2 . . . . . 62 D1
Wells BA5 . . . . . 203 D4
West Coker BA22 . . . . . 197 A8
Weston-super-Mare BS23 . . 48 D8
Weston-super-Mare, Worle BS22 . . . . . 31 E2
Williton TA4 . . . . . 202 D2
Wincanton BA9 . . . . . 216 C4
Winford BS40 . . . . . 38 A7
Winsham TA20 . . . . . 194 E1
Wiveliscombe TA4 . . . . . 210 C4
Wookey BA5 . . . . . 139 D8
Wookey Hole BA5 . . . . . 203 A8
Woolley BA1 . . . . . 27 F6
Wrington BS40 . . . . . 35 D2
Yatton BS49 . . . . . 34 C8
Yenston BA8 . . . . . 189 F8
Yeovil BA20 . . . . . 219 B4
Highview BA2 . . . . . 228 A1
High View BS20 . . . . . 2 A4
High View Dr TA7 . . . . . 156 B8
Highwall La BS14, BS31 . . . 23 F1
HIGHWAY 185 E7
Highwoods Cl TA14 . . . . . 185 F2
Higson Cl BA22 . . . . . 186 D3
Hilary Rd TA1 . . . . . 212 D3
Hildesheim Bridge BS23 . . 48 F7
Hildesheim Cl BS23 . . . . . 48 F6
Hildeshiem Ct 9 BS23 . . . 48 E7
Hilhouse BS9 . . . . . 5 C6
Hill Ave BA2 . . . . . 44 F1
Hillborne Gdns BA21 . . . . . 218 C5
Hillbrook Ct DT9 . . . . . 225 D4
Hill Brow DT9 . . . . . 225 B2
Hill Cl BA9 . . . . . 216 D4
Hillclose La TA19 . . . . . 221 F2
HILL CORNER 120 E6
Hillcote Est BS24 . . . . . 67 B8
Hillcrest
Crowcombe TA4 . . . . . 151 B7
Peasedown St John BA2 . . 79 C7
Pensford BS39 . . . . . 40 E3
Hillcrest Cl
Bristol BS13 . . . . . 22 B6
Nailsea BS48 . . . . . 8 E1
Yeovil BA21 . . . . . 219 C7
Hillcrest Dr BA2 . . . . . 44 C4
Hillcrest Rd
Nailsea BS48 . . . . . 8 E1
Portishead BS20 . . . . . 1 E4
Templecombe BA8 . . . . . 176 E1
Hill Crest Rd BA21 . . . . . 219 C6
Hillcroft Cl BS22 . . . . . 31 A2
Hill Cross BA22 . . . . . 196 F6
Hill Ct BS39 . . . . . 77 E6
Hilldale Rd BS48 . . . . . 19 B5
Hill Dr BS8 . . . . . 10 C3
HILL END 196 F6
Hillend BS22 . . . . . 31 E3
HILLFARRANCE 167 E3
Hillfield BS27 . . . . . 90 B7
Hill Gay Cl BS20 . . . . . 1 F4
Hill Ground BA11 . . . . . 119 E5
Hillgrove Ave BA20 . . . . . 218 F2
Hillgrove Cl TA6 . . . . . 208 E5
Hillgrove Rd BA5 . . . . . 93 C1
Hillgrove St N BS2 . . . . . 227 A4
Hillgrove St BS2 . . . . . 227 B4
Hillgrove Terr BS23 . . . . . 48 D1
Hill Head BA6 . . . . . 206 D3
Hill Head Cl
Glastonbury BA6 . . . . . 206 D3
Taunton TA1 . . . . . 213 A3
Hillhead Cotts TA2 . . . . . 212 C8
Hillhead Cross TA24 . . . . . 128 D3
Hillhouse EX14 . . . . . 192 D3
Hill House Cl DT9 . . . . . 225 E5
Hillier's La
Churchill BS25 . . . . . 52 D4
Yarley BA5 . . . . . 139 C8
Hillingdon Ct BA21 . . . . . 218 C6
Hill La
Bicknoller, Culverhays TA4 . . . . . 133 A1
Bicknoller TA4 . . . . . 132 F2
Brent Knoll TA9 . . . . . 86 B3
Carhampton TA24 . . . . . 131 A4
Chipstable TA4 . . . . . 165 C6
Clevedon BS21 . . . . . 7 C4
Draycott BS27 . . . . . 90 C2
Portishead BS20 . . . . . 1 F1
Rodney Stoke BS27 . . . . . 91 B2
Rowberrow BS25 . . . . . 53 A1
Shepton Mallet BA4 . . . . . 205 B6
Waterrow TA4 . . . . . 165 E5
West Quantoxhead TA4 . . . 132 F4
Hill Lea Gdns BS27 . . . . . 90 B8
Hillmead
Churchill BS40 . . . . . 53 A5
Shepton Mallet BA4 . . . . . 205 B6
Hillmer Rise BS29 . . . . . 50 F3
Hill Moor BS21 . . . . . 6 E2
Hillpath BS29 . . . . . 51 B2
Hill Pk BS49 . . . . . 34 E5
Hill Rd
Allerford TA24 . . . . . 124 E4
Clevedon BS21 . . . . . 6 D4
Dundry BS41 . . . . . 21 D2
Minehead TA24 . . . . . 125 B4
Sandford BS25 . . . . . 52 A3
Weston-super-Mare BS23 . . 48 F8
Weston-super-Mare, Worle BS22 . . . . . 31 E2
Hill Rd E BS22 . . . . . 31 E2
Hillsboro TA7 . . . . . 136 E4
Hillsborough BS8 . . . . . 226 A2
Hillsborough Gdns TA8 . . . 85 B1
Hillsborough Ho BS23 . . . . . 49 A4
Hills Cl BS31 . . . . . 25 A5
Hills Cotts TA4 . . . . . 167 A7
Hillsdon Rd BS9 . . . . . 5 F8
HILLSIDE
Axbridge 70 C2
Midsomer Norton 96 E8
Hillside
Bristol BS6 . . . . . 226 C4
Chard TA20 . . . . . 223 B4
Horrington BA5 . . . . . 113 A2
Portbury BS20 . . . . . 3 D3
Puriton TA7 . . . . . 136 C4
West Pennard BA6 . . . . . 140 B1
Hillside Ave
Frome BA11 . . . . . 119 F2
Midsomer Norton BA3 . . . . . 96 F8
Hillside Cl
Curry Rivel TA10 . . . . . 171 D4
Paulton BS39 . . . . . 77 F6
Hill Side Cl BA5 . . . . . 203 C5
Hillside Cres
Midsomer Norton BA3 . . . . . 96 E8
Puriton TA7 . . . . . 136 C4
Hillside Dr
Frome BA11 . . . . . 120 B4
Puriton TA7 . . . . . 136 C4
Hillside Fst Sch BS22 . . . . . 31 E2
Hillside Gdns
Bishop Sutton BS39 . . . . . 57 C3
Weston-super-Mare BS22 . . 31 B1
Hillside Gr TA1 . . . . . 212 C1
Hillside Ho BA11 . . . . . 119 F3
Hillside Rd
Backwell BS48 . . . . . 19 A4
Bath BA2 . . . . . 44 D4
Bleadon BS24 . . . . . 67 B8
Clevedon BS21 . . . . . 6 D3
Long Ashton BS41 . . . . . 11 B2
Midsomer Norton BA3 . . . . . 96 F8
Portishead BS20 . . . . . 1 D4
Hillside Terr BA21 . . . . . 219 C5
Hillside View
1 Barwick BA22 . . . . . 197 F8
Midsomer Norton BA3 . . . . . 78 A3
Peasedown St John BA2 . . 79 C8
Yeovil BA22 . . . . . 219 D1
Hillside W BS24 . . . . . 49 F2
Hill's La 10 TA12 . . . . . 185 E6
Hills Orch 9 TA12 . . . . . 185 E6
Hill St
Bristol BS1 . . . . . 226 C2
Stogumber TA4 . . . . . 150 D8
Hill Terr TA1 . . . . . 212 A4
Hill The
Freshford BA3 . . . . . 64 C5
Langport TA10 . . . . . 172 A5
Hill Top BS20 . . . . . 2 A4
Hilltop La TA5 . . . . . 133 D6
Hilltops TA8 . . . . . 65 F6
Hillview
Midsomer Norton BA3 . . . . . 96 E7
Timsbury BA2 . . . . . 60 B1
Hill View
Brean TA8 . . . . . 65 E2
Bristol BS8 . . . . . 226 B2
Brompton Ralph TA4 . . . . . 150 C3
Farrington Gurney BS39 . . . 77 B3
Marksbury BA2 . . . . . 42 B1
Mudford BA21 . . . . . 187 D6
Priston BA2 . . . . . 61 A5
Queen Camel BA22 . . . . . 174 F4
Yeovil BA21 . . . . . 219 C5
Hillview Ave BS21 . . . . . 6 D2
Hillview Cl TA24 . . . . . 200 D7
Hill View Cl
Ilton TA19 . . . . . 183 F4
7 Stoke sub Hamdon TA14 . . . . . 185 F4
West Chinnock TA18 . . . . . 196 B8
Hill View Ct
Evercreech BA4 . . . . . 141 E1
Weston-super-Mare BS22 . . 49 D8
Hill View Cvn Pk BS40 . . . . . 20 B1
Hillview Gdns BS40 . . . . . 37 C8
Hill View Park Homes BS22 . . . . . 49 D8
Hillview Rd
Loxton BS26 . . . . . 68 C4
Minehead TA24 . . . . . 200 D7
Hill View Rd
Bath BA1 . . . . . 28 B2
Bristol BS13 . . . . . 22 A8
Carhampton TA24 . . . . . 131 A5
Weston-super-Mare BS23 . . 49 A7
Hillview Terr TA12 . . . . . 185 D5
Hill View Terr
Ilminster TA19 . . . . . 221 B4
Lyng TA3 . . . . . 170 C7
Hill View Trad Est TA4 . . . 151 E4
Hillway TA11 . . . . . 173 E7
Hillworth Ho 26 BA4 . . . . . 205 B6
Hillyfield Rd BS13 . . . . . 22 A6
Hillyfields
Taunton TA1 . . . . . 213 C2
Winscombe BS25 . . . . . 70 B8
Hillyfields Way BS25 . . . . . 70 A8
Hilly Head TA21 . . . . . 222 B5
Hilly Pk TA2 . . . . . 168 B5
Hinam Cross TA22 . . . . . 163 B7
Hinckley Cl BS22 . . . . . 32 C4
Hincombe Hill BA4 . . . . . 142 E2
Hindhayes Inf Sch BA16 207 D5
Hindhayes La BA16 . . . . . 207 D6
Hind Pitts BS25 . . . . . 70 F7
Hine Rd TA1 . . . . . 212 B1
Hinkley Point Nature Trail* TA5 . . . . . 134 C8
Hinkley Point Visitor Ctr* TA6 . . . . . 208 F4
HINTON 187 D7
Hinton BS24 . . . . . 49 A2
HINTON BLEWETT 75 F6
HINTON CHARTERHOUSE 63 E1
Hinton Cl
Bath BA2 . . . . . 43 F6
Hinton St George TA17 . . . 195 D7
Saltford BS31 . . . . . 25 E3
Hinton Cross BA22 . . . . . 187 D7
Hinton Dr TA1 . . . . . 212 E1
Hinton Hill BA2, BA3 . . . . . 63 A1
Hinton La 12 BS8 . . . . . 11 F6
Hinton Rd TA18 . . . . . 224 B8
HINTON ST GEORGE 195 D7
Hinton St George CE Sch TA17 . . . . . 195 C7
Hinton Villas BA2 . . . . . 63 E1
Hippisley Dr BS26 . . . . . 70 D2
Hippisley Ho BA5 . . . . . 113 A1
Hiscocks Dr BA2 . . . . . 44 E4
Hiscocks La BA8 . . . . . 176 E2
Hitchen TA16 . . . . . 195 F7
Hitchen Cl SN14 . . . . . 13 F8
Hitchen Hill BA4 . . . . . 140 F3
Hitchings La TA3 . . . . . 170 B7
Hitchin La BA4 . . . . . 205 A5
Hither Acre TA19 . . . . . 221 A4
Hither Bath Bridge BS4 . . 23 C8
Hither Gn BS21 . . . . . 6 F2
Hither Green Ind Est BS21 . . 6 F2
Hither Mead TA4 . . . . . 167 F8
Hittsford La EX36 . . . . . 162 A1
Hoare's La BA11 . . . . . 98 B3
Hobart Rd BS23 . . . . . 48 F3
Hobbiton Rd BS22 . . . . . 32 A4
Hobbs Ct 1 BS48 . . . . . 8 F2
Hobbs La BS48 . . . . . 20 E3
Hobb's La BS1 . . . . . 226 C2
Hobbs Mead 7 TA4 . . . . . 167 F8
Hobbs Rd BA4 . . . . . 205 D3
HOBB'S WALL 59 E5
Hob La TA2 . . . . . 168 E8
Hobwell La BS41 . . . . . 11 C2
Hoccombe Ford TA4 . . . . . 150 F1
Hocken Cl TA20 . . . . . 223 D6
HOCKHOLLER 180 E8
HOCKHOLLER GREEN 180 E8
Hockley Ct BA1 . . . . . 27 D1
Hockley La BA22 . . . . . 175 E5
Hockpitt La TA5 . . . . . 134 A2
HOCKWORTHY 178 D6
Hodder's Cl BA11 . . . . . 119 E5
Hodders La BS22 . . . . . 32 D6
Hodges Barton TA11 . . . . . 211 C4
Hodshill BA2 . . . . . 62 F6
Hoecroft BA3 . . . . . 96 D2
Hoecroft Gdns BA3 . . . . . 96 D3
Hogarth Mews BS22 . . . . . 32 A3
Hogarth Wlk BS22 . . . . . 32 A3
HOGGINGTON 83 D4
Hoggington La BA14 . . . . . 83 E3
Hogues Wlk BS13 . . . . . 22 B4
Holbeach Way BS14 . . . . . 23 A2
HOLBEAR 223 D2
Holbear TA20 . . . . . 223 D2
Holbrook Cres BS13 . . . . . 22 D4
Holbrook Pk TA13 . . . . . 220 C5
Holburne Museum & Crafts Study Ctr* BA2 . . . . . 45 B7
HOLCOMBE 116 C8
Holcombe BS14 . . . . . 23 A5
Holcombe Cl BA2 . . . . . 28 F1
Holcombe Gn BA1 . . . . . 27 B2
Holcombe Gr BS31 . . . . . 24 D5
Holcombe Hill BA3 . . . . . 116 C7
Holcombe La
Bathampton BA2 . . . . . 28 F1
Doulting BA4 . . . . . 141 E4
HOLCOMBE ROGUS 178 F5
Holcombe Vale BA2 . . . . . 28 F1
Holden's Way
Curry Rivel TA10 . . . . . 171 C3
Curry Rivel TA10 . . . . . 171 D3
Holders Wlk BS41 . . . . . 20 F8
Holdfast La TA14 . . . . . 185 D1
Holditch Court La TA20 . . 198 E5
Holditch La EX13, TA20 . . 198 E5
Holdscroft La DT6 . . . . . 199 B1
Holeground Villas BA5 . . . 203 A8
Holemore Cross EX14 . . . 191 F5
Holes La BA11 . . . . . 118 B6
Holes Sq TA24 . . . . . 130 B5
HOLFORD 133 D4
Holford Cl BS48 . . . . . 8 E1
Holford Ct BS14 . . . . . 23 B5
Holford La TA4 . . . . . 151 C5
Holford Rd
Bridgwater TA6 . . . . . 208 B4
Taunton TA2 . . . . . 212 E8
Hollam Cross TA22 . . . . . 163 E7
Hollam Dr TA22 . . . . . 163 D6
Hollam La TA22 . . . . . 163 D7
Holland Ct BA16 . . . . . 207 D7
Holland Rd
Bath BA1 . . . . . 28 B1
Clevedon BS21 . . . . . 6 B1
HOLLANDS 219 A7
Holland's La TA4 . . . . . 149 E1
Holland St BS23 . . . . . 49 A8
Holland's Wash Dro TA20 . . . . . 193 C5
Holleys Cl TA20 . . . . . 198 D8
Hollies Cl
Martock TA12 . . . . . 185 D5
Middlezoy TA7 . . . . . 155 B3
Shepton Mallet BA4 . . . . . 205 C6
Hollies La BA1 . . . . . 29 A6
Hollies The
Crewkerne TA18 . . . . . 224 C4
Midsomer Norton BA3 . . . . . 78 A1
Yeovil BA21 . . . . . 219 C7
Hollis Ave BS20 . . . . . 2 C3
Hollis Cl
Halstock BA22 . . . . . 197 D3
Long Ashton BS41 . . . . . 21 A8
Hollis Cres BS20 . . . . . 2 C3
Hollister's Dr BS13 . . . . . 22 D4
Hollis Way
Halstock BA22 . . . . . 197 D3
Southwick BA14 . . . . . 83 F3
Holloway
Bath BA2 . . . . . 228 B1
Lopen TA13 . . . . . 185 A1
Minehead TA24 . . . . . 200 F7
Holloway Rd TA7 . . . . . 155 B2
Holloway St TA24 . . . . . 200 F7
Holloway The TA21 . . . . . 179 E7
HOLLOW BROOK 57 C6
Hollowbrook La BS39, BS40 . . . . . 57 D6
Hollowell Hill
Norton Sub Hamdon TA14, TA18 . . . . . 185 E1
West Chinnock TA18 . . . . . 196 B8
Hollow La
Baltonsborough BA6 . . . . . 158 B8
Dinnington TA17 . . . . . 195 B7
Lopen TA13 . . . . . 185 A1
Montacute TA15 . . . . . 186 B3
Wembdon TA5, TA6 . . . . . 208 C7
Weston-super-Mare BS22 . . 31 F3
Hollow Marsh La BA3, BS39 . . . . . 76 B4
Hollowmead BS49 . . . . . 34 E8
Hollowmead Cl BS49 . . . . . 34 F8
Hollow Rd
Shepton Beauchamp TA19 . . . . . 184 D3
Shipham BS25 . . . . . 70 F8
Hollow The
Bath BA2 . . . . . 44 B4
Corsley Heath BA12 . . . . . 144 E8
Dunkerton BA2 . . . . . 61 D4
Westbury-sub-Mendip BA5 110 D7
Hollway Cl BS14 . . . . . 23 E5
Hollway Rd BS14 . . . . . 23 E5
HOLLY BROOK 110 F5
Hollybush Cl BA15 . . . . . 64 E7
Hollybush La
Bristol BS9 . . . . . 5 E5
Bristol BS9 . . . . . 5 F4
Leigh u M BA3 . . . . . 117 A2
Holly Cl
Bridgwater TA6 . . . . . 209 E5
Nailsea BS48 . . . . . 9 A3
7 North Petherton TA6 . . 153 F3
Taunton TA1 . . . . . 213 C1
Weston-super-Mare BS22 . . 32 A1
Holly Ct
Bristol BS2 . . . . . 226 C4
Frome BA11 . . . . . 120 B7
Holly Dr BA2 . . . . . 62 D8
Holly Gr TA18 . . . . . 224 D7
Holly Hill BA4 . . . . . 142 C1
Hollyhock Cl TA6 . . . . . 208 E1
Holly La
Clevedon BS21 . . . . . 6 F6
Drimpton DT8 . . . . . 199 F8
Shepton Mallet BA4 . . . . . 205 C4
Hollyman Wlk 5 BS21 . . . . . 6 F3
Hollymead La BS9 . . . . . 5 E4
Hollyridge BS14 . . . . . 23 C6
Holly Ridge BS20 . . . . . 2 A5
Holly Terr
Chard TA20 . . . . . 223 C4
Odcombe BA22 . . . . . 186 C2
Holly Tree Wlk BA20 . . . . . 218 E3
Holly Wlk
Keynsham BS31 . . . . . 24 D4
Radstock BA3 . . . . . 78 E1
Holman Cl BA6 . . . . . 206 E6
HOLMAN CLAVEL 181 E3
Holman's BA6 . . . . . 157 E4
Holmbury Cl BA11 . . . . . 120 D6
Holmbush TA24 . . . . . 128 E8
Holm Cl TA8 . . . . . 104 B5
Holmlea
Portishead BS20 . . . . . 2 F5

Holmlea *continued*
1 Wookey BA5 139 D8
Holmoak Rd BS31 24 C4
Holm Oaks BA6 157 E4
Holm Rd BS24 49 E2
Holms Rd BS23 49 A5
Holm Vw TA23 202 D7
Holsom Cl BS14 23 F6
Holsom Rd BS14 23 F6
Holst Gdns BS4 22 D7
Holt Ball Steep TA24 129 D7
Holten's La BA22 196 E6
Holt Hill DT9 189 C1
Holt La
Halstock BA22 197 F3
South Perrott DT8 196 D1
Stourton Caundle DT9, DT10 189 E1
West Pennard BA6 140 D2
HOLTON 176 C5
Holton Cross BA9 176 C6
Holton St BA9 176 C5
Holt Rd
North Brewham BA11 161 E8
Witham Friary BA11 143 D1
Holtsdown La BA1 28 F7
Holvert La TA20 194 F1
HOLWAY
Sherborne 188 D7
Taunton 213 C2
Thorncombe 199 C6
Holway
North Petherton TA6 153 F4
Tatworth TA20 198 D8
Holway Ave TA1 213 B3
Holway Deane TA1 213 D2
Holway Gn TA1 213 C2
Holway Hill TA1 213 B2
Holway House Pk TA19 183 E2
Holway Park Com Prim Sch TA1 213 C3
Holway Rd TA1 213 B3
HOLWELL 143 B8
Holwell Cl BS39 77 E4
Holwell Hill BA11 143 B7
Holwell La BS27 89 F8
Holworthy La TA22 148 E2
Holy Moor Cross EX36 162 C1
Holy Moor La EX36 162 C1
Holyoake St TA21 222 C7
Holyrood Com Sch (Lower) TA20 223 C4
Holyrood Com Sch (Upper) TA20 223 C5
Holyrood St TA20 223 C3
Holy Tree Cross TA14 185 E3
Holy Trinity CE Prim Sch
Taunton TA1 213 A3
Yeovil BA20 218 E2
HOLYWELL 197 C8
HOLYWELL LAKE 179 E7
Holy Well Rd TA7 137 C2
Homberg Way TA6 208 E6
Homeavon Ho BS31 24 F5
Homecanton Ho BA9 216 C4
Homecastle Ho 2 TA6 208 F5
Homechime Ho BA5 203 D3
Home Cl
Westbury-sub-Mendip BA5 110 E6
West Camel BA22 174 D3
Wrington BS40 35 E3
Homeclose La EX13, TA20 198 A8
Home Cotts TA1 212 D5
Home Dr
Wincanton BA9 216 C3
Yeovil BA21 218 E5
Home Farm Cl BA2 79 B7
Home Farm La BA22 188 A8
Home Farm Pk TA19 183 E2
Home Farm Rd BS8 11 B8
Home Farm Way TA19 183 E2
Homefield
Bishops Lydeard TA4 167 E8
Congresbury BS49 34 E3
Locking BS24 50 A5
Timsbury BA2 60 C2
Wellington TA21 222 E4
Homefield Cl
Beckington BA11 101 E4
Creech St Michael TA3 169 D4
Locking BS24 50 A5
Saltford BS31 25 E3
Winscombe BS25 51 F1
Home Field Cl TA11 157 B4
Homefield Ct BA22 174 F1
Homefield Ind Est BS24 50 A5
Homefield Rd BS31 25 F3
Homefields BA5 110 E6
Home Fields BA4 205 C4
Homeground BS21 6 F2
Home Ground BS11 4 D7
Homelea Pk E BA1 44 A7
Homelea Pk W BA1 44 A7
Home Mdw TA24 200 D7
Homemead BA2 43 A8
Home Mead BS4 22 E7
Home Orch
Chew Stoke BS40 56 D8
Hatch Beauchamp TA3 183 A7
Homestead BS20 1 E3
Homestead Pk BA5 203 A7
Homestead The
Clevedon BS21 6 C3
Homestead The *continued*
Keynsham BS31 24 F2
Homestead Way BS25 70 A8
Homeville Ho BA20 219 A4
Home Way Cnr BA6 138 B4
Hone Cross EX16 164 F5
Hone La TA22 147 F4
Honeycombe Rise DT9 225 B2
Honey Crock La TA7 155 E8
Honeygar La BA6 138 B5
Honey Garston Cl BS13 22 B4
Honey Garston Rd BS13 22 B4
HONEY HALL 52 C7
Honeyhall La BS49 52 D7
Honeyhurst La BS27 109 F8
Honeylands
Curry Rivel TA10 171 D4
Portishead BS20 2 C3
Honeymead
Bristol BS14 23 C6
Croscombe BA5 204 B8
Honey Mead La BA6, TA11 158 B4
Honeypot La TA11 158 C1
Honey Pot La BA11 144 A4
Honey Row La TA4 132 E2
Honeysuckle Pl BS24 50 A8
Honeywell La BA3 94 F4
Honiton 9 BS22 32 A2
Honiton Rd
Clevedon BS21 6 E1
Taunton TA3 168 D1
Hood Cl BA6 206 E3
Hood Rd BA21 219 F8
HOOK
Chard 198 B8
Timsbury 60 D2
Hookedmead La BS26 88 A1
Hook Hill BA2 60 D2
Hook La
Hinton Blewett BA3, BS39 75 E4
North Cheriton BA9 176 C5
Hooks Batch BS40 54 C4
Hookway Hill TA24 123 A3
Hooper Ave BA5 112 E1
Hooper Cl
Burnham-on-S TA8 104 D5
Highbridge TA9 104 F4
Hooper Rd
Bristol BS14 23 D5
Street BA16 207 B5
Hoopers Barton 9 BA11 119 E5
Hooper's Cl TA1 212 B2
Hoopers Cross EX16 164 D3
Hooper's La
East Coker BA22 197 F7
Fordgate TA7 154 E3
HOOPERS POOL 83 D1
Hopcott Cl TA24 200 E6
Hopcott Rd TA24 200 F5
Hopcott Terr TA24 201 A5
Hopechapel Hill 10 BS8 11 F6
Hope Cl BA5 203 C4
Hope Corner Cl TA2 212 E8
Hope Corner La TA2 212 F8
Hope Cote Lodge BA2 45 C1
Hope Cotts
Highbridge TA9 104 D3
Kingston Seymour BS21 16 B2
Hope Cross SP8 177 D3
Hope Ct BS1 226 B1
Hope Sq BS8 11 F6
Hope Terr BA3 78 B1
Hopewell Gdns BS11 4 F7
Hopewell St TA6 208 D5
Hopkins Ct BA9 216 C2
Hopkins Ho BA22 218 A5
Hopkins St BS23 48 E8
Hopton Ct BA4 141 E1
Horesham Gr BS13 22 C5
Horfield Rd BS2 227 A4
HORN ASH 199 D7
Hornbeam Cl
Bridgwater TA6 209 D5
Frome BA11 120 C6
Taunton TA1 213 D2
Hornbeam Wlk BS31 24 C3
HORNBLOTTON 158 F5
Horne Cl BA3 96 F1
HORNER 129 B8
Horner Nature Trails★ TA24 129 B8
Horner Rd TA2 213 B7
HORNINGSHAM 144 C4
Horningsham Prim Sch BA12 144 D4
Horn La TA20 194 B2
HORNSBURY 223 E7
Hornsbury Hill TA20 223 E8
Hornsey La TA20 182 B1
Horns La BA9 160 B2
Horn's La BS26 70 B2
Horn St BA11 143 B8
Hornswell DT9 189 D4
HORRINGTON 113 A1
Horrington Prim Sch BA5 113 B3
HORSECASTLE 17 A2
Horsecastle Cl BS49 17 A1
Horsecastle Farm Rd BS49 17 A1
Horsecastle La DT9 225 C3
Horsecastles DT9 225 D3
Horse Cl BA11 101 D5
Horsecombe Brow BA2 45 A1
Horsecombe Gr BA2 45 A1
Horsecombe Vale BA2 45 A1
Horsecroft La TA3 170 B4
Horsefair The BS1 227 B3
Horseham La TA5 134 E8
Horsehill La BA4 142 D2
Horse La DT9 176 A2
Horseland La TA24 131 A5
Horseleaze La BS25 52 D1
Horsemans Mews BA6 206 D5
Horse Mill Cross DT6 199 D3
Horse Mill La TA11 211 E4
Horsepark La TA24 130 A4
Horse Pond La TA6 208 F4
Horsepool Rd BS13 21 E3
Horse Race La BS8 10 A6
Horse Rd TA24 130 F5
Horseshoe Cotts TA12 185 E7
Horseshoe Dr BS9 5 C4
Horseshoe Rd TA20 199 A6
Horseshoe Wlk BA2 45 B5
HORSEY 136 C2
Horsey La
Horsey TA7 136 C2
Langport TA10 172 B4
Yeovil BA20 219 A4
Horsey Rdbt BA20 219 A3
HORSINGTON 176 D2
Horsington CE Prim Sch BA8 176 D3
Horsington Ho BA8 176 E2
Horstmann Cl 2 BA1 44 B7
Hortmead La TA19 183 E3
HORTON 183 C1
Horton Cl BA21 218 D6
HORTON CROSS 183 D2
Horton Ho BA2 228 C4
Horton St
Bristol BS2 227 C3
Frome BA11 119 D5
Horton Way TA7 136 E4
Horts Rd TA1 212 C1
Horwood Rd BS48 8 F1
Hosegood Dr BS24 49 C4
Hosey Wlk BS13 22 A5
Hoskins Cl TA10 171 C4
Hospital La
Sherborne DT9 225 D4
South Petherton TA13 220 D5
Hospital Rdbt BA20 219 A5
Host St BS1 227 A3
Hot Bath St 6 BA1 228 B2
Hotwell Rd BS8 226 B1
HOTWELLS 226 A1
Hotwells Prim Sch BS8 11 F6
Houlgate Way BS26 70 B1
Houlton St BS2 227 C4
Houndsmill BA8 176 E2
HOUNDSMOOR 167 A4
Houndsmoor La TA4 167 A4
Hound St DT9 225 D4
HOUNDSTONE 218 A6
Houndstone Bsns Pk BA22 218 B6
Houndstone Cl BA21 218 C5
Houndstone Cnr BA22 218 A5
Houndstone Ct BA22 218 A5
Houndstone Pk BA22 218 A5
Houndstone Ret Pk BA22 218 B5
Houndwood Cl BA16 207 A6
Houndwood Dro BA16 207 A6
HOUNSLEY BATCH 38 A3
House Gate Rd BA11 143 F2
House's La TA20 193 F1
Housman Rd BA16 207 D5
Houston Way BA11 119 D5
Hoveland Cres TA1 212 D2
Hoveland Ct TA1 212 E2
Hoveland Dr TA1 212 D1
Hoveland La TA1 212 C2
Howard Cl
Burnham-on-S TA8 104 C7
Saltford BS31 25 D3
Howard Rd
Wellington TA21 222 D7
Yeovil BA21 219 E6
Howards Row TA20 223 C4
Howecroft Ct BS9 5 E4
Howecroft Gdns BS9 5 E4
Howell Hill BA22 174 D4
Howell's La TA2, TA6 153 D1
Howgrove Hill La BS40 37 C2
How Hill BA2 44 A6
Howitt Way 1 BS24 49 F7
Howleigh La TA3 181 C5
HOWLEY 192 F4
Hownel La TA22 147 F2
Hoyles Cl TA21 222 E4
Hoyles Rd TA21 222 E4
Hozzard La BS28 107 E2
Huckeymead La BA4 158 F7
Huddleston Ct 10 BA5 203 D4
Hudson St TA8 104 B6
Hudson Way TA2 212 C6
Huett Cl TA8 65 F3
Hugdole La TA7 137 D2
Hughenden Rd BS23 49 A8
Hughes Cl 6 TA6 209 B4
Hughes Ct BA11 101 E8
Hugh Sexey CE Mid Sch BS28 107 E3
Hugo St TA1 213 A4
Huish BA20 219 A5
Huish Ball Steep TA24 129 D7
HUISH CHAMPFLOWER 165 F8
Huish Cl
Highbridge TA9 104 D4
Taunton TA1 213 D4
Huish Cleeve TA4 165 E7
Huish Ct BA3 79 B2
HUISH EPISCOPI 172 B5
Huish Episcopi Acad TA10 172 A5
Huish Episcopi Prim Sch TA10 172 A5
Huish Gdns 2 BA20 219 A5
Huish La
Alweston DT9 189 B2
Washford TA23 131 E4
Wyke Champflower BA10 215 C4
Huish Mdw TA23 131 E4
Huish Park (Yeovil Town FC) BA22 218 B7
Huish Prim Sch BA20 219 A5
Huish Rd TA11 173 C7
Huish Row TA24 129 A8
Hukeley Head Cross EX16 164 D3
Hulk Moor Dro BA16, BA16 207 C8
Hulkshay La TA6 153 E3
Hull La DT9, BA8 176 B3
Humber Gr TA1 213 D3
Humberstan Wlk BS11 4 E8
Humphreys Rd TA21 222 E7
Humphry Davy Way 6 BS8 11 F5
Humpy La DT9 189 A1
Hundredstone Cl BA21 219 B8
Hundry La TA10 184 C8
HUNGERFORD 131 E3
Hungerford Cl BS4 23 E8
Hungerford Gdns BS4 23 E8
Hungerford Rd
Bath BA1 44 C7
Bristol BS4 23 E8
Hungerford Terr BA2 62 D1
Hung Rd BS11 4 E5
HUNSTRETE 41 D2
Hunstrete La BS39 41 B4
Hunstrete Rd BA2 59 F7
Huntash La TA4 167 A4
Huntenhull Gn BA13 121 C3
Huntenhull La BA13 121 D4
Hunter's Hill EX15 179 E1
Hunters Moon Touring Pk EX13 198 E1
Hunters Rest Miniature Rlwy★ BS39 59 A5
Hunter's Way EX15 179 E1
Huntham Cl TA3 170 E6
Huntham La TA3 170 E5
Huntham Rd TA3 170 D4
Huntingham Rd BS13 21 F4
Huntley Cl EX13 198 A2
Huntley Gr BS48 9 A1
Huntley La
Chardstock EX13 198 A8
Tatworth EX13, TA20 193 D1
HUNTSCOTT 129 E6
HUNTSHAM 178 A7
Hunts La TA5 133 D5
Hunt's La BS49 34 E8
Huntsmans Ridge BS27 90 C7
Hunts Mead DT9 225 B2
HUNTSPILL 136 B8
Huntspill Rd TA9 104 D2
Huntspill River National Nature Reserve★ TA9 136 D6
HUNTSTILE 153 C4
HUNTWORTH 154 B5
Huntworth Bsns Pk TA6 154 A5
Huntworth La
Fordgate TA7 154 C5
North Petherton TA6 153 F4
HURCOTT 173 C8
Hurcott Cross TA19 184 D3
Hurcott La TA19 184 D4
Hurdle Way TA1 213 A3
Hurd's Bldgs BA11 119 F4
Hurley La TA4 151 B8
Hurlstone Pk TA24 124 B3
Hurmans Cl TA7 156 B8
Hurn Dro BA5 139 B6
Hurn La
Berrow TA8 84 F7
Keynsham BS31 25 A3
Pitcombe BA7 215 A1
Shepton Montague BA7 160 A2
Hurn Rd BS21 6 F2
Hursley Hill
Bristol BS14 40 D8
Whitchurch BS14 23 D1
Hursley La BS14 23 E1
HURST 185 D5
Hurst TA12 185 D5
Hurst Dro
Compton Dundon TA11 157 A3
Hambridge TA10, TA12 184 E8
Hurst Mews TA12 185 D5
Hurston Rd BS4 22 D7
Hurst Pk TA12 185 D5
Hurst Rd
Bristol BS4 22 F8
Weston-super-Mare BS23 49 A6
Hurst Wlk BS4 22 F8
Hussey's DT10 190 F5
Hutchings's La TA4 167 D4
Hutchin's La BA10 160 F8
HUTTON 49 E2
Hutton CE Prim Sch BS24 49 E2
Hutton Cl
Bristol BS9 5 E7
Keynsham BS31 25 A2
Hutton Hill BS24 49 F2
Hutton Moor La BS22, BS24 49 C6
Hutton Moor Pk BS24 49 C6
Hutton Moor Rd BS22 49 C7
Hutton Moor Rdbt BS22 49 C7
Huxham La BA4 158 F7
Hyacinth Terr TA21 222 C5
Hyatt Pl BA4 204 F5
Hyatts Wood Rd BS48 19 E1
Hyde Ct BA21 218 C6
Hyde La
Monkton Heathfield TA2 169 C5
Taunton TA2 213 F6
Hyde Lane Cotts TA2 169 C5
Hyde Park Ave 4 TA6 153 E3
Hyde Pk 5 TA6 153 E3
Hyde Rd
Minehead TA24 200 E6
Montacute TA15 186 B4
Hyde's La SN14 13 A6
Hyde The
Clevedon BS21 16 C8
Keynsham BS31 24 F6
Hyland Gr BS9 5 F8
Hylton Cl TA2 212 F8
Hynicombe La TA4 165 D6
Hythe La BS27 89 E5

I

Iberry La TA3 183 E8
ICELTON 32 C8
Idwal Cl BA2 79 C8
Iford Cl BS31 25 E3
Iford Fields BA15 64 E2
Iford Hill BA15 64 E2
Iford La BA3, BA15 64 C3
ILCHESTER 173 E1
Ilchester Com Prim Sch (Inf) BA22 173 E2
Ilchester Com Prim Sch (Jun) BA22 173 E2
Ilchester Cres BS13 22 B8
Ilchester La TA10 172 F4
ILCHESTER MEAD 173 D1
Ilchester Mead BA22 173 D1
Ilchester Mus★ BA22 173 E1
Ilchester Rd
Bristol BS13 22 B8
Charlton Mackrell TA11 173 F6
Chilthorne Domer BA21, BA22 186 F6
Yeovil BA21 218 F8
Ile Ct TA19 221 C4
Ilex Ave BS21 6 E2
Ilex Cl
Bristol BS13 21 F6
Huntspill TA9 136 B8
Ilex La BS25 51 F1
ILFORD 184 A4
Ilford Ct TA1 212 C2
Illustrious Cres BA22 173 E2
ILMINSTER 221 C4
Ilminster BS24 49 A2
Ilminster Ave BS4 22 F8
Ilminster Ave E-ACT Acad BS4 23 A8
Ilminster Cl
Clevedon BS21 6 E2
Nailsea BS48 18 D8
Ilminster Rd TA1 213 D4
Ilsyn Gr BS14 23 D7
ILTON 183 E4
Ilton Bsns Pk TA19 183 F5
Imbercourt Cl BS14 23 B8
Immenstadt Dr TA21 222 D4
Imperial Pk BS13 22 C6
Imperial Rd BS14 23 C8
Imperial Way
Bridgwater TA6 136 B2
Frome BA11 120 D7
Improvement Pl 5 TA21 222 D5
Inchalloch 19 BA1 28 A1
Incline The TA19 221 B3
Inclosures The 5 BS22 49 F8
INGLESBATCH 61 C8
Ingleton Dr BS22 32 A4
Ingrams Mdw TA23 202 C6
Inkerman Ct TA1 213 A3
Inman Ho BA1 228 C4
INMAN'S BATCH 38 A5
Inn Cotts BS11 5 A7
Inner Circ TA1 213 D5
Inner Elm Terr BA3 78 C1
Inner Gullands TA1 212 D3
Innicks Cl BS40 55 D1
Innox Gdns BS13 22 A5
Innox Gr BA2 43 F2
INNOX HILL 119 F6
Innox Hill BA11 119 E6
Innox La BA1 28 B5
Innox Rd BA2 44 B5
Inns Court Ave BS4 22 D7
Inns Court Dr BS4 22 D6
Inns Court Gn BS4 22 D7
Innsmead La TA7 137 B1
Instow 7 BS22 32 A2
Instow Rd BS4 22 E8
Instow Wlk BS4 22 E8
International Coll Sherborne Sch DT9 225 D5
Inverness Rd BA2 44 C6
Inwood Rd TA6 208 C5
Irene Cl TA6 209 D7
Ireson Cl BA9 216 D4
Ireson La BA9 216 D4
Irnham Rd TA24 201 A7
Iron Dish La TA13 184 E6
Iron Mill La BA11 101 A1
Ironmould La BS31 24 A8

Iron Post TA22 . . . . 163 B5
Irons Way BS24 . . . . 50 C8
Irvine Cl TA2 . . . . 212 C6
Irving Cl BS21 . . . . 6 F3
Irving Ho BS1 . . . . 226 C3
Irving Rd TA11 . . . . 158 A1
Irwell Rd TA1 . . . . 213 D4
Isaacs Cl BA16 . . . . 207 B4
Island The BA3 . . . . 78 A1
ISLE ABBOTTS 183 F7
ISLE BREWERS 184 A8
Islemoor Dro TA3 . . . . . . 184 A8
Islemoor La TA13 . . . . 220 B6
Islemoor Rd TA3 . . . . 183 F8
Isleport Bsns Pk TA9 . . . . 104 F4
Isleport Rd TA9 . . . . 104 F3
Isles La
  East Coker, Lyatts BA22 . . 197 C6
  East Coker, Sutton Bingham
  BA21 . . . . 197 D6
Ivel Ct BA21 . . . . 219 C5
Ivel Gdns BA22 . . . . 173 E1
Ivel Sq BA20 . . . . 219 B5
Ivelway TA18 . . . . 224 C5
Ivo Peters Rd BA2 . . . . . . 228 A2
Ivors Way TA6 . . . . 153 E4
Ivy Ave BA2 . . . . 44 C4
Ivy Bank Pk BA2 . . . . 44 F2
Ivybridge 8 BS22 . . . . 32 A2
Ivy Cl BS48 . . . . 8 D1
Ivy Cotts TA3 . . . . 181 E3
Ivy Cross TA21 . . . . 179 D7
Ivy Ct BS20 . . . . 1 F5
Ivy Gn TA20 . . . . 223 C3
Ivy Gr BA2 . . . . 44 C4
Ivy Grove Cl TA6 . . . . 209 D7
Ivy Ho
  Chard TA20 . . . . 223 B4
  Wellington TA21 . . . . . . 222 C6
Ivy House Cotts BS29 . . . . 50 D7
Ivy House Pk TA3 . . . . . . 169 C2
Ivy La BS24 . . . . 50 A8
Ivyleaf Rd TA11 . . . . 211 C4
Ivy Pl BA2 . . . . 44 C4
Ivythorn Cl BA16 . . . . 207 C4
Ivythorn Rd BA16 . . . . . . 207 C4
Ivywell Rd BS9 . . . . 5 E3
Ivy Wlk
  Banwell BS29 . . . . 50 E4
  Midsomer Norton BA3 . . . 97 B8
  Yeovil BA20 . . . . 218 E3
IWOOD 35 A3
Iwood La BS40 . . . . 35 A2

J

Jack Price Cl BS13 . . . . 22 C3
Jack's Dro BS28 . . . . 137 F8
Jack's La
  Croscombe BA5 . . . . 204 C7
  Frome BA11 . . . . 119 D7
Jackson's La TA5 . . . . 134 A2
Jack White's Gibbet BA9 176 B8
Jacobs Cl BA6 . . . . 206 E5
Jacob's Ct BS1 . . . . 226 C2
Jacobs Mdw BS20 . . . . 2 F4
Jacob St
  Bristol BS2 . . . . 227 B3
  Bristol BS2 . . . . 227 C3
Jacob's Wells Rd BS8 . . . 226 B2
Jagaar Ct TA7 . . . . 137 D5
Jaguar Ho 3 BA1 . . . . . . 228 B3
Jamaica St BS2 . . . . 227 B4
James Cl
  Holcombe BA3 . . . . 116 C8
  Shepton Mallet BA4 . . . . 205 C4
James La EX14 . . . . 192 F2
James Lane Cross EX13 193 A1
James St W BA1 . . . . 228 B2
James's Hill BA10 . . . . . . 161 A8
James St BS5 . . . . 227 C4
Jane Austin Centre The★
  BA1 . . . . 228 B3
Janson Cl TA6 . . . . 209 D6
Japonica Cl TA6 . . . . 209 D5
Jarman Way TA20 . . . . . . 223 D6
Jarmany Hill BA6 . . . . . . 157 F3
Jarmyns TA1 . . . . 212 A3
Jarvis Cl DT10 . . . . 190 B4
Jarvis La TA9 . . . . 86 D4
Jarvis Way DT10 . . . . 190 B4
Jasmine Cl
  Bridgwater TA6 . . . . 208 D1
  Crewkerne TA18 . . . . . . 224 D7
  Highbridge TA9 . . . . 104 D4
  Weston-super-Mare BS22 . 32 A1
  Yeovil BA20 . . . . 218 B5
Jasmine Ct 8 BS23 . . . . . . 48 E8
Jasmine La BS49 . . . . 17 F2
Jasmine Way BS24 . . . . . . 32 A1
Jay Cl BA11 . . . . 120 B6
Jaycroft Rd TA8 . . . . 104 B6
Jay View BS23 . . . . 49 A5
Jeffreys' Way TA1 . . . . . . 212 A2
Jeffries Cl TA19 . . . . 183 C4
Jeffs Way 3 EX13 . . . . . . 198 A1
Jellalabad Ct TA1 . . . . . . 212 F3
Jellicoe Ct BS22 . . . . 31 E4
Jena Ct BS31 . . . . 25 D3
Jenson Ave BA11 . . . . 120 D8
Jesmond Rd
  Clevedon BS21 . . . . 6 C3
  Weston-super-Mare BS22 . 32 C4
Jesse Hughes Ct BA1 . . . . 28 C2
Jessop Ct BS1 . . . . 227 B2
Jessop Underpass BS3 . . . 11 F4

Jews La
  Bath BA2 . . . . 44 C6
  Churchill BS25 . . . . 52 F4
  Wiveliscombe TA4 . . . . . 210 B5
Jill Dando Memorial
  Garden★ 8 BS23 . . . . . . 48 D8
Jill's Cl BA1 . . . . 142 A6
Jim O'Neil Ho BS11 . . . . 4 D7
Jocelin Dr BS22 . . . . 31 F4
Jocelin Rd BA6 . . . . 206 F5
Jocelyn Dr BA5 . . . . 203 B3
John Beales Hill BA4 . . . . 140 F3
John Cabot Ct BS1 . . . . . 226 A1
John Carr's Terr BS8 . . . . 226 B2
John Cozens Ho 6 BS2 . . 227 C3
John Grinter Way TA21 . . 222 D4
John Gunn Cl TA20 . . . . . 223 C5
John Hall Cl BS14 . . . . 23 B7
John St S TA8 . . . . 104 A7
John Slessor Ct BA1 . . . . 228 B4
Johnson Cl
  East Brent TA9 . . . . 86 D5
  Wells BA5 . . . . 203 F5
Johnson Flats BA21 . . . . . 219 C5
Johnson's Ctyd DT9 . . . . 225 D3
John St
  Bath BA1 . . . . 228 B3
  Bristol BS1 . . . . 227 A3
  Burnham-on-S TA8 . . . . 104 A7
  Weston-super-Mare TA8 . 104 D3
Johnstone Ct BA16 . . . . . 207 B3
Johnstone St BA2 . . . . . . 228 C2
John Wesleys Chapel★
  BS1 . . . . 227 B3
Joles La BA11 . . . . 120 F1
Jones Cl BS49 . . . . 17 A1
Joselin Ct DT9 . . . . 225 D5
Joyden Ct TA20 . . . . 223 D2
Joy Hill BS8 . . . . 11 F6
Juan's La SP8 . . . . 177 E1
Jubilee Cl
  Bridgwater TA6 . . . . 209 C4
  Castle Cary BA7 . . . . 214 C6
  Chard TA20 . . . . 223 C3
  Midsomer Norton BA3 . . . 97 A8
Jubilee Cotts 10 BA11 . . . 119 F4
Jubilee Ct
  8 Wellington TA21 . . . . 222 D5
  Weston-super-Mare BS23 . 48 F8
Jubilee Dr BS8 . . . . 10 B4
Jubilee Gdns
  Milverton TA4 . . . . 167 A4
  South Petherton TA13 . . 220 C4
Jubilee La BS40 . . . . 53 A6
Jubilee Path BS22 . . . . 31 C1
Jubilee Pl
  Bristol BS1 . . . . 227 A1
  Clevedon BS21 . . . . 6 D1
  Yeovil BA21 . . . . 218 D5
Jubilee Rd
  Axbridge BS26 . . . . 70 C2
  Radstock BA3 . . . . 78 D1
  Street BA16 . . . . 207 C4
  Weston-super-Mare BS23 . 48 E7
Jubilee St
  Bristol BS2 . . . . 227 C2
  Burnham-on-S TA8 . . . . 104 B6
  Taunton TA1 . . . . 212 E6
Jubilee Terr
  Frome BA11 . . . . 119 E5
  Hemington BA3 . . . . 99 C7
  Paulton BS39 . . . . 77 E6
Jubilee Way BS22 . . . . 32 C3
Judy's Orch TA7 . . . . 154 F5
Julian Cl
  Bristol BS9 . . . . 5 E3
  Shepton Mallet BA4 . . . . 205 C4
Julian Ct BS9 . . . . 5 E3
Julian Rd
  Bath BA1 . . . . 228 B3
  Bristol BS9 . . . . 5 E3
Julian's Acres TA8 . . . . . . 84 F4
Julier Ho BA1 . . . . 228 C4
Jumpers Combe TA23 . . . 148 E8
Junction Ave BA2 . . . . . . 228 A1
Junction Dro TA3 . . . . . . 170 C2
Junction Rd BA2 . . . . 228 A1
Juniper Cl
  Bridgwater TA6 . . . . 209 E4
  Yeovil BA20 . . . . 218 F3
Juniper Pl BS22 . . . . 31 F4
Juniper Rd TA1 . . . . 213 C2
Jurston La
  Wellington TA21 . . . . . . 222 E6
  Wellington TA21 . . . . . . 222 F5
Jury Hill TA22 . . . . 163 E6
Jury Rd TA22 . . . . 163 E6
Justice Ave BS31 . . . . 25 E3
Justice La BA11 . . . . 119 F5

K

Kale St BA4 . . . . 142 D2
Kale Street Cotts BA4 . . . 142 D2
Karen Cl BS48 . . . . 19 A4
Karen Dr BS48 . . . . 19 A5
Kaynton Mead BA1 . . . . . . 44 B7
Keats Ho 4 BS23 . . . . 48 F4
Keats Rd
  Radstock BA3 . . . . 97 C8
  Taunton TA1 . . . . 213 C4
Kebby's Farm Cl TA4 . . . 202 E3
Keble Ave BS13 . . . . 21 F5
Keeds La BS41 . . . . 10 F1
Keedwell Hill BS41 . . . . . 10 F1
Keel Ave BS20 . . . . 2 F7
Keel's Hill BA2 . . . . 79 C8

Keene's Way BS21 . . . . 6 C2
Keens Cl BA16 . . . . 207 D5
Keen's Elm La BA16 . . . . 207 E4
Keens La TA7 . . . . 155 C2
KEENTHORNE 134 D2
Keep St BA22 . . . . 174 D3
Keep The BS22 . . . . 32 A3
Keg Store The BS1 . . . . . 227 B2
KEINTON MANDEVILLE . . 158 B1
Keinton Mandeville Prim Sch
  TA11 . . . . 158 A1
Kellways BA16 . . . . 19 A4
Kelson's La BS28 . . . . 108 B3
Kelso Pl BA1 . . . . 44 D7
Kelso Villas BA1 . . . . 44 D7
KELSTON 26 C3
Kelston Cl BS31 . . . . 25 D4
Kelston Gdns BS22 . . . . . . 32 B5
Kelston Rd
  Bath BA1 . . . . 26 E1
  Keynsham BS31 . . . . 24 D8
  Weston-super-Mare BS22 . 32 B5
Kelston View BA2 . . . . 44 A5
Kelting Gr BS21 . . . . 6 F2
Keltings TA6 . . . . 208 C6
Kelway Rd TA21 . . . . 222 F7
Kember's Hill BA22, DT9 . 175 C3
Kemble Cl BS48 . . . . 9 A1
Kemble Gdns BS11 . . . . 4 F5
Kemm Cl BS27 . . . . 90 B6
Kempe's Cl BS41 . . . . 11 A2
Kempe Way BS24 . . . . 49 E7
Kemps La TA24 . . . . 147 B7
Kemp's La BA11 . . . . 120 F7
Kemps Way TA22 . . . . 163 D6
Kempthorne La BA2 . . . . . 44 E1
Ken Cl
  Chard TA20 . . . . 223 D3
  Wells BA5 . . . . 140 C8
Kencot Wlk BS13 . . . . 22 B3
Kendale Rd TA6 . . . . 208 E6
Kendall Cl TA3 . . . . 169 D6
Kendrick Ct 1 BA5 . . . . . 203 D4
Kenelm Cl BS13 . . . . 22 B3
Kenilworth Cl BS31 . . . . . 24 D4
Kenilworth Ct BA1 . . . . . . 45 B8
Kenmare Rd BS4 . . . . 22 E8
Kenmeade Cl BS25 . . . . . . 70 E8
Kenmore Dr BA21 . . . . . . 219 B6
KENN 16 F7
Kennard Cl BA6 . . . . 206 F3
Kennard Moor Dro
  Butleigh BA6 . . . . 157 E7
  Glastonbury BA6 . . . . . . 206 F1
Kennaway Rd BS21 . . . . . . 6 E2
Kenn Bsns Pk BS21 . . . . . 16 E8
Kenn Cl BS23 . . . . 49 A5
Kenn Court BS4 . . . . 22 E7
Kennedy Cl TA9 . . . . 104 E4
Kennel Batch BA5 . . . . . . 111 D4
Kennel La
  Compton Bishop BS26 . . . 68 E3
  East Pennard BA4 . . . . . 158 F8
  Langport TA10 . . . . 172 A6
  West Bagborough TA4 . . 151 D4
Kennel Lodge Rd BS3 . . . 11 E4
Kenn Est BS21 . . . . 16 E5
Kennet Gr TA1 . . . . 213 D4
Kennet Ho 10 BA1 . . . . . . 228 B2
Kennet Pk BA2 . . . . 28 E1
Kennet Rd BS31 . . . . 25 A4
Kennford 6 BS22 . . . . 31 F2
Kennington Rd BA1 . . . . . 44 B7
Kennion Cl TA20 . . . . 223 D3
Kennion Rd BA5 . . . . 203 C5
Kenn Moor Dr BS21 . . . . . 6 F1
KENN MOOR GATE 17 F4
Kennmoor Rd BS21 . . . . . 17 A6
Kenn Moor Rd BS49 . . . . 17 F1
Kenn Rd BS21 . . . . 16 F6
Kenn St BS21 . . . . 16 F7
KENNY 183 B4
Kensington Ct
  Bath BA1 . . . . 28 B2
  Bristol BS8 . . . . 226 A3
Kensington Fields BA14 . . 83 F7
Kensington Gdns
  Bath BA1 . . . . 28 B1
  Bridgwater TA6 . . . . 209 D6
Kensington Gr TA24 . . . . 200 E6
Kensington Pl
  Bath BA1 . . . . 28 B1
  Bristol BS8 . . . . 226 A3
Kensington Rd BS23 . . . . 48 F5
Kent Ave
  Bridgwater TA6 . . . . 209 A2
  Weston-super-Mare BS24 . 50 C8
  Weston-super-Mare BS24 . 50 D8
Kentisworth Rd DT10 . . . 190 F5
Kent La
  Shapwick TA7 . . . . 137 F1
  Shepton Mallet BA4 . . . . 205 C4
Kent Rd
  Congresbury BS49 . . . . . 34 D5
  Tatworth TA20 . . . . 198 D8
Kent's Bglws TA20 . . . . . 198 D8
Kent's Cl TA20 . . . . 198 C8
Kent's Cotts TA20 . . . . . . 198 D8
Kentshare La BS40 . . . . . . 38 B6
Kents La TA20 . . . . 198 D8
Kent's Orch TA20 . . . . . . 198 D8
Kent St BS27 . . . . 71 B1
Kent Way TA6 . . . . 32 B4
Kenwyn Cl TA1 . . . . 213 D3
Keppel Cl BS31 . . . . 25 D2
Kerry Croft BA11 . . . . . . 143 C3
Kersey Ct BA11 . . . . 119 C5
Kersham La TA24 . . . . . . 130 A1

Kestrel Cl TA6 . . . . 209 C3
Kestrel Dr BS22 . . . . 31 E1
KEWARD 203 C2
Keward Ave BA5 . . . . 203 B3
Keward Cl BA5 . . . . 203 B3
Keward Mill Trad Est
  BA5 . . . . 203 B2
Keward Wlk BA5 . . . . 203 C5
Kew Rd BS23 . . . . 30 E1
Kewside BS22 . . . . 31 B4
KEWSTOKE 31 B4
Kewstoke Prim Sch BS22 . 31 B3
Kewstoke Rd
  Bath BA2 . . . . 45 A2
  Bristol BS9 . . . . 5 E4
  Weston-super-Mare BS22 . 31 C3
Kew Wlk BS4 . . . . 23 C8
Keyes Path BS22 . . . . 31 F4
KEYFORD 119 F3
Keyford BA11 . . . . 119 F3
Keyford Cotts 15 BA11 . . 119 F3
Keyford Ct BA11 . . . . 119 F2
KEYFORD FIELD 119 F2
Keyford Field Cotts
  BA11 . . . . 119 F2
Keyford Gdns BA11 . . . . . 119 F4
Keyford Pl BA11 . . . . 119 F4
Keyford Rdbt BA22 . . . . . 197 E8
Keyford Terr BA11 . . . . . 119 F4
Keyhaven Bglws BS22 . . . 31 B4
Key Hill BA22 . . . . 197 E8
KEYNSHAM 24 E7
Keynsham By-Pass BS31 . 24 E7
Keynsham Rd BS30, BS31 . 25 A8
Keynsham Sta BS31 . . . . . 24 F6
Keyton Hill BS28 . . . . 107 E2
Kicks Hill TA7 . . . . 155 B4
Kicks Hill La TA7 . . . . . . 155 B4
Kidder Bank BA5 . . . . 203 F5
Kiddles BA21 . . . . 219 C5
Kidd's La BA4 . . . . 141 C6
Kid Gate Dro TA9, BS28 . 137 D8
Kidner Cl TA7 . . . . 136 E4
Kidsbury Rd TA6 . . . . 208 E5
Kielder Dr BS22 . . . . 31 F3
Kilbirnie Rd BS14 . . . . 23 A3
Kilburn Dr TA6 . . . . 209 D6
Kildare BA2 . . . . 45 B7
Kildare Gdns TA24 . . . . . 200 F6
Kildare Rd BS13 . . . . 22 D8
Kilkenny Ave 5 TA2 . . . . 212 F6
Kilkenny Ct TA2 . . . . 212 F6
Kilkenny La
  Bath BA2 . . . . 62 B8
  Wraxall BA4 . . . . 159 A6
Kilkenny Pl BS20 . . . . 2 C6
Killams Ave
  Staplehay TA3 . . . . 181 F8
  Taunton TA1 . . . . 168 F1
Killams Cl TA1 . . . . 168 F1
Killams Cres TA1 . . . . . . 168 F1
Killams Dr TA1 . . . . 168 F1
Killams Gn TA1 . . . . 168 F1
Killams La TA1 . . . . 168 F1
Killarney Ave TA8 . . . . . . 104 C6
Killick Way TA4 . . . . 202 D3
KILLING'S KNAP 97 B4
KILMERSDON 98 B5
Kilmersdon CE Prim Sch
  BA3 . . . . 98 A6
Kilmersdon Hill BA3 . . . . . 98 A5
Kilmersdon Rd
  Bristol BS13 . . . . 22 B4
  Radstock BA3 . . . . 97 E8
KILMINGTON 161 F7
KILMINGTON COMMON . . 161 F6
Kilminster Rd BS11 . . . . . . 4 D7
Kilmorie Cl TA1 . . . . 212 C2
Kiln Cl TA5 . . . . 135 B5
Kiln Dr
  Evercreech BA4 . . . . 141 E1
  Highbridge TA9 . . . . 104 D3
Kiln Pk BS23 . . . . 49 A6
KILTON 133 E6
Kilton Cross TA5 . . . . 133 E5
KILVE 133 C6
Kilve BS24 . . . . 49 A2
Kilve Cl TA2 . . . . 212 F7
Kilve Cres TA2 . . . . 212 F7
Kilve Ct TA5 . . . . 133 C5
Kilver St BA4 . . . . 205 D6
Kilver Street Hill BA4 . . . 205 D7
Kimber Cl TA9 . . . . 104 D3
Kimberley Rd 6 . . . . 6 C2
Kimberley Terr TA6 . . . . . 209 B7
Kinber Cl BA1 . . . . 27 A3
Kinforde TA20 . . . . 223 C6
King Alfred Cl 3 TA4 . . . 153 F4
King Alfred Sch The TA9 104 C5
King Alfreds Ctyd 7
  BA5 . . . . 203 D4
King Alfreds Way BS28 . . 108 B4
King Alfred Way BA15 . . . 64 D7
King Arthur Dr BA21 . . . . 218 D7
King Arthur's Com Sch
  BA9 . . . . 216 A4
King Athelstan Dr TA20 . 223 D2
King Ceol Cl TA20 . . . . . . 223 D2
King Cerdic Cl TA20 . . . . 223 D2
Kingcott Mill Farm Cvns
  BS48 . . . . 20 B8
King Cuthred Cl TA20 . . . 223 D2
King Cuthred Dr TA20 . . . 223 C2
Kingdom BA5 . . . . 113 A4
Kingdom La TA2 . . . . 168 A4
Kingdom Mead TA3 . . . . 169 D4
KINGDON 37 D5

Kingdown Rd BS40 . . . . . . 37 C5
King Edward Cl BS14 . . . . 23 A6
King Edward Rd
  Bath BA2 . . . . 44 D5
  Minehead TA24 . . . . 201 A6
King Edward's Jun Sch
  BA2 . . . . 45 C7
King Edward's Pre-Prep Sch
  BA1 . . . . 44 C8
King Edward's Sch BA2 . . 45 C7
Kingfisher Cl TA6 . . . . . . 209 C3
Kingfisher Cl BA20 . . . . . 218 D3
Kingfisher Cl BA3 . . . . 64 C6
Kingfisher Dr BA3 . . . . 97 B8
Kingfisher Rd
  Portishead BS20 . . . . 2 F7
  Portishead BS20 . . . . 3 A7
  Weston-super-Mare BS22 . 49 F8
Kingfisher Wy BS21 . . . . . 1 B1
King George Ave TA6 . . . 208 F2
King George Cl TA6 . . . . . 209 A2
King George Rd TA24 . . . 201 A6
King George's Rd
  Bath BA2 . . . . 44 C6
  Bristol BS13 . . . . 21 F5
King George St 2 BA20 . 219 B4
King George V Pl 7 BS1 . 227 A2
King Ina Rd TA11 . . . . . . 211 D4
King Ine Cl N TA20 . . . . . 223 C2
King Ine Cl S TA20 . . . . . 223 C2
King La BS39 . . . . 58 F4
Kinglake Villas TA6 . . . . . 209 C4
King Rd BS49 . . . . 52 C6
Kingsacre BA7 . . . . 214 B5
Kings Acre TA4 . . . . 151 B5
KINGSBRIDGE 148 E8
KINGSBURY EPISCOPI . . 185 A8
Kingsbury Episcopi Prim Sch
  TA12 . . . . 185 A6
KINGSBURY REGIS 217 D3
Kings Castle Bsns Est
  TA6 . . . . 209 A6
King's Castle Rd BA5 . . . 112 E1
Kings Cl
  Shepton Mallet BA4 . . . . 205 B5
  Taunton TA1 . . . . 213 A2
Kingscliffe Terr TA6 . . . . 209 A2
King's Cnr TA22 . . . . 163 D6
King's Coll TA1 . . . . 213 B2
Kingscombe BA3 . . . . 114 E6
Kingscourt Cl BS14 . . . . . 23 A4
Kings Cres DT9 . . . . 225 D5
Kings Croft BS41 . . . . 10 E1
Kings Ct
  Bath BA1 . . . . 228 B2
  Bristol BS1 . . . . 227 A2
  Bristol, St Pauls BS1 . . . 227 B4
  2 Bristol, Withywood BS13 21 F4
  Sherborne DT9 . . . . 225 D6
  Yeovil BA21 . . . . 219 C6
KINGSDON 173 E4
Kingsdon CE Prim Sch
  TA11 . . . . 173 D5
Kingsdon Hill TA11 . . . . . 173 D5
Kingsdon Manor Sch
  TA11 . . . . 173 D4
KINGSDOWN
  Box 29 F3
  Bristol 227 A4
Kingsdown Cl TA6 . . . . . . 209 D6
Kingsdown Gr SN13 . . . . . 29 F3
Kingsdown Par BS6 . . . . . 227 A4
Kingsdown View 16 BA1 . 28 A1
Kings Dr
  Bridgwater TA6 . . . . 209 D8
  Westonzoyland TA7 . . . . 154 E6
Kingsettle Hill BA10 . . . . 161 B5
Kingsfield BA2 . . . . 44 C3
Kingsford Gate Cross
  TA24 . . . . 145 B7
Kingsford Hill TA24 . . . . . 145 C7
King's Hall Sch TA2 . . . . 168 E6
Kingshams BA22 . . . . 173 E3
King's Head La BS13 . . . . 21 F7
Kingshill BS48 . . . . 8 C2
Kings Hill BA22 . . . . 186 E6
King's Hill BA3 . . . . 94 F7
Kingshill CE Prim Sch
  BS48 . . . . 8 C1
Kingshill Gdns BS48 . . . . . 8 C1
Kingshill La BS40 . . . . 56 C4
Kingsholme Ct BS23 . . . . 30 C1
Kings La TA7 . . . . 156 B8
King's La
  Binegar BA3 . . . . 95 E1
  Clevedon BS21 . . . . 6 D5
  6 Weston-super-Mare
  BS23 . . . . 48 E8
Kingsland TA23 . . . . 202 D7
Kingsland Grange 1
  BA21 . . . . 218 C6
Kingsland La TA24 . . . . . . 148 D5
Kingsland Rd BA4 . . . . . . 205 B5
Kingsland Trad Est BS2 . . 227 C3
Kings Lear TA19 . . . . 183 F4
Kingsley Cl TA1 . . . . 212 C1
Kingsley Ho BS2 . . . . 227 C2
Kingsley Rd
  Clevedon BS21 . . . . 6 D2
  Radstock BA3 . . . . 78 C3
  Weston-super-Mare BS23 . 48 F3
KINGSMEAD 228 A2
Kingsmead BS48 . . . . 8 C2
Kingsmead Cl
  Holcombe BA3 . . . . 116 C8

Kingsmead Cl continued
Wiveliscombe TA4 . . . . 210 C3
Kingsmead Com Sch
TA4 . . . . 210 C3
Kingsmead Ct 8 BA1 . . . 228 B2
Kingsmead N BA1 . . . . . 228 B2
Kingsmead Sq BA1 . . . . . 228 B2
Kingsmead St BA1 . . . . . 228 B2
Kingsmead W BA1 . . . . . 228 B2
Kingsmill BS9 . . . . 5 D5
King's Mill Rd DT10 . . . 190 D3
Kingsmoor Prim Sch
TA7 . . . . 136 E2
Kings Oak Mdw BS39 . . . 58 E2
Kings of Wessex Com Sch
The BS27 . . . . 90 B7
King's Pl TA6 . . . . . . 208 F5
King Sq
Bridgwater TA6 . . . . . 208 F5
Bristol BS2 . . . . 227 A4
King Square Ave BS2 . . . 227 A4
Kings Rd
Sherborne DT9 . . . . . 225 D5
Stoke sub Hamdon TA14 . 185 F5
Wells BA5 . . . . 140 C8
Wrington BS40 . . . . . 35 D1
King's Rd
Bristol BS8 . . . . 226 A3
Clevedon BS21 . . . . . 6 D5
Doulting BA4 . . . . . . 141 F4
Portishead BS20 . . . . 1 F4
Kings Ride TA20 . . . . . 223 B6
King's Sch BA10 . . . . 215 E6
Kings Sq BS30 . . . . . . 25 D8
King St
Bridgwater TA6 . . . . . 209 A5
Bristol BS1 . . . . 227 A4
Frome BA11 . . . . 119 F5
Glastonbury BA6 . . . . 206 D5
Highbridge TA9 . . . . 104 D3
Yeovil BA21 . . . . . . 219 B6
Kingston BA20 . . . . . 219 A5
Kingston Ave
Clevedon BS21 . . . . . 6 E3
Saltford BS31 . . . . . 25 C3
Kingston Bldgs 5 BA1 . 228 C2
Kingston Cl
Street BA16 . . . . . . 207 D6
Taunton TA2 . . . . . . 212 E7
Kingston Dr BS48 . . . . 18 C8
KINGSTONE 221 E2
Kingstone Cross TA19 . . 221 F2
Kingstone Hill TA19 . . . 221 F2
Kingston La
Felton BS40 . . . . . . 37 F8
Maiden Bradley BA12 . . 144 C1
Kingston Mead BS40 . . . 37 F7
Kingston Mews 3 TA2 . 212 F6
Kingston Rd
Bath BA1 . . . . 228 C2
Nailsea BS48 . . . . . 18 C8
Taunton TA2 . . . . . . 212 E7
KINGSTON ST MARY . . . 168 E8
Kingston St Mary CE Prim
Sch TA2 . . . . 168 D8
KINGSTON SEYMOUR . . . 16 C2
Kingston View BS21 . . . 219 B6
Kingston Way BS48 . . . 18 C8
Kingston Well La TA20 . 194 C2
KINGSWAY 44 C3
Kingsway
Bath BA1 . . . . 44 C3
Holcombe BA3 . . . . . 116 C8
Mark BS26, TA9 . . . . 87 D3
Portishead BS20 . . . . 1 F4
Taunton TA1 . . . . . . 168 F1
Kingsway Ctr BA11 . . . 119 F4
Kingsway Rd TA8 . . . . 104 B7
Kingswear 3 BS22 . . . 32 A2
Kings Weston Ave BS11 . 4 E8
Kings Weston La BS11 . . 5 A8
Kings Weston Rd BS9 . . 5 B8
Kingsweston Sch BS11 . . 5 A8
Kings Wlk BS13 . . . . . 21 E7
KINGSWOOD 150 E8
Kingswood Chase BA14 . 83 F6
Kingswood Prep Sch BA1 27 E1
Kingswood Rd TA18 . . . 224 C4
Kingswood Sch BA1 . . . 27 E2
KINGTON MAGNA 177 E2
Kington View BA8 . . . . 176 E1
Kingwell View BS39 . . . 59 D2
KINGWESTON 157 E2
Kingweston Rd
Butleigh BA6 . . . . . 157 E3
Charlton Mackrell TA11 . 173 E8
King William Ave BS1 . . 227 A2
King William Rd TA7 . . 137 D2
Kinsale Rd BS14 . . . . 23 C7
Kinvara Rd BS4 . . . . . 22 E8
Kinver Terr TA8 . . . . . 104 A7
Kipling Ave BA2 . . . . . 44 F4
Kipling Rd
Radstock BA3 . . . . . . 78 C1
Weston-super-Mare BS23 . 49 A3
Kippax Ave BA5 . . . . . 203 F5
Kipscombe Cross EX35 . 122 A6
Kirk Dr TA7 . . . . 154 E6
Kirkham St TA11 . . . . 211 E4
Kirlegate BA6 . . . . . . 138 C4
Kissing Batch BA11 . . . 119 C6
KITBRIDGE 198 A6
Kitchener Rd TA2 . . . . 168 A6
Kitchens La TA13 . . . . 185 A1

Kite La BA4 . . . . 159 C6
Kites Croft BA5 . . . . . 110 E7
Kite's Nest La SP8 . . . 161 F1
Kithill TA18 . . . . . . 224 D4
Kitley Hill BA3 . . . . . 78 C4
Kitridge La TA24 . . . . 146 B7
Kitrow La TA24 . . . . . 131 A6
Kit's La TA4 . . . . . . 166 A6
Kitswall La TA24 . . . . 130 D5
Kitt Hill DT9 . . . . . . 225 C4
KITTISFORD 166 B1
Kitton La DT9 . . . . . . 188 A4
Kitts TA21 . . . . 222 D4
Kittwake Dr
6 Portishead BS20 . . . . . 2 F6
Portishead BS20 . . . . 2 F7
KITTWHISTLE 199 D6
Knacker's Hole La
Churchinford TA3 . . . 192 A6
Thorncombe DT6, TA20 . 199 C4
Knap Hill BA3 . . . . . 117 B2
KNAPP 169 F4
Knapp TA16 . . . . . . 195 F7
Knapp Cotts TA4 . . . . 151 E1
Knapp Hill Cl BA5 . . . 113 A2
Knapp La
Bishops Lydeard TA4 . . 151 E1
North Curry TA3 . . . . 170 B4
Knapp Rd
Creech St Michael TA3 . 169 F4
North Curry TA3 . . . . 170 A4
Knapps Cl BS25 . . . . . 69 F8
Knapps Dr BS25 . . . . . 69 F8
Knapps La
Chard TA20 . . . . 194 C4
Langport TA10 . . . . . 172 B5
Knapp The TA24 . . . . 130 A4
Knap The BA8 . . . . . 176 E1
Knaptons Hill BA11 . . . 118 C6
Kneller Cl BS11 . . . . . 5 A8
Knight Cl BS22 . . . . . 32 A5
KNIGHTCOTT 50 F3
Knightcott BS29 . . . . . 50 F3
Knightcott Gdns BS29 . 50 F3
Knightcott Ind Est BS29 . 50 F3
Knightcott Pk BS29 . . . 51 A3
Knightcott Rd
Abbots Leigh BS8 . . . 10 F8
Banwell BS29 . . . . . . 50 F3
Knightlands La TA10 . . 172 F4
KNIGHTON 184 D7
Knighton TA5 . . . . . . 134 B7
Knighton Dro TA10 . . . 184 D7
Knightsbridge Pk BS13 . 22 E4
Knightsbridge Way TA6 209 D6
Knight's Cross TA21 . . 181 A5
Knight's Ct BA11 . . . . 119 F4
Knight Shute La TA20 . 193 D6
Knight's La
Axminster EX13 . . . . 198 A4
Higher Chillington TA19 . 194 E5
Knights Rd TA21 . . . . 180 D8
Knights Templar CE Meth
Com Sch TA23 . . . . 202 D6
Knightstone La BS13 . . 169 D3
Knightstone Cl
Axbridge BS26 . . . . . 70 C1
Kingsbury Episcopi TA12 . 185 B8
Peasedown St John BA2 . 79 B8
Knightstone Cswy BS23 . 48 C8
Knightstone Ct
Burnham-on-S TA8 . . . 104 B6
Clevedon BS21 . . . . . 6 D1
Stalbridge DT10 . . . . 190 B4
Taunton TA2 . . . . . . 213 A6
Weston-super-Mare BS23 . 30 D1
Knightstone Gn BS23 . . 48 E6
Knightstone Ho
1 Bristol BS2 . . . . . 227 A4
Weston-super-Mare BS23 . 48 D8
Knightstone Hts BA11 . 119 F3
Knightstone Mead TA22 148 A3
Knightstone Pk 4 BS23 . 48 E5
Knightstone Pl
Bath BA1 . . . . 27 B1
7 Weston-super-Mare
BS22 . . . . 31 F2
Knightstone Rd BS23 . . 48 C8
Knightstone Sq BS14 . . 23 C5
Knightstone Wlk BS2 . . 226 C4
Knights Yd BA7 . . . . . 214 C5
Knobsbury Hill BA3 . . . 98 D6
Knobsbury La BA3 . . . 98 C7
KNOLE 173 A4
Knole Cswy
Knole TA10 . . . . 173 A4
Long Sutton TA10 . . . 172 F4
Knole Pit La TA10 . . . 173 A4
Knoll Ct BS9 . . . . . . 5 D3
Knoll Green La TA5 . . . 134 F2
Knoll Hill BS9 . . . . . 5 D3
Knoll Hill View BA11 . . 143 C6
Knoll Ho 5 BA11 . . . . 119 F4
Knoll La BA4 . . . . . . 142 E3
Knoll Pk TA8 . . . . . . 65 F2
Knoll The BS20 . . . . . 2 D7
Knoll View
Burnham-on-S TA8 . . . 104 C8
4 Frome BA11 . . . . . 119 F4
Knotcroft La TA2 . . . . 153 D1
Knotts Paddock DT9 . . 225 E4
KNOWLE 136 D2
Knowle Cross DT8 . . . 199 F6
Knowle Dro
Middlezoy TA7 . . . . . 155 A4
Westonzoyland TA7 . . . 154 F5
Knowle End TA7 . . . . 136 E3

Knowle La
Chard TA20 . . . . 194 B6
Dunster TA24 . . . . . . 201 B1
Misterton DT8, TA18 . . 224 E2
Shepton Mallet BA4 . . . 204 C5
Wookey BA5 . . . . . . 110 E1
Knowle Moor Dro BA5 . 110 C2
Knowle Rd TA6 . . . . . 209 C6
KNOWLE ST GILES . . . 194 B6
Knowles Rd BS21 . . . . 6 C2
Knowleyards Rd TA7 . . 155 B4
KNOWSTONE 162 A2
Korresia Wlk TA6 . . . . 208 D1
Kuching Rd BA22 . . . . 174 A2
Kylross Ave BS14 . . . 23 B5
Kyrle Gdns BA1 . . . . . 28 F3
Kyte Rd BA4 . . . . . . 205 C5

L

Labbott The BS31 . . . . 24 E5
Labourham Dro BS27 . . 90 B5
Labourham Way BS27 . . 90 B6
Laburnum Cl
Bridgwater TA6 . . . . 209 D4
Frome BA11 . . . . 120 B7
Midsomer Norton BA3 . . 96 F8
Somerton TA11 . . . . . 211 D4
Laburnum Cotts 7 TA21 222 D6
Laburnum Cres TA18 . . 224 D7
Laburnum Ct
7 Taunton TA1 . . . . 213 A4
Weston-super-Mare BS23 . 49 B7
Laburnum Dr TA11 . . . 211 D4
Laburnum Gr BA3 . . . 96 F8
Laburnum Lodges TA9 . 136 A8
Laburnum Rd
Wellington TA21 . . . . 222 E5
Weston-super-Mare BS23 . 49 B7
Laburnum St TA1 . . . . 213 A4
Laburnum Terr
Batheaston BA1 . . . . 28 F3
Creech St Michael TA3 . 169 D4
Laburnum Way BA20 . . 218 D2
Laburnum Wlk BS31 . . 24 C3
Lacey Rd BS14 . . . . . 23 F6
La Ciotat Ho TA6 . . . . 209 A4
Ladd Cl TA9 . . . . . . 104 D3
Ladies Mile BS8 . . . . 5 F1
Ladman Gr BS14 . . . . 23 E6
Ladman Rd BS14 . . . . 23 E5
Ladycroft 5 BS21 . . . . 6 B1
Ladye Bay BS21 . . . . 6 D7
Ladye Wake BS22 . . . 31 F4
Lady Harriet Acland's Dr
TA22 . . . . 164 A8
Lady Lawn TA3 . . . . . 168 D1
Ladymead BS20 . . . . . 2 F5
Ladymead Cl TA6 . . . . 208 B4
Ladymeade
Backwell BS48 . . . . . 19 A7
Ilminster TA19 . . . . . 221 B3
Ladymead Ho BA1 . . . 228 C3
Ladymead La BS40 . . . 52 F5
Ladymead Rd TA2 . . . 168 F6
Lady St TA22 . . . . . . 163 D7
Lady Victoria's Dr TA22 . 163 E6
Ladywell BS40 . . . . . 35 D2
Laggan Gdns BA1 . . . . 27 E1
Laggan Ho BA1 . . . . . 27 E1
Lagger Hill TA5 . . . . . 133 C5
Lahs Pl BA11 . . . . . . 101 E4
Lakefields BA22 . . . . 197 B8
Lakemead Gdns 3 BS13 . 21 F4
Lakemead Gr BS13 . . . 21 F6
Lake Mews BA22 . . . . 219 B1
Lake Rd BS20 . . . . . . 2 D7
Lake Shore Dr BS13 . . 22 C6
Lakeside TA9 . . . . . . 104 E4
Lakeside Cl BS40 . . . . 55 D5
Lakeside Ct BS24 . . . . 32 B1
Lakeside Pk
Bridgwater TA6 . . . . 209 A3
Vobster BA11 . . . . . . 117 E8
Lakeview Cres TA9 . . . 104 E3
Lake Wall TA7 . . . . . 154 E4
Lambert Cl DT9 . . . . . 217 C2
Lambert Ct DT9 . . . . . 217 C2
Lambert La TA19 . . . . 194 F5
Lambert Pl BS4 . . . . . 22 D6
Lambert's Hill BA4 . . . 204 F3
Lamberts Marsh BA14 . 83 E2
Lamb La TA6 . . . . . . 208 F4
Lambourne Ct TA18 . . 224 D7
Lambourne Way BS20 . 2 F5
Lambourn Rd BS31 . . . 25 A4
Lambpark Ct TA3 . . . . 191 F6
LAMBRIDGE 28 C2
Lambridge 6 BA1 . . . . 28 C1
Lambridge Bldgs 1 BA1 28 C1
Lambridge Grange 6
BA1 . . . . 28 C2
Lambridge Mews 5 BA1 . 28 C1
Lambridge Pl BA1 . . . 28 C1
Lambridge St BA1 . . . 28 C1
Lambrok Cl BA14 . . . . 83 F6
Lambrok Rd BA14 . . . 83 F6
Lambrook Cl TA1 . . . . 213 B4
Lambrook Gate TA13 . . 184 F5
Lambrook Ho BA9 . . . 216 C4
Lambrook Rd
Shepton Beauchamp
TA19 . . . . 184 E4
Taunton TA1 . . . . . . 213 B4
Lambrook St BA6 . . . . 206 E4
Lambrook Way TA1 . . 213 C4
Lambs Field DT9 . . . . 225 E5

Lamb St BS2 . . . . . . 227 C3
Lamington Cl BS13 . . . 21 F6
Lamont Ho 7 BA1 . . . 28 C1
Lampard's Bldgs BA1 . 228 B4
Lamparts Way TA19 . . 183 C2
Lampeter Rd BS9 . . . . 5 F7
Lampley Rd BS21 . . . . 16 D2
Lampreys La TA13 . . . 220 C3
Lampton Ave BS13 . . . 22 E3
Lampton Gr BS13 . . . 22 E3
Lampton Rd BS41 . . . 10 F1
LAMYATT 159 F6
Lancaster Cl TA6 . . . . 136 B2
Lancaster House Sch
BS23 . . . . 48 F8
Lancer Ct TA21 . . . . . 222 D6
Lanch La SP8 . . . . . . 177 F5
Lancock St TA21 . . . . 222 A5
Lancombe La BA10 . . . 215 C3
Landacre La TA24 . . . 146 A7
Landemann Cir BS23 . . 30 E1
Landemann Path 2 BS23. 48 E8
Landing Lights BS14 . . 22 E5
Landlord's Hill TA21 . . 179 E7
Landmark Ct BS1 . . . 226 C1
Landmead BA6 . . . . . 206 D5
Landmoor La TA10 . . . 172 D4
Landsdown Mews BA11 . 119 D5
Landseer BA8 . . . . . . 176 D4
Landseer Cl BS22 . . . 31 F3
Landseer Rd BA2 . . . 44 B6
Landshire La
Charlton Horethorne
DT9 . . . . 176 A1
Chilton Polden TA7 . . 137 A3
Henstridge BA8 . . . . 190 C6
Odcombe BA22 . . . . 186 C1
LANE END 144 D8
Lane End BA12 . . . . . 144 D8
Lane Foot TA24 . . . . 129 D7
Lane Head TA24 . . . . 123 E4
Lanesborough Rise BS14 . 23 D7
Lanes End Hill BA11,
BA12 . . . . 144 D8
Laneys Dro BS24 . . . . 49 E5
LANGALLER 169 C6
Langaller Hill TA22 . . . 163 D4
Langdon Cl TA20 . . . . 223 D6
Langdon Rd BA2 . . . . 44 B4
Langdons DT9 . . . . . 225 E5
Langdons Way TA20 . . 198 C8
Langdown St BS14 . . 23 E5
Langer's La TA19 . . . 194 E5
LANGFORD 212 A8
LANGFORD BUDVILLE . . 166 E2
Langford Budville CE Prim
Sch TA21 . . . . 166 F1
Langford Cl TA3 . . . . 170 F1
Langford Ct BA11 . . . 143 F4
Langford Ct Cotts BS40 . 53 E5
Langford Gate TA4 . . 166 F2
Langford La
Fivehead TA3 . . . . . 170 F2
Lower Langford BS40 . 53 E5
Norton Fitzwarren TA2 . 168 C6
Langford Rd
Bristol BS13 . . . . . . 21 F8
Lower Langford BS40 . 53 E5
Weston-super-Mare BS23 . 49 A6
Langfords La BS39 . . . 77 C8
Langford's La BS39 . . . 59 D1
LANGHAM
Chard 223 C7
Gillingham 177 F4
Langham Dr TA1 . . . . 212 C1
Langham Gdns TA1 . . 212 C1
Langham La SP8 . . . . 177 F5
Langham Pl BA11 . . . 82 F1
Langhill Ave BS4 . . . . 22 D7
Langland La TA7 . . . . 137 D2
Langlands 8 TA14 . . . 185 F4
Langlands La TA3 . . . 169 F2
Langland's La TA9 . . . 104 B1
LANGLEY 210 C6
Langley Cres BS3 . . . 11 E1
Langley Cross TA4 . . . 210 B6
LANGLEY MARSH 210 A7
Langleys Cotts BA3 . . 96 B8
Langley's La BA3, BS39 . 77 C1
Langmead Dro
Middlezoy TA7 . . . . . 155 A4
Westonzoyland TA7 . . . 154 F5
Langmead La TA7 . . . 155 A4
Langmead Pl TA18 . . 224 C4
Langmead Rd TA18 . . 224 C4
Langmead Sq TA18 . . 224 C4
Langmoor La EX13 . . . 198 D2
LANGPORT 172 B5
Langport Gdns BS48 . . 18 E4
Langport Rd
Long Sutton TA10 . . . 172 E5
Middlezoy TA7 . . . . . 155 B4
Somerton TA11 . . . . . 211 B4
Weston-super-Mare BS23 . 48 E5
Lang Rd TA18 . . . . . 224 C4
LANGRIDGE 27 E7
Langridge La BA1 . . . 27 D8
Lang's Cnr TA19 . . . . 183 B1
Langton Ho 9 BS2 . . . 227 C3
Langworthy Orch TA19 . 183 C1
LANSDOWN
Bath 27 E1
Langridge 27 B6
Lansdown Cres
2 Bath BA1 . . . . . . 27 F1
Timsbury BA2 . . . . . 60 C2
Lansdown Ct BS23 . . . 48 F8
Lansdowne Pl BA9 . . 216 C4

Lansdowne Rd TA2 . . . 213 A6
Lansdown Gdns BS22 . 32 B5
Lansdown Gr BA1 . . . 28 A1
Lansdown Grove Ct BA1. 228 B4
Lansdown Grove Lodge
BA1 . . . . 228 B4
Lansdown Ho BA1 . . . 27 F1
Lansdown Hts BA1 . . 27 F1
Lansdown La
Bath BA1 . . . . 27 B4
Upton Cheyney BS30 . . 26 D8
Lansdown Mans BA1 . . 228 B4
Lansdown Pk BA1 . . . 27 E3
Lansdown Pl
Bristol BS8 . . . . 226 A3
Frome BA11 . . . . 119 D5
High Littleton BS39 . . 59 D1
Lansdown Pl E BA1 . . 228 B4
Lansdown Pl W 1 BA1 . 27 F1
Lansdown Rd
Bath BA1 . . . . 27 E2
Bristol BS8 . . . . 226 A3
Saltford BS31 . . . . . 25 E3
Lansdown View
Bath BA2 . . . . 44 C5
Faulkland BA3 . . . . . 80 D1
Timsbury BA2 . . . . . 60 C2
Tunley BA2 . . . . 61 B4
Lanthony Cl BS24 . . . 50 A8
Lapwing Cl
Minehead TA24 . . . . 201 C5
Portishead BS20 . . . . 2 F6
Lapwing Gdns BS22 . . 31 F1
Larch Ave TA20 . . . . 223 B5
Larch Cl
Bridgwater TA6 . . . . 209 D6
Churchill BS40 . . . . . 53 A5
Nailsea BS48 . . . . . 9 A2
Taunton TA1 . . . . . . 213 D2
Larch Ct BA3 . . . . . . 97 D8
Larches The BS22 . . . 32 A3
Larchfield Cl BA11 . . . 120 B7
Larchfield Trad Est TA19. 221 B1
Larchgrove Cres BS22 . 31 F1
Larchgrove Wlk BS22 . 31 F1
Larchwood Ct BA3 . . . 79 A3
Lark Cl BA3 . . . . . . 97 B8
LARKHALL 28 C2
Larkhall Pl BA1 . . . . 28 C2
Larkhall Terr BA1 . . . 28 C2
Larkhill Rd
Locking BS24 . . . . . 50 B6
Yeovil BA21 . . . . . . 218 D7
Lark Pl BA1 . . . . . . 44 D7
Lark Rd BS22 . . . . . 31 F1
Larks Mdw DT10 . . . . 190 C4
Larkspur Cl TA1 . . . . 213 C1
Larkspur Cres BA21 . . 218 D7
Larkspur Ct TA2 . . . . 212 D7
Larspur Rd TA6 . . . . 208 E1
Larviscombe Cl TA4 . . 202 D4
Larviscombe Rd TA4 . . 202 D4
Lasbury Gr BS13 . . . . 22 C5
Lascot Hill BS28 . . . . 108 C5
LATCHAM 108 F4
Latcham Dro BS27, BS28 . 109 A4
Latches La BS27 . . . . 90 D3
Latchmoor Ho BS13 . . 22 A8
Late Broads BA15 . . . 64 D7
LATTIFORD 176 D5
Lauder Ct DT9 . . . . . 217 D2
LAUNCHERLEY 140 B5
Launcherley Cross BA5. 140 A6
Launcherley Rd BA4, BA5 140 B5
Launder Cl BA6 . . . . 206 E4
Laura Pl BA2 . . . . . . 228 C3
Laurel Ave TA9 . . . . 86 A2
Laurel Cl
East Coker BA22 . . . 197 B8
Frome BA11 . . . . 120 B7
Taunton TA1 . . . . . . 213 C1
Laurel Dr
Nailsea BS48 . . . . . 8 F2
Paulton BS39 . . . . . 77 E5
Weston-super-Mare BS23 . 48 E2
Laurel Gdns
Chard TA20 . . . . 223 B5
Timsbury BA2 . . . . . 60 B1
Yatton BS49 . . . . . 17 B1
Laurel La BA22 . . . . 174 F3
Laurel St BA6 . . . . . 140 A1
Laurels The
Churchill BS25 . . . . 52 F4
Crewkerne TA18 . . . . 224 D7
Wembdon TA6 . . . . . 208 C6
Weston-super-Mare BS23 . 48 E2
Westwood BA15 . . . 64 F3
Laurel Terr BS49 . . . . 17 B1
Lavender Cl BS22 . . . 32 A5
Lavender Ct
Frome BA11 . . . . 120 B7
Street BA16 . . . . . . 207 B4
Lavender Gr TA1 . . . 212 C3
Lavender Wlk TA6 . . . 208 D1
LAVERLEY 140 C2
Laverley Cotts BA6 . . . 140 C2
Laverock Ct TA1 . . . . 212 E5
Lavers Ct TA12 . . . . . 186 A7
Laver's La TA20 . . . . 198 F5
Lavers Oak TA12 . . . 185 E7
LAVERTON 100 F7
Lavington Cl BS21 . . . 6 B1
Lavinia Wy TA6 . . . . 208 D5
LAWFORD 151 E7
Lawfords Gate BS2 . . 227 C3
Lawfords Gate Ho 17
BS2 . . . . 227 C3
Lawford St BS2 . . . . 227 C3

Law La
Drayton TA10 171 F3
Langport TA10 172 A3
Lawn La
Galhampton BA22 175 D8
Shapwick TA7 137 F1
Lawn Mdw TA3 169 C3
Lawnmoor La TA10 184 C6
Lawn Rd TA2 212 C8
Lawnside BS48 19 B5
Lawns The
Bristol BS11 4 E7
Combe St Nicholas TA20 193 D6
Weston-super-Mare BS22 32 B3
Yatton BS49 17 A1
Lawn The [1] TA21 222 D6
Lawpool Ct [12] BA5 203 D4
Lawrence Cl
Burnham-on-S TA8 104 D5
Highbridge TA9 104 F4
Somerton TA11 211 D3
Weston-super-Mare BS22 31 E2
Lawrence Hayes BA9 216 D3
Lawrence Hill BA9 216 A2
Lawrence Hill Bsns Ctr BA9 216 B3
Lawrence Mews BS22 31 E2
Lawrence Rd
Coleford BA3 116 F7
Weston-super-Mare BS22 31 E2
Wrington BS40 35 E2
Laws Dr BS24 49 F7
Lawson Cl
[5] Martock TA12 185 E6
Saltford BS31 25 C2
Lawyer's Hill TA5 152 C7
Lax Ct BA5 203 B4
Laxton Cl TA1 213 D5
Laxton Rd TA1 213 E5
Laxton Way BA2 79 D7
Laycock Hill DT9 217 D7
Layfield La TA3 170 C3
LAYMORE 199 C7
Layne Terr TA18 196 B8
Lays Bsns Ctr BS31 24 C4
Lays Dr BS31 24 C5
Lays La BS40 54 D4
Lays The BA11 101 E5
Leach Cl BS21 6 D1
Leaches Cl BA22 186 B6
Leach Rd TA20 223 D7
Leach's Field TA2 168 D8
Lea Cl BA21 219 B8
Lea Croft BS13 22 A4
Leading Edge The BS8 226 B2
Leadon Gr TA1 213 D4
Leafield Cl TA2 168 B5
Leafy Way BS24 50 B4
Lea Grove Rd BS21 6 C4
Leaholme Gdns BS14 23 A3
Lear's La BA9 177 C6
Leat The [8] TA4 167 F8
Leawood Ct [3] BS23 30 C1
Leaze Cl BA11 119 D5
Leaze Dro BA5 139 A7
Leaze Ho BA11 119 D5
Leaze House Mews BA11 119 D5
Leaze La
Blagdon BS40 72 E8
West Chinnock TA18 196 B8
Yeovil BA21 219 F4
Leazemoor La TA10 172 B8
Leaze Rd BA11 119 D5
Leaze The
Radstock BA3 97 D8
Rode BA2 82 C1
Leazeway Dro TA7 155 C1
Lecher La DT8, TA18 196 B1
Leda Ave BS14 23 A7
Leedham Rd BS24 50 C5
LEEFORD 122 B5
Leeford La EX35 122 B5
Leeming Way BS11 4 C8
Lee Pk TA21 180 F7
Leeside BS20 2 C5
Leet Ct DT9 225 B2
Leeward Cl TA6 209 C4
Leewood Rd BS23 30 F1
Leffman Ct TA11 211 C4
Leggar The TA6 209 A6
Legion Rd BA21 218 F6
Leg La BS40 54 B3
Leg Of Mutton Rd BA6 206 E6
Leg Sq BA4 205 C6
Leg Square Ct BA4 205 C6
Leigh Cl BA1 28 A2
Leigh Court Bsns Ctr BS8 5 A2
Leigh Furlong Rd BA16 207 B4
Leigh La
Cold Ashton BA1 13 B3
Crowcombe TA4 151 A7
Halstock BA22 197 C3
Winsford TA22 147 C2
Winsham TA20 199 A8
LEIGHLAND CHAPEL 149 C7
Leigh-on-Mendip Fst Sch BA3 117 A3
Leigh Rd
Bristol BS8 226 B4
Leigh u M BA11 117 C2
Street BA16 207 C5
Taunton TA2 213 B8
Leigh St BA3 116 F3
LEIGHTON 142 E6
Leighton Cl BA4 141 E1
Leighton Cres BS24 67 A8
Leighton La BA4 141 E1
Leighton Lane Ind Est BA4 141 E1
Leighton Rd BA1 27 A3
LEIGH UPON MENDIP 116 F3
Leigh View Rd BS20 2 E7
Leighwood Dr BS48 8 B1
LEIGH WOODS 11 D6
Leigh Woods Forest Walks* BS8 5 C1
Leigh Woods National Nature Reserve* BS8 11 D8
Leinster Ave BS4 22 D8
Lemon La BS2 227 C4
Lenover Gdns BS13 22 B4
Lenthay Cl DT9 225 C2
Lenthay Ct DT9 225 C3
Lenthay Rd DT9 225 B2
Leonard Houlden Ct [7] TA2 213 A8
Leonard La BS1 227 A3
Leonard's Barton BA11 119 E6
Leopold Bldgs BA1 228 C4
Lerburne The BS28 108 D4
Leslie Ave TA2 212 E6
Leslie Rise BA15 64 F3
Les Rosiers Gdns BA9 216 C4
Lester Dr BS22 32 A3
Lester La DT9 176 A2
Letham Ct TA19 221 B4
Lethbridge Pk TA4 151 D1
Lethbridge Rd BA5 203 C4
Level La DT9 176 A2
Level View TA10 172 C5
Leversedge Rd BA11 120 A7
LEWCOMBE 197 E2
Lewins Mead BS1 227 A3
Lewis Cres BA11 119 F6
Lewisham Gr BS23 49 A8
Lewis Rd
Bristol BS13 22 A8
Taunton TA2 212 E7
Lewis's Dro BA5 138 E7
Lewmond Ave BA5 203 F5
Leycroft Cl TA1 213 B4
Leycroft Gr TA1 213 B4
Leycroft Rd TA1 213 B4
Leyland Wlk BS13 21 F4
Leys Hill BA11 120 A6
Leys La BA11 119 F7
Leys The BS21 6 B1
Leystone Cl BA11 120 A6
Leyton Dr TA6 209 D6
Lias Rd BA16 207 B4
Liberty Gdns BS1 226 C1
Liberty La BS40 54 E2
Liberty Pl TA6 209 B4
Liberty The BA5 203 E5
Lidden Hill TA18 195 C5
Liddymore La
Watchet TA23 202 D5
Williton TA4, TA23 202 E4
Liddymore Rd TA23 202 C6
Lightermans Cl TA24 201 B7
Lightgate TA13 220 D5
Lightgate La TA13 220 D4
Lightgate Rd TA13 220 D4
Lilac Cl TA1 213 C2
Lilac Ct BS31 24 C4
Lilac Terr BA3 78 C2
Lilac Way BS22 32 A5
Lilian Terr BS39 77 E5
Lillebonne Cl TA21 222 F6
Lillebonne Wy TA21 222 D7
Lillesdon Terr TA3 170 A2
Lilliana Wy TA6 208 E1
Lillington Cl BA3 79 B2
Lillington Rd BA3 79 B2
Lillington Way TA20 223 C5
Lilly Batch BA11 119 F7
Lillycombe La TA3, EX15 191 B8
Lillypool Cheese & Cider Farm* BS25 70 F6
LILSTOCK 133 F7
Lily La BA8 176 E1
Limber Rd BA22 218 A6
Limbers La BA5 139 B8
Limbury [2] TA12 185 E6
Limbury Cotts [3] TA12 185 E6
Limebreach Wood BS48 8 D3
Limeburn Hill BS40 38 E5
Lime Cl
Frome BA11 120 B7
Locking BS24 50 B4
Minehead TA24 200 D7
Street BA16 207 C5
Weston-super-Mare BS22 32 A1
Lime Cres TA1 213 C2
Lime Ct BS31 24 C4
Lime Gr
Bath BA2 45 B6
Shepton Mallet BA4 205 A6
Lime Grove Gdns BA2 45 B6
Lime Kiln BA21 218 C5
Limekiln La
Bath BA2 45 F4
Chard, Forton TA20 223 D1
Chard, Lydmarsh TA20 194 C3
Cricket St Thomas TA20 194 E2
Leigh u M BA11 117 C3
Oakhill BA3 114 E5
Stoke St Michael BA3 115 F4
Tatworth TA20 193 F1
Lime Kiln La
Castle Cary BA7 214 E4
Clevedon BS21 6 D3
Henstridge BA8 190 A6
Wookey Hole BA5 203 B7
Lime Kiln Rd BS1 226 B2
Limekilns Cl BS31 24 F5
Limepits La TA10 172 D5
Limerick Cl DT9 217 D2
Limerick La BA11 101 F2
Limes Cl TA4 202 E3
Lime St
Nether Stowey TA5 134 B2
Stogursey TA5 134 C6
Limestone Hill TA5 135 C1
Lime Terr BA3 78 D1
Lime Tree Ave BA20 218 E2
Lime Tree Cl TA6 209 D4
Lime Tree Gr BS20 4 D3
LIMINGTON 174 A1
Limington Rd BA22 173 E1
Limousin Way TA6 209 A1
Limpetshell La TA4 202 E3
LIMPLEY STOKE 64 A6
Limpley Stoke Rd BA15 64 D6
Linch La BA4 142 D2
Lincoln Hill TA19 184 E4
Lincoln Cl BS31 24 C4
Lincoln La BS23 49 B4
Lincombe Rd BA3 97 D8
Lincott View BA2 79 C8
Linden Ave BS23 49 B8
Linden Cl
Bridgwater TA6 209 C4
Bristol BS14 23 E6
Frome BA11 119 D5
Radstock BA3 97 E8
Linden Ct BS21 6 D4
Linden Gdns BA1 44 D8
Linden Gr TA1 212 E5
Linden Hill TA21 222 A6
Linden Rd
Clevedon BS21 6 D4
Yeovil BA20 218 F5
Lindens The BS22 31 E4
Lindisfarne Cl BA15 64 E6
Lindsey Cl BS20 1 F4
Lindsey Cres [1] TA6 153 F3
Linemere Cl BS48 19 D6
Linen Wlk BA1 28 C2
Lines Way BS14 23 C3
Liney Rd TA7 154 F6
Lingfield Ave BA21 219 D7
Linham Rd TA6 208 F6
Linhay Cl EX15 179 E1
Linkhay TA20 198 D8
Linkhay Cl TA20 198 D8
Link La
Burrington BS40 53 F3
Monkton Farleigh BA15 46 F8
Linkmead BA3 96 F2
Link Rd
Nailsea BS48 8 F2
Portishead BS20 2 C5
Links Ct BS23 48 D4
Links Gdns TA8 84 F3
Linkside BS21 6 E6
Links Rd BS23 48 C2
Link The BS27 90 B8
Linley Cl
Bath BA2 44 A5
Bridgwater TA6 209 D7
Linleys The BA1 44 C7
Linne Ho BA2 44 A5
Linnet Cl
Taunton TA1 212 B4
Weston-super-Mare BS22 31 E1
Linnet Gdns [5] BS20 2 F6
Linnet Way
Frome BA11 120 B6
Midsomer Norton BA3 97 B8
Linsvale Cl BA11 120 C5
Linsvale Dr BA11 120 C5
Lintern Cl BA4 159 C7
Linton's Wlk BS14 23 A7
Lion Cl BS48 8 D2
Lion D'angers TA4 210 D4
Lion Ho [20] BA4 205 B6
Lion Mews TA11 211 E4
Lipe Hill La TA3, TA4 168 B1
Lipe La TA3 169 C3
Lipgate Pl BS20 2 D3
Lippetts Way TA7 137 D1
Lippiat Hill BA3 80 C3
Lippiatt La
Cheddar BS27 90 C7
Shipham BS25 70 F8
Timsbury BA2 60 B3
Lippiatt The BS27 90 C8
LIPYEATE 97 E1
Lisieux Ct TA1 213 D2
Lisieux Way TA1 213 C3
Lisle Rd BS22 32 B4
Listercombe Cl TA19 221 C2
Lister Gr BA15 64 F3
Lister's Hill TA19 221 C2
LISTOCK 170 C2
Litfield Pl BS8 11 F7
Litfield Rd BS8 11 F8
Litt Hill BA3 75 F2
Little Ann St BS2, BS5 227 C4
Little Birch Croft BS14 23 A3
Little Bishop St BS2 227 B4
Littlebrook BS39 77 E6
Little Brooks La BA4 205 C4
Little Burrow Dro TA7 155 A1
Little Caroline Pl [4] BS8 11 F5
Little Cl TA2 212 C8
Little Elm Rd TA7 155 C4
Little England TA7 155 C2
Little Entry BA5 203 F5
Littlefield DT9 225 B3
Littlefield Cl BA16 156 E7
Littlefield La TA10 172 E4
Little Field La BA5 110 F7
Littlefields Ave BS29 51 B3
Littlefields La TA19 184 F3
Littlefields Rd BS29 51 B3
Littlefields Rise BS29 51 B3
Little George St
Bristol BS2 227 C4
Weston-super-Mare BS23 48 E7
Little Gn BA5 111 A4
LITTLE GREEN 118 B6
Little Halt BS20 1 E4
Little Ham BS21 16 C8
Littleham Cotts TA3 181 E6
Little Headley Cl BS13 22 B7
LITTLE HILL 192 F8
LITTLE KEYFORD 119 E1
Little Keyford La BA11 119 E1
Little King St BS1 227 A2
Little La
Farmborough BA2 60 A6
Kingsbury Episcopi TA12 185 A7
Little Leaze La TA7 137 D2
Little Lester TA19 221 C2
LITTLE LONDON 114 F3
Little Marston Rd BA22 174 F1
Little Mdw
[6] Bishops Lydeard TA4 167 F8
Ilchester BA22 173 E2
Little Mead TA14 185 F2
Little Mead Cl BS24 49 E3
Little Meadow End BS48 18 E8
Little Moor Rd TA9 106 F3
Littlemore Dro TA7 154 C3
LITTLE NORTON 186 A2
Little Orch
Cheddar BS27 90 C8
Street BA16 207 D7
Weston-super-Mare BS23 48 D1
Little Orchard [34] TA12 185 E6
Little Paul St BS2 226 C4
Little Pen TA8 84 F5
Little Plover Cl TA24 201 C5
Little Sammons BA22 186 E5
Little Silver Ct TA23 202 C7
Little Silver La TA21 222 D2
Little St TA14 185 E2
Little Stanhope St BA1 228 A2
Little Stoke Rd BS9 5 E4
Little Thatch Cl BS14 23 C6
LITTLETON 38 D4
Littleton Hill TA11 211 E6
Littleton La
Wellow BA2 80 C7
Winford BS40 38 D5
Little Trumps BA22 186 B7
LITTLE WESTON 175 B4
Little Withey Mead BS9 5 F5
Little Wiveliscombe La TA4 165 D6
Littlewood BA11 143 C4
Littlewood Cl BS14 23 B3
Littlewood La BS49 18 C2
LITTON 75 F2
Litton BS24 49 A2
Liver Moor Dro TA11 156 E2
Livingstone Rd BA2 44 D5
Livingstone Terr BA2 228 A1
Livingstone Way TA2 212 B6
Llewellyns Almshouses [6] BA5 203 D4
Llewellyn Way BS22 32 B3
Lloyd Cl TA1 212 B1
Load La TA7 154 E5
Load Pool TA7 155 C2
Lobelia Cl TA9 104 D5
Lockemor Rd BS13 22 F4
Lockes Paddock BS22 32 C3
Locketts Barton TA3 170 D7
Lockey Rd BA4 205 B4
Lock Gdns BS13 21 E7
LOCKING 50 A4
Locking Farm Ind Est BS24 50 A5
Locking Head Dro
Locking BS24 49 F5
Weston-super-Mare BS24 50 A6
Locking Moor Rd
Locking BS24 50 B5
Weston-super-Mare BS22 49 D8
Locking Prim Sch BS24 50 B4
Locking Rd BS22, BS23 49 B7
Lockingwell Rd BS31 24 D5
LOCKSBROOK 44 B6
Locksbrook Ct [8] BA1 44 B6
Locksbrook Rd
Bath BA1 44 C6
Weston-super-Mare BS22 32 B5
Locksbrook Trad Est [7] BA1 44 B6
Lock's Hill BA11 119 F3
Lockside BS20 2 E7
Lockside Sq BS20 2 E7
Lock's La BA9 216 C4
Locks Way TA7 136 F3
Lockswell TA7 136 E4
Lockswell Cotts BA4 141 B1
Lockwood Ct [4] BA21 218 F7
Lockyer Dro TA7 156 A5
Lodes La TA2 168 E8
Lodge Cl
Taunton TA1 212 A2
Wellington TA21 222 D6
Yatton BS49 34 B8
Lodge Cotts TA3 181 D6
Lodge Ct
Bristol BS9 5 E4
Castle Cary BA7 214 B4
Lodge Dr
Long Ashton BS41 11 B2
Weston-super-Mare BS23 31 A1
Lodge Gdns BA2 44 D1
Lodge Hill
Berkley BA11, BA13 120 F5
Bratton Seymour BA9 176 A7
Somerton TA11 211 F4
Westbury-sub-Mendip BA5 110 D5
Yarlington BA9 175 F7
Lodge Hill Ind Pk BA5 110 D5
Lodge La
Axminster EX13 198 B2
Tudhay EX13 198 C3
Wraxall BS48 9 B2
Lodge Pl BS1 226 C3
Lodge Rd
Horningsham BA12 144 D4
Kingsdon TA11 173 D4
Lodge Rocks TA24 131 D3
Lodge St BS1 226 C3
Lodges The BA3 96 D1
LODWAY 4 B5
Lodway BS20 4 C4
Lodway Cl BS20 4 C5
Lodway Gdns BS20 4 C4
Lodwells Orch TA3 170 B4
Lombardy Cl [5] BS22 49 E8
London Cross TA4 151 E4
London Dro BA6, BS28 138 D7
London Ho TA4 210 C4
London Rd
Bath BA1 228 C4
Milborne Port DT9 217 E1
London Rd E BA1 29 A3
London Rd W BA1 28 E2
London Sq
[28] Martock TA12 185 E6
Portishead BS20 2 E7
London St BA1 228 C4
Longacre BS21 16 B8
Long Acre BA4 205 C4
Longacre Cl TA2 212 E7
Longacre Dro TA7 154 D7
Long Acre Ho BA1 228 C4
Longacre La TA19 194 F6
Long Acre Rd BS14 23 A3
Long Acres Cl BS9 5 D7
LONGALLER 168 B4
LONG ASHTON 11 A1
Long Ashton Bsns Pk BS41 11 B1
Long Ashton Rd BS41 11 B2
Long Ave BS21 6 B2
Long Barnaby BA3 78 A2
Longbottom BS25 71 A6
Longbridge [16] BA4 205 B6
Longbrook Trad Est BS3 11 E3
Long Cl
Ilminster TA19 221 C2
Yeovil BA21 218 C5
Longcombe Dr BA12 144 F6
LONGCROFT 219 A8
Longcroft Rd BA21 219 C6
LONG CROSS 37 D7
Long Cross
Bristol BS11 4 F8
Doulting BA4 141 F8
Felton BS40 37 D7
Nether Stowey TA5 134 A3
Long Cross Bottom
Doulting BA3 142 A8
Stoke St Michael BA3 116 A1
Long Cross Prim Sch BS11 4 F8
Longdown Dr BS22 32 B4
Long Dro
Broadway TA19, TA20 183 A2
Buckland St Mary TA20 182 F2
Glastonbury BA5 139 E4
Westbury-sub-Mendip BS27 110 A4
Long Eaton Dr BS14 23 B7
Longfellow Ave BA2 44 F4
Longfellow Rd BA3 97 C8
Longfield BA11 118 A7
Longfield Cl TA4 202 E2
Longforth Rd TA21 222 D6
Longforward Hill
Dinnington TA17 195 A8
Seavington St Mary TA19 184 D1
Longforward La
Dinnington TA17 195 B8
Seavington St Mary TA19 184 D1
Long Furlong La
East Coker BA22 197 C8
Long Sutton TA10 172 E5
Long Ground BA11 119 F3
Long Hay Cl BA2 44 B5
LONGHEDGE 144 E7
Long Hill
Clewer BS28 89 D2
Shepton Mallet BA4 141 C8
Long Holcombe Cross EX36 145 E6
Longhorn Dr [7] TA6 209 A1
LONGHOUSE 61 D5
Long La
Backwell BS48 19 C2
Bourton SP8 161 D1
Cucklington BA9 177 D5
Dinder BA5 140 D7
Felton BS40 37 B5
Fishpond Bottom DT6 199 B1
Walton BA16 156 D7
Wanstrow BA4 142 F5

Long La *continued*
West Chinnock TA18 . . . . . 196 B7
Wheddon Cross TA24. . . . . 129 C2
Wootton Courtenay TA24. . 129 E8
Wrington BS40 . . . . 36 B2
Long Lakes TA4. . . . . 202 E4
Longlands La
East Coker BA22 . . . . 197 C8
Westbury-sub-Mendip BA5 110 E7
Longleat Cl BA11. . . . . 119 F3
Longleat Ct BA11 . . . . 119 E4
Longleat Forest Holiday Village★ BA12 . . . . 144 F5
Longleat House★ BA12. . 144 D6
Longleat La BA3 . . . . 116 C8
Longleat Rd BA3. . . . . 116 B8
Longleat Rly★ BA12. . . . . 144 C6
Longleat Safari & Adventure Park★ BA12 . . . . 144 D6
Longleaze Gdns BS24 . . . . 49 F3
LONG LOAD. 172 E2
Long Load Rd TA12 . . . . . 185 E8
Longman's Lea BA4. . . . . . 159 C7
Longmarsh La TA10 . . . . . 172 E6
Longmead TA4 . . . . 165 E8
Long Mead BA21. . . . . 218 C5
Longmead Cl
Norton St Philip BA2 . . . . . . 81 F4
Taunton TA1. . . . . 212 D2
Wellington TA21. . . . . 222 B8
Longmead Cotts TA21 . . . 222 B8
Longmead Croft BS13. . . . 21 F4
Longmeadow Rd BS31 . . . 24 C4
Longmead Way TA1. . . . . 212 D2
Long Moor Dro TA7, TA9 . 137 A7
Long Orchard Hill TA19 . 221 E3
Longreach Gr BS14 . . . . . . 23 D6
Long Ride Dro BA6. . . . . . 157 F3
Longridge Way BS24 . . . . . 49 F7
Long Row BS1 . . . . 227 B2
Long Run BA22 . . . . 186 C2
Longrun La TA1. . . . . 212 D4
Longs Field TA3 . . . . 170 C4
Long St
Croscombe BA5. . . . . 204 B7
Galhampton BA22 . . . . 175 E8
High Ham TA10 . . . . 156 A1
Sherborne DT9 . . . . 225 E4
Williton TA4 . . . . 202 E3
Longstone Ave TA6 . . . . . 209 C5
Longstone Cl TA5. . . . . . . 134 B2
Longstrings La TA18 . . . . 224 C8
LONG SUTTON 172 F4
Long Sutton CE Prim Sch TA10 . . . . 172 E4
Long-Thorn BS48. . . . . 18 F6
Longthorne Pl BA2. . . . . . . 44 F2
Long Thorn La BS40. . . . . . 55 E7
Longton Grove Rd 3 BS23 . . . . 48 E8
Longton Ind Est BS23 . . . . 48 F6
Long Valley Rd BA2 . . . . . . 43 F5
Longvernal BA3. . . . . 77 F1
Longvernal Prim Sch BA3 77 F1
Longway Ave BS13, BS14. . 22 F4
Longwood Ho BS8 . . . . 10 D4
Longwood La
Burlescombe TA21. . . . . . . 179 C4
Long Ashton BS8, BS41. . . . 10 F4
Lonsdale Ave BS23. . . . . . . 48 F4
Lonsdale Rd TA5. . . . . 135 C2
Look's La BA6 . . . . 157 C6
Looseall La TA22. . . . . 163 D8
LOPEN 185 A1
Lopen Head TA13 . . . . 220 A1
Lopen La TA13. . . . . 220 C1
Lopen Rd TA13, TA17. . . . . 195 D8
Lordsleaze La TA20 . . . . . 223 D3
Lords Meadow La 5 EX16. . . . . 164 B1
Lords Way TA6. . . . . 208 E6
Loretto Gdns 5 EX13 . . . . 198 A1
Loretto Rd EX13 . . . . 198 A1
Lorne Pl BA5 . . . . 203 E5
Lorne Rd BA2. . . . . 44 D6
Lotment Hill TA11. . . . . . . 173 D5
LOTTISHAM. 158 D5
Lottisham La BA4, BA6. . . . 158 D6
Lottisham Rd BA6. . . . . . . 158 C6
Lotts' Ave BS48 . . . . 19 B5
Lotus Ct BS22. . . . . 31 C1
Lotus Dr TA6 . . . . 208 D1
Louisa Gate TA22 . . . . 163 F7
Louisa St BS2. . . . . 227 C2
Loundshay La TA4 . . . . . . 167 A4
Lovugine Cl TA8 . . . . 104 C7
Love La
Burnham-on-S TA8. . . . . . . 104 C7
Ilminster TA19. . . . . 221 C3
Marnhull DT10. . . . . 190 F6
Shepton Beauchamp TA19. 184 E4
Wincanton BA9 . . . . 216 F5
Lovelands DT2. . . . . 197 A1
Lovelinch Gdns BS41. . . . . 10 F1
Lovell Dr BS39. . . . . 57 C4
Lovells Mead DT10. . . . . . . 190 F6
Lovells Mill BS39. . . . . 57 D4
Lovells The BS20. . . . . 4 B4
Loveridge La TA20 . . . . . . 198 D8
Lovers La BA3, BS39 . . . . . . 78 A5
Lovers Wlk BA5. . . . . 203 D5
Lovers' Wlk
4 Cannington TA5 . . . . . . 135 B2
Weston-super-Mare BS23. . 48 D8
Loves Hill BA2 . . . . 60 A1
Loves La BA14 . . . . 83 C7
Love's La BA2. . . . . 59 F6
LOVINGTON 158 F1
Lovington CE Prim Sch BA7. . . . . 158 F2
Lowbourne BS14. . . . . 22 F6
Lower Acreman St 3 DT9 . . . . 225 D3
Lower Actis BA6 . . . . 206 E3
LOWER AISHOLT 152 C6
Lower Ansford BA7 . . . . . 214 B7
Lower Backway BA10 . . . . 215 E6
Lower Batch BS40 . . . . 39 B3
Lower Bath Rd TA6 . . . . . 209 B6
Lower Beadon TA16. . . . . . 195 F7
Lower Borough Walls BA1 . . . . 228 C2
Lowerbourne Terr TA24 . 124 A3
Lower Boyston La DT9 . . 188 F5
Lower Bristol Rd
Bath BA2 . . . . 44 B6
Clutton BS39 . . . . 58 F4
Lower Burlington Rd BS20. . 2 E7
LOWER BURROW. 184 F7
Lower Camden Pl BA1 . . 228 C4
LOWER CANADA 49 F2
Lower Castle St BS1 . . . . 227 B3
Lower Chapel Ct BA5. . . . 113 A1
Lower Cheriton La BA8. . 176 D4
LOWER CHILTON CANTELO 187 C8
Lower Church La BS2 . . . 227 A3
Lower Church Rd BS23 . . . 48 D8
LOWER CLAVERHAM 17 F2
Lower Claverham BS49. . . 17 F3
Lower Clifton Hill BS8. . . 226 B2
Lower College St BS1 . . . 226 C2
Lower Coombses TA20 . . 198 D8
Lower Cross EX15. . . . . . . 179 C1
Lower Down Rd BS20 . . . . . 2 B5
LOWER DOWNSIDE 205 C7
LOWER DURSTON 169 F7
Lower East Coker Rd BA20 . . . . 218 F1
Lower East Hayes BA1. . . . 45 B8
LOWER FAILAND 10 A8
Lower Fairfield TA4 . . . . . 166 F5
Lower Fairmead Rd BA21 . . . . 219 D8
Lower Fallow Cl BS14 . . . . 22 F3
Lower Farm DT9. . . . . 187 E4
Lower Farm La BA2 . . . . . . 43 B7
Lowerfield La TA19 . . . . . 184 E1
Lower Foxmoor Rd TA21 222 B5
Lower Gay St BS2. . . . . . . 227 A4
LOWER GODNEY 138 F5
Lower Guinea St BS1. . . . 227 A1
Lower Gully Dro BS28 . . . . 89 F3
Lower Gunville DT9 . . . . . 217 D2
LOWER HALSTOCK LEIGH 197 B2
LOWER HARMSWELL. 12 C3
Lower Hedgemead Rd BA1 . . . . 228 C4
Lower High St BS11 . . . . . . 4 D7
LOWER HOLDITCH 198 D5
Lower Holway Cl TA1 . . . 213 D2
Lower Hyde Rd TA15 . . . . 186 B4
Lower Innox BA11. . . . . . . 119 E6
LOWER KEYFORD. 119 F3
Lower Keyford BA11 . . . . 119 F3
Lower Kingsbury DT9 . . . 217 D3
Lower Kingsdown Rd SN13 . . . . 29 F3
Lower Knowles Rd BS21. . . 6 C2
Lower La
Shepton Mallet BA4. . . . . . 205 C6
Weston Town BA4 . . . . 142 E5
Lower Lamb St BS1 . . . . . 226 C2
LOWER LANGFORD 53 C5
LOWER LEIGH. 207 C6
Lower Linden Rd BS21 . . . . 6 D3
Lower Lodfin EX16 . . . . . . 164 B2
Lower Marshfield Rd TA24 . . . . 201 B6
LOWER MARSTON 143 E7
Lower Maudlin St BS1. . . 227 A3
Lower Mdw TA19 . . . . 221 A4
Lower Meadow Rd TA24. 201 B5
LOWER MERRIDGE 152 C5
Lower Middle St TA1. . . . . 212 F4
LOWER MILTON 203 B8
Lower New Rd BS27. . . . . . 90 A7
Lower Northend BA1. . . . . . 28 F5
Lower North St BS27 . . . . . 90 B8
Lower North Town La BA22 . . . . 175 D7
Lower Norton La
Weston-super-Mare BS22 . . 31 E4
Weston-super-Mare, Norton BS22 . . . . 31 C4
Lower Notlake Dro BS28 . . 89 E4
LOWER ODCOMBE 186 D2
Lower Odcombe BA22. . . 186 C2
Lower Oldfield Pk BA2 . . 228 A1
Lower Orch TA19 . . . . 184 C5
Lower Parade Ground Rd BS24 . . . . 50 C5
Lower Park La TA24. . . . . 129 E1
Lower Park Row BS1. . . . . 227 A3
LOWER PEASEDOWN 79 B8
Lower Pk TA24. . . . . 200 E7
Lower Queen's BS21 . . . . . . 6 D3
Lower Rd
Hinton Blewett BS39 . . . . . . 75 E6
Horsington BA8 . . . . 176 D3
Kingsdon TA11. . . . . 173 D5
Stalbridge DT10. . . . . 190 C4
Lower Rd *continued*
Woolavington TA7 . . . . 136 E4
Lower Ream BA21 . . . . . . 218 C5
LOWER ROADWATER 131 D1
Lower Rocke's Cotts BA6 . . . . 157 D4
LOWER RUDGE. 102 D4
Lower Severalls Gdn★ TA18 . . . . 196 A6
Lowerside La BA6. . . . . . . 206 D7
Lowerside Rd BA6 . . . . . . 206 E6
Lower Silk Mill BA4 . . . . . 204 F6
LOWER SOMERTON. 211 E3
Lower Somerton TA11. . . 211 F3
Lower St
Buckland Dinham BA11 . . . 100 A2
Carhampton TA24. . . . . 131 B4
Chewton Mendip BA3 . . . . . 94 F7
Curry Mallet TA3 . . . . 183 C8
Merriott TA16. . . . . 195 F7
Pilton BA4 . . . . 140 F3
Rode BA11. . . . . 101 E8
Upton Noble BA4. . . . . 142 F2
West Chinnock TA18 . . . . . 196 B8
Lower Stoke BA2, BA3 . . . . 64 A8
LOWER STRATTON 220 E1
LOWER STRODE. 56 A8
Lower Strode BS40. . . . . . . 56 A7
Lower Strode Rd BS21 . . . . 16 A7
LOWER SWAINSWICK 28 C3
LOWER TIPPACOTT 122 A4
Lower Touches TA20 . . . . . 223 E5
Lower Town
Montacute TA15. . . . . 186 B4
Sampford Peverell EX16 . . 178 D1
Lower Turners Barn La BA20 . . . . 218 F2
LOWER VELLOW. 132 D1
Lower Vellow TA4 . . . . 132 D2
LOWER VEXFORD. 150 F6
LOWER WEACOMBE 132 E3
LOWER WEARE. 88 D8
LOWER WESTFORD 222 A6
LOWER WESTHOLME 140 C3
Lower Westholme Rd BA4 . . . . 140 D3
LOWER WESTON 44 C7
LOWER WHATLEY 118 D3
Lower Whitelands BA3 . . . . 79 B3
Lower Woodcock St BA7 214 C5
LOWER WOOLSTON. 175 F6
Lower Wraxhill Rd BA20. 218 F1
LOWER WRITHLINGTON . . . 79 C3
LOW HAM 172 B8
Low Ham Rd TA10. . . . . . . 172 B8
Lowlands Terr TA1. . . . . . . 212 B4
Lowman Cross EX16. . . . . . 178 B2
Lowmoor Ind Est TA21. . . 222 B8
Low's Hill La DT9 . . . . 188 B3
Lowsome La DT9. . . . . 188 A5
Lowther Rd BA21 . . . . 219 E7
LOWTON 181 B5
Lowtrow Cross TA4 . . . . . 165 A8
LOW WATER 119 E6
Loxhams TA10 . . . . 156 B2
Loxleigh Ave TA6 . . . . 209 B4
Loxleigh Gdns TA6 . . . . . . 209 B4
Loxley Batch TA7 . . . . 156 A8
Loxley Gdns BA2 . . . . 44 C4
Loxley Terr TA6. . . . . 208 F7
LOXTON. 68 C4
Loxton Dr BA2 . . . . 44 B6
Loxton Rd BS23 . . . . 48 F2
Loxton Sq BS14. . . . . 23 A6
Lubborn La BA6. . . . . 158 B5
LUCCOMBE. 129 D7
Lucerne Cres TA6. . . . . 208 D1
Luckes La TA4 . . . . 132 E3
Luckington Cross BA11. . . . 98 B2
Lucklands Rd BA1. . . . . 27 C1
Luckley Ave BS13 . . . . 22 C5
LUCKWELL BRIDGE 129 C1
Luckwells La TA24 . . . . . . 129 E2
Lucott Cross TA24 . . . . 128 C6
Ludbourne Rd DT9. . . . . . . 225 E3
Ludlow Ave TA2 . . . . 213 A8
Ludlow Cl
Bridgwater TA6 . . . . 209 A2
Frome BA11. . . . . 120 C6
Keynsham BS31. . . . . 24 D5
LUDNEY 194 F7
Ludney Cross TA19. . . . . . . 194 F7
Ludney La
Dinnington TA17. . . . . 195 A8
Ilminster TA19. . . . . 194 F7
Ludwells Orch BS39. . . . . . . 77 E5
LUFTON 186 D3
Lufton Heights Commerce Pk BA22. . . . . 218 A7
Lufton Trad Est BA22 . . . . 218 A7
Lufton Way BA22. . . . . 218 A6
Luggard's Cross BS21 . . . . . 8 C4
Lugshorn La TA11. . . . . . . 211 C8
Luke's Cl BA3. . . . . 78 F3
Lukes Gdn TA24. . . . . 131 B4
Luke St EX16 . . . . 164 B1
LULLINGTON. 101 A4
Lullington La BA11. . . . . . . 101 B3
LULSGATE BOTTOM 37 A8
Lulsgate Rd BS13 . . . . 22 A8
Lulworth Rd BS31 . . . . 24 E4
Lundy Dr TA8 . . . . 104 B5
Luns Hill BA6 . . . . 157 F1
Lunty Mead BS48 . . . . 18 F6
Lupin Way BA22 . . . . 218 B5
LUPPITT 191 B1
Lush Path DT9. . . . . 225 E4
Lusty Gdns BA10. . . . . 215 E5
Luttrell Cl TA2. . . . . 213 B8
Luttrell Gdns TA24 . . . . . . 200 F6
Luttrell Wy TA24 . . . . 201 C6
Luvers La BS40 . . . . 54 D1
LUXBOROUGH 148 E8
Luxborough Rd TA6 . . . . . 208 B4
Lux Furlong BS9 . . . . 5 B7
Luxhay Cl TA2 . . . . 213 B8
LUXTON. 192 A6
Luxton's La BA3, BA4 . . . . 116 F1
Lyatt La BA5 . . . . 140 E8
LYATTS 197 B6
Lyatts Hill BA22. . . . . 197 B6
Lychgate Pk BS24. . . . . 50 A4
Lyddieth Ct BA15. . . . . 64 E7
Lyddon Cl TA21 . . . . 222 D4
Lyddon Rd BS22 . . . . 32 B3
Lyddon's Hill TA22 . . . . . . 148 A1
Lyddons Mead TA20. . . . . . 223 E4
Lydeard Cross TA5 . . . . 152 E3
Lydeard Down Hill TA4 . . 151 B4
Lydeard Mead TA4 . . . . 167 E8
LYDEARD ST LAWRENCE 151 B3
Lydeard St Lawrence Com Prim Sch TA4 . . . . 151 A3
Lyde Ct BA21 . . . . 219 E6
Lyde Gn BA2. . . . . 81 E5
Lyde La BA21 . . . . 219 F6
Lyde Rd BA21 . . . . 219 E7
LYDFORD FAIR PLACE. . . . 158 C3
LYDMARSH. 194 C3
Lydon La TA4 . . . . 165 D5
LYE CROSS 36 C1
Lye Cross Rd BS40 . . . . 36 C1
Lyefield Rd BS22. . . . . 31 E4
LYE HOLE 36 E2
Lye Hole La BS40 . . . . 36 D2
Lye La BA4 . . . . 158 F6
Lye Mead BS40 . . . . 38 A6
LYE'S GREEN 121 B1
Lyes The BS49 . . . . 34 D3
Lyewater TA18. . . . . 224 B6
Lyme Gdns BA1 . . . . 44 B7
Lyme Rd
Axminster EX13. . . . . 198 A1
Bath BA1 . . . . 44 B7
Crewkerne TA18. . . . . 224 B4
Lymore Ave BA2 . . . . 44 C5
Lymore Cl BA2. . . . . 44 C5
Lymore Gdns BA2. . . . . 44 C5
Lymore Terr BA2. . . . . 44 C4
LYMPSHAM. 67 B1
Lympsham CE Fst Sch BS24. . . . . 67 B1
Lympsham Gn BA2. . . . . 62 D8
Lympsham Rd BS24 . . . . 67 B1
Lynbrook BS41. . . . . 10 F1
Lynbrook La BA2. . . . . 44 F3
Lynch Cl BS22 . . . . 31 F3
Lynchcombe La BA5 . . . . . 110 F6
Lynch Cres BS25 . . . . 69 F7
Lynch Hill BA3. . . . . 96 A3
Lynch La
Cheddar BS27 . . . . 90 C8
Hardington Mandeville BA22. . . . . 197 A6
Westbury-sub-Mendip BA5 110 D8
Lynchmead BS25. . . . . 70 A7
Lynch The BS25. . . . . 69 F7
Lyncombe Hall BA2 . . . . 45 A4
LYNCOMBE HILL 45 A4
Lyncombe Hill BA2. . . . . . . 228 C1
LYNCOMBE VALE. 45 A3
Lyncombe Vale BA2. . . . . . . 45 B4
Lyncombe Vale Rd BA2. . . 45 A4
Lyndale Ave
Bridgwater TA6 . . . . 208 E5
Bristol BS9. . . . . 5 D5
Lynde Cl BS13 . . . . 22 B4
Lyndhurst Cres TA6 . . . . . . 208 C5
Lyndhurst Gr TA12 . . . . 185 D7
Lyndhurst Rd
Bath BA2. . . . . 44 C6
Bristol BS9. . . . . 5 F7
Keynsham BS31. . . . . 24 F3
Midsomer Norton BA3. . . . . . 97 B8
Weston-super-Mare BS23. . 48 E4
Lyndhurst Terr BA1 . . . . . 228 C4
Lynfield Pk BA1. . . . . 27 C1
Lynfield Rd BA11. . . . . 119 D5
Lynford La TA11 . . . . 158 C1
LYNFORD-ON-FOSSE 158 C2
LYNG 170 C7
LYNGFORD 213 A7
Lyngford Cres TA2 . . . . 213 A7
Lyngford La TA2 . . . . 168 F6
Lyngford Park Prim Sch TA2. . . . . 213 B8
Lyngford Pl TA2 . . . . 213 A7
Lyngford Rd TA2. . . . . 213 A7
Lyngford Sq TA2 . . . . 213 A7
Lynmouth Cl BS22 . . . . 32 A2
Lynor Cl TA1. . . . . 213 D3
Lynton Cl BS20 . . . . 2 E4
Lynton Rd
Burnham-on-S TA8. . . . . 104 B6
Midsomer Norton BA3. . . . . . 97 B8
Lynwood Cl
Frome BA11. . . . . 119 D4
Midsomer Norton BA3. . . . . . 97 A8
Lynx Cres BS24 . . . . 49 B2
Lynx Trad Est BA20. . . . . . . 218 D3
Lynx West Trad Est BA20. . . . . 218 C3
Lyons Court Rd BS14 . . . . . . 23 D7
Lyons Ct BS23 . . . . 48 F7
Lype La TA22 . . . . 147 E4
Lypstone Cl BS24 . . . . 50 A8
Lypyatt La BA6. . . . . 206 F4
Lysander Rd BA20. . . . . 218 E3
Lysander Ret Pk BA20. . . . 219 A3
Lysander Road Rdbt BA20 . . . . 218 C3
Lyster Cl BA22 . . . . 173 E1
Lyster Gdns BA22 . . . . 173 E1
Lyte's Cary★ TA11. . . . . 173 F5
Lytes Cary Rd BS31. . . . . 25 A3
Lytton Gdns BA2 . . . . 44 B4
Lytton Gr BS31. . . . . 25 A5
Lyveden Gdns BS13 . . . . 22 B5
Lyvedon Way BS41 . . . . 11 B1

M

McAdam Way BS1 . . . . 11 F5
Macaulay Bldgs BA2 . . . . . 45 C4
McCrae Rd BS24 . . . . 50 B5
McCreath Cl 3 TA6. . . . . . 153 F3
Mc Creery Rd DT9 . . . . . . 225 D6
Macey's Rd BS13. . . . . 22 D3
Macfarlane Chase BS23 . . 49 A5
Machine Cross TA22 . . . . . 163 F6
Macies The BA1 . . . . 27 B3
MACKHAM 191 A4
McKinley Terr TA23 . . . . . 131 E4
Mackley La BA2. . . . . 81 E3
Macleod Cl BS21. . . . . 6 A2
Macquarie Farm Cl BS49 . 17 A1
Macrae Rd BS20 . . . . 4 E4
Madam La
Weston-super-Mare BS22 . . 31 F2
Weston-super-Mare BS22 . . 32 A3
Weston-super-Mare BS22 . . 32 A4
Madam's Paddock BS40. . . 39 B3
Madden Cl TA8 . . . . 104 C7
Maddocks Pk BA9. . . . . . . 216 C3
Maddocks Slade TA8. . . . . 104 A8
Madeira Ct BS23. . . . . 48 C8
Madeira Rd
Clevedon BS21. . . . . 6 D3
Weston-super-Mare BS23 . . 30 C1
Madgeon La TA20. . . . . . . 192 E8
Madison Ct 5 TA18 . . . . . 224 C6
Madwoman's La BS28 . . . . 108 B2
Maesbury Rd BS31 . . . . 25 A2
Maesdown Cl BA4. . . . . . . 141 E2
Maesdown Cotts BA4 . . . 141 E2
Maesdown Hill BA4 . . . . . 141 E3
Maes Down Ho 10 BA4 . . 205 B6
Maesdown Rd
Doulting BA4 . . . . 141 E4
Evercreech BA4. . . . . 141 E2
Maesknoll La BS14, BS39. . 40 B8
Magdalana Ct BS1 . . . . . . 227 B1
Magdalen Ave BA2. . . . . . . 228 B1
Magdalene Cl BA6 . . . . . . 206 D4
Magdalene Ct 9 TA1 . . . . 212 F4
Magdalene La 10 TA1 . . . 212 F4
Magdalene Rd BA3. . . . . . . 79 C2
Magdalene St
Glastonbury BA6 . . . . 206 D4
Taunton TA1. . . . . 212 F4
Magdalen La BA14 . . . . 83 B7
Magdalen Rd BA2. . . . . . . 228 B1
Magdalen Way BS22 . . . . . 32 A3
Magellan Cl BS22 . . . . 31 F4
Maggs Folly BS39. . . . . 59 D2
Maggs Hill BA2 . . . . 60 B2
Maggs La
Castle Cary BA7. . . . . 214 C7
Whitchurch BS14. . . . . 23 C4
Maglands Rd TA23 . . . . . . 202 D6
Magna Cl BA21 . . . . 219 D8
Magnolia Ave BS22 . . . . . . 32 A1
Magnolia Cl
Frome BA11. . . . . 120 C7
Weston-super-Mare BS22 . . 49 E7
Magnolia Rd BA3 . . . . 78 E1
Magnolia Tree Rd TA6 . . 209 E5
Magpie Cl
Burnham-on-S TA8. . . . . 85 B1
Weston-super-Mare BS22. . 49 E8
Maiden Beech Mid Sch TA18 . . . . 224 B4
MAIDEN BRADLEY 144 C1
MAIDENBROOK 213 D7
Maidenbrook La TA2 . . . . 169 A6
Maiden Croft La BA6 . . . 139 D2
MAIDEN HEAD 21 F1
Maidenhead Cross EX16. 179 C2
Maidenhead Rd BS13. . . . . 22 D3
Maiden Way BS11. . . . . 4 C8
Maidstone Gr BS24. . . . . . . 49 A1
Maincombe Cl TA18. . . . . 224 C4
MAINES BATCH 35 E3
Main Rd
Brockley BS49 . . . . 18 D2
Burrowbridge TA7 . . . . 154 F1
Cannington TA5 . . . . 135 C1
Coxley BA5. . . . . 139 E6
Flax Bourton BS48. . . . . 19 F7
Huntspill TA9 . . . . 136 B8
Hutton BS24 . . . . 49 E2
Kilve TA5 . . . . 133 C5
Lyng TA3, TA7. . . . . 170 C7
Middlezoy TA7 . . . . 155 B3
Othery TA7. . . . . 155 B2
Shapwick TA7. . . . . 155 F8
Westhay BA6. . . . . 138 B5
Westonzoyland TA7 . . . . . . 154 F5
Main St
Babcary TA11. . . . . 174 C7
Barton St David TA11. . . . . 158 A3
Chilthorne Domer BA22. . . 186 E6

Main St *continued*
Farrington Gurney BS39 ... 77 A4
Martock TA12 .... 185 F7
Walton BA16 .... 156 D7
Malago Wlk BS13 .... 21 E4
Malden Mead BS14 .... 23 A5
Malherbie Ct TA20 ...... 194 B6
Malin Par BS20 .... 2 F6
Mallard Pl TA1 .... 104 C4
Mallard Rd TA24 .... 201 C5
Mallard Way TA6 .... 209 B4
Mallard Wlk ❼ BS22 ..... 49 E8
Mallory Cl TA2 .... 212 C6
Mallow Cl BS21 .... 6 C2
Mall The
Bath BA1 .... 228 C2
Bristol, Clifton BS8 .... 11 F7
Malmesbury Ct ❻ BA21 .. 218 C6
Malmesbury Way BA21 .. 218 C6
MALMSMEAD 122 C4
Mal's Mead La TA20 ..... 194 C3
Malta Way BA22 .... 174 A2
Malt Ho The TA4 .... 210 C4
Malthouse Cl BA9 .... 216 C4
Malthouse Ct
Frome BA11 .... 119 E3
Taunton TA1 .... 212 A4
Malthouse La DT9 .... 187 F5
Malthouses TA21 .... 167 A1
Maltings Ind Est The BA1. 44 B6
Maltings The
Chard TA20 .... 223 C3
Frome BA11 .... 119 F4
Midford BA2 .... 63 C5
Sherborne DT9 .... 225 E4
Weston-super-Mare BS22.. 31 F2
Maltlands BS22 .... 49 D8
Malvern Bldgs BA1 .... 28 A2
Malvern Cl TA6 .... 209 D6
Malvern Ct BA21 .... 218 D6
Malvern Rd BS23 .... 48 E5
Malvern Terr
❹ Bath BA1 .... 28 A1
Taunton TA2 .... 212 F6
Malvern Villas ❸ BA1 .... 28 A1
Mamsey La TA4 .... 202 C3
Manchester Cotts BS22... 31 E3
Mancroft Ave BS11 .... 4 F7
Mandarin Cl TA6 .... 209 B4
Mandy Mdws BA3 .... 77 F1
Mangle Cave Hill TA18 .. 195 C5
Manilla Cres
Weston-super-Mare BS23 .. 30 C1
❷❶ Weston-super-Mare
BS23 .... 30 C1
Manilla Pl BS23 .... 30 C1
Manilla Rd BS8 .... 226 A3
Manleaze Cvn Pk BA4 ... 205 D3
Manleys Cotts TA2 ...... 168 C6
Manmoor La BS21 .... 7 A1
Manning Cl BA5 .... 203 F5
Manning Rd TA4 .... 167 E6
Manning's La BA3 .... 94 F3
Manor Barton TA14 ..... 185 E2
Manor Bldgs TA18 ...... 196 C4
Manor Cl
Berrow TA8 .... 84 F6
Bradford Abbas DT9 ..... 187 E1
Chard TA20 .... 223 C2
Charlton Horethorne DT9. 176 A2
Cossington TA7 .... 136 F3
Ditcheat BA4 .... 159 C7
East Brent TA9 .... 86 D5
Easton-in-G BS20 .... 4 A4
Farrington Gurney BS39 ... 77 A3
Glastonbury BA6 .... 206 D5
Kingsdon TA11 .... 173 D5
Portishead BS20 .... 2 A5
South Perrott DT8 ...... 196 C1
Sparkford BA22 .... 175 A4
Taunton TA1 .... 212 E3
Templecombe BA8 .... 189 E8
Wellow BA2 .... 62 D1
Manor Cl The BS8 .... 11 A8
Manor Copse Rd BA3 ..... 79 C2
Manor Court Com Prim Sch
TA20 .... 223 C3
Manor Ct
Backwell BS48 .... 19 A5
Burnham-on-S TA8 ...... 104 B7
Cossington TA7 .... 136 F3
Easton BA5 .... 111 A4
Horsington BA8 .... 176 D2
Locking BS24 .... 50 B4
Sherborne DT9 .... 225 D5
Stawell TA7 .... 137 A1
Weston-super-Mare BS23.. 49 A8
Manor Dr
Bathford BA1 .... 29 C2
Berrow TA8 .... 84 F6
Chedzoy TA7 .... 154 D8
East Coker BA22 .... 197 B8
❶❶ Merriott TA16 ...... 195 F7
Staplegrove TA2 .... 212 C4
Taunton TA1 .... 212 E3
Manor Farm
Chard TA20 .... 223 C3
East Coker BA22 .... 197 B8
Manor Farm Barns TA7.. 169 E5
Manor Farm Cl
Paulton BS39 .... 77 D6
Tatworth TA20 .... 198 C8
Weston-super-Mare BS24.. 49 B2
Manor Farm Cres BS24... 49 B2
Manor Furlong BA11 .... 119 E2
Manor Gdns
Farmborough BA2 .... 59 F6
Farrington Gurney BS39 ... 77 A3

Manor Gdns *continued*
Ilchester BA22 .... 173 E1
Locking BS24 .... 50 A4
Weston-super-Mare BS22.. 31 B4
Manor Gn EX14 .... 191 F2
Manor Grange BS24 .... 67 B7
Manor Ho BS2 .... 226 C3
Manor House Gdns BA6 .. 206 D5
Manor House Rd BA6 .... 206 D5
Manor La
Abbots Leigh BS8 .... 10 F8
Wedmore BS28 .... 108 A5
Manor Mews TA2 .... 212 D8
Manor Orch TA1 .... 212 D2
Manor Park Cl BA3 .... 79 C2
Manor Pk
Bath BA1 .... 44 B8
Keinton Mandeville TA11.. 158 B1
Norton Fitzwarren TA2 ... 168 B4
Pawlett TA6 .... 135 F6
Radstock BA3 .... 79 C2
Weston-super-Mare BS23.. 48 E1
Manor Pl TA11 .... 158 B1
Manor Rd
Abbots Leigh BS8 .... 10 F7
Bath BA1 .... 27 C1
Bridgwater TA6 .... 209 B1
Bristol, Bishopsworth BS13. 22 A6
Burnham-on-S TA8 ...... 104 B7
Chedzoy TA7 .... 154 D8
Cossington TA7 .... 136 F3
Edington TA7 .... 137 D2
Frome BA11 .... 119 E2
Isle Abbotts TA3 .... 183 F7
Kingsdon TA11 .... 173 D5
Milborne Port DT9 ...... 217 C3
Minehead TA24 .... 201 B4
Pawlett TA6 .... 135 F6
Radstock BA3 .... 79 C2
Saltford BS31 .... 25 C2
Staplegrove TA2 .... 212 C8
Taunton TA1 .... 212 D3
Weston-super-Mare BS23.. 49 A8
Yeovil BA20 .... 219 A4
Manor Ride TA9 .... 86 B2
Manor St BA22 .... 197 A8
Manor Terr BA3 .... 79 C2
Manor Valley BS23 .... 31 A1
Manor View
Crewkerne TA18 .... 224 C4
Golsoncott TA23 .... 131 D1
Manor Villas BA1 .... 27 C1
Manor Way
Berrow TA8 .... 84 F6
Failand BS8 .... 10 C4
Frome BA11 .... 119 E2
Manse La TA7 .... 136 C4
Mansel Cl BS31 .... 25 C3
Mansfield Ave BS23 ...... 49 B8
Mansfield Rd TA1 .... 213 A3
Manshay La DT6 .... 199 D1
Manship Gn BA4 .... 205 B6
Manston Cl BS14 .... 23 C7
Mantle St TA21 .... 222 C5
Mantle VC Rd BA22 ..... 174 A2
Manvers St BA1 .... 228 C1
Manworthy Cross TA4.... 166 C4
MAPERTON 176 B5
Maperton Rd DT9 .... 176 A2
Maple Cl
Bristol BS14 .... 23 D5
Evercreech BA4 .... 141 F1
North Petherton TA6 .... 153 F3
Puriton TA7 .... 136 C4
Street BA16 .... 207 C5
Taunton TA2 .... 213 A4
Weston-super-Mare BS23.. 49 A8
Wincanton BA9 .... 216 C2
Maple Ct
Bridgwater TA6 .... 209 D6
Bristol BS9 .... 226 A3
Frome BA11 .... 120 A7
❾ Weston-super-Mare
BS23 .... 30 C1
Maple Dr
Bristol BS9 .... 5 C4
Burnham-on-S TA8 ...... 104 B5
Crewkerne TA18 .... 224 D7
Radstock BA3 .... 78 E1
Yeovil BA20 .... 218 F3
Maple Gdns BA2 .... 44 E4
Maple Gr BA2 .... 44 E4
Maple Ho BS2 .... 227 A4
Maple Leaf Ct BS8 ...... 226 A3
Maple Rd
Curry Rivel TA10 .... 171 D4
Langport TA10 .... 172 A6
Maple Rise BA3 .... 79 B2
Maples The
Nailsea BS48 .... 8 C1
Shepton Mallet BA4 ..... 205 C6
Maplestone Rd BS14 ..... 23 A3
Maple Tree Ct TA7 ...... 136 F3
Maple Wlk BS31 .... 24 D4
Mapstone Cl BA6 .... 206 B3
Marchant Holliday Sch The
BA8 .... 176 C5
Marchant's Hill BA3 ...... 95 F2
Marchants Pass BA1 .... 228 C1
Marchfields Way BS23 ... 49 A5
March La BA22 .... 175 D8
Marconi Cl BS23 .... 49 B7
Marconi Dr TA9 .... 104 D5
Marconi Rd BS20 .... 1 F5
Marden Gr TA1 .... 213 D3
Marden Rd BS31 .... 25 A4
Mardi's La TA11 .... 158 C2
Mardyke Ferry Rd BS1 .. 226 B1

Mare La TA13 .... 220 C5
Mares La BA5 .... 110 E7
Margaret Cres TA8 ..... 104 A5
Margaret Rd ❹ BS13 .... 21 F4
Margaret's Bldgs BA1 ... 228 B3
Margaret's Hill BA1 .... 228 C4
Margery Fish Gdns★
TA13 .... 220 C8
Marguerite Rd BS13 ..... 21 F7
Marina Row TA6 .... 209 B4
Marindin Dr BS22 .... 32 B4
Marine Ct BA21 .... 219 D5
Marine Dr TA8 .... 104 B5
Marine Hill BS21 .... 6 C5
Marine Par
Clevedon BS21 .... 6 C4
Pill BS20 .... 4 C5
Weston-super-Mare BS23.. 30 B1
Weston-super-Mare BS23.. 48 D6
Mariners Cl
Backwell BS48 .... 19 A6
Bridgwater TA6 .... 209 A5
Minehead TA24 .... 201 B7
Mariner's Cl BS22 .... 31 D1
Mariners Ct TA6 .... 209 A5
Mariners Dr
Backwell BS48 .... 19 A6
Bristol BS9 .... 5 D4
Mariner's Path BS9 .... 5 E3
Mariners Way TA23 ..... 202 D6
Mariner's Way BS20 ...... 4 C5
Maritime Heritage Ctr★
BS1 .... 226 B1
Marjoram Way BS20 ...... 2 F5
MARK 106 D4
MARK CAUSEWAY 106 A3
Mark CE Fst Sch TA9 ... 106 A4
Mark Coll TA9 .... 106 E4
Mark Cswy TA9 .... 106 B4
Market Ave BS20 .... 32 C5
Market Cl
❹ Bampton EX16 .... 164 B1
Brushford TA22 .... 163 E4
Market Ct
❽ Bridgwater TA6 ...... 208 F5
❷ Crewkerne TA18 ..... 224 C6
Market Ent Ctr The TA24. 129 E1
Market Gate BS2 .... 227 C3
Market House La TA24 .. 200 F7
Market House Mus The★
TA23 .... 202 C7
Market Ind Est BS49 ..... 17 B1
Market La BS23 .... 48 D8
Market Pl
Burlescombe EX16 ...... 179 B4
Castle Cary BA7 .... 214 C5
Frome BA11 .... 119 F5
Glastonbury BA6 .... 206 D4
Ilchester BA22 .... 173 E1
Radstock BA3 .... 78 F2
❷❸ Shepton Mallet BA4 .. 205 B6
Somerton TA11 .... 211 E4
Wells BA5 .... 203 E4
Wincanton BA9 .... 216 C4
Winford BS40 .... 37 F7
Wiveliscombe TA4 ...... 210 C4
Market Pl The BA11 .... 143 B8
Market Sq
Crewkerne TA18 .... 224 C6
South Petherton TA13 .. 220 C4
Market St
Bridgwater TA6 .... 208 F5
Crewkerne TA18 .... 224 C6
Highbridge TA9 .... 104 E3
Watchet TA23 .... 202 C7
Wells BA5 .... 203 D4
Yeovil BA20 .... 219 B5
Market Terr TA9 .... 104 E3
Mark La BS1 .... 226 C2
Marklands BS9 .... 5 E3
Mark Rd
Burtle TA7 .... 137 D6
Highbridge TA9 .... 105 A2
MARKSBURY 42 B1
Marksbury CE Prim Sch
BA2 .... 42 B2
Marks Cl TA3 .... 169 C4
Marksmead DT8 .... 199 F8
Marksview Bsns Ctr
BA21 .... 219 F7
Marlborough Ave TA6 ... 209 A2
Marlborough Bldgs
Bath BA1 .... 228 A3
Langport TA10 .... 171 F5
Marlborough Cl TA6 .... 209 A2
Marlborough Ct TA8 ..... 85 B1
Marlborough Dr BS22 .... 32 B2
Marlborough Flats ❽
BS2 .... 227 A4
Marlborough Hill BS2 ... 227 A4
Marlborough Hill Pl BS2 227 A4
Marlborough La BA1 .... 228 A3
Marlborough Rd BA21 ... 219 E6
Marlborough St
Bath BA1 .... 228 A4
Bristol BS2 .... 227 A4
Marl Cl BA21 .... 218 E7
Marle Ground TA19 ..... 184 E2
Marlepit Gr BS13 .... 21 F6
Marley Cl TA24 .... 201 A5
Marley's Row TA24 ..... 124 A3
Marleys Way BA11 ...... 119 C5
Marlfield Wlk BS13 ...... 21 E7
Marling Ho TA24 .... 201 B7
Marl La DT9 .... 187 E3
Marlowe Ho ❸ BS23 ..... 48 F4
Marl Pits ❶ BS48 .... 19 A6
Marl Pits La BA11 ...... 143 C7

Marne Cl BS14 .... 23 D5
MARNHULL 190 F5
Marnhull Cl DT10 ...... 190 F6
Marriage La DT10 ...... 190 F3
Marron Cl BS26 .... 70 C2
Marsa Wy ❶❶ TA6 ...... 209 B4
Marsden Rd BA2 .... 44 B3
MARSH 192 E5
MARSHALL'S ELM 207 D2
Marshall Way BA11 ..... 120 D8
Marshall Wlk BS4 .... 22 D7
MARSHALSEA 199 C3
Marshalsea Est DT6 .... 199 C3
Marshbridge Cross TA22 163 C7
Marshclose Hill TA22.... 146 E2
Marsh Cross TA24 ...... 200 D1
MARSHFIELD 13 E8
Marshfield Rd TA24 .... 201 B5
Marshfield Way BA1 ..... 28 A1
Marsh Hill TA22 .... 163 C8
Marsh La
Barrington TA19 .... 184 E5
Barton St David TA11 ... 158 A4
Bridgwater TA6 .... 209 B1
Buckhorn Weston BA9 ... 177 C4
Cannington TA5 .... 135 C2
Dunster TA24 .... 201 E3
Easton-in-G BS20 .... 4 A4
Farrington Gurney BS39 .. 77 A3
Henstridge BA8 .... 190 B7
Holcombe BA3 .... 116 C5
Penselwood BA9 .... 161 D2
Pitney TA10 .... 172 D7
Portbury BS20 .... 3 F6
South Cheriton BA8 ..... 176 E4
Temple Cloud BS39 ...... 59 A1
Tintinhull BA22 .... 186 A5
Yeovil BA21 .... 218 F8
Yeovil Marsh BA21 ...... 187 A5
Marsh Lane Ind Est BS20 .. 3 F7
Marsh Pottinson Ho ❶❻
BA20 .... 219 B4
Marsh Rd
Bristol BS3 .... 11 F3
Rode BA11 .... 82 F1
Standerwick BA11 ...... 102 D1
Yatton BS49 .... 34 B8
Marsh St
Avonmouth BS11 .... 4 C8
❹ Bristol BS1 .... 227 A2
Dunster TA24 .... 201 E3
MARSH STREET 201 F3
Marshway TA3 .... 170 D1
MARSHWOOD 199 C2
Marshwood CE Prim Sch
DT6 .... 199 C2
Marshwood Cross DT6 .. 199 E1
Marson Rd BS21 .... 6 D3
MARSTON BIGOT 143 D3
Marston Cl
Frome BA11 .... 119 D2
Taunton TA1 .... 212 C1
MARSTON GATE 119 C1
Marston La BA11 .... 119 D2
MARSTON MAGNA 174 F1
Marston Mead BA11 .... 119 D2
Marston Rd
Frome BA11 .... 119 D1
Nunney BA11 .... 143 D8
Sherborne DT9 .... 225 B5
Marston Trad Est BA11 .. 119 E1
Martcombe Rd BS20 ...... 4 C2
Martha's Orch BS13 ..... 21 E7
Martindale Ct BS22 ...... 49 D8
Martindale Rd BS22 ...... 49 D8
Martingale Wy BS20 ...... 2 E6
Martins TA3 .... 169 C4
Martins Bldgs ❹ TA21 .. 222 D5
Martins Cl
Evercreech BA4 .... 141 E1
Wellington TA21 .... 222 D5
Wells BA5 .... 203 B3
Martin's Cl TA8 .... 85 A3
Martins Gr BS22 .... 31 E2
Martins La BA4 .... 205 E5
Martins Paddock BA4 ... 142 A6
Martin St BA6 .... 158 A5
Martins The BS20 .... 3 A6
Martland Cl TA7 .... 136 E3
Martlet Rd TA24 .... 200 F7
Martock 185 D6
Martock BS24 .... 67 B7
Martock Bsns Pk TA12 ... 185 D7
Martock CE Prim Sch
TA12 .... 185 D6
Martock La TA12 .... 185 F7
Martock Rd
Keynsham BS31 .... 25 A3
Long Sutton TA10 ...... 172 E4
Mart Road Ind Est TA24 . 201 B6
Mart The ❻ BS23 .... 48 E5
Martyn Cl TA5 .... 135 B5
Marwin Cl TA12 .... 185 E7
Marwood Cl TA8 .... 104 C8
Marwood Rd BS4 .... 22 E8
Mary Brown Davis La ❻
BA5 .... 139 D8
Marybush La BS2 .... 227 B3
Mary Elton Prim Sch BS21.. 6 B1
Mary Hart Cl BA16 ..... 207 C4
Mary La ❶❶ EX16 .... 164 B1
Mary Rd BA5 .... 203 C5
Mary St
Taunton TA1 .... 212 F3
Yeovil BA20 .... 219 B5
Masefield Ho BS23 .... 49 A4
Mason La TA15 .... 186 B4

Masons Way BA11 .... 119 C1
Mason's Way BS27 .... 90 C7
Mason Way BA4 .... 205 A4
Massingham Pk TA2 ..... 213 B6
Materman Rd BS14 .... 23 E5
Matfurlong Cl TA12 .... 185 D5
Matthews Cl BS14 .... 23 F6
Matthews Rd
Taunton TA1 .... 212 B1
Yeovil BA21 .... 219 C5
Mattock's Tree Hill TA3. 169 E1
Matt's La TA14 .... 185 F4
Mattys Cross EX14 ..... 191 D3
MAUDLIN 199 C8
Maudlin Cross TA20 .... 199 C8
Maudlin La TA20 .... 199 C8
Maudslay Field BA22 ... 197 C8
MAUNDOWN 165 F7
Maunsell Rd BS24 .... 49 E7
Maunsel Rd TA7 .... 153 F1
Max Mill La BS25 .... 69 C8
Maxwell Rd BA4 .... 205 B4
Maxwell St TA2 .... 212 E6
Maybrick Rd BA2 .... 44 D5
Mayfair Ave BS48 .... 8 F1
Mayfield Ave BS22 .... 31 E1
Mayfield Cl BA22 .... 175 D8
Mayfield Dr TA6 .... 208 B4
Mayfield Rd
Bath BA2 .... 44 D5
Yeovil BA21 .... 219 D6
Mayfields BS31 .... 24 E5
Mayfield Terr TA4 ...... 210 C4
Mayflower Cl TA6 ...... 209 D5
Mayflower Ct TA6 ...... 104 E4
Mayflower Gdns BS48 .... 9 A2
May La BA1 .... 44 B8
Maynard Cl
Bristol BS13 .... 22 C5
❹ Clevedon BS21 .... 6 F3
Maynard Rd BS13 .... 22 C5
Maynard Terr BS39 ...... 58 F3
Maypole Cl BS39 .... 58 E3
MAY POLE KNAP 211 C4
May Pole Knap TA11 .... 211 C4
Maysfield Cl BS20 .... 2 D3
Maysgreen La BS24 ...... 33 B3
May's La BS24 .... 33 C3
Maysmead La BS40 .... 53 C6
May Terr BA22 .... 131 E3
Maytree Ave BS13 .... 22 B7
Maytree Cl
Bristol BS13 .... 22 B7
Frome BA11 .... 120 B7
May Tree Cl BS48 .... 8 C1
May Tree Rd BA3 .... 78 E1
May Tree Wlk BS31 ...... 24 C3
Mdwhayes TA24 .... 124 A3
Mead Ave BA22 .... 218 B6
Mead Cl
Bath BA2 .... 44 E3
Bristol BS11 .... 4 E6
Cheddar BS27 .... 90 B6
East Huntspill TA9 ..... 136 E8
Stoke St Michael BA3 ... 116 B2
Mead Com Prim Sch The
BA14 .... 83 C6
Meade Cl TA6 .... 153 F3
Meade Ho BA2 .... 44 A5
Meade La TA19 .... 184 E1
MEADGATE EAST 60 E2
MEADGATE WEST 60 D2
Mead La
Blagdon BS40 .... 54 E3
Lydford Fair Place TA11 . 158 C3
Saltford BS31 .... 25 F4
Sandford BS25 .... 51 E4
Stocklinch TA19 .... 184 C4
Wanstrow BA4 .... 142 F4
West Pennard BA6 ...... 140 C2
Meadlands BA2 .... 43 B7
Meadowbank BS22 .... 31 F3
Meadow Cl
Backwell BS48 .... 19 B6
Chilton Trinity TA5 ..... 135 F2
Farrington Gurney BS39 .. 77 A3
Henstridge BA8 .... 190 A7
Highbridge TA9 .... 104 D4
Kingston St Mary TA2 ... 168 E8
Langport TA10 .... 172 A6
Nailsea BS48 .... 8 E3
Nether Stowey TA5 .... 134 A2
Stalbridge DT10 .... 190 B4
Street BA16 .... 207 B4
Wincanton BA9 .... 216 D3
Meadow Cotts TA24 .... 131 B4
Meadow Croft BS24 ...... 49 B2
Meadowcroft Dr TA8 ... 104 C8
Meadow Ct BA1 .... 44 A7
Meadow Dr
Bath BA2 .... 62 D8
Locking BS24 .... 50 B4
Portishead BS20 .... 1 F1
Meadow Gdns
Bath BA1 .... 27 A1
Stogursey TA5 .... 134 C6
Meadow Gr BS11 .... 4 D7
Meadow La
Bathampton BA2 .... 28 D1
Walton BA16 .... 156 E7
Meadowland BS49 .... 17 A1
Meadowlands BS22 ...... 32 C2
Meadowlands Ave TA6 .. 208 E6
Meadow Pk
Bathford BA1 .... 29 B3

Meadow Pk *continued*
Wembdon TA6 . . . 208 C5
Meadow Pl BS22 . . . 32 D3
Meadow Rd
Clevedon BS21 . . . 6 E3
Frome BA11 . . . 119 F7
Paulton BS39 . . . 77 F4
Yeovil BA21 . . . 219 E7
Meadow Rise BA4 . . . 205 B7
Meadows Cl BS20 . . . 1 F5
Meadows End BS25 . . . 52 D4
Meadowside
Carhampton TA24 . . . 131 A5
Rockwell Green TA21 . . . 222 B5
Meadowside Cl TA1 . . . 212 B4
Meadowside Dr BS14 . . . 23 A3
Meadows Prim Sch The BS30 . . . 25 D8
Meadow St
Axbridge BS26 . . . 70 C2
Weston-super-Mare BS23 . . 48 E7
Meadows The
2 Bourton SP8 . . . 161 F1
Drayton TA10 . . . 171 E3
Porlock TA24 . . . 124 A3
Meadow Terr TA24 . . . 201 A5
Meadow View
2 Bampton EX16 . . . 164 B1
4 Barwick BA22 . . . 197 F8
East Coker BA22 . . . 197 C8
Glastonbury BA6 . . . 206 E3
Long Sutton TA10 . . . 172 E1
Radstock BA3 . . . 79 A1
Timberscombe TA24 . . . 130 B5
Meadow View Cl BA1 . . . 44 A8
Meadow Villas 14 BS23 . . . 48 E8
Mead Rd BS20 . . . 2 C2
Meads Ct TA6 . . . 208 E3
Meads Droveway TA3 . . . 169 D5
Mead St BS3 . . . 227 C1
Meads The DT9 . . . 217 D2
Mead Terr BS40 . . . 54 E2
Mead The
Clutton BS39 . . . 58 E3
Dundry BS41 . . . 21 D2
East Brent TA9 . . . 86 E5
Farmborough BA2 . . . 60 A6
Henstridge BA8 . . . 190 A6
Holcombe BA3 . . . 116 C8
Ilchester BA22 . . . 173 D1
Ilminster TA19 . . . 221 B3
Keynsham BS31 . . . 24 E3
Paulton BS39 . . . 77 D5
Rode BA11 . . . 101 E8
14 Shepton Mallet BA4 . . . 205 B6
Shipham BS25 . . . 70 E8
Stoke St Michael BA3 . . . 116 B2
Stratton-on-t F BA3 . . . 96 F2
Street BA16 . . . 207 D7
Timsbury BA2 . . . 60 C3
Winsley BA15 . . . 64 E7
Mead Vale BS22 . . . 49 E8
Mead Vale Com Prim Sch BS22 . . . 31 E1
Meadway
Bristol BS9 . . . 5 C6
Farmborough BA2 . . . 60 A6
Temple Cloud BS39 . . . 58 E1
Woolavington TA7 . . . 136 E4
Mead Way TA2 . . . 169 B6
Meadway Ave BS48 . . . 8 D2
Mearcombe La BS24 . . . 67 F6
Meardon Rd BS14 . . . 23 E6
MEARE . . . 138 D4
Meare BS24 . . . 48 F2
MEARE GREEN
Hatch Beauchamp . . . 169 F1
Stoke St Gregory . . . 170 D5
Meare Rd
Bath BA2 . . . 45 A2
Glastonbury BA6 . . . 206 B6
Meare Village Prim Sch BA6 . . . 138 D4
Meareway BA6 . . . 138 C5
MEARNS . . . 59 E2
Mearn's Cross BA3 . . . 94 B6
Mede Cl BS1 . . . 227 B1
Medical Ave BS2, BS8 . . . 226 C3
Medway Cl
Keynsham BS31 . . . 25 A3
Taunton TA1 . . . 213 D4
Medway Dr BS31 . . . 25 A3
Meetinghouse La BS49 . . . 18 A1
Melbourne House Mews BA5 . . . 203 D4
Melbourne Pl TA6 . . . 209 B6
Melbourne Terr 2 BS21 . . . 6 D2
Melcombe Ct BA2 . . . 44 D4
Melcombe La TA6 . . . 153 E3
Melcombe Rd BA2 . . . 44 D4
Mellanby Cl BA16 . . . 207 D5
Mellent Ave BS13 . . . 22 C3
MELLS . . . 118 B7
Mells CE Sch BA11 . . . 118 A6
Mells Cl BS31 . . . 25 A2
MELLS GREEN . . . 118 A6
Mells La BA3 . . . 79 B1
Melrose Ave
Bristol BS8 . . . 226 B4
Wells BA5 . . . 203 C4
Melrose Ct 3 BA5 . . . 203 C4
Melrose Gr BA2 . . . 44 B3
Melrose Pl BS8 . . . 226 B4
Melrose Rd BA21 . . . 219 B6
Melrose Terr BA1 . . . 28 A2
Melsbury La BA5 . . . 139 E6
Memorial Ave TA18 . . . 224 C5
Memorial Rd
Wrington BS40 . . . 35 E2
Yeovil BA22 . . . 218 B6
Mendip Ave
Shepton Mallet BA4 . . . 205 E4
Weston-super-Mare BS22 . . 31 F2
Mendip Bsns Pk BS26 . . . 87 A6
Mendip Cl
Axbridge BS26 . . . 70 D2
Frome BA11 . . . 120 A7
Keynsham BS31 . . . 24 D5
3 Nailsea BS48 . . . 8 E1
Paulton BS39 . . . 77 E4
Yatton BS49 . . . 34 B7
Mendip Dr BA11 . . . 120 A7
Mendip Edge BS24 . . . 66 F8
Mendip Fields BA3 . . . 96 C2
Mendip Gdns
Bath BA2 . . . 62 D8
Frome BA11 . . . 120 B7
Yatton BS49 . . . 34 B7
Mendip Ho TA1 . . . 212 F3
Mendip Lea Cl BS27 . . . 90 F2
Mendip Lodge BS25 . . . 70 A8
Mendip Rd
Bridgwater TA6 . . . 209 C4
Locking BS24 . . . 50 D4
Portishead BS20 . . . 2 B5
Rooks Bridge BS26 . . . 87 A6
Stoke St Michael BA3 . . . 116 A2
Weston-super-Mare BS23 . . 49 A7
Yatton BS49 . . . 34 B7
Mendip Rise BS24 . . . 50 B4
Mendip Vale BA3 . . . 116 E7
Mendip Vale Sta* BA4 . . 205 F3
Mendip Vale Trad Est BS27 . . . 90 A7
Mendip View
Coleford BA3 . . . 116 F7
Street BA16 . . . 207 B7
Mendip Villas
Cheddar BS27 . . . 71 A1
Compton Martin BS40 . . . 73 F7
Emborough BA3 . . . 95 E3
Mendip Way
Burnham-on-S TA8 . . . 104 B7
Radstock BA3 . . . 78 F3
Menlea BS40 . . . 54 D3
Mercer Ct BS14 . . . 23 B8
Merchants' Acad
Bristol BS13 . . . 22 A4
Bristol BS13 . . . 22 A5
Merchants Almshouses 6 BS1 . . . 227 A2
Merchants' Barton 3 BA11 . . . 119 F4
Merchants Barton Ind Est BA11 . . . 119 F4
Merchants Ct BS8 . . . 226 A1
Merchant Sq BS20 . . . 2 E6
Merchants Quay BS1 . . . 227 A1
Merchants Rd
Bristol BS8 . . . 226 A3
Bristol, Hotwells BS8 . . . 226 A1
Merchants Row BS1 . . . 226 C1
Merchant St BS1 . . . 227 B3
Meredith Cl BA22 . . . 197 C3
Meredith Ct BS1 . . . 226 A1
Merevale Way BA21 . . . 218 C7
Meriden BA1 . . . 44 D8
Meridian Pl BS8 . . . 226 B3
Meridian Vale BS8 . . . 226 B3
Meriet Ave BS13 . . . 22 B4
Merino Way 7 TA6 . . . 154 A5
Merle Cl TA6 . . . 209 B4
Merlin Cl
Bristol BS9 . . . 5 F8
1 Weston-super-Mare BS22 . . . 49 E8
Merlin Dr BA5 . . . 203 B5
Merlin Ind Pk TA2 . . . 213 B6
Merlin Pk BS20 . . . 2 A4
Merrick Ct BS1 . . . 227 A1
Merrick Rd BA6 . . . 206 E7
MERRIDGE . . . 152 D5
Merridge Cl TA6 . . . 208 A4
Merridge Hill TA5 . . . 152 D6
Merrifields TA4 . . . 167 E6
Merriman Gdns BA16 . . . 207 C5
Merriman Rd BA16 . . . 207 C5
Merrimans Rd BS11 . . . 4 D8
MERRIOTT . . . 195 E7
Merriott Fst Sch TA16 . . . 195 F7
Merriott Rd
Hinton St George TA17 . . . 195 D7
Merriott TA16 . . . 195 F6
MERRIOTTSFORD . . . 195 F7
Merry-field BA3 . . . 116 E8
Merryfield La
Doulting BA4 . . . 141 F5
Ilton TA19 . . . 183 E4
Merryfield Lane Halt* BA4 . . . 141 F5
Merryfield Rd BS24 . . . 50 B6
Merryfields TA9 . . . 106 D5
Merry La TA9 . . . 136 F8
Merthyr Guest Cl BA8 . . . 176 E1
Merton Dr BS24 . . . 50 A8
Mervyn Ball Cl TA20 . . . 223 C5
Methwyn Cl BS22 . . . 49 C7
Metropole Ct TA24 . . . 201 A7
Metropolitan The BS1 . . . 227 B1
Mews The
Bath BA1 . . . 44 A8
5 Bridgwater TA6 . . . 209 B4
East Coker BA22 . . . 197 C7
Mews The *continued*
Minehead TA24 . . . 201 A7
Wiveliscombe TA4 . . . 210 C4
Mewswell Dr BS27 . . . 71 B1
Mezellion Pl 14 BA1 . . . 28 B1
Mianda Terr TA19 . . . 221 C3
Michaels Mead BA1 . . . 27 B2
Midas Ct TA11 . . . 211 D3
Middle Ave BS1 . . . 227 A2
Middle Brooks BA16 . . . 207 C3
MIDDLE BURNHAM . . . 104 D8
MIDDLE CHINNOCK . . . 196 C8
Middlecombe Cross TA24 . . . 200 C6
Middle Dro
Baltonsborough BA6 . . . 158 B4
Compton Dundon TA11 . . . 156 F3
Glastonbury BA6 . . . 206 B5
Hambridge TA10, TA12 . . . 184 F8
Lydford Fair Place TA11 . . . 158 C3
Rodney Stoke BS27 . . . 109 C6
Street BA6 . . . 157 C7
Middlefield La
Barrington TA10 . . . 184 D6
Norton Sub Hamdon TA13, TA16 . . . 185 D1
West Chinnock TA16 . . . 196 A8
Middle Field La DT9 . . . 188 B7
Middlefield Rd TA10 . . . 172 C7
Middleford Ho BS13 . . . 22 C4
Middle Gate TA10 . . . 172 D8
Middlegate Rd TA10 . . . 172 C7
MIDDLE GREEN . . . 222 D3
Middle Green Rd TA21 . . 222 E3
Middle La
Bath BA1 . . . 28 B1
Kingston Seymour BS21 . . . 15 F4
Middle Leaze Dro TA12 . . 185 F7
MIDDLE LEIGH . . . 207 C4
Middle Leigh BA16 . . . 207 C5
MIDDLE LUXTON . . . 191 F5
Middlemead BA3 . . . 96 F3
Middlemoor Dro TA7 . . . 154 A1
Middle Moor Drove TA5 . 134 D7
Middle Moor La BS27 . . . 89 E7
Middlemoor Water Pk* TA7 . . . 136 F5
Middle Path TA18 . . . 224 B5
Middlepiece La BA2, BS31 . 42 B7
Middle Rd TA7 . . . 137 A3
Middle Ridge La DT9 . . . 175 D1
Middleroom Dro TA3 . . . 182 E4
Middle's La BA4 . . . 140 C4
Middle St
Ashcott TA7 . . . 156 B7
Burnham-on-S TA9 . . . 85 E5
East Harptree BS40 . . . 74 F4
East Lambrook TA13 . . . 220 C8
Galhampton BA22 . . . 175 D8
Kingsdon TA11 . . . 173 D5
Martock TA12 . . . 185 D4
Minehead TA24 . . . 200 F8
Misterton TA18 . . . 224 F3
Montacute TA15 . . . 186 B3
North Perrott TA18 . . . 196 C4
Puriton TA7 . . . 136 C4
Rimpton BA22 . . . 188 A8
Shepton Beauchamp TA19 . 184 E3
Taunton TA1 . . . 212 F4
Yeovil BA20 . . . 219 B4
Middle Stoke BA3 . . . 64 A6
MIDDLE STOUGHTON . . . 108 A8
Middle Stream Cl TA6 . . . 208 D2
Middleton La
Clatworthy TA4 . . . 149 C2
Shepton Mallet BA4 . . . 205 B4
Middleton Rd BS11 . . . 4 F8
Middle Touches TA20 . . . 223 E5
Middleway TA1 . . . 212 E2
Middle Way TA11 . . . 157 B4
Middleway Ct TA1 . . . 212 E2
Middleway Rd BA4 . . . 158 E8
Middlewood Cl BA2 . . . 44 C2
Middle Yeo Gn BS48 . . . 8 D3
MIDDLEZOY . . . 155 B3
Middlezoy Prim Sch TA7 . 155 B3
Midelney Rd TA10 . . . 171 E2
MIDFORD . . . 63 C6
Midford BS24 . . . 48 F2
Midford Hill BA2, BA3 . . . 63 C5
Midford La BA2, BA3 . . . 63 E7
Midford Rd
Southstoke BA2 . . . 63 B7
Taunton TA1 . . . 213 B4
Midhaven Rise BS22 . . . 31 E4
MID LAMBROOK . . . 220 A8
Midland Bridge Rd BA1, BA2 . . . 228 A2
Midland Mews BS2 . . . 227 C3
Midland Rd
Bath BA1 . . . 44 D7
Bristol BS2 . . . 227 C3
Midland St BS2 . . . 227 C2
Midleaze DT9 . . . 225 A3
Midney La BA9 . . . 177 D8
Midsomer Ent Pk BA3 . . . 78 C2
MIDSOMER NORTON . . . 78 B3
Midsomer Norton Prim Sch BA3 . . . 78 B1
Midsomer Norton South* BA3 . . . 97 A8
Midsummer Bldgs BA1 . . . 28 B2
MIDWAY . . . 115 E2
MILBORNE PORT . . . 217 E2
Milborne Port Bsns Ctr DT9 . . . 217 D2
Milborne Port Prim Sch DT9 . . . 217 D2
MILBORNE WICK . . . 217 B6
Milburn Rd BS23 . . . 48 F7
Milbury Gdns BS22 . . . 31 C2
Mildmay Dr BA22 . . . 174 F3
Mildmay's Rd TA10 . . . 155 F1
Mildred Rd BA16 . . . 156 E7
Miles Cl BS20 . . . 4 E3
Miles's Bldgs BA1 . . . 228 B3
Miles St BA2 . . . 228 C1
Milestone Cl TA6 . . . 153 F4
Milestone Ct BS22 . . . 32 D2
Mile Wlk BS14 . . . 23 A6
Milford Inf Sch BA21 . . . 219 B7
Milford Jun Sch BA21 . . . 219 B7
Milford Pk BA21 . . . 219 C7
Milford Pl 3 TA1 . . . 213 A4
Milford Rd BA21 . . . 219 C7
Milking La BS27 . . . 90 E2
Milk St
Bath BA1 . . . 228 B2
Frome BA11 . . . 119 E5
Millands La TA5 . . . 133 C6
Millands The TA11 . . . 211 E4
Millards Ct BA3 . . . 78 B3
Millards Hill BA3 . . . 78 B3
Millard's Hill
Batcombe BA4 . . . 142 D2
Midsomer Norton BA3 . . . 78 C3
Mill Ave BS1 . . . 227 A2
Millbatch BA6 . . . 138 C4
Mill Batch Farm Ind Est TA9 . . . 86 F4
Mill Bay TA6 . . . 153 E4
Millbourn Cl BA15 . . . 64 D7
Millbourne Rd BS27 . . . 90 C7
Millbridge Gdns TA24 . . . 200 F7
Millbridge Rd TA24 . . . 200 E7
MILLBROOK . . . 198 A1
Millbrook BA20 . . . 219 A4
Millbrook Cross 1 EX13 . 198 A1
Millbrook Ct BA2 . . . 228 C1
Millbrook Dale EX13 . . . 198 A1
Millbrook Gdns BA7 . . . 214 B5
Millbrook Pl BA2 . . . 228 C1
Mill Cl
Cannington TA5 . . . 135 B2
East Coker BA22 . . . 197 C8
Frome BA11 . . . 119 F6
Nether Stowey TA5 . . . 134 A2
Portbury BS20 . . . 3 D2
Mill Cotts
Creech St Michael TA3 . . . 169 D4
Saltford BS31 . . . 25 F2
Millcross BS21 . . . 16 C8
Mill Cross
Halstock BA22 . . . 197 C3
Kingston St Mary TA2 . . . 168 E7
Mill Ct
Midsomer Norton BA3 . . . 78 A1
Watchet TA23 . . . 202 B7
Millennium Cl BA3 . . . 116 A3
Millennium Sq BS1 . . . 226 C2
Miller Cl BS23 . . . 48 F8
Miller Ho BS8 . . . 226 A2
Millers Cl
Bourton SP8 . . . 161 F1
Pill BS20 . . . 4 C4
Millers Ct BS21 . . . 16 E8
Millers Gdns BA5 . . . 203 E5
Miller's Hill DT9 . . . 217 A5
Millers Orch TA3 . . . 170 F1
Millers Pl BA1 . . . 28 E3
Millers Rise BS22 . . . 32 A4
Millers Way 11 TA4 . . . 167 F8
Miller Way DT9 . . . 225 E5
Miller Wlk BA2 . . . 28 F1
Milletts Cl 2 TA24 . . . 131 A5
Mill Farm Hill TA5 . . . 134 F1
Millfield
Chard TA20 . . . 223 D3
Ilchester BA22 . . . 173 E2
Midsomer Norton BA3 . . . 96 F8
Millfield Cl TA20 . . . 223 D3
Millfield Ind Est TA20 . . . 223 E3
Millfield Prep Sch BA6 . . 139 D1
Millfield Sch BA16 . . . 207 E5
Millford La BA4 . . . 159 C6
Mill Gdns TA24 . . . 201 D1
Millgreen Cl TA9 . . . 136 B8
Millground Rd BS13 . . . 21 F5
Millham La TA22 . . . 163 D6
MILLHAYES . . . 180 C1
Mill Hill BA2 . . . 62 E1
Mill Ho BS1 . . . 227 A2
Mill House Ct BA11 . . . 119 F5
Millier Rd BS49 . . . 35 B8
Milliman Cl BS13 . . . 22 C5
Milliner Ct BA4 . . . 205 B5
Mill La
Alhampton BA4 . . . 159 C5
Axminster EX13 . . . 198 F3
Batcombe BA4 . . . 142 C1
Bathampton BA2 . . . 28 F2
3 Bath BA2 . . . 44 B6
Beckington BA11 . . . 101 D5
Bishops Lydeard TA4 . . . 167 F8
Bitton BS30 . . . 25 E8
Bourton SP8 . . . 161 F1
Bradford Abbas DT9 . . . 187 E1
Bruton BA10 . . . 215 E6
Butcombe BS40 . . . 55 A8
Cannington TA5 . . . 135 B2
Chard TA20 . . . 223 C3
Chard, Wambrook TA20 . . 193 C2
Charlton Mackrell TA11 . . 173 E7
Chew Stoke BS40 . . . 56 D8
Clatworthy TA4 . . . 149 E2
Compton Dando BS39 . . . 41 A5
Mill La *continued*
Compton Martin BS40 . . . 74 A7
Congresbury BS49 . . . 34 D4
Corfe TA3 . . . 181 F6
Corsley Heath BA11, BA12 144 C8
Creech St Michael TA3 . . . 169 D4
Crewkerne, Misterton TA18 . . . 196 B3
Crewkerne TA18 . . . 224 D5
Dinnington TA17 . . . 195 B8
Dowlish Wake TA19 . . . 194 E7
Dunster TA24 . . . 201 D1
East Coker BA22 . . . 197 C7
East Coker, Holywell BA22 . 197 B8
East Huntspill TA9 . . . 136 D8
Exford TA24 . . . 128 C2
Halstock BA22 . . . 197 C3
Higher Chillington TA19 . . . 194 E5
Ilchester BA22 . . . 173 F1
Ilminster TA19 . . . 221 B7
Kingstone TA19 . . . 221 F1
Lopen TA13 . . . 185 A1
Lynford-on-F TA11 . . . 158 C2
Maiden Bradley BA12 . . . 144 B3
Marnhull DT10 . . . 190 F6
Milverton TA4 . . . 167 A5
Monkton Combe BA2 . . . 63 E8
Nether Stowey TA5 . . . 134 A2
North Wootton BA4 . . . 140 D5
Othery TA7 . . . 155 C2
Pitcombe BA10 . . . 215 C3
Porlock TA24 . . . 124 A3
Portbury BS20 . . . 3 E3
Priston BA2 . . . 61 A7
Shapwick TA7 . . . 155 F8
Shepton Mallet BA4 . . . 204 E4
Somerton TA11 . . . 211 D2
South Petherton TA13 . . . 220 E6
Stoke St Michael BA3 . . . 116 B3
Stone Allerton BS26 . . . 88 D4
Taunton TA3 . . . 168 D1
Thurloxton TA2 . . . 153 D1
Timsbury BA2 . . . 60 B1
Trent DT9 . . . 187 F5
Watchet TA23 . . . 202 C7
Wedmore BS28 . . . 108 E3
Wells BA5 . . . 203 A1
West Monkton TA2 . . . 169 D8
Wiveliscombe TA4 . . . 210 C4
Wrington BS40 . . . 53 F8
Yeovil BA20 . . . 219 B4
Mill Lane Cl TA3 . . . 168 D1
Mill La Trad Est BA20 . . . 219 C4
Mill Leat BA6 . . . 157 F5
Mill Leg BS49 . . . 34 D4
Millmead Ho BS13 . . . 22 C4
Millmead Rd BA2 . . . 44 C5
MILLMOOR . . . 179 E1
Millmoot La TA7 . . . 136 F3
Mill on the Brue* BA10 215 D5
Millpill Cl BS9 . . . 5 D5
Mill Rd
Barton St David TA11 . . . 158 A3
Radstock BA3 . . . 79 B2
Mill Rise
Bourton SP8 . . . 161 F1
Staplegrove TA2 . . . 212 B7
Mill Road Ind Est BA3 . . . 79 B3
Mills Dr TA21 . . . 222 F7
Mill St
Carhampton TA24 . . . 131 B4
North Petherton TA6 . . . 153 F3
Rimpton BA22 . . . 188 A8
Watchet TA23 . . . 202 C7
Wells BA5 . . . 203 D4
Wincanton BA9 . . . 216 C4
Millstream Cl TA24 . . . 200 F6
Mill Stream Cl BS26 . . . 70 C1
Mill Stream Gdns TA21 . . 222 B7
Mill Street Cl BA9 . . . 216 C4
Millthorn Ho 2 BA16 . . . 207 C5
Millward Terr BS39 . . . 77 E6
Millway
Chard TA20 . . . 193 C2
Rodney Stoke BS27 . . . 110 B8
Millway Rise Ind Est EX13 . . . 198 A2
Millwey Ave EX13 . . . 198 A2
MILLWEY RISE . . . 198 A2
Mill Wlk TA7 . . . 136 E3
Millwood Cl TA6 . . . 208 E2
Milne Cl TA6 . . . 208 F7
Milsom Pl TA4 . . . 167 F6
Milsom St BA1 . . . 228 B3
MILTON
Martock . . . 185 E8
Weston-super-Mare . . . 31 C2
Milton Ave
Bath BA2 . . . 44 F4
Weston-super-Mare BS23 . . 49 A8
Milton Brow BS22 . . . 31 B2
Milton Cl
Nailsea BS48 . . . 8 E3
Taunton TA1 . . . 213 C3
Yeovil BA21 . . . 218 C6
MILTON CLEVEDON . . . 160 A8
Milton Ct BA4 . . . 205 B7
Milton Gn BS22 . . . 31 C1
Milton Hill
Monkton Heathfield TA2 . . 213 E7
Weston-super-Mare BS22 . . 31 B2
Milton Ho BA21 . . . 187 D6
Milton La
Martock TA12 . . . 185 E8
Wells BA5 . . . 203 D5
Wookey Hole BA5 . . . 203 B8
Milton Leaze TA10 . . . 172 E2

Milton Lodge Gdns★ BA5 203 D7
Milton Park Prim Sch BS22 31 C1
Milton Park Rd BS22 31 C1
Milton Pl TA6 208 E4
Milton Rd
Radstock BA3 78 C1
Taunton TA1 213 C3
Weston-super-Mare BS22, BS23 49 B8
Milton Rise BS22 31 C1
Miltons Cl BS13 22 D4
Milton Terr BA5 203 A8
MILVERTON 166 F4
Milverton BS24 48 F2
Milverton Com Prim Sch TA4 166 F4
Milverton Rd TA21 222 B8
Milward Rd BS31 24 E6
Minchington's Cl TA14 185 F2
MINEHEAD 201 A8
Minehead Com Hospl TA24 201 B5
Minehead Ent Pk TA24 201 B5
Minehead First Sch TA24 200 F6
Minehead La TA22 164 A7
Minehead Mid Sch TA24 201 A6
Minehead Rd
Bishops Lydeard TA4 167 E8
Bristol BS4 23 A8
Minehead Sta★ TA24 201 B7
Miners Cl BS41 10 F2
Minerva Ct BA2 228 C3
Minerva Gdns BA2 44 C4
Minnows The TA20 223 C3
Minsmere Rd BS31 25 A4
Minster Cl TA1 212 C1
Minster Ct TA1 212 C1
Minster Way BA2 45 C8
Minton Cl BS14 23 B5
Mintons TA20 223 B3
Mintons Orch TA20 223 B3
Mint The BA11 119 E5
Misburg Cl BA4 204 F6
MISTERTON 224 E3
Misterton CE Fst Sch TA18 224 F3
Mistletoe La BA4 205 D3
Mitchell Gdns TA20 223 B3
Mitchell La BS1 227 B2
Mitchell's Pool TA21 222 E6
Mitchell's Row BA22 175 D6
Mitchell St TA21 222 C7
Mitchell Terr BA5 112 E1
Mitchelmore Rd BA21 219 B5
Mitford-Slade Ct BS49 34 C7
Mitre Ct TA1 213 B4
Mizzymead Cl 1 BS48 8 D1
Mizzymead Rd BS48 8 E1
Mizzymead Rise BS48 8 E1
Moffats Dr BA5 113 A2
Molesworth Cl BS13 22 A4
Molesworth Dr BS13 22 A4
Molly Cl BS39 76 E8
Monarch Ctr TA2 213 C6
Monday's Court La TA10 172 E5
Money Pit La EX13 193 A1
Monger Cotts BS39 77 F4
Monger La
Midsomer Norton BA3 78 A3
Paulton BS39 78 A4
Monington Rd BA6 206 E6
Monk Barton Cl BA21 218 C7
Monk Cross TA24 128 D1
Monkley La BA11 83 C1
Monks Cl
Rooks Bridge BS26 87 B5
Taunton TA1 213 B5
Monks Dale BA21 218 D6
Monksdale Rd BA2 44 D4
Monks Dr TA7 137 F1
Monks Ford BA5 139 D8
Monksford La BA5 139 C8
Monks Hill BS22 31 B3
MONKSILVER 150 A8
Monks' Path TA23, TA24 131 E4
Monkstone Dr TA8 84 F5
Monkstone Gdns 6 EX13 198 A1
Monksway TA23 131 E4
Monks Way TA8 104 B6
Monkton Ave BS24 49 A2
MONKTON COMBE 45 F1
Monkton Combe Jun Sch BA2 45 C1
MONKTON FARLEIGH 46 F7
MONKTON HEATHFIELD 213 E8
Monkton La TA5 134 D5
Monkton Prep Sch BA2 63 E8
Monkton Sen Sch BA2 45 E1
Monmouth Cl
Chard TA20 223 E4
Glastonbury BA6 206 D5
Portishead BS20 1 F4
Westonzoyland TA7 154 F6
Monmouth Ct
Bath BA1 228 A2
Chard TA20 223 E4
Pill BS20 4 C5
Monmouth Dr BA11 120 B6
Monmouth Farm Cl TA6 135 F5
Monmouth Paddock BA2 81 E5
Monmouth Pl BA1 228 B2
Monmouth Rd
Keynsham BS31 24 D5
Monmouth Rd *continued*
Pill BS20 4 C5
Shepton Mallet BA4 205 A5
Taunton TA1 213 B5
Westonzoyland TA7 154 F6
Yeovil BA21 219 D7
Monmouth St
Bath BA1 228 B2
Bridgwater TA6 209 A5
MONTACUTE 186 B3
Montacute Cir 4 BS22 49 F8
Montacute House★ TA15 186 B4
Montacute Rd
Montacute TA14, TA15 186 B4
Tintinhull BA22 186 B6
Montacute TV, Radio & Toy Mus★ TA15 186 C4
Montague Ct 4 BS2 227 A4
Montague Flats 6 BS2 227 A4
Montague Gdns BA7 214 B5
Montague Hill BS2 227 A4
Montague Hill S 5 BS2 227 A4
Montague Ho 8 BA1 28 C1
Montague Pl BS6 227 A4
Montague Rd
Saltford BS31 25 D2
Shoscombe BA2 79 E5
Montague St BS1 227 A4
Montague Way TA20 223 C3
Monteclefe CE Jun Sch TA11 211 E3
Montepelier BS23 48 F8
Montgomery Ct BA11 120 A4
Montpelier E BS23 30 F1
Montrose Cotts BA1 27 C1
Montrose Rd BA21 219 E7
Montrose Villas BS27 90 C7
Montsurs Cl BA3 96 D3
Monument Cl TA21 222 E4
Monument Rd TA21 222 E3
MOOLHAM 221 C1
Moolham La
Ilminster TA19 194 D7
Kingstone TA19 221 D1
Moondown La TA13 220 B2
Moonhayes Cross EX14 191 F4
Moon La TA7 153 E1
Moonraker Cl 8 TA6 209 B4
Moon's Dro TA7 155 A1
Moons Hill BA3 116 B4
Moonshill Cl BA3 116 A3
Moonshill Cotts BA3 116 A3
Moonshill Rd BA3 116 A3
Moon St BS2 227 B4
MOOR 220 C3
Moor Cl
Compton Dundon TA11 156 F2
Langport TA10 172 A6
Wincanton BA9 216 C3
Moorclose Dro TA7 137 C3
Moorclose La BA4 158 E6
Moor Croft Rd BS24 49 E3
Moor Dro TA7 155 F6
Moorend Gdns BS11 4 F7
Moor End Spout BS48 8 D2
Moore's La TA5, TA6 208 C7
Moores Yd BA14 83 C6
Moorfield Gdn TA24 146 C6
Moorfield Rd BS48 19 A6
Moorfields Cl BA2 44 D3
Moorfields Ct BS48 8 D2
Moorfields Dr BA2 44 D4
Moorfields Ho BS48 8 D2
Moorfields Rd
Bath BA2 44 D4
Nailsea BS48 8 D2
Moor Gate BS20 2 F4
Moor Gn BS26 70 C1
Moor Gr BS11 5 A8
Moorgrove Ho BS9 5 C7
Moorham Rd BS25 52 A1
MOORHAYNE 192 D2
Moorhouse La TA4 165 A8
Moor House La TA5 133 E4
Moorings The
Bath BA2 45 B6
Pill BS20 4 C4
Moor La
Alhampton BA4 159 C5
Backwell BS48 18 F6
Batcombe BA4 142 D1
Brushford TA22 163 F4
Churchinford TA3 192 A7
Clapton in G BS20 2 E1
Clevedon BS21 6 E2
Clevedon BS21 7 A2
Cucklington SP8 177 E5
Draycott BS27 90 F1
East Coker BA22 197 D7
Hardington Mandeville BA22 197 A7
Higher Chillington TA20 194 F5
Hutton BS24 49 D3
North Curry TA3 170 B4
South Petherton TA13 220 B3
Tickenham BS21 7 F4
Walton in G BS21 7 C6
Westbury-sub-Mendip BA5 110 C5
Weston-super-Mare BS24 49 F7
Wincanton BA9 216 C2
Moorland Cl TA1 213 C5
Moorland Cotts BS26 69 F2
Moorland Pk BS24 33 E5
Moorland Pl TA1 213 C5
Moorland Rd
Bath BA2 44 D5
Bridgwater TA6 209 D4
Moorland Rd *continued*
Street BA16 207 B7
Taunton TA1 213 C5
Weston-super-Mare BS23 48 E4
MOORLANDS 44 D3
Moorlands TA4 167 F8
Moorlands Cl
16 Martock TA12 185 E6
Nailsea BS48 8 D2
Moorlands Ct TA16 195 F7
Moorlands Inf Sch BA2 44 D4
Moorlands Jun Sch BA2 44 D3
Moorlands Pk 18 TA12 185 E6
Moorlands Pk Sh Ctr 19 TA12 185 E6
Moorlands Rd TA16 195 E6
Moorland St BS26 70 C1
Moorlands The BA2 44 D3
Moorland Way TA6 209 D5
Moor Lane Cl TA3 170 B4
Moorlay Cres BS40 37 F8
MOORLEDGE 39 E1
Moorledge La BS39, BS40 57 F7
Moorledge Rd BS40 39 B1
MOORLINCH 155 E7
Moorlinch Right Dro TA7 155 D6
Moor Park Rd TA10 171 F5
Moor Pk
Clevedon BS21 6 E2
Langport TA10 171 F5
Moor Rd
Banwell BS29 51 B5
Middlezoy TA7 155 B4
Minehead TA24 200 E8
Moorlinch TA7 155 D7
Sutton Mallet TA7 155 B8
Yatton BS49 17 B2
Moorsfield BS39 58 F3
Moor Sherd BS28 110 C1
Moorside BS49 17 B1
Moorside Ct BS21 6 E2
Moorside Villas BS21 6 E2
Moortown La TA10 171 B2
Moorview Cl BA6 138 C4
Moor Villas TA13 220 B3
Moorway La DT9 188 C6
Moots La TA6 209 D4
Morangis Way TA20 223 B6
Moravia Cl TA6 208 E6
Morden Wlk BS14 23 D7
MOREBATH 164 B3
Moreton Cl BS14 23 A4
Moreton La BS40 56 E2
Moreton Mans 5 BS23 30 C1
Morford St BA1 228 B4
Morgan Cl
Saltford BS31 25 D2
Weston-super-Mare BS22 50 B8
Morgan Pl BS48 20 B8
Morgans Bldgs BS20 8 F8
Morgans Hill Cl BS48 18 D8
Morgan's La
East Harptree BS40 74 F2
8 Frome BA11 119 E5
Morgans Rise TA1 212 A3
Morgan Way BA2 79 E7
Morland Rd
Glastonbury BA6 206 B3
Highbridge TA9 104 D4
Morlands Ent Pk BA6 206 B3
Morlands Ind Pk TA9 104 D4
Morley Terr
Bath BA2 44 D6
Radstock BA3 79 A3
Mornington Pk TA21 222 E5
Morpeth Rd BS4 22 D8
Morrell's Cross EX16 164 B4
Morrell's La EX16 178 B6
Morris Cl TA19 184 C5
Morris La BA1 29 B3
Morston Ct BS22 49 C7
Mortimer Cl
Bath BA1 27 B2
Woolavington TA7 136 E4
Mortimer Rd BS8 226 A3
Morton's La TA10 156 C1
Moseley Gr BS23 48 E2
Moss Cl TA6 209 C6
Moss La TA3 169 C3
Mosterton Down La DT8 196 A1
Moulton Cl BA4 205 A4
Mound The BA6 206 C4
Mounsdon Cl BA6 157 E4
Mountain Ash BA1 27 D1
Mountain's La BA2 59 E6
Mountain Wood BA1 29 C2
Mountbatten Cl
Burnham-on-S TA8 85 A1
Weston-super-Mare BS22 31 E4
Mountbatten Ho TA6 209 C5
Mount Beacon BA1 28 A1
Mount Beacon Pl 3 BA1 27 F1
Mount Beacon Row 1 BA1 28 A1
Mounters Cl DT10 190 F5
Mounter's Hill EX13, TA20 193 B2
Mountery Cl BA5 203 D5
Mountery Rd BA5 203 D5
Mountfields Ave TA1 213 B1
Mountfields Pk TA1 213 B1
Mountfields Rd TA1 213 B1
Mount Gr BA2 44 B3
Mount Hey TA11 211 E3
Mount Hindrance Cl TA20 223 D6
Mount Hindrance La TA20 223 D6
Mount Ho TA1 212 F3
Mount La
Charlton Horethorne DT9 176 A1
Golsoncott TA23, TA24 131 C1
Mount Nebo TA1 212 E2
Mount Pleasant
Bath BA2 45 D1
Castle Cary BA7 214 C5
Crewkerne TA18 224 D6
Frome BA11 119 F2
Kilmington BA12 161 F6
Pill BS20 4 D4
Pilton BA4 140 F3
Radstock BA3 79 B2
Yeovil BA21 219 C5
Mount Pleasant Ave BA5 203 B5
MOUNT RADFORD 208 C6
Mount Rd
Bath BA1 228 B4
Bath, Southdown BA2 44 B3
Nether Stowey TA5 134 A2
Mountsfield BA11 120 A2
Mount St
Bishops Lydeard TA4 167 E8
Bridgwater TA6 208 F5
Taunton TA1 212 F3
Mount Terr TA1 213 A3
MOUNT THE 119 F2
Mount The
Frome BA11 119 F2
Taunton TA1 212 F3
Yatton BS49 34 C8
Mount View
Bath, Beacon Hill BA1 28 A1
Bath, Southdown BA2 44 B3
Woolavington TA7 136 E4
Mount View Terr TA6 135 F6
Mountway TA1 213 A3
Mountway Cl TA1 212 C4
Mountway La TA1 212 C4
Mountway Rd TA1 212 C4
Movey La BA22 173 F1
Mow Barton
Bristol BS13 21 F6
8 Martock TA12 185 E6
Mow Barton Rd TA11 173 D5
Mowbray Rd BS14 23 C7
Mowcroft Rd BS13 22 D4
Mowes La DT10 190 F4
Mowground La TA7 137 A3
Mowleaze 11 BA22 197 F8
Mowlems The BA14 83 F3
Mowries Ct TA11 211 D4
Moxham Dr BS13 22 C4
M Shed★ BS1 227 A1
MUCHELNEY 172 B3
Muchelney Abbey★ TA10 172 A3
MUCHELNEY HAM 172 B2
Muchelney Hill BA6 158 B5
Muchelney Ho TA19 221 B3
Muchelney Pottery & The John Leach Gall★ TA10 172 B2
Muchelney Way BA21 218 C7
Muckleditch La TA19 184 D3
Muddicombe Cross TA24 128 B2
Muddicombe La TA24 128 B2
Muddyford La TA4 151 A3
Muddy La BS22 32 A8
MUDFORD 187 D6
Mudford Hill BA21 187 C5
Mudford Rd BA21 219 B8
MUDFORD SOCK 187 B6
MUDGLEY 138 D8
Mudgley Cross Roads BS28 108 F1
Mudgley Hill BS28 108 E1
Mudgley Rd
Rooks Bridge BS26 87 A4
Wedmore BS28 108 E3
Mud La BS49 17 D2
Mulberry Ave BS20 2 E5
Mulberry Cl
Backwell BS48 19 A6
Portishead BS20 2 F5
Taunton TA1 213 C2
Weston-super-Mare BS22 32 A1
Mulberry Ct BA11 120 B7
Mulberry Farm BA6 140 B1
Mulberry Gdns
4 Crewkerne TA18 224 C5
Sherborne DT9 225 C5
Mulberry La
Bleadon BS24 67 C6
Stoke Sub Hamdon TA14 186 A4
Mulberry Rd BS49 34 E3
Mulberry Tree Cl TA6 209 D5
Mulberry Wlk BS9 5 C8
Mulholland Way TA9 104 D5
Mullins Cl BA5 203 B3
Mullins Way BA7 214 B6
Mundays Mead BA9 216 D3
Munden's La DT9 189 A1
Murford Ave BS13 22 B4
Murford Wlk BS13 22 B4
Murhill BA3 64 C6
Muriel Terr BA5 203 D3
Murray-Smith Dr BA22 218 A6
Murray Way BA9 216 B3
Murtry Hill La BA11 100 C2
Musbury Cl DT10 190 F6
Musbury La DT10 190 F6
Muscovy Dr 1 TA6 154 A5
Museum of Somerset★ TA1 212 F4
Museum of South Somerset★ BA20 219 B4
Musgraves TA22 163 E6
Musgrove Pk Hospl TA1 212 C3
Musgrove Rd TA1 212 C3
Musmoor La BA22 174 F7
Mus of Bath at Work★ BA1 228 B4
Mus of East Asian Art★ BA1 228 B3
Mutton La BS28 108 D4
Mutton St DT6 199 D1
Mux's La TA4 151 B3
Myrtleberry Mead BS22 32 A5
Myrtle Cl TA6 209 D5
Myrtle Dr
Bristol BS11 4 E5
Burnham-on-S TA8 104 A7
Myrtle Gdns BS49 34 C8
Myrtle Hill BS20 4 C5
Myrtle La TA21 179 E7
Myrtle Rd
Bristol BS2 226 C4
22 Martock TA12 185 E6
Myrtles The BS24 49 D2
Myrtle Tree Cres BS22 31 A6
Myrtlle Cotts TA3 182 D7

N

Nag's La TA18 195 B1
NAILSBOURNE 168 D7
NAILSEA 8 E3
Nailsea and Backwell Station BS48 18 F7
Nailsea Cl BS13 22 A7
Nailsea Com Sch BS48 8 E1
Nailsea Moor La BS48 17 F7
Nailsea Park Cl BS48 8 F2
Nailsea Pk BS48 8 F2
Nailsea Wall BS21 17 C8
Nailsea Wall La BS48 17 E7
NAILWELL 61 D6
Naishes Ave BA2 79 D7
Naish Farm BA3 96 D3
Naish Hill BS20 2 F1
Naish Ho BA2 44 A6
Naish La BS48 20 D3
Naisholt Rd BA4 204 F6
Naish Rd TA8 85 A3
Naish's Cross BA3 96 D3
Naish's St BA11 119 E5
Nalder Cl BA4 205 D4
Nanga-gat Rd BA22 174 A2
Nanny Hurn's La BS39 58 A1
Napier Ct
Bristol BS1 226 B1
Sherborne DT9 225 B2
Napier Miles Rd BS11 5 A8
Napier Rd BA1 27 A3
Naples View TA6 208 E7
NARFORD'S 193 C1
Narfords La TA20 193 C1
Narrow Plain BS2 227 B2
Narrow Quay BS1 227 A2
NASH 197 C8
Nash Barton BA22 197 C8
Nash Cl BS31 25 A5
Nash Dr TA21 222 F6
Nash Gn TA2 212 B7
Nash La
Dinnington TA17, TA19 195 A6
East Coker BA22 197 C7
Marshwood DT6 199 B2
Yeovil BA20 218 D1
Nates La BS40 35 F1
Nathan Cl BA20 218 D2
Naunton Way BS22 31 B2
Neale's Way BA4 141 E2
Neathem Rd BA21 219 C7
Neat La BA4 204 D1
Nedge Cnr BA3 94 D4
Nedge Hill BA3 94 D3
Nedge La BA3 94 C4
Needhams Patch TA4 167 E6
NEIGHBOURNE 115 C5
Nelson Bldgs BA1 228 C4
Nelson Ct
Bridgwater TA6 208 F5
Weston-super-Mare BS22 31 E4
Nelson Ho
Bath BA1 228 A3
5 Bristol BS1 227 A3
Nelson Pl BA1 228 C4
Nelson Pl E BA1 228 C4
Nelson Pl W BA1 228 A2
Nelson St BS1 227 A3
Nelson Terr BA1 228 C4
Nelson Villas BA1 228 A2
Nempnett St BS40 55 D5
NEMPNETT THRUBWELL 55 D5
Neroche Prim Sch TA19 183 C2
Neroche View TA3 183 A7
Nerrols Dr TA2 213 C7
Neston Wlk BS4 22 F8
NETHERCLAY 182 B7
Netherclay TA1 212 A4
Netherclay La TA3 182 B7
NETHER COMPTON 187 F4
Nethercoombe La DT9 225 C5
NETHERCOTT 151 C3
Nethercott La TA4 151 C3
Nethercott Way TA4 151 A3
NETHERHAY 199 F8

Netherhay La DT8 199 F8
Nethermoor Rd TA7 155 B3
NETHERSTOKE 197 D3
Netherstoke La BA22 197 C3
NETHER STOWEY 134 B3
Nether Stowey CE Prim Sch
TA5 134 A2
Netherton Cross BA22 197 E6
Netherton La
East Coker BA22 197 F6
Marston Magna BA22 175 A1
Netherton Rd BA21 219 D7
Netherton Wood La BS48 18 A6
Netherways BS21 6 B1
Netley BA21 218 D6
NETTLEBRIDGE 115 D6
Nettlebridge Hill BA3 115 D5
NETTLECOMBE 149 F8
Nettlecombe Hill
Castle Cary BA7 214 F6
Pitcombe BA7 215 A2
Nettlecombe Ho BA5 113 A1
Nettlecombe Park Rd
Monksilver TA4 132 A1
Sticklepath TA4 149 F7
Nettle Combe View BA5 113 A2
Neva Rd BS23 48 E6
Neville Cl 1 TA11 173 F7
Neville Pk BA6 158 A5
Nevys La TA4 150 E8
Newark St BA1 228 C1
Newbarn Park Rd TA1 212 B1
Newberrys Patch TA3 192 A7
Newbery Cl 4 EX13 198 A1
Newbery La TA18 224 F3
New Bldgs
3 Bampton EX16 164 C1
Dunwear TA7 209 D1
Frome BA11 119 F3
Ilminster TA19 221 B1
North Perrott TA18 196 C4
Oake TA4 167 C4
Peasedown St John BA2 79 B8
New Bond St BA1 228 C2
New Bond Street Pl BA1 228 C2
Newbourne Rd BS22 49 C8
NEWBRIDGE 44 B8
Newbridge Ct BA1 44 B7
Newbridge Dro TA9 105 A1
Newbridge Gdns BA1 44 A8
Newbridge Hill BA1 44 B7
Newbridge Ho BS9 5 C4
Newbridge La TA9 104 F1
Newbridge Prim Sch BA1 44 B7
Newbridge Rd BA1, BA2 44 B7
New Bristol Rd BS22 31 E1
New Buildings La BA11 119 F3
New Bungalows TA20 223 C3
NEWBURY
Coleford 98 B1
Horningsham 144 E4
Newbury BA12 144 E4
Newbury Cotts BA3 117 A8
Newbury Terr 3 BA21 218 F7
Newchester Cross TA16 195 E7
New Church Rd BS23 48 D2
New Cl
Bourton SP8 161 F1
Haselbury Plucknett TA18 196 B5
Horrington BA5 113 A4
Street BA16 207 B4
Newclose La BS40 56 D1
Newclose Terr TA14 185 E4
Newcombe Cvn Pk TA8 104 B8
Newcombe Dr BS9 5 C4
Newcombe La BS25 70 B7
Newcombe Rd BS9 5 F7
Newcot Cross EX15 191 A5
NEWCOTT 192 C3
New Cotts
Milton Clevedon BA4 160 A8
West Chinnock TA18 196 B8
NEW CROSS 184 F6
New Cross TA11 211 C3
New Cross Hill
Barrington TA12, TA13 184 F6
Kingsbury Episcopi TA12 185 A6
New Cut BA5 203 D7
New Cut Bow BS21 16 A6
Newditch La BS40 20 C1
Newell DT9 225 C4
Newfield TA4 166 F4
Newfields BS40 72 C8
New Fosseway Rd BS14 23 B6
New Fosseway Sch BS13 22 E4
Newfoundland Rd BS2 227 C4
Newfoundland St BS2 227 C4
Newfoundland Way
Bristol BS2 227 C4
Portishead BS20 2 E6
New Friary Cotts BA11 143 C3
Newgate BS1 227 B3
Newgate Cross TA22 163 D7
Newgate La TA4 210 C5
Newhaven Pl BS20 1 E4
Newhaven Rd BS20 1 D4
New Hill TA11 211 E4
Newhouse La TA4 165 E6
Newington Cl BA11 119 E3
Newington Terr BA11 119 E4
New Kingsley Rd BS2 227 C2
New King St BA1 228 B2
New La
Bampton EX16 163 F2
Charlton Horethorne DT9 176 A1
New La *continued*
Creech St Michael TA3 169 D5
Cricket St Thomas TA20 194 E4
Haselbury Plucknett TA18 196 C6
Tatworth TA20 198 C8
Witham Friary BA11 143 C4
Newland DT9 225 E4
Newland Cross TA24 128 B1
Newland Dr BS13 22 A4
Newland Flats 5 DT9 225 E4
Newland Gdn 8 DT9 225 E4
Newland Ho BA1 27 F1
Newland Rd
Bristol BS13 22 A3
Weston-super-Mare BS23 48 F6
Newlands Cl BS20 2 C5
Newlands Cres TA3 169 C3
Newlands Gn BS21 6 E1
Newlands Gr TA3 169 C3
Newlands Hill BS20 2 C4
Newlands Rd
Keynsham BS31 24 D4
Ruishton TA3 169 C3
Newland Wlk BS13 22 A3
Newlyn Ave BS9 5 D5
Newlyn Cres TA7 136 B4
Newman Cl BA6 206 E6
Newmans La
East Huntspill TA9 105 C1
Timsbury BA2 60 B2
Newmarket Ave 9 BS1 227 A3
New Mdws BS14 23 A6
Newnham Cl BS14 23 D7
New Orchard St BA1 228 C2
New Park Ho BS21 6 D5
New Pit Cotts BA2 60 F1
New Pk EX16 162 E4
NEWPORT 170 B2
Newport Cl
Clevedon BS21 6 C2
Portishead BS20 1 F4
Newport Hill TA3 170 B2
Newport Rd BS20 4 C5
Newquay Rd BS4 22 F8
New Rd
Banwell BS29 50 E4
Barwick BA22 197 F8
Bathford BA1 29 D2
Bawdrip TA7 136 D2
Bridgwater TA6 209 A5
Burrowbridge TA3, TA7 170 E8
Cannington TA5 135 C1
Carhampton TA24 131 A5
Chapel Allerton BS26 88 C2
Chard Junction TA20 198 F8
Churchill BS25 52 F4
Clevedon BS21 6 D2
Combe St Nicholas TA20 193 D6
Crewkerne TA18 195 B4
Crickham BS28 108 D8
Draycott BS27 91 C3
East Huntspill TA9 136 D8
Freshford BA3 64 B5
Frome BA11 120 B4
Hambridge TA12 184 E7
Haselbury Plucknett TA18 196 E6
High Littleton BS39 59 C3
Hinton St George TA17 195 C7
Ilminster TA19 221 B4
Kilmersdon BA3 98 E4
Kilmington BA12 161 E7
Lyng TA3 170 B6
North Wootton BA4 140 A4
Norton Sub Hamdon, Chiselborough TA14 185 F1
Norton Sub Hamdon TA14 185 E3
Oare EX35 122 D4
Odcombe BA22 186 D3
Othery TA7 155 C2
Pensford BS39 40 D3
Pill BS20 4 C4
Porlock TA24 123 E3
Rawridge EX14 191 E1
Redhill BS40 37 A4
Seavington St Mary TA19 184 E1
Sherborne DT9 225 E3
Shipham BS25 52 E1
South Cadbury BA22 175 E4
Stalbridge DT10 190 B4
Staple Fitzpaine TA3 182 D5
Taunton TA3 168 D1
West Bagborough TA4 151 E4
Weston Town BA4 142 D5
Wiveliscombe TA4 166 A6
Yeovil BA22 218 A5
New Road Gate EX35 122 D5
New Rock Ind Est BA3 96 D2
Newsome Ave BS20 4 C4
New Sq BA5 113 A2
New St
Bath BA1 228 B2
Bristol BS2 227 C3
Long Sutton TA10 172 E4
Marnhull DT10 190 F5
Mells BA11 118 B7
North Perrott TA18 196 C4
Somerton TA11 211 E4
Wells BA5 203 D5
New Street Flats 4 BS2 227 C3
New Thomas St BS2 227 C2
NEWTON
Combe St Nicholas 193 A7
Watchet 132 E1
Newton Cl
Burnham-on-S TA8 85 A2
West Harptree BS40 74 E6
Newton Ct 14 EX16 164 B1
Newton Gn BS48 18 C8
Newton La
Bicknoller TA4 132 E1
Corfe TA3 181 F6
Newton Rd
Barwick BA22 197 F8
Bath BA2 43 F6
North Petherton TA6 153 F3
Taunton TA1 213 E4
Weston-super-Mare BS23 48 E6
Yeovil BA20 219 D3
NEWTON ST LOE 43 D6
Newton Sq 8 EX16 164 B1
Newton's Rd
Weston-super-Mare BS22 31 E3
Weston-super-Mare BS22 31 E4
NEWTOWN
Axbridge 69 D2
Bridgwater 208 E6
NEW TOWN
Bishop Sutton 57 D7
Freshford 81 F8
Hatch Beauchamp 182 E4
Kington Magna 177 E1
Milborne Port 217 B2
Paulton 77 D6
Wedmore 138 E8
Yeovil 219 C6
Newtown TA12 185 E7
Newtown La BA6 140 A1
Newtown Pk TA10 172 A6
Newtown Rd
Highbridge TA9 104 D3
Langport TA10 172 A6
New Way TA10 172 B7
Nibley Rd BS11 4 E5
Nicholas Cl TA22 163 E4
Nicholls Cl TA6 208 D4
Nichol Pl TA4 167 F6
Nichol's Rd BS20 1 F5
Nick Reed's La EX15 180 D1
Nidon La TA7 137 D3
Nigel Pk BS11 4 E7
Nightingale Acre TA3 183 A7
Nightingale Ave BA11 120 B6
Nightingale Cl
1 Bridgwater TA6 209 C4
Burnham-on-S TA8 85 B1
Wells BA5 203 B3
Weston-super-Mare BS22 31 E1
Nightingale Ct
16 Taunton TA1 213 A4
Weston-super-Mare BS22 31 E1
Nightingale Gdns BS48 8 D2
Nightingale Gr BA4 205 C5
Nightingale La BA22 174 F6
Nightingale Rise BS20 1 F3
Nightingales TA4 167 E6
Nightingale Way BA3 97 B8
Nile St BA1 228 A2
NIMMER 223 C8
Nine Acre Dro TA7 138 B2
Nine Acre La TA3 170 C4
Nine Barrows La BA5 92 E4
Nippors Way BS25 69 F8
Nithsdale Rd BS23 48 E4
Nixon Trad Units BS24 49 A3
No 1 Royal Cres Mus★
BA1 228 B3
Noah's Ark Zoo Farm★
BS48 9 B7
Noah's Hill TA2 169 B7
Noake Rd DT9 225 B3
Noble St TA1 213 B4
Noel Coward Cl TA8 104 C6
Nomis Pk BS49 34 E2
No Place La TA5 152 E5
Norbins Rd BA6 206 D5
Nordens Mdw TA4 210 D4
Nordrach La BS40 73 D5
Nore Gdns BS20 2 C6
Nore Park Dr BS20 1 F5
Nore Rd BS20 2 A6
Norfolk Ave BS2 227 B4
Norfolk Bldgs BA1 228 A2
Norfolk Cl TA6 209 C3
Norfolk Cres BA1 228 A2
Norfolk Gr BS31 24 C4
Norfolk Hts 10 BS2 227 B4
Norfolk Rd
Portishead BS20 2 E4
Weston-super-Mare BS23 48 F5
Norland Rd BS8 11 F8
Norlet Ct BA6 206 D5
Normandy Ave TA23 202 E6
Normandy Dr TA1 213 C3
Normandy Ho BA16 207 B6
Norman La TA7 156 B7
Norman Rd BS31 25 E3
Normans The BA2 28 F1
Normans Way BS20 3 E7
Norrington Way TA20 223 D2
Northam Farm Cvn Pk & Camp Site TA8 65 F4
Northampton Bldgs BA1 228 B4
Northampton Ho BS48 9 D3
Northampton St BA1 228 B4
Northanger Ct 5 BA2 228 C3
North Ave TA9 104 C4
NORTHAY
Combe St Nicholas 193 B6
Hawkchurch 199 A3
Northay Cross EX13 199 B3
Northay La
Axminster EX13 199 A3
Combe St Nicholas TA20 193 B6
North Bank BA5 203 A8
NORTH BARROW 175 A8
NORTH BREWHAM 161 A7
Northbrook Dr TA7 137 F1
Northbrook Rd
Cannington TA5 135 C2
Shapwick TA7 138 A1
Yeovil BA21 219 D7
NORTH CADBURY 175 D6
North Cadbury CE Prim Sch
BA22 175 D6
NORTH CHERITON 176 C4
North Chew Terr BS40 39 B3
North Chine Dro BA5 138 D8
North Cl BS27 90 F3
NORTH COKER 197 D8
Northcombe La TA22 163 E7
Northcote Cres BA11 120 A7
Northcote Rd BS8 5 F1
North Cres DT9 217 D3
North Croft TA4 202 D3
NORTH CURRY 170 C4
North Curry CE Prim Sch
TA3 170 B3
North Down Cl BS25 70 F8
North Down La BS25 70 F8
Northdown Rd BA3 78 E5
North Dro BS48 8 A2
NORTHEND 28 F5
NORTH END
Clutton 58 E5
Millmoor 179 E3
Taunton 169 D5
Yatton 16 F3
North End
Charlton Horethorne DT9 176 A2
Creech St Michael TA3 169 D5
Midsomer Norton BA3 78 B2
North End Rd BS49 16 F3
Northern Path BS21 6 F3
Northern Way BS21 6 F3
NORTHFIELD
Bridgwater 208 C4
Radstock 79 B1
Somerton 211 C5
Northfield
Bridgwater TA6 208 E4
Radstock BA3 79 A3
Somerton TA11 211 C4
Timsbury BA2 60 C3
Winsley BA15 64 F7
Northfield Ave TA1 212 E4
Northfield Cl TA5 134 C6
Northfield Gdns TA1 212 E5
Northfield Ho
Bath BA1 27 F1
Glastonbury BA6 206 E4
Northfield La
Dinnington TA17 195 B8
South Petherton TA13 220 C2
Northfield Rd
Minehead TA24 201 A8
Portishead BS20 1 E3
Taunton TA1 212 E4
Northfields
Bath BA1 27 F1
Taunton TA1 212 B3
Northfields Cl BA1 27 F1
Northfield Way TA11 211 C5
NORTHGATE 210 C5
Northgate
Bridgwater TA6 208 F5
Wiveliscombe TA4 210 C5
Northgate St BA1 228 C2
North Gr
Pill BS20 4 C4
Wells BA5 203 E5
North Green St 11 BS8 11 F6
North Hill Mews BA11 119 F5
North Hill Rd TA24 200 F8
North Hills Cl BS24 49 B2
North Hill Woodland Trail★
TA24 125 B4
North La
Bath BA2 45 D5
Berrow TA8 65 F1
Challacombe EX31, TA24 126 B4
East Coker BA22 197 A7
Nailsea BS48 8 B1
Othery TA7 155 C2
Stogursey TA5 134 C7
2 Weston-super-Mare BS23 48 E7
Yeovil BA20 219 B5
Northleach Wlk BS11 4 F5
North Leaze BS41 11 B2
Northleaze CE Prim Sch
BS41 11 B2
Northleaze Ho BA16 207 C6
North Leaze La BA22 175 C7
Northleigh Ave BS22 31 C1
Northleigh Rd TA1 213 B3
Northload Bridge BA6 206 C5
Northload Bridge Rdbt
BA6 206 D5
Northload Dro BS28 109 E2
Northload La BS28 109 D1
Northload St BA6 206 D5
Northload Terr BA6 206 D5
North Mdws BA2 79 E8
Northmead Ave BA3 77 F2
Northmead Cl BA3 77 F2
Northmead Dro TA3 170 A1
Northmead Rd BA3 77 F2
North Mills La TA13 220 C5
Northmoor La TA3 170 C7
Northmoor Rd
Dulverton TA22 163 D7
Othery TA10 155 D1
NORTH NEWTON 153 F2
North Newton Com Prim Sch
TA7 153 F2
NORTHOVER
Glastonbury 206 B3
Ilchester 173 E2
Northover Bldgs BA6 206 B3
Northover Dr TA20 223 B5
Northover Farmhouse
BA6 207 D8
North Par
Bath BA2 228 C2
Frome BA11 119 F5
North Parade Bldgs 8
BA1 228 C2
North Parade Pas 7
BA1 228 C2
North Parade Rd BA2 45 B6
NORTH PERROTT 196 C4
North Perrott Rd TA18 196 C5
NORTH PETHERTON 153 F4
North Petherton Com Prim Sch TA6 153 F3
North Rd
Banwell BS29 51 A3
Bath, Bathwick BA2 45 C6
Bath, Combe Down BA2 45 B2
Charlton Horethorne DT9 176 A2
Easterton BS24 67 D2
Leigh Woods BS8 11 D7
Midsomer Norton BA3 78 A1
Minehead TA24 201 A7
Sherborne DT9 225 E5
Timsbury BA2 60 C2
Wells BA5 203 E5
Williton TA4 202 D4
Northside
Castle Cary BA7 214 C6
Rockwell Green TA21 222 B5
North Side Rd BS48 36 F8
North Somerset Mus★
BS23 48 E8
North St
Babcary TA11 174 C7
Bradford Abbas DT9 187 E1
Bridgwater TA6 208 E4
Bristol BS1 227 B4
Castle Cary BA7 214 C5
Crewkerne TA18 224 C7
Drayton TA10 171 E3
Haselbury Plucknett TA18 196 C6
Ilminster TA19 221 C4
Langport TA10 172 A5
Martock TA12 185 E6
Milborne Port DT9 217 D2
Milverton TA4 167 A4
Nailsea BS48 8 B1
North Petherton TA6 153 E4
Norton St Philip BA2 81 E4
Norton Sub Hamdon TA14 185 E1
Shepton Beauchamp TA19 184 E4
Somerton TA11 211 E4
South Petherton TA13 220 C5
Stoke sub Hamdon TA14 185 F4
Taunton TA1 212 F4
Wellington TA21 222 D6
Weston-super-Mare BS23 48 E8
Williton TA4 202 D3
Wincanton BA9 216 C4
Wiveliscombe TA4 210 B4
NORTH STOKE 26 C6
North Stoke La BS30 26 B8
North Terr BA21 219 C6
NORTH TOWN
North Cadbury 175 C7
North Wootton 140 D5
Taunton 212 E5
North Town TA11 173 D5
North Town Com Prim Sch
TA1 212 E4
Northtown La
North Wootton BA4 140 C4
Taunton TA1 212 E4
North Town Mews TA1 212 E5
Northumberland Bldgs 1
BA1 228 B2
Northumberland Pl 1
BA1 228 C2
North View BA3 79 B2
North View Cl BA2 44 B5
North View Dr BS29 51 A2
North Villas TA4 167 F6
North Way
Bath BA2 44 A5
Midsomer Norton BA3 78 A1
NORTH WESTON 2 C2
NORTHWICK 105 F6
NORTH WICK 39 D8
Northwick Gdns BS39 57 D4
Northwick Rd
Chew Magna BS39, BS41 39 D7
Mark TA9 106 B5
NORTH WIDCOMBE 57 B1
Northwood Cl TA2 168 B4
Northwood Dro BA6 158 A6
NORTH WOOTTON
Sherborne 188 F1
Wells 140 C4
NORTON 31 D4
Norton Cl
Chew Magna BS40 39 B3
Shepton Mallet BA4 205 A5
Norton Dro TA12 185 B8
NORTON FITZWARREN 168 B4
Norton Fitzwarren CE Com Prim Sch TA2 168 B5
Norton Grange BA2 81 E5
NORTON HAWKFIELD 39 F6
NORTON HILL 97 B7

Norton Hill Sch BA3 .... 97 B8
Norton Ho **7** BS1.. 227 B1
Norton La
Chew Magna BS39, BS40 .. 39 D5
Wellow BA2 .... 81 B7
Weston-super-Mare BS22.. 31 C4
Whitchurch BS14 .... 23 C2
NORTON MALREWARD ... 40 B7
Norton Radstock Coll BA3 78 F2
Norton Rd TA14 .... 185 E3
NORTON ST PHILIP 81 F4
Norton St Philip CE Fst Sch
BA2 .... 81 E4
NORTON SUB HAMDON .. 185 F3
Norton sub Hamdon CE Prim
Sch TA14 .... 185 F3
NORTON'S WOOD 7 C5
Nortons Wood La BS21... 7 A5
Norville La BS27 .... 90 B8
Norville La BS27 .... 90 B8
Norwich Cl TA1 .... 212 C1
Norwich Ct TA1 .... 212 D2
Norwood Ave BA2 .... 45 E5
Norwood Gr BS20 ....1 F5
Notaro Wy TA7 .... 154 A4
Notgrove Cl BS22 ...... 31 B2
Notlake Dro BS27 ...... 89 E4
Notting Hill Way BS26... 88 D6
Nova Quarter BA16...... 207 B5
Nova Scotia Pl BS1..... 226 A1
Novers Cres BS4 .... 22 C8
Novers Hill BS4 .... 22 C8
Novers La BS4 .... 22 D7
NOVERS PARK 22 C8
Novers Park Dr BS4 .... 22 C8
Novers Park Rd BS4..... 22 D8
Novers Rd BS4 .... 22 C8
Nowers La TA21 .... 222 C3
Nowhere La BS48 .... 9 A1
Number 15 BA21....... 219 F7
NUNNEY 143 C8
Nunney Barton BA11 ... 119 D4
Nunney Castle ★ BA11 .. 143 B8
NUNNEY CATCH 143 B7
Nunney Catch Rbt BA11 . 143 B7
Nunney Cl
Burnham-on-S TA8....... 85 C1
Keynsham BS31......... 25 A2
Nunney Fst Sch BA11 ... 143 B8
Nunney Rd BA11 .... 119 D4
Nurcott La TA24 .... 147 C7
Nursery Cl TA5 .... 135 B5
Nursery Gdns TA20..... 223 E4
Nursery La BA9 .... 216 C4
Nursery Rd BA20....... 219 A3
Nursery Rise BA3 ...... 96 E4
Nursery Terr TA6 ...... 208 E5
Nursery Villas TA20 .... 223 E4
Nutgrove La BS40 ...... 39 A4
Nutshole La TA20 ...... 194 B2
Nut Tree Cl TA9....... 136 E8
Nut Tree La TA18 ...... 224 D7
Nutts La BA11.......... 101 F8
Nutwell Rd BS22 ...... 31 C4
Nutwell Sq BS22 ...... 31 E2
Nydon The TA7 .... 137 D3
NYE 51 E8
Nye Cl BS27 .... 90 C7
Nye Dro BS24 .... 51 E5
Nye Rd BS25.......... 51 F5
NYLAND 90 C1
Nyland Dro BS27 ...... 90 B1
Nyland La BA8 .... 190 C8
Nyland View BS27...... 90 F3
NYNEHEAD 167 C1
Nynehead Hollow TA21.. 167 C1
Nynehead Rd
Nynehead TA21 .... 167 C1
Wellington TA21........ 222 F8
Nythe Rd TA7.......... 156 A5

O

Oak Apple Dr TA6....... 208 D6
Oak Ave BA2.......... 44 C3
Oak Cl TA24 .... 200 D7
Oak Ct
Bristol BS14........... 23 A5
Weston-super-Mare BS22.. 32 C3
Oakdale Gdns BS22 .... 31 F2
Oakdale Rd BS14....... 23 A8
Oak Dr
Crewkerne TA18......... 224 D7
Portishead BS20 .... 2 B4
OAKE 167 D4
Oake Acres TA4........ 167 D4
Oake, Bradford & Nynehead
CE Prim Sch TA4...... 167 D4
Oake Cl TA4 .... 167 D4
Oake Gn TA4 .... 167 D4
Oak End Way TA20..... 223 C5
Oaken Ground TA21.... 222 B5
Oakfield Acad BA11..... 119 D4
Oakfield Cl
Bath BA1............. 44 D8
Frome BA11........... 119 D5
Oakfield Gr BS8....... 226 B4
Oakfield Pk TA21 ..... 222 E4
Oakfield Pl BS8....... 226 B4
Oakfield Rd
Bridgwater TA6........ 208 C4
Bristol BS8........... 226 B4
Frome BA11........... 119 D4
Keynsham BS31......... 24 F2
Street BA16........... 207 B4
Oakford Ave BS23...... 48 F8
Oakford La BA1........ 29 A8

Oak Gr BS20 .... 4 C5
Oakgrove Way TA6..... 209 D6
OAKHILL 115 A3
Oakhill BS24.......... 49 A2
Oakhill CE Prim Sch BA3 115 B3
Oakhill Cl BS48........9 B1
Oakhill Ct BA3 .... 116 E3
Oakhill Rd BA2 .... 44 F2
Oak Ho
Brean TA8 .... 65 E2
Bristol BS13.......... 22 D4
Oakhurst Rd BS9........5 F5
Oak La
East Anstey TA22...... 162 E6
Rodhuish TA24........ 131 A3
Taunton TA1 .... 212 F6
Oakland Ct TA12 ...... 185 E7
Oakland Dr
Hutton BS24 .... 49 E3
Martock TA12......... 185 E7
Oakland Rd TA12...... 185 E7
Oaklands
Cheddar BS27 .... 90 A8
Clevedon BS21......... 6 C4
Paulton BS39.......... 77 E4
Temple Cloud BS39..... 58 E1
Oaklands Ave TA20..... 223 F4
Oaklands Rd BA21 .... 219 D7
Oakleigh BA20........ 218 D2
Oakleigh Cl BS48...... 19 B5
Oakley
Bath BA2............. 45 E5
Clevedon BS21......... 16 B8
Oakley Cl TA7......... 154 F5
Oakley La BA22........ 186 F6
Oak Lodge Cres TA24 .. 200 F7
Oakmear Rd TA6...... 208 C3
Oak Rd
Nether Stowey TA5 ..... 134 B2
Winscombe BS25........ 70 A8
Oakridge Cl BS25...... 70 B7
Oakridge La BS25...... 70 C6
Oakridge Pk BA21...... 219 A6
Oaksey Gr BS48........ 9 A1
Oak St BA2 .... 228 B1
Oaks The
Nailsea BS48.......... 9 A2
Taunton TA1.......... 213 C1
Wembdon TA6......... 208 C6
Winford BS40 .... 37 F7
Oak Terr BA3 .... 78 D1
Oak Tree Arena (Somerset
Speedway) ★ TA9 .... 105 A5
Oak Tree Cl EX14 ..... 191 F2
Oaktree Ct BS11 ....4 E7
Oaktree Gdns BS13..... 21 E5
Oak Tree Ho **13** TA14... 185 F4
Oaktree Pk 49 E5
Oaktree Pl BS22 ...... 32 C3
Oak Tree Pl TA8 ...... 85 A3
Oak Tree Way TA5 ..... 135 B2
Oak Tree Wlk BS31..... 24 D3
Oak Vale La BA8 ...... 190 A6
Oak Way BA22 .... 218 A7
OARE 122 E4
OAREFORD 122 F3
Oare Post TA24 .... 123 B3
Oasis Acad Brightstowe
BS11................4 E7
Oasis Acad John Williams
BS14................ 23 B7
Oasis Acad New Oak BS14 23 B7
Oatfield BS48......... 19 F1
OATHILL 199 E8
Oathill Cotts BA4 ..... 140 F3
Oathill La
Clapton TA18 .... 195 C1
Winsham TA18......... 199 E8
Oatlands Ave BS14..... 23 A6
Oatley La TA5......... 134 F2
Oborne Rd DT9 .... 225 F5
OBRIDGE 213 A6
Obridge Cl TA2 .... 213 A6
Obridge Cres TA2...... 213 A6
Obridge La TA2 .... 213 A6
Obridge Rd TA2....... 213 A6
Obridge Viaduct TA2... 213 B6
Observatory Field BS25.. 70 B8
Observatory The BS22... 31 D3
Ocean Way BA22....... 174 B3
Octagon The **5** TA1... 212 F4
Octavia Cl TA20....... 208 E2
ODCOMBE 186 D2
Odcombe Hollow BA22.. 196 B4
ODD DOWN 44 D2
Odeon Bldgs BS23..... 48 E7
Odins Rd BA2......... 44 D1
Olands Rd TA1........ 212 D6
Old Acre Rd BS14...... 23 A3
Old Airfield Cvn Pk The
TA7................ 155 A4
Old Ansford Inn BA7 ... 214 C6
Old App BA7.......... 159 A3
Old Banwell Rd BS24.... 50 B4
Oldbarn La
Bampton EX16......... 163 E1
Compton Martin BS40.... 56 D1
Old Barn La
Felton BS40.......... 37 A5
Hatch Beauchamp TA3... 182 F6
Old Barn Way BA20 ... 218 E3
Old Barrow Hill BS11.... 4 D7
Old Basin TA6........ 209 B2
Oldberry La BA22...... 163 D6
Old Bond St **4** BA1... 228 B2
Old Bowden Way DT9... 217 D4
Old Bread St BS2 ..... 227 C2

Old Brewery Ind Est The
TA4................ 210 C4
Old Brewery Rd TA4.... 210 C4
Old Brewery The
6 Frome BA11........ 119 F4
Rode BA11 .... 101 E8
Old Brewhouse The BA1.. 27 B2
Old Bridge Cl BA6...... 206 D5
Oldbridge Rd BS14..... 23 C3
Old Bristol Rd
East Brent TA9......... 86 E4
Oakhill BA3, BA4...... 114 E1
Priddy BA5, BS40....... 93 A6
Shepton Mallet BA4..... 141 C8
Wells BA5 .... 112 B5
Weston-super-Mare BS22.. 32 A2
Oldbroach La TA3...... 213 F2
Old Bull La BA4....... 141 F7
Old Burnham Rd TA9.... 104 D4
Old Chapel BA1........ 228 C4
Old Chapel Ct TA10.... 172 A6
Old Chapel La BS48..... 17 F7
Old Chapel Rd TA7..... 155 B3
Old Chelsea La BS8..... 10 C4
Old Church Rd
Axbridge BS26......... 70 C1
Clevedon BS21......... 6 C3
Nailsea BS48.......... 18 D8
Weston-super-Mare BS23.. 48 D2
OLD CLEEVE 131 E4
Old Cleeve CE Sch TA23 131 E4
Old Coach Rd BS26..... 69 C2
Old Combe Hill TA3.... 181 F5
Old Co-op Cotts BA3.... 117 A7
Old Dairy Ct BS21........6 E3
Old Dairy The BA2 .... 44 D4
OLD DITCH 110 E4
Old Ditch BS5 .... 110 E4
Old Ditch La TA7...... 155 E7
OLD DOWN 95 F3
Old Down La BA4...... 142 A6
Old Drill Hall The BS2.. 227 C3
Old England Way BA2... 79 E8
Old Farm DT9......... 225 C4
Old Farm Cl TA24..... 200 E6
Old Farm Ct
Blackford BS28........ 107 E4
Queen Camel BA22..... 174 F3
Old Farm Pl TA17..... 195 C7
Old Farm Rd
Minehead TA24........ 200 E6
Nether Stowey TA5...... 134 B2
Old Ferry Rd BA2...... 44 C6
Oldfield BS21..........6 E1
Oldfield La BA2....... 44 E4
OLDFIELD PARK 44 E4
Oldfield Park Inf Sch BA2 44 D6
Oldfield Park Jun Sch
BA2................ 44 C4
Oldfield Park Sta BA2 .. 44 D6
Oldfield Pl BS8....... 11 F5
Oldfield Rd
Bath BA2............. 228 A1
Bristol BS8........... 226 A1
Oldfield Sch BA1...... 26 F1
OLDFORD 101 B1
Oldford Hill BA11..... 101 B1
Oldford Residential Pk
BA11............... 101 B1
Old Forge The BA2..... 61 B4
Old Forge Way BA2 .... 79 E8
Old Fosse Rd
Bath BA2............. 44 C1
Clandown BA3......... 78 E4
Old Frome Rd
Bath BA2............. 62 E8
Doulting BA4.......... 141 E8
Horrington BA5......... 113 D3
Oakhill BA3, BA4....... 115 B1
Old Glove Factory The
BA22............... 186 B6
Old Gore La BA3....... 95 E3
Old Green The **2** DT9.. 225 D4
Old Ham TA5......... 133 D6
Old Hill
Wincanton BA9 .... 216 C5
Winford BS40 .... 37 D6
Wrington BS40........ 35 F3
Old Hitchen **5** TA16.. 195 F7
Old Ho The BA5....... 64 C5
Old Junction Rd BS23... 49 B5
Old King St BA1....... 228 B3
Old King Street Ct BS1.. 227 B3
Old La
Farmborough BA2....... 60 A6
Nailsea BS21........... 8 C4
Porlock TA24......... 124 B3
Old Main Rd TA6...... 135 F5
Old Malt Ho BS2...... 227 C4
Old Maltings The BA3... 115 A3
Old Manor Est BA3 .... 116 C8
Old Market **6** TA12... 185 E6
Old Market Ct BA6..... 206 D5
Old Market Mews DT10.. 190 B4
Old Market Rd BA4..... 205 B6
Old Market Rdbt BS2.... 227 C3
Old Market St BS2 .... 227 C3
Oldmead La BS26...... 87 C5
Oldmead Wlk BS13..... 21 E7
Old Midford Rd BA2.... 63 A6
Old Millard's Hill BA3... 78 B3
Old Mill Rd
Portishead BS20 .... 2 D5
Woolavington TA7 ...... 136 B4
Old Mill Road Ind Est BS20 .2 E6
OLD MILLS 77 D3
Old Mills Ind Est BS39... 77 D3
Old Mills La BS39...... 77 D3

Old Mill Way
Wells BA5 .... 203 B2
Weston-super-Mare BS24.. 50 A8
OLDMIXON 49 B1
Oldmixon Cres BS24.... 49 A3
Oldmixon Prim Sch BS24. 49 A2
Oldmixon Rd BS24..... 49 B1
Old Mixon Rd BS24.... 49 C1
Old Newbridge Hill BA1.. 44 A6
Old Oaks Cl TA6...... 208 D5
Old Orch TA20........ 223 F1
Old Orchard BA1...... 228 C3
Old Orchard Cl TA19... 183 F4
Old Orchards TA20..... 223 E4
Old Orchard St BA1.... 228 C2
Old Orchard The TA19... 221 A5
Old Orch The TA13.... 220 D4
Old Park Hill BS2 .... 226 C3
Old Park Rd
Bristol BS11........... 4 D7
Clevedon BS21......... 6 E4
Old Pawlett Rd TA9 ... 136 A7
Old Pit Rd BA3........ 97 C8
Old Pit Terr BA3...... 78 E4
Old Pk BS2 .... 226 C3
Old Police Station The
BA9................ 216 C4
Old Post Office Cotts
TA7................ 153 F2
Old Post Office La BS23.. 48 D8
Old Pound Ct SP8...... 161 E1
Old Print Works **6** BA11 119 E5
Old Print Works Rd BS39. 77 D6
Old Priory Rd BS20.......4 B4
Old Quarry BA2....... 44 D2
Old Quarry Rd BS11......4 E7
Old Quarry Rise BS11....4 E7
Old Rd
North Petherton TA6 ... 153 F4
Odcombe BA22 .... 186 C2
Pensford BS39......... 40 E3
Radstock BA3......... 79 C1
South Cadbury BA22.... 175 E4
Old Rd The BA8....... 189 D6
Old Rectory The TA9 ... 86 C4
Oldrey La TA24....... 147 C8
Old Saw Mills The BA3.. 117 A3
Old Sawmill The BA12.. 161 F6
Old School Cl
Alweston DT9......... 189 A1
Ashcott TA7.......... 156 B8
Churchill BS25........ 52 F4
Yeovil BA21.......... 218 C5
Old School Hill BA2.... 62 F7
Old School Ho BA21.... 219 C5
Old School Ho The
Bath BA1............. 228 B4
Whatley BA11......... 118 A3
Old School La
Bleadon BS24 .... 67 C6
Catcott TA7.......... 137 D2
Clifton Wood BS8...... 226 B2
Lynford-on-F TA11..... 158 C2
Old School Pl
Sherborne DT9 .... 225 D3
Wells BA5 .... 203 E5
Old School The BA11... 119 E4
Oldshute La TA22...... 163 C7
Old Sneed Ave BS9..... 5 D4
Old Sneed Cotts BS9.... 5 E4
Old Sneed Pk BS9...... 5 D4
Old Sneed Rd BS9..... 5 D4
Old St BS21............6 E3
Old Station Cl
Cheddar BS27 .... 90 A7
Wrington BS40........ 35 D1
Old Station Ct TA20.... 223 D5
Old Station Gdns BA8 .. 190 A7
Old Station La BA10.... 215 C4
Old Station Rd BA20.... 219 C4
Old Station Way BA20... 219 C4
Old Stream Farm TA10.. 171 E3
Old Street La BA5...... 204 B7
Old Tannery The **20** BS2. 227 C3
Old Tarnwell BS39..... 40 B2
Old Taunton Rd TA6.... 209 A4
Old Threshing Mill The
BA4................ 141 B2
Old Tiverton Rd EX16... 164 C1
Old Tk BA2 .... 63 F7
Old Town TA20........ 223 C3
Old Vicarage Cl TA7.... 137 B2
Old Vicarage Ct BS14... 23 C4
Old Vicarage Gdns TA13. 220 C4
Old Vicarage Gn BS31... 24 E6
Old Vicarage La TA4.... 167 B8
Old Vicarage The TA21.. 222 E6
Oldville Ave BS21...... 6 D2
Old Walcot Sch The BA1. 228 B3
Old Wall BS24........ 66 D5
Old Water Gdns The BS40 54 E2
OLD WAY 184 A4
Old Way
Chipstable TA4........ 165 D6
Stogumber TA4........ 150 D8
Oldway Ho TA21....... 222 F4
Oldway La TA3........ 183 A8
Oldway Pk TA9........ 222 F4
Oldway Pl TA9........ 104 D4
Oldway Rd
East Anstey TA22...... 162 F5
Wellington TA21....... 222 E4
OLDWAYS END........ 162 E3
Old Wells Rd
Bath BA2............. 44 F3
Croscombe BA5........ 204 D6
Doulting BA4......... 142 A8
Glastonbury BA6...... 206 F6

Old Wells Rd continued
Leigh u M BA3, BA4, BA11 117 B2
Shepton Mallet BA4..... 205 A5
Old Weston Rd
Congresbury BS49...... 34 B5
Flax Bourton BS48...... 20 B8
Old Yarn Mills The DT9. 225 D2
Oliver Brooks Rd BA3... 96 E3
Oliver's La TA19....... 183 B2
Olivier Cl TA8........ 104 C6
One Elm TA10........ 172 B7
Onega Ctr BA1........ 228 A3
Onega Terr BA1........ 228 A3
Oolite Gr BA2......... 44 D1
Oolite Rd BA2 .... 44 D1
Orange Gr BA1........ 228 C2
Orange St BS2 .... 227 C4
Orchard Ave
Bristol BS1........... 226 C2
Midsomer Norton BA3... 77 F1
Portishead BS21 .... 7 E4
Orchard Cl
Banwell BS29......... 51 B3
Bishop Sutton BS39..... 57 C3
Bradford On Tone TA4... 167 F1
Bristol, Westbury on T BS9 ..5 F5
Carhampton TA24...... 131 B5
Castle Cary BA7....... 214 B7
Cheddar BS27 .... 90 B8
Coleford BA3.......... 117 A7
Congresbury BS49...... 34 D4
Cossington TA7....... 137 A3
Coxley BA5........... 139 E6
Drimpton DT8 .... 199 F8
East Brent TA9........ 86 E4
East Chinnock BA22..... 196 E8
East Huntspill TA9 .... 136 E8
Felton BS40.......... 37 C8
Flax Bourton BS48..... 20 A8
Frome BA11.......... 119 D4
Highbridge TA9 .... 104 E4
Keynsham BS31........ 24 D6
Long Sutton TA10...... 172 E4
3 North Petherton TA6 .. 153 E3
Odcombe BA22 .... 186 C2
Portishead BS20 .... 2 D5
Queen Camel BA22..... 174 F3
Rockwell Green TA21.... 222 A5
South Petherton TA13... 220 C5
Sparkford BA22....... 175 A5
Taunton TA1.......... 168 D1
Wedmore BS28........ 108 C4
West Coker BA22...... 197 A8
Weston-super-Mare, Kewstoke
BS22............... 31 B3
Weston-super-Mare, Worle
BS22............... 31 F2
Westwood BA15....... 64 F3
Wincanton BA9........ 216 D3
Wrington BS40........ 35 E2
Yeovil Marsh BA21..... 187 A5
Orchard Cl The BS24.... 49 F4
ORCHARD COMMON ... 182 A8
Orchard Cotts
Croscombe BA5........ 204 B7
Timsbury BA2......... 60 F1
Orchard Cres BS11..... 4 D7
Orchard Ct
Claverham BS49....... 17 F1
Highbridge TA9 .... 104 E3
Minehead TA24....... 201 B4
Street BA16.......... 207 C6
Wellington TA21....... 222 E6
Orchard Dr
Bristol BS13.......... 22 A6
Sandford BS25........ 52 A4
Southwick BA14........ 83 E3
Taunton TA1.......... 212 A3
Orchard End BS40..... 74 F4
Orchard Gdns
Paulton BS39......... 77 E6
West Buckland TA21.... 180 F7
Orchard Gn TA2....... 212 F8
Orchard Ho
Weston-super-Mare BS22.. 31 F2
Yeovil BA21.......... 219 A6
Orchard La
Allerford TA24........ 124 B4
Bristol BS1........... 226 C2
Chewton Mendip BA3... 94 F6
Crewkerne TA18....... 224 C6
Evercreech BA4....... 141 E1
Kingsbury Episcopi TA12 . 185 B8
Thorncombe TA20 .... 199 B6
Wembdon TA6........ 208 D5
Orchard Lea
Coxley BA5........... 139 E7
Pill BS20 .... 4 D4
Wells BA5 .... 203 C5
Orchardleigh BA11..... 196 E8
Orchardleigh View BA11 119 D6
Orchard Lodge BA2 ... 45 F8
Orchard Mead TA19.... 183 C1
Orchard Paddock BA5... 203 A7
Orchard Pk
Bristol BS14.......... 23 D4
West Camel BA22...... 174 D3
Orchard Pl
Aller TA10........... 171 D8
1 Weston-super-Mare
BS23............... 48 E7
Orchard Rd
Axbridge BS26........ 70 C1
Backwell BS48........ 19 A6
Carhampton TA24...... 131 B5

Orchard Rd *continued*
Clevedon BS21 . . . 6 D2
Hutton BS24 . . . 49 E2
Long Ashton BS41 . . . 10 F1
Milborne Port DT9 . . . 217 C2
Minehead TA24 . . . 200 F8
Nailsea BS48 . . . 8 D1
Paulton BS39 . . . 77 E6
Somerton TA11 . . . 211 B4
Street BA16 . . . 207 C6
Orchard Rise
Crewkerne TA18 . . . 224 C5
Fivehead TA3 . . . 170 F2
Porlock TA24 . . . 124 A3
Ruishton TA3 . . . 169 C4
Orchards Sh Ctr TA1 . . . 212 F3
Orchard St
Bristol BS1 . . . 226 C2
Frome BA11 . . . 119 E5
Weston-super-Mare BS23 . . 48 E8
Yeovil BA20 . . . 219 A4
Orchards The
Bristol, Shirehampton BS11 . 4 E6
Horrington BA5 . . . 113 A2
Stocklinch TA19 . . . 184 C4
Orchard Terr
5 Bath BA2 . . . 44 B6
Glastonbury BA6 . . . 206 D5
Orchard The
Banwell BS29 . . . 51 A3
Bath, Combe Down BA2 . . . 45 B1
Batheaston BA1 . . . 28 F5
Bath, Newbridge BA1 . . . 44 A7
Chard TA20 . . . 223 D2
Corston BA2 . . . 43 B8
Freshford BA3 . . . 64 C5
Holywell Lake TA21 . . . 179 E7
Locking BS24 . . . 50 A5
Meare BA6 . . . 138 D4
Pensford BS39 . . . 40 E4
Pill BS20 . . . 4 C4
Ruishton TA3 . . . 169 C2
Upper Stanton Drew BS39 . 40 A2
Orchard Vale
Ilminster TA19 . . . 221 B3
Langport TA10 . . . 172 A5
Midsomer Norton BA3 . . . 77 F1
Orchard View
Baltonsborough BA6 . . . 158 B6
Haselbury Plucknett TA18 . 196 C6
Orchard Way
Charlton Horethorne DT9 . . . 176 A2
Cheddar BS27 . . . 90 B8
Keinton Mandeville TA11 . . 158 A1
Misterton TA18 . . . 224 F3
Peasedown St John BA2 . . . 79 D7
Shapwick TA7 . . . 137 F1
Taunton TA1 . . . 213 D5
Timberscombe TA24 . . . 130 B5
Williton TA4 . . . 202 E4
Woolavington TA7 . . . 136 E3
Orchard Wlk
Churchill BS25 . . . 52 E4
Milborne Port DT9 . . . 217 C2
Orchard Wyndham★ TA4 . . . 132 B2
Orchid Cl TA1 . . . 169 A1
Orchid Dr
Bath BA2 . . . 44 C2
Keynsham BS31 . . . 24 E3
Orchids The TA8 . . . 85 A2
Orchid Wy TA6 . . . 208 E1
Oriel Dr BA6 . . . 206 D4
Oriel Gdns BA1 . . . 28 C2
Oriel Gr BA2 . . . 44 B4
Oriel Rd BA16 . . . 207 C5
Orme Dr BS21 . . . 6 D5
Ormerod Rd BS9 . . . 5 E5
Orneage Cl BA11 . . . 101 E8
Orwell Dr BS31 . . . 25 A4
Osborne Ave BS23 . . . 48 F7
Osborne Gr TA1 . . . 212 E3
Osborne Pl TA16 . . . 195 F7
Osborne Rd
Bath BA1 . . . 44 B7
Bridgwater TA6 . . . 208 F6
Bristol BS3 . . . 226 C1
Weston-super-Mare BS23 . . 48 F7
Yeovil BA20 . . . 219 A5
Osborne's La BA1 . . . 27 A3
Osborne Villas BS2 . . . 226 C4
Osborne Wallis Ho BS8 . . 226 A1
Osborne Way TA1 . . . 212 E3
Osborne Wlk TA8 . . . 104 C6
Osmond Dr BA5 . . . 203 B3
Osmond Rd 2 BS24 . . . 49 F7
Osprey Ct BS14 . . . 22 D5
Osprey Gdns BS22 . . . 31 F1
Ostlings La BA1 . . . 29 B2
Ostrey Mead BS27 . . . 90 B7
Otago Terr 5 BA1 . . . 28 C2
OTHERY . . . 155 B2
Othery Village Prim Sch TA7 . . . 155 C2
Ottawa Rd BS23 . . . 48 F3
OTTERFORD . . . 181 E1
Otterford Cl BS14 . . . 23 B5
Otterford Gypsy Pk TA3 . 181 D2
Otterford Lakes Nature Reserve★ TA3 . . . 192 B8
Otterford Lakes Nature Trail★ TA3 . . . 181 E1
Otterham La TA3 . . . 183 F8
OTTERHAMPTON . . . 135 A6
Otterhampton Prim Sch TA5 . . . 135 B5
Otter Rd 1 BS21 . . . 6 E1
Otter Vale Cl EX14 . . . 191 F1
Ottery La DT9 . . . 225 C3
Our Lady of Mount Carmel RC Prim Sch BA9 . . . 216 C3
Our Lady of the Rosary RC Prim Sch BS11 . . . 5 A8
Outer Circ TA1 . . . 213 D5
Outer Gullands TA1 . . . 212 D2
OVAL THE . . . 44 C4
Oval The BA2 . . . 44 C4
Overbrook Bsns Ctr BS28 . . . 107 D4
Overcombe BA8 . . . 189 E8
OVER COMPTON . . . 187 F4
Overdale
Clandown BA3 . . . 78 E5
Peasedown St John BA2 . . . 60 F3
Overhill BS20 . . . 4 D4
Over Innox BA11 . . . 119 F6
Overland La TA3 . . . 170 C3
Overlands
North Curry TA3 . . . 170 C4
Ruishton TA3 . . . 169 C4
OVERLEIGH . . . 207 C3
Overleigh
Street BA16 . . . 207 C3
Street BA16 . . . 207 C4
Overstables La BS21 . . . 6 D3
OVER STOWEY . . . 134 A1
OVER STRATTON . . . 220 D1
OVERTON . . . 169 C7
Overton BA9 . . . 216 D4
Owen Dr BS8 . . . 10 B4
Owen St TA21 . . . 222 C6
Owlaborough La EX36 . . . 162 B2
Owl St
South Petherton TA13 . . . 220 B8
Stocklinch TA19 . . . 184 C3
Owsley Cotts TA19 . . . 184 E4
Oxendale BA16 . . . 207 B5
Oxen La TA3 . . . 170 B3
OXENPILL . . . 138 C4
Oxenpill BA6 . . . 138 C4
Oxen Rd TA18 . . . 224 C6
Oxford Pl
Bath BA2 . . . 45 C2
19 Bristol, Clifton BS8 . . . 11 F6
10 Taunton TA2 . . . 213 A8
Weston-super-Mare BS23 . . 48 D7
Oxford Rd BA21 . . . 219 E7
Oxford Row BA1 . . . 228 B3
Oxford Sq BS24 . . . 50 B6
Oxford St
Bristol BS2 . . . 227 C2
Bristol, Tyndall's Park BS2 226 C4
Burnham-on-S TA8 . . . 104 B6
Evercreech BA4 . . . 141 E1
Weston-super-Mare BS23 . . 48 D7
Oxford Terr 4 TA6 . . . 209 B4
Oxhayes DT8 . . . 199 F8
Oxhouse La
Failand BS8 . . . 10 B6
Winford BS40 . . . 37 D6
Oxleaze
5 Bishops Lydeard TA4 . . 167 F8
Bristol BS13 . . . 22 D4
Oxleaze La BS41 . . . 21 E3
Oxley Cotts DT9 . . . 225 C4
Ozenhay BS39 . . . 75 E6

P

Packers' Way TA18 . . . 196 B3
Pack Horse La BA2 . . . 62 F7
PACKSADDLE . . . 119 F7
Packsaddle Way BA11 . . . 119 F7
Pacquet Ho BS20 . . . 4 D5
Paddles La BA11 . . . 119 D1
Paddock Cl TA3 . . . 169 D5
Paddock Dr TA9 . . . 104 D4
Paddock Gdn BS14 . . . 22 F4
Paddock Park BS22 . . . 32 B2
Paddocks Cvn Pk The BS26 . . . 87 A7
Paddocks The
Bath BA2 . . . 45 B1
Ilchester BA22 . . . 173 E1
Sandford BS25 . . . 52 C4
Wellington TA21 . . . 222 E5
Weston-super-Mare BS23 . . 48 D2
Paddock The
Banwell BS29 . . . 51 A3
Clevedon BS21 . . . 6 D2
Corston BA2 . . . 43 B7
Dulverton TA22 . . . 163 D6
Galhampton BA22 . . . 175 D8
Portishead BS20 . . . 2 D4
Taunton, Dowsland TA1 . . 168 F1
Taunton, Trull TA3 . . . 168 D1
Paddock Wlk DT9 . . . 217 C2
Paddock Woods BA2 . . . 45 D2
Paddons Farm TA5 . . . 134 C6
Padfield Cl BA2 . . . 44 B5
Padfield Gn BA4 . . . 141 E6
Padleigh Hill BA2 . . . 44 B2
Padstow Rd BS4 . . . 22 F8
Paganel Cl TA24 . . . 200 F6
Paganel Rd TA24 . . . 200 F6
Paganel Rise TA24 . . . 200 E6
Paganel Way TA24 . . . 200 E6
Pagans Hill BS40 . . . 38 D2
Pageant Dr DT9 . . . 225 D3
Page La BA6 . . . 140 A2
Page's Ct BS49 . . . 34 C8
Page's Hill BA16 . . . 207 C1
Pages Mead BS11 . . . 4 C8
PAINTMOOR . . . 194 B4
Paintmoor La TA20 . . . 194 B4
Palace Ct BA5 . . . 203 D3
Palace Gdns TA4 . . . 210 C4
Palace Yard Mews BA1 . . 228 B2
Palfrey's La TA20 . . . 193 D3
Palmer Cl TA6 . . . 208 F2
Palmer Row 7 BS23 . . . 48 E8
Palmers Cl TA8 . . . 104 D8
Palmer's Elm BS24 . . . 33 B4
Palmer's End La TA12 . . . 184 F7
Palmers La BA2 . . . 61 B3
Palmers Rd BA6 . . . 206 D4
Palmer St
Frome BA11 . . . 119 F4
South Petherton TA13 . . . 220 C4
Weston-super-Mare BS23 . . 48 E8
Palmerston Rd TA1 . . . 212 D5
Palmer's Way BS24 . . . 49 D2
Palm Tree Cl TA6 . . . 209 E5
PANBOROUGH . . . 138 F8
Panborough Dro BA5 . . . 138 F8
Panoramic The BS1 . . . 226 C3
Paper La BS39 . . . 77 D6
Parade Nurseries TA24 . . 200 F7
Parade The
1 Bath BA2 . . . 44 B6
Bristol, Bishopsworth BS13 . 22 A6
Bristol, Shirehampton BS11 . 4 E6
Chardstock EX13 . . . 198 A7
Minehead TA24 . . . 200 F7
Paradise Cres BA4 . . . 141 E2
Paradise La
Croscombe BA5 . . . 204 B7
Glastonbury BA6 . . . 139 D2
Langport TA10 . . . 172 A7
Tatworth TA20 . . . 193 F1
Paradise Rd BA6 . . . 206 D5
Paradise Row BS39 . . . 41 A6
Paragon Ct 13 BS23 . . . 30 C1
Paragon Rd BS23 . . . 30 C1
Paragon Sch The BA2 . . . 45 A3
Paragon The
Bath BA1 . . . 228 C3
Bristol BS8 . . . 11 F6
Paray Dr BA5 . . . 203 F5
PARBROOK . . . 158 D7
Parbrook Ct BS14 . . . 23 B5
Parbrook La BA6 . . . 158 D7
Parcroft Gdns BA20 . . . 218 F5
PARDLESTONE . . . 133 C5
Pardlestone La TA5 . . . 133 C5
Parfields BA20 . . . 218 F5
Parish Brook Rd BS48 . . . 8 B2
Parish Hill BA22 . . . 175 D5
Parish Land La TA5 . . . 152 D5
Parish Mews BA20 . . . 218 C5
PARK . . . 156 D1
Park Ave
Bath BA2 . . . 228 B1
Bridgwater TA6 . . . 208 D4
Castle Cary BA7 . . . 214 B4
Yatton BS49 . . . 17 B1
Park Barn La TA19 . . . 183 C4
Park Batch BS40 . . . 54 F3
Park Bglws EX16 . . . 179 B3
Park Cl
Barton St David TA11 . . . 158 A3
Cossington TA7 . . . 136 F3
Keynsham BS31 . . . 24 D5
Paulton BS39 . . . 77 D5
Staplehay TA3 . . . 181 D8
Street BA16 . . . 207 C5
Park Cnr
Hambridge TA3 . . . 184 B7
Leigh u M BA11 . . . 117 D3
PARK CORNER . . . 64 A4
Park Cotts TA20 . . . 223 B5
Park Cres
Chard TA20 . . . 223 B5
Cossington TA7 . . . 136 F3
Park Ct 5 BS23 . . . 48 E5
Park End BS29 . . . 50 E4
Parker Cl TA21 . . . 222 E6
Parkes Ave BS24 . . . 50 D4
Parkes Rd BS24 . . . 50 C5
Park Farm BA6 . . . 206 C4
Park Farm Rd BA6 . . . 206 C4
Parkfield Cl TA6 . . . 153 F4
Parkfield Cres TA1 . . . 212 D2
Parkfield Dr TA1 . . . 212 D3
Parkfield Gdns BS39 . . . 57 D3
Parkfield Prim Sch TA1 . . 212 D3
Parkfield Rd
Axbridge BS26 . . . 70 D1
Taunton TA1 . . . 212 D3
Parkfields Orch BA6 . . . 157 E4
Parkfields Residential Home BA6 . . . 157 E4
Park Gate TA2 . . . 168 F7
Parkgate La BA11 . . . 101 E7
Park Gdns
Bath BA1 . . . 44 D8
Yeovil BA20 . . . 219 A5
Park Gr DT10 . . . 190 B4
Park Hayes BA3 . . . 116 F3
Park Hill
Bristol BS11 . . . 4 F6
Mells BA11 . . . 118 C7
Pilton BA4 . . . 140 E3
Park Hill Dr BA11 . . . 119 F6
Park Ho BA2 . . . 44 E4
Parkhouse La BS31 . . . 24 C2
Parkhouse Rd TA24 . . . 200 E7
Parkhurst Rd BS23 . . . 49 A7
Park La
Barton St David TA11 . . . 158 A3
Bath BA1 . . . 44 D7
Blagdon BS40 . . . 54 F3
Bristol BS2 . . . 226 C3
Cannington TA5 . . . 135 B3
Carhampton TA24 . . . 131 A5
Castle Cary BA7 . . . 214 D7
Combe St Nicholas TA20 . . 193 C6
Downhead BA4 . . . 117 A1
Faulkland BA3 . . . 80 B1
Goathurst TA5 . . . 153 C4
Henstridge BA8 . . . 190 A8
High Ham TA10 . . . 156 D1
Ilminster TA19 . . . 183 E1
Kingsdon TA11 . . . 173 E5
Kingston St Mary TA2 . . . 168 C8
Langport TA10 . . . 171 E4
Montacute BA22, TA15 . . . 186 B3
North Newton TA7 . . . 154 A3
North Petherton TA6 . . . 153 F4
Seavington St Mary TA19 . . 184 C1
Thorncombe TA20 . . . 199 A7
Wellington TA21 . . . 222 C1
West Buckland TA21 . . . 180 E7
Yenston BA8 . . . 189 F8
Park La Cl TA24 . . . 131 A5
Parklands BS39 . . . 59 D2
Parklands Ave BS22 . . . 32 A4
Parklands Rd
Bristol BS3 . . . 11 E4
Wellington TA21 . . . 222 D7
Parklands Rise TA24 . . . 200 D7
Parklands Way TA11 . . . 211 B4
Parkland Wlk TA18 . . . 224 C4
Park Lodge BA20 . . . 219 A5
Parkmead TA2 . . . 213 E8
Park Pl
Bath BA1 . . . 228 A4
Bristol BS2 . . . 226 C3
Bristol BS8 . . . 226 B3
Castle Cary BA7 . . . 214 C5
Weston-super-Mare BS23 . . 48 D8
Park Rd
Bath BA1 . . . 44 B7
Bridgwater TA6 . . . 208 D4
Bristol BS3 . . . 226 B1
Bristol, Shirehampton BS11 . . 4 F6
Bruton BA10 . . . 215 E5
Chard TA20 . . . 223 C4
Clevedon BS21 . . . 6 D4
Congresbury BS49 . . . 34 E3
Frome BA11 . . . 119 E4
Henstridge BA8 . . . 190 A6
Keynsham BS31 . . . 24 E4
Paulton BS39 . . . 77 D5
Shepton Mallet BA4 . . . 205 B5
Stalbridge DT10 . . . 190 B4
Street BA16 . . . 207 C5
Yeovil BA20 . . . 219 B5
Park Row BS1 . . . 226 C3
Park Sch The BA20 . . . 219 A5
Parks Cotts TA2 . . . 168 D8
Parkside Ct 1 TA6 . . . 209 B4
Parks La
Brompton Ralph TA4 . . . 150 C3
Minehead TA24 . . . 200 F7
Park St
Bath BA1 . . . 228 A4
Bristol BS1 . . . 226 C3
Castle Cary BA7 . . . 214 C5
Dunster TA24 . . . 201 D1
Exford TA24 . . . 128 D1
Minehead TA24 . . . 200 F7
Taunton TA1 . . . 212 E3
Yeovil BA20 . . . 219 B4
Parks The
Bridgwater TA6 . . . 208 D4
Minehead TA24 . . . 200 E7
Parkstone Ave TA6 . . . 209 A2
Park Street Ave BS1 . . . 226 C3
Park Street Mews BA1 . . 228 A4
Parks View TA24 . . . 124 A4
Parksway Ct TA24 . . . 200 E7
Park Terr
Chard TA20 . . . 223 B6
Glastonbury BA6 . . . 206 D4
Minehead TA24 . . . 200 F7
Park The
Castle Cary BA7 . . . 214 B4
Keynsham BS31 . . . 24 E6
Portishead BS20 . . . 2 F5
Yatton BS49 . . . 17 B1
Yeovil BA20 . . . 219 A5
Park View
Axminster EX13 . . . 198 A3
Bath BA2 . . . 44 D6
Cotford St Luke TA4 . . . 167 F6
Crewkerne, Misterton TA18 . . . 196 B3
Crewkerne TA18 . . . 224 C4
Montacute TA15 . . . 186 B3
Stogursey TA5 . . . 134 C5
Park Villas BS23 . . . 48 D8
Park Wall BA10 . . . 215 F5
Park Wall Dro TA7 . . . 209 F4
Park Water La DT8 . . . 199 F5
Parkway
Bridgwater TA6 . . . 209 C5
Timsbury BA2 . . . 60 E2
Park Way
Bruton BA10 . . . 215 E5
Midsomer Norton BA3 . . . 97 A8
Ruishton TA3 . . . 169 C3
Park Way BS22 . . . 32 B1
Parkway La BA2 . . . 60 D3
Park Wlk BS20 . . . 4 D4
Park Wood Cl BS14 . . . 22 F4
Parlour Ho TA1 . . . 213 B5
Parmin Cl TA1 . . . 213 C3
Parmin Way TA1 . . . 213 C3
Parnell Rd BS21 . . . 6 D3
Parnell Way TA8 . . . 104 B8
Parrett Cl TA10 . . . 171 F5
Parrett Mead
South Perrott DT8 . . . 196 C1
Taunton TA1 . . . 213 D3
Parrett Way TA6 . . . 209 B3
Parrett Works Cotts TA12 . . . 220 F8
Parricks La EX13 . . . 198 D3
Parrocks La TA20 . . . 198 C8
Parry Cl BA2 . . . 44 B4
Parry's Cl BS9 . . . 5 E5
Parrys Gr BS9 . . . 5 E5
Parry's La BS9 . . . 5 F5
Parsonage Cl
Langport TA10 . . . 172 A5
Somerton TA11 . . . 211 E3
West Harptree BS40 . . . 74 E6
Winford BS40 . . . 37 F6
Parsonage Cotts
Kingston St Mary TA2 . . . 168 D8
West Camel BA22 . . . 174 D3
Parsonage Cres BA7 . . . 214 B6
Parsonage Ct
Puriton TA7 . . . 136 B4
Taunton TA1 . . . 212 A4
Parsonage Hill TA11 . . . 211 E3
Parsonage La
Ashill TA19 . . . 183 C4
Axbridge BS26 . . . 70 E2
Bath BA1 . . . 228 B2
Charlton Musgrove BA9 . . . 161 B1
Chilcompton BA3 . . . 96 C4
Kingston St Mary TA2 . . . 168 D8
Milverton TA4 . . . 167 A4
Pensford BS39 . . . 40 D6
Staple Fitzpaine TA3 . . . 182 C4
Winford BS40 . . . 37 F6
Parsonage Pl TA10 . . . 171 D4
Parsonage Rd
Berrow TA8 . . . 84 F5
Long Ashton BS41 . . . 11 C2
West Camel BA22 . . . 174 D3
Parson's Batch BA4 . . . 140 E3
Parsons Cl
Bicknoller TA4 . . . 132 F2
Long Sutton TA10 . . . 172 F4
Nether Stowey TA5 . . . 134 A3
Parson's Dro BS28 . . . 138 C7
Parsons Gate BA7 . . . 214 B7
Parsons Gn
Clevedon BS21 . . . 16 C8
Weston-super-Mare BS22 . . 32 A3
Parson's La TA11 . . . 173 D5
Parsons' La TA5 . . . 152 A7
Parsons Mead BS48 . . . 19 F7
Parsons Paddock BS14 . . . 23 A7
Parsons Pen BS27 . . . 90 B7
Parsons Rd TA9 . . . 104 C4
Parson's St TA24 . . . 124 A3
Parsons Way
Wells BA5 . . . 203 B4
Winscombe BS25 . . . 69 E6
Partis Coll BA1 . . . 44 A8
Partis Way BA1 . . . 44 A8
Partition St BS1 . . . 226 C2
Partman's Hill BA3 . . . 116 B3
Partridge Cl
Moorlinch TA7 . . . 155 F7
Weston-super-Mare BS22 . . 31 F1
Partway La
Chard Junction TA20 . . . 198 F6
East Chinnock BA22 . . . 196 F7
Passage Leaze BS11 . . . 4 D6
Passage St BS2 . . . 227 B2
Pastures Ave BS22 . . . 32 C3
Pastures The BA15 . . . 64 E3
Patch Croft BS21 . . . 16 C8
Pathe Rd TA7 . . . 155 B1
Pathfinder Terr 3 TA6 . . 209 B4
Patrick's Way TA3 . . . 181 D8
Patrum Cl TA1 . . . 212 B1
Patson Hill La DT9 . . . 188 B5
Patterson Ho 8 BS1 . . . 227 B1
Pattinson Cl BA21 . . . 219 D6
Pattons TA3 . . . 169 C1
Patwell La BA10 . . . 215 E6
Patwell St BA10 . . . 215 E6
Paullet EX16 . . . 178 C1
Paulls Cl TA10 . . . 172 A6
Paull's La TA19 . . . 183 B2
Paulman Gdns BS41 . . . 20 F8
Paulmont Rise BS39 . . . 58 E1
Paul's Cswy BS49 . . . 34 D4
Pauls Rd TA11 . . . 211 C3
Paul St
Bristol BS2 . . . 226 C4
Frome BA11 . . . 119 F5
Shepton Mallet BA4 . . . 205 B6
Taunton TA1 . . . 212 F3
Paulto' Hill BA3, BS39 . . . 78 B6
PAULTON . . . 77 F5
Paulton Inf Sch BS39 . . . 77 E5
Paulton Jun Sch BS39 . . . 77 E5
Paulton La BA2, BA3 . . . 78 D7
Paulton Memorial Hospl BS39 . . . 77 F4
Paulton Rd
Farrington Gurney BS39 . . . 77 B4
Hallatrow BS39 . . . 77 B7
Midsomer Norton BA3 . . . 77 F1
Paulwood Rd BS39 . . . 58 E1
Pavement The TA3 . . . 170 B4
Pavey Cl BS13 . . . 22 C4

Pavey Rd BS13. . . . . 22 C4
Pavyotts La BA22 . . . . . . 197 E8
Pawelski Cl BA4. . . . . 142 B7
PAWLETT 136 A5
Pawlett BS24 . . . . 49 A2
Pawlett Mead Dro TA6 . . 136 A5
Pawlett Prim Sch TA6 . . . 135 F5
Pawlett Rd
  Bristol BS13. . . . . 22 C3
  Walpole TA6. . . . . 136 A4
  West Huntspill TA6, TA9. . 136 A7
Pawlett Almshouses
  TA5. . . . . 134 C5
Pawlett Wlk BS13. . . . . . . 22 C3
Paybridge Rd BS13. . . . . . 21 F4
Payne Rd BS24. . . . . 49 D2
Payne Ho 17 BS23. . . . . . . 48 E8
Paynes La TA7. . . . . 155 C2
Payne's La TA12. . . . . 185 E8
PAYTON. 179 F7
Payton Rd
  Holywell Lake TA21. . . . . 179 F7
  Rockwell Green TA21. . . . 222 A5
Peace Cl TA6 . . . . 209 D6
Peacehay La TA21. . . . . . 179 E4
Peach Tree Cl TA6. . . . . . 209 E5
Peacocks Cl TA21. . . . . . . 180 F7
Peacocks Hill TA11. . . . . 158 A3
Peadon La TA5 . . . . 134 C4
Peak La
  Compton Dundon TA11. . . 157 A2
  Shepton Beauchamp TA19 184 D3
PEAR ASH 161 E2
Pear Ash La BA9. . . . . 161 E2
Pearce Dr TA9. . . . . 104 D4
Pearmain Rd BA16. . . . . . 207 B4
Pearse Cl BS22 . . . . 32 B5
Pearson Ho BA21 . . . . 219 A6
Peart Cl BS13. . . . . 21 E5
Peart Dr BS13. . . . . 21 E4
Pear Tree Ave BS41 . . . . . . 20 E8
Peartree Cl BS13. . . . . 22 B4
Pear Tree Cl
  Bridgwater TA6 . . . . 209 D4
  Westleigh EX16 . . . . 179 A4
Peartree Field BS20. . . . . . . 2 F5
Peartree Gdns BS4 . . . . . . 67 C6
Pear Tree Ind Est BS40 . . 53 C4
Pear Tree Way TA21 . . . . 222 F4
Peartwater Hill TA5 . . . . 152 D8
Peartwater Rd TA5. . . . . . 152 D7
PEASEDOWN ST JOHN . . . 79 C8
Peasedown St John Prim Sch
  BA2. . . . . 79 C7
PEASMARSH. 194 B7
Pebbles Orch TA19. . . . . . 184 E4
PECKING MILL 159 D8
Pecking Mill Rd BA4. . . . 141 E1
Pedder Rd BS21 . . . . 6 D1
Peddles Cl TA10 . . . . 171 D8
Peddles La TA11 . . . . 173 E8
Pedlars Gr
  Chapmanslade BA13 . . . . . 121 C4
  Frome BA11. . . . . 119 C4
PEDWELL 156 A7
Pedwell Cvn Pk TA7. . . . . 156 A7
Pedwell Hill TA7. . . . . . . 156 A7
Pedwell La TA7. . . . . 156 A7
Peel Ct TA23. . . . . 202 C7
Peel St BS5. . . . . 227 C4
Peerage Ct TA24. . . . . 201 A6
Pegasus Ct 17 BA20 . . . . . 219 B4
Peggy's La TA18. . . . . 196 C5
Peile Dr TA2. . . . . 212 E7
Peir Cl BS20. . . . . 2 E7
Pelham Ct TA6. . . . . 209 D7
Pelican Cl BS22. . . . . 49 F8
Pelting Dro BA5. . . . . 92 D1
Pembroke Ave BS11. . . . . . . 4 E6
Pembroke Cl
  Burnham-on-S TA8 . . . . . . 85 B1
  Taunton TA1 . . . . 212 C1
  Yeovil BA21 . . . . 219 E7
Pembroke Ct BS21. . . . . 6 C4
Pembroke Gr BS8. . . . . . . 226 A3
Pembroke Ho 1 BS23. . . . 30 C1
Pembroke Mans BS8. . . . 226 A4
Pembroke Pl BS8 . . . . 226 A1
Pembroke Rd
  Bridgwater TA6 . . . . 209 C3
  Bristol BS8. . . . . 226 A4
  Bristol, Shirehampton BS11 . 4 E6
  Portishead BS20. . . . . 1 E4
  Weston-super-Mare BS23 . . 48 F4
Pembroke St BS2. . . . . . . 227 B4
Pembroke Vale BS8. . . . . 226 A4
Pemswell Rd TA24. . . . . . 200 F8
Penarth Dr BS24. . . . . 49 A1
Penarth Rd TA6. . . . . 208 D4
Pen Cross BA22. . . . . 197 B5
Pendle Cl BS25 . . . . 70 A7
Pendlesham Gdns BS23 . . 31 A1
PENDOMER. 197 B5
Pendomer Rd BA22. . . . . 197 B5
Pendragon Pk BA6. . . . . . 206 D5
Pen Elm Cotts TA2 . . . . . 168 B5
Pen Elm Hill TA2. . . . . . . 168 B6
Penel Orlieu TA6. . . . . . . 208 F4
Penfield BA21 . . . . 219 C5
Pen Hill BA9. . . . . 161 C4
Penlea Ave TA6. . . . . 208 B5
Penlea Cl TA6 . . . . 208 E2
Penlea Ct BS11. . . . . 4 D7
Pen Mill Hill SP8, BA12. . 161 F2
Pen Mill Inf Sch BA21 . . 219 D6
Pen Mill Trad Est BA21 . 219 F6
Penmoor Pl TA8 . . . . 84 F5
Penmoor Rd TA8. . . . . 84 F5

Penmore Rd BA22, DT9 . . 188 B7
Pennant Pl BS20. . . . . 2 F7
Pennard BS24 . . . . 49 A2
Pennard Ct
  Bath BA2. . . . . 44 A6
  Bristol BS14. . . . . 23 B5
Pennard Gn BA6. . . . . 44 A6
Pennard La BA6. . . . . 140 A2
Penn Cl
  Cheddar BS27 . . . . 90 C7
  Wells BA5. . . . . 112 E2
Penn Ct BS26 . . . . 70 C1
Penneys Piece BA11 . . . . 120 C6
Penn Gdns BA1. . . . . 44 A8
Penn Hill BA20. . . . . 219 B4
Penn Hill Pk BA20. . . . . . 219 B4
Penn Hill Rd BA1. . . . . 27 A1
Pennine Gdns BS23 . . . . . 31 A1
Penn La BA22. . . . . 197 A6
Pennlea BS13. . . . . 22 C7
Penn Lea Ct BA1. . . . . 44 B8
Penn Lea Rd BA1. . . . . 44 B8
PENN MILL. 219 E6
Pennon Rise BS1. . . . . . . 226 C1
Penn Rd BS27 . . . . 90 C7
Penn St BS1. . . . . 227 B3
Penns The BS21 . . . . 6 E2
PENNSYLVANIA 12 F7
Penn View BA9. . . . . 216 D4
Penn Way BS26. . . . . 70 C1
Penny Batch La BA5. . . . . 139 E8
Penny Cl TA21. . . . . 222 D7
Pennycress BS22. . . . . 49 D7
Pennycress Wy TA6. . . . . 208 E1
Penny Lea TA23. . . . . 202 C6
Pennyquick BA2. . . . . 43 D6
Pennyquick View BA2. . . . 43 F6
Penny's Meade TA13 . . . . 183 F4
Pennywell Est 3 BS21 . . . . 6 D2
Pennywell Rd BS2. . . . . . 227 C4
Penpole Ave BS11. . . . . 4 E6
Penpole Cl BS11. . . . . 4 D7
Penpole La BS11. . . . . 4 E7
Penpole Pk BS11. . . . . 4 E7
Penpole Pl BS11 . . . . 4 E6
Penrice Cl BS22. . . . . 31 C2
Penrose BS14. . . . . 22 F7
Penrose Sch TA6. . . . . . . 208 E4
PENSELWOOD 161 C2
PENSFORD 40 E4
Pensford Ct BS14. . . . . 23 D5
Pensford Hill BS39. . . . . . 40 D5
Pensford La BS39. . . . . . . 40 A3
Pensford Old Rd BS39. . . 40 D4
Pensford Prim Sch BS39 . 40 D4
Pensford Way TA6. . . . . . 120 D7
Pentagon The BS9. . . . . 5 B5
Penthouse Hill BA1. . . . . . 28 F3
Pentire Ave BS13. . . . . 22 A6
Pentridge La DT10 . . . . . . 190 E2
Penzoy Ave TA6. . . . . 209 B4
Pepperall Rd TA9. . . . . . . 104 E4
Peppershells La BS39 . . . . 41 C6
Pepys Ct BS31. . . . . 25 D2
Pera Pl BA1. . . . . 228 C4
Pera Rd BA1. . . . . 228 C4
Perch Hill BA5. . . . . 110 E6
Percivale Rd BA21 . . . . . . 218 D7
Percival Rd BS8. . . . . 11 F8
Percy Pl 13 BA1. . . . . 28 B1
Percy Rd BA21. . . . . 219 D6
Percy Terrace BA2. . . . . . . 44 D6
Peregrine Cl BS22 . . . . 31 F1
Perfect View BA1. . . . . 28 A1
PERITON. 200 D6
Periton Cross TA24 . . . . . 200 D6
Periton Ct TA24. . . . . 200 D6
Periton La TA24. . . . . 200 D7
Periton Mead Sch TA24. . 200 D6
Periton Rd TA24 . . . . 200 D6
Periton Rise TA24. . . . . . . 200 D6
Periton Way TA24. . . . . . 200 D6
Perkins La BA5. . . . . 203 B4
Perley La TA23. . . . . 148 D8
Perrett Ho 22 BS2. . . . . . 227 C3
Perretts Ct BS1. . . . . 226 C1
Perrett Way BS20 . . . . 4 E4
Perridge Hill BA4. . . . . . . 140 D4
Perrin Cl BS39. . . . . 76 E8
Perrings The BS48. . . . . . . 18 E8
Perrott Hill Sch TA18. . . 196 B4
Perrow La BS28. . . . . 89 C2
Perry Cl BA3. . . . . 78 D1
Perry Court Prim Sch
  BS14. . . . . 23 A4
Perrycroft Ave BS13. . . . . 22 A6
Perrycroft Rd BS13. . . . . . 22 A6
PERRY GREEN 208 B8
Perry Hill TA11. . . . . 174 D8
Perry Hill Rd TA11 . . . . . 211 D2
Perry La TA9. . . . . 106 F5
Perry Lake La BS13 . . . . . 139 B7
Perrymans Cl BS30. . . . . . 12 A8
PERRYMEAD 45 B3
Perrymead
  Bath BA2. . . . . 45 B3
  Weston-super-Mare BS22 . . 32 B5
Perrymead Ct BA2. . . . . . . 45 B4
Perrymead Pl BA2. . . . . . . 45 B4
Perry New Rd TA22 . . . . . 163 E4
Perry Pl BA21. . . . . 219 C5
Perry Rd
  Blackford TA9. . . . . 107 A6
  Bristol BS1. . . . . 227 A3
  Long Ashton BS41 . . . . 20 F8
Perry's Cider Mills★
  TA19 . . . . 194 E7

Perry's Cl BS27 . . . . 90 A7
Perry St TA20. . . . . 198 D8
PERRY STREET 198 E8
Pesley Cl BS13. . . . . 22 A4
Pesters La TA11. . . . . 211 E3
Pestlefield La TA3. . . . . . . 170 C1
Petercole Dr BS13 . . . . . . 22 A6
Peter's Gore DT6. . . . . . . 199 B1
Peterside BS29. . . . . 76 E8
Peterson Ave 2 BS13. . . . 22 C4
Peterson Sq BS13. . . . . . . 22 C3
Peter St
  Shepton Mallet BA4. . . . . 205 B6
  Taunton TA2. . . . . 212 F6
  Yeovil BA20 . . . . 219 B4
Petherton Gdns BS14. . . . 23 B7
Petherton Rd
  Bristol BS14. . . . . 23 B7
  North Newton TA7. . . . . . 153 F2
Pethick Ho BS4. . . . . 22 F8
Peto Garden at Iford Manor
  The★ BA15. . . . . 64 E3
Peto Gr BA15. . . . . 64 F3
Petrel Cl TA6. . . . . 209 D7
Petter's Way BA20 . . . . . 219 B4
Petticoat La BA4. . . . . . . 205 B6
Pettitts Cl DT9. . . . . 187 E1
PETTON. 165 A3
Petton Cross EX16. . . . . . 165 A3
Petvin Cl BA16. . . . . 207 D4
Petvins Ct TA18. . . . . 196 C5
Pevensey Wlk BS4 . . . . . . 22 D7
Pharmacy Flats The
  DT10. . . . . 190 F6
Pheasant The TA19 . . . . . 184 E1
Phelps Cl TA20. . . . . 223 D6
Philippa Cl BS14. . . . . 23 A7
Philips Ho 2 BS2. . . . . . . 227 B4
Phillip Ho TA6. . . . . 208 F2
Phillips Cl TA6. . . . . 208 D4
Phillip's Dro TA3. . . . . . . 170 D7
Phillips Rd BS23. . . . . 49 A6
Phillis Hill BS39. . . . . 77 F4
Phippen St 1 BS1. . . . . . 227 B1
Phoenix Cl
  Frome BA11. . . . . 119 D4
  Taunton TA1. . . . . 212 F3
Phoenix Ho
  Bath BA1. . . . . 228 B4
  Frome BA11. . . . . 119 D4
Phoenix Rd TA6. . . . . 209 B3
Phoenix Terr TA8 . . . . . . 104 B6
Phoenix Way BS20. . . . . 2 F6
Piazza Ct BA16. . . . . 207 B5
PIBSBURY 172 C5
Piccadilly Pl BA1. . . . . 45 B8
Piccadilly Ho 13 BA4. . . . 205 B6
Pickeridge Cl TA2. . . . . . . 213 B7
Picket La DT8. . . . . 196 C1
Pickett La BA21. . . . . 219 A7
PICKNEY. 168 B8
Pickney La TA2. . . . . 168 B7
Pickpurse La TA4 . . . . 150 E8
Pickwick Rd BA1. . . . . 28 A2
PICT'S HILL. 172 B6
Piece TA19. . . . . 184 E4
Piece La TA19 . . . . 184 E4
Piece Rd DT9 . . . . 217 C3
Piece The 2 TA16. . . . . . . 195 F7
Pier Rd BS20. . . . . 2 E7
Pierrepont Pl 9 BA1 . . . . 228 C2
Pierrepont St BA1 . . . . . . 228 C2
Piers Rd BA4. . . . . 142 A6
Pier St TA6. . . . . 104 A6
Piffin La TA4. . . . . 167 E8
Pigeon House Dr BS13 . . 22 B4
Pigeon La BS40. . . . . 36 E1
Pig Hill BA22. . . . . 197 A7
Pightley La TA5. . . . . 152 F6
Pightley Rd TA5. . . . . 152 E7
Pig La TA7. . . . . 154 D8
Pig Market La TA1. . . . . . 212 F3
Pigott Ave BS13. . . . . 22 A4
Pigs Hill La TA5. . . . . 134 D1
Pike Cl BA6. . . . . 206 C5
Pike Hill BA4. . . . . 205 A7
Pike La BA4. . . . . 205 B6
Pikes Cres
  Dunster TA24. . . . . 201 D2
  Taunton TA1. . . . . 212 E1
Pilcorn St BS28. . . . . 108 C4
Pile La
  Curry Mallet TA3. . . . . . . 183 C8
  Stourton Caundle DT10 . . . 189 F3
Piley La TA21. . . . . 179 D8
Pilgrims Way
  Bristol BS11. . . . . 4 C7
  Chew Stoke BS40 . . . . 56 D8
  Lovington BA7 . . . . 158 E3
  Weston-super-Mare BS22 . . 31 E3
Pilgrim's Way TA6. . . . . . 135 F5
PILL. 4 C4
Pillar La BA22. . . . . 99 D4
Pill Bridge La BA22. . . . . 173 D1
Pill Head La TA18 . . . . . . 196 C4
Pill Mdw SP8. . . . . 177 E2
Pillmead La BS28. . . . . . . 108 D5
Pillmoor Dro BA5. . . . . . . 139 F6
Pillmoor La BA5. . . . . 139 F6
Pillmore La
  Highbridge TA9. . . . . 105 A4
  Watchfield TA9. . . . . 105 C4
Pill Rd
  Abbots Leigh BS8. . . . . 4 F1
  Pill BS20. . . . . 4 E2
  Rooks Bridge BS26, TA9 . . 87 C2
Pill St BS20. . . . . 4 D4
Pill Way BS21. . . . . 6 B2

Pilots Helm TA6 . . . . 153 E4
PILSDON. 199 F2
Pilsdon La DT6 . . . . 199 F3
PILTON 140 F3
Pilton Hill BA4. . . . . 140 C4
Pilton Manor Vineyard★
  BA4. . . . . 140 E3
Pimms La BS22. . . . . 31 B3
Pimm's La BS22. . . . . 31 B2
Pimpernel Cl BA16. . . . . . 207 B7
Pince's Knap TA20 . . . . . 198 F5
Pinchay La BS40. . . . . 38 A4
Pinching Cl BA5. . . . . 203 E3
Pinckney Gn BA15. . . . . . . 46 E5
Pincushion Cnr BA22. . . . 197 E6
Pine Ave TA20. . . . . 223 C5
Pine Cl
  Street BA16. . . . . 207 B3
  Taunton TA1. . . . . 213 D2
  Weston-super-Mare BS22 . . 31 F1
Pinecroft
  Bristol BS14. . . . . 22 F7
  Portishead BS20. . . . . 1 F6
Pine Ct
  Chew Magna BS40. . . . . . . 39 B3
  Frome BA11. . . . . 120 B7
  Keynsham BS31. . . . . 24 C4
  Radstock BA3. . . . . 79 A2
Pine Hill BS22. . . . . 31 D2
Pine Lea BS24. . . . . 67 B6
Pine Ridge Cl BS9. . . . . 5 C4
Pines The
  Chilcompton BA3. . . . . 96 D3
  Wincanton BA9. . . . . 216 C3
Pines Residential Site The
  BA11. . . . . 120 D8
Pines Way
  Bath BA2. . . . . 228 A2
  Radstock BA3. . . . . 79 A2
Pines Way Ind Est BA2 . . 228 A2
Pine Tree Ave BA20 . . . . 218 F3
Pine Tree Cl TA6. . . . . . . 209 D4
Pinetree Rd BS24. . . . . . . 50 D4
Pine Wlk BA3. . . . . 78 E1
Pinewood TA11 . . . . 211 D4
Pinewood Ave BA3. . . . . . 77 F1
Pinewood Dr TA11. . . . . . 211 D4
Pinewood Gr BA3. . . . . . . 77 F1
Pinewood Rd BA3. . . . . . . 77 F1
Pinewood Way TA8 . . . . . 65 F3
Pinford La DT9 . . . . 188 F3
Pinhay Rd BS13. . . . . 22 B6
Pinkham Hill TA20 . . . . . 194 B6
Pinkhams Twist BS14 . . . 23 A5
Pink Knoll Hollow DT9 . . 188 C8
Pinksmoor La TA21 . . . . . 179 E7
Pinkwood La BA10. . . . . . 160 E7
Pinmore BS11 . . . . 119 E2
Pinney Cl TA1. . . . . 212 B1
Pinnockscroft TA8. . . . . . . 84 F5
Pintail Rd TA24. . . . . 201 C5
Pinter Cl TA8. . . . . 104 C6
Pioneer Ave BA2. . . . . 44 F1
Pipehouse BA2. . . . . 63 E4
Pipehouse La BA2. . . . . . . 63 E4
Pipe La BS1. . . . . 226 C2
Piper's Alley TA19 . . . . . . 221 B4
Pipers Cl BS26. . . . . 88 E6
Pipers Pl EX14. . . . . 191 F2
Pippard Cl BA16. . . . . 207 E5
Pippin Cl BA2. . . . . 79 D7
Pippins The
  Portishead BS20. . . . . 2 F5
  Wembdon TA6. . . . . 208 D6
Pipplepen La DT8, TA18. . 196 B2
Pitchcombe Gdns BS9. . . . 5 D7
Pitcher's Hill TA2 . . . . . . 168 F7
Pitching The
  Castle Cary BA7. . . . . 214 C5
  Chilcompton BA3. . . . . 96 D5
Pitch & Pay La BS9. . . . . . . 5 E3
Pitch & Pay Pk BS9. . . . . . . 5 E3
PITCOMBE. 215 D3
Pitcombe Hill BA10. . . . . 215 B2
Pitcombe La BA4. . . . . . . 165 B5
Pitcombe Rock BA10. . . . 215 C3
PITCOT. 115 F7
Pitcot La BA3. . . . . 115 F7
Pitfield Cnr BA22. . . . . . . 188 A7
Pitfour Terr BA2. . . . . 60 B2
Pithay Ct BS1. . . . . 227 A3
Pithay The
  Bristol BS1. . . . . 227 A3
  Paulton BS39. . . . . 77 E6
Pit Hill TA17 . . . . 195 B7
Pit Hill La TA7 . . . . 155 C7
Pit La
  Backwell BS48. . . . . 19 A4
  Sticklepath TA23 . . . . 149 D7
  Sutton Mallet TA7. . . . . . 155 D7
  Ubley BS40. . . . . 55 F5
Pitman Ct BA1. . . . . 28 C2
Pitman Ho BA2. . . . . 44 D4
Pitman Rd BS23. . . . . 48 E6
PITMINSTER. 181 E6
PITNEY. 172 C7
Pitney Hill TA10. . . . . . . 172 C6
Pit Rd
  Dinnington TA17. . . . . . . 195 C7
  Midsomer Norton BA3. . . . 78 B1
PITSFORD HILL. 150 E1
Pitsham La TA4. . . . . 164 E6
Pitt Ct TA10. . . . . 171 B3
Pitten St BA3. . . . . 116 E3
Pitt La
  Huish Champflower TA4. . . 165 E8
  Porlock Weir TA24. . . . . . 123 C3
  Waterrow TA4. . . . . 165 F5

Pitts Cl TA1. . . . . 212 C1
Pitts La TA3 . . . . 183 F7
Pitt's La BS40. . . . . 39 B1
Pitway TA13 . . . . 220 D5
Pitway Cl BS39. . . . . 76 F4
Pitway Hill TA13. . . . . . . 220 D6
Pitway La BS39. . . . . 76 E4
Pixash Bsns Ctr BS31 . . . 25 B5
Pixash La BS31. . . . . 25 C5
Pix La TA4. . . . . 167 B4
Pixton Way TA22. . . . . . . 163 E6
Pizey Ave
  Burnham-on-S TA8. . . . . . 85 A1
  Clevedon BS21. . . . . 6 B2
Pizey Ave Ind Est BS21 . . . 6 C2
Pizey Cl BS21. . . . . 6 B2
Place Dro TA7. . . . . 154 F4
Placket La BA20. . . . . 218 D1
Plain Pond TA4. . . . . 210 C5
PLAINSFIELD 152 B7
Plain The BA2 . . . . 81 E4
Plais St TA2 . . . . 212 F6
Plantaganet Chase BA20 218 D2
Plantagenet Pk BA20. . . 218 E3
Platterwell La (East Town La)
  BA4. . . . . 141 B3
Players La TA8. . . . . 85 A1
Playfield Cl 2 BA8. . . . . . 190 A6
Playford Gdns BS11. . . . . . 4 E8
Playses Gn TA10. . . . . . . 184 D8
PLEAMORE CROSS. 222 A2
Pleasant Pl BA1. . . . . 29 D2
Pleshey Cl BS22. . . . . 31 D2
Plimsoll Ho 3 BS1. . . . . . 227 B1
Plot La DT9. . . . . 187 F5
Plott La BA8. . . . . 190 B7
Plough Cl BA16. . . . . 207 A4
Ploughed Paddock BS48 . . 8 D1
Plover Cl
  Milborne Port DT9. . . . . . 217 C2
  Minehead TA24. . . . . 201 C5
  Weston-super-Mare BS22 . . 31 F1
Plover Ct BA21. . . . . 218 D6
Plover Rd DT9 . . . . 217 C2
Plovers Rise BA3. . . . . 79 A3
Plowage La BA22 . . . . . . 174 D3
Plox BA10. . . . . 215 E6
Plox Gn BA10. . . . . 215 E6
Plucknett Row BA20 . . . 218 D5
Plud St BS28. . . . . 108 B3
Plumber's Barton 9
  BA11. . . . . 119 F4
Plumers Cl 4 BS21 . . . . 6 E1
Plum La TA6. . . . . 209 C2
Plumley Cres BS24. . . . . . 50 A4
Plumley Ct BS23. . . . . 48 D4
PLUMMER'S HILL. 77 E6
Plummer's La BA5. . . . . . . 92 D5
Plum Orch DT9 . . . . 187 F4
Plumptre Ave BA5 . . . . . 203 F5
Plumptre Cl BS39. . . . . . . 77 E5
Plumptre Rd BS39. . . . . . . 77 E5
Plumtree Cl BS25. . . . . . . 52 A1
Plum Tree Cl TA6. . . . . . . 209 E5
Plum Tree Rd BS22. . . . . . 49 E8
Plunder St BS49. . . . . 35 B7
Plunging Dr BA6. . . . . . . 206 F1
Plymor Rd TA9. . . . . 136 A8
Poachers End TA24 . . . . . 201 C4
Pococks Yd TA10. . . . . . . 171 F5
Podgers Dr BA1. . . . . 27 B2
Podger's La TA19. . . . . . . 183 F4
PODIMORE. 174 A3
Podium Sh Ctr The 2 BA2 228 C2
Poets Cnr BA3. . . . . 97 C8
Polden Bsns Ctr The
  TA6. . . . . 136 B2
Polden Cl BS48. . . . . 8 E1
Polden Ct TA6. . . . . 209 B5
Polden Rd
  Portishead BS20. . . . . 2 B5
  Weston-super-Mare BS23 . . 48 F8
Polden St TA6. . . . . 209 B5
Polden View BA6. . . . . . . 206 E3
Polden Wlk TA7. . . . . 136 E3
Pole Rue La TA20. . . . . . . 193 C6
POLESHILL 166 C1
Polestar Way BS24. . . . . . 50 A8
Polham La TA11 . . . . 211 D3
Police La BS39. . . . . 40 E3
Polkes Field TA3. . . . . 170 F6
Pollard Rd
  Bridgwater TA6. . . . . 209 D6
  Weston-super-Mare BS22 . . 49 E8
Pollards Ct TA24. . . . . . . 124 A3
Pollard's La TA21. . . . . . . 180 F7
Pollards Way TA1. . . . . . . 212 E4
POLSHAM. 139 D5
Polygon Rd BS8. . . . . 226 A2
Polygon The 15 BS8. . . . . 11 F6
Pomeroy La BA14. . . . . . . 83 B6
Pomfrett Gdns BS14 . . . . 23 E5
Pond Cl 5 BA8. . . . . 190 A6
Pond Cotts BA3. . . . . 80 D2
Pond Head BS20. . . . . 4 D4
Pondhead Cross TA4. . . . 202 E3
Pond La TA21. . . . . 179 D3
Pond Orch TA4. . . . . 150 B8
Pondpool La TA3 . . . . 170 C3
Pond Wlk DT10 . . . . 190 B4
Ponsford Rd
  Bristol BS14. . . . . 23 B8
  Minehead TA24. . . . . 201 A6
Pookfield Cl BA11. . . . . . 143 B7
Poolbridge Rd BS28. . . . . 107 C4

Pool Cl TA7. . . . . 136 C4
POOLE. 222 F8
Poole Cl BS13. . . . . 22 C5
Poole Hill TA22. . . . . 163 B5
Poole Ho BA2. . . . . 43 F5
Poole Ind Est TA20. . . . . . 222 F8
Pooles Cl TA5. . . . . 134 A2
Pooles La TA20. . . . . 194 E1
Poole St BS11. . . . . 4 B8
Pooles Wharf BS8. . . . . . 226 A1
Pooles Wharf Ct BS8. . . 226 A1
Pool Hill TA21. . . . . 165 E1
Pool La BS40. . . . . 38 A2
POOLTOWN. 148 E8
Poop Hill TA18. . . . . 196 C8
Poop Hill La TA18. . . . . . 196 C8
Poor Hill BA2. . . . . 59 F6
Poorhouse La DT6. . . . . . 199 E1
Pope Cl TA1. . . . . 168 D1
Popery La TA24. . . . . 129 E1
Pope's La
  Milborne Port DT9. . . . 217 D2
  Rockwell Green TA21. . . 222 B4
Pope's Wlk BA2. . . . . 45 B3
Popham Cl
  Bridgwater TA6. . . . . . . 209 D5
  East Brent TA9. . . . . 86 D5
Popham Flats TA21. . . . . 222 D6
Popham Rd TA21. . . . . . . 222 F7
Pop La EX13, TA20. . . . . . 198 B8
Poplar Ave BS9. . . . . 5 D6
Poplar Cl
  Bath BA2. . . . . 44 D4
  Frome BA11. . . . . 120 B7
Poplar Dr BA21. . . . . 218 C7
Poplar Est TA9. . . . . 104 D3
Poplar Farm BA5. . . . . . . 111 A4
Poplar La
  Catcott TA7. . . . . 137 D1
  Mark TA9. . . . . 105 E3
Poplar Pl **16** BS23. . . . . . . 48 E8
Poplar Rd
  Bath BA2. . . . . 62 D8
  Bridgwater TA6. . . . . . . 209 D7
  Bristol, Highridge BS13. . 21 F7
  Burnham-on-S TA8. . . . 104 A8
  Street BA16. . . . . 207 C3
  Taunton TA1. . . . . 213 D2
Poplars Cl BA21. . . . . 187 A5
Poplars The
  Easton-in-G BS20. . . . . . . 4 B4
  Porlock TA24. . . . . 124 A3
  Weston-super-Mare BS22. 32 A1
Poplar Tree La BA14. . . . . 83 C2
Poplar Wlk BS24. . . . . 49 E5
Poples Bow TA9. . . . . 104 E5
Pople's La BA11. . . . . 117 F8
Pople's Well TA18. . . . . . 224 B6
Poppy Cl
  Weston-super-Mare BS22. 32 A5
  Yeovil BA22. . . . . 218 B5
Porch EX13. . . . . 198 A3
Porch Cl BA5. . . . . 206 E3
Porchestall Dro BA6. . . . 206 B4
PORLOCK. 124 A4
Porlock Cl
  3 Clevedon BS21. . . . . . . 6 E1
  Weston-super-Mare BS23. . 48 F2
Porlock Dr TA1. . . . . 212 C1
PORLOCKFORD. 123 F4
Porlock Gdns BS48. . . . . . . 8 E1
Porlock Hill TA24. . . . . . 123 F3
Porlock Rd
  Bath BA2. . . . . 45 A1
  Minehead TA24. . . . . . . 200 C7
Porlock Visitor Ctr★
  TA24. . . . . 124 A3
PORLOCK WEIR. 123 D4
Portal Rd BS24. . . . . 50 D4
PORTBURY. 3 D3
Portbury Comm BS20. . . . . . 2 E4
Portbury Gr BS11. . . . . 4 D6
Portbury Hundred The
  BS20. . . . . 3 C4
Portbury La BS20. . . . . 9 E7
Portbury Way BS20. . . . . . 3 E5
Portbury Wlk BS11. . . . . . . 4 D6
Portcullis Rd TA10. . . . . 172 A6
Porter's Hatch BA6. . . . . 138 D4
PORTFIELD. 171 E5
Portfield La TA10. . . . . . . 171 F5
PORTISHEAD. 2 B4
Portishead Bsns Pk BS20. . 2 E5★
Portishead Lodge BS20. . . 2 D6
Portishead Prim sch BS20. . 2 D4
Portishead Rd BS22. . . . . 32 B4
Portishead Way BS3. . . . . 11 E3
Port La TA22. . . . . 164 A5
PORTLAND. 207 A6
Portland Cl
  Cannington TA5. . . . . . . 135 B2
  Nailsea BS48. . . . . 8 D1
Portland Ct BS1. . . . . 226 A1
Portland Dr BS20. . . . . 2 E4
Portland Grange **6** TA1. 212 E4
Portland Lofts **8** BS2. . 227 B4
Portland Mans **9** BS2. . 227 B4
Portland Pl
  Bath BA1. . . . . 228 B4
  Brent Knoll TA9. . . . . 86 B1
  Bridgwater TA6. . . . . . . 208 D5
  Frome BA11. . . . . 119 D5
Portland Rd
  Bath BA1. . . . . 228 B4

Portland Rd continued
  Frome BA11. . . . . 119 D5
  Langport TA10. . . . . 172 B5
  Street BA16. . . . . 207 A6
Portland Sq BS2. . . . . 227 B4
Portland St
  Bristol, Clifton BS8. . . . . 11 F7
  Taunton TA1. . . . . 212 E4
Portland Terr
  Bath BA1. . . . . 228 B4
  Watchet TA23. . . . . 202 C7
Portman Cres **9** TA6. . . . 153 F3
Portman Ct BA22. . . . . . . 196 E8
Portman Dr TA6. . . . . 153 E3
Portman Rd TA6. . . . . 153 E3
Portmans TA3. . . . . 170 B3
Portman St TA2. . . . . 212 F6
Portmeade Dro BS26. . . . . 70 C1
Portmeirion Cl BS14. . . . . 23 B5
Portnell's La BA12. . . . . . 161 F2
Portobello Bldgs TA20. . 223 B4
Portreeve Dr BA21. . . . . . 219 B6
Port View BS20. . . . . 4 C5
Portview Rd BS11. . . . . 4 B8
Portview Trad Est BS11. . . 4 B7
Portwall Dro TA7. . . . . . . 209 F5
Portwall La BS1. . . . . 227 B1
Portwall La E **10** BS1. . . . 227 B1
PORTWAY. 207 D4
Portway
  Bristol, Shirehampton BS11. 4 C6
  Bristol, Sneyd Park BS8. . . 5 C3
  Frome BA11. . . . . 120 A4
  Holford TA5. . . . . 133 D4
  Street BA16. . . . . 207 D4
  Wells BA5. . . . . 203 C4
Portway Ave BA5. . . . . . . 203 D4
Portway Hill
  Batcombe BA4. . . . . 142 C1
  Bruton BA4. . . . . 159 F6
Portway La
  Binegar BA3. . . . . 95 E1
  Holford TA5. . . . . 133 E4
Portway Lodge **1** BA5. . 203 C4
Portway Rdbt BS11. . . . . . . 4 C8
Portway Villas BA11. . . . 120 A4
Positano **2** TA6. . . . . . . 208 F7
Poskitt Ho TA6. . . . . 208 F6
Post Cl TA21. . . . . 222 E4
Post La
  Malmsmead EX35. . . . . . 122 C4
  Skilgate TA4. . . . . 164 E1
Post Office La
  Blagdon BS40. . . . . 54 D3
  Flax Bourton BS48. . . . . . 19 F7
  Minehead TA24. . . . . . . 200 F7
  Tatworth TA20. . . . . 198 C8
Post Office Rd BS24. . . . . 50 C5
Post Office Yd DT8. . . . . 199 F7
Poston Way BA15. . . . . . . 64 E7
Pot La BA11. . . . . 120 F8
Potter's Cross TA4. . . . . . 165 C7
POTTERS HILL. 20 B1
Potters Ho **1** BA4. . . . . . 205 B6
Potterton Cl TA6. . . . . . . 208 F1
Pottery Cl BS23. . . . . 49 A6
Pottery Rd TA19. . . . . . . 183 C1
Pottery View TA19. . . . . 183 C1
Pottle St BA12. . . . . 144 D3
Potts Cl BA1. . . . . 28 F3
Poulett Cotts TA17. . . . . 195 D7
POUND. 220 F2
Pound Cl
  Glastonbury BA6. . . . . . 206 D5
  Stalbridge DT10. . . . . . 190 B4
  Yeovil BA21. . . . . 218 C5
Pound Farm Cl TA6. . . . . 208 D3
Poundfield Rd TA24. . . . . 200 E6
Pound Fold TA4. . . . . 151 E3
Pound Hill TA21. . . . . . . 179 A5
Poundisford Cl TA1. . . . . 212 D1
Pound La
  Bishops Lydeard TA4. . . . 151 F1
  Buckland St Mary TA20. . 193 A8
  Downhead BA4. . . . . . . 117 A1
  Easton BA5. . . . . 111 A4
  Lydford Fair Place TA11. 158 C3
  Martock TA12. . . . . 185 D6
  Nailsea BS48. . . . . 8 D3
  Oakhill BA3. . . . . 115 B5
  Rawridge EX14. . . . . . . 191 F1
  Yarcombe EX14. . . . . . . 192 E2
  Yarlington BA9. . . . . . . 175 F8
  Yeovil BA22. . . . . 218 A2
Pound Mead BS40. . . . . . . 37 C8
Pound Orch TA4. . . . . 151 C7
Pound Pool TA11. . . . . . . 211 C4
Pound Rd
  Axminster EX13. . . . . . . 198 F2
  Broadway TA19. . . . . . . 183 B2
  Pawlett TA6. . . . . 135 F5
Poundsclose TA4. . . . . . . 163 E4
Pound Terr **3** TA21. . . . . 222 D5
Pound The BS40. . . . . 36 D3
Pound Way TA10. . . . . . . 172 B3
Pounsell La TA10. . . . . . . 172 B5
Powell Cl TA3. . . . . 169 D4
Powell Ct BA5. . . . . 203 B4
Powells Acres BS21. . . . . . 6 E3
Powis Cl BS22. . . . . 31 C2
Powlett Cl BA2. . . . . 45 B7
Powlett Rd BA2. . . . . 45 B8
Pow's Hill BA3. . . . . 78 D5
Pow's Orch BA3. . . . . 78 A1
Powy's Gn DT9. . . . . 225 C4
Powy's La DT9. . . . . 225 C4
POYNTINGTON. 188 E6

Poyntz Rd BS4. . . . . 22 F8
Prankerds Rd DT9. . . . . . 217 C2
Preachers Vale BA3. . . . . 116 F7
Preanes Gn BS22. . . . . 32 A2
Precinct The BS20. . . . . . . 2 D5
Prescot Cl BS22. . . . . 31 B2
PRESCOTT. 179 C1
Prescott Rd EX15. . . . . . . 179 D1
PRESTLEIGH. 141 D3
Prestleigh La BA4. . . . . . . 141 E4
Prestleigh Rd BA4. . . . . . 141 E2
PRESTON. 150 E6
PRESTON BOWYER. 167 B5
Preston CE Prim Sch
  BA21. . . . . 218 C7
Preston Cross TA4. . . . . . 150 E6
Preston Gr BA20. . . . . 218 F5
Preston La TA4. . . . . 150 E6
PRESTON PLUCKNETT. . . 218 D4
Preston Rd
  Yeovil BA20. . . . . 218 E5
  Yeovil, Houndstone BA22. 218 B3
Preston Road Rdbt BA21 218 C5
Preston Sch BA21. . . . . . . 218 D5
Prestor **9** BS13. . . . . 198 A1
Pretwood Cl TA19. . . . . . 221 C3
Prewett St BS1. . . . . 227 B1
Prey La TA3. . . . . 182 C3
Preywater Rd BA5. . . . . . 139 D8
Prices Ave TA21. . . . . 222 D7
Prices Bldgs TA6. . . . . . . 209 A4
Priddles La TA20. . . . . . . 193 C8
PRIDDY. 92 D3
Priddy Cl
  Bath BA2. . . . . 44 B5
  Frome BA11. . . . . 120 C7
Priddy Ct BS14. . . . . 23 B5
Priddy Dr BS14. . . . . 23 B5
Priddy Nine Barrows★
  BA5. . . . . 92 F4
Priddy Prim Sch BA5. . . . 92 D3
Priddy Rd BA5. . . . . 112 B3
Priddy Veal La BA5. . . . . 111 A5
Priestlands DT9. . . . . 225 D5
Priestlands La DT9. . . . . 225 D5
Priestley Way TA8. . . . . . 104 C5
Priest Row BA5. . . . . 203 D4
Priest's House★ TA10. . . 172 A3
Priest St TA4. . . . . 202 C2
Priests Way BS22. . . . . . . 31 D2
Prigg La TA13. . . . . 220 C4
Primmerfield La BA3. . . . . 94 C8
PRIMROSE HILL. 27 D1
Primrose Hill
  Bath BA1. . . . . 27 D1
  Charlton Mackrell TA11. . 173 F7
  East Coker BA22. . . . . . 197 B2
  Nunney BA11. . . . . 143 B8
Primrose Hill Pk Homes
  TA11. . . . . 173 F7
Primrose La
  Midsomer Norton BA3. . . 78 B1
  Yeovil BA21. . . . . 187 D5
Primrose Wlk TA6. . . . . . 208 D1
Prince Philip Cl TA20. . . . 223 B3
Princes Bldgs BA1. . . . . . 228 B3
Prince's Bldgs **17** BS8. . . 11 F6
Prince's Cl **11** TA14. . . . 185 E4
Princes' La BS8. . . . . 11 F6
Princes Rd BA5. . . . . 203 D4
Prince's Rd
  Clevedon BS21. . . . . 6 D3
  Shepton Mallet BA4. . . . 205 C6
  Street BA16. . . . . 207 B6
Princess Anne Rd BA11. . 120 A7
Princess Cl
  Keynsham BS31. . . . . . . 24 E4
  12 North Petherton TA6. . 153 F4
Princess Rd TA1. . . . . 212 D2
Princess Row BS2. . . . . . 227 A4
Princess St TA8. . . . . 104 B7
Princes St
  Bath BA1. . . . . 228 B2
  Taunton TA1. . . . . 213 B4
  Yeovil BA20. . . . . 219 B5
Prince's St
  Bristol BS2. . . . . 227 C4
  Clandown BA3. . . . . 78 E5
Princess Victoria St BS8. . 11 F6
Prince St BS1. . . . . 227 A1
Prince Street Rdbt BS1. . 227 A2
Printers Ct **32** TA12. . . . 185 E6
Prior Park Bldgs BA2. . . . . 45 B5
Prior Park Coll BA2. . . . . . 45 C2
Prior Park Cotts BA2. . . . 228 C1
Prior Park Gdns BA2. . . . . 45 B5
Prior Park Landscape Gdn★
  BA2. . . . . 45 C3
Prior Park Rd BA2. . . . . . . 45 B4
Priors Hill BA2. . . . . 60 A2
Prior's Wlk TA1. . . . . 212 F4
PRIORSWOOD. 213 B7
Priorswood Ind Est TA2 213 B7
Priorswood Pl **8** TA2. . . 213 A8
Priorswood Prim Sch
  TA2. . . . . 212 F6
Priorswood Rd TA2. . . . . 213 A6
Priory Ave TA1. . . . . 213 A4
Priory Bridge Rd TA1. . . 213 A5
Priory Cl
  Bath BA2. . . . . 45 B2
  Cannington TA5. . . . . . . 135 C2
  Castle Cary BA7. . . . . . . 214 B5
  Chilton Polden TA7. . . . 137 B2
  Ilchester BA22. . . . . 173 E1
  Midsomer Norton BA3. . . 78 A1
  Yeovil BA20. . . . . 218 D1

Priory Com Sch BS22. . . . 32 B3
Priory Ct
  Bridgwater TA6. . . . . . . 208 F4
  9 Stoke sub Hamdon
  TA14. . . . . 185 F4
  5 Taunton TA1. . . . . . . 213 A5
  Wellington TA21. . . . . . 222 E7
Priory Farm Trad Est BS11. . 3 D3
Priory Fields TA1. . . . . . . 213 A5
Priory Fields Ret Pk TA1 213 A5
Priorygate Ct BA7. . . . . . 214 B6
Priory Gdns
  Bristol, Shirehampton BS11. . 4 D7
  Burnham-on-S TA8. . . . 104 B6
  Easton-in-G BS20. . . . . . . 4 B4
  Wellington TA21. . . . . . 222 E6
Priory Glade BA21. . . . . . 218 C6
Priory Gn TA24. . . . . 201 E2
Priory Hill TA5. . . . . 134 C5
Priory Hospl BA5. . . . . . . 203 C3
Priory Mead BA6. . . . . . . 215 F8
Priory Mews BS23. . . . . . . 49 B7
Priory Path BA7. . . . . 214 C5
Priory Pl BA5. . . . . 203 D3
Priory Rd
  Bristol BS8. . . . . 226 C4
  Bristol, Shirehampton BS11. . 4 D6
  Chilton Polden TA7. . . . 137 B2
  Easton-in-G BS20. . . . . . . 4 B4
  Ilchester BA22. . . . . 173 E1
  Keynsham BS31. . . . . . . 24 E7
  Portbury BS20. . . . . 3 D3
  Wells BA5. . . . . 203 D3
  Weston-super-Mare BS23. . 49 A7
Priory Sch The TA2. . . . . 213 B7
Priory View TA1. . . . . 214 B6
Priory Villas BA9. . . . . . . 216 C3
Priory Way TA1. . . . . 213 B5
Priory Way Ind Est TA1 . 213 B5
Priory Wlk
  Portbury BS20. . . . . 3 D3
  Taunton TA1. . . . . 213 A5
PRISTON. 61 B5
Priston Cl BS22. . . . . 32 B5
Priston La BA2, BA3. . . . . 61 A5
Priston Rd BA2. . . . . 61 D6
Pritchard St BS2. . . . . . . 227 B4
Private Rd
  North Brewham BA11. . . 161 E8
  Staplegrove TA2. . . . . . 212 D7
Privet Dr BS13. . . . . 22 C5
Proctor Dr BS23. . . . . 49 B4
Proctor Ho BS1. . . . . 227 B1
Prophet's La TA14. . . . . . 185 E3
Prospect Cl
  East Brent TA9. . . . . 86 E5
  Shepton Mallet BA4. . . . 205 A6
Prospect Gdns BA1. . . . . . 28 F5
Prospect Ho BS22. . . . . . . 31 E3
Prospect Pl
  Bath, Beacon Hill BA1. . . 28 A1
  Bathford BA1. . . . . 29 D2
  Bath, Weston BA1. . . . . . 27 C2
  9 Weston-super-Mare
  BS23. . . . . 48 E8
Prospect Rd BA2. . . . . 45 C4
Prospect Row TA18. . . . . 224 F3
Prospect Terr TA1. . . . . . 212 F5
Prospect Villas BA4. . . . . 159 C7
Protheroes Ho BS1. . . . . 226 C2
Proud Cross BS40. . . . . . . 74 E4
Providence La BS41. . . . . . 10 F2
Providence Pl
  Bristol BS2. . . . . 227 C2
  Bruton BA10. . . . . 215 D6
PROVIDENCE PLACE. 77 F1
Providence Rise BS41. . . . 10 F2
Providence View BS41. . . 11 A1
Provident Pl TA6. . . . . . . 208 E5
Prowle's Cross BA22. . . . 197 F5
Prowse La TA2. . . . . 106 C7
Prowse's La BS26. . . . . . . 70 A1
Prowses Mdw TA2. . . . . . 168 A4
PUBLOW. 40 F4
Publow La BS39. . . . . 40 E5
PUCKINGTON. 184 B5
Pud Brook DT9. . . . . 217 D1
Pudding Pie Cl BS40. . . . . 53 A5
Pudding Pie La BS40. . . . . 53 A6
Puddle Town TA18. . . . . . 196 B5
Puddy's La TA9. . . . . 105 D4
PUDLEIGH. 223 B8
Pudleigh La TA20. . . . . . . 223 B8
Puffin Cl
  Minehead TA24. . . . . . . 201 C5
  Weston-super-Mare BS22. 49 F8
Pullen Ct BA4. . . . . 205 B4
Pulmans La TA18. . . . . . . 224 C5
Pulpitsway Dro TA12. . . 185 A8
Pulteney Ave BA2. . . . . . . 45 B6
Pulteney Bridge BA2. . . . 228 C2
Pulteney Gdns BA2. . . . . . 45 B6
Pulteney Gr BA2. . . . . 45 B6
Pulteney Mews **4** BA2. . 45 B7
Pulteney Rd BA2. . . . . 45 B6
Pulteney Terr BA2. . . . . . . 45 B6
Pump La
  Bathford BA1. . . . . 29 B2
  Bristol BS1. . . . . 227 B1
  Redhill BS40. . . . . 36 D2
Pump Sq BS20. . . . . 4 D5
Punnet Cl BS27. . . . . 90 B7
Puppy Cross Ways BA3. . . 94 F5
Puppy La BA3. . . . . 94 F5
Purcell Wlk BS4. . . . . 22 D7
Purdue Cl BS22. . . . . 32 B3
Purewell TA7. . . . . 136 C4
PURITON. 136 C4

Puriton Hill TA7. . . . . . . 136 C3
Puriton Manor TA7. . . . . 136 C4
Puriton Pk TA7. . . . . 136 C4
Puriton Prim Sch TA7. . . 136 C4
Puriton Rd
  Pawlett TA6. . . . . 136 A5
  West Huntspill TA9. . . . 136 B7
Purlewent Dr BA1. . . . . . . 27 C1
Purley Dr TA6. . . . . 209 D6
PURN. 67 A7
Purnell Wy BS39. . . . . 77 D6
Purn La BS24. . . . . 67 A8
Purn Rd BS24. . . . . 66 F8
Purn Way BS24. . . . . 67 B7
PURSE CAUNDLE. 189 D4
Purse Caundle Manor
  House★ DT9. . . . . 189 D4
Pursey Ave BA16. . . . . . . 207 E5
PURTINGTON. 195 A4
Purving Row BS24. . . . . . . 67 C1
Purving Row La BS24. . . . 67 C1
Putham La TA24. . . . . 129 F1
Putsham Hill TA5. . . . . . . 133 D5
Putsham Mead TA5. . . . . 133 D5
Puttingthorpe Dr BS22. . 49 C7
Putts La DT9. . . . . 175 D1
Putt's La DT9. . . . . 188 D8
Puxley Cl BS14. . . . . 23 E6
PUXTON. 33 D3
Puxton La BS24. . . . . 33 D3
Puxton Moor La BS24. . . . 33 E2
Puxton Park (Adventure
  Park)★ BS24. . . . . 33 B3
Puxton Rd BS24. . . . . 33 C2
Pyde La TA10. . . . . 184 D6
Pye Cnr
  Churchill BS25. . . . . 52 D4
  Merriott TA16. . . . . 195 F6
  Somerton TA11. . . . . . . 211 D4
Pye La TA20. . . . . 198 E8
PYLEIGH. 151 B1
Pyleigh La TA4. . . . . 151 A1
Pyle La BA22. . . . . 174 A2
Pyles Thorne TA21. . . . . 222 E5
Pyles Thorne Cl TA21. . . 222 E5
Pyles Thorne Rd TA21. . . 222 E4
Pylewell La BS25. . . . . 52 D1
Pyle Well La TA11. . . . . . 174 E8
PYLLE. 141 B1
Pylle Hill BA4. . . . . 141 A1
Pylle La BA4. . . . . 141 B1
Pylle Rd BA4. . . . . 141 A2
Pyncombe La TA4. . . . . . . 210 B3
Pyne Point BS21. . . . . 6 C3
Pynne Cl BS14. . . . . 23 F5
Pynne Rd BS14. . . . . 23 F5
Pyracantha Wlk BS14. . . . 23 A6
PYRLAND. 213 A8
Pyrland Ave TA2. . . . . . . 212 F8
Pyrland Pl TA2. . . . . 213 A8
Pyrland Wlk TA6. . . . . . . 208 B4

Q

Quab La
  Alston Sutton BS26. . . . . 88 F3
  Wedmore BS28. . . . . . . 108 B5
Quab Lane Cl BS28. . . . . 108 B4
Quaish La BA4. . . . . 140 C4
Quaker's La TA4. . . . . 210 C3
Quakinghouse La TA4. . . 166 E5
Quantick Gdns TA24. . . . 201 B5
Quantock Ave TA6. . . . . . 208 D4
Quantock Cl
  Burnham-on-S TA8. . . . 104 B7
  North Petherton TA6. . . 153 E4
Quantock Ct
  Burnham-on-S TA8. . . . 104 A5
  Ilminster TA19. . . . . . . 221 C4
  Street BA16. . . . . 207 B5
  Williton TA4. . . . . 202 D2
Quantock Gr TA4. . . . . . . 202 E2
Quantock Ho TA6. . . . . . . 153 E4
Quantock Mdw TA6. . . . . 208 C5
Quantock Par TA6. . . . . . 153 E4
Quantock Rd
  Bridgwater TA5, TA6. . . 208 B5
  Cannington TA5. . . . . . . 135 C1
  Portishead BS20. . . . . . . 2 B5
  Taunton TA2. . . . . 212 E8
  Watchet TA23. . . . . 202 C6
  Wellington TA21. . . . . . 222 D7
  Weston-super-Mare BS23. . 48 E4
Quantock Rise
  Kingston St Mary TA2. . . 168 E8
  Pawlett TA6. . . . . 135 F5
Quantocks BA2. . . . . 45 A1
Quantock Terr TA6. . . . . . 209 A6
Quantock View
  Bishops Lydeard TA4. . . . 167 F8
  Highbridge TA9. . . . . . . 104 D3
  Kilve TA5. . . . . 133 C6
Quantock Way
  Bridgwater TA6. . . . . . . 208 C5
  Kingston St Mary TA2. . . 168 D8
Quaperlake St BA10. . . . 215 F7
Quarante-Ans BA4. . . . . 142 B7
Quarme La TA24. . . . . . . 147 E7
QUARR. 177 E5
Quarr BA4. . . . . 205 C6
Quarr Cross SP8. . . . . 177 E4
Quarr Dr DT9. . . . . 225 D6
Quarr La DT9. . . . . 225 D6
Quarr Lane Pk DT9. . . . . . 225 D6
Quarry Batch
  Street BA16. . . . . 207 A5
  Walton BA16. . . . . 156 E7

Quarry Cl
Bath BA2 . . . . . 44 F1
Limpley Stoke BA3 . . . . . 64 D6
Minehead TA24 . . . . . 201 B5
Quarry Cotts BA22 . . . . . 197 F8
Quarry Hay BS40 . . . . . 56 D8
Quarry Hill BA22 . . . . . 175 F4
Quarry La
Blagdon Hill TA3 . . . . . 181 D4
Bradford Abbas DT9 . . . . . 187 E1
Butleigh BA6 . . . . . 157 D3
Combe St Nicholas TA20 . . 193 D6
Kingston St Mary TA2 . . . . 168 F7
Quarrylands La BS26 . . . . . 88 B4
Quarrymans Ct BA2 . . . . . 45 B1
Quarry Rd
Bath BA2 . . . . . 45 D6
Kingsdon TA11 . . . . . 173 D5
Portishead BS20 . . . . . 2 C4
Sandford BS25 . . . . . 52 A2
Street BA16 . . . . . 207 B4
Washford TA23 . . . . . 131 F4
Quarry Rise BS24 . . . . . 66 F8
Quarry Rock Gdns BA2 . . 45 D4
Quarry Vale Cotts BA2 . . . . 45 B1
Quarry Way BS48 . . . . . 8 D2
Quartley Hill EX16 . . . . . 164 E4
Quartly Dr TA1 . . . . . 212 A3
Quay La TA24 . . . . . 201 A8
Quays Ave BS20 . . . . . 2 E5
Quayside TA6 . . . . . 208 F5
Quay St
Bristol BS1 . . . . . 227 A3
Minehead TA24 . . . . . 201 A8
Quays The BS1 . . . . . 226 C1
Quay W TA24 . . . . . 125 D4
Quebec BA2 . . . . . 44 A6
Quedam Sh Ctr 6 BA21 . 219 B5
Queen Anne Ct TA24 . . . . 200 F7
QUEEN CAMEL 174 F3
Queen Charlotte St BS1 . 227 A2
QUEEN CHARLTON 24 B3
Queen Charlton La BS14 . . 23 E2
Queen Elizabeth Ct
Bridgwater TA6 . . . . . 209 A5
Street BA16 . . . . . 207 C6
Queen Elizabeth's Hospital Sch BS8 . . . . . 226 B3
Queen Quay BS1 . . . . . 227 A2
Queen's Ave
Bristol BS8 . . . . . 226 B3
Portishead BS20 . . . . . 2 C5
Queens Cl TA20 . . . . . 223 B2
Queen's Coll TA1 . . . . . 212 D1
Queen's Coll Jun Sch TA1 . . . . . 212 D1
Queenscote BS20 . . . . . 2 F5
Queens Cres TA14 . . . . . 185 F5
Queen's Ct BS8 . . . . . 226 B3
Queen's Down TA3 . . . . . 169 C4
Queens Dr TA1 . . . . . 168 D1
Queen's Dr BA2 . . . . . 45 A2
Queens Gate BS9 . . . . . 5 D5
Queens Gate Terr TA1 . . . 213 A3
Queens Gr BA9 . . . . . 161 E2
Queens Par BS1 . . . . . 226 C2
Queen's Par BA1 . . . . . 228 B3
Queen's Parade Pl BA1 . . 228 B3
Queens Pl BA2 . . . . . 45 B5
Queen Sq
Bath BA1 . . . . . 228 B2
Bristol BS1 . . . . . 227 A2
North Curry TA3 . . . . . 170 B4
Saltford BS31 . . . . . 25 F3
Queen Square Ave 10 BS1 . . . . . 227 A2
Queen Square Pl BA1 . . . 228 B3
Queens Rd
Banwell BS29 . . . . . 51 A3
Bradford Abbas DT9 . . . . . 187 E1
Frome BA11 . . . . . 119 D4
Keynsham BS31 . . . . . 24 D4
Minehead TA24 . . . . . 201 A6
Nailsea BS48 . . . . . 8 D1
Portishead BS20 . . . . . 1 E4
Somerton TA11 . . . . . 211 D4
Street BA16 . . . . . 207 B5
Wellington TA21 . . . . . 222 E4
Queen's Rd
Bridgwater TA6 . . . . . 208 F2
Bristol, Bishopsworth BS13, BS41 . . . . . 21 F4
Bristol BS8 . . . . . 226 B3
Clevedon BS21 . . . . . 6 D3
Evercreech BA4 . . . . . 141 E2
Radstock BA3 . . . . . 79 B2
Shepton Mallet BA4 . . . . . 205 A5
Weston-super-Mare BS23 . . 30 D1
Queens Row BS27 . . . . . 90 C8
Queens Sq TA9 . . . . . 104 C4
Queen St
Bath BA1 . . . . . 228 B2
Bridgwater TA6 . . . . . 208 F5
Bristol BS2 . . . . . 227 B3
Keinton Mandeville TA11 . . 158 A1
North Petherton TA6 . . . . 153 F4
Taunton TA1 . . . . . 213 B4
Tintinhull BA22 . . . . . 186 B7
11 Wells BA5 . . . . . 203 D4
Yarlington BA9 . . . . . 175 F8
Queens Terr TA1 . . . . . 213 A3
Queen's Terr
Sherborne DT9 . . . . . 225 D6
Wiveliscombe TA4 . . . . . 210 C4
Queensway
Taunton TA1 . . . . . 212 B1
Yeovil BA20 . . . . . 219 A4
Queens Way BS20 . . . . . 1 E4
Queen's Way BS22 . . . . . 31 F4
Queensway Cl TA9 . . . . . 106 E5
Queensway Ctr BS22 . . . . 32 B2
Queensway Pl BA20 . . . . 219 A4
Queenswood Rd TA6 . . . . 208 C4
Queenwood Ave BA1 . . . . 28 A1
Quicksilver Rdbt BA20 . . 218 F2
Quickthorn Cl BS14 . . . . . 23 A6
Quiet St BA1 . . . . . 228 B2
Quilter Gr BS4 . . . . . 22 D7
Quirke St TA24 . . . . . 200 F7

R

Raby Mews BA2 . . . . . 45 B7
Raby Pl BA2 . . . . . 45 B7
Rackclose Gdns TA20 . . . 223 A4
Rackclose Ho TA20 . . . . 223 A4
Rackclose Pk TA20 . . . . 223 B4
Rackfield TA21 . . . . . 222 A5
Rackfield Pl BA2 . . . . . 44 B6
Rackhay BS1 . . . . . 227 A2
Rackley La
Buckland St Mary TA20 . . 182 B1
Compton Bishop BS26 . . . 69 B2
Rackstile TA20 . . . . . 223 A7
Rackvernal Ct BA3 . . . . . 78 B1
Rackvernal Rd BA3 . . . . . 78 B1
RADDINGTON 165 B4
Raddon Cl BA4 . . . . . 205 B6
RADFORD 78 C8
Radford Hill
Camerton BA2, BA3 . . . . . 78 C7
Timsbury BA2 . . . . . 60 C1
Radigan La TA3, TA19 . . . 183 C5
RADLET 134 C1
Radlet Cl TA2 . . . . . 213 B7
Radnidge La EX16 . . . . . 162 D4
RADSTOCK 78 E1
Radstock & District Mus★ BA3 . . . . . 78 F2
Radstock Rd BA3 . . . . . 78 C2
Ragged Dro BA6 . . . . . 158 A7
Rag Hill BA3 . . . . . 79 D5
Rag La
Babcary BA22 . . . . . 174 B6
Yarcombe EX14 . . . . . 192 D2
Raglan Cl
Bridgwater TA6 . . . . . 209 D7
Chilcompton BA3 . . . . . 96 C4
Raglan Ct 4 TA2 . . . . . 212 F6
Ragland La BA1 . . . . . 28 A2
Ragland St BA1 . . . . . 28 A2
Raglan La BS40 . . . . . 37 E7
Raglan Pl 20 BS23 . . . . . 30 C1
Raglan's Cross TA4 . . . . 202 F2
Raglan Terr
Bath BA1 . . . . . 28 A2
Yeovil BA21 . . . . . 218 F7
Raglan Wlk BS31 . . . . . 24 D4
Railford Hill BA11 . . . . . 118 B3
Railway Arches BS2 . . . . 227 C2
Railway Cotts BA11 . . . . 143 C3
Railway La BA2 . . . . . 62 D1
Railway Pl BA1 . . . . . 228 C1
Railway St
Bath BA1 . . . . . 228 C1
Taunton TA2 . . . . . 212 F6
Railway Terr BA2 . . . . . 79 E4
Railway View Pl BA3 . . . . 78 B2
Rainbow La TA3 . . . . . 191 C7
Rainham Ct 2 BS23 . . . . . 30 C1
Rains Batch BS40 . . . . . 72 E6
Raisey La TA20 . . . . . 193 C7
Raleigh Cl
Bridgwater TA6 . . . . . 209 C5
Saltford BS31 . . . . . 25 D2
Raleigh Ct
Sherborne DT9 . . . . . 225 E4
3 Weston-super-Mare BS23 . . . . . 48 E5
Raleigh Ho TA6 . . . . . 209 C5
Raleigh Rd DT10 . . . . . 190 B4
Raleigh Rise BS20 . . . . . 2 B5
Raliegh Pl DT9 . . . . . 225 D2
Ralph Allen Dr BA2 . . . . . 45 B3
Ralph Allen Sch BA2 . . . . 45 E2
Ralston Ct BA9 . . . . . 216 C4
Rambler Way TA6 . . . . . 208 E6
Ramon Ave TA23 . . . . . 202 D7
Ramsay Cl BS22 . . . . . 31 E4
Ramsay Way TA8 . . . . . 104 C8
Ramscombe Forest Wlks★ TA5 . . . . . 151 E8
Ramscombe La BA1 . . . . . 28 F6
Ramsey La TA21 . . . . . 179 F8
Ramshorn Cl TA1 . . . . . 212 C2
Ramshorn Gn TA1 . . . . . 212 D2
Ramshorn Pl TA1 . . . . . 212 D3
Ranchways BS20 . . . . . 1 F4
Randall Rd BS8 . . . . . 226 B2
Randolph Ave BS13 . . . . . 22 B5
Randolph Cl BS13 . . . . . 22 B5
Randolph Rd BA11 . . . . . 119 F4
Ranger Rd BA6 . . . . . 206 C3
Rangoon Rd TA23 . . . . . 202 E6
Rankers La BS39 . . . . . 41 C5
Rank The
Coxley BA5 . . . . . 139 F6
Maiden Bradley BA12 . . . 144 C2
Vobster BA3 . . . . . 117 D6
Ranscombe Ave BS22 . . . . 31 D2
Ransford BS21 . . . . . 6 B1
Raphael Ct BS1 . . . . . 227 B1
Rapide Wy
Weston-super-Mare BS24 . . 49 B4
Weston-super-Mare BS24 . . 49 C4
RAPPS 183 D3
Raps Cl TA1 . . . . . 213 E5
Raps Gn TA1 . . . . . 213 E5
Rashwood La BA11 . . . . . 118 B6
Ratleigh La DT9 . . . . . 188 A3
Rattigan Cl TA8 . . . . . 104 C6
Rattle Row TA24 . . . . . 131 B4
Raven Cl BS22 . . . . . 31 E1
Raven Ct BS9 . . . . . 5 F8
Ravenhead Dr BS14 . . . . . 23 B8
Ravensmead TA20 . . . . . 223 C5
Ravenswood Special Sch BS48 . . . . . 8 D3
Ravensworth Terr TA8 . . 104 B7
Rawle's Bldgs TA24 . . . . 124 A3
Rawlings La BS26 . . . . . 88 E2
Rawlins Ave BS22 . . . . . 32 A5
RAWRIDGE 191 F1
Rayens Cl BS41 . . . . . 10 F1
Rayens Cross Rd BS41 . . . 10 F1
Rayleigh Rd BS9 . . . . . 5 E7
Raymar Flats TA19 . . . . 221 A4
Raymond St TA2 . . . . . 212 E6
Raymore Rise BS41 . . . . . 10 F1
Rayneswood BS23 . . . . . 48 F8
Read Mead BA6 . . . . . 206 E3
Reakes Cl BA5 . . . . . 203 C4
Rebels Way BA6 . . . . . 206 D5
Reckleford BA20, BA21 . . 219 B5
Reckleford Inf Sch BA21 219 C5
Rector's Cl TA8 . . . . . 65 F3
Rector's Way BS23 . . . . . 48 F6
Rectory Cl
Farmborough BA2 . . . . . 60 A6
6 North Petherton TA6 . . 153 E3
Staplegrove TA2 . . . . . 212 C8
Wraxall BS48 . . . . . 9 A2
Rectory Ct TA20 . . . . . 193 D6
Rectory Dr
Burnham-on-S TA8 . . . . . 104 B8
Staplegrove TA2 . . . . . 212 C7
Yatton BS49 . . . . . 34 C7
Rectory Farm Cl BA22 . . . 174 F3
Rectory Gdns TA20 . . . . 193 D6
Rectory Hill
Chapel Allerton BS26 . . . . 88 D2
Pitney TA10 . . . . . 172 C7
South Cadbury BA22 . . . . 175 C3
Rectory La
Bleadon BS24 . . . . . 67 C6
Compton Martin BS40 . . . . 74 B6
Hardington Mandeville BA22 . . . . . 197 A6
Horsington BA8 . . . . . 176 E2
Norton Sub Hamdon TA14 . 185 F2
Shalford BA9 . . . . . 216 E6
Sparkford BA22 . . . . . 175 A3
Timsbury BA2 . . . . . 60 B2
Rectory Lawn TA8 . . . . . 104 B8
Rectory Pl TA8 . . . . . 104 C8
Rectory Rd
Ashbrittle TA21 . . . . . 178 F8
Burnham-on-S TA8 . . . . . 104 B8
Easton-in-G BS20 . . . . . 4 B3
Norton Fitzwarren TA2 . . . 168 B5
Shepton Mallet BA4 . . . . . 205 B6
Staplegrove TA2 . . . . . 212 C8
Rectory Way
Lympsham BS24 . . . . . 66 F2
Yatton BS49 . . . . . 34 C7
Recurium Lodge BS26 . . . . 70 B2
Redacre BS40 . . . . . 36 D3
RED BALL 179 C4
Red Barn La TA20 . . . . . 193 D4
Redcliff Backs BS1 . . . . 227 B2
REDCLIFFE BAY 1 E4
Redcliffe Cl BS20 . . . . . 1 E3
Redcliffe Par E BS1 . . . . 227 A1
Redcliffe Par W BS1 . . . . 227 A1
Redcliffe Sixth Form Ctr The BS1 . . . . . 227 B1
Redcliffe St BS27 . . . . . 90 C7
Redcliffe Way BS1 . . . . . 227 B1
Redcliff Hill BS1 . . . . . 227 B1
Redcliff Mead La BS1 . . . 227 B1
Redcliff St BS1 . . . . . 227 B2
Red Cotts
Blagdon BS40 . . . . . 54 D6
Corsley Heath BA12 . . . . 144 E8
Redcroft BS40 . . . . . 36 D3
Redcross Mews 14 BS2 . . 227 C3
Redcross St BS2 . . . . . 227 C3
Redding Pit La BS40 . . . . 37 E4
Reddings The BS40 . . . . . 74 B7
Redfield Gr BA3 . . . . . 97 A8
Redfield Rd BA3 . . . . . 97 A8
Redford Cres BS13 . . . . . 21 F3
Redford Trad Est BS3 . . . . 22 C8
Redford Wlk BS13 . . . . . 21 F3
Redgate Pk TA18 . . . . . 224 C8
Redgates Rd TA24 . . . . . 200 E7
Redgate St TA6 . . . . . 209 B4
REDHILL 36 D3
Red Hill
Peasedown St John BA2 . . . 60 E1
Redhill BS40 . . . . . 36 D2
West Monkton TA2 . . . . . 169 B7
Redhill La BA3 . . . . . 95 A2
Red Hill La TA7 . . . . . 155 E7
Redhole La DT9 . . . . . 225 D8
Red House La BS9 . . . . . 5 E6
Red House Rd TA9 . . . . . 86 D5
Red La
Churchinford TA3 . . . . . 191 F7
Hemyock EX15 . . . . . 180 E3
Seaborough DT8 . . . . . 195 E1
Staplehay TA3 . . . . . 181 E8
Redlake Dr TA1 . . . . . 213 D3
Redland Ave BS20 . . . . . 3 F6
Redland La TA3 . . . . . 183 C8
Redland Pk BA2 . . . . . 43 F6
Redlands La TA7 . . . . . 137 C2
Redlands Terr BA3 . . . . . 96 F8
Redland Terr BA11 . . . . . 119 F3
REDLANE 191 F7
Red Lion Ct
3 Crewkerne TA18 . . . . . 224 C6
Somerton TA11 . . . . . 211 E4
Wellington TA21 . . . . . 222 E6
Red Lodge Bsns Pk BS24 . 32 D1
REDLYNCH 160 D4
Redlynch Cross BA10 . . . 160 E4
Redlynch La BS31 . . . . . 24 D2
Redmans Hill BS28 . . . . . 107 E4
Redpoll Dr BS20 . . . . . 3 A6
RED POST 79 B7
Red Post
Chard TA20 . . . . . 193 D3
Isle Abbotts TA3 . . . . . 183 E7
Porlock TA24 . . . . . 124 B3
Red Post Cross TA11 . . . 173 D4
Red Post Ct BA2 . . . . . 79 B7
Red Rd
Berrow TA8 . . . . . 85 A7
Brean TA8 . . . . . 66 A2
Redshard La BS40 . . . . . 53 B7
Redstart Prim Sch The TA20 . . . . . 223 C5
Redstart Rd TA20 . . . . . 223 C6
Redway TA24 . . . . . 124 A3
Red Way The BA12 . . . . . 144 F6
Redwing Dr BS22 . . . . . 31 F1
Red Wing Rd DT9 . . . . . 217 C2
Redwood Cl
Nailsea BS48 . . . . . 9 A2
Radstock BA3 . . . . . 97 E8
Redwood Ho BS13 . . . . . 22 D3
Redwood La BS48 . . . . . 20 C7
Redwood Rd BA21 . . . . . 219 E8
Reed Cl
Bridgwater TA6 . . . . . 208 F2
Chard TA20 . . . . . 223 D6
Watchet TA23 . . . . . 202 D6
Reedley Rd BS9 . . . . . 5 F5
Reedmoor Gdns TA6 . . . . 208 E7
Reeds Dr TA7 . . . . . 136 F4
Reed Way BS22 . . . . . 32 C3
Rees Way BS26 . . . . . 87 E7
Reeves Cl BS27 . . . . . 90 F2
Regal Rd BA4 . . . . . 205 B6
Regal Way 24 BA4 . . . . . 205 B6
Regency Cl TA8 . . . . . 85 A2
Regency Ct BA5 . . . . . 203 C4
Regency Wlk BA11 . . . . . 119 E4
Regent Ct BA22 . . . . . 173 E2
Regent Gn TA4 . . . . . 167 F1
Regent Mews TA20 . . . . . 223 C3
Regent St
Bradford On Tone TA4 . . . . 167 F1
Bristol BS8 . . . . . 226 A2
Burnham-on-S TA8 . . . . . 104 A7
Weston-super-Mare BS23 . . 48 E7
Regents The
Cotford St Luke TA4 . . . . . 167 E6
Keynsham BS31 . . . . . 24 F6
4 Yeovil BA21 . . . . . 218 C6
Regents Way TA24 . . . . . 200 E6
Regent Way TA6 . . . . . 209 A2
REGIL 37 F2
Regil La BS40 . . . . . 38 A6
Regil Rd BS40 . . . . . 37 F3
Regina The BA1 . . . . . 228 B3
Reid Ct BA5 . . . . . 203 B4
Remalard Ct BA7 . . . . . 214 B5
Rendcomb Cl BS22 . . . . . 31 B2
Rennison Ct BS23 . . . . . 48 E4
Reservoir La BA5 . . . . . 203 C6
Retford Ho BA2 . . . . . 45 E5
Retreat Cvn Pk The TA8 . . 85 A2
Retreat The
Foxcote BA3 . . . . . 79 E3
Frome BA11 . . . . . 120 B4
Taunton TA2 . . . . . 168 F6
Weston-super-Mare BS23 . . 30 C1
Reubens Ct BS22 . . . . . 31 F3
Rex Rd BA22 . . . . . 186 C2
Rex's La
Barwick BA22 . . . . . 197 F8
Yeovil BA22 . . . . . 219 C1
Rexton La TA4 . . . . . 150 F5
Reynald's Way
Butleigh BA6 . . . . . 157 C4
Street BA16 . . . . . 207 D1
Reynolds TA21 . . . . . 166 F2
Reynolds Cl BS31 . . . . . 25 A5
RHODE 153 D5
Rhode Cl BS31 . . . . . 25 A3
Rhode La TA6 . . . . . 208 E2
Rhodes Cl TA2 . . . . . 212 C7
Rhodyate BS40 . . . . . 54 D2
Rhodyate Hill BS49 . . . . . 34 F6
Rhodyate La BS49 . . . . . 35 A7
Rhodyate The BS29 . . . . . 51 C1
Rhydderch Way TA18 . . . 224 C5
Rhyll Gate Cross TA22 . . 162 E7
Rhymes Pl BA1 . . . . . 28 C3
Rhyne Bridge 9 TA6 . . . 209 A1
Rhyne Terr BS23 . . . . . 48 D2
Rhyne View BS48 . . . . . 8 B1
Richard Beadon Cl TA4 . . 210 B4
Richard Huish Coll TA1 . . 213 A2
Richards Cl
Wellington TA21 . . . . . 222 C8
Weston-super-Mare BS22 . . 32 B4
Richards Cres TA2 . . . . . 169 B6
Richmond Cl
Bath BA1 . . . . . 27 F1
Bridgwater TA6 . . . . . 208 F7
Keynsham BS31 . . . . . 24 D4
Minehead TA24 . . . . . 200 E6
Portishead BS20 . . . . . 2 E5
Sampford Peverell EX16 . . 178 D1
Sherborne DT9 . . . . . 225 C3
Richmond Ct BA22 . . . . . 173 E2
Richmond Gn
Nailsea BS48 . . . . . 8 F1
Sherborne DT9 . . . . . 225 C4
Taunton TA1 . . . . . 212 D5
Richmond Hill
Bath BA1 . . . . . 27 F1
Bristol BS8 . . . . . 226 B3
Richmond Hill Ave BS8 . . 226 B3
Richmond Ho
Crewkerne TA18 . . . . . 224 C6
9 Shepton Mallet BA4 . . . 205 B6
Yeovil BA20 . . . . . 219 A4
Richmond Hts
Bath BA1 . . . . . 27 F2
Bristol BS8 . . . . . 226 B3
Richmond La
Bath BA1 . . . . . 27 F1
Bristol BS8 . . . . . 226 B3
Richmond Mews BS8 . . . . 226 A3
Richmond Park Rd BS8 . . 226 A3
Richmond Pk TA1 . . . . . 212 C4
Richmond Pl BA1 . . . . . 27 F1
Richmond Rd
Bath BA1 . . . . . 27 F1
2 Frome BA11 . . . . . 119 E3
Sherborne DT9 . . . . . 225 C3
Taunton TA1 . . . . . 212 D5
Yeovil BA20 . . . . . 219 A4
Richmond St BS23 . . . . . 48 D7
Richmond Terr BS8 . . . . . 226 A3
Richmond Villas BA6 . . . . 206 E4
Richmond Way BA21 . . . . 218 C6
Rich's Farmhouse Cider Farm★ TA9 . . . . . 105 D3
RICH'S HOLFORD 151 C4
Ricketts La BS22 . . . . . 32 A2
RICKFORD 54 B3
Rickford La BS40 . . . . . 54 A3
Rickford Rd BS48 . . . . . 8 F1
Rickford Rise BS40 . . . . . 54 A3
Rickhayes BA9 . . . . . 216 B4
Rickhay Rise TA18 . . . . . 196 B8
Ricklands The BS40 . . . . . 38 A6
Ricksey Cl TA11 . . . . . 211 B3
Ricksey La TA11 . . . . . 211 B3
Ricksmead Dro TA7 . . . . 155 B2
Rickyard Rd BS40 . . . . . 35 E2
RIDGE 74 C5
Ridge Cl BS20 . . . . . 2 A4
Ridge Cres BS40 . . . . . 74 E6
Ridge Green Cl BA2 . . . . . 62 D8
Ridge Highway TA4 . . . . . 166 A3
Ridge Hill TA4 . . . . . 210 D5
Ridge La
Corton Denham DT9 . . . . . 175 D1
East Chinnock BA22 . . . . . 196 F8
East Coker BA22 . . . . . 197 A7
Pitcombe BA7, BA10 . . . . 215 A2
Ridge BS40 . . . . . 74 D5
Shepton Mallet BA4 . . . . . 205 B3
Ridgemead BA20 . . . . . 218 D2
Ridgemeade BS14 . . . . . 23 B4
Ridgemount Gdns BS14 . . 23 B5
Ridge Rd
Croscombe BA4, BA5 . . . . 204 D5
West Anstey TA22 . . . . . 162 D7
Ridge The
Bristol BS11 . . . . . 4 E7
Porlock TA24 . . . . . 124 B3
Poyntington DT9 . . . . . 188 F7
Yatton BS49 . . . . . 34 B8
Ridgeview BS41 . . . . . 11 B2
Ridgeview Ho BS20 . . . . . 2 E3
RIDGEWAY 143 C7
Ridgeway
Ashcott TA7 . . . . . 156 B8
Nailsea BS48 . . . . . 8 C1
Nunney BA11 . . . . . 143 C8
Sherborne DT9 . . . . . 225 B3
Ridgeway Ave BS23 . . . . . 48 E6
Ridgeway Cl BS40 . . . . . 74 E6
Ridgeway Ct BS14 . . . . . 23 C5
Ridgeway Gdns
Bristol BS14 . . . . . 23 C5
Glastonbury BA6 . . . . . 206 F5
Ridgeway La
Bristol BS14 . . . . . 23 B5
Moorlinch TA7 . . . . . 155 F7
North Cadbury BA22 . . . . 175 D6
Nunney BA11 . . . . . 143 C8
Shillingford EX16 . . . . . 164 D2
Stolford TA5 . . . . . 134 E8
Ridgeway Rd BS41 . . . . . 11 A2
Ridgeway The BS22 . . . . . 31 B2
Ridgewood BS9 . . . . . 5 D3
Ridgewood Cross EX15 . . 191 B8
Ridgewood La EX15 . . . . . 191 A8
Ridgway TA18 . . . . . 196 B8
Ridgway Cross EX36 . . . . 145 K1
RIDING GATE 177 B8
Ridings The BS13 . . . . . 21 E4
Ridley Cnr TA10 . . . . . 171 C5
Ridley Hill TA10 . . . . . 171 E8
Riec-Sur-Belon Way TA19 . . . . . 221 A4
Rigg La DT9 . . . . . 187 F5

Rigg Lane Cotts DT9 187 F5
Riggles Cross EX14 191 D3
RIMPTON 188 A8
Rimpton Hill BA22 188 A7
Rimpton Rd BA22 174 F1
Ringdown La EX15 180 F2
Ringolds Way BA16 207 B4
Ringspit La BS14, BS39 40 E8
Ring St DT10 190 B4
Ringstone TA9 136 B8
Ringswell Gdns BA1 28 B1
Ringwell BA2 81 E4
Ringwell Hill TA12 185 D4
Ringwell La BA2 81 E4
Ringwood Gr BS23 31 A1
Ringwood Rd
  Bath BA2 44 C5
  Bridgwater TA6 209 A2
Riphay Cross TA22 163 E3
Rippleside BS20 2 C5
Rippleside Rd BS21 6 E5
Ripple The BS21 8 D4
Risdale Rd BS3 11 F1
Risdon Rd TA23 202 C6
Risedale Cl TA6 208 C5
Risedale Rd BS25 70 A8
Risemoor Rd TA6 208 E2
Ritchie Rd BA22 218 A5
Rivendell BS22 32 A4
Riverbed Ho TA9 104 D3
River Dro TA7 155 E4
River La TA7 209 E1
Riverland Dr BS13 21 F5
Riverleaze
  Bristol BS9 5 C5
  Portishead BS20 1 F6
River Mead BS21 16 D8
River Pl BA2 44 B6
River Rd
  East Huntspill TA7 137 B8
  Mark TA9 106 D1
  Pawlett TA6 135 F5
  Portbury BS20 3 F8
Riversgate BS1 227 C2
RIVERSIDE
  Midsomer Norton 96 F7
  Wellington 222 B6
Riverside
  Banwell BS24, BS29 51 B5
  Bridgwater TA6 208 F6
  Burrowbridge TA7 154 F1
  Combwich TA5 135 C5
  Dinder BA5 140 D7
  Horton TA19 183 C2
  Meare BA5 138 F5
  Taunton TA1 212 E4
  Wellington TA21 222 B7
Riverside Cl
  Bridgwater TA6 208 F7
  Bristol BS11 4 F5
  Clevedon BS21 6 B1
  Midsomer Norton BA3 96 F7
  Weston-super-Mare BS22 32 C3
Riverside Cotts BA3 79 A2
Riverside Ct BA2 228 B1
Riverside Gdns
  Bath BA1 228 B2
  Dunster TA24 201 E3
  Midsomer Norton BA3 96 F7
Riverside Pl 2 TA1 212 F4
Riverside Rd
  Bath BA2 228 B2
  Midsomer Norton BA3 96 F7
Riverside Row TA24 124 A3
Riverside Terr BA11 119 F5
Riverside Wlk BA3 96 F7
Rivers Rd
  Bath BA1 28 A1
  Bath BA1 228 C4
  Yeovil BA21 219 D8
Rivers Reach BA11 120 A5
Rivers St BA1 228 B3
Rivers Street Mews BA1 228 B3
River St BS2 227 C3
River Street Pl 5 BA1 228 B3
River Terr BS31 24 F5
Riverton Rd TA7 136 B4
River View
  Bridgwater TA6 208 F6
  Combwich TA5 135 B5
  Exebridge TA22 163 F3
Riverway BS48 8 F3
River Wlk BS22 32 D2
Roachill Cross EX36 162 C1
Road Hill
  Alcombe SN13 29 E8
  Langford Budville TA4 166 B3
ROADWATER 131 C1
Roath Rd BS20 2 D5
Robbins Cl SN14 13 F8
Robert Blake Science Coll
  TA6 208 F3
Robert Ct BS8 11 D7
Roberts Dr TA6 209 A2
Roberts Rd TA2 168 A6
Robert St TA4 202 D2
Robin Cl
  Bristol BS14 23 D6
  Midsomer Norton BA3 97 B8
  Taunton TA1 212 B4
  Weston-super-Mare BS22 49 E8
Robin Dr BS24 49 E2
Robinia Wlk BS14 23 A7
Robin La BS21 6 D5
Robin Pl BS20 3 A6
Robins Ct
  Chard TA20 223 C5
  Frome BA11 119 D5
Robins Dr
  Bridgwater TA6 209 A6
  Burtle TA7 137 D6
Robins La
  Burtle TA7 137 C6
  Frome BA11 119 D5
  Shepton Beauchamp TA19 184 E4
Robinson Cl BS48 19 A5
Robinson Hts DT10 190 B4
Robinson Way BS48 19 A5
Rob-Lynne Ct BS25 69 F8
Roche Cl BA21 218 C7
Rochester Cl BS24 49 A1
Rochester Rd TA2 213 A8
Rochfort Ct BA1 45 B8
Rock Ave BS48 8 C2
Rock Cotts BS20 4 E4
Rockeries Dr BS25 69 F8
Rockeries The BS25 69 F8
Rockery Pk BA2 45 C2
Rocketts Cl TA3 169 D4
Rocketts Cotts TA3 169 C4
Rockfield Cotts TA21 179 F7
Rock Hall Cotts BA2 45 B1
Rockhall Ho 10 BS23 30 C1
Rock Hall Ho BA2 45 B1
Rock Hall La BA2 45 B1
Rock Hill TA3 170 C1
Rockhill Est BS31 24 F4
Rockingham Gdns BS11 5 A8
Rockingham Gr BS23 31 A1
Rock La
  Bath BA2 45 B1
  Exford TA24 128 D1
  West Bagborough TA4 151 E5
Rockleaze
  Bristol BS9 5 E2
  Evercreech BA4 141 E2
Rockleaze Ave BS9 5 E3
Rockleaze Ct BS9 5 E3
Rockleaze Mans 12 BS23 30 C1
Rockleaze Rd BS9 5 E3
Rockliffe Ave BA2 45 B8
Rockliffe Rd BA2 45 B8
Rock Rd
  Chilcompton BA3 96 D2
  Keynsham BS31 24 E5
  Midsomer Norton BA3 78 B2
  Yatton BS49 34 C7
Rock's Dro BA16 138 F3
Rocks La BS40 20 E1
Rocks St BA5 204 C7
Rocks The BA4 142 B7
Rock Terr BA3 116 F6
Rockway TA3 170 C1
Rockwell Gate TA21 222 B5
ROCKWELL GREEN 222 B5
Rockwell Green CE Prim Sch
  TA21 222 B5
Rocky Hill TA11 173 D5
Rocky La TA23 131 E2
Rodber Cl BA9 216 B4
Rodber Gdns BA9 216 B4
Roddenbury Cl BA11 120 B5
Roddenbury View BA12 144 D8
Rodden Rd BA11 120 A5
RODE 101 F8
Rode Hill
  Rode BA11 82 E1
  Southwick BA11 83 A1
Rode Methodist Fst Sch
  BA11 101 E8
Rodfords Mead BS14 23 A7
RODGROVE 177 C3
RODHUISH 131 B2
Rodhuish Cross TA24 131 B3
Rodhuish Hill La TA24 131 A3
Rod La TA19 183 F4
Rodmead La BA5 110 E4
Rodmead Wlk BS13 22 A4
Rodmoor Rd BS20 2 D6
Rodmore Cres BA4 141 E1
Rodmore Rd BA4 141 E1
Rodney BS24 49 A2
Rodney Ct BA22 218 A5
Rodney Ho BA2 44 A6
Rodney Pl BS8 226 A3
Rodney Rd
  Backwell BS48 19 A6
  Saltford BS31 25 E2
RODNEY STOKE 91 A1
Rodney Stoke National
  Nature Reserve* BS27 91 B2
RODWAY 135 B3
Rodway TA5 135 B3
Rodwell La TA13 184 E5
Roe Ave BA22 218 A5
Roebuck Cl BS22 32 B4
Roebuck Gate La TA4 151 B6
Roe Cl TA6 209 D4
Roe La BA22 188 B8
Roemead La BA3 114 C5
Roemead Rd BA3 114 C4
Rogers Cl
  Buckland Dinham BA11 100 A3
  Clutton BS39 58 E3
  North Petherton TA6 153 F3
Rogers Wlk TA4 167 E6
Roland Cl TA1 212 C2
ROLSTONE 32 F2
Roman Baths The* BA1 228 C2
Roman Ct BA21 219 D6
Roman Farm Rd BS4 22 E7
Roman Ho BA1 228 C4
Roman La TA6 208 C3
Roman Rd
  Batheaston BA1 29 C7
  Bleadon BS24 67 C8
  Sandford BS25 51 F4
  Taunton TA1 213 C5
Roman Villas BA4 205 E4
Roman Way
  Bristol BS9 5 C4
  Coleford BA3 116 F7
  Paulton BS39 77 C6
  Peasedown St John BA2 79 E7
  Watchet TA23 202 C7
Roman Way The BA6 206 C3
Romney Mead TA1 213 D4
Romney Rd 2 TA6 154 A5
Romsey Rd BA21 219 E8
Ron Jones Ho 3 BS1 227 B4
Rookery Cl
  Puriton TA7 136 C4
  Rooks Bridge BS26 87 A6
  Weston-super-Mare BS22 31 E3
Rookery La
  Croscombe BA5 204 B7
  Drimpton DT8 199 F6
Rookery Terr TA21 222 C5
Rookery The BA5 140 D7
Rookery Way BS14 22 F4
ROOKHAM 112 B5
Rook La BA11 119 F4
ROOKS BRIDGE 87 C5
Rooksbridge Rd BS24,
  BS26 87 B6
Rooksbridge Wlk BA2 44 B5
Rooks La BA11 120 E7
Rook's Meade La TA19 184 E1
ROOK'S NEST 150 C4
Room Hill Rd TA24 146 D7
Roper's La BS40 35 E3
Rope Walk Ho 23 BS2 227 C3
Ropewalk The TA20 223 B5
Rope Wk TA24 201 B7
Rope Wlk
  Backwell BS48 19 A5
  Bridgwater TA6 209 A5
  Coleford BA3 116 E8
  Evercreech BA4 141 E1
  14 Martock TA12 185 E6
  Wellington TA21 222 C4
Rope Wlk The TA23 202 C7
Roping Rd BA21 219 B6
Rosary Dr TA6 208 B4
Rosa Wy TA6 208 E1
Rosebank Rd TA4 167 A4
Roseberry Cotts BA3 117 A7
Roseberry Pl BA2 44 C6
Roseberry Rd BA2 44 C6
Roseberry Terr TA1 212 D5
Rosebery Ave
  Bridgwater TA6 209 B5
  Yeovil BA21 219 D6
Rosebery St TA2 212 E7
Rosebery Terr BS8 226 B2
Rose Cotts
  Taunton TA1 213 B3
  Weston-super-Mare BS22 32 C2
Rose & Crown Cotts BA3 116 F6
Rose Ct
  Keinton Mandeville TA11 158 A1
  Shepton Mallet BA4 205 B6
Rosedale Ave BS23 49 A7
Rose Dale Wlk BA11 119 F6
Rose Gdns BS22 32 B4
Rose Hill
  Bath BA1 28 C3
  Portishead BS20 2 C6
  Spaxton TA5 152 F2
Rose La
  Crewkerne, Misterton
  TA18 196 B3
  Crewkerne TA18 224 B6
  Purtington TA20 195 A3
Roseland Cl BA1 28 C3
Roselyn Cres DT9 189 A1
Rosemary Cres BS20 2 F5
Rosemary La
  Dulverton TA22 163 D6
  Freshford BA3 64 B4
ROSEMARY LANE 180 D1
Rosemarylane Cross
  EX15 180 D1
Rosemary St DT9 217 C2
Rose Meadow Vw BS3 11 E1
Rose Meare Gdns BS13 21 E7
Rose Mills Ind Est TA19 183 E2
Rosemont Terr BS8 226 A2
Rosemount La BA2 45 B4
Rosemount Rd BS48 20 B8
Roseneath Ave TA8 84 F4
Rose Terr
  Bath BA2 45 C2
  Bristol BS8 226 B3
Rose Tree Paddock TA8 84 F4
Rosette Cotts TA12 185 B7
Rosevean Cl TA6 209 D7
Rose Villas TA5 135 B2
Rosewarn Cl BA2 44 A4
Rosewell Ct BA1 228 B2
Rosewood Ave TA8 104 C6
Rosewood Cl TA8 104 C7
Rosewood Dr TA8 104 C6
Roslyn Ave BS22 31 C1
Rossendale Cl BS22 31 F3
Rosshayne La EX14 192 C2
Rossiter Grange 5 BS13 21 F4
Rossiter Rd BA2 228 C1
Rossiter's Hill BA11 119 F3
Rossiter's Rd BA11 119 E3
Rosslyn Cl 1 BA1 44 B7
Rosslyn Rd BA1 44 B7
ROTCOMBE 59 D2
Rotcombe La BS39 59 D2
Rotcombe Vale BS39 59 D2
Rotton Row TA4 210 C4
Roughmoor TA4 202 E4
Roughmoor Cl TA1 212 D5
Roughmoor Cotts TA1 212 D5
Roughmoor Cres TA1 212 D5
Roughmoor Ind Est TA4 202 E4
Roughmoor La BA5 110 C7
ROUNDHAM 195 D4
Roundhill Gr BA2 44 B3
Roundhill Pk BA2 44 A4
Roundmoor Cl BS31 25 D3
Roundmoor Gdns BS14 23 D7
Roundoak Gdns TA21 167 C2
Round Oak Gr BS27 90 A8
Round Oak Rd BS27 90 A8
Round Pool La TA4 151 B7
Roundwell Cl BA4 204 F6
Roundwell St TA13 220 C4
Rowacres
  Bath BA2 44 B3
  Bristol BS14 22 F6
Rowan Cl
  Nailsea BS48 9 A2
  Puriton TA7 136 C4
  Wincanton BA9 216 D2
Rowan Ct
  Frome BA11 120 B7
  Radstock BA3 78 E1
Rowan Dr
  Berrow TA8 84 F5
  Taunton TA1 213 D1
Rowan Ho BS13 22 D4
Rowan Pl BS24 32 B1
Rowans Cl TA6 209 C6
Rowans The BS20 2 B4
Rowan Way
  Churchill BS40 53 A5
  Yeovil BA20 218 F3
Rowan Wlk BS31 24 C4
Rowbarrow Hill
  Rimpton DT9 188 A7
  Trent DT9 187 F6
ROWBARTON 212 E7
Rowbarton Cl TA2 212 F7
ROWBERROW 53 A1
Rowberrow BS14 22 F7
Rowberrow La BS25 70 F8
Rowberrow Way BS48 8 E1
Rowcliffe Cotts TA21 178 F8
Rowdells Orch TA19 184 D1
Rowden Mill La DT10 189 F1
Rowdens Rd BA5 203 D3
Rowditch La TA5 133 D5
Rowe Cl TA21 222 A4
Rowe's Hill BA12 144 E4
ROWFORD 168 F6
Row La
  Keinton Mandeville TA11 158 A1
  Laverton BA2 100 D8
Rowlands Cl BA1 29 B2
Rowlands Rise TA7 136 C4
Rowley Rd BA6 206 E5
Rowls La BA9 177 E6
Rowmarsh La TA10 172 D5
Rownham Cl BS3 11 E4
Rownham Ct BS8 226 A1
Rownham Hill BS8 11 E6
Rownham Mead BS8 226 A1
Row Of Ashes La BS40 36 F4
Rows La EX16 164 A1
Rows The BS22 31 E2
Row The
  Hambridge TA10 184 D8
  Langport TA10 172 B3
Royal Ave BA1 228 B3
Royal Cl BA21 219 C6
Royal Cres* BA1 228 A3
Royal Cres BS23 48 D8
Royal Ct BS23 48 D4
Royal Dr TA6 136 B2
Royal Fort Rd BS2, BS8 226 C3
Royal High School Bath Jun
  Sch The BA1 27 D1
Royal High School Bath The
  BA1 27 F2
Royal Ho 4 BA4 205 B6
Royal National Hospl for
  Rheumatic Diseases
  BA1 228 B2
Royal Par
  Bristol BS8 226 B3
  Weston-super-Mare BS23 48 D8
Royal Park Mews BS8 226 A3
Royal Pk BS8 226 A3
Royal Portbury Dock Rd
  BS20 3 E5
Royal Prom BS8 226 B3
Royal Sands BS23 48 D4
Royal United Hospl BA1 44 B8
Royal West of England Acad
  BS8 226 B3
Royal York Cres BS8 11 F6
Royal York Ho 7 BS8 226 A2
Royal York Mews 6
  BS8 226 A2
Royal York Villas BS8 226 A2
Royces La TA19 184 C5
Roynon Way BS27 90 B7
Roys Pl TA2 213 F7
Royston Lodge BS23 48 D6
Royston Rd TA3 192 A7
ROYSTON WATER 192 B7
Rozel Ho 14 BS23 30 C1
Rubbery La TA11 158 D1
Rubens Cl BS31 25 A5
Ruborough Rd TA6 209 C4
Ruckley Ford BA3 80 A2
Ruddock Cl BA22 197 B8
Ruddock Way BA22 197 B8
Ruddymead BS21 6 D2
RUDGE 102 D5
Rudge Hill BA11 102 D5
Rudge La
  Beckington BA11 102 B6
  Standerwick BA11 102 D3
Rudge Rd BA11 102 B2
Rudgeway Rd BS39 77 E4
Rudgewood Cl BS13 22 D4
Rudgleigh Ave BS20 4 C4
Rudgleigh Rd BS20 4 C4
Rudhall Gn BS22 32 B3
Rudmore Pk BA1 44 A7
Rue La
  Alweston DT9 189 C2
  Hambridge TA3 184 B7
Ruett La BS39 77 B4
Rugg's Dro
  Chedzoy TA7 154 D7
  West Huntspill TA9 136 B7
Rugg's Hill TA22 148 E2
Rughill BS28 108 D8
Rugosa Dr TA8 84 F4
RUISHTON 169 C3
Ruishton CE Prim Sch
  TA3 169 C3
Ruishton La TA3 169 C3
Ruishton Lane Cotts TA3 169 C3
RUMWELL 168 B2
RUNNINGTON 179 F8
Runnymede Rd BA21 219 D8
Runway The BS24 49 C4
Rupert St
  Bristol BS1 227 A3
  Taunton TA2 212 E6
Rusham BS13 21 F4
Rush Ash La BA3 116 E8
Rushgrove Gdns BS39 57 C4
RUSH HILL 44 B2
Rush Hill
  Bath BA2 44 C2
  Farrington Gurney BS39 76 F3
Rush Hill La BS28 107 F3
Rushmoor BS21 6 A1
Rushmoor Gr BS48 19 A5
Rushmoor La BS48 19 A5
Rushway BS40 53 F4
Ruskin Cl TA1 213 C4
Ruskin Rd BA3 78 C1
Ruskway La TA10 184 C6
Russell Ave BS24 50 C5
Russell Cl BS40 38 A6
Russell Pl
  Bridgwater TA6 208 F6
  Milborne Port DT9 217 C3
Russell Pope Ave TA20 223 D2
Russell Rd
  Clevedon BS21 6 C3
  Locking BS24 50 C6
Russell's TA4 210 C4
Russell's Barton BA11 143 B8
Russell St BA1 228 B3
Russet Cl TA21 222 F7
Russets The BS20 2 F4
Russett Cl BS48 19 B6
Russett Gr BS48 18 C8
Russett Rd
  Street BA16 207 C4
  Taunton TA1 213 E5
Russet Way
  Peasedown St John BA2 79 D7
  Yeovil BA20 218 D2
Russ La BS21 16 E4
Russ St BS2 227 C2
Rusty Well BA20 218 F3
Rusty Well Pk BA20 218 F3
Ruthven Rd BS4 22 E8
Rutland Cl BS22 49 C8
Rutter's La TA19 221 B4
Ryalls Ct BA21 219 C5
Ryburn Cl TA1 213 D3
Rydal Ave BS24 50 A4
Rydal Rd BS23 48 F4
RYDON 169 E8
Rydon Cres TA5 135 C2
Rydon La
  Lopen TA13 185 A1
  South Petherton TA13 220 A5
  Taunton TA2 212 F8
Rye TA7 136 C4
Rye Cl BS13 21 E6
Ryecroft Ave BS22 31 E2
Ryecroft Rise BS41 11 B1
Ryefields Cl BA22 197 B8
Rye Gdns BA20 218 D2
Rye La TA7 155 C2
Ryelands Farm Ind Est
  TA21 222 B3
Ryeleaze BS11 4 E5
Ryepool TA4 167 F8
Ryesland Way TA3 169 D4
Rye Water La DT2 197 A1
Rylands BA11 101 E4
Rylands Cl TA4 202 D2
Rylestone Gr BS9 5 F5
Rysdale Rd BS9 5 F6

Sabrina Way BS9 . . . . 5 C4
Sackmore Gn DT10. . . . . . 190 F6
Sackmore La DT10 . . . . . . 190 F5
Saco Ho BS1. . . . . 227 B2
Sadborow La TA20 . . . . . . 199 B4
Sadborow Pound TA20 . . 199 B5
Sadbury Cl BS22 . . . . 32 B4
Sadler St BA5. . . . . 203 D4
Sadlier Cl BS11. . . . . 5 A8
Saffin Ho TA2 . . . . 213 F8
Saffron Cl TA1 . . . . 168 F1
Saffron Ct
  Bath BA1. . . . . 228 C4
  Sherborne DT9 . . . . 225 E4
Saffron Ho 10 BS23 . . . . . 48 E8
Saffrons The 7 BS22. . . . . 32 B4
Sage Cl BS20 . . . . 1 E4
Sage's La BA3 . . . . 94 D6
Sainsbury Cl TA24. . . . . . . 200 D7
Sainsbury Rd TA24 . . . . . . 200 D7
St Agnes Cl BS48. . . . . 9 A1
St Albans Pl TA2 . . . . 212 F8
St Aldhelm's CE Prim Sch
  BA4. . . . . 141 E6
St Aldhelm's Cl BA11. . . . . 119 D4
St Aldhelms Ct BA11 . . . . . 119 D4
St Aldhelm's Rd DT9 . . . . 225 D6
St Algars Yd BA11. . . . . . . 144 A4
St Andrew's CE Jun Sch
  Burnham-on-S TA8 . . . . 104 B7
  Congresbury BS49. . . . . . 34 C4
St Andrew's CE Prim Sch
  Bath BA1. . . . . 228 B4
  Chardstock EX13 . . . . . . 198 A7
  Taunton TA2 . . . . 212 F6
St Andrews Cl
  Castle Cary BA7. . . . . . . 214 B7
  Nailsea BS48. . . . . 9 A1
  Weston-super-Mare BS22 . . 31 F3
St Andrew's Cl
  Congresbury BS49. . . . . . 34 C4
  Curry Rivel TA10 . . . . . . 171 D4
  High Ham TA10 . . . . 156 A2
St Andrews Ct TA24 . . . . . 200 F7
St Andrew's Ct BA5 . . . . . 203 F5
St Andrews Dr EX13 . . . . . 198 A2
St Andrews La TA24 . . . . . 200 F7
St Andrews Mews 4
  BA5 . . . . 203 C3
St Andrew's Par 1 BS23 . . 48 F4
St Andrews Pk BA5 . . . . . 203 D3
St Andrews Rd
  Backwell BS48. . . . . 19 B5
  Cheddar BS27 . . . . 90 C7
  Yeovil BA20 . . . . 218 F5
St Andrew's Rd
  Burnham-on-S TA8 . . . . 104 B7
  Stogursey TA5 . . . . 134 C5
  6 Taunton TA2 . . . . 212 F6
St Andrew St BA5 . . . . . . 203 E4
St Andrew's Terr BA1 . . . . 228 B3
St Andrews View TA2 . . . . 212 F6
St Andrews Wlk 5 BA5. . . 203 C3
St Anne's Ave BS31 . . . . . . 24 D6
St Anne's CE Prim Sch
  BS24 . . . . 33 B5
St Anne's Cl BA5 . . . . 158 A5
St Anne's Ct BS31. . . . . 24 D6
St Anne's Gdns BA21 . . . . 218 E6
St Ann's Cl TA2 . . . . 212 E7
St Ann's Dr TA8 . . . . 85 A1
St Ann's Pl BA1 . . . . 228 B2
St Ann's Way BA2. . . . . 45 C6
St Anthony's Cl BA3. . . . . . 78 A2
St Antonys Sq 1 DT9 . . . . 225 D3
St Aubyn's Ave BS23 . . . . . 48 D2
St Audries Cl TA5 . . . . 134 C6
St Audries Ct TA23 . . . . . . 202 B7
*St Augustine of Canterbury
  Sch The TA2* 213 A7
St Augustines Ct 1 TA1. . 213 A4
St Augustine's Par BS1. . . 227 A4
St Augustine's Pl 1 BS1. . 227 A2
St Augustine St TA1. . . . . 213 A4
St Austell Cl BS48. . . . . 19 A8
St Austell Rd BS22 . . . . 49 B8
St Barnabas Cl BA3 . . . . . . 78 B3
St Bartholomew's CE Fst Sch
  TA18. . . . . 224 D5
St Benedict's CE Jun Sch
  BA6. . . . . 206 D4
St Benedict's Cl BA6 . . . . . 206 D4
St Benedict's RC Prim Sch
  BA3. . . . . 97 C7
St Bernadette RC Prim Sch
  BS14 . . . . 23 B6
St Bernadette RC Sch
  BS14 . . . . 23 B6
St Bernard's RC Prim Sch
  BS11 . . . . .4 E6
St Bernard's Rd BS11 . . . . . .4 E6
St Brides Cl BA6 . . . . 206 D5
St Bridges Cl BS22. . . . . . . 31 A6
St Bridges Ct BS22. . . . . . . 31 A6
St Bridget's Cl TA8. . . . . . . 65 F5
St Cadoc Ho BS31. . . . . . . 24 F5
ST CATHERINE 13 F1
St Catherine's Cl BA2 . . . . . 45 C6
St Catherine's Cres DT9 . 225 B3
St Catherine's Ct 10
  BA11. . . . . 119 E5
St Catherines Hill BA10. . 119 E5
St Catherine's Mead BS20 . 4 D3
St Catherine's Way DT9 . 225 B3

St Chad's Ave BA3 . . . . . . 78 A1
St Chad's Gn BA3 . . . . . . 97 A8
St Charles Cl BA3 . . . . 78 A2
St Christophers Cl BA2. . . 45 C8
St Christopher's Ct BS21. . . 6 C5
St Christopher's Way TA8 85 A2
ST CLEERS 211 C3
St Cleers TA11. . . . . 211 C3
St Cleer's Orch TA11 . . . . 211 C3
St Cleers Way TA11 . . . . . 211 C3
St Clements Ct
  Bath BA1. . . . . 27 C1
  Bristol BS2. . . . . 227 C4
  Clevedon BS21. . . . . 6 C4
  Keynsham BS31. . . . . 24 E4
  2 Weston-super-Mare
  BS22. . . . . 32 A2
St Clements Rd BS31. . . . . 24 F4
St Congars Wy BS49. . . . . 34 B4
St Cuthbert Ave BA5 . . . . 203 B5
St Cuthbert's CE Inf Sch
  BA5. . . . . 203 C3
St Cuthbert's Lodge 3
  BA5 . . . . 203 D4
St Cuthbert St BA5. . . . . . 203 D4
St Cuthbert's Villas BA5. . 203 A5
St Cuthbert Way BA5. . . . 203 B5
St Davids Cl EX13 . . . . . . 198 A2
St David's Cl
  Glastonbury BA6 . . . . . . 206 E4
  Taunton TA2. . . . . 213 A8
  Weston-super-Mare BS22 . 31 B2
St David's Cres BA21 . . . . 219 B7
St Davids Ct TA6. . . . . . . 209 D3
St David's Ct BS21. . . . . . . 16 E8
St David's Dr EX13 . . . . . 198 A2
St Davids Gdns TA2. . . . . 212 F8
St Davids Mews BS1 . . . . 226 C2
St Davids Pl BA10 . . . . . . 215 E7
ST DECUMANS 202 B6
St Decuman's Rd TA23 . . 202 C7
St Dubricius CE First Sch
  TA24. . . . . 124 A3
St Dunstans Cl
  Glastonbury BA6 . . . . . . 206 D5
  Keynsham BS31. . . . . 24 E6
St Dunstan's Com Sch
  BA6. . . . . 206 D5
St Dunstan's Pk BA6 . . . . 158 A5
St Edmund's Rd BA6 . . . . 206 D5
St Edmunds's Rd BA6 . . . 206 E5
St Edmund's Terr BA3. . . . 117 C7
St Edward's Cl TA7. . . . . . 137 B2
St Edward's Rd BS8. . . . . 226 B2
St Edyth's Rd BS9. . . . . 5 C6
St Elizabeth's Way TA13. 220 C4
SS Peter & Paul RC Cath*
  BS8. . . . . 226 A4
SS Peter & Paul RC Prim Sch
  BS8. . . . . 226 C4
St Francis Prim Sch BS48 . .8 F1
St Francis Rd BS31. . . . . . . 24 D6
St George CE Prim Sch
  BS1. . . . . 226 B2
ST GEORGES. 32 D3
St Georges Ave EX13 . . . . 198 A2
St George's Ave
  Taunton TA2 . . . . 212 F8
  Yeovil BA21 . . . . 219 B7
St Georges Bldgs BA1. . . 228 A3
St George's CE Sch, Bourton
  SP8. . . . . 161 E1
St George's Cl TA24. . . . . 201 D2
St George's Cross BA11 . . 101 E1
St Georges Ct BA6 . . . . . . 206 E5
St George's Hill
  Bath BA2. . . . . 45 D8
  Easton-in-G BS20. . . . . . . 4 A3
St George's Ho BS8 . . . . . 226 B2
St Georges La BS20 . . . . . . .4 B4
St Georges Mews TA1 . . . 212 F3
St Georges Pl BA1 . . . . . . 228 A3
St George's Pl TA1. . . . . . 212 F3
St Georges Prim Sch
  BS22. . . . . 32 D3
St George's RC Prim Sch
  TA1. . . . . 213 A3
St Georges Rd BS1. . . . . . 226 C2
St George's Rd
  Keynsham BS31. . . . . 24 D6
  Portbury BS20 . . . . 3 E7
St Georges Sq TA1. . . . . . 212 F3
St George's St TA24. . . . . 201 D2
St George's Way TA1 . . . . 212 E2
St Gildas TA20 . . . . 223 D4
St Gilda's Cl TA10 . . . . . . 172 A5
St Gildas Ct TA10 . . . . . . 172 A5
St Gildas Rd Prim Sch
  BA21. . . . . 219 B5
St Gilda's Way BA6 . . . . . 206 D4
St Gregory's CE Prim Sch
  DT10. . . . . 190 F5
St Gregory's RC Sch BA2 . 62 D8
St Helens BA22 . . . . 175 D8
St Hilary Cl BS9. . . . . 5 D5
St Ives Cl BS48. . . . . 9 A1
St Ives Rd BS23 . . . . 49 A5
St James' Barton BS1. . . . 227 B4
St James Cl TA1 . . . . 212 F4
St James Ct
  Bridgwater TA6 . . . . 209 D3
  4 Taunton TA1 . . . . 212 F4
St James Mews TA13. . . . . 220 C4
St James's Cl BA21. . . . . . 218 D5
St James's Par BA1 . . . . . 228 B2
St James's Pk
  Bath BA1. . . . . 228 B4
  Yeovil BA20 . . . . 218 C5

St James' Sq BA6 . . . . . . 157 D4
St James's Sq BA1 . . . . . . 228 A4
St James's St
  Bath BA1. . . . . 228 B4
  South Petherton TA13 . . . 220 C4
St James St
  Taunton TA1 . . . . 212 F4
  Weston-super-Mare BS23. . 48 D7
St James Terr BA22 . . . . . 197 A2
St John's BA1 . . . . 44 B8
*St John & St Francis CE Prim
  Sch TA6* 209 D4
St John's Ave BS31. . . . . . . 6 D3
St John's Bridge 4 BS1. 227 A3
St John's CE Fst Sch
  BA11. . . . . 119 F4
St John's CE Inf Sch BA6 206 E5
St John's CE Prim Sch
  Keynsham BS31. . . . . 24 E5
  Midsomer Norton BA3. . . . 78 A2
  Wellington TA21. . . . . . . 222 E6
St Johns Cl TA21. . . . . . . 222 E6
St John's Cl
  Peasedown St John BA2. . . 79 B7
  Skilgate TA4. . . . . 164 E6
  Weston-super-Mare BS23. . 30 D1
St John's Cres
  Midsomer Norton BA3. . . . 78 A2
  Trowbridge BA14. . . . . . . 83 F6
St Johns Ct
  Axbridge BS26. . . . . 70 B2
  Bath BA2. . . . . 228 C3
  Keynsham BS31. . . . . 24 E6
  Wells BA5 . . . . 203 D3
St Johns Ho 3 BA20 . . . . 219 B5
St John's Pl BA1 . . . . 228 B2
*St John's RC Prim Sch
  (Annexe) BA2*. 44 D4
St Johns Rd BA2 . . . . 60 B1
St John's Rd
  Backwell BS48. . . . . 19 B5
  Bath BA2. . . . . 44 D3
  Bath, Lower Weston BA1. . 44 C7
  Burnham-on-S TA8 . . . . 104 B7
  Clevedon BS21. . . . . 6 D3
  Frome BA11. . . . . 120 B5
  Taunton TA1. . . . . 212 E3
  Yeovil BA21 . . . . 219 D7
St Johns Ret Pk TA1 . . . 213 B5
St John's Sq BA6 . . . . 206 D5
St John St
  Bridgwater TA6 . . . . 209 B4
  Wells BA5 . . . . 203 D4
St John's Terr BA11. . . . . . 119 E3
St Johns Wlk BA6. . . . . . . 206 D5
*St John the Evangelist CE
  Prim Sch BS21*. 6 C1
*St Joseph & St Teresa RC
  Prim Sch BA5*. 203 D4
St Josephs Field TA1. . . . 213 A3
St Joseph's RC Prim Sch
  Bridgwater TA6 . . . . 208 D4
  Burnham-on-S TA8 . . . . 104 B6
  Portishead BS20 . . . . 2 D4
St Joseph's Rd BS23 . . . . . 30 E1
St Judes Ho 21 BS2 . . . . . 227 C3
St Jude's Terr BS2. . . . . . . 31 C1
St Julian's CE Prim Sch
  BA2. . . . . 62 E1
St Julian's Cl BS39. . . . . . . 77 E4
St Julian's Rd BA2 . . . . 79 F5
St Juthware Cl BA22 . . . . 197 C3
St Katherine's CE Prim Sch
  BS40 . . . . 37 A7
St Katherine's Sch BS20. . . 4 E3
St Kenya Ct BS31. . . . . 24 F5
St Keyna Prim Sch BS31. . 24 D5
St Keyna Rd BS31. . . . . 24 F5
St Kilda's Rd BA2 . . . . 44 D5
St Ladoc Rd BS31 . . . . 24 D6
St Laud Cl BS9. . . . . 5 D5
St Lawrence Ct BS11 . . . . . .4 E8
St Lawrence's CE Prim Sch
  BA5 . . . . 110 E6
St Leonards Ct BA20 . . . . 219 A4
St Loe Cl BS14 . . . . 22 F3
St Louis RC Prim Sch
  BA11. . . . . 119 E5
St Luke's Cl TA8 . . . . 104 B7
St Lukes Mews TA4 . . . . . 167 E6
St Luke's Rd BA11 . . . . . . 101 E5
St Luke's Rd
  Bath BA2. . . . . 44 F3
  Midsomer Norton BA3. . . . 77 F2
St Margarets Cl BS48. . . . . 19 A5
St Margaret's Cl BS31. . . . 24 D6
St Margarets Ct TA1 . . . . 213 B4
St Margaret's La TA20 . . . 198 C8
St Margaret's La BS48. . . . . 19 A5
St Margaret's Rd BA22 . . 186 B6
St Margaret's Sch BA22 . 186 C6
St Margaret's Terr BS23. . . 48 D8
St Mark's CE Sch BA1 . . . 28 B2
St Marks Cl
  Chedzoy TA7. . . . . 154 E8
  Keynsham BS31. . . . . 24 E6
St Marks Ct TA6. . . . . 209 D3
*St Mark's Ecumenical CE/
  Methodist Prim Sch*
  BS22. . . . . 31 F4
St Marks Gdns BA2. . . . . 228 C1
St Mark's Rd
  Bath BA2. . . . . 228 C1
  Burnham-on-S TA8 . . . . 104 B8
  Midsomer Norton BA3. . . . 78 A2
  Weston-super-Mare BS22. . 32 A3
St Martins
  Clevedon BS21. . . . . 6 C5

St Martins *continued*
  Long Ashton BS41. . . . . . 11 A1
St Martin's CE Prim Sch
  BS22. . . . . 31 D2
St Martin's Cl
  Fivehead TA3 . . . . 170 F1
  Zeals BA12. . . . . 161 F3
St Martins Ct BS22 . . . . . . 31 E3
St Martin's Ct BA2 . . . . . . 44 D4
St Martin's Garden Prim Sch
  BA2. . . . . 44 D1
St Martin's La SN14. . . . . . 13 F8
St Martin's Pk SN14. . . . . . 13 F8
St Martins Way BA2. . . . . 44 D4
St Mary CE Prim Sch BA2 45 C8
*St Mary Redcliffe & Temple
  CE Sch BS1*. 227 B1
*St Mary & St Peter's CE VC
  Prim Sch*
  Barrington TA19. . . . . . . 184 D5
  Ilton TA19 . . . . 183 E4
St Mary's Bldgs BA2. . . . 228 B1
St Mary's CE Prim Sch
  Bradford Abbas DT9 . . . . 187 E1
  Bridgwater TA6 . . . . 208 C4
  Radstock BA3 . . . . 79 C1
  Thorncombe TA20 . . . . . 199 B6
  Timsbury BA2 . . . . 60 C3
St Marys Cl
  Hutton BS24 . . . . 49 D2
  Seavington St Mary TA19. . 184 D1
  Wedmore BS28 . . . . 108 C3
St Mary's Cl
  10 Axminster EX13 . . . . 198 A1
  Bath BA2. . . . . 45 B6
  Chard TA20. . . . . 223 C2
  Cossington TA7 . . . . 136 F3
  Timsbury BA2 . . . . 60 B2
St Mary's Cres
  Chard TA20. . . . . 223 C3
  13 North Petherton TA6 . . 153 F4
  Yeovil BA21 . . . . 219 C8
St Marys Ct TA6. . . . . 153 E4
St Mary's Ct
  1 Bridgwater TA6. . . . . 208 F4
  Weston-super-Mare BS24. . 49 A1
St Mary's Gdns BS40 . . . . 53 B5
St Mary's Gr BS48. . . . . . . 18 C8
St Mary's La BA4. . . . . . . 140 E3
St Mary's Park Rd BS20 . . 2 C4
St Mary's Pk
  Langport TA10 . . . . 172 A5
  Nailsea BS48. . . . . 18 C8
St Marys Pl BA4. . . . . 142 F4
St Mary's Prim Sch BS26 . .3 E3
St Mary's RC Prim Sch
  Axminster EX13. . . . . . . 198 A1
  Bath BA1 . . . . 27 B1
St Mary's Rd
  Bristol BS11. . . . . 4 D7
  Burnham-on-S TA8 . . . . 104 B7
  Frome BA11. . . . . 120 B5
  Hutton BS24 . . . . 49 D2
  Leigh Woods BS8. . . . . . . 11 D6
  Meare BA6. . . . . 138 D4
  Oxenpill BA6 . . . . 138 C4
  Portishead BS20 . . . . 2 C4
  Sherborne DT9 . . . . 225 B3
  Westonzoyland TA7 . . . . 154 F5
St Marys Rise BA3 . . . . . . 79 C2
St Mary's St BS26. . . . . 70 C2
St Mary St
  Bridgwater TA6 . . . . 208 F4
  Nether Stowey TA5. . . . . 134 B2
St Mary's View BA22 . . . . 196 F7
St Mary's Wlk BS11 . . . . . . 4 D6
St Mathew's Pl BA2 . . . . . 45 B5
St Mathias Ho BS2 . . . . . 227 C3
St Matthew's Cl BS23 . . . . 30 D1
St Matthew's Field TA6. . 208 E4
St Matthews Gn TA6 . . . . 208 E4
St Matthew's Rd BS6. . . . 227 A4
St Matthias Pk BS2. . . . . . 227 C3
St Medard Rd BS28 . . . . . 108 C4
St Michael Cl TA3. . . . . . . 169 D4
*St Michael on the Mount CE
  Prim Sch BS2*. 226 C4
St Michael Rd BA3 . . . . . . 169 D4
St Michael's Ave
  Clevedon BS21. . . . . 6 D1
  Weston-super-Mare BS22. . 32 A3
  Yeovil BA21 . . . . 219 C7
St Michael's CE First Sch
  TA24 . . . . 200 F7
St Michael's CE Jun Sch
  BA2. . . . . 44 A6
St Michaels Cl
  Nether Compton DT9. . . . 187 F3
  Stoke St Michael BA3 . . . 116 B3
St Michael's Cl
  Buckland Dinham BA11. . . 100 A3
  Glastonbury BA6 . . . . . . 206 E3
  Nether Stowey TA5. . . . . 134 A2
St Michael's Cres TA2 . . . 213 A8
St Michaels Ct
  Bawdrip TA7. . . . . 136 E2
  Walton BA16 . . . . 156 D7
  Yeovil BA21 . . . . 219 C8
St Michael's Ct BA2. . . . . . 63 E8
St Michael's Gdns TA13 . 220 D5
St Michael's Hill
  Bristol BS2. . . . . 226 C4
  Milverton TA4. . . . . 167 A4
St Michael's Hospl BS2 . 226 C4
St Michael's Pk BS2. . . . . 226 C4
St Michael's Pl BA1 . . . . . 228 B2
St Michaels Rd BA2 . . . . . 44 A5

St Michael's Rd
  Bath BA1. . . . . 44 D7
  Burnham-on-S TA8. . . . . 104 B7
  Minehead TA24 . . . . 200 F8
  Yeovil BA21 . . . . 219 D6
St Michael's View TA15 . 186 B4
St Nicholas Almshouses 5
  BS1 . . . . 227 A2
St Nicholas CE Prim Sch
  Combe St Nicholas TA20 . . 193 D6
  Henstridge BA8. . . . . . . 190 A7
St Nicholas' CE Prim Sch
  BA3. . . . . 79 A2
*St Nicholas Chantry CE Prim
  Sch BS21*. 6 E3
St Nicholas Cl
  4 Henstridge BA8 . . . . 190 A6
  Winsley BA15. . . . . 64 D7
  Yeovil BA20 . . . . 219 B4
St Nicholas Ct BA2. . . . . . 28 C1
St Nicholas Pk BA20. . . . . 219 B4
St Nicholas Rd
  Bristol BS2. . . . . 227 C4
  Weston-super-Mare BS23. . 48 D2
  Whitchurch BS14. . . . . . . 23 C4
St Nicholas St BS1 . . . . . . 227 A2
St Nicholas Way BS48. . . . 18 D2
St Oswald's Ct BS13. . . . . . 22 A8
St Patricks Cl 3 TA2. . . . 213 A8
St Patricks Ct BS13. . . . . . 24 C5
St Patrick's Ct BA2. . . . . . 45 B6
St Patrick's Rd
  Taunton TA1. . . . . 213 A8
  Yeovil BA21 . . . . 218 D7
ST PAULS 227 C4
St Paul's CE Jun Sch
  BA4. . . . . 205 B5
St Pauls Cl TA13. . . . . 220 D4
St Paul's Cl DT9 . . . . 225 E6
St Pauls Ct TA6. . . . . 209 D3
St Paul's Flats DT9. . . . . . 225 E6
St Paul's Gn DT9. . . . . . . 225 E6
St Pauls Pl
  Bath BA1. . . . . 228 B2
  Midsomer Norton BA3. . . . 78 A2
St Paul's Rd
  Bristol BS8. . . . . 226 B4
  Burnham-on-S TA8. . . . . 104 B7
  Weston-super-Mare BS23. . 48 E5
St Paul St BS2 . . . . 227 B4
St Paul's Terr BA5 . . . . . . 111 A4
St Peter's Ave BS23 . . . . . 30 D1
St Peter's CE Fst Sch
  TA4. . . . . 202 D4
St Peters CE Prim Sch
  BS20. . . . . 2 D4
St Peter's CE Prim Sch
  BS13 . . . . 21 F6
St Peters Cl
  Ilton TA19 . . . . 183 F4
  Staple Fitzpaine TA3 . . . 182 C5
  Williton TA4 . . . . 202 D2
St Peter's Cl
  Horton TA19. . . . . 183 C1
  Taunton TA1. . . . . 213 B7
St Peters Ct TA6 . . . . 209 D3
St Peter's Ct BS8. . . . . . . 226 B2
St Peters Lodge BS20 . . . . 2 D4
St Peters Rd
  Portishead BS20 . . . . 2 D4
  Shepton Mallet BA4. . . . 205 A6
St Peter's Rd
  Burnham-on-S TA8. . . . . 104 B7
  Radstock BA3 . . . . 97 C8
St Peter's Rise
  Bristol BS13. . . . . 22 B7
  South Petherton TA13 . . 220 D4
St Peters Terr 21 BA4 . . . 205 B6
St Peter's Terr BA2. . . . . . . 44 D6
St Philip's CE Prim Sch
  BA2. . . . . 44 D2
St Philips Rd BS2 . . . . . . 227 C3
St Pius X RC Prim Sch
  BS13 . . . . 22 A5
St Quintin Pk TA2. . . . . . 213 E6
St Rayn Hill TA17 . . . . . . 195 B4
St Saviour's Ave TA6. . . . 209 A4
St Saviour's CE Inf Sch
  BA1. . . . . 28 B2
St Saviour's CE Jun Sch
  BA1. . . . . 28 B2
St Saviour's Rd BA1. . . . . 28 C2
St Saviour's Terr 10 BA1. . 28 B1
St Saviours Way BA1 . . . . 28 C1
St Stephen's Ave 3 BS1. 227 A2
St Stephen's CE Jun Sch
  BA1. . . . . 27 F1
St Stephen's Cl BA1. . . . . 228 B4
St Stephen's Ct BA1. . . . . 228 B4
St Stephen's Pl BA1 . . . . . 228 B4
St Stephen's Rd BA1 . . . . 228 B4
St Stephen's St BS1 . . . . . 227 A2
St Swithins Cl DT9 . . . . . 225 E4
St Swithin's Pl BA1 . . . . . 228 C4
St Swithin's Rd DT9 . . . . 225 E4
St Swithin's Yd BA1 . . . . 228 B4
St Thomas Cross BA21 . . 219 C5
St Thomas Ct TA6. . . . . . 209 D3
St Thomas' Ct BA5 . . . . . 203 F5
St Thomas Mews BA5 . . . 203 F5
St Thomas Pl BS1. . . . . . . 227 B2
St Thomas Rd BA3 . . . . . . 78 B2
St Thomas St E BS1. . . . . 227 B2
St Thomas St
  Bristol BS1. . . . . 227 B2

St Thomas St *continued*
Dunster TA24 201 E2
Wells BA5 203 E5
St Thomas Terr BA5 203 F5
St Vigor & St John CE Prim Sch BA3 96 E3
St Vincent's Rd BS8 226 A2
St Whytes Rd BS4 22 D8
St Winifreds Dr BA2 45 D2
Salcombe Gdns BS22 32 A2
Salcombe Rd BS4 23 A8
Salerno Cl BA22 173 E2
Sales Ho [15] BA4 205 B6
Salisbury Rd
Bath BA1 28 B2
Burnham-on-S TA8 104 C7
Paulton BS39 77 F4
Weston-super-Mare BS22 31 C1
Salisbury St TA2 212 E6
Salisbury Terr
Castle Cary BA7 214 B5
[4] Frome BA11 119 E3
Gurney Slade BA3 114 E8
Weston-super-Mare BS23 48 D7
Sally Hill BS20 2 E7
Sally In The Wood BA1, BA15 46 D6
Sally Lovell's La BA8 189 F8
Sally Lunn's Kitchen Mus★ BA1 228 C2
Sallysmead Cl BS13 22 B4
Salmon Par TA6 209 A4
SALTFORD 25 D2
Saltford CE Prim Sch BS31 25 E2
Saltford Ct BS31 25 E3
Salthouse Ct BS21 6 B2
Salthouse La BA20 219 A4
Salthouse Rd BS21 6 B2
Saltings Cl BS21 6 B2
Saltlands TA6 208 F7
Saltlands Ave TA6 208 F7
Saltlands Ho TA6 208 F7
Saltry La TA24 131 A6
Saltwell Ave BS14 23 C5
Salway Cl BS40 38 E1
Salway Gdns [11] EX13 198 A1
Samarate Way BA20 218 D4
Sambourne La BS20 4 C4
SAMPFORD ARUNDEL 179 E5
Sampford Arundel Com Prim Sch TA21 179 E5
SAMPFORD BRETT 202 E1
SAMPFORD MOOR 179 F5
SAMPFORD PEVERELL 178 E1
Sampford Peverell CE Prim Sch EX16 178 C1
Sampford Rocks TA4 202 F1
Sampsons Rd BS13 22 D4
Samuel Ct BA8 176 F1
Samuels Ct TA2 212 E6
Samways Cl BA22 218 B5
Sanctuary Gdns BS9 5 D3
Sanctuary La TA22 148 A2
SAND 108 C2
Sandalwood Ride TA6 153 F5
Sandbrook La BA22 175 D7
Sandburrows Rd BS13 21 F6
Sandburrows Wlk BS13 21 F6
Sandcroft BS14 22 F6
Sandcroft Ave BS23 48 D2
Sandene Cl TA2 212 C8
Sanderling BS20 2 F6
Sanderling Pl [7] BS20 2 F6
Sand Farm La BS22 31 A6
SANDFORD 52 A3
SANDFORD BATCH 51 F2
Sandford Cl [2] BS21 6 B1
Sandford Hill TA5, TA6 208 A6
SANDFORD ORCAS 188 C7
Sandford Orcas Manor Ho★ DT9 188 C8
Sandford Orcas Rd DT9 225 B7
Sandford Pk BA14 83 F7
Sandford Prim Sch BS25 52 B4
Sandford Rd
Bristol BS8 226 A1
Weston-super-Mare BS23 49 A7
Winscombe BS25 51 F1
Sandhill La TA24 131 C4
Sandhills Dr TA8 84 F4
Sandhurst Rd BA20 218 F1
Sanding's La
Chapel Leigh TA4 167 A8
Fitzhead TA4 166 F8
Lydeard St Lawrence TA4 151 A1
Sandlewood Cl BA21 219 E8
Sandmead Rd BS25 52 A4
Sandown Cl
Bridgwater TA6 209 A2
[3] Yeovil BA20 219 A5
Sandpiper Cl
Bridgwater TA6 209 A4
Minehead TA24 201 C5
Sandpiper Dr BS22 31 F1
Sandpiper Rd TA6 209 A4
Sandpits Rd BA6 206 F5
Sand Rd
Wedmore BS28 108 C3
Weston-super-Mare BS22 31 B5
Sandringham Cl TA6 209 C7
Sandringham Ct [2] BS23 48 F5
Sandringham Rd
[1] Weston-super-Mare BS23 48 F5
Sandringham Rd *continued*
Yeovil BA21 219 E6
Sandrocks La TA24 131 B3
Sandscross La BA11 100 A3
Sand St TA4 166 F4
Sandy Cl TA9 104 D4
Sandy Hole TA16 195 F7
Sandy La
Beckington BA11 101 E4
Cannington TA5 135 A3
Chew Magna BS40 39 C3
Easton-in-G BS8 10 A8
Failand BS8 10 C7
Stanton Drew BS39, BS40 39 E3
Wiveliscombe TA4 210 C7
Sandyleaze BS9 5 E7
Sandy's Hill La BA11 119 E1
Sandy's La EX14 191 F2
Sandys Moor TA4 210 D4
Sandy View BA11 101 E4
Sandyway Cross EX36 145 H4
Sansome's Hill DT9 217 D2
Sansom's Cross DT6 199 F1
Sarabeth Dr BA2 61 A4
Saracen St BA1 228 C3
Saunder's Piece La TA18 224 A7
Saunters Cl BA9 216 B4
Saunton Wlk BS4 22 E8
Savannah Dr [3] TA6 154 A5
Savernake Rd BS22 31 F3
Savery or Cottage Row TA1 213 B3
Saviano Way TA6 208 E7
Saville Cres BS22 49 C8
Saville Gate Cl BS9 5 F4
Saville Mews BS6 227 A4
Saville Pl BS8 226 A2
Saville Rd
Bristol BS9 5 F3
Weston-super-Mare BS22 49 C8
Saville Row BA1 228 B3
Savoy The BS11 4 E6
Saw Cl BA1 228 B2
Sawmill Cotts BA11 143 B8
Sawmill Gdns BA3 96 D3
Sawpit La BA6 140 C2
Sawpits Cl TA4 150 D8
Sawyers Cl
Chilcompton BA3 96 D3
Wraxall BS48 9 A2
Sawyers Ct BS21 6 E3
SAWYER'S HILL 180 E7
Sawyers Leigh TA2 168 D8
Sawyers Mill EX16 164 E2
Saxby Cl
Clevedon BS21 6 B1
Weston-super-Mare BS22 32 B4
Saxon Cl
Oake TA4 167 D4
Watchet TA23 202 B7
Saxon Ct
Ilminster TA19 221 B4
Weston-super-Mare BS22 32 D3
Saxondale Ave TA8 85 A3
Saxon Gn TA6 209 C4
Saxon Pl BS27 90 B7
Saxon Rd
Bridgwater TA6 209 C4
Weston-super-Mare BS22 49 C8
Saxon Ridge TA23 202 B7
Saxon St BS40 53 D6
Saxonvale BA11 119 F4
Saxon Way
Cheddar BS27 90 B6
Peasedown St John BA2 79 E8
Wedmore BS28 108 C4
Wincanton BA9 216 B3
Winsley BA15 64 F7
Saxony Pl [3] TA6 209 A1
Says La BS40 53 B4
Scadden's La BS27 91 B1
Scafell Cl
Taunton TA1 212 C1
Weston-super-Mare BS23 31 A1
Scamel Ho [11] BA4 205 B6
Scaurs The BS22 31 F2
School Cl
Bampton EX16 164 B1
Banwell BS29 51 B3
Bristol, Whitchurch BS14 22 F4
Tintinhull BA22 186 C6
Watchet TA23 202 C7
School Cotts
[13] East Coker BA22 197 F8
Enmore TA5 153 A5
Taunton TA2 168 F6
School Dr DT9 225 E5
School Fields
Cannington TA5 135 C2
[2] North Petherton TA6 153 F3
School Hill
Ashcott TA7 156 B8
Cucklington BA9 177 D6
Misterton TA18 224 F3
South Perrott DT8 196 C1
Westbury-sub-Mendip BA5 110 E6
Wookey Hole BA5 203 A8
SCHOOL HOUSE 199 A5
School La
Barrow Gurney BS48 20 D5
Batheaston BA1 28 F4
Blackford BS28 107 D4
Burrowbridge TA7 154 F1
Chew Stoke BS40 56 D8
Combwich TA5 135 B5
Compton Dundon TA11 157 A3
Doulting BA4 141 E6
Draycott BS27 90 F3
School La *continued*
Drimpton DT8 199 E6
Farrington Gurney BS39 77 A4
Horrington BA5 113 A1
Kilmersdon BA3 98 A6
Lopen TA13 185 A1
[7] North Petherton TA6 153 F4
Rowberrow BS25 53 A1
Seavington St Michael TA19 184 E2
Shapwick TA7 137 F1
Sherborne DT9 225 D3
Somerton TA11 211 E3
Tatworth TA20 198 C8
Templecombe BA8 176 E1
Wick St Lawrence BS22 32 B7
Woolavington TA7 136 E4
School of Christ the King RC Prim BS4 22 E8
School Rd
Kingsdon TA11 173 D5
Monkton Heathfield TA2 213 F8
Parbrook BA6 158 C7
Westonzoyland TA7 154 E5
Wrington BS40 35 E2
School St
Curry Rivel TA10 171 D4
Drayton TA10 171 E3
School View BS48 9 B1
Schooner Pl TA24 201 B7
Scimitar Rd BA22 218 B6
Scobell Rise BS39 59 C2
Score La BS40 54 E2
Score The BS40 54 E2
Scornfield La BS40 56 D7
Scotch Horn Cl BS48 8 F2
Scotch Horn Way [5] BS48 8 F2
Scot Cl TA6 135 F5
Scot Elm Dr
Weston-super-Mare BS24 32 D1
Weston-super-Mare BS29 50 D8
Scot La BS40 38 D1
Scotland La
Axbridge BS26 107 D8
Chapel Allerton BS26 107 D8
Rudge BA11 102 C4
Stockwood Vale BS4, BS14 24 A7
Scots Pine Ave [3] BS48 8 F2
Scott Cl TA2 212 C6
Scott Rd
Frome BA11 119 F5
Highbridge TA9 104 D3
Weston-super-Mare BS23 49 A4
Scotts Cl BA3 116 C8
Scott's Hill
Huish Champflower TA4 165 E8
Seavington St Mary TA19 184 D1
Scotts La TA7 137 D1
Scott's La
Baltonsborough BA6 158 A8
Wellington TA21 222 E6
Scotts Way TA18 196 B8
Scouse Cross EX13 198 E2
Scouse La EX13 198 E2
Scrapton La TA20 193 D5
Scruibbitts La TA7 137 B2
Scumbrum La BS39 59 C2
SEABOROUGH 195 E1
Seaborough View TA18 224 C4
Seabrook Rd BS22 31 D1
Sea King Rd BA20 218 D3
Sea La
Carhampton TA24 131 A7
Dunster TA24 201 F4
Kilve TA5 133 C6
Watchet TA23 132 D5
Sealey Cl BS27 90 F3
Sealey Cres BA5 112 E1
Sealeys Cl TA9 136 A8
SEA MILLS 5 B6
Sea Mills Inf Sch BS9 5 C7
Sea Mills La BS9 5 C5
Sea Mills Prim Sch BS9 5 B5
Sea Mills Sta BS9 5 B4
SeaQuarium★ BS23 48 D6
Searle Cres BS23 49 A6
Searle Ct
Clevedon BS21 6 E2
Somerton TA11 211 D3
Seat La BA4 142 D1
Seaton Ct BA20 219 A4
Seaton Rd BA20 218 F4
Seavale Mews BS21 6 C4
Seavale Rd BS21 6 C4
Seaview Rd
Portishead, Redcliffe Bay BS20 1 F4
Portishead, West Hill BS20 1 F6
Sea View Rd TA8 104 A8
SEAVINGTON ST MARY 184 D1
SEAVINGTON ST MICHAEL 184 F2
Seawalls BS9 5 D2
Seawalls Rd BS9 5 D2
Seaward Dr TA6 208 F6
Seaward Way TA24 201 C6
Second Ave
Axminster EX13 198 A2
Bath BA2 44 D5
Bristol BS14 23 B7
Radstock BA3 97 C7
Second Dro TA7 155 D3
Secret World Wildlife Rescue★ TA9 136 C8
SECTOR 198 B1
Sector Hill EX13 198 B1
Sector La EX13 198 A1
Sedge Cl TA6 208 F2
Sedge Dro TA7 137 C3
Sedge Mead BA11 119 F7
Sedgemoor Cl
Nailsea BS48 18 E8
Yeovil BA21 219 D7
Sedgemoor Dro
Sutton Mallet TA7 155 A6
Wrantage TA3 170 B2
Sedgemoor Hill Dr TA7 155 B7
Sedgemoor Manor Com Jun Sch TA6 209 C6
Sedgemoor Manor Inf Sch TA6 209 D5
Sedgemoor Rd
Bath BA2 44 F2
Bridgwater TA6 209 C3
Weston-super-Mare BS23 30 F1
Woolavington TA7 136 E3
Sedgemoor Way
Glastonbury BA6 206 D5
Woolavington TA7 136 E3
Sedgemount Ind Pk TA6 136 A2
Sedgewick Ho BS11 4 E7
Seeley Cres BA16 207 B3
Sefton Sq BS24 50 A8
Selbourne Cl BA1 44 A8
Selbourne Pl TA24 200 F6
Selbourne Rd BS23 48 E4
Selden Rd BS14 23 E5
Sellbed Cross TA24 146 A8
Selley Wlk BS13 22 A5
Selway Ct BA2 45 B2
Selwood TA20 223 C5
Selwood Acad BA11 120 B6
Selwood Cl BS22 49 C7
Selwood Cres BA11 120 A7
Selwood Rd
Frome BA11 119 E5
Glastonbury BA6 206 F6
Selwood St BA11 118 B7
SELWORTHY 124 D3
Selworthy Cl
Bridgwater TA6 208 F1
Keynsham BS31 24 D5
Selworthy Gdns [4] BS48 8 E1
Selworthy Ho BA2 44 F2
Selworthy Rd
Taunton TA2 213 B8
Weston-super-Mare BS23 49 A4
Selworthy Specl Sch TA2 213 A8
Selworthy Terr BA2 44 F2
Semington Cl TA1 213 D4
Septimus Bldgs BS14 22 D5
Serbert Cl BS20 2 E5
Serbert Rd BS20 2 E5
Serbert Way BS20 2 E5
Sercombe Pk BS21 6 E1
Serel Dr BA5 203 B3
Serenity Rise BA16 207 B5
Serlo Ct BS22 32 A4
Serotines The TA10 171 D8
Sevenacres TA11 211 C3
Seven Acres La BA1 28 F5
Seven Acres The [3] BS24 49 F7
SEVEN ASH 151 D4
Seven Dials BA1 228 B2
Seventh Ave BS14 23 A7
Seven Thorns EX35 122 D5
Severalls Park Ave TA18 224 C5
Severn Ave BS23 48 E5
Severn Cl TA6 209 D7
Severn Dr TA1 213 C4
Severn Gr TA8 104 B5
Severnleigh Gdns BS9 5 F3
Severnmeade BS20 1 F5
Severn Rd
Bristol BS11 4 D6
Pill BS20 4 C5
Portishead BS20 2 C5
Weston-super-Mare BS23 48 E5
Severn Terr TA23 202 C7
Severn Way BS31 25 A5
Sevier Rd BS26 68 C3
Seville Ct
Portishead BS20 2 E7
Taunton TA1 212 D2
Seville Rd BS20 2 E7
Seward Terr BA3 79 C2
Sewell Ho BS25 70 A8
Sexey's Hospl BA10 215 E6
Sexey's Hospl (Almshouses) BA10 215 E6
Sexey's Rd BS28 107 E4
Sexey's Sch BA10 215 D5
Seymour Cl
Clevedon BS21 6 E3
Wells BA5 203 C5
Weston-super-Mare BS22 31 F4
Seymour Rd
[5] Bath BA1 28 A1
Bridgwater TA6 209 D5
Street BA16 207 D4
Seymour St TA21 222 C6
Shackel Cross EX15 191 B8
Shadow Wlk BS24 50 C3
Shadwell Ct BA9 216 C4
Shadwell La BA9 216 C4
Shaftesbury Ave [2] BA1 44 C7
Shaftesbury Cl BS48 18 D8
Shaftesbury La BA9 177 B6
Shaftesbury Mews [7] BA2 44 D5
Shaftesbury Rd
Bath BA2 44 D5
Henstridge BA8 190 C8
Weston-super-Mare BS23 49 B8
Shaftesbury Terr BA3 79 A3
Shaftgate Ave BA4 205 A6
Shaft Rd BA2 45 E1
Shakespeare Ave
Bath BA2 44 F4
Taunton TA1 213 C3
Shakespeare Ct BS23 48 F2
Shakespeare Rd BA3 78 C1
Shaking Dro TA9 137 B6
SHALFORD 216 D8
Shalford La
Charlton Musgrove BA9 161 A2
Shalford BA9 216 D8
Shallows The BS31 25 F3
Shambles The TA3 170 B4
Sham Castle La BA2 45 C7
Shannon Wlk BS20 2 F6
Shapcott La EX36 162 C2
Shapcott Wood Hill EX36 162 A2
Shaplands BS9 5 F4
Shapway TA19 184 F3
Shapway Cross TA19 184 F3
Shapway La BA4 141 F2
Shapway Rd BA4 141 E2
SHAPWICK 137 F1
Shapwick Heath National Nature Reserve★ TA7 137 F4
Shapwick Hill TA7 155 F8
Shapwick Prep Sch TA7 137 D6
Shapwick Rd BA6 138 A4
Shapwick Right Dro TA7 155 C6
Shapwick Sch TA7 137 F1
Sharland Cl BS9 5 E3
Sharland Gr BS13 22 C4
Sharlands TA19 184 C5
Sharpenton La TA7 155 D6
Sharpham Dro BA16 138 E1
Sharpham La
Glastonbury BA16 138 D1
Stoke St Gregory TA3 170 E5
Sharpham Rd
Cheddar BS27 89 F7
Glastonbury BA6 206 F7
SHARPSTONE 64 A4
Shatterwell Cotts BA9 216 C4
Shatt La TA5 152 F3
Shatwell La
Castle Cary BA9 214 F1
Yarlington BA9 175 F8
Shaulders The TA2 213 C7
Shave Cross DT6 199 F1
Shave Hill SP8 177 D4
Shave La
Crewkerne TA18 224 A3
Donyatt TA19 183 D1
Horton TA19 183 C1
South Brewham BA10 161 A6
SHAWFORD 101 D7
Shawford La BA11 101 D7
Shaw Gdns BS14 23 A8
Shaw Path TA8 104 C6
Shaws Way BA2 43 F5
Sheafhayne Cross EX14 192 E4
Shearing Cross TA20 199 A5
Shearn La TA8 104 B7
Shearwater Cl TA6 209 D3
Shedrick Hill TA20 199 B8
Sheepfair La SN14 13 F8
Sheephouse Cvn Pk BS20 3 E7
Sheeplands La DT9 225 B5
Sheeplands The DT9 225 B5
Sheeps Croft BS13 22 A5
Sheepstealing La TA4 150 E5
SHEEPWAY 3 B5
Sheepway BS20 3 B5
Sheep Way TA19 184 E3
Sheepway La BS20 3 C5
Sheldon Cl BS21 6 F2
Sheldon Ct TA1 212 E4
Sheldon Dr BA5 203 C3
Sheldon Mill [3] BA5 203 C3
Sheldon's La TA22 163 A7
Shelduck Cl TA24 201 C5
Shelley Ave BS21 6 D2
Shelley Cl
Burnham-on-S TA8 85 A2
Yeovil BA21 218 D6
Shelley Dr TA8 85 B2
Shelley Gr TA1 213 B3
Shelley Rd
Bath BA2 44 F4
Radstock BA3 78 C1
Weston-super-Mare BS23 49 A4
Shell's La
Chard TA20 193 A3
Shepton Beauchamp TA19 184 E4
Shellthorn Gr TA6 208 F2
Shelthorn Hill TA5 152 F3
Shelway La TA19 184 C4
Shepherds Cl TA6 208 D6
Shepherd's Cl TA11 157 A4
Shepherd's Cnr TA23 131 E4
Shepherds Cross BA8 176 C5
Shepherd's Dro TA7 155 A3
Shepherd's Hay TA1 212 C2
Shepherd's Hill SP8 177 E4
Shepherd's La
Chard TA20 223 B4
Frome BA11 144 B7
Hemyock EX15 180 F1
Shepherds Way BS22 32 C2
Shepherd Wlk BA2 45 A1
Sheppard's Barton [11] BA11 119 E5
Sheppard's Cnr TA5 153 B5
Sheppards Gdns BA1 27 B1
Sheppards Wlk BA3 96 D3

Sheppy's Cider Farm Centre★ TA4 167 F1
Sheppy's Mill BS49 34 D5
Shepton BS24 49 A2
SHEPTON BEAUCHAMP 184 E3
Shepton Beauchamp CE Prim Sch TA19 184 E4
SHEPTON MALLET 205 D6
Shepton Mallet Com Hospl BA4 204 F6
Shepton Mallet Inf Sch BA4 205 C6
SHEPTON MONTAGUE 160 B2
Shepton Old Rd
Croscombe BA5 204 A6
Dinder BA5 140 D7
Shepton Rd BA4, BA5 204 D7
SHERBORNE
Litton 75 D3
Milborne Port 225 C6
Sherborne Abbey★ DT9 225 D3
Sherborne Abbey CE Prim Sch DT9 225 B2
Sherborne Castle★ DT9 225 F3
Sherborne Girls Sch DT9 225 C4
Sherborne Hill DT9 225 E1
Sherborne Mus★ DT9 225 D4
Sherborne Old Castle★ DT9 225 F4
Sherborne Prep Sch DT9 225 D3
Sherborne Prim Sch DT9 225 E5
Sherborne Rd
Milborne Port DT9 217 C2
Yenston BA8 189 E6
Yeovil BA21 219 D5
Sherborne Sch DT9 225 D4
SHERFORD 212 E1
Sherford Rd TA1 212 E1
Sherford Terr TA1 212 E1
Sheridan Cl TA6 209 D3
Sheridan Gdns BA14 83 F6
Sheridan Rd
Bath BA2 43 F5
Burnham-on-S TA8 104 C6
Sherlands 4 TA16 195 F7
Sherlands Gdns 3 TA16 195 F7
Sherring Rd BA4 205 D4
Sherrin Way BS13 21 E3
Sherston Cl BS48 9 A1
Shervage Ct TA6 209 C5
Sherwood Cl BS31 24 E5
Sherwood Cres BS22 31 F3
Sherwood Rd BS31 24 E5
Shetland Way BS48 9 A1
Shickle Gr BA2 44 D1
Shiller's La DT9 188 C7
SHILLINGFORD 164 E2
Shiners Elms BS49 34 B8
SHIPHAM 70 F7
Shipham CE Fst Sch BS25 70 E8
Shipham Cl
Bristol BS14 23 B5
Nailsea BS48 18 F8
Weston-super-Mare BS23 49 A7
Shipham La BS25 52 B1
Shipham Rd BS27 71 A3
Ship La
Bristol BS1 227 B1
Combwich TA5 135 B5
SHIPLATE 67 F6
Shiplate Rd BS24 67 E6
Shipney La DT10 190 C5
Shircombe La TA22 147 F2
Shire Gdns BS11 4 D8
SHIREHAMPTON 4 E7
Shirehampton Prim Sch BS11 4 D6
Shirehampton Rd BS9 5 C6
Shirehampton Sta BS11 4 D5
Shiremoor Hill TA16 195 F7
Shire St
Bridgwater TA6 209 A1
13 Bridgwater TA7 154 A5
Shires The TA24 201 C5
Shires Yd BA1 228 B3
SHOCKERWICK 29 F5
Shockerwick La BA1 29 D4
Shoe La
Paulton BS39 77 D6
Slape Cross TA7 209 E7
Shoot Hill TA17 195 C8
Shophouse Rd BA2 44 B5
Shop La
Pilton BA4 140 E3
Wingfield BA14 83 C6
Shopland Ho 8 BS21 6 C2
SHOPNOLLER 151 E3
SHOREDITCH 169 A1
Shoreditch BS40 56 C7
Shoreditch Rd
Stoke St Mary TA3 169 A1
Taunton TA1 213 B1
Shoredown La DT9, BA8 217 E6
Short Dro
Mudgley BS28 138 C7
Westbury-sub-Mendip BA5, BS27 110 B4
Short La
Draycott BS27 90 E3
Litton BA3 75 F2
Long Ashton BS41 11 A2
Stone Allerton BS26 88 C2
Shortland La BS28 108 C3
Shortmarsh La BA22 196 F4
SHORT STREET 121 F6
Short Way BS8 10 B4
Shortwood Rd BS13 22 E3
Shortwood Wlk BS13 22 E3
SHOSCOMBE 79 E6
Shoscombe CE Prim Sch BA2 79 F5
Shoscombe Gdns BA11 120 C7
SHOSCOMBE VALE 79 E5
Shovel La TA6 153 E3
Showell Pk TA2 212 B7
Showering Cl BS14 23 D5
Showering Rd BS14 23 D5
Showground Bsns Pk The TA6 209 B1
Showground Rd TA6 209 B1
Shrewsbury Bow BS24 50 A8
Shrewsbury Rd BA22 218 B7
Shrubbery Ave BS23 30 D1
Shrubbery Cl TA8 84 E8
Shrubbery Rd BS23 30 D1
Shrubbery Terr 11 BS23 30 C1
Shrubbery Wlk BS23 30 D1
Shrubbery Wlk W BS23 30 D1
Shudrick La TA19 221 C3
Shums Ct 3 BA1 228 C2
Shurtland La TA4 150 C3
SHURTON 134 C7
Shurton La TA5 134 C6
Shute La
Bruton BA10 215 D6
Huish Champflower TA4 165 C8
Long Sutton TA10 172 E4
Shute Lake La TA18 224 D5
Shuteleigh TA21 222 E5
Shutemead TA1 212 A4
Shute Row TA21 222 E5
Shuter Rd BS13 21 E5
Shute's La SP8 177 E4
Shutewater Cl TA1 212 A4
Shutewater Hill TA1 212 A4
Shutewater Orch TA1 212 A3
Shutgate Mdw TA4 202 D3
Shuttern 2 TA1 212 E3
Shuttern Bridge 3 TA1 212 E3
Shutwell La BA4 140 E3
Shyners Terr 8 TA16 195 F7
SIDBROOK 169 B6
SIDCOT 70 C7
Sidcot Dr BS25 70 A7
Sidcot La BS25 70 A7
Sidcot Sch BS25 70 B7
Sideland Cl BS14 23 E6
Sidelings The BS40 73 D8
Side Wood La EX36 162 A1
Sidings The DT10 190 C4
Sidmouth Cl TA8 104 C8
Sidney Hill Cottage Homes BS25 52 E4
SIGWELLS 175 E2
Silbury Rd BS3 11 E2
Silbury Rise BS31 25 A2
Silcox Rd BS13 22 C4
Silk Cl BA4 205 B7
Silk House Barton DT10 190 B4
Silklands Gr BS9 5 C6
Silk Mills La TA2 212 B6
Silk Mills Rd TA1 212 B4
Silton Rd 1 SP8 161 F1
Silverberry Rd BS22 32 A1
Silvercombe 1 BS23 48 E5
Silver Ct BS48 8 C2
Silverdale Cl
Brushford TA22 163 E4
Wembdon TA6 208 C5
Silverdown Hill TA4 150 C7
Silver La BA11 144 B7
Silverlake Cotts DT9 188 B2
Silverlow Rd BS48 8 D2
Silvermead TA24 201 B5
Silver Mead BS49 34 D2
Silvermead Ct TA24 201 B5
Silver Moor La BS29 50 F7
Silver Rd BA16 207 C5
Silver Springs TA19 184 E3
Silver St
11 Bampton EX16 164 B1
Barrington TA19 184 D5
Barton St David TA11 158 A3
Barwick BA22 197 F8
Bridgwater TA6 208 F4
Bristol BS1 227 A3
Bruton BA10 215 E6
Chard TA20 223 C3
Cheddar BS27 90 B8
Chew Magna BS40 39 B3
Congresbury BS49 34 D2
Crewkerne TA18 196 B3
Curry Mallet TA3 183 C8
Ditcheat BA4 159 C7
East Lambrook TA13 220 C8
Fivehead TA3 170 F1
Glastonbury BA6 206 E4
Holcombe BA3 97 C1
Huntspill TA9 136 A8
Ilminster TA19 221 B4
Kilmersdon BA3 98 B5
Kingsbury Episcopi TA12 185 B8
Kingsdon TA11 173 D5
Langport TA10 172 A3
Midsomer Norton BA3 97 A7
Milverton TA4 167 A4
Nailsea BS48 8 D2
Portishead BS20 1 F1
Shepton Beauchamp TA19 184 E3
South Petherton TA13 220 D5
Taunton TA1 213 A3
Wells BA5 203 E3
West Buckland TA21 180 F7
Silver St *continued*
Wincanton BA9 216 C4
Wiveliscombe TA4 210 C4
Wrington BS40 35 E2
Yeovil BA20 219 B5
Silverstone Way BS49 34 D3
SILVER STREET 180 F8
Simbriss Rd BA3 114 F5
Simmental St TA6 209 A1
Simmons Cl BA16 207 D5
SIMONSBATH 127 B2
SIMONSBURROW 180 C3
Simons Cl BS22 32 A2
Simon's Cl BS39 77 F5
Simons Mews
Chard TA20 223 E4
3 Weston-super-Mare BS23 48 F7
Simons Rd DT9 225 D5
Sinclair Ho BS8 226 A2
Singapore Rd BS23 48 E3
Singer Ct BA11 119 F5
Singer's Knoll BA11 119 F4
SINGLE HILL 80 A5
Single Hill BA2 79 F5
Singleton Ct BA5 203 C5
SION HILL 27 E1
Sion Hill
Bath BA1 27 E1
Bristol BS8 11 F7
Sion Hill Pl BA1 27 E1
Sion La BS8 11 F7
Sion Pl
Bath BA2 45 B6
Bristol BS8 11 F7
Sion Rd BA1 27 E1
Sir Bevil Grenville's Mon★ BA1 12 A1
Sir Gilbert Scott Ct TA4 202 E3
Sirius Wood BA2 44 B2
Siskin Wlk BS22 49 F8
Sisters The BA4 205 A6
Six Acres Cl TA1 213 C5
Sixpence BS39 59 D2
Six Streams BA1 27 B2
Sixteen Acre La TA20 193 D8
Sixth Ave BS14 23 A7
Sixty Acres Cl BS8 10 B4
Six Ways BS21 6 C4
SKILGATE 164 E6
Skillgate La TA14 185 E1
Skimmerton La TA5, TA6 208 A5
Skinner's Hill BA2 78 F7
Skinners La BS25 52 F4
Skinner's La TA14 185 F2
Skitmoor Dro BS28 109 C2
Skylark Ave BS21 1 B1
Slab Dro TA7 155 A1
Sladacre La BS40 54 E2
Sladebrook Ave BA2 44 C3
Sladebrook Ct BA2 44 C3
Sladebrook Rd BA2 44 B4
Slade Cl TA4 150 E8
Slade La
Barrow Gurney BS48 20 C4
Golsoncott TA23 131 E1
Hawkridge TA22 146 D1
Lympsham BS24 67 B1
Rimpton BA22 188 A7
Rooks Bridge BS26 87 E4
West Anstey EX36 162 B6
Slade Rd BS20 2 D5
Slade's Cross TA20 193 D7
Slades Ct 2 BS48 19 A6
Slades Hill BA8 176 E1
Slades Orch TA19 183 C1
Slade Way TA4 202 E4
Slait Hill BA4 142 C7
Slait La BA9 216 C7
SLAPE CROSS 209 F6
Slapes Cl TA2 168 F6
Slate La BS14, BS31 41 B7
Sleep La BS14 23 D3
Sleight Cl BA21 218 C6
Sleight La BA5 140 E8
Slingsby Gdns BS24 49 C4
Slippery Batch TA11 211 A6
Sloe Cl BS22 49 D8
Slopers La BA9 176 D5
SLOUGH GREEN 182 D7
Slough Green Cvn Pk TA3 182 D8
Slough Hill TA3 182 D6
Slough La
Cold Ashton SN14 12 F5
Crowcombe TA4 151 A8
North Wootton BA4 140 B3
Stoke St Gregory TA3 170 F6
Upottery EX14 191 F5
Sloway La TA6, TA9 136 A8
Slow Court La BA22 174 D3
Slowland La BA5 110 D8
Slugg Hill BA16 207 C3
Smallacombe Hill EX16, EX36 162 D4
Smallbrook La BS39 41 B6
Smallcombe Cl BA3 78 E5
Smallcombe Rd BA3 78 E4
Small Down End BS25 51 F2
Small Down La BA4 142 B2
Small La EX16 179 B2
Small Mead Dro BA6 157 F4
Smallmoor Chase BA16 156 E7
Smallmoor Dro TA7 155 C3
Small Moor La BA16 156 E7
Smallridge Rd EX13 198 A4
Smalls Mead 2 TA11 173 F7
Small St BS1 227 A3
SMALL WAY 214 B2
Smallway BS49 34 D5
Small Way La BA22 214 C1
Smallways La TA7 137 B3
Smallwood View BA3 96 E7
SMEATHARPE 191 E5
Smeathy La EX15 180 F3
Smeaton Rd BS1 11 F5
Sminhays Cnr TA23 149 B5
SMITHAM HILL 74 D2
Smithfield Rd BA16 207 B4
Smithick's La BA11 143 E6
Smithmead BS13 22 B5
Smiths Cl BS27 91 A1
Smith's Forge Ind Est BS49 16 F3
Smith's Hill TA18 196 C8
Smith's La BA4 159 C6
Smith's Row TA15 186 B4
Smith's Terr BA21 219 C6
Smith Way TA9 104 D3
Smithy TA1 212 B3
Smithyard La TA4, TA23 202 A3
Smithy La BA11 119 E4
Smokeham La TA4 151 D5
Smoky Hole La TA18 185 F1
Smurl La TA9 104 C1
Smythe Croft BS14 23 A3
Smythes Cross EX15 191 C7
Snagg La BA4 159 D5
Snag La BA9 216 E3
Snake La BS28 109 C1
Snakelake Hill BA10 160 C7
Snap Hill TA11 173 D8
Snathe Lea 4 TA4 167 F8
Snedden Gr TA1 213 B5
SNEYD PK 5 D3
Snipefield La BS28 108 A6
Snowberry Cl
Bridgwater TA6 208 E2
Weston-super-Mare BS22 32 A1
Snowberry Ct TA1 213 C2
Snowdon Cottage La TA20 223 B4
Snowdon Hts TA20 223 B4
Snowdon Vale BS23 31 A1
Snowdrop Cl BS22 32 A5
Snow Hill
Bath BA1 28 A1
Bath BA2 228 C4
Snow Hill Ho BA1 228 C4
Society Rd BA4 205 A6
SOCKETY 196 D1
Sock Hill BA21 187 C6
Sock La BA21 187 C6
Sock's La BA10 160 F8
SOHO 117 A5
Soho BA2 81 E5
Solomon's Hollow TA3 169 F2
Solon Ct BS13 21 F5
Solsbury Ct BA1 28 F3
Solsbury La BA1 28 F4
Solsbury View 11 BA1 28 A1
Solsbury Way BA1 28 A2
Somer Ave BA3 77 F2
Somer Cl BA3 96 F8
Somer Ct BA3 78 B1
SOMERDALE 24 E7
Somerdale Ave
Bath BA2 44 D2
Bristol BS4 22 F8
Weston-super-Mare BS22 49 C8
Somerdale Cl BS22 49 C8
Somerdale Rd BS31 24 F7
Somerdale Rd N BS30, BS31 24 F8
Somerdale View BA2 44 C2
Somer Ho BA3 78 A1
Somerhouse Orch BA6 206 E5
Somer Lea BA3 96 D5
Somerleaze Cl BA5 203 B3
Somer Rd BA3 77 F2
Somerset Ave
Taunton TA1 212 B2
Weston-super-Mare BS22, BS24 50 A8
Somerset Brick & Tile Mus★ TA6 209 A6
Somerset Bridge Prim Sch TA6 209 A1
Somerset Cl
Martock TA12 185 E7
Shepton Mallet BA4 205 C5
Somerset Coll of Arts & Tech TA1 212 D4
Somerset Ct BA21 219 A6
Somerset Cty Cricket Gd★ TA1 212 F4
Somerset Distillery The★ TA12 184 F7
Somerset & Dorset Joint Rly★ BA3 97 A8
Somerset & Dorset Rlwy Trust Mus★ TA23 131 E4
Somerset Fire HQ TA2 169 A7
Somerset Folly BA2 60 B2
Somerset Gdns TA6 209 C3
Somerset Ho
Bath BA2 44 D3
12 Bristol BS2 227 C3
Somerset La BA1 27 E1
Somerset Levels National Nature Reserve★ TA7 155 C6
Somerset Mews BS23 48 F6
Somerset Pl
Bath BA1 27 E1
Taunton TA1 213 B4
Yeovil BA20 219 A3
Somerset Rd
Bridgwater TA6 209 C3
Clevedon BS21 6 E3
Frome BA11 119 E4
Portishead BS20 1 F5
Somerset Rural Life Mus★ BA6 206 E4
Somerset Shire Horses★ TA7 156 C6
Somerset Sq
Bristol BS1 227 B1
3 Nailsea BS48 8 E2
Somerset St
Bath BA1 228 C1
Bristol BS1 227 B1
Bristol, Kingsdown BS2 227 A4
Somerset Way
Highbridge TA9 104 E3
Paulton BS39 77 E6
Somer's Hill BA11 117 D3
SOMERTON 211 D3
Somerton BS24 49 A2
Somerton Bsns Pk TA11 211 B5
Somerton Cl TA6 209 D4
Somerton Door Dro
Compton Dundon TA11 156 E1
Somerton TA11 211 A7
Somerton Dro TA11 156 E1
Somertonfield Rd TA11 172 E7
Somerton Gdns BA11 120 C7
Somerton Hill
Langport TA10 172 E7
Somerton TA11 211 A3
Somerton Inf Sch TA11 211 C4
SOMERTON RANDLE 173 C7
Somerton Rd
Clevedon BS21 6 E1
Langport TA10 172 A6
Street BA16 207 D4
Somervale Rd BA3 78 E2
Somervale Sch BA3 78 A1
Somerville Cl
Saltford BS31 25 E2
Shepton Mallet BA4 205 D4
Somerville Cotts BA5 204 B8
Somerville Rd
Sandford BS25 52 A4
Wells BA5 203 C5
Somerville Way TA6 209 D3
Soper Gdns BS4 22 D7
Sopers Field TA20 223 D2
Sophia Gdns BS22 32 B4
Sorrel Dr TA6 208 E1
Sorrel Gdns BS20 2 F5
Southampton Row 5 TA2 213 A8
South Ave
Bath BA2 44 D5
Highbridge TA9 104 C4
Portishead BS20 2 D6
Sherborne DT9 225 B2
SOUTHAY 185 B6
Southay Cross TA20 193 A4
Southay La TA20 192 F4
South Bank
Castle Cary BA7 214 B3
Wookey Hole BA5 203 A8
SOUTH BARROW 175 A6
Southbourne Gdns BA1 28 B1
Southbourne Ho TA6 208 E4
Southbourne Mans BA2 228 C2
South Brent Cl TA9 85 F3
SOUTH BREWHAM 161 A6
South Bristol Bsns Pk BS4 22 E7
South Bristol Com Hospl BS14 22 F5
South Bristol Trad Pk BS3 11 F3
Southbrook TA5 135 C2
Southbrook Cl TA5 135 C2
Southbrook Cotts BA9 216 F4
SOUTH CADBURY 175 C4
South Cary La BA7 214 A5
SOUTH CHARD 198 C8
SOUTH CHERITON 176 D3
South Cl
Draycott BS27 90 E2
Lympsham BS24 86 B8
Walton BA16 156 E7
South Combe BS24 67 B6
Southcombe Way BA22 186 B6
SOUTH COMMON 198 A4
South Common La EX13 198 A5
Southcot Pl BA2 228 C1
South Croft BS25 51 F2
Southcroft Dr BA13 121 D4
South Ct DT9 225 B3
South Dene BS9 5 E6
SOUTHDOWN 44 B4
SOUTH DOWN 191 F6
Southdown
Charlton Horethorne DT9 176 A1
Weston-super-Mare BS22 31 F4
Southdown Ave BA2 44 B3
Southdown Com Inf Sch BA2 44 B3
Southdown Cross EX16 179 B2
Southdown Jun Sch BA2 44 B3
Southdown Rd
Bath BA2 44 B4
Bristol BS9 5 F8
South Dro
Curry Rivel TA10 171 B4
North Curry TA3 170 D2

Southend Gdns TA9 . . . . **104** E5
Southend Rd BS23 . . . . **48** E4
Southernhay BS8 . . . . . **226** B2
Southernhay Ave BS8 . . **226** B2
Southernhay Cres BS8 . . **226** B2
Southern Lea Rd TA8. . . **104** C8
Southern Ring Path 4
　BS21 . . . . **.6** B1
Southern Way BS21 . . . . . **6** C1
South Espl TA8 . . . . **104** A5
Southey Rd BS21 . . . . **6** D2
SOUTHFIELD **79** A2
Southfield
　Cheddar BS27 . . . . **90** B8
　Norton St Philip BA2 . . . **81** F4
　Radstock BA3 . . . . **79** A2
　Southwick BA14 . . . . **83** F2
　Wiveliscombe TA4 . . . . . **210** C3
Southfield Cl
　Nailsea BS48 . . . . **8** E3
　Taunton TA2 . . . . **168** E8
　Weston-super-Mare BS23 . . **48** D2
　Woolavington TA7 . . . . . **136** E3
Southfield Rd Trad Est
　BS48 . . . . **8** F3
Southfield Farm Cvn Pk &
　Camp Site TA8 . . . . **65** F4
Southfield Hill BA3. . . . . **99** A6
Southfield Rd
　Nailsea BS48 . . . . **.8** F3
　Shepton Mallet BA4. . . . . **205** A5
Southfield Rd Trad Est
　BS48 . . . . **8** F3
Southfields
　Frome BA11. . . . . **120** A2
　Ilminster TA19 . . . . **183** E2
South Fields BA6 . . . . . . **206** E3
Southgate
　Bath BA1 . . . . **228** C2
　Frome BA11. . . . . **120** D7
　Wiveliscombe TA4 . . . . . **210** C3
Southgate Ave TA6. . . . . **209** A3
Southgate Dr BA9. . . . . . **216** C3
Southgate Rd BA9 . . . . . **216** C3
Southgate Sh Ctr BA1. . . **228** C2
South Gr BS20 . . . . **4** C4
South Green St 8 BS8 . . **11** F6
South Harp TA13. . . . . . . **220** E1
South Hele Cross EX16 . . **165** C1
SOUTH HILL **211** A1
South Hill BS25 . . . . **51** F2
South La
　Challacombe EX31. . . . . . **126** A3
　Nether Stowey TA5 . . . . . **134** B2
Southlands
　Bath BA1 . . . . **27** B1
　Carhampton TA24. . . . . . **131** B5
Southlands Dr BA2. . . . . . **60** B2
Southlands Way BS49 . . . **34** E5
South Lawn BS24 . . . . **49** F4
South Lawn Cl BS24. . . . . **49** F4
South Lea Rd BA1 . . . . . . **44** A8
Southleaze BS25. . . . . **70** A6
Southleaze Orch BA16. . **207** C6
Southleaze Rd BA16. . . . **207** B6
Southleigh BS25 . . . . **69** F8
Southleigh Rd
　Bristol BS8. . . . . **226** B4
　Taunton TA1 . . . . **213** B3
SOUTHMARSH **161** B1
South Mdw BA5. . . . . **113** A1
South Mdws BS40. . . . . . . **35** E2
Southmead
　West Camel BA22 . . . . . . **174** D3
　Winscombe BS25. . . . . . . **70** A8
Southmead Cres TA18. . . **224** C5
Southmead La BA8. . . . . **190** A6
Southmead Rd BS22 . . . . **49** B7
Southmead Terr TA18. . . **224** C5
South Molton Rd EX16 . . **164** B1
South Moors La TA7 . . . . **137** B2
Southover BA5. . . . . **203** D3
Southover Rd BS39. . . . . . **59** D1
South Par
　Bath BA2 . . . . **228** C2
　Chew Magna BS40. . . . . . **39** B3
　Frome BA11. . . . . **119** E4
　Weston-super-Mare BS23 . . **48** D8
South Parade Cotts BA2. . **45** C1
SOUTH PERROTT **196** C1
SOUTH PETHERTON **220** C4
South Petherton Com Hospl
　TA13. . . . . **220** D5
South Petherton Inf Sch
　TA13. . . . . **220** C4
South Petherton Jun Sch
　TA13. . . . . **220** D3
South Pk TA24. . . . . **200** D6
South Rd
　Brean TA8 . . . . **65** F3
　Lympsham BS24. . . . . **67** B1
　Midsomer Norton BA3. . . . **78** B1
　Portishead BS20 . . . . **2** D7
　Taunton TA1. . . . . **213** A2
　Timsbury BA2 . . . . **60** B2
　Watchet TA23. . . . . **202** C6
　Weston-super-Mare BS23 . . **30** C1
Southridge Hts BS24 . . . . **67** A8
South Road Villas BA9 . . **216** C3
South Rock Ind Est BA3 . . **96** D1
Southside BS23 . . . . **48** E8
South Side BS49 . . . . **34** E5
Southside Cl BS9 . . . . **.5** B8
Southside Cres BS22 . . . . **31** A4
South St
　Burnham-on-S TA8. . . . . **104** A6
　Castle Cary BA7. . . . . . . **214** B4

South St continued
　Crewkerne TA18. . . . . . . **224** D5
　Hinton St George TA17 . . **195** D7
　Holcombe Rogus TA21 . . **178** F5
　Kington Magna SP8. . . . . **177** E1
　Milborne Port DT9. . . . . **217** D2
　Montacute TA15. . . . . . . **186** B3
　Sherborne DT9 . . . . **225** E3
　South Petherton TA13 . . **220** D4
　Stratton-on-f BA3. . . . . . **96** F2
　Taunton TA1. . . . . **213** A3
　Walton BA16 . . . . **156** E7
　Wellington TA21. . . . . . . **222** E5
　Wells BA5 . . . . **203** D4
　West Camel BA22 . . . . . . **174** D3
　Wincanton BA9 . . . . **216** C3
　Wiveliscombe TA4 . . . . . **210** C4
　Yeovil BA20 . . . . **219** B4
SOUTHSTOKE **62** E7
Southstoke La BA2. . . . . . **62** F8
Southstoke Rd BA2. . . . . . **44** F1
South Terr
　Burnham-on-S TA8. . . . . **104** B6
　Weston-super-Mare BS23 . . **48** D8
SOUTHTOWN **183** C3
Southtown La BA6. . . . . . **158** B8
SOUTH TWERTON **44** C5
Southview TA3 . . . . **168** D1
South View
　12 Barwick BA22. . . . . . . **197** F8
　Bawdrip TA7. . . . . **136** C2
　Bradford Abbas DT9 . . . . **187** E1
　Broadway TA19 . . . . **183** C2
　Clandown BA3 . . . . **78** E5
　Ditcheat BA4 . . . . **159** C6
　Horrington BA5. . . . . **113** A1
　Lynford-on-f TA11 . . . . . **158** C1
　Monkton Combe BA2. . . . **45** E1
　Paulton BS39. . . . . **77** E6
　Portishead BS20 . . . . **2** D7
　Queen Camel BA22 . . . . . **174** F3
　Timsbury BA2 . . . . **60** B2
　Westleigh EX16 . . . . **179** A3
Southview Cl
　Hutton BS24 . . . . **49** E2
　Westonzoyland TA7 . . . . **154** F5
South View Pl BA3. . . . . . **78** B2
Southview Rd TA7 . . . . . **154** F5
South View Rd
　Bath BA2 . . . . **44** D6
　Milborne Port DT9. . . . . **217** C3
South View Terr
　Taunton TA3 . . . . **168** D1
　Yatton BS49 . . . . **17** B1
South Villas TA4 . . . . . . **167** F6
Southville BA21. . . . . **219** C5
Southville Rd BS23. . . . . . **48** E4
Southville Terr BA2 . . . . . **45** B4
SOUTHWAY **139** D5
Southway Cl BA21. . . . . . **218** F6
Southway Cres BA21 . . . . **218** F6
Southway Ct BS21 . . . . . . **6** D1
Southway Dr BA21 . . . . . **218** F6
Southwell TA3. . . . . **168** D1
Southwell Cl TA3 . . . . . . **168** D1
Southwell Cres TA9 . . . . **104** E3
Southwell Ct TA9 . . . . . . **104** E3
Southwell St BS2 . . . . . . **226** C4
South Western Bsns Pk
　DT9. . . . . **225** D3
South Western Terr
　BA20 . . . . **219** C4
SOUTHWICK
　Trowbridge **83** F2
　Watchfield **105** C2
Southwick CE Prim Sch
　BA14. . . . . **83** F3
Southwick Ctry Pk★ BA14 **83** F5
Southwick Rd TA9 . . . . . **106** C1
SOUTH WIDCOMBE **75** C6
Southwood BA4 . . . . **159** D8
Southwood Ave BS9. . . . . . **5** C8
Southwood Dr BS9. . . . . . **.5** B8
Southwood Dr E BS9 . . . . . **5** C8
Southwood Gr TA1. . . . . **212** C2
Southwoods BA20. . . . . . **219** A3
Southwood Way TA3 . . . **181** C5
Sovereign Rd TA6. . . . . . **209** D7
Sovereign Sh Ctr BS23 . . . **48** D8
Sowden Hill TA5 . . . . . . **134** D4
Spanish Hill TA6. . . . . . . **153** F2
Spargrove La BA4. . . . . . **142** B1
SPARKFORD **175** A5
Sparkford Hill La BA22. . **175** A4
Sparkford Rd BA22. . . . . **175** A6
Sparkhayes La TA24. . . . **124** A3
Sparks Way TA9 . . . . **104** D3
Sparrow Hill Way BS26. . . **88** E6
Sparrow La
　Portbury Wharf BS20. . . . . **3** A6
　Withypool TA24. . . . . . . **146** C7
Sparrow Rd BA21 . . . . . . **219** B6
Spartley Dr BS13. . . . . . . **21** F6
Spartley Wlk BS13 . . . . . . **21** F6
SPAXTON **152** E8
Spaxton CE Prim Sch
　TA5. . . . . **152** E7
Spaxton Cl TA8 . . . . **104** C8
Spaxton Rd TA5. . . . . **153** C7
Spearcey Cl TA3 . . . . **181** D8
Spearcey La TA3 . . . . **181** D8
Spearhay La TA20. . . . . . **198** F5
Spear Mead DT8 . . . . **199** F7
Spears La TA4 . . . . **166** A4
Specket La DT8. . . . . **199** E5
SPECKINGTON **174** C2
Speckington La BA22. . . **174** B2
Specklemead BS39. . . . . . **77** D5

Speedwell Ind Est 1 BS21 **6** C2
Speke Cl
　Ilminster TA19 . . . . **221** B4
　Merriott TA16. . . . . **195** F7
　Staplegrove TA2. . . . . . . **212** B6
Speke Ct TA19 . . . . **221** B4
Spencer Ave TA2 . . . . . . **212** E6
Spencer Cl TA6. . . . . **209** D3
Spencer Dr
　Midsomer Norton BA3. . . . **78** A2
　Weston-super-Mare BS22. . **32** B3
Spencer Ho 6 BS1. . . . . **227** B1
Spencer Rd BA4 . . . . **205** C3
Spencers Belle Vue BA1. . **228** B1
Sperring Ct BA3 . . . . **96** F8
Sperry Cross TA4 . . . . . . **149** B1
Spicer Way TA20. . . . . . . **223** D2
SPIKE ISLAND. **226** B1
Spike Island★ BS3 . . . . . **226** B1
Spillers Cl TA6. . . . . **208** E2
Spindleberry Cl BS48 . . . . **9** A2
Spiningmill Cotts 3
　BA11. . . . . **119** E5
Spinners End BS22. . . . . . **32** B4
Spinners Ho 5 BA4. . . . . **205** B6
Spinney Croft BS13 . . . . . **21** F5
Spinneyfield TA4 . . . . . . **167** F7
Spinney Rd BS24. . . . . . . **50** D4
Spinney The
　Ashcott TA7 . . . . **156** A8
　Portishead BS20 . . . . **2** C4
　Taunton TA1. . . . . **212** D8
　Weston-super-Mare BS24 . . **48** F1
　Yeovil BA20 . . . . **218** D2
Spire Cross TA24. . . . . . . **147** A4
SPLATT **152** E8
Splatt La TA5 . . . . **152** E8
Splott BS26. . . . . **88** F6
Spoonbill Rd TA6 . . . . . . **209** B4
Spratts Bridge BS40. . . . . **39** A3
Sprigg Dr BS20 . . . . **1** F1
Springbok Cl BA16. . . . . **207** D7
Spring Cres BA2. . . . . . . **228** C2
Springer's Hill BA3. . . . . **116** E6
Springfield
　Ilminster TA19 . . . . **221** B2
　Norton St Philip BA2. . . . . **81** E4
　Peasedown St John BA2 . . **79** C7
　Street BA16. . . . . **207** B5
Springfield Ave
　Bridgwater TA6 . . . . **208** C3
　Bristol, Shirehampton BS11 . . **4** D6
　Weston-super-Mare BS22 . . **31** D1
Springfield Bldgs
　Midsomer Norton BS39. . . . **77** D2
　Radstock BA3 . . . . **79** A3
Springfield Cl
　Bath BA1 . . . . **44** B5
　Cheddar BS27 . . . . **90** A8
　Cross BS26 . . . . **69** F2
Springfield Cotts
　Upton Cheyney BS30. . . . **26** A8
　Winsford TA24. . . . . **147** A6
Springfield Cres BA3. . . . . **79** A3
Spring Field Cres DT9. . . **225** C3
Springfield Ct BA4 . . . . . **205** A5
Springfield Dr BS28. . . . . **108** C3
Springfield Flats TA20. . **223** C4
Springfield Gdns BS29 . . . **51** A3
Springfield Ho
　Bristol BS6. . . . . **226** C4
　Portishead BS20 . . . . **2** C4
Springfield Hts BA3 . . . . . **78** E4
Springfield Lawn BS11 . . . . **4** D6
Springfield Pl
　Bath BA1 . . . . **27** F1
　Clandown BA3 . . . . **78** E4
　Yeovil BA21 . . . . **218** E7
Springfield Rd
　Cheddar BS27 . . . . **90** A8
　3 Highbridge TA9. . . . . **104** E4
　Highbridge TA9. . . . . . . **104** E4
　Milborne Port DT9. . . . . **217** D3
　Pill BS20 . . . . **4** C4
　Portishead BS20 . . . . **2** B5
　Wellington TA21. . . . . . . **222** C7
　Wincanton BA9 . . . . **216** B4
　Yeovil BA21 . . . . **218** E7
Springfields
　East Chinnock BA22. . . . **196** E8
　Stalbridge DT10. . . . . . . **190** C4
Springfield Terr
　Street BA16. . . . . **207** B5
　Tatworth TA20. . . . . **198** D8
SPRING GARDENS **119** D8
Spring Gardens Rd BA2 . . **228** C2
Spring Gdns
　Minehead TA24 . . . . **201** B5
　Wiveliscombe TA4 . . . . . **210** C5
Spring Ground Rd BS39 . . **77** E5
Spring Hill
　Bristol BS2. . . . . **227** A4
　Weston-super-Mare BS22 . . **31** D2
Springhill Cl BS39. . . . . . **77** C6
Spring Hill Dr BS22 . . . . . **31** E1
Spring La
　Bath BA1 . . . . **28** B2
　Dundry BS41 . . . . **22** A1
　Sandford Orcas DT9 . . . . **188** C7
Springley Rd TA6. . . . . . **209** D6
Springmead BA20. . . . . . **223** B3
Springmead Sch BA11 . . . **101** E4
Spring Rd BA11 . . . . **119** F6
Spring Rise
　Portishead BS20 . . . . **2** C3
　Puriton TA7 . . . . **136** C4
　Wells BA5 . . . . **203** C3

Spring Terr
　Frome BA11. . . . . **119** D2
　Weston-super-Mare BS22. . **31** C2
Spring Vale BA1 . . . . **28** B2
Spring Valley BA1. . . . . . . **27** F2
Springway Ind Est TA7 . . **155** A5
Spring Wood Gdns BS24. . **49** E3
Spruce Way
　Bath BA2 . . . . **62** E8
　Weston-super-Mare BS22. . **49** E8
Spurwells TA19 . . . . **183** F4
Squares Rd TA5 . . . . **135** F2
Square The
　Axbridge BS26 . . . . **70** C2
　Banwell BS29. . . . . **51** B3
　Bath BA2 . . . . **228** B1
　Edington TA7 . . . . **137** C2
　Maiden Bradley BA12 . . . **144** C2
　Shipham BS25 . . . . **70** E7
　Taunton TA1. . . . . **213** C2
　Temple Cloud BS39 . . . . . **58** E1
　Wellow BA2 . . . . **62** D1
　Westbury-sub-Mendip BA5 **110** E6
　Winscombe BS25. . . . . . . **69** E6
　Wiveliscombe TA4 . . . . . **210** C4
　Woolavington TA7 . . . . . **136** E4
Squibbs Cl TA6. . . . . **209** D5
Squibbs Ho TA6. . . . . . . **208** F5
Squire La BS40 . . . . **55** C1
Squirrel Ct TA21 . . . . . . **222** D5
Stabbins Cl BS22. . . . . . . **32** B5
Stables The BA3 . . . . **98** B5
Stable Yd BA2. . . . . **44** D6
Stacey's Ct TA10. . . . . . . **171** F5
Staddlestones BA3. . . . . . **96** F7
Staddonhill Rd TA24 . . . **146** F8
Stafford Pl BS23 . . . . **48** E8
Stafford Rd
　Bridgwater TA6 . . . . **209** C3
　Portishead BS20 . . . . **2** E4
　Weston-super-Mare BS23 . . **48** F7
STAFFORD'S GREEN **188** D8
Stagman La TA7, BA16 . . **156** C8
Stag Mill Cross EX16 . . . **178** B3
Stag Way BA6 . . . . **206** C4
Stainer Cl BS4 . . . . **22** D7
Staker's Cross TA20 . . . . **195** B2
Staker's Cross La TA18,
　TA20 . . . . **195** B2
STALBRIDGE. **190** C4
Stalbridge Cl DT10 . . . . . **190** B4
Stalbridge La
　Marnhull DT10. . . . . **190** F2
　Sturminster Newton DT10. **190** F1
Stalbridge Pk DT10 . . . . **190** A4
Stalbridge Prim Sch
　DT10. . . . . **190** B5
Stalbridge Rd
　Henstridge BA8 . . . . **190** A6
　Stalbridge Weston DT10. **190** A3
　Stourton Caundle DT10 . . **189** F2
STALBRIDGE WESTON . . **190** A3
Stalcombe La BA2 . . . . . . **42** B4
Staling Way BA4 . . . . . . **205** C4
Stallards TA21 . . . . **222** C3
STALLEN **188** A3
Stallgrove La BA16. . . . . **207** D3
Stall St BA1. . . . . **228** C2
Stalls The BA12 . . . . **144** D7
Stambrook Pk BA1. . . . . . **29** A5
Stammery Hill EX13 . . . . **198** C1
Stanchester Com Sch
　TA14. . . . . **186** A4
Stanchester Way TA10 . . **171** D4
Stancombe La
　Flax Bourton BS48. . . . . . **19** E7
　Westbury-sub-Mendip BA5 **110** F8
Standards Rd TA7. . . . . . **154** E5
Standards The TA7. . . . . **137** D2
STANDERWICK **102** C2
Standerwick Cross BA11 **102** B2
Standerwick Orch TA19 . **183** C2
Standfast Pl TA2. . . . . . . **213** C8
Standhill Rd TA10. . . . . . **155** F2
Standish Ct TA1. . . . . . . **212** F4
Standish St TA6. . . . . **208** F7
Stane Way BS11 . . . . **4** C7
Stanford Pl BS4. . . . . **22** D7
Stanhope Pl BA1. . . . . . . **228** A2
Stanhope Rd BS23 . . . . . . **48** E3
Stanier Cl BA11 . . . . **120** D6
Stanier Rd BA2 . . . . **228** A2
Stankley View TA19 . . . . **184** F4
Stanley Cl
　Bridgwater TA6 . . . . **208** F2
　Staplegrove TA2. . . . . . . **212** C6
Stanley Ct BA3. . . . . **78** B2
Stanley Gr BS23 . . . . **48** F7
Stanley Rd 2 BS23. . . . . . **48** F7
Stanley Rd W BA2. . . . . . . **44** D5
Stanley Terr BA3. . . . . . . **79** A3
Stanley Villas 12 BA1. . . . **28** A1
Stanmoor Rd TA7 . . . . . . **170** F8
Stanshalls Cl BS40. . . . . . **37** C8
Stanshalls Dr BS40. . . . . . **37** C8
Stanshalls La BS40. . . . . . **37** C8
STANTON DREW **39** F2
Stanton Drew Prim Sch
　BS39. . . . . **40** A2
Stanton Drew Stone Circles★
　BS39. . . . . **40** A3
Stanton La BS39. . . . . **40** D4
STANTON PRIOR **42** E2
Stanton Rd BS40. . . . . **39** B3
STANTON WICK **58** D8
Stanton Wick La BS39. . . . **40** B1
Stant Way TA20. . . . . . . **193** C6

Stanway Cl
　Bath BA2 . . . . **44** D1
　Taunton TA2 . . . . **212** D7
Staple Cl TA4 . . . . **132** E4
Staplecombe Vineyard★
　TA2. . . . . **168** C6
STAPLE FITZPAINE **182** C5
Staplegate EX16 . . . . **178** A3
Staple Gr BS31. . . . . **24** D5
STAPLEGROVE **212** C8
Staplegrove CE Prim Sch
　TA2 . . . . **212** C7
Staplegrove Manor TA2 . **212** D8
Staplegrove Rd
　Staplegrove TA2. . . . . . . **212** C7
　Taunton TA1, TA2. . . . . . **212** E5
STAPLEHAY **181** D8
Staple Hill TA3. . . . . **182** C5
Staple La TA4. . . . . **132** E4
STAPLE LAWNS **182** B5
Staples Cl BS21. . . . . **6** E1
Staples Gn BS22 . . . . **32** B3
Staples Hill BA3. . . . . **64** C4
Staples Mdw TA20 . . . . . **198** D8
STAPLETON **185** E8
Stapleton Cl TA12. . . . . . **185** E7
Stapleton Cross TA12 . . . **185** E7
Stapleton Rd TA12 . . . . . **185** E7
STAPLEY **191** D8
Stapley Cross TA3 . . . . . **181** B1
Stapling La TA24. . . . . . . **130** F3
STAR **52** D1
Starcross Rd BS22 . . . . . . **32** A2
Star La BS20. . . . . **4** D4
Starling Cl BS22 . . . . **49** E8
Starrs Cl BS26. . . . . **70** B2
Stars La BA20. . . . . **219** C4
Statham Cl
　Cheddar BS27 . . . . **90** B7
　Taunton TA1. . . . . **212** D1
Statham Gr TA1. . . . . **212** C2
STATHE **171** B8
Stathe Cotts TA7. . . . . . . **171** B7
Stathe Rd TA7 . . . . **171** A8
Station App
　Bristol BS1. . . . . **227** C1
　Frome BA11. . . . . **120** A4
　Ilminster TA19 . . . . **183** E1
　Pensford BS39. . . . . **40** D5
　Weston-super-Mare BS23 . . **48** E7
Station Cl
　Backwell BS48. . . . . **18** F7
　Congresbury BS49. . . . . . **34** C4
Station Lodge 8 BS23 . . . **48** E7
Station Mead BA3. . . . . . . **96** D3
Station Path TA11. . . . . . **211** D3
Station Rd
　Ashcott TA7 . . . . **156** B8
　Axbridge BS26 . . . . **70** C2
　Backwell BS48. . . . . **19** A6
　Bampton EX16. . . . . **164** B1
　Bath BA1 . . . . **28** F2
　Bath BA1 . . . . **44** C7
　Binegar BA3 . . . . **114** D7
　Bishops Lydeard TA4 . . . **167** E8
　Blagdon BS40 . . . . **54** E3
　Bristol, Shirehampton BS11 . . **4** D5
　Bristol, Shirehampton BS11 . . **4** E6
　Bruton BA10 . . . . **215** F6
　Burlescombe EX16. . . . . **179** B3
　Burnham-on-S TA9. . . . . **85** F3
　Burtle TA7 . . . . **137** D6
　Castle Cary BA7. . . . . . . **214** B6
　Chard Junction TA20 . . . **198** D8
　Cheddar BS27 . . . . **90** B7
　Clevedon BS21. . . . . **6** D3
　Clutton BS39 . . . . **58** E3
　Congresbury BS49. . . . . . **34** C4
　Cossington TA7 . . . . **136** F3
　Draycott BS27 . . . . **90** E2
　Dunster TA24. . . . . **201** E4
　Flax Bourton BS48. . . . . . **20** A8
　Freshford BA3. . . . . **64** C5
　Hatch Beauchamp TA3 . . **183** A7
　Ilminster TA19 . . . . **221** A4
　Keynsham BS31. . . . . **24** E6
　Meare TA7 . . . . **138** C1
　Midsomer Norton BA3. . . . **78** B2
　Milborne Port DT9. . . . . **217** D4
　Milverton TA4. . . . . **167** A5
　Misterton TA18 . . . . **224** E4
　Nailsea BS48. . . . . **8** F2
　Norton Fitzwarren TA2. . **168** B4
　Pill BS20 . . . . **4** C4
　Portbury BS20. . . . . **3** D3
　Portishead BS20 . . . . **2** D6
　Sandford BS25. . . . . **51** F4
　Shapwick TA7. . . . . **137** F2
　Shepton Mallet BA4. . . . **205** B5
　Sherborne DT9 . . . . **225** E3
　Stalbridge DT10. . . . . . . **190** B4
　Stogumber TA4 . . . . **150** D8
　Taunton TA1. . . . . **212** F5
　Templecombe BA8. . . . . **176** E1
　Walpole TA6. . . . . **136** B3
　Wanstrow BA4. . . . . **142** F4
　Washford TA23 . . . . **131** E4
　Wellington TA21. . . . . . . **222** C7
　Wellow BA2 . . . . **62** D1
　Westbury-sub-Mendip BA5 **110** E5
　Weston-super-Mare BS23 . . **48** E7
　Weston-super-Mare, St Georges
　BS22. . . . . **32** D2
　Weston-super-Mare, Worle
　BS22. . . . . **31** F2
　Williton TA4. . . . . **202** E3
　Wincanton BA9 . . . . **216** C3
　Wiveliscombe TA4 . . . . . **210** C4

Sta–Sun 269

Station Rd *continued*
Wrington BS40 35 D2
Yatton BS49 17 B1
Station Rd (Blackmoor La)
BA8 190 A7
Station Rd Ind Est BA10 215 F6
Station Road Bsns Pk
DT10 190 B5
Station Terr TA24 201 A7
Station Vw BA3 96 F8
Station Way BA4 141 E1
Station Wlk TA9 104 E3
Staundle La TA3 183 B8
Staunton Fields BS14 23 C4
Staunton La
Minehead TA24 201 A4
Whitchurch BS14 23 D3
Staunton Rd TA24 201 A5
Staunton Rise TA24 201 A5
Staunton Way BS14 23 D4
Stavordale Gr BS14 23 B6
STAWELL 137 A1
Stawell Rd TA7 137 B1
STAWLEY 166 A1
Stawley Prim Sch TA21 179 B8
Steamalong TA3 183 E7
Steam Mills BA3 96 F8
Steam Packet Terr 2
TA6 209 B4
STEANBOW 140 D2
Steanbow Cotts BA4 140 D3
STEART
Babcary 174 C6
Combwich 135 D8
Steart Ave TA8 104 B6
Steart Cl TA8 104 B6
Steart Cotts TA3 169 C3
Steart Ct TA8 104 A7
Steart Dr TA8 104 A6
Steart Dro TA10 156 D1
Steart Gdns TA8 104 B6
Steart Hill BA22 174 D5
Steart La
Babcary TA11 174 B6
Wheddon Cross TA24 129 F3
Stedhams Cl TA21 222 D7
Steeds Terr BA3 115 D6
Steel La TA7 137 D2
Steel Mills BS31 24 F4
Steel's La BA9 161 D2
Steel Well La BA8 190 A6
Steep La TA22 164 C8
Steeple View BA3 116 A3
Steep The TA24 147 C5
Steevens Ho (Almshouses)
13 BS2 227 C3
STEMBRIDGE 185 A7
Stembridge Rd TA10 156 B1
Stembridge Tower Mill★
TA10 156 B1
Stembridge Way TA2 168 B4
Stephen's Hill TA10 172 E4
Stephenson Dr BA11 120 D6
Stephenson Rd TA24 201 B6
Stephen St TA1 213 A4
Stephen Way 6 TA1 213 A4
Steppes Cres 13 TA12 185 E6
Steppes Mdw TA12 185 E6
Steps La BA2 100 E7
Stert Dro TA5 135 B7
Steven's Cl BA4 205 A5
Stevens La
Frome BA11 119 F3
Lympsham BS24 67 C3
Stewart Ct EX13 198 A2
Steway La BA1 29 B6
STEWLEY 183 B5
Stibbear La TA19 194 A8
Stiby Ct BA21 218 F7
Stiby Rd BA21 218 E7
Stickland BS21 6 C1
Stickleball La BA4, BA6 140 D1
Stickle Hill TA4 151 B7
STICKLEPATH
Combe St Nicholas 193 D7
Monksilver 149 E7
Stickle Path EX16 165 C1
STICKLINCH 140 C1
Sticklinch Rd BA6 140 C2
Stilemead La BS40 55 D1
Stiles Ct BA5 203 B4
STILEWAY 138 E3
Stileway BA6 138 E4
Stileway Bsns Pk BS21 16 B8
Stiling Cl TA9 104 D4
Stillingfleet Rd BS13 22 C5
Stillington Cl BA5 203 B3
Stillman Cl BS13 21 E4
Stirling Way
Frome BA11 120 C6
Keynsham BS31 24 E4
Stirtingale Ave BA2 44 C3
Stirtingale Rd BA2 44 C3
Stitching La BS28 138 C8
Stitchings La BA2 61 D7
Stitchings Shord La BS39 57 C4
Stoate Cl TA23 202 C5
Stoberry Ave BA5 203 E5
Stoberry Cres BA5 203 E5
Stoberry Park Sch BA5 203 E5
STOCK 53 B8
Stockbridge TA17 195 D7
Stockbridge La BA6 140 B2
Stockditch Rd TA12 185 B7
Stockers Cl TA4 210 B4
Stockham Cross TA4 151 D5
Stockham Hill TA22 163 E8
Stock Hill BA3 115 B8
Stockhill Cl BA3 96 C3
Stock Hill Ct BA3 117 B7
Stockhill Rd BA3 96 C2
Stock La
Buckhorn Weston SP8 177 F5
Lower Langford BS40 53 A7
STOCKLAND BRISTOL 135 A6
Stockland Hill EX14 192 A1
Stockland Manor TA5 134 F6
STOCKLINCH 184 B4
STOCKLINCH
OTTERSEY 184 C4
STOCKLINCH ST
MAGDALEN 184 C4
Stockman La TA20 198 C7
Stockmead BS40 53 B5
Stockmoor Cl TA6 209 A2
Stockmoor Dr
10 Bridgwater TA6 154 A5
Bridgwater TA6 209 A1
Stock Moor Dro TA6 209 A1
Stock's La
Hatch Beauchamp TA3,
TA19 183 B6
Leigh u M BA3 116 E3
North Wootton BA4 140 C4
Stockstyle La EX13 198 A8
Stockton Cl BS14 22 F4
Stock Way N BS48 8 F2
Stock Way S BS48 8 E2
Stockwitch Cross BA22 174 B3
STOCKWOOD 23 E5
Stockwood Bsns Pk BA4 141 C2
Stockwood Hill BS31 24 C7
Stockwood La BS14 23 E5
STOCKWOOD VALE 24 C6
Stockwood Vale BS31 24 C6
Stodden's La TA8 104 E8
Stodden's Rd TA8 85 C1
Stodden's Wlk TA8 104 B8
Stodeleigh Cl BS22 32 B3
STOFORD 197 F8
Stoford La
Broadway TA19 183 C2
West Buckland TA21 181 A7
Stoford Pl TA19 183 C2
STOGUMBER 150 D8
Stogumber CE Prim Sch
TA4 150 D8
Stogumber Sta★ TA4 150 E8
STOGURSEY 134 C5
Stogursey CE Prim Sch
TA5 134 B5
Stogursey La TA5 134 A3
STOKE BISHOP 5 E5
Stoke Bishop CE Prim Sch
BS9 5 D5
Stoke Cotts BS9 5 E4
Stoke Cres BA3 116 A2
Stoke Cross 10 TA14 185 F4
Stoke Gr BS9 5 E6
Stoke Hamlet BS9 5 F6
Stoke Hill
Bristol BS9 5 E3
Chew Stoke BS40 56 D7
Stoke St Mary TA3 169 D1
Stoke St Michael BA3 116 A2
Stoney Stoke BA9 160 E3
Stoke La
Bristol, Westbury on T BS9 5 F6
Stoke St Mary TA3 169 A1
Wincanton BA9 216 F5
Yarlington BA9 175 E7
Stokeleigh Wlk BS9 5 C5
Stoke Mead BA2 63 F7
Stoke Moor Dro BS27 109 D6
Stoke Paddock Rd BS9 5 D6
Stoke Park Rd BS9 5 F4
Stoke Park Rd S BS9 5 E3
STOKE PERO 128 F6
Stoke Rd
Bristol BS9 5 F3
Martock TA12 185 E5
North Curry TA3 170 C4
Portishead BS20 2 D5
Ruishton TA3 169 C2
Stoke St Mary TA3 169 B1
Street BA16 207 E6
Taunton TA1 213 B1
Westbury-sub-Mendip BA5 110 D6
STOKE ST GREGORY 170 E6
Stoke St Gregory CE Prim
Sch TA3 170 E6
STOKE ST MARY 169 C1
STOKE ST MICHAEL 116 B2
Stoke St Michael Prim Sch
BA3 116 A3
Stokes Croft BS1 227 B4
Stokes La DT10 189 F2
Stoke St BS27 110 B8
STOKE SUB HAMDON 185 F5
Stoke sub Hamdon Castle
Prim Sch TA14 185 F4
Stoke sub Hamdon Priory★
TA14 185 F4
STOKE TRISTER 177 B7
STOLFORD 134 F8
Stolford Hill TA22 148 A4
Stonage La TA18 196 C5
Stoneable Rd BA3 79 A3
Stoneage La BA2 61 B1
STONE ALLERTON 88 C3
Stone Allerton Dro BS26 88 B2
STON EASTON 95 E8
Stonebarrow La EX13 198 F2
Stoneberry Rd BS14 23 B3
STONEBRIDGE
Banwell 51 A4
STONEBRIDGE *continued*
Frome 120 A7
Stonebridge BS21 6 D1
Stonebridge Dr BA11 120 B7
Stonebridge Rd BS23 48 F4
Stonechat Green BS20 3 A6
Stone Cl TA1 168 D1
Stone Cross TA24 128 E1
Stonedene DT9 225 D6
Stone Down La BA6 139 D1
STONE-EDGE BATCH 8 D4
Stonegallows TA1 212 A3
Stonehenge La BS48 8 E4
STONE HILL 207 A4
Stonehill
South Cadbury BA22 175 C3
Stoke Sub Hamdon TA14 186 A4
Street BA16 207 B5
Stone Hill Ct TA24 200 F7
Stone Hill La TA4 166 D3
Stonehouse Cl BA2 45 B2
Stonehouse La BA2 45 B2
Stone La
Durnfield BA22 186 B8
East Pennard BA4 158 E6
Exford TA24 128 E1
Winsford TA24 147 E6
Yeovil BA21 187 B5
Stoneleigh
Chew Magna BS40 39 B3
Wellington TA21 222 B8
Stoneleigh Cl
Burnham-on-S TA8 104 C8
Staplegrove TA2 212 C8
Stoneleigh Ct
Bath BA1 27 E3
Taunton TA1 212 C1
Stoneleigh Mews BA21 218 C7
Stoneleigh Rise BA11 120 A6
Stone Mead La TA10 173 A4
Stone Rd TA8 104 D5
Stoneridge La TA4 165 D5
Stones Cross BA3 78 B2
Stonesfield TA18 196 B5
Stones Paddock BA3 116 C7
Stonewall Terr BA11 119 F2
Stonewell Dr BS49 34 D3
Stonewell Gr BS49 34 D3
Stonewell La BS49 34 D3
Stonewell Park Rd BS49 34 D3
Stoneyard La BA3 75 D2
Stoney Cl TA24 129 F6
Stoneyfield Cl BS20 4 B5
Stoneyfields BS20 4 B4
Stoney Furlong TA2 213 B8
Stoney Head Cvn Pk TA3 169 F1
Stoneyhurst Dr TA10 171 C3
Stoney La
Bishops Lydeard TA4 167 E8
Curry Rivel TA10 171 C3
East Coker BA22 197 D6
Stocklinch TA19 184 C4
Stoney Lane Cross EX16 178 B3
Stoney Littleton Long
Barrow★ BA2 80 C7
Stoney St TA24 129 C7
Stoney Steep
Portishead BS20 2 C6
Wraxall BS48 9 A5
STONEY STOKE 160 F3
STONEY STRATTON 141 F2
STONY HEAD 169 F1
Stonyhead Hill TA3 169 F1
STONY KNAPS 199 D7
Stony La
Axminster EX13 198 A1
Hawkridge TA22 146 E3
Whatley BA11 118 A2
STONY LITTLETON 80 B6
Stony St BA11 119 F5
STOODHAM 220 D6
Stoodham TA13 220 D5
Stoodly La
North Wootton BA4 140 D4
Pilton BA4 204 A2
Stooper's Hill TA20 193 C6
STOPGATE 192 C4
Stopgate Cross EX14 192 C4
Stoppard Rd TA8 104 C6
Stopper's La BA5 139 F6
Stormont Cl BS23 48 F3
Stormore BA13 121 F8
Storridge La
Axminster EX13 198 B6
Brompton Regis TA22 148 A1
Storridge View TA22 148 A2
Stothert Ave
Bath BA2 228 A2
East Twerton BA2 44 D6
STOUGHTON CROSS 108 B8
Stourhead Gardens★
BA12 161 F5
Stourhead House★ BA12 161 F5
Stour Hill SP8 177 E1
Stour Hill Pk SP8 177 F1
STOURTON 161 F5
STOURTON CAUNDLE 189 F2
Stourton Cl BA11 119 E3
Stourton Gdns 1 BA11 119 E3
Stourton La BA12 161 F6
Stourton View BA11 119 E3
Stourton Way BA21 218 D6
STOUT 156 B2
Stout Cross EX14 192 C5
Stout's Way La
Luxborough TA23 148 F8
Rodhuish TA24 131 A1
Stowborough Cotts BA2 79 C7
STOWELL 176 C1
Stowell Hill DT9 176 C1
Stowell La TA20 198 D8
Stowers Row 31 TA12 185 E6
STOWEY 57 F4
Stowey Bottom BS39 57 E5
Stowey Cross Rds BS39 57 F5
Stowey La
Curry Mallet TA3 183 E8
Fivehead TA3 170 E1
Stowey Pk BS49 34 D7
Stowey Rd
Pitney TA10 172 D7
Taunton TA2 212 E8
Yatton BS49 34 C8
Stow Ho BS11 4 E5
Stradling Ave BS23 48 F5
Stradling Cl TA7 137 B2
Stradling's Hill TA5 135 B3
Stradlings Yd BS2 226 C4
Straight Dro
Burrowbridge TA7 155 B1
Chilton Trinity TA5 135 F2
West Huntspill TA9 136 B7
Woolavington TA9 137 A6
Straight La BA11 101 D7
Straightmead BA3 75 F1
Straight St BS2 227 C2
Strap La
Ston Easton BA3 95 F7
Upton Noble BA4, BA10 143 A1
Stratford Cl BS14 22 F3
Stratford Ct BS9 5 F8
Stratford La BS40 56 E1
Stratford Rd BA21 218 D5
Stratheden BS8 226 A4
Stratton Cl TA6 209 D3
STRATTON-ON-THE
FOSSE 96 F1
Stratton Rd
Holcombe BA3 116 B8
Saltford BS31 25 E3
Strawberry Bank TA19 221 C4
Strawberry Cl BS48 8 D1
Strawberry Field BS26 70 D2
Strawberry Gdns BS48 18 D8
Strawberry Hill
Clevedon BS21 6 F4
Street BA16 207 B7
Strawberry La BS13, BS41 21 E3
Strawberry Way BA5 203 C4
Strawberry Way Rdbt
BA5 203 D3
Streaked La TA3 170 C6
STREAM 132 A2
Streamcombe La TA22 163 B5
Streamcross BS49 17 D1
Streamleaze BS40 39 B3
Streamside
Chew Magna BS40 39 B3
1 Clevedon BS21 6 F3
Taunton TA1 213 C2
STREET
Chard 194 C2
Glastonbury 207 C7
STREET ASH 193 C8
Street Ash La TA20 193 C8
Street Dro
Street BA16 207 E7
Street, Marshall's Elm
BA16 207 B1
STREET END 54 D3
Street End BS40 54 D2
Street End La BS40 54 D2
Street Ho TA19 221 B3
Street La
Odcombe BA22 186 C2
South Brewham BA10 161 A7
STREET ON THE FOSSE 141 C2
Street Rd
Compton Dundon TA11 157 A4
Glastonbury BA6 206 D3
Street BA6 207 D8
Street Rdbt BA16 207 D7
Street Shoe Mus★ BA16 207 C6
Street The
Bishop Sutton BS39 57 D4
Chew Stoke BS40 56 D8
Chilcompton BA3 96 D5
Compton Martin BS40 74 B7
Draycott BS27 90 F2
Farmborough BA2 59 F6
Kilmington BA12 161 F6
Radstock BA3 78 F2
Stowey BS39 57 F4
Ubley BS40 55 D1
Wanstrow BA4 142 F4
West Monkton TA2 169 C7
Winford BS40 37 F1
Stretcholt La TA6 135 F6
Stretford La TA19 194 F7
Stringfellow Cres TA20 223 D5
Stringfellow Mews TA20 223 C3
Stringland's La TA24 131 B2
STRINGSTON 133 F5
STRODE 55 E7
Strode Coll BA16 207 D6
Strode Ho 7 BA4 205 B6
Strode Rd
Clevedon BS21 6 C2
Street BA16 207 D6
Strode Way
Clevedon BS21 6 B1
Shepton Mallet BA4 205 A5
Stroud Rd BS11 4 E5
Stroud Way BS24 49 E7
Strowland La BS24 86 F6
Strowlands BS24, TA9 86 E6
Struthers Cl BA16 207 B7
Strutter's Hill BA10 215 D2
Stuart Ho BS23 30 D1
Stuart Pl BA2 44 D6
Stuart Rd BS23 49 A5
Stuarts Cl BA5 203 D3
Stubb's La BA11 101 D4
STUDLEY GREEN 83 F6
Studley La BA4 142 F4
Studley Mdws BA4 142 F4
Stump Cross
Pitcombe BA7 215 A1
Shepton Mallet BA4 204 D5
STURFORD 144 F7
Sturford La BA12 144 E7
Sturmey Way BS20 4 E3
Sturminster Cl BS14 23 D6
Sturminster Lodge BS14 23 D5
Sturminster Rd BS14 23 D7
Stutts End TA4 167 E6
Style Flats TA4 210 C5
Style Rd TA4 210 C5
Styles Ave BA11 120 C4
Styles Cl BA11 120 B4
Styles Hill BA11 120 B4
Styles Mdw BA11 120 C5
Styles Pk BA11 120 B4
Sub Rd BA6 157 D4
Suffolk Cl TA6 209 C3
Suffolk Cres TA1 212 C1
Suffolk Ct TA1 212 C1
Suffolk Ho BA1 44 C8
Sugg's La TA19 183 C2
Sulis Manor Rd BA2 62 D8
Sullivan Cl BS4 22 D6
Sully Cl TA6 209 D6
Sumerleaze Cres TA2 213 C8
Sumerlin Dr BS21 6 F3
Summer Ct BS8 226 B3
Summerfield BS22 32 A3
Summerfield Ave TA21 180 D8
Summerfield Cl TA7 154 F5
Summerfield Ct TA1 212 E4
Summerfield Rd BA1 28 A1
Summerfields BA8 190 A7
Summerfields Rd TA20 223 C3
Summerfield Terr BA1 28 A1
Summerfield Way TA21 180 D8
Summer Ground Dr BS13 22 A5
Summerhedge Cres TA7 155 C2
Summerhedge Rd TA7 155 C1
Summer Hill
Frome BA11 119 F3
Hinton St George TA17 195 D7
Summerhill Rd BA1 27 D1
Summerhouse BS21 8 D4
Summer House Terr
BA20 219 B4
Summerhouse View
BA21 219 C6
Summer La
Banwell BS29 50 E5
Chard TA20 194 C4
Hinton St George TA13,
TA17 195 C8
Monkton Combe BA2 63 D8
Weston-super-Mare BS22,
BS24 32 B1
Weston-super-Mare BS29 50 B8
Weston-super-Mare BS29 50 D7
Summer La N BS22 32 A2
Summerland Ave TA24 201 A7
Summerland Pl TA24 200 F7
Summerland Rd TA24 200 F7
SUMMERLANDS 218 F6
Summerlands
Backwell BS48 19 B5
Yeovil BA21 218 E6
Summerlands Hospl
BA21 218 F6
Summerlands Park Ave
TA19 221 B4
Summerlands Park Cl
TA19 221 B4
Summerlands Park Dr
TA19 221 B4
Summerlands Rd BS23 49 B8
Summer Lane Cvn Pk
BS29 50 E3
Summer Lane Park Homes
BS29 50 E4
Summerlays Ct BA2 45 B6
Summerlays Pl BA2 45 B6
Summerlea BA2 61 A5
Summerleaze BS31 24 E7
Summerleaze Cres TA2 213 C7
Summerleaze Pk BA20 218 F5
Summer Shard TA13 220 C4
Summers Hill La BA4 204 C2
Summerville Terr TA8 104 B6
Summerway TA24 129 E1
Summerway Dro TA7 209 E4
Summerwood Rd BA16 207 B4
Sun Batch BS27 91 A3
Sunderland Pl BS8 226 B3
Sunderland St 2 BA2 228 C3
Sundew Cl TA1 213 C1
Sunfield Rd BS24 49 E3
Sunningdale BS8 226 B4
Sunningdale Cl BS48 9 A1
Sunningdale Rd
Weston-super-Mare BS22 31 F3
Yeovil BA21 219 C6
Sunnybank BA2 45 B4
Sunny Bank TA4 150 B8

Sunnybank Ct BS24 . . . . . . 32 B1
Sunnybank Rd TA6 . . . . . . 208 E2
Sunnybank Way BS24 . . . . 32 B1
Sunnybrow Cl 10 TA6 . . . 153 F4
Sunny Cl TA9 . . . . 136 B8
Sunny Hill
Bristol BS9 . . . . 5 C7
Pitcombe BA10 . . . . 215 C4
Sunnyhill Dr BS11 . . . . 4 E6
Sunnyhill Ho E BS11 . . . . . . 4 E6
Sunnyhill Ho W BS11 . . . . . . 4 E6
Sunny La BA10 . . . . 215 C4
Sunnymead
Bridgwater TA6 . . . . 208 E2
Keynsham BS31 . . . . 24 F3
Midsomer Norton BA3 . . . . . 77 F2
Oakhill BA3 . . . . 114 F3
Stratton-on-t F BA3 . . . . 96 F2
Sunnymeade BA6 . . . . 138 C4
Sunnymede Rd BS48 . . . . . . 8 D3
Sunnyside
Barrington TA19 . . . . 184 C5
Bristol BS9 . . . . 5 E5
Burlescombe EX16 . . . . 179 C2
Clatworthy TA4 . . . . 149 F1
Clutton BS39 . . . . 59 B4
Farrington Gurney BS39 . . . 77 B3
Frome BA11 . . . . 119 F3
Sunnyside Cotts TA24 . . . 129 A8
Sunnyside Cres BS21 . . . . . . 6 D3
Sunnyside Farm Trad Est
BS20 . . . . 4 C2
Sunnyside Gdns BA2 . . . . . 60 B2
Sunnyside Pl BA11 . . . . . . 119 F3
Sunnyside Rd
Clevedon BS21 . . . . 6 D3
Weston-super-Mare BS23 . . 48 E5
Sunnyside Rd N BS23 . . . . 48 E6
Sunnyside Terr 6 DT9 . . . 225 E4
Sunnyside View BA2 . . . . . 79 C7
Sunnyvale
Camerton BA2 . . . . 78 E8
Clevedon BS21 . . . . 6 B1
Sunridge Cl BA3 . . . . 96 F8
Sunridge Pk BA3 . . . . 96 F8
Sunset Cl BA2 . . . . 79 C7
Sun St BA11 . . . . 119 E5
Suprema Ave TA7 . . . . 137 C2
Suprema Est TA7 . . . . 137 D2
Surrey St BS2 . . . . 227 B4
Susanna's Cross BA3 . . . . 116 B2
Susanna's La BA3 . . . . 116 C2
Sussex Ave TA6 . . . . 209 B3
Sussex Cl TA6 . . . . 209 B3
Sussex Lodge TA1 . . . . . . 212 F5
Sussex Pl BA2 . . . . 228 C1
Sutherland Ave TA8 . . . . . 104 B6
Sutherland Cl TA1 . . . . 212 C1
Sutherland Ct TA1 . . . . 212 C1
Sutherland Dr BS24 . . . . . . 49 D2
SUTTON 159 B4
SUTTON BINGHAM 197 D6
Sutton Cl
Frome BA11 . . . . 120 B7
Weston-super-Mare BS22 . . 49 E8
Sutton Cross TA10 . . . . . . 172 F4
Sutton Grange BA21 . . . . 218 C6
Sutton Hill
East Coker BA22 . . . . 197 D6
Long Sutton TA10 . . . . 172 E3
Sutton Hill Rd BS39 . . . . . . 57 D4
Sutton La
Redhill BS40 . . . . 36 F1
Walton BA16 . . . . 156 D6
SUTTON MALLET 155 B7
SUTTON MONTIS 175 C3
Sutton Pk BS39 . . . . 57 D4
Sutton Rd TA11 . . . . 211 C2
Sutton St BA2 . . . . 45 B7
Sutton View TA10 . . . . 172 E2
SUTTON WICK 57 B2
Swains TA21 . . . . 222 D4
Swains La TA21 . . . . 222 D4
Swain St TA23 . . . . 202 C7
Swainswick BS14 . . . . 22 F6
Swainswick CE Prim Sch
BA1 . . . . 28 B5
Swainswick Gdns BA1 . . . . 28 C2
Swainswick La BA1 . . . . . . 28 D4
Swallow Cl BA3 . . . . 97 B8
Swallowcliffe Ct 5
BA20 . . . . 219 A5
Swallowcliffe Gdns
BA20 . . . . 219 A5
Swallow Ct BS14 . . . . 23 F6
Swallow Ct EX16 . . . . 178 F1
Swallow Dr BA11 . . . . 120 B6
Swallow Gdns BS22 . . . . . . 49 E8
Swallow Hill TA10 . . . . 172 A6
Swallow St BA1 . . . . 228 C2
Swallows The BS22 . . . . . . 49 D7
Swan Cl BS22 . . . . 49 E8
Swancombe
Blagdon BS40 . . . . 54 E2
Clapton in G BS20 . . . . 8 E8
Swan Down TA20 . . . . 194 E4
Swane Rd BS14 . . . . 23 F6
Swan Hill TA18 . . . . 196 C5
Swan Ho 3 BA4 . . . . 205 B6
Swanmead Com Sch
TA19 . . . . 221 C3
Swan Prec TA19 . . . . 221 C3
Swanshard La BA5 . . . . . . 139 D6
Swans La BS27 . . . . 90 F2
Swan Yd DT9 . . . . 225 D4
Swedish Hos TA13 . . . . . . 220 D1
Sweetgrass Rd BS24 . . . . . 50 A8
Sweethay Cl TA3 . . . . 181 D8
Sweethay Cross TA3 . . . . 181 C8
Sweethay La TA3 . . . . 181 C8
Sweetleaze BA3 . . . . 116 A2
SWELL 171 A2
Swell Cl TA9 . . . . 136 B8
Swell La TA3 . . . . 171 A2
Swiddacombe La EX36 . . 162 C7
Swift Cl BS22 . . . . 31 F1
Swift Lodge BA20 . . . . . . 219 A4
Swifts TA21 . . . . 166 F1
Swillbridge Cvn Pk TA23 202 F6
SWINEFORD 26 A7
Swingbridge TA2 . . . . 213 E7
Swiss Dr BS3 . . . . 11 F2
Swiss Rd
Bristol BS3 . . . . 11 F1
Weston-super-Mare BS23 . . 48 F7
Sycamore Cl
Bridgwater TA6 . . . . 209 D5
Burnham-on-S TA8 . . . . . . 104 A5
Nailsea BS48 . . . . 8 E2
Shipham BS25 . . . . 70 E8
Taunton TA1 . . . . 213 C2
Weston-super-Mare BS23 . . 49 A8
Weston-super-Mare, Locking
BS24 . . . . 49 E5
Westonzoyland TA7 . . . . . 154 E5
Sycamore Ct TA20 . . . . . . 223 C5
Sycamore Dr
Crewkerne TA18 . . . . 224 D7
Frome BA11 . . . . 120 B7
Langport TA10 . . . . 172 A6
Yeovil BA20 . . . . 218 F2
Sycamore Rd
Minehead TA24 . . . . 200 D7
Radstock BA3 . . . . 79 B2
Sycamores BS23 . . . . 30 E1
Sycamore Sq TA20 . . . . . . 223 C5
Sycamore Wlk TA3 . . . . . . 169 D4
SYDENHAM 209 C5
Sydenham Bldgs BA2 . . . 228 A2
Sydenham Cl
Bridgwater TA6 . . . . 209 C6
Porlock TA24 . . . . 124 B4
Sydenham Rd
Bath BA2 . . . . 228 A2
Bridgwater TA6 . . . . 209 C6
Sydenham Terr BA2 . . . . . . 45 C1
Sydling Rd BA21 . . . . 219 D6
Sydnalls La BA12 . . . . 144 E8
Sydney Bldgs BA2 . . . . 45 B6
Sydney Ho BA2 . . . . 45 B7
Sydney Mews BA2 . . . . 45 B7
Sydney Pl BA2 . . . . 45 B7
Sydney Rd BA2 . . . . 45 B7
Sydney Row BS1 . . . . 226 B1
Sydney Wharf BA2 . . . . 45 B7
Sylvan Rd TA21 . . . . 222 E5
Sylvan Way
Bristol BS9 . . . . 5 B7
Monkton Heathfield TA2 . . 213 E8
Symes Ave BS13 . . . . 22 C4
Symes Cl
Chard TA20 . . . . 223 C4
North Perrott TA18 . . . . . . 196 C4
Symes Pk BA1 . . . . 27 A2
Symons Way
Bridgwater TA6 . . . . 209 A6
Cheddar BS27 . . . . 90 C7
Syndercombe La TA4,
TA23 . . . . 149 D2
SYNDERFORD 199 C6

T

Tabernacle La 4 BA20 . . 219 B4
TACKER STREET 149 C8
TADHILL 116 F2
Tadhill La BA3 . . . . 116 D2
TADWICK 12 E1
Tadwick La BA1 . . . . 28 A6
Tail Mill TA16 . . . . 195 F7
Tailor's Ct 7 BS1 . . . . 227 A3
Talbot Cl TA9 . . . . 104 D3
Tallis Gr BS4 . . . . 22 D6
Tallowood BA4 . . . . 205 D5
Tamar Ave TA1 . . . . 213 B1
Tamar Dr BS31 . . . . 25 A4
Tamar Rd BS22 . . . . 32 A2
Tamblyn Cl BA3 . . . . 79 A3
Tamsin Ct BS31 . . . . 24 F5
Tamworth Rd BS31 . . . . 24 E4
Tancred St TA1 . . . . 213 A4
TANGIER 212 E4
Tangier TA1 . . . . 212 E4
Tankard's Cl BS8 . . . . 226 C3
Tankey's Cl BA11 . . . . 120 A7
Tan La SP8 . . . . 161 F1
Tanner Cl BA3 . . . . 97 C8
Tanner's Hill TA4 . . . . 165 E7
Tanners La SN14 . . . . 13 F8
Tanners Wlk
Bath BA2 . . . . 43 F5
Marshfield SN14 . . . . 13 F8
Tannery Cl BA16 . . . . 207 C5
Tannery Ct TA18 . . . . 224 C7
Tanorth Cl BS14 . . . . 23 A3
Tanorth Rd BS14 . . . . 22 F3
Tansee Hill TA20 . . . . 199 B6
Tansey BA4 . . . . 142 A6
Tansey Ct TA6 . . . . 208 E1
Tansy La BS20 . . . . 2 F5
Tanyard
Broadway TA19 . . . . 183 C2
Tanyard continued
Nether Stowey TA5 . . . . . . 134 B2
Tanyard Cotts TA24 . . . . . 131 A5
Tanyard La
Langport TA10 . . . . 172 A5
North Wootton BA4 . . . . . . 140 C4
North Wootton, Lower
Westholme BA4 . . . . 140 D3
Tan Yard La TA13 . . . . 184 F5
Tanyards BA10 . . . . 215 F7
Tanyard The BA16 . . . . . . 207 C5
Tape La BA3 . . . . 114 F7
Taphouse La DT6 . . . . 199 E1
Tapmoor Rd TA7 . . . . 155 C8
Tappers La 2 TA6 . . . . . . 153 E3
Tapps La TA7 . . . . 136 E4
Tapstone Rd TA20 . . . . 223 D4
Taranto Hill BA22 . . . . 173 E2
Taranto Way BA22 . . . . . . 174 A2
Target La TA12 . . . . 185 D4
TARNOCK 87 D6
Tarnock Ave BS14 . . . . 23 A7
Tarnwell BS39 . . . . 40 A2
Tarragon Pl BS20 . . . . 2 F5
Tarrant La BA20 . . . . 218 F1
Tarratt La
East Coker BA22 . . . . 197 E8
Yeovil BA20, BA22 . . . . 219 A1
Tarratt Rd BA20 . . . . 218 F1
Tarr Post TA22 . . . . 146 C1
Tarr Steps★ TA22 . . . . 146 E3
Tarr Steps National Nature
Reserve★ TA22 . . . . 146 E3
Tarr Water Cotts TA23 . . . 148 E8
Tatham Ct TA1 . . . . 212 D4
TATWORTH 198 C8
Tatworth Prim Sch TA20 198 C8
Tatworth Rd TA20 . . . . 223 C2
Tatworth St TA20 . . . . 198 C8
Tauntfield Cl TA1 . . . . 213 A3
TAUNTON 212 D5
Taunton Acad The TA2 . . . 168 E6
Taunton Nuffield Health
Hospl TA2 . . . . 212 B7
Taunton Rd
Ashcott TA7 . . . . 156 B7
Bishops Lydeard TA4 . . . . . 167 F7
Bridgwater TA6 . . . . 209 A3
North Petherton TA6 . . . . . 153 F4
Thurloxton TA6 . . . . 153 E2
Wellington TA21 . . . . 222 E7
Weston-super-Mare BS22 . . 32 B4
Wiveliscombe TA4 . . . . 210 D4
Taunton Sch TA2 . . . . 212 D6
Taunton Sta TA1 . . . . 212 F5
Taunton Third Way TA1 . 212 F4
Taunton Trad Est TA2 . . . . 212 A7
Taunton Vale Pk TA2 . . . . 213 F8
Taunusstein Way 12
BA20 . . . . 219 B4
Taveners Wlk BS48 . . . . 8 F3
Taverner Cl BS4 . . . . 22 D7
Taverners Cl 6 BS23 . . . . . 48 F4
TAVERN SCOTT 38 D1
Tavistock Rd BS22 . . . . 32 A2
Tawny Way BS22 . . . . 49 F8
Taylor Cl TA2 . . . . 168 B5
Taylor Ct
Bridgwater TA6 . . . . 209 A5
Weston-super-Mare BS22 . . 32 B4
Taylor Gdns BS13 . . . . 21 F4
Taylor Ho TA19 . . . . 221 B3
Taylor's Meade TA20 . . . . 193 D6
Taylor's Orch TA14 . . . . . . 185 E1
Tayman Ridge BS30 . . . . . . 25 D8
Teagle Cl BA5 . . . . 203 F5
Teak Cl TA6 . . . . 209 D6
Teal Cl
Bridgwater TA6 . . . . 209 A4
Weston-super-Mare BS22 . . 31 F1
Tealham Moor Dro BS28 137 E8
Teal Rd TA24 . . . . 201 C5
Teals Acre 8 TA5 . . . . 135 B2
Teal Way BS20 . . . . 2 F6
Teapot Lane (Worms Lane)
BA6 . . . . 158 B6
Teasel Wlk BS22 . . . . 49 D7
Technical St TA8 . . . . 104 B6
Teck Hill TA6 . . . . 153 E2
Teckhill La TA6 . . . . 153 E2
Teddington Cl BA2 . . . . 44 C4
Teesdale Cl BS22 . . . . 49 D8
Teeside BA14 . . . . 83 F4
Teeswater Way 9 TA6 . . . 154 A5
Teign Ct BA16 . . . . 156 D7
Teignmouth Rd BS21 . . . . . . 6 E3
Telephone Ave BS1 . . . . . 227 A2
Telford Ho
Bath BA2 . . . . 44 D3
Leigh Woods BS8 . . . . 11 E7
Tellis Cross BA22 . . . . 197 D8
TELLISFORD 82 E4
Tellisford La BA2 . . . . 81 F4
Tellis La BA3 . . . . 114 D8
Temblett Gn TA6 . . . . 208 C5
Templars Barton BA8 . . . 176 E1
Templars Ct
Long Sutton TA10 . . . . 172 E1
1 Weston-super-Mare
BS22 . . . . 49 D7
Templars Pl BA8 . . . . 176 E1
Templars Way BS25 . . . . . . 70 E7
TEMPLE 144 E7
Temple Back BS1 . . . . 227 B2
Temple Back East BS1 . . 227 C2
Temple Bridge Bsns Pk
BS39 . . . . 76 F7
Temple Circus Giratory
BS1 . . . . 227 C1
TEMPLE CLOUD 58 E1
TEMPLECOMBE 176 E1
Templecombe La SP8 . . . 177 C3
Templecombe Sta BA8 . . 176 E1
Temple Ct BS31 . . . . 24 E5
Temple Field TA23 . . . . . . 202 C6
Temple Gate BS1 . . . . 227 B1
Temple Inn La BS39 . . . . . . 58 E1
Temple La BA8 . . . . 176 F1
Templeland Rd BS13 . . . . . 21 F5
Temple of Harmony★
TA5 . . . . 153 B5
Temple Rose St BS1 . . . . 227 B2
Temple St
Bristol BS1 . . . . 227 B2
Keynsham BS31 . . . . 24 F5
Temple Way BS2 . . . . 227 B2
Temple Way Underpass
BS2 . . . . 227 C3
Tenby Rd BS31 . . . . 24 D4
Tengore La TA10 . . . . 172 C6
Tennis Corner Dro BA11 102 D2
Tennis Court Ave BS39 . . . 77 D5
Tennis Court Rd BS39 . . . . 77 D5
Tennyson Ave BS21 . . . . 6 B2
Tennyson Cl BS31 . . . . 24 F6
Tennyson Rd
Bath BA1 . . . . 44 D7
Weston-super-Mare BS23 . . 49 A3
Tenterk Cl BS24 . . . . 67 B6
Tents Hill BA11 . . . . 118 B6
TERHILL 151 F3
Terhill La TA4 . . . . 151 F3
Termare Cl BA22 . . . . 218 B6
Terrace The
Minehead TA24 . . . . 201 A5
Shipham BS25 . . . . 70 E7
Terrace View DT9 . . . . 225 E5
Terrace Wlk BA1 . . . . 228 C2
Terrell St BS2 . . . . 227 A4
Terry Hill BA3 . . . . 98 D8
Terry Ho BS1 . . . . 226 C3
Tetbury Gdns BS48 . . . . 9 A1
Tetton Cl TA6 . . . . 208 B4
Teviot Rd BS31 . . . . 25 A4
Tewkesbury BA21 . . . . 218 D6
Tewther Rd BS13 . . . . 22 D3
Teyfant Com Sch BS13 . . . 22 E4
Teyfant Rd BS13 . . . . 22 E4
Teyfant Wlk BS13 . . . . 22 E4
Thackeray Ave BS21 . . . . . . 6 E4
Thackeray Ho BS23 . . . . . . 49 A5
Thackeray Rd BS21 . . . . 6 E4
Thames Dr TA1 . . . . 213 D4
Thatcham Cl 2 BA21 . . . . 218 F7
Thatcham Ct 1 BA21 . . . . 218 F7
Thatcham Pk BA21 . . . . . . 218 F7
Thatch Cotts TA20 . . . . . . 194 E1
Thatcher Cl BS20 . . . . 2 D4
Thatch The TA11 . . . . 211 C4
Theaks Mews TA1 . . . . 213 A3
THEALE 109 C1
Theatre Royal BS1 . . . . . . 227 A2
Theillay Cl TA5 . . . . 134 A3
There-and-Back-Again La
BS1 . . . . 226 C3
Theynes Croft BS41 . . . . . . 11 B1
THICKET MEAD 77 F3
Thicket Mead BA3 . . . . 78 A2
Thickthorn Cross TA19 . . 183 C3
Thimble La DT9 . . . . 217 D2
Third Ave
Bath BA2 . . . . 44 D5
Bristol BS14 . . . . 23 B7
Radstock BA3 . . . . 97 D7
Thirlmere Rd BS23 . . . . 49 A4
Thistledoo Vine TA7 . . . . 136 F2
Thistle Pk TA6 . . . . 209 B1
Thomas Bunn Cl BA11 . . . 120 A7
Thomas Cl BS29 . . . . 51 A3
Thomas Ct BS1 . . . . 227 B2
Thomas La BS1 . . . . 227 B2
Thomas Lane Appartments
BS1 . . . . 227 B2
Thomas Pl TA21 . . . . 222 D7
Thomas St
Bath BA1 . . . . 228 C4
Bristol BS2 . . . . 227 B4
Taunton TA2 . . . . 212 F6
Thomas Way BA6 . . . . 206 B4
Thomas Way Ind Est
BA6 . . . . 206 B4
Thompson Cl TA6 . . . . 209 D6
Thompson Rd
Bristol BS14 . . . . 23 E6
Wells BA5 . . . . 203 D3
Thompson Way BS24 . . . . . 50 C8
Thomson Dr TA18 . . . . 224 D5
Thong La TA10 . . . . 184 D6
Thornash Cl TA2 . . . . 213 F8
Thornbank Ct DT9 . . . . . . 225 E4
Thornbank Pl BA2 . . . . . . 228 A1
Thornbury Dr BS23 . . . . 48 D2
Thornbury Rd BS23 . . . . . . 48 C2
Thornbush Cross TA4 . . . 150 F3
Thorn Cl BS22 . . . . 32 B2
THORNCOMBE 199 B6
Thorncombe Cres TA6 . . 209 C5
Thorncombe Thorn
TA20 . . . . 199 B5
Thorndale BS8 . . . . 226 A4
Thorndale Cl BS22 . . . . 49 D8
Thorndale Mews BS8 . . . . 226 A4
Thorndun Park Dr TA20 . 223 D6
THORNE COFFIN 218 A8
Thorne Cross BA22 . . . . . . 218 B7
Thorne Cross Way TA21 . 178 D8
Thorne Gdns BA21 . . . . . . 218 C7
Thorne La
Wheddon Cross TA24 . . . . 147 C8
Winsford TA24 . . . . 147 C8
Yeovil BA21 . . . . 218 C8
Thorne Pk TA8 . . . . 104 B5
THORNE ST MARGARET . . 179 D8
THORNEY 172 A1
Thorneymoor La TA10 . . . 172 A3
Thorney Rd TA12 . . . . 185 B8
THORNFALCON 169 E2
Thornhill Dro TA12 . . . . . . 173 A1
Thornhill Rd DT10 . . . . 190 B4
Thorn La TA3 . . . . 169 D2
Thornton Rd BA21 . . . . . . 218 D7
Thornwell La BA9 . . . . 216 D3
Thornwell Way BA9 . . . . . 216 C3
Thorny La BA21 . . . . 187 E8
Thornymarsh La BA7 . . . . 175 B8
THOULSTONE 121 F4
THREE ASHES
North Cadbury 175 C7
Oakhill 115 E1
Three Ashes DT8 . . . . 199 D7
Three Ashes La TA11 . . . . 157 B4
Three Corner Mead
BA21 . . . . 218 C5
Three Gates Cross TA22 . 163 C6
Three Hill View BA6 . . . . . 206 E5
Three Horse Shoes Hill
TA5 . . . . 152 C4
Three Oaks Cross TA19 . . 183 C4
Three Queens' La BS1 . . . 227 B2
Three Ways Sch BA2 . . . . . 62 E8
Three Wells Rd BS13 . . . . . 21 F4
Thrift Cl DT10 . . . . 190 C4
Throgmorton Rd BS4 . . . . . 22 F8
Throop Rd BA8 . . . . 176 F1
Thrubwell La BS40 . . . . 37 B4
Thrupe La BA5 . . . . 114 A2
Thrush Cl 4 BS22 . . . . 49 E8
Thumb La BA4 . . . . 158 E7
THURLBEAR 182 C8
Thurlbear CE Prim Sch
TA3 . . . . 182 C8
Thurlestone BS14 . . . . 23 A6
Thurlocks BA22 . . . . 186 B6
THURLOXTON 153 D1
Thyme Cl BS20 . . . . 2 F5
Thynne Cl BS27 . . . . 90 B6
Tibbott Rd BS14 . . . . 23 D5
Tibbott Wlk BS14 . . . . 23 D5
Tichborne Rd BS23 . . . . 30 E1
TICKENHAM 7 F4
Tickenham CE Prim Sch
BS21 . . . . 7 F4
Tickenham Hill BS48 . . . . . . 8 E4
Tickenham Rd BS21 . . . . 7 A4
Tide Gr BS11 . . . . 5 A8
Tides Reach TA24 . . . . 125 C4
Tiffany Ct BS1 . . . . 227 B1
Tiledown BS39 . . . . 58 E1
Tiledown Cl BS39 . . . . 58 F1
Tile Hill BA10 . . . . 161 A7
Tile House Rd
East Huntspill TA7 . . . . 137 B8
Mark TA9 . . . . 106 C1
Tilery EX14 . . . . 192 D3
Tilham St BA6 . . . . 158 B6
Tilley Cl
Farmborough BA2 . . . . 60 A5
Keynsham BS31 . . . . 25 A2
Tilley La BA2 . . . . 60 A5
Tilleys Dro BA5 . . . . 138 F7
TILLWORTH 198 D3
Tilsey La TA4 . . . . 150 C5
Tilton Ct 5 DT9 . . . . 225 D3
TIMBERSCOMBE 130 C4
Timberscombe CE First Sch
TA24 . . . . 130 B5
Timberscombe Way TA6 . 208 B4
Timberscombe Wlk BS14 . 23 C5
Timbers The BA3 . . . . 97 B7
Timberyard TA7 . . . . 137 F1
Timewell Hill EX16 . . . . . . 164 C4
TIMSBURY 60 B1
TIMSBURY BOTTOM 60 A1
Timsbury Rd
Farmborough BA2 . . . . 60 B5
High Littleton BS39 . . . . 59 D1
Timsbury Village Workshops
BA2 . . . . 59 F3
Tin Bridge Rdbt BA6 . . . . 139 D3
Tinker's La
Compton Martin BS40 . . . . . 74 B7
Cucklington BA9 . . . . 177 D7
Halse TA4 . . . . 167 C6
Kilmersdon BA11 . . . . 98 B1
Tinneys La DT9 . . . . 225 E4
Tintagel Cl BS31 . . . . 24 D4
Tintagel Rd BA21 . . . . 218 D7
Tintern BA21 . . . . 218 C6
TINTINHULL 186 C6
Tintinhull Gdn★ BA22 . . . 186 C6
Tintinhull Rd BA21 . . . . . . 186 F5
Tipcote Hill 17 BA4 . . . . . . 205 B6
Tipnoller Hill TA4 . . . . 210 F7
Tippacott La EX35 . . . . 122 A4
Tiptoft 3 TA14 . . . . 185 F4
Tirley Way BS22 . . . . 31 B2
Titan Barrow BA1 . . . . 29 C2
Tithe Barn Cross EX15 . . . 179 D2
Tithe Ct BA20 . . . . 218 D5
Tithe Mdw TA4 . . . . 167 A7
Tithill La TA4 . . . . 167 F7
Titlands La BA5 . . . . 203 A7
Titus Wy BS31 . . . . 24 F7

Tiverton Gdns BS22 32 A2
Tiverton Rd
Bampton EX16 164 C1
2 Clevedon BS21 6 E1
TIVINGTON 129 F8
Tivington Cross TA24 129 F8
Tivoli Ho BS23 48 E8
Tivoli La BS23 48 E8
Toghill La BS30 12 A8
Tolbury La BA10 215 D6
Tolbury Mill BA10 215 E6
TOLLAND 150 E3
Tolland BS24 49 A2
Tolland Cross TA4 150 E3
Toll Bridge Rd BA1 28 E3
Tolley's La TA20 194 C3
Toll Gate TA4 210 C4
Toll House Rd 1 TA5 135 B2
Toll Rd
Porlock TA24 124 A3
Weston-super-Mare BS23 66 F8
Toms Cl TA20 223 B3
Tomtit's La TA11 211 C3
TONE 222 A8
TONEDALE 222 B7
Tonedale Bsns Pk TA21 222 B7
Tonedale Ind Est TA21 222 B8
Tone Dr TA6 209 B3
Tone Gn TA4 167 E2
Tone Hill TA21 222 B8
Tone Rd BS21 6 D1
Toneway TA2 213 C6
Toose The BA21 218 C6
Top Hill BA4 142 F2
Top La
Gasper BA12 161 E4
Mells BA11 118 B6
Top Rd
Charlton Adam TA11 173 F7
Cheddar BS27 90 E5
Shipham BS25 70 F7
Westbury-sub-Mendip BA5 110 E6
Top St
Kingsdon TA11 173 D5
Pilton BA4 140 F3
Top Wood BA3 116 B7
Torbay Cl BA7 214 B5
Torbay Rd BA7 214 A5
Torbay Road Ind Est BA7 214 A5
Torbay Villas BA7 214 A5
Tor Cl BS22 32 A2
Torhill La BA5 203 F4
Torhole Bottom BA3 94 A4
Tori Green 2 TA6 209 A1
Tormynton Rd BS22 31 E3
Torre Cider Farm★ TA23 131 E3
Torre Rocks TA23 131 E2
Torres Vedras Dr TA21 222 F7
Torre The BA21 218 C6
Torridge Mead TA1 213 D4
Torridge Rd BS31 25 A4
Torrington Ave BS4 22 F8
Torrington Cres BS22 32 A3
Tor St BA5 203 E4
Tor View
Cheddar BS27 90 C7
Woolavington TA7 136 E4
Tor View Ave BA6 206 D3
Tor Wood View BA5 203 E5
T'OTHER SIDE THE HILL 115 B7
Totnes Cl BS22 32 A2
Totney Dro BS28 137 E8
Totshill Dr BS13 22 E4
Totshill Gr BS13 22 E4
Tottenham Pl BS8 226 B3
Totterdown La
Pilton BA4 204 B1
Weston-super-Mare BS24 49 A1
Totterdown Rd BS23 48 F4
Touches La TA20 223 E5
Touches Mdw TA20 223 E5
Touching End La SN14 13 F8
Touch La TA10 156 C1
Touchstone Cl TA20 223 B4
Touchstone La TA20 223 B4
Toulouse Rd 5 TA6 209 A1
TOULTON 152 A2
Tout Hill BA9 216 C3
Tout La BA22,TA11 174 A6
Tovey Cl BS22 31 E4
Tower Cl
Cheddar BS27 90 B6
Stoke St Michael BA3 116 A3
Tower Farms Ind Units TA4 151 A4
TOWERHEAD 51 D4
Towerhead Rd BS29 51 D3
Tower Hill
Bristol BS2 227 B3
Bruton BA10 215 D6
Holcombe Rogus TA21 178 D5
Horsington BA8 176 E2
Locking BS24 50 D4
Stogursey TA5 134 B5
Stoke St Michael BA3 116 A3
Williton TA4 202 E2
Tower Hill Rd TA18 224 B5
Tower House La BS48 9 A4
Tower La
Bristol BS1 227 A3
Taunton TA1 212 E4
Towerleaze BS9 5 D3
Tower Rd
Kilmington BA12 161 D6
Portishead BS20 2 A4
Stawell TA7 137 B1
Yeovil BA21 219 C8
Tower St
Bristol BS1 227 B2
Taunton TA1 212 E4
Tower The BS1 227 B2
Tower View
Frome BA11 119 F2
South Cheriton BA8 176 D3
Wanstrow BA4 142 E4
Tower Wlk BS23 30 D1
Town Barton BA2 81 F4
Town Cl
North Curry TA3 170 B4
Stogursey TA5 134 B6
Town End BA2 81 F4
Townend Villas TA14 185 F2
Town Farm TA3 170 B4
Townhall Bldgs BA5 203 E4
Town Hill EX36 162 C6
Town La BA4 205 C6
Town Marsh TA22 163 D7
Townrise 15 BA20 219 B4
TOWNSEND 92 D4
TOWNS END 77 E4
TOWN'S END 116 E3
Townsend
East Harptree BS40 75 A5
Ilminster TA19 221 D3
Marston Magna BA22 174 F1
Middlezoy TA7 155 C3
Montacute TA15 186 B3
Shepton Mallet BA4 205 B5
Westonzoyland TA7 154 F5
Williton TA4 202 E3
Townsend Cl
Bristol BS14 23 F5
Bruton BA10 215 F7
Townsend Cotts TA24 147 C5
Townsend Gn 10 BA8 190 A6
Townsend La
Chilton Polden TA7 137 B2
Emborough BA3 95 B2
Theale BS28 109 A2
Townsend Orch
Merriott TA16 195 F8
Street BA16 207 B5
Townsend Pk BA10 215 F7
Townsend Rd
Bristol BS14 23 F5
Minehead TA24 201 A6
Townsend Rise BA10 215 F7
Townsend Sh Pk BA4 205 B5
Townshend Rd BS22 32 B5
Town St BA4 205 B6
Town Tree Farm Nature Trail★ TA12 185 C8
Town Tree La TA10, TA12 185 D8
TRACEBRIDGE 179 A8
Tracey Cl TA7 209 E8
Trackfordmoor Cross TA22 163 B3
Tracy Cl BS14 22 F7
Trafalgar Rd BA1 27 B1
Traits La BA22 174 E4
Trajan's Way BA4 205 E5
Tramshed The BA1 228 C3
Transform Ind Est TA6 209 A6
Transom Ho BS1 227 B2
Transom Pl TA24 201 B7
Travers Cl BS4 22 D6
Trawden Cl BS23 31 A1
Treasure Ct TA8 85 A1
Treasurer's Ho★ TA12 185 E6
TREBLE'S HOLFORD 151 C4
TREBOROUGH 149 A7
Treborough Cl TA2 213 B8
Treefield Rd BS21 6 D2
Tregarth Rd BS3 11 F1
Tregelles Cl TA9 104 C4
Tregonwell Rd TA24 201 A7
Trelawn Cl BS22 32 D2
Trelissick Gdns 3 BS22 49 F8
Trellech Ct 3 BA21 218 C6
Tremes Cl SN14 13 F8
Tremlett Mews 3 BS22 32 B4
Trenchard Rd
Locking BS24 50 D4
Saltford BS31 25 D3
Trenchard St BS1 226 C3
Trendle La
Bicknoller TA4 132 F2
Stoney Stoke BA9 160 E3
Trendle Rd TA1 212 B1
Trendle St DT9 225 D3
Trendlewood Way BS48 9 A1
Trenleigh Dr BS22 32 A2
TRENT 187 F5
Trent Cl BA21 219 E8
Trent Ct TA1 213 D4
Trent Gr BS31 25 A4
Trent Mdw TA1 213 E4
Trent Path La DT9 225 A5
Trent Young's CE Prim Sch DT9 187 F5
Tresco Spinney BA21 218 C6
Trescothick Cl BS31 24 E6
Trevanna Rd BS3 11 F1
Trevelyan Rd BS23 48 F7
Trevett Rd TA1 212 C2
Trevithick Cl BA11 120 C6
Trevor Rd TA6 209 C6
Trevor Smith Pl TA1 213 A3
Trewartha Cl BS23 48 F8
Trewartha Pk BS23 48 F8
Trewint Gdns BS4 22 F8
Triangle Ct 2 BA2 44 D5
Triangle Ctr The BS21 6 D3
Triangle E BA2 44 D5
Triangle N BA2 44 D5
Triangle S BS8 226 B3
Triangle The
Castle Cary BA7 214 C5
Clevedon BS21 6 D3
North Curry TA3 170 A4
Paulton BS39 77 E6
Portishead BS20 2 B5
Somerton TA11 211 D4
Wrington BS40 35 D2
Triangle Villas 1 BA2 44 D5
Triangle W
Bath BA2 44 D5
Bristol BS8 226 B3
Tribunal & Lake Village Mus★ BA6 206 D4
Trickey Warren La TA3 181 C1
Trim Bridge 3 BA1 228 B2
Trim St BA1 228 B2
Trinder Rd BS20 4 B4
Trindlewell La TA18 196 C4
TRINITY 119 E5
Trinity Bsns Ctr TA1 213 A3
Trinity CE Fst Sch BA11 119 C4
Trinity Cl
Bath BA1 228 B2
Blackford BS28 107 D4
Burnham-on-S TA8 85 A1
Wellington TA21 222 C5
Trinity Coll BS9 5 E4
Trinity Ct
Bridgwater TA6 208 F6
Nailsea BS48 8 C1
13 Yeovil BA20 219 B4
Trinity Gate TA1 213 A3
Trinity Mews 15 BS2 227 C3
Trinity Pl
3 Bristol BS8 226 A2
4 Weston-super-Mare BS23 30 C1
Trinity Prim Sch BS20 2 F5
Trinity Rd
Bath BA2 45 B2
Nailsea BS48 8 D1
Taunton TA1 213 B3
Weston-super-Mare BS23 30 C1
Trinity Rise TA8 85 A1
Trinity Row
Frome BA11 119 E5
Wellington TA21 222 C5
Trinity St
Bath BA1 228 B2
Frome BA11 119 E5
Taunton TA1 213 B3
Trinity Way
Bridgwater TA6 208 E6
Minehead TA24 201 B7
Trinity Wlk
Bristol BS2 227 C3
Frome BA11 119 E5
Trin Mills BS1 227 A1
Tripps Cnr BS49 34 D7
Tripps Dro BA5 139 A6
Tripps Row BS41 11 A1
TRISCOMBE 151 D6
Triscombe Ave TA6 208 D4
Triscombe Gate TA24 147 D8
Triscombe Ho TA4 151 D5
Triscombe Rd TA2 212 E8
Tristram Dr TA3 169 D4
Tropical Bird Garden★ TA8 47 F2
Tropiquaria Zoo★ TA23 131 F4
Trossachs Dr BA2 45 D8
Trotts La TA19 183 B2
Trottsway Cross TA24 129 C2
TROWBRIDGE 83 F7
Trowbridge Cl TA9 104 D4
Trowell La TA4 165 E4
Trow La BA12 144 C2
Truckwell La TA4 150 D4
TRUDOXHILL 143 C6
TRULL 168 D1
Trull CE Prim Sch TA3 168 D1
Trull Green Dr TA3 168 D1
Trull Rd TA1 212 E2
Trumps Cross EX16 178 E3
Truro Cl TA8 104 C7
Truro Rd BS48 9 A1
Trym Bank BS9 5 D7
Trym Cross Rd BS9 5 C5
Trymleaze BS9 5 C5
Trym Side BS9 5 C5
Trymwood Par BS9 5 D6
Tucker's Cross DT9 188 A4
Tuckers La BA7 214 B7
Tucker's La
Baltonsborough BA6 157 F6
Ubley BS40 73 E8
Tucker's Moor Cross EX16 162 F3
Tucker St BA5 203 C4
TUCKERTON 169 F8
Tuckerton La TA7 153 F1
TUCKING MILL 63 C8
Tuckingmill La BS39 41 E5
Tuckmarsh La BA11 143 E7
Tuckmill BS21 6 B1
Tudballs TA24 128 D1
Tuddington Gdns BA5 203 B4
TUDHAY 198 C3
Tudor Ct
Chard TA20 223 C6
Yeovil BA20 219 A4
Tudor Rd
Portishead BS20 2 E4
Weston-super-Mare BS22 32 A4
Tudor Way TA6 209 A1
Tudway Cl BA5 203 C4
Tufton Ave BS11 5 A8
Tugela Rd BS13 21 F7
Tuggy's La BA2 63 E1
Tulip Tree Rd TA6 209 E5
Tulse Hill BA12 161 F2
Tunbridge Cl BS40 39 B2
Tunbridge Rd BS40 39 B2
Tuncombe La TA18 195 D4
Tundra Walk 5 TA6 154 A5
TUNLEY 61 B3
Tunley Hill BA2 60 E2
Tunley Rd BA2, BA3 61 D5
Tunnel La BA3 96 F5
Tunnell La 14 TA14 185 F4
Tunnel The TA24 128 B2
Tunscombe La BA4 142 D8
Tunstall Cl BS9 5 E4
Turin Path 4 TA6 208 E7
Turkey Ct 5 TA1 212 E3
TURLEIGH 64 F6
Turnbury Ave BS48 9 A1
Turnbury Cl BS22 31 F3
Turner Cl
Bridgwater TA6 209 A4
Keynsham BS31 25 A5
Turner Ct
Wells BA5 203 D3
Weston-super-Mare BS22 31 F3
Turner Rd TA2 212 E7
Turner's Barn La BA20 218 F2
Turner's Court La BA3 114 D8
Turner's La DT6 199 B2
Turner's Twr BA3 80 A1
Turner Way BS21 6 B1
Turn Hill TA10 155 F2
Turnhill Rd TA10 156 A2
Turnock Gdns BS24 50 D8
Turnpike
Milverton TA4 167 A4
Sampford Peverell EX16 178 C1
Turnpike Cl TA18 196 B3
Turnpike Cnr BA3 95 B8
Turnpike Cross TA14 185 E2
Turnpike Cvn Pk TA20 193 A4
Turnpike Gn TA18 196 B3
Turnpike La BA4 142 B6
Turnpike Rd
Cross BS26 69 E1
Shipham BS25 70 E8
Turnstone 3 BS20 2 F6
Turstin Rd BA6 206 F6
Turtlegate Ave BS13 21 E4
Turtlegate Wlk BS13 21 E4
Tut Hill DT9 189 C1
Tutton Way BS21 6 D1
Tuttors Hill BS27 71 C1
Tuxwell La TA5 152 C8
Tweed Rd BS21 6 C1
Tweed Rd Ind Est 2 BS21 6 C1
Tweentown BS27 90 B8
Twelve Acre Post TA22 163 A4
Twelve Acres DT9 225 B5
Twelve Acres Cl BS39 77 D6
TWERTON 44 A5
Twerton Farm Cl 2 BA2 44 B6
Twerton Inf Sch BA2 44 A5
Twinell La TA5 152 D7
Twines Cl BA22 175 A5
Twinhoe La BA2 62 E2
Twistgates La EX14 192 A4
Twitchen Ball Cnr EX36 145 G3
Twitchens La BS27 90 F2
Two Acres Cvn Pk BS21 1 B1
Two Acres Rd BS14 23 A7
Two Ash Hill TA20 193 F1
Two Ash La TA20 194 A1
Two Elms BA21 187 E8
Two Tower La BA22 219 B2
Two Trees BS40 72 E8
Twyford Pl TA21 222 D5
Tydeman Rd BS20 2 F5
Tyler Gn 2 BS22 32 B4
Tylers End TA9 104 F3
Tyler's La TA4 167 A7
Tyler Way TA9 104 D3
Tyndall Ave BS8 226 C4
Tyndall Ho 5 BS2 227 C3
TYNDALL'S PARK 226 C4
Tyndalls Park Mews BS2 226 C4
Tyndall's Park Rd BS8 226 C4
Tyne Gr 10 BS20 2 F6
Tyne Pk TA1 213 D3
TYNING
Radstock 79 B3
Timsbury 60 A2
Tyning Cl BS14 23 A7
Tyning Cotts BA3 116 C7
Tyning End BA2 45 B5
Tyning Hill
Hemington BA3 99 C8
Radstock BA3 79 B3
Tyning La BA1 28 B1
Tyning Pl BA2 45 C2
Tyning Rd
Bathampton BA2 28 F2
Bath BA2 45 C2
Peasedown St John BA2 79 D7
Saltford BS31 25 E2
Winsley BA15 64 E7
Tynings BS39 58 D3
Tynings La BA5 203 C8
Tynings Mews BS23 48 E4
Tynings Rd BA16 207 B4
Tynings The
Clevedon BS21 6 A1
Portishead BS20 1 F1
Tynings Way
Clutton BS39 58 E3
Tynings Way *continued*
Westwood BA15 64 F3
Tyning Terr 15 BA1 28 A1
Tyning The
Bath BA2 45 B5
Freshford BA3 64 B4
Tynte Ave BS13 22 E3
Tynte Rd TA6 209 D6
Tyntesfield House (NT)★ BS48 9 F4
Tyntesfield Rd BS13 22 A8
Tyrone Wlk BS4 22 E8
TYTHERINGTON 143 E8
Tytherington La BA11 143 E8
TYTHERLEIGH 198 C6
Tythe St BA6 206 E3
Tythings Com Ctr The BA9 216 C3
Tythings Ct TA24 200 F7
Tything Way BA9 216 D3

U

UBLEY 55 E1
Ubley CE Prim Sch BS40 55 D1
Ubley Dro BS40 73 B7
UBLEY SIDELING 73 D8
UDLEY 35 C4
ULLCOMBE 192 A4
Ullcombe La EX14 191 F4
Ullswater Cl BS23 49 A4
Ullswater Dr BA1 28 A2
Uncombe Cl BS48 19 D7
Underbanks BS20 4 D4
Underdown BA21 219 F5
Underdown Ho BS1 227 A1
Underdown Hollow
Bradford Abbas DT9 187 E2
Yeovil BA21 219 F4
Underdown La DT9 225 F6
Underhill
Gurney Slade BA3 114 E7
Hambridge TA10 184 D8
Penselwood BA9 161 D1
Underhill Ave BA3 77 F2
Underhill Cl BA16 207 B5
Underhill Dr BS23 48 D1
Underhill La
Midsomer Norton BA3 77 F2
Staple Fitzpaine TA3 182 B4
Underhill Rd BA16 207 B5
Under Knoll BA2 79 E8
Under La BS40 36 D1
Underleaf Way BA2 79 D7
Undertown BS40 74 A7
Undertown La BS40 74 A7
Under Way TA20 193 D6
Underwood Ave BS22 31 B1
Underwood Bsns Pk BA5 203 B6
Underwood End BS25 52 A4
Underwood La TA10 172 C8
Underwood Rd
Glastonbury BA6 206 D6
Kingsdon TA11 173 D5
Portishead BS20 2 C3
Union Dro TA10 172 B6
Union La TA4 202 E4
Union Pas BA1 228 C2
Union Pl BS23 48 D7
Union St
Bath BA1 228 C2
Bridgwater TA6 209 B6
Bristol BS1 227 B3
Cheddar BS27 90 B7
Dulverton TA22 163 D6
Nailsea BS48 8 C1
Wells BA5 203 D4
Weston-super-Mare BS23 48 D7
Yeovil BA20 219 B4
Unite Ho BS1 226 C2
Unity Ct BS31 25 A5
Unity Rd BS31 25 A6
Unity St BS1 226 C2
University Cl BS9 5 F4
University of Bristol Dorothy Hodgkin Bldg BS1 227 A4
University Rd BS8 226 C3
University Wlk BS8 226 C3
Univ of Bath BA2 45 E5
Univ of Bristol BS8 226 C3
Univ of Bristol Dept of Ed BS8 226 C3
Univ of Bristol Langford House Sch of Veterinary Science BS40 53 B6
Univ of Bristol Sch of Veterinary Science BS2 226 C4
Univ of the West of England BS3 11 E4
Upcot Cres TA1 212 B2
UPCOTT 168 B3
Upcott La
Bicknoller TA4 132 F1
Winsford TA24 147 D7
Upcott Rd TA1, TA4 168 B3
UPHILL 48 C2
Uphill Ct BS23 48 D2
Uphill Dr BA1 28 B2
Uphill Farm Cvn Pk BS23 48 E1
Uphill Prim Sch BS23 48 D2
Uphill Rd N BS23 48 D4
Uphill Rd S BS23 48 D2
Uphills BA10 215 E7

Uphill Way BS23 48 D1
Upjohn Cres BS13 22 D3
Uplands
Bratton Seymour BA9 176 B8
Mark TA9 106 E4
Uplands Cl BA2 63 F7
Uplands Dr BS31 25 F2
Uplands Rd BS31 25 F2
Uplands Terr BA22 197 B8
Uplands The BS48 18 C8
UPLOWMAN 178 B2
Uplowman CE Prim Sch EX16 178 B2
UP MUDFORD 187 D5
UPOTTERY 191 F2
Upottery Prim Sch EX14 191 F2
Upper Belgrave Rd BS8 5 F1
UPPER BENTER 115 C7
Upper Berkeley Pl BS8 226 B3
Upper Bloomfield Rd BA2 44 D1
Upper Borough Walls BA1 228 C2
Upper Breach BA5 113 A2
Upper Bristol Rd
Bath BA1 44 D7
Clutton BS39 58 D3
Weston-super-Mare BS22 31 B1
Upper Byron Pl BS8 226 B3
Upper Camden Pl BA1 228 C4
UPPER CHEDDON 168 F7
Upper Church La
Bristol BS2 226 C3
Hutton BS24 49 D2
Upper Church Rd BS23 30 D1
Upper Church St BA1 228 B3
UPPER COXLEY 139 F6
Upper Crannel Dro BA6 139 C4
Upper Ct BA3 97 C8
Upper East Hayes BA1 28 B1
Upper Farm Cl BA2 81 F4
Upper Flowerfield BA11 143 B7
Upper Furlong BA2 60 B3
UPPER GODNEY 139 A6
Upper Green La BS40 55 B7
Upper Hedgemead Rd BA1 228 B4
Upper High St
Castle Cary BA7 214 C5
Taunton TA1 212 F3
Upper Holway Rd TA1 213 C2
Upper Kewstoke Rd BS23 30 B1
Upper Lambridge St BA1 28 C2
UPPER LANGFORD 53 C3
UPPER LANGRIDGE 27 B7
Upper Lansdown Mews BA1 27 F1
UPPER LITTLETON 38 B6
Upper Maudlin St BS2 227 A3
Upper Merrifield BA3 116 E8
Upper Merryfield BA3 97 E1
UPPER MILTON 203 D7
Upper Mount Pleasant BA3 64 A4
Upper Myrtle Hill BS20 4 C4
Upper New Rd BS27 90 A8
Upper North St BS27 90 B8
Upper Oldfield Pk BA2 228 A1
Upper Pitching BA3 96 D5
UPPER RADFORD 78 B8
Upper Rd BS39 75 E6
Upper Stanton BS39 40 A2
UPPER STANTON DREW 40 B2
Upper Strode BS40 55 F7
UPPER SWAINSWICK 28 B8
Upper Town La BS40 37 C8
UPPER VOBSTER 117 D8
Upper Wells St BS1 226 C2
UPPER WESTHOLME 140 D4
UPPER WESTON 27 A3
UPPER WESTWOOD 100 F8
Upper Whatcombe BA11 119 E6
Upper Wood St TA1 212 E4
Upper York St BS2 227 B4
UPPOTERY 191 F2
UPTON
Langport 172 D5
Skilgate 164 F8
Upton BS24 49 A2
UPTON CHEYNEY 26 B8
Upton Cotts BS41 38 F8
Upton La
Dundry BS41 39 A8
Seavington St Michael TA19 184 E2
UPTON NOBLE 142 F2
Upton Noble CE Prim Sch BA4 142 F2
Urchinwood La BS49 34 F4
URGASHAY 174 C3

V

VAGG 186 F5
Vagg Hill BA22 186 E5
Vagg La BA22 186 F5
Vagg Pk BA22 186 F5
Valda Rd BS22 31 C2
Vale Cl TA18 224 C4
Vale Cres BS22 32 C2
Vale Ct BS8 226 A4
Vale End BS48 8 D1
Vale La BS3 22 C8
Vale Mill Way BS24 49 F8
Valentine Cl BS14 23 B5
Valentines TA22 163 E6
Vale Rd
Stalbridge DT10 190 B4
Yeovil BA21 219 E6
Valerian Cl BS11 4 F6
Vale St BA8 190 A6
Valetta Cl BS23 48 F3
Valetta Pl TA6 208 F5
Vale View
Aller TA10 171 E8
Henstridge BA8 190 A7
Radstock BA3 79 A2
Wincanton BA9 216 F5
Vale View Cotts TA4 151 E4
Vale View Gdns BA9 216 C2
Vale View Pl 16 BA1 28 B1
Vale View Terr BA1 28 F3
Valley Cl
6 Nailsea BS48 8 E2
Wells BA5 203 C4
Yeovil BA21 219 B6
Valley Ct BS20 1 E3
Valley Gdns BS48 8 E2
Valley Line Ind Pk BS27 90 A7
Valley Rd
Bristol, Bedminster Down BS13 22 A8
Clevedon BS21 6 F5
Crewkerne TA18 224 C4
Leigh Woods BS8 11 C7
Portishead BS20 2 A2
Taunton TA1 213 C5
Valley View
8 Axminster EX13 198 A1
Chilcompton BA3 96 D3
Clutton BS39 58 E3
Frome BA11 119 D6
Millmoor EX15 179 E1
Morebath EX16 164 B3
Valley View Cl BA1 28 B3
Valley View Rd
Bath BA1 28 C3
Paulton BS39 77 E6
Valley Way Rd BS48 8 E3
Valley Wlk BA3 78 B2
Vallis Ct 7 BA11 119 E5
Vallis Fst Sch BA11 119 E5
Vallis Rd BA11 119 D5
Vallis Trad Est BA11 119 D5
Vallis Way BA11 119 E5
Vanbrugh Gdns BS11 4 F8
Van Diemen's La BA1 27 F2
Vandyck Ave BS31 24 F6
Vane St 7 BA2 45 B7
Vanguard Ct BA22 218 A5
Varsity Way BS24 50 B6
Vaughan Ct BA5 203 B4
Veales DT10 189 F2
Veale The BS24 67 C6
Veal La
Horrington BA5 113 B2
Walton BA16 156 E6
Vedal Dro TA10 172 D4
Vee La BS40 37 D8
Vellore La BA2 45 C7
Vellow Rd TA4 150 D8
Vellow Wood La TA4 132 D1
Vemplett's Cross TA23 131 E1
Venford Hill
East Anstey TA22 162 E8
Hawkridge TA22 146 D1
Venland Bsns Pk TA24 201 B6
Venland Ind Pk TA24 201 A6
Venn Cl TA4 167 E6
Venn Cross TA4 165 D3
Venn Hill DT6, TA20 199 C6
Venniford Cross TA24 129 F8
Vennland Way TA24 201 A6
Venns Cl BS27 90 B7
Venns Gate BS27 71 A1
Venture 7 BA20 218 C3
Venture 20 BA20 218 C3
Venture Eleven The TA2 213 B6
Venture Way TA2 213 B6
Venus La BS39 58 E3
Venus St BS49 34 E2
Vera St TA2 212 F7
Verbena Way BS22 32 A1
Verbena Wlk TA6 208 E1
Verdun Terr TA23 131 E4
Vereland Rd BS24 49 E3
Verlands BS49 34 E5
Vernal La BA11 119 D6
Vernalls Rd DT9 225 D5
Vernham Gr BA2 44 C1
Vernhamwood Cl BA2 44 C1
Vernon Cl BS31 25 D3
Vernon La BS26 69 B3
Vernon Pk BA2 44 C6
Vernon Terr BA2 44 C6
Vernslade BA1 27 A2
Verriers 10 TA6 153 E3
VERRINGTON 216 A5
Verrington La BA9 216 B5
Verrington Park Rd BA9 216 B4
Vesey's Hole Hill SP8 177 E4
Vestry Cl BA16 207 C5
Vestry Ct 1 BA16 207 C5
Vestry La BS5 227 C4
Vestry Rd BA16 207 C5
Vian End BS22 31 F4
Vicarage Cl
Chard TA20 223 C3
Coxley BA5 139 E6
Creech St Michael TA3 169 D4
8 Frome BA11 119 F4
Stogursey TA5 134 C6
Weston-super-Mare BS22 32 A3
Vicarage Cl *continued*
Westonzoyland TA7 154 F5
Vicarage Ct
Burnham-on-S TA8 104 A7
Timberscombe TA24 130 B5
Vicarage Gdns BA2 79 B7
Vicarage Hill
Combe St Nicholas TA20 193 D6
Dulverton TA22 163 D6
Vicarage La
Barrow Gurney BS48 20 C6
Compton Bishop BS26 69 B3
Compton Dando BS39 41 D6
Creech St Michael TA3 169 D4
Draycott BS27 90 F3
Mark TA9 106 E5
Norton St Philip BA2 81 E4
Pawlett TA6 135 F5
Shapwick TA7 137 F1
7 Wookey BA5 139 D8
Vicarage Lawns TA3 169 D4
Vicarage Rd
Bristol, Bishopsworth BS13 22 A6
Carhampton TA24 131 B5
Leigh Woods BS8 11 D6
Minehead TA24 200 F8
Stogursey TA5 134 C6
Wookey BA5 139 E8
Woolavington TA7 136 E4
Vicarage St
Burnham-on-S TA8 104 A7
Frome BA11 119 F4
Tintinhull BA22 186 C6
6 Yeovil BA20 219 B4
Vicarage Wlk BA20 219 B5
Vicar's Cl BA5 203 E5
Vicars La TA6 208 D5
Vicar's La TA12 184 F7
Vickery Cl
Bridgwater TA6 208 D3
Curry Rivel TA10 171 D4
Victoria Art Gall The* BA2 228 C2
Victoria Ave TA20 223 D4
Victoria Bldgs
Bath BA2 44 D6
Glastonbury BA6 206 E4
Victoria Bridge Ct BA1 228 A3
Victoria Bridge Rd BA1, BA2 228 A2
Victoria Bsns Pk TA20 223 D4
Victoria Cl
Bath BA2 44 C5
Portishead BS20 2 D5
Yeovil BA21 219 D6
Victoria Cotts BA2 62 F7
Victoria Ct
Castle Cary BA7 214 B5
Chard TA20 223 D4
Frome BA11 120 A4
Ilminster TA19 221 C4
Portishead BS20 2 D5
Victoria Gate TA1 213 B4
Victoria Gdns
Batheaston BA1 28 F3
Castle Cary BA7 214 B6
15 Henstridge BA8 190 A6
Victoria Gr BA4 205 D5
Victoria Ho
Bath BA1 44 D8
Keynsham BS31 24 F4
Victoria Jubilee Homes BS40 53 C6
Victoria La BA4 141 E1
Victoria Lodge BS22 31 E2
Victoria Mews BA7 214 B5
VICTORIA PARK 226 B3
Victoria Park Bsns Ctr BA1 44 D7
Victoria Pk
Castle Cary BA7 214 B5
Weston-super-Mare BS23 30 D1
Victoria Pl
Bath, Combe Down BA2 45 C1
2 Bath, Lambridge BA1 28 C1
Chardstock EX13 198 A7
Highbridge TA9 104 D3
Paulton BS39 77 D5
Weston-super-Mare BS23 48 D8
Victoria Quadrant BS23 48 E8
Victoria Rd
Avonmouth BS11 4 B7
Bath BA2 44 D6
Bridgwater TA6 208 E5
Castle Cary BA7 214 B5
Clevedon BS21 6 C3
Frome BA11 120 A4
Minehead TA24 201 A5
Saltford BS31 25 D3
Yeovil BA21 219 D6
Victoria Sh Mews TA18 224 C6
Victoria Sq
Bristol BS8 226 A3
Crewkerne TA18 224 B6
Evercreech BA4 141 E1
Portishead BS20 2 D5
Weston-super-Mare BS23 48 D7
Victoria St
Bristol BS1 227 B2
Burnham-on-S TA8 104 A7
Taunton TA1 213 B4
Wellington TA21 222 D6
Victoria Terr
Bath BA2 44 D6
14 Bristol, Clifton BS8 11 F6
14 Henstridge BA8 190 A6
Paulton BS39 77 E6
Victoria Way TA5 152 E7
Victory Rd TA2 213 A7
Vienna Way 4 TA6 154 A5
Vigor Rd BS13 22 B5
Viking Cl TA23 202 D7
Vilberie Cl TA2 212 A7
Village Rd TA3 182 F6
Villa Rosa 16 BS23 30 C1
Villes La TA24 124 A4
Villice La BS40 74 A7
Vincent Cl TA8 104 C7
Vincent Pl BA20 219 B5
Vincents Cl DT9 189 A1
Vincent St 5 BA20 219 B5
Vine Gdns
Frome BA11 119 F6
Weston-super-Mare BS22 32 A2
Vine Gr BA8 176 E1
Vine House Gdns TA20 223 C3
Vinery The BS25 70 A7
Vine St BA8 176 E1
Vineyards BA1 228 C3
Viney Bridge Mills TA18 224 D5
Viney La EX14 191 F1
Viney St TA1 213 B3
Viney's Yd BA10 215 F6
Vining's Hill BA4 142 D1
Vinney La BA11 143 F8
Violet La DT9 176 A2
Virginia Cl 1 BA8 190 A6
Virginia Orch TA3 169 C3
Viscount Sq TA6 208 E7
Vivary Ct TA1 212 E3
Vivary Gate TA1 212 F3
Vivary Hts TA1 212 E2
Vivary Rd TA1 212 E3
Vivien Ave BA3 78 A2
Vixen Cl BA22 174 A3
VOBSTER 117 C7
Vobster Cross BA3 117 D7
Vobster Hill BA3 117 D7
VOLE 106 B8
Vole Rd
Brent Knoll TA9 86 D1
Mark TA9 106 B7
Volis Cross TA5 152 F1
Volis Hill TA2 168 F8
Vowell Cl BS13 22 B4
Vowles Cl BS48 9 A3
VOXMOOR 222 F1
Vulcan Ho BA2 228 C3
Vulcan Rd TA24 201 B6
Vynes Cl BS48 9 A1
Vynes Ind Est BS48 9 A3
Vynes Way BS48 9 A1
Vyvyan Rd BS8 226 A3
Vyvyan Terr BS8 226 A3

W

WADBROOK 198 C4
Wadbrook Cross EX13 198 C4
WADBURY 118 D7
WADDICOMBE 162 E6
Wade Cl TA7 154 E6
WADEFORD 193 D5
Wadeford Hill TA20 193 D5
Wade St BS2 227 C3
Wadham Cl
Bridgwater TA6 209 D6
Ilminster TA19 221 A4
Wadham Com Sch TA18 224 D7
Wadham Cross
Knowstone EX36 162 A2
West Anstey EX36 162 A4
Wadham Hill EX36 162 A2
Wadham's Almshouses TA19 183 E4
Wadham St BS23 48 D8
WAGG 172 B5
Wagg Dro TA10 172 B5
WAGGS PLOT 198 B4
Waggs Plot EX13 198 B4
Wagon And Horses Hill BA4 141 E8
Wagtail Cres BS20 3 A6
Wagtail Gdns BS22 49 E8
Wains Cl 3 BS21 6 C2
Wainwright Cl 5 BS22 32 B4
Wainwright Ct BA4 205 B4
Wainwright Dr BA11 120 C7
Waits Cl BS29 50 F3
Wakedean Gdns BS49 17 A1
WALCOMBE 203 E7
Walcombe La BA5 203 E6
Walcot Bldgs
Bath BA1 45 B8
Bath BA1 228 C4
Walcot Ct BA1 228 C4
Walcot Gate BA1 228 C4
Walcot Ho BA1 228 C4
Walcot Par BA1 228 C4
Walcot St BA1 228 C3
Walcot Terr BA1 228 C4
Waldegrave Rd BA1 27 E1
Waldegrave Terr BA3 79 A3
Walden Rd BS31 25 A4
Waldock Barton TA13 220 D4
Waldron's Cross TA21 165 E1
WALES 174 E3
Wales La BA22 174 E3
WALFORD 169 D7
Walford Ave BS22 32 C3
Walford Cross Ind Pk TA2 169 D6
Walford Cross Roads TA2 169 D7
Walker Rd BA11 120 A3
Walkers Dr BS24 49 F7
Walkers Gate TA21 222 D5
Walker St BS2 226 C4
Walk La TA13 184 F1
WALLACE 74 E3
Wallace La BS40 74 E3
Wallace Rd BA1 28 B1
Wallace Wells Rd TA8 104 D5
Wallbridge BA11 120 B4
Wallbridge Ave BA11 120 A4
Wallbridge Gdns BA11 120 A4
Wallbridge Ho BA11 120 A4
Wallbridge Ind Est BA11 120 B4
Wall Ditch La TA16 196 A8
Wallenge Cl BS39 77 F6
Wallenge Dr BS39 77 F6
Walley La BS40 57 B7
Wall Gn BS26 70 C1
Wallingford Rd BS4 22 D7
Wallington Way BA11 119 D6
Walliscote Grove Rd 11 BS23 48 E7
Walliscote Prim Sch BS23 48 E7
Walliscote Rd BS23 48 D6
Walliscote Rd S BS23 48 D4
WALL MEAD 60 C4
Walls La BS28 108 B8
Walls The TA7 137 C2
Wall The TA9 106 D5
Wally Court Rd BS40 56 E8
Walmsley Terr 4 BA1 28 B1
Walnut Bldgs BA3 79 A3
Walnut Cl
Axbridge BS26 70 B1
Cheddar BS27 90 B7
Easton-in-G BS20 4 A3
Keynsham BS31 24 C4
Nailsea BS48 18 E8
Puriton TA7 136 C4
Rode BA11 101 E8
Taunton TA1 212 B4
Weston-super-Mare BS24 49 B2
Walnut Dr
Bath BA2 44 E4
Bridgwater TA6 209 D3
Somerton TA11 211 D4
Walnut Gr BA4 205 C4
Walnut La TA7 136 F3
Walnut Rd TA10 172 A6
Walnuts The TA7 137 B2
Walnut Tree Cl
Ubley BS40 55 D1
Wells BA5 203 C5
Walnut Tree Cnr TA23 131 F4
Walnut Tree Ct BS49 34 D4
Walnut Tree Dr TA24 131 A5
Walnut Wlk
Bristol BS13 22 A6
Frome BA11 120 B7
Keynsham BS31 24 C4
WALPOLE 136 B4
Walridge Cross TA4 166 A4
Walrond Ct TA19 221 B3
Walrond's Pk TA3 184 B7
WALROW 105 C2
Walrow TA9 104 E3
Walrow Ind Est TA9 104 F2
Walrow Terr TA9 104 E3
Walscombe Cl 1 TA14 185 F4
Walsh Ave BS14 23 A7
Walsh Cl BS24 49 B2
Waltham End BS24 50 A8
WALTON 156 E7
Walton BS24 49 A2
Walton Bay House Park Homes BS21 1 B1
Walton CE Prim Sch BA16 156 E7
Walton Cl
Bridgwater TA6 209 D5
Keynsham BS31 24 D4
Walton Cres BS40 37 F8
Walton Cross BS21 7 B7
Walton Ct TA24 201 A7
Walton Dro BA16 156 D5
WALTON IN GORDANO 7 B7
Walton Rd
Bristol BS11 4 D6
Clevedon BS21 6 F4
WALTON ST MARY 6 E5
Walton St
Portishead BS21 1 A1
Walton in G BS21 7 A8
Walwyn Cl BA2 44 A6
Walwyn Gdns BS13 22 C3
WAMBROOK 193 C3
Wambrook Cl TA1 212 E1
Wand Rd BA5 203 C2
Wansbeck Gn TA1 213 D3
Wansbeck Rd BS31 25 A4
Wansbrough Rd BS22 32 B4
Wansdyke Bsns Ctr BA2 44 D4
Wansdyke Ct BS14 23 B5
Wansdyke Prim Sch BS14 22 F4
Wansdyke Rd BA2 44 D1
Wansdyke Workshops
Keynsham BS31 25 A6
Peasedown St John BA2 79 D6
WANSTROW 142 F4
Wapping Rd BS1 227 A1
Warden Rd TA24 200 F6
Ward La TA7 154 E8
Wardleworth Way TA21 222 C7
Wardour Rd BS4 22 D8
Wareham Cl BS48 8 D1
Wareham Cross EX13 198 E1
Wareham Rd EX13 198 E2

Wares La TA6 208 D6
Waring Ho BS1 227 A1
WARLEIGH 46 C6
Warleigh Cl BA11 119 D4
Warleigh Dr BA1 29 A3
Warleigh La BA1 46 C5
Warleys La BS24 32 C1
Warman Cl BS14 23 F6
Warman Rd BS14 23 F6
War Memorial Hospl TA8 104 B7
Warmington Rd BS14 23 C8
Warminster Rd
Beckington BA11 101 E4
Claverton BA2, BA3 46 B5
Frome BA11 120 B4
Warne Pk BS23 49 A6
Warner Cl BS49 35 A7
Warne Rd BS23 49 A6
Warren Cl
Bridgwater TA6 208 F6
Bruton BA10 215 E6
Charlton Horethorne DT9 176 A2
Fenn's Wood BS41 10 E1
Hutton BS24 49 D2
Warren Farm Cvn Pk & Camp Site TA8 65 F5
Warren Gdns BS14 23 F5
Warren La BS41 20 E8
Warren Rd
Brean TA8 65 F6
Minehead TA24 201 B7
Warren's Cl BS27 71 B1
Warrens Hill BS27 71 B1
Warrens Hill Rd BS27 71 D4
Warren St TA21 222 A4
Warrens Way BA5 113 A1
Warren The BA16 207 A5
Warres Rd TA2 213 C8
Warrilow Cl BS22 32 B5
Warrior Ave BA22 218 B6
Warry Cl BS48 9 B2
Warth La BS22 32 A8
Warwick Ave TA6 209 C3
Warwick Cl BS22 49 C8
Warwick Gdns
Burnham-on-S TA8 85 B1
Clutton BS39 58 D3
Taunton TA1 213 C2
Warwick Rd
3 Bath BA1 44 B7
Keynsham BS31 24 D4
Taunton TA2 213 A8
(was BS22 31 E1
WASHBROOK 89 A1
Washcross La TA19 184 E3
WASHFORD 131 F4
Washford Cross TA23 131 F3
Washford Hill TA23 202 A5
Washford Sta TA23 131 E4
Washingpool DT9 188 E7
Washing Pound La
Bristol BS14 23 B4
Nailsea BS48 8 B4
Washington Gdns TA6 208 E5
Washington Terr TA20 223 B5
Wash La TA15 186 B4
Washpool La BA2 43 F2
Wassail Cl 5 TA24 131 A5
Wassail View TA2 168 B4
WATCHET 202 B6
Watchet Boat Mus* TA23 202 C7
Watchet Sta TA23 202 C7
WATCHFIELD 105 D2
Watch House Pl BS20 2 E7
Watch House Rd BS20 4 D4
Watchill Ave BS13 21 F6
Watchill Cl BS13 21 F6
Watchwell Dro BA6 157 D7
Waterbridge Rd BS13 21 F4
Watercombe Hts BA20 218 D2
Watercombe La
Yeovil BA20 218 C2
Yeovil, Preston Plucknett BA20 218 D5
Watercombe Pk BA20 218 D3
Watercress Cl BS48 9 B2
Waterfield Cl TA1 212 B3
Waterfield Dr TA1 212 B3
Waterford Beck BA14 83 F6
Waterford Cl TA6 209 A2
Waterford Pk BA3 78 E1
Waterfront Ho BA2 228 B1
WATERGORE 220 B2
Water Hill TA4 150 F7
Waterhouse La BA2 63 F8
Water La
Bristol BS1 227 B2
Butleigh BA6 157 E4
Charlton Horethorne DT9 176 A2
Crowcombe TA4 151 A7
Frome BA11 119 E3
Horningsham BA12 144 D4
Keenthorne TA5 134 C1
Lopen TA13 185 A1
Nether Stowey TA5 134 A1
Paulton BA3, BS39 78 A4
Pill BS20 4 C4
Somerton TA11 211 C3
Stogumber TA4 150 F7
Waterlake DT10 190 B4
Waterlake Rd TA20 198 C8
Waterlands La TA18 224 C8
Waterleaze TA2 213 D7
WATERLIP 142 A7
Waterlip BA4 141 F7
Waterloo
Frome BA11 119 F5
Puriton TA7 136 C4
Waterloo Bldgs 4 BA2 44 B6
Waterloo Cl TA7 136 C4
Waterloo Cotts TA1 212 B4
Waterloo Cres DT9 176 A1
Waterloo Ho BS20 4 D5
Waterloo La
Stalbridge DT10 190 A1
Yeovil BA20 219 A4
Waterloo Pl 19 BS2 227 C3
Waterloo Rd
Bristol BS2 227 C3
Radstock BA3 79 A2
Shepton Mallet BA4 205 B7
Wellington TA21 222 C6
Waterloo St
Bristol BS2 227 C3
9 Bristol, Clifton BS8 11 F7
Weston-super-Mare BS23 48 E8
Waterloo Terr DT9 225 F4
Watermans Mdw TA6 208 E6
Watermead TA20 198 D8
Watermead Cl 9 BA1 228 B2
Water Path TA21 222 A5
WATERROW 165 F4
Waters Edge BS20 2 E7
WATERSIDE 78 E1
Waterside Cres BA3 78 D1
Waterside La BA3 98 A6
Waterside Pk BS20 1 D4
Waterside Rd
Radstock BA3 78 D1
Wincanton BA9 216 C4
Waterside Way BA3 97 D8
Waters La BS27 90 C8
Watersmeet Cl
Golsoncott TA23 131 D1
Rooks Bridge BS26 87 B5
Water St
Barrington TA19 184 D5
Curry Rivel TA10 171 C4
East Harptree BS40 74 F4
East Lambrook TA13 220 C8
Hambridge TA10 171 D1
Lopen TA13 185 A1
Martock TA12 185 D5
Seavington St Michael TA19 184 E1
Watery Combe BA3 94 E7
Watery La
Axminster EX13 198 A3
Bath BA2 44 A6
Broadway TA19 194 B8
Charlton Horethorne DT9 176 C1
Clatworthy TA4 149 C2
Coultings TA5 134 E3
Doynton BS30 12 A8
Halstock BA22 197 D3
Hewish TA18 195 D3
Langford Budville TA4, TA21 166 C2
Minehead TA24 200 F7
Nailsea BS48 8 B2
North Petherton TA6 153 E4
Spaxton TA5 152 F4
Stogursey TA5 134 C5
Stratton-on-t F BA3 97 A3
Williton TA4 202 E4
Winford BS40 38 B4
Wiveliscombe TA4 210 C6
Watling St BA21 218 D7
Watling Way BS11 4 D7
Watsons La TA6 209 A5
Watts Corner BA6 206 F7
Watts La TA4 151 E1
Watts's Quarry La TA10, TA11 173 A5
Watts's Rd TA7 137 D8
Waveney Rd BS31 25 A3
Wavering Down Rise BS26 70 A3
Waverley TA11 211 C4
Waverley Cl
Frome BA11 120 C6
Somerton TA11 211 C4
Waverley Rd
Backwell BS48 19 A7
Bridgwater TA6 208 F6
Bristol, Shirehampton BS11 4 E6
Weston-super-Mare BS23 48 F4
Waverly Ct BS49 34 D3
Waverney Cl TA1 213 D3
Wayacre Dro BS24 66 E6
Wayclose La BA9 177 D5
Waycroft Acad BS14 23 E5
Waydown Cross TA24 130 A4
Waydown La TA24 130 A4
Wayfield Gdns BA1 28 F4
WAYFORD 195 B1
Wayford Cl BS31 25 A3
Wayford Hill TA18 195 C1
Wayland Rd BS22 31 E3
Waysdown La TA4 149 D1
Wayside
Staplehay TA3 181 D8
Weston-super-Mare BS22 31 D2
Wayside Cl BA11 120 C6
Wayside Dr BS21 6 E5
WAY WICK 32 E1
WCA Ho BS1 227 A2
WEACOMBE 132 F3
Weacombe Rd
Bridgwater TA6 209 C5
Taunton TA2 212 F7
Weal Terr BA1 27 B2
Weal The BA1 27 C2
WEARE 88 E6
Weare CE Fst Sch BS26 88 D7
Weare Ct BS1 226 A1
Weares La TA7 137 D2
WEARNE 172 A7
Weatherley Dr BS20 1 F3
Weatherly Ave BA2 44 D2
Weavers Cl
Crewkerne TA18 224 D5
Shepton Mallet BA4 205 D4
Weavers Ct BA11 119 E3
Weavers Orch BA2 62 D1
Weaver's Reach TA21 222 B7
Weavers The BA11 101 E4
Webber Rd BA4 205 D4
Webbers TA4 167 F7
Webbers CE Prim Sch TA21 178 F5
Webbers Cl TA21 222 E4
Webbers Way TA7 136 B4
WEBBINGTON 68 E4
Webbington Rd BS26 69 C3
Webb's Cl BA5 203 D3
Webb's Hill BA11 119 B5
Webbs Mead
Beckington BA11 101 E4
Chew Stoke BS40 56 D8
Wedgwood Cl BS14 23 B5
Wedgwood Rd BA2 44 A5
Wedlakes TA23 202 C6
Wedlands TA2 212 F7
Wedlock Way BS3 11 F3
WEDMORE 108 D3
Wedmore Cl
Bath BA2 44 A3
Burnham-on-S TA8 104 C8
Frome BA11 120 C7
Weston-super-Mare BS23 48 F2
Wedmore Fst Sch BS28 108 B4
Wedmore Pk BA2 44 A3
Wedmore Rd
Cheddar BS27 90 A7
Clevedon BS21 6 B1
Nailsea BS48 18 E8
Saltford BS31 25 D4
Weekesley La BA2 60 D1
Weekes Mdw TA21 179 E6
Week La TA22 147 D4
WEEKMOOR 167 B3
Weetwood Rd BS49 34 E5
Weind The BS22 31 D2
Weir Cl BS39 77 D6
Weirfield Gn TA1 212 D5
Weirfield Rd TA24 201 A8
Weir Head Cotts TA22 163 D7
Weir La
Abbots Leigh BS8 10 F5
Marshfield SN14 13 F8
Pilton BA4 140 E3
Yeovilton BA22 174 A1
Weir Rd BS49 34 E3
Welbeck Rd BA21 219 E7
WELHAM 160 A2
Welland Cl TA1 213 D4
Welland Rd
Keynsham BS31 24 F4
Yeovil BA21 219 D7
Wellard Cl 1 BS22 32 B4
Well Cl
Long Ashton BS41 11 B1
Weston-super-Mare BS24 49 B2
Winscombe BS25 70 A8
Wellesley Ct TA1 212 C1
Wellesley Gn BA10 215 E6
Wellesley Park Prim Sch TA21 222 E4
Wellesley Pk TA21 222 D4
Wellesley St TA2 212 F6
Wellesley Way TA3 192 A7
Wellfield Hill DT6, EX13 199 B2
Well House Cl BS9 5 E3
Wellhouse La BA6 206 F4
Wellings Cl TA20 198 C8
WELLINGTON 222 D7
Wellington Bldgs BA1 27 B2
Wellington Com Hospl TA21 222 D5
Wellington Ct BS21 6 C5
Wellington Flats BA20 219 A4
Wellington Hill TA21 222 F2
Wellington Jun Sch TA21 222 E5
Wellington Mews BS11 4 D5
Wellington Monument* TA21 180 B4
Wellington Mus TA21 222 D6
Wellington New Rd TA1 212 B3
Wellington Pl
Cheddar BS27 90 B7
Weston-super-Mare BS23 48 D7
Wellington Rd
Bridgwater TA6 209 B5
Bristol BS2 227 C4
Taunton TA1 212 D4
Wellington Sch TA21 222 E5
Wellington Sq TA24 200 F7
Wellington Terr
18 Bristol BS8 11 F6
Clevedon BS21 6 D5
Wiveliscombe TA4 210 C5
WELLISFORD 179 D8
Well La
Banwell BS29 50 E3
Purse Caundle DT9 189 D4
Timberscombe TA24 130 A5
Yatton BS49 34 C8
WELLOW 62 D1
Wellow Brook Ct BA3 78 B3
Wellow Brook Mdw BA3 78 B2
Wellow Dr BA11 120 C7
Wellow La
Hinton Charterhouse BA2 63 D1
Norton St Philip BA2 81 D5
Peasedown St John BA2 79 C6
Shoscombe BA2 79 E6
Wellow Mead BA2 79 B7
Wellow Rd BA2 80 B8
Wellow Tyning BA2 79 D7
Well Pk BS49 34 E4
WELLS 203 E4
Wells Cathedral* BA5 203 E4
Wells Cathedral Jun Sch BA5 203 E5
Wells Cathedral Sch BA5 203 E5
Wells Central CE Jun Sch BA5 203 C3
Wells Cl
Bristol BS14 23 C5
Burnham-on-S TA8 104 C7
Nailsea BS48 9 B1
Taunton TA2 213 A8
Wellsea Gr BS23 49 B7
Wellshead La TA24 128 A3
Wells & Mendip Mus* BA5 203 E4
WELLSPRINGS 212 F8
Wellsprings Prim Sch TA2 212 F8
Wellsprings Rd TA2 212 F7
Wells Rd
Bath BA2 228 B1
Bristol BS14 23 C7
Chilcompton BA3 96 F4
Clevedon BS21 6 D1
Corston BA2 43 B7
Dundry BS40, BS41 38 F7
Glastonbury BA6 206 E6
Glastonbury, Southway BA5, BA6 139 D4
Hallatrow BS39 77 B7
Norton St Philip BA2, BA3 81 C3
Priddy BA5 92 E2
Radstock BA3 78 E2
Rodney Stoke BS27 91 B1
Shepton Mallet BA4 204 E6
Theale BS28 109 B1
Westbury-sub-Mendip BA5 110 E6
Wookey Hole BA5 203 A7
Yarley BA5 139 C8
Wells Road Trad Est BA6 206 F7
Wells Sq BA3 78 D1
Wellsway
Bath BA2 44 F3
Keynsham BS31 24 F3
Wells Way BS28 107 F3
Wellsway Pk BA2 62 D8
Wellsway Sec Sch BS31 25 A5
Well The TA21 222 B5
Welsford Ave BA5 203 C5
Welsford Cl BA5 203 B5
Welsh Back BS1 227 A2
Welsh Ct BA5 203 B4
WELSHMILL 119 F6
Welshmill La BA11 119 F5
Welshmill Rd BA11 119 F5
WELTON 78 B2
Welton Gr BA3 78 B3
WELTON HOLLOW 78 D2
Welton Prim Sch BA3 78 C2
Welton Rd BA3 78 E2
Welton Vale BA3 78 B2
WEMBDON 208 C6
Wembdon Ct TA6 208 E4
Wembdon Hill TA6 208 C6
Wembdon Orch TA6 208 C6
Wembdon Rd TA6 208 E4
Wembdon Rise TA6 208 D5
Wembdon St George's CE Prim Sch TA6 208 C6
Wemberham Cres BS49 17 A1
Wemberham La BS49 33 E8
Wendick Dro TA10 171 E3
Wentwood Dr BS24 49 A1
Wentworth Cl BS22 32 A3
Wentworth Rd BA21 219 E7
Werren Cl TA23 202 B7
Wesley Ave BA3 78 C1
Wesley Cl
Brean TA8 65 F3
Frome BA11 119 F4
Southwick BA14 83 E2
Taunton TA1 212 C1
Wanstrow BA4 142 F4
Wesley Ct BS23 48 F8
Wesley Dr BS22 32 A3
Wesley La BA14 83 E2
Wesley Mews BS27 90 B7
Wesley Rd BA3 78 D1
Wesley Slope 13 BA11 119 F4
Wesley Villas
Coleford BA3 116 F6
12 Frome BA11 119 F4
Wessex Bldgs TA11 211 B5
Wessex Bsns Ctr BS27 90 A7
Wessex Cl
Bridgwater TA6 209 C4
Chard TA20 223 C2
Street BA16 207 D6
Wessex Ct 4 DT9 225 D3
Wessex Dr DT9 187 E1
Wessex Fields BA11 119 D2
Wessex Fields Ret Pk BA11 119 D2
Wessex Ho 10 BS2 227 C3
Wessex Pk TA11 211 B5
Wessex Rd
Stalbridge DT10 190 C4
Taunton TA1 168 E1
Weston-super-Mare BS24 49 B2
Yeovil BA21 218 D8
Wessex Rise TA11 211 E3
Wessex Way BA9 216 B3
Westacre BA16 207 A4
Westacre Cl BS27 90 B8
Westacre Rd BS27 90 B8
WEST ANSTEY 162 C6
West Anstey School Cross EX36 162 C5
West Approach Rd TA7 136 D4
West Ave
Bath BA2 44 C5
Highbridge TA9 104 C4
Westaway Cl BS49 34 C7
Westaway Pk BS49 34 D7
WEST BAGBOROUGH 151 F4
West Bank BA5 203 A8
Westbourne Ave
Clevedon BS21 6 B2
Keynsham BS31 24 E5
Westbourne Cl BA20 218 E5
Westbourne Cres BS21 6 B2
Westbourne Gr BA20 218 E5
Westbourne Ho BA2 228 C2
Westbourne Pl BS8 226 B3
WEST BOURTON 177 E8
West Bourton Rd SP8 177 E8
West Bower La TA5 153 C7
West Bow Ho TA6 208 E4
WEST BRADLEY 158 C7
Westbridge Pk DT9 225 B2
West Brook BA21 218 D6
Westbrook Ct BA4 141 E1
Westbrooke Ct BS1 226 A1
Westbrook Pk BA1 27 A2
Westbrook Rd
Bristol BS4 23 D8
Evercreech BA4 141 E1
Weston-super-Mare BS22 31 D1
Westbrook Vale BA4 141 E1
WEST BUCKLAND 180 F7
West Buckland Com Prim Sch TA21 180 F7
West Buckland Rd TA21 180 D7
Westbury
Bradford Abbas DT9 187 E1
Sherborne DT9 225 D3
Westbury Court Rd BS9 5 F7
Westbury Cres BS23 48 F2
Westbury Gdns BA22 186 C2
Westbury La BS9 5 C7
WESTBURY ON TRYM 5 F7
WESTBURY-SUB-MENDIP 110 D6
Westbury Terr
Dunkerton BA2 61 E5
2 Sherborne DT9 225 D3
Westbury View BA2 79 E8
WEST CAMEL 174 D3
West Camel Farm BA22 174 E3
West Camel Rd BA22 174 E3
West Charlton TA11 173 E7
WEST CHINNOCK 196 B8
West Chinnock CE Prim Sch TA18 196 B8
West Cl
Bath BA2 44 A5
Dunster TA24 201 D2
WEST COKER 197 A8
West Coker CE Prim Sch BA22 197 A8
West Coker Rd BA20 218 E2
WESTCOMBE
Batcombe 142 B2
Somerton 172 E7
Westcombe BA8 176 E1
Westcombe Hill BA4 142 C2
Westcombe Rd
Evercreech BA4 141 F2
Westcombe BA4 142 A2
Westcombes EX13 198 B7
Westcombe Trad Est TA19 183 E1
WEST COMPTON 204 C3
West Compton La BA4 204 E3
West Coombe
Bristol BS9 5 D6
Yeovil BA21 218 D6
West Coombe La TA4 165 D8
West Cornmoor Dro TA9 136 D7
Westcott Cl BA11 120 C6
Westcott Cross TA23 130 D1
Westcott La TA4 148 F2
Westcott Mead TA24 128 E1
West Cotts TA24 127 A2
West Cres TA19 221 B2
West Croft
Blagdon BS40 54 E2
Clevedon BS21 6 B2
West Ct
Horrington BA5 112 F1
Portishead BS20 2 D4
Templecombe BA8 176 E1
West Dene BS9 5 E6
West Dro TA7 137 D4
West Dundry La BS41 21 E2
WEST END
Blagdon 54 E3
Chewton Mendip 93 F6
Clevedon 6 B2
Frome 119 F5

WEST END *continued*
Nailsea 17 F7
Somerton 211 C3
West End
Bristol BS3 226 C1
Bristol, Kingsdown BS2 227 A4
Frome BA11 119 F5
Lower Weare BS26 88 D8
Marston Magna BA22 174 E1
Somerton TA11 211 C4
Street BA16 207 B5
Wedmore BS28 108 C3
West End Cl
Somerton TA11 211 C4
South Petherton TA13 220 B4
West End Ct
Chedzoy TA7 136 D1
South Petherton TA13 220 B4
West End Farm Cvn Pk BS24 49 E4
Westend La BA11 143 C6
West End La BS48 18 A8
West End Trad Est BS48 8 B1
West End View
Barrington TA19 184 C5
South Petherton TA13 220 B4
West End Way TA13 220 B4
Westerkirk Gate TA2 212 C7
Westerleigh Rd
Bath BA2 45 B1
Clevedon BS21 6 B2
Westerly Ct TA19 221 B4
Western Approaches BA22 174 A2
Western Ave BA21 218 B6
Western Ct
Clevedon BS21 6 D3
Shepton Mallet BA4 205 B6
Western Dr BS14 22 E6
Western Gate TA10 172 C7
Western La
East Quantoxhead TA5 133 A5
Minehead TA24 200 F7
Ridge BS40 74 C3
Western Retreat BA5 203 B5
Western St DT9 187 E4
Western Way
Bridgwater TA6 208 F7
Winsham TA20 194 E1
Westex Ho BS23 49 B5
WESTFIELD 97 C8
Westfield
Bruton BA10 215 D5
Clevedon BS21 16 D8
Curry Rivel TA10 171 C3
Shepton Mallet BA4 205 A6
Sherborne DT9 225 B2
Westfield Ave BA21 218 E6
Westfield Cl
Backwell BS48 19 A6
Bath BA2 44 E3
Bridgwater TA6 208 E4
Burnham-on-S TA8 104 B8
Keynsham BS31 24 C5
Weston-super-Mare BS23 48 D2
West Field Cl TA1 212 A2
Westfield Com Sch BA21 218 E6
Westfield Cres
Banwell BS29 51 A3
Yeovil BA21 218 F6
Westfield Ct TA8 104 B8
Westfield Dr
Backwell BS48 19 A6
Burnham-on-S TA8 104 B8
Westfield Est BA12 161 F2
Westfield Gr BA21 218 F6
Westfield Ho
Bath BA2 44 E3
Bridgwater TA6 208 E4
Westfield Ind & Trad Est BA3 97 C7
Westfield Inf Com Sch BA21 218 E6
Westfield La
Curry Rivel TA10 171 C3
Draycott BS27 90 E3
North Curry TA3 170 C3
Rodney Stoke BS27 110 C8
Street BA6, BA16 207 E2
West Field Lawn TA8 104 B8
Westfield Pk BA1 44 A7
Westfield Pk S BA1 44 A7
Westfield Pl
Bristol BS8 11 F7
Yeovil BA21 218 E6
Westfield Prim Sch BA3 97 C8
Westfield Rd
Backwell BS48 19 A6
Banwell BS29 51 A3
Burnham-on-S TA8 104 B8
Frome BA11 119 D3
Wells BA5 203 C4
Weston-super-Mare BS23 48 D2
Yeovil BA21 218 F6
Westfields TA19 184 C5
Westfield Terr BA3 78 D1
WESTFORD 179 F7
Westford Cl TA21 222 A5
Westford Ct TA21 222 A5
Westford Dr TA21 222 A5
West Garston BS29 51 A3
Westgate BS1 226 B1
Westgate Bldgs BA1 228 B2
Westgate St
Bath BA1 228 B2

Westgate St *continued*
4 Taunton TA1 212 E3
Westhall Rd BA1 44 D7
WESTHAM 107 C2
WEST HARPTREE 74 E6
West Harptree Rd BS40 74 F5
WEST HATCH 182 E7
West Hatch La TA3 182 F8
Westhaven Cl BS48 19 A6
Westhaven Sch BS23 48 D2
WESTHAY 138 A5
Westhay Broad Dro TA7 137 E6
Westhay Cross EX13 198 F3
Westhay Moor Dro BA5, BA6 138 D6
Westhay Rd BA6 138 C4
West Hay Rd BS40 35 C3
West Hendford BA20 218 F3
WEST HEWISH 33 A5
WEST HILL
Nailsea 9 A5
Portishead 2 A5
Wincanton 216 B4
West Hill
Milborne Port DT9 217 D2
Nailsea BS48 9 A5
Portishead BS20 2 B5
Wincanton BA9 216 B4
West Hill Ct BS20 2 C6
WEST HILL GARDENS 78 E1
Westhill Gdns BS20 2 C5
West Hill Gdns
Radstock BA3 78 D1
Radstock BA3 78 E1
Westhill La TA9 105 C2
West Hill Rd BA3 78 D1
Westholm Rd TA11 211 B4
West Howetown La TA24 147 D5
WEST HUNTSPILL 136 A7
West Huntspill Com Prim Sch TA9 104 C1
West La
Alhampton BA4 159 C5
Alweston DT9 189 A2
Barrington TA13 184 F5
Croscombe BA5 140 F8
Felton BS40 37 C8
Lynford-on-F TA11 158 D2
Sherborne DT9 188 F1
Westlake Cl TA7 155 C2
WEST LAMBROOK 184 F5
Westland Rd BA20 218 F4
Westlands Distribution Pk BS24 49 B3
West Lea Rd BA1 27 A1
West Leaze BA16 207 B6
WESTLEIGH 179 A4
WEST LEIGH 150 F1
Westleigh Gdns BA4 205 A6
West Leigh Inf Sch BS48 19 A6
Westleigh Pk BS14 23 B8
Westleigh Rd TA1 213 B3
Westley Mews BS24 32 C1
West Links BS23 48 D2
West Links Cl BS22 31 B3
West Littleton Rd SN14 13 F8
West Lodge BA4 205 A5
WEST LUCCOMBE 124 C3
WEST LYDFORD 158 C2
WEST LYNG 170 B7
West Lynne BS27 90 B8
West Mall BS8 11 F7
Westmans Est TA8 104 C7
Westmarch Way BS22 32 A4
Westmead BA3 96 D3
Westmead Gdns BA1 27 A2
West Mendip Com Hospl BA6 139 D3
Westmere Cres TA8 104 C8
West Mill La
Marnhull DT10 190 D6
Sherborne DT9 225 C2
Westminster BA21 218 C7
Westminster Bldgs DT10 190 B4
Westminster Cotts DT10 190 B4
Westminster St BA20 219 A4
Westminster Way TA6 136 B2
WEST MONKTON 169 C7
West Monkton CE Prim Sch TA2 213 F8
Westmoor Dro TA10, TA12 184 E7
Westmoor La TA10 184 D8
Westmoreland Dr BA2 228 A2
Westmoreland Rd BA2 228 A1
Westmoreland St BA2 228 A2
Westmoreland Station Rd BA2 228 A1
WEST MUDFORD 187 C7
WEST NEWTON 169 F8
WESTON 27 B1
Weston All Saints CE Prim Sch BA1 27 A2
WESTON BAMPFYLDE 175 B3
Weston Bsns Pk BS24 49 E5
Weston Cl
Bristol BS9 5 C7
East Chinnock BA22 196 E8
Weston Coll BS48 8 E2
Weston College BS23 48 D8
Weston Coll South West Skills Campus BS22 49 C8
Weston Coll Uni Campus BS23 48 F2
Weston Ct BS24 49 B3
Weston Dro BS20 7 F8
Weston Euro Pk BS24 49 B4

Weston Express Bsns Pk BS22 49 C6
Weston Farm La BA1 27 C2
Weston Gateway Tourist Pk BS24 32 C1
Weston General Hospl BS23 48 E2
Weston Hill SP8 177 D3
Westonia BS22 31 E2
Westonian Ct BS9 5 C4
Weston Ind Est BS24 49 B2
WESTON IN GORDANO 1 F1
Weston La
Bath BA1 44 C8
Christon BS26 68 C7
East Coker BA22 197 E5
Halstock DT2 196 F1
Weston Lock Ret BA2 44 C6
Weston Lodge BS23 48 D8
Weston Milton Sta BS22 49 C7
Weston Miniature Rly★ BS23 48 D5
WESTON PARK 27 C1
Weston Park Ct BA1 27 D1
Weston Pk BA1 27 C1
Weston Pk E BA1 27 D1
Weston Pk W BA1 27 C1
Weston Rd
Bath BA1 44 D8
Brean TA8 66 A5
Congresbury BS49 34 B5
East Brent BS24, TA9 86 D6
Failand BS8 10 C3
Long Ashton BS41 20 D8
Weston Ret Pk BS23 49 A6
Weston St
Buckhorn Weston SP8 177 D3
East Chinnock BA22 196 E8
WESTON-SUPER-MARE 48 B7
Weston-super-Mare Sta BS23 48 E7
WESTON TOWN 142 E5
Weston Town BA4 141 E1
Weston Way BS24 49 F2
Weston Wlk BA11 119 C6
Weston Wood Rd BS20 2 C3
WESTONZOYLAND 154 E5
Westonzoyland Prim Sch TA7 154 F5
Westonzoyland Pumping Sta★ TA7 154 D3
Westonzoyland Rd TA6, TA7 209 E4
Westover
Frome BA11 119 D4
Nunney BA11 143 B7
Westover Ct BA11 119 D4
Westover Gdns BS9 5 F8
Westover Gn TA6 208 E4
Westover Green Com Sch TA6 208 E4
Westover La
Crewkerne TA18 224 B7
Martock TA12 185 F8
Westover Rd BS9 5 F8
Westover's Cnr BS28 108 B4
Westover Trad Est TA10 171 F5
Westover View TA18 224 C7
WESTOWE 151 A3
Westowe Hill TA4 151 A3
West Par BS9 5 C7
Westpark TA21 180 D7
Westpark TA21 180 D7
Westpark 26 TA21 180 D7
West Park Cl TA24 200 E7
WEST PENNARD 140 B1
West Pennard CE Prim Sch BA6 140 B1
West Pk
Bristol BS8 226 B4
Butleigh BA6 157 E4
Castle Cary BA7 214 B6
Minehead TA24 200 E7
Yeovil BA20 218 F5
WEST PORLOCK 123 F4
WESTPORT 184 C7
Westport La TA3, TA10 184 B7
WEST QUANTOXHEAD 132 E4
West Quay TA6 208 F5
West Rd
East Brent BS24, TA9 86 B7
Lympsham BS24 67 B1
Midsomer Norton BA3 78 A3
Wiveliscombe TA4 210 B4
Yatton BS49 34 B7
Westridge DT9 225 C3
Westridge Way TA4 167 E7
West Rocke Ave BS9 5 D6
West Rolstone Rd BS24 33 A1
West Sedgemoor Nature Reserve★ TA3 170 F3
West Sedgemoor Rd TA3 170 D3
WEST SHEPTON 205 A4
West Shepton BA4 205 A5
West Somerset Com Coll The TA24 201 B5
West Somerset Community College Farm TA24 201 D4
West Somerset Railway★ TA4 150 F7
West Somerset Rly★ TA4 151 C4
West Somerset Rural Life Mus★ TA24 124 C4
West St
Ashcott TA7 156 B8
Axbridge BS26 70 B2

West St *continued*
Bampton EX16 164 B1
Banwell BS29 51 A3
Banwell BS29 51 B3
Bishops Lydeard TA4 167 E8
Bridgwater TA6 208 E4
Bristol BS2 227 C3
Carhampton TA24 131 B4
Crewkerne TA18 224 B6
Dunster TA24 201 D1
Hinton St George TA17 195 C7
Ilchester BA22 173 E1
Ilminster TA19 221 B4
Kington Magna SP8 177 E1
Martock TA12 185 E8
Minehead TA24 200 E6
Seavington St Mary TA19 184 D1
Somerton TA11 211 D4
South Petherton TA13 220 B4
Stoke sub Hamdon TA14 185 E3
Templecombe BA8 189 E8
Watchet TA23 202 B7
Wells BA5 203 C3
Weston-super-Mare BS23 48 D8
Wiveliscombe TA4 210 C4
Yarlington BA9 175 F7
Yeovil BA20 218 F4
WEST STOKE 185 E4
WEST STOUGHTON 107 E6
West Terr BA2 82 C1
WEST TOWN
Backwell 18 F5
Baltonsborough 157 F6
Ubley 55 B6
West Town Gr BS4 23 D8
West Town La
Baltonsborough BA6 157 F5
Bristol BS4, BS14 23 C8
West Town Pk BS4 23 D8
West Town Rd
Backwell BS48 19 A5
Bristol BS11 4 C7
West Tyning BA2 42 B1
Westview BS39 77 C5
West View
Creech St Michael TA3 169 D5
Long Sutton TA10 172 E4
Milborne Port DT9 217 D3
Queen Camel BA22 174 F4
South Cadbury BA22 175 D4
West Monkton TA2 169 D8
West View Cl TA7 155 B4
Westview Orch BA3 64 B5
West View Rd
Batheaston BA1 29 A3
Keynsham BS31 24 E5
West Villas TA4 167 F6
Westville BA21 219 C5
Westward BS41 11 B2
Westward Cl BS40 35 D2
Westward Dr BS20 4 C4
Westward Gdns BS41 11 B2
Westward Rd BS13 21 F7
Westway
Nailsea BS48 8 E2
Street BA16 207 B6
West Way BS21 6 C3
Westway Ctr BA11 119 F5
Westway La BA4 205 B4
West Ways BA22 196 E8
West Well La BS28 109 C1
WEST WICK 32 C1
West Wick BS24 32 C1
West Wick Rdbt BS22, BS24 50 B8
WESTWOOD 64 E3
Westwood BA2 45 E6
Westwood Ave BS39 59 C2
Westwood Cl 2 BS22 31 F2
Westwood Cotts BA8 176 E1
Westwood Dr BA11 119 C4
Westwood Dro TA11 158 C3
WEST WOODLANDS 143 F6
Westwood Rd
Bridgwater TA6 209 D7
Bristol BS4 23 D8
Westwoods BA1 29 B3
Westwood with Iford Prim Sch BA15 64 F3
Wetherell Pl BS8 226 B3
Wet La BS27 90 F2
Wetlands La BS20 2 C3
Wetlands & Willows Visitor Ctr★ TA3 170 D5
Wetmoor La
Langport TA10 172 C2
Westbury-sub-Mendip BA5 110 E1
Wexford Rd BS4 22 D8
WEYCROFT 198 B2
Weycroft Ave EX13 198 A2
Weylands BA11 119 E6
Weymont Cl TA7 155 B3
Weymouth Ct BA1 45 B8
Weymouth Rd
Evercreech BA4 141 E1
Frome BA11 119 E4
Weymouth St BA1 45 B8
Whaddon Hill BA10 160 C7
Wharf Cotts TA21 222 B8
Wharf Ho TA19 221 B4
Wharf La
Ilminster TA19 221 B3
Portbury BS20 3 B5
Wharfside BS24 66 E3
Wharnecliffe Cl BS14 23 B5
Wharnecliffe Gdns BS14 23 B5
Whatcombe Rd BA11 119 E6
Whatcombe Terr BA11 119 E6

WHATLEY
Frome 118 D4
Winsham 194 C1
Whatley TA10 171 F5
Whatley Cross TA20 194 C1
Whatley La
Buckland St Mary TA20 192 D7
Langport TA10 172 A5
Tatworth TA20 194 C1
Winsham TA20 199 A8
Whatley Mews TA10 171 F5
Whatley Vineyard & Herb Gdn★ BA11 118 D4
Wheatfield Dr BS22 32 A5
Wheatfield La BA3 95 A6
Wheathill Cl
Keynsham BS31 24 D5
Milborne Port DT9 217 D2
Wheathill La DT9 217 E3
Wheathill Way DT9 217 D2
Wheatleigh Cl TA1 212 E2
Wheatley Cres TA1 213 B5
Wheatstones 10 TA4 167 F8
WHEDDON CROSS 129 E1
Wheeler Gr BA5 203 B4
Wheelers Cl BA3 78 D2
Wheelers Dr BA3 78 C2
WHEELER'S HILL 78 C2
Wheelers Rd BA3 78 D2
Wheel House La TA20 199 B7
Whellers Mdw TA12 185 E7
Whetham Mill Cross DT8 199 F5
Whetham Mill La DT8 199 F6
Whetstones Almshouses TA19 183 F4
Whimbrel Ave 2 BS20 2 F6
WHIPCOTT 179 B5
Whippington Ct BS1 227 B3
Whirligg La 15 TA14 185 F4
Whirligig La TA1 212 F4
Whirligig Pl 7 TA1 212 F4
Whistley La BS40 74 F6
Whitbourne Moor BA12 144 E8
WHITBOURNE SPRINGS 144 F7
Whitbourne Springs BA12 144 F7
Whitchey Dro TA9 137 A5
WHITCHURCH 23 D4
Whitchurch District Ctr BS14 23 A5
Whitchurch La
Bristol, Bishopsworth BS13 22 B5
Bristol, Hartcliffe BS13 22 C5
Bristol, Whitchurch BS14 22 E5
Dundry BS41 22 C1
Henstridge BA8 190 A7
Yenston BA8 189 F8
Whitchurch Prim Sch BS14 23 C4
Whitchurch Rd BS13 22 A6
Whitchurch Trad Est BS14 22 F5
WHITCOMBE 175 D2
Whitcombe Farm La DT9 175 D2
Whitcross 10 BA22 197 F8
White Ash La TA20 193 A5
WHITE BALL 179 D6
Whitebeam Cl TA6 209 D5
Whitebrook La BA2 79 A8
Whitebrook Terr TA21 178 F5
White Cats Cotts BA8 176 E3
Whitechapel La BA11 101 C1
Whitecroft TA4 202 E4
WHITECROSS 171 E3
WHITE CROSS
Bishop Sutton 57 E1
Burnham-on-Sea 105 B8
Hallatrow 76 F6
Zeals 161 F3
White Cross
Brent Knoll TA9 105 C8
Exford TA24 128 B1
Whitecross Ave BS14 23 C6
White Cross Gate BS39 76 F6
Whitecross La
Banwell BS29 51 A4
Minehead TA24 200 E7
Whitecross Rd
East Harptree BS40 74 F4
Weston-super-Mare BS23 48 F6
Whitecross Way TA24 200 E7
Whitedown Cross EX15 191 B4
WHITEFIELD 210 B8
Whitefield Cl BA1 29 B4
White field Cross EX36 162 D3
Whitefield La TA19 184 D4
Whitefield Rocks TA4 150 B1
WHITE GATE 194 B1
Whitegate Cl
Bleadon BS24 67 B6
Minehead TA24 201 A6
Whitegate Rd TA24 201 A6
Whitegates Gdns TA24 200 F6
WHITEHALL 180 A1
Whitehall
Taunton TA1 212 F5
Watchet TA23 202 B7
Whitehall Cl TA13 220 D4
Whitehall Ct TA18 224 C7
Whitehall Rd TA6 136 B2
White Hart La TA21 222 D6
WHITE HILL 79 F6
White Hill
Langport TA10 172 A7
Shoscombe BA2 79 F6
White Hill Dro TA20 193 C5
Whitehole Hill BA3 116 E4

White Horse Dr BA11 .... 120 C6
White Horse La BS28 .... 138 D8
White Horse Rd BA15 .... 64 E7
Whitehouse Ctr (PRU) BS13 .... 22 C5
Whitehouse La
Litton BA3 .... 75 D3
Wraxall BS48 .... 9 A6
White House La
East Huntspill TA9 .... 136 E7
Loxton BS26 .... 68 A3
Whitehouse Rd BS49 .... 34 F8
White House Rd TA5, TA6 .... 135 D5
WHITELACKINGTON 184 C2
Whiteladies Rd BS8 .... 226 B4
Whitelands Hill BA3 .... 79 B3
Whiteleaze La
Thurloxton TA2 .... 153 C1
West Monkton TA2 .... 169 D8
White Lodge Pk BS20 .... 2 D6
White Mead BA21 .... 218 D6
Whitemill La BA11 .... 119 C3
Whitemoor Hill TA20 .... 194 C4
Whitemoor La TA4 .... 150 F3
Whitemore Ct BA1 .... 29 A4
Whiteoak Way BS48 .... 18 D8
White Oxmead La BA2 .... 61 E1
White Ox Mead La BA2 .... 61 F1
White Post
Midsomer Norton BA3 .... 97 B6
Twitchen EX36 .... 145 K2
Whitepost Gate DT9 .... 188 D6
Whites Cl TA6 .... 208 E2
White's Dro BA5 .... 138 F7
Whitesfield Ct BS48 .... 8 D2
Whitesfield Rd BS48 .... 8 D1
White's La TA4 .... 133 A1
Whitesome's Dro BS27 .... 109 C6
White St
Bristol BS5 .... 227 C4
Creech St Michael TA3 .... 169 E4
Horningsham BA12 .... 144 E4
North Curry TA3 .... 170 C4
WHITESTAUNTON 193 B5
Whitestaunton Cross TA20 .... 193 B5
Whitestone Rd BA11 .... 120 B6
Whitewall Cnr TA3 .... 181 D2
WHITEWAY 44 A4
Whiteway TA20 .... 193 E6
Whiteway Rd BA2 .... 44 A3
Whitewell Pl BA11 .... 119 E3
Whitewell Rd BA11 .... 119 E3
Whitewells Rd BA1 .... 28 A2
Whitewick La TA5 .... 134 F8
Whitfield Rd TA6 .... 209 D6
Whitford Hill
Corfe TA3 .... 182 A4
Pitminster TA3 .... 181 F5
Whitford La TA3 .... 182 A4
Whithys The BA16 .... 207 C7
Whiting Cl BA4 .... 205 C4
Whiting La 1 TA6 .... 153 E3
Whiting Rd
Bristol BS13 .... 22 A4
Glastonbury BA6 .... 206 F5
Whiting Way BA5 .... 203 D4
Whitland Ave BS13 .... 22 B5
Whitland Rd BS13 .... 22 B5
WHITLEY BATTS 40 F2
Whitley La BA16 .... 156 D7
Whitley Rd TA7, BA16 .... 156 C8
Whitling St BS40 .... 38 A2
Whitmead Gdns BS13 .... 22 C4
Whitmore La TA2 .... 212 D8
Whitmore Rd TA2 .... 212 E8
WHITNAGE 178 C2
Whitnage La EX16 .... 178 C2
WHITNELL 134 D2
Whitnell Cnr BA5 .... 113 F6
Whitnell La
Binegar BA3 .... 114 B8
Keenthorne TA5 .... 134 D2
Whitney Cres BS24 .... 49 C5
Whitney Hill TA19 .... 193 F8
Whitson Ho 1 BS2 .... 227 C3
Whitson St BS1 .... 227 A4
Whitstone BA4 .... 205 C5
Whitstone Cl BA4 .... 205 C6
Whitstone Cnr BA4 .... 205 D1
Whitstone Ct BA4 .... 205 D5
Whitstone Hill BA4 .... 204 C1
Whitstone La BA4 .... 205 E1
Whitstone Rd BA4 .... 205 D4
Whitstone Rise BA4 .... 205 D4
Whitsweil Steep TA24 .... 130 D4
Whittakers Ho 6 BA4 .... 205 B6
Whitting Rd BS23 .... 48 E4
Whittington Dr BS22 .... 31 D2
Whittock Rd BS14 .... 23 D6
Whittock Sq BS14 .... 23 D7
Whittox La BA11 .... 119 E5
Whitwell Rd BS14 .... 23 B8
Whitworth Rd
Frome BA11 .... 119 F2
Minehead TA24 .... 200 D7
WICK
Burnham-on-Sea 85 E8
Glastonbury 139 E2
Stogursey 134 D7
Wicketsbeer Rd BA22 .... 197 C6
Wickfield BS21 .... 6 C1
Wickham Ct BS21 .... 6 C3
Wickham Rise BA11 .... 119 F6
Wickham's Cross or Beggar's Grave BA6 .... 157 C3
Wickham Way
East Brent TA9 .... 86 D4
Shepton Mallet BA4 .... 205 A6
Wick Hill
Charlton Horethorne DT9 .... 176 A1
Milborne Port DT9 .... 217 B6
Wickhill Rd TA10 .... 171 D5
Wick Hollow BA6 .... 206 F5
Wick House Cl BS31 .... 25 D3
Wick La
Burnham-on-S TA9 .... 85 E6
Glastonbury BA6 .... 139 E2
Lympsham BS24 .... 66 E1
Norton Fitzwarren TA2 .... 168 A6
Peasedown St John BA2, BA3 .... 60 F1
Pensford BS39 .... 40 D3
Upton Cheyney BS30 .... 26 A8
WICKLANE 61 A1
Wicklow Rd BS4 .... 22 E8
Wick Moor Dro TA5 .... 134 C7
Wick Rd
Bishop Sutton BS39 .... 57 C3
Lympsham BS24 .... 66 D2
Milborne Port DT9 .... 217 C4
Wick St Lawrence BS22 .... 32 B7
WICK ST LAWRENCE 32 B7
WIDCOMBE 45 C4
Widcombe BS14 .... 23 A6
Widcombe CE Jun Sch BA2 .... 45 B5
Widcombe Cres BA2 .... 45 B5
Widcombe Hill BA2 .... 45 C4
Widcombe Inf Sch BA2 .... 45 B5
Widcombe Par BA2 .... 228 C1
Widcombe Rise BA2 .... 45 B5
Widcombe Terr BA2 .... 45 B5
Wideatts Rd BS27 .... 90 A7
Widmore Gr BS13 .... 22 B5
WIGBOROUGH 220 F1
Wigeon Cl TA24 .... 201 C5
Wight Row BS20 .... 2 F6
Wigmore Gdns BS22 .... 31 D2
Wiindsor Cres TA20 .... 223 B3
Wilbye Gr BS4 .... 22 D7
Wildcountry La BS48 .... 20 E6
Wilde Cl TA8 .... 104 C6
Wilder Ct BS2 .... 227 B4
Wilderness Dro BA16 .... 138 E2
Wilderness The 9 DT9 .... 225 E4
Wilder St BS2 .... 227 B4
Wildmoor La TA21 .... 180 F6
Wild Oak Ho TA3 .... 168 D1
Wild Oak La TA3 .... 168 D1
Wilfred Rd TA1 .... 213 A4
Wilfrid Rd BA16 .... 207 D6
Wilkins Cl TA20 .... 223 E4
Wilkins Rd TA6 .... 209 D5
WILKINTHROOP 176 C2
WILLAND 191 E8
Willan Pl BS24 .... 32 C1
Willcocks Cl 6 TA21 .... 222 D5
Willcox Cl BA6 .... 206 E5
Willet Cl TA9 .... 104 D3
Willet's La BA3 .... 94 D6
WILLETT 150 E4
Willett Hill Cross TA4 .... 150 D5
Willey Rd TA3 .... 170 E6
WILLHAYNE 223 A8
William Daw Cl BS29 .... 50 F3
William Jessop Wy BS14 .... 22 E4
William Reynolds Ho BA16 .... 207 D7
William St
Bath BA2 .... 228 C3
Taunton TA2 .... 212 F6
Williamstowe BA2 .... 45 C1
William's Yd BS40 .... 38 A7
Willie Gill Ct TA1 .... 212 E4
Willinton Rd BS4 .... 22 F8
Willis Hay DT9 .... 225 D3
Willis's La TA18 .... 196 C4
WILLITON 202 D3
Williton Com Hospl TA4 .... 202 D3
Williton Cres BS23 .... 48 F3
Williton Ind Est TA4 .... 202 E4
Williton Sta TA4 .... 202 F4
Will La TA4 .... 151 A3
Willmott Cl BS14 .... 22 F3
Willmotts Cl TA7 .... 137 B2
Willoughby Cl BS13 .... 22 B7
Willoughby Pl TA20 .... 223 D3
Willoughby Rd TA6 .... 208 C4
Willowbank TA24 .... 130 B4
Willow Cl
Bath BA2 .... 62 E8
Clevedon BS21 .... 6 E3
East Huntspill TA9 .... 136 E7
Langport TA10 .... 172 A6
Long Ashton BS41 .... 10 F1
Portishead BS20 .... 2 C4
Radstock BA3 .... 78 E2
Taunton TA1 .... 213 D1
Weston-super-Mare, St Georges BS22 .... 32 D2
Weston-super-Mare, Uphill BS23 .... 48 E2
Westonzoyland TA7 .... 154 E5
Williton TA4 .... 202 E3
Willow Ct TA6 .... 209 D5
Willowdown BS22 .... 31 E4
Willowdown Prim Acad TA6 .... 209 C8
Willow Dr
Bleadon BS24 .... 67 C6
Hutton BS24 .... 49 E2
Shepton Mallet BA4 .... 205 A6
Willow Dr *continued*
Weston-super-Mare BS24 .... 49 E5
Willowfalls The BA1 .... 28 E3
Willow Gdns BS22 .... 32 D2
Willow Gn
Bath BA2 .... 44 D4
Chedzoy TA7 .... 154 D8
Willow Gr TA23 .... 131 E4
Willow Ho BS13 .... 22 D4
Willow La EX15 .... 180 F2
Willow Rd
Street BA16 .... 207 B3
Yeovil BA21 .... 218 F6
Willows The
Brent Knoll TA9 .... 86 A2
Nailsea BS48 .... 8 F3
Willow The BA3 .... 96 F2
Willow Tree Cl BA22 .... 174 A4
Willow Vale BA11 .... 119 F5
Willow Way TA18 .... 224 D7
Willow Wlk
Bridgwater TA6 .... 209 C4
Keynsham BS31 .... 24 D4
Wills Ind Est TA6 .... 209 A4
Wills Rd TA6 .... 208 F1
Wills Way BS4 .... 22 D6
Willway St BS2 .... 227 C3
WILMINGTON 43 A1
Wilmots Way BS20 .... 4 D4
Wilsham Cross EX35 .... 122 A5
Wilsham La EX35 .... 122 A5
Wilson Cl BA5 .... 203 C2
Wilson Gdns BS24 .... 32 C1
Wilson Pl BS2 .... 227 C4
Wilsons Cl TA5 .... 134 B2
Wilson St BS2 .... 227 C4
WILSTOCK VILLAGE TA6 .... 153 F5
WILTON 212 F2
Wilton Cl
Burnham-on-S TA8 .... 104 C8
Street BA16 .... 207 D5
Taunton TA1 .... 212 E3
Wilton Ct BS23 .... 48 D7
Wilton Gdns BS23 .... 48 D7
Wilton Gr TA1 .... 212 E3
Wilton Orch
Street BA16 .... 207 D5
Taunton TA1 .... 212 E2
Wilton Rd BA21 .... 219 E8
Wiltons BS40 .... 35 D2
Wilton St TA1 .... 212 E3
WILTOWN
Curry Rivel 171 C3
Wellington 180 F3
Wiltown TA10 .... 171 D3
Wiltown La EX15 .... 180 F3
Wiltshire Cl TA1 .... 212 C2
Wiltshire Ct TA1 .... 212 C2
Wiltshires Barton 4 BA11 .... 119 E5
Wiltshire Way BA1 .... 28 A2
Wilway La TA22 .... 163 C6
Wimblestone Rd BS25 .... 51 F2
Wimborne Cl TA1 .... 213 D3
Wimborough La BA22 .... 196 F6
Winash Cl BS14 .... 23 D7
WINCANTON 216 A4
Wincanton Bsns Pk BA9 .... 216 B3
Wincanton Cl BS48 .... 9 B1
Wincanton Com Hospl BA9 .... 216 B4
Wincanton Mus★ BA9 .... 216 C4
Wincanton Prim Sch BA9 .... 216 C3
Winchcombe Cl BS48 .... 19 A8
Winchcombe Gr BS11 .... 4 F5
Winchester Cotts TA19 .... 184 E1
Winchester Gdns BA21 .... 219 C7
Winchester Ho 2 TA1 .... 213 A4
Winchester Rd
5 Bath BA2 .... 44 D5
Burnham-on-S TA8 .... 104 C7
Winchester St TA1 .... 213 A4
Windball Hill TA22 .... 163 B7
Windcliff Cres BS11 .... 4 E7
Wind Down Cl TA6 .... 208 C4
Windermere Ave BS23 .... 48 F4
Windermere Cl BA20 .... 218 F2
Windmill TA3 .... 170 F5
Windmill Bsns Pk BS21 .... 16 E8
Windmill Cl TA9 .... 105 B7
Windmill Cotts TA15 .... 186 C4
Windmill Cres TA7 .... 136 E3
WINDMILL HILL 183 B3
Windmill Hill
Hutton BS24 .... 50 A2
Wrantage TA3 .... 170 A2
Windmill Hill La
Ashill TA19 .... 183 B3
Westbury-sub-Mendip BA5 .... 110 D4
Windmill Hill Rd BA6 .... 206 E5
Windmill La
Langport TA10 .... 172 C5
Montacute TA15 .... 186 C4
West Pennard BA6 .... 140 C1
Windmill Rd
Clevedon BS21 .... 16 E8
High Ham TA10 .... 156 A1
Windmill Rise TA18 .... 224 C7
Windrush Cl BA2 .... 43 F4
Windrush Gn BS31 .... 25 A4
Windrush Rd BS31 .... 25 A4
Windsbatch Hill BA11 .... 101 C1
Windsbatch La BA11 .... 101 B1
Windsor Ave BS31 .... 24 E4
Windsor Bridge Rd BA1, BA2 .... 44 D7
Windsor Castle BA1 .... 44 D7
Windsor Cl
Burnham-on-S TA8 .... 85 B1
Clevedon BS21 .... 6 D2
Minehead TA24 .... 200 E6
Taunton TA1 .... 212 C1
Windsor Cres BA11 .... 120 A5
Windsor Ct
4 Bath BA1 .... 44 C7
13 Bristol, Clifton BS8 .... 11 F6
Windsor Dr
Bridgwater TA6 .... 209 D7
Nailsea BS48 .... 8 E2
Windsor Hill La BA4 .... 141 B8
Windsor Ho TA6 .... 209 C5
Windsor La TA14 .... 186 A4
Windsor Pl
5 Bath BA1 .... 44 C7
Bristol, Clifton BS8 .... 11 F6
Windsor Rd
Bridgwater TA6 .... 209 D7
Weston-super-Mare BS22 .... 31 C2
Windsor Terr
Bristol, Clifton BS8 .... 11 F6
17 Henstridge BA8 .... 190 A6
Paulton BS39 .... 77 E5
Windsor Villas 3 BA1 .... 44 C7
Windway Hill TA4 .... 164 D6
Windwhistle Circ BS23 .... 48 F4
Windwhistle La
Sticklepath TA4 .... 149 F6
Weston-super-Mare BS23 .... 48 E3
Windwhistle Prim Sch BS23 .... 48 F3
Windwhistle Rd BS23 .... 48 D3
Windy Ridge TA17 .... 195 D7
Windyridge La TA11 .... 211 B1
Wine St
Bath BA1 .... 228 C2
Bristol BS1 .... 227 A3
Frome BA11 .... 119 E4
Yeovil BA20 .... 219 B4
WINFORD 37 F7
Winford CE Prim Sch BS40 .... 37 F7
Winford Cl BS20 .... 2 E4
Winford Gr BS13 .... 22 A8
Winford La BS41 .... 21 C1
Winford Rd BS40 .... 38 F3
Winford Rural Workshops BA22 .... 197 A2
Winford Terr
Bridgwater TA6 .... 209 B6
Bristol BS41 .... 21 C5
Wingard Cl BS23 .... 48 D2
Wingard Ct 6 BS23 .... 48 E5
Wingate Ave BA21 .... 219 C7
WINGFIELD 83 C6
Wingfield Rd DT9 .... 225 C3
Winifred Cliff Ct 1 EX16 .... 164 B1
Winifred's La BA1 .... 27 E1
Winkworth Way TA1, TA2 .... 213 A5
Winnibrook La TA24 .... 131 A5
Winnowing End BS25 .... 52 A3
Winpenny La TA2 .... 168 E8
Winsbeer La
Rockwell Green TA21 .... 222 A6
Runnington TA21 .... 179 F8
Winsbury View BA2 .... 42 B1
WINSCOMBE 69 F7
Winscombe Cl BS31 .... 24 D6
Winscombe Ct BA11 .... 120 B5
Winscombe Dro
Shipham BS25 .... 70 D6
Winscombe BS25 .... 70 A5
Winscombe Hill BS25 .... 69 F5
Winscombe Rd BS23 .... 49 A7
Winscombe Woodborough Prim Sch BS25 .... 70 A8
WINSFORD 147 C5
WINSHAM 194 D1
Winsham Cl BS14 .... 23 B5
Winsham Prim Sch TA20 .... 194 E1
Winslade Cl TA2 .... 213 B7
WINSLEY 64 D7
Winsley CE Prim Sch BA15 .... 64 E7
Winsley Hill BA3 .... 64 B6
Winsley Rd BA15 .... 64 F7
Winsors La TA24 .... 131 A5
Winstitchen Cross TA24 .... 127 C2
Winstitchen La TA24 .... 127 C2
Winston Cl TA2 .... 212 E6
Winston Dr BA21 .... 218 F8
Winstone Ct BS2 .... 226 C3
Winterfield TA18 .... 196 B5
Winterfield Pk BS39 .... 77 E4
Winterfield Rd BS39 .... 77 E5
WINTERHAY GREEN 221 A5
Winterhay La TA19 .... 221 A5
WINTERHEAD 70 D8
Winter La DT9 .... 188 C8
Winters Cross TA4 .... 165 C8
Winters Field TA1 .... 213 A5
Winters Hill La BA4 .... 204 C3
Winters La BS40 .... 36 D6
Winter's La TA4 .... 150 C3
Winters Orch TA3 .... 169 C1
Winterstoke Commercial Ctr BS23 .... 49 A6
Winterstoke Rd
Bristol BS3 .... 11 F3
Weston-super-Mare BS23, BS24 .... 49 B4
Winterstoke Underpass BS3 .... 11 F4
WINTER WELL 182 C7
Winterwell La BA4 .... 141 F4
Winter Wlk BS14 .... 23 C6
Wint Hill BS29 .... 51 B2
WINYARD'S GAP 196 E1
Winyards View TA18 .... 224 D4
Wireworks Est The TA6 .... 136 A2
Wirral Park Rd BA6 .... 206 C3
Wirral Park Rdbt BA6 .... 206 C3
Wirral Park Trad Est BA6 .... 206 B3
Wirral Pk Ind Est BA6 .... 206 B4
Wishford Mews BA3 .... 78 C2
Wisley Wlk BS22 .... 49 F7
Wisteria Ave BS24 .... 49 D2
Wisteria Cl BA22 .... 218 B5
Wiston Cross EX36 .... 162 D2
Witches Wlk TA6 .... 208 E2
Witch Hazel Rd BS13 .... 22 E3
WITCOMBE 185 F8
Witcombe Dro TA12 .... 172 F1
Witcombe La TA12 .... 185 F8
Witham Cl TA1 .... 213 D3
WITHAM FRIARY 143 C3
Witham Rd BS31 .... 25 A3
Withers La 1 BS13 .... 22 C4
Withey Cl E BS9 .... 5 F6
Withey Cl W BS9 .... 5 F5
Witheys The BS14 .... 23 C4
Withial Hill BA4 .... 158 D8
Withiel Dr TA5 .... 135 B2
WITHIEL FLOREY 148 E4
Withiel Hill TA24 .... 148 F6
Withies La BA3 .... 97 A8
Withies Pk BA3 .... 96 F8
Withies Wy BA3 .... 96 F8
Withmoor Dro TA10 .... 172 E4
Withybed La BA9 .... 177 E6
WITHYBROOK 115 E3
Withy Cl BS48 .... 8 F3
WITHYCOMBE 131 B4
Withycombe Cross TA24 .... 131 C4
Withycombe Hill TA5 .... 135 A5
Withycombe Hill Gate TA24 .... 130 F4
Withycombe La TA24 .... 131 B5
Withy Cotts BA3 .... 115 C5
WITHYDITCH 61 C3
Withyditch La BA2 .... 61 C4
Withy Gr TA9 .... 136 C7
Withy Grove Cl TA6 .... 209 D7
Withy Hays Rd 3 TA11 .... 173 F7
Withy La
Barton St David TA11 .... 158 A3
Clatworthy TA4 .... 149 B2
Hemyock EX15 .... 180 B1
Oakhill BA3 .... 115 C5
Withymead BS49 .... 17 F1
WITHY MILLS 78 A7
WITHYPOOL 146 C6
Withypool Cross
Hawkridge TA22 .... 146 C2
Twitchen EX36 .... 145 J4
Withypool Gdns BS14 .... 23 B5
Withy Rd TA9 .... 136 C7
Withys The BS20 .... 4 D4
Withywine La TA22 .... 164 C5
WITHYWOOD 22 A4
Withywood Gdns 1 BS13 .... 21 F4
Withy Wood La BA4 .... 142 C5
Withywood Rd BS13 .... 21 F4
Witney Cl BS31 .... 25 D3
Witney La
Chard TA20 .... 223 B8
Tatworth TA20 .... 193 F1
Wittey's La TA20 .... 199 B6
WIVELISCOMBE 210 B4
Wiveliscombe Prim Sch TA4 .... 210 B5
Wivenhoe Ct BA11 .... 120 C6
Woburn Rd BA21 .... 219 E7
Wolfester Terr BA22 .... 174 F4
Wollens Cl BA6 .... 206 C4
Wolmer Cl TA6 .... 208 E2
Wolsey Cl BA5 .... 203 B3
Wolverlands BA22 .... 175 A6
Wolvershill Ind Units BS29 .... 50 C6
Wolvershill Pk BS29 .... 51 A3
Wolvershill Rd
Banwell BS29 .... 50 E6
Weston-super-Mare BS24 .... 50 C8
WONDERSTONE 67 D6
Wonhouse Dro BS28 .... 138 B6
Woodacre BS20 .... 2 E7
Woodadvent La TA23 .... 131 E1
Woodbarton TA4 .... 166 F4
Woodbirds Hill La TA10 .... 172 C8
WOODBOROUGH 70 B8
Woodborough Cres BS25 .... 70 A7
Woodborough Ct BS25 .... 70 A8
Woodborough Dr BS25 .... 70 A8
Woodborough Hill Cotts BA2 .... 79 C4
Woodborough La BA3 .... 79 A4
Woodborough Mill La BS39 .... 41 B5
Woodborough Rd
Radstock BA3 .... 79 A3
Winscombe BS25 .... 69 F8
Woodburn Cross EX16 .... 162 F2
Woodburn Hill EX16 .... 162 F2
Woodburn Water Cross EX16 .... 162 F1
Woodbury Ave BA5 .... 203 F5
Woodbury Cl BA5 .... 203 F5
Woodbury Rd TA6 .... 208 D4
Wood Cl BA5 .... 203 B4

Woodcliff Ave BS22 . . . . . . 31 C1
Woodcliff Rd BS22 . . . . 31 C1
Wood Close La TA17 . . . . 195 A8
Woodcock St BA7 . . . . 214 C5
Woodcock Way EX13 . . . . 198 B7
WOODCOMBE 200 C8
Woodcombe Brake TA24 200 D7
Woodcombe Cotts TA24 . 200 C8
Woodcombe La TA24 . . . . 200 C8
Woodcote BA20 . . . . 218 D2
Woodcroft BS39 . . . . 57 C3
Woodcroft Mdws TA20 . . 192 E7
Wooddene BS25 . . . . 70 A8
Wood Dro TA10 . . . . 171 E8
Wood End TA4 . . . . 167 D6
Wood End Wlk BS9 . . . . 5 C6
Wood Farm Cotts TA5 . . . 134 E4
Woodfield Cl TA8 . . . . 104 C5
WOODFORD
Watchet 132 A1
Wells 140 A6
Woodford Cl BS48 . . . . 9 A1
Woodford Cotts TA4 . . . . 132 A1
Woodford Ct 2 BS23 . . . . . 48 E5
Woodford La
Coxley BA5 . . . . 139 F6
Wells BA5 . . . . 203 B1
Woodford Rd BA5 . . . . 140 A6
Woodfords Gn BA7 . . . . . . 214 B6
WOODGATE 179 E2
Woodhayes BA8 . . . . 190 A6
Woodhayes Ct 19 BA8 . . . 190 A6
Woodhayes Ho 12 BA8 . . 190 A6
Woodhayes Rd BA11 . . . . 120 C6
Woodhenge BA22 . . . . 218 B5
WOODHILL
Portishead 2 D7
Stoke St Gregory 170 F6
Woodhill BS49 . . . . 34 E6
Woodhill Ave BS20 . . . . 2 D6
Woodhill Ct BS20 . . . . 2 D6
Wood Hill Pk BS20 . . . . 2 D7
Woodhill Rd BS20 . . . . 2 D6
Woodhill Terr TA3 . . . . . . 170 F6
Woodhill Views BS48 . . . . 8 F3
Woodhouse Cross SP8 . . 177 F6
Woodhouse La
Axminster EX13 . . . . 198 D1
Chard TA20 . . . . 194 B6
Marston Magna BA22 . . . . 175 B1
Montacute TA15 . . . . 186 C3
Woodhouse Rd
Axminster EX13 . . . . 198 D1
Bath BA2 . . . . 44 A6
Woodhurst Rd BS23 . . . . . . 49 A7
Woodington Rd BS21 . . . . . . 6 C1
Wood Kilns The BS49 . . . . 17 A1
Wood La
Axbridge BS26 . . . . 70 D2
Blue Anchor TA24 . . . . 131 C6
Butleigh BA6 . . . . 157 C4
Carhampton TA24 . . . . 131 B4
Chapmanslade BA13 . . . . . 121 D4
Clapton in G BS20 . . . . 8 E8
Crowcombe TA4 . . . . 151 C7
Drimpton DT8 . . . . 199 E7
High Ham TA10 . . . . 155 E1
Marnhull DT10 . . . . 190 F2
Moorlinch TA7 . . . . 155 E8
North Perrott TA18 . . . . . . 196 D3
Rodney Stoke BS27 . . . . 91 B1
South Cheriton BA8 . . . . . . 176 C4
Stalbridge DT10 . . . . 190 B4
Stawell TA7 . . . . 137 A1
Stogumber TA4 . . . . 150 D7
Weston-super-Mare BS23 . . . 30 F1
Woodland Ave TA7 . . . . . . 154 F5
Woodland Cl
6 Carhampton TA24 . . . . . 131 A5
Failand BS8 . . . . 10 B4
Woodland Cotts BA3 . . . . . 64 D6
Woodland Ct BS9 . . . . 5 C3
Woodland Glade BS21 . . . . . 6 E5
Woodland Gr
Bath, Bushey Norwood BA2 . . . . 45 E5
Bath, Weston Park BA1 . . . . 27 C1
Bristol BS9 . . . . 5 D6
Yeovil BA20 . . . . 219 B4
Woodland Pl BA2 . . . . 45 D5
Woodland Rd
Bristol BS8 . . . . 226 C4
Frome BA11 . . . . 119 F4
Nailsea BS48 . . . . 8 E3
Taunton TA2 . . . . 213 A7
Watchet TA23 . . . . 202 C6
Weston-super-Mare BS23 . . 48 D4
WOODLANDS 183 E6
Woodlands
Axbridge BS26 . . . . 70 D2
Wellington TA21 . . . . 222 F3
Weston-super-Mare BS23 . . 30 D1
Woodlands Bsns Pk EX16 . . . . 179 C3
Woodlands Court Bsns Pk TA6 . . . . 136 B2
Woodlands Ct BS11 . . . . 4 E5
Woodlands Dr
Ruishton TA3 . . . . 169 C3
Winsley BA3 . . . . 64 B6
Woodlands La
Holcombe BA3 . . . . 116 B7
Isle Abbotts TA3 . . . . 183 E6
Woodlands Mead DT10 . . 190 F6
Woodlands Pk BA1 . . . . 28 C2
Woodlands Rd
Baltonsborough BA6 . . . . . 158 A8
Clevedon BS21 . . . . 6 C4
Portishead BS20 . . . . 2 D8
Woodlands The
Peasedown St John BA2 . . . 60 F3
Shepton Mallet BA4 . . . . . . 205 D5
Woodland Way
Failand BS8 . . . . 10 B4
Frome BA11 . . . . 120 D7
Woodleaze BS9 . . . . 5 B6
Woodleigh Gdns BS14 . . . . 23 C6
Woodmarsh Cl BS14 . . . . . 23 A4
Woodmead Gdns BS13 . . . 22 C4
Woodmill BS49 . . . . 17 A1
Woodmill Cl DT10 . . . . 190 B5
Woodpecker Ave BA3 . . . . 97 B8
Woodpecker Dr BS22 . . . . 49 E8
Woodram La TA3 . . . . 181 E5
Wood Rd
Ashill TA19 . . . . 183 B4
High Ham TA10 . . . . 172 A8
Woodridge Mead TA4 . . . 167 F8
Wood Rock EX36 . . . . 162 C5
Woodrush Cl TA1 . . . . 213 C1
Woods Batch BA16 . . . . . . 207 B6
Woods Cnr TA11 . . . . 173 E8
Wood's Cross EX36 . . . . . 162 C5
Woods Hill BA3 . . . . 64 A6
Woodside
Bristol BS9 . . . . 5 D3
Midsomer Norton BA3 . . . . . 77 E1
Woodside Ave BS24 . . . . . . 49 B2
Woodside Cl TA24 . . . . . . 200 D7
Woodside Ct BS23 . . . . 49 A8
Woodside Gdns BS20 . . . . . . 1 E5
Woodside Rd BS21 . . . . 6 E5
Woodspring Ave BS22 . . . . 31 B3
Woodspring Cres BS22 . . . 31 A3
Woodspring Mus★ BS23 . . 48 E8
Woodspring Priory★ BS22 . . . . 14 C1
Woods Rd BA16 . . . . 207 A6
Wood St
Bath BA1 . . . . 228 B2
Bath, Beechen Cliff BA2 . . 228 B1
Milverton TA4 . . . . 166 F5
Taunton TA1 . . . . 212 E4
Woodstock Rd
Taunton TA1 . . . . 212 E5
Weston-super-Mare BS22 . . 49 B8
Yeovil BA21 . . . . 219 C7
Woodview
Chilcompton BA3 . . . . 96 E5
2 Clevedon BS21 . . . . 6 F3
Paulton BS39 . . . . 77 C5
Wells BA5 . . . . 203 E5
Woodview Cl BS11 . . . . 4 E7
Woodview Dr BS49 . . . . 35 B8
Woodview Rd BS27 . . . . . . 90 C7
Woodview Terr
Nailsea BS48 . . . . 8 F2
Weston-super-Mare BS23 . . 49 A6
Wood Way EX35 . . . . 122 D4
Woodwell Rd BS11 . . . . 4 E5
WOOKEY 139 E8
Wookey Cl BS48 . . . . 18 F8
WOOKEY HOLE 203 A7
Wookey Hole Cave★ BA5 . . . . 111 E5
Wookey Hole Papermill & Mus★ BA5 . . . . 203 A8
Wookey Hole Rd BA5 . . . . 203 B5
Wookey Prim Sch BA5 . . . 139 D8
WOOLAVINGTON 136 F4
Woolavington Hill TA7 . . 136 E3
Woolavington Rd TA7 . . . 136 D4
Woolavington Right Dro TA7 . . . . 154 D6
Woolavington Village Prim Sch TA7 . . . . 136 E4
Woolcott La SP8 . . . . 161 E1
Wooler Rd BS23 . . . . 48 E8
Wooley La TA19, TA20 . . . 194 C6
Woolhayes La TA20 . . . . . 223 A8
WOOLLARD 41 A6
Woollard La
Bristol BS14, BS39 . . . . 41 A7
Whitchurch BS14 . . . . 23 E1
Woollen La BA22 . . . . 174 F1
WOOLLEY 27 F5
Woolley La BA1 . . . . 28 A4
Woolley Rd BS14 . . . . 23 E5
WOOLMINSTONE 195 B3
Woolpit La TA24 . . . . 146 B7
Woolshed Cl TA24 . . . . . . 129 E1
WOOLSTON
North Cadbury 175 E6
Watchet 132 D2
Woolstone La TA5 . . . . . . 134 F7
Woolston Rd BA22 . . . . . . 175 E6
Woolvers Way BS24 . . . . . . 50 B6
WOOLVERTON 82 C1
Wooton Hill BA6 . . . . 157 C5
WOOTTON COURTENAY . . 129 F6
Wootton Cross EX13 . . . . 198 F1
Wootton Gr DT9 . . . . 225 E5
Wootton St BA6 . . . . 157 C6
Wootton Vineyard★ BA4 140 C5
Worberry La BA3 . . . . 95 B7
Worcester Bldgs BA1 . . . . 28 B2
Worcester Cl BA2 . . . . 79 D7
Worcester Cres BS8 . . . . . 226 A4
Worcester Ct BS8 . . . . 226 A4
Worcester Gdns BS48 . . . . 18 C8
Worcester Pk BA1 . . . . 28 B2
Worcester Pl BA1 . . . . 28 B2
Worcester Rd BS8 . . . . . . 226 A4
Worcester Terr
Bath BA1 . . . . 28 B2
Bristol BS8 . . . . 226 A4
Wordsworth Ave TA6 . . . . 208 E6
Wordsworth Cl TA8 . . . . . . 85 B2
Wordsworth Dr TA1 . . . . . 213 B3
Wordsworth Rd
Clevedon BS21 . . . . 6 C2
Weston-super-Mare BS23 . . 49 A3
World's End La BS31 . . . . . 25 C5
WORLE 31 F2
WORLEBURY 31 A2
Worlebury CE Fst Sch BS22 . . . . 31 B3
Worlebury Cl BS22 . . . . 31 B3
Worlebury Hill Rd BS22, BS23 . . . . 31 B2
Worlebury Park Rd BS22 . 31 A2
Worle Com Sch BS22 . . . . . 31 E1
Worle Ct BS22 . . . . 31 F3
Worle Ind Est BS22 . . . . 32 B2
Worle Moor Rd BS24 . . . . . 49 E7
Worle Sta BS22 . . . . 32 B1
Wormcliff La SN13 . . . . 29 F3
WORMINSTER 140 C5
Worminster Batch BA4 . . 140 D5
Worston La TA8 . . . . 104 C5
Worston Orch TA9 . . . . . . 104 E4
Worston Rd TA9 . . . . 104 E5
WORTH 139 D8
Worthings The BS24 . . . . . 67 B1
Worthington Cl BS28 . . . . 108 D5
Worth La TA22, TA24 . . . . 146 C4
WORTHY 123 E5
Worthy Cres BS24 . . . . 67 B1
Worthy La
Creech St Michael TA3 . . . . 169 D5
Pilton BA4 . . . . 140 F3
5 Weston-super-Mare BS23 . . . . 48 E8
West Pennard BA4, BA6 . . 140 D1
Worthy Pl 4 BS23 . . . . 48 E8
Worthy Toll Rd TA24 . . . . 123 D4
Wouldham Rd TA23 . . . . . 202 D6
Wrangcombe La TA21 . . . 180 A4
Wrangcombe Rd TA21 . . . 180 A4
Wrangle Farm Gn BS21 . . . . 6 E2
WRANGLE THE 74 A5
Wrangle The 5 BS24 . . . . . 49 F7
WRANGWAY 180 A4
Wrangway Rd EX15 . . . . . 180 A3
WRANTAGE 170 A1
WRAXALL
Ditcheat 159 A7
Nailsea 9 C3
Wraxall CE Prim Sch BS48 . 9 B4
Wraxall Cross Rds BA4 . . 159 A7
Wraxall Gr BS13 . . . . 22 A8
Wraxall Hill
Ditcheat BA4 . . . . 159 A8
Wraxall BS48 . . . . 9 C5
Wraxall Rd BA4 . . . . 159 B7
Wraxall Vineyard★ BA4 . . 159 A7
Wraxhill Cl BA16 . . . . 207 D5
Wraxhill Rd
Street BA16 . . . . 207 C5
Yeovil BA20 . . . . 218 E1
WREATH 194 C3
Wreath La TA20 . . . . 194 B3
Wren Cl
Frome BA11 . . . . 120 B6
Taunton TA1 . . . . 212 C4
Weston-super-Mare BS22 . . 49 D8
Wren Gdns BS20 . . . . 3 A7
Wrenmoor Cl TA6 . . . . 209 C3
WRINGTON 35 E1
Wrington CE Prim Sch BS40 . . . . 35 E2
Wrington Cres BS13 . . . . . . 22 A7
Wrington Hill BS40 . . . . 35 F5
Wrington La BS49 . . . . 34 E5
Wrington Mead BS49 . . . . . 34 E5
Wrington Rd BS49 . . . . 34 F4
Wristland Rd TA23 . . . . . . 202 D7
WRITHLINGTON 79 C2
Writhlington Ct BA3 . . . . . . 79 C2
Writhlington Sch BA3 . . . . 79 C1
Writh Rd DT9 . . . . 189 B1
Wroughton Dr BS13 . . . . . . 22 D4
Wroughton Gdns BS13 . . . 22 D4
Wry La TA4 . . . . 149 F2
Wyatt Ave BS13 . . . . 21 F5
Wyatt Cl BS13 . . . . 21 F5
Wyatt's Cl BS48 . . . . 8 D2
Wyatts Ct TA17 . . . . 195 C7
Wyatts Field TA3 . . . . 168 D1
Wyatts Way TA19 . . . . 183 C4
Wych Ct EX13 . . . . 198 E3
Wych Elm Rd BA11 . . . . . 120 C6
Wydford Cl DT9 . . . . 225 B3
Wydon La TA24 . . . . 124 F3
Wye Ave TA6 . . . . 209 D3
Wyedale Ave BS9 . . . . 5 C7
WYKE CHAMPFLOWER . . . 215 A6
Wyke La
Wyke Champflower BA10 . . . . 215 A5
Wyke Champflower BA10 . . . . 215 A6
Wyke Rd
Castle Cary BA7, BA10 . . . 214 E7
Wyke Champflower BA10 . . . . 215 C6
Wylds Rd TA6 . . . . 209 A7
Wylds Road Ind Est TA6 . 209 A7
Wyllie Ct BS22 . . . . 32 A5
Wymbush Cres BS13 . . . . . 22 C5
Wymbush Gdns BS13 . . . . 22 C5
Wyndam Ct BS2 . . . . 227 B4
Wyndeats La TA5 . . . . 134 B5
Wyndham Cres BS20 . . . . . . 4 B4
Wyndham Ct BA21 . . . . . . 219 C5
Wyndham Rd
Bridgwater TA6 . . . . 209 C6
Taunton TA2 . . . . 212 E7
Watchet TA23 . . . . 202 C6
Wyndham's TA4 . . . . 210 C4
Wyndham St BA20 . . . . . . 219 C5
Wyndham View BA21 . . . . 219 D5
Wyndham Way BS20 . . . . . . 2 E5
Wyndham Way Ret Pk BS20 . . . . 2 D5
Wynford Rd BA11 . . . . 120 B5
Wynnes Cl DT9 . . . . 225 C3
Wynnes Rise DT9 . . . . 225 C3
Wynsome St BA14 . . . . 83 F3
Wynter Cl BS22 . . . . 32 A3
Wyrral Cl BA6 . . . . 206 D3
Wytch Gn EX13 . . . . 198 E3
Wythburn Rd BA11 . . . . . . 120 C5
Wyvern Cl
Bruton BA10 . . . . 215 F7
Weston-super-Mare BS23 . . 48 F7
Yeovil BA20 . . . . 218 C1
Wyvern Ct TA18 . . . . 224 C6
Wyvern Mews 5 BS23 . . . . 48 F7
Wyvern Rd TA1 . . . . 168 E1
Wyville Rd BA11 . . . . 120 C6

Y

Yadley Cl BS25 . . . . 70 A7
Yadley La BS25 . . . . 70 A6
Yadley Way BS25 . . . . 70 A7
Yallands Hill TA2 . . . . 213 E8
YALWAY 153 A1
Yanel La BS25 . . . . 52 B5
Yanhey Hill EX16 . . . . 162 E4
Yanleigh Cl BS13 . . . . 21 D6
YANLEY 21 C8
Yanley La BS41, BS13 . . . . . 21 C7
Yarbury Way BS24 . . . . 32 B1
YARCOMBE 192 D3
YARDE 132 A2
Yarde Pl TA1 . . . . 212 F4
Yard La
Marshwood DT6 . . . . 199 F3
Wiveliscombe TA4 . . . . . . 210 C6
Yardleigh Cross EX13 . . . 198 D4
Yard The BA11 . . . . 143 C4
Yardwall Rd TA9 . . . . 106 A3
YARFORD 168 C8
YARLEY 139 C8
Yarley Cross BA5 . . . . 139 C8
Yarley Field La BA5 . . . . . 139 B7
Yarley Hill BA5 . . . . 139 C7
YARLINGTON 175 F8
Yarlington Cl TA2 . . . . 168 B4
Yarnbarton BA8 . . . . 176 E1
Yarn Barton BA20 . . . . 219 A4
YARROW 106 E3
Yarrow Ct BS22 . . . . 32 A5
Yarrow Rd TA9 . . . . 106 D3
YATTON 34 C8
Yatton Cl BS13 . . . . 21 F8
Yatton Jun & Inf Schs BS49 . . . . 34 C8
Yatton Station BS49 . . . . . . 17 A1
YEABRIDGE 220 E2
Yeabsleys Way BA7 . . . . . 214 C6
Yealscombe La TA24 . . . . 128 B2
Yeamen's Ho BS1 . . . . 227 B1
Yeap's Dro BA5 . . . . 139 A7
Yearmoor La TA5 . . . . 134 F8
Yearnor Mill La
Oare TA24 . . . . 122 F5
Porlock Weir TA24 . . . . 123 B5
Yeates Ct BS21 . . . . 6 E3
Yeatman Cl BS39 . . . . 57 D4
Yeatman Hospl DT9 . . . . . 225 D4
Yellingmill La BA4 . . . . . . 141 C8
Yellowcombe La TA24 . . . . 147 C5
Yellow Rose Cvn Pk TA20 . . . . 193 D6
Yellow Way Rd
Maiden Bradley BA11, BA12 . . . . 144 A3
Witham Friary BA11 . . . . . 143 F3
Yellow Wood Cross TA4 132 D2
YENSTON 189 F8
Yenston Hill BA8 . . . . 189 F8
Yeo Bank La BS21 . . . . 15 F1
Yeo Cl
Cheddar BS27 . . . . 90 B6
Weston-super-Mare BS23 . . 49 A5
Yeo Ct
Clevedon BS21 . . . . 6 C2
Congresbury BS49 . . . . 34 D4
Yeo La
Bridgwater TA6 . . . . 209 B2
Long Ashton BS41 . . . . 10 F1
Yeolands Dr BS21 . . . . 6 B1
Yeo Leisure Pk★ BA20 . . 219 C4
Yeomanry Way BA4 . . . . . 205 D5
Yeomans Cl BS9 . . . . 5 D5
Yeomanside Cl BS14 . . . . . 23 C5
Yeomans Lodge BA11 . . . 119 C4
Yeomans Orch BS40 . . . . . 35 E3
Yeomead BS48 . . . . 8 F3
Yeomeads BS41 . . . . 10 F1
Yeo Mill Cross EX36 . . . . . 162 C5
Yeo Moor BS21 . . . . 6 E2
Yeo Moor Dro BS27, BS28 . . . . 109 D3
Yeo Moor Inf Sch BS21 . . . . 6 E2
Yeo Moor Jun Sch BS21 . . . . 6 E2
Yeo Rd TA6 . . . . 209 B2
Yeo Valley 2 BA22 . . . . . . 197 F8
Yeo Valley Way BS48 . . . . . . 9 B2
YEOVIL 218 E4
Yeovil Bsns Ctr BA21 . . . . 219 F7
Yeovil Coll BA21 . . . . 219 A6
Yeovil District Hospl BA21 . . . . 219 B5
Yeovil Innovation Centre BS22 . . . . 218 B7
Yeovil Junction Sta BA22 . . . . 219 E1
YEOVIL MARSH 187 A6
Yeovil Marsh Pk BA21 . . . 187 A5
Yeovil Pen Mill Sta BA21 219 E5
Yeovil Railway Ctr★ BA22 . . . . 219 D1
Yeovil Rd
Crewkerne TA18 . . . . 224 E7
Halstock BA22 . . . . 197 D3
Montacute TA15 . . . . 186 B3
Sherborne DT9 . . . . 225 C4
Tintinhull BA22 . . . . 186 C6
Yeovil BA22 . . . . 218 F1
Yeovil Small Bsns Ctr BA22 . . . . 218 B6
YEOVILTON 174 A1
Yeovil Trinity Foyer 7 BA20 . . . . 219 B4
Yeoward Rd BS21 . . . . 6 E1
Yeo Way BS21 . . . . 6 B2
Yet Mead La BS27 . . . . 110 B7
Yewcroft Cl BS14 . . . . 23 A4
Yewtree Batch BS40 . . . . . 37 A1
Yew Tree Cl
Bishop Sutton BS39 . . . . 57 D4
Lower Langford BS40 . . . . . 53 E6
Nailsea BS48 . . . . 8 C1
Yeovil BA20 . . . . 218 E2
Yew Tree Cotts BS40 . . . . . 54 E3
Yew Tree Ct BS14 . . . . 23 B5
Yew Tree Dr BS22 . . . . 50 B8
Yew Tree Gdns
Nailsea BS48 . . . . 8 C1
Pill BS20 . . . . 4 C4
Sandford BS25 . . . . 52 A4
Yew Tree La
Compton Martin BS40 . . . . . 74 A7
Kingston Seymour BS21 . . . 16 B1
Taunton TA2 . . . . 213 E6
Yew Tree Pk BS49 . . . . 34 D3
Yomede Pk BA1 . . . . 44 A7
Yonder Dro TA10 . . . . 184 E8
Yonder Hill Cotts TA20 . . 198 E7
Yonder Mead TA4 . . . . 167 F7
York Bldgs TA6 . . . . 208 F5
York Cl
Axminster EX13 . . . . 198 A1
Weston-super-Mare BS22 . . 32 A4
York Ct BS2 . . . . 227 B4
York Gdns BS8 . . . . 11 F6
York Lodge 4 BA20 . . . . . 219 A5
York Pl
Bath BA1 . . . . 45 B8
Bristol, Brandon Hill BS1 . . 226 C2
Bristol, Victoria Park BS8 . 226 B3
Yeovil BA20 . . . . 219 A5
York Rd
Bridgwater TA6 . . . . 208 F2
Bristol BS2 . . . . 227 C1
Taunton TA1 . . . . 213 C5
York's La BA3 . . . . 94 B6
York St
Bath BA1 . . . . 228 C2
Bristol BS2 . . . . 227 B4
5 Frome BA11 . . . . 119 E5
Weston-super-Mare BS23 . . 48 D7
Youngwood La BS48 . . . . . 18 D7

Z

ZEALS 161 F2
Zeals Rise BA12 . . . . 161 F2
Zembard La TA20 . . . . 223 C4
Zeta Cl TA7 . . . . 209 E8
Zig Zag BS21 . . . . 6 D4
Zion Hill
Midsomer Norton BA3 . . . . . 96 B7
Oakhill BA3 . . . . 115 A3
18 Shepton Mallet BA4 . . . 205 B6